c. 1993

W9-AVG-065

Peace and War

READINGS FOR WRITERS

Peace and War

READINGS FOR WRITERS

Dennis Okerstrom
Park College

Sarah Morgan
Park College

ALLYN AND BACON
Boston   London   Toronto   Sydney   Tokyo   Singapore

Executive Editor: Joseph Opiela
Editorial Assistant: Brenda Conaway
Production Administrator: Marjorie Payne
Editorial-Production Service: York Production Services
Cover Administrator: Linda Dickinson
Composition Buyer: Linda Cox
Manufacturing Buyer: Megan Cochran

Copyright © 1993 by Allyn and Bacon
A Division of Simon & Schuster, Inc.
160 Gould Street
Needham Heights, MA 02194

All rights reserved. No part of the material protected by this copyright notice may be reproduced or utilized in any form or by any means, electronic or mechanical, including photocopying, recording, or by any information storage and retrieval system, without the written permission of the copyright owner.

Library of Congress Cataloging-in-Publication Data

Okerstrom, Dennis.
    Peace and war : readings for writers / Dennis Okerstrom, Sarah Morgan.
      p. cm.
    ISBN 0-205-13603-6 (alk. paper)
    1. Readers—War. 2. Readers—Peace. 3. College readers. 4. English language—Rhetoric. 5. War—Problems, exercises, etc. 6. Peace—Problems, exercises, etc. I. Morgan, Sarah, 1953–   . II. Title.
PE1127.W3034 1993
808'.0427—dc20
                                          91-43825
                                              CIP

This book is printed on
recycled, acid-free paper.

This book is printed on recycled acid-free paper.

Printed in the United States of America

10 9 8 7 6 5 4 3 2 1   98 97 96 95 94 93

Credits

Chapter 1

Page 5. "Gauging the Winds of War" Reprinted with permission from *Science News,* the weekly news magazine of science, copyright 1991 by Science Service, Inc.

Page 13. "Causes of Wars" Reprinted by permission of the publishers from *The Causes of Wars* by Michael Howard. Cambridge, Mass.: Harvard University Press, Copyright © 1983 by Michael Howard.

Page 26. "Lawful Wars" Reprinted with permission from *Foreign Policy* 72 (Fall 1988). Copyright 1988 by Carnegie Endowment for International Peace.

Credits continued on page 470, which constitutes an extension of the copyright page.

For Joan Sargeant and her Yank—D. R. O.

For Howard Morgan and his—S. J. M.

Contents

1 Why War?   1

Rhetorical Contents

The following divisions include both aims or purposes of discourse (exposition, narration, description, argument, and persuasion) and ways of thinking, developing ideas, and organizing material (the four "aims" as well as the more specific methods of cause/effect, comparison/contrast, definition, division and classification, exemplification, and process analysis). No text settles neatly into any single category, however, so we've listed each piece according to its dominating characteristics. Some pieces make such full use of the range of possibilities that they appear in several categories.

Cause/Effect

Comparison/Contrast

Definition

Description

Division/Classification

Exemplification

Exposition

Narration

Persuasion/Argument

Process Analysis

Preface

IN JANUARY, 1991, the war in the Persian Gulf began. As the prelude to battle unfolded, as more and more questions were raised about the cause and possible results of the war, we began to feel that perhaps the general issue of war was one that needed a great deal of study by college students if we are to have any hope for a peaceful future. Then one of our students, an Army reservist, was called to active duty and sent to the Gulf, and our small campus was fairly abuzz as concerned students and teachers wondered what the war would bring next and whom it would take.

Each day, students dropped by our offices to talk about the war or raised questions in class about the ongoing hostilities a half-world away. As we tried to stay current on the Persian Gulf war, we realized that there always are more questions than answers about such hostilities and that the issues in even a limited war are far more complex than most of us realize.

Last year, those of us who grew up during the Cold War were fairly agog at the apparent ending of that ideological conflict, a potential nuclear sword of Damocles that had hung suspended over the globe for four decades. But with the unraveling of what had been the Soviet Union, the threat of nuclear war seemed both further away and more possible than ever. Who would control the 27,000 nuclear warheads scattered across the new Commonwealth of Independent States? Would a coup by hardliners place the button within reach of some Russian or Ukrainian Dr. Strangelove?

Even the aversion or end of war creates problems.

The essays and articles in this book provide no easy solutions to such problems, nor do they cover more than a fraction of the issues and perspectives of them that arise in any conflict. Rather, *Peace and War: Readings for Writers* attempts to direct attention to enduring and universal concerns about causes and effects of war, about who fights the battles, about who or what are legitimate targets, about how the public is informed about a war as it is fought. This book's coverage is neither exhaustive nor all-inclusive; it is a starting point for further discussion and research. We hope it will help its readers explore these issues and that it perhaps will suggest ways for readers to develop and deepen their understanding of war and its complexities.

Each of the eight chapters opens with an introduction that focuses on the chapter's topic, providing context and suggesting related causes and consequences. Headnotes before each selection build upon that context and ask readers to contribute to its continuing construction. The selections in each chapter are followed by a short series of questions for discussion or writing; each chapter concludes with a longer list of discussion, writing, and research suggestions that ask the reader to connect the selections in various ways for various purposes as well as to bring in new information. Questions at the end of Chapters 7 and 8 also suggest connections to essays from previous chapters.

No book is entirely the result of the efforts of those whose names appear on the cover. The time, energy, and talent of many people went into this one, and we would like to acknowledge them.

For their help in researching the issues of war, we want to extend our appreciation to students Roger Hughlett, Tami Loos, Rachel Allen, Lance Brashear, Ligia Bramlett, Connie Espinoza, Brandi Brobst, Jennifer Jones, Pamela Moore, Maurice Oelklaus, Kim White, and April Flowers. Deborah Lale was helpful in clerical matters. Kevin Bowen of the William Joiner Center for the Study of War and Social Consequences in Boston, Massachusetts, was kind enough to offer suggestions. For their discussion and enthusiasm, thanks also to Catherine Thompson, Terry and Ellen Morris, and Keith and Lolly Snyder. Ann Schultis, research librarian at Park College, was invaluable as a resource and for providing unfailing good humor and encouragement when we sorely needed both. Richard Jenseth of Lehigh University, C. Jerial Howard of Northeastern Illinois State University, David Schwalm of Arizona State University, and Louis Smith of the University of Massachusetts, Boston offered helpful advice in the initial stages of this book.

None of this would have been possible without the advice and good sense of our friend and editor at Allyn and Bacon, Joseph Opiela. Words are not nearly enough thanks for the patience and help given by our spouses, Michael Vivion and Jeanette Okerstrom, both teachers also, who suffered through another project.

Introduction

ONE AFTERNOON ALYCE LORENZ turned the corner by the drugstore in the small Michigan town where she lived and saw a huge military truck bouncing up the hill. The teenager stopped to let it pass. Watching, she suddenly realized that the young men in the truck's bed were POWs, German soldiers who were to be confined in a nearby camp. She stared from the sidewalk, struck by her first look at the enemy with whom her country was at war.

"They looked just like us," she says, a trace of wonder still in her voice almost fifty years later. "Somehow, I never thought the enemy would be human."

But the enemy always is.

Precisely because only humans go to war, war becomes at once the most dreadful of occurrences, the most destructive of human life and achievement, and the most human of activities. While we pride ourselves on our high civilizations, these civilizations are often founded by war or fears of war. We marvel at the technology of war but spend our lives concerned that we will one day have to face equivalent weaponry. Fear leads to arms races; arms races rush headlong to combat. In all of history, that seems always to be the case.

Some wars seem almost to be a battle of wills; one nation acts in a way that another cannot or will not abide, or it imposes conditions that another nation believes will hurt it or harm its interests. Each nation sends its women, men, and metal to force the other to bend to its will. After enough soldiers, civilians, and metal have been twisted into nothingness, one side surrenders, or all nations sign an agreement calling it quits—until next time.

Other wars seem to be a battle of ills. One nation embarks upon activities so unjust, illegal, or cruel that another nation attempts to persuade it to cease. It may levy economic sanctions against the offender or apply political pressure, turning only as a last resort to war. War is a strong persuader for the defeated.

The start of the Persian Gulf war prompted us to consider what college students today know about war. We watched as several of our students either joined the military or were called to active duty by their Reserve units, and the topic became for several months the abiding concern of much of the United States. In discussing the war in our classes, we realized just how broad the issue is. This book is the result of our wanting to present for students some of those issues in the hope that a greater understanding of war and its various elements will ensue.

War is much more than combat. It is politics, both international and domestic. In the lining up of allies, of friends, of choosing sides, sometimes a nation that wishes to remain aloof from a war cannot. Loyalties change. Which of the United States' World War II enemies are now its allies? Which of its friends of the 1960s and 1970s have become its enemies? At home, the person in the White House Oval Office seems to have a major part in whether we fight, and then a whole host of political considerations enter.

Also complicating the matter are the civilians, more of whom die in modern war than combatants. Civilians have always suffered in war, but the ratio of civilian casualties to combatant casualties has risen astronomically in the twentieth century. The increase results partly from the frightening technology that human knowledge has refined into weapons powerful enough to shatter entire nations. Efforts to understand war are also complicated by the difficulty of finding truth among all the reports, images, and opinions that war engenders; of deciding who will be asked to do the fighting and how such decisions are made in a democracy; of what happens after war, when it seems that much has changed but few problems have been solved. What, too, is the individual's responsibility in war, in peace?

If there is to be any hope for a future of peace, war is an activity that must be studied carefully and understood clearly. We must get away from jingoism, from glorification of war, and seek to resolve international disputes without combat. Advances in communication and transportation have not only made the earth a much smaller place but also have made possible the swift resolution of conflicts. Or escalation and destruction.

It's a world so small that it hasn't room for battlefields.

1

Why War?

LT. GEORGE FRANKLIN, a fighter pilot in World War II, related a mission over occupied France in 1944. Flying a P-47 Thunderbolt on a "mission of opportunity"—military jargon for a mission to harass the enemy at the pilot's discretion—Franklin spotted a lone American B-24 heading back to England, flying low and slow and with one of its four engines out, its propeller feathered.

He radioed the pilot of the bomber, who asked him to fly around the crippled aircraft and look for obvious damage that might mean not making back to its home field. Franklin checked it below, from all sides, and saw no leaking fuel, no wisps of smoke, no obvious damage except numerous bullet holes. He reported back to the bomber pilot, and agreed to escort the bomber home as protection against roving German fighters. For twenty minutes, the two men who had never met flew alongside each other silently. When Franklin saw they were approaching the coast of France, he pressed his throat microphone to pass the information to the bomber crew, ten men no doubt anxious for any good news.

In the middle of Franklin's sentence, the bomber exploded. The sky filled with smoke and flame, tiny bits of metal, a red mist. Ten men had just vaporized. Franklin's reaction? Numbness. Then he put it from his mind. If he had ever once stopped to think about death, he said, he would not have been able to fly again. Fighting would have been impossible.

That, of course, is just the point. War is not just technology and ideals and victories and parades. War is death, both of combatants and of civilians, of grandparents and babies, of teenagers and mothers and fathers and frightened soldiers. It is grisly, it is numbing. It has been so for thousands of years, with each war more gruesome than the last. Yet despite all of the philosophy, the art, the intricate social and political and economic structures engendered by civilization, humans continue to resort to war to settle disputes.

Wars have been studied by historians, psychologists, lawyers, soldiers, diplomats, anthropologists, and other interested and concerned humans. Despite centuries of debate and inquiry, we are always left with the question: Why?

Many studies have suggested that aggression is innate in humans and that war is a natural outgrowth of this inner drive. Anthropologists cite various contemporary primitive cultures in which warriors are constantly battling other groups, other villages, other warriors, for prestige, booty, mates. The implication seems to be that wars among more complex nation-states are based on the same fairly clear-cut and simple reasons. One child has something the other wants. One nation has something another wants.

But is it really that simple? Some studies, with equally vehement advocates, hold that peace is the norm for humans, and war the aberration.

Sometimes the debate seems to hinge on definitions. Exactly what is war? Is raiding by simple nomads the same as war by nuclear powers? Why was World War II called a *war,* and the Korean Conflict a *police action?* Ultimately it comes down to law and nations. When one nation is officially at armed conflict with another, it is called *war.* Even if the two sides are not shooting, as in the Cold War, if conflict is a distinct possibility it wins the title *War.* Lesser conflicts are usually officially called something else, although they generally are called *war* by most people. Such semantics seem spurious; they trivialize situations in which people die by armed conflict.

Modern nations seldom take their citizens to war on a whim. Scholars today say that war is a reasoned response to a perceived threat, that nations go to war when the failure to do so will result in something even worse than combat. If that is so, war cannot possibly be as simple as children's squabbles. A whole gamut of possibilities must be weighed, and a plethora of factors will affect a decision to go to war: economics, politics, psychology, fear, pride.

For the United States, war has had a tumultuous history. The framers of the Constitution divided the duties and responsibilities of government among three branches, and specifically gave the power to declare war to Congress. However, the President was given power over the armed forces as Commander-in-Chief, a curious position that has eroded the power of Congress in matters of war. Since 1776, the United States has engaged in armed conflicts more than 200 times; in each instance, casualties were suffered on both sides. However, only five of those actions were wars declared by Congress: The War of 1812, the Mexican War, the Spanish-American War, and World Wars I and II. All of the others, including Korea, Vietnam, Lebanon, Grenada, Panama, and the Persian Gulf war, have been carried out at the order of the President. (After troops were already committed, Congress did vote to support the action in the Persian Gulf, but stopped short of declaring war on Iraq.)

This situation—presidential fiat to start wars—clearly throws a wrench into the works of trying to explain war on the simple basis of "want-have." The psychological and experiential makeup of each chief executive has been a fundamental factor in decisions to go to war, short-circuiting the pluralism of American society reflected in Congress. After the debacle in Vietnam, when Presidents Kennedy, Johnson, and Nixon successively ordered more troops, more bombings of other Southeast Asian nations (a wider front), Congress approved in 1973 the War Powers Act that sought to severely limit what the President could do in committing troops to combat. Essentially, except for troops defending themselves against attack, the President was limited to sending troops into potential combat situations for only sixty days unless Congress approved.

Presidents since Nixon have simply ignored the War Powers Act, claiming it encroached on their executive power, and the result has been that U.S. troops have continued to be placed in combat without Congressional approval.

In a democracy, is such a system desirable? Should the most serious of decisions, that of committing soldiers to combat, of possibly exposing civilians to retaliatory attack, be solely in the hands of one person?

The debate goes on; questions continue. For what reasons should the United States ever go to war? Is it possible to never again wage war? Should economic reasons—including, for instance, threatened oil supplies—be cause enough for war? Should the United States act solely out of concern for human rights? What about secret wars, the covert operations that occasionally come to light when they are bungled, such as the Iran-Contra affair? Is the selling of weapons to other nations an invitation for them to go to war?

In the fifth century, Augustine wrote a doctrine of "just war" in which specific factors, based on Christian principles, had to be met before a nation could justly wage a war. Should the United States adhere strictly to the Augustinian model or should pragmatism rule in the decision to go to war? In a democracy, how much should an individual citizen have to say about such a decision?

As you read this chapter, try to form your own conclusions about war, about its causes, about its future. Attempt to formulate your own response to being ordered to fight. Under what conditions would you do so? When would you refuse? How do you balance your responsibilities as a citizen with strongly held beliefs that may be contrary to a national policy?

BRUCE BOWER

Gauging the Winds of War

What is the ultimate cause of war—biological or cultural? Anthropologists have sought the answer to that question for decades, often studying primitive cultures, and coming up with conflicting answers. Some still insist on an innate human aggressiveness, but many today hold that wars stem from conflicts arising out of competition for scarce commodities, societal goals, prestige accorded warriors or other socially determined factors.

Bruce Bower, a writer for Science News, *presents a synopsis of current thinking on the causes of war in an article that first appeared in that journal on February 9, 1991. Before reading, reflect on what you believe to be the fundamental causes of war and whether your belief holds room for hope that wars may one day be eliminated or whether wars will always be a part of human existence.*

IN A 1971 MOTOWN HIT SINGLE, Edwin Starr posed the musical question, "War—what is it good for?" His gruff response: "Absolutely nothin'." 1

Despite the grimly predictable tragedies of armed conflict, almost all ancient and modern societies studied by anthropologists have engaged in at least periodic bouts of warfare. The ubiquity of organized fighting between human groups—currently brought home by the war in the Middle East—has fired up the scientific study of warfare over the last 30 years and has sparked some bruising academic skirmishes. 2

A handful of warfare researchers described their findings and theories at last November's meeting of the American Anthropological Association in New Orleans. These investigators do not praise fighting, but they assume that anything so common in human experience serves some purpose. They search for the "absolutely somethin' " that lights the fuse of violence in bands of foragers, tribes of hunter–gatherers, rudimentary political states and modern nations alike. 3

In the 1960s, as U.S. involvement in Vietnam deepened, anthropological theories of war's causes and consequences flourished, numbering at least 16 by 1973, observes Keith F. Otterbein of the State University of New York at Buffalo. However, he says, only about half of those theories still receive strong scientific support, and no persuasive new theories have emerged. 4

Current notions about the roots of war stem mainly from studies   5
of nonindustrial societies lacking centralized political power and extensive military organizations. In Otterbein's view, all of these theoretical
approaches focus on three themes:

- "ultimate" causes of war that influence the goals people fight   6
  for, such as competition within a society for scarce resources or
  mates, and intense divisions between groups of related men.

- "proximate" causes of war, such as a society's military prepar-   7
  edness and the goals of its leaders, often centering on the desire
  for land, natural resources or control of trade routes.

- consequences of war that influence further conflict, including   8
  population decline, improved access to resources, and increased
  prestige and power accorded to victorious warriors.

Although some anthropologists and sociobiologists contend that a   9
genetic tendency toward physical violence greases the human war machine, theories of innate aggression attract few advocates today, Otterbein maintains. Nevertheless, disputes over the alleged biological roots
of combat continue to erupt, ignited in many cases by the work of
Napoleon A. Chagnon of the University of California, Santa Barbara,
whose studies of warfare have become the most widely publicized research in this field.

Since 1964, Chagnon has conducted fieldwork among the 15,000   10
Yanomamo Indians who inhabit some 200 villages in the Amazonian
jungle of Brazil and Venezuela. He has long stressed the ferocity and
frequency of combat between Yanomamo villages. Some other anthropologists who have studied the jungle tribe argue that Chagnon empha-
sizes a misleading slice of Yanomamo life.

Chagnon's latest report, in the Feb. 26, 1988 SCIENCE, concludes   11
that revenge fuels protracted, bloody battles between groups of men
from different Yanomamo villages. Competition for food, water, territory or women creates the initial friction, he says. Minor bow-and-
arrow confrontations ensue, escalating rapidly when a death results and
the victim's male relatives exact revenge through raids on the offending
village.

Blood vengeance apparently raises the social status and reproduc-   12
tive success of Yanomamo warriors, who represent nearly half of the
men in the tribe, Chagnon maintains. On average, killers have more
than twice as many wives and three times as many children as their
peaceable counterparts.

Chagnon refrains from arguing that warfare generally proves bi-   13 ologically advantageous among the Yanomamo or in any other culture. He does contend, however, that reproductive success and fighting prowess probably go hand-in-hand in many human groups, and that this may help explain the great prestige attached to military conquest in both modern and ancient states.

Even if Chagnon's Yanomamo data hold up, responds anthropol-   14
ogist John H. Moore, successful warriors in similar tribal societies some-times contribute few genes to subsequent generations. Moore, of the University of Oklahoma in Norman, cites the 19th century Cheyenne Indians of the North American plains as a case in point. The Cheyenne, with a population of about 3,000 divided into bands of 150 to 400 in-dividuals, engaged in fierce warfare with other Indian tribes as well as with U.S. military forces, achieving historical notoriety with their de-feat of Custer at the battle of Little Big Horn. In addition to seven warrior bands led by numerous war chiefs, Cheyenne society included 44 peace chiefs, sometimes more than one to a band, who led polygy-nous extended families.

U.S. Census data collected in 1880 and 1892 reveal that men in   15
the Cheyenne peace bands had a striking reproductive advantage over warriors, reports Moore in the June 1990 CURRENT ANTHROPOLOGY. The war chiefs stressed celibacy and ritual suicide, while the peace chiefs had numerous wives and children, he notes.

Moore asserts that many societies without centralized political sys-   16
tems, including the Cheyenne, undergo periodic cultural reorganiza-tions, and he says researchers have no evidence suggesting that recent Yanomamo behavior reflects all or most of human prehistory, or even the Yanomamo of several generations ago.

Another critic of Chagnon's research, Marvin Harris of the Uni-   17
versity of Florida in Gainesville, theorizes that war occurs among hunter-gatherers and other "band-and-village" peoples when population growth creates increasingly intense competition for food, especially protein-rich game. He maintains that warfare, for all its brutality, effectively prunes these populations, preventing malnutrition and hunger among survi-vors—whether the combatants hail from Yanomamo villages or from horticultural groups in Papua New Guinea.

"Band-and-village societies must pay a heavy price for keeping   18
population and food supply in balance, and warfare is part of that price," Harris writes in *Our Kind* (1989, Harper & Row, New York). Conflicts sometimes veer out of control, wiping out more lives than malnutrition would have claimed, but "no system is fail-safe," he notes.

Harris' theory may help explain widespread fighting among North   19
America's Anasazi Indians around 700 years ago, says Jonathan Haas of the Field Museum of National History in Chicago. Although Anasazi

culture extended back at least to 500 A.D., Haas points out that burnt houses, decapitated skeletons and other archaeological evidence of warfare date only to the second half of the 13th century A.D. At that time, the ingredients for war coalesced, he says: A burgeoning population fostered the emergence of distinct cultural groups with an "us versus them" mentality, and periodic droughts reduced crop yields and drained food reserves.

When the Anasazi abandoned their population centers at the end   20
of the 13th century and the droughts also eased, warfare again diminished, Haas observes.

"Tribal peoples cycle in and out of warfare because of environ-   21
mental stress," he says. "Warfare has increased with the evolution of states because environmental stresses are more unrelenting now."

The nearly unrelenting warfare of most early states, which spread   22
throughout the world from 3200 B.C. until around 1800 A.D., often reflects the "predatory accumulation" practiced by rulers sitting atop centralized political hierarchies, asserts Stephen P. Reyna of the University of New Hampshire in Durham. However, early or "archaic" states possessed nowhere near the political complexity or destructive means of modern "nation-states," he notes.

A violent conflict in the Chad Basin of north central Africa around   23
200 years ago illustrates the dynamics of warfare between archaic states, Reyna says. A leader of one state accused a neighboring leader of a crime against Islam—incest with his daughter—and the charge sparked a war. But the real problem stemmed from the rapid growth of both states due to a brutal type of arms race, Reyna holds. These leaders had engaged in constant warfare with weaker neighbors to accumulate wealth and larger armies. In a vicious cycle, each victory enabled them to accumulate even more means of destruction to wage more successful wars, he says. Eventually their "fields of empire" overlapped, and war between the two soon followed.

Reyna notes that the incest charge, though probably unfounded,   24
served a strategic purpose: it led to the defection of several generals aligned with the accused ruler, undermining his army and helping to seal his eventual defeat.

Such hostilities grew out of a long history of warfare among hu-   25
man groups, says Robert L. Carneiro of the American Museum of Natural History in New York City. In his view, war played a critical role in the evolution of large political and social systems.

The origins of war probably stretch back through a couple of mil-   26
lion years to Stone Age times, Carneiro contends. Stone Age battles— fought to avenge murders, wife-stealing or other trespasses often ob-

served among modern hunter-gatherers—served to push small bands of humans apart and keep them separate.

But around 10,000 years ago, the nature of warfare changed, he 27 maintains. The spread of agriculture increased permanent settlements and human populations. Adjacent villages then began to fight over access to farmland. Instead of pushing the communities apart in traditional Stone Age fashion, these wars forged the emergence of the chiefdom, a forced coalition of several formerly independent villages under the control of a paramount chief. With chiefdoms came district chiefs, village chiefs, advisers and other early representatives of social and political complexity.

Archaeological signs of war, such as the number of weapons found 28 in graves and heavily fortified occupation sites, increase with the growth of chiefdoms, Carneiro observes. The push from chiefdoms to even larger state-societies did not occur swiftly or irreversibly throughout the world, he says, but early hotbeds of state growth appeared where limited areas of prime farmland prevented vanquished villagers from fleeing to greener pastures. Prime examples include Mesopotamia, the Nile valley and the Peruvian coast.

"War was the one instrument capable of surmounting autonomous 29 villages and deserves careful study as a cause of social evolution," Carneiro says.

Perhaps the most wide-ranging warfare study to date was conducted during the 1980s by Carol R. Ember and Melvin Ember of Human Relations Area Files, a privately funded research organization in New Haven, Conn. The team analyzed anthropological descriptions of 186 nonindustrial societies, virtually all of which operated on a much smaller scale than modern nation-states. Descriptions ranged from 18th-century writings on Native American tribes to recent accounts of African hunter-gatherers.

Two independent coders read the voluminous literature and rated 31 the presence and frequency of warfare, aggressive acts, natural disasters and other social and psychological factors, focusing on a 25-year period in each society.

The Embers say their unpublished findings offer a tentative theory 32 of war, at least among "simple" societies: The societies that engage in the most warfare express considerably more fear of food shortages caused by expected but unpredictable natural disasters, such as drought, flood or infestation. The fear of others—indicated by child-rearing practices stressing mistrust of neighbors—further fuels the tendency to fight, the researchers say.

Their data provide no backing for other explanations of warfare. 33

For example, the Embers found that societies already experiencing chronic food and protein shortages did not engage in excessive fighting. The study also failed to support the idea that a shortage of women stimulates warfare and regulates population.

Some researchers have suggested a penchant for warfare among   34
sexually restrictive societies and among societies with high levels of interpersonal aggression, as reflected in elevated rates of murder and theft. The Embers' study showed no such links.

Parents in warlike societies do tend to encourage toughness and   35
aggression among boys, but warfare apparently *causes* this practice rather than vice versa, the Embers argue. When these societies lose wars and come under the control of outside forces, harsh child-rearing methods diminish sharply, they found.

Three-quarters of the sample's "simple" societies fought wars every   36
two years, Carol Ember notes, although "this doesn't mean war is inevitable."

The Embers hope to expand their analyses to modern nation-states.   37
In the meantime, they suspect that the link between the risk of war and the fear of unpredictable disasters extends to a wide variety of situations.

Several researchers say contact with Westerners has whipped up   38
local conflicts in Africa and elsewhere since the early days of European colonialism.

More than a century ago, for example, Tuareg tribes of northern   39
Africa limited their attacks to small-scale raids on caravans passing through their territory, says Candelario Saenz of the State University of New York at Purchase. The Tuareg extorted camels and other goods from the caravans to support their pastoral way of life, Saenz says. But when France took control of Algeria in the late 1800s, it imposed numerous restrictions on trade in the region. Tuareg groups soon entered into a period of nearly constant warfare among themselves as they competed for the rapidly decreasing supply of goods passing along traditional trade routes, Saenz says.

Another instance of Western contact helping to foment violence   40
occurred more recently in the ethnically mixed African nation of Mauritania, says Michael M. Horowitz of the State University of New York at Binghamton, who has conducted fieldwork there for the past four years.

The completion of a large dam on the Senegal River several years   41
ago expanded farmable floodplains and drew the promise of considerable outside investment by Western agricultural companies, Horowitz says. But the local population, long dependent on farming this fertile river valley, already occupied much of the area.

"The Mauritanian government is now killing and torturing these   42 people to get the land," Horowitz says. "In the process, they've created 100,000 refugees and intensified violence between ethnic groups."

Whether stimulated by Western contact or not, most of the 120 wars documented since the end of World War II similarly pit large states against smaller nations or ethnic groups the states claim to represent, says Jason Clay of Cultural Survival, a public-interest organization in Cambridge, Mass.

In the aftermath of the international conflict sparked by the aggressions of the Axis powers, he notes, dictatorships and one-party states ironically solidified their power in many parts of the world, including Africa, the Soviet Union and Eastern Europe. Diverse nations and groups of people with separate languages and cultural histories were yoked to the goals of unresponsive, unelected leaders of both the political right and left, Clay says.

Moreover, those leaders socked away whatever taxes, internal resources, foreign aid and international loans they could extract for themselves, leaving the rest of the populace destitute, he maintains.

"The destruction of social and political life at the local level and the stripping away of resources by modern one-party states has led to longer, more widespread wars," Clay argues. "We'll have more violence at the regional level and the settling of old scores as states fall apart in the post-Cold War world."

Although Clay's dire prediction gathers support from the bloody Soviet crackdown on Lithuania's independence movement and the increasing tensions in other Soviet republics, anthropological research provides room for optimism, says R. Brian Ferguson of Rutgers University in Newark, N.J.

"War is not the natural human condition," Ferguson says. "Research shows that war varies over time due to factors such as trade, population growth and outside contacts."

Often, leaders must paint the enemy as inhuman in order to motivate people to kill, he says—and even then, many soldiers come out of combat with severe psychological aftereffects.

"We need to dispense with the idea that people love violence and are doomed to fight," Ferguson concludes.

Content Considerations

1. Bower writes that investigators assume of war "that anything so common in human experience serves some purpose" (paragraph 3). Most studies seem to be of primitive or nonindustrial cultures. Would their conclusions be different if industrial nations were the object of their study? Why?

2. Robert L. Carneiro is credited in this essay as advancing the theory that war was crucial in the evolution of large political and social systems (paragraph 25). Does this theory seem viable to you? Why or why not?

3. Research by Melvin Ember and Carol R. Ember seems to dispute many theories about causes of war and to support others. Why do so many scholars find so many apparently contradictory explanations for phenomena such as war? How does one evaluate all of the conflicting data?

The Causes of Wars

Wars have been studied and written about since the Greek historian Thucydides recorded the events of the Peloponnesian War. However, according to Michael Howard, a British historian and professor at Oxford University, many modern historians have tended to concentrate on the study of peace, assuming that war was not an aberration but the norm, and the real challenge is in preventing conflict. War is the result of modern states—but those same states also preserve the peace, Howard writes in this essay, the first chapter of his 1984 book of the same title.

Wars arise because of conscious actions by political entities, Howard asserts, and from a belief that they can achieve more by going to war than by staying at peace. All wars ultimately are fought on that principle, he says.

Before reading this, list all the wars you can recall, then write the causes as you know them. Do you agree with Howard? Why or why not?

NO ONE CAN DESCRIBE the topic that I have chosen to discuss as 1 a neglected and understudied one. How much ink has been spilled about it, how many library shelves have been filled with works on the subject, since the days of Thucydides! How many scholars from how many specialties have applied their expertise to this intractable problem! Mathematicians, meteorologists, sociologists, anthropologists, geographers, physicists, political scientists, philosophers, theologians and lawyers are only the most obvious of the categories that come to mind when one surveys the ranks of those who have sought some formula for perpetual peace, or who have at least hoped to reduce the complexities of international conflict to some orderly structure, to develop a theory that will enable us to explain, to understand and to control a phenomenon which, if we fail to abolish it, might well abolish us.

Yet it is not a problem that has aroused a great deal of interest in 2 the historical profession. The causes of specific wars, yes: these provide unending material for analysis and interpretation, usually fuelled by plenty of documents and starkly conflicting prejudices on the part of the scholars themselves. But the phenomenon of war as a continuing activity within human society is one that as a profession we take very much for granted. The alternation of war and peace has been the very stuff of the past. War has been throughout history a normal way of conducting disputes between political groups. Few of us, probably, would go along with those socio-biologists who claim that this has been so because man is 'innately aggressive'. The calculations of advantage and risk, sometimes careful, sometimes crude, that statesmen make before committing their countries to war are very remotely linked, if at all, to the displays of tribal *machismo* that we witness today in football crowds. Since the use or threat of physical force is the most elementary way of asserting power and controlling one's environment, the fact that men have frequently had recourse to it does not cause the historian a great deal of surprise. Force, or the threat of it, may not settle arguments, but it does play a considerable part in determining the structure of the world in which we live.

Indeed historians are usually less interested in the causes of war   3
than they are in the causes of peace; in the way in which peaceful communities, controlled by legitimized authorities, have developed and sustained themselves at all. The great scholars who a hundred years ago gained the study of history its primacy of place in British universities, men such as Stubbs, Maitland and Tout, devoted themselves to discovering how a society so peaceful and so law-abiding as that within which they lived had come into existence. They examined the interaction between power and consent, freedom and obligation, State and community, that has made possible the emergence of that humdrum condition of political life that we know as peace. In international affairs the occasions for rivalries, whether dynastic, religious, economic, political or ideological, have been so self-evident that historians have found it more interesting to study the work of those statesmen whose skill *avoided* conflict—the Castlereaghs, the Cannings, the Salisburys, even the Palmerstons—than those whose ineptitude failed to prevent it. The breakdown of international order does not, on the whole, strike us as a pathological aberration from the norm. On the contrary, the maintenance of that order and its peaceful adjustment to changing circumstances appears as a task presenting a continuous challenge to human ingenuity, and our wonder, like Dr. Johnson's at women preaching, is not that it is done so imperfectly, but that it is under the circumstances ever done at all.

I spoke a moment ago about the multiplicity of books that have   4
been written about the causes of war since the time of Thucydides. In fact I think we would find that the vast majority of them had been written since 1914, and that the degree of intellectual concern about the causes of war to which we have become accustomed has existed only since the First World War. In view of the damage which the war did to the social and political structure of Europe, this is understandable enough. But there has been a tendency to argue that because that war caused

such great and lasting damage, because it destroyed three great empires and nearly beggared a fourth, it must have arisen from causes of peculiar complexity and profundity, from the neuroses of nations, from the widening class struggle, from a crisis in industrial society. I have argued this myself, taking issue with Mr A. J. P. Taylor on the subject,[1] but now I wonder whether on this, as on so many other matters, I was not wrong and he was not right.

It is true, and it is important to bear in mind in examining the problems of that period, that before 1914 war was almost universally considered an acceptable, perhaps an inevitable and for many people a desirable way of settling international differences, and that the war generally foreseen was expected to be, if not exactly *frisch und fröhlich,* then certainly brief; no longer, certainly, than the war of 1870 that was consciously or unconsciously taken by that generation as a model. Had it not been so generally felt that war was an acceptable and tolerable way of solving international disputes, statesmen and soldiers would no doubt have approached the crisis of 1914 in a very different fashion.

But there was nothing new about this attitude to war. Statesmen had always been able to assume that war would be acceptable at least to those sections of their populations whose opinion mattered to them, and in this respect the decision to go to war in 1914—for Continental statesmen at least—in no way differed from those taken by their predecessors of earlier generations. The causes of the Great War are thus in essence no more complex or profound than those of any previous European war, or indeed than those described by Thucydides[2] as underlying the Peloponnesian War: 'What made war inevitable was the growth of Athenian power and the fear this caused in Sparta.' In Central Europe there was the German fear that the disintegration of the Habsburg Empire would result in an enormous enhancement of Russian power—power already becoming formidable as French-financed industries and railways put Russian manpower at the service of her military machine. In Western Europe there was the traditional British fear that Germany might establish a hegemony over Europe which, even more than that of Napoleon, would place at risk the security of Britain and her own possessions; a fear fuelled by the knowledge that there was within Germany a widespread determination to achieve a world status comparable with her latent power. Consideration of this kind had caused wars in Europe often enough before. Was there really anything different about 1914?

Ever since the eighteenth century, war had been blamed by intellectuals upon the stupidity or the self-interest of governing elites (as it is now blamed upon 'military-industrial complexes'), with the implicit or explicit assumption that if the control of state affairs was in the hands of sensible men—businessmen, as Cobden thought, the workers, as Jean

Jaurès thought—then wars would be no more. By the twentieth century
the growth of the social and biological sciences was producing alternative explanations. As Quincy Wright expressed it in his massive *Study
of War,* 'Scientific investigators . . . tended to attribute war to imma-
turities in social knowledge and control, as one might attribute epidem-
ics to insufficient medical knowledge or to inadequate public health
services.'[3] The Social Darwinian acceptance of the inevitability of struggle, indeed of its desirability if mankind was to progress, the view,
expressed by the elder Moltke but very widely shared at the turn of the
century, that perpetual peace was a dream and not even a beautiful dream,
did not survive the Great War in those countries where the bourgeois-
liberal culture was dominant, Britain and the United States. The failure
of these nations to appreciate that such bellicist views, or variants of
them, were still widespread in other areas of the world, those dominated
by Fascism and by Marxism-Leninism, were to cause embarrassing misunderstandings, and possibly still do.

For liberal intellectuals war was so self-evidently a pathological
aberration from the norm, at best a ghastly mistake, at worst a crime.
Those who initiated wars must in their view have been criminal, or
sick, or the victims of forces beyond their power to control. Those who
were so accused disclaimed responsibility for the events of 1914, throwing it on others or saying the whole thing was a terrible mistake for
which no one was to blame. None of them, with their societies in ruins
around them and tens of millions dead, were prepared to say coura-
geously: 'We only acted as statesmen always have in the past. In the
circumstances then prevailing, war seemed to us to be the best way of
protecting or forwarding the national interests for which we were responsible. There was an element of risk, certainly, but the risk might
have been greater had we postponed the issue. Our real guilt does not
lie in the fact that we started the war. It lies in our mistaken belief that
we could win it.'

The trouble is that if we are to regard war as pathological and
abnormal, then all conflict must be similarly regarded; for war is only
a particular kind of conflict between a particular category of social groups,
sovereign states. It is, as Clausewitz put it, 'a clash between major interests that is resolved by bloodshed—that is the only way in which it
differs from other conflicts'.[4] If one had no sovereign states one would
have no wars, as Rousseau rightly pointed out—but, as Hobbes equally
rightly pointed out, we would probably have no peace either. As states
acquire a monopoly of violence, war becomes the only remaining form
of conflict that may legitimately be settled by physical force. The mechanism of legitimization of authority and of social control that makes it
possible for the state to moderate or eliminate conflicts within its bor-

ders or at the very least to ensure that these are not conducted by competitive violence—the mechanism to the study of which historians have quite properly devoted so much attention—makes possible the conduct of armed conflict with other states, and on occasion—if the state is to survive—it makes it necessary. These conflicts arise from conflicting claims, or interests, or ideologies, or perceptions; and these perceptions may indeed be fuelled by social or psychological drives that we do not fully understand and that one day we may learn rather better how to control. But the problem is the control of social conflict *as such;* not simply of war. However inchoate or disreputable the motives for war may be, its initiation is almost by definition a deliberate and carefully considered act and its conduct, at least at the more advanced levels of social development, a matter of very precise central control. If history shows any record of 'accidental' wars, I have yet to find them. Certainly statesmen have sometimes been surprised by the nature of the war they have unleashed, and it is reasonable to assume that in at least fifty per cent of the cases they got a result they did not expect. But that is not the same as a war begun by mistake and continued with no political purpose.

Statesmen in fact go to war to achieve very specific ends, and the 10
reasons for which states have fought one another have been categorized and recategorized innumerable times. Vattel the lawyer divided them into the necessary, the customary, the rational and the capricious. Jomini the strategist identified ideological, economic and popular wars, wars to defend the balance of power, wars to assist allies, wars to assert or to defend rights. Quincy Wright the political scientist divided them into the idealistic, the psychological, the political and the judicial. Bernard Brodie in our own times has refused to discriminate: 'Any theory of the causes of war in general or any war in particular that is not inherently eclectic and comprehensive,' he stated, ' . . . is bound for that very reason to be wrong.'⁵ Another contemporary analyst, Geoffrey Blainey, is on the contrary unashamedly reductionist. All war-aims, he wrote, 'are simply varieties of power. The vanity of nationalism, the will to spread an ideology, the protection of kinsmen in an adjacent land, the desire for more territory . . . all these represent power in different wrappings. The conflicting aims of rival nations are always conflicts of power.'⁶

In principle I am sure that Bernard Brodie was right: no single 11
explanation for conflict between states, any more than for conflict between any other social groups, is likely to stand up to critical examination. But Blainey is right as well. Quincy Wright provided us with a useful indicator when he suggested that 'while animal war is a function of instinct and primitive war of the *mores,* civilized war is primarily a

function of state politics'.[7] Medievalists will perhaps bridle at the application of the term 'primitive' to the sophisticated and subtle societies of the Middle Ages, for whom war was also a 'function of the mores', a way of life that often demanded only the most banal of justifications. As a way of life it persisted in Europe well into the seventeenth century, if no later. For Louis XIV and his court war was, in his early years at least, little more than a seasonal variation on hunting. But by the eighteenth century the mood had changed. For Frederick the Great war was to be preeminently a function of *Staatspolitik,* and so it has remained ever since. And although statesmen can be as emotional or as prejudiced in their judgements as any other group of human beings, it is very seldom that their attitudes, their perceptions and their decisions are not related, however remotely, to the fundamental issues of *power;* that capacity to control their environment on which the independent existence of their states and often the cultural values of their societies depend.

And here perhaps we do find a factor that sets inter-state conflict somewhat apart from other forms of social rivalry. States may fight— indeed as often as not they do fight—not over any specific issue such as might otherwise have been resolved by peaceful means, but in order to acquire, to enhance or to preserve their capacity to function as independent actors in the international system at all. 'The stakes of war,' as Raymond Aron has reminded us, 'are the existence, the creation or the elimination of States.'[8] It is a somber analysis, but one which the historical record very amply bears out.

It is here that those analysts who come to the study of war from the disciplines of the natural sciences, particularly the biological sciences, tend, it seems to me, to go astray. The conflicts between states which have usually led to war have normally arisen, not from any irrational and emotive drives, but from almost a superabundance of analytic rationality. Sophisticated communities (one hesitates to apply to them Quincy Wright's word, 'civilized') do not react simply to immediate threats. Their intelligence (and I use the term in its double sense) enables them to assess the implications that any event taking place anywhere in the world, however remote, may have for their own capacity, immediately to exert influence, ultimately perhaps to survive. In the later Middle Ages and the Early Modern period every child born to every prince anywhere in Europe was registered on the delicate seismographs that monitored the shifts in dynastic power. Every marriage was a diplomatic triumph or disaster. Every stillbirth, as Henry VIII knew, could presage political catastrophe. Today the key events may be different, the pattern remains the same. A malfunction in the political mechanism of some remote African community, a *coup d'état* in a miniscule Caribbean republic, an insurrection deep in the hinterland of South-East Asia, an assassination in some emirate in the Middle East—all these will be subjected to the kind of anxious examination and calculation that was devoted a hundred years ago to the news of comparable events in the Balkans: an insurrection in Philippopolis, a *coup d'état* in Constantinople, an assassination in Belgrade. To whose advantage will this ultimately redound, asked the worried diplomats, ours or *theirs?* Little enough in itself, perhaps, but will it not precipitate or strengthen a trend, set in motion a tide whose melancholy withdrawing roar will strip us of our friends and influence and leave us isolated in a world dominated by adversaries deeply hostile to us and all that we stand for?

There have certainly been occasions when states have gone to war   14
in a mood of ideological fervour like the French in 1792; or of swaggering aggression like the Americans against Spain in 1898 or the British against the Boers a year later; or to make more money, as did the British in the War of Jenkins' Ear in 1739; or in a generous desire to help peoples of similar creed or race, as perhaps the Russians did in 1877 and the British dominions certainly did in 1914 and 1939. But in general men have fought during the past two hundred years neither because they are aggressive nor because they are acquisitive animals, but because they are reasoning ones: because they discern, or believe that they can discern, dangers before they become immediate, the possibility of threats before they are made.

The Habsburg Monarchy might have shattered into a dozen pieces,   15
the Russian railway system might have linked every corner of the Empire with rapid transit communications, without a single Bavarian farmer or Ruhr factory-hand necessarily having his way of life disturbed. But were German statesmen and soldiers being totally paranoid in their fear that, in a Europe where the Russians could deploy so vast a superiority of military power and were supported not only by France but by a string of client Slav successor states in the Balkans, those farmers and factory-hands would indeed be very seriously at risk? And if our answer is that they were indeed being paranoid, and that that paranoia was induced, as many historians would now have us believe, by internal social tensions, what are we to say about British perceptions of German power in the 1930s? Why should the British people of that generation have felt disturbed by the revival of German military capabilities and the extension of their hegemony over Eastern Europe when German leaders were at the time quite sincerely disclaiming any intention of threatening either Britain herself or her control over her Empire? Was this also paranoia? Those historians who have suggested that it was are not popular with their colleagues.

But be this as it may, in 1914 many of the German people, and in   16
1939 nearly all the British, felt justified in going to war, not over any

specific issue that could have been settled by negotiation, but *to maintain their power;* and to do so while it was still possible, before they found themselves so isolated, so impotent, that they had no power left to maintain and had to accept a subordinate position within an international system dominated by their adversaries. 'What made war inevitable was the growth of Athenian power and the fear this caused in Sparta.' Or, to quote another grimly apt passage from Thucydides:

> The Athenians made their Empire more and more strong . . .   17
> [until] finally the point was reached when Athenian strength at-
> tained a peak plain for all to see and the Athenians began to en-
> croach upon Sparta's allies. It was at this point that Sparta felt the
> position to be no longer tolerable and decided by starting the pres-
> ent war to employ all her energies in attacking and if possible de-
> stroying the power of Athens.[9]

You can vary the names of the actors, but the model remains a   18
valid one for the purposes of our analysis. I am rather afraid that it still does.

Something that has changed since the time of Thucydides, how-   19
ever, is the nature of the power that appears so threatening. From the time of Thucydides until that of Louis XIV there was basically only one source of political and military power—control of territory, with all the resources in wealth and manpower that this provided. This control might come through conquest, or through alliance, or through marriage, or through purchase, but the power of princes could be very exactly computed in terms of the extent of their territories and the number of men they could put under arms.

In seventeenth-century Europe this began to change. Extent of   20
territory remained important, but no less important was the effective-ness with which the resources of that territory could be exploited. Ini-tially there were the bureaucratic and fiscal mechanisms that transformed loose coagulations of territorial authority into highly structured central-ized states whose armed forces, though not necessarily large, were per-manent, disciplined and paid. Then came the political transformations of the revolutionary era which made available to these state-systems the entire manpower of their country; or at least as much of it as the ad-ministrators were able to handle. And finally came the revolution in transport, the railways of the nineteenth century that turned the revo-lutionary ideal of the 'Nation in Arms' into a reality. By the early twen-tieth century military power—on the Continent of Europe, at least —was seen as a simple combination of military manpower and railways. The quality of armaments was of secondary importance, and political

intentions were virtually excluded from account. The growth of power was measured in terms of the growth of populations and of communications; of the number of men who could be put under arms and transported to the battlefield to make their weight felt in the initial and presumably decisive battles. It was the mutual perception of threat in those terms that turned Europe before 1914 into an armed camp, and it was their calculations within this framework that reduced German staff officers increasingly to despair and launched their leaders on their catastrophic gamble in 1914.

But already the development of weapon technology had introduced yet another element into the international power calculus, one that has in our own age become dominant. It was only in the course of the nineteenth century that technology began to produce weapons-systems—initially in the form of naval vessels—that could be seen as likely in themselves to prove decisive, through their qualitative and quantitative superiority, in the event of conflict. But as war became increasingly a matter of competing technologies rather than competing armies, so there developed that escalatory process known as the 'arms race'. As a title the phrase, like so many coined by journalists to catch the eye, is misleading. 'Arms races' are in fact continuing and open-ended attempts to match power for power. They are as much means of achieving stable or, if possible, favourable power balances as were the dynastic marriage policies of Valois and Habsburg. To suggest that they in themselves are causes of war implies a naïve if not totally mistaken view of the relationship between the two phenomena. The causes of war remain rooted, as much as they were in the pre-industrial age, in perceptions by statesmen of the growth of hostile power and the fears for the restriction, if not the extinction, of their own. The threat, or rather the fear, has not changed, whether it comes from aggregations of territory or from dreadnoughts, from the numbers of men under arms or from missile systems. The means which states employ to sustain or to extend their power may have been transformed, but their objectives and preoccupations remain the same.

'Arms races' can no more be isolated than wars themselves from the political circumstances that give rise to them, and like wars they will take as many different forms as political circumstances dictate. They may be no more than a process of competitive modernization, of maintaining a *status quo* that commands general support but in which no participant wishes, whether from reasons of pride or of prudence, to fall behind in keeping his armoury up to date. If there are no political causes for fear or rivalry this process need not in itself be a destabilizing factor in international relations. But they may on the other hand be the result of a quite deliberate assertion of an intention to *change* the *status quo,* as was, for example, the German naval challenge to Britain at the beginning of this century.

This challenge was an explicit attempt by Tirpitz and his associates   23
to destroy the hegemonial position at sea which Britain saw as essential to her security, and, not inconceivably, to replace it with one of their own. As British and German diplomats repeatedly explained to the German government, it was not the German naval programme in itself that gave rise to so much alarm in Britain. It was the intention that lay behind it. If the *status quo* was to be maintained, the German challenge had to be met.

The naval race could quite easily have been ended on one of two   24
conditions. Either the Germans could have abandoned their challenge, as had the French in the previous century, and acquiesced in British naval supremacy; or the British could have yielded as gracefully as they did, a decade or so later, to the United States, and abandoned a status they no longer had the capacity, or the will, to maintain. As it was, they saw the German challenge as one to which they could and should respond, and their power position as one which they were prepared if necessary to use force to preserve. The British naval programme was thus, like that of the Germans, a signal of political intent; and that intent, that refusal to acquiesce in a fundamental transformation of the power balance, was indeed a major element among the causes of war. The naval competition provided a very accurate indication and measurement of political rivalries and tensions, but it did not cause them; nor could it have been abated unless the rivalries themselves had been abandoned.

It was the general perception of the growth of German power that   25
was awakened by the naval challenge, and the fear that a German hegemony on the Continent would be the first step to a challenge to her own hegemony on the oceans, that led Britain to involve herself in the continental conflict on the side of France and Russia. 'What made war inevitable was the growth of *Spartan* power', to paraphrase Thucydides, 'and the fear which this caused in *Athens.*' In the Great War that followed, Germany was defeated, but survived with none of her latent power destroyed. A 'false hegemony' of Britain and France was established in Europe that could last only so long as Germany did not again mobilize her resources to challenge it. German rearmament in the 1930s did not of itself mean that Hitler wanted war (though one has to ignore his entire philosophy if one is to believe that he did not); but it did mean that he was determined, with a great deal of popular support, to obtain a free hand on the international scene, *so oder so,* as he was in the habit of saying. With that free hand he intended to establish German power on an irreversible basis; this was the message conveyed by his armament programme. The armament programme which the British reluctantly

adopted in reply was intended to show that, rather than submit to the hegemonial aspirations they feared from such a revival of German power, they would fight to preserve their own freedom of action. Once again to paraphrase Thucydides:

> Finally the point was reached when German strength attained   26
> a peak plain for all to see, and the Germans began to encroach upon
> Britain's allies. It was at this point that Britain felt the position to
> be no longer tolerable and decided by starting this present war to
> employ all her energies in attacking and if possible destroying the
> power of Germany.

What the Second World War established was not a new British   27 hegemony, but a Soviet hegemony over the Euro-Asian land mass from the Elbe to Vladivostok; and what was seen, at least from Moscow, as an American hegemony over the rest of the world; one freely accepted in Western Europe as a preferable alternative to being absorbed by the rival hegemony. Rival armaments were developed to define and preserve the new territorial boundaries, and the present arms competition began. But in considering the present situation, historical experience suggests that we must ask the fundamental question: *what kind of competition is it?* Is it one between powers which accept the *status quo,* are satisfied with the existing power-relationship, and are concerned simply to modernize their armaments in order to preserve it? Or does it reflect an underlying instability in the system?

My own perception, I am afraid, is that it is the latter. There was   28 a period for a decade after the war when the Soviet Union was probably a *status quo* power but the West was not; that is, the Russians were not seriously concerned to challenge the American global hegemony, but the West did not accept that of the Russians in Eastern Europe. Then there was a decade of relative mutual acceptance between 1955 and 1965; and it was no accident that this was the heyday of disarmament/arms-control negotiations. But thereafter the Soviet Union has shown itself increasingly unwilling to accept the Western global hegemony, if only because many other peoples in the world have been unwilling to do so either. Reaction against Western dominance has brought the Soviet Union some allies and many opportunities in the global arena, and she has developed naval power to be able to assist the former and exploit the latter. She has aspired in fact to global power status, as did Germany before 1914; and if the West complains, as did Britain about Germany, that the Russians do not *need* a Navy for defence purposes, the Soviet Union can retort, as did Germany, that she needs it to make clear to the world the status to which she aspires; that is, so that she can operate on

the world scene by virtue of her own power and not by permission of
anyone else. Like Germany, she is determined to be treated as an equal,
and armed strength has appeared the only way to achieve that status.

The trouble is that what is seen by one party as the breaking of an   29
alien hegemony and the establishment of equal status will be seen by
the incumbent powers as a striving for the establishment of an alternate
hegemony, and they are not necessarily wrong. In international politics,
the appetite often comes with eating; and there really may be no way
to check an aspiring rival except by the mobilization of stronger military
power. An arms race then becomes almost a necessary surrogate for
war, a test of national will and strength; and arms control becomes
possible only when the underlying power balance has been mutually
agreed.

We would be blind therefore if we did not recognize that the causes   30
which have produced war in the past are operating in our own day as
powerfully as at any time in history. It is by no means impossible that
a thousand years hence a historian will write—if any historians survive,
and there are any records for them to write history from—'What made
war inevitable was the growth of Soviet power and the fear which this
caused in the United States.' But times *have* changed since Thucydides.
They have changed even since 1914. These were, as we have seen, bellicist societies in which war was a normal, acceptable, even a desirable
way of settling differences. The question that arises today is, how widely
and evenly spread is that intense revulsion against war that at present
characterizes our own society? For if war is indeed now *universally* seen
as being unacceptable as an instrument of policy, then all analogies drawn
from the past are misleading, and although power struggles may continue, they will be diverted into other channels. But if that revulsion is
not evenly spread, societies which continue to see armed force as an
acceptable means for attaining their political ends are likely to establish
a dominance over those which do not. Indeed they will not necessarily
have to fight for it.

My second and concluding point is this. Whatever may be the   31
underlying causes of international conflict, even if we accept the role
of atavistic militarism or of military-industrial complexes or of socio-
biological drives or of domestic tensions in fuelling it, wars begin with
conscious and reasoned decisions based on the calculation, made by *both*
parties, that they can achieve more by going to war than by remaining
at peace.[10] Even in the most bellicist of societies this kind of calculation
has to be made and it has never even for them been an easy one. When
the decision to go to war involves the likelihood, if not the certainty,
that the conflict will take the form of an exchange of nuclear weapons
from which one's own territory cannot be immune, then even for the

most bellicist of leaders, even for those most insulated from the pressures of public opinion, the calculation that they have more to gain from going to war than by remaining at peace and pursuing their policies by other means will, to put it mildly, not be self-evident. The odds against such a course benefiting their state or themselves or their cause will be greater, and more *evidently* greater, than in any situation that history has ever had to record. Society may have accepted killing as a legitimate instrument of state policy, but not, as yet, suicide. For that reason I find it hard to believe that the abolition of nuclear weapons, even if it were possible, would be an unmixed blessing. Nothing that makes it easier for statesmen to regard war as a feasible instrument of state policy, one from which they stand to gain rather than lose, is likely to contribute to a lasting peace.

Content Considerations

1. Howard is a historian. Why does he disagree with writers in other disciplines who look for causes of war other than political (paragraph 13)?

2. Wars are not accidental but are the result of "conflicting claims, or interests, or ideologies, or perceptions" (paragraph 9), according to Howard. List some existing forces today that are likely to result in future wars.

3. Weapons technology has emerged in the twentieth century as a dominant force in international relations, Howard says (paragraph 21). How might fear of such technology affect future wars?

ENDNOTES

1. See 'Reflections on The First World War' in my *Studies in War and Peace* (Temple Smith, 1970), p. 99.
2. *History of the Peloponnesian War* (trans. Rex Warner, Penguin, 1954), p. 25.
3. Quincy Wright, *A Study of War* (Chicago 1941) vol. II, p. 733.
4. Karl von Clausewitz, *On War* (Princeton University Press, 1976), p. 149.
5. Bernard Brodie, *War and Politics* (Macmillan, New York, 1973), p. 339.
6. Geoffrey Blainey, *The Causes of War* (London, 1973), p. 149.
7. Wright, *op. cit.* II, 144.
8. Raymond Aron, *Peace and War: a Theory of International Relations* (London, 1966), p. 7.
9. Thucydides, *op. cit.,* p. 77.
10. See Blainey, *op. cit.,* p. 128.

MORTON H. HALPERIN

Lawful Wars

Wars are generally thought of as necessary for the continued existence of a society, entered into reluctantly after careful consideration by a nation's leaders and fought by a united citizenry. However, many wars and quasi-wars are conducted clandestinely, usually without the knowledge of citizens and often without the knowledge of elected officials. Morton H. Halperin charges that U.S. presidents have often engaged in covert military operations against foreign powers without informing Congress. Some officials defend the practice as necessary for the secrecy that is vital to keeping agents alive; others denounce the practice as inimical to democratic ideals.

Writing in the fall, 1988, Foreign Policy, Halperin takes issue with the practice of covert operations such as the Iran-Contra affair under President Ronald Reagan. He calls for Congress to reaffirm its powers in foreign policy and to take the "covert" out of covert action.

Consider before reading this essay whether you believe that secrecy is necessary in certain operations involving the security of the United States. To what extent should secrecy prevail?

THE IRAN-*CONTRA* AFFAIR and the U.S. naval presence in the Persian Gulf reveal a system-wide breakdown in the democratic control of American foreign policy. In a country founded on the principle of shared powers in foreign affairs, the president has come to assert a unilateral authority over the use and support of military force by the United States. The officials behind the Iran-*contra* affair, in which arms were sold to Iran in exchange for American hostages held in Lebanon and the profits diverted to the Nicaraguan rebels, completely by-passed every democratic check placed upon the president. Their actions vividly demonstrate the deep incongruity and dangers that unauthorized covert action poses to a democracy. Similarly, President Ronald Reagan's introduction of naval forces to the Persian Gulf in violation of the War Powers Resolution of 1973 risked an unauthorized war. These abuses by the Reagan administration suggest a need to re-evaluate the role of covert action and unilateral military action in U.S. foreign policy. [1]

The next administration will have both an opportunity and a responsibility to restore democracy and accountability to the foreign-policy process. Historically this issue has transcended party lines; it has [2] never been one of Democrat versus Republican but rather one of the president versus Congress. Although all postwar presidents have shown extreme reluctance to allow Congress a role in formulating military policy, that need not be the case. The time has come to begin a new relationship between the two branches over national security and military policy.

There was a time when few would contest the principle that the president could not commit the United States to military intervention without the support of the American people and the approval of Congress. While some presidents certainly violated this principle, they knew that their actions transgressed the constitutional norm requiring congressional authorization. Consequently, those presidents preferred to cover up their actions rather than challenge the congressional role in the process.

Following World War II, however, presidents arrived at a new claim—that they did not need Congress's assent to commit the country to a military conflict. Whether by an overt use of the military—as in Korea, Vietnam, and Grenada—or by a covert operation by the CIA—as in Iran, Guatemala, the Dominican Republic, Laos, Chile, Angola, Afghanistan, and Nicaragua—presidents now assert an inherent constitutional right through their executive power as commander in chief to act as they see fit. Those who support this view tend to base their position on historical practice. In the latest exegesis on this claim, the November 1987 Minority Report of the congressional Iran-*contra* investigation stated, "Presidents historically have had not only the power to negotiate and communicate, but also to deploy force overtly—sometimes for major campaigns involving significant loss of life—without Congressional approval."

The turnabout occurred sometime between 1947 and 1950. In 1947, when President Harry Truman wanted to send military aid to Greece and Turkey to prevent communist takeovers, he asked for and received authorization from Congress. Three years later, however, when Truman wanted to send the army to aid South Korea against the North Korean attack, he completely by-passed Congress; instead he sought approval from the United Nations Security Council. And in 1953, when President Dwight Eisenhower wanted Iranian leader Mohammad Mossadeq removed from power, he took the matter wholly unto himself by going underground through the CIA. These episodes represent a progressive decline in congressional participation in the decision to make a military commitment from specific approval to unauthorized war and finally to secret war.

This presidential unilateralism is usually couched in terms of constitutional prerogative or national security imperative. But the underlying reason has a more telling label: power politics. Presidents deliberately exclude Congress because they do not want Congress involved and because members will ask too many questions and might actually oppose presidential actions. As former national security adviser Robert McFarlane said pointedly in his May 11, 1987, testimony at the Iran-*contra* hearings, the president and his advisers "turned to covert action [in Nicaragua] because they thought they could not get Congressional support for overt activities."

Yet it is a rare case when congressional participation jeopardizes   7
the success of a covert operation or undermines the effectiveness of U.S. foreign policy. On the contrary, congressional participation enhances and is essential to—constitutionally as well as practically—a successful American foreign policy. The benefits of public consensus on military action far outweigh the conceivable loss of some opportunities stemming from public debate and congressional approval. As a matter of constitutional law America's democratic system demands that all major policy decisions—especially those concerning war—be made publicly and through the legislative process. And from a practical perspective, no major military policy will succeed without public and congressional approval. Then Secretary of Defense Caspar Weinberger accepted this latter tenet in 1984 when he articulated standards requiring clear congressional and public support before the engagement of U.S. troops. His standards should apply as fully to covert paramilitary operations as they do to overt war. Further, these standards should be secured in a legal framework that ensures congressional participation in every kind of military engagement.

Thus the next administration should work closely with Congress   8
to establish a regime of prior notice, consultation, and approval for all uses of military force. The framework already exists for conducting military activities, whether overt or covert, in accordance with publicly enunciated standards. The War Powers Resolution of 1973 by its terms applies to overt use of force whenever the armed forces are sent "into hostilities or into situations where imminent involvement in hostilities is clearly indicated by the circumstances." Likewise, the Intelligence Oversight Act of 1980 applies to all covert paramilitary operations.

Congress and the next president should work together to amend   9
the War Powers Resolution in two fundamental ways: first, by creating a special leadership committee from both houses of Congress with which the president could consult about any military situation, and second, by requiring advance congressional approval of any military action, except when defending against attacks on U.S. territory, troops, and facilities abroad and rescuing American hostages. The first proposal was introduced in the Senate in May 1988 by Robert Byrd (D.-West Virginia),

Sam Nunn (D.-Georgia), John Warner (R.-Virginia), and George Mitchell (D.-Maine) as part of a comprehensive redrafting of the War Powers Resolution. The second proposal was part of the original version of the War Powers Resolution passed by the Senate in 1973, but it was then reworked into its present form in a compromise with the House of Representatives.

The next president should endorse both proposals. And he should   10 also support a parallel structure for covert paramilitary activities requiring prior consultation and approval. Finally, anytime the president is unsure under which category a contemplated action falls, he should consult the leadership committee. Taken together, an amended War Powers Resolution and a prior-approval requirement for use or support of paramilitary operations would solidify the current war powers framework and help eliminate the conflict often deemed inherent in conducting foreign military operations in a democratic society.

THE TROUBLE WITH SECRET WARS

The Iran-*contra* scandal illustrates what invariably happens when a   11 president tries to circumvent public debate and approval. The effort to supply the *contras* despite an express congressional ban on such activity nearly led to a constitutional crisis. Reagan fostered a policy and an environment where he was not accountable to Congress or the American people and where his advisers on the National Security Council (NSC) and in the CIA were not even accountable to him. The NSC operated outside the Constitution and the law to implement a policy that Congress had rejected through its undisputed power of the purse. And the NSC staff performed the operation covertly not because the foreign-policy objectives required that the U.S. role remain undetected, but simply to keep Congress in the dark.

But a protracted covert paramilitary operation has little chance of   12 success without public and congressional support. McFarlane learned this lesson the hard way, testifying on May 11, 1987, that "it was clearly unwise to rely on covert activity as the core of our policy [because] you cannot get popular and Congressional support for such policy." He added, "It is virtually impossible, almost as a matter of definition, to rally the public behind a policy you cannot even talk about."

The Iran-*contra* affair has resurrected the issue of whether covert   13 action is an effective instrument of U.S. foreign policy. The *Report of the Congressional Committees Investigating the Iran-Contra Affair*, while raising the question whether covert action can "be authorized and conducted in a manner compatible with the American system of democratic government and the rule of law," never analyzed that fundamental prob-

lem. Instead, the Iran-*contra* report simply asserted that "covert operations are a necessary component of our Nation's foreign policy."

On December 16, 1987, following the release of the Iran-*contra*   14
committees' conclusions, former Secretary of Defense Clark Clifford
testified before Congress that "on balance covert activities have harmed
this country more than they have helped us," because of the "repeated
instances of embarrassing failures—where the goals of the operations
themselves were not fulfilled and unforeseen setbacks occurred instead."
Clifford concluded that "unless we can control overt activities once and
for all, we may wish to abandon them."

His assessment contravenes generally accepted lore that covert op-   15
erations are a necessary and positive option in the U.S. foreign-policy
retinue. Covert operations retain a certain romantic attractiveness among
both the populace and politicians that squarely contradicts the reality of
their failure. Not only do they require the use of unsavory tactics by
American agents, but they also have tended to promote regimes that
practice the worst kinds of repression.

In 1976 the Select Committee to Study Governmental Operations   16
with Respect to Intelligence Activities, known as the Church committee, conducted a thorough analysis of covert paramilitary operations, or
"secret wars," following revelations of widespread abuse at home and
abroad by the CIA, the FBI, and other U.S. intelligence agencies. The
Church committee's review of nearly 30 years of secret wars concluded
that "on balance, . . . the evidence points toward the failure of paramilitary activity as a technique of covert action." While finding it difficult to make judgments as to "success" or "failure," the committee
found that covert operations have tended to be successful only "when
covert operations have been consistent with, and in tactical support of,
policies which have emerged from a national debate and the established
processes of government."

The Church committee also reiterated testimony it heard that "co-   17
vert action can be a success when the objective of the project is to support an individual, a party, or a government in doing what that
individual, party or government wants to do—and when it has the will
and capacity to do it. Covert action cannot build political institutions
where there is no local political will to have them." Additionally, the
committee pointed out that the cumulative long-term effects of a covert
operation tended to undermine whatever short-term success it may have
achieved, and it noted that the U.S. operatives and policymakers rarely
considered the long-term consequences of past or pending operations.

The Church committee fell just short of making the ultimate pro-   18
posal of "a ban on *all* forms of covert action." In preserving the option
of covert action, the committee stressed as its "most basic conclusion"

that "covert action must be seen as an exceptional act, to be undertaken only when the national security requires it and when overt means will not suffice." But Congress's failure to enact this standard into law enabled the Reagan administration to initiate a whole new wave of the kinds of operations that the Church committee had sought to prevent.

The 12 years since the Church committee issued its final report have only served to confirm its assertion that covert paramilitary activity has not been successful. Such operations fail to adhere to the procedures established in the Constitution that guarantee an open and accountable system of government. They avoid precisely the democratic process in the United States that most of them are ostensibly designed to promote in other countries. 19

Secret wars also make for bad foreign policy. The results of even "successful" secret wars have been the empowerment of dictators wholly inimical to American political values. The greatest "successes"—Iran in 1953, Guatemala in 1954, and Chile in 1973—spawned some of the worst oppression of the postwar era. Clearly it was not intended, nor is it necessary, in the words of the Church committee, to "adopt tactics unworthy of a democracy [or] reminiscent of the tactics of totalitarian regimes" to protect U.S. national security. 20

Restoring Congress's constitutional role demands that Congress activate its full share of authority over paramilitary operations by taking the "covert" out of covert action. The common perception of prohibiting paramilitary operations focuses on the operational level: stopping the CIA, or any other intelligence agency, from engaging in these activities. However, the issue can also be approached procedurally: requiring that any covert paramilitary activity be legally authorized by Congress and the president. The new phenomenon of "overt covert" paramilitary operations—as in Nicaragua and Afghanistan—complies in a general sense with this procedure to the extent that the operational details have been kept secret while the policies have been debated and authorized publicly. These two operations actually fail to conform, however, because they were launched before public debate and congressional authorization. 21

Supporters of covert operations contend that the concern for constitutional procedure is irrelevant when vital issues of national security are at stake. They say that any kind of public acknowledgment of covert operations inhibits America's ability to conduct necessary foreign-policy initiatives. But inadvertent or intentional leaks have occurred in almost every major covert operation carried out over the last 40 years. It is virtually certain that all significant and prolonged paramilitary programs will become public during the course of the operation. If the press alone does not ferret out the policy, then the operatives themselves—U.S. 22

government officials or the people in the field—will be hard pressed not to reveal the policy. As then Representative and now Senator Wyche Fowler, Jr. (D.-Georgia) commented on the Nicaragua operation on September 22, 1983: "A paramilitary operation of the size being conducted was impossible to be kept covert. . . . We knew that from the beginning, and we found that within 3 or 4 weeks the participants were themselves announcing their thanks to the people of the United States for giving them the resources to try to overthrow a government down there."

Moreover, covert operations are not stopped simply because they are exposed but because they have no popular or congressional support. Where support was sufficient or opposition indifferent, public disclosures did not undermine the outcome of the project. When the initial covert operation, which was started in December 1981, became public in 1982, the operation was not stopped. Rather, Congress continued to appropriate funds for the next 2 years and then renewed aid in 1986 after a 15-month prohibition. Indeed, even after the Iran-*contra* diversion was exposed in November 1986, aid to the *contras* continued.   23

Other examples from the past also illustrate how public attitudes can affect covert operations that have been revealed. When news of the U.S. covert effort to remove Guatemalan President Jácobo Arbenz Guzmán leaked in 1954, the press dismissed it as communist propaganda; in the political climate of that time policymakers and the public supported activity against perceived communist regimes in the Western Hemisphere and did not doubt the government's denials. Consequently, the operation rolled along unscathed.   24

President John Kennedy is often quoted as having said that he wished the 1961 Bay of Pigs invasion of Cuba had been leaked to the press so that it might have been prevented. But, as with the Guatemalan operation, enough public information existed prior to the invasion to expose it; the operation proceeded unaffected because the general political atmosphere in Congress and around the country supported the goal of overthrowing Cuban leader Fidel Castro. The press in that era simply did not report such information because the people accepted on faith the government's denials that it was engaged in unauthorized and unsavory behavior. Because of the American experiences in the Vietnam War and the Watergate scandal, however, the press now reports such information; and the people believe it more readily, or at least treat the government's denials with much greater skepticism.   25

In 1975 the United States began to provide substantial covert assistance to one group in a three-sided civil war in the newly decolonized African state of Angola. Then President Gerald Ford made an intelli-   26 gence "finding" and notified the appropriate congressional committees of his action. But since public pronouncements and greater press coverage made it impossible to keep the operation secret, the effect of the administration's "plausible denial" was lost completely. With the operation already public, Ford simply went to Congress in 1976 for public authorization, as he should have done in the first place. At that time Congress saw fit to deny the president funds and stop the operation; it also imposed an absolute ban on all covert assistance directed against Angola, the so-called Clark amendment, named for then Iowa Democratic Senator Richard Clark.

Congress rightly played an instrumental role in assessing whether   27
the United States should continue to intervene in Angola. When in 1985 Congress repealed the Clark amendment, Representative Lee Hamilton (D.-Indiana), chairman of the House Intelligence Committee, gave assurance that such a repeal "should not be construed as approval by the Congress" of renewed .covert assistance to rebel leader Jonas Savimbi's National Union for the Total Independence of Angola (UNITA). The administration nevertheless went on to initiate a covert operation to provide paramilitary support to UNITA. In response, Senator Bill Bradley (D.-New Jersey) introduced a bill in July 1987 that would "require that any United States Government support for military or paramilitary operations in Angola be openly acknowledged and publicly debated." A parallel effort was made in the House to add similar language to the Intelligence Authorization Act. This language conforms exactly to the proposal here to eliminate the "covert" aspect of paramilitary operations.

In another relevant example, the CIA had been funneling hundreds   28
of millions of dollars of "secret" military assistance to rebel forces, or *mujahedeen,* opposing the Soviet invasion of Afghanistan. Operational details such as sources and methods, shipment times, and the means of implementation were kept secret; but U.S. involvement was well known to Congress, the media, the American public, and the world. Similarly, Pakistan's participation in the effort, though not officially acknowledged by the U.S. government, was widely known. Despite the assertion that this was a covert activity, the CIA operation was publicly authorized on October 4, 1984, by a concurrent resolution expressing Congress's opposition to the Soviet invasion and calling for "effective support" for the Afghan rebels.

The Afghan assistance operation provides the most useful insights   29
into the proper means for American engagement in or support for paramilitary operations. Although when the operation began it was truly covert, Congress subsequently debated the issue openly and authorized

the administration to aid the rebels; far from preventing the United States from supporting the *mujabedeen,* this public process led to a larger and more effective operation.

Another objection to expanding congressional control over covert   30
operations is that it intrudes, in practical terms if not constitutionally, on the president's ability to conduct foreign policy. Critics recite the old phrase that America cannot have 535 secretaries of state. This argument finds comfort in the general state of inefficiency pervading congressional action, especially in foreign-policy matters. For example, Congress was unable to apply the War Powers Resolution to Reagan's order for U.S. naval escort of reflagged Kuwaiti oil and gas tankers in the Persian Gulf.

But Congress would not be so inefficient in responding to presi-   31
dential initiatives if the president included it in the decision-making process. Indeed, congressional tactics in large part have developed in response to presidential efforts to minimize Congress's role, a role that is essential to the constitutional system of checks and balances. Congressional opposition need not be dismissed as an intrusion upon the operation; rather, it should be seen as a barometer measuring the political efficacy of a plan. At any rate, the president cannot under the Constitution exclude Congress simply to gain a freer hand on policy. Covert operations are attractive to presidents largely as short cuts around the procedural hassles inherent in a democratic system. But mere inconvenience, unlike threats to national survival, does not excuse illegal or unconstitutional conduct. As the Supreme Court stated in its 1983 decision in the case of *Immigration and Naturalization Service* v. *Chadba:*

> There is no support in the Constitution for the proposition that   32
> the cumbersomeness and delays often encountered in complying
> with explicit constitutional standards may be avoided, either by the
> Congress or by the President. . . . With all the obvious flaws of
> delay, untidiness, and potential for abuse, we have not yet found a
> better way to preserve freedom than by making the exercise of
> power subject to the carefully crafted restraints spelled out in the
> Constitution.

The Church committee and the Iran-*contra* investigations showed   33
that even the strictest provisions controlling covert operations inevitably are abused. The only way to stop this pattern is to impose an absolute requirement of public approval to bar paramilitary operations that are covert. But such a restriction does not require inaction in the face of a real threat to national security. In emergencies where a president feels he must take paramilitary action he can do so in conformity with the War Powers Resolution or under his implied constitutional power to

"repel sudden attacks." If he felt compelled to take actions others might judge illegal or unauthorized, he would be obliged later to explain why and then to accept the political consequences, be they a drop in his opinion poll ratings, an election loss, or even impeachment. Yet if a president did come clean in this way, the political fallout probably would be minimal.

Finally, critics contend that including Congress in deliberations over possible paramilitary operations will inhibit agents from acting for fear that congressional leaks will expose the operation and risk their lives. They maintain that Congress does not have a "need to know." But on the contrary, Congress, as the legislative branch of government, has an essential need to know the substance of all military initiatives. This does not mean that Congress needs to know the operational details—who is going precisely where and when. But it should know and approve the substantive goals of the operation. Further, given the political and legal fallout that ensues when a secret war is exposed, agents in the field will want an absolute assurance that the operation is fully authorized.

Requiring public debate and congressional approval would not prevent the president from conducting military activities whose details must be kept secret. But it would ensure a democratic basis for the operation's policy objective. The quantity and quality of the assistance, as well as the names of involved third countries, can remain secret, or at least not be confirmed publicly. The same standards applied to all other national security secrets—a balance between the government's legitimate interest in secrecy and the public's right to know, with a presumption in favor of disclosure—should apply equally to covert paramilitary operations.

The three most recent paramilitary efforts, at least in their later stages, comport with this approach. The United States conducted major paramilitary operations against governments in Afghanistan, Angola, and Nicaragua. Although the administration initially attempted to keep each operation covert, in whole or in part, they were quickly revealed in the media and by the foreign operatives themselves. Yet all three proceeded unhindered, though they did face public and congressional opposition. Countries that wished to assist the United States without officially revealing their involvement were not forced to do so even though their involvement was well known. In all, no operational purpose was served in pursuing any of these operations "covertly."

These three operations are indicative of the problems endemic to the existing system of conducting covert actions. Initiated covertly, the *contra* and Afghanistan operations were approved by Congress only after the administration presented Congress with a fait accompli and left it with the ominous burden of bearing the blame of whatever "failure" might follow if it stopped the operations.

As when forces are committed abroad overtly, it is very difficult   38 for Congress to pull the plug once U.S. commitments, resources, and personnel are on the line. The prohibition proposed here, like the War Powers Resolution before it, is designed to give Congress an opportunity to act before an operation begins and the political pressure mounts. Indeed, the present and proposed intelligence oversight statutes require prior notification of all covert operations, except in the most extreme circumstances when time is of the essence, for precisely the same reason.

Congress has the constitutional authority and the statutory means   39 to prohibit the use or support of covert paramilitary actions. What it lacks is the political will. As the Iran-*contra* report concluded, the present sentiment on Capitol Hill continues to favor retaining the covert option. Even the strongest advocates of tighter congressional oversight have been unwilling to take the next step of supporting a procedural ban on paramilitary operations. They are reluctant to give up a policy tool that has come to be seen as a middle ground between military intervention and diplomacy. But as David Aaron, former deputy assistant national security adviser in the Carter administration, stated in testimony before the House Intelligence Committee on September 22, 1983: "One of the tragedies about covert action is that it is often an excuse for doing something without really doing it. It is something that a policy maker does because he does not have anything else [to] do."

Once covert paramilitary operations are removed from common   40 practice and relegated to last-resort status, as the Church committee recommended, requiring their public approval will not seem so drastic. Moreover, public authorization will not necessarily eliminate the "middle option" as a U.S. foreign-policy option; it simply will transfer it to the public sphere where all major policy decisions of a democratic society belong.

THE FOREIGN AFFAIRS POWER STRUGGLE

Secret war covers only one-half of the problem of employing military force abroad. Executive supremacy also extends to the overt use   41 of military force, the war power. Reagan has involved the U.S. Navy in a hostile situation in the Persian Gulf. Assigned to escort Kuwaiti oil tankers since July 1987, the navy has taken hostile fire and engaged in retaliatory strikes against Iranian military and economic targets. The president has refused to sit down with Congress to work out a specific and coherent policy on the U.S. presence in the area that Congress could approve.

Since the escort operation began, a small number of senators have   42
struggled unsuccessfully to invoke the War Powers Resolution. This law
was intended to prevent a president from ever again excluding Congress
in decisions to use military force. It requires the president to submit a
report to Congress within 48 hours after U.S. armed forces are introduced into a "hostile" situation. If Congress does not approve the president's action within 60 days "after a [presidential] report is submitted,"
the forces must withdraw no later than 90 days from the date of introduction. But if the president fails to make a report, Congress itself must
establish that "hostilities" exist and that a report was "required to be
submitted."

No Congress has ever made such a move, despite the insistence of   43
a few impassioned senators. In particular, Lowell Weicker (R.-Con-
necticut) and Brock Adams (D.-Washington) have argued that as long
as the War Powers Resolution is on the books, it must be obeyed. But
Congress has turned a deaf ear. Most recently, on June 6, 1988, the
Senate rejected an effort to invoke the resolution. Congress's inaction
and Reagan's refusal to make a report or consult Congress in a meaningful way have motivated a number of key senators to propose changes
in the current law that would allow for closer consultation between the
two branches while removing the automatic withdrawal provision. This
proposal represents a significant step forward and provides a basis from
which to institute a more comprehensive reform that would more effectively ensure a role for Congress in deciding war issues.

The Constitution clearly confronted the question of which branch   44
should control the war power: "The Congress shall have power . . .
to declare war." Although the precise interpretation of that power has
been in dispute ever since the Constitution was ratified, the basic meaning is clear: The president may not introduce the United States into a
military situation without the consent of Congress. This applies whether
the war is declared or undeclared, whether it is gradual or immediate,
and whether the commitment is with money or with blood. Congress's
constitutional power to "grant letters of marque and reprisal" is the
historical and legal equivalent of today's low-intensity conflict. The
Constitution's framers were not unaware of the phenomenon of undeclared war. Just as the conduct of war is too important to be left to the
generals, the decision to go to war is too important to be left to the
president.

The foreign affairs power struggle has raged for two centuries and   45
remains no closer to resolution than when it started. The general structure of the foreign affairs power as laid out in the Constitution has been
refined subsequently through legislation, executive order, and institutional practice, as well as through the attestations of the Founding Fa-

thers, the *Federalist Papers,* and the published exchanges of James Madison and Alexander Hamilton. The documentary evidence—the Constitution itself and the notes of the constitutional conventioneers—favors Congress's view that the president is limited to executing the war powers authorized by Congress, except for repelling attacks upon U.S. territory and making treaties and appointing ambassadors. (The latter two still require Senate approval.) But the historical evidence favors the president as the dominant, and sometimes exclusive, authority over foreign policy. This is due both to the practical necessity of having a single representative for the country in the world community and, until recent times, to Congress's general deferral to the president, save when he commits a blatant blunder.

But even 200 years of historical precedent and political convenience   46
cannot override the Constitution. Thus the words of Supreme Court Justice Robert Jackson in the 1952 steel seizure case *Youngstown Sheet and Tube* v. *Sawyer* ring equally true today to this constitutional logjam: "[P]artisan debate and scholarly speculation yields no net result but only supplies more or less apt quotations from respected sources on each side of any question."

A shared foreign affairs power does not on its own inhibit the   47
conduct of foreign policy; it merely requires that all such conduct be properly authorized by Congress. Many foreign-policy conflicts between the president and Congress have much less to do with the substance of the policies than with the procedure through which they are carried out. Congress's attempts to invoke the War Powers Resolution whenever a president engages U.S. troops in hostile situations have stirred more divisiveness between the two branches than the actual troop engagements. Even after U.S. ships came under attack in the Persian Gulf, Congress generally concurred that Reagan should continue to help protect the shipping lanes from attacks by Iraq and Iran. A major conflict arose, however, when he refused to report the incident in accordance with the War Powers Resolution.

Congress enacted the War Powers Resolution over President Rich-   48
ard Nixon's veto to reassert its exclusive constitutional responsibility to declare war. Many castigate the resolution as a knee-jerk reaction to the Vietnam War, during which Congress found itself unable to check the president's incremental escalation of involvement. Vietnam certainly sparked the resolution's genesis, but its substance grew from a much deeper source. Its drafters sought to rearticulate for the 20th century the relationship originally envisaged between Congress and the president in matters of war. They wanted to bring Congress back into the decision-making process while preserving the president's inherent powers to act in self-defense in true national emergencies and in protection of Amer-

ican citizens. As one of the resolution's cosponsors, then Senator William Hathaway (D.-Maine), stated at the time, "[it] is a bill to make clear to a future Executive that he is authorized by Congress to act in a situation of real emergency, but if he should try to move from that emergency situation into a nightmarish situation of war without the consent of Congress, not only will he have to abuse the Constitution; he will have to violate the mandate of law."

Ironically, the War Powers Resolution ended up relinquishing as much of Congress's war power as it sought to reclaim. The resolution is most remarkable for the flexibility it gives the president. In effect it is an advance 90-day declaration of war. It permits the president unilaterally to engage in war, or in any military activity short of war, anywhere in the world, for any reason at any time, for up to 90 days (60 days plus an additional 30 days to withdraw the troops). It requires only that whenever possible he consult with Congress prior to making such a move and that he report to Congress the reasons and legal authority for the action and its duration and scope. It does, of course, require that the president withdraw U.S. troops within 90 days if Congress has not passed a bill extending the authorization. 49

The claim that the 60–90-day withdrawal requirement constitutes an unconstitutional legislative veto is totally unfounded. The War Powers Resolution does, in fact, include a legislative veto: Section 5(c) requires the president to remove U.S. forces when "the Congress so directs by concurrent resolution." Such legislative vetoes were held to be void by the Supreme Court in the *Chadba* decision. But the 60–90-day requirement is a different matter. It is an affirmative, statutory authorization that is capped with a sunset provision similar to that found in many other laws, where Congress authorizes the president to perform a given action for a specified period subject to Congress's reauthorization when the time runs out. 50

Ninety days is plenty of time for the president to persuade Congress of the merits of his actions and for Congress to vote on them. Critics of the resolution claim that it actually foments hostilities by encouraging the adversary to refuse to settle the dispute in the hope that the troops will have to be withdrawn within 90 days. But such a withdrawal would happen only if a majority of Congress voted against the authorizing bill. The resolution itself provides expedited procedures to ensure that Congress will vote on the bill within 60 days after the president files his report. If a majority of Congress cannot come to an agreement with the president to continue the military involvement in "hostilities," then probably there is no consensus to continue the action. As the Congressional Report accompanying the resolution states, "Refusal to act affirmatively by the Congress within the specified time pe- 51 riod respecting emergency action to repel an attack could only indicate the most serious questions about the bona fides of the alleged attack or imminent threat of an attack." And if Congress does not support the president's use of force, then it is hardly fair to expect an adversary to accede to the president's demands either.

Moreover, an adversary does not need the War Powers Resolution   52
to play a wait-and-see game. Any unilateral action by the president invites a congressional challenge as soon as it becomes known. If Congress has serious objections to the operation, it is fully capable of undercutting the president through its normal legislative powers, without relying on the War Powers Resolution.

But it is inconceivable that Congress would fail to support any   53
reasonably prudent presidential action. The purpose of the resolution is to incorporate the congressional perspective into military policy. Certainly Congress might not accept the president's view at face value, especially since Congress's essential function is to formulate policy for the president to execute. As with the budget or other policy proposals initiated by the president, Congress will give due deference to the executive's desire while retaining the option to make modifications.

In almost every episode calling for the War Powers Resolution,   54
Congress has been fully prepared to sign on to the president's policy. In Lebanon, Grenada, and the Persian Gulf, Congress challenged the president only with respect to his refusal to recognize Congress's right to have some say in the process. Members voiced very little objection to the actual substance of those actions. Indeed, invoking the War Powers Resolution would very likely have brought more support to the president's actions than they already enjoyed, albeit probably with some greater clarity of purpose. It also would have provided an additional means for disengaging from the hostilities—at the behest of Congress—should that have been necessary.

The presidential refusal to abide by the War Powers Resolution   55
stems from a penchant within the executive branch to carry out policies free of outside scrutiny and opposition. Even after the engagement of troops reveals an administration's program, most presidents still would prefer to proceed unimpeded: hence the continued refusal to accept the resolution. But Congress can give the president a much needed "second opinion" before he proceeds with a risky operation. The decision to go to war demands the greatest reflection and deliberation from all perspectives. In the exclusive company of hand-picked advisers, the president is too easily insulated from views different from his own. The potential for making mistakes or abusing power increases when the number of alternative views declines.

Advance congressional approval would also legitimate military ac- 56
tions, whether overt or covert, to the outside world once an operation
actually had begun. Such a course would foster bipartisanship in foreign
policy, allowing the United States to present to allies and adversaries
alike a unified front committed to achieving its goals. And it would
further weaken any attempts by an adversary to defeat the president
through Congress.

Advance approval would also help to prevent the backlash from 57
Congress that inevitably follows a foreign-policy failure. Indeed, Congress's investigation of the Iran-*contra* affair focused extensively on the
Reagan administration's failure to keep Congress informed about the
arms sales to Iran, as was required under the intelligence oversight procedures in effect. (The president's violation of the ban on funding the
contras was a separate problem.) Had the appropriate members of Congress been informed, they would have had far less to complain about
once the operation was revealed. While Congress still may have voiced
strong objections to the operation on a variety of grounds (and perhaps
even dissuaded him from undertaking the operation at all), the president
at least would have satisfied the existing—though deficient—legal
requirements.

The drafters of the War Powers Resolution—at least those in the 58
Senate—originally intended that the law would prevent the president
from using force without congressional approval except in certain defined emergencies. The Senate bill in 1973 articulated only three exceptions under which a president could act unilaterally: to repel attacks
against U.S. territory, to repel attacks against U.S. armed forces located
outside U.S. territory, and to rescue American citizens. The Senate saw
these exceptions as the broadest interpretation of the framers' intent to
preserve for the president the inherent power to respond to sudden attacks on U.S. territory. As Madison noted, Congress's power was
changed from "to make war" to "to declare war" in order to leave "to
the Executive the power to repel sudden attacks."

The original Senate language seems the best vehicle for instituting 59
a prior-approval requirement on all uses of overt military force. It puts
the war power back where it belongs, in Congress, but leaves the president the necessary latitude to take immediate action to defend the United
States and its citizens. These same requirements also should apply to
covert paramilitary action—advance congressional approval except to
repel attack and rescue citizens. Indeed, all military action—whether
overt or covert, direct or indirect—should be treated on the same terms.
This article has discussed covert paramilitary action separately from overt
war powers because they have been treated as different entities for so

long and because they currently operate under different legal regimens. From a policy perspective, conceptually they need not be treated separately.

Even in situations where the president does not need advance   60
congressional approval he should consult in advance with a special leadership committee of Congress both to give notice of the operation and to get feedback about it. Consultation, in the words of Senator Byrd, means the "exploration of a consensus prior to a decision to commit U.S. forces in a situation." The president should also consult this committee about any definitionally ambiguous operation that could conceivably fall through the crack between war powers and covert action. Only when time is of the essence should the president carry out an action without at least consulting the leadership committee in advance. The new law will require prior notice of all covert operations. The 48-hour exception will apply only when time is critical and for no other reason. This is the standard as written in the proposed Intelligence Oversight Act of 1988.

Following the latest failure to apply the War Powers Resolution,   61
Congress began to take steps to establish a body that can perform the function that has been contemplated. In May 1988 Byrd, Nunn, Warner, and Mitchell introduced a bill to make the War Powers Resolution "more workable." Their bill would remove the 60–90-day automatic cutoff, which they view as tying the president's hands. They recognized that "presidents have refused to acknowledge the constitutionality of the statute." Presidents have also used this provision as an excuse for not complying with the reporting and consultation requirements.

Therefore, the bill would set up a "permanent consultative body"   62
of 6 persons—the majority and minority leaders of both houses, the Speaker of the House, and the president pro tempore of the Senate— whom the president would always have to consult before using force. In addition, the bill would create an expanded group of 18, consisting of the core 6 plus the chairman and the ranking minority members of the House and Senate armed services, foreign affairs, and intelligence committees. This group would join in consultation with the president and discuss among themselves an appropriate legislative response to the situation at hand.

An additional requirement should be added to the bill: that the   63
president must also discuss with the consultative body any contemplated covert paramilitary action or support and any other mission, such as hostage rescue or military assistance to allies engaged in a military conflict, that does not fall clearly into one category or another. Then the whole Congress should consider the action, unless it is one of the three

exceptions established in the original Senate version of the War Powers Resolution.

Taken together, these proposals would mark a significant turn away 64 from accepting the president's right to take the country into combat, overtly or covertly, without the participation of Congress or the public. They would strengthen not only America's democratic system but also its foreign policy.

Content Considerations

1. Halperin points out an aspect of American governance that has created discord between the executive and legislative branches regarding foreign policy. Discuss how the Constitution, in its delegation of powers, has made this conflict almost certain to happen.

2. Halperin lists throughout this essay various covert operations by the United States since World War II. What have been the results of such actions? Do they support the author's contention that covert actions either fail or else empower dictators "wholly inimical to American political values" (paragraph 20)?

3. How does Halperin build his case for eliminating covert operations?

The Declaration of Independence

One of the most famous documents in history is the colonies' defiant procla-
mation of independence and list of grievances against George III, King of
England. Thomas Jefferson, the well-born son of a Virginia planter, was only
33 when he wrote the Declaration for the Continental Congress. Jefferson, a
lawyer, used many sources for his masterpiece including Jean Jacques Rousseau
and John Locke.

The Declaration presents the political philosophy of the colonial elite of
Jefferson's day then concludes with a lengthy compilation of alleged abuses of
the American colonists by the English King. The language is majestic, but
also precise: When it says "all men" that is exactly what was meant. Some
have called this document a superb example of propaganda.

You have all read this many times. Please read it again, in the context
of a declaration of war. How would the Declaration have to be worded today?

In Congress, July 4, 1776
The unanimous Declaration of the thirteen united States of
America,

WHEN IN THE Course OF HUMAN EVENTS, it becomes necessary 1
for one people to dissolve the political bands which have connected them
with another, and to assume among the powers of the earth, the separate
and equal station to which the Laws of Nature and of Nature's God
entitle them, a decent respect to the opinions of mankind requires that
they should declare the causes which impel them to the separation.

We hold these truths to be self-evident, that all men are created 2
equal, that they are endowed by their Creator with certain unalienable
Rights, that among these are Life, Liberty and the pursuit of Happiness.
That to secure these rights, Governments are instituted among Men,
deriving their just powers from the consent of the governed. That
whenever any Form of Government becomes destructive of these ends,
it is the Right of the People to alter or to abolish it, and to institute a
new Government, laying its foundation on such principles, and organizing its powers in such form, as to them shall seem most likely to effect
their Safety and Happiness. Prudence, indeed, will dictate that Governments long established should not be changed for light and transient

causes; and accordingly all experience hath shewn, that mankind are more disposed to suffer, while evils are sufferable, than to right themselves by abolishing the forms to which they are accustomed. But when a long train of abuses and usurpations, pursuing invariably the same Object, evinces a design to reduce them under absolute Despotism, it is their right, it is their duty, to throw off such Government, and to provide new Guards for their future security. Such has been the patient sufferance of these Colonies; and such is now the necessity which constrains them to alter their former Systems of Government. The history of the present King of Great Britain is a history of repeated injuries and usurpations, all having in direct object the establishment of an absolute Tyranny over these States. To prove this, let Facts be submitted to a candid world:

He has refused his Assent to Laws, the most wholesome and necessary for the public good. 3

He has forbidden his Governors to pass Laws of immediate and pressing importance, unless suspended in their operation till his Assent should be obtained; and when so suspended, he has utterly neglected to attend to them. 4

He has refused to pass other Laws for the accommodation of large districts of people, unless those people would relinquish the right of Representation in the Legislature, a right inestimable to them and formidable to tyrants only. 5

He has called together legislative bodies at places unusual, uncomfortable, and distant from the depository of their public Records, for the sole purpose of fatiguing them into compliance with his measures. 6

He has dissolved Representative Houses repeatedly, for opposing with manly firmness his invasions on the rights of the people. 7

He has refused for a long time, after such dissolutions, to cause others to be elected; whereby the Legislative powers, incapable of Annihilation, have returned to the People at large for their exercise; the State remaining in the mean time exposed to all the dangers of invasion from without, and convulsions within. 8

He has endeavoured to prevent the population of these States; for that purpose obstructing the Laws for Naturalization of Foreigners; refusing to pass others to encourage their migrations hither, and raising the conditions of new Appropriations of Lands. 9

He has obstructed the Administration of Justice, by refusing his Assent to Laws for establishing Judiciary powers. 10

He has made Judges dependent on his Will alone, for the tenure of their offices, and the amount and payment of their salaries. 11

He has erected a multitude of New Offices, and sent hither swarms of Officers to harass our people, and eat out their substance. 12

He has kept among us, in times of peace, Standing Armies, with- 13
out the Consent of our legislatures.

He has affected to render the Military independent of and superior 14
to the Civil power.

He has combined with others to subject us to a jurisdiction foreign 15
to our constitution, and unacknowledged by our laws; giving his Assent
to their Acts of pretended Legislation:

> For quartering large bodies of armed troops among us:

> For protecting them, by a mock Trial, from punishment for any
> Murders which they should commit on the Inhabitants of these
> States:

> For cutting off our Trade with all parts of the world:

> For imposing Taxes on us without our Consent:

> For depriving us in many cases of the benefits of Trial by Jury:

> For transporting us beyond Seas to be tried for pretended offences:

> For abolishing the free System of English Laws in a neighboring
> Province, establishing therein an Arbitrary government, and en-
> larging its Boundaries so as to render it at once an example and
> fit instrument for introducing the same absolute rule into these
> Colonies:

> For taking away our Charters, abolishing our most valuable Laws
> and altering fundamentally the Forms of our Governments:

> For suspending our own Legislatures, and declaring themselves
> invested with power to legislate for us in all cases whatsoever.

He has abdicated Government here by declaring us out of his Pro- 16
tection and waging War against us.

He has plundered our seas, ravaged our Coasts, burnt our towns, 17
and destroyed the lives of our people.

He is at this time transporting large Armies of foreign Mercenaries 18
to compleat the works of death, desolation and tyranny, already begun
with circumstances of Cruelty & perfidy scarcely paralleled in the most
barbarous ages, and totally unworthy the Head of a civilized nation.

He has constrained our fellow Citizens taken Captive on the high 19
Seas to bear Arms against their Country, to become the executioners of
their friends and Brethren, or to fall themselves by their Hands.

He has excited domestic insurrections amongst us, and has endea- 20
voured to bring on the inhabitants of our frontiers, the merciless Indian
Savages, whose known rule of warfare is an undistinguished destruction
of all ages, sexes and conditions.

In every stage of these Oppressions We have Petitioned for Redress 21 in the most humble terms. Our repeated Petitions have been answered only by repeated injury. A Prince, whose character is thus marked by every act which may define a Tyrant, is unfit to be the ruler of a free people.

Nor have We been wanting in attentions to our British brethren. 22 We have warned them from time to time of attempts by their legislature to extend an unwarrantable jurisdiction over us. We have reminded them of the circumstances of our emigration and settlement here. We have appealed to their native justice and magnanimity, and we have conjured them by the ties of our common kindred to disavow these usurpations, which would inevitably interrupt our connections and correspondence. They too have been deaf to the voice of justice and of consanguinity. We must, therefore, acquiesce in the necessity, which denounces our Separation, and hold them, as we hold the rest of mankind, Enemies in War, in Peace Friends.

WE THEREFORE the Representatives of the UNITED STATES OF 23 AMERICA, in General Congress, Assembled, appealing to the Supreme Judge of the world for the rectitude of our intentions, do, in the Name and by Authority of the good People of these Colonies, solemnly publish and declare, That these United Colonies are and of Right ought to be FREE AND INDEPENDENT STATES; that they are Absolved from all Allegiance to the British Crown, and that all political connection between them and the State of Great Britain, is and ought to be totally dissolved; and that as FREE AND INDEPENDENT STATES, they have full Power to levy War, conclude Peace, contract Alliances, establish Commerce, and to do all other Acts and Things which INDEPENDENT states may of right do. AND for the support of this Declaration, with a firm reliance on the protection of divine Providence, we mutually pledge to each other our Lives, our Fortunes and our sacred Honor.

Content Considerations

1. The Declaration of Independence amounted to a declaration of war. In what ways does Jefferson assure that the American colonies are viewed in the most favorable light?
2. Consider the organization of Jefferson's document. How does the arrangement of the sections contribute to its effectiveness?
3. What might have been the King's reply to this document had he written one?

How Presidents Take the Nation Into War

Although the Constitution gives Congress the power to declare war, it is usually the president as Commander-in-Chief of the armed forces who ultimately decides whether to commit troops to combat or place them in hazardous areas. The reasons for their doing so are many, according to journalist and historian Barbara Kellerman. Writing in the January 20, 1991, New York Times, *she avows that the personality of the president is as much a factor in decisions of war as the issues themselves.*

In 1973, Congress adopted the War Powers Resolution, which sought to limit presidential power in matters of war. The resolution limits to 60 days the time for which the chief executive may commit troops to potential or actual combat; the president must seek approval from Congress to order troops to remain longer.

Consider the personalities of various individuals, including politicians, and reflect on what their response to a perceived threat might be if they were president. Why do you think Congress enacted the War Powers Resolution?

IN THE EARLY DAYS of the Republic, George Washington declared 1 that "it is our own true policy to steer clear of permanent alliances with any portion of the foreign world." However, since the Presidency of Woodrow Wilson, the United States has frankly abandoned its professed proclivity for isolationism.

America's attempt to make the world safe for democracy by en- 2 tering the Great War paved the way for what at least since the Second World War has been the role Americans have frequently played: world policeman. As a consequence, while Americans still cherish the notion that they are a peace-loving people, the fact is that the United States is quite often at war.

For all the recurrent wrangling about whether it is the executive 3 or the legislature that has the power to decide to fight, in modern American history it has been the President who has assumed nearly total responsibility for determining the nation's role in world affairs.

Executive decisions to enter into combat inevitably invoke a na- 4 tional ideology shaped by the belief that the United States is different from, and even superior to, the other nations of the world. Americans have considered it their mission to spread—usually by example but sometimes by direct intervention—freedom and justice around the world. There is no overestimating this essentially moral imperative: It provided the underpinning for decisions by at least three of the last ten presidents to engage in military adventures, and by four others to lead America into major wars.

It was John F. Kennedy who was responsible for escalating, over two years, the number of military personnel in South Vietnam from 948 to 16,000. It was Richard M. Nixon who decided, without the knowledge of Congress or the American people, to expand the Vietnam War into Laos and Cambodia. And when Ronald Reagan decided to send soldiers and marines to Grenada, he did no more than notify Congress once the invasion was under way.

In the last 50 years, four other Presidents have committed the American people to all-out war: Franklin D. Roosevelt, Harry S. Truman, Lyndon B. Johnson and now George Bush. How does the Commander in Chief determine that the benefits of combat are likely to outweigh the cost in young lives? The virtue of the mission is a necessary precondition. But it does not fully explain how Presidents decide to put others at risk—particularly when the number of casualties is likely to be high. While the immediate circumstances were very different, in each case a few key elements explain the President's decision to fight.

The individual. Like everyone, Presidents make decisions based on who they are. Life history matters: Lyndon Johnson was the first Congressman to enlist in the armed forces, one day after Pearl Harbor, and George Bush was the youngest pilot in the United States Navy. World view matters: When America was still reluctant to drink of "the hell broth that is brewing in Europe" (Hemingway's phrase), Franklin Roosevelt declared that "the world has grown so small and weapons of attack so swift, that no nation can be safe." President Truman, a voracious reader of history, believed that a threat demanded a strong response, swiftly executed: he "was not brought up to run from a fight," he liked to say. Skills, capacities and interests also matter, as do deep-seated motives, impulses, and values.

The event. Presidents go to war in response to an event or series of events that seems to them to threaten world order in general, and American interests in particular. War engulfs Europe and later Pearl Harbor is attacked: North Korea invades South Korea; the destroyer Maddox is fired on by North Vietnamese torpedo boats in the Gulf of Tonkin; Iraq seizes oil-rich Kuwait as its "19th province." Since Mun-

ich, such marker events inevitably elicit from Presidents a powerful impulse to avoid appeasement. As President Truman puts it, "If we are
tough enough now there won't have to be any next step."

The enemy. The fiend, the "other," is identified and labeled, and   9
becomes in time an object to be obliterated at all costs. Nazis, Hitler,
swastika; Commies, Stalin, hammer and sickle; Red China, North Ko-
reans, Viet Cong; and recently a new nemesis, the swaggering, suddenly
familiar figure of Saddam Hussein. Presidents become persuaded that
their antagonists are genuinely evil, and thereby justify the violence of
their campaign against them to the American people.

The environment. Presidents operate in domestic and international   10
contexts that may or may not favor strong Presidential action. President
Bush, in cobbling together the international coalition against Iraq, benefited mightily from the enormously improved relations between the
United States and the Soviet Union.

Moreover, once the war option is on the table, there are other
major players, domestic and foreign, with whom Presidents, lacking the
authority of kings, have to contend. Well into 1941, Franklin Roosevelt
had to reckon not only with isolationists in Congress, but also with pro-
Nazis like Father Coughlin and Socialists like Norman Thomas. And
Lyndon Johnson's escalation in Vietnam was undermined by domestic
protests almost from the start.

Of course, the environment contains friendly voices too. F.D.R.'s   12
special relationship with Winston Churchill spurred the President into
action before America's declaration of war. "The voice and force of the
United States may count for nothing if they are withheld too long,"
wrote the Prime Minister to the President in 1940. (Fifty years later
another Prime Minister whispered virtually the same words into the ear
of another President.) For their part, Presidents Truman and Bush sought,
and received, cover and support for their own hawkish impulses from
both Congress and the United Nations.

The decision-making process. Once the precipitating event takes   13
place a machinery is established to fashion a response. A small decision-
making group is called together, comprising the President's most trusted
advisors; the group that makes initial recommendations tends to play a
key role for the duration. When Japan attacked Pearl Harbor, Franklin
Roosevelt brought his Cabinet in for consultation; they were soon joined
by 10 members of Congress. The group decided that the President would
go before Congress the next day and ask for a formal declaration of
war. When North Korea invaded South Korea, Harry Truman promptly
summoned the nation's top military and diplomatic leadership. Over
dinner, they agreed on a firm stand to help Korea. Lyndon Johnson's
gradual escalation in Vietnam was decided on by about eight top Gov-

ernment officials whose work, despite some changes in memberships, was more or less continuous. The men, who met at noon on Tuesdays, called themselves the Tuesday lunch group or the Tuesday cabinet. And since August 2, President Bush has been at the center of a very small decision-making group that includes James A. Baker 3d, Dick Cheney, Brent Scowcroft and Gen. Colin L. Powell.

Given who George Bush is; given Iraq's invasion of Kuwait and [14] the demonization of Saddam Hussein; given the high degree of Soviet-American cooperation during the Gulf crisis and the apparently unanimous support from his advisors for the decision to fight, it comes finally as no surprise that last week the Commander in Chief ordered the start of warfare in Iraq and Kuwait. Along with one of his heroes, Henry Stimson, George Bush has always believed that by the end of the Roosevelt era the United States could never again be "an island to herself."

Content Considerations

1. Summarize the reasons that Kellerman gives for Presidential decisions to commit troops to combat.
2. How does the American system of going to war contribute to the ease of committing troops to combat?
3. Describe your own "world view," and write how it would affect any decision regarding war if you were President. What events in your life have shaped your world view?

Unlocking the Promise of Freedom

U.S. and U.N. coalition forces walked over the Iraqi army in four days of ground war in the Persian Gulf war, and within weeks contingents of U.S. troops were headed home. Parades, speeches, and tearful hugs awaited them; celebrations abounded, which many saw as somehow linked to the lack of recognition given Vietnam veterans. Later, many questions would arise about what had been accomplished in the war with Iraq, but the earliest welcome home ceremonies were euphoric paeans to the valor and ability of U.S. troops.

George Bush delivered the following speech on April 13, 1991, at Maxwell Air Force Base in Alabama to returning Air Force men and women. Here he not only paid the usual homage to the coalition forces but also articulated his vision for the future and the role the United States would have in its formation.

Before reading this, write down what you know about the "New World Order," a phrase that was repeated often during the Gulf war.

THANK YOU ALL very, very much for that warm welcome. General Boyd and General McPeak, the distinguished members of the Congress with us—Senators Heflin, Shelby, and Bill Dickinson. Mayor Folmar, a nonpartisan event, but I'm glad to see some friends of long-standing over here, who were enormously helpful to me in getting to be President of the United States. 1

It is my great pleasure to look out across what essentially is a sea of blue, to meet this morning with the men and women of the Air University—the Air War College, the Air Command and Staff School, the Squadron Officers School, and of course, the NCO Academy. And I'm glad to see democracy in action, I see a Navy guy here or there, or maybe a Coast Guardsman, maybe the Marines, maybe the Army over here. And I think I recognize some friends from overseas, members of our coalition who helped us so much in achieving our objectives halfway around the world. They're more than welcome. 2

The history of aviation has been shaped here since the Wright brothers brought their strange new mechanical bird to Montgomery, and housed it in a hangar not far from where we stand. This institution from its early days as the Air Corps Tactical School has defined the 3 nation's air strategy and tactics that have guided our operations over the fields of Europe and the seas of the Pacific, from the first World War to the thousand hours of Desert Storm.

It falls to all of you to derive the lessons learned from this war. ⁴ Desert Storm demonstrated the true strength of joint operations. Not the notion that each service must participate in equal parts in every operation in every war, but that we use the proper tools at the proper time. In Desert Storm, a critical tool was certainly air power. And every one of you can take pride in that fact. Our technology and training ensured minimal losses, and our precision, your precision, spared the lives of innocent civilians.

But our victory also showed that technology alone is insufficient. ⁵ A warrior's heart must burn with the will to fight. And if he fights but does not believe, no technology in the world can save him. We and our allies had more than superior weapons; we had the will to win.

I might say parenthetically, this will is personified by the man who ⁶ leads you. I know that General Boyd often speaks about what he calls the unlimited liability of the military profession. He knows because he's put it all on the line. As a veteran of Vietnam, he flew 105 combat missions before being shot down over Hanoi. And he spent almost seven years, 2,500 cruel days, in captivity. And yet he emerged brave, unbroken. He kept the faith to himself and to his nation.

And let me just say a word about this man over here on my left, ⁷ General McPeak. I remember early on a meeting up at Camp David with Tony McPeak. Secretary Cheney was there; General Powell was there; Brent Scowcroft, other chiefs. The other chiefs, I believe, were with us, Tony. And in a very laid-back way, typical of him with his modesty, but with total confidence, he told me exactly what he felt air power could do. And after he left, I don't mean to show my native skepticism, but I turned to my trusted National Security Advisor, who's standing over here, General Brent Scowcroft, and I said,

"Brent, does this guy really know what he's talking about?"

And Lieutenant General Scowcroft—Air Force Lieutenant General, ⁸ said,

"Yes."

And General McPeak did. ⁹

And to be doubly sure then, and he'll remember this, just before ¹⁰ the war started, I invited General McPeak and Secretary Cheney to join me and General Scowcroft upstairs at the residence in the White House— quiet lunch there. And I asked Tony, I think he'd come back then from the theater, the other theater. And I put the question to him, I think this is exactly what I said,

"Are you as certain now as you were up at Camp David?"

And he said,

"Even more so."

And the war started just a few days later, and history will record that General McPeak was 100 percent right, right on target.

Here at Air University it's your business to read the lessons of the past with an eye on the far horizon. And that's why I wanted to speak to you today about the new world taking shape around us, about the prospects for a new world order now within our reach. For more than four decades we've lived in a world divided, East from West; a world locked in a conflict of arms and ideas called the Cold War. Two systems, two superpowers, separated by mistrust and unremitting hostility.

For more than four decades, America's energies were focused on containing the threat to the free world from the forces of communism. That war is over. East Germany has vanished from the map as a separate entity. Today in Berlin, the wall that once divided a continent, divided a world in two, has been pulverized, turned into souvenirs. And the sections that remain standing are but museum pieces. The Warsaw Pact passed into the pages of history last week. Not with a bang, but with a whimper, its demise reported in a story reported on page A16 of *The Washington Post.*

In the coming weeks I'll be talking in some detail about the possibility of a new world order emerging after the Cold War. And in recent weeks, I've been focusing not only on the Gulf, but on free trade, on the North American Free Trade Agreement, the Uruguay Round trade negotiations, and the essentiality of obtaining from the United States Congress a renewal of Fast-Track authority to achieve our goals. But today I want to discuss another aspect of that order, our relations with Europe and the Soviet Union.

Twice this century, a dream born on the battlefields of Europe died after the shooting stopped. The dream of a world in which major powers worked together to ensure peace; to settle their disputes through cooperation, not confrontation. Today a transformed Europe stands closer than ever before to its free and democratic destiny. At long last, Europe is moving forward, moving toward a new world of hope.

At the same time, we and our European allies have moved beyond containment to a policy of active engagement in a world no longer driven by Cold War tensions and animosities. You see, as the Cold War drew to an end we saw the possibilities of a new order in which nations worked together to promote peace and prosperity. I'm not talking here of a blueprint that will govern the conduct of nations or some supernatural structure or institution. The new world order does not mean surrendering our national sovereignty or forfeiting our interests. It really describes a responsibility imposed by our successes. It refers to new ways of working with other nations to deter aggression and to achieve stability, to achieve prosperity and, above all, to achieve peace.

It springs from hopes for a world based on a shared commitment among nations large and small, to a set of principles that undergird our relations. Peaceful settlements of disputes, solidarity against aggression, reduced and controlled arsenals, and just treatment of all peoples. 18

This order, this ability to work together got its first real test in the Gulf war. For the first time, a regional conflict, the aggression against Kuwait, did not serve as a proxy for superpower confrontation. For the first time, the United Nations Security Council, free from the clash of Cold War ideologies, functioned as its designers intended, a force for conflict resolution in collective security. 19

In the Gulf, nations from Europe and North America, Asia and Africa and the Arab world joined together to stop aggression, and sent a signal to would-be tyrants everywhere in the world. By joining forces to defend one small nation, we showed that we can work together against aggressors in defense of principle. 20

We also recognized that the Cold War's end didn't deliver us into an era of perpetual peace. As old threats recede, new threats emerge. The quest for the new world order is, in part, a challenge to keep the dangers of disorder at bay. 21

Today, thank God, Kuwait is free. But turmoil in that tormented region of the world continues. Saddam's continued savagery has placed his regime outside the international order. We will not interfere in Iraq's civil war. Iraqi people must decide their own political future. 22

Looking out here at you and thinking of your families, let me comment a little further. We set our objectives. These objectives, sanctioned by international law, have been achieved. I made very clear that when our objectives were obtained that our troops would be coming home. And, yes, we want the suffering of those refugees to stop, and in keeping with our nation's compassion and concern, we are massively helping. But, yes, I want our troops out of Iraq and back home as soon as possible. 23

Internal conflicts have been raging in Iraq for many years. And we're helping out and we're going to continue to help these refugees. But I do not want one single soldier or airman shoved into a civil war in Iraq that's been going on for ages. And I'm not going to have that. 24

I know the coalition's historic effort destroyed Saddam's ability to undertake aggression against any neighbor. You did that job. But now the international community will further guarantee that Saddam's ability to threaten his neighbors is completely eliminated by destroying Iraq's weapons of mass destruction. 25

And as I just mentioned, we will continue to help the Iraqi refu- 26

gees, the hundreds and thousands of victims of this man's, Saddam
Hussein's, brutality. See food and shelter and safety and the opportunity
to return unharmed to their homes. We will not tolerate any interference
in this massive international relief effort. Iraq can return to the community of nations only when its leaders abandon the brutality and
repression that is destroying their country. With Saddam in power, Iraq
will remain a pariah nation, its people denied moral contacts with most
of the outside world.

We must build on the successes of Desert Storm to give new shape　27
and momentum to this new world order, to use force wisely and extend
the hand of compassion wherever we can. Today we welcome Europe's
willingness to shoulder a large share of this responsibility. This new
sense of responsibility on the part of our European allies is most evident
and most critical in Europe's eastern half.

The nations of Eastern Europe, for so long the other Europe, must　28
take their place now alongside their neighbors to the west. Just as we've
overcome Europe's political division, we must help to ease crossover
from poverty into prosperity.

The United States will do its part, we always have. As we have　29
already in reducing Poland's official debt burden to the United States
by 70 percent; increasing our assistance this year to Eastern Europe by
50 percent. But the key, the key to helping these new democracies develop is trade and investment.

The new entrepreneurs of Czechoslovakia and Poland and Hun-　30
gary aren't looking to government, their own or others, to shower them
with riches. They're looking for new opportunities, a new freedom for
the productive genius strangled by 40 years of state control.

Yesterday, my esteemed friend, a man we all honor and salute,　31
President Vaclav Havel of Czechoslovakia called me up. He wanted to
request advice and help from the West. He faces enormous problems.
You see, Czechoslovakia wants to be democratic. This man is leading
them toward perfecting their fledgling democracy. Its economy is moving from a failed socialist model to a market economy.

We all must help. It's not easy to convert state-owned and operated　32
weapons plants into market-driven plants to produce consumer goods.
But these new democracies can do just exactly that with the proper
advice and help from the West. It is in our interest, it is in the interest
of the United States of America, that Czechoslovakia, Poland, and Hungary strengthen those fledgling democracies and strengthen their fledgling market economies.

We recognize that new roles and even new institutions are natural　33
outgrowths of the new Europe. Whether it's the European Community
or a broadened mandate for the CSCE, the U.S. supports all efforts to

forge a European approach to common challenges on the continent and in the world beyond, with the understanding that Europe's long-term security is intertwined with America's, and that NATO remains the best means to assure it.

And we look to Europe to act as a force for stability outside its 34 own borders. In a world as interdependent as ours, no industrialized nation can maintain membership in good standing in the global community without assuming its fair share of responsibility for peace and security.

But even in the face of such welcome change, Americans will re- 35 main in Europe in support of history's most successful alliance, NATO. America's commitment is the best guarantee of a secure Europe, and a secure Europe is vital to American interests and vital to world peace. This is the essential logic of the Atlantic Alliance which anchors America in Europe.

This century's history shows that America's destiny and interests 36 cannot be separate from Europe's. Through the long years of Cold War and conflict, the United States stood fast for freedom in Europe. And now, as Eastern Europe is opening up to democratic ideas, true progress becomes possible.

The Soviet Union is engaged in its own dramatic transformation. 37 The policies of confrontation abroad, like the discredited dogma of communism from which those policies sprang, lies dormant, if not mortally wounded. Much has changed. The path of international cooperation fostered by President Gorbachev and manifested most clearly in the Persian Gulf marks a radical change in Soviet behavior. And yet, the course of change within the Soviet Union is far less clear.

Economic and political reform there is under severe challenge. So- 38 viet citizens, facing the collapse of the old order while the new still struggles to be born, confront desperate economic conditions; their hard-won freedoms in peril. Ancient ethnic enmities, conflict between republics and between republics and the central government add to these monumental challenges that they face.

America's policy toward the Soviet Union in these troubled times 39 is, first and foremost, to continue our efforts to build the cooperative relationship that has allowed our nations and so many others to strengthen international peace and stability. At the same time, we will continue to support a reform process within the Soviet Union aimed at political and economic freedom. A process we believe must be built on peaceful dialogue and negotiation. This is a policy that we will advocate steadfastly, both in our discussions with the central Soviet government and with all elements active in Soviet political life.

Let there be no misunderstanding, the path ahead for the Soviet 40

Union will be difficult and, at times, extraordinarily painful. History weighs heavily on all the peoples of the U.S.S.R., liberation from 70 years of communism, from a thousand years of autocracy. It's going to be slow. There will be setbacks. But this process of reform, this transformation from within must proceed. If external cooperation and our progress toward true international peace is to endure, it must succeed. Only when this transformation is complete will we be able to take full measure of the opportunities presented by this new and evolving world order.

The new world order really is a tool for addressing a new world   41
of possibilities. This order gains its mission and shape not just from shared interests, but from shared ideals. And the ideals that have spawned new freedoms throughout the world have received their boldest and clearest expression in our great country the United States. Never before has the world looked more to the American example. Never before have so many millions drawn hope from the American idea. And the reason is simple: Unlike any other nation in the world, as Americans, we enjoy profound and mysterious bonds of affection and idealism. We feel our deep connections to community, to families, to our faiths.

But what defines this nation? What makes us America is not our   42
ties to a piece of territory or bonds of blood; what makes us American is our allegiance to an idea that all people everywhere must be free. This idea is as old and enduring as this nation itself, as deeply rooted, and what we are as a promise implicit to all the world in the words of our own Declaration of Independence.

The new world facing us, and I wish I were your age, it's a won-   43
derful world of discovery. A world devoted to unlocking the promise of freedom. It's no more structured than a dream; no more regimented than an innovator's burst of inspiration. If we trust ourselves and our values; if we retain the pioneer's enthusiasm for exploring the world beyond our shores; if we strive to engage in the world that beckons us, then and only then, will America be true to all that is best in us.

May God bless our great nation, the United States of America.   44
And thank you all for what you have done for freedom and for our fundamental values. Thank you very much.

Content Considerations

1. President Bush addressed an audience that was overwhelmingly military. How did that fact affect the tone of his speech?
2. With very few exceptions, Presidential speeches are not long remembered. Is there anything about this address that makes you believe it will live alongside Lincoln's Gettysburg Address?

3. Summarize Bush's vision of a "New World Order." List those items that you believe are attainable. Is such a vision possible without future wars?

The Justness of the Iraqi Position

All wars, of course, have two sides, and in the Persian Gulf war the Iraqis claimed to be in the right. Every nation in a war is able to justify its position, sanctify its actions; many often invoke prayers and other religious rites. Leaders of nations usually refer in glowing terms to the courage of its soldiers, and to the glorious cause for which the war is being fought.

Saddam Hussein, who for many Americans was the embodiment of evil—"another Hitler" in George Bush's words—was no exception to invoking the favor of God, singing the praises of his troops, and stressing the justness of Iraq's position. The following was a radio address to the Iraqi people delivered on Baghdad Radio on February 21, 1991, just a few days before the start of the ground war.

Before you read this, write an outline of what you would expect the leader of a nation at war to say to his people.

O GREAT PEOPLE; O stalwart men in our valiant armed forces; O 1
faithful, honest Muslims, wherever you may be; O people wherever faith in God has found its way to your hearts, and wherever it found what embodies it in the sincerity of your intentions and deeds; O lovers of humanity, virtue, and fairness, who reject aggressiveness, injustice, and unfairness. In difficult circumstances and their events, some people, more often than not, lose the connection with the beginning and preoccupy themselves with the results, or forget, when there are resemblances, the connection between any result and the reasons that gave rise to those events, and on whose basis those results were based.

Furthermore, in difficult circumstances, which difficulty is hard to 2
describe, the mind and consciousness are generally preoccupied with what influences the life of the individual concerned with that circumstance. Thus, he bases his opinion and position on it without connecting every individual case with what is collective. The future is even absent at times, or not given very great importance as an indispensable weight for assessing the [inaudible] of each case, regardless of whether that case, or individual item that is being assessed, is connected to the past and present or to the reasons and beginnings, or whether it is part of the results; and regardless of whether it was part of the simple results and individual items, with limited effect, or of the major results that have a

comprehensive effect that go beyond the individual, a number of individuals, or only a specific sector in the society, to the society as a whole and where it goes beyond the transient and quick moving present to the future as a whole.

Some have either completely forgotten those influential facts in the   3
life of man, whether in this or that direction, or the presence of these facts in their minds has become weak. Many facts between causes and effects, or between the prelude to and the results of the circumstances and events that preceded 2 August and what took place on 2 August and afterward, have been missed.

This description was in most cases applicable to some Arabs and   4
to many foreigners so that some of them could not remember what Zionism and U.S. imperialism have done against Iraq, beginning with the Irangate plot or the Iran–Contra scandal in 1986 until the first months of 1990, when the plot against Iraq reached its dangerous phases when U.S. and Western media began to prepare for the Israeli aggression against us, but which we confronted in the statement of 8 April 1990; when the Americans cut off bread from Iraq and canceled the grain deal concluded with U.S. companies in the third month of the same year, that is 1990; and when they raised the slogan of an economic, technologic, and scientific boycott of Iraq and worked to make Europe and Japan do the same.

We know that recalling the preludes and causes leading up to the   5
results, and recalling the grounds for an event or events in a permanent manner and in all [inaudible] is not an easy undertaking. This is because doing so requires a high degree of awareness, or because this requires a vital connection between those recalling the backgrounds and preludes to these events, and the kind of immediate and long-term suffering produced by their causes and effects.

Those whom we describe as forgetful or being unaware of the   6
connection between a given cause and a given effect do not all enjoy the same degree of awareness that provides the elements of [inaudible] what is required. Most of them have not suffered the causes and effects of the circumstances, especially in the world arena. Therefore, we have faced serious difficulties in making them understand that what happened on 2 August, despite the clarity of the entirely just historic dimension, is basically not a cause within the course of the conflict between Iraq, as a bastion of faith and honorable aspiration, and Zionism and U.S. imperialism. The events of that day are one aspect of the results of the battle or the conflict that preceded 2 August. The measure taken on the glorious day of the call is a means of self-defense, and one aimed at defending all honorable principles and values of Iraq. Although [inaudible] an offensive form, an account of the events of this day should not be

taken out from the general context of developments. A correct account of this requires that it be placed within its comprehensive framework.

The failure of some world circles, especially among politicians who   7
are [inaudible] against the Arabs [inaudible] to understand has been boosted by the fact that, regardless of the details, the objective of these circles is to harm Iraq's accomplishments.

Some tyrannical Arab rulers, who betrayed the nation's principles   8
and aspirations of their peoples, cooperated with and stooped to this tendency. They accepted degradation and humiliation, even inside the palaces and seats of their rule. They chose the path of obeying the tendentious foreigner and his evil, hostile intentions.

This flood of media campaigns officially conducted against us by   9
30 countries further complicated the prospect of establishing a link between causes and effects, and between what happened to the Arabs and to the Iraqis prior to 2 August, what happened on the day of the call to glory, and what happened after 2 August. All the accumulated extensions and influences of these countries accompany these campaigns, and are affected by them. Nevertheless, the noble person has remained noble, and is guided by the facts, not merely through what he sees and hears, but through that which his heart and his faithful empathy with jihad and his destiny with the Iraqi stance lead him.

This is the stance of the people in this nation. What has guided   10
them in this direction has been their long suffering at the hands of the ranks of injustice, the unjust, and the Arab rulers who are their allies and who betrayed the nation and sold out honor and religion to the foreigner. Some of those rulers chose this course as an indispensable path to assuming their places on the seat of power, and undeservedly impose themselves on their people. It was the advance price for their agentry. Other rulers stooped to this after they discovered that there was no other way to keep the seat of power, taking into account the nature of rule they have chosen, except by complying with the will of the U.S. intelligence services. This applies without exception to the Arab rulers who are siding with the United States today and supplying its aggression under the Arab cover and with funds it needs, and with the false and fraudulent talk of Arab ability. Evil is what they are doing.

Traitor Fahd, the betrayer of the two mosques, and lightheaded   11
Hosni, the ruler with which noble Arab Egypt has been afflicted, stand at the head of the list. Faced with this state of affairs, we found that the enemy media and the enemy policy dropped a heavy screen on every event, stand, or cause that preceded 2 August 1990 that could shed some light on these incidents and explain their true nature. Palestine, whose just cause dates back more than 40 years, as well as its future and the positions on it has been one of the most important pillars of the con-

spiracy in which the oil rulers have participated as conspirators against Iraq, led by the agent sheiks of Kuwait and the Saudi rulers.

Biased people have even tried to neglect the fate of Palestine as being one of the causes of these events. The tendentious media, which have widespread influence and impact, and the suspect politicians and those who seek personal objectives, backed by Zionism everywhere, began to focus on the 2 August events to depict them as having taken place without any basis or background and as though our attention were being devoted only to these events. They even issued orders to silence voices and prevent them from mentioning any historical background that would explain to the foreigner or the Arab what he does not know about the reality of the relationship that exists between Kuwait and Iraq, and that Kuwait is part of Iraq, but was annexed following the partitioning conspiracy to weaken the Arab nation, harm its status and role, and weaken every Arab country that has some kind of leverage. 12

In view of this deluge of the falsification of facts, and of this large number of countries participating in the aggression, or those who have been confused about the real reasons for the results, it is insufficient to respond and clarify through media and political statements alone, in view of our modest influence. Measures and actions are inevitable in order to place the innocent, who do not know the [inaudible] before a rational debate that bypasses the smokescreens and misinformation launched by hostile information media. 13

Something must be done to place the enemies in an embarrassing situation or in an impasse, something that will drive them to behavior and positions that will make those who have been anesthetized by hostile media wake up to new facts or new [inaudible] that will reveal to them the facts, free from covers, so that they can appear as they are: crystal clear. Thus came the 15 February initiative, which the Revolution Command Council statement fired at the enemy goal, to use the terms of sports and athletics, so as to shake the nets of the enemy court. 14

Either an acceptance that pleases friends, or rejection that annoys the enemies. This may divide their ranks, which are founded on rancor and rallied around wrong. Certain people who have been misled will discover what will help them to realize that what has happened, and the root of what has happened, was not caused by 2 August and what followed. What preceded 2 August does not go back to 1990, its events, and circumstances alone, but goes back to every iota of dignity and pride, faith and tenacity toward right, rejection of the wrong, and hostility to criminal usurper Zionism, support for the poor, and the fight against injustice and corruption. These stands are the qualities of Iraqis or what has been revived in them by the revolutionary leadership. 15

The rancor against Iraq has been created over time. With every 16 aspect of capability added to it or created, to become a serious pillar of its characteristics and potential, with steadfastness in the face of its characteristics and potential, with steadfastness in the face of the aggression exposing the weakness of some of the Arabs vis-à-vis the aggression of Zionism and the ambitions of the Americans, with every book that has been written with the sweat in support of the blood of struggle, with every effort and every stage of building in Iraq's lofty edifice with every floor in the building of its new civilization or a wheel in every factory or plant which has been built as a symbol of loftiness and as an introduction to a new happy and prosperous life under firm faith in God, the homeland, and the nation, and with the slogan of the poor have a right in the wealth of the rich, because they are members of the same people or members of the same nation, and all of them are the sons of Adam and Eve.

To those who ask about the rancor of Hosni and others like him   17
toward the leadership and people of Iraq, and to those who were alarmed by this rancor harbored by those who ate and drank under Iraqi hospitality and were given attention which they do not deserve: We say that we do not regret the hospitality and good intentions accorded by us or the people of Iraq toward people whom we wanted, at the time, to be brothers of the Iraqis, when they stood in the ranks of the faithful, with noble convictions, and honorable intentions. But since they have committed treason, no one will feel sorry for them. May God's curse be upon them until the day of judgment. We say that these misled people have derived their rancor against you, O Iraqis, and against your leadership, from the attributes which you possess and which have characterized your leadership. These misled people have apparently found in every call for honor and purity of intention, and in every call stating that the ruler or leader should be part of his people, an insult aimed against him personally by the people of Iraq and its leadership.

Each placard you raised when you went out to receive them, those   18
who rejected the Zionist scheme and U.S. imperialism and denounced their agents, was viewed by them as a placard directed against them. Each word said about the importance of the fairness of the ruler or leader, and about his lightweight guilt when the money he carries is lightweight, was considered a personal attack against them. Each denunciation of weakness, submissiveness, and the acceptance of humiliation was an insult to them.

Yes, noble mujahedeen sons in Iraq: That group of Arabs, and   19
maybe other rulers, and even some foreigners, have found that every positive feature in you and your structure reflects, in a shining mirror, their shortcomings and defects before the people and the nation. Each call for power, invincibility, faith, capability, nobility, pride, dignity,

courage, liberation from the foreigner, abstinence, and the liberation of the soul from the ill-gotten money; and each attempt to highlight the correct qualities of an official, in accordance with Arab and Muslim standards, was considered an instigation against them and a call to and indoctrination of their peoples to triumph over them.

It seems this is why some Arab rulers were filled with hatred against you. This, along with covetous designs, is also the reason that may fill some foreigners with hatred against you. But, brothers and sons, stalwart and honest men, and glorious women, what more can we do? Would anything other than this have left even a grain of honor, faith, glory, and pride; or would it have left a gift that we would take pride in and a future towards whose doors and shining promises we race?

Would any action to the contrary—in which we would follow the heels of the foreigner in the direction that he wants—leave a drop of honor for the men and free women? Would any such act leave faith and its rites anything but decaying bones and fine dust that meets no need? Is there [inaudible] that our great Iraqi people and glorious nation takes pride in other than this course? We will all maintain our character and will demand anything else that will boost and entrench faith and cleanse souls to the satisfaction of [inaudible] and the nation.

There is no other course than the one we have chosen, except the course of humiliation and darkness, after which there will be no bright sign in the sky or brilliant light on earth. We have chosen this course. The Iraqis have chosen this course in an era where many characteristics became manifest. They continue to ask and work for what will make them more brilliant, faithful, and lofty. There is no other course. We will protect it with our souls, funds, and hearts. We will proceed on this course, irrespective of the nature of the political efforts which we are exerting and whose formulation and directions Tariq Aziz carried to Moscow, and which, if rejected, will expose all the covers and will only maintain the premeditated intentions of the aggression against us without any cover and without any slogans that will lead to intermingling.

After the 15 February 1991 initiative sprang from its sister initiative of 12 August 1990, what did Bush say, and what did his servant Fahd say? Bush rejected it, and regarded it as a cruel hoax before he understood it. Fahd, who chews his words just as camels chew the grass of their pastures, became an eloquent orator to say the war against Iraq will continue until Iraq does this and that. Note, O observers; note, O people who have been distracted by the 2 August 1990 events from the real intentions of the aggression; note and examine that which you have overlooked. The Iraqis and good people became aware of it at an early date.

Note how Bush and Fahd have designs regarding matters that were not included among their slogans, either before or after 2 August, and not until a short time ago. Note how they now have ambitions for greater things—lightheaded Hosni speaks in the same strain—in order to reveal their true intentions and not accept the 15 February initiative. Remember how in the period that preceded the announcement of the initiative, they and others in the West used to say that as soon as the word withdrawal is said, everything will be possible afterward.

Note how they now have revealed their greed more clearly than they did—even in the moment preceding the announcement of the initiative. Note what their media are talking about now. These media are speaking about depriving Iraq of strength and capability, and of the manifestations of progress, honor, and good example. They want to deprive Iraq of every quality characterizing truly faithful people and good sons who are faithful to their people, homeland, and nation. Shame on them, and shame on their cowardly act, and all they do. 25

Note how those who at one stage of the struggle wanted to make of the word withdrawal an introduction to the undermining of our Armed Forces' determination and resolve and to sow disarray in their ranks no longer are interested in such a word now—or so they claim. They have started to neglect it and to talk about what is new, now that this has become a gratuitous gain, as they believe. 26

They forgot that our people and armed forces—in addition to their evident great determination for jihad, which is a dowry to the wedding of jihad and sacrifice—are also fully aware that every step we make should be countered by what it deserves in terms of guarantees and by an action that keeps the future open before the Iraqis and the Arabs and all the faithful who reject injustice in the world and that the word withdrawal has been placed by the Iraqis, the Arabs, and the good men of this world within this context and within the proper framework. 27

From this premise, and in the context of the comprehensive approach, it is the entire 15 February initiative, as a new beginning, that will make the Iraqis more determined and more resolved if the initiative is rejected. Their armed forces will become more capable. This will result from the exposure of pretexts and disclosure of the true nature of the premeditated intentions. All this will make them more patient and steadfast and better prepared for the battle which God blesses and which good men support—after which there will be only a glorious conclusion, where a brilliant sun will clear the dust of battle, and where the clouds of battles will be dispelled to make room for a brilliant moon surrounded by a halo, whose size will be commensurate with the sacrifices that are required by the duties and conditions of victory and by the practice that God Almighty expects from the people of holy war. 28

O brothers, O people: Note how those who feared a ground battle 29 have now avoided the showdown for over a month. They have persisted further in killing civilians [inaudible] and destroying property with their long-range aircraft and missiles with rancor that dwarfs that of Hulegu [grandson of the Mongol ruler Genghis Khan]. They are doing this in an [inaudible] to cover up their inability to confront our land forces in southern Iraq. Note how they, and certain people who do not know the Iraqis' faith and capability, now portray matters as though the mere fact of not launching the land offensive is a gain to Iraq that the Iraqis should respond to it with further concessions that would harm their principles, dignity, and rights, as well as the Arab nation's rights and security. Notice how they are indulging in illusions. With any initiative, Iraq does not seek a temporary truce or capitulation which the failures and shameful people want or have illusions about the possibility of achieving.

O fair people, note all this, as the Iraqis have noted, acknowl- 30 edged, and concluded. Note all this so as to excuse the Iraqis from any subsequent action, and to understand the justness of the Iraqi position. God is great. Mercy and immortality for our martyrs and our nation. Dignity, glory, and victory for the heroes of this path, the sons of our nation and mankind. God is great, God is great; accursed be the lowly.

Content Considerations

1. In what way does Saddam Hussein attempt to reinforce Iraqi loyalty to the war with the U.S. and U.N. forces? List specific examples.
2. Hussein's speech is much more flowery than that of George Bush in the previous reading. Are there similarities in the phrases used by both leaders? What is the tone of both speeches?
3. Who was Hussein's audience? If the audience had been primarily military, how might this speech have been different?

— *Ideas for Discussion, Writing, and Research* —

1. Kellerman writes about the ways presidents decide to take the country to war. Using the speech by Bush, as well as other information you can gather, write a paper in which you support or refute Kellerman's contention of individual bias and experience in making that decision.

2. Bower details theories of sociologists and anthropologists for the causes of war, theories that Howard says miss the mark. Using these two readings, as well as others you find elsewhere, write a paper in which you formulate your own theory of the ultimate causes of war.

3. Halperin presents the arguments for and against covert operations, secret wars, or activities that are intended to promote the welfare or security of the United States. Learn more about one of the covert operations he mentions, and write a paper supporting the use of covert operations or urging their complete halt.

4. Bush and Hussein both invoked grand visions for their nations in their speeches in this chapter. Read additional wartime speeches by national leaders on both sides of any conflict. How are they similar? How do they differ? What makes the difference in wartime speeches?

5. Howard lists several common reasons cited for wars, but advocates that, despite the rhetoric, all wars are calculated political decisions. Interview veterans from the World Wars, and the conflicts in Korea, Vietnam, and the Gulf about what they believe were the reasons for their war. Write a paper in which you support or refute Howard's position.

6. Kellerman relates how presidents take the nation to war; Halperin writes that Congress must reassert its power to authorize combat under the Constitution. Investigate one of the undeclared wars in which the United States has been involved and determine whether Congress approved or disapproved of the war. How was it possible to wage war without Congressional approval?

7. Learn more about the War Powers Resolution of 1973, which was intended to restrict presidential war-making powers. Has it worked? Why or why not?

8. Write letters to your Congressman and Senators asking for their positions on presidential and Congressional war powers. Incorporate their replies into a paper about the history of "Presidents' Wars."

9. Research the topic of presidential wars to learn the first instance of a president sending troops into a potential combat situation. What was Congress's reaction?

10. Wars are often described as political diversions, something to prop up the sagging popularity of a president. Write a paper in which you take a stand for or against this notion, citing public opinion polls, election results, and political rhetoric.

2

Who Fights, Who Dies?

WILLIE JONES WAS A POOR factory worker from the area of Forty-Sixth Street and Tenth Avenue in New York City. His name would doubtless be lost to history but for one thing: his was the first name drawn in the New York Draft Lottery of 1863.

His selection and that of other draftees for the Union Army from New York ultimately set off riots that killed from 300 to 1,200 persons, left large sections of New York City in smoldering ruins, and lasted several days until put down by troops returning from the bloody battlefield at Gettysburg.

The Civil War today is among the most popular of American wars: re-enactors skirmish on weekends using authentic uniforms, weapons, and tactics; writers continue to churn out fiction and history books by the score; a public television series draws millions of viewers. But by 1862, the Civil War was anything but popular in the North. When Abraham Lincoln was unable to continue the battles with volunteers in blue, he ordered the institution of conscription—the first national draft, signed into law on July 17. It called for states to furnish specific numbers of troops. It didn't work, and so in March, 1863, a new federal draft law was passed, which placed authority directly in the hands of the national government. The law was extremely unpopular—and outrageous by today's standards: it called for all men between 20 and 45 to register, then names were drawn, lottery-style. However, any man selected could either hire another in his place or pay the government $300 for an exemption. Since that was the equivalent of a year's pay for many, it meant that the poor would have to fight and the rich would not if they so chose.

Willie Jones and virtually every other man drawn in that first New York lottery were poor factory workers, and that fact was not lost on them. Already incensed over the prospect of fighting to free slaves whom they feared would compete with them for scarce jobs, the New Yorkers exploded in a paroxysm of violence that included lynching every black they could find. But in the end, the troops prevailed, draftees reported for induction, and the Civil War continued.

Conscription was common to European nations in the nineteenth century, but for Americans, the idea of being forced into the armed services was anathema. And despite the continued use of a national draft in the twentieth century, the paradox of involuntary service in a free society continues to plague Americans. That argument was joined, after Vietnam, by questions regarding the essential fairness and effectiveness of an all-volunteer armed service.

The issues are many: Should the country rely on an all-volunteer force, or would a draft even in peacetime ensure more of a cross-section of society? Should women be subject to a draft? Should women serve in combat zones, or is their presence downgrading the effectiveness of the services? Should sexual preference be a factor in joining the armed services—and should avowal of homosexual tendencies be enough to disqualify someone from a possible draft? Should individual conscience take precedence over national policy?

Since World War I, the concept of a "just" war has caused individual Americans to speak out—and sometimes to suffer the consequences. Eugene V. Debs, a four-time Socialist Party candidate for president, urged men not to register for the draft on the grounds that the war that was raging in Europe was unjust and not America's concern. For his views, Debs was convicted of violation of the Sedition Act of 1918 and sentenced to ten years in prison. He was pardoned in 1921.

World War II saw nearly universal conscription as thirteen million men—and women—served in the U.S. military. (All of the women, it should be noted, were volunteers.) It wasn't until Vietnam, and the civil unrest that the war engendered, that the fairness of a draft was questioned. Haunting questions about who fights and who dies in a democratic society were raised as it was pointed out that the war in the jungles and highlands of Southeast Asia was being fought largely by the poor, the young, the black. Deferments were issued to those with enough money to go to college or otherwise to qualify for exemptions, and the outcry, even after a lottery system was instituted, led to the dismantling of the draft in 1973.

However, serious questions have since been raised about the effectiveness and the fairness of an all-volunteer service. Despite being 12 to 14 percent of the overall population, blacks represented 29 percent of the army in the Persian Gulf in 1990–1991. Should blacks, purportedly denied civilian job opportunities, be expected to be the defenders of America? Should a draft with no deferments be reinstituted, thus ensuring that the sons of America's wealthy and elite will also serve? Would American leaders be less likely to urge war if their own children would be doing the fighting? Who should be responsible, ultimately, for defending U.S. interests, which sometimes include business and economic interests, not just philosophical ideals? The answers are not easy.

Women in the military seems a safe and relatively noncontroversial issue, particularly after the war in the Persian Gulf: Women were taken prisoner, women were killed in SCUD missile attacks, women flew helicopters in the combat zone. But the questions linger: Should women be drafted if conscription becomes necessary in the future? Should women be assigned to combat duty? What about women with small children? What happens if women become pregnant? And perhaps more controversial, have women weakened the armed services?

Gays are barred from serving in the military. As recently as 1990, the Supreme Court upheld the constitutionality of the military's decision neither to recruit nor retain homosexuals, and to discharge anyone in the service discovered to be gay. However, as one writer in this chapter points out, the unambiguous language of the military provision barring gays leaves a giant loophole in a future draft: Anyone may simply claim to be gay and be permanently exempt from serving in the military. Should the ban against homosexuals be lifted?

The age of soldiers is an issue that has generated little controversy in the United States military: enlistees must be at least 17, and must have parental consent if they are not 18. But in many countries, children as young as 8 or 9 are drafted, and U.S. soldiers might easily find themselves facing enemy soldiers not even teenagers yet. The average age of U.S. soldiers in Vietnam was 19: Today, those draftees could not legally buy a beer anywhere in the United States. How old is too young to die?

The case of Army Reserve Capt. Yolanda Huet-Vaughan, a medical doctor, drew much attention because of her declaration of conscientious objection to the war in the Persian Gulf. Is selective conscientious objection possible? Are all wars equal and equally just or moral? What criteria should be used in granting conscientious objector status?

In this chapter, a variety of writers offers a variety of opinions on the subject of who should serve—and possibly die—in America's wars.

Muddling the Issue
of Women in War

*Although some women in the armed forces are often quoted as insisting upon
their right to participate in combat, other officers and enlisted women do not
want to exercise that right. They and many members of the general public
believe that women are less suited—physically, mentally, emotionally—than
men for combat roles. But these beliefs are in part formed by traditional social
or cultural roles. Many, many women in the United States have always worked
outside their homes, often because of economic need rather than career aspirations. These women were usually, however, also wives and mothers, and,
although American culture seems to have become less rigid about women's
place, women are usually seen as the strength of the family and the children it
includes.*

*Thus many people view the prospect of women as combat soldiers as
dangerous to American tradition and harmful to American culture. In the next
essay, writer Suzanne Fields looks at the changes that could occur if women
were not excluded from combat duty. Before you read it, write a few paragraphs
developing your ideas about how the entry of women into the armed forces may
have changed American culture and how our culture may change further if
women serve in combat.*

WHO CAN FORGET the soldier in Desert Storm who carried her   1
baby's photograph on her helmet?

Who can forget the pictures of departing women caressing infants   2
who would have been suckling at their breasts if their Moms hadn't had
more important things to do, like driving a truck?

Who can forget the children, whose first words to Mommy were   3
"bye, bye."

This is national policy that inflicts havoc on our children, destroy-   4
ing the fabric of family, and in another time, every man would agree
that this is a strange way to fight a war to protect hearth and home. But
some people in Washington were trying last week to make sure that
young women will be put in harm's way the next time we fight a war.

The Defense Advisory Committee on Women in the Services   5
(DACOWITS, in the military jargon), appointed by the secretary of

defense (who gives them office space in the Pentagon) to make recommendations to the Pentagon, voted overwhelmingly to repeal the combat exclusion for women.

Most of the DACOWITS military strategists are well-to-do Republican women who have never held a gun and who no doubt earnestly hope they'll never have to. They've listened to hundreds of female officers talk about "glass ceilings," promotions and career opportunities.   6

DACOWITS panelists, who talked a lot about "combat readiness," think they've got the Big Mo for equal opportunity misery in war time, and now they're taking their message to Congress.   7

A few courageous DACOWITS voices tried to debate the issue, to talk about the implications and consequences for the American family. They wanted hard facts from the Gulf War, not stirring anecdotes. They wanted to meet the enlisted women who testified before the House Armed Services Committee last year that they didn't want combat.   8

They wanted to talk about the 10 percent of military women who are pregnant at any given time, the emotional and financial costs of day-care for combat mothers in a long war. These skeptics got only three minutes to raise questions.   9

This was considerably less than the time allotted to a woman who complained that tampons and sanitary napkins were scarce in the desert, and that it was difficult for women to keep their minds on their jobs when they were thinking about their menstrual cycles.   10

The subject of differences in physical strength of men and women was studiously ignored, as was discussion of how the armed services, including the academies, have created double standards for physical tests to accommodate women.   11

The panelists dismissed as irrelevant the impact of what the repeal of the combat exclusion may be on any future draft. A 1981 Supreme Court decision upheld the exemption of women from the draft by reasoning that the draft existed to supply troops for combat. Since women were exempt from combat, they were exempt from the draft.   12

Once this exclusion is removed, it's difficult to see how conscription would not apply to all young women if it applied to all young men.   13

A powerful argument against women in combat was made by a colonel in the Marines and a Vietnam veteran.   14

"Why," he asked, "do these women in the service want to trade the best of what it means to be a woman for the worst of what it means to be a man?"   15

Content Considerations

1. Reread and respond to the last sentence of Fields's essay, focusing on what the speaker could mean by "best."
2. Construct an argument establishing your own fitness for combat duty and share it with your class. Then write a counter-argument demonstrating why you are unfit for such duty.
3. What is the author's position toward giving women combat duty? How does she express it? Do you agree with her?

Soldier Boys, Soldier Girls

The notion that women are not strong enough for combat duty has long prevailed; now, however, that women are proving their strength in the military and in other fields, many critics are saying that strength alone does not make the soldier. A soldier needs to be aggressive: a soldier needs to fit into the military unit. Women may not have the hormones for aggression, and the hormones they do have (or can attract) may disrupt the operation of the military.

The following article, taken from a February, 1990, issue of The New Republic, *discusses the qualities needed for combat and whether women possess them. Write a few paragraphs about what those qualities might be, then decide whether you believe those qualities are possessed by men, women, or either.*

DURING THE U.S. INVASION OF PANAMA, a female solider who   1
had been driving a truck for hours, ferrying troops into a combat zone
amid sporadic enemy fire, was about to be pressed back into service
when she started crying. Another woman, who had been performing
the same job, approached her and, by some accounts, started crying too.
Both were relieved of their duties—whether at their request or not remains unclear.

After news of the incident reached the press, the Army took pains   2
to convey that the women had not disobeyed orders or been derelict in
their duty. On the contrary, according to an Army official quoted in
The Washington Post, "They performed superbly."

There are a number of sympathetic and truthful things you can   3
say about these two women. But to call the performance of a soldier
who breaks down and cries during combat "superb" is ludicrous and
patronizing.

This utterance embodies a particular form of disingenuousness that   4
has clouded the debate over opening combat positions to women. Within
the Pentagon there is deep opposition to the idea, but it almost never
gets honestly expressed.

The shallowness of the resulting debate is by itself a good argu-   5
ment for proceeding with Rep. Pat Schroeder's interesting plan to open
some Army units in every type of combat specialty to women on a
four-year test basis. Mere public discussion of the issue, it seems, is not
going to get us very far.

The only valid reason to keep women out of combat is if their presence is debilitating to what military types call "the mission." This is a real possibility, but so far it hasn't been illuminated by much honest discussion. Opponents of the combat exclusion rule often act as if the only reasonable doubts about female soliders have to do with physical strength and stamina.

If so, of course, the solution is simple. Women who pass all rele- 6 vant physical tests can go to war. Thus, a woman who can march, say, 10 hours with a 100-pound pack would be eligible for the infantry; a woman who can readily lift and load heavy artillery shells would be admitted to the field artillery. The number of women passing relevant strength tests should grow over the years, as strength, in the increasingly technological military, declines in relevance.

But strength and stamina are not the only pertinent biological dif- 7 ferences between men and women. Men are, statistically speaking, more aggressive than women, and at least some of this difference is inherent— due to the effect of testosterone on the brain's development and its daily functioning. It is less clear whether other observed differences are also genetically based. But the aggression gap alone means that, even if the military were entirely gender-blind, and physical strength were irrelevant, full parity would be highly unlikely; barring genetic engineering, there will never be as many women who want to kill, and are good at it, as men.

As with physical strength, aggregate differences between the sexes 8 in aggressiveness or bravery needn't stand in the way of individual women; insufficiently aggressive women (and, for that matter, insufficiently aggressive men) can, in principle, be weeded out. There is now no systematic effort to gauge such psychological factors in basic training, but some such tests may be useful adjuncts to the Schroeder plan.

The ultimate test of such tests, though, can only come in combat. 9 If, after the best feasible attempts to screen for the physical and behavioral components of effective fighting, women who reach certain combat positions have a markedly higher rate of failure under fire, then women will have to be barred from those jobs.

The second big issue that cannot be definitively settled without 10 bloodshed is the effect of women on previously all-male groups. The hypothesis, advanced by some anthropologists and evolutionary biologists, that men are genetically predisposed to fight in groups remains controversial. It is unclear whether the intense bonds formed during war, and all the valor and sacrifice they inspire, result from "male-bonding" or simply "person-under-fire bonding." Either way, there is no doubt that introducing a woman into a previously all-male platoon will change the group dynamics.

One source of change, of course, is romance. Another possible   11
problem is the patronizing of women. The question, in the end, is simple: After all the adjustments have been made, and the group has found
some new equilibrium, will the change have been for the better, the
worse or neither?

The only way to find out for sure is amid live ammunition: Open   12
some Army combat units to women and wait for the next Panama.
(Pains will have to be taken to ensure the candor of the postmortem—
by, for example, guaranteeing anonymity to all soldiers interviewed.
Some officers complain off the record that political pressure has long
discouraged negative assessments of the present degree of sexual
integration.)

The issue of women in combat may end up being much ado about   13
very little. Surveys suggest that few of the 192,000 enlisted women in
the military are yearning for combat duty. (The case is different for the
33,000 female officers, who know that their exclusion from combat
commands hurts their careers.)

West Point, like the other service academies, was integrated barely   14
more than a decade ago. And this year the first captain (the top-ranking
cadet in the senior class) was a woman. Still, the zenith, so far, for
women in the military was probably reached in Panama. The now-
famous assault by Capt. Linda Bray's military police unit on the Pana-
manian guard-dog kennel was not, it turns out, quite as heroic or bloody
as first advertised. But it nonetheless appears to be the first time a woman
has commanded a military unit in combat. And by all accounts she
didn't bat an eyelash, much less shed a tear.

Content Considerations

1. What arguments against women in combat does this editorial consider?
   What is its conclusion? How is it expressed?
2. What proposal is made as a means of determining women's fitness for
   battle? What do you think of the proposal?
3. Discuss the idea of "bonding" and its importance in the military. How
   might women soldiers affect that bonding?

Drafting Daughters

So far in the United States, only men have been drafted and only men must register for the draft. Why not women?

Boston Globe columnist Ellen Goodman contemplates such an occurrence in the following essay. For many Americans, the idea of drafting women dashes too far off the path of tradition; others believe that fairness and democracy demand that if men register, so must women. Some see this difference in treatment as a perpetuation of social ills or a continuation of an unsupportable cultural attitude. Others think that women just aren't fit for military duty and thus should neither serve nor register.

Goodman, who was awarded the Pulitzer Prize in 1980, writes a syndicated column carried by newspapers across the country. In the following selection (February, 1980) she writes about the issue of drafting women, about what it indicates, about its morality. Write a short statement that explains your own position on this issue and your reasons for holding it before you begin reading.

1   My DAUGHTER IS ELEVEN, and as we watched the evening news, she turns to me seriously and says, "I don't like the way the world is doing things." Neither do I.

2   My daughter is eleven years and eight months old, to be precise, and I do not want her to grow up and be drafted. Nor does she.

3   My daughter is almost twelve, and thinks about unkindness and evil, about endangered species and war. I don't want her to grow up and be brutalized by war—as soldier or civilian.

4   As I read those sentences over, they seem too mild. What I want to say is that I am horrified by the very idea that she could be sent to fight for fossil fuel or fossilized ideas. What I want to say is that I can imagine no justification for war other than self-defense, and I am scared stiff about who has the power to decide what is "defense."

5   But now, in the last days before President Carter decides whether we will register young people and whether half of those young people will be female, I wonder about something else. Would I feel differently if my daughter were my son? Would I be more accepting, less anguished, at the notion of a son drafted, a son at war?

6   Would I beat the drums and pin the bars and stars on his uniform

with pride? Would I look forward to him being toughened up, be proud of his heroism, and accept his risk as a simple fact of life?

I cannot believe it.   7

So, when I am asked now about registering women for the draft   8
along with men I have to nod yes reluctantly. I don't want anyone registered, anyone drafted, unless it is a genuine crisis. But if there is a draft, this time it can't just touch our sons, like some civilized plague that leaves daughters alone to produce another generation of warriors.

We may have to register women along with men anyway. Women   9
may not have won equal rights yet, but they have "won" equal responsibilities. A male-only draft may be ruled unconstitutional.

But at a deeper level, we have to register women along with men   10
because our society requires it. For generations, war has been part of the rage so many men have held against women.

War is in the hard-hat yelling at an equal rights rally, "Where were   11
you at Iwo Jima?" War is in the man infuriated at the notion of a woman challenging veterans' preference. War is in the mind of the man who challenges his wife for having had a soft life.

War has often split couples and sexes apart, into lives built on   12
separate realities. It has been part of the grudge of self-sacrifice, the painful gap of understanding and experience between men's and women's lives. It is the stuff of which alienation and novels are written.

But more awesomely, as a male activity, a rite of passage, a test   13
of manhood, war has been gruesomely acceptable. Old men who were warriors have sent younger men to war as if it were their birthright. The women's role until recently was to wave banners and sing slogans, and be in need of protection from the enemy.

We all pretended that war was civilized. War had rules and battle-   14
grounds. War did not touch the finer and nobler things, like women.

This was, of course, never true. The losers, the enemies, the vic-   15
tims, the widows of war were as brutalized as the soldiers. Under duress and in defense, women always fought.

But, perhaps, stripped of its maleness and mystery, its audience   16
and cheerleaders, war can be finally disillusioned. Without the last trappings of chivalry, it can be seen for what it is: the last deadly resort.

So, if we must have a draft registration, I would include young   17
women as well as young men. I would include them because they can do the job. I would include them because all women must gain the status to stop as well as to start wars. I would include them because it has been too easy to send men alone.

I would include them because I simply cannot believe that I would   18
feel differently if my daughter were my son.

Content Considerations

1. Paraphrase Goodman's argument and the reasons she gives for her position. Write a response in which you evaluate the soundness of those reasons.

2. In what ways does warfare affect the relationship between men and women? Between parents and children?

3. Explore the notion that war is one of "the last trappings of chivalry" (paragraph 16).

SONIA SHAH

Racial Inequity in the Military

A government can choose any of several ways to fill the ranks of its military. It can draft or conscript citizens, requiring them to serve full-time for a specified number of years. In that system, it can choose to require service of all citizens or just those who meet certain age, education, and physical requirements. It can rely mostly on reserves, bringing units together for only a few days each year. Or the government can call for volunteers to the armed forces, taking only those who wish to join. The United States instituted such a voluntary system after it abolished the draft in 1973.

To some, the volunteer system seemed ideal. No one was forced to join, so it was assumed that only those with an interest would volunteer. But others were more critical, saying that the interest that prompts many recruits was socioeconomic. Often they are members of lower classes who could not find jobs elsewhere, largely because they were minorities, they lacked educational op-portunities, or they were poor. Thus the volunteer army is sometimes viewed as an example of racism and discrimination.

Sonia Shah discusses this perspective in the following article, reprinted from the Spring 1991 Nuclear Times, *the magazine of which she is managing editor. Before reading her comments, write several paragraphs about the ways in which a volunteer army could perpetuate racial inequity.*

AS WITH MOST national crises, the situation in the Persian Gulf threatens to bear heavily on the underdogs of our society, the poor and the nonwhite.

One such imbalance is in the composition of the armed forces. According to the Joint Chiefs of Staff, 29 percent of the army personnel in the gulf are African-American, compared with only 12 percent of the overall U.S. population. This is not surprising since the military actively perpetuates race and class inequity, mostly due to the enlistment prob-lems the all-volunteer service has suffered since its inception.

Congress ended the draft in 1973, but by 1980 the poor quality of recruits forced legislators to set standards for enlistment, including one requiring high school diplomas for at least 65 percent of enlistees. By 1989, however, both the army and navy were hard put to fill their quotas and consequently resorted to lowering their aptitude and edu-cational standards. Although the army significantly decreased its numbers, its desperation to find enlistees had permeated recruitment practice and policy.

One investigation directed by the military, cited in a December 1989 *Hartford Courant* series, found 189 recruitment violations in the army and navy over just two years. The fouls included forged diplomas, concealed criminal records, and fraudulent aptitude tests. The General Accounting Office calculates that recruitment fraud costs taxpayers over $750 million yearly, based on the number of discharged recruits and their replacement costs. 4

MANIPULATIVE PRACTICES

An additional $2.1 billion of taxpayers' money is pumped into slick television and magazine recruitment advertisements designed to entice underprivileged kids with the benefits of military life by exploiting their lack of opportunity in the civilian world. For example, the Youth Attitude Tracking Study, commissioned by the military, proposed that enlistment quotas be filled during times of both economic sluggishness and fewer 18- to 26-year-olds by targeting lower-income youth. 5

The tactics are shamelessly manipulative. "Need college money? Job training?" television ads ask. "Join the army. Be all that you can be." In reality, however, few veterans are eligible for benefits. The cost-saving New GI Bill dictates, among other things, that honorable discharges are required to qualify for the advertised benefits. Yet, according to the Youth and Militarism program of the American Friends Service Committee, one of every three servicepeople does not garner the distinction of honorable discharge, even fewer for African-Americans and Latinos. Ultimately, around 40 percent of all veterans are ineligible for benefits, the AFSC says. 6

Claims of job-training opportunities are also overstated since assignments are made according to the results of standardized tests, and only those with the highest scores receive the management and technical positions that offer skills having any value in the civilian world. The lower scorers end up as "atomic demolition experts," military double-talk for those who carry and load bombs. The procedure works as a tracking system for minority servicepeople, who by and large end up carrying rifles and staffing transportation units. 7

Yet the military seems a better and better opportunity for minorities. The demand for unskilled labor, once a source of employment for the underprivileged, has diminished as cheap offshore workforces in areas such as South Korea and Taiwan are being tapped. The administration continues to slash financial aid and minority scholarships, further chipping away at the already slim chance for a college education. These 8 trends, coupled with aggressive recruitment practices, induce many youths to enter the military for lack of better options and with hope for employment opportunities.

This is not necessarily the case for white enlistees, who generally   9
have less education than their black counterparts in the service, according to a 1989 National Research Council study. Perhaps whites who hold the educational levels of black soldiers simply don't need to enlist.

While trends in education and employment affect all Americans, it   10
may be that they impact the lowest-class tiers of the black community such that they do not have enough energy, support, or motivation to make it even to the military. Conversely, the lowest-class tiers of the white community do make it to the military. It may be that for white soldiers the military *is* more a last resort than a better option.

While the criminal justice system imprisons, jails, probates, or paroles 25 percent of all black males between the ages of 20 and 29, members of the community with greater promise, the potential lawyers, doctors, and teachers—that is, over 40 percent of all black males passing military physical and aptitude tests—are being enlisted into the military. There, despite their relatively higher educational levels, they are concentrated in support roles, slightly underrepresented in combat arms, and greatly underrepresented in technical fields.

And although 30 percent of the army was black in 1986, only 10   12
percent of army officers were black and only 7 percent were generals. The military's shallow but seductive claims of opportunity wield the double-edged sword of disillusionment and wasted potential for the African-American community. The manipulation may actually be more devastating than a direct offer of a last resort option.

ACTIVISTS RESPOND

This gradual but systematic degradation of minority communities   13
is brought into sharp relief with the potential for bloodshed facing troops in the Middle East. Because now, what black soldiers can expect is not merely a military ghetto but a military graveyard.

The crisis has galvanized a clear and loud antiwar cry from minority communities and civil-rights activists. The newly formed African-American Network Against U.S. Intervention in the Middle East and its coalition members, such as the National Alliance of Third World Journalists and the National Rainbow Coalition, are organizing low-income and minority groups to demand an end to the war in the Persian Gulf and to use the funds earmarked for war for the betterment of the nation's poorer communities.

The African-American Network is working to reclaim Martin Lu-   15 ther King Jr.'s legacy with nationwide teach-ins, speaking caravans, and rallies in lower-income and minority neighborhoods. And they mobilized their memberships to participate in the national January 26 demonstration against the war.

Their ongoing protest focuses on the drain war imposes on minority communities and that an antiwar stand is a necessary condition of an antiracist agenda. The argument runs that Western-style racism, the tool of oppression in this country, also shapes American imperialism in Third World countries, a notion that stems less from a natural camaraderie between people of color globally than a shared fate as objects of Western racism.

"This is another racist military adventure," says Jack O'Dell, international affairs director of the National Rainbow Coalition. "There is a philosophy that life is cheap in Asia," he says, speculating that "there would be no military buildup in a white country." Many consider the Middle East part of Asia.

The two white superpowers consistently played out their Cold War struggle on the backs of the poorer, darker countries of the world, activists say. Now, asks Bernard Dreano, a French peace activist involved in the 1980s East-West dialogue, "will this reunification of whites in the First and Second Worlds be made without consideration for the interests of the Third World, or even against those interests?" Activists argue that the answer, embodied in the current situation in the Persian Gulf, seems to be yes, and the so-called "new world order" may just be a revamped Cold War structure in which attention is focused directly on the Third World.

Given this historical context and its social costs, American people of color must act now, activists say. But they may have a more difficult time making themselves heard than they did during the Vietnam War. "At least then people were trying to deal with racial inequality," says Kathy Flewellen of the African-American Network. "Today people are saying that there is no problem."

Since the 1960s, the news media have disguised racism, rarely showing it as a divisive national issue. One recent example is how the complex problem of racial imbalance in the military has been framed as a simplistic black-on-black dispute between black civil-rights activists and Chair of the Joint Chiefs of Staff, African-American Colin Powell. Another case is how opinion polls, like the *New York Times*/CBS poll which reported that 55 percent of black respondents oppose Persian Gulf intervention compared to 27 percent of white respondents, are cursorily explained by racial imbalance in the military, effectively making it acceptable for blacks and whites to hold very different political views without having to investigate any of the reasons why.

Progressive people of color are most compelled by the fact that on   21
almost every level, and in most any U.S. military endeavor, minorities
stand to lose the most.

"It is injustice that leads to war," says Flewellen. "The issue of   22
having a pool of people whose labor and lives are invisible and accustomed to supporting the power and privilege of others is the same dichotomy in this country that you see the North doing to the South. If
activists don't understand the centrality of that dilemma, then their solution is only a partial solution."

Content Considerations

1. According to Shah, what is wrong with the military's recruitment of
    the underprivileged? Do you agree?
2. What is your position regarding the idea that "an antiwar stand is a
    necessary condition of an antiracist agenda" (paragraph 16)?
3. To what extent is it necessary for the American military to reflect the
    racial proportions of the nation? Write an argument presenting your
    conclusion. (Consider: Same ratio of males and females? Geographical
    and socioeconomic distribution? Age balances?)

Black Leaders vs. Desert Storm

The onset of the Persian Gulf war was prefaced by antiwar demonstrations and speeches; the antiwar activities continued during the war. Many black leaders were adamantly against the war and cited many reasons for their opposition: one was that, although blacks comprise about 13 percent of the country's population, they comprised 20 percent of the forces sent to the Gulf. The leaders saw that blacks might suffer casualties disproportionate to their numbers and thus bear more of the burden of war than other racial groups.

The following appeared in Commentary *in May, 1991. Arch Puddington, a writer who is active in civil rights, examines the antiwar sentiment expressed about the Gulf War and then takes a close look at how issues concerning voluntary military service played a part in that sentiment.*

Try to recall what you know about civil rights and military service. With classmates, list the information, and, as you read, add to or modify the list.

ON THE SURFACE, the controversy over the role of black service-men in the Gulf War revolved around complaints that black men and women were "disproportionately" represented among the troops assigned to Operation Desert Storm. Although blacks make up just 13 percent of the American population and approximately 15 percent of the age group from which most servicemen are drawn, their percentage in the armed forces is higher: 20 percent throughout the services; 33 percent in the Army; 20 percent in the Marines; and 15 percent in the Navy and Air Force. As for Operation Desert Storm, blacks were some 25 percent of total forces and 30 percent of the ground units thought to be most vulnerable to heavy casualties.

Again and again, black elected officials, clergymen, editors, educators, and community activists pointed to these figures in opposing the war, and most Americans thus came to perceive the issue of disproportionality as central to the relative lack of black support for President Bush's policy as indicated by every opinion poll taken during the crisis. Black leaders were not, of course, the only prominent Americans to object to that policy in the days prior to the outbreak of hostilities. But with the possible exception of the mainline Protestant clergy, black leaders stood out for the uniformity and intensity of their opposition to the use of force in the liberation of Kuwait. Black leadership was also notable for the stridency of its criticism and for its willingness to attack America's prosecution of the war after hostilities had been initiated. At least one prominent figure, Martin Luther King, III, the son of the martyred civil-rights leader, went so far as to urge black troops to refuse to fight. "We've been fighting a war we've been told to fight, and right here we don't have rights," King told a Chicago audience several days after the war had begun. "Every black soldier ought to say, 'You all do what you want to. I'm not going to fight. This is not my war.' "

While King's advocacy of mutiny by soldiers in time of war represented an extreme position, his claim that blacks are systematically denied equal rights was often reiterated in commentaries which invariably cited President Bush's veto of the 1990 Civil Rights Act as justification for black coolness toward the war. Yet it should not be thought that the antiwar attitudes of the black leadership were solely, or even primarily, motivated by narrowly racial concerns like the veto of the civil-rights measure or the high percentages of black combat troops. In fact, the statements of black leaders often dwelt on such broad, nonracial questions as the nation's role in the post–cold-war world, the nature of the Kuwaiti government, America's alliance with Israel, even the legitimacy of war under any circumstances. And on these central foreign-policy concerns, the views of black leaders often proved radically at variance with the views of the American people.

This was especially true of the Democratic members of the Congressional Black Caucus. That only the lone Republican member of the Caucus, Gary Franks of Connecticut, should have supported the Solarz-Michel resolution giving President Bush sanction for the use of force comes as little surprise, considering the antiwar sentiment which prevailed among all but a few Democratic liberals in the days prior to the war. However, a clear difference between black and white liberals was revealed, in stark terms, several days *after* the war began, when the House of Representatives took up a resolution supporting the troops and commending President Bush in his role as commander-in-chief. While before the war 183 House members had opposed authorizing the President to use military force, only twelve voted "no" or merely "present" on the measure commending the troops and the President after the war had begun. Of those dozen Congressmen, ten were black; the two others were Henry Gonzalez, Democrat of Texas, and Bernard Sanders, Vermont's freshman Socialist Congressman.

Nor did the war's quick conclusion, or the fact that American casualties were minimal, or the fact that black combat deaths (at 15 percent) were proportionately much lower than the black troop presence in Desert Storm, or the glowing national tributes to black military performance, move the black congressional delegation from its all-out antiwar stance. This was vividly demonstrated by the response of black Congressmen to yet a third measure relating to the Desert Storm operation, a routine $15-billion supplementary appropriation overwhelmingly approved after the war's successful conclusion. Of only eighteen Congressmen who opposed the appropriation, fully fifteen were members of the Black Caucus.

Aside from their votes, black Congressmen were also notable for the harshness of their attacks on the war—and on President Bush personally—and, at the same time, for their seeming lack of concern about Saddam Hussein's occupation of Kuwait, the plight of the Kuwaiti people, the threat posed by Iraq to Israel and other friendly nations in the region, or the implications of Saddam's past use of chemical weapons and his drive to acquire a nuclear potential.

Like other critics, most black Congressmen saw the war as hinging almost exclusively on control of the Gulf's oil wealth. Congressman Charles Rangel of New York declared that the crisis was the result of "dipstick diplomacy that says we must expose our young people to death for oil." Congressman Floyd Flake, also of New York, asserted that "American blood should not be spilled for not [*sic*] one drop of oil." Congresswoman Maxine Waters of California went a step further, advancing the thesis that the war was about America's "having the ability to leverage this country against the European [oil] market . . . and Japan." A more radical note was struck by Congressman Gus Savage of Illinois, who argued that the real problem was not Saddam Hussein's aggression but rather

> resource exploitation . . . where developed nations exploit the resources of undeveloped nations so that the undeveloped nations suffer increasing poverty . . . while the developed nations with the Eurocentric culture, the capitalist economy, prosper.

Another favored, if worn-out, cliché dragged in during the congressional debate was the notion of war as nothing more than the young being dispatched to slaughter by tired old men for the enrichment of elites or to further a pointless geopolitical goal. Congressman Ron Dellums of California stated that, in the end, "old men will sit down around a table to solve political problems after young men have died." To which Congressman Charles Hayes of Illinois added his opposition to the idea that "a bunch of old men should be determining whether our young men should risk their lives in an attempt to preserve revenue for mega-rich oil companies and Arab royalty."

Some Black Caucus members seemed close to embracing a pacifist stance. "Only a madman would want to go to war," Dellums said, "because war is killing, death, and destruction, nothing more, nothing less." Congressman Major Owens of New York saw war as useless slaughter: "My conscience tells me that if I vote for all this unnecessary killing, this mass murder, I become an accessory to murder." (Owens cannot be accused of inconsistency: after the war, he charged the United States with having behaved "almost the way we behaved at Hiroshima and Nagasaki.")

As for the fate of Kuwait, then groaning under Iraqi control, in speeches during the crucial debate prior to the war authorization, most Black Caucus members simply avoided the subject—an unusual omission given that this was the very issue which had provided the basis for the approval by the UN Secretary Council of the use of force. But several spoke of the Kuwaitis in tones of derision. "Two of the most undemocratic, oppressive nations on the face of the earth," was the description of Saudi Arabia and Kuwait given by William Clay of Missouri, while Kweisi Mfume of Maryland noted that "Kuwait by no means represented Jeffersonian democracy." And Hayes, after dismissing Kuwaitis as "wealthy people who inherited their wealth," managed to sneer at the foreigners, including hundreds of Americans, who had been held hostage by Saddam Hussein during the first months of the crisis as "people who were over there, making money." 11

It is, of course, true that neither Kuwait nor Saudi Arabia qualifies as a democracy. But Kuwait had made important concessions to democratic forces in the year prior to its occupation, and had earned a reputation as one of the more tolerant societies in the Middle East. In any event, the same black Congressmen who held Kuwait's human-rights record up to scorn were hardly known in the past for applying strict democratic standards to third-world countries. The Black Caucus, for instance, had been an enthusiastic supporter of Grenada's New Jewel Movement, an organization openly disdainful of parliamentary niceties, and individual members of the Caucus—among them Ron Dellums and Gus Savage—have expressed highly favorable opinions of Fidel Castro despite the Cuban dictator's totalitarian rule and the pervasive militarism of Cuban life. 12

In contrast to the confused logic and the double standards which marked their comments on the nature of the various Middle Eastern countries involved in the crisis, prominent blacks seemed genuinely moved by the prospect of heavy American casualties, especially during a ground campaign. Such fears were understandable in view of the widespread, and, as we now know, widely inaccurate predictions of tens of thousands of dead and wounded American soldiers issued both by the antiwar movement and by various military analysts. And the sincerity of black fears stood in notable contrast to the hypocrisy of peace-move- 13 ment spokesmen as *they* anticipated massive U.S. combat deaths: how often did we hear one or another antiwar leader link the success of his cause to the return of thousands of body bags?

Yet even on this score there were hints that blacks, too, were not   14
above exploiting war casualties to further political objectives. Thus, an activist black clergyman was quoted in the Washington *Post* as suggesting that black war dead might fuel a revival of the civil-rights protest movement:

> Funerals become by nature political events, similar to what has   15
> happened in South Africa, and there would be tremendous growth in the antiwar movement in the black community [in response to massive black casualties].

And, in fact, the Reverend Jesse Jackson and other well-known figures   16
shamelessly used the occasion of a funeral for a black New Jersey soldier killed in action as a forum to attack the government's prosecution of the war and to demand enactment of civil-rights legislation.

In general, for blacks of a leftist or strongly black-nationalist bent,   17
the war functioned as a convenient weapon for the advancement of any number of ideologies or causes. Jesse Jackson told a rally that every bomb dropped on Baghdad deprived blacks of roads and schools. For Jack O'Dell, international-affairs director of Jackson's Rainbow Coalition, the war's lesson was that "racism has become the central ingredient in the idea of national chauvinism." Ron Daniels, former national director of the Rainbow Coalition, viewed the conflict through both nationalist and Marxist prisms, a perspective which led him to praise Saddam Hussein. Saddam, Daniels wrote, was being put down because he had tried to "break the back" of colonialism in the Middle East, in the course of which he had become a threat to "Uncle Tom" regimes like Kuwait. For Daniels, President Bush's New World Order amounted to "a new system of global white power and supremacy with the United States at the helm." As for Molefi Asante, an influential figure in the movement for an Afrocentric curriculum, Iraq was the latest in a long line of third-world victims of American imperialism. Meanwhile, the *Amsterdam News,* New York's leading black newspaper, managed to link the war to a plan to "re-whiten America by luring more and more Eastern Europeans to these shores, thereby reducing employment opportunities for black Americans."

Probably no group opposed to the war could equal the black clergy   18
for bitterness and moral castigation. The Reverend Calvin O. Butts, III, the pastor of the Abyssinian Baptist Church, Harlem's most prestigious parish, told his congregants that President Bush had lied about the war,

and he accused the media of working with the government to conceal the facts. The Reverend Herbert Daughtry called President Bush "the invader," and said the U.S. was a "greater monster" than Saddam Hussein. Father Lawrence Lucas declared at an antiwar rally that "there is no reason to justify the killing of people by George Bush because of oil." And a statement issued by a group of black leaders, but spearheaded by activist clergymen, described the war as "immoral and unspiritual" as well as "wrong, unnecessary, unprincipled, and dirty."

America was not the only target of criticism; a number of black [19] clergy and other high-visibility black figures seized the opportunity to restate their distaste for Israel and for Israel's close ties to the United States. Father Lucas, for example, theorized that the war had been declared in order to "improve U.S. support to Israel," while the Reverend Ben Chavis, executive director of the Commission on Racial Justice of the United Church of Christ, declared that blacks should be in solidarity with Palestinians because "undergirding the whole conflict in the Gulf is the unresolved issue of the rights of the Palestinian people." In New York, Mayor David Dinkins drew sharp criticism from a number of prominent blacks for having joined Congressman Rangel in a wartime visit to Israel, a step Dinkins explained as a gesture of solidarity during a period when Israel was under Iraqi missile assault. Dinkins, it should be stressed, had strongly opposed the war, but this fact was deemed irrelevant by critics like Reverend Butts, who accused the mayor of being more concerned with New York's Jewish voters "than with his own community," or like the radical attorney Colin Moore, who blasted Dinkins for having failed to visit "South Africa or other countries on the [African] continent where people are involved in liberation struggles." Congressman Rangel, a consistent and outspoken opponent of the war, was nevertheless forced to end his speech prematurely at a Harlem rally after he was jeered for defending Israel.

In the midst of hostilities, Jesse Jackson was heard to complain that [20] the views of black leaders were being ignored by the Bush administration in its making of war policy. Whether Jackson was serious in suggesting that Bush consult with those who share the global outlook of Dellums, Butts, or Jackson himself is unclear. In the past, of course, wartime presidents did meet with civil-rights leaders over the denial of basic rights suffered by the country's black citizens. But during World War II, the issues which Walter White and A. Philip Randolph raised with President Franklin D. Roosevelt were altogether crucial for blacks and for the successful prosecution of the war; one of those issues, ironically, was securing the right of the black soldier to fight for his country. To be sure, Randolph threatened a protest march in response to the widespread exclusion of black workers from defense-industry jobs. But

Randolph was also committed to an Allied victory; and he acted in the hope that in addition to gaining crucial rights for blacks, his wartime crusades would strengthen the patriotic bonds between blacks and their country. The message of Randolph's generation of civil-rights leader— "Give us our rights and we will gladly fight for our country"—was far different from the embittered refrain of today's black leadership: "This is not our war."

Jesse Jackson, of course, believes he should be recognized as a   21 foreign-policy expert as well as a protest leader. Yet statements he made before and during Desert Storm suggest his grasp of world affairs remains essentially the same as in 1984, when as a presidential candidate he delivered himself of absurd chants which likened Fidel Castro and Daniel Ortega to Christ. "There were no troops in Canada on our border about to bomb us," Jackson said shortly after the war began, summing up his grasp of the Middle East. To an antiwar rally, Jackson screamed that "When that war breaks out, our youth will burn first." And in the most tortured reasoning, Jackson announced that the establishment of the January 15 deadline for an Iraqi withdrawal "makes no sense" since President Bush "did not confirm a date for the liberation of South Africa or the liberation of Central America."

Unfortunately, the perspective on world affairs revealed in Jack-   22 son's various pronouncements prevails among those within the black political establishment who focus attention on foreign-policy issues. Insofar as there exists a distinctly black global view, it is not merely at variance with the American people's concept of their country's place in the world, but wildly so. The assumptions which instruct this mindset are a jumbled and often contradictory combination of selective pacifism, profound mistrust of American goals, and lingering identification with radical, anti-democratic third-world regimes and liberation movements. These assumptions led during the 1980's to a harshly critical response to the invasion of Grenada (heedless of the action's popularity in Grenada itself), an unrelenting animus toward defense spending, and an opposition to American support for anti-Communist insurgencies, including the struggle against the Soviet occupation of Afghanistan.

In a sense, then, the passionate opposition to the Gulf War con-   23 forms to a pattern of hostility to the exercise of American power, whatever the context. Nevertheless, the unrelenting opposition to the war remains highly unsettling due to its fervor and near-unanimity. Of generally recognized black leaders, only a few—Congressman William Gray of Pennsylvania, John E. Jacob of the Urban League, and Benjamin Hooks of the NAACP were among the most prominent—acknowledged the moral and political importance of responding to Saddam Hussein's aggression. Furthermore, segments of the leadership seemed to find the issue of black military "overrepresentation" less a cause for complaint than a weapon in the promotion of an anti-interventionist foreign policy.

The question of who fights for America is, in fact, worthy of   24
serious examination. Blacks, Hispanics, and whites from modest economic backgrounds predominate in today's armed forces, and will continue to do so as long as America opts for a volunteer military. Although the awesome performance of U.S. forces in Desert Storm should go a long way toward resolving the debate over the battlefield effectiveness of the volunteer force, an argument against the current arrangement can still be made on the grounds that a volunteer force is incompatible with the country's democratic traditions.

But the alternative remains a reinstitution of the draft, an option   25
which no black leader, or any antiwar stalwart, has endorsed. Here it is worth recalling that blacks were among the most fervent champions of the volunteer force during the debates which preceded its adoption in 1973 and which then focused on its troubled first years. In response to misgivings expressed by white politicians and military authorities that the composition of a volunteer army might be "too black," prominent blacks, like then-Congresswoman Shirley Chisholm, responded with barely concealed rage. Mrs. Chisholm, herself no hawk, fumed: "All this talk about a volunteer army being poor and black is not an indication of 'concern' for the black and the poor, but rather of the deep fear of the possibility of a black army." As for the critical question of how black troops might react to suffering "disproportionate" casualties, Ron Dellums, no less, issued a statement distinguished by an uncompromising emphasis on individual responsibility:

> Black volunteers understand what joining the military means.   26
> If, through exercise of free choice by individuals, there are [proportionately] more blacks in the military than in the population, we should expect a proportionately greater sacrifice. The whole idea of a volunteer army is that the individual will take this risk and this responsibility by his or her free choice.

Speaking around the same time, the civil-rights leader Vernon Jordan   27
detected a double standard in white fears about the possibility of high black casualty rates:

> It is interesting that while American servicemen were fighting   28
> and dying in Vietnam there was little concern about the disproportionate numbers of blacks in front-line combat units and the

casualty lists. Criticisms of the armed forces should be based on real issues, not on false racial concerns.

Black leaders were equally adamant on the sensitive issue of how 29 black soldiers would react if assigned to "restore order" in riot-torn American inner cities, or in some controversial third-world setting, such as a civil war in Africa or Latin America. Margaret Bush Wilson, then-chairman of the NAACP, regarded suggestions that blacks might balk at such assignments as a "smokescreen thrown up by more subtle, sophisticated racists." Similarly, Clifford L. Alexander, Jr., who served as Jimmy Carter's Secretary of the Army, dismissed as racist the notion that blacks would refuse duty in certain parts of the world, including even South Africa.

Thus, right up until the Gulf crisis, the public posture of America's 30 black leadership toward the volunteer army was one of wholehearted endorsement. In part, this was due to the fact that the volunteer military functioned as an instrument of upward mobility for thousands of black youths. There was also an understandable defensiveness over the subtle and sometimes not-so-subtle mutterings that a heavily black military would be an inferior or even disloyal military. In 1978, for example, then-Congressman Paul N. McCloskey, Jr. told an audience of Stanford alumni that it was "dangerous to have an all-black army," and added, by way of amplification, that "the Mafia was able to maintain its political and financial success by infiltrating the New York police department." Blacks, of course, were all too aware that the apprehensions which McCloskey was injudicious enough to express in a semi-public forum were being echoed, *sotto voce,* by other political and military officials.

There was, however, something a bit too glib in the assertions of 31 Chisholm, Jordan, and others that the racial composition of the military was a subject not worthy of discussion. Jordan was not altogether accurate in declaring that the country had been unconcerned with the rates of black casualties during the Vietnam war. In fact, after civil-rights groups complained about the high percentages of black casualties suffered during the war's early years, military authorities took measures affecting the assignment of combat troops which substantially reduced those rates.

Nor were black leaders guiltless of obstructing the military's ef- 32 forts at racial harmony. Martin Luther King, Jr., in addition to deploring Vietnam as a distraction from President Johnson's domestic agenda, came to accept the interpretation of that war as a form of racist imperialism, and urged blacks to boycott it. There were, as well, the demagogues of Black Power, ready to charge, as Stokely Carmichael did, that the war's hidden purpose was to "get rid of black people in the ghettos" by using them as "cannon fodder." While the degree to which Black Power ideology infected the troops is unclear, both black and white observers agree it was a force during the war's later years, particularly among black draftees from the Northern inner cities. At the same time, white-supremacist groups also gained a disturbingly wide following in the Army and Marines.

In contrast to all this, today, in the wake of Desert Storm's success, the military is being hailed as the most successfully integrated institution in American society. "The Army is the only place in America where a white will routinely be bossed around by black superiors," comments Charles Moskos, an authority on military-society relations. Journalists investigating the state of race relations in Desert Storm found a level of cooperation that was an inspirational story in itself. Repeatedly, black servicemen and -women stressed that in the armed forces they were treated with respect; that prejudice, if it existed, was much less significant than in civilian life; and that those assigned to Desert Storm had been too busy doing their jobs to worry about matters like skin color.   33

An obvious question is whether American society can learn anything from the military's success in race relations. Some civil-rights leaders have already announced the lesson: affirmative action works, and what is needed is passage of the latest version of the Civil Rights Restitution Act.   34

Now, it is true that the military has adopted a number of measures specifically designed to stimulate integration and tolerance: modest efforts to encourage the promotion of minorities into the officer ranks, special race-relations training courses for officers, and a strict policy of not tolerating prejudice within the various forces. These measures have been important, particularly as they send a reassuring signal to minorities about the atmosphere awaiting them during their service.   35

Ultimately, however, the military has become a racial success story primarily because of certain characteristics inherent in a volunteer service. To begin with, the abolition of the draft has eliminated those who resented service or the close interracial cooperation which the military demands. More to the point, the enhanced pay, benefits, and educational opportunities ensured that the military would draw better-educated, highly motivated enlistees, something which in turn has enabled it to strengthen already tough enlistment standards. If affirmative action has played a modest role in the successful integration of the armed forces, a much greater share of the credit belongs to the military's commitment to merit and standards, a quality sharply at odds with the logic of affirmative action. Black servicemen, in fact, boast higher educational credentials than white enlistees, and there are no special racial or ethnic   36 admissions tracks of the type which have contributed to the unhealthy state of race relations on the nation's college campuses.

Reflecting on the controversy over the role of black troops in the Gulf, Edwin Dorn of the Brookings Institution has observed: 37

> Man for man and woman for woman, this military is much better than the draft-era military of Vietnam—and I say that to address all those who think blacks and women have ruined standards in the military. The fact is that if you go out and talk to those soldiers at the 82nd Airborne or talk to the soldiers in the tank units at Fort Knox, they don't think of themselves as cannon fodder or victims, they think of themselves as professionals doing a job they are very well trained to do. 38

The *esprit de corps* which impresses Dorn, and which was vividly on display in interviews with Gulf War participants, reflects more than anything else pride in an institution which demands a high level of performance and rewards it when delivered. When asked their attitude toward military service, black troops invariably mention the opportunity to accomplish a mission they consider important; they mention fair treatment and an atmosphere of relative equality; they mention self-respect. They do not mention affirmative-action programs, racial preference, or reverse discrimination. Nor does anyone think that affirmative action is responsible for the emergence of such high-ranking black officers as the commandant of West Point, the deputy commander of Desert Storm, and, of course, Colin Powell, chairman of the Joint Chiefs of Staff. 39

By any standard, Powell would seem an ideal figure of inspiration for black youth. The son of Jamaican immigrants, both of whom worked in New York's garment district, Powell received his early military training not at West Point or Virginia Military Institute but through the ROTC program at the City College of New York. Although officially integrated, the military Powell entered during the 50's was by no means the equal-opportunity employer of today, and Powell encountered his share of discrimination during stints at Southern bases like Fort Bragg, North Carolina and Fort Benning, Georgia. Yet Powell's credo on racial matters has been to regard his color as other people's problem, not his— an optimistic philosophy which helps explain his rise within the military. 40

For many black leaders, however, General Powell's commanding and articulate presence has posed something of a dilemma. By all accounts greatly respected by America's black population, Powell was generally ignored by black war opponents, many of whom in other forums have bitterly lamented the dearth of strong, successful, black 41 men who could serve as examples for troubled youth. But the problem presented by Powell's highly visible role went much deeper than his association with a war of which black leaders disapproved. For as we have seen, many black leaders considered that war not just wrong, but immoral. By extension, Powell might well be regarded as a war criminal; he was not, after all, an infantryman just following orders, and if he did not make the political decision to declare war against Iraq, he was a crucial participant in the formulation of war-fighting tactics and strategy, including the bombing of Iraqi cities, the very thing Congressman Owens must have had in mind when he compared America's tactics in the Gulf to the use of atomic weapons against Japan.

Powell was also unsympathetic to complaints about the high per-   42
centage of blacks in the armed forces. Typically, he did not shy away from the possible consequences once war broke out:

> If one out of four, roughly one out of five, is black, if the   43
> whole force accepts casualties, what would you wish me to do?
> Move the blacks from the positions they're in so that they will have
> a lower percentage of casualties? Every part of the force, whether
> it's Hispanic American, Pacific American, or lower-income white
> soldiers will probably sustain casualties in relationship to the per-
> centage that they represent in the overall force.
>
> What you keep wanting me to say is that this is disproportion-
> ate or wrong. I don't think it's disproportionate or wrong. I think
> it's a decision the American people made when they said have a
> volunteer army and allow those to serve who want to serve.

Powell also tartly noted that some of those complaining about   44
disproportionality had, a few months before the crisis, complained to
him that proposed reductions in the post-cold-war armed forces would
disproportionately injure blacks by denying them the opportunity for
advancement through military careers. And as for the argument that the
high black military presence was due to a semi-involuntary "economic
draft," Powell noted that blacks, as well as other groups (he might have
mentioned poor Southern whites), had traditionally favored military careers for such reasons as education, advancement, "adventure," and simply because the military life appealed to them.

This was so even though, historically, blacks were treated no bet-   45
ter by the military than by other American institutions. Throughout the
first half of this century, quotas ensured a relatively low percentage of
black troop representation, few blacks were promoted to the officer
ranks, and no black officer was placed in command of white subordi-
nates. Influenced by its strong Southern traditions, the military accepted

as fact just about every racial myth of the day: that blacks were lazy and insensitive to racial slurs, that they preferred white to black officers, could not be taught to fly, or lacked the reflexes for armored combat (a special prejudice of General George Patton). As one historian put it, the prevailing attitude of the military establishment at the beginning of World War II could be summed up in the crude motto: "You know how niggers are."

Testimony to the depth of such prejudice is the shameful treatment   46
of retired General Benjamin O. Davis, Jr. during his years at West Point, from which he was the first black to graduate in this century. Davis, who went on to become the commander of the Black Eagles, the legendary World War II flying unit, has just published his memoirs. In them he recounts that, while at West Point, for no other reason than race, he was subjected to "silencing," a practice otherwise reserved for cadets found guilty of honor-code violations. Except as required in the course of duty, no cadet would speak to Davis, and no one would share his room. After graduation, Davis's encounters with racial discrimination continued. A commanding officer encouraged him to enroll in law school and seek a political career; it was not "logical," the officer explained, for a black to command whites.

Infatuated with airplanes, Davis was initially rejected for training   47
as a pilot since it was Army policy that blacks not be admitted to flight school; once, an Army doctor invented a history of epilepsy to justify rejecting Davis. Eventually, however, a group of black flyers was trained and sent into action in North Africa and Europe. Still, recalcitrant commanders attempted to have the unit reassigned to non-combat duty, reasoning, as a report from a high Army Air Corps official stated, that "The Negro type has not the proper reflexes to make a first-class fighter pilot." In spite of everything, however, Davis and his comrades prevailed, and their record of distinguished service was ultimately hailed throughout America.

The heroism of the black flyers, Davis believes, advanced both the   48
Allied cause and the cause of the Negro, whose just demands for equality were growing more insistent as the war progressed. And there was a third cause to which Davis was deeply and personally attached: the cause of blacks in the military. Bolstered by an unyielding personal code which forbade his reacting with bitterness to acts of prejudice, Davis nevertheless remembers every insult, and he candidly admits to a preference for overseas assignments because of the American racial environment. At the same time he remains devoted to the military; in his view there is no more honorable profession. And he believes that America, with all its faults, is worth fighting for.

Davis and his Black Eagles served as an inspiration to past gener-   49 ations, and Colin Powell and the black troops of the Gulf conflict stand as a source of national pride today. As Haynes Johnson of the Washington *Post* wrote: "Black combat veterans [can serve] not only as role models for other blacks but also for whites." Yet few black leaders seem to have been shaken from their fixation on the theme of blacks as cannon fodder, or as victims of an economic "draft." No wonder, then, that one already sees evidence of black military resentment at the lack of support from black civilian leaders. Hearing criticism where they strongly believe that praise is warranted, black military men are beginning to ask, as the deputy commander of Desert Storm, General Calvin Waller, did: "What are our leaders doing in our communities to get our young black men off drugs? What are they doing to keep them in school or from dying in the streets?"

There has been much speculation about the broad political and cultural repercussions of the American military performance in the Gulf. President Bush's assertion that the war has enabled America to get out from under the Vietnam syndrome implies much more than a renewed respect for the military. Broadly speaking, the Vietnam syndrome entailed a reduced faith in America, in its world role, its key institutions, in its ability to solve its domestic ills, of which race relations counts as among the most important. Certainly one positive effect will be a diminution of negative views about blacks among whites. Future opinion polls will probably not find, as did a National Opinion Research Center poll taken before the war, that 51 percent of white Americans question the patriotism of blacks.

We do not know to what degree the whites in that poll were responding to statements by the nation's black leaders, although it seems reasonable to suppose that this was a significant factor. Unfortunately, a change in the perspective of the current black political leadership is highly unlikely. In contrast to many Americans who initially opposed the war but eventually came to identify with the goal of freeing Kuwait and handing Saddam Hussein a resounding setback, most black leaders seemed as dismayed by America's winning the war as with its having entered it in the first place. On the other hand, while polls showed blacks consistently less supportive of the war than other Americans, ordinary blacks were much more likely to support it than were their leaders. Indeed, an ABC-Washington *Post* poll taken after the war registered a stunning 77-percent black approval rating for President Bush, a figure which principally reflects deep pride in identifying with an *American* victory and a repudiation of the slogan: "This is not our war."

That this pride is not shared by most black leaders is tragic—tragic mainly because it reflects blindness to signs of positive change and also because it betrays a view of world affairs preposterous in many of its essentials and ultimately irrelevant to the future course of American political life.

Content Considerations

1. What is Puddington's criticism of the foreign policy beliefs often espoused by black leaders? How do those beliefs connect to the question of who fights America's wars?
2. What evidence does Puddington offer that the military has been a "success in race relations"?
3. What arguments in favor of a volunteer army does this article present? Use them as well as others of your own devising in a written statement of your position.

The Fairness Doctrine

The question of who serves in the military, who fights the wars and dies in them, gains an edge during times of war. A volunteer army may be fine in peacetime, according to some views, because it provides opportunities that enlistees may not find in the civilian workforce. But when war begins, those who have volunteered may die serving their country—while the rest of the country is at home as usual. At that point, critics are likely to become more severe, for the ones that serve may be from among the disadvantaged; thus they serve, are wounded, and perhaps die while those who already enjoy the best of America are free to continue enjoying.

The following essay examines the fairness of a volunteer army. Taken from the British publication The Economist, *the piece was written during the war in the Persian Gulf and speculates that the draft could be resurrected if the war lasted long enough. That did not happen, of course, but those who would like to see a draft replace the volunteer system still voice the criticisms that the essay advances.*

Before you read them, write about what kind of conscription you think would be most fair if the draft were to be resumed.

FEW WORDS ARE AS LOADED—or brandished as freely—as "fairness". During last autumn's budget ordeal, it was the Democratic euphemism-of-choice, meaning that the rich were not paying their fair share of taxes. 1

Now similar class-tinged appeals are beginning to be heard in the debate over the Gulf. The rich, it is said, are not doing their fair share of military service and should therefore be made to serve. In this revised version of the term, fairness implies the need for conscription. 2

Arguments in favour of reviving the draft are not new. Those who advocate compulsory "national service" schemes have long complained that America's military is made up disproportionately of the poor and the black; rich whites, they say, are shirking their duty to the common defence. In peace, such concerns seemed exaggerated. The prospect of war has changed that. 3

America's is not, in fact, a poor-man's military. According to studies done by the Congressional Budget Office and the Defence Department, recruits in recent years have been roughly representative (measured 4

by family earnings and education levels) of the enlistment-age population. In 1987, for example, about 45% of active-duty recruits came from
families with above-average incomes. More than 90% of them finished
secondary school, compared with 75% of all Americans. Indeed, because of the rising education standards demanded of recruits, the underclass is, in effect, excluded from military service.

But if the poor are not substantially over-represented, blacks are.   5
Though they make up just 14% of the enlistment-age population, blacks
account for nearly 22% of the active-duty recruits. In the Army, which
would probably suffer the most casualties should war come, that number is 28%. The rich, by contrast, are unlikely to suffer much: the children of the top 15% of earners have joined at a rate one-fifth the national
average. Among enlisted servicemen, only about 20% have a parent
who has graduated from university.

Such disparities, argue defenders of the all-volunteer forces, are   6
unavoidable. Because it offers job-training and education, the military
will draw in those who cannot get them elsewhere; because it is seen as
truly meritocratic, it will be attractive to blacks. The problem, they say,
is a lack of opportunity in civilian life. In return for a ready solution,
those who join accept certain obligations—and certain risks. So long as
those risks are shared by a force that is broadly representative of society,
its legitimacy cannot be questioned.

Proponents of a draft, such as James Webb, a former secretary of   7
the Navy, and Charles Peters, the editor of the *Washington Monthly,*
disagree. They say the absence from Saudi Arabia of the offspring of
the "elite"—only two congressmen, and no members of the Bush cabinet, have children in the Gulf—has insulated these leaders from the
consequences of their decisions and opinions. And that, they argue, has
blunted domestic dissent and made war more likely.

Those views, like so many others applied to the Gulf war-in-wait-   8
ing, are vestiges of Vietnam. Then, the draft system—especially the
exemptions from it—was grossly unfair: by granting liberal deferrals to
those enrolled in university, it effectively allowed the clever and the rich
to avoid service, while condemning the rest—mainly blacks and blue-
collar whites—to fight and, often, die. Even within the services, the
proportion of blacks in combat roles was higher than in non-combat
roles (something that is not true of today's forces).

Its inequities acknowledged, the Vietnam draft was done away   9
with in 1973 and replaced by an all-volunteer force. Since then, military
planners have agreed that a draft—a random one, without exemptions—
would probably be reinstated in the event of a big conflict. For now,
the Pentagon says it has no such intentions. A draft started today would,
in any case, take about nine months to deliver soldiers to the Gulf and

would, even then, have a negligible effect on the force's representative-ness. War, it is said, will not be long or bloody enough to warrant one.

Perhaps. Hitler said that war is like entering a darkened room; a nation never knows what lies inside until it walks in and turns on the lights. Yet even as America prepares to take those steps, talk of a draft is increasing. In a recent poll, almost 60% of those asked said they favoured the idea. And Les Aspin, the chairman of the House Armed Services Committee, will soon hold hearings on the matter. Mr. Aspin's thoughts are not yet known. But others on Capitol Hill believe that if war lasts more than a month, or casualties reach 5,000, the pressure for a draft will be hard to resist.

10

Content Considerations

1. What groups are over-represented in the U.S. military? Why does it matter?
2. Respond to the assertion that the governing elite are removed from the effects of their decisions because so few of their children serve in the military. How could such a situation have "blunted domestic dissent and made war more likely"?
3. In what ways is the military "meritocratic"? Why might a meritocratic system be especially attractive to minorities?

The Rich Don't Serve—So What?

Charles Peters, editor in chief of The Washington Monthly, *is known for declaring his opinions and conclusions with great force and certainty. One of his opinions is that the United States should dispense with the volunteer army and return to a conscription system. In the next essay,* The New Republic *editor Michael Kinsley argues against such a return, espousing instead the value of the volunteer system.*

Although it has always been the case that citizens could volunteer for military service, the change to an all-volunteer army has meant that the military has had to improve its image in order to be perceived by potential enlistees as a desirable occupation or career. Its standards—the basic requirements for employment—have improved, thus attracting those with higher ability and potential. Its benefits and pay have increased.

Before you read Kinsley's argument (from The Washington Monthly, *March, 1989), write several paragraphs on the value of a voluntary military to the United States' social and economic structure. As you read, compare the values you found to those Kinsley discusses.*

ONE CHAPTER OF the Gospel According to *The Washington Monthly* that I have some trouble with is Charles Peters's enthusiasm for a military draft. This bad idea in its own right also reflects two characteristic defects of the Peters's Gospel generally. First, a slight authoritarian streak: a too-casual willingness to say that something ought to be required just because it would be nice (such as Charlie's notorious proposal for a law banning banks from the ground floor of office buildings). Second, an occasional failure to think through the practical difficulties of achieving some desirable end through a seemingly simple policy initiative (such as the idea of giving a capital gains break to "new" and "productive" investments only). 1

It certainly would be nice if the armed services represented a cross section of the population; if every citizen made a patriotic contribution to America before going off on his or her own life course; if there were one guaranteed occasion of social class mixing in our increasingly stratified society. These are the advantages Charlie sees in a draft, based on his own experience in World War II. (These, plus saving the government money.) But telling people they must give up two years of their 2 lives is a major infringement on freedom, for which there ought to be a major reason. "The defense of our country" is, of course, a major reason, but the defense of our country is not at stake. It is being defended adequately without a draft, by people who are in the military because they wish to be there. The people who make defense policy are not merely satisfied with current arrangements—they actively prefer a volunteer force to a draft, for obvious reasons. Are the genuine but amorphous spiritual reasons for bringing back a draft more important?

Nicholas Von Hoffman put the practical case against a draft in a nutshell many years ago when he wrote: "Draft old men's money, not young men's bodies." One way to look at a draft is as a tax on the difference between what the Army pays you and what it would take to entice you into the Army voluntarily. At some level of pay and benefit, the military can meet its manpower needs without resorting to this tax. Von Hoffman's point was: why not pay for this national defense by taxing the people who can best afford it?

Look at this economic point another way. Today, we actually are paying enough to fill the Army without a draft (though, of course, we are borrowing the money instead of taxing ourselves to raise it—a different problem). No more soldiers are needed. A draft, therefore, would be pointless unless it accompanies a reduction in pay and benefits to get rid of some of those volunteers and make room for the draftees. That might well make the Army more socially representative. But what would happen to those who join up voluntarily under current policies? One of two things. Either they would be in the Army anyway (as volunteers or draftees), only earning a lot less; or they would be doing something else (or possibly nothing else) when they'd rather be in the Army under current arrangements. In short, however "unfair" it may seem to fill the Army with volunteers, it's no favor to would-be volunteers to shut off this option in order to put others unwillingly in their place.

In fact, today's volunteer military is reasonably socially diverse. There aren't a lot of Groton graduates, and the poorest of the underclass aren't wanted or needed. But between these two extremes, it's fairly representative of society as a whole. And to the extent it isn't, so what? Why should the military be a perfect social cross section? In particular, if black Americans find in the armed services an especially good opportunity for self-advancement with less discrimination, and as a result are disproportionately represented there, I think that's something America can be reasonably proud of rather than the reverse. In a way, it's insulting to those who have chosen military service, either as a career or as a useful life experience that will lead somewhere else, to say that what they're doing is so undesirable that others who aren't interested should be forced to do it in their place.

Even if military service is made so undesirable that there are no 6
volunteers, there will still be the practical problem of what to do with
all the draftees. The military needs only a small fraction of any age
cohort. What about the rest? The Vietnam-era solution was a wildly
generous and unfair system of exemptions. Since this episode was precisely one origin of the Monthly's draft enthusiasm, that option's presumably out. There are only two others: a lottery and a system of
universal service that would include worthy nonmilitary work such as
the Peace Corps and teaching in the inner city and so on.

A lottery would still be unfair, of course. It would just be unfair 7
at random, rather than on perceived race and class grounds. If the volunteer army (as opposed to the old draft-with-exemptions) were truly
unfair, that would be an improvement. But to snatch two years from
just a small fraction of the population against their will, and to make
room for them by reducing opportunity for people who want it, all in
the name of "fairness," seems insane. As for drafting everybody and
then finding work for them to do, that surely would wipe out any
conceivable savings from underpaying soldiers. You don't have to be a
neoconservative to predict that it would be a bureaucratic nightmare.
And you don't need to be overly pessimistic about human nature to
doubt that involuntary time-servers are going to put their hearts into
their assigned tasks.

Having made the case, now let me backtrack. First, I'm talking 8
about a peacetime draft. Obviously, soldiers are needed only in peacetime because of the risk of war, and as a deterrent to war. But there's a
difference between that risk and the much larger and more immediate
risk to life and limb that comes from actually being in a war. If we ever
find ourselves in an extended land war again—hard to imagine—that's
the time for a draft. Whether having a draft already in place would make
starting and pursuing such a war harder—as the Gospel assumes—or
easier is, at the very least, unclear.

Second, a new spirit of patriotic service of the sort Charles longs 9
for, in contrast to the reigning spirit of the Reagan years, is an attractive
vision. You can imagine a culture where it was more or less assumed
that everybody would do a year to two of military or civilian service
after high school or college before heading off into "the real world." It
wouldn't even offend my libertarian principles too much if kids were
given a slight nudge through provisos in student loans and so on. But
it seems to me that encouraging voluntary service is a more promising
way to create such a new spirit than telling young people: "OK, buddy,
it's either work with Alzheimer's victims, go to jail, or move to Canada."

Content Considerations

1. According to Kinsley, why is a volunteer force preferable to a conscripted one?
2. Discuss the benefits and drawbacks of a volunteer force, a lottery draft, a universal service requirement, and a draft that includes deferments. Explain which you think is preferable and why you find it so.
3. Visit a recruitment office, examine the literature, and interview members of the military in order to gather perspectives on the value of the current volunteer system.

Claim You're Gay, Avoid the Military

The issue of sexual preference is one associated with many concerns; central to them all is whether sexual preference affects the quality of one's work and the morality of one's decisions. The American "standard" is heterosexuality; persons who do not fit that description have often claimed that they are discriminated against in areas such as employment and housing. Gays are forbidden to serve in the armed forces.

In the following essay, writer Randy Shilts points out some possible consequences of the U.S. military's current policy toward homosexuals. While some people might view being excluded from military service a blessing, others wish to serve or are already serving and do not want their careers jeopardized. Shilts, author of And the Band Played On, *a history of AIDS in America, is currently writing a book on gays in the military. Before you read what he has to say, make a list of the possible effects that the military's policy toward homosexuals could create.*

THE LARGE-SCALE BUILD-UP of American troops in the Persian Gulf has led many to call for reinstatement of the military draft. Some experts believe that if a shooting war lasted longer than a few months, the military may need more troops than are now available among both active duty and reserve personnel. Shortages might have to be made up from conscription.

Amid this discussion, one central point has been overlooked: Under current Pentagon policies, enforcing a draft will be virtually impossible.

The reason is Department of Defense regulation 1332.14, which states that "homosexuality is incompatible with military service." Lesbians and gay men—or anyone who says they might be gay at some point in the unspecified future—are banned from serving in the armed forces.

Initially, this policy may seem a marginal, even trivial, concern as we consider whether to go to war. Think again. According to the policy, "homosexual means a person, regardless of sex, who engages in, or intends to engage in homosexual acts."

The Pentagon's all-inclusive language allows for no exceptions or flexibility. In fact, the military routinely dismisses people who have only said they are gay—even though no evidence exists as to whether they've ever had gay sex. In other words, 1332.14 offers an extraordinarily easy way out to anybody who wants to evade military service.

"Gay deceivers" were a major headache for the Selective Service 6 system during the Vietnam War, even when getting deferred because of homosexuality was an arduous process. To successfully claim homosexuality back then, some prospective draftees were required to furnish signed affidavits from sexual partners attesting to homosexual activity.

After courts questioned the ambiguities in the wording of the mil- 7 itary's policy, the Department of Defense instituted its new ironclad, anti-gay regulations in 1981. These proscriptions were upheld by the Supreme Court in February 1990.

To understand how this could bring turmoil to any new military 8 draft, consider how much society has changed since the Vietnam era.

To claim you were gay 25 years ago meant jeopardizing your fu- 9 ture. Most professional accreditation organizations, including those for doctors, dentists and lawyers, barred gays from practicing on the grounds of "moral turpitude."

Today, however, this has changed. For much of America, ho- 10 mosexuality is not the bugaboo it once was. In 1965, dodging the draft through claims of homosexuality might have meant disgrace. In 1990, it would probably do little more than earn one a slot on "Geraldo" or "Sally Jessy Raphael."

Given this, and the fact that going to war might mean getting on 11 the wrong end of Saddam Hussein's mustard gas, I'd wager that when faced with the draft, a fair number of young heterosexual men will just say "gay." It won't even take a large number of prospective draftees claiming homosexuality to throw Selective Service into disarray.

Add to this the number of draft age men facing combat who ac- 12 tually are gay and who will be far less reluctant to tell this to their draft boards than their Vietnam era counterparts, and the armed services will be in serious trouble.

Already, worried lesbian and gay reservists are considering leaving 13 the reserves now rather than face the prospect of separation or even court martial in Saudi Arabia. Secrets, they fear, will be much harder to keep in the close quarters of the Arabian desert than in their once monthly training weekends.

According to lawyers at gay advocacy groups, some reserve com- 14 manders are newly reluctant to base a discharge solely on a reservist's claims of homosexuality. They want more proof. Suddenly, they're realizing they may lose some of their best people when they're needed most.

What the commanders are also learning, however, is that the pol- 15 icy now cuts both ways, allowing for no exceptions and absolutely no consideration of the quality of service offered by homosexual personnel.

Gay rights advocates have long argued that the regulation's Draconian stance victimizes lesbian and gay soldiers who have often proved to be both unquestionably patriotic and among the military's top performers. What any return to the draft might prove, however, is that the ultimate victim of regulation 1332.14 is the military itself.

Content Considerations

1. How is the military's policy of excluding gays from military service connected to implementing and enforcing a draft?
2. What importance does the passage of time between Vietnam and the Gulf war have to the issue of gays in the military?
3. Explain your own position regarding homosexuals serving in the military by conscription or by choice.

JOHN COURTNEY MURRAY, S.J.

War and Conscience

In every war, some people refuse to serve, claiming conscientious objector sta-tus. What this means, of course, is that they object to serving because to do so is against the beliefs they hold. They may believe that war is never justified, that the killing and destruction that is war has no grounds, ever. Or they may believe that a particular war is wrong, that the nation's reasons for going to war are not sound and thus refuse to enlist or to follow deployment orders.

Selective conscientious objection is this second kind; some people hold that the only reason to fight a war is if a nation is directly threatened. Such a situation has happened rarely in the United States, so conscientious objectors have claimed that the stated reasons for a particular war are immoral, and they have refused to serve.

In the next selection, written and published during the Vietnam War, John Courtney Murray, S.J., examines what it means to be a conscientious objector. One of the points in his essay is that "the whole relation of the person to society is involved in this issue" (paragraph 2). Write several paragraphs about the relations between a citizen and his or her society before you begin.

THE NATION IS CONFRONTED today with the issue of selective conscientious objection, conscientious objection to particular wars or, as it is sometimes called, discretionary armed service.

The theoretical implications of the issue are complex and subtle. The issue raises the whole question of war as a political act and the means whereby it should be confined within the moral universe. The issue also raises the question of the status of the private conscience in the face of public law and national policy. In fact, the whole relation of the person to society is involved in this issue. Moreover, the practical implications of the issue are far reaching. Selective conscientious objec-tion, as Gordon Zahn has pointed out, is an "explosive principle." If once admitted with regard to the issue of war, the consequences of the principle might run to great lengths in the civil community.

My brief comments on this far-reaching principle are here directed, for reasons that will appear, both to the academic community, especially the student community, and to the political community and its representatives.

A personal note may be permissible here. During the deliberations

112

of the President's Advisory Commission on Selective Service, on which I was privileged to serve, I undertook to advocate that the revised statute should extend the provisions of the present statute to include not only the absolute pacifist but also the relative pacifist; that the grounds for the status of conscientious objector should be not only religiously or non-religiously motivated opposition to participation in war in all forms, but also to similarly motivated opposition to participation in particular wars.

This position was rejected by the majority of the Commission. No   5
Presidential recommendation was made to the Congress on the issue. There is evidence that the Congress is not sympathetic to the position of the selective objector and is not inclined to accept it. This does not mean that the issue has been satisfactorily settled. The public argument goes on and must go on. It is much too late in the day to defend the theory of General Hershey that "the conscientious objector by my theory is best handled if no one hears of him." The issue is before the country and it must be kept there.

It is true that the issue has been raised by a small number of people,   6
chiefly in the academic community—students, seminarians, professors, not to speak of ministers of religion. But this group of citizens is socially significant. It must be heard and it must be talked to. I recognize that in many respects the issue has been raised rather badly, in ways that betray misunderstandings. Moreover, mistakes have been made about the mode of handling the issue. Nevertheless, the student community is to be praised for having raised a profound moral issue that has been too long disregarded in American life.

The American attitude toward war has tended to oscillate between   7
absolute pacifism in peacetime and extremes of ferocity in wartime. Prevalent in American society has been an abstract ethic, conceived either in religious or in secularized terms, which condemns all war as immoral. No nation has the *jus ad bellum*. On the other hand, when a concrete historical situation creates the necessity for war, no ethic governs its conduct. There are no moral criteria operative to control the uses of force. There is no *jus in bello*. One may pursue hostilities to the military objective of unconditional surrender, and the nation may escalate the use of force to the paroxysm of violence of which Hiroshima and Nagasaki are forever the symbols, even though they were prepared for by the fire-bomb raids on Tokyo and by the saturation bombing of German cities. And all this use of violence can somehow be justified by slogans that were as simplistic as the principles of absolute pacifism.

These extreme alternatives are no longer tolerable. Our nation must   8
make its way to some discriminating doctrine—moral, political, and military—on the uses of force. Perhaps the contemporary agitation in

the academic community over selective conscientious objection may help in this direction. It has contributed to a revival of the traditional doctrine of the just war, whose origins were in Augustine and which was elaborated by the medieval Schoolmen and furthered by international jurists in the Scholastic tradition and by others in the later tradition of Grotius.

This doctrine has long been neglected, even by the churches; now 9 we begin to witness its revival. We are also beginning to realize that it is not a sectarian doctrine. It is not exclusively Roman Catholic; in certain forms of its presentation, it is not even Christian. It emerges in the minds of all men of reason and good will when they face two inevitable questions. First, what are the norms that govern recourse to the violence of war? Second, what are the norms that govern the measure of violence to be used in war? In other words, when is war rightful, and what is rightful in war? One may indeed refuse the questions, but this is a form of moral abdication, which would likewise be fatal to civilization. If one does face the questions, one must arrive at the just war doctrine in its classical form, or at some analogue or surrogate, conceived in other terms.

The essential significance of the traditional doctrine is that it insists, 10 first, that military decisions are a species of political decisions, and second, that political decisions must be viewed, not simply in the perspectives of politics as an exercise of power, but of morality and theology in some valid sense. If military and political decisions are not so viewed, the result is the degradation of those who make them and the destruction of the human community.

My conclusion here is that we all owe some debt of gratitude to 11 those who, by raising the issue of selective conscientious objection, have undertaken to transform the tragic conflict in South Vietnam into an issue, not simply of political decision and military strategy, but of moral judgment as well.

The mention of South Vietnam leads me to my second point. The 12 issue of selective conscientious objection has been raised in the midst of the war in Southeast Asia. Therefore, there is danger lest the issue be muddled and confused, or even misused and abused. In South Vietnam we see war stripped of all the false sanctities with which we managed to invest World War I and World War II, and to a lesser extent even Korea. The South Vietnamese war is not a crusade. There is not even a villain of the piece, as the Kaiser was, or Hitler, or Hirohito. Not even Ho Chi Minh or Mao Tse-tung can be cast in the role of the man in the black hat. We have no easy justifying slogans. We cannot cry "On to Hanoi," as we cried "On to Berlin" and "On to Tokyo." This war does not raise the massive issue of national survival. It is a limited military action for limited political aims. As we view it in the press or on television it almost seems to fulfill Hobbes's vision of human life in the state of pure nature, "nasty, brutish, and short" except that the war in South Vietnam will not be short. In the face of the reality of it, all our ancient simplisms fail us. The American people are uncomfortable, baffled, and even resentful and angry.

To state the problem quite coldly, the war in South Vietnam is 13 subject to opposition on political and military grounds, and also on grounds of national interest. This opposition has been voiced, and voiced in passionate terms. It has evoked a response in the name of patriotism that is also passionate. Consequently, in this context, it is difficult to raise the moral issue of selective conscientious objection. There are even some to whom it seems dangerous to let the issue be raised at all.

At this juncture I venture to make a recommendation in the com- 14 mon interest of good public argument. The issue of selective conscientious objection must be distinguished from the issue of the justice of the South Vietnam war. If this distinction is not made and enforced in argument, the result will be confusion and the clash of passions. The necessary public argument will degenerate into a useless and harmful quarrel. The distinction can be made. I make it myself. I advocate selective conscientious objection in the name of the traditional moral doctrine on war and also in the name of traditional American political doctrine on the rights of conscience. I am also prepared to make the case for the American military presence and action in South Vietnam.

I hasten to add that I can just about make the moral case. But so 15 it always is. The morality of war can never be more than marginal. The issue of war can never be portrayed in black and white. Moral judgment on the issue must be reached by a balance of many factors. To argue about the morality of war inevitably leads one into gray areas. This is the point that was excellently made by Mr. Secretary Vance in his thoughtful address to the Annual Convention of the Episcopal Diocese of West Virginia on May 6th, 1967. It is evident here that our national tradition of confused moral thought on the uses of force does us a great disservice. It results in a polarization of opinion that makes communication among citizens difficult or even impossible. As Mr. Vance said, "In America today one of the greatest barriers to understanding is the very nature of the dialogue which has developed over the issue of Vietnam. It is heated and intolerant. The lines on both sides are too sharply drawn." I agree.

By the same token rational argument about selective conscientious 16 objection will be impossible if public opinion is polarized by all the passions that have been aroused by the South Vietnam war. The two issues, I repeat, can and must be separated.

Another difficulty confronts us here. The issue about conscientious 17 objection seems to have been drawn between the academic community and the political community—if you will, between poets and politicians, between scientists and statesmen, between humanists and men of affairs, between the churches and the secular world. It is, therefore, no accident that the dialogue at the present moment is in a miserable state. One may seek the reason for the fact in the differences in the climate of thought and feeling that prevail in the two distinct communities, academic and political. In consequence of this difference in climate each community, in a different way, can become the victim of the intellectual and moral vice that is known as the selective perception of reality.

It has been observed that the commitment of the intellectual today 18 is not simply to the search for truth, but also to the betterment of the world—to the eradication of evil and to the creation of conditions of human dignity, first among which is peace. One might say that he has assumed a prophetic role, not unlike that of the churches. This is most laudable. The danger is lest the very strength of the moral commitment—to peace and against war—may foreclose inquiry into the military and political facts of the contemporary world—the naked facts of power situations and the requirements of law and order in an imperfect world, which may justify recourse to the arbitrament of arms. The problem is compounded if the so-called "norms of nonconformism" begin to operate. In that case opposition to war becomes the test of commitment to the ideals of the academic community.

On the other hand, the politician is no prophet. He may and should 19 wish to shape the world unto the common desire of the heart of man which is peace with freedom and justice. But he is obliged to regard the world as an arena in which historical alternatives are always limited. He must face enduring problems, which may seem intractable, and which demand continuing decisions and acts. His actions cannot be based on absolute certainties or on considerations of the ideal, but on a careful balancing and choosing between the relativities that are before him.

In a word, for the prophets and for the intellectual, war is simply 20 evil. For the politician it may well appear to be the lesser evil. This too is a conscientious position, but it is very different from the prophetic position, even though the choice of the lesser evil is part of the human pursuit of the good. In any event, it is not surprising that the politician and the prophet fail to communicate. It must also be remembered that the politician creates the situation within which the prophetic voice may be safely heard. There is much wisdom in the statement of Paul Ramsey: "The right of pacifist conscientious objection can be granted for the fostering of the consciences of free men, only because in national emergencies there are a sufficient number of individuals whose political discretion has been instructed in the need to repel, and the justice of repelling, injury to the common good."

I might add a practical point. The intellectual, whether he be stu- 21 dent or professor, sets a premium on being provocative. His task is to challenge all certainties, especially easy certainties, and therefore to challenge the authorities on which certainties may depend. He wants evidence, not authority, and he sets a high value on dissent. All this is excellent and necessary. But there is danger in thrusting this scale of evaluation into the political community. It is not merely that the intellectual provokes reaction; he provokes an over-reaction on the part of the representatives of the political community, and thus he may easily defeat his own cause.

The advocacy of selective conscientious objection in the midst of 22 the South Vietnamese war is provocative, and the political response to it has been an over-reaction. If you want the evidence you need only read the record of the hearings in the Congress, both Senate and House, on the revision of the Selective Service Act, when the issue of conscientious objection was brought up. The claim that the selective objector should be recognized was met with the response that all conscientious objection should be abolished.

All this amounts simply to saying that we face a most difficult 23 issue. It might be of some value to try to locate some of the sources of the difficulty. Strictly on grounds of moral argument, the right conscientiously to object to participation in a particular war is incontestable. I shall not argue this issue. The practical question before all of us is how to get the moral validity of this right understood and how to get the right itself legally recognized, declared in statutory law. (I leave aside the question whether the right is a human right, which ought to receive sanction in the Bill of Rights as a constitutional right.)

I have made one practical suggestion already. The issue of selective 24 conscientious objection must be argued on its own merits. It is not a question of whether one is for or against the war in Vietnam, for or against selective service, much less for or against killing other people. The worst thing that could happen would be to use the issue of conscientious objection as a tactical weapon for political opposition to the war in Vietnam or to the general course of American foreign policy. This would not be good morality and it would be worse politics. Perhaps the central practical question might be put in this way: Do the conditions exist which make possible the responsible exercise of a right of selective conscientious objection? The existence of these conditions is the prerequisite for granting legal status to the right itself.

There are two major conditions. The first is an exact understand- 25 ing of the just-war doctrine, and the second is respect for what Socrates called "the conscience of the laws." I offer two examples, from among many, where these conditions were not observed.

Not long ago a young man in an anti-Vietnam protest on tele-   26
vision declared that he would be willing to fight in Vietnam if he knew that the war there was just, but since he did not know, he was obliged to protest its immorality. This young man clearly did not understand the just-war doctrine and he did not understand what Socrates meant by the "conscience of the laws."

Similarly, in a statement issued by a Seminarians' Conference on   27
the Draft held not long ago in Cambridge, there appears this statement: "The spirit of these principles [of the just-war doctrine] demands that every war be opposed until or unless it can be morally justified in re-lation to these principles." Socrates would not have agreed with this statement nor do I. The dear seminarians have got it backward.

The root of the error here may be simply described as a failure to   28
understand that provision of the just-war doctrine which requires that a war should be "declared." This is not simply a nice piece of legalism, the prescription of a sheer technicality. Behind the provision lies a whole philosophy of the State as a moral and political agent. The provision implies the recognition of the authority of the political community by established political processes to make decisions about the course of its action in history, to muster behind these decisions the united efforts of the community, and to publicize these decisions before the world.

If there is to be a political community, capable of being a moral   29
agent in the international community, there must be some way of pub-licly identifying the nation's decisions. These decisions must be declared to be the decisions of the community. Therefore, if the decision is for war, the war must be declared. This declaration is a moral and political act. It states a decision conscientiously arrived at in the interests of the international common good. It submits the decision to the judgment of mankind. Moreover, when the decision-making processes of the com-munity have been employed and a decision has been reached, at least a preliminary measure of internal authority must be conceded by the cit-izens to this decision, even by those citizens who dissent from it. This, at least in part, is what Socrates meant by respect for the "conscience of the laws." This is why in the just-war theory it has always been main-tained that the presumption stands for the decision of the community as officially declared. He who dissents from the decision must accept the burden of proof.

The truth, therefore, is contrary to the statement of the seminari-   30
ans. The citizen is to concede the justness of the common political de-cision, made in behalf of the nation, unless and until he is sure in his

own mind that the decision is unjust, for reasons that he in turn must be ready convincingly to declare. The burden of proof is on him, not on the government or the administration or the nation as a whole. He does not and may not resign his conscience into the keeping of the State, but he must recognize that the State too has its conscience which informs its laws and decisions. When his personal conscience clashes with the conscience of the laws, his personal decision is his alone. It is valid for him, and he must follow it. But in doing so he still stands within the community and is subject to its judgment as already declared.

Only if conceived in these terms can the inevitable tension between   31 the person and the community be properly a tension of the moral order. Otherwise, it will degenerate into a mere power struggle between arbitrary authority and an aggregate of individuals, each of whom claims to be the final arbiter of right and wrong.

This is the line of reasoning which led me to argue before the   32 National Advisory Commission on Selective Service that one who applies for the status of selective conscientious objector should be obliged to state his case before a competent panel of judges. I was also following the suggestion of Ralph Potter that the concession of status to the selective objector might help to upgrade the level of moral and political discourse in this country. It is presently lamentably low. On the other hand, Paul Ramsey has recently suggested that the matter works the other way round. "A considerable upgrading of the level of political discourse in America is among the conditions of the possibility of granting selective conscientious objection. At least the two things can and may and must go together." He adds rather sadly: "The signs of the times are not propitious for either." I agree.

Those who urge the just-war doctrine as the ground for selective   33 conscientious objection must understand the doctrine itself. They may not naïvely or cynically employ it as a device for opting out from under the legitimate decisions of the political community, or as a tactic for political opposition to particular wars. Rightly understood, this doctrine is not an invitation to pacifism, and still less to civil disobedience. There is a further requisite for legal recognition of selective conscientious objection. It is the prior recognition of the difference between moral objection to a particular war and political opposition to a particular war. This seems to be the sticking point for the political community. It brings into question the whole ethos of our society in the matter of the uses of force.

Historically, we have been disposed to regard the intuitive verdict   34 of the absolute pacifist that all wars are wrong as having the force of a moral imperative. The same moral force is not conceded to the judgment of the conscientious man, religious or not, who makes a reflective and discriminating judgment on the war in front of him. The general disposition is to say that objection to particular wars is and can only be political and, therefore, cannot entitle anyone to the status of conscientious objector.

Here again there is a misunderstanding of the just-war doctrine. 35 In fact there seems to be a misunderstanding of the very nature of the moral reasoning. The just-war doctrine starts from the moral principle that the order of justice and law cannot be left without adequate means for its own defense, including the use of force. The doctrine further holds that the use of force is subject to certain conditions and its justice depends on certain circumstances. The investigation of the fulfillment of these conditions leads the conscientious man to a consideration of certain political and military factors in a given situation. There is the issue of aggression, the issue of the measure of force to be employed in resisting it, the issue of probable success, the issue of the balance of good and evil that will be the outcome. The fact that his judgment must take account of military and political factors does not make the judgment purely political. It is a judgment reached within a moral universe, and the final reason for it is of the moral order.

There is some subtlety to this argument. But that is not, I think, 36 the reason why the political community refuses to assimilate or accept it. The reasons are of the practical order. The immediate reason is the enormous difficulty of administering a statute that would provide for selective conscientious objection. The deeper reason is the perennial problem of the erroneous conscience. It may be easily illustrated.

Suppose a young man comes forward and says: "I refuse to serve 37 in this war on grounds of the Nuremberg principle." Conversation discloses that he has not the foggiest idea what the Nuremberg principle really is. Or suppose he understands the principle and says: "I refuse to serve because in this war the United States is committing war crimes." The fact may be, as it is in South Vietnam, that this allegation is false. Or suppose he says, "I refuse to serve because the United States is the aggressor in this war." This reason again may be demonstrably false. What then is the tribunal to do?

Here perhaps we come to the heart of the difficulty and I have 38 only two things to say. First, unless the right to selective objection is granted to possibly erroneous consciences it will not be granted at all. The State will have to abide by the principle of the Seeger case, which does not require that the objection be the truth but that it be truly held. One must follow the logic of an argument wherever it leads. On the other hand, the political community cannot be blamed for harboring the fear that if the right to selective objection is acknowledged in these sweeping terms, it might possibly lead to anarchy, to the breakdown of society, and to the paralysis of public policy.

Second, the reality of this fear imposes a further burden on the 39 consciences of those who would appeal to freedom of conscience. Selective objection is not a trivial matter. As Ralph Potter has said: "The nation is ultimately a moral community. To challenge its well-established policies as illegal, immoral, and unjust is to pose a threat, the seriousness of which seems at times to escape the critics themselves, whether by the callousness of youth or the callousness of usage." It must be recognized that society will defend itself against this threat, if it be carelessly wielded.

The solution can only be the cultivation of political discretion 40 throughout the populace, not least in the student and academic community. A manifold work of moral and political intelligence is called for. No political society can be founded on the principle that absolute rights are to be accorded to the individual conscience, and to all individual consciences, even when they are in error. This is rank individualism and to hold it would reveal a misunderstanding of the very nature of the political community. On the other hand, the political community is bound to respect conscience. But the fulfillment of this obligation supposes that the consciences of the citizens are themselves formed and informed.

Therefore, the final question may be whether there is abroad in 41 the land a sufficient measure of moral and political discretion, in such wise that the Congress could, under safeguard of the national security, acknowledge the right of discretionary armed service. To cultivate this power of discretion is a task for all of us.

Content Considerations

1. Discuss how Murray believes military decisions should be viewed. What might be the consequences of viewing them as he suggests?
2. Respond to the assertion that "In a word, for the prophets and for the intellectual, war is simply evil" (paragraph 20). Explain whether you agree. What other groups exist that might find war evil? That would not?
3. What does Murray conclude about selective conscientious objection? Construct your own argument to answer his.

— *Ideas for Discussion, Writing, and Research* —

1. What issues concerning women in military service do the essays by the editors of *The New Republic,* Suzanne Fields, and Ellen Goodman focus on? What issues that you believe are important do they neglect?

2. The pieces written by Sonia Shah, Arch Puddington, *Economist* editors, and Michael Kinsley concern the possible disproportion of minorities in the military to the general population. How do the selections differ regarding the significance of such a disproportion? What is your own position regarding the idea that the racial composition of the military should reflect that of the country's population?

3. Randy Shilts examines the military policy that forbids homosexuals from serving in the military. What is the reasoning behind this policy? Explain whether it is convincing to you, and to what degree.

4. John Courtney Murray, S.J., weaves into his argument the idea of a "just war." What does that term mean? What does it have to do with the conscientious objection to war?

5. What is the history of conscientious objection in American wars? How have the conditions of granting conscientious objection been modified during the years? (It may be a good idea to work with others on this; divide the research and compare information in order to draw conclusions.)

6. What evidence exists that supports or undermines the military's decision to forbid homosexuals from joining the service? Using that information, argue for or against the Department of Defense regulation 1332.14.

7. Using the pieces by Goodman, Shah, Puddington, *The Economist,* Kinsley, and several sources of your selection, argue for the merits of a conscripted or a volunteer army.

8. The institution of a volunteer army affects areas besides military ones. Explore the effects it has on American economics, upward mobility, class structure, education, family structure, politics, or an ethnic or racial minority group.

9. Discover the roles women have filled during wartime for one period of history in the country of your choice. Use what you discover to examine the controversies concerning women in combat.

10. What happens to a family when one of its members goes off to war? Gather information from interviews and oral histories as well as written sources.

3

Hand-axes to Smart Bombs: Technology of War

"QUEENIE" WAS SHEATHED in polished aluminum, a glittering sliver in a pale blue sky over the islands of Japan. No effort was made to camouflage the B-29: How do you hide the biggest airplane ever made (to that time)? But the crewmen aboard Queenie were confident: the Boeing Superfortress was not only the biggest airplane in the world, it could, they were told, fly higher than the anti-aircraft fire that the Japanese could shoot, and higher and faster than most Japanese fighters. It had a sophisticated defense system, including guns directed by radar and fired remotely; it was pressurized, so even at the highest altitude the crewmen were comfortable; it could carry an enormous load of bombs over thousands of miles and return, without refueling.

The B-29 was the logical weapon to deliver the atom bomb to Hiroshima and Nagasaki in August, 1945.

For Lynn Johnston, born and reared on a small farm in northern Missouri, riding at 35,000 feet over the Pacific Ocean was, indeed, a long way from home. For sixty-three missions, Johnston and his fellow crewmen lifted off from airstrips on islands across the Pacific and dropped tons of high-explosives on targets across Japan and Southeast Asia. Near the end of the war, on the island of Tinian in the Marianas, one end of the base was sealed off from everyone. No one could penetrate the tight defensive line around the Superforts parked inside.

The B-29s beyond the line were no different from Queenie, but Johnston and every airman on Tinian knew something big was up. On August 6, one of the B-29s lifted off the steel-mat runway, and the world was changed forever. The age of the atomic bomb had arrived.

As sophisticated as the B-29 had seemed to be in the 1940s, it was quickly decommissioned as ever-more complicated and deadly aircraft were built, followed shortly by missiles that could deliver death without the guidance of a human pilot.

The history of war technology has been the history of killing humans ever more remotely, ever more dispassionately. This chapter considers the technology and its consequences, as well as the moral and ethical questions that accompany such sophisticated weaponry. They prompt such questions as: Do high-tech weapons make war more acceptable by creating a wall between the warriors and the targets? Do scientists and doctors have any moral responsibility when developing technology that will be used to kill? Should advanced technology be limited to only a few "responsible" nations? Is the environment a legitimate target in war?

The first weapons were undoubtedly rocks and sticks; they required close physical proximity. Paleolithic warriors had to see the faces of their enemies, had to look into the eyes of those they were about to kill. For thousands, perhaps tens of thousands, of years there was little advance. A rock was tied to a stick to make a more effective club; sharpened stones were attached to shafts to make a spear. Perhaps the greatest technological advance in military weaponry in the first million years or so of human warfare was the bow: the simple expedient of tying a line to both ends of a flexible limb created an awesome weapon, capable of killing foes a hundred yards away.

Henry V at Agincourt proved the efficacy of the longbow; in a three-hour battle, his archers decimated French forces using swords and other close fighting weapons. When the French finally fled the field, the carnage was simply too ghastly to comprehend: perhaps 10,000 dead Frenchmen, no more than 100 dead Englishmen (Shakespeare says 30).

But of course, every advance in martial weaponry has meant a corresponding advance in defensive tools. Against the club, the sword, and the spear was held the shield. As protection against the bow, unwieldy armour for both warriors and horses was developed. With the invention of firearms, however, armour and hand-to-hand combat were quickly outmoded. Now, with a single hand-held weapon, a warrior could dispatch an enemy from several hundred yards—far enough so that he could not see his face, nor look into his eyes. It was a perfect weapon for the squeamish or the softhearted.

Up through the nineteenth century, warfare had been largely a matter of large numbers of lightly armed troops trying to overwhelm a similar opposing force. While it is true that thousands of soldiers, and as many civilians, were killed in these clashes, the basic facts of warfare had changed little since Agincourt: one soldier could kill, individually, several enemy troops; if enough on one side could also accomplish this, that side won.

But technology intervened once more near the end of the nineteenth century, and World War I saw the use on a massive scale of horrible new weapons: machine guns, airplanes, tanks, submarines, hand grenades, chemicals. And for the first year of that horrible conflict, the old generals stuck by old tactics. Gallant charges across "no-man's land" were nothing more than attempts to wear out machine guns with young men's chests.

Here at last, in the trenches that zigged and zagged across the French countryside, twentieth-century war technology was born. Now a single soldier, often quite far removed from his targets, could kill or maim hundreds of enemy troops and never even see the results.

Strategic bombing aircraft such as Queenie, often decorated with buxom females painted on the noses to humanize them for the young pilots, resulted in wholesale destruction of entire cities during World War II. Except for two occasions—Hiroshima and Nagasaki—that destruction was accomplished by thousands of high-explosive bombs, today called *conventional* weapons.

Vietnam was a throwback. While pilots in sophisticated aircraft dropped more tons of bombs than all the bombs dropped in World War II, Vietnam was essentially a ground war, fought by "Grunts," infantrymen using M-16s.

It was the *blitzkrieg* war in the Persian Gulf that carried technology one step further, one step removed from the reality of death. Each night, millions of us Americans sat as prisoners in front of our television sets watching Pentagon briefers and officers in Saudi Arabia describe the latest success of a Patriot missile or a "smart bomb." We were mesmerized by the grainy images of a building in downtown Baghdad caught in the cross-hairs of an American bomb-sight: "Right down the stack," the general chirps. And the building explodes in surreal slow motion, the windows and doors blowing outward, the walls collapsing inward, the entire multi-storied building sinking slowly on itself like a torpedoed ship. Time after time, we watched rockets and missiles home in on Iraqi tanks, watched the turrets blow off, flames erupt.

It was the ultimate video game. Our technology against theirs, and ours won. A virtually bloodless war.

Or was it? Only late did we learn of the true horror: perhaps 100,000 Iraqi conscripts shredded by cluster bombs dropped, à la World War II, by B-52s. Hundreds of civilians cremated when their bomb shelter was obliterated by a not-so-smart bomb. Inside the tanks were charred Iraqi soldiers in grotesquely stiff poses, their eyes boiled from their heads, their mouths permanent rictuses emitting voiceless screams.

Nintendo technology, it turns out, was only part of the story of the Persian Gulf war. Computer-age weapons with the capacity to hit a precise target comprised less than 8 percent of the weapons expended in the war; conventional, high-explosive or flame-dealing bombs were the overwhelming weapons of choice.

In the chapter that follows, you will read about the technology of war, from conventional weaponry to biological and chemical warfare, to atomic and nuclear bombs. What should be the ultimate purpose of advanced technology? What seems to have been the result thus far? What limits can be imposed on weapons of destruction? Should chemical and biological weapons be stockpiled, even if we never intend to use them?

WILLIAM L. LAURENCE

Atomic Bombing of Nagasaki Told by Flight Member

On August 9, 1945, the United States dropped a second atomic bomb on Japan, this time on the city of Nagasaki. Reporter William L. Laurence was on that flight; he was, in fact, the only member of the press who knew about the earlier secret testing of the bomb. In this article, printed in the New York Times *one month after the Nagasaki mission, he describes preparations for the bombing, the drop, and the first few minutes after the bomb hit its target.*

Before you read his account, imagine what procedures flight crews follow before missions. Using those procedures to establish a chronology, write a paragraph about what emotions you would feel if you were a member of such a crew. Then, as you read, note the emotions Laurence expresses about the bombing mission through his writing.

WITH THE ATOMIC-BOMB MISSION to Japan, August 9 (Delayed)—We are on our way to bomb the mainland of Japan. Our flying contingent consists of three specially designed B-29 Superforts, and two of these carry no bombs. But our lead plane is on its way with another atomic bomb, the second in three days, concentrating in its active substance an explosive energy equivalent to twenty thousand and, under favorable conditions, forty thousand tons of TNT. 1

We have several chosen targets. One of these is the great industrial and shipping center of Nagasaki, on the western shore of Kyushu, one of the main islands of the Japanese homeland. 2

I watched the assembly of this man-made meteor during the past two days and was among the small group of scientists and Army and Navy representatives privileged to be present at the ritual of its loading in the Superfort last night, against a background of threatening black skies torn open at intervals by great lightning flashes. 3

It is a thing of beauty to behold, this "gadget." Into its design went millions of man-hours of what is without doubt the most concentrated intellectual effort in history. Never before had so much brain power been focused on a single problem. 4

This atomic bomb is different from the bomb used three days ago with such devastating results on Hiroshima. 5

I saw the atomic substance before it was placed inside the bomb. By itself it is not at all dangerous to handle. It is only under certain conditions, produced in the bomb assembly, that it can be made to yield up its energy, and even then it gives only a small fraction of its total contents—a fraction, however, large enough to produce the greatest explosion on earth.

The briefing at midnight revealed the extreme care and the tremendous amount of preparation that had been made to take care of every detail of the mission, to make certain that the atomic bomb fully served the purpose for which it was intended. Each target in turn was shown in detailed maps and in aerial photographs. Every detail of the course was rehearsed—navigation, altitude, weather, where to land in emergencies. It came out that the Navy had rescue craft, known as Dumbos and Superdumbos, stationed at various strategic points in the vicinity of the targets, ready to rescue the fliers in case they were forced to bail out.

The briefing period ended with a moving prayer by the chaplain. We then proceeded to the mess hall for the traditional early-morning breakfast before departure on a bombing mission.

A convoy of trucks took us to the supply building for the special equipment carried on combat missions. This included the Mae West, a parachute, a lifeboat, an oxygen mask, a flak suit, and a survival vest. We still had a few hours before take-off time, but we all went to the flying field and stood around in little groups or sat in jeeps talking rather casually about our mission to the Empire, as the Japanese home islands are known hereabouts.

In command of our mission is Major Charles W. Sweeney, twenty-five, of 124 Hamilton Avenue, North Quincy, Massachusetts. His flagship, carrying the atomic bomb, is named *The Great Artiste,* but the name does not appear on the body of the great silver ship, with its unusually long, four-bladed, orange-tipped propellers. Instead, it carries the number 77, and someone remarks that it was "Red" Grange's winning number on the gridiron.

We took off at 3:50 this morning and headed northwest on a straight line for the Empire. The night was cloudy and threatening, with only a few stars here and there breaking through the overcast. The weather report had predicted storms ahead part of the way but clear sailing for the final and climactic stages of our odyssey.

We were about an hour away from our base when the storm broke. Our great ship took some heavy dips through the abysmal darkness around us, but it took these dips much more gracefully than a large commercial air liner, producing a sensation more in the nature of a glide than a "bump," like a great ocean liner riding the waves except that in this case the air waves were much higher and the rhythmic tempo of the glide was much faster.

I noticed a strange eerie light coming through the window high above the navigator's cabin, and as I peered through the dark all around us I saw a startling phenomenon. The whirling giant propellers had somehow become great luminous disks of blue flame. The same luminous blue flame appeared on the plexiglas windows in the nose of the ship, and on the tips of the giant wings. It looked as though we were riding the whirlwind through space on a chariot of blue fire.   13

It was, I surmised, a surcharge of static electricity that had accumulated on the tips of the propellers and on the di-electric material of the plastic windows. One's thoughts dwelt anxiously on the precious cargo in the invisible ship ahead of us. Was there any likelihood of danger that this heavy electric tension in the atmosphere all about us might set it off?   14

I expressed my fears to Captain Bock, who seems nonchalant and unperturbed at the controls. He quickly reassured me.   15

"It is a familiar phenomenon seen often on ships. I have seen it many times on bombing missions. It is known as St. Elmo's fire."   16

On we went through the night. We soon rode out the storm and our ship was once again sailing on a smooth course straight ahead, on a direct line to the Empire.   17

Our altimeter showed that we were traveling through space at a height of seventeen thousand feet. The thermometer registered an outside temperature of thirty-three degrees below zero Centigrade, about thirty below Fahrenheit. Inside our pressurized cabin the temperature was that of a comfortable air-conditioned room and a pressure corresponding to an altitude of eight thousand feet. Captain Bock cautioned me, however, to keep my oxygen mask handy in case of emergency. This, he explained, might mean either something going wrong with the pressure equipment inside the ship or a hole through the cabin by flak.   18

The first signs of dawn came shortly after five o'clock. Sergeant Curry, of Hoopeston, Illinois, who had been listening steadily on his earphones for radio reports, while maintaining a strict radio silence himself, greeted it by rising to his feet and gazing out the window.   19

"It's good to see the day," he told me. "I get a feeling of claustrophobia hemmed in this cabin at night."   20

He is a typical American youth, looking even younger than his twenty years. It takes no mind reader to read his thoughts.   21

"It's a long way from Hoopeston," I find myself remarking.   22

"Yep," he replies, as he busies himself decoding a message from outer space.   23

"Think this atomic bomb will end the war?" he asks hopefully.   24

"There is a very good chance that this one may do the trick," I   25
assured him, "but if not, then the next one or two surely will. Its power
is such that no nation can stand up against it very long." This was not
my own view. I had heard it expressed all around a few hours earlier,
before we took off. To anyone who had seen this manmade fireball in
action, as I had less than a month ago in the desert of New Mexico, this
view did not sound overoptimistic.

By 5:50 it was really light outside. We had lost our lead ship, but   26
Lieutenant Godfrey, our navigator, informs me that we had arranged
for that contingency. We have an assembly point in the sky above the
little island of Yakushima, southeast of Kyushu, at 9:10. We are to circle
there and wait for the rest of our formation.

Our genial bombardier, Lieutenant Levy, comes over to invite me   27
to take his front-row seat in the transparent nose of the ship, and I accept
eagerly. From that vantage point in space, seventeen thousand feet above
the Pacific, one gets a view of hundreds of miles on all sides, horizon-
tally and vertically. At that height the vast ocean below and the sky
above seem to merge into one great sphere.

I was on the inside of that firmament, riding above the giant   28
mountains of white cumulus clouds, letting myself be suspended in infinite space. One hears the whirl of the motors behind one, but it soon
becomes insignificant against the immensity all around and is before
long swallowed by it. There comes a point where space also swallows
time and one lives through eternal moments filled with an oppressive
loneliness, as though all life had suddenly vanished from the earth and
you are the only one left, a lone survivor traveling endlessly through
interplanetary space.

My mind soon returns to the mission I am on. Somewhere beyond   29
these vast mountains of white clouds ahead of me there lies Japan, the
land of our enemy. In about four hours from now one of its cities,
making weapons of war for use against us, will be wiped off the map
by the greatest weapon ever made by man: In one tenth of a millionth
of a second, a fraction of time immeasurable by any clock, a whirlwind
from the skies will pulverize thousands of its buildings and tens of thousands of its inhabitants.

But at this moment no one yet knows which one of the several   30
cities chosen as targets is to be annihilated. The final choice lies with
destiny. The winds over Japan will make the decision. If they carry
heavy clouds over our primary target, the city will be saved, at least for
the time being. None of its inhabitants will ever know that the wind of
a benevolent destiny had passed over their heads. But that same wind
will doom another city.

Our weather planes ahead of us are on their way to find out where 31
the wind blows. Half an hour before target time we will know what
the winds have decided.

Does one feel any pity or compassion for the poor devils about to 32
die? Not when one thinks of Pearl Harbor and of the Death March on
Bataan.

Captain Bock informs me that we are about to start our climb to 33
bombing altitude.

He manipulates a few knobs on his control panel to the right of 34
him, and I alternately watch the white clouds and ocean below me and
the altimeter on the bombardier's panel. We reached our altitude at nine
o'clock. We were then over Japanese waters, close to their mainland.
Lieutenant Godfrey mentioned to me to look through his radar scope.
Before me was the outline of our assembly point. We shall soon meet
our lead ship and proceed to the final stage of our journey.

We reached Yakushima at 9:12 and there, about four hundred feet 35
ahead of us, was *The Great Artiste* with its precious load. I saw Lieutenant Godfrey and Sergeant Curry strap on their parachutes and I decided
to do likewise.

We started circling. We saw little towns on the coastline, heedless 36
of our presence. We kept on circling, waiting for the third ship in our
formation.

It was 9:56 when we began heading for the coastline. Our weather 37
scouts had sent us code messages, deciphered by Sergeant Curry, informing us that both the primary target as well as the secondary were
clearly visible.

The winds of destiny seemed to favor certain Japanese cities that 38
must remain nameless. We circled about them again and again and found
no opening in the thick umbrella of clouds that covered them. Destiny
chose Nagasaki as the ultimate target.

We had been circling for some time when we noticed black puffs 39
of smoke coming through the white clouds directly at us. There were
fifteen bursts of flak in rapid succession, all too low. Captain Bock
changed his course. There soon followed eight more bursts of flak, right
up to our altitude, but by this time were too far to the left.

We flew southward down the channel and at 11:33 crossed the 40
coastline and headed straight for Nagasaki, about one hundred miles to
the west. Here again we circled until we found an opening in the clouds.
It was 12:01 and the goal of our mission had arrived.

We heard the prearranged signal on our radio, put on our arc 41
welder's glasses, and watched tensely the maneuverings of the strike
ship about half a mile in front of us.

"There she goes!" someone said.   42

Out of the belly of *The Great Artiste* what looked like a black object   43
went downward.

Captain Bock swung to get out of range; but even though we were   44
turning away in the opposite direction, and despite the fact that it was
broad daylight in our cabin, all of us became aware of a giant flash that
broke through the dark barrier of our arc welder's lenses and flooded
our cabin with intense light.

We removed our glasses after the first flash, but the light still   45
lingered on, a bluish-green light that illuminated the entire sky all around.
A tremendous blast wave struck our ship and made it tremble from nose
to tail. This was followed by four more blasts in rapid succession, each
resounding like the boom of cannon fire hitting our plane from all
directions.

Observers in the tail of the ship saw a giant ball of fire rise as   46
though from the bowels of the earth, belching forth enormous white
smoke rings. Next they saw a giant pillar of purple fire, ten thousand
feet high, shooting skyward with enormous speed.

By the time our ship had made another turn in the direction of the   47
atomic explosion the pillar of purple fire had reached the level of our
altitude. Only about forty-five seconds had passed. Awe-struck, we
watched it shoot upward like a meteor coming from the earth instead
of from outer space, becoming ever more alive as it climbed skyward
through the white clouds. It was no longer smoke, or dust, or even a
cloud of fire. It was a living thing, a new species of being, born right
before our incredulous eyes.

At one stage of its evolution, covering millions of years in terms   48
of seconds, the entity assumed the form of a giant square totem pole,
with its base about three miles along, tapering off to about a mile at the
top. Its bottom was brown, its center was amber, its top white. But it
was a living totem pole, carved with many grotesque masks grimacing
at the earth.

Then, just when it appeared as though the thing had settled down   49
into a state of permanence, there came shooting out of the top a giant
mushroom that increased the height of the pillar to a total of forty-five
thousand feet. The mushroom top was even more alive than the pillar,
seething and boiling in a white fury of creamy foam, sizzling upward
and then descending earthward, a thousand Old Faithful geysers rolled
into one.

It kept struggling in an elemental fury, like a creature in the act of   50
breaking the bonds that held it down. In a few seconds it had freed itself
from its gigantic stem and floated upward with tremendous speed, its

momentum carrying it into the stratosphere to a height of about sixty thousand feet.

But no sooner did this happen when another mushroom, smaller   51
in size than the first one, began emerging out of the pillar. It was as though the decapitated monster was growing a new head.

As the first mushroom floated off into the blue it changed its shape   52
into a flowerlike form, its giant petals curving downward, creamy white outside, rose-colored inside. It still retained that shape when we last gazed at it from a distance of about two hundred miles. The boiling pillar of many colors could also be seen at that distance, a giant mountain of jumbled rainbows, in travail. Much living substance had gone into those rainbows. The quivering top of the pillar was protruding to a great height through the white clouds, giving the appearance of a monstrous prehistoric creature with a ruff around its neck, a fleecy ruff extending in all directions, as far as the eye could see.

Content Considerations

1. Explain how Nagasaki became the target for the bomb dropped during this mission.
2. In what ways does Laurence's treatment of the preparation and flight differ from his treatment of the aftermath of the bombing?
3. Using information from this article and your own knowledge, discuss how the bomb was "a living thing, a new species of being" for the crew. How was it "a living thing, a new species of being" for all people on Earth?

Thank God for the Atom Bomb

Much of what we believe has its roots in our experience; the events of our lives, what has happened, where we have been, what we have done, all lead us to certain conclusions about the world and its realities. That idea is one that author Paul Fussell brings to this essay about the ethics of war.

What are the ethics of war? What are the rules? In modern times, such rules have been set by the Geneva Convention, by various policies and resolutions emanating from governments and organizations. Before reading Fussell's essay, work with classmates to list reasons why rules of war are needed and then work on a list of how the very notion of war makes such rules senseless. Then write a couple of paragraphs outlining your own conclusions about the necessity for rules of war.

MANY YEARS AGO in New York I saw on the side of a bus a whiskey ad I've remembered all this time. It's been for me a model of the short poem, and indeed I've come upon few short poems subsequently that exhibited more poetic talent. The ad consisted of two eleven-syllable lines of "verse," thus:

1

> In life, experience is the great teacher
> In Scotch, Teacher's is the great experience.

For present purposes we must jettison the second line (licking our lips, to be sure, as it disappears), leaving the first to register a principle whose banality suggests that it enshrines a most useful truth. I bring up the matter because, writing on the forty-second anniversary of the atom-bombing of Hiroshima and Nagasaki, I want to consider something suggested by the long debate about the ethics, if any, of that ghastly affair. Namely, the importance of experience, sheer, vulgar experience, in influencing, if not determining, one's views about that use of the atom bomb.

The experience I'm talking about is having to come to grips, face to face, with an enemy who designs your death. The experience is common to those in the marines and the infantry and even the line navy, to those, in short, who fought the Second World War mindful always that their mission was, as they were repeatedly assured, "to close with the enemy and destroy him." *Destroy,* notice: not hurt, frighten, drive away, or capture. I think there's something to be learned about that war, as well as about the tendency of historical memory unwittingly to resolve ambiguity and generally clean up the premises, by considering the way testimonies emanating from real war experience tend to complicate attitudes about the most cruel ending of that most cruel war.

"What did you do in the Great War, Daddy?" The recruiting poster deserves ridicule and contempt, of course, but here its question is embarrassingly relevant, and the problem is one that touches on the dirty little secret of social class in America. Arthur T. Hadley said recently that those for whom the use of the A-bomb was "wrong" seem to be implying "that it would have been better to allow thousands on thousands of American and Japanese infantrymen to die in honest hand-to-hand combat on the beaches than to drop those two bombs." People holding such views, he notes, "do not come from the ranks of society that produce infantrymen or pilots." And there's an eloquence problem: most of those with firsthand experience of the war at its worst were not elaborately educated people. Relatively inarticulate, most have remained silent about what they know. That is, few of those destined to be blown to pieces if the main Japanese islands had been invaded went on to become our most effective men of letters or impressive ethical theorists or professors of contemporary history or of international law. The testimony of experience has tended to come from rough diamonds—James Jones is an example—who went through the war as enlisted men in the infantry or the Marine Corps.

Anticipating objections from those without such experience, in his book *WWII* Jones carefully prepares for his chapter on the A-bombs by detailing the plans already in motion for the infantry assaults on the home islands of Kyushu (thirteen divisions scheduled to land in November 1945) and ultimately Honshu (sixteen divisions scheduled for March 1946). Planners of the invasion assumed that it would require a full year, to November 1946, for the Japanese to be sufficiently worn down by land-combat attrition to surrender. By that time, one million American casualties was the expected price. Jones observes that the forthcoming invasion of Kyushu "was well into its collecting and stockpiling stages before the war ended." (The island of Saipan was designated a main ammunition and supply base for the invasion, and if you go there today you can see some of the assembled stuff still sitting there.) "The assault troops were chosen and already in training," Jones reminds his readers, and he illuminates by the light of experience what this meant:

3

4

What it must have been like to some old-timer buck sergeant or staff sergeant who had been through Guadalcanal or Bougainville or the Philippines, to stand on some beach and watch this huge war machine beginning to stir and move all around him and know that he very likely had survived this far only to fall dead on the dirt of Japan's home islands, hardly bears thinking about.

Another bright enlisted man, this one an experienced marine destined for the assault on Honshu, adds his testimony. Former Pfc. E. B. Sledge, author of the splendid memoir *With the Old Breed at Peleliu and Okinawa,* noticed at the time that the fighting grew "more vicious the closer we got to Japan," with the carnage of Iwo Jima and Okinawa worse than what had gone before. He points out that

> what we had *experienced* [my emphasis] in fighting the Japs (pardon the expression) on Peleliu and Okinawa caused us to formulate some very definite opinions that the invasion . . . would be a ghastly bloodletting. . . . It would shock the American public and the world. [Every Japanese] soldier, civilian, woman, and child would fight to the death with whatever weapons they had, rifle, grenade, or bamboo spear.

The Japanese pre-invasion patriotic song, "One Hundred Million Souls for the Emperor," says Sledge, "meant just that." Universal national kamikaze was the point. One kamikaze pilot, discouraged by his unit's failure to impede the Americans very much despite the bizarre casualties it caused, wrote before diving his plane onto an American ship, "I see the war situation becoming more desperate. All Japanese must become soldiers and die for the Emperor." Sledge's First Marine Division was to land close to the Yokosuka Naval Base, "one of the most heavily defended sectors of the island." The marines were told, he recalls, that

> due to the strong beach defenses, caves, tunnels, and numerous Jap suicide torpedo boats and manned mines, few Marines in the first five assault waves would get ashore alive—my company was scheduled to be in the first and second waves. The veterans in the outfit felt we had already run out of luck anyway. . . . We viewed the invasion with complete resignation that we would be killed— either on the beach or inland.

And the invasion was going to take place: there's no question about that. It was not theoretical or merely rumored in order to scare the Japanese. By July 10, 1945, the prelanding naval and aerial bombardment of the coast had begun, and the battleships *Iowa, Missouri, Wisconsin,* and *King George V* were steaming up and down the coast, softening it up with their sixteen-inch shells.

On the other hand, John Kenneth Galbraith is persuaded that the Japanese would have surrendered surely by November without an invasion. He thinks the A-bombs were unnecessary and unjustified because the war was ending anyway. The A-bombs meant, he says, "a difference, at most, of two or three weeks." But at the time, with no indication that surrender was on the way, the kamikazes were sinking American vessels, the *Indianapolis* was sunk (880 men killed), and Allied casualties were running to over 7,000 per week. "Two or three weeks," says Galbraith. Two weeks more means 14,000 more killed and wounded, three weeks more, 21,000. Those weeks mean the world if you're one of those thousands or related to one of them. During the time between the dropping of the Nagasaki bomb on August 9 and the actual surrender on the fifteenth, the war pursued its accustomed course: on the twelfth of August eight captured American fliers were executed (heads chopped off); the fifty-first United States submarine, *Bonefish,* was sunk (all aboard drowned); the destroyer *Callaghan* went down, the seventieth to be sunk, and the Destroyer Escort *Underhill* was lost. That's a bit of what happened in six days of the two or three weeks posited by Galbraith. What did he do in the war? He worked in the Office of Price Administration in Washington. I don't demand that he experience having his ass shot off. I merely note that he didn't.

Likewise, the historian Michael Sherry, author of a recent book on the rise of the American bombing mystique, *The Creation of Armageddon,* argues that we didn't delay long enough between the test explosion in New Mexico and the mortal explosions in Japan. More delay would have made possible deeper moral considerations and perhaps laudable second thoughts and restraint. "The risks of delaying the bomb's use," he says, "would have been small—not the thousands of casualties expected of invasion but only a few days or weeks of relatively routine operations." While the mass murders represented by these "relatively routine operations" were enacting, Michael Sherry was safe at home. Indeed, when the bombs were dropped he was going on eight months old, in danger only of falling out of his pram. In speaking thus of Galbraith and Sherry, I'm aware of the offensive implications *ad hominem.* But what's at stake in an infantry assault is so entirely unthinkable to those without the experience of one, or several, or many, even if they possess very wide-ranging imaginations and warm sympathies, that experience is crucial in this case.

In general, the principle is, the farther from the scene of horror, the easier the talk. One young combat naval officer close to the action

wrote home in the fall of 1943, just before the marines underwent the
agony of Tarawa: "When I read that we will fight the Japs for years if
necessary and will sacrifice hundreds of thousands if we must, I always
like to check from where he's talking: it's seldom out here." That was
Lieutenant (j.g.) John F. Kennedy. And Winston Churchill, with an
irony perhaps too broad and easy, noted in Parliament that the people
who preferred invasion to A-bombing seemed to have "no intention of
proceeding to the Japanese front themselves."

A remoteness from experience like Galbraith's and Sherry's, and a   8
similar rationalistic abstraction from actuality, seem to motivate the re-
action of an anonymous reviewer of William Manchester's *Goodbye
Darkness: A Memoir of the Pacific War* for *The New York Review of Books*.
The reviewer naturally dislikes Manchester's still terming the enemy
Nips or Japs, but what really shakes him (her?) is this passage of
Manchester's:

> After Biak the enemy withdrew to deep caverns. Rooting them
> out became a bloody business which reached its ultimate horrors
> in the last months of the war. You think of the lives which would
> have been lost in an invasion of Japan's home islands—a staggering
> number of Americans but millions more of Japanese—and you thank
> God for the atomic bomb.

Thank God for the atom bomb. From this, "one recoils," says the reviewer. One does, doesn't one?

And not just a staggering number of Americans would have been   9
killed in the invasion. Thousands of British assault troops would have
been destroyed too, the anticipated casualties from the almost 200,000
men in the six divisions (the same number used to invade Normandy)
assigned to invade the Malay Peninsula on September 9. Aimed at the
reconquest of Singapore, this operation was expected to last until about
March 1946—that is, seven more months of infantry fighting. "But for
the atomic bombs," a British observer intimate with the Japanese defenses notes, "I don't think we would have stood a cat in hell's chance.
We would have been murdered in the biggest massacre of the war. They
would have annihilated the lot of us."

The Dutchman Laurens van der Post had been a prisoner of the   10
Japanese for three and a half years. He and thousands of his fellows,
enfeebled by beriberi and pellagra, were being systematically starved to
death, the Japanese rationalizing this treatment not just because the prisoners were white men but because they had allowed themselves to be
captured at all and were therefore moral garbage. In the summer of 1945
Field Marshal Terauchi issued a significant order: at the moment the

Allies invaded the main islands, all prisoners were to be killed by the prison-camp commanders. But thank God that did not happen. When the A-bombs were dropped, van der Post recalls, "This cataclysm I was certain would make the Japanese feel that they could withdraw from the war without dishonor, because it would strike them, as it had us in the silence of our prison night, as something supernatural."

In an exchange of views not long ago in *The New York Review of Books,* Joseph Alsop and David Joravsky set forth the by now familiar argument on both sides of the debate about the "ethics" of the bomb. It's not hard to guess which side each chose once you know that Alsop experienced capture by the Japanese at Hong Kong early in 1942, while Joravsky came into no deadly contact with the Japanese: a young, combat-innocent soldier, he was on his way to the Pacific when the war ended. The editors of *The New York Review* gave the debate the tendentious title "Was the Hiroshima Bomb Necessary?" surely an unanswerable question (unlike "Was It Effective?") and one precisely indicating the intellectual difficulties involved in imposing *ex post facto* a rational and even a genteel ethics on this event. In arguing the acceptability of the bomb, Alsop focuses on the power and fanaticism of War Minister Anami, who insisted that Japan fight to the bitter end, defending the main islands with the same techniques and tenacity employed at Iwo and Okinawa. Alsop concludes: "Japanese surrender could never have been obtained, at any rate without the honor-satisfying bloodbath envisioned by . . . Anami, if the hideous destruction of Hiroshima and Nagasaki had not finally galvanized the peace advocates into tearing up the entire Japanese book of rules." The Japanese plan to deploy the undefeated bulk of their ground forces, over two million men, plus 10,000 kamikaze planes, plus the elderly and all the women and children with sharpened spears they could muster in a suicidal defense makes it absurd, says Alsop, to "hold the common view, by now hardly challenged by anyone, that the decision to drop the two bombs on Japan was wicked in itself, and that President Truman and all others who joined in making or who [like Robert Oppenheimer] assented to this decision shared in the wickedness." And in explanation of "the two bombs," Alsop adds: "The true, climactic, and successful effort of the Japanese peace advocates . . . did not begin in deadly earnest until *after* the second bomb had destroyed Nagasaki. The Nagasaki bomb was thus the trigger to all the developments that led to peace." At this time the army was so unready for surrender that most looked forward to the forthcoming invasion as an indispensable opportunity to show their mettle, enthusiastically agreeing with the army spokesman who reasoned early in 1945, "Since the retreat from Guadalcanal, the Army has had little opportunity to engage the enemy in land battles. But when we meet in Japan proper, our Army will demonstrate its invincible superiority." This possibility foreclosed by the Emperor's post-A-bomb surrender broadcast, the shocked, disappointed officers of one infantry battalion, anticipating a professionally impressive defense of the beaches, killed themselves in the following numbers: one major, three captains, ten first lieutenants, and twelve second lieutenants.

David Joravsky, now a professor of history at Northwestern, argued on the other hand that those who decided to use the A-bombs on cities betray defects of "reason and self-restraint." It all needn't have happened, he says, "if the U.S. government had been willing to take a few more days and to be a bit more thoughtful in opening up the age of nuclear warfare." I've already noted what "a few more days" would mean to the luckless troops and sailors on the spot, and as to being thoughtful when "opening up the age of nuclear warfare," of course no one was focusing on anything as portentous as that, which reflects a historian's tidy hindsight. The U.S. government was engaged not in that sort of momentous thing but in ending the war conclusively, as well as irrationally Remembering Pearl Harbor with a vengeance. It didn't know then what everyone knows now about leukemia and various kinds of carcinoma and birth defects. Truman was not being sly or coy when he insisted that the bomb was "only another weapon." History, as Eliot's "Gerontion" notes,

> . . . has many cunning passages, contrived corridors
> And issues, deceives with whispering ambitions,
> Guides us by vanities. . . .
>
>   Think
> Neither fear nor courage saves us.
>   Unnatural vices
> Are fathered by our heroism. Virtues
> Are forced upon us by our impudent crimes.

Understanding the past requires pretending that you don't know the present. It requires feeling its own pressure on your pulses without any *ex post facto* illumination. That's a harder thing to do than Joravsky seems to think.

The Alsop-Joravsky debate, reduced to a collision between experience and theory, was conducted with a certain civilized respect for evidence. Not so the way the scurrilous, agitprop *New Statesman* conceives those justifying the dropping of the bomb and those opposing. They are, on the one hand, says Bruce Page, "the imperialist class-forces acting through Harry Truman" and, on the other, those representing "the humane, democratic virtues"—in short, "facists" as opposed to "populists." But ironically the bomb saved the lives not of any imperialists but only of the low and humble, the quintessentially democratic huddled masses—the conscripted enlisted men manning the fated invasion divisions and the sailors crouching at their gun-mounts in terror of the Kamikazes. When the war ended, Bruce Page was nine years old. For someone of his experience, phrases like "imperialist class forces" come easily, and the issues look perfectly clear.

He's not the only one to have forgotten, if he ever knew, the unspeakable savagery of the Pacific war. The dramatic postwar Japanese success at hustling and merchandising and tourism has (happily, in many ways) effaced for most people the vicious assault context in which the Hiroshima horror should be viewed. It is easy to forget, or not to know, what Japan was like before it was first destroyed, and then humiliated, tamed, and constitutionalized by the West. "Implacable, treacherous, barbaric"—those were Admiral Halsey's characterizations of the enemy, and at the time few facing the Japanese would deny that they fit to a T. One remembers the captured American airmen—the lucky ones who escaped decapitation—locked for years in packing crates. One remembers the gleeful use of bayonets on civilians, on nurses and the wounded, in Hong Kong and Singapore. Anyone who actually fought in the Pacific recalls the Japanese routinely firing on medics, killing the wounded (torturing them first, if possible), and cutting off the penises of the dead to stick in the corpses' mouths. The degree to which Americans register shock and extraordinary shame about the Hiroshima bomb correlates closely with lack of information about the Pacific war.

And of course the brutality was not just on one side. There was much sadism and cruelty, undeniably racist, on ours. (It's worth noting in passing how few hopes blacks could entertain of desegregation and decent treatment when the U.S. Army itself slandered the enemy as "the little brown Jap.") Marines and soldiers could augment their view of their own invincibility by possessing a well-washed Japanese skull, and very soon after Guadalcanal it was common to treat surrendering Japanese as handy rifle targets. Plenty of Japanese gold teeth were extracted—some from still living mouths—with Marine Corps Ka-Bar knives, and one of E. B. Sledge's fellow marines went around with a cut-off Japanese hand. When its smell grew too offensive and Sledge urged him to get rid of it, he defended his possession of this trophy thus: "How many Marines you reckon that hand pulled the trigger on?" (It's hardly necessary to observe that a soldier in the ETO would probably not have dealt that way with a German or Italian—that is, a "white person's"—hand.) In the Pacific the situation grew so public and scan-

14

15

dalous that in September 1942, the Commander in Chief of the Pacific
Fleet issued this order: "No part of the enemy's body may be used as a
souvenir. Unit Commanders will take stern disciplinary action. . . ."

Among Americans it was widely held that the Japanese were really   16
subhuman, little yellow beasts, and popular imagery depicted them as
lice, rats, bats, vipers, dogs, and monkeys. What was required, said the
Marine Corps journal *The Leatherneck* in May 1945, was "a gigantic task
of extermination." The Japanese constituted a "pestilence," and the only
appropriate treatment was "annihilation." Some of the marines landing
on Iwo Jima had "Rodent Exterminator" written on their helmet covers,
and on one American flagship the naval commander had erected a large
sign enjoining all to "KILL JAPS! KILL JAPS! KILL MORE JAPS!"
Herman Wouk remembers the Pacific war scene correctly while analyzing Ensign Keith in *The Caine Mutiny:* "Like most of the naval executioners of Kwajalein, he seemed to regard the enemy as a species of
animal pest." And the feeling was entirely reciprocal: "From the grim
and desperate taciturnity with which the Japanese died, they seemed on
their side to believe that they were contending with an invasion of large
armed rats." Hiroshima seems to follow in natural sequence: "This ob-
liviousness of both sides to the fact that the opponents were human
beings may perhaps be cited as the key to the many massacres of the
Pacific war." Since the Jap vermin resist so madly and have killed so
many of us, let's pour gasoline into their bunkers and light it and then
shoot those afire who try to get out. Why not? Why not blow them all
up, with satchel charges or with something stronger? Why not, indeed,
drop a new kind of bomb on them, and on the un–uniformed ones too,
since the Japanese government has announced that women from ages of
seventeen to forty are being called up to repel the invasion? The intelligence officer of the U.S. Fifth Air Force declared on July 21, 1945,
that "the entire population of Japan is a proper military target," and he
added emphatically, *"There are no civilians in Japan."* Why delay and
allow one more American high school kid to see his own intestines
blown out of his body and spread before him in the dirt while he screams
and screams when with the new bomb we can end the whole thing just
like that?

On Okinawa, only weeks before Hiroshima, 123,000 Japanese and   17
Americans *killed* each other. (About 140,000 Japanese died at Hiroshima.) "Just awful" was the comment on the Okinawa slaughter not
of some pacifist but of General MacArthur. On July 14, 1945, General
Marshall sadly informed the Combined Chiefs of Staff—he was not
trying to scare the Japanese—that it's now "now clear . . . that in order
to finish with the Japanese quickly, it will be necessary to invade the

industrial heart of Japan." The invasion was definitely on, as I know because I was to be in it.

When the atom bomb ended the war, I was in the Forty-fifth 18 Infantry Division, which had been through the European war so thoroughly that it had needed to be reconstituted two or three times. We were in a staging area near Rheims, ready to be shipped back across the United States for refresher training at Fort Lewis, Washington, and then sent on for final preparation in the Philippines. My division, like most of the ones transferred from Europe, was to take part in the invasion of Honshu. (The earlier landing on Kyushu was to be carried out by the 700,000 infantry already in the Pacific, those with whom James Jones has sympathized.) I was a twenty-one-year-old second lieutenant of infantry leading a rifle platoon. Although still officially fit for combat, in the German war I had already been wounded in the back and the leg badly enough to be adjudged, after the war, 40 percent disabled. But even if my leg buckled and I fell to the ground whenever I jumped out of the back of a truck, and even if the very idea of more combat made me breathe in gasps and shake all over, my condition was held to be adequate for the next act. When the atom bombs were dropped and news began to circulate that "Operation Olympic" would not, after all, be necessary, when we learned to our astonishment that we would not be obliged in a few months to rush up the beaches near Tokyo assault-firing while being machine-gunned, mortared, and shelled, for all the practiced phlegm of our tough façades we broke down and cried with relief and joy. We were going to live. We were going to grow to adulthood after all. The killing was all going to be over, and peace was actually going to be the state of things. When the *Enola Gay* dropped its package, "There were cheers," says John Toland, "over the intercom; it meant the end of the war." Down on the ground the reaction of Sledge's marine buddies when they heard the news was more solemn and complicated. They heard about the end of the war

> with quiet disbelief coupled with an indescribable sense of relief. We thought the Japanese would never surrender. Many refused to believe it. . . . Sitting in stunned silence, we remembered our dead. So many dead. So many maimed. So many bright futures consigned to the ashes of the past. So many dreams lost in the madness that had engulfed us. Except for a few widely scattered shouts of joy, the survivors of the abyss sat hollow-eyed and silent, trying to comprehend a world without war.

These troops who cried and cheered with relief or who sat stunned by the weight of their experience are very different from the high-minded, guilt-ridden GIs we're told about by J. Glenn Gray in his sensitive book *The Warriors*. During the war in Europe Gray was an interrogator in the Army Counterintelligence Corps, and in that capacity he experienced the war at Division level. There's no denying that Gray's outlook on everything was admirably noble, elevated, and responsible. After the war he became a much-admired professor of philosophy at Colorado College and an esteemed editor of Heidegger. But *The Warriors,* his meditation on the moral and psychological dimensions of modern soldiering, gives every sign of error occasioned by remoteness from experience. Division headquarters is miles—*miles*—behind the line where soldiers experience terror and madness and relieve those pressures by crazy brutality and sadism. Indeed, unless they actually encountered the enemy during the war, most "soldiers" have very little idea what "combat" was like. As William Manchester says, "All who wore uniforms are called veterans, but more than 90 percent of them are as uninformed about the killing zones as those on the home front." Manchester's fellow marine E. B. Sledge thoughtfully and responsibly invokes the terms *drastically* and *totally* to underline the differences in experience between front and rear, and not even the far rear, but the close rear. "Our code of conduct toward the enemy," he notes, "differed drastically from that prevailing back at the division CP." (He's describing gold-tooth extraction from still-living Japanese.) Again he writes: "We existed in an environment totally incomprehensible to men behind the lines . . .," even, he would insist, to men as intelligent and sensitive as Glenn Gray, who missed seeing with his own eyes Sledge's marine friends sliding under fire down a shell-pocketed ridge slimy with mud and liquid dysentery shit into the maggoty Japanese and USMC corpses at the bottom, vomiting as the maggots burrowed into their own foul clothing. "We didn't talk about such things," says Sledge. "They were too horrible and obscene even for hardened veterans. . . . Nor do authors normally write about such vileness; unless they have seen it with their own eyes, it is too preposterous to think that men could actually live and fight for days and nights on end under such terrible conditions and not be driven insane." And Sledge has added a comment on such experience and the insulation provided by even a short distance: "Often people just behind our rifle companies couldn't understand what we knew." Glenn Gray was not in a rifle company, or even just behind one. "When the news of the atomic bombing of Hiroshima and Nagasaki came," he asks us to believe, "many an American soldier felt shocked and ashamed." Shocked, OK, but why ashamed? Because we'd destroyed civilians? We'd been doing that for years, in raids on Hamburg and Berlin and Cologne and Frankfurt and Mannheim and Dresden, and Tokyo, and besides, the two A-bombs wiped out 10,000 Japanese troops, not often thought of now, John Hersey's kindly physicians and Jesuit priests being more touching. If around division headquarters some of the people Gray talked to felt ashamed, down in the rifle companies no one did, despite Gray's assertions: "The combat soldier," he says,

> knew better than Americans at home what those bombs meant in suffering and injustice. The man of conscience realized intuitively that the vast majority of Japanese in both cities were no more, if no less, guilty of the war than were his own parents, sisters, or brothers.

I find this canting nonsense. The purpose of the bombs was not to "punish" people but to stop the war. To intensify the shame Gray insists we feel, he seems willing to fiddle the facts. The Hiroshima bomb, he says, was dropped "without any warning." But actually, two days before, 720,000 leaflets were dropped on the city urging everyone to get out and indicating that the place was going to be (as the Potsdam Declaration has promised) obliterated. Of course few left.

Experience whispers that the pity is not that we used the bomb to   19
end the Japanese war but that it wasn't ready in time to end the German one. If only it could have been rushed into production faster and dropped at the right moment on the Reich Chancellery or Berchtesgaden or Hitler's military headquarters in East Prussia (where Colonel Stauffenberg's July 20 bomb didn't do the job because it wasn't big enough), much of the Nazi hierarchy could have been pulverized immediately, saving not just the embarrassment of the Nuremberg trials but the lives of around four million Jews, Poles, Slavs, and gypsies, not to mention the lives and limbs of millions of Allied and German soldiers. If the bomb had only been ready in time, the young men of my infantry platoon would not have been so cruelly killed and wounded.

All this is not to deny that like the Russian Revolution, the atom-   20
bombing of Japan was a vast historical tragedy, and every passing year magnifies the dilemma into which it has lodged the contemporary world. As with the Russian Revolution, there are two sides—that's why it's a tragedy instead of a disaster—and unless we are, like Bruce Page, simple-mindedly unimaginative and cruel, we will be painfully aware of both sides at once. To observe that from the viewpoint of the war's victims-to-be the bomb seemed precisely the right thing to drop is to purchase no immunity from horror. To experience both sides, one might study the book *Unforgettable Fire: Pictures Drawn by Atomic Bomb Survivors,* which presents a number of amateur drawings and watercolors of the Hiroshima scene made by middle-aged and elderly survivors for a

peace exhibition in 1975. In addition to the almost unbearable pictures, the book offers brief moments of memoir not for the weak-stomached:

> While taking my severely wounded wife out to the river bank . . ., I was horrified indeed at the sight of a stark naked man standing in the rain with his eyeball in his palm. He looked to be in great pain but there was nothing that I could do for him. I wonder what became of him. Even today, I vividly remember the sight. I was simply miserable.

These childlike drawings and paintings are of skin hanging down, breasts torn off, people bleeding and burning, dying mothers nursing dead babies. A bloody woman holds a bloody child in the ruins of a house, and the artist remembers her calling, "Please help this child! Someone, please help this child. Please help! Someone, please." As Samuel Johnson said of the smothering of Desdemona, the innocent in another tragedy, "It is not to be endured." Nor, it should be noticed, is an infantryman's account of having his arm blown off in the Arno Valley in Italy in 1944:

> I wanted to die and die fast. I wanted to forget this miserable world. I cursed the war, I cursed the people who were responsible for it, I cursed God for putting me here . . . to suffer for something I never did or knew anything about.

(A good place to interrupt and remember Glenn Gray's noble but hopelessly one-sided remarks about "injustice," as well as "suffering.")

"For this was hell," the soldier goes on,

> and I never imagined anything or anyone could suffer so bitterly. I screamed and cursed. Why? What had I done to deserve this? But no answer came. I yelled for medics, because subconsciously I wanted to live. I tried to apply my right hand over my bleeding stump, but I didn't have the strength to hold it. I looked to the left of me and saw the bloody mess that was once my left arm; its fingers and palm were turned upward, like a flower looking to the sun for its strength.

The future scholar-critic who writes *The History of Canting in the Twentieth Century* will find much to study and interpret in the utterances of those who dilate on the special wickedness of the A-bomb-droppers. He will realize that such utterance can perform for the speaker a valuable double function. First, it can display the fineness of his moral weave.

And second, by implication it can also inform the audience that during the war he was not socially so unfortunate as to find himself down there with the ground forces, where he might have had to compromise the purity and clarity of his moral system by the experience of weighing his own life against someone else's. Down there, which is where the other people were, is the place where coarse self-interest is the rule. When the young soldier with the wild eyes comes at you, firing, do you shoot him in the foot, hoping he'll be hurt badly enough to drop or mis-aim the gun with which he's going to kill you, or do you shoot him in the chest (or, if you're a prime shot, in the head) and make certain that you and not he will be the survivor of that mortal moment?

It would be not just stupid but would betray a lamentable want of human experience to expect soldiers to be very sensitive humanitarians. The Glenn Grays of this world need to have their attention directed to the testimony of those who know, like, say, Admiral of the Fleet Lord Fisher, who said, "Moderation in war is imbecility," or Sir Arthur Harris, director of the admittedly wicked aerial-bombing campaign designed, as Churchill put it, to "de-house" the German civilian population, who observed that "War is immoral," or our own General W. J. Sherman: "War is cruelty, and you cannot refine it." Lord Louis Mountbatten, trying to say something sensible about the dropping of the A-bomb, came up only with "War is crazy." Or rather, it requires choices among craziness. "It would seem even more crazy," he went on, "if we were to have more casualties on our side to save the Japanese." One of the unpleasant facts for anyone in the ground armies during the war was that you had to become pro tem a subordinate of the very uncivilian George S. Patton and respond somehow to his unremitting insistence that you embrace his view of things. But in one of his effusions he was right, and his observation tends to suggest the experiential dubiousness of the concept of "just wars." "War is not a contest with gloves," he perceived. "It is resorted to only when laws, which are rules, have failed." Soldiers being like that, only the barest decencies should be expected of them. They did not start the war, except in the terrible sense hinted at in Frederic Manning's observation based on his front-line experience in the Great War: "War is waged by men; not by beasts, or by gods. It is a peculiarly human activity. To call it a crime against mankind is to miss at least half its significance; it is also the punishment of a crime." Knowing that unflattering truth by experience, soldiers have every motive for wanting a war stopped, by any means.

The stupidity, parochialism, and greed in the international mismanagement of the whole nuclear challenge should not tempt us to misimagine the circumstances of the bomb's first "use." Nor should our well-justified fears and suspicions occasioned by the capture of the nu-

21

22

clear-power trade by the inept and the mendacious (who have fucked up the works at Three Mile Island, Chernobyl, etc.) tempt us to infer retrospectively extraordinary corruption, imbecility, or motiveless malignity in those who decided, all things considered, to drop the bomb. Times change. Harry Truman was not a fascist but a democrat. He was as close to a genuine egalitarian as anyone we've seen in high office for a long time. He is the only President in my lifetime who ever had experience in a small unit of ground troops whose mission it was to kill people. That sort of experience of actual war seems useful to presidents especially, helping to inform them about life in general and restraining them from making fools of themselves needlessly—the way Ronald Reagan did in 1985 when he visited the German military cemetery at Bitburg containing the SS graves. The propriety of this visit he explained by asserting that no Germans who fought in the war remain alive and that "very few . . . even remember the war." Reagan's ignnorance or facile forgetfulness are imputed by Arthur Schlesinger to his total lack of serious experience of war—the Second World War or any other. "Though he often makes throwaway references to his military career," says Schlesinger, "Mr. Reagan in fact is the only American president who was of military age during the Second World War and saw no service overseas. He fought the war on the film lots of Hollywood, slept in his own bed every night and apparently got many of his ideas of what happened from subsequent study of the *Reader's Digest.*"

Truman was a different piece of goods entirely. He knew war, and   23
he knew better than some of his critics then and now what he was doing and why he was doing it. "Having found the bomb," he said, "we used it. . . . We have used it to shorten the agony of young Americans."

The past, which as always did not know the future, acted in ways   24
that ask to be imagined before they are condemned. Or even simplified.

Content Considerations

1. Fussell says that the purpose of a combatant is to destroy the enemy (paragraph 2). Respond to his assertion and then explore its implications. How do rules apply?
2. Paraphrase Fussell's argument, examine the support he provides for it and evaluate its effectiveness. Is there other evidence he could have provided?
3. What ethics do you believe should be followed in wartime regarding combatants? Regarding civilians? Regarding prisoners of war? Explain why you think so.

The U.S. Was Wrong

The United States twice dropped atomic bombs on Japan—on Hiroshima on August 6, 1945, and on Nagasaki on August 9, 1945. Hundreds of thousands of civilians were killed or injured. Survivors suffered burns and wounds; their bodies were torn, melted, scattered. Many who were seemingly unharmed later developed diseases linked to atomic radiation. Some evidence suggests that the damage caused by the bomb altered genetic composition so that the children born to survivors also suffered higher rates of birth defects and illness.

Popular belief holds that the bombings were necessary to end the carnage that had become World War II, but here writer Gar Alperovitz argues against the truth of that belief. A former congressional assistant and U.S. Senate staff member, Alperovitz suggests other reasons for the bombings. Before you read this argument, recall what you know about the atomic bomb and the bombings of Hiroshima and Nagasaki, including any pictures or films with which you may be familiar. Write a few paragraphs about the circumstances that justify the using of such a weapon.

THOUGH IT HAS NOT YET received broad public attention, there exists overwhelming historical evidence that President Harry S. Truman knew he could almost certainly end World War II without using the atomic bomb: The United States had cracked the Japanese code, and a stream of documents released over the last forty years show that Mr. Truman had two other options.

The first option was to clarify America's surrender terms to assure the Japanese we would not remove their emperor. The second was simply to await the expected Soviet declaration of war—which, United States intelligence advised, appeared likely to end the conflict on its own.

Instead, Hiroshima was bombed August 6, 1945, and Nagasaki on August 9. The planned date for the Soviet Union's entry into the war against Japan was August 8.

The big turning point was the emperor's continuing June–July decision to open surrender negotiations through Moscow. Top American officials—and, most critically, the president—understood the move was extraordinary: Mr. Truman's secret diaries, lost until 1978, call the key intercepted message "the telegram from Jap Emperor asking for peace."

Other documents—among them newly discovered secret memo-

149

randums from William J. Donovan, director of the Office of Strategic Services—show that Mr. Truman was personally advised of Japanese peace initiatives through Swiss and Portuguese channels as early as three months before Hiroshima. Moreover, Mr. Truman told several officials he had no objection in principle to Japan's keeping the emperor, which seemed the only sticking point.

American leaders were sure that if he so chose "the Mikado could stop the war with a royal word"—as one top presidential aide put it. Having decided to use the bomb, however, Mr. Truman was urged by Secretary of State James F. Byrnes not to give assurances to the emperor before the weapon had been demonstrated. [6]

Additional official records, including minutes of top-level White House planning meetings, show the president was clearly advised of the importance of a Soviet declaration of war: It would pull the rug out from under Japanese military leaders who were desperately hoping the powerful Red Army would stay neutral. [7]

General George C. Marshall in mid-June told Mr. Truman that "the impact of Russian entry on the already hopeless Japanese may well be the decisive action levering them into capitulation at that time or shortly thereafter if we land." [8]

A month later, the American-British Combined Intelligence Staffs advised their chiefs of the critical importance of a Red Army attack. As the top British general, Sir Hastings Ismay, summarized the conclusions for Prime Minister Winston Churchill: "If and when Russia came into the war against Japan, the Japanese would probably wish to get out on almost any terms short of the dethronement of the Emperor." [9]

Mr. Truman's private diaries also record his understanding of the significance of this option. On July 17, 1945, when Stalin confirmed that the Red Army would march, Mr. Truman privately noted: "Fini Japs when that comes about." [10]

There was plenty of time: The American invasion of Japan was not scheduled until the spring of 1946. Even a preliminary landing on the island of Kyushu was still three months in the future. [11]

General Dwight D. Eisenhower, appalled that the bomb would be used in these circumstances, urged Mr. Truman and Secretary of War Henry L. Stimson not to drop it. In his memoirs, he observed that weeks before Hiroshima, Japan had been seeking a way to surrender. "It wasn't necessary," he said in a later interview, "to hit them with that awful thing." [12]

The man who presided over the Joint Chiefs of Staff, Admiral William D. Leahy, was equally shocked: "The use of this barbarous weapon at Hiroshima and Nagasaki was of no material assistance in our [13] war against Japan. The Japanese were already defeated and ready to surrender."

Why, then, was the bomb used?   14

American leaders rejected the most obvious option—simply wait-   15
ing for the Red Army attack—out of political, not military, concerns.

As the diary of one official put it, they wanted to end the war   16
before Moscow got "in so much on the kill." Secretary of the Navy
James V. Forrestal's diaries record that Mr. Byrnes "was most anxious
to get the Japanese affair over with before the Russians got in."

United States leaders had also begun to think of the atomic bomb   17
as what Secretary Stimson termed the "master card" of diplomacy. President Truman postponed his Potsdam meeting with Stalin until July 17,
1945—one day after the first successful nuclear test—to be sure the atomic
bomb would strengthen his hand before confronting the Soviet leader
on the shape of a postwar settlement.

To this day, we do not know with absolute certainty Mr. Tru-   18
man's personal attitudes on several key issues. Yet we do know that his
most important adviser, Secretary of State Byrnes, was convinced that
dropping the bomb would serve crucial long-range diplomatic purposes.

As one atomic scientist, Leo Szilard, observed: "Mr. Byrnes did   19
not argue that it was necessary to use the bomb against the cities of
Japan in order to win the war. Mr. Byrnes' . . . view [was] that our
possessing and demonstrating the bomb would make Russia more
manageable."

Content Considerations

1. Summarize Alperovitz's position on the bombings of Hiroshima and
   Nagasaki; compare or contrast it with your own.
2. Discuss how political concerns may have influenced military decisions
   in the atomic bombings. What relations exist between the areas of politics and the military?
3. What evidence do you see in this article that the enemy is depersonalized
   in times of war? What effect might such depersonalization have on decisions, on soldiers, on nations?

War's New Science

Much of the latest technology in weaponry suggests that people may soon become superfluous, that weapons guided by computers could fight the wars that now must be carried out by military personnel. Some experts talk about saving lives; the public and the media have been quick to latch on to the idea of Nintendo wars fought by remote control, the victor being the one left with the most unexpended weaponry.

How probable is such a war? Published in Newsweek *February 18, 1991, the next article looks at the possibility and compares weapons it calls* evolutionary *and* revolutionary. *Before you read it, write a few paragraphs about what the consequences of a war fought completely with machines might be.*

A COST-FREE VICTORY. A push-button, remote-control war won 1
without casualties. Surgical strikes that wipe out military targets while
sparing civilians. Anyone with a television set, watching videos of
American bombs sailing through Iraqi doorways and down air shafts,
must wonder: if these weapons were just a little more gee-whiz, couldn't
the grunts and their ground assaults be dispensed with altogether? With
a lethal land battle looming in the Persian Gulf, the fantasy of war made
bloodless by science is all the more beguiling.

The results of the Persian Gulf showdown, when they finally come 2
in, will fuel an old quarrel over the virtues of high tech versus low tech,
especially if some smart weapons turn out to be duds. But that debate
may miss the point. The fact is that future weapons will have to be high
tech to survive. The real question is, just how high tech—and what
kind of weapons? For planners and policymakers, the issue is whether
to build ever more sophisticated airplanes and tanks—"manned platforms," in the military jargon—or whether to build better unmanned
weapons to do the job instead. The choice is between evolution and
revolution.

The most revolutionary weapon to land on Saddam is the cruise 3
missile. In Baghdad, one Western correspondent watched in awe as a
Tomahawk passed overhead, seemed to pause for a moment—and turned
left, toward the Ministry of Defense. Who needs pilots when missiles
have minds of their own? Yet the workhorse of the war so far is a plane

that began rolling off the assembly line back when American cars had fins. The B-52 has unloaded more bombs on the Iraqi forces than any warplane in the allied arsenal. The old plane is a model of the evolutionary approach. It has been rebuilt and reequipped a half-dozen times over the past three decades to run missions at night and through bad weather. In all, the apparent success of American weaponry in the gulf still owes more to slow and often painful trial and error than any sudden breakthrough. Most of the technology is vintage 1970s. Kennedy-era airframes like the F-4 and F-111 have been stuffed full of high-tech gear—microprocessors, laser guiding devices, electromagnetic jammers, infrared sensors.

Inside the so-called Iron Triangle—the Pentagon, Congress and   4
the defense industry—tech can almost never be too high. The military has spent billions perfecting "stealth" technology to allow airplanes to slip past enemy defenses. Already the Pentagon is using the performance of the F-117A Stealth fighter in the gulf to seek congressional support for the B-2 Stealth bomber, endangered on Capitol Hill by its high price tag (at least $850 million apiece). The F-117A Stealth fighter has been a success—but in a more specialized role than the Pentagon acknowledges. The Stealth does not pack much punch. Yet because it is invisible to enemy radar, it can loiter over the target. In the gulf, the F-117A has been used mostly as a spotter plane, circling on high, training a laser "designator" on the target. Old-fashioned conventional aircraft—like the F-15, F-111 and Tornado—swoop in behind to actually deliver the bombs. It is a case study of how new high tech can be combined with old tech to get the job done.

The Pentagon would like to build a whole new generation of air-   5
craft with truly revolutionary technology. Although Defense Secretary Dick Cheney canceled the Navy's A-12 after massive cost overruns, the Navy will undoubtedly need to build a new attack plane to replace the aging A-6. The Air Force, meanwhile, forges ahead with the ATF— Advanced Tactical Fighter. The ATF will not only be stealthy, it will be equipped with ever more sophisticated computers to help the pilot fly the plane—and, if need be, fly it for him. The Air Force is experimenting with a Virtual Reality Helmet that projects a cartoonlike image of the battlefield for the pilot, with flashing symbols for enemy planes, and a yellow-brick road leading right to the target. Additionally, if the "Gs" from the tight-turning, fast-climbing plane make the pilot pass out, then a new computer, delicately called the pilot's associate, would take over.

So why have pilots at all? Why not just build a plane that delivers   6
weapons by remote control? There are, in fact, such planes on the drawing boards. Their backers call them RPVs—"remotely piloted vehicles."

Pilots, who do not want to be put out of business, call them "drones" (as in "dull" or "stupid"). The Air Force has been slow to develop drones for anything more ambitious than target practice.

Parochialism aside, there are other real problems in designing weapons that find targets without human guidance. It is one thing for an infrared—heat seeking—missile to pick a target out of the cold clear sky, but quite another to spot one on the warm and cluttered ground. Development of these "brilliant" weapons takes years of trial and error. The Pentagon is still struggling to perfect a radar-guided, "fire and forget" missile called the AMRAAM that has been in development for more than a decade.

Soaring costs: The greatest obstacle to the high-tech revolution is money. As the costs of these weapons soar (the B-2 costs roughly 10 times as much as the old B-52), the resources available to the Pentagon will shrink, especially if the American economy remains shaky. Some defense experts, like Armed Services Committee chairman Sam Nunn, argue that the United States should continue to produce tried-and-true planes, but arm them with ever-smarter munitions, which are far cheaper to build than airplanes. The old planes need not be able to penetrate right to the target. The idea is to launch bombs and missiles from "platforms" that would "stand off" out of the range of enemy fighters and antiaircraft. The old could be married to the new: a B-52, for instance, can launch a cruise missile.

Americans have always looked to science for their answers, in war as in everything else. The H-bomb was supposed to make war too awful to contemplate, and Star Wars was intended to make it impossible to win. Now science seeks to leave the fighting to machines. It is unlikely that high technology will ever entirely remove men from the loop, however—nor should it. War is too unpredictable to be left to Dr. Strangelove's computer. Yet the promise of high-tech warfare still beckons: to slowly move men farther and farther from the killing fields.

Content Considerations

1. According to the authors, what is the difference between evolutionary and revolutionary weapons? What appear to be the advantages of each kind?
2. Discuss how wars might be affected if technology continues "to slowly move men farther and farther from the killing fields."
3. Explore the ways in which the public's attitude toward conventional weapons differs from its attitude toward high-tech weapons. What might be responsible for the differences?

— PAUL F. WALKER AND ERIC STAMBLER —

. . . *And the Dirty Little Weapons*

For many Americans watching television screens or reading the newspapers, the Persian Gulf war looked clean. High-tech weapons sought military targets and removed them; "smart missiles" tracked and hit SCUDs, exploding them in a shower of sparks and smoke. But other, more conventional weapons were also used. The authors of this essay say that 92.6 percent of the tonnage dropped during the war was the conventional kind, no more advanced than air raids by B-17s in World War II. These conventional weapons caused immense casualties, perhaps as many as 100,000 Iraqi conscripts.

If so, the Gulf war fell far short of the Nintendo and Star Wars ideal that seems to have been made of it. Before you begin the essay by Paul F. Walker and Eric Stambler, both of whom are with the Institute for Peace and International Security in Cambridge, Massachusetts, compile a list of what you know about the weapons that the United States and its allies used in the Gulf. Then write for a few minutes about why high-tech weapons often seem less warlike than most conventional ones.

THE FIRST IMAGES of the 43-day Persian Gulf War mesmerized 1
television viewers: nighttime pictures of Iraqi bunkers and buildings, many in downtown Baghdad, being "surgically" destroyed by precision-guided bombs dropped from stealthy aircraft. Coalition forces undertook thousands of aircraft sorties and missile strikes in the first days of the war, and a select number of the successful laser-guided bomb strikes were portrayed daily back home on the news. Similarly, American technical prowess was graphically displayed as Patriot air–defense missiles intercepted Iraq's modified versions of Soviet Scud missiles launched against Saudi Arabia and Israel. High-tech warfare had come of age.

These images created the impression that the war was a bloodless, 2
push-button battle in which only military targets were destroyed. Pentagon officials stressed in daily briefings that coalition war planners were taking great pains to match weapon to target in order to minimize "collateral damage," that is, harm to civilians in Iraq and Kuwait, particularly in cities. Halfway through the war journalist Gregg Easterbrook described the conflict as a "robowar"; that is, "the raids are intense, unremitting, and conducted with the world's most advanced non-nu-

clear weaponry, but it is unlikely they have caused the sort of general destruction being anticipated by commentators—vast expanses of carnage, smoking craters, and blackened obliteration." He went on to explain that in the first five days of Desert Storm, coalition air forces dropped some 15,000 tons of explosives on Iraq, but Iraq reported only 41 civilian deaths. "Despite public perceptions, the recent history of high-tech conventional warfare has been toward steadily reduced general destruction."[1] The January 21 *Wall Street Journal* editorialized that "advanced weapons spare civilians," while the *Washington Post* quoted U.S. officials on February 18 suggesting that Iraq could be faking destruction in a play for international sympathy.

U.S. and allied press briefings emphasized that most targets were military—air and ground weaponry and the Iraqi field army. Clearly there was no carpet bombing of downtown Baghdad. Yet, the briefers and ground observers also noted that targets of the air campaign were spread throughout Iraq and Kuwait, far beyond border military deployments. Many sites had civilian functions and were located in civilian populated areas—electrical power plants and grids, communications facilities, air defense and missile sites, airports and runways, military and political command centers—making it difficult, if not impossible, to preclude noncombatant casualties. These are the areas where the U.S. government has claimed "surgical" bombing and has been completely unwilling to provide target lists and casualty and damage assessments. Thus, the full extent of Iraqi civilian, as well as military, casualties from the Gulf War remains unknown. [3]

The strikingly low loss of life on the U.S. side—and the fact that neither side used nuclear, chemical, or biological weapons except for some Iraqi chemical mines—contributed to the perception that casualties were limited in the war. But early first-hand accounts gave a different glimpse of what was happening in Iraq. Capt. Steve Tate, pilot of an F-15 jet fighter which escorted the first wave of bombers and who was the first American to shoot down an Iraqi plane, described his bird's-eye view of Baghdad after the first hour of allied bombardment: "Flames rising up from the city left some neighborhoods lit up like a huge Christmas tree. . . . The entire city was just sparkling at us." Fellow F-15 pilot Lt. Col. Don Klein, commander of the 27th Tactical Fighter Squadron which participated in the first attacks, exclaimed that Baghdad "looked awesome. . . . There were things going off all over the place. There were a bunch of explosions, quick as they were going off. I couldn't count. . . . If you saw any of the footage from World War II, that's exactly what it looks like." [4]

The raids described above do not suggest "surgical" or "precision" strikes in urban areas. And the amount of ordnance used there has not [5] been distinguished from the overall tonnage dropped. Gen. Merrill "Tony" McPeak, air force chief of staff, proclaimed in a March 15 briefing that the war marked "the first time in history that a field army has been defeated by air power" and estimated that some 88,500 tons of bombs had been dropped in 109,876 aircraft sorties. At 59,000 tons a month, this is considerably more intense than the 34,000 tons per month dropped during the Vietnam War and the 22,000 tons per month dropped during the Korean War. In Vietnam, deaths averaged one for every two tons of explosive; in Korea, nearly four per ton. Gen. H. Norman Schwarzkopf has talked of over 100,000 casualties in the Gulf; U.S. military officials say damage assessment is continuing. But the outbreak of civil war has made that assessment more difficult, if not impossible.

Before the Gulf War, American commanders in Saudi Arabia in December portrayed an "air-land battle" which would include bombing and strafing of Iraqi command and control centers, troops, and supply lines; carpet-bombing by B-52 bombers based in Diego Garcia to clear Iraqi minefields; dense artillery fire, including laser-guided Copperhead shells and the new multiple launch rocket system; Cobra and Apache attack helicopters firing dozens of missiles and rockets; A-10 attack planes belching 4,000 rounds per minute of 30-millimeter cannon fire; navy battleships firing 2,000-pound shells from the Gulf; and both surface ships and submarines launching Tomahawk cruise missiles with 1,000-pound homing warheads.   6

One general commented: "When you concentrate that kind of firepower, you can kill an entire regiment in less than five minutes." Other officials said the air campaign would turn the area between Basra and the Kuwait border into a "parking lot." Gen. Thomas Kelly commented concisely on February 23 that by the time the Iraqi army was forced out of Kuwait, "there won't be many of them left." While much of this rhetoric may have been aimed at intimidating Saddam Hussein, the war as it was fought was probably closer to these plans than most televised pictures suggested.   7

In fact, one of the most horrifying images of the war was the "parking lot" created when aircraft, helicopters, and ground forces attacked Iraqi troops fleeing on highways out of Kuwait City February 25 and 26. Over 1,500 Iraqi tanks, armored vehicles, trucks, jeeps, ambulances, and automobiles were destroyed along several miles of highway running between Kuwait City and Umm Qasr in Iraq, victims of several hours of air attacks. In contrast to the emotionally remote TV pictures of smart bombs, these photos showed hundreds of charred and twisted bodies among the ruins.   8

Military troops and equipment were the primary targets—and by most accounts the highway casualties consisted largely of retreating Iraqi   9 forces. Yet it is clear from preliminary post-war damage assessments that destruction went far beyond military facilities and personnel. Many of the critical targets in Baghdad and other cities were civilian, although not so defined by the military: telephone and other communication centers, utilities and power grids, bridges and highways. Some 50 railroad and highway bridges between Basra and Baghdad were damaged or rendered inoperable by air bombardment. Highways and surrounding areas were bombed in the air force search-and-destroy missions against Iraqi mobile missile launchers. A U.N. report issued in mid-March described "near apocalyptic" damage to Iraq's infrastructure which has relegated the country to a "pre-industrial age." According to the survey team report, the destruction of 9,000 homes has left some 72,000 Iraqis homeless.

As General McPeak explained in his briefing on retreating Iraqi 10 forces, "When enemy armies are defeated, they retreat, often in disorder, and we have what is known in the business as the exploitation phase. It's during this phase that the true fruits of victory are achieved from combat. . . . It's a tough business. . . . It often causes us to do very brutal things—that's the nature of war."

But another major reason for the widespread damage lies in the 11 type of weapons used. Precision-guided munitions—the Mavericks, Hellfires, TOWs, and other such missiles—were used against selected targets such as tanks, armored personnel carriers, and other "hard targets." But the strikes against ground troops, armored formations, widespread defenses, and other large targets, many located in civilian areas, were undertaken with less discriminating weapons.

One little-known fact is that of the 88,500 tons of bombs dropped, 12 only 6,520 tons—7.4 percent—were precision-guided ordnance, according to official Pentagon figures. Most of the weapons used were conventional, and very destructive, bombs and artillery. The military has not provided a breakdown of the weapons used but an air force spokesman has acknowledged that the "full complement of tactical munitions was employed throughout Desert Storm" and that he "wouldn't disagree with" a long list of destructive air-launched ordnance presented to him for confirmation that they were used in the war. This list included all the weapons mentioned below. Recent press reports of postwar military and civilian casualties caused by unexploded "bomblets" appear to confirm wide use of antipersonnel weapons.

One of the most common "workhorse" weapons was the "cluster 13 bomb unit" (CBU). These weapons have been gradually refined over the last three decades to deliver explosions lethal to personnel and equipment over expanded areas. Instead of a single large explosion, these bombs contain dozens, hundreds, and sometimes thousands of bomblets called BLUs (bomb live units), essentially high-tech grenades designed to spread devastation over wide areas.

Today's aircraft may carry a cluster bomb unit filled with 1,800 one-pound bomblets such as the BLU-26 Sadeye—a cast steel shell with aerodynamic vanes and 0.7 pound of TNT in which 600 razor-sharp steel shards are embedded. The Sadeye can be equipped with fuses to explode upon impact, several yards above ground, or some time after landing. It is lethal up to about 40 feet. Thus a container of 1,800 Sadeyes, called a CBU-75, disperses destruction over more than double the territory of the standard 2,000-pound bomb. A typical bomb is the 2,000 pound Mk-84, developed in the 1950s. The Mk-84 creates a crater 50 feet in diameter and 36 feet deep or, exploding before it hits the ground, disperses shrapnel to a lethal radius of 400 yards.

A wide variety of cluster bombs has been developed since they were first designed in the 1960s as successors to simpler fragmentation or antipersonnel bombs. The bomblets can be dropped en masse to disperse themselves with their aerodynamic fins, or they can be spewed out by compressed air in streams behind the plane. Some use parachutes or drogues to slow their descent; some are equipped with shaped charges for use against hardened targets such as tanks. Others can bounce 10 feet or more after impact to scatter antipersonnel shrapnel. Some are designed to disperse smoke, napalm, or chemical agents, and other models are mines with delayed fuses or acoustic or seismic sensors for use against tanks.

The Rockeye II is a 750-pound unit carrying 717 antitank fragmentation bomblets which can distinguish between soft and hard targets; one F-15E fighter/bomber can carry as many as 22 Rockeyes. The CBU-58 carries 650 Sadeyes; the CBU-52/B carries 254. The striking feature all share is their wide area coverage: the CBU-52/B can cover 1.3 million square feet, equal to over 22 football fields. The CBU-75 covers the equivalent of 157 football fields.

One 950-pound cluster bomb, the CBU-87/B, was described by air force officials as the weapon of choice in the Middle East. This "combined effects munition" carries 202 bomblets, the BLU-97/B. Each 3.4-pound bomblet carries a triple punch: a prefragmented antipersonnel casing to spray deadly shrapnel; a hollow-charge antitank warhead; and a disc of incendiary zirconium to add a fiery finishing touch. The air force claims one such bomblet will disable heavy vehicles over a 50-foot radius and aircraft over a 250-foot radius. Troops would be still more vulnerable at greater ranges.

A single B-52 strategic bomber can carry 40 such cluster bombs, with a total of 8,080 bomblets. Theoretically, assuming a danger radius of 250 feet, one B-52 could carpet-bomb over 176 million square yards, equal to 27,500 football fields. The 28 B-52s which reportedly dropped 470 tons of explosives on Iraqi ground forces on one day, January 30, could have obliterated 1,600 square miles, an area one-third the size of Connecticut.

Fuel-air explosives were another group of weapons used against Iraq. The U.S. Central Command says they were used to clear mine-fields in Kuwait throughout the war, although it is reluctant to identify the specific weapons used. [19]

Predecessors to fuel-air explosives were incendiary or fire bombs, weapons filled with highly flammable material such as thermite, mag-nesium powder, or napalm—a mixture of gasoline and benzene with aluminum or polystyrene soap as a thickener. These weapons would spread fire over wide areas and, when ignited in restricted areas such as bunkers, would consume so much oxygen that victims who were not burned to death would suffocate. [20]

Fuel-air explosives form highly gaseous mixtures which, when detonated, produce much more blast than fire. For their size and weight, they provide a much larger blast than any other weapon except for nuclear devices; in fact, the blast can mimic a small nuclear explosion. They were first widely used in Vietnam to destroy Vietcong tunnels and to clear heavily wooded areas for helicopter landing sites. Some are launched from aircraft, others from helicopters or ground vehicles. [21]

For example, the appropriately named MAD FAE (mass air deliv-ery fuel-air explosive) consists of 12 containers of ethylene oxide or propylene oxide trailed behind utility helicopters. The containers release a cloud of highly volatile vapors which, when mixed with air and det-onated, can cover an area over 1,000 feet long with blast pressures five times that of TNT. A surface unit consists of an armored vehicle with 30 launch tubes for five-inch Zuni rockets equipped with fuel-air mu-nitions to detonate mine fields. U.S. inventories also include an air-dropped unit of three 100-pound canisters filled with ethylene oxide. A proximity fuse bursts the canisters 30 feet above ground and disperses an aerosol cloud more than 2,500 cubic yards in volume which is det-onated a few inches above ground by a second charge. The blast over-pressures of 300 pounds per square inch will flatten everything within a 60-foot radius and kill any troops nearby, both above and below ground. Just a few pounds overpressure is lethal for humans. [22]

One "favorite of the Marine Corps" in the Mideast, according to an anonymous Pentagon spokesman, was the BLU-82, known as "Big Blue 82" or "Daisy Cutter." Last used in Vietnam by U.S. Special Forces for clearing helicopter landing sites, the 15,000-pound bomb is filled with an aqueous mixture of ammonium nitrate, aluminum pow-der, and polystyrene soap. It can only be launched from a cargo aircraft, [23] the MC–130 Hercules, by rolling it out the rear cargo door. The bomb descends by parachute and detonates just above ground, producing blast overpressures of 1,000 pounds per square inch and disintegrating everything within hundreds of yards. It can be used to clear minefields or against concentrations of troops, aircraft, and equipment. How many of these blockbusters were actually used is still unknown.

Another widely used weapon was the multiple launch rocket system (MLRS), a mainstay of ground force operational plans: the army has purchased almost 500,000 of these rockets over the past decade and deployed them to Europe and Korea. The MLRS is a sophisticated artillery gun capable of firing more deadly warheads faster, farther, and more accurately than its predecessors. About 115 were deployed and "several thousand rockets fired" in the Gulf War, according to U.S. military officials. The tracked vehicle carries 12 rockets, each containing 644 submunitions: small antipersonnel bomblets not much larger than a 35-millimeter film canister which individually can saturate an area 220 yards in diameter, according to the manufacturer. A full 12-rocket volley can spread more than two tons of firepower over an area the size of six football fields in one minute.

The full extent of war damage in Iraq and Kuwait will not be known for some time, if ever. But much of what we know now challenges the assumption that the war was an antiseptic Nintendo game, an impersonal conflict with little "collateral" damage, or a contest dominated by selective, precision-guided munitions which discriminated between human beings in and out of military uniform. Large amounts of explosive tonnage were dropped in the region, over 90 percent in the form of weapons that were not precision guided—and we do not have accurate information on the success and reliability of precision-guided ordnance. The intense air campaign, with over 2,500 sorties flown on average per day, and the high-tech destructive weapons must have wreaked incredible damage.

We have some first-hand descriptions from war refugees and returning Americans that bear this out, as well as a few gruesome examples that appeared on television screens and in news photos. Still, the human face of this war, to use John Keegan's term from *The Face of Battle,* must be better revealed before it can be properly understood and appropriate lessons drawn for history. This was not a surgical war; it was a slaughter. History may judge high technology the winner, but human beings were certainly the victims.

ENDNOTES

1. Gregg Easterbrook, "Robowar," *New Republic* (Feb. 11, 1991), p. 17.

2. Philip Shenon, "Allied Fliers Jubilantly Describe Their Command of Iraqi Skies," *New York Times,* Jan. 18, 1991, p. A10.
3. Quoted in George J. Church, "If War Begins," *Time* (Dec. 10, 1991), pp. 29–30.
4. Quoted in Michael Kinsley, "TRB from Washington: Dead Iraqis," *New Republic* (March 18, 1991), p. 6.

Content Considerations

1. Explain the evidence the authors offer to establish that the Persian Gulf war was not "a bloodless, push-button battle in which only military targets were destroyed." Did you find the evidence surprising? Why?
2. If the authors are correct about the kinds of weapons used in the war, what destruction must have occurred? How did the media present the destruction?
3. Discuss the concept of "collateral damage" in wartime. Can such damage be avoided? When is it justified?

Victor W. Sidel, M.D.

Biological Weapons Research and Physicians: Historical and Ethical Analysis

Biological warfare is by no means a new concept or practice. The following article by Dr. Victor W. Sidel notes a siege in 1346 during which one army threw disease-ridden cadavers over a city's walls in order to infect and weaken its enemy. In such warfare, living organisms or their products are used as weapons to hurt, kill, or "incapacitate" opponents. Although some doctors and scientists around the world have denounced the practice of developing such deadly weapons and have refused to conduct bioweapon research or divulge the results of such research, others believe that any assistance they can provide their country during war or peace is justified.

Dr. Sidel, Distinguished University Professor of Social Medicine at the Montefiore Medical Center, Albert Einstein College of Medicine, Bronx, New York, presents a brief history of biological warfare and then examines the ethical questions that such warfare raises. Before you begin his article, published in Physicians for Social Responsibility Quarterly *in March, 1991, write about whether biological weapons are worse than any other kind. Is an anthrax bomb worse than a conventional high-explosive missile?*

Analysis of the historical and ethical elements of the role of scientists and physicians in weapons research, of the history and nature of biological weapons, and of the ethical issues posed by the research leads to the conclusion that biological weapons research by physicians is unethical, even for a "just war." Furthermore, since so-called defensive research on such weapons under military sponsorship is widely viewed as highly ambiguous, provocative, and strongly suggestive of offensive goals, it is urged that physicians refuse participation in such research as well. Instead, it is advocated that physicians and others undertake a series of specific efforts to end the biological arms race and to prevent the militarization of biology. PSRQ 1991;1:31–42

163

PARTICIPATION OF PHYSICIANS in research on biological weapons [2] raises issues relevant to three overlapping areas: the ethics of research, the ethics of medicine, and the ethics of war. Review of history and ethics in these areas will begin with discussion of the role of scientists and physicians in weapons research, proceed to examine the history and nature of biological weapons, the reasons for the universal abhorrence in which they are held, and the ethics of biological weapons research, and conclude by consideration of the special issues raised by the physician's role in research and action on biological weapons.

THE ROLE OF SCIENTISTS AND PHYSICIANS IN RESEARCH ON WEAPONS OF WAR

Scientists throughout history have been called upon to play a role [3] in preparation for war or in support of the conflict[1,2]. Archimedes used his skills on behalf of Dionysius of Syracuse to construct an arsenal in preparation for war against the Romans[3], Leonardo da Vinci designed fortifications for the Duke of Milan[4], and Galileo calculated trajectories of projectiles for the Grand Duke of Tuscany[5]. In this century, Fritz Haber, who was awarded the 1919 Nobel Prize in Chemistry for his synthesis of ammonia, is known as the father of Germany's chemical weapons program of World War I. In his Nobel Prize acceptance speech, Haber declared poison gas "a higher form of killing"[6]. Indeed this century is replete with examples of scientist participation in research on weapons: chemists have worked on explosives and poison gases; physicists worked on nuclear weapons in World War II; biologists worked on herbicides for use in the Vietnam War; and for at least the past 50 years, biologists, biomedical scientists, and physicians have worked on biological weapons.

There have also been numerous examples of scientists who refused [4] to work on the development of weapons of war. While da Vinci was willing to trade design of fortifications for the patronage of his Duke, he was not willing to "publish or divulge" his design for a submarine "on account of the evil nature of men"[4]. During the Crimean War, the British government consulted the noted physicist Michael Faraday on the feasibility of developing poison gases; Faraday responded that it was entirely feasible, but that it was inhuman and he would have nothing to do with it[7]. Other scientists, such as Alfred Nobel, Albert Einstein, and Leo Szilard, participated in the development of weapons or in scientific or theoretical advances that led to weapons and, then based on a realization of what these weapons could do, tried to prevent the weapons they helped develop from being used[8].

SOCIAL RESPONSIBILITY OF THE SCIENTIST

The ethical issues that lie behind the decision of a scientist to participate or to refuse to participate in research are part of the spectrum of issues that relate to the responsibility of scientists for the social consequences of their work[9-13]. At one end of the ethical spectrum lies the view that research (in contrast to development) is value-free and the scientist therefore has no social or moral responsibility for the ways in which his or her scientific work is applied. This argument was stated explicitly by the sociologist Lundberg and his colleagues in 1929:

> It is not the business of a chemist who invents a high explosive to be influenced in his task by considerations as to whether his product will be used to blow up cathedrals or to build tunnels through the mountains[14].

This view of the amorality of science and the freedom from responsibility of the scientist for its consequences followed in part from the assumptions that 1) scientific progress was the road to human perfection, and 2) that science was "an autonomous force working for man's welfare in contrast to the disruptive force of politics"[15].

The assumptions that scientific work is value free and that scientific findings invariably lead to progress were increasingly challenged in the 1930s and 1940s. Applications of science by Nazi Germany shocked many scientists. Other questions were raised about the role of U.S. physicists in research on nuclear weapons, both by the physicists themselves within the constraints of secrecy of the work during World War II, and later publicly by them and many others[16].

Some scientists have maintained in recent years that the realm of value-free science includes not only work in pure science, such as the original discovery of chlorine or the development of the special theory of relativity, long before there was any application for them in war, but also applied science work on what is clearly intended to be a weapon of war. Professor Louis Fieser, for example, had been leader of a team of Harvard University scientists who developed napalm—jellied gasoline used as an incendiary weapon—during World War II. When asked in 1967 about the use of napalm in that war and later in the Indochina War, he said that he felt free of guilt:

> You don't know what's coming. That wasn't my business. That is for other people. I was working on a technical problem that was considered pressing. . . . I distinguish between developing a munition of some kind and using it. You can't blame the outfit

that put out the rifle that killed the President. I'd do it again, if called upon, in defense of the country[17].

Fieser, midway in his comment, seems to shift his argument somewhat from absence of any responsibility for the use of the weapon to a justification of his work on the basis of its usefulness "in defense of the country." Many other scientists who explicitly recognize the ethical conflicts involved in work on weapons argue that a higher ethical principle—the imperative of defending one's country or of helping to curb what is perceived as evil or destructive, leads to a decision to participate in such work. The German, later American, rocket scientist Wernher von Braun wrote in a letter in 1968:   11

> While right from the beginning I deeply deplored the war and the misery and suffering it spread all over the world, I found myself caught in a maelstrom in which I simply felt that, like it or not, it was my duty to work for my country at war[18].   12

Dr. Theodor Rosebury, who worked on biological weapons during World War II, explained his participation in a different way. His argument relied not on the defense of his country, but on danger to the world and on his belief that crisis circumstances, expected to pass in a limited time, required that he act as he did. "We were fighting a fire, and it seemed necessary to risk getting dirty as well as burnt," he later wrote[19].   13

Many of the U.S. and British scientists who worked in the development of controlled nuclear fission for use in weapons shared this sense that their role was to save the world from a greater evil. After it became clear that Nazi Germany had not developed nuclear weapons, a number of scientists felt the work should be suspended and raised objections as it became clear the weapon they helped develop would be used against Japan. Following the nuclear bombing of Hiroshima and Nagasaki, a recognition of the destruction and of the potential future consequences led many of those who had participated to initiate public discussion of the morality of what they had done. J. Robert Oppenheimer wrote in 1949, "the physicists have known sin" and, in 1956, "we did the Devil's work"[18]. The founding of the *Bulletin of the Atomic Scientists* and of the Federation of American Scientists after World War II reflected this moral concern[8,20].   14

Other scientists who recognized an ethical dilemma in work on weapons resolved it by arguing that their work was designed to reduce the devastation of war. For example, Dr. Knut Krieger, while working on "nonlethal" chemical and biological weapons in the 1960s, argued in   15 defense of his work that the research would lead to decreased fatalities: " . . . if we do indeed succeed in creating incapacitating systems and are able to substitute incapacitation for death it appears to me that, next to stopping war, this would be an important step forward"[18].

Paradoxically, other scientists argued that development of horrible new weapons made war less likely and was therefore a contribution to lessening its devastation. In 1892 Albert Nobel defended his development of dynamite by predicting that "on the day that two army corps can mutually annihilate each other in a second, all civilized nations will surely recoil with horror and disband their troops"[18]. This concept that research on highly destructive weapons would lead to a lessening of the probability of war was expressed in 1958 by Professor Hans Bethe, a physicist who had worked on the development of the hydrogen bomb. He argued that scientists must help preserve the precarious balance of armament that would make it disastrous for either side to start a war, the basis for the current U.S. strategic nuclear policy of mutually assured destruction (MAD). "Only then," Bethe reasoned, "can we argue for and embark on more constructive ventures like disarmament and international cooperation which may eventually lead to a more definite peace"[21]. 16

Some scientists who felt on ethical grounds they should participate in weapons research in a particular war refused to participate when that war was over. Dr. Rosebury, who believed during World War II that his work on the development of biological weapons, although "dirty," could be morally justified because of the special moral imperative of the fight against Hitler, shortly after the end of the war refused any further participation in such work[22]. Many of the nuclear physicists who began to question work on nuclear weapons after it became clear Germany had no such weapons, or after they were used in Japan, refused to do any further work on them. 17

The most all-encompassing expression of the view that it is the responsibility of scientists to refuse to participate in any research on weapons of war was given in an oath proposed by one of the participants in the 1962 Pugwash Conference on Science and World Affairs, one of a series of meetings of scientists from different countries to discuss problems of disarmament and world peace: 18

> Under no circumstances shall I work for war, neither directly nor through any advice. Only those who take the same oath shall be admitted to my laboratory and to any learned societies of which I am a member[23]. 19

The Society for Social Responsibility in Science cites the following among its principles: 20

> To foster throughout the world a . . . tradition of personal [21]
> moral responsibility for the consequences for humanity of profes-
> sional activity, with emphasis on constructive alternatives to mili-
> tarism; to embody in this tradition the principle that the individual
> must abstain from destructive work and devote himself to con-
> structive work, according to his own moral judgment; to ascertain
> . . . the boundary between constructive and destructive work to
> serve as a guide for individual and group decisions and action[24].

Along with the decision whether or not to participate in weapons [22]
research is the ethical responsibility to inform and warn the public, and
this responsibility is shared by both pure and applied scientists. Those
who assert this responsibility note that scientists are often in a unique
position to warn the public of specific dangers that special scientific
knowledge permits them to perceive earlier or more clearly than others.
Debate arises, however, on whether scientists should simply state the
facts (which in itself involves deciding what is a fact, which facts to
present, and how and where to present them) or should go beyond the
facts to state their opinions on the courses of action to which they have
been led by their analysis of the facts. Furthermore, many scientists, like
others in the community, do not carefully distinguish between fact and
opinion in their statements. Since the expertise of scientists in most
societies often lends considerable weight to their views, and since there
are usually elements of the analysis that lie outside purely scientific expertise, the propriety of public policy statements by scientists has at
times been questioned. On the other hand, silence by scientists on urgent public policy issues on which they have relevant technical information has also been questioned as evasion of moral responsibility. The
problem of how to avoid scientists' undue power to influence societal
decisions, while at the same time maintaining responsibility for the consequences of scientific work is still unsolved.

In summary, we see a spectrum of views on ethical responsibilities [23]
of scientists in relation to work on weapons: complete denial of moral
responsibility for the consequences of any scientific work including work
directly contributing to weapons development; recognition of moral responsibility for the consequences of work leading to weapons, but citing
of competing obligations that require such work, such as doing one's
country's bidding whatever the consequences, or reducing the possibility of war or its devastation; recognition of moral responsibility by refusing any work on weapons; and responsibility to inform or to lead
public opinion on policies related to the weapons the scientist helped
develop.

SOCIAL RESPONSIBILITY OF THE PHYSICIAN

Narrowing the focus from a consideration of the work of scientists in general in the development of weapons to a consideration of the specific case of the physician-scientist or physician-technologist, the question that first arises is whether it is constructive to view certain ethical responsibilities as peculiar to the physician's social role. The view that appears to be most prevalent holds that along with sharing the moral responsibilities of all scientists and indeed of all people, the physician has special additional ethical responsibilities because of his or her role in preserving life and health[19,25]. Others argue that to assert a special form of medical ethics is arrogant, elitist, and in some ways destructive to the role of the physician, because it conveys increased power and adds social distance between physician and patient.

As evidence for the view that many physicians feel they have special ethical responsibilities, Rosebury described the response to physician participation in work on biological weapons during World War II: "There was much quiet but searching discussion among us regarding the place of doctors in such work . . . a certain delicacy concentrated most of the physicians into principally or primarily defensive operations"[19]. Rosebury goes on to point out that the modifiers principally and primarily are needed "because military operations can never be exclusively defensive," a point which will be discussed below.

The special responsibility of physicians is perceived largely as an ethical responsibility not to use their power to do harm (primum non nocere). Although only a very small percentage of U.S. medical students now swear to a literal translation of the Hippocratic Oath, this code for physicians is often cited as an expression of their special responsibility: "I will apply dietetic measures for the benefit of the sick according to my ability and judgment; I will keep them from harm and injustice. I will neither give a deadly drug to anybody if asked for it, nor will I make a suggestion to this effect"[26]. While the oath as written seems to apply to the relationship of the physician to an individual patient, its meaning has been broadened by many to proscribe physician participation in actions harmful to others.

A modern version of the Hippocratic Oath, the Declaration of Geneva, developed and regularly revised by the World Medical Association, is sworn to by more graduating U.S. medical students than is the original oath. The relevant portion reads:

> I will not permit considerations of religion, nationality, race, party politics, or social standing to intervene between my duty and my patient; I will maintain the utmost respect for human life from

24

25

26

27

28

its beginning even under threat and I will not use my medical knowledge contrary to the laws of humanity[27].

In the Prayer of Maimonides, also read at some medical school [29] commencements, the physician beseeches, "Preserve the strength of my body that I may be able to restore the strength of the rich and the poor, the good and the bad, the friend and the foe. Let me see in the sufferer the man alone"[28]. More directly to the point, the Regulations in Time of Armed Conflict adopted by the World Medical Association states:

> The primary task of the medical profession is to preserve health [30] and save life. Hence it is deemed unethical for physicians to: 1) give advice or perform prophylactic, diagnostic, or therapeutic procedures that are not justifiable in the patient's interest, 2) weaken the physical and mental strength of a human being without therapeutic justification, 3) employ scientific knowledge to imperil health or destroy life[29].

Presumably these special proscriptions on the work of physicians [31] are necessary because of the doctor's special skills and special opportunities, both to do good and to do harm. In this context it may be of interest that in Greek mythology, at least until the emergence of Chiron, a good centaur with healing skills, and his pupil Asklepios, a god/human who practiced both protection of health and treatment of disease, the power to heal was closely bound up with the power to harm. Indeed the first deity appealed to in the Hippocratic Oath, "Apollo the Physician," appeared to derive his healing powers in part from the ability he and his twin sister Artemis had to cause acute illness and sudden death by shooting their arrows at mortals. They also had gentle darts that brought the death of old age. Apollo's son, Asklepios, who is the next to be cited in the Hippocratic Oath and whose healing work is mentioned in the *Iliad,* used his skills only for good and is called a "blameless physician" by Homer[30].

In summary, there seems to be a general consensus that physicians [32] participate in weapons research at their ethical peril, even if their country demands it or they think it useful for deterrence or other preventive purposes. Because of the ambiguity of "defensive" work on biological weapons, the dilemma for the physicians is not easily resolved even for those who believe that defensive efforts are ethically permissible.

THE NATURE OF BIOLOGICAL WEAPONS

The horrors of biological weapons are expressed by one of only [33]

10 Genoese and Venetian travellers out of 1,000 who survived a 1346 siege of the walled city of Caffa (now called Feodosia), a seaport on the east coast of the Crimea:

> "The Tartars, fatigued by such a plague and pestiforous dis-
> ease, stupefied and amazed, observing themselves dying without
> hope of health, ordered cadavers placed on their hurling machines
> and thrown into the city of Caffa, so that by means of these intol-
> erable passengers the defenders died widely. Thus there were pro-
> jected mountains of dead, nor could the Christians hide or flee, or
> be freed from such disaster. . . . And soon all the air was infected
> and the water poisoned, corrupt and petrified, and such a great
> odor increased. . . . So great and so much was the general mor-
> tality that great shouts and clamor arose from Chinese, Indians,
> Persians, Nubians, Ethiopians, Egyptians, Arabs, Saracens, Greeks,
> who cried and wept, and suspected the extreme judgment of God"[31].

Equally evocative is the definition of biological warfare published in 1959 by what was then called the U.S. Department of Health, Education and Welfare:

> Biological warfare is the intentional use of living organisms or
> their toxic products to cause death, disability or damage in man,
> animals, or plants. The target is man, either by causing sickness or
> death, or through limitation of his food supplies or other agricul-
> tural resources. Man must wage a continuous fight to maintain and
> defend himself, his animals, and his plants in competition with
> insects and micro-organisms. The object of biological warfare is to
> overcome these efforts by deliberately distributing large numbers
> of organisms of native and foreign origin, or their toxic products,
> taking full advantage of the ability to utilize more effective methods
> of dissemination and unusual portals of entry. Biological warfare
> has been aptly described as public health in reverse[32].

When the Geneva Protocol was negotiated in 1925, prohibition of use of "bacteriological methods of warfare" was added to what had originally been envisaged as purely a chemical weapons treaty. Many of the nations ratifying the Protocol reserved the right to use such weapons in retaliation if they were first used against them, and the Protocol became essentially a no-first-use treaty. Furthermore, the Protocol did not in any way limit the development, production, testing, or stockpiling of either chemical or biological weapons, only their use[33].

Despite the Protocol, there is evidence that both chemical and biological weapons were used in the wars of the 1930s and 1940s[34]. It is reliably reported, for example, that in the 1930s invading Japanese troops brought into China rice and wheat mixed with fleas carrying plague, resulting in plague in areas of China that had not experienced plague before. Extensive experiments were conducted in Japanese laboratories on prisoners of war from a number of different countries testing a wide variety of agents including anthrax, plague, gas gangrene, encephalitis, typhus, typhoid, hemorrhagic fever, cholera, smallpox, and tularemia[35]. The U.S. required this information after the end of the war but unlike the 1949 Soviet prosecution of 12 of those involved in work, the U.S. never tried any of the participants. Instead, U.S. researchers met with Japanese biological warfare experts in Tokyo and urged that the experts be "spared embarrassment" so the U.S. could benefit from their knowledge[36–38].

According to testimony at the Nuremberg trials prisoners at Ger- [39] man concentration camps such as Buchenwald were infected to test response to biological agents. The British are known to have released anthrax spores on Gruinard Island off the coast of Scotland to demonstrate the spread of the disease to the animal population of the island; the island remained uninhabitable for many years. Churchill is said to have considered anthrax as a weapon, although it was never used. In the U.S., work on anthrax and brucellosis as weapons was performed and a plant was constructed in southern Indiana for the production of anthrax bombs; only a prototype was actually produced and tested in Utah[39].

Since World War II there have been numerous allegations of bio- [40] logical weapons development and even use, although every one of the reports of actual hostile use are unsubstantiated. In the United States it was revealed in 1969 that in the 1950s and 1960s the University of Utah had, under contract, conducted secret experiments at the U.S. Army Dugway Proving Ground involving large-scale field testing of biological warfare agents including tularemia, Rocky Mountain spotted fever, plague, and Q fever. In 1950, U.S. Navy ships in the San Francisco Bay area released large quantities of aerosolized Serratia marcescens and Bacillus globigii (Bacillus subtilis variant niger), believed to be nonpathogenic, to test dispersal efficiency. Subsequent infections and deaths from Serratia, particularly among immunologically compromised individuals, were later attributed by some analysts to this release. During the 1950s and 1960s, the U.S. conducted 239 top-secret open-air disseminations of simulants, involving such areas as the New York City subways and Washington National Airport[40]. During the 1950s and 1960s, a large infrastructure of laboratories, test facilities, and production plants related to chemical and biological weapons was constructed in the U.S., and by the end of the 1960s, the U.S. government had at least 10 different biological and toxin weapons available[41].

In 1969 the Nixon Administration, with the concurrence of the Defense Department, which declared that "biological weapons lacked military usefulness," unconditionally renounced U.S. development, production, stockpiling, and use of biological weapons, and announced that the U.S. would unilaterally dismantle its biological weapons program. In 1972, the U.S.S.R. ended its opposition to a separate biological weapons treaty (it had urged a more comprehensive treaty) and the Convention on the Prohibition of the Development, Prevention, and Stockpiling of Bacteriological (Biological) and Toxin Weapons and on Their Destruction was negotiated[42]. The Biological Weapons Convention (BWC) prohibits the development or acquisition of biological agents or toxins, as well as weapons carrying them and means of their production, stockpiling, transfer, or delivery, except for "prophylactic, protective, and other peaceful purposes." The BWC was ratified by the U.S. Senate in 1975 (the same year in which the Senate belatedly ratified the Geneva Protocol of 1925). As of December 31, 1987, 110 nations had ratified the BWC and an additional 25 nations had signed but not yet ratified it[43]. Until the 1988 Intermediate Nuclear Force Treaty, it was the only treaty in modern times to prohibit possession as well as use of weapons.

Invoking the specter of possible new biological weapons produced by genetic engineering techniques, and unproved allegations of aggressive biological weapons programs in other countries, as well as the absence of proscription of defensive efforts by the BWC, the Reagan Administration initiated intensive efforts to conduct "defensive" research. The budget for the U.S. Army Biological Defense Research Program (BDRP), which sponsors programs in a wide variety of academic, commercial, and government laboratories, increased from $15.1 million in 1981 to $60 million in 1988 and the basic research component of BDRP activities increased 60-fold from 1981 to 1986. Much of this research work is medical in nature, including the development of immunizations and of treatment against organisms that might be used as weapons[44].

Even though offensive work on biological weapons has been internationally outlawed, it is important to reiterate the special ethical issues involved in their development and potential use. First, these are weapons of indiscriminate mass destruction. If noncombatants are specific targets, as they have been in recent years for chemical weapons, civilians constitute the most vulnerable and least protected segment of the population and widespread civilian casualties would likely result. Even if attempts are made to target only hostile military forces, biological agents spread through populations in highly unpredictable ways and could cause vast unintended damage to both combatants and noncombatants. Examples of such unpredictability can be found even among naturally occurring diseases. The measles virus, although usually relatively benign, can cause extremely high case fatality rates under certain conditions. A measles epidemic in Fiji in 1875 killed 20–25% of the unprotected islanders, and an epidemic in Boer concentration camps in 1900 caused many deaths among the weakened women and children[45]. In short, because of their potential impact on noncombatants and their inherent failure to limit destructiveness to the minimum necessary to achieve a defined military purpose, use of these weapons cannot be justified even in what has been defined ethically as a "just" war.

Second, development or use of biological weapons systems may lead to further attrition of international law. The Geneva Protocol of 1925, which outlawed their use, has been weakened. In 1969, for example, the majority of nations party to the Protocol declared via their positions on United Nations General Assembly resolution 2603A (XXIV), that the use of harassing incapacitants is forbidden by the Protocol. Yet the U.S. used such weapons, calling them riot control agents, and stated that it considered them outside the scope of the Protocol[46]. More recently weapons that are unquestionably covered by the Protocol have been used with impunity by several nations. For example, the use of mustard gas, nerve gas, and perhaps other chemical weapons by Iraq in its war with Iran, and against its own Kurdish population evoked no effective protest by the U.S. or by the world community. With regard to the BWC, it has been recently conjectured that Iran is developing biological weapons[47] and that less developed nations and terrorists may be capable of producing and using them[48,49]. The more biological weapons are developed, and the more widespread the knowledge of them becomes, the weaker the BWC will become. Damage to these existing arms control treaties threatens all arms control and disarmament efforts[50].

Turning from the ethical issues posed by offensive research to those of defensive research, a number of concerns about defensive research have been raised.

1. There is ample precedent for masking the work of facilities developing biological weapons by calling them preventive laboratories. The Japanese laboratory established in 1933 for developing such weapons was called the Epidemic Prevention Laboratory. One of its activities was supplying vaccines for troops bound for Manchuria, but its major work was developing and testing weapons[38]. Military forces today could knowingly conduct research on offensive use of biological weapons under the cover of defensive research since, as we have noted, offensive

and defensive research are inextricably joined for at least some phases of the work. During the parts of the work in which offensive and defensive efforts parallel each other, it is possible (indeed probable, if military researchers are conscientiously working to explore forms of organisms against which defenses might be needed) that new forms of organisms may be found or developed that would be *more* effective as biological weapons. Indeed, it is difficult to imagine testing medical defenses against organisms not ordinarily found in nature except by producing such organisms. There may be a temptation to test the defense by trying it out against the offensive organism. And someone in a military-sponsored laboratory may be tempted, ostensibly in the interest of defense, to go further in the study of more virulent or more stable or more easily disseminated organisms.

The possibility that offensive work is being done in the U.S. under the cover of defensive work has been denied by the leadership of the BDRP, who point out the divergence between the two types of research[51]. Nonetheless, critics of the BDRP programs raise questions about the ambiguity of the BDRP defensive research[52]. Piller and Yamamoto, for example, argue that "these efforts are highly ambiguous, provocative and strongly suggestive of offensive goals"[44]. Given what is known of the secrecy and duplicity of military efforts in many nations, it is surely possible that a physician-scientist in some nation might either consent to or be misled into work intended for offensive use under the guise of recruitment for defensive work. 47

2. Analysts believe that biological weapons research, even if truly defensive in intent, may be dangerous to surrounding communities if virulent infectious organisms are accidentally released, although no examples of such release have yet been convincingly documented. Concern has been raised about the safety of several aspects of the work of the BDRP. The proposals for construction of a Biosafety Level 4 Laboratory in Utah for testing aerosols of virulent organisms were modified, as a result of protest, to a proposal for a Biosafety Level 3 Laboratory at which testing of the most dangerous aerosols would be prohibited[44]. Research on anthrax being conducted under BDRP sponsorship at the University of Massachusetts has been the subject of intense protest[53,53a]. 48

3. Biological weapons research, even if truly defensive in intent, can be viewed by a potential military adversary as an attempt to develop protection for a nation's military forces against an organism that the nation itself might wish to use for offensive purposes, thus permitting that nation to protect its own personnel in a biological first strike. Adversaries know that any nation secretly preparing a stockpile of biolog- 49

ical weapons for use in war (whether intended as deterrence, retaliation, or first use) would be likely to prepare vaccines and other defensive measures to protect its own troops and population. Indeed, the reason military leaders are likely to give for the preparation of any form of altered bacilli or viruses, in order to give the appearance of compliance with the BWC, is that these organisms are needed for preparation of defenses. It is impossible for adversaries to determine whether a nation's defensive efforts are part of preparation for offensive use of weapons.

Many of the fears of other nations (shared by a number of analysts 50 in the U.S.) are based on the military sponsorship of defensive research. Other nations may view with suspicion, even if the research is relatively open, the intense interest of military forces (in contrast to civilian medical researchers) in vaccines or treatment against specific organisms, particularly organisms that are not found in nature or cause few problems unless purposely spread. Such fears about the work of the BDRP, as well as concern about defensive programs in other nations, help feed a continuing arms race in biological weapons. Just as the U.S. Army supports its requests for appropriation of funds in this area by citing suspicions and possible exaggerations of what others are doing, so the armies of other countries try to maximize their resources by casting not unreasonable suspicions on what the U.S. is doing. Indeed it was Dr. Shiro Ishii's 1930 report, almost certainly untrue, but unfortunately very plausible, that the most powerful Western countries were secretly studying biological weapons that led to Japan's embrace of biological weapons research and eventual use[37].

Concern has also been expressed about the militarization of genetic 51 engineering and of biology in general, just as much of physics was militarized during World War II. Characterization of biological weapons as "public health in reverse," may therefore have an even broader and more sinister meaning than simply the use of specific forms of disease in military armamentaria. The entire field of biology—and particular aspects of it such as the Human Genome Research Project—may be in danger of military subversion to destructive ends[54,55].

What Should Be the Physician's Role?

Some proponents of defensive research on biological weapons have 52 argued that it is entirely ethical that physicians work on the defensive aspects of biological weapons, and in fact that responsibility demands it[56]. Advocates for the BDRP support this argument with the possibility of the use of such weapons against the U.S., and their opinion that work on defenses may also be useful in developing protection against naturally occurring disease, both diseases we already face and those that may arise in the future. Huxsoll, Orient, and others believe it is the obligation of physicians and other medical scientists to work on such defensive measures and argue there is no ethical reason for this work not to be done within the BDRP[51,57].

Many other analysts, including the author of this paper, take a different position[58–60]. Joining Piller and Yamamoto in viewing the BDRP program as "highly ambiguous, provocative and strongly suggestive of offensive goals," we believe it unethical for physicians to play a role in it. Such work, we believe, rather than reducing the possibility of the use of biological weapons or reducing the consequences of their use, has a strong potential for intensifying a biological arms race and helping to militarize the science of biology, thereby increasing the risk of the use of biological weapons and the destructiveness of their effects if they are used.

The question is where on the slippery slope of physician participation in preparing for war or in binding up the wounds should physicians draw the line? Should physicians, as Ryle suggested in the 1930s, refuse all participation, including noncombatant treatment roles, thus making war more horrible to contemplate and therefore less likely to occur[61]? Should physicians refuse to participate in civil defense planning for nuclear war because these efforts too are ambiguous, provocative and, when conducted in a nation with first-strike nuclear potential, suggestive of offensive goals[62]? Whatever the physician's answer to these questions, which appear to represent even broader potential refusals to participate in preparation for war or in binding up its wounds, we believe it ethically necessary for physicians to draw a line short of participation in military-sponsored defensive research on biological weapons. If physicians engage in civilian-sponsored research that carries an obligation to report all findings in the open literature, even if the research may have implications for defense against biological weapons, we believe physicians who participate cannot be ethically faulted. It is when physicians engage in military-sponsored research, in which the openness of reporting has been disputed and the purposes may be ambiguous, that they cannot be distinguished ethically from those who work on the development or production of weapons.

Fortunately, there is a way to de-escalate the biological arms race, the trend toward militarization of biology, and the ethical dilemmas for physicians. As we have noted, the BWC prohibits any "development, production, stockpiling, transfer, or acquisition of biological agents or toxins" except for "prophylactic, protective, and other peaceful purposes." The responsibility for governmentally sponsored medical research for prophylactic, protective, and other peaceful purposes in the

53

54

55

U.S. lies largely with the National Institutes of Health (NIH) and the Centers for Disease Control (CDC). The NIH or the CDC should therefore be given the responsibility, and the resources, for medical research of this type. The U.S. Army may still want to conduct nonmedical research and development on defense against biological weapons, such as work on detectors, protective clothing, and other barriers to the spread of organisms, but such research is less likely to be seen as offensive, and is less likely to provoke a biological weapons race, less likely to pervert the science of biology and, for our purposes most importantly, less likely to involve physicians.

In addition to the ethical dilemmas involved in these decisions, it   56
may also be unethical for physicians simply to ignore the issue of biological weapons. One of the greatest dangers of these weapons may be the apathy of the medical profession toward them. The fact that biological weapons are the ones with which physicians may become engaged and one about which they have specialized knowledge, gives physicians a special responsibility not only to refuse to work on them, but also actively to work to reduce the threat of biological weapons development or use. Such efforts might include support of measures to strengthen the BWC through introduction of more restrictive interpretations to eliminate ambiguities and of new verification proposals that will be considered at the Third BWC Review Conference scheduled for 1991. U.S. physicians may also wish to support legislation to transfer all medical aspects of biological defense from the military to the NIH or the CDC.

More broadly, physicians may wish to explore the connection be-   57
tween production of nuclear weapons and production of chemical or biological weapons. It has been argued that as the nuclear powers refuse to reduce substantially their vast stockpiles of nuclear weapons and refuse to agree to verifiable cessation of nuclear weapons testing and production, nonnuclear powers contemplate development and production of chemical or biological weapons for deterrence against nuclear weapons. The U.S. Defense Intelligence Agency has reported that " . . . third world nations view chemical weapons as an attractive and inexpensive alternative to nuclear weapons"[63], a view confirmed by statements by Saddam Hussein, President of Iraq[64]. There is much physicians can do, through Physicians for Social Responsibility in the U.S. and the International Physicians for the Prevention of Nuclear War, to reduce the provocation and the proliferation of weapons of mass destruction caused by the nuclear arms race.

Individual physicians and scientists can also add to the awareness   58
of the dangers of biological weapons by signing the pledge, sponsored by the Council for Responsible Genetics (186 South Street, Boston, MA 02111), "not to engage knowingly in research and teaching that will

further development of chemical and biological warfare agents." Physicians may also wish to help awaken the medical profession to the danger of biological, chemical, or nuclear war by adding a clause to the oath taken by medical students at graduation from medical school. This method has already been used in the U.S.S.R. for alerting students to the dangers of nuclear war. All Soviet students are required to sign upon graduation an oath that begins: "Upon having conferred on me the high calling of physician, and entering medical practice I do solemnly swear . . ." In 1983 a clause was added to the oath that reads: "Recognizing the danger that nuclear weapons present for mankind, to struggle tirelessly for peace and for the prevention of nuclear war"[65]. A modified form could be used in the U.S., with wording along the lines of: "Recognizing that nuclear, chemical, and biological arms are weapons of indiscriminate mass destruction and threaten the health of all humanity, I will refuse to play any role that might increase the risk of use of such weapons and will, as part of my professional responsibility, work actively for peace and for the prevention of their use."

ACKNOWLEDGMENTS

Portions of the first section of this paper were adapted from a paper written in 1978 with Mark Sidel, cited as reference 1; I am grateful to him for permission to use that material. During the past 25 years many other colleagues have been extremely helpful in my understanding of the facts that the issues related to biological weapons. Among those to whom I am most indebted are Gordon Burck, Leonard Cole, Robert Cook-Deegan, Paul Epstein, Naomi Franklin, Jack Geiger, Robert Goldwyn, Ira Helfand, Jay Jacobson, Jonathan King, Meryl Nass, Richard Novick, Theodor Rosebury, Barbara Hatch Rosenberg, William Sayres, Susan Wright, and Raymond Zilinskas.

REFERENCES

1. Sidel VW, Sidel M. Biomedical science and war. In: Reich WT, ed. Encyclopedia of bioethics. New York: Free Press, 1978: 1699–1704.
2. Roland A. Haphaestus and history: scientists, engineers, and war in Western experience. In: Mitcham C, Siekevitz P, eds. Ethical issues associated with scientific and technological research for the military. Ann NY Acad Sci 1989;577:50–60.
3. Ferrill A. The origins of war: from the Stone Age to Alexander the Great. London: Thames and Hudson, 1985. Cited by Roland A: Haphaestus and history: scientists, engineers, and war in Western experience. In: Mitcham C, Siekevitz P, eds. Ethical issues associated with scientific and technological research for the military. Ann NY Acad Sci 1989;577:50–60.
4. da Vinci L. The notebooks of Leonardo da Vinci. New York: Reynal and

Hitchcock, 1962. Cited by Roland A: Haphaestus and history: scientists, engineers, and war in Western experience. In: Mitcham C, Siekevitz P, eds. Ethical issues associated with scientific and technological research for the military. Ann NY Acad Sci 1989;577:50–60.

5. Drake S. Galileo at work: his scientific biography. Chicago: University of Chicago Press, 1978. Cited by Roland A: Haphaestus and history: scientists, engineers, and war in Western experience. In: Mitcham C, Siekevitz P, eds. Ethical issues associated with scientific and technological research for the military. Ann NY Acad Sci 1989;577:50–60.

6. Harris R, Paxman J. A higher form of killing: the secret story of chemical and biological welfare. New York: Hill and Wang, 1982.

7. Russel B. Facts and fiction. New York: Simon and Schuster, 1962.

8. Rhodes R. The making of the atomic bomb. New York: Simon and Schuster, 1986.

9. Bernal JD. Science in history. London: C. A. Watts & Co., 1954.

10. Brown M, ed. The social responsibility of the scientist. New York: Free Press, 1971.

11. Dinegar RH. The moral arguments for military research. In: Mitcham C, Siekevitz P, eds. Ethical issues associated with scientific and technological research for the military. Ann NY Acad Sci 1989;577:10–20.

12. Roth B. The moral arguments against military research. In: Mitcham C, Siekevitz P, eds. Ethical issues associated with scientific and technological research for the military. Ann NY Acad Sci 1989;577:21–33.

13. Sinsheimer RL. The responsibility of scientists. In: Wright S, ed. Preventing a biological arms race. Cambridge, MA: MIT Press, 1990;71–77.

14. Merton RK. Social theory and social structure. Glencoe, IL: Free Press, 1957.

15. Gilpin R. American scientists and nuclear weapons policy. Princeton: Princeton University Press, 1962.

16. Chalk R. Drawing the line: an examination of conscientious objection in science. In: Mitcham C, Siekevitz P, eds. Ethical issues associated with scientific and technological research for the military. Ann NY Acad Sci 1989;577:61–74.

17. Napalm inventor discounts guilt. Harvard chemist would "do it again" for the country. New York Times, December 27, 1967;8.

18. Reid RW. Tongues of conscience: weapons research and the scientists' dilemma. New York: Walker & Co., 1969.

19. Rosebury T. Medical ethics and biological warfare. Perspect Biol Med 1963;6:312–323.

20. Janck R. Brighter than a thousand suns: a personal history of the atomic scientists. Translated by James Cleugh. New York: Harcourt, Brace & Co., 1958.

21. Bethe HA. Review of brighter than a thousand suns. Bulletin of the Atomic Scientists 1958;14:426–428.

22. Rosebury T. Peace or pestilence: biological warfare and how to avoid it. New York: Whittlesey House, 1949.

23. Magat M. Some remarks concerning the responsibility of scientists. Scientists and World Affairs. London: Pugwash Conference on Science and World Affairs, 1962. Cited by Sidel VW, Sidel M. Biomedical science and war. In: Reich WT, ed. Encyclopedia of bioethics. New York: Free Press, 1978:1699–1704.

24. Bry I, Doe J. War and men of science. Science 1955;122:911–913.

25. Lappe M. Ethics in biological warfare research. In: Wright S, ed: Preventing a biological arms race. Cambridge, MA: MIT Press, 1990:78–99.

26. Ludwig E: The Hippocratic oath. Bulletin of the History of Medicine, Supplement 1. Baltimore: Johns Hopkins Press, 1943:3.

27. Declaration of Geneva. Handbook of declarations. Geneva: World Medical Association, 1983:3.

28. Friedenwald H. Translation of Maimonides, Bulletin of the Johns Hopkins Hospital 1917;28:260–261. Daily prayer of a physician. In: Reich WT, ed. Encyclopedia of Bioethics. New York, The Free Press, 1978:1, 737.

29. Regulations in time of armed conflict. Handbook of declarations. Geneva; World Medical Association, 1983:5.

30. Sigerist HE. A history of medicine. Vol. 2. Early Greek, Hindu and Persian medicine. New York: Oxford University Press, 1961:20.

31. Derbes VJ. DeMussis and the great plague of 1348: a forgotten episode of bacteriological warfare. JAMA 1966:196:179.

32. U.S. Department of Health, Education and Welfare. Effects of biological warfare agents. Washington, DC: US Government Printing Office, 1959.

33. Text of the 1925 Geneva Protocol. Appendix B. In: Wright S, ed. Preventing a biological arms race. Cambridge, MA: MIT Press, 1990:368–369.

34. Sidel VW, Goldwyn RM. Chemical and biological warfares: a primer. New Engl J Med 1966:274:21–27.

35. Burck GM. Biological, chemical and toxin warfare agents. Appendix A. In: Wright S, ed. Preventing a biological arms race. Cambridge, MA: MIT Press, 1990:368–369.

36. Powell JW. Japan's germ warfare: the US cover-up of a war crime. Bulletin of Concerned Asian Scholars 1980:12(4):2–17.

37. Powell JW. A hidden chapter in history. Bulletin of the Atomic Scientists 1981;37(8):45–49.

38. Williams P, Wallace D. Unit 731: the Japanese army's secret of secrets. London: Hodder and Stoughton, 1989.

39. Bernstein BJ. Churchill's secret biological weapons. Bulletin of the Atomic Scientists 1987;(Jan/Feb):46–50.

40. Cole LA. Clouds of secrecy: the army's germ warfare tests over populated areas. Totowa, NJ: Rowman and Littlefield, 1988.

41. Wright S. Evaluation of biological warfare policy 1945–1990. In: Wright S, ed: Preventing a biological arms race. Cambridge, MA: MIT Press, 1990:26–68.

42. Text of the 1972 Biological Weapons Convention. In: Wright S, ed: Preventing a biological arms race. Cambridge, MA: MIT Press, 1990:370–376.

43. States parties to the 1925 Geneva Protocol and the 1972 Biological Weapons

Convention. In: Wright S, ed. Preventing a biological arms race. Cambridge, MA:MIT Press, 1990:379–383.

44. Piller C, Yamamoto KR. The U.S. Biological Defense Research Program in the 1980s: a critique. In: Wright S, ed. Preventing a biological arms race. Cambridge, MA: MIT Press, 1990:133–168.

45. Brincker JAH. Historical, epidemiological, and etiological study of measles (morbilli; rubeola). Proc Roy Soc Med 1938;31:807–828.

46. Robinson JPP. Incapacitants: a proposal for their treatment in a CW convention. Presented at the Third Pugwash CW Workshop; April 12–14, 1976, London, England. Cited in Sidel VW: Weapons of mass destruction: the greatest threat to public health. JAMA 1989;262:680–682.

47. Carus WS. The genie unleashed: Iraq's chemical and biological weapons production: Policy Paper 14. Washington, DC: Washington Institute for Near East Policy, 1989.

48. Zilinskas RA. Biological warfare and the third world. Politics and the Life Sciences 1990;9:59–76.

49. Zilinskas RA. Terrorism and biological weapons: inevitable alliance? Perspect Biol Med 1990;34:44–72.

50. Falk R. Inhibiting reliance on biological weaponry: the role and relevance of international law. In: Wright S, ed. Preventing a biological arms race. Cambridge, MA: MIT Press, 1990:243–266.

51. Huxsoll DL, Parrott CD, Patrick WC. Medicine in defense against biological warfare. JAMA 1989;262:677–678.

52. Wright S, Ketcham S. The problem of interpreting the US Biological Defense Research Program. In: Wright S, ed. Preventing a biological arms race. Cambridge, MA: MIT Press, 1990:169–196.

53. Foreman J. Army funding spurs germ warfare fears. Boston Sunday Globe, October 21, 1990:1.

53a. Nass M. The labyrinth of biological defense. The PSR Quarterly 1991;1:24–30.

54. Piller C, Yamamoto KR. Gene wars: military control over the new genetic technologies. New York: William Morrow, 1988.

55. King J, Strauss H. The hazards of defensive biological warfare programs. In: Wright S, ed. Preventing a biological arms race. Cambridge, MA: MIT Press, 1990:120–132.

56. Crozier D. The physician and biologic warfare. New Engl J Med 1971;284:1008–1011.

57. Orient JM. Chemical and biological warfare: should defenses be researched and developed? JAMA 1989;262:644–648.

58. Jacobson JA, Rosenberg BH. Biological defense research: charting a safer course. JAMA 1989;262:675–676.

59. Sidel VW. Proliferation of biological weapons. Public Health Comments 1989;3(11):3–6.

60. Sidel VW. Weapons of mass destruction: the greatest threat to public health. JAMA 1989;262:680–682.

61. Ryle JA. Forward. In: Joules H, ed. The doctor's view of war. London: C. Allen & Unwin, 1983:7.
62. Leaning J, Keyes L., eds. The counterfeit ark: crisis relocation for nuclear war. Cambridge, MA: Ballinger, 1984.
63. Chemical warfare progress and problems in defensive capability. A report to the Chairman, Committee on Foreign Affairs, U.S. House of Representatives, 1986, Washington, DC: U.S. General Accounting Office, GAO/PEMD-86-11. Cited by Zilinskas RA. Biological warfare and the third world. Politics and the Life Sciences 1990;9:59–76.
64. Raviv D, Melman Y. Iraq's arsenal of horrors. Washington Post, April 8, 1990; B1. Cited in Zilinskas RA: Biological warfare and the third world. Politics and the Life Sciences 1990;9:59–76.
65. Cassel CK, Jameton AL, Sidel VW, Storey PB. The physician's oath and the prevention of nuclear war. JAMA 1985;254:653–654.

Content Considerations

1. What are the ethical issues for physicians who are involved in or have been asked to participate in the development of biological weapons?
2. Explain the differences between offensive and defensive research and the ethical questions associated with each. Does one seem more justifiable than the other?
3. Summarize the historical instances of biological warfare and discuss how likely it is that such warfare will be practiced in the future.

Battlefields of Ashes and Mud

In the following article, published November, 1990, in Natural History, writer Bernard Nietschmann considers ecoterrorism, a name given to environmental warfare. Such warfare is also known as ecocide and is far from modern; accounts of destruction through attacks on the environment reach back thousands of years.

During times of war, enemies can do much to weaken and even destroy each other by tampering with water and air supplies, destroying crops and forests, burning or spraying large areas of country and city. Human loss of life may be as immediate as the loss of land and species, but some effects of ecoterrorism may linger for scores of years.

Write a page about the kinds of environmental destruction that can be practiced during war; recall what you have read or seen and include what you can imagine.

THE ENVIRONMENT HAS always been both a military target and a 1
casualty of war. An enemy's habitat provides food, refuge, cover, and a staging ground for attacks. In prehistoric times, fire-drives deprived an enemy of game animals and cover. Some 3,000 years ago, Abimelech's forces spread salt on the conquered city of Shechem (Judg. 9:45), near Nablus, Jordan—perhaps the first recorded use of chemicals to destroy an enemy's territory.

Scorched earth tactics were used by the North against the Confed- 2
eracy in the American Civil War, by Britain against the Mau Mau insurgency in Kenya (1950–1956), by France against Algerian independence forces (1949–1962), and by the Soviet Union against mujaheddin communities, their crops and sanctuaries in Afghanistan (1979–1989). This strategy is now the weapon of choice by government forces against insurgents in southern Sudan, Eritrea, Tigray, Chittagong Hill Tracts, Kawthoolei, East Timor, El Salvador, and Guatemala.

In Vietnam, the United States elevated environmental damage to 3
a primary tactic in its fight against the peasant guerrilla forces of the National Liberation Front, or Vietcong, and the lightly armed and highly mobile North Vietnamese army. United States forces bombed and shelled 30 percent of South Vietnam's territory, leaving a moonlike landscape pockmarked by an estimated 250 million craters. Planes sprayed herbi-

cides on 10 percent of the country, destroying 8 percent of the crop-lands, 14 percent of the forests, and 50 percent of the mangroves. "Rome plow" bulldozers and ship anchor chains cleared vegetation. The war in Vietnam left in its wake extensive impoverished grasslands instead of forests, widespread erosion and dust storms, major declines in fresh-water and coastal fisheries, and severe losses of wildlife, especially from the forest canopy—wounds from which the land may not recover for a hundred years. (In France, shell craters from the 1916 Battle of Verdun are still present and thinly vegetated seventy-five years later.) In Viet-nam, war-damaged environments fostered the spread of bamboo thick-ets and the tenacious *Imperata cylindrica* grass, rodent populations, and "bomb crater malaria."

Almost all of the world's current wars (some one hundred in more than forty, mostly Third World countries) are between conventional state forces and guerrilla insurgents or nationalists. Environmental "interdiction"—meaning destruction—is a very popular tactic. Com-paratively inexpensive, it does not expose often poorly trained and unmotivated government troops to guerrilla ambushes in unfamiliar terrain. As R. Kipp, chief historian of the Strategic Air Command (1967–1968), wrote, "Guerrillas are not fought with rifles, but rather are lo-cated and then bombed to oblivion."

A main guerrilla objective is to remain invisible to government forces. Locating guerrillas in a forest or a community presents a needle-in-a-haystack problem. The solution is to bomb the haystack. In El Salvador, rebel-controlled areas are frequently napalmed, shelled with artillery, and hit with 500- and 750-pound bombs. In Guatemala, some 500 communities, their fields, and nearby forests have been burned and leveled to deprive left-wing insurgents of recruits, food, and shelter. In Tigray and Eritrea, the Ethiopian occupation forces destroy crops and vegetation to induce famine. And in 1988, the Iraqi occupation army used poison gas against Kurdistan to kill guerrillas and civilians and to contaminate vegetation, forcing some 400,000 Kurds to flee the oil-rich territory. (This summer the largest concentration of conventional weap-ons seen anywhere since World War II was deployed in and around Iraq.)

Elsewhere, fauna and flora become casualties of war. Lebanon's historic cedar forests are disappearing under the demand for camouflage and firewood for armies and fuel-starved civilians; the teak forests in the Shan and Karen nations (perhaps 80 percent of the world's total) may be gone in three years through exploitation as a war crop by both the Myanmar (Burmese) occupation forces and the Karen and Shan resis-tance forces; Myanmar is also defoliating croplands and forest sanctu-aries of Shan and other indigenous peoples' resistance forces under the pretext of opium poppy destruction; Bangladesh is deforesting the war-torn Chittagong Hill Tracts; and the confluence of the biologically rich Tigris-Euphrates rivers—the cradle of civilization—was the main theater of the recent destructive war between Iran and Iraq.

Preparations for war may be as environmentally destructive as war itself. Training exercises, bombing and artillery practice, weapons testing, and refuse disposal affect many environments continuously, unlike actual war.   7

The production and testing of nuclear weapons are the most environmentally destructive war-preparation activities. The mining and processing of radioactive ore, weapons assembly, and disposal of radioactive wastes contaminate extensive areas used by the world's nuclear weapons powers. Weapons testing takes place in the most isolated (and therefore the least disturbed) environments, contaminating soils, plants, animals, and groundwater for thousands of years. Since 1963 the United States and Great Britain have exploded more than 670 nuclear weapons and "devices" in the Nevada desert, on land claimed by the Western Shoshone Nation. In this same region, the United States is constructing a high-level nuclear waste disposal center. Between 1946 and 1958, the United States detonated sixty-six atomic and hydrogen bombs on Bikini and Enewetok atolls in the Pacific. The radioactive cleanup will cost $200 million.   8

Elsewhere in the Pacific, the United States and Britain exploded 34 atomic and hydrogen bombs on Christmas Island (1957–1962); Britain set off 12 nuclear weapons on eleven Aboriginal nations in northwestern and central Australia (1952–1957); beginning in 1966, France detonated 132 nuclear weapons on Moruroa and Fangatuafa atolls in the South Pacific. On Moruroa the bombing created fissures a half mile long and eighteen inches wide in the coral base, blew large pieces out of its sides, collapsed the entire atoll until it is barely awash above the sea, and produced more than one million leaking bags and barrels of radioactive waste. The destruction of the coral reef may have led to the proliferation of single-celled organisms that produce toxins ingested by many species of fish. Ciguatera fish poisoning is now a public health and economic problem on many Pacific islands where people depend on fish for food and income. On Johnston Island, the United States is planning to incinerate expired-date chemical and biological weapons materials despite the protests of island peoples living downwind and downstream.   9

Similar environmental damage has been done by the Soviet Union and China, and to a lesser extent, India.   10

Ironically, in the midst of war and war preparation, environments and species may be inadvertently protected. In World War I the presence of German submarines shut down the North Atlantic fishing industry,   11 which rejuvenated the fisheries and led to postwar bumper catches. The demilitarized zone between North and South Korea is effectively a wild-life preserve. Wildlife has also had a resurgence in many other cold- and hot-war borderlands, such as along the Iron Curtain, between the USSR and China, and between Libya and Chad. In Nicaragua two decades of back-to-back Sandinista and Contra wars and almost a decade of resis-tance by the indigenous peoples in eastern Nicaragua, known as the Yapti Tasba, have sharply reduced hunting, logging, cattle ranching with its attendant forest-to-pasture conversion, and exploitation of coastal and sea resources.

Armed conflicts between state armies and guerrilla insurgents and 12 nationalists make up 90 percent of today's wars, and they are all in the biotically rich but economically poor Third and Fourth worlds. Instead of using the expensive counter-insurgency "hearts and minds" strategy, gaining the allegiance of their people through aid and propaganda, many Third World governments prefer to use the cheaper "ashes and mud" environment interdiction approach, which produces immediate results and requires no government reforms or concessions. But in these Third World wars, no international standards exist to monitor, control, or prohibit environmental warfare (ecocide) or, for that matter, any of these internal wars (the Geneva Conventions apply only to international states at war with each other).

Ultimately, ashes and mud counter-insurgency policies will be 13 counterproductive. Degraded land and resources are as much a reason for taking up arms as are repression, invasion, and ideology.

Content Considerations

1. What is the author's position on environmental warfare? How does he express it?
2. Of what significance to the environment is the fact that most current wars are between conventional state forces and guerrilla insurgents or nationalists?
3. Working with a group of classmates, identify instances of ecoterrorism and arrange them chronologically. Do later instances appear more harmful than earlier ones? What do you conclude?

Environmental Destruction Is an Ancient Tool of War

Perhaps destroying the environment is a part of war, a part no different or unusual than firing weapons or taking prisoners. Such destruction has occurred for centuries in the name of warfare; only recently have terms such as ecoterroism *or* ecocide *or* bioweaponry *been coined to describe acts of war whose targets are primarily land, water, trees, plants—complete ecosystems. That humans suffer when their habitat is destroyed or poisoned seems almost incidental. But is it?*

Here Jessica Matthews, vice president of World Resources Institute, raises questions about the direct and indirect results of environmental attacks, most specifically those that occurred during the Persian Gulf war. Before you read her comments, write a few paragraphs about ecocide as military strategy.

WASHINGTON—Saddam Hussein did not commit ecoterrorism. Whoever in the White House coined the phrase deserves a pat on the back for propaganda impact, but not for accuracy. 1

Terrorism consists of acts of violence committed against innocent individuals chosen to represent a broad class of people. This broader group is intended to be so frightened that they will force their government to change its policies. 2

Random violence without a political purpose is not terrorism. Nor are acts of war between combatants. Nor, especially, is wholesale environmental destruction, which is an ancient tool of war and perhaps its inevitable consequence. 3

In 146 B.C., the Romans destroyed the Carthaginians' fields by spreading salt on them. Genghis Khan wrecked Mesopotamia's irrigation system. Medieval armies hurled the corpses of diseased animals over the walls of besieged towns to pollute their water supply. The Chinese flooded vast areas in order to stop the advance of Japanese armies, as did the Dutch to slow the Germans in 1940. And the United States sprayed poisonous herbicides over Vietnam with arguably greater impact on crops and civilians than on the Viet Cong. 4

Civil War Union Gen. Philip Sheridan, who knew whereof he spoke, explained the strategy: "Reduction to poverty brings prayers for 5 peace more surely and more quickly than does the destruction of human life.''

Iraq's intentional oil spills and its bombing of Kuwait's oil wells 6 fall squarely within this long tradition. Moreover, these acts could have had direct military utility. Had the ground war lasted and had the wind and tides quickly carried the oil to Saudi desalinization plants, the spill could have affected U.S. troops' water supply.

Iraq may also have been contemplating setting fire to the spill as 7 a defense against an amphibious attack. Winston Churchill considered such a tactic as a defense against a possible German invasion of Britain.

President Bush's comment at the time, "It doesn't measure up to 8 any military doctrine of any kind. It's kind of sick," helped to demonize Saddam Hussein, but did not reflect the Pentagon's concern about Iraq's threats. Smoke has often been used to obscure battlefields. Presumably, heat-seeking devices on smart weapons could be confounded by billow- ing fires.

Months before the war began, the Department of Defense com- 9 missioned a then-secret study to evaluate such impacts, as well as broader effects on climate and the regional environment. Those and subsequent analyses suggest that global climate probably will not be affected. The smoke and soot are not rising high enough into the atmosphere. But locally and regionally, the lasting effects may be catastrophic.

Tiny particles of soot pouring down on Kuwait and parts of Iraq 10 and Iran lodge in the respiratory system, where they damage tissue and efficiently deliver toxic gases to the body. One class of these, a type of hydrocarbon likely to be produced by the fires, is known to be carcin- ogenic. High levels of sulfur dioxide, a precursor of acid rain whose impact could reach as far as Pakistan, is another likely result.

Monitoring is drastically inadequate, including the effort by a U.S. 11 team whose preliminary results were released last week. No one knows what the direct consequences for people, livestock and other species will be, or the indirect ones through drinking contaminated water. But given what is known about long-term exposure to much milder pollution, there is every reason to fear that the effects could be awful—especially for children.

The suggestion that something new—ecoterrorism—has been 12 practiced obscures the truth that war is usually terrible for the environ- ment. Modern war can be more terrible, just as it can be more destruc- tive of people and everything else.

Saddam Hussein bears the blame, but the U.S. shares responsibil- 13 ity, as it does for refugees' suffering. At a minimum, that means an honest effort—not the minimalist one made so far—to find out exactly what harm has been done.

Content Considerations

1. What is the author's argument? What evidence does she offer in its support? To what extent do you agree with her?

2. Discuss the truth of Gen. Philip Sheridan's comment that "Reduction to poverty brings prayers for peace more surely and more quickly than does the destruction of human life." What is your position regarding reduction to poverty as a military strategy?

3. Environmental destruction usually occurs during a war even if the environment has not been specifically targeted. Investigate an instance of such incidental harm and determine the extent to which the harm has been remedied.

ROBERT JERVIS

Arms Control, Stability, and Causes of War

Technology, according to Robert Jervis, had little to do with the development and stockpiling of armament. It has created fearsome weapons, many so devastating that countries have so far refrained from using them, but a nation's drive to arm itself results from general concerns for security and defense. Proposals to control arms, to limit their number and kind through limits on production, inventory, and purchasing, therefore often meet with mixed reaction. Probably few countries want to blow up the world or a sizable portion of it but most want to protect what they see as their own interests from those of other countries. And all countries want a sound defense against invasion.

Robert Jervis, Adlai E. Stevenson Professor of International Relations and a member of the Institute of War and Peace Studies at Columbia University, explores the connections among arms control, international and domestic stability, and the causes of war. The connections are complex. You may want to skim the article once and then return to it for a thorough reading. Before you do so, however, write about how the topics of arms control, stability, and causes of war could be related. As you read, compare your ideas to Jervis's.

IF THE MAIN OBJECTIVE of arms control is to make war less likely, then any theory of arms control must rest on a theory of the causes of war.[1] Most analysts start with the premise that the anarchial nature of the international system is crucial: armed conflicts occur because no higher authority can prevent them.[2] This is consistent with the realist tradition, which has dominated American thinking since World War II and which informed the thinking of those who contributed to the Fall 1960 issue of *Daedalus*, even those who rejected much of this perspective. The central assumptions are that states are the main actors in international affairs, that the external environment is more important in determining states' behavior than their domestic characteristics, that this behavior was conditioned by the absence of an international sovereign, and that in this context states must be preoccupied with their own security.

Although this framework does not specify exactly when and where armed conflict will occur, it does give general directions to arms control. First, it tells us that we cannot eliminate the possibility of war without creating world government. Second, it points to states rather than individuals, economic classes, interest groups, bureaucracies, or transnational organizations as the sources of conflict and cooperation in international politics. Third, it could lead analysts to think about which kinds of systems are more war-prone than others. Indeed, there has been a great deal of research on whether bipolar or multipolar systems are more conducive to war.[3] But because this factor cannot be altered, arms control analysts were drawn to the ways in which states' security policies can produce wars that are inadvertent in the sense that they could have been avoided without sacrificing the states' core values.

It is now almost trivial to note that arms control is made possible   3
by the fact that the superpowers have common as well as conflicting interests even—or especially—in the military arena and that cooperation and conflict are so closely linked that we can hardly analyze one without paying attention to the other. In the political and intellectual atmosphere of the late 1950s, however, this perspective did not come naturally. Memories of McCarthyism were still vivid; the claim that the United States had common interests with the Soviet Union could be seen as dangerously close to being "soft on Communism"; partly because the Soviet Union seemed to be gaining on the West in almost all respects, most members of the American elite were preoccupied with the task of competing with the Communist adversaries. Indeed, while liberals scorned the ideological rhetoric of the Eisenhower administration, they criticized it as much for its failure to develop a vigorous military posture as for its diplomatic clumsiness.

In this era, military policy and disarmament were considered quite   4
separate, if not antithetical. Most of those who were concerned with disarmament believed either that such efforts could only follow a general reduction of conflict between the superpowers or, more frequently, that disarmament would produce such desired political changes. Thus, the linked arguments of the emerging arms control community that each superpower should be concerned about the other's military posture for reasons of mutual safety as well as for competitive advantage, and the view that disarmament and arms control were aspects of security policy, not alternatives to it, were major intellectual and political contributions.

ARMS CONTROL POSTULATES

Thomas Schelling emphasized "the possibility that one can simul   5
taneously think seriously and sympathetically about our military posture and about collaborating with our enemies to improve it."[4] He and Morton Halperin similarly introduced *Strategy and Arms Control* as follows: "The essential feature of arms control is the recognition of the common

interest, of the possibility of reciprocation and cooperation even between potential enemies with respect to their military establishments."[5] Note that the claim is not merely that the United States and the Soviet Union have some interests in common. Even the most hardened cold warriors were willing to see some areas where the superpowers could negotiate. But the stronger and less obvious argument is that it is in the area of military policy, where common sense and much previous discussion had located the highest degree of conflict, that the superpowers had major reasons to cooperate. In significant measure this argument rested on the broader development of deterrence theory and the claim that, in Brodie's familiar words: "Thus far the chief purpose of our military establishment has been to win wars. From now on its chief purpose must be to avert them. It can have almost no other useful purpose."[6] A shift in the way war was viewed opened a space for arms control. Measures which were in both sides' military interests were precluded as long as people thought that wars were absolute struggles in which each side tried only to weaken, thwart, and harm the other and believed that the state could best prevent wars by being in the best position to defeat the other should war occur. As we will see later, many of the criticisms of arms control rest on this conception of deterrence.

By contrast, arms control rests on the theory that wars can occur because states have failed to realize the cooperation which their interests actually entail. For its centrality as well as its disagreement with previous views, the claim that hostile states almost always have important interests of military policy in common can be called the fundamental postulate of arms control. Although perhaps only one side can win a war, both could lose it in the sense of there having been at least one if not several outcomes that would have been mutually preferred to fighting. I use the word *realize* in two senses: to understand and to put into practice. Because the purpose of arms control research was not only academic, the two senses of *realize* were linked: it was hoped that as the intellectual explanation for the potential common interest gained plausibility, the superpowers would act on their improved understanding.

Closely related to this theme is the second postulate of arms control: arms control and security policy are not opposed to each other. "What we have tried to emphasize more than anything else," Schelling and Halperin noted in concluding *Strategy and Arms Control*, "is that arms control, if properly conceived, is not necessarily hostile to, or incompatible with, or an alternative to, a military policy properly conceived."[7] "There is hardly an objective of arms control, that is not equally a continuing urgent objective of national military strategy—of our unilateral military plans and policies."[8] In the context of the 1950s, the idea of common interest between scholars concerned with avoiding war and the military was as surprising to some as the idea of common interest with the Soviet Union was to others. In fact, the two conceptions are linked. For if US-Soviet military relations were zero-sum, then it would have been difficult to find overlap between arms control and military policy. Again, what is central is the conception of war and how it might be prevented. To say that there is no conflict between intelligent arms control and intelligent unilateral military policy means that there must be significant common interest between the two sides, and that winning war in the sense of defeating the other's army can no longer be the dominant goal. Once one argues that conflict is inhibited because both sides realize that to engage in it is to leave them both worse off than if they had been more restrained, arms control is compatible with good military policy because our conception of what makes military policy good has changed. But—and these are troublesome points to which we will return—this claim was not made fully explicit, is subject to rebuttal on both theoretical and practical grounds, and has been the focus for later arguments, although not always couched in these terms.

CRISIS STABILITY

Although there are several ways in which arms control might help realize Soviet-American common interest and shape the conception of proper American military policy, the central contribution of the 1960 *Dædalus* writers was to emphasize the importance of crisis stability. Indeed, this has remained the focus of the theory and, to a lesser extent, the practice of arms control ever since. The basic idea is that even if both sides prefer peace to war, war could result through "the reciprocal fear of surprise attack" to use Schelling's well-known phrase.[9] Thus Schelling and Halperin declare: "The most mischievous character of today's strategic weapons is that they may provide an enormous advantage, in the event that war occurs, to the side that starts it."[10] A first-strike advantage, coupled with the belief that war is very likely, if not inevitable, would make it rational for a state to attack even if it was peaceful because the alternative to attacking would be seen, not as peace, but as being attacked. Under these circumstances, the state's efforts to deter the adversary or protect itself in case of war would make war more likely. Observing the state's preparations, the adversary would see the danger of war increasing and would itself make ready to strike. While it was not much mentioned in the early literature, the obvious case which seemed to fit this model was the outbreak of World War I, although the relevant history is actually quite ambiguous and has been subject to fierce dispute. The crucial variables that the arms controllers focused on were the relative advantage of first as compared to a second strike (that is, the vulnerability of weapons systems and their associated apparatus) and the perceived likelihood of war. (We will return to a significant omission—the states' expectations about the value of a world that stays at peace.) Unlike some causes of war, these are manipulable by policy and so are particularly appropriate for a theory that can lead to actions.

DOES THE STATE WANT THE ADVERSARY'S FORCES TO BE VULNERABLE?

While it is clear then that the state should seek to keep the peace by decreasing the adversary's incentives to attack, should it decrease its own incentives to do so? That is, does it want the adversary's forces to be invulnerable and therefore its own population to be vulnerable? The first arms control postulate certainly implies that this could be the case: just because the adversary wants to reduce its vulnerability does not mean that this posture would be bad for the state. Indeed, the logic of crisis stability implies that the danger of war will be reduced if both sides are immune to surprise attack. But the early arms control literature rarely declared that the United States would be better off if the Soviet strategic forces were difficult to destroy.

There are three ways in which this argument might be joined that derive from different, but not conflicting, ways of analyzing the causes of wars. First, one can claim that crisis instability can cause wars without asserting that this is the *only* cause of war, or even the most important one. Schelling and Halperin imply pride of place to this danger when, in the sentence quoted above, they refer to first-strike advantage as "the most mischievous character of today's strategic weapons,"[11] and the impression of importance is underlined by the lengthy discussion of the topic. But this position could only be justified by comparing this danger to others, which little arms control literature did. Furthermore, it is interesting that Schelling and Halperin do not say that the first-strike advantage poses the greatest danger of war, but rather that this is the most troublesome aspect "of today's strategic weapons." There then may be greater dangers arising from sources other than the weapons. The obvious questions are what these other dangers might be, whether concentrating on crisis stability distracts us from dealing with them and, indeed, whether increasing crisis stability, especially by decreasing the vulnerability of Soviet strategic forces, magnifies these other dangers.

These questions can be approached through a second avenue. The theory of war that focuses on crisis instability can be seen as a part of a more general theory that stresses the security dilemma and the spiral model of conflict. The security dilemma arises because many of the ways in which states try to increase their security have the unintended consequence of decreasing the security of others. The spiral model of conflict sees the resulting action-reaction dynamic as accelerated by each side's inability to understand the other or to see how the other is interpreting its own behavior. These processes generate and magnify conflict, leading to unnecessary wars.[12] But wars can also start through the failure to deter the adversary: if threats led to insecurity and war in 1914, the British policy of conciliation and of taking full account of the supposed security needs of the other side produced war twenty-five years later.[13] Deterrence theory, in brief, argues that wars are caused by states failing to develop the military strength and credible threats necessary to dissuade others from challenging the status quo. Furthermore, threats are most likely to be believed when the state can carry them out at reasonable cost, which in turn is more likely to be the case when the state can protect its own population (that is, if the adversary's strategic forces are vulnerable).

Deterrence theory and the spiral model then make very different   12
arguments about the relationship between threats and vulnerability on the one hand and war on the other. Yet, the community of deterrence theorists overlaps very heavily with the community of arms controllers. And in some ways, deterrence and arms control are compatible, if not complementary. Both point to the importance of credibility and argue that threats and promises must be contingent; that is, the state must show the other that it can and will take actions the other does not want *if and only if* the other takes prohibited actions. But the two paths to war are quite different and in practice, although not in theory, the policy prescriptions often contradict each other. Arms control stresses the dangers that arise when reassurances and promises—especially the promise not to strike—are either not made or are not believed; deterrence stresses the dangers that arise when threats are absent or dismissed. Thus, when Schelling writes on arms control, he talks of the danger of inadvertent war and the necessity for reassurances that show the adversary that the state will refrain from attacking if the adversary will. When he writes on deterrence, he argues that war can occur if the state appears weak, and that it must show that it will not back down in the face of threats.

NATURE AND INTENTIONS OF THE ADVERSARY

To go further we need to turn to the third avenue and question of   13
whether the state wants the other side's forces to be vulnerable. Classic arms control, like classic realism, sees the actors as essentially identical; discussions of crisis stability are couched in terms of two interchangeable actors. But other theories—those of Kant, Marx, and Wilson, for

example—see the causes of war as lying within particular kinds of states. Far from ignoring domestic characteristics and treating all states as identical "billiard balls,"[14] these theories assert that certain states cause wars by being aggressive. This is implicitly true for much deterrence theory. The language there often posits one side that is defending the status quo and another that is challenging it. The implication is that aggressive states cause wars and the problem is how to halt aggression rather than how to cope with offense-dominant technology and the security dilemma.

To see the prime cause of wars as stemming from the aggressive tendencies of some states is not automatically to dismiss the danger of crisis instability. Even if the adversary is highly aggressive, a mutually undesired war could come about through the reciprocal fear of surprise attack. To put the point more generally, even if the degree of conflict between the two sides is quite high, there is still room for some cooperation (that is, the first postulate of arms control can still hold). Indeed, even during World War II there were some restraints (on bombing cities at the start of the war and on not using poison gas throughout), although these may have been abetted by one side or the other miscalculating its own interests. Once nuclear weapons come on the scene, furthermore, the area of common interests expands because both sides need to avoid all-out war. Nevertheless, if one or both sides is highly aggressive, the range of applicability of the second postulate must be questioned. In many areas, good military policy will not be good arms control, and the attempt to render Soviet forces vulnerable might be an example.

The belief that the main cause of war is aggressive states is often linked to the claim that aggressiveness is correlated with, if not caused by, domestic repression. Although for years dismissed if not ridiculed by many arms controllers, this argument receives more than a little support from recent events. It is not likely to be an accident that unprecedented progress in arms control has occurred at the same time that the Soviet system has undergone unprecedented liberalization. Obstacles which were enormous when Brezhnev and his predecessors were in power have vanished with the Gorbachev revolution. This is not to say that all dangers have passed, or that nothing would have been possible without extensive changes within the Soviet Union, but it does appear that the success of arms control has been driven less by technological breakthroughs, intellectual ingenuity, and shifts in the balance of power than by internal changes which have affected the entire range of Soviet foreign policies.

INTERESTS, DOCTRINES, AND STABILITY

Those who argued that the United States should have extensive counterforce capability pointed out that not only can wars start through aggression, but also that although avoiding war is the central American interest, it is not the only American interest. The most obvious other American interest that could be threatened by invulnerable Soviet nuclear forces is Western Europe. The United States needs to deter against attacks on allies—"extended deterrence." The problem arises because of what Glenn Snyder has called the "stability-instability paradox."[15] If there is great stability at the strategic nuclear level, then there is little credibility in either side's threat to launch an all-out attack in response to anything other than an unlimited strike against it.[16] The straightforward inference is that, in Colin Gray's words, "The United States cannot afford the crisis stability that precludes first use of strategic nuclear weapons."[17]

It seems intuitively obvious that if there is crisis stability, neither side can credibly threaten to start an all-out war in response to a limited provocation. But this misstates the situation. It would be an accurate formulation if levels of violence were hermetically sealed off from each other, if undesired escalation were impossible.[18] In fact, most statesmen realize that whenever violence is set in motion, no one can be sure where it will end up. Because events can readily escape control, limited responses carry with them some probability that the final, although unintended, result will be all-out war. A state that begins a confrontation or responds to one invokes what Schelling called "the threat that leaves something to chance."[19] What then brings pressure to bear on the adversary—and on the state as well—is less the immediate product of the action than the fear of where both states could end up.

The fact that the limited response would not automatically lead to all-out war means that the state can rationally carry it out under some circumstances, and that the threat to do so can be credible; the fact that the outcome could be mutual suicide means that the pressure generated is considerable. During the Cuban Missile Crisis, for example, both sides feared that the confrontation, although managed extremely carefully, could escalate to nuclear war. According to Arthur Schlesinger, Kennedy's sense of urgency toward the end of the crisis was "based on fear, not of Khruschev's intention, but human error, of something going terribly wrong down the line."[20] Indeed, the incident that convinced the president that the situation was too dangerous to be permitted to continue was the shooting down of the U-2 over Cuba, which we now know actually represented an instance of these mechanisms because it was carried out by a local Soviet military officer against the wishes of Moscow.[21]

There are two implications for arms control. First, crisis stability need not leave allies dangerously exposed to threats. The fact that nu-

17

18

19

clear war could grow out of a conventional one means that even if the Soviets believed that they could win the latter, they could be deterred by the possibility of the former, whose occurrence would not depend on the vulnerability of their forces. Second, effective counterforce targeting is not necessary for deterrence. Arms controllers can argue for the virtues of mutual invulnerability without arguing against an effective military policy; the second arms control postulate is not invalidated by the state's need to protect its allies.

IMPORTANCE OF DOCTRINE

But if the need for extended deterrence need not disturb arms control, military doctrine can. The applicability of the fundamental arms control postulate is questionable if American leaders believe that in order to be secure, the United States must be able to insure that the Soviet Union—or any other adversary—could not gain a military lead over the United States in any kind of limited warfare. It can be argued that, even if unfortunate, deterrence indeed does impose such a requirement: if the United States were not able to match Soviet military power at all levels, the Soviet Union could be tempted to start a limited war. The stability-instability paradox would hold escalation in check; advantage at lower levels of violence could be turned into meaningful victory in war or coercion in peacetime. This view of military affairs is heavily zero-sum. Soviet and American security would be incompatible because only one side could have military superiority and only that side could be secure. 20

At the highest levels of violence, strong counterforce doctrines similarly conflict with the possibility, if not the desirability, of crisis stability. As long as both sides believe that all-out war would result in mutual devastation, first-strike incentives are negligible and crisis stability is relatively easy to attain. This is not true, however, if decision makers believe that there are real advantages to be gained by destroying more of the adversary's strategic forces than the state is losing. Because of multiple warheads, and, even more, because of the vulnerability of command and control facilities, a first strike will almost surely be advantageous in purely counterforce terms. A state that is preoccupied with counting surviving warheads, especially those with counterforce capability, will have significant incentives to strike first. While these incentives would not likely be high enough to be a menace in times of calm, they could be sufficient to create instability in periods of heightened tension and perceived likelihood of war. Theoretically, this need not be true, even if both sides adopted counterforce targeting. In principle, weapons and command systems could be so invulnerable that 21 attacking would use up more warheads than it would destroy. But it appears that while the vulnerability of command and control systems can be reduced, it cannot be eliminated. In practice, then, it is probably true that the only thing worse than starting a counterforce war would be having to fight one after receiving the first blow.

To the extent that either or both sides believe that wars are only—   22
or even are best—deterred by having a counterforce capability superior to that of the adversary, arms control is pointless or even dangerous. A status quo power with extensive commitments could seek crisis stability only if it had the ability to defend its allies on the nonnuclear level. But crisis stability itself would be hard to achieve because of the offensive advantage in a counterforce war. By contrast, if what deters is the risk of escalation and the threat that leaves something to chance, then both arms control postulates have a great deal of validity.

This perspective also reveals the limits of arms control. While both   23
sides have an interest in eliminating extreme crisis instability, they need to see that there is some chance that events could get out of control once violence is employed because this is the main generator of caution and the primary means of exerting pressure on the other side. Given the complexity of large-scale military organizations and the unpredictability of human affairs, it is doubtful that arms control could succeed too well and produce arrangements that would drive the danger of undesired escalation close to zero. Furthermore, decision makers would probably ensure that this does not happen. That is, if crisis stability seemed to greatly reduce risks, it would permit, if not require, statesmen to take bolder actions during a crisis in order to produce the desired level of danger.[22] Similarly, if decision makers believed confrontations were quite safe, they would feel freer to provoke them (that is, to challenge the adversary's important interests). If crisis management were seen as easy, there would be less pressure on statesmen to try to prevent crises from arising in the first place. (It is striking that we have gone more than a quarter of a century since the last major superpower crisis—this is longer than the main rivals stayed at peace in most of the prenuclear era.) If security is linked in part to the danger of inadvertent war, then too much stability could make the world safe for coercion and violence. Successful arms control is, then, at a certain distant point, self-limiting.

Unless and until this point is reached, however, the fundamental   24
and secondary arms control postulates are compatible with the role of force and threats with the nuclear age. But this does not mean that they meet the greatest dangers of war. The focus on vulnerability and first-strike incentives is excessively mechanistic. States start wars for political objectives, not because they see an opportunity or fear that the other side does. Indeed, it is hard to find even a single war that was inadver-

tent in the sense that, immediately after it started, both sides would have preferred to return to peace on the basis of the status quo ante. Of course the question is not one of either/or. Crisis instability can interact with political conflict, arms controllers never suggested that the former in the absence of the latter would yield war. They did not worry that British forces were vulnerable to an American, or even to a French, attack; but by concentrating on the dangers of offensive advantages and assuming rather than examining the political context, they may have both exaggerated the danger of crisis instability and generated excessive hope that technical arms control could bring peace, if not cooperation. There is much validity to the old Soviet criticism of American arms control as preoccupied with the military causes of war at the expense of considering the broader relations between the two countries. If relations remain extremely bad, war can occur even if strategic weapons are not vulnerable; if relations greatly improve, vulnerabilities will not be a major source of danger.

Wars are caused predominantly by conflicts of political interests. 25 Clashing security requirements are not the only and, perhaps, not the most important sources of such conflicts. Incompatible desires for territory and dominance, hostile nationalisms and other ideologies, and assorted calculations that fighting can be of benefit are common causes of wars that lie beyond the ameliorative reach of arms control. As I noted earlier, crisis instability is an extreme and fast-acting example of the security dilemma. When the offense is dominant, states cannot make themselves secure without menacing—or even attacking—the adversary. But arms control theorists did not build on this insight and raise the question of whether American military and foreign policy was unnecessarily decreasing Soviet security and heightening Soviet-American conflict, probably because they shared the prevailing belief that the Soviet Union was driven more by the desire to expand than by the fear that the West would attack it. Concentrating on the danger of preemption and immediate desperation, arms control paid less attention to a preventive war which could be produced by the perception that the other side is steadily eroding the state's security.

The standard formula for crisis stability focuses on the size of the 26 gap between the payoffs for striking first and for striking second. But this neglects the expected evaluation of a world in which war does not occur, which is irrelevant only when war is judged to be completely certain. As long as the state believes that there is a chance that war can be avoided, its decisions will be strongly influenced by how well it thinks it will do if peace is maintained. Thus, a state which is satisfied with the status quo and is optimistic about its future prospects will seek to preserve the peace and may refrain from striking even in the face of crisis instability. By contrast, a state which is highly dissatisfied and/or which believes that its position is likely to deteriorate badly if current trends continue can rationally strike even when the offense has only a slight advantage.[23] Furthermore, one side's misguided military policy can contribute to the other's sense of threat and belief that its future fate is bleak unless it fights. While the fundamental and second arms control postulates still apply, the focus on military instability is too narrow, if not misleading.

When the costs of war are enormous, it is hard to see how one can start unless one or both sides believe that war is inevitable and that striking first is preferable to striking second. The theory that underlies most American arms control thinking then has a large measure of validity. But it excludes the broad political considerations which usually play such a large role in decisions to fight. Both the danger of aggression and the possibility of long-run spirals of hostility and fear have been more potent causes of war than has crisis instability.

ACKNOWLEDGEMENTS

I am grateful to Emanuel Adler, Barry Posen, and Steve Weber for comments.

ENDNOTES

1. For good discussions on the causes of war, see Geoffrey Blainey, *The Causes of War* (New York: Free Press, 1973); and Jack Levy, "The Causes of War: A Review of the Theories and Evidence," in Philip Tetlock, et al., eds., *Behavior, Society and Nuclear War,* vol. 1 (New York: Oxford University Press, 1989), 209–333. Bernard Brodie argued that because the danger of Soviet-American war was so slight and because the destruction of such a war could not be limited, arms control should concentrate on its third objective of saving money: Bernard Brodie, "On the Objectives of Arms Control," *International Security* 1 (1) (Summer 1976): 17–36. There is quite a bit to be said for this view—and arms control may have contributed to the stability that Brodie noted.

2. The classic statement is from Kenneth Waltz, *Man, the State, and War* (New York: Columbia University Press, 1954).

3. Kenneth Waltz, *Theory of International Politics* (Reading, Mass.: Addison-Wesley, 1979).

4. Thomas Schelling, "Reciprocal Measures for Arms Stabilization" *Dœdalus* 89 (4) (Fall 1960): 892.

5. Thomas Schelling and Morton Halperin, *Strategy and Arms Control* (New York: Twentieth Century Fund, 1961), 2.

6. Bernard Brodie, *The Absolute Weapon* (New York: Harcourt Brace, 1946), 76.

7. Schelling and Halperin, 141.
8. Ibid., 4.
9. Thomas Schelling, *The Strategy of Conflict* (Cambridge: Harvard University Press, 1960), chap. 9; Schelling, *Arms and Influence* (New Haven: Yale University Press, 1966), chap. 6.
10. Robert Powell argues that under most plausible assumptions, the situation is not as dangerous as one might think: see "Crisis Stability in the Nuclear Age," *American Political Science Review* 83 (1) (March 1989): 61–76. I have argued that standard analysis neglects important psychological processes and dynamics: *The Meaning of the Nuclear Revolution* (Ithaca: Cornell University Press, 1989), chap. 5.
11. Schelling and Halperin, 9.
12. See John Herz, "Idealist Internationalism and the Security Dilemma," *World Politics* 2 (2) (January 1950): 157–80; Herbert Butterfield, *History and Human Relations* (London: Collins, 1951), 19–20; Arnold Wolfers, *Discord and Collaboration* (Baltimore: Johns Hopkins University Press, 1962), 83–86; Waltz, *Man, the State and War*, 198–223; and Robert Jervis, *Perception and Misperception in International Politics* (Princeton: Princeton University Press, 1976), 62–90.
13. In fact, the history of neither case carefully matches the models that bear their names: see Robert Jervis, "War and Misperception," *Journal of Interdisciplinary History* 18 (4) (Spring 1988): 685–89.
14. The billiard ball analogy comes from Wolfers, 4–19.
15. Glenn Snyder, "The Balance of Terror and the Balance of Power" in Paul Seabury, ed., *The Balance of Power* (San Francisco: Chandler, 1964), 184–201. Similarly, Schelling and Halperin say: "If one of the things that prevents local wars is the fear of both sides that it will spiral to total war, then agreements which make it less likely that this will happen may end up making local war more likely. On the other hand this could be a reasonable price for greater insurance that local war will not go to total war." Schelling and Halperin, 31; see also 62–3.
16. In this discussion I will put the latter possibility aside, both because it is hard to imagine the circumstances which could lead to such a Soviet attack and because the problem is analytically parallel to that of extended deterrence. I will also assume that the conventional balance in Europe would permit the Soviets to conquer the continent if nuclear weapons were not used, and that both sides realize this is the case. In fact, this is hotly disputed.
17. Colin Gray, "Strategic Stability Reconsidered," *Dædalus* 109 (4) (Fall 1980): 147.
18. There is an important link between crisis instability and events getting out of control, although this connection was not explicitly drawn even by those who developed the concepts. When offensive advantage is slight (i.e., when even striking first will lead to disaster) it is hard to see how an all-out nuclear war could start. Thus Herman Kahn argued that while crisis instability could be troublesome, "I have put this possibility low on the list of possible cause of war . . . because of the belief that as long as decision makers are

consciously in control of events, they are very much more likely to draw back from pressing buttons and accept any resulting risks, than to do something which would make war inevitable—particularly, if this war were to occur at a time and under circumstances not of their choosing." But as Kahn recognizes, a great deal rides on the proviso that "decision makers are consciously in control of events." Herman Kahn, "The Arms Race and Some of Its Hazards," *Dædalus* 89 (4) (Fall 1960): 760.

19. Schelling, *Strategy of Conflict*, 187–203.
20. Arthur Schlesinger, Jr., *Robert F. Kennedy and His Times* (Boston: Houghton Mifflin, 1978), 529. For more extended discussion of these fears and why they were well grounded, see Jervis, *Implications of the Nuclear Revolution*, 82–95.
21. Richard Bernstein, "Meeting Sheds New Light on Cuban Missile Crisis," *New York Times,* 14 October 1987.
22. For further discussion, see Jervis, *The Meaning of the Nuclear Revolution*, 96; and Barry Nalebuff, "Brinkmanship and Deterrence: The Neutrality of Escalation," *Conflict Management and Peace Science* 9 (2) (Spring 1986): 19–30.
23. Under these circumstances, statesmen may also exaggerate the chances that war will bring victory. See Richard Ned Lebow, *Between Peace and War* (Baltimore: Johns Hopkins University Press, 1981).

Content Considerations

1. What theories of the causes of war does Jervis present? With classmates, use your knowledge to identify wars fought for the causes presented. Then write about which causes seem most likely to bring about future wars.
2. According to Jervis, how are arms control, stability, and the causes of war related? Comment on his argument and conclusions.
3. What prevents peace?

— *Ideas for Discussion, Writing, and Research* —

1. William Laurence, Paul Fussell, and Gar Alperovitz write about the atomic bombing of Japanese cities during World War II. How and why do their views differ? What is your own position?

2. The creation and use of nuclear weaponry is sometimes viewed as an achievement that changed people's views of themselves and the world forever. How could it have done so? Use the pieces by Laurence, Fussell, and Alperovitz but also gather information from written and oral sources.

3. Research the development of the atomic bomb, concentrating on the testing it received, the ethical questions of the researchers involved, the conditions that made its development possible, the current state of atomic technology, or current efforts to control its use.

4. The pieces by Evan Thomas and John Barry, Paul Walker and Eric Stambler, and Victor W. Sidel discuss conventional and advanced weapon technology. Using information from their essays and elsewhere, define conventional and advanced weapons. What dangers do the various weapons present? What dangers do they decrease or eliminate?

5. Victor W. Sidel, Bernard Nietschmann, and Jessica Mathews write about destruction of the environment, both deliberate and incidental. What dangers does war pose for particular environments? Are the dangers inevitable? What kinds of environmental destruction should war rules forbid, if any? Why?

6. With classmates, gather more information about wartime ecocide. After sharing information, determine the kinds of dangers such environmental practices present to humans.

7. How do Robert Jervis's comments about arms control relate to the pieces written by Laurence, Fussell, and Alperovitz?

8. Research the issue of arms control in order to reach your own conclusions about what kinds of weapons should be forbidden or limited. Who makes such decisions on the international level and how are they enforced?

9. Victor W. Sidel discusses the ethics of biological weapons research. Relate his comments to those made in any other three selections in this chapter.

10. Using this chapter and information gleaned from other sources for background and support, address the idea that the use of certain kinds of weapons during war is moral, but the use of other kinds of weapons is not. In other words, is all fair during war? No holds barred? What is your position?

4

Target: Civilians

WORLD WAR II BEGAN in September, 1939, and the most destructive war in history was to last for six long, bloody years. Mary Joan
Sargeant was nearly 13 when she heard the somber voice of Winston
Churchill, British Prime Minister, inform the British of the state of war.
She lived with her mother in Manchester, which became a major Luftwaffe target the following year, and they faced the terrors and incon-
veniences of civilians in a war zone: rousted out nightly to sleep in air
raid shelters; numbed by the incessant wail of sirens, day and night,
warning of more waves of enemy bombers; terrified by the dull thuds
of exploding bombs throughout the city.

Eventually, the strain of living in a prime target industrial city
proved too great, and Joan, as she was called, moved with her mother
to Shrewsbury, a small village away from the industrial centers that
attracted German bombers. But there was no real escape. One moonlit
night, a lone bomber apparently saw a reflection on the glass roof of
the local greenhouse and dropped a single high-explosive bomb. The
explosion killed an elderly woman and her granddaughter. Shortly after
than, when Joan was 16, she took a job as a bomb fuse inspector, stamping her initials in brass fuses that soon would be dropped on Germany.

A U.S. Army air base was built outside the town, and Joan began dating a Yank stationed there. She appreciated the little gifts her Yank brought her: candy bars, canned peaches, fruit. Across England, food was severely rationed for civilians—one egg each month, four ounces of meat monthly, a pint of milk every week. The Americans seemed always to have plenty of everything.

With her girlfriends, she managed to make fashionable the required equipment of war. Ugly and cumbersome gas masks were mandatory and had to be carried everywhere, constant reminders that the nation was at war. Teenage girls made colorful bags to disguise the hideous masks. But the memory remains: "I'll never forget the smell and taste of vulcanized rubber. The horror of those gas masks, and what they meant, will stay with me forever."

Eventually, Joan Sargeant married her Yank, and a year after the close of the war moved to the United States. Food was everywhere, rich food, in unlimited supply. Unused to such fare, she was hospitalized for a week shortly after her arrival. "I couldn't remember when I wasn't hungry during the war."

Civilians, of course, have always suffered in wars. Accounts in the Bible detail what happened to the Amalekites, losers to Saul and the Israelites: "And he took Agag the king of the Amalekites alive, and utterly destroyed all the people with the edge of the sword" (I Sam. 15:8). The Romans did the same thing with the Carthaginians. In more recent times, civilians have also been targets. Consider the murder of six million Jews by Hitler's Nazis; the slaughter of perhaps a million or more Cambodians by the Khmer Rouge; the gassing of the Kurds by Saddam Hussein's forces in Iraq.

Richard Rhodes, of the Massachusetts Institute of Technology, recently wrote in the *Journal of the American Medical Association* that the ferocity of the past notwithstanding, civilian deaths have actually increased, especially in the twentieth century. Since 1700, wars have claimed some 100 million lives; 90 percent of those deaths occurred since 1900. Moreover, the ratio of civilian deaths to combatants has also risen. Historically, about 50 percent of war deaths have been civilians; by the 1980s, that figure had climbed to 85 percent.

Perhaps Americans have grown complacent about civilian deaths, because since the Civil War there has been no war fought on American soil (excluding the attack on Pearl Harbor and the campaign in the Aleutian Islands during World War II). Other countries, including Joan Sargeant's England, have periodically suffered the horrors of war.

This chapter deals with civilians in wartime. The issue is essentially bi-polar: either civilians are legitimate targets in war, or they are not. Almost no one suggests that there will not be accidental deaths in any armed conflict, or that civilians will not suffer from hunger, sickness, or cold. The opinions diverge on whether in a war entire nations are at conflict, or only opposing soldiers.

The question is not as easy to answer as it first appears. First, every nation relies on civilians to manufacture the armament of its warriors. Are they therefore as culpable as combatants? Second, it is often difficult to tell the civilians from the combatants, especially in a guerrilla war such as the Vietnam war. Third, military centers and strategic targets often are located in heavily populated areas, sometimes for convenience, often to discourage attacks by opposing forces. If civilians are to be targeted, does that include young children? How can civilians and combatants be separated?

As a nation, the United States has little moral ground to stand on in the issue of targeting civilians. We remain the only country ever to have dropped atomic bombs on population centers. But is there any moral difference in dropping a single bomb on Hiroshima and in dropping tens of thousands of bombs on Dresden, Germany, in World War II? In Dresden, the bombs created a fire that swept through the city and killed upwards of 100,000 people. Of course, German bombers targeted London in an effort to terrorize the British into surrender.

Other issues must also be considered. Racism appears to have been a factor in the wartime decision to intern 120,000 Japanese Americans living on the West Coast. The United States was at war with Japan, certainly; it was also at war with Germany and Italy, but German Americans and Italian Americans were not sent to concentration camps, or relocation centers.

But all things pale in comparison to the Holocaust, the systematic murder of six million Jewish men, women, and children by the Germans in World War II. The events, individually and collectively, are numbing in their ferocity, their magnitude, their seeming lack of any shred of humanity. For half a century, Germans and the world have struggled to find answers. Why? Was the murder of civilians an aberration, a unique set of circumstances that will never be repeated? Or was it something deeper, more sinister, more universal?

As you read the essays in this chapter about the fate of civilians during wartime, consider how you would respond if the United States were a warzone. Consider the eagerness of 16-year-old Joan Sargeant to stamp her initials in bomb fuses, whose possible targets were German civilians. Would your response be any different?

Killing Civilians

*A veteran of the Spanish Civil War, Eric Blair (1903–1950), wrote numer-
ous essays, novels (Animal Farm, 1984), and other works under the pseu-
donym George Orwell. One of his particular concerns was language—with
how language is used and abused in politics and society in order to shape belief
and action. In the following essay, written in response to a popular World
War II British pamphlet condemning the bombing of civilian areas, Orwell
addresses the meaning—or lack of meaning—behind catchwords or phrases.*

*Jingoism is a word once used for what we might now refer to as popular
wisdom or slogans—words used, passed around, and believed with little or no
examination but usually held chauvinistically. Before you read Orwell's comments on such words, write a couple of paragraphs on the notion that civilians
are legitimate targets during times of war.*

MISS VERA BRITTAIN'S PAMPHLET, *Seed of Chaos,* is an eloquent 1
attack on indiscriminate or "obliteration" bombing. "Owing to the RAF
raids," she says, "thousands of helpless and innocent people in German,
Italian and German-occupied cities are being subjected to agonising forms
of death and injury comparable to the worst tortures of the Middle
Ages." Various well-known opponents of bombing, such as General
Franco and Major-General Fuller, are brought out in support of this.
Miss Brittain is not, however, taking the pacifist standpoint. She is willing and anxious to win the war, apparently. She merely wishes us to
stick to "legitimate" methods of war and abandon civilian bombing,
which she fears will blacken our reputation in the eyes of posterity. Her
pamphlet is issued by the Bombing Restriction Committee, which has
issued others with similar titles.

Now, no one in his senses regards bombing, or any other opera- 2
tion of war, with anything but disgust. On the other hand, no decent
person cares tuppence for the opinion of posterity. And there is something very distasteful in accepting war as an instrument and at the same
time wanting to dodge responsibility for its more obviously barbarous
features. Pacifism is a tenable position, provided that you are willing to
take the consequences. But all talk of "limiting" or "humanising" war
is sheer humbug, based on the fact that the average human being never
bothers to examine catchwords.

The catchwords used in this connection are "killing civilians," 3
"massacre of women and children" and "destruction of our cultural
heritage." It is tacitly assumed that air bombing does more of this kind
of thing than ground warfare.

When you look a bit closer, the first question that strikes you is: 4
Why is it worse to kill civilians than soldiers? Obviously one must not
kill children if it is in any way avoidable, but it is only in propaganda
pamphlets that every bomb drops on a school or an orphanage. A bomb
kills a cross section of the population; but not quite a representative
selection, because the children and expectant mothers are usually the
first to be evacuated, and some of the young men will be away in the
army. Probably a disproportionately large number of bomb victims will
be middle-aged. (Up to date, German bombs have killed between six
and seven thousand children in this country. This is, I believe, less than
the number killed in road accidents in the same period.) On the other
hand, "normal" or "legitimate" warfare picks out and slaughters all the
healthiest and bravest of the young male population. Every time a German submarine goes to the bottom about fifty young men of fine phy-
sique and good nerve are suffocated. Yet people who would hold up
their hands at the very words "civilian bombing" will repeat with satisfaction such phrases as "We are winning the Battle of the Atlantic."
Heaven knows how many people our blitz on Germany and the occupied countries has killed and will kill, but you can be quite certain it
will never come anywhere near the slaughter that has happened on the
Russian front.

War is not avoidable at this stage of history, and since it has to 5
happen it does not seem to me a bad thing that others should be killed
besides young men. I wrote in 1937: "Sometimes it is a comfort to me
to think that the aeroplane is altering the conditions of war. Perhaps
when the next great war comes we may see that sight unprecedented in
all history, a jingo with a bullet hole in him." We haven't yet seen that
(it is perhaps a contradiction in terms), but at any rate the suffering of
this war has been shared out more evenly than the last one was. The
immunity of the civilian, one of the things that have made war possible,
has been shattered. Unlike Miss Brittain, I don't regret that. I can't feel
that war is "humanised" by being confined to the slaughter of the young
and becomes "barbarous" when the old get killed as well.

As to international agreements to "limit" war, they are never kept 6
when it pays to break them. Long before the last war the nations had
agreed not to use gas, but they used it all the same. This time they have
refrained, merely because gas is comparatively ineffective in a war of
movement, while its use against civilian populations would be sure to
provide reprisals in kind. Against an enemy who can't hit back, e.g. the

Abyssinians, it is used readily enough. War is of its nature barbarous, it is better to admit that. If we see ourselves as the savages we are, some improvement is possible, or at least thinkable.

Content Considerations

1. What exactly is Orwell objecting to in this essay? What reasons does he give for his objection?
2. Orwell claims that "the average human being never bothers to examine catchwords." With classmates, determine what he means. Then find current examples of catchwords, examine them, and write about the assumptions they include.
3. Near the end of the essay (paragraph 5), Orwell says that "one of the things that have made war possible" is "the immunity of the civilian." Is he right? How might the immunity of the civilian make war possible?

Barkinson's Law on Bombing

Perhaps no more famous ironic essay can be found than Jonathan Swift's "A Modest Proposal." There, Swift proposes that Irish babies be used as food for the starving masses, a proposal met with horror and consternation by many in eighteenth century England who failed to see the irony.

Edgar Snow, an American who lived for many years in China, wrote "Barkinson's Law on Bombing" in 1967 in reaction to the widespread bombing in Vietnam. In the essay, he makes some rather macabre suggestions about targeting civilians, suggestions that might have appealed to George Orwell but that Snow obviously found abhorrent. Despite the irony of this essay, the real irony, Snow later wrote, was that U.S. policy seemed to follow his "Law."

As you read this, consider how effective is the use of irony. For another example of it, read Mike Royko's essay in the chapter on Media. Think of times in your everyday life when you say exactly the opposite of what you mean.

V. CHESTERTON BARKINSON[1]

MUCH CONFUSION and needless heartache are caused by misleading statements originating with officials to the effect that people, and especially mothers and children, are not legitimate or intended targets of bombing. Whether officials believe that or not, such statements result in a militarily unsound view that bombing inanimate targets is a good thing but that bombing humans is not only a bad thing but a waste of taxes. Barkinson's infallible law on bombing teaches us otherwise.

To begin with Barkinson's basic law, both precision and strategic bombing "expand so as to fill the area available. . . . " In laymen's language that means that what begins as selective bombing can only be completed by saturation bombing.

Unfortunately, in civilized democracies, the process of expanding bombing to its natural culmination is agonizingly prolonged by efforts to avoid arousing clergymen, etc., at the outset. That is done by assurances that inanimate objects are the main and even only (!!) admissible targets. When the tender Christian conscience comes to accept this routine bombing as a painless affair, targets can gradually be expanded to include domestic animals or even elephants—once elephants are sus-

pected of transporting enemy goods. One is then soon logically reconciled to the elimination of all burden bearers, including human porters.

As the tempo and area expand, bombing and burning may be   4
officially allowed to include men, women, and children illegally domi-
ciled near dangerous farms, oil depots, railways, jungles, mountains,
bridges, forests, factories, roads, waterways, barracks, munitions plants
(often camouflaged as schools and hospitals) or other objects which may
resemble weapons or potential weapons. Public acceptance of this progress may be accelerated if one or two elder statesmen, preferably ex-
Presidents, explain that irrational living habits of the natives make their
incidental extermination unavoidable. The killing of those who may
dwell near objects struck through pilot's error or wind deflection is now
also seen as necessary. From time to time it is useful for military spokesmen to emphasize to mothers that their boys' lives might be lost through
ground interference (antiaircraft fire, etc.) if pilots waste time trying to
place their loads accurately on foggy days.

Gradually bombing reaches a stage when overt evidence causes the   5
more canny taxpayers to suspect the profound truth. They do not wish
to be told it in so many words, and need not be. As anyone who has
experienced bombing knows, the truth is simply that even if *all* "legitimate" (inanimate) military targets are taken out the result can scarcely
touch the enemy's heartbase (Barkinson's all-inclusive term for morale
factors), which alone makes possible continued resistance to the efforts
of the bombers. Realists will understand at last that all weapons and all
non-human means of war are in themselves quite innocent and harmless.
It is only men—for example, Vietnamese Communists—who make
weapons a menace. Here Barkinson is beautifully clear: *it is men that
make war, not weapons.* What makes Vietnamese Communists? Men!
Where do men come from? They come from children. What is the means
of their production? Women!

In order quickly to eliminate interference with the work, primary   6
bombing targets should be women, children, and men—and in that
order—while all weapons and means of production should be of secondary or tertiary priority, according to Barkinson.[2] Unhappily, means
of production—even magnificent forests and jungles—are often found
near *people,* but their burning at current rates *could* be avoided, as indicated below.

Empirical evidence in support of this basic law in bombing prior-   7
ities came to Barkinsonian research workers recently from an eyewitness
freshly returned from Vietnam. An American lady who accompanied a
peace mission to Hanoi told the American press (although she probably
had never even heard of Barkinson's law) that she had seen that our
bombing is, indeed, killing many civilians. But, she added, she found

"no *innocent people* there"! All were opposed to the bombing, all were resisting it by whatever means available, and hence all shared war guilt in the primary degree.

The classic fulfillment of Barkinson's law on bombing priorities   8
to date was, of course, the primitive Hiroshima bomb which killed outright only 78,000 people. At Hiroshima we were unable to avoid much incidental property damage, and there were instances of partial incineration and its untidy human reminders. Today's sophisticated antipersonnel bombs, however, can leave buildings and weapons intact, and do no injury beyond killing all living things—without leaving unsightly remnants such as result from vulgar uses of napalm. Minor structural damage would still be entailed, of course, by the removal of personnel targets sheltered in high-yield buildings such as obstetrical and gynecological hospitals, clinics, maternity homes, crèches, nurseries, and kindergartens.

Once adoption of natural bombing priorities had ended interfer-   9
ence in the North, the same methods could eliminate both living and future Viet Cong, by eradicating their embryonic bases. Useful rural installations such as the more substantial housing constructed with American AID, concrete pig pens, certain launching pads (to be designated by General Westmoreland), a few churches, temples, and the new John Steinbeck memorial libraries, could probably be preserved. Vietnam and the free world could then make the scene together (after the soil had been decontaminated).

It is only in theory, of course, that intelligent target planning of   10
this sort can be realized fully. For no one can guarantee that the above program would not, in one way or another, lead to the end of bombers and bombing for all time, eliminating future work to be done! Thus, Barkinson effectively demonstrates the practical impossibility of perfection in any such extreme degree.

In a related science, C. Northcote Parkinson's celebrated parallel   11
law on the proliferation of bureaucracies teaches us that administrations inevitably expand to fill the time available, and that the expansion has nothing to do with the value or completion of the work assigned. To the contrary: the two, four, eight, sixteen, etc., bureaucrats hired to assist one administrator will never complete the work which that official originally was capable of doing alone. For them to do so would be to eliminate themselves.

Similarly, the administration of the American Vietnam program,   12
which began with only one noncombatant advisor to Saigon pilots, now includes tens of thousands of bombardiers and support personnel on aircraft carriers and airfields that stretch throughout Southeast Asia to

the Philippines, Taiwan, Okinawa, Japan, Korea, Guam, and beyond—
to the whole of what President Eisenhower called the "military-industrial complex" inside the U.S.—all directed by countless new general
officers. They are thoroughly committed to hold down, under the able
strategic leadership of Commander Buz Sawyer, ever-expanding base
real estate from India to the Antipodes. Bombing administrators for
Vietnam have now unloaded more tons of explosives there than were
dropped on Germany throughout World War II, but there is no sign
that the available space has been exhausted. The law is that these gentle-
men will never declare themselves redundant, nor abandon their mul-
tibillion-dollar base establishments in Asia, by "completing the work"
which Mr. Walt Whitman Rostow was handling, all alone, until he
expanded his work by inventing the Green Berets.

Barkinson's Subsidiary Law on Punitive Bombing foresees, more-   13
over, a final solution to the old "guns or butter" dilemma. "Butter here
and bombs abroad" is a viable check and balance system whereby the
welfare or butter bureaucracy expands its work but is checked by the
bomber bureaucracy from going to extremes (such as promoting brains
before bombs), while the bomber bureaucracy is held in balance by the
butter bureaucracy so as to avoid excesses which could cause the extermination of both bureaucracies. Some support is given to this view in
the recent pregnant thesis of McGeorge Bundy, entitled "An End to
Either/Or," which refutes contentions that what he euphemistically terms
"wide foreign activities" are incompatible with welfare "work at home."

Barkinson also teaches that Punitive Bombing is the highest   14
expression of responsible power, simply because the bomber bureaucracy is least affected by mob instincts—sometimes described as "international (spare the mark!) laws." For example, Senator Morse contends
that armed occupation and bombing by United States forces of even an
insignificant country like Vietnam amount to war crimes in violation of
the Kellogg-Briand Peace Pact, the Geneva Accords of 1954, the UN
Charter, the Nuremberg International Judgments on War Crimes, and
the United States Constitution!

Only a more intensive punishment program (as Senator Edward   15
P. Brooke finally concluded) can expose such archaic illusions and lead
to appropriate reforms. Despite repeated protests, one of the most notorious transgressions against Barkinson still appears in the U.S. Army
Field Manual, which states: "Any person, whether a member of the
Armed Forces or a civilian, who commits an act which constitutes a
crime under international law, is responsible therefore, and liable to
punishment. Such offenses in connection with war . . . comprise: (a)
Crimes against peace, (b) Crimes against humanity, (c) War crimes."[3]

It is not enough that such regulations are in practice ignored. They must be totally stricken from the record along with all other obsolete "either/or" concepts which interfere with the natural laws of bombing.

Anyway, that is what we Barkinsonians believe. If we are right, those who shudder at the prospect of an early conclusion to the Vietnam war may forget their fears. The Administration is, as President Johnson has lately reiterated, permanently attached to the principles of "the most careful and self-limited war in history." Here, once again, Barkinson is helpful: his law on the "self-limited war" is that it can end only in self-determined peace—as confirmed by Mr. Johnson's swift rejection of Hanoi's February proposal to exchange peace talks for a cessation of bombing. There is thus no scientific reason to doubt that the air punishment of Vietnam will continue in accordance with the natural laws of bombing—limited, to be sure, by the area available to the bombers in which to fill the available time with new workers and new work to be done.[4]

16

ENDNOTES

1. V. Chesterton Barkinson's remarkable studies on the natural laws of bombing should not be confused with the equally remarkable (and remarkably coincidental) *Parkinson's Law,* by D. Northcote Parkinson (N.Y., 1957), a work which V. Chesterton Barkinson often uses for extensive documentation in the course of his own investigations.
2. Barkinson—a happily married man—is, of course, no misogynist. Sentiment has no influence on the work of a scientist.
3. Department of the Army, Field Manual, July 18, 1956, Section 498.
4. Originally intended as a macabre exaggeration of the possible, this article by 1968 seemed tragic reality rather more than ironic spoof. For evidence that Barkinson's laws on bombing were in fact being widely implemented—through the saturation sowing of cluster bombs and far more deadly napalm, in operations amounting to genocide—consult an eyewitness report, by a correspondent recommended for his veracity by the U.S. Air Force: *Air War: Vietnam,* by Frank Harvey (Bantam Books, New York, 1967). EDGAR SNOW

Content Considerations

1. What kind of tone is Snow using? How effective is it in helping make his point? What is his point?
2. Snow compares bombings to bureaucracies. What purposes does such a comparison serve?
3. Examine the assertions Snow makes about civilians in wartime. With which of them do you agree? Why?

MARTIN HARWIT

Smart Versus Nuclear Bombs

The kinds of weapons wielded in war affect civilians as well as combatants. Although a target is usually selected because of its military value—a bridge, a factory, an air strip—civilians who live near targeted areas as well as those who work in them may become casualties. Thus weapons precise enough to locate and hit a target directly could spare the lives of civilians and possibly reduce damage to the areas where they live.

Such praise has been heaped upon the "smart" bombs used in the Persian Gulf war; technology made it possible for very specific buildings, structures, and even vehicles to be precisely bombed, sparing surrounding areas and people. "Collateral damage" was kept low. Martin Harwit, the director of the National Air and Space Museum, writes about such damage, comparing it to the destruction caused by carpet bombing and nuclear bombs of previous wars. Before you read, write a paragraph about how smart bombs could possibly reduce the threat of nuclear war; write another about how civilians might benefit from such a reduction.

IN THE EARLY DAYS of World War II, U.S. air power doctrine aimed at destroying an adversary's ability to wage war by destroying his military production and supply system. This meant strategic bombing targeted specifically at aircraft factories and armament industries crucial to providing the machinery of war, and later concentrated on oil refineries and munitions factories required to keep that machinery in action and on bridges and railroad junctions essential for supplying those resources to fighting men.

In the course of the war, the British rejected this doctrine, and the United States silently allowed it to lapse, as thousand-bomber raids first devastated whole cities in Germany and later leveled most of the major population centers in Japan. In the face of fighters and flak, precision bombing turned out to be almost impossible. At the start of the war, a typical bomb fell up to three miles away from its intended target in daytime and up to five miles away at night. Toward the end of the war, that circle of error had been reduced to about a thousand yards. But that still meant devastating a whole square mile of a city in order to be certain of destroying a single important military target. And it took vast fleets of bombers to fully cover that big an area.

The crews in those armadas of bombers suffered horrendous losses, 3
particularly over Europe, in the early days of the war, when German
fighters, day after day, night after night, rose to attack and destroy the
unescorted, heavily laden, lumbering aircraft. Only in the last 18 months
of the war in Europe were long-range fighter escorts available to keep
German attackers at bay.

These difficulties made the atomic bomb developed at Los Alamos, 4
New Mexico, seem like an incomparably more efficient weapon. It could
be delivered by a single airplane and was capable of immense destruction. And within a few years after Hiroshima and Nagasaki, military
doctrine began to evolve in the direction of huge nuclear arsenals.

A challenge to the nuclear doctrine may now have been offered up 5
by the war in the Gulf. The smart bombs employed there showed a
remarkable ability to hit individual buildings and even rapidly moving
tanks, while keeping civilian casualties substantially lower than in any
previous wars of comparable magnitude.

In effect, the war in the Gulf returned to the original doctrine of 6
concentrating on military targets and showed that the doctrine could
now be successfully implemented in combat.

If we genuinely adhere to this revived doctrine and its greater con- 7
cern for minimizing casualties among civilian populations, how do we
deal with the huge nuclear arsenals amassed over four decades of cold
war? It makes no sense to target a nuclear weapon for delivery to a
single building or even a tank battalion. These weapons of mass destruction vaporize, rather than merely destroy, the intended target, and they
wipe out large surrounding regions as well.

If smart weapons can so successfully take care of all purely military 8
requirements, are nuclear weapons to be kept in our arsenals only to
pose a nihilistic retaliatory threat to any enemy contemplating first use?
And if so, how many such weapons would we need to retain for adequate defense?

Answers to such questions will not be found quickly. Military 9
analysts will need to think through all of the ramifications of the Gulf
war before deciding on a new nuclear strategy. But if that strategy were
to involve a dramatic reduction of the world's nuclear arsenals, all of us
would breathe a little easier for our children and grandchildren.

Wars inevitably claim innocent victims. If the lessons learned from 10
the Gulf war could enable us to lower the nuclear threat that has hung
over the world now for nearly half a century, we would at least have
gained something from all those "smart" bombs besides just one more
set of sophisticated weapons.

Content Considerations

1. What is the "nuclear doctrine"? How did it develop? What danger does it pose for civilians?
2. Paragraph eight consists of two questions. How do you answer them?
3. Are smart bombs more humane than other types? Construct an argument for or against their use in decreasing the numbers of civilian casualties in war.

War at Nine Years Old

Born in Berlin in 1935, Kamilla Chadwick, known as Anna, spent her early childhood years being shuttled back and forth from Berlin to the countryside to escape the bombing of her native city. In her book The War According to Anna: A Paean to My Mother, *Chadwick describes a childhood full of movement, of secrecy and lies and propaganda, of parents who taught her what could be spoken aloud and what must be lied about in order to survive Hitler's Germany. When she was eight, she and her family were evacuated to an area that was absorbed by Poland, having lost their home and subsequent temporary lodging during air raids.*

When she was nine years old, Chadwick and her family and the village in which they lived were evacuated as the Russians drew near. The selection that follows explains what happened when the train filled with evacuees was stopped in the midst of a battle between German and Russian forces.

Write a few paragraphs about how a nine-year-old child might view the events of war—separation from parents, air raids, a home destroyed by bombs, a series of evacuations, the final threat of falling into the hands of the enemy.

THEY'VE TAKEN MOTHER

OUR GROUP OF REFUGEES from the train was told to follow a 1
Russian soldier. I felt like a sheep in the bleating herd that a shepherd
had led by my Aunt Marie's house every morning. During our summer
visits, I used to watch the sheep every day; there was always a black
one among them. Now I felt like I was a little black sheep carrying
Erich, while Mother pushed Lisa in her carriage and Dieter carried the
suitcases.

I can't remember whether I was afraid. Perhaps I had shut off the 2
"feeling" part of me. I do remember some of my thoughts: Why are
we all following a Russian who has his back turned to us and isn't even
looking to see how many are following? If we were going to run away,
where would we hide, and how long would it take until they found us
again? Or would we get bombed, and this time all be killed?

Now I thought Dieter was stupid, carrying those suitcases. Mother 3
had told him to leave them behind. And it seemed as though Erich were
putting on weight by the minute as we marched behind the Russian,

who didn't even seem to care if we followed him or not. I wondered what they would do with us, and why I heard so much machine gun fire. I hadn't seen a single German soldier.

I also wondered about something Mother had said to Hilda just a   4
few days before: "To the victor, the spoils. It's always been like that. The tools of war may change, but the rewards remain the same."

I hadn't been able to figure out what "the spoils" were, since   5
everyone I knew had buried his treasure. Spoils were things pirates got. Pirates stole other people's ships and robbed the women of their jewels. They killed all the sailors and then burned the ships while they stood on their own deck, grinning from ear to ear and looking satisfied.

Pirates attacked ships full of innocent people and lots of treasure.   6
The Russians were the pirates. But I knew that we had started the war. That made us pirates, too. So the whole thing was nothing more than a bunch of pirates fighting it out over a country instead of a boat.

I felt much more comfortable thinking about what was going on   7
in terms of something I knew about. It didn't matter that this knowledge came from the movies. I knew what was going to happen next: They would rob the women of their jewels, while the victims wept and pleaded: "No, please, not my wedding band." The prettiest of the women would be put into a special room to be saved for later, when the fighting was over. Sometimes the women would go quietly, looking heroic, and other times they screamed and had to be dragged by the hair to that special room.

What happened in the special room was pretty dreadful, but still I   8
didn't know what it was. I knew beautiful girls were part of the spoils and I felt glad I wasn't one of them. It never once entered my mind that Mother might be. I knew she was beautiful, because people said so, but I didn't think of her as being part of the spoils of war.

I don't remember how long we followed that soldier; it seemed a   9
long way from the station. In a way, that was good, because the railway yards were still being bombed by somebody. I didn't care any longer whose bombs they were. Bombs are bombs.

When we came to a farmhouse, we were told to go into the cellar   10
and stay there. The cellar was a long dark tunnel, with a dirt floor. There was nothing to sit on—not at all like our basements in Berlin.

The door leading into the cellar was left open, and I noticed for   11
the first time that day that the sun was shining. It might even be warm out there, I thought. Light filtered into the cellar and I noticed that we had a man among us. He had only one hand, which he kept waving about, urging the crowd to be quiet and stop carrying on like crazy people.

I thought him very rude and resented his being there. One hand   12 or not, he was a man and shouldn't have been there with us. Father wasn't, so why that man?

I went outside to see what was going on and to warm up a little. 13 I took Erich with me. Outside, I could see the farmhouse and adjoining buildings, which were built around a square cobblestone courtyard, just like Aunt Marie and Uncle Wilhelm's place; even the compost heap was in the same position, next to the outhouse.

Then some Russian soldiers arrived, so I picked up my brother 14 and rushed back into the cellar. The Russians came in just behind me.

I didn't see any guns or knives or anything that could be used to 15 kill people. Still, they looked dangerous and terrifying. They shouted at us and made the women give them their watches and jewelry, including their wedding bands. Mother gave them her rings and wristwatch. The women in the back didn't even wait until they were ordered to hand over their things; they just passed them to me and I gave them to the soldiers. I noticed how dirty the soldiers' hands and fingernails were, but not a single Russian was wounded or walked with a bloodsoaked bandage or broken arm in a sling. They were young and strong—and dirty.

The looting went on until there was nothing left to be taken from 16 us. Soldiers who came too late for any spoils went away disappointed and angry. They suspected the women of having jewelry hidden in their clothing, and one promised they would come back later and search us properly. Now the women really cried! But not Mother. She just seemed to draw into herself. Yet she was calm and comforting to us children.

"Don't worry," she said, hugging us, "it will all work out 17 somehow."

"Are they going to kill us?" 18

"No. Why should they?" 19

I really think now that Mother didn't believe in anybody killing 20 anybody else. She thought there was something good in every person. I remembered all those awful things I had been told about the Russians, but so far I hadn't seen them kill anybody. I was beginning to hope that maybe they really weren't that bad, and Mother was right.

Around noon, we were ordered to leave the cellar and go into the 21 courtyard, where we were made to stand in a line. Maybe now was the time! Maybe now we were to be shot! Instead, two soldiers came and gave us soup and bread, and milk for the little children. Their hands were clean. That seemed very important. I was never allowed to eat while I had dirty hands and fingernails, and I certainly was not allowed to accept food from somebody else's dirty hands.

I had just finished my soup, when I saw some women pouring 22 their soup and milk onto the cobblestones. "It's been poisoned!" they screamed. "It's all a trick. They are poisoning us!" I looked at my mother trying to get some soup into Erich, and she looked back at me and said, "Don't worry." The two Russians who had handed out the food looked upset and angry.

"No, no," they told us, "it's good!"   23

It *was* good and I wished I could have more. Now I didn't believe   24
anybody, just my mother. She was always right and wouldn't let us be poisoned.

I stood around, trying not to worry, when suddenly a man jumped   25
over a gate and came toward me. He wore a black leather coat and carried a long sword with a thin blade in his right hand, held up high into the air. He looked straight at me.

I remember looking at him, knowing that this was a Russian Jew,   26
the most terrible person in the whole world. I don't remember what happened next.

Mother said I screamed and screamed, and when she came rushing   27
out, she saw this man with a sword standing in front of me. He didn't know what to do; he tried to help but that only made matters worse.

The Russian left and Mother calmed me down. Afterward I thought   28
I would never again feel afraid of anything. Everything was happening differently from what I had been told to expect. The whole world seemed upside down. The Russians had not killed or tortured anyone. They had taken us to a safe place and given us good food. Nothing was poisoned and the Russian Jew had not stuck his sword into me, but had tried to help me.

Nonetheless, from the moment I saw the Russian Jew I began to   29
stutter.

In a while two Russian officers approached—the first Russian of-   30
ficers I had seen. I stared at them closely, without feeling I was being rude. Being rude belonged to another time.

The officers looked splendid. It was hard to think of them as the   31
enemy. They were clean, well-dressed and well-polished, wore ribbons as decorations and had pistols dangling in holsters. They looked us over, then told my mother to come with them. Mother wore a gray flannel suit and a black fur coat, but somehow everything about her suddenly looked white. There were tears in her eyes when she told me to look after the children. Then she whispered, "Remember Aunt Marie and Uncle Wilhelm," and kissed each one of us. It was like saying goodbye before going on a long journey.

Now I began to feel the threat of yet another terror. I recalled my   32
pirate theory and the part about pretty ladies being "spoils." The other

women were silent now. Everyone watched Mother being taken across the yard and through the door of the farmhouse. It was a white house, with lace curtains fluttering through broken windows.

An elderly lady came to stand with us, saying, "You poor children." I don't know how long we all stood there looking at the door through which Mother had disappeared. We were all listening. We could hear some shooting in the distance, but it was almost peaceful where we stood. Except that Mother was in that house with two Russian officers.   33

Mother had been scared; I knew that.   34

She had told me to remember Aunt Marie and Uncle Wilhelm.   35
Why? As far as I knew, nothing like this had ever happened to them. All the women were quiet, shrinking back as though they were not there. What was happening inside that house? What were they doing to my mother?

Mother didn't know any secrets for which she could be tortured.   36
In the movies, women with secrets had their breasts cut off to make them talk. They were screaming all the time because it hurt so much.

"Oh God, You must help her now," I told Him. There was nothing I could do to protect her this time. "Please, let her come back," I prayed silently.   37

If she were raped, whatever that was, would she die? Ladies who were being raped screamed. And what was rape? I vaguely knew it had something to do with having all your clothes ripped off and being thrown to the ground. I had seen that in the movies, too, but never what followed. One heard screams while it was going on, and then later on one would see a woman's body. It was clear that something awful had happened, and it was always done by the enemy. It never occurred to me that a German man might rape a German woman.   38

I wished I knew more—and I wished I didn't know as much as I knew. Nothing I had learned at school had prepared me for my mother being taken away by the Russians. I wondered what Father would have done. What could he have done? Nothing, I thought.   39

Just when I couldn't stand it any longer and began to feel sick, the door opened again. Mother walked out, fully dressed, fur coat and all, with a Russian officer at each side. She was smoking a cigarette with a whole packet in her hand. She was smiling and talking to them. Then they left and she came toward us, still smoking her cigarette, her eyes twice as large as usual. She looked and acted as though she hadn't been hurt. The terror was over. Or was it? I still felt unsure. Something was different. She was so terribly calm, and so white. When she kissed and hugged us, her breath smelled of alcohol and cigarettes. Then she walked over to the other women.   40

I saw the man with the only one hand put his arms around her 41
and she put her head on his shoulder and closed her eyes. All the other
women milled about her, asking questions. I had a terrible time hearing
anything.

She said the Russians had not touched her, but only because she 42
managed to convince them that now wasn't a good time for it—that
evening would be better. She had promised to go with them later, and
they had said they'd be back for her.

"None of us will be safe by evening," she told the group. "As 43
soon as it gets dark, this place will be pure hell for everyone. They
already have begun their drinking."

ESCAPE

After a great deal of loud, confused chatter about drunken soldiers, 44
rape, abuse of children—and even murder—there seemed to be a consensus among the frightened women that any attempt to escape would
almost certainly bring on terrible retribution. "If we just be quiet and
go back into our cellar . . . "

Mother stood firm. "No!" 45

A woman said maybe Mother was so scared because she hadn't 46
told the truth about what had happened in the house; maybe she had
been raped and now was willing to endanger her children by trying to
run away. They refused to listen to Mother's warning, but they didn't
try to stop her when she gathered up our few belongings.

Not even the Russians tried to stop us. There were all sorts of 47
soldiers about, but they acted as if we were invisible. Were the soldiers
all drunk by this time? Am I remembering what really happened? Or
had my brain gone numb?

I think my memory is correct, because I remember Mother saying 48
we were "ghosts." She moved Lisa a little and put Erich into the bottom
end of the baby carriage. She told Dieter and me to leave the two suitcases, but Dieter refused, so I carried one for him.

As we walked down the road away from the farm I kept remem- 49
bering what Mother had whispered to us about "remembering Aunt
Marie and Uncle Wilhelm." Somehow I knew she was thinking about
them now and intended to get us to them.

Soon we came to the main street leading back into town. We kept 50
well into the middle of the road but still we could not avoid the rubble
and debris from gutted and burned buildings. As we walked past the
still-smoking ruins we came to an area where there had been heavy
fighting. We saw piles of dead German soldiers along the side of the
road. Mother told us not to look, but we looked anyway. I never had

seen dead German soldiers before. They no longer looked brave and victorious—only like broken toy soldiers, left to be swept up and thrown away. Maybe they were put there for the garbage truck, I thought.

"Know what?" Dieter asked. "Dead soldiers don't look like people any more." I had the same thought.   51

Suddenly we weren't invisible. We seemed to become a real nuisance. We constantly were being shouted at by the Russians. They pointed their guns at us, waving us out of the way. Mother smiled and waved back. I wondered why she wasn't afraid any longer. She smiled and went on—there was no stopping her. Dieter and I smiled and waved, too, even though we didn't feel like it. Somehow, smiling and waving at the enemy kept us from getting hurt or captured again.   52

I don't know where we were, but it wasn't a very large town. As we left what might once have been its center, we came to some houses untouched by bombs or fire. They were nice two-story houses with fenced front yards. Most of them had open doors, and bits of clothing, bicycles, toys and even dishes were strewn about the yards. "Looted," Mother said.   53

Dieter spotted a children's wagon and wanted to take it for the suitcases. I said no, because that was stealing. Mother stopped to hear our argument and she said to Dieter, "That's a good idea, my child," and smiled. He was terribly pleased. Then she said to me, "Don't worry." But I couldn't help it. We had stolen something, and Mother was acting as if stealing suddenly was allowed.   54

While we were living in Berlin, Dieter had a friend, Sonny, who would call for him to come and play in the park. Only they didn't go to the park. Sonny would take Dieter to one of the big stores where they would steal things. When Mother found out, Sonny disappeared, and there was a big fuss with punishments. Dieter had to promise never to steal anything again in his whole life. And now he had done it again— and Mother called it "a good idea." Life was getting stranger and stranger.   55

But it was good not to have to carry those suitcases. We put them into the wagon and pulled them easily. As we pushed on, I saw lots of clothes and toys lying about. I longed for some of them, but I never said a word. I still had a feeling it wasn't right.   56

Sometime in the afternoon we left all the houses and ruins behind. We were walking along a road lined with burning German tanks and trucks. Some of them were standing upright with smoke pouring from them, some had fallen onto their sides, and some looked as if a giant had turned them on their backs. There was a horrible smell in the air.   57

I told Mother I had to go to the bathroom, and she said to go behind the nearest tank, but to hurry. Dead German soldiers were everywhere and black crows hovered over them. I had to walk a little   58 farther than I had intended, to be out of sight. When I had finished, a voice that sounded full of pain suddenly called out, "Here, girl, come here. Here, Here." I felt a terrible embarrassment. Someone had been watching me. I started to run and then saw the man. He was a young German soldier under a tank. Half of his body looked mashed and badly burned. He smelled sickeningly awful; one hand moved just a little. He pointed to a revolver and begged me to put it to his head and pull the trigger.

"It's not difficult," he whispered, when he saw how horrified I 59 was. I hesitated, not knowing what to do. I looked at him and smelled the awful stench and saw the crows picking at the dead bodies. I thought crows ate grain, not people.

"Please, please," the soldier whispered. He seemed so young. "Do 60 something good for me." He pointed at the revolver once again. It was awful. What was I supposed to do?

I was afraid to call Mother. She had changed so much since Father 61 left us at the train, I hardly knew her. Her acceptance of Dieter stealing the wagon still bothered me. Would she tell me it was a good idea to shoot the soldier?

I knew my Ten Commandments. One of them was, "Thou shalt 62 not kill," and if one broke that commandment, one would go to Hell. That wasn't where I wanted to go. Then I heard Mother and Dieter calling me. I grabbed the revolver and put it into the man's hand. Then I turned and shouted, "I a-a-a-m c-c-c-c-oming," and ran. I never told Mother about the soldier, not even when she scolded me for having taken so long.

I thought about that soldier for a very long time. I wondered if he 63 had managed to shoot himself, and whether it was the right thing to do. I had nightmares about him, but I always stopped just in time. Even in my dreams I didn't want to find out what happened.

As we walked along, Mother pushing, Dieter and I pulling, I 64 thought about war. Why did so many men seem to think war was good and honorable? Why did they march to their deaths singing and smiling? I wondered whether they all had been tricked and been lied to. Or were men really so stupid as to believe killing and dying was fun and exciting? And what about women? Why didn't women stop it? Why didn't they say to their husbands and sons, "No, you can't go; I won't let you." I knew Mother would never have allowed Dieter to go. If the rulers of two countries wanted war, let them fight each other. The winner would get the loser's country. It was such an easy solution!

I also thought a lot about my sudden stuttering. When Erich began 65 to stutter, I felt so sorry for him. I thought it was another one of his illnesses, one I would never catch. And now I had caught it, too. I thought Erich's stuttering came after he had had a high temperature for so long. But I wasn't sick, and here I was, stuttering. It began after I saw that Russian Jew with the sword and thought he was going to kill me. Dieter had seen it all, too, so why didn't he stutter? I decided I had been scared out of my wits, and now that I wasn't scared any longer, the stuttering would stop. So I began practicing. I started with my name. "A–a–a–a–nna." Over and over again. I couldn't say it without the most awful stammer. Then I tried, "My name is Anna," and that was all right. I tried, "I c–c–c–an do it." The "can" didn't work either, nor did: "I think I can do it." The German word for "thinking" begins with a "d," and that was a problem, too.

After a while, Dieter got bored with listening.   66

"See if you can still sing," he suggested. "I'll help you."   67

At first I thought he was out of his mind, but I tried it and it   68
worked. I could sing without a single stutter. So Dieter and I pulled our little wagon, singing songs about peaceful meadows and birds, and the sounds of different instruments, and a mill that stood in a valley in the Black Forest. Finally our voices began to give out and I called ahead to ask Mother where we were going.

"Somewhere away from the Russians," she called back.   69

"B–b–b–b–ut," I said, "They are everywhere. You said so yourself.   70
The war is almost over and the Russians have won it."

"They can't be everywhere," Mother reassured us. "They are   71
sticking close to the main highways first."

"Why?"   72

"The roads are better and it keeps them from getting lost. That   73
means they can't be in every nook and cranny at the same time."

Dieter got the point at once. "Then we are getting out of here to   74
find a nook or cranny."

Still, I wasn't sure. "'B–b–b–b–but won't they catch up with us in   75
the end?"

"Not us," said Mother. "We'll let the Americans catch up with   76
us. Not the Russians."

I had forgotten the Americans and the British and the French.   77

Just then we saw columns of trucks slowly moving toward us. We   78
were walking on the right side of the road, going one way, the trucks were on the left side, going the other. They were filled with happy Russian soldiers.

"Smile," Mother ordered. 'Smile and wave to them."   79

So once again we smiled and waved at the enemy, and they laughed   80
and waved back. Now and then, a soldier would jump from a truck and come over to inspect us. I smiled so much, it hurt. They looked much

cleaner and not so tired; their uniforms were all straight and unwrinkled, and they didn't carry machine guns. Most of them had beards. I never had seen so many men with beards before. Everyone wanted to look at Lisa, who looked back at them with big blue eyes under blond curly hair. Every time Father came near her, she cried. But now, confronted by bearded Russian soldiers, she smiled.

All the men had to touch Lisa. It seemed as if they couldn't help 81 themselves. One by one they took a fat little finger and made funny noises—some sort of Russian baby talk. Their hands were not too clean; I looked at my mother, expecting her to tell them, "Go and wash your hands first," but she never did. She really had changed. "Djetochka," they'd call Lisa. The rest of us were ignored. I decided Lisa must look like a Russian baby and that's why she got all that attention.

The Russians gave us loaves of bread. I couldn't understand why 82 they were so friendly and why they didn't try to stop us from running away. Later, Mother explained.

"First of all, we were going to where they had been already. That 83 means we couldn't escape. Secondly, we were friendly and non-threatening, and third, we must look utterly ridiculous and totally out of place."

I didn't like the part about utterly ridiculous. 84

"Incongruous," Mother explained, holding up the arm of her 85 beautiful and expensive fur coat—bedraggled now, but still beautiful. "Incongruous" was not yet in my vocabulary, but I did see what she meant: A displaced person with a baby carriage, four very tired and dirty children—and a fur coat.

Dieter didn't like the part about looking non-threatening. 86

"What if we had a bomb in that carriage, instead of Lisa and Er- 87 ich?" he asked.

Mother gave him one of her long looks. "What if?" she asked. 88 "We'd all be killed and would only kill a few Russians. What would be the point of that?"

Dieter had no answer, but he muttered his disgruntlement. Then 89 came a distraction. A plane was coming over and flying low. "Run," Mother shouted. She grabbed up Lisa and I took Erich. We ran into an open field and fell flat. The plane was above us in an instant, spraying bullets all over the place, trying to hit the Russian trucks and soldiers.

The Russians had abandoned their vehicles and also lay flat in our 90 field. The plane left as suddenly as it had come. We got back on the road and found the baby carriage and wagon undamaged. Dieter was disgusted. "I could have done better with my air rifle."

Mother put Lisa back in her carriage and I lifted Erich into the 91 wagon with the suitcases. Again, Mother suggested we leave them behind. "No!" Dieter said, "Never." Mother shook her head and took off her fur coat to cover Erich.

A Russian officer was coming toward us. Mother watched him   92
approach. She was ever so still and her eyes got big. Was he going to take her with him? But he saluted instead, and told her, in very good High German, that we should take a route where there were no troop movements. He said this route was too dangerous for women and children. Then he gave Mother a map and showed her where we were.

"Thank you very much indeed." Her relief was apparent to all   93
of us.

Content Considerations

1. In what ways do Anna's first experiences with the enemy surprise her? How had her expectations been formed?
2. Respond to Chadwick's narrative by focusing on the parts that seemed most frightening or horrible or unbelievable.
3. How are the dangers and hardship Chadwick's family faced as civilians similar to that experienced by combatants? How are the experiences different?

February 16, 1942

Enemy Aliens: Scare on the Coast

The United States declared war on Japan on December 8, 1941, after the Japanese attacked Pearl Harbor. Declarations of war upon the United States by Germany and Italy soon followed; within days the United States was fully immersed in World War II. With that immersion, people of German, Italian, or Japanese ancestry became the objects of increased scrutiny in the United States. The group that received the closest attention was the Japanese, many of whom were born in the United States or had become naturalized citizens.

President Franklin D. Roosevelt signed Executive Order 9066 in February, 1942; it authorized the military to issue the orders and proclamations it deemed necessary to protect military areas from sabotage and espionage. Through such authority Japanese Americans were subjected to curfews and were prevented from leaving their homes except during the day. Through such authority 120,000 Japanese Americans were forced to live in detention camps until the war was over. Entire towns were declared "Military Areas," thus preventing Japanese Americans from residing in them or even entering them. Americans of German or Italian descent were not affected.

The following article appeared in Time; *the news it reports may give some indication of America's attitudes and fears. Before you read it, recall what you already know about this incident in U.S. history; then write a paragraph about what the incident suggests regarding racism, expediency, and civilian loyalties in wartime.*

AT DAWN ONE MORNING FBI men raided Terminal Island, a dis-   1
ordered conglomeration of tiny wooden houses, fish nets, rabbit war-
rens, where 2,000 Japanese lived right in the middle of Los Angeles
Harbor, a stone's throw from the Navy's Reeves Field. Agents blocked
the bridge, rooted through the narrow lanes of fishermen's huts, carted
off 383 men for "investigations."

All along the West Coast the presence of enemy aliens became a   2
suddenly, sinisterly glaring fact: Japanese and Italian fishermen along the
water front, Japanese who worked all day on hands and knees in geo-
metrically perfect truck gardens which sometimes overlay oil pipelines,
Japanese settlements near big airplane plants and military posts.

Attorney General Francis Biddle marked off 135 restricted zones   3

from which all enemy aliens must move by Feb. 24. No one could say
how many thousands would have to pack up and go. Nor did anyone
know where they would go to. (The Government considered the idea
of setting up big farm camps in the interior.) Francis Biddle also set up
a curfew zone, covering a fourth of California, where all remaining
aliens must be in their houses from 9 p.m. to 6 a.m., must never travel
more than five miles from home.

No citizen of a democracy could be happy about some of the pa-   4
thetic situations which these orders created. For every potential fifth
columnist, hundreds of innocent aliens would suffer. In industrial Pittsburg, near San Francisco, old Italian women who had lived in the same
houses for 30 years, who had sons and daughters working in Pittsburg's
factories, prayed at Mass that they would not have to leave home.

Luciano Maniscalco, a San Francisco fisherman for 40 years, sat   5
glumly in his bunting-draped home, surrounded by snapshots of his
twelve children: one in the Navy, one in the Army, one in the Merchant
Marine, one a Red Cross ambulance driver. Complained old Maniscalco, "I wanta be citizen, wanta fish. What I do now? Can't get job.
Not a citizen. Can't get papers, can't write. My head she too damn
hard."

The orders would also play hob with West Coast agriculture. In   6
the Los Angeles area, Japanese produce more than half the truck crops—
especially celery, spinach, beets, string beans—vegetables which take
infinite work and patience. In Santa Cruz County, a $500,000 crop of
sprouts and artichokes awaited harvesting by Italians. Most of California's tomato crop, which accounts for a fourth of U.S. canned tomatoes,
has been grown by Japanese farmers.

But the West Coast valued safety more than vegetables, more than   7
the comfort or livelihood of foreigners who might be innocent but were
still foreigners. Francis Biddle's measures struck most West Coast citizens, indeed, as wishy-washy, especially in giving aliens one to three
weeks of grace to move from restricted zones. From California's Attorney General Earl Warren, from 100 sheriffs and district attorneys and
from Los Angeles' Mayor Fletcher Bowron came a demand that all
enemy aliens be removed at least 200 miles inland. The Los Angeles
County Defense Council wanted them all interned.

By week's end the coast was sure that its fears were not hysterical.   8
FBI agents continued their raids. In one of them, made on "very definite
suspicions of espionage," at Vallejo, Calif. near the Navy's Big Mare
Island yard, they seized Navy signal flags and flares, arrested nine Japs.

Content Considerations

1. Characterize the tone of this news report. How does the writer view the events it contains?
2. What fears prompted the internment of Japanese Americans? Gather more information about the reasons given by government and military officials at the time as well as reactions from civilians of both Japanese and non-Japanese ancestry.
3. What rules or policies should govern the treatment of citizens whose ancestry relates them to an enemy country?

Korematsu v. United States

*As a result of Executive Order No. 9066, Japanese Americans living on the
West Coast were subject to many orders regarding curfews and evacuation from
certain areas. Forced to leave their homes, they were relocated, detained in
camps, and forced to remain there until the end of World War II. As one might
expect, some Japanese Americans objected to those orders; some refused to
follow them. Some sought relief in the courts.*

In the case of Korematsu v. United States, *petitioner Korematsu was
an American citizen whose parents had been born in Japan. Korematsu violated
a military order issued by General DeWitt, Civilian Exclusion Order No. 34
of the Commanding General of the Western Command, U.S. Army. Korematsu's case came before the Supreme Court; the Court decided against him in
1944.*

*Excerpts of that ruling follow. Before you read them, write a paragraph
on the reasons one could give for upholding an order such as Exclusion Order
No. 34 and the reasons one could give for judging it invalid. Then, as you
read the majority opinion by Justice Black, a concurring opinion by Justice
Frankfurter, and dissenting opinions by Justices Murphy and Jackson, be aware
of the reasons they give for their decisions.*

Korematsu *v.* United States
H. Black, F. Frankfurter, F. Murphy, and R.H. Jackson

Source: 323 U.S. 214

MR. JUSTICE BLACK delivered the opinion of the court.

The petitioner, an American citizen of Japanese descent, was con- 1
victed in a Federal District Court for remaining in San Leandro, California, a "Military Area," contrary to Civilian Exclusion Order No. 34
of the Commanding General of the Western Command, U.S. Army,
which directed that after May 9, 1942, all persons of Japanese ancestry
should be excluded from that area. No question was raised as to petitioner's loyalty to the United States. The Circuit Court of Appeals af-

firmed, and the importance of the constitutional questions involved caused us to grant certiorari.

It should be noted, to begin with, that all legal restrictions which curtail the civil rights of a single racial group are immediately suspect. That is not to say that such restrictions are unconstitutional. It is to say that courts must subject them to the most rigid scrutiny. Pressing public necessity may sometimes justify the existence of such restrictions; racial antagonism never can.

In the instant case, prosecution of the petitioner was begun by information charging violation of an Act of Congress, of March 21, 1942, 56 Stat. 173, which provides that:

Whoever shall enter, remain in, leave, or commit any act in any military area or military zone prescribed, under the authority of an executive order of the President, by the secretary of war, or by any military commander designated by the secretary of war, contrary to the restrictions applicable to any such area or zone or contrary to the order of the secretary of war or any such military commander, shall, if it appears that he knew or should have known of the existence and extent of the restrictions or order and that his act was in violation thereof, be guilty of a misdemeanor and upon conviction shall be liable to a fine of not to exceed $5,000 or to imprisonment for not more than one year, or both, for each offense.

Exclusion Order No. 34, which the petitioner knowingly and admittedly violated, was one of a number of military orders and proclamations, all of which were substantially based upon Executive Order No. 9066, 7 Fed. Reg. 1407. That order, issued after we were at war with Japan, declared that "the successful prosecution of the war requires every possible protection against espionage and against sabotage to national-defense material, national-defense premises, and national-defense utilities. . . . "

One of the series of orders and proclamations, a curfew order, which, like the exclusion order here was promulgated pursuant to Executive Order 9066, subjected all persons of Japanese ancestry in prescribed West Coast military areas to remain in their residences from 8 P.M. to 6 A.M. As is the case with the exclusion order here, that prior curfew order was designed as a "protection against espionage and against sabotage." In *Hirabayashi v. United States,* 320 U.S. 81, we sustained a conviction obtained for violation of the curfew order. The *Hirabayashi* conviction and this one thus rest on the same 1942 congressional act and the same basic executive and military orders, all of which orders were aimed at the twin dangers of espionage and sabotage.

The 1942 act was attacked in the *Hirabayashi* case as an unconstitutional delegation of power; it was contended that the curfew order and other orders on which it rested were beyond the war powers of the Congress, the military authorities, and of the President, as commander in chief of the Army; and, finally, that to apply the curfew order against none but citizens of Japanese ancestry amounted to a constitutionally prohibited discrimination solely on account of race. To these questions, we gave the serious consideration which their importance justified. We upheld the curfew order as an exercise of the power of the government to take steps necessary to prevent espionage and sabotage in an area threatened by Japanese attack.

In the light of the principles we announced in the *Hirabayashi* case,   8 we are unable to conclude that it was beyond the war power of Congress and the executive to exclude those of Japanese ancestry from the West Coast war area at the time they did. True, exclusion from the area in which one's home is located is a far greater deprivation than constant confinement to the home from 8 P.M. to 6 A.M. Nothing short of apprehension by the proper military authorities of the gravest imminent danger to the public safety can constitutionally justify either. But exclusion from a threatened area, no less than curfew, has a definite and close relationship to the prevention of espionage and sabotage. The military authorities, charged with the primary responsibility of defending our shores, concluded that curfew provided inadequate protection and ordered exclusion. They did so, as pointed out in our *Hirabayashi* opinion, in accordance with congressional authority to the military to say who should and who should not remain in the threatened areas.

In this case the petitioner challenges the assumptions upon which   9 we rested our conclusions in the *Hirabayashi* case. He also urges that by May 1942, when Order No. 34 was promulgated, all danger of Japanese invasion of the West Coast had disappeared. After careful consideration of these contentions, we are compelled to reject them.

Here, as in the *Hirabayashi* case, *supra,* at p. 99,   10

> We cannot reject as unfounded the judgment of the military authorities and of Congress that there were disloyal members of that population, whose number and strength could not be precisely and quickly ascertained. We cannot say that the warmaking branches of the government did not have ground for believing that in a critical hour such persons could not readily be isolated and separately dealt with, and constituted a menace to the national defense and safety, which demanded that prompt and adequate measures be taken to guard against it . . .

It is said that we are dealing here with the case of imprisonment   11 of a citizen in a concentration camp solely because of his ancestry, without evidence or inquiry concerning his loyalty and good disposition toward the United States. Our task would be simpler, our duty clear, were this a case involving the imprisonment of a loyal citizen in a concentration camp because of racial prejudice. Regardless of the true nature of the assembly and relocation centers—and we deem it unjustifiable to call them concentration camps with all the ugly connotations that term implies—we are dealing specially with nothing but an exclusion order. To cast this case into outlines of racial prejudice, without reference to the real military dangers which were presented, merely confuses the issue.

Korematsu was not excluded from the Military Area because of   12
hostility to him or his race. He *was* excluded because we are at war with the Japanese Empire, because the properly constituted military authorities feared an invasion of our West Coast and felt constrained to take proper security measures, because they decided that the military urgency of the situation demanded that all citizens of Japanese ancestry be segregated from the West Coast temporarily, and, finally, because Congress, reposing its confidence in this time of war in our military leaders—as inevitably it must—determined that they should have the power to do just this.

There was evidence of disloyalty on the part of some, the military   13
authorities considered that the need for action was great, and time was short. We cannot—by availing ourselves of the calm perspective of hindsight—now say that at the time these actions were unjustified.

MR. JUSTICE FRANKFURTER, concurring:

According to my reading of Civilian Exclusion Order No. 34, it   14
was an offense for Korematsu to be found in Military Area No. 1, the territory wherein he was previously living, except within the bounds of the established Assembly Center of that area. Even though the various orders issued by General DeWitt be deemed a comprehensive code of instructions, their tenor is clear and not contradictory. They put upon Korematsu the obligation to leave Military Area No. 1, but only by the method prescribed in the instructions, i.e., by reporting to the Assembly Center. I am unable to see how the legal considerations that led to the decision in Hirabayashi v. United States, 320 U.S. 81, fail to sustain the military order which made the conduct now in controversy a crime. And so I join in the opinion of the Court, but should like to add a few words of my own.

The provisions of the Constitution which confer on the Congress   15
and the President powers to enable this country to wage war are as much

part of the Constitution as provisions looking to a nation at peace. And
we have had recent occasion to quote approvingly the statement of former Chief Justice Hughes that the war power of the government is "the
power to wage war successfully." *Hirabayashi* v. *United States, supra* at
93; and see *Home Bldg. & L. Assn.* v. *Blaisdell,* 290 U.S. 398, 426. Therefore, the validity of action under the war power must be judged wholly
in the context of war. That action is not to be stigmatized as lawless
because like action in times of peace would be lawless. To talk about a
military order that expresses an allowable judgment of war needs by
those entrusted with the duty of conducting war as "an unconstitutional
order" is to suffuse a part of the Constitution with an atmosphere of
unconstitutionality.

The respective spheres of action of military authorities and of judges   16
are of course very different. But within their sphere, military authorities
are no more outside the bounds of obedience to the Constitution than
are judges within theirs. "The war power of the United States, like its
other powers . . . is subject to applicable constitutional limitations,"
Hamilton v. *Kentucky Distilleries Co.,* 251 U.S. 146, 156. To recognize
that military orders are "reasonably expedient military precautions" in
time of war and yet to deny them constitutional legitimacy makes of
the Constitution an instrument for dialectic subtleties not reasonably to
be attributed to the hard-headed framers, of whom a majority had had
actual participation in war.

If a military order such as that under review does not transcend   17
the means appropriate for conducting war, such action by the military
is as constitutional as would be any authorized action by the Interstate
Commerce Commission within the limits of the constitutional power
to regulate commerce. And being an exercise of the war power explicitly
granted by the Constitution for safeguarding the national life by pros-
ecuting war effectively, I find nothing in the Constitution which denies
to Congress the power to enforce such a valid military order by making
its violation an offense triable in the civil courts. Compare *Interstate
Commerce Commission* v. *Brimson,* 154 U.S. 447; 155 U.S. 3, and *Mon-
ongabela Bridge Co.* v. *United States,* 216 U.S. 177. To find that the
Constitution does not forbid the military measures now complained of
does not carry with it approval of that which Congress and the executive
did. That is their business, not ours.

MR. JUSTICE MURPHY, dissenting.

It must be conceded that the military and naval situation in the   18
spring of 1942 was such as to generate a very real fear of invasion of
the Pacific Coast, accompanied by fears of sabotage and espionage in

that area. The military command was therefore justified in adopting all reasonable means necessary to combat these dangers. In adjudging the military action taken in light of the then apparent dangers, we must not erect too high or too meticulous standards; it is necessary only that the action have some reasonable relation to the removal of the dangers of invasion, sabotage, and espionage. But the exclusion, either temporarily or permanently, of all persons with Japanese blood in their veins has no such reasonable relation. And that relation is lacking because the exclusion order necessarily must rely for its reasonableness upon the assumption that *all* persons of Japanese ancestry may have a dangerous tendency to commit sabotage and espionage and to aid our Japanese enemy in other ways. It is difficult to believe that reason, logic, or experience could be marshaled in support of such an assumption.

That this forced exclusion was the result in good measure of this [19] erroneous assumption of racial guilt rather than bona fide military necessity is evidenced by the Commanding General's Final Report on the evacuation from the Pacific Coast area. In it he refers to all individuals of Japanese descent as "subversive," as belonging to "an enemy race" whose "racial strains are undiluted," and as constituting "over 112,000 potential enemies . . . at large today" along the Pacific Coast. In support of this blanket condemnation of all persons of Japanese descent, however, no reliable evidence is cited to show that such individuals were generally disloyal, or had generally so conducted themselves in this area as to constitute a special menace to defense installations or war industries, or had otherwise by their behavior furnished reasonable ground for their exclusion as a group.

Justification for the exclusion is sought, instead, mainly upon ques- [20] tionable racial and sociological grounds not ordinarily within the realm of expert military judgment, supplemented by certain semi-military conclusions drawn from an unwarranted use of circumstantial evidence. Individuals of Japanese ancestry are condemned because they are said to be "a large, unassimilated, tightly knit racial group, bound to an enemy nation by strong ties of race, culture, custom and religion." They are claimed to be given to "emperor-worshipping ceremonies." Japanese language schools and allegedly pro-Japanese organizations are cited as evidence of possible group disloyalty, together with facts as to certain persons being educated and residing at length in japan. It is intimated that many of these individuals deliberately resided "adjacent to strategic points," thus enabling them "to carry into execution a tremendous program of sabotage on a mass scale should any considerable number of them have been inclined to do so."

The need for protective custody is also asserted. The report refers [21] without identity to "numerous incidents of violence" as well as to other admittedly unverified or cumulative incidents. From this, plus certain other events not shown to have been connected with the Japanese Americans, it is concluded that the "situation was fraught with danger to the Japanese population itself" and that the general public "was ready to take matters into its own hands." Finally, it is intimated, though not directly charged or proved, that persons of Japanese ancestry were responsible for three minor isolated shellings and bombings of the Pacific Coast area, as well as for unidentified radio transmissions and night signaling.

The main reasons relied upon by those responsible for the forced   22
evacuation, therefore, do not prove a reasonable relation between the group characteristics of Japanese Americans and the dangers of invasion, sabotage, and espionage. The reasons appear, instead, to be largely an accumulation of much of the misinformation, half-truths, and insinuations that for years have been directed against Japanese Americans by people with racial and economic prejudices—the same people who have been among the foremost advocates of the evacuation. A military judgment based upon such racial and sociological considerations is not entitled to the great weight ordinarily given the judgments based upon strictly military considerations. Especially is this so when every charge relative to race, religion, culture, geographical location, and legal and economic status has been substantially discredited by independent studies made by experts in these matters.

The military necessity which is essential to the validity of the evac-   23
uation order thus resolves itself into a few intimations that certain individuals actively aided the enemy, from which it is inferred that the entire group of Japanese Americans could not be trusted to be or remain loyal to the United States. . . .

No adequate reason is given for the failure to treat these Japanese   24
Americans on an individual basis by holding investigations and hearings to separate the loyal from the disloyal, as was done in the case of persons of German and Italian ancestry. See House Report No. 2124 (77th Cong., 2d Sess.) 247-52. It is asserted merely that the loyalties of this group "were unknown and time was of the essence." Yet nearly four months elapsed after Pearl Harbor before the first exclusion order was issued; nearly eight months went by until the last order was issued; and the last of these "subversive" persons was not actually removed until almost eleven months had elapsed. Leisure and deliberation seem to have been more of the essence than speed. And the fact that conditions were not such as to warrant a declaration of martial law adds strength to the belief that the factors of time and military necessity were not as urgent as they have been represented to be.

Moreover, there was no adequate proof that the Federal Bureau of   25

Investigation and the military and naval intelligence services did not have the espionage and sabotage situation well in hand during this long period. Nor is there any denial of the fact that not one person of Japanese ancestry was accused or convicted of espionage or sabotage after Pearl Harbor while they were still free, a fact which is some evidence of the loyalty of the vast majority of these individuals and of the effectiveness of the established methods of combatting these evils. It seems incredible that under these circumstances it would have been impossible to hold loyalty hearings for the mere 112,000 persons involved—or at least for the 70,000 American citizens—especially when a large part of this number represented children and elderly men and women. Any inconvenience that may have accompanied an attempt to conform to procedural due process cannot be said to justify violations of constitutional rights of individuals.

I dissent, therefore, from this legalization of racism. Racial discrimination in any form and in any degree has no justifiable part whatever in our democratic way of life. It is unattractive in any setting but it is utterly revolting among a free people who have embraced the principles set forth in the Constitution of the United States. All residents of this nation are kin in some way by blood or culture to a foreign land. Yet they are primarily and necessarily a part of the new and distinct civilization of the United States. They must accordingly be treated at all times as the heirs of the American experiment and as entitled to all the rights and freedoms guaranteed by the Constitution. **26**

MR. JUSTICE JACKSON, dissenting.

Korematsu was born on our soil, of parents born in Japan. The **27** Constitution makes him a citizen of the United States by nativity and a citizen of California by residence. No claim is made that he is not loyal to this country. There is no suggestion that apart from the matter involved here he is not law-abiding and well disposed. Korematsu, however, has been convicted of an act not commonly a crime. It consists merely of being present in the state whereof he is a citizen, near the place where he was born, and where all his life he has lived.

Even more unusual is the series of military orders which made this **28** conduct a crime. They forbid such a one to remain, and they also forbid him to leave. They were so drawn that the only way Korematsu could avoid violation was to give himself up to the military authority. This meant submission to custody, examination, and transportation out of the territory, to be followed by indeterminate confinement in detention camps.

A citizen's presence in the locality, however, was made a crime **29** only if his parents were of Japanese birth. Had Korematsu been one of four—the others being, say, a German alien enemy, an Italian alien enemy, and a citizen of American-born ancestors convicted of treason but out on parole—only Korematsu's presence would have violated the order. The difference between their innocence and his crime would result, not from anything he did, said, or thought different than they but only in that he was born of different racial stock.

Now, if any fundamental assumption underlies our system, it is 30 that guilt is personal and not inheritable. Even if all of one's antecedents had been convicted of treason, the Constitution forbids its penalties to be visited upon him, for it provides that "no attainder of treason shall work corruption of blood or forfeiture except during the life of the person attainted." But here is an attempt to make an otherwise innocent act a crime merely because this prisoner is the son of parents as to whom he had no choice and belongs to a race from which there is no way to resign. If Congress in peacetime legislation should enact such a criminal law, I should suppose this Court would refuse to enforce it.

But the "law" which this prisoner is convicted of disregarding is 31 not found in an act of Congress but in a military order. Neither the act of Congress nor the executive order of the President, nor both together, would afford a basis for this conviction. It rests on the orders of General DeWitt. And it is said that if the military commander had reasonable military grounds for promulgating the orders, they are constitutional and become law, and the Court is required to enforce them. There are several reasons why I cannot subscribe to this doctrine.

It would be impracticable and dangerous idealism to expect or 32 insist that each specific military command in an area of probable operations will conform to conventional tests of constitutionality. When an area is so beset that it must be put under military control at all, the paramount consideration is that its measures be successful rather than legal. The armed services must protect a society, not merely its Constitution. The very essence of the military job is to marshal physical force, to remove every obstacle to its effectiveness, to give it every strategic advantage. Defense measures will not, and often should not, be held within the limits that bind civil authority in peace. No court can require such a commander in such circumstances to act as a reasonable man; he may be unreasonably cautious and exacting. Perhaps he should be. But a commander in temporarily focusing the life of a community on defense is carrying out a military program; he is not making law in the sense the courts know the term. He issues orders, and they may have a certain authority as military commands, although they may be very bad as constitutional law.

But if we cannot confine military expedients by the Constitution, 33 neither would I distort the Constitution to approve all that the military may deem expedient. That is what the Court appears to be doing, whether consciously or not. I cannot say, from any evidence before me, that the orders of General DeWitt were not reasonably expedient military precautions, nor could I say that they were. But even if they were permissible military procedures, I deny that it follows that they are constitutional. If, as the Court holds, it does follow, then we may as well say that any military order will be constitutional and have done with it. . . .

A military order, however unconstitutional, is not apt to last longer   34
than the military emergency. Even during that period a succeeding commander may revoke it all. But once a judicial opinion rationalizes such an order to show that it conforms to the Constitution, or rather rationalizes the Constitution to show that the Constitution sanctions such an order, the Court for all time has validated the principle of racial discrimination in criminal procedure and of transplanting American citizens. The principle then lies about like a loaded weapon ready for the hand of any authority that can bring forward a plausible claim of an urgent need. Every repetition imbeds that principle more deeply in our law and thinking and expands it to new purposes. All who observe the work of courts are familiar with what Judge Cardozo described as "the tendency of a principle to expand itself to the limit of its logic." A military commander may overstep the bounds of constitutionality and it is an incident. But if we review and approve, that passing incident becomes the doctrine of the Constitution. There it has a generative power of its own, and all that it creates will be in its own image. Nothing better illustrates this danger than does the Court's opinion in this case. . . .

I should hold that a civil court cannot be made to enforce an order   35
which violates constitutional limitations even if it is a reasonable exercise of military authority. The courts can exercise only the judicial power, can apply only law, and must abide by the Constitution, or they cease to be civil courts and become instruments of military policy.

Content Considerations

1. How do the opinions of dissenting Justices Murphy and Jackson answer those of Justices Black and Frankfurter? On what points did the Korematsu decision seem to rest?
2. What part did racial prejudice have in the internment? What part did expediency play?
3. What conclusions do you draw about the treatment of Japanese American civilians in the United States during World War II?

On Patrol

The United States became involved with conflicts in Vietnam in the 1940s, siding with France in the French-Indochinese war and providing funds for its war costs. By 1959, after the Communist Party of North Vietnam announced that it would "liberate" South Vietnam from imperialist powers, the United States had sent about 2,000 military men to act as "advisors" to the South Vietnamese. By 1963, President Kennedy had sent 17,000 military personnel; under President Johnson that number grew to more than 500,000, falling to about 69,000 by 1972. The Paris Peace Accords resulted in a cease-fire on January 30, 1973; United States' official presence in Vietnam ended April 29, 1975.

Ron Kovic enlisted in the Marines after graduating from high school in 1963. During his second tour of duty in Vietnam he was wounded—paralyzed below the chest. His first book, Born on the Fourth of July, *from which the following is excerpted, was published in 1976; others have followed.*

The excerpt describes what happened one night in a Vietnamese village when the soldiers were out on patrol. Before you begin reading, write about how soldiers might feel about the civilian population in a country where they have been sent to fight.

HE WENT OUT ON PATROL with the others the night of the ambush at exactly eight o'clock, loading a round into the chamber of his weapon before he walked outside the tent and into the dark and rain. As usual he had made all the men put on camouflage from head to toe, made sure they had all blackened their faces, and attached twigs and branches to their arms and legs with rubber bands.

One by one the scouts moved slowly past the thick barbed wire and began to walk along the bank of the river, heading toward the graveyard where the ambush would be set up. They were moving north exactly as planned, a line of shadows tightly bunched in the rain. Sometimes it would stop raining and they would spread out somewhat more, but mostly they continued to bunch up together, as if they were afraid of losing their way.

There was a rice paddy on the edge of the graveyard. No one said a word as they walked through it and he thought he could hear voices from the village. He could smell the familiar smoke from the fires in the huts and he knew that the people who went out fishing each day must have come home. They were the people he watched every morning moving quietly in their small boats down toward the mouth of the river, heading out to the sea. Some of the older men reminded him of his father, going to work each morning and coming back home every night to sit by their fires with their children cooking their fish. They must talk about us sometimes, he thought. He wondered a lot what it was they thought about him and the men.

He remembered how difficult it had been when he had first come 4 to the war to tell the villagers from the enemy and sometimes it had seemed easier to hate all of them, but he had always tried very hard not to. He wished he could be sure they understood that he and the men were there because they were trying to help all of them save their country from the communists.

They were on a rice dike that bordered the graveyard. The voices 5 from the huts nearby seemed quite loud. He looked up ahead to where the lieutenant who had come along with them that night was standing. The lieutenant had sent one of the men, Molina, on across the rice dikes almost to the edge of the village. The cold rain was still coming down very hard and the men behind him were standing like a line of statues waiting for the next command.

But now something was wrong up ahead. He could see Molina 6 waving his hands excitedly trying to tell the lieutenant something. Stumbling over the dikes, almost crawling, Molina came back toward the lieutenant. He saw him whisper something in his ear. And now the lieutenant turned and looked at him. "Sergeant," he said, "Molina and I are going to get a look up ahead. Stay here with the team."

Balancing on the dike, he turned around slowly after the lieutenant 7 had gone, motioning with his rifle for all of the men in back of him to get down. Each one, carefully, one after the other, squatted along the dike on one knee, waiting in the rain to move out again. They were all shivering from the cold.

They waited for what seemed a long time and then the lieutenant 8 and Molina appeared suddenly through the darkness. He could tell from their faces that they had seen something. They had seen something up ahead, he was sure, and they were going to tell him what they had just seen. He stood up, too excited to stay kneeling down on the dike.

"What is it?" he cried. 9

"Be quiet," whispered the lieutenant sharply, grabbing his arm, 10 almost throwing him into the paddy. He began talking very quickly and much louder than he should have. "I think we found them. I think we found them," he repeated, almost shouting.

He didn't know what the lieutenant meant. "What?" he said. 11

"The sappers, the sappers! Let's go!" The lieutenant was taking over now. He seemed very sure of himself, he was acting very confident. "Let's go, goddamn it!"   12

He clicked his rifle off safety and got his men up quickly, urging them forward, following the lieutenant and Molina toward the edge of the village. They ran through the paddy, splashing like a family of ducks. This time he hoped and prayed it would be the real enemy. He would be ready for them this time. Here was another chance, he thought. He was so excited he ran straight into the lieutenant, bouncing clumsily off his chest.   13

"I'm sorry, sir," he said.   14

"Quiet! They're out there," the lieutenant whispered to him, motioning to the rest of the men to get down on their hands and knees now. They crawled to the tree line, then along the back of the rice paddy through almost a foot of water, until the whole team lay in a long line pressed up against the dike, facing the village.   15

He saw a light, a fire he thought, flickering in the distance off to the right of the village, with little dark figures that seemed to be moving behind it. He could not tell how far away they were from there. It was very hard to tell distance in the dark.   16

The lieutenant moved next to him. "You see?" he whispered. "Look," he said, very keyed up now. "They've got rifles. Can you see the rifles? Can you see them?" the lieutenant asked him.   17

He looked very hard through the rain.   18

"Can you see them?"   19

"Yes, I see them. I see them," he said. He was very sure.   20

The lieutenant put his arm around him and whispered in his ear. "Tell them down at the end to give me an illumination. I want this whole place lit up like a fucking Christmas tree."   21

Turning quickly to the man on his right, he told him what the lieutenant had said. He told him to pass the instructions all the way to the end of the line, where a flare would be fired just above the small fire near the village.   22

Lying there in the mud behind the dike, he stared at the fire that still flickered in the rain. He could still see the little figures moving back and forth against it like small shadows on a screen. He felt the whole line tense, then heard the WOOOORSHH of the flare cracking overhead in a tremendous ball of sputtering light turning night into day, arching over their heads toward the small fire that he now saw was burning inside an open hut.   23

Suddenly someone was firing from the end with his rifle, and now the whole line opened up, roaring their weapons like thunder, pulling their triggers again and again without even thinking, emptying every-   24 thing they had into the hut in a tremendous stream of bright orange tracers that criss-crossed each other in the night.

The flare arched its last sputtering bits into the village and it be- 25 came dark, and all he could see were the bright orange embers from the fire that had gone out.

And he could hear them. 26

There were voices screaming. 27

"What happened? Goddamn it, what happened?" yelled the 28 lieutenant.

The voices were screaming from inside the hut. 29

"Who gave the order to fire? I wanna know who gave the order 30 to fire."

The lieutenant was standing up now, looking up and down the 31 line of men still lying in the rain.

He found that he was shaking. It had all happened so quickly. 32

"We better get a killer team out there," he heard Molina say. 33

"All right, all right. Sergeant," the lieutenant said to him, "get 34 out there with Molina and tell me how many we got."

He got to his feet and quickly got five of the men together, leading 35 them over the dike and through the water to the hut from where the screams were still coming. It was much closer than he had first thought. Now he could see very clearly the smoldering embers of the fire that had been blown out by the terrific blast of their rifles.

Molina turned the beam of his flashlight into the hut. "Oh God," 36 he said. "Oh Jesus Christ." He started to cry. "We just shot up a bunch of kids!"

The floor of the small hut was covered with them, screaming and 37 thrashing their arms back and forth, lying in pools of blood, crying wildly, screaming again and again. They were shot in the face, in the chest, in the legs, moaning and crying.

"Oh Jesus!" he cried. 38

He could hear the lieutenant shouting at them, wanting to know 39 how many they had killed.

There was an old man in the corner with his head blown off from 40 his eyes up, his brains hanging out of his head like jelly. He kept looking at the strange sight, he had never seen anything like it before. A small boy next to the old man was still alive, although he had been shot many times. He was crying softly, lying in a large pool of blood. His small foot had been shot almost completely off and seemed to be hanging by a thread.

"What's happening? What's going on up there?" The lieutenant 41 was getting very impatient now.

Molina shouted for the lieutenant to come quickly. "You better   42
get up here. There's a lot of wounded people up here."

He heard a small girl moaning now. She was shot through the   43
stomach and bleeding out of the rear end. All he could see now was
blood everywhere and he heard their screams with his heart racing like
it had never raced before. He felt crazy and weak as he stood there
staring at them with the rest of the men, staring down onto the floor
like it was a nightmare, like it was some kind of dream and it really
wasn't happening.

And then he could no longer stand watching. They were people,   44
he thought, children and old men, people, people like himself, and he
had to do something, he had to move, he had to help, do something.
He jerked the green medical bag off his back, ripping it open and grabbing for bandages, yelling at Molina to please come and help him. He
knelt down in the middle of the screaming bodies and began bandaging
them, trying to cover the holes where the blood was still spurting out.
"It's gonna be okay. It's gonna be okay," he tried to say, but he was
crying now, crying and still trying to bandage them all up. He moved
from body to body searching in the dark with his fingers for the holes
the bullets had made, bandaging each one as quickly as he could, his
shaking hands wet with the blood. It was raining into the hut and a cold
wind swept his face as he moved in the dark.

The lieutenant had just come up with the others.   45

"Help me!" he screamed. "Somebody help!"   46

"Well goddamn it, sergeant! What's the matter? How many did   47
we kill?"

"They're children!" he screamed at the lieutenant.   48

"Children and old men!" cried Molina.   49

"Where are their rifles?" the lieutenant asked.   50

"There aren't any rifles," he said.   51

"Well, help him then!" screamed the lieutenant to the rest of the   52
men. The men stood in the entrance of the hut, but they would not
move. "Help him, help him. I'm ordering you to help him!"

The men were not moving and some of them were crying now,   53
dropping their rifles and sitting down on the wet ground. They were
weeping now with their hands against their faces. 'Oh Jesus, oh God,
forgive us."

"Forgive us for what we've done!" he heard Molina cry.   54

"Get up," screamed the lieutenant. "What do you think this is?   55
I'm ordering you all to get up."

Some of the men began slowly crawling over the bodies, grabbing   56
for the bandages that were still left.

By now some of the villagers had gathered outside the hut. He 57
could hear them shouting angrily. He knew they must be cursing them.

"You better get a fucking chopper in here," someone was yelling. 58

"Where's the radio man? Get the radio man!" 59

"Hello, Cactus Red. This is Red Light Two. Ahhh this is Red 60
Light Two. We need an emergency evac. We got a lot of wounded . . .
ahh . . . friendly wounded. A lot of friendly wounded out here." He
could hear the lieutenant on the radio, trying to tell the helicopters where
to come.

The men in the hut were just sitting there crying. They could not 61
move, and they did not listen to the lieutenant's orders. They just sat
with the rain pouring down on them through the roof, crying and not
moving.

"You men! You men have got to start listening to me. You gotta 62
stop crying like babies and start acting like marines!" The lieutenant
who was off the radio now was shoving the men, pleading with them
to move. "You're men, not babies. It's all a mistake. It wasn't your
fault. They got in the way. Don't you people understand—they got in
the goddamn way!"

When the medivac chopper came, he picked up the little boy who 63
was lying next to the old man. His foot came off and he grabbed it up
quickly and bandaged it against the bottom stump of the boy's leg. He
held him looking into his frightened eyes and carried him up to the open
door of the helicopter. The boy was still crying softly when he handed
him to the gunner.

And when it was all over and all the wounded had been loaded 64
aboard, he helped the lieutenant move the men back on patrol. They
walked away from the hut in the rain. And now he felt his body go
numb and heavy, feeling awful and sick inside like the night the corporal
had died, as they moved along in the dark and the rain behind the
lieutenant toward the graveyard.

Content Considerations

1. What conditions led to the horror Kovic describes? Could it have been avoided? Who is to blame?
2. What attitudes toward noncombatants do the soldiers on patrol seem to have? What does this piece suggest about civilian lives in wartime?
3. Respond by focusing on the narrator and the "he" of the story. What are the effects of this night's events on the unnamed soldier? Putting yourself in his place, how would the events have affected you?

— *Ideas for Discussion, Writing, and Research* —

1. Using information from any five essays in this chapter, discuss the possible fates of civilians during wartime.

2. How do the views of Orwell and Snow differ regarding civilian casualties? How are they similar?

3. Using the selections by Harwit, Chadwick, and Kovic, explore the ways that war technology affects civilians.

4. What is a war crime? Is there such a thing? Review the pieces written by Chadwick, Orwell, Snow, and Kovic as well as "Enemy Aliens" and "Korematsu v. United States," then investigate other sources to help you form your position.

5. Answer George Orwell's question: "Why is it worse to kill civilians than soldiers?" (page 210). Use any four of the readings in this chapter as well as your own reasoning and beliefs to support your answer.

6. Construct an argument supporting or opposing the way people of Japanese ancestry were treated by the U.S. government during World War II. Gather information from other sources to help you do so.

7. What kinds of attitudes do the soldiers in the pieces by Chadwick and Kovic display toward civilians?

8. Using any three pieces in this chapter (as well as any other sources you need), explore the attitudes civilians of various types display toward war. How do their attitudes affect their behavior? How do their attitudes affect war?

9. To what extent do "Enemy Aliens," "Korematsu v. United States," and the "War at Nine Years Old" suggest that racial or ethnic prejudice affects the treatment of civilians during wartime? To what extent might such prejudice be necessary to war?

10. If all civilians were somehow safe from all dangers during wartime, could a war be waged? What would it be like? Explore the possibility that war could not exist if no civilian lives would be endangered by it.

5

Who Needs to Know?

IT WAS COMPELLING. Addictive, even. Night after night, images of super high-tech weapons cleanly, surgically, removing targets: bridges, command centers, incoming SCUD missiles. CNN's Peter Arnett and others showing us the night sky over Baghdad streaked with a pyrotechnic display that made even the largest July Fourth celebration look timid. Those jubilant pilots of returning jet fighter-bombers, faces flushed and radiant, exclaiming repeatedly about taking out their targets while jinking around hose-streams of triple A (antiaircraft artillery). And those Marines. The few, the proud. Their young, earnest faces looking straight into the cameras, trying to look fierce.

All the big names in journalism showed up, at least briefly, to don a bush jacket, sling a gas mask over one shoulder, and interview a general or a private or another journalist.

We were saturated with news of the Persian Gulf war. Day and night, every television station, every newspaper, every news magazine inundated us with ink and images of the slow buildup and lightning conclusion of the battle. It was the mother of all news events.

During the troop deployment, the initial skirmishes, and the final four-day battle, there were occasional bleats of protest from the news media, protests that the military command was not allowing reporters freedom to report. Reporters charged that they were denied access to "grunts," the front-line foot soldier on whom the brunt of the war would necessarily fall. Others railed at the choreographed military briefings, long on jargon and jingoism, they said, but very short on facts. Still others insisted that the media was being used by the government as a public relations arms: good news only, let's all rally behind the troops. Throughout the protests of the media, polls showed the public solidly behind the Pentagon—and opposed to the media. An interesting fact, considering the First Amendment.

The Gulf war was not the first war in which the news media was in conflict with the government and the military. In fact, the nation was founded on a belief that government and press must necessarily be adversaries: The First Amendment to the Constitution was a recognition of the importance of a free press to a free people and a belief that any government would attempt to muzzle it. That belief proved correct very quickly. In 1798, Federalist supporters of George Washington and Alexander Hamilton pushed through Congress the Alien and Sedition Acts, which made it a federal offense to criticize the government or any official. Even Thomas Jefferson, the ultimate liberal, tried to invoke the provisions of the act, before reversing himself and seeking the repeal of the laws.

During the Civil War, Abraham Lincoln used Executive Authority to imprison newspaper editors critical of the war effort. In 1898, William Randolph Hearst's chain of newspapers virtually carried the United States into war with Spain, as he published daily accounts of supposed atrocities against the Cubans. Americans in World War I rushed to embrace Woodrow Wilson's "war to make the world safe for democracy," and they allowed no criticism of governmental policies.

Americans approached World War II with a no-nonsense, sleeves-rolled-up attitude, intent on ending a massively destructive enterprise. The reporting from correspondents such as Edward R. Murrow, Walter Cronkite, and Ernie Pyle was just as straightforward. Not often critical of U.S. policy or of the military, the media often were used as vehicles for propaganda, but in general were left alone to report any news that didn't deal directly with troop movements or intended maneuvers.

In fact, few questioned the role of the press until the war in Vietnam.

And even then, in what was the first "television war" in history, there were few hard questions in the beginning. Each evening, television anchormen devoted three or four minutes to the war in Southeast Asia, three or four edited minutes that excised most of the blood and shredded viscera of the casualties of the war. Major newspapers editorialized about the threat of Communism, pushed for Americans to support their troops. Eventually, after several years of war in which little progress was seen despite the rosy briefings by military officers, some journalists began to question the causes and goals of the conflict.

It was not until after the fall of Saigon in 1975 that anyone began asking hard questions about the role of the press. A few blamed the outcome of the war on the media, but the Army's own official history of the war in Vietnam denies the charge (see the chapter on Vietnam).

The questions lingered, however. What is the role of news media in a war? How free should reporters be to report what they see and discover, short of revealing important information to the enemy? Is television reporting, by its very nature (remember Marshall McLuhan?), essentially different from print media? Should the military dole out the news at briefings or is that merely self-serving propaganda? If news organizations are strictly controlled by the military or government, where do we get unbiased information about the war? Should reporters be allowed to broadcast from the capital of the enemy?

All of these queries moved to prime time during the Persian Gulf war.

There, in a carefully orchestrated series of events, the media were muzzled. Whether you believe that was good or bad depends of course on your attitudes toward the media, toward the war, toward the military, and toward the government. There was no question that the military press briefers put the best face on all news: extensive civilian casualties during an errant bombing attack were blandly described as "collateral damage."

News organizations, primarily print media, were outraged by what they saw as control of the news by the Pentagon. Broadcast news officials were more sanguine. Print journalists (who historically have had little good to say about electronic media types) said that the Gulf war was custom-made for television: Lots of showmanship in the high-tech gadgetry; plenty of soundbites of camouflage-clad generals with colorful language; screens filled with the exploding night sky viewed from Riyadh rooftops. But what was really happening over in the desert? Was war a better choice than sanctions? What were the goals of the war? What was the likely post-war scenario? What was happening to the Iraqis in Baghdad, and to those in the front lines who were being carpet-bombed by B-52s? No one, it seemed, was asking those questions.

Only since the end of the 100-hour war, as the nation welcomed home its "heroes"—most of whom never fired a shot—have other questions about the role and the performance of journalists been raised.

The questions should trouble us all. No one has ever suggested that journalists should have unlimited access and no restrictions on their stories. Clearly, matters of individual safety of soldiers, sailors, and fliers are not subject to debate, nor are matters of clearly identifiable national harm.

But what exactly is the role of news media in wartime? Once the shooting starts, should they "support the troops" and save the investigative stories for the end of the war? Should a free society depend solely on the news releases of its government, including the military? Should pictures of dead and badly wounded civilians or soldiers be shown? Are all wars political and, therefore, subject to scrutiny of political motives?

Keep these questions in mind as you read the selections in this chapter about the media, and formulate others as you compare readings.

The First Casualty

Phillip Knightley takes the title of his book The First Casualty *from a line attributed to Senator Hiram Johnson in 1917: "The first casualty when war comes is truth." A casualty is something injured, lost, or destroyed; thus soldiers and civilians, values and beliefs, property and livelihood may be among those things that are harmed by war. The truth of what happened and why, of decisions and motives, of results and consequences might indeed be the first casualty of war.*

During war, most people—often combatants as well as civilians—depend upon the media for the truth. Who are the men and women that report on war? Why them? How do they gain the position of reporting their perceptions and interpretations to millions of other people?

Where do their stories come from? Secrecy and security are by-words of war; so are public relations and propaganda. War correspondents attempt to find truth, to see it and report it, but their attempts may sometimes conflict with the desires or requirements of the people who fight, command, or decide.

In the following selection, a chapter from The First Casualty *(1975), Knightley considers the history of war reporting and the part Vietnam had in that history. Before you read his discussion, write several paragraphs about what the public needs from the media during war.*

A GALLUP POLL IN MID-1967 revealed that half of all Americans had no idea what the war in Vietnam was about. Just after the Tet offensive in 1968, the chairman of the Appropriations Committee of the House of Representatives, without whose consent there would be no money for the war, genuinely seeking enlightenment, asked the Chief of Staff of the United States Army: "Who would you say is our enemy in this conflict?"

Clearly, those charged with the responsibility of informing the United States public about Vietnam had not fulfilled their task. Given that the issues were complex and the facts unpalatable, this failure has never been satisfactorily explained. True, the whole story did come out in the end, but the feeling of the American reader that he was not getting a satisfactory running story of the war still concerns those correspondents who did their best to provide it. The most likely theory is that the combination of low understanding of the war at home and high

drama in Vietnam created a challenge that few correspondents were able
to meet. And when such correspondents were present, too often their
efforts were frustrated by the attitude of their editors in the United
States.

All sorts of correspondents, from all sorts of publications, went to   3
Vietnam. There were specialist writers from technical journals, trainee
reporters from college newspapers, counter-insurgency experts from
military publishers, religious correspondents, famous authors, small-town
editors, old hands from Korea, even older hands from the Second World
War, and what Henry Kamm of the *New York Times* called "proto-
journalists," men who had never written a professional word or taken
a professional photograph in their lives until the war brought them to
Saigon. They all wrote stories that were used and presumably read or
took photographs that were bought and reproduced. Michael Herr, who
went to Vietnam for *Esquire,* estimated that, at a time when there were
between 600 and 700 accredited correspondents, "only fifty gave journalism a better name than it deserved, particularly in Vietnam."

Ambition, principally, had brought them all there. The war was   4
the biggest story in the world at the time—"the longest-running front-
page story in history," as a United Press man put it; "the best story
going on anywhere in the world at the moment," said Peter Arnett—
and there was no better place for a young reporter to put a gloss on a
new career or an old reporter to revitalise a fading one. Herbert Matthews had made it sound better in the pre-Second World War days: "If
you have not seen a battle, your education has been somewhat neglected—for after all, war has ever been one of the primary functions
of mankind, and unless you see men fight you miss something fundamental." But what it comes down to is that war provides rich material
for a correspondent, and Vietnam was the richest ever. "You see these
things, these terrible things," said Charles Mohr, "but in an odd way
they're good stories."

The mechanics of becoming accredited were straightforward. The   5
correspondent applied to his nearest South Vietnamese embassy for an
entry visa. It was usually granted. In Saigon, the correspondent reported
to the U.S. authorities with a letter from his newspaper requesting accreditation and accepting responsibility for him. If he wished to be accredited as a free-lance, he needed letters from two organisations saying
that they were prepared to buy his dispatches. The correspondent was
then issued an accreditation card identifying him and stating: *"The bearer
of this card should be accorded full co-operation and assistance . . . to assure
the successful completion of his mission. Bearer is authorised to rations and
quarters on a reimbursable basis. Upon presentation of this card, bearer is entitled
to air, water, and ground transportation under a priority of 3. . . ."*

The correspondent signed an agreement to abide by a set of fifteen   6
ground rules, dealing mainly with preserving military security, and was
on his way. Some got a tailor to run up a safari jacket—Saigon tailors
called it a "CBS jacket"—with matching trousers, which looked vaguely
like a uniform, not, in most cases, out of any sense of commitment, but
so as to be less conspicuous in a military situation. On his army fatigues
he could sew his official identification, his name and organisation, thus:
JOHN SHAW, TIME, or, to the disbelief of most GIs, in his particular
case, ALAN WILLIAMS, QUEEN.

The MACV card would admit the correspondent to the daily brief-   7
ing on the war's progress given at the Joint United States Public Affairs
Office (JUSPAO), which had been created to handle press relations and
psychological warfare. ("I never met anyone there," claimed one correspondent, "who seemed to realise that there was a difference.") If he
was prepared to believe JUSPAO, a correspondent could cover the war
simply by attending the briefings each day. Most correspondents considered them a waste of time, but one, Joe Fried of the *New York Daily
News,* built up a reputation, during his nine years and eight months in
Vietnam—"longer than anyone and without a vacation"—by his daily,
persistent, and provocative questioning, sometimes driving the briefing
officer into revealing an item of genuine news value.

For the correspondent who preferred to spend more time in the   8
field, the problem was not in finding material, but in the risk of being
overwhelmed by it. Murray Sayle wrote to me saying: "I arrived here
as everyone else does, hoping to sum it all up in 1,000 crisp words. I
wind up in the hotel on Friday nights trying to make some sense out of
a great whirl of experience—the ghastly sights you see and your own
feelings of fear and loneliness."

Sayle, then working for the *Sunday Times* of London, wrote an   9
article on April 28, 1968, describing a day in his life in Vietnam. It is
worth looking at as an example of the "whirl of experience" a correspondent could expect to face as he tried to follow the war. "I begin the
day at sea approaching the mouth of the Perfume River aboard the
American landing craft Universal No. 70, bound for Hue with 190 tons
of reinforcing sheet for runways. I am trying to get to Camp Evans,
north of Hue, where it is unofficially reported that a big battle is developing—but it is impossible to fly direct from Da Nang."

Sayle leaves the boat and sets out to walk to Phu Bai, a big Amer-   10
ican base, seven and half miles away. Crossing a floating bridge, he is
overtaken by an American and two South Vietnamese soldiers escorting
four barefoot Vietcong prisoners, three boys and a girl, all about seventeen years old. He is mistaken for part of the escort and finds himself
in the interrogation room at the headquarters of the South Vietnamese

First Infantry Division, where the proceedings open with the interro-
gating officer kicking one of the prisoners in the stomach "with his well-
polished, heavy military boots."

At this point the American soldier realises that Sayle is a corre-   11
spondent and asks him to leave. Sayle, feeling shaken, has a cup of coffee
at the Cercle Sportif, or what is left of it, and then hitches a ride with
a convoy of United States army trucks, "many of which are decorated
with little rows of two, three, or four yellow figures wearing conical
hats and sandals, each one neatly crossed out."

As he nears Phu Bai, there is a tremendous explosion, followed   12
by leaping sheets of orange flame and billowing smoke—a helicopter
has shed a rotor blade and crashed into the base ammunition dump.
While he waits for a helicopter to take him to Evans, Sayle watches a
Vietnamese engraving mottoes on the soldiers' cigarette lighters. "Fa-
vourites are 'Make war, not work' and 'I pass through the Valley of
Death unafraid, for I am the meanest bastard in the valley.' " At Evans,
Sayle joins the officers' chow line for dinner: deep-frozen shrimps, grilled
steak, plum tart, and coffee. Then the colonel whose battalion is to make
the first air assault in the morning outlines his plan to fourteen correspondents and photographers, who draw straws for the order in which
they will go. Sayle draws the first wave, with a French news agency
man and an Italian photographer. He fills two water bottles, collects a
C ration, and finds an empty stretcher in the press tent, which turns out
to be alongside a battery of two 175-millimetre guns firing two rounds
of harassment and interdiction at nothing in particular every half-hour
through the night. "Thinking about copy deadline, I suddenly remember the date—tomorrow is Anzac Day and the day after is the fourteenth
anniversary of the Geneva agreements which ended the French war in
Vietnam."

As well as trying to assess the significance of so varied a day,   13
correspondents faced other major difficulties. Covering the war was
highly dangerous, and Vietnam had no respect for reputations. Forty-
five war correspondents were killed in Vietnam and eighteen listed as
missing. Those killed included such experienced correspondents as Larry
Burrows, Dickey Chapelle, Marguerite Higgins (who died in the United
States of a tropical disease contracted in Vietnam), François Sully, and
the author and historian Bernard Fall. They died in helicopter crashes,
from stepping on land-mines, and, in one instance, directly at the hands
of the Vietcong. This occurred in May 1968, when five correspondents
driving in Cholon were attacked, and, although the one survivor said
they had shouted *"Bao chi"* ("press"), they were machine-gunned. The
next day, a United Press photographer called Charlie Eggleston took a

weapon and announced that he was going out on a mission of revenge. He, too, was shot dead, but as the story in Saigon went, not before he had first killed three Vietcong.

There was some argument among correspondents, after the Cho- 14 lon incident, about the wisdom of carrying arms. The difficulty was that if even one correspondent continued to go armed, this entitled the Vietcong to assume—as perhaps they had in the Cholon case—that all the correspondents were armed, and to react accordingly. Nothing came of the discussions, and many correspondents continued to carry personal weapons, ranging from Sean Flynn's pearl-handled twenty-two-calibre pistol in a shoulder holster to Peter Arnett's Mauser machine pistol. Ward Just noted that most of these weapons were seldom fired, "save for one legendary American correspondent who lived in the field with the First Cavalry Division and left Vietnam with three notches in his belt." This was Charlie Black, a correspondent for the *Columbus Inquirer,* of Columbus, Georgia, home of the First Cavalry. Black has not denied the charge. "I'm not really a Wyatt Earp, but if some guy comes after me I answer back."

Another daily difficulty was that not all military authorities wel- 15 comed correspondents or understood their function. In fact, some actively hated them. These ranged from officers who felt that correspondents were undermining the war effort—"My Marines are winning this war and you people are losing it for us in your papers"—to GIs who resented the correspondents' freedom to choose whether and when to risk their lives. "Those bastards," one rifleman said, watching a jeep-load of correspondents drop Michael Herr and drive away. "I hope they die." This visible enmity and the recurring accusation that they were doing a lousy job of reporting the war—"Why don't you guys tell it like it really is?"—caused considerable introspection among correspondents. What should be their attitude to the war, and how should they report it? Peter Arnett's method was to get out with the units doing the actual fighting.

From the time Arnett arrived in Vietnam in 1962, a tough twenty- 16 seven-year-old New Zealander, until the war's end thirteen years later, he spent more time in the field than any other correspondent. "It's essential that a reporter see for himself those thousands of little battles at the lowest command levels to begin to comprehend what it is all about. With luck, with enough small definitions, he might be able to begin to generalise, but to stand off and take a long-range view has been proved erroneous time and again." In the field, as elsewhere, Arnett determined to "observe with as much professional detachment as possible, to report a scene with accuracy and clarity." Above all, he never became *involved* in what he was reporting or photographing, and that made him, according to the author Marina Warner, "as hardboiled as a Chinese thousand-year-old egg."

Arnett has described his standing one hot noon outside the Saigon   17
market and seeing a Buddhist monk squat on the pavement, squirt gasoline over himself from a rubber bottle, flick a cigarette lighter, and turn himself in a matter of minutes into a blackened corpse. "I could have prevented that immolation by rushing at him and kicking the gasoline away. As a human being I wanted to, as a reporter I couldn't."
So Arnett photographed the monk ablaze, beat off the Vietnamese secret police trying to grab his camera, raced back to the Associated Press office, and sent his photograph and story round the world.

Other correspondents, particularly photographers, tended to agree   18
with this view of their rôle. (Television was in a class of its own here and must be dealt with as such.) Even Philip Jones Griffiths, whose portrayal of suffering Vietnamese civilians forms perhaps the best photographic testament of the war, has said, "Your job is to record it all for history. You can't not feel involved, but you have to steel yourself and do your job, take your photographs. That's what you're there for. It's no use crying. You can't focus with tears in your eyes. It's better to do the breaking down later in the darkroom."

Clearly, this emotional detachment came more easily to some cor-   19
respondents than to others. Clare Hollingworth of the *Daily Telegraph,* who had been reporting wars since 1939, was intrigued by the conflict in Vietnam. "The Americans were fighting a war with fantastic weaponry. I made it my business to know what weapons, planes, etc, were being used there. I love weapons and know a fair amount about them. I daresay I can take a machine-gun apart and put it together again, and as fast as any man. The tactical side appealed to me immensely. My emotions weren't really involved." To remain as detached as this, it was necessary for a correspondent to keep aloof from debate on the origins of the war. As Julian Pettifer of the BBC said, "There is simply no point in arguing whether the war is right or wrong. You're always left with the fact that it is there and it's your job to cover it."

But, while most correspondents saw their rôle in terms as clear   20
and uncomplicated as this, others went through deep and sometimes agonising examination of their motives and began to question whether it was possible to cover the war with an untroubled conscience. Usually, the first serious doubt appeared under pressure. Alec Shimkin of *Newsweek* was on Route 1, near the village of Trang Bang, in 1972, when the Vietnamese air force dropped napalm on their own side and burned two infants to death. Shimkin came back down the roadway towards a group of correspondents, who were hoping to get from him an eye-

witness account of what had happened. But Shimkin was temporarily crazed with fury and grief, and he shouted, "Goddamn you! Leave me alone. Get the hell out," at the correspondents who approached him. Whether the incident would have had any lasting effect on Shimkin must remain speculation, because he was reported soon afterwards as missing, presumed dead, at Quang Tri.

Marina Warner, reporting at the time for the *Spectator,* recalls the   21
effect on her of her first encounter with civilian casualties. "I saw this old woman coming down the road with a child in her arms. The child's flesh was falling off. I said to myself, 'My God, I've seen all this before.' I had. On television. Somehow seeing it before on television took away some of the reality and I wasn't as shocked as I had expected to be. But later, when the horror sank in, I stood on the roadway exposing myself to fire when I didn't need to. And I stood there longer than I needed to. It was some sort of expiation. I had the feeling that if I could have been wounded it would have taken away the guilt I felt about the burnt child, the guilt I felt about Vietnam."

Murray Sayle went out on the "body detail" that brought back   22
the bodies of the four correspondents killed in the attack in Cholon in 1968. He wrote to me: "There's a strange calm about the dead, they don't feel any pain. You look at them and then look away and when you look back they look exactly the same. When you see people badly hit you feel very healthy and you think, when I get out of here without a scratch I will have beaten the system and nothing can ever be as bad as hearing the shooting and that second or two before you know if it is you or not. Then, when it's not you, you feel like an impostor, an intruder, crouching off to the side, notebook in hand. I sometimes feel I am engaging in some clinical investigation of my own motives at the expense of other people."

Those correspondents sufficiently frank to admit it agree that there   23
are moments in war when the exhilaration compensates for all the horror, all the doubt. Some of them look for historical or psychological justification. Tim Page, who worked for *Life,* says, "War has always been glamorous. And I don't care who he is, if you put a gun into a man's hand, then he feels bigger." Others simply accept it without question. "I can't explain it," says Peter Gill of the *Daily Telegraph,* "but there is something fantastically exhilarating about being terrified out of your wits." Chris Dobson of the *Daily Mail* agrees. "When I'm actually taking part in an action it's always as though I'm three martinis up. I'm in another, a higher gear, and it's marvellous." And Horst Faas, the Associated Press photographer, for whom war has become a way of life, says, in his urban German accent, "Vot I like eez boom boom. Oh yes."

This fascination for violence and death, along with the struggle   24
the more sensitive correspondents had in trying to reconcile their hatred
of war with their very real enjoyment of it, puzzled and annoyed some
observers. "It is impossible to realize how much of Ernest Hemingway
still lives in the hearts of men until you spend time with the professional
war correspondents," wrote Nora Ephron in *New York* magazine. "Most
of the Americans are stuck in the Hemingway bag and they tend to
romanticize war, just as he did. Which is not surprising: unlike fighting
in the war itself, unlike big-game hunting, working as a war correspondent is almost the only classic male endeavor left that provides
physical danger and personal risk without public disapproval and the
awful truth is that for correspondents, war is not hell. It is fun."

It would be hard to disagree with Nora Ephron's accusation when   25
applied to most correspondents in most wars. But, just as the First
World War marked a turning point in the history of war correspondents—never again could a war be reported so badly—so Vietnam stands
out, for it was there that correspondents began seriously to question the
ethics of their business. Photographers were particularly troubled, because their craft is by its nature more obviously voyeuristic and intrusive
than that of a writer. So in Vietnam, while one found photographers
who, like Horst Faas, enjoyed taking hard-news pictures of violent events,
and for whom death and atrocity held no horror, there were also men
like Larry Burrows, who began to wonder what it was all about.

Burrows, a Londoner, who lived in Hong Kong and worked for   26
Life, was described by the former *Picture Post* editor Tom Hopkinson as
"the greatest war photographer there has ever been." When he first went
to Vietnam, in 1962, he was able to rationalise his attitude: "It's an
important time in history and if I can convey a little of what goes on,
then it's a good reason to be here." But later he began to shield his
readers from the horror of the war. "I was trying to take a shot of this
guy who was dying in the helicopter. I never took his face. I don't like
making it too real. I've wondered about that point quite a lot. I think if
the pictures are too terrible, people quickly turn over the page to avoid
looking. So I try to shoot them so that people will look and feel, not
revulsion, but an understanding of war." The more Burrows thought
about the soldier in the helicopter series—"Yankee Papa 13"—the more
it appears to have worried him. "I was torn between being a photographer and the normal human feelings. It is not easy to photograph a
pilot dying in a friend's arms and later to photograph the breakdown of
the friend. I didn't know what to do. Was I simply capitalising on someone else's grief?" He felt the troops' resentment more keenly. "They
look up from their dying friends and see me shooting pictures. They

feel that I am capitalising on their misery and get very angry." Burrows was killed in a helicopter crash in February 1971, and so we will never know where this self-questioning would have led him. But we have an indication, from an encounter with Burrows described by *Esquire* writer Michael Herr.

Burrows and Herr were on a landing zone when a Chinook heli-   27
copter arrived. Burrows ran down and photographed the crew, the soldiers coming down an incline to get on board, three wounded being carefully lifted up, six corpses in closed body bags. Then he took one picture each of the helicopter rearing, settling, and departing. "When it was gone," Herr wrote, "he looked at me and he seemed to be in the most open distress. 'Sometimes one feels like such a bastard,' he said."

Herr said that correspondents discussed the problem often, and in   28
the end "there's no way around it; if you photographed a dead marine with a poncho over his face and got something for it, you were some kind of parasite. But what were you if you pulled the poncho back first to make a better shot, and did that in front of his friends? . . . What were you if you stood there watching it, making a note to remember it later in case you might want to use it?"

If a photographer puzzled over his professional ethics too long, he   29
risked missing a picture. Harri Peccinotti spent weeks in Vietnam, for *Nova,* a London magazine, waiting for one particular photograph—a South Vietnamese woman loading her husband's body into a body bag and onto a helicopter taking the dead and wounded from a place where there had been a battle. Eventually, the circumstances were right photographically, even better than Peccinotti had hoped for: the woman had her child with her. But, at the moment he could have taken the picture, the helicopter crew asked for Peccinotti's help in getting the wounded on board. "I had to make a choice. I went to help the wounded and I never got the photograph."

In 1967, Donald McCullin of the *Sunday Times* said he would like   30
to do war photography every day of the week. "I used to be a war-a-year man, but now that's not enough. I need two a year now. When it gets to be three or four, then I'll start to be worried." McCullin admitted that he tended to romanticise war, but insisted that "photographically war can be very beautiful." In 1970 he was wounded and was taken from the front, with other casualties, in the back of a truck. "I knew the man next to me had died when his toes next to my face went lifeless and began to move with the jolting . . . it's incredible to see somebody not alive. I don't want to be maimed, but why them and not me?" McCullin recovered and went back to photographing in Vietnam. Now he became less reckless and much more calculating—"I know just what photograph justifies what risk"—and, although he still found danger

exhilarating, he noticed that his detachment had gone. "Almost without realising it, I found myself getting involved with helping wounded and carrying stretchers and that sort of thing. And my photography started to suffer. It started to come second."

The most intrusive medium in Vietnam was television, and, as the   31
war went on, the hunger of editors for combat footage increased. "Before they were satisfied with a corpse," Richard Lindley, a British television reporter, said. "Then they had to have people dying in action." Michael Herr described a truck carrying a dying ARVN soldier that stopped near a group of correspondents. The soldier, who was only nineteen or twenty, had been shot in the chest. A television cameraman leaned over the Vietnamese and began filming. The other correspondents watched. "He opened his eyes briefly a few times and looked back at us. The first time he tried to smile . . . then it left him. I'm sure he didn't even see us the last time he looked, but we all knew what it was that he had seen just before that." The Vietnamese had seen the zoom lens of a sixteen-millimetre converted Auricon sound camera capturing his last moments of life on film that, if the flight connections worked and the editors back at the network liked it, would be shown in American living rooms within forty-eight hours.

This little item would not be exceptional. During the Tet offen-   32
sive, a Vietnamese in a checked shirt appeared on television being walked—that is, dragged—between two soldiers. The soldiers took him over to a man holding a pistol, who held it to the head of the man in the checked shirt and blew his brains out. All of it was seen in full colour on television (and later in a memorable series of photographs taken by Eddie Adams of the AP).

Any viewer in the United States who watched regularly the tele-   33
vision reporting from Vietnam—and it was from television that 60 percent of Americans got most of their war news—would agree that he saw scenes of real-life violence, death, and horror on his screen that would have been unthinkable before Vietnam. The risk and intrusion that such filming involved could, perhaps, be justified if it could be shown that television had been particularly effective in revealing the true nature of the war and thus had been able to change people's attitudes to it. Is there any evidence to this effect?

The director of CBS News in Washington, William Small, wrote: 34
"When television covered its 'first war' in Vietnam it showed a terrible truth of war in a manner new to mass audiences. A case can be made, and certainly should be examined, that this was cardinal to the disillusionment of Americans with this war, the cynicism of many young people towards America, and the destruction of Lyndon Johnson's tenure of office." A *Washington Post* reporter, Don Oberdorfer, amply doc-

uments, in his book *Tet,* the number of commentators and editors (including those of Time Inc.) who had to re-examine their attitudes after extensive television—and press—coverage brought home to them the bewildering contradictions of a seemingly unending war.

Television's power seems to have impressed British observers even more than American. The director-general of the Royal United Service Institution, Air Vice-Marshal S. W. B. Menaul, believes that television had "a lot to answer for [in] the collapse of American morale in relation to the Vietnam war." The then editor of the *Economist,* Alistair Burnet, wrote that the television reporting of Vietnam had made it very difficult for two American administrations to continue that war, "which was going on in American homes," irrespective of the merits or demerits of why the United States was actually involved in Vietnam. Robin Day, the BBC commentator, told a seminar of the Royal United Service Institution that the war on colour-television screens in American living rooms had made Americans far more anti-militarist and anti-war than anything else: "One wonders if in future a democracy which has uninhibited television coverage in every home will ever be able to fight a war, however just. . . . The full brutality of the combat will be there in close up and colour, and blood looks very red on the colour television screen." And the Director of Defence Operations, Plans and Supplies at the Ministry of Defence, Brigadier F. G. Caldwell, said that the American experience in Vietnam meant that if Britain were to go to war again, "we would have to start saying to ourselves, are we going to let the television cameras loose on the battlefield?"

All this seems very persuasive, and it would be difficult to believe that the sight, day after day, of American soldiers and Vietnamese civilians dying in a war that seemed to make no progress could not have had *some* effect on the viewer. Yet a survey conducted for *Newsweek* in 1967 suggested a remarkably different conclusion: that television had encouraged a majority of viewers to *support* the war. When faced with deciding whether television coverage had made them feel more like "backing up the boys in Vietnam" or like opposing the war, 64 per cent of viewers replied that they were moved to support the soldiers and only 26 per cent to oppose the war. A prominent American psychiatrist, Fredric Wertham, said, in the same year, that television had the effect of conditioning its audience to accept war, and a further *Newsweek* enquiry, in 1972, suggested that the public was developing a tolerance of horror in the newscasts from Vietnam—"The only way we can possibly tolerate it is by turning off a part of ourselves instead of the television set."

Edward Jay Epstein's survey of television producers and news editors, for his book *News from Nowhere,* showed that more than two-thirds of those he interviewed felt that television had had little effect in changing public opinion on Vietnam. An opinion commonly expressed was that people saw exactly what they wanted to in a news report and that television only served to reinforce existing views. *The New Yorker's* television critic, Michael J. Arlen, reported, on several occasions, that viewers had a vague, unhappy feeling that they were not getting "the true picture" of Vietnam from the medium. So if it was true that television did not radically change public opinion about the war, could it have been because of the quality of the coverage?

Television is a comparatively new medium. There were 10,000 sets 38 in the United States in 1941; at the time of Korea there were 10 million, and at the peak of the Vietnam War 100 million. There was some television reporting in Korea, a lot of it daring—an American general had to order the BBC cameraman Cyril Page to get down off the front of a tank to which he had tied himself so as to get a grandstand view of the battle as the tank went into action. But, until Vietnam, no one knew what problems the prolonged day-by-day coverage of a war by television would produce. The first was surprising—a lack of reality. It had been believed that when battle scenes were brought into the living room the reality of war would at last be brought home to a civilian audience. But Arlen was quick to point out, in *The New Yorker,* that by the same process battle scenes are made less real, "diminished in part by the physical size of the television screen, which, for all the industry's advances, still shows one a picture of men three inches tall shooting at other men three inches tall." Sandy Gall of ITN found shooting combat footage difficult and dangerous, and the end result very disappointing. "I think you lose one dimension on television's small screen and things look smaller than life; the sound of battle, for example, never coming across. I am always let down when I eventually see my footage and think, Is that all? The sense of danger never comes across on television and you, the correspondent, always look as though you had an easy time of it."

For many Americans in Vietnam, there emerged a strange side to 39 the war that became directly related to television—the fact that the war seemed so unreal that sometimes it became almost possible to believe that everything was taking place on some giant Hollywood set and all the participants were extras playing a remake of *Back to Bataan*. GIs— and even correspondents—brought up on Second World War movies shown on television, used to seeing Errol Flynn sweeping to victory through the jungles of Burma or Brian Donlevy giving the Japanese hell in the Coral Sea, tended to relate their experiences in Vietnam to the Hollywood version of America at war. Michael Herr, making a dash, with Davis Greenway of *Time,* from one position at Hué to another, caught himself saying to a Marine a line from a hundred Hollywood war films: "We're going to cut out now. Will you cover us?" One should not be surprised, therefore, to find that GIs sometimes behaved, in the presence of television cameras, as if they were making *Dispatch from Da Nang*. Herr describes soldiers running about during a fight because they knew there was a television crew nearby. "They were actually making war movies in their heads, doing little guts and glory Leatherneck tap dances under fire, getting their pimples shot off for the networks."

So it is not difficult to understand how, when seen on a small 40 screen, in the enveloping and cosy atmosphere of the household, sometime between the afternoon soap-box drama and the late-night war movie, the television version of the war in Vietnam could appear as just another drama, in which the hero is the correspondent and everything will come out all right at the end. Jack Laurence of CBS, an experienced war correspondent, who spent a lot of time in Vietnam, had this possibility brought home to him in Israel during the 1973 conflict. He was in a hotel lobby, and a couple who had just arrived from the United States recognised him and said, "We saw you on television and we knew everything was going to be all right because you were there." There is not much a television correspondent can do about such a situation as that; it seems inherent in the nature of the medium. However, correspondents, or, more fairly, their editors, do have something to answer for in their selection of news in Vietnam.

Years of television news of the war have left viewers with a blur 41 of images consisting mainly of helicopters landing in jungle clearings, soldiers charging into undergrowth, wounded being loaded onto helicopters, artillery and mortar fire, air strikes on distant targets, napalm canisters turning slowly in the sky, and a breathless correspondent poking a stick microphone under an army officer's nose and asking, "What's happening up there, Colonel?" (The only honest answer came, in 1972, from a captain on Highway 13. "I wish the hell I knew," he said.) The networks claimed that combat footage was what the public wanted; that concentrating on combat prevented the film's being out of date if it was delayed in transmission; that it was difficult to shoot anything other than combat film when only three or four minutes were available in the average news program for events in Vietnam; and that the illusion of American progress created by combat footage shot from only one side was balanced by what the correspondent had to say.

This is simply not true. To begin with, combat footage fails to 42 convey all aspects of combat. "A cameraman feels so inadequate, being able to record only a minute part of the misery, a minute part of the fighting," said Kurt Volkert, a CBS cameraman. "You have to decide what the most important action is. Is it the woman holding her crying baby? Is it the young girl cringing near her house because of the exploding grenades? Or is it the defiant looking Vietcong with blood on his face just after capture?" When the cameraman's thirty minutes of combat footage are edited down to three minutes—not an unusual editing ratio—the result is a segment of action that bears about as much relation to the reality in Vietnam as a battle scene shot in Hollywood does. In fact, the Hollywood version would probably appear more realistic.

The American viewer who hoped to learn something serious about Vietnam was subjected, instead, to a television course in the techniques of war, and he was not sufficiently exposed either to what the war meant to the people over whose land it was being fought, or to the political complexities of the situation, or even to the considered personal views of reporters who had spent years covering the situation. Yet, even by the networks' own standards, the limited aspects of the war that the viewer was permitted to see could produce excellent television. One of the most dramatic pieces of film on the war was shot by a CBS team on Highway 13 late in April 1972. A South Vietnamese mine, intended to stop advancing enemy tanks, had caught a truck loaded with refugees. The film showed dead children, distressed babies, and a woman weeping over the body of her son. The reporter, Bob Simon, described what had happened and then, with perhaps the best sign-off line from Vietnam, said simply, "There's nothing left to say about this war, nothing at all." "Morley Safer's Vietnam," an hour-long report by the CBS correspondent in Saigon, was Safer's own explicit view, and was hailed by *The New Yorker's* critic, Michael J. Arlen, as "one of the best pieces of journalism to come out of the Vietnam war in any medium." But film like this was rare.

Competition for combat footage was so intense that it not only forced American television teams to follow each other into what the BBC's correspondent Michael Clayton called "appallingly dangerous situations," but it also made editors reluctant to risk allowing a team the time and the freedom to make its own film of the war. Where were the television equivalents of Martha Gellhorn's series on Vietnamese orphanages and hospitals, or Philip Jones Griffiths' searing book on the nature of the war, *Vietnam Inc.?* True, television was handicapped by its mechanics—a three-man, or even a two-man, team loaded with camera, sound equipment, and film is less mobile and more dependent on military transport, and in a dangerous situation more vulnerable, than a journalist or a photographer. In its presentation, too, television is sometimes handicapped by its commercial associations. The Vietnamese cameraman Vo Suu filmed the brutal shooting of a Vietcong suspect by General Nguyen Ngoc Loan during the Tet offensive. NBC blacked out

43

44

the screen for three seconds after the dead man hit the ground, so as to provide a buffer before the commercial that followed. (What television *really* wanted was action in which the men died cleanly and not too bloodily. "When they get a film which shows what a mortar does to a man, really shows the flesh torn and the blood flowing, they get squeamish," says Richard Lindley. "They want it to be just so. They want television to be cinema.")

American television executives showed too little courage in their   45
approach to Vietnam. They followed each other into paths the army had chosen for them. They saw the war as "an American war in Asia—and that's the only story the American audience is interested in," and they let other, equally important, aspects of Vietnam go uncovered.

All this said, attempts to film the war from the other side were   46
even less successful. James Cameron, Romano Cagnoni, and Malcolm Aird went to North Vietnam in 1965. They went as an independent team—Cameron to report, Cagnoni to take photographs, and Aird to make a film—paying their own expenses. Although the North Vietnamese had given them visas, they were not freely welcomed. "We were treated with considerable suspicion," Aird said, "and it took not just days but weeks to break this down. Even then, we were not able to film all the things we naïvely supposed we would be able to film—stuff like bombs falling and American prisoners. But in 1965 any film at all out of North Vietnam was news." The film Cameron and Aird made, before the North Vietnamese suddenly and without explanation asked them to leave, presented a sympathetic view of the country. "It was interesting to see how quickly you are on the side you are working with," Aird said. "In North Vietnam the Americans to us were the enemy."

The North Vietnamese themselves had no correspondents as we   47
understand the word. They followed the progress of the war as best they could from party newspapers, government broadcasts, and large wall posters. The flavour of the news presentation in the North can best be had by extracts from wall posters appearing in Hanoi on March 21, 1975, as the North Vietnamese army pushed south towards Saigon: "The South attacks and rises. Very big victories. Nearly a million countrymen have risen to be their own masters. Complete liberation of five provinces." Then followed a list of casualties inflicted and equipment captured. The posters ended with "Long live the victory of the soldiers and people of the western region."

Western correspondents were allowed into the North only if the   48
North Vietnamese government could see some advantage to itself from the visit. This is not to say that the North Vietnamese dictated what the correspondents wrote, but it does help to explain why Western corre-

spondents who went to the North were looked upon with suspicion in their own countries. They had to be prepared for attacks on their reliability, their competence, and their professional ability. "The kindest thing anyone could say of me," said Cameron, "was that I was a misguided, gullible Commie tool."

Harrison E. Salisbury of the *New York Times,* the first correspondent from a major United States newspaper to go to North Vietnam, writing from Hanoi in December 1966, said: "Whatever the explanation, one can see that United States planes are dropping an enormous weight of explosives on purely civilian targets." This forced the administration to concede that American pilots had accidentally struck civilian areas while attempting to bomb military targets, and made Salisbury a much-hated figure in Washington. Secretary of State Dean Rusk asked the *New York Times'* publisher how long Salisbury planned to stay in Hanoi. The Pentagon called him "Ho Chi Salisbury of the *Hanoi Times.*" The *Washington Post* alleged that the casualty figures he gave after one raid that he reported were exactly the same as those in Communist propaganda pamphlets, and a *Post* article said that Salisbury was Ho Chi Minh's new weapon in the war. William Randolph Hearst, Jr., reminded his readers of the treasonable war-time broadcasts by Lord Haw-Haw and Tokyo Rose. The columnist Joseph Alsop wrote: "Whether a United States reporter ought to go to an enemy capital to give the authority of his by-line to enemy propaganda figures is an interesting question." Some of his critics accused Salisbury of being politically naïve, of not giving proper attribution of his sources, and, as in Cameron's case, of being duped by the Communists. The Pulitzer Prize jury recommended him for a prize by a vote of four to one, but the Pulitzer Advisory Board rejected the recommendation by six votes to five. Being a war correspondent on the enemy side was clearly not the easiest way to advance one's career.

Others who went to Hanoi later included Mary McCarthy, Anthony Lewis, Michael MacLear from the Canadian Broadcasting Corporation, and R. K. Karanjia from India, and Agence France Presse maintained a bureau there throughout the war. But to be a war correspondent with the Vietcong in South Vietnam was a much rarer occurrence.

Wilfred Burchett, the Australian who had sent the first story to the West from Hiroshima and who had reported the Korean peace talks from the North Korean side, began reporting the Vietnam war in 1963, free-lancing for the Japanese *Mainichi* group, the British Communist daily *Morning Star,* and the American *National Guardian,* and working from the Vietcong side. Burchett made no pretence about where his sympathies were—"The US puppet regime, no matter what new personalities the puppet masters may push to the top in the endless cycle of coup and counter-coup, is doomed." But his reports on Vietcong schools, arsenals, hospitals, the administrative structure, transport, and commissary made intriguing reading: "Hunting teams attached to every unit ensured that there was always something to go with the rice. The 'something' varied from elephant steaks—the Americans bombed and strafed them from the air as potential 'supply vehicles'—to jungle rats, with monkey, wild pig, porcupine, civets, and other wild creatures in between."

Burchett travelled mainly on foot or by bicycle, occasionally on 52 horseback or by motorised sampan. He was several times within a few miles of Saigon and appeared to have no trouble in traversing at night even the Saigon-controlled areas. But, although he wore the typical native black pajamas and conical straw hat, his bulk, his colouring, and his features clearly distinguished him as non-Vietnamese, and the United States forces soon heard rumours of a "white man" working with the Vietcong. (Madeleine Riffaud of the French Communist paper *L'Humanité* was travelling with Burchett at this stage, but, being slight and dark, she was able to pass as a Vietnamese.) Burchett has said that the American military authorities' reaction to his presence was to try to kill him. "My size and grey hair probably showed up on reconnaissance photographs, because four planes came over one morning, headed straight for our overnight camp, and bombed it, one after the other. Fortunately, the guards with us had dug shelters immediately on our arrival the previous night and the first blast almost blew us into the holes. The first string landed within two or three hundred yards, but the jungle absorbed most of the blast and the shrapnel."

Madeleine Riffaud was the only woman correspondent with the 53 Vietcong, but there were many with the American forces, either on brief visits or on long-term assignments. Jillian Robertson, of the *London Sunday Express,* went on a bombing mission in South Vietnam in a B-57—"Before, I had just been a spectator of this war, now I was part of it." Patricia Penn wrote in the *New Statesman* about amputees at a Quaker limb centre at Quang Ngai—"Ho Min, who's seven, lost his parents when he lost his leg. He sits crying alone in a corner, soaking his stump in a bucket of antiseptic. Now and then he lifts it out of the liquid, stares at it puzzled, and then—as if for an answer—looks at me." Victoria Brittain, a resident correspondent for *The Times* of London, mixed straight reporting with articles on child victims—"Even a 'relatively good' orphanage is chaotic, filthy, stuffed with children so starved of adult contact that the moment you step inside the courtyard your whole lower body and legs are covered with small exploring hands." Gloria

Emerson of the *New York Times* wrote a fine series of articles on refugees, mentioning in one of them Richard Hughes, a former correspondent, who had abandoned journalism in Vietnam to run four orphanages.

Lest this concentration on personal experience and human-interest   54
reporting give the wrong impression, it should be noted that there were
also women writers who were interested in the political, cultural, and
historical background of the war, Frances FitzGerald probably being the
best known.

There were also women combat correspondents. Catherine Leroy,   55
a French photographer in her early twenties, was captured at Hué and
photographed the Vietcong troops in action before they released her.
She had mixed feelings about the war: "I want people who see my
pictures to hate war as I do. But although I am afraid, I have to be there
when the killing starts." Oriana Fallaci, an Italian correspondent, said
she wanted to report a war because "I was a little girl in the Second
World War and my father was a partisan. So I went to Vietnam because
it was the war of our time." She interviewed General Vo Nguyen Giap,
commander-in-chief of the North Vietnamese army, and, in the South,
President Thieu—"He was very passionate, and he even cried. They
were real tears. I really liked him." Kate Webb, a New Zealander, worked
for the United Press and saw more action than most men did. She was
among the first correspondents into the compound of the United States
Embassy after the Vietcong had occupied it during the Tet offensive in
1968. She described it later: "It was like a butcher shop in Eden, beautiful but ghastly. The green lawns and white ornamental fountains were
strewn with bodies."

Kate Webb was captured by North Vietnamese troops in Cam-   56
bodia in April 1971 and held for twenty-five days before being released—"I was asked, 'If you really are an objective reporter, as you
say, you must want to stay with us, having spent so much time with
the other side. Do you want to go back to your family or stay with us?'
I thought of my own dictum—dead men don't write stories. Then I
answered seriously, 'I'd like to stay with you a few weeks and then
return home.' " She could describe in graphic terms what it was like
being on patrol in Vietnam: "The first time I went out, there was a bit
of a fire fight and I was so scared that I wet my pants. I hoped the GIs
would think that it was sweat and that no one would notice. Then I
saw that some of the GIs had wet pants, too, and it didn't matter any
more."

What Henry Kamm of the *New York Times* called proto-journalists   57
were the non-professionals, who "come without real involvement, come

with the vocation of being onlookers, of mixing with those, like the press, who have a safe share in the war." Some of these went on to become correspondents or photographers. (One of them, Tim Page, prefers the description "mercenary journalists.") Some correspondents have objected to being bracketed with them, on the grounds that they were not serious professionals, interested in reporting the war, but "thrill seekers," gun-carrying hippies, who smoked pot and used acid and sometimes heroin, and that, although they looked young and harmless, they were really old and deadly. "Tim Page was twenty-three when I first met him," wrote Michael Herr. "And I can remember wishing that I'd known him when he was still young."

But the accreditation system in Vietnam made it possible for any- 58
one calling himself a free-lance journalist to get an MACV card. All he needed were two letters from agencies or newspapers saying that they would be prepared to buy his material. The Associated Press, for one, would lend virtually anyone a camera, complete with film, light metre, and brief instructions on its use, promise to pay a minimum of $15 for any acceptable picture, and provide a letter to help the new man get his accreditation. A local or home-town newspaper would usually be prepared to provide the second letter. After that, the correspondent was on his own. Transport was free, he could live on C rations, and in the field he was not likely to be charged for accommodations. If he was prepared to take risks, he could find himself comparatively rich overnight.

Tim Page was twenty when he first arrived in Vietnam. At the 59
end of a hippie trip across Asia, he found himself in the middle of a battle at Chu Lai. A series of his photographs appeared in *Life* on September 3, 1965, covering six pages, and for these *Life* paid him $6,000. Over the next eighteen months, mostly by taking photographs where other photographers were not prepared to go, Page made $28,000—not a lot by professional standards, but a lot of money for an orphan boy from a London suburb. Page, Eddie Adams, Sean Flynn, Steve Nerthup, John Steinbeck, Jr., and Simon Dring moved around together. Page and Flynn used to ride in and out of some combat areas on Honda motor-cycles. They had a flip, throwaway attitude to the war, but some of it was quite perceptive. "No one wants to admit it," Page says, "but there is a lot of sex appeal and a lot of fun in weapons. Where else but in Vietnam would a man get a chance to play with a supersonic jet, drive a tank, or shoot off a rocket, and even get highly paid for it?"

Page was slightly wounded in the fighting at Chu Lai, and then 60
more seriously during the Buddhist riots in 1966, receiving shrapnel in the head, chest, and arms. In 1967, a B-57 mistook a United States coast guard cutter, in which Page was travelling, for a Vietcong vessel, and in nine strafing and bombing runs sank the ship, killed three of the crew,

and wounded eight. Page received multiple wounds, and needed twelve operations and weeks in hospital to recover. In 1969, he got out of a helicopter near Cu Chi to help pick up two wounded. The sergeant with him stepped on a mine, which blew off the sergeant's legs and sent a two-inch piece of shrapnel through Page's forehead, above the right eye, and deep into the base of his brain. For some time he was close to death; he recovered sufficiently to be moved to a hospital in Japan, then to the Walter Reed Army Hospital, in Washington, D.C., and finally to the Institute of Rehabilitation Medicine, in New York. He was eighteen months recovering. *Time* and *Life* had bought most of his photographs, and they undertook to pay his hospital bills. They came to $136,000.

While he was still receiving treatment, he had a letter from a British publisher asking him to write a book to be called *Through with War,* which would "once and for all take the glamour out of war." Page remembers his bewilderment. "Jesus! Take the glamour out of war. How the hell can you do that? You can't take the glamour out of a tank burning or a helicopter blowing up. It's like trying to take the glamour out of sex. War is *good* for you." 61

The type of war that Page and others found glamorous—the ground war of attrition against the North Vietnamese and the Vietcong—began to wind down from 1969 on. The American public had been aware of the war in Vietnam in proportion to the number of American combat troops involved and the level of casualties they suffered. President Nixon's policy became, therefore, steadily to withdraw these troops, to pass the ground war over to the Vietnamese, to order the remaining GIs to fight as little as possible, and to switch the weight of the American attack to the air. Since the bombing campaign was not very evident to the American public, the war seemed to fade away. Correspondents attuned to battle reporting found fewer battles to report, editors and producers became less willing to devote space and time to a war that the administration assured them was as good as over, and those reporters who went digging for other stories about Vietnam found that the army had suddenly become extremely obstructive and had started "administering the news with an eye-dropper," as *Time* magazine's correspondent Jonathan Larsen wrote. 62

There were two main reasons for this. The military authorities did not want reported the sad state of the United States Army, and they wanted to encourage public apathy about the war by keeping as secret as possible the escalation of the bombing. They were not successful on the first count. The year 1971 saw a series of stories revealing the massive heroin problem among United States troops (about one in ten was 63 addicted), the "fragging," or blowing up by grenades, of unpopular officers (forty-five killed, 318 wounded in 1971), the staggering desertion rate, the number of combat refusals, and the growing tendency to regard an order simply as a basis for discussion. The *Washington Post* headed its series on the problem ARMY IN ANGUISH, and Colonel Robert Heinl, a military historian, wrote in the *Armed Forces Journal* that conditions in Vietnam among the American forces "have only been exceeded in this century by the French Army's Nivelle mutinies in 1917 and the collapse of the Tsarist armies in 1916 and 1917." GIs were photographed carrying peace symbols, a picture appeared in *Newsweek* of a helicopter with a sign on the side saying "My God! How'd we get into this mess?" and CBS News ran film of GIs smoking pot from a gun barrel.

There was less success in revealing the new emphasis in the war—the intensified bombing of North Vietnam, Laos, and Cambodia. There can be some excuse for the correspondents' failure here, because reporters and photographers were not allowed on air strikes and the official concealment operation was massive—*Newsweek* described it as "the most systematic military cover-up in the history of America's role in the Indo-Chinese war." A former United States Air Force major later revealed—and an embarrassed Pentagon later confirmed—that the United States, over a period of fourteen months in 1969–70, had conducted a clandestine bombing campaign against Cambodia, whose neutrality Washington then professed to respect. Scores of American pilots took part in the cover-up by making fictitious reports, and the Pentagon did its bit by falsifying statistics. What the military was so anxious to conceal was that the bombing of Indo-China was on a scale far greater than anything previously known. During the whole of the Second World War, less than 80,000 tons of bombs fell on Britain. In Indo-China, the United States dropped more than 4 million tons—fifty times as much. Or, put another way, the United States used explosives cumulatively equal to hundreds of the nuclear weapon used at Hiroshima. 64

The military successfully hid the real extent of this bombing campaign behind a screen of lies, evasions, and "newspeak." The Pentagon insisted that its air operations were announced daily by MACV in Saigon. To see how informative these announcements were, it is necessary to quote only one. On March 10, 1972, MACV's release 70-10 said: "Yesterday U.S. aircraft, including U.S. Air Force B-52s, continued air operations along the Ho Chi Minh trail in Laos. In addition, U.S. aircraft flew combat missions in support of Royal Laotian forces in Laos. Yesterday, U.S. aircraft, including U.S. Air Force B-52s, continued air operations against enemy forces and their lines of supply in Cambodia." How many aircraft? How many tons of bombs? What, exactly, was 65 attacked? Were any of the targets (as revealed in classified American military documents quoted in *Air War in Indo-China*) civilian villages that the air force was ordered to destroy—in the mind-boggling "newspeak" phrase—"so as to deprive the enemy of the population resource"? William Shawcross, writing in the *New Statesman,* quoted a Pentagon spokesman as saying, "We do not hit civilian targets. Correction. We do not target civilian targets." To explain how targets that were clearly civilian came to be hit, the spokesman produced explanations involving terms such as "collateral damage" and "circular error probability."

The correspondents did their best. At briefings in Saigon, they pressed for details of targets in North Vietnam. Had the civilian population been attacked? Had Hanoi airport been attacked? Were pilotless aircraft being used? Peter Hazelhurst of *The Times* reported a briefing in Saigon in December 1972 at which the spokesman refused to answer a single question. Frustrated American correspondents said angrily, "Aren't you ashamed of America? The North Vietnamese, the Russians, and the Chinese know what targets have been hit. It's happened. They all know, except the American public." Their protests were useless. The surge in the air war in Indo-China remained poorly reported, and what *was* revealed passed with amazingly little outcry. Shawcross wrote: "One day Nixon and his [bombing] philosophy will be as despised as the Spanish inquisitors are today. But given the Americans' apparently total lack of interest in what their country is doing, now that they themselves are not dying doing it, that will be a long time yet." 66

American reaction might well have been different if the same attention that had been paid to the ground conflict in Vietnam had been given to the air war, if the reader had been told graphically and at the time about the bombing of Indo-China. In the face of official obstruction—at one stage of the surge in the war, the military authorities imposed an embargo on the news and then an embargo on the embargo—how could this have been achieved? 67

There is reason to believe that much, if not all, of the major news about Vietnam could have come out at the time. Even the information eventually revealed in the Pentagon Papers was available or could have been deduced at the time, as I. F. Stone demonstrated, by diligently ploughing through government reports and transcripts of open hearings, and by reading between the lines. It must also have been possible to do this in connection with the bombing of Indo-China, as the experience of Tom Oliphant, a Washington correspondent for the *Boston Globe,* illustrates. 68

Oliphant discovered in 1972 that, although the total tonnage of 69 bombs dropped on Indo-China each month was not announced, the figure was available on enquiry at the South-East Asia Section of the Public Information Office of the Defense Department. No national newspaper, no wire service, no network took advantage of this to present the figures every month and compare them with previous months' totals. So Oliphant began to do it himself. True, there was no breakdown of the figure for South Vietnam, North Vietnam, Laos, or Cambodia, and no other detail to make the stark figure more easily understandable. But it was a beginning, and if other correspondents had supported Oliphant by making similar enquiries, there is no telling what they might have been able to squeeze out of the Defense Department. Oliphant wrote in *Ramparts,* in November 1972: "The press *can* find a way to gather information which the MACV never mentions. If it does, and if the information starts to flow on a regular day-in-day-out basis, the great mass of Americans will draw the appropriate conclusions."

In the end, the Vietnam War was better reported than any of the   70
other wars examined here. But this is not saying a lot. True, there was no censorship, and correspondents were free to move around at will. However, as journalist Murray Kempton has reminded us, with a million-dollar corps of correspondents in Vietnam the war in Cambodia was kept hidden for a year.

There have been many suggestions as to what went wrong. Drew   71
Middleton, the military correspondent of the *New York Times,* blames the very fact that there were no censors. "On three trips to Vietnam," he said in a letter to the author, "I found generals and everyone else far more weary of talking to reporters precisely because there was no censorship. Their usual line with a difficult or sensitive question was 'You must ask the public relations people about that.' The latter, usually of low rank, clammed up, and the reporter and the public got less. . . . Comparing the Second World War and Vietnam, I think there was a hell of a lot more original reporting in the first and not so much sitting around in bars—although there was plenty of drinking—and conning each other on stories."

David Halberstam wrote to me: "The problem was trying to cover   72
something every day as news when in fact the real key was that it was all derivative of the French Indo-China war, which is history. So you really should have had a third paragraph in each story which would have said, 'All of this is shit and none of this means anything because we are in the same footsteps as the French and we are prisoners of their experience.' But given the rules of newspaper reporting you can't really do that. Events have to be judged by themselves, as if the past did not

really exist. This is not usually such a problem for a reporter, but to an
incredible degree in Vietnam I think we were haunted and indeed im-
prisoned by the past."

Was it possible that, as Michael Herr wrote in *Esquire*, "conven-   73
tional journalism could no more reveal this war than conventional firepower could win it"? "All it could do was view the most profound
event of the American decade and turn it into a communications pud-
ding, taking its most obvious, undeniable history and making it into a
secret history." More than one correspondent felt that journalism was
not the best medium for capturing the real war. Gavin Young, one of
the best British reporters to cover the war, wrote: "Correspondents are
bound to be haunted by the feeling that there is probably only one way
to work the various elusive aspects of the war into one wholly satisfactory picture. Apart from the aid programmes, the military operations,
the political ups and downs, how can one depict the human facets of
such a complete tragedy? What of the thoughts and feelings of the Vietnamese? How has the war affected their lives and art, their outlook
on foreigners, and different cultures? How if at all, have the Americans
been changed by contact with the Vietnamese?" Young concluded, "The
Vietnamese War awaits its novelist."

So in the reporting of Vietnam each day's news was swiftly con-   74
sumed by the next day's. Too few correspondents looked back and tried
to see what it added up to, too few probed beyond the official version
of events to expose the lies and half-truths, too few tried to analyse
what it all meant. There were language problems: few correspondents
spoke French, much less Vietnamese. There were time problems: Kevin
Buckley's investigation into "Operation Speedy Express" took two men
two and a half months. And there were cultural problems: apart from
Bernard Fall's and Frances FitzGerald's, there were no serious attempts
to explain to Americans something about the people they were fighting.
On the whole, writers for nondaily publications came out better than
most of their colleagues, because, free from the tyranny of pressing
deadlines, they could look at the war in greater depth—reporters like
Tom Buckley in the *New York Times Magazine,* Jonathan Schell of *The
New Yorker,* and Sol Sanders of *U.S. News & World Report* are examples,
apart from those already mentioned, that spring to mind.

It was a frustrating war for correspondents, with no neat, no sim-   75
ple, no easily drawn conclusions. Nicholas Tomalin of the *Sunday Times,*
later killed in the Middle East, caught the frustration particularly well
in an article he wrote, in March 1969, on the battle of Bien Hoa. Tomalin set out the circumstances of the battle in some detail: 500 Vietcong
and North Vietnamese soldiers attacked the American air base at Bien
Hoa in broad daylight, after infiltrating nearby villages. Following a

fierce fight, the Americans repulsed them, inflicting heavy casualties. During the battle, the hamlet of Thai Hiep, built specifically for Roman Catholic refugees from Hanoi, and thus regarded as staunchly anti-Communist, was levelled by American air strikes because the enemy had made a stand there. "Except that it was fought in daylight, it was an archetype of virtually all the significant battles in Vietnam. The side that won Bien Hoa wins the war." But when Tomalin came to tell his readers who *had* won the battle, he found himself unable to decide. He quoted Radio Hanoi as claiming a victory because the battle had proved that even the "most secure" areas of Vietnam were still totally vulnerable and that Communist troops could be defeated only by blasting Vietnamese villages and civilians into oblivion. He quoted a United States army information officer who "after telling me what a famous victory Bien Hoa was . . . paused and said reflectively, 'I'm not sure why I'm giving you all this crap. I'm a VC supporter myself.' " In the end, clearly dissatisfied that he could do no better, Tomalin reached a conclusion that eventually applied equally well to the 1973 cease-fire. No one had won.

Of the many correspondents involved in reporting Vietnam, few   76
remained untouched by the experience. Of the principal characters in the My Lai story, Seymour Hersh won a Pulitzer Prize; Ronald Haeberle decided to go back to being a photographer, but found that when prospective employers learned that he was the man who had taken the massacre pictures, no one wanted to employ him. Other correspondents moved to other wars—there were noisy reunions in Bangladesh and later in Tel Aviv. Few believed that the cease-fire in Vietnam would last, and when the North Vietnamese attacked in April 1975, forcing the South Vietnamese army to retreat in confusion, many old Vietnam hands hurried back to the front. They were not as welcome as in earlier days. The South Vietnam army newspaper, *Tien Tuyen,* called them "the enemy within," and said that their reporting was playing a major part in the Communist successes. When Saigon finally fell, on April 30, and the war was at long last over, some correspondents found it hard to believe. Peter Arnett's comment summed up their feelings: "I never thought I'd live to see the day I'd watch a North Vietnamese platoon . . . in the square in front of the Rex Movie Theatre."

But in between the cease-fire and the North Vietnamese drive to   77
victory, other correspondents had second thoughts about their job, and some became uncertain whether they wanted to continue. Jack Laurence of CBS had worrying nightmares. "One I always have is seeing myself jump out of a window. I was starting to worry about whether I could keep my head straight. . . . Maybe people like Horst Faas have some kind of steel inside them that psychologically shuts out the horror and

prevents them from being affected emotionally. I'm not saying everyone is unaffected by it. I don't know what other people's nightmares are. I only know mine."

Content Considerations

1. According to Knightley, how did television coverage affect public perception of the Vietnam War? To what extent does his argument persuade you of its soundness?

2. How might the personal characteristics and biases of a journalist affect the way he or she selects which news to report? How might they affect the way he or she reports it?

3. Using Knightley's essay as well as your own experience, work with classmates to determine what a viewer or reader should keep in mind while watching or reading news reports. How does an individual become a critical consumer of news?

The Media in Vietnam

The American media are often blamed for the outcome of the Vietnam War. Their coverage, the charge goes, focused on the sensational, demonstrated a definite antiwar bias, and resulted in undermining public support for the war. Without that support victory was impossible, and thus the military could not win the war.

In United States Army in Vietnam, *however, a 1988 publication of the U.S. Army Center of Military History, Army historians suggest that the blame was misplaced. Although it found some fault with coverage of the war, the Center's report claims that the media covered the war fairly and that their reports represented the war more accurately than those prepared by the administration. The Center cites other causes for the decline in American support for the war.*

Before you read the Center's evaluation, write several paragraphs discussing what could cause a nation's citizens to cease its support of a war. As you read, compare the reasons you thought of with those presented.

MOST OF THE public affairs problems that confronted the United States in South Vietnam stemmed from the contradictions implicit in Lyndon Johnson's strategy for the war. The president was convinced that the conflict was necessary but believed that the American public and Congress lacked the will, without very careful handling, to carry it to a successful conclusion. Accordingly, he sought to move the country toward an acceptance of war, but in so doing to alienate as few Americans as possible. A policy of gradually increasing pressures against North Vietnam seemed the best approach. Besides minimizing public relations problems and preserving as much leeway as possible for his domestic agenda, it would reduce the chance of a major confrontation with North Vietnam's allies, the Soviet Union and Communist China, and might persuade Hanoi to abandon its aggression against South Vietnam before all-out war erupted. At the very least, it would introduce the American public and Congress to the war by degrees while buying time for the military to prepare a proper base of action in South Vietnam. Doing just enough to placate scattered but vocal prowar elements in Congress and the news media, it would also preserve options for the president that might disappear if the so-called hawks gained ascendancy.

Johnson had his way, but at the cost of his own credibility. By 2
postponing some unpopular decisions while making others only after
weighing how the press and public might react, he indeed hardened the
American people and Congress to the necessity for military action, enabled the armed services to build up strength in South Vietnam, and
kept the hawks largely at bay. Yet in the process he also peppered the
public record with so many inconsistencies and circumlocutions that he
prompted one commentator to observe that the record of his administration's "concealments and misleading denials . . . is almost as long as
its impressive list of achievements."[1]

Once the United States had become fully committed to the war, 3
major flaws in the administration's strategy created more public relations problems. Given the restrictions and limited goals Johnson had
adopted—no extension of the ground war to North Vietnam, no invasion of Laos or Cambodia, no action that would induce Communist
China to enter the war—the practical initiative rested with the enemy.
He could choose when or where to fight. If American or South Vietnamese forces delivered a serious blow, he could withdraw into his
sanctuaries to mend and regroup. All the while, his adherents could hide
among the South Vietnamese, subverting the military and civilian bureaucracies and preparing for the day when the United States would tire
and withdraw. Under the circumstances, the only viable option open to
the United States was to convince the enemy that there was no hope
for the Communist cause. To do that, however, the administration had
first to convince the American people that South Vietnam was either
worth a prolonged war of attrition or that U.S. forces could win in the
end without a major sacrifice of lives and treasure.

Neither alternative was possible. For many reasons—political im- 4
maturity brought on by years of French misrule; a corrupt, entrenched
bureaucracy; a lack of initiative aggravated by the "can do" impatience
of the U.S. military; a basic American failure to understand the oriental
mentality—the South Vietnamese were unreceptive to the sort of reforms that might have made their cause attractive to the American public. As for the enemy, with the Soviet Union and Communist China
replenishing his materiel losses and with the number of young men
coming of age every year in North Vietnam outpacing his battlefield
casualties, he could lose every battle and still win. He had only to endure
until the cost of the war for the United States increased to levels intol-
erable over the long term. Although there were moments of insight—
Westmoreland's reflections on the "political attrition" the Johnson
administration was inflicting upon itself and the military, Ward Just's
article on the marines' programs in the I Corps Tactical Zone—neither

the administration nor the press appears to have recognized the implications and potential consequences of the president's strategy.

As the war progressed, the frustrations endemic to the conflict nevertheless found their way into the press with disconcerting regularity. While capable of victories, reporters claimed, the South Vietnamese Army was all too ready to surrender the burden of the fighting to the United States. In the same way, they noted, American forces won on the battlefield but made little progress toward a satisfactory settlement of the war. Meanwhile, corruption remained rampant within the South Vietnamese bureaucracy, and the pacification program appeared either to make little headway or, as at Ben Suc, to be counterproductive.

The Johnson administration responded with public relations campaigns to demonstrate that the South Vietnamese were indeed effective, that pacification was working, and that American forces were making progress. The press dutifully repeated every one of the president's assertions. Yet as the Saigon correspondents continually demonstrated, each official statement of optimism about the war seemed to have a pessimistic counterpart and each statistic showing progress an equally persuasive opposite. When General Westmoreland commented at the National Press Club in November 1967 that the enemy could no longer conduct large-unit operations near South Vietnam's cities, his statement received wide, mostly straightforward coverage in the press. Then, only two months later, the Tet offensive established that Communist forces retained the ability to attack the cities and to confound even the most astute advertising claims.

As the war progressed, information officers found themselves caught between the president's efforts to bolster support and their own judgment that the military should remain above politics. Beginning with General Wheeler's decision to disregard the advice of the Honolulu information conference that the Military Assistance Command should leave justification of the war to elected officials in Washington, they found themselves drawn progressively into politics, to the point that by late 1967 they had become as involved in "selling" the war to the American public as the political appointees they served. 6

Complicating the situation further was a conflict in Saigon between the American press and the military. With censorship politically impossible, the military had to make do with a system of voluntary guidelines that largely eliminated security problems but left reporters free to comment on the inconsistencies that plagued the U.S. effort. Believing that the press had in most cases supported official policies in earlier American wars, especially World War II, many members of the military expected similar support in Vietnam. When the contradictions 7

engendered by President Johnson's strategy of limited war led instead
to a more critical attitude, the military tended increasingly to blame the
press for the credibility problems they experienced, accusing television
news in particular of turning the American public against the war.

In so doing, critics of the press within the military paid great at-   8
tention to the mistakes of the news media but little to the work of the
majority of reporters, who attempted conscientiously to tell all sides of
the story. They also misassessed the nature of television coverage, which,
despite isolated instances to the contrary—the burning of Cam Ne, General Loan's execution of the Viet Cong officer—was most often banal
and stylized. What alienated the American public, in both the Korean
and Vietnam Wars, was not news coverage but casualties. Public support for each war dropped inexorably by 15 percentage points whenever
total U.S. casualties increased by a factor of ten.[2]

The news media, for their part, responded in kind. Citing the   9
clandestine bombing of Laos, the slowness with which information from
the field reached Saigon, and instances of perceived dissembling, reporters accused the military of attempting to mislead the American public. Yet even as they leveled this charge, they yielded far too readily to
the pressures of their profession. Competing with one another for every
scrap of news, under the compulsion of deadlines at home, sacrificing
depth and analysis to color, they created news where none existed—
Arnett's story about the use of tear gas, Webster's report on the severing
of an enemy's ear, a whole string of stories on the dire position of the
marines at Khe Sanh—while failing to make the most of what legitimate
news did exist. The good and bad points of the South Vietnamese Army
and government, the wars in Laos and Cambodia, the policies and objectives of Hanoi and the National Liberation Front, the pacification
program—all received less coverage in the press, positive or negative,
than they probably should and could have. It is undeniable, however,
that press reports were still often more accurate than the public statements of the administration in portraying the situation in Vietnam.

In the end, President Johnson and his advisers put too much faith   10
in public relations. Masters of the well-placed leak, adept at manipulat-
ing the electorate, they forgot at least two common-sense rules of effective propaganda: that the truth has greater ultimate power than the
most pleasing of bromides and that no amount of massaging will heal
a broken limb or a fundamentally flawed strategy. Even if Zorthian,
Bankson, Sidle, and the others had managed to create the sort of objec-
tivity they sought in the press, they would have failed in their larger
purpose. For as long as the president's strategy prevailed, the enemy
would hold the initiative and casualties would continue, inexorably, to
rise.

ENDNOTES

1. Charles Roberts, "LBJ's Credibility Gap," *Newsweek,* 19 Dec 66.
2. John Mueller, *War, Presidents, and Public Opinion* (New York: Wiley, 1973).

Content Considerations

1. What public relations strategy was devised to win support of the war? How effectively did it work? Why?
2. What military strategies made good public relations difficult? How were these strategies related to public support of the war?
3. What made the press critical of the war? What might the media have done to provide better coverage?

Read Some About It

Issues that cluster around the media's role during wartime have to do with access—access to information, to places, to people. Their role is one that has changed as technology has changed. Having instant communication via satellite changes the role from what it was in the past when correspondents sent their reports through the mail or by courier. Planes and automobiles can move correspondents farther and faster than ships and horses. Such speed sometimes complicates the relationship between the media and the military, for it makes even more delicate the balance between telling enough and telling too much.

But the basic issue of access has always been present. The military may censor information for security reasons or in efforts to form public opinion. The media may demand information that could hurt military effectiveness or embarrass officials, and they, too, may attempt to form public opinion as well as inform the public.

Journalist Arthur Lubow supplies a brief history of wartime censorship in the following article, first printed in the March 18, 1991, issue of the New Republic. *Before you begin reading, write a few paragraphs about how public opinion and support may be shaped by information provided by both the media and the military.*

EVER SINCE ORGANIZED war reporting began, belligerent nations 1 have been trying to muzzle war correspondents. The stated purpose is always to keep secrets from the enemy. The unstated purpose, when the war, unlike the Gulf conflict, goes badly, is to keep secrets from the citizens back home. Although civil libertarians may see a yawning gulf between these two motivations, for a military commander the two overlap. It is easier to prosecute a war if the enemy is befuddled and the home front is bamboozled.

William Howard Russell, the first war correspondent, quickly dis- 2 covered the dynamic that would govern his profession. Sent to the Crimea in the winter of 1854–55 by *The Times* of London, Russell described the suffering of British troops and the idiocy of their leaders. At Balaclava, he wrote: "The commonest accessories of a hospital are wanting; there is not the least attention paid to decency or cleanliness—the stench is appalling—the fetid air can barely struggle out to taint the atmosphere, save through the chinks in the walls and roofs, and, for all I can observe, these men die without the least effort being made to save them." Lord Raglan, the commanding general, urged *The Times* to suppress Russell's reports on the grounds that they aided the enemy. In fact, the Russians knew how bad conditions were at the front. It was the Britons back home who were in the dark. Once they were enlightened, the Cabinet fell; and at the front Britain belatedly introduced military censorship.

In those days, however, censorship was crude and tentative. The latter half of the nineteenth century was in fact the golden age of the war correspondent. The exploits of these men are legendary. Archibald Forbes sneaked in and out of starving, besieged Paris near the end of the Franco-Prussian War in 1871, to report in the London *Daily News:* "I had brought in, stowed in a wallet on my back, some five pounds of ham. The servants of the place where I stayed put the meat on a dish with a cover over it, and showed it up and down the Rue du Faubourg St. Honore as a curiosity, charging a sou for lifting the cover." In 1872, pursued by hostile Cossacks across the frigid steppes, J. A. MacGahan rode 400 miles to catch up with the Russian army; and then, finding that the army had advanced, he continued the same distance through what was said to be impassable desert to Khiva. In 1898, witnessing a bloody rebellion against the British Lancers at Omdurman in the Sudan, George W. Steevens wrote for the London *Daily Mail:* "The last dervish stood up and filled his chest; he shouted the name of his God and hurled his spear. Then he stood quite still, waiting. It took him full; he quivered, gave at the knees, and toppled with his head on his arms and his face turned towards the legions of his conquerors." These heroic sagas have long nourished the souls of war correspondents in the way that tales of Sitting Bull comfort the reservation-bound Sioux.

Progress in communications doomed the old-fashioned war correspondent. Because telegraph facilities were scarce and expensive, the early correspondents had relied on the mails; their dispatches were published too late to be of strategic use to the enemy. By the time of the Spanish-American War in 1898, however, the cable was cheap and available. The American authorities installed censors at the telegraph offices where reporters filed (first in Tampa and Key West, later in Cuba) and at the receiving stations in New York. On the battlefield, however, reporters were still perfectly free.

It was the Japanese, in their 1904–05 conflict with Russia, who turned the ratchet of censorship to the squeaking point by introducing what today we call "pooling." Promising Western correspondents a trip to the front, the Japanese authorities kept them bottled up in Tokyo for months. When a handful of reporters were at last selected to go to

Manchuria, they were detained under tight escort at a risible distance
from the fighting. The Japanese were censoring what reporters could
see as well as what they could write. Frederick Palmer covered both the
Spanish-American and the Russo-Japanese wars, and he lived to read of
the Korean War a half-century later. As an old man he declared that the
Russo-Japanese War was the beginning of the end: "It was the start of
the secrecy, which in the world wars to come barred reporters from the
front lines, so that no public should ever know the truth."

For a democracy, total censorship on the Japanese model was   6
thought to be too brutal. An added refinement was required. It arrived
with the First World War. Recognizing the need to disseminate helpful
news as well as to suppress the unhelpful, upon entering the First World
War the U.S. government created a bureau under Colorado publicist
George Creel that would not only administer censorship but also supply
war news. By the Second World War these functions had evolved distinctly enough for President Roosevelt to create the straightforwardly
named Office of Censorship and Office of War Information. As an index
of the success of these sister bureaus, one remembers that, thanks to
total censorship in Honolulu and misleading official statements in Washington, for a year the United States concealed the extent of the damage
at Pearl Harbor. The Japanese knew what their bombers had accomplished. Americans did not. However, correspondents were allowed to
accompany the troops, and they witnessed the critical battles, including
the landings at Guadalcanal, North Africa, and Normandy.

Unlike the two world wars, the conflict in Korea engulfed the   7
United States without warning. Lacking official guidance, correspondents at the start of the war vividly described the panicked, desperate,
under-equipped GIs falling back before the onslaught from the north.
Marguerite Higgins of the *New York Herald Tribune* quoted a young
lieutenant: "Are you correspondents telling people back home the truth?
Are you telling them that out of one platoon of twenty men we have
three left? Are you telling them that we have nothing to fight with, and
that it is an utterly useless war?" General MacArthur's staff branded the
reporters traitors and threatened to revoke their credentials, but
MacArthur waited six months before imposing formal censorship. By
that time most of the reporters actually favored formal censorship over
the self-censorship that they had been observing. (One described the
procedure as "you-write-what-you-like-and-we'll-shoot-you-if-we-don't-
like-it.") Although on paper the code was harsh—no "'derogatory comments" about United Nations commanders or troops, and no unauthorized disclosures about the impact of enemy fire, for example—in

practice the censors were lenient in letting copy through and lax in punishing infractions.

In Korea, as in the world wars, Washington coupled misinfor- 8
mation to censorship in a flagging effort to control American opinion. Near the end of the war, for instance, in the midst of peace negotiations, an embarrassed White House contradicted accurate accounts that it was about to accede to a divided Korea. As *The New York Times*'s James Reston wrote, "The official art of denying the truth without actually lying is as old as government itself." Censorship and misinformation, both in moderation, were part of the game. The reporters were content, or as content as reporters are temperamentally able to be.

But everything went haywire in Vietnam. That war trampled the 9
delicate pas de deux of the previous half century, in which the government imposed censorship and prettified the truth, while the press tested the censorship and challenged the obfuscations. The peculiar situation of the press in Vietnam stemmed from the unprecedented circumstances of the conflict. It was not a declared war and therefore the president could not impose military censorship. Since the war proceeded largely as a counterinsurgency, it would have been hard in any event to make the face-saving argument that censorship was essential to preserve strategic secrets, rather than to sway opinion back home. With government assistance, reporters in Vietnam traveled easily to the battlefield and, except for minimal restrictions (no identification of casualties until the families had been informed, for instance), described what they saw.

In this first American war of the television era, TV correspondents 10
could record the sorts of images that *The New Yorker*'s Michael Arlen described in one "routine film clip": "Scenes of men moving in to attack, and attacking—scenes, in fact, of men living close to death and killing—with one heart-rending sequence of a young soldier being carried out, his leg apparently smashed, screaming to his comrades, 'It hurts! It hurts!' " Not since the golden age had war correspondents been so free to move.

Without censorship the government was like a man who has lost 11
one arm: it overdeveloped its remaining limb, propaganda. Military prestidigitators in Saigon invented figures to show how well the war was going. Back home, officials from the president on down strong-armed editors and publishers into suppressing and distorting the reports from the field. At Otto Feuerbringer's *Time,* editors privy to the "big picture" from Pentagon brass assiduously rewrote the files provided by their correspondents in Vietnam. At *The New York Times* the new publisher, Arthur Ochs Sulzberger, was summoned in October 1963 to a

White House meeting with President Kennedy, who suggested that young David Halberstam had gotten too close to the story in Vietnam and would benefit from a transfer. (Sulzberger declined to transfer him.)

Unable despite these efforts to squelch pessimistic reporting, 12 Washington tried to smother it by inviting dozens of correspondents (Joseph Alsop and Marguerite Higgins were the two most famous) to make quick, escorted tours of the war zone and return with predictions of American victory. What everyone now remembers is the widening credibility gap that eventually swallowed the Johnson administration. But for a time the military's propaganda prevailed. The perception at home was that the war would be won.

However, the policy of letting the reporters see everything and 13 then denying everything they saw ultimately backfired. In this country (and even more in others) the war correspondent has traditionally regarded himself as a loyal auxiliary to his nation's armed forces. In the two world wars American correspondents even wore military uniforms. Although reporters are supposed to be noncombatants, from Richard Harding Davis at Las Guasimas to Charles Mohr at Hue they have carried weapons and joined in assaults. Over the course of the Vietnam War, this partiality to the home team was slowly and painfully eroded. "There gets to be a point when the question is, Whose side are you on?" Dean Rusk told a group of reporters after the Tet offensive. "Now, I'm the secretary of state of the United States and I'm on our side." Even when they favored the American mission of "fighting communism" (and, especially before 1968, most did), American reporters lost their team spirit as they struggled to get their stories heard over the static of misleading bureaucrats. The officials, in turn, grew convinced that the reporters were on "the other side," and blamed the press for souring the American public on the war effort. It was an extreme case of the old dynamic.

To put matters in perspective, consider this incident from the 14 Spanish-American War. Following their triumph at San Juan hill, American troops hunkered down in front of Santiago. They were soaked by torrential rains, raked by Spanish bullets, and racked by tropical fevers. After three days of this, Richard Harding Davis, the most celebrated correspondent of his day, wrote a story for the *New York Herald* that conveyed the desperation, and concluded: "Truthfully, the expedition was prepared in ignorance and conducted in a series of blunders. . . . This is written with the sole purpose that the entire press of the country will force instant action at Washington to relieve the strained situation." When the story appeared, some accused Davis of treason, and the commanding general later said that had he read it in Cuba, he would have arrested and deported Davis immediately. However, between the time that these words were written and published, the Spanish fleet was destroyed, assuring an American victory. There was no need to accuse Davis and his brethren journalists of stabbing their country in the back, of draining America's will to fight. America had won.

Vietnam was a different story—an unprecedented defeat. One lesson in press relations that American authorities took from Vietnam to the current war in the Gulf is that the less said, the better. They are providing almost no information, true or false. Instead, they are relying on a censorship that is almost as rigid as the Japanese variety of 1904–05. Generals prefer to fight with no one watching. For the political leadership, however, a war that lasts more than a few days requires public consent, and the public demands at least some information. The journalists, for their part, are already nostalgic for the good old days of Vietnam, when they could go virtually everywhere and see virtually everything. Both the press and the military are burdened with the memory of Vietnam, but their memories should be longer. Vietnam was an anomaly. In modern war, reporters must be permitted at the front, and they must submit to sensible censorship. Mutual mistrust is part of the shared heritage of soldiers and journalists in time of war. So is mutual accommodation.

Content Considerations

1. Summarize the history Lubow presents. How have the roles and practices of the media changed since William Howard Russell (paragraph 2) reported war?
2. How are misinformation and censorship used to form public opinion during wartime? To whom does public opinion matter? Why?
3. Lubow claims that "reporters must be permitted at the front, and they must submit to sensible censorship" (paragraph 15). To what extent do you agree? How do you define *sensible*?

Eyeballing the Nintendo Apocalypse

Christopher Dickey reported the following about the first days of the American bombing of Iraq from Amman, Jordan. Published in Rolling Stone *March 7, 1991, his story centers on television coverage of the war and what such coverage meant to journalists, civilians, and the governments of the opposing nations.*

When the bombing began, regular network television programming stopped. For hours an American viewer could watch live war coverage, coverage dominated by interviews and commentary but punctuated by spectacular images of bombs locating targets and destroying them. As the days passed, the coverage became less constant on most channels, but the images remained. The impression created by those images is one that bears examination, especially because television viewers tend to watch passively, questioning little, accepting as truth whatever flickers on the screen before them.

What flickered on the screen was, according to most journalists and many military, a highly censored and sanitized representation of war. How can such a representation shape beliefs about warfare?

OF THE LAST TO STAY, Sebastian Rich and Nigel Baker were 1
among the first to leave. Rich, a British cameraman who had been through many wars and had heard many bombs, heard enough on the first night of the American war on Iraq to make him believe it was time to head for the Jordanian border. Baker, his producer, agreed. They were a curious pair working together. Rich was a wild-haired swashbuckler in a leather jacket with a teddy bear in his pocket, a talisman from his kids. Baker was a teddy bear himself: round, amiable, serious.

The morning after that first night of hovering lights and deafening 2
blasts, Baker drove around Baghdad to look at the damage and discovered the world's first surgical Armageddon. Missiles had flown in windows and blasted interiors, shaved off communications dishes, imploded the insides of office buildings. But houses were left standing, bus stations were still open. The first night of bombing had been like hell, but the American bombs and cruise missiles had, like Milton's Satan, found darkness visible. They had hit only what they had wanted. The people in Baghdad discovered with the sunrise that the inferno was not as bad as it sounded. Rich, who was in Beirut when the Israelis laid it waste in 1982, said he looked around and saw "the safest bombing raid I've

ever been in." But still, it was time to leave. They had pictures to get out, and they wanted out themselves.

On the road it was dark, and the six-lane highway stretched in   3
front of them, empty, moonless, invisible beyond the taxi's headlights. Western Iraq, on the way to Jordan, is a wasteland without relief. Sand gives way to sand, and the stars disappear into a flat horizon. Rich put one of his cassettes in the tinny stereo: the Eagles. "Heartache Tonight." For years, first in one gulf war, now in this one, journalists had found in the song a kind of anthem. "Somebody's gonna hurt someone/Before the night is through," it begins. "Somebody's gonna come undone/ There's nothing we can do." All you could do as war loomed and broke, after all, was watch or—as some reporters put it—bear witness.

The driver began to nod. Nod off. Drive off the road. The car   4
skidded to a stop in a small cloud of dust. Rich took the wheel. They went on, faster now. There had been a kind of convoy of six cars when they began. Now they were alone. The others had gone on, and Rich was speeding, pushing ninety miles an hour. A tire blew. Again, dust swirled through the headlights as the car ran off the road not far from sites marked clearly on the highway: H2 and H3. Every newspaper map and countless military briefings had identified those landmarks as the sites of Iraq's Scud-missile bases threatening Israel. Somewhere overhead there were American night eyes watching this place, homing in on it, as they dragged the spare tire from the back, fumbled with the jack, alone on the desert highway with no cover.

The delays put them at the border, at last, at about 10:30 that   5
night. The paperwork was processed. But there was no gas to be found and not enough in the tank to make it across no man's land to Jordan's checkpoint. Reluctantly, they turned back into Iraq and were heading again for H2 and H3 when the horizon flamed up like sheet lightning. The Americans were hitting again.

It was midmorning when Rich and Baker finally got to Amman,   6
and I, comfortably ensconced at the Intercontinental Hotel, ran into them. The ABC videotape Rich brought out with him held the first clear images of the war. He'd stuffed it in his crotch like a tight-wound third testicle to evade searches at the border.

Now it was in a machine, airing all over the world: stunning foot-   7
age shot through a starlight scope that gathered every pixel of luminosity in that terrible night, illuminating the Baghdad skyline in aquamarine, making each tracer, each missile, glow like a close encounter of the third kind. My god, we thought, looking at the scenes unfold on little Sony monitors, it was just as the pilots landing after their missions said it had been. It looked like the Fourth of July. Only better. Because, after all, this meant something.

I was trying to figure out what. Did these awesome images mean   8
we'd won already? Everything we had heard, everything we had seen
on the screen, told us Saddam was all but vanquished. The world was
enthralled by the wizardry of the air war. Even military experts who
had warned days before about the limited effectiveness of bombing now
became effusive in its praise. The Kuwaiti front, after all, was a relatively small area, one opined on the *Today* show. When the B-52s got
through with it, it would look like "a waffle."

There is, on first impression, nothing so authoritative or imme-   9
diate as a television picture. Add to it the high-tech gloss of a starlight
scope or, as we saw later, the cross hairs guiding smart bombs and
missiles to impact and the war you see on the screen becomes as pristine
and precise as a computer simulation. This was the war being brought
into the living rooms of America and the world—a Nintendo apocalypse.

But even on the first day, a cleareyed old Palestinian leaning on   10
his cane in an Amman grocery cautioned me against too much faith in
images. He was sixty-four. He'd seen five wars firsthand in this corner
of the world. He was waiting to see and to hear more. "The defeat is
not complete yet,'" he said. "We are still under the spell of the achievement of the first attack." Saddam had some surprises left, he suggested—and indeed, that night the first Scuds hit Tel Aviv. It was the
same night Rich and Baker saw the attack that was supposed to have
stopped the Scuds from flying and yet hadn't. There was, it seemed, a
glitch in the video game.

Over the next couple of days, all the rest of the Western TV cor-   11
respondents in Baghdad—but one—came out. The Iraqis didn't want
them there and left them no choice. The only reporter allowed to stay
was Peter Arnett of CNN. His network had special privileges, better
access, better connections. It was the only news organization in the
world allowed by the tight Iraqi security to have an open four-wire
telephone line operating twenty-four hours a day between Baghdad and
Atlanta. This had been the key to its triumph reporting impressions and
sounds the first few hours of the bombing. All other communications
were cut. "What we need," said an editor from one of the other American networks as he watched in competitive despair, "is a pinpoint,
surgical strike on that four-wire."

But CNN had something no one else could or would have: the   12
Baghdad ratings. Saddam, in his bunker somewhere, was tuning in.
And even before Saddam started watching, there was the audience in
the White House. The dictator and the president communicated with
each other on a worldwide party line—so publicly that there was never
any room for quiet diplomacy, so quickly that each nuance of policy
was stored on tape before embassies and emissaries working for peace

even knew what was happening. CNN was "better than a diplomatic bag," Bush's spokesman would proclaim as the war went on. Diplomats, despairing, were left to infer their orders and send their responses through television's satellite dishes and correspondents. "CNN's been driving policy since the outset," said an American well familiar with operations of American diplomacy in the region. Diplomats "could send a cable in saying whatever [they] liked, and nobody would believe it 'til they'd seen it on CNN."

Oddly, as the conflict and the coverage widened, the focus of the   13
information coming out of Iraq, Saudi Arabia and Israel was narrowing. Arnett began reporting like the hostage of Baghdad. The Americans bombed a factory they said made biological weapons. The Iraqis said it made baby formula. There were the officially sanctioned pictures: cans of baby milk and a sign. The Iraqis occasionally released tapes they had shot, at times and in places that no one could confirm, of Saddam, of soldiers and finally of wounded, dead and dying civilians. The tapes were Saddam's answer to broadcasts from Tel Aviv showing the damage his rockets had wrought on a civilian neighborhood there. Saddam is always answering Israel, one way or another, and he would have seen the censored Israeli tapes himself on CNN.

Who knew how to get at the truth of this war? It began to strike   14
me, as I talked to Arab friends, that they had an advantage over those of us who grew up in the West. Americans were used to accepting, more or less, what they saw and heard on the screen. The wiser of the Arabs were used to disbelieving everything. A young Palestinian businessman in Amman despaired, at first, each time he heard Radio Baghdad claim scores of planes had been shot down. He wanted Saddam to score an Arab victory, but he remembered the crushing defeat of the Six Day War: "In '67 my uncle from Ramallah drove up to our house in a Volkswagen as a refugee, and on the radio—I remember I was seven—we were liberating Palestine." The Yom Kippur War: "In '73 my father said, 'We lost,' when the Israelis surrounded Egypt's Third Army. And here, people were still celebrating the victory. Up until now people still believe we won the '73 war."

Now it was happening again. But all sides were playing the same   15
game. On the first day, allied commanders claimed to have "annihilated" Saddam's Republican Guard. The second day, they had "decimated" it. The third day they were merely "attacking."

Some of us rolled up to the Iraqi border to talk to refugees emerg-   16
ing from the action. But they told wild and contradictory stories. The most that could be gleaned with confidence was that the war was growing more brutal, the civilians suffering greater hardships than anyone had seen those first few days in Baghdad. But the battlefield, as it really

was, was beyond our field of view. The war the world saw and heard was reduced to flashes of light in the sky, censored videos, dueling communiqués, pool reports and monitored broadcasts delivered by bellboys to the rooms of correspondents in Amman or Dhahran. "It's another fax war," said Tim Llewellyn of the BBC. The thunder of battle was limited, as he put it, to "the rustle of filch under the door."

Indeed, those of us who had spent some time in the Middle East   17 had seen—or rather, not seen—this kind of war before. The fight between Iraq and Iran lasted eight horrid years, and it was allowed to endure endlessly, it seemed, because no one could ever capture the reality of the battle. The most one saw was a carefully guided tour of the aftermath.

Screams and stench, the suffocating dust of crumbled buildings   18 and glutinous slicks of congealed gore were everywhere at the front. Reporters were not. And the fighting, separated from the reality of suffering, was allowed to go on and on. Somewhere, somehow, close to a million people had died. The numbers had just kept rolling over like the score on a pinball machine.

As the American administration tried, in the second week of the   19 war, to reduce expectations of a quick victory, a sense of helplessness set in among reporters trying to tell the story. To explain what was happening, a correspondent could say a lot about politics and context, peace initiatives and diplomacy. But about the war itself there was little to know for sure except that somebody was going to hurt someone before each night was through. Somewhere. Out in the darkness. Invisible.

Content Considerations

1. Throughout this piece Dickey speaks of searching for the truth of the war. Why does he keep searching? What does he find? What hampers his search?

2. What are the consequences of unquestioning acceptance of what one sees and hears on television?

3. Dickey suggests that the war between Iraq and Iran had lasted so long "because no one could ever capture the reality of the battle" (paragraph 18). How important is it that the reality of battle be captured? For whom is it important? How is such reality captured?

DANIEL HALLIN

TV's Clean Little War

Although the idea may be hard to grasp, a civilian can learn as much about war events by what is not told or shown as from what is. A civilian can learn much by examining the approach a broadcast takes to the war events it airs, by examining the language it uses, the graphics it pictures on the screen, the symbols and logos with which it identifies. These elements of television coverage may tell the viewer much more than the actual news report, for these elements may have a more powerful effect on viewers than a recitation of factual information—especially since factual information in wartime often undergoes repeated revision.

Writing in the May, 1991, issue of the Bulletin of the Atomic Scientists, *Daniel Hallin examines some of the elements of the Persian Gulf war news coverage that combined to create a single effect. Hallin is the author of* The "Uncensored War": The Media and Vietnam *(1986) and teaches communications at the University of California, San Diego. Before you join him in his examination, write a few paragraphs about how American culture views war and discuss any shifts that you detect in those views.*

IN THE INTRODUCTION to *Living-Room War,* a book about television coverage of the Vietnam War, Michael Arlen wrote: "I can't say I completely agree with people who think that when battle scenes are brought into the living room the hazards of war are necessarily made 'real' to the civilian audience. It seems to me that by the same process they are also made less 'real'—diminished, in part, by the physical size of the television screen, which, for all the industry's advances, still shows one picture of men three inches tall shooting at other men three inches tall, and trivialized, or at least tamed, by the enveloping cozy alarums of the household."

But Arlen knew that what diminished and prettified television's portrayal of Vietnam was more than the size of the television screen and its location in the domestic space of the home. The nature of television journalism and its relation to its audience, its military sources, and the wider American culture also pushed strongly in this direction. Americans went into Vietnam with a romantic view of war derived largely from the representation of World War II in popular culture. For readers of the *New York Times* and the *Washington Post* the war may have been above all a political policy, part of the global struggle between East and West; television accepted the political rationale, but its focus was different. On television, war was an arena of individual action, a place where men—there was no room for women—could show courage and mastery in a way that was rarely possible in everyday life.

Eventually Vietnam forced a more sober view of war into American culture. *Combat* gave way to *M★A★S★H*, and *The Green Berets* to *Full Metal Jacket*. Older images lived on in such films as *Rambo* but they no longer dominated the culture. But television coverage of the war in the Persian Gulf has brought back much of the guts and glory tradition. And this may prove one of the second living-room war's greatest costs: that it restored war to a place of pride in American culture. 3

Five interconnected images dominated television coverage of the Gulf War: 4

Technology.   Surely the most powerful images of this war were of triumphant technology: smart-bomb videos, tanks rolling across the desert, cruise missiles flaming into the sky in a graceful arc, the homely but lovable A-10 Warthog. "Deadly streaks of fire in the night sky," ABC's Sam Donaldson reported on January 21. "A Scud missile is headed for Dhahran in eastern Saudi Arabia. And rising to intercept it, a U.S. Patriot missile. Bull's eye! No more Scud!" 5

The pictures were compelling: it is hard to imagine better video than the explosion of a mine-clearing line charge. And the technical accomplishments were stunning enough to impress journalists, as when CNN anchor David French was "honored" by the air force with a ride on an F-15E Strike Eagle and gushed about its high-tech effectiveness. 6

The pictures would be different if the cameras were on the ground, where the bombs landed. But in a technological war, especially one in which most of the dying is on one side, this is rarely possible. Even if Iraq had granted the media full freedom to cover the war from its side, journalists would not be interested in experiencing a B-52 attack firsthand. So technological war appears "clean" most of the time, more so when both sides exercise military restrictions on coverage. 7

Network coverage of the aftermath of the Gulf War, when journalists finally could see its human results, often seemed tamer than print coverage, which was full of references to charred and dismembered bodies. In Vietnam, self-censorship was also significant. Network policies limited the use of the most graphic footage, particularly of American casualties. 8

Experts.   These appeared in two guises. First there were the 9 military briefers, standing calm and assured before the clamoring throng of reporters. Their role was much more important in the Gulf War than in Vietnam, where the daily press briefing in Saigon was grist for wire stories but rarely shown on television. It is not hard to see why—military control of the media in the Gulf, especially restrictions on movement, gave journalists there few other channels of information. In Vietnam, journalists were free to visit any unit that would have them and to travel without an official escort. In the Gulf, until the last days of the war when the pool arrangement broke down, small numbers of reporters were shepherded around under carefully controlled conditions. The military managed the media much as a modern presidential campaign does, releasing carefully controlled doses of information, setting up carefully planned photo opportunities, and minimizing reporters' access to any other source of information.

It is interesting that despite complaints and finally evasion by reporters in the field, major news organizations declined to join in legal challenges to the rules. The networks may well have been so wary of appearing adversarial that they were happy to be able to put on the screen, "Cleared by the U.S. Military." 10

The tightness of these restrictions was by no means purely a matter of protecting military security. According to a number of reviews of the press in Vietnam, including studies by the Twentieth Century Fund and the army's Office of Military History, the looser rules that prevailed in Vietnam worked well for that purpose. Journalists in Vietnam accepted guidelines for restricting sensitive information as a condition of accreditation to accompany troops in the field. But they neither had to submit their copy for censorship nor travel in pools organized and supervised by the military. 11

The networks also had their own experts, retired military and Defense Department officials for the most part, whose function was to put the war "into context." This meant that the war was seen from the strategist's point of view, in essentially technical terms sanitized from reference to violence or death. "We have the initiative in the air," reported ABC consultant Tony Cordesman on January 21. Cordesman is a military specialist who has also served as an aide to Republican Sen. John McCain of Arizona. "We can use our aircraft as long as we think we can keep finding valuable targets and killing them before we commit the land forces." (Killing targets is different from killing people.) "We're going to wait . . . as we let air power take what is an inevitable toll and we can undermine and almost destroy the cohesiveness of Iraq's forces." Cordesman stumbled for a moment before saying "destroy" as though he were uncomfortable with a word that connoted violence. 12

Journalists quickly picked up the language. "From the air, sea, and 13 with artillery they pounded Iraqi troops and armor concentrations in southern Kuwait for three hours," NBC's Tom Brokaw said on February 12. "It was the real thing, yet it was also a useful test of the complexities of mounting an all-out attack with so many forces from many different nations." Again there is the parallel with coverage of presidential elections, the focus on candidates' "game plans" which keeps journalists clear of divisive questions of ideology and policy. The parallel to sports reporting is also clear: one of the most prominent visuals of the Gulf War was the computerized "chalkboard," used to diagram military strategies as it is used to diagram football plays.

The fighting men and women. On August 23 Dan Rather opened the *CBS Evening News* broadcast with a report on the First Tactical Air Wing of the U.S. Air Force: "These are the warplanes and these are the fighting men and women who are the heart of the massive U.S. military buildup in the area. We'll show it to you up close and from the inside on tonight's broadcast." The central characters in television's drama of war, in the Gulf as in Vietnam, were the American soldiers, and their moods set the tone of the reporting. 14

Troops went into Vietnam with high morale, and the gung-ho attitude pervaded the living-room war in the early years. Later, as the troops began to sour on the war, television's image of the war became more negative. In the Gulf crisis the reverse was true. During the troop buildup, soldiers in the Gulf would often be heard expressing doubts about the prospect of war. Once policymakers decided to go to war, however, the troops put aside doubts and focused on doing their job. "Can't wait to do it," said one marine in a typical report on the impending ground war (CBS, January 28). "This is what we have been training for—myself for 13 years." Television reflected and celebrated their enthusiasm, and the war came to be identified with them. 15

War brings out "valor and grit," in the melodramatic phrase Rather invoked repeatedly the night President Bush announced a cease-fire. But it also brings out hatred—more intensely in a war like Vietnam which had substantial casualties on both sides—and cold indifference to human life. But television cannot speak of this other side of the war culture, because it would show disrespect to the fighting men and women. 16

A gunner on the battleship *Wisconsin* said with a big laugh to CBS correspondent Eric Engberg on February 9: "The 16-inch is of course a great counter to the other guy's firepower weapon. It's an anti-materiel weapon. And we prefer shooting at their artillery, their structures. Don't waste the 16-inch on people; you can do that with other things!" But his attitude had to be assimilated to the image of skill and bravery, and its moral implications passed over. 17

There is an important connection between the images of the fight- 18
ing men and women and technology. The troops took pride in their
mastery of technology, and their skill was an important theme in news
coverage. But mastering technology generally means accepting its logic,
and the soldiers often added to the chorus of sanitized, technological
language.

The enemy. War reporting usually turns the enemy into the 19
incarnation of absolute evil, and one of the reasons the Gulf War played
so well in the media is that Saddam Hussein's regime fit the image better
than most. Nevertheless, the tendency to portray war as good versus
evil distorted Gulf coverage in important ways.

The enemy is considered to practice a kind of evil we could never 20
practice: his actions and ours belong to different moral orders. Reporting
on the release of oil into the Gulf, Alan Pizzey of CBS said on January
28: "This is the first time in history that nature has been a direct target."
He forgot that the United States defoliated nearly five million acres of
forest during the Vietnam War, spraying almost half of South Vietnam's
forest area at least once.

Although the presence of television cameras in Iraq added a new 21
dimension to this second living-room war, the effect on public opinion
in the West was probably minimal. Images of dead and grieving Iraqis
filled the television screens for a few brief but powerful minutes in the
aftermath of the bombing of the shelter in Baghdad in which many
civilians died. But those images were sandwiched between, and overwhelmed in volume of coverage by, other images: the experts, assuring
us that we, unlike the enemy, care about human life; and the fighting
men and women, expressing gratitude that planes, not they, were doing
the fighting.

If the war had dragged on, Iraq might have taken on a human face 22
different from that of its hated leader. Television has the power to do
that, and more so as it becomes a more global institution whose presence
is accepted across political lines. American TV never had the kind of
access to North Vietnam that CNN had to Iraq.

The flag. The flag never figured prominently in television cov- 23
erage of Vietnam, in an era when patriotism—or nationalism—was taken
for granted. Those who questioned the war were excoriated, but only
very late in the war did part of the public feel the need to, literally, wave
the flag.

For television, the flag is as sacred as the fighting men and women. 24
These symbols are close to the hearts of ordinary Americans, to whose
sentiments television is closely tuned. The flag must be celebrated and

is above politics. The patriotism stories were often found at the end of the news and treated with a heavy dose of symbolic visuals, even becoming part of the network's signature. NBC sent a reporter to Mount Rushmore on Presidents Day to interview people about the war, closing the evening news with their unanimous expressions of support for it and for the president, and a lingering shot of the "American shrine."

Producers of network news shows were no doubt sincerely caught up, like most of the nation, in the wave of community feeling, closely connected to solidarity with the troops, which was labeled patriotism. But the flag was also a convenient political protection from charges that the networks were helping the enemy by reporting from Baghdad. [25]

And the flag provided an upbeat closing to the news, something apparently of concern to advertisers. Despite the increase in viewing during the war, advertisers were reluctant to sponsor war news. The *New York Times* reported on February 7: "CBS executives had even offered advertisers assurances that . . . war specials could be tailored to provide better lead-ins to commercials. One way would be to insert the commercials after segments that were specially produced with upbeat images like patriotic views from the home front." Advertisers, according to the *Times,* were not impressed. But the networks' preoccupation with this problem may partly explain the flag's prominence in coverage. [26]

NBC adopted as its logo a picture of a fighter/bomber superimposed on the American flag with the words, "America at War." This is a good summary of the Gulf War on television: the good feelings and sacred aura of the flag have been attached once again to war. There has been much commentary about the Gulf War "exorcising the ghosts of Vietnam," as ABC's Jeff Greenfield put it the day after the cease-fire, and this is assumed to be a good thing. But the nation learned a good deal of value from Vietnam, and if exorcising the ghosts means forgetting that war is not a parade, this is a dangerous turn for American culture. [27]

Content Considerations

1. What images dominated television war broadcasts? How might these images have shaped public perception of the war?
2. How did you receive information about the Persian Gulf war during its duration? Record your own experience and draw some conclusions from it or interview classmates, friends, and family to see how media coverage affected their perceptions of the war.

3. What point is the author making about war? As you form an answer, respond to Hallin's comments in paragraph 3 about pride, then relate them to the last paragraph of the article, especially the phrase "war is not a parade."

MICHAEL MASSING

Another Front

What constitutes good media coverage of combat? Factual information? Solid statistics of how many are dead, how many are missing, how many are wounded? Photographs and film footage of the front, of battle, of bombings? These may all be a part of what the public needs to know during war, but access to such information seemed limited during the Gulf war.

But access to other information was unlimited. In the following article, Michael Massing, a contributing editor of the Columbia Journalism Review *as well as a writer for other publications, looks at the kinds of reporting done and the kinds that could have been done. Before you read, work with classmates to compile a list of questions you think reporters should find answers to in order to keep the public informed.*

THE WAR MAY BE OVER, but the battle over press access rages. In 1
a U.S. District Court in New York City, an eclectic group of news organizations, including *The Nation, Harper's,* and *The Village Voice,* is pressing a suit against the Defense Department, charging it with imposing unconstitutional restrictions during the gulf conflict.

In the current climate, the outcome of any contest between *The* 2
Nation and the nation would seem foreordained. Yet the effort certainly seems worthwhile: if Dick Cheney and Colin Powell go unchallenged now, there's no telling what they or their successors might attempt in the future.

Looking back at the gulf conflict, though, it seems clear that access 3
was not really the issue. Yes, the pools, the escorts, the clearance procedures were all terribly burdensome, but greater openness would not necessarily have produced better coverage.

Consider, for instance, the case of *New York Times* reporter Mal- 4
colm W. Browne. A veteran war correspondent, Browne was highly critical of the Pentagon's restrictions. "Each pool member," he declared in an article in the *Times Magazine,* "is an unpaid employee of the Department of Defense, on whose behalf he or she prepares the news of the war for the outer world." To illustrate the point, Browne recounted his own experience as part of a pool taken to interview F-117A pilots returning from bombing raids over Iraq. In one dispatch, Browne's description of the F-117A as a "fighter-bomber" was changed to

"fighter"; in another, a colleague's characterization of the pilots as "giddy" was changed to "proud." Browne was also kept from filing a story about the bombing of Iraq's nuclear weapons development plants, only to have General Norman Schwarzkopf make the information public two days later.

Browne's pique is understandable. But what does all this add up to? A sanitized adjective, an altered airplane description, a story delayed for a day. Not exactly the Pentagon Papers.

Of course, had Browne not been forced to join a pool, he might have turned up far more interesting material. I doubt it, though, judging from the work of those reporters who did manage to slip their minders and make it to the front. Telling of loneliness and boredom, cold nights and bad food, their stories offered moving glimpses of soldiers preparing for battle. Unfortunately, they added little to our understanding of the war itself.

Too often, American correspondents seemed to be fighting the last war. Where there was sand, they saw rice paddies, and, like latter-day David Halberstams, they instinctively headed for the front. This was no guerrilla war, however, but a high-intensity, fully conventional conflict, and it required something other than traditional on-the-ground reporting. In particular, it required an ability to digest and make sense of the huge amount of data generated by the conflict.

Take the air war. The general lack of access to Iraq made gathering firsthand information all but impossible. And the press briefings in Riyadh and Washington, with their *Top Gun* videos, offered little help. Yet the sheer number of bombing raids indicated that something extraordinary was going on over Iraq. The Pentagon insisted it was targeting only military-related facilities, but the attacks on power plants, oil refineries, and other elements of the country's infrastructure suggested a far more destructive plan—one designed to return Iraq to "a pre-industrial age," as a U.N. report subsequently put it. What was the Pentagon's purpose in all this? And was it consistent with the U.N. resolution authorizing the use of force to liberate Kuwait? Reporters—busy talking their way through military checkpoints—never bothered to ask.

Nor did they ponder the extent of the killing being carried out by allied forces. True, it was mostly enemy soldiers who were being killed, and that's what war is all about. Yet many of the victims were hapless conscripts sent to the front against their will, and the policy of slaughtering them seemed to demand some analysis. This was not a simple task, given the refusal of U.S. briefers to estimate enemy KIAs. Yet, by extrapolating from the number of sorties flown, the amount of ordnance dropped, and the "killing box" strategy pursued by the B-52s and other aircraft, reporters could have offered some rough estimates of their own. Busy interviewing grunts at the front, they just didn't have the time.

Similarly, the press failed to scrutinize the types of weapons de-   10
ployed by the allies. While reporting endlessly on the chemical-weapons threat from Iraq—a threat that never materialized—correspondents showed little interest in America's own fearsome weapons. Like napalm. For the first time since Vietnam, the U.S. forces used this flesh-searing substance, mostly to kill Iraqi troops in bunkers. In light of the outcry over the use of napalm in Vietnam, one might have expected questions to be raised about its use in the gulf. Yet the few stories that mentioned the subject seemed entirely perfunctory in nature. ALLIES ARE SAID TO CHOOSE NAPALM FOR STRIKES ON IRAQI FORTIFICATIONS ran the head-line over a story in *The New York Times* on February 23. Only eight paragraphs long, the article explained that

> a wave of napalm-fueled fire splashed across the mouths of a system   10
> of caves or trenchworks may fail to burn the occupants but can remove so much oxygen from the air that the defenders suffocate. For this reason, some opponents of its use have argued that napalm should be classified as a chemical weapon and banned.
>
> Nevertheless, napalm remains a mainstay of armies and air   10
> forces throughout the world, and has been used in many wars and minor conflicts since it was introduced in World War II. . . .

That article was written by Malcolm Browne.   10

To get at the real story in the gulf, reporters did not have to travel   11
to the front. They did not even have to travel to Saudi Arabia. Most of the information they needed was available in Washington. All that was required was an independent mind willing to dig into it. In short, this war needed fewer David Halberstams and more I.F. Stones.

Content Considerations

1. What is Massing's evaluation of news coverage of the war? How does he make his opinion known? To what extent do you agree with him?
2. Massing says that the Gulf war "required an ability to digest and make sense of the huge amount of data generated by the conflict" (paragraph 7). Explore his assertion, discussing what kind of news reports might have resulted from such an undertaking.
3. What point does the author make through his examples involving *New York Times* reporter Malcolm W. Browne? What does Massing believe should be the aim of war correspondents? What do you believe their objective should be?

M★U★S★H★

As writer and painter Margaret Spillane reminds readers in the next piece, published in the February 25, 1991, issue of the Nation, *coverage of the Gulf war was not confined to news shows. Talk shows, daytime and late-night, sent their reporters out to interview the public, discussed war events and attitudes, hosted experts. Columnists, broadcasters, retired military personnel, actors, and scholars had their say in various ways and in various contexts.*

The result of such coverage, according to Spillane, was not good. The war became a television production, and not just because of military censorship. Before you read her comments, write a few paragraphs about television as a medium: What are the characteristics of a television broadcast on almost any subject? How are news and entertainment related?

Q: What do Hiroshima, Nagasaki and Baghdad have in common?

A: Nothing . . . yet.

JAY LENO,
The Tonight Show, January 15

WHAT A SHOCK. I'd just spent the first two weeks of 1991 in   1
Ireland, and was beginning to take for granted that country's deeply researched and reasoned media coverage of the massing tensions in the Persian Gulf. But when I got home, switched on the TV and saw the first bombs dropping on Baghdad, it was clear that the Irish, in their overwhelming support for a diplomatic solution, were missing the point: A Middle East peace conference could never have realized the goals of those Desert Stormtroopers in the White House—namely, to tie a yellow ribbon round the grim picture of a bank-busted, recessionary economy and bury it deeper than Saddam Hussein's bunker.

Television demonstrates what a relief this war has offered to many   2
public figures. George Bush has lost his lockjaw look and picked up some Reaganesque by-golly, as in his reference to "the darndest search-and-destroy effort that has ever been undertaken." Now he's on a first-name basis with the enemy, wrapping just enough of his fake homefolks accent around the word Saddam so that it sometimes sounds like Sodom, sometimes Satan.

George Will looks visibly relieved as well. All those years of Sunday-mannered conservatism have paid off: With current events absolving him, the choirboy can start lobbing those stored-up cherry bombs. Less than thirty hours after the first shot was fired on Iraq, Will showed up on *Nightline,* his eyes flashing with a possessed, triumphant light. "Someone should send Saddam Hussein the PBS series on the Civil War!" spake the hyperventilating Will in a voice so like Dr. Strangelove's that I expected to see one of his hands leap forward to keep the other from rocketing skyward. Three days later on *This Week With David Brinkley,* Will was lyrical and fervent as he prophesied: "There's more to S.D.I. than the Patriot, as you will learn to your pleasure sooner or later!" And what delight to see consumer-advocate ninnies eating crow at the vindication of "the military-industrial complex, much maligned since Eisenhower coined the phrase. . . . It turns out they make some pretty good products." Only a party pooper would show Will stories by Fred Kaplan in *The Boston Globe* demonstrating that U.S. infantry fighting vehicles are frighteningly inadequate for desert showdowns.

Life's been a lot easier for the anchors, too, who no longer have to pretend attentiveness to the fine points of Third World culture. Hear Jingo Belle Deborah Norville ask no one in particular, "I wonder what language they speak in Kuwait?" Hear Neo-Nativist Bryant Gumbel giggle on camera when asking Norville, after a Colonel Yacoub finished offering his views on the Middle East, "Did you understand a word he said? I didn't!" Gumbel then went on to tell a story from the Afghan war, when he was sent a guest he'd been assured was "high, high up in the mujahedeen" ("a big muckety-muck," offered Norville). Well, continued Gumbel, they got this guy on camera and "he proceeded to talk and . . ." (Gumbel makes a face of astonished incomprehension). What language was he speaking? asked Norville. Gumbel: "I have NO idea!" Norville: "Blubbedyblubbedyblubbedy!" Gumbel: "You're just trying to restrain yourself from laughing!" Infidels say the darndest things.

This ecumenical embrace was aired on Monday morning, January 21—the holiday honoring Nobel Peace Prize laureate Martin Luther King, Jr. King was conspicuously absent from NBC's programming: I watched the network's news from 6 A.M., and King's name was not heard until a brief snippet of video at 9:35 A.M., showing Coretta Scott King delivering the annual "State of the Dream" address. But they didn't bother to air Coretta's voice declaring, "In 1991 we have to work closer together to protest and march and speak out more often, until preparing for education is a greater priority in every nation than preparing for war." Instead, on the heels of the King item they aired one of those appalling public service announcements that, under the slogan "The more you know . . . ," offers some of the kind of cheery, quick-fix, no-cash solutions to the education crisis (play games with your kids, count the stars together, etc.) that Poppy had in mind when he called himself the Education President. (Speaking of commercials, it would have been interesting to have spent the past five months on Madison Avenue, finding out how products were being packaged to get maximum bang for their war bucks. A number of commercials have been gulf-streamed into P.S.A.s. One features a preachy-dad voiceover reminding you how much petroleum you waste because your foot won't Just Say No to the accelerator: "Let's put our energy into saving it," says another quick-fix apostle, as the logo for Texaco floats over the screen.

The silencing of Coretta Scott King is one of the more egregious   6 insults by a TV news-reporting establishment that, in the face of massive censorship by the military of all Middle East war coverage, has been only too eager to show the Pentagon how well it behaves on the home front as well. On *Donahue,* Phil cited *The New York Times'*s foreign correspondent Malcolm Browne, who likened the new cut-to-Pentagon-standards media corps to Propaganda Kompagnien, Goebbels's troop of war journalists specially trained to make Nazi military exploits look ever fresh and glorious. Fairness & Accuracy in Reporting's recent media survey exposes the networks as having snuggled into Poppy's back pocket for some time now, virtually suppressing news of popular opposition since August. And it's not just an absence of protest footage; FAIR reports that "none of the foreign policy experts associated with the peace movement—such as Edward Said, Noam Chomsky or the scholars of the Institute for Policy Studies—appeared on any nightly network news program." Of the nominal TV coverage accorded to Jesse Jackson's trip to Iraq, "none of these stories included any quotes from Jackson." The networks have undergone a Moonie-style mass conversion to the doctrine that the only true expert is a general with a pension. Look at the Hannibal of the Ho Chi Minh Trail, Gen. William Westmoreland, on *Good Morning America,* referring to the Iraqi leader as "Sadat Hussein": Put a burnoose over their heads and they're all the same.

Clearly, untold amounts of network energy have gone into mak-   7 ing this one a breathtakingly telegenic war, from the snappy America-at-War graphics to the strict policing of the East-West sartorial frontier: stateside correspondents almost metallically smooth and hard looking, with crisp haircuts and sharp suits; gulf correspondents rough-and-ready in tousled hair, wearing something very Banana Republic—open-necked with epaulettes—even if they don't caravan any farther than the hotel bar. A recent David Letterman comment about one NBC war correspondent reinforces the new dogma that never the frontline/anchor twain shall meet. "Arthur Kent won't get Tom Brokaw's job—he hasn't got the hair. Kent's got field hair."

The word "antiseptic" has been applied to the Pentagon's warfare   8
style thus far: what a break for network chiefs, who have to contend with the fact that far more Americans have color TV sets today than at the outset of the Vietnam War. What could make the networks' war-design departments happier than military briefers like Rear Adm. Conrad Lautenbacher? "This is not a video game," admonishes Lautenbacher, as he proceeds to show us a video game. The admiral knows that America wants no more maimed bodies served nightly on the news. Here's something you can watch while you eat your dinner: no soldier bleeding copiously into a Southeast Asian jungle, but a neat electronic colorfield painting in which a red blot flowers against green geometry. Both the image and the explanation—"That was a strategic target which I prefer to identify as a strategic target"—are nonspecific enough to be soothing. When pundits and generals talk about "the mistakes of Vietnam," messy, distressing news is at the top of their list.

One way to avoid messiness is to avoid broadening the discus-   9
sion—hence the small pool of military pensioners as the experts, and virtually no coverage of dissent. But an even more effective tool is velocity: keep the segments short, go for the yes-or-no answer and banish even the tiniest opportunity for pause and reflection. Cut-to-commercial music is being used with far greater frequency to snuff the sentences of those who can't keep it snappy.

While such breathless charging through current events has been   10
the American TV standard for years, in the past few weeks the acceleration has been dramatic. One place where it's well on display, along with the networks' cynicism and opportunism, is in the ubiquitous instant programming segments with names like "Kids Ask About War" and "The Littlest Victims." On the day after the war started, *Good Morning America's* Miriam Hernandez was in an eighth-grade classroom in Arlington, Virginia, sticking a microphone in each child's face and asking what she or he thought about the war. Woe to the children who didn't understand the principle of the soundbite; before their sentences ended they were cut off with a crisp "Thank you."

Anyone who's at home all day can tell you that news reports and   11
commentary go on not just in the standard morning and evening slots but throughout the day on a variety of talk and magazine-format shows. As in newsland, the keep-it-moving protocol rules. On ABC's *Home* show, Mexican-American actor Edward James Olmos was permitted to talk on acceptable Latino-makes-good topics (teaching kids how to avoid barrio warfare and drugs). But with the gulf war just a few days old,

Olmos was concerned about another minority. "Now that this war has started," he said, "how are we going to look at Americans who are Arab or Muslim?" "That's a question that's gonna take some time to answer," offered host Gary Collins. "Let's take a break." But instead of an answer, after the commercials we got the Harlem Globetrotters.

Sally Jessy Raphael did her bit for the war: Twenty women whose 12 men got shipped out to Saudi Arabia were given makeovers. Their guys in the gulf will then receive the before-and-after photos. The show— two-thirds of which was pre-empted by military briefings—managed to give a lot of weeping women in new hairdos a chance to air their feelings to the tune of about seven words apiece. Here's a taste:

> *Sally:* Hold it together, Amy. You okay? . . . There are not 13 a lot of men who have . . . women as beautiful as you. . . .
>
> *Amy:* They pampered us a lot. . . .
>
> *Sally:* (points to photos): That's the old Amy and this is the new. Do you think you can keep that up?
>
> *Amy:* . . . I don't think so, without them at home.

Tabloid TV products like *A Current Affair* manage to sandwich in 14 plenty of human-interest gulf stories between their usual serving of "Funny Man Murder Mystery" and "Pasta al Porno." *A Current Affair* allows such savvy war profiteers as Dr. Joyce Brothers to telescope nimbly a thirty-second housecall into instant War and Remembrance. To a 10-year-old girl whose uncle had just left for Desert Storm, a war only five days old at that point, Brothers inquired, "Do you think this war has made you grow up too soon?"

And instant oral-history projects too: As soon as the war com- 15 menced, *Hard Copy* dispatched correspondents to America's six time zones to see how The People were living with an hours-old war 6,000 miles away. In Los Angeles, correspondent Dean Vallas thrust a microphone at men in a shelter for the homeless, demanding, "Are you supporting your country?" "The American voice was as one," exulted *Hard Copy*'s reporter Barry Nolan, who was corroborated by a man in Anchorage who declared the war "great" and pronounced his response to be "every true American's opinion. . . . And anybody who doesn't like it shouldn't be here." In Greenwich Village, an entire station house of police officers attached yellow ribbons to their badges. There were no reports of reprimands for this violation of uniform code—I wonder if superior officers would gaze so mildly if officers dangled pink ACT UP triangles from their badges.

Only one dissenting voice wiggled through the loud patriot cho- 16 rus. Traveling across the Southwest by train, an elderly woman told *Hard Copy*'s correspondent Rafael Abramovitz: "I don't want to lose my grandsons. . . . It's a whole way of life [in the Middle East] that we don't understand. And we are imposing ourselves on them."

Joan Rivers's early contributions to the war effort included her reporting the fact that actress Margot Kidder had announced her opposition to the bombing of Iraq. Joan then added the utter falsehood that Margot had backed down on her antiwar position with the words, "I'm a kidder." 17

Joan's gulfward comic aim hasn't strayed from the easy bull's-eye of Saddam-bashing ("He's sixty feet underground? I'd be happy if it was just six feet! . . . Do you believe how ugly he is? And in his country they make the *women* wear veils"). Jay Leno's been delivering much of the same to *Tonight Show* audiences: "I just found out that in 1969, Saddam Hussein got a degree in law. . . . If we'd known he was a lawyer, we would have killed him back in August! . . . More bad news for Saddam Hussein: Rand McNally just came out with the 1991 atlas— and Iraq is not in it." 18

It wasn't too much of a surprise that *Saturday Night Live*'s very first show after Bush launched the gulf war would not risk alienating its beer-boy constituency with any daring takeoffs on the U.S. forces' mad-dog Commander in Chief. One *SNL* segment—a satire on John McLaughlin's Sunday-morning news squabbles—had terrific potential. This time it was called "The Sinatra Report." So why didn't *SNL* go bananas on the gulf and let Old Blue Eyes take the blame? Instead of letting Frankie flay peaceniks and caress warheads, they had him take uncharacteristically safe shots at Milli Vanilli and MTV. 19

Most disappointing of all was the guest host: Sting, who's written songs against nuclear holocaust and had photo ops with Amazon Indian chiefs to save the rain forest, uttered not a syllable against the war. 20

But "Wayne's World," *SNL*'s regular sendup of public-access programming, provided an ingenious summation of the war issues that truly preoccupy the network brass. "Wayne's World" usually finds two adolescent boys, Wayne and his sidekick, Garth, doing their community cable broadcast from Wayne's parents' basement. On the Saturday after the first bombs fell on Iraq, they've been awake for three days straight, drinking Jolt cola in a room filled with televisions, doing nonstop monitoring of all the networks' war coverage. Now they're ready to announce their "Best/Worst List of Media Coverage." Among the picks were, Best name of a correspondent: Brit Hume ("Sounds like James Bond"). Best military hardware name: Scud. Worst map: *Nightline*'s ("I built a volcano in the third grade that was better than that"). Worst cut- 21 to-commercial music: CNN's ("It's just drums! Hey, spend some money: It's a war").

Content Considerations

1. To whom was the war a relief, according to Spillane? Evaluate the support she provides for this claim. Do you agree with her?
2. What is the harm of the "breathless charging through current events" (paragraph 10) and "the keep-it-moving protocol" (paragraph 11) of which Spillane accuses television? Use your own experience as well as her comments to explain the answer you construct.
3. What is the author's tone in this essay? What is her attitude toward television coverage of the Gulf war? Toward the Gulf war itself? How do you know?

New & Improved Postwar Press Guidelines

People who practice a particular occupation or profession often have a view of their jobs different from an outsider. Their familiarity with and opinion of its demands and responsibilities, its limitations and mitigations, often differ from those of one who spends his or her days in some other pursuit. Journalism is certainly one of those professions whose practitioners form definite ideas of their jobs. Foremost among these ideas are the protection of free speech and the public's right to know.

In the following piece, published just after the Gulf war, columnist Mike Royko considers the responsibility of the press and its relations with the public. During that war, the media were unhappy with military restrictions on news. The public was unhappy with media coverage but did not mind that the military had imposed restrictions.

Before you read Royko's column, write a couple of paragraphs about what you expect from the press in several areas, not just war coverage. Then write a paragraph about the press's responsibility to truth.

CHICAGO—Because of the widespread anger at press coverage of the Iraq war, the National Association of Newspapers has voted to radically modify the way newspapers cover all news. 1

You've probably already heard about the changes, which are the most sweeping in journalistic history. They are expected to be adopted and rigidly observed by every paper in America within a few days. 2

But for those who may have missed the story, this is the way it was outlined by A.D. Hinkstain, president of the association. 3

"It has become clear that most Americans were dissatisfied with the way the press tried to cover the war. At the same time, polls showed most Americans were pleased by the way the government successfully prevented the press from covering the war. 4

"We believe the press should be responsive to public opinion. Therefore, the National Association of Newspapers has established new guidelines that will be adhered to by the American press." 5

Here are the main points in the NAN's guidelines: 6

All stories about government agencies or individuals will be printed 7 exactly as they are provided to the press by official government spokes-persons. This applies to all branches of government: federal, state and local. Reporters will be limited to asking only two questions:

1. "Is there anything you want to tell us today?"
2. "Do we have your permission to print this?"

To assure accuracy, all stories will be submitted to government censors for review and approval before they are published. If a story is not approved, the reporter will be required to write a letter of apology to the censor for having wasted his time.   8

Investigative reporting of political figures, governmental agencies, and individuals and corporations that do business with government will cease. Those persons who call or write newspapers with complaints or tips about alleged governmental mistreatment, misconduct or injustice will be advised to write a letter to their congressman and to fly a flag on all patriotic holidays. And their names will be turned over to the FBI.   9

No editorials critical of elected officials will be permitted, espe-cially if public opinion polls show that the official has a high approval rating. Those officials with high approval ratings are to be described as being blessed with courage, wisdom, cleanliness and godliness. How-ever, if polls show an official's approval rating has slipped below 25 percent, and he is assured of being defeated in the next election, edito-rials are permitted to describe him as contemptible, low-down, immoral and so on.   10

Unpleasant news is to be avoided in all sections of newspapers. Stories should accentuate the positive and eliminate the negative. For example, an accurate story would begin: "A governmental official dis-closed today that more than half of all savings and loan institutions are in fine shape." Or: "The president signed a new tax law today. He said Americans will still have lots and lots of spending money and that the government will use the taxes wisely and we will all be very happy." Or: "The latest official unemployment figures were released today and they showed that most people have jobs, TV sets, air conditioning and love their president."   11

People are upset about crime. To avoid adding to their stress, crime news is not to be printed. However, to fulfill an obligation to inform, newspapers can publish stories that say: "The latest law enforce-ment figures show that more than 99 percent of all Americans were not murdered this week."   12

The subject of death is also discouraged, since it can be depressing.   13

So it is suggested that stories be written with an uplifting tone, such as: "More than 120 people went to a better life, in a joyful place, to eternal bliss and happiness when they had the good fortune to be aboard an airliner that nicked a mountain, the lucky souls."

Under these guidelines, financial news will be revised. Stock tables will list only those stocks that have gone up in value. The words "bankruptcy," "recession" and "loss" are barred from all financial pages. Why cause readers to hyperventilate? It weakens our national resolve. 14

Political campaigns will no longer be covered by reporters. Campaign strategists, speech writers and pollsters will submit daily statements to newspapers, which will print them without comment. However, should polls show that one candidate is unbeatable and his opponent is clearly a whipped dog, editorialists are permitted to flail the pathetic also-ran as boldly as they choose. 15

Should we be forced to engage in another war to preserve democracy, newspapers will no longer send reporters to the battle zone. Instead, they will be given a statement each day by the commander in chief (a videotape for TV, which services the reading- and thinking-impaired). The commander in chief's statement will be printed on the front page with his official photograph, in color and suitable for framing. Anyone caught leaving that page on a bus or subway, or lining a bird cage with it, will be subject to charges of treason, insurrection, perversion and mopery with intent to gawk. 16

Future wars will be covered by radio talk shows, with officially designated hosts. And sponsored, of course, by Boeing. Under these new guidelines, we will have a happier society. This will be the mother of all journalistic changes. 17

As Mr. Hinkstain put it: "We are finally recognizing and bowing to the public's right not to know." 18

Content Considerations

1. Characterize Royko's tone. Is it effective in helping him make his point?
2. With classmates, summarize the kinds of reporting Royko targets in this piece. What would be the result for each kind if the recommendations were followed?
3. Respond to the column's last paragraph. Is what it suggests about the public true? To what extent?

— *Ideas for Discussion, Writing, and Research* —

1. Using any four pieces in this chapter, discuss how the public seems to regard the media.
2. The pieces by Knightley, Massing, and Lubow focus on reporting war. What do their discussions tell you about the nature of war correspondence?
3. How has television affected the reporting of war? What issues has television technology raised for war correspondence? Use information from the essays by Knightley, Dickey, and Spillane as well as other sources you find useful.
4. Using any four of the selections in this chapter for background and support, propose your own guidelines for war correspondence.
5. Truth is an issue in journalism; how do the selections in this chapter address that issue?
6. What do you believe is the purpose of the press? What are its responsibilities? Use at least three of the selections in this chapter and two additional sources in forming your response.
7. What is your opinion of the media? What good does the press serve?
8. "Media in Vietnam" as well as the essays by Knightley, Massing, Lubow, and Royko examine the conflicts between government and journalism. Characterize the nature of those conflicts. What resolution to the conflicts might you suggest?
9. How does the freedom of a country and its citizens relate to the freedom of the press? Use any four of the pieces in this chapter to help you form or support your position.
10. How does the press shape public opinion, belief, and perception about war? To what extent does this shaping benefit the public? To what extent does it harm?

6

The War Is Over—Now What?

THE WAR IN EUROPE had ended more than a dozen years earlier. Those who had marched to the drums of military bands, who had faced months of misery in trenches across France, who had been exposed to mustard gas and machine guns, disease and destruction, had returned triumphant to parades and promises. In 1920, Congress approved a bonus to be paid in 1945 to these World War I veterans who had braved the tanks and aeroplanes of the Great War.

But within a decade, the world was plunged into a huge depression, and thousands of the ex-soldiers were thrown out of work. Unable to feed their families, they organized, and twenty thousand marched on Washington, D.C., demanding an early payment of the promised bonus for war service.

For weeks in the steaming heat of the summer of 1932, the veterans with their families camped out in a make-shift city of tents and cardboard shacks, a cankerous reminder of the state of the economy. Congress turned down their request for an early payment but had authorized passage home for the veterans. Most left; several thousand stayed, and Washington began to look like an armed camp. Finally, exasperated, President Herbert Hoover told the army to remove the Bonus City and its residents.

Chief of Staff Gen. Douglas MacArthur, along with Maj. Dwight Eisenhower and Maj. George Patton, ordered their troops to forcibly eject the world-war veterans from abandoned buildings near the White House. It was not a proud moment in American history: uniformed soldiers with fixed bayonets scuffling with bedraggled war veterans, their families watching. In the end, the veterans were forced to leave, but there were many injuries, and one youngster later died. The War to End All Wars had eventually pitted one generation of soldiers against another.

The horrendous incident received blaring headlines around the world, and Hoover, already embattled in the White House, lost the election to Franklin D. Roosevelt. Many pundits blamed Hoover's fight with the Bonus Marchers for his defeat. By most accounts a decent and honorable man, Hoover had been director of Belgian Relief and U.S. Food Administrator after the war. But war is strange; its aftermath is usually not what is envisioned at the time of the shooting.

The results and consequences of wars range over the entire spectrum of human experience: personal, political, economic, environmental. And despite the fact that wars have been waged for thousands of years, about the only thing we seem to learn from them is how to fight and kill more efficiently; the consequences are realized only much later.

Has the modern intensity and horror of war become too much for sane humans to endure? War has no peacetime equivalent, so there is no way to prepare for the psychological trauma of witnessing death and destruction on a mass scale, no defense mechanism to ward off the impact of seeing one's friends killed, maimed, mutilated. Yet only recently has the phenomenon of the psychological cost of war on its participants been recognized and studied. The strain of continued exposure to combat may manifest itself years later, or it may debilitate a soldier immediately. In any event, it is now recognized that it is virtually impossible to escape unscarred from the terrors and uncertainties of combat. Years after a war ends, a nation and its citizens may still be psychological victims of war.

What happens to those in a war who are uprooted, whose entire way of life has been destroyed or forever transformed? Following World War II, hundreds of thousands of persons became nationless, refugees from the storm that changed the political boundaries and internal configurations of their countries. These people—displaced persons, D.P.'s—spent years in camps originally built for the German army before being admitted to various nations not always eager to accept them. Following the war in Vietnam, thousands of Boat People sought to flee the new regime, floating on packed vessels often for weeks or months before being picked up by passing ships. It is estimated that in Cambodia, following the Khmer Rouge victory there, millions of dissidents and intellectuals, along with their families, were systematically killed. In Iraq, at least two million Kurds fled their homes after being urged by President Bush to rise up and overthrow Saddam Hussein. They tried, but were overwhelmed by Hussein's troops; they settled in camps in northern Iraq and died by the thousands from disease and starvation.

What is the responsibility of victorious nations toward displaced persons in a war? Is it possible to foresee the disasters to civilians that are a probable result of war?

An endless chain of political and economic consequences that follow wars seems never to prompt any solutions or considerations before the next war. Following World War I, the economic future of Europe hinged on reparations demanded from Germany, a shattered nation with no possible means of repayment except to borrow from the United States. Bankers were eager to lend money to Germany to pay reparations to Europe so Europe could pay off loans to the United States. The whole scheme was a house of cards that blew down in the first gust of recessionary wind, and the world was plunged into a miserable decade of depression before squaring off once more for war.

Economic collapse was forecast once more after World War II, when war-financed industries would have to shut down, but another unforetold occurrence kept the country's industrial wheels turning: the Cold War. Former wartime allies turned on each other, and mutual distrust and lack of communication meant that hundreds of billions of dollars would be pumped into armaments. These high-tech weapons were sold to client nations and anyone else with enough money to purchase them and inevitably would be used in a regional war, sometimes against the very nations that sold them.

In some cases, the aftermath of the war continues much longer than the war itself. In Kuwait, Saddam Hussein released an enormous oil slick that threatens to vastly alter marine life in the Persian Gulf for generations. Before withdrawing, he torched hundreds of oil wells that continued to burn, spilling dense smoke and tons of emissions into the air, with results that even the most highly regarded scientists can only speculate about.

Many post-war scenarios were postulated for the Persian Gulf region by a variety of experts. The most common prediction was that the overthrow of Hussein and crushing defeat of Iraq would leave a power vacuum in the region, enticing others to fight to fill it. Another prediction was that the balance of power would shift to Iran, creating perhaps a climate of dangerous instability. More rosy pictures had the major players in the alliance making peace with Israel. Indeed, after much wrangling, peace talks were scheduled to take place during the last week of October, 1991. It may not be known for many years how successful these would prove to be. What no one predicted was that Hussein would still be in power, that the Kurds would become D.P.'s, and that a major environmental disaster was in the making. At war's end, the United States did little in the region to ensure future peace; in fact, some factors such as the plight of the Kurds work against stability.

What is the answer to the unforeseen problems that arise in the aftermath of wars? We offer none. But as you read the selections here, consider what might have been done to prevent such occurrences. Was any preventive action possible?

As the Bonus Marchers of 1932 learned in their unsuccessful siege of Washington, there are no bonuses in the aftermath of war.

Okinawa:
The Bloodiest Battle of All

Emotions created during a particular event may remain strong long after the event itself is over. Such is often the case with war experiences, as William Manchester suggests in the next essay as he illustrates the strength of emotion and vivid memory created by war.

A Marine in World War II who fought in Okinawa, "the last and bloodiest battle of the Pacific war," Manchester was among the 20 percent of his regiment to survive the battle. After the war he completed his B.A. and M.A. degrees and became a reporter, editor, and professor. He has written several books on politics, journalism, and history. The essay that follows appeared in the New York Times Magazine *in 1987. In it Manchester considers the dedication of a monument to the American, Japanese, and Okinawan soldiers who fought in Okinawa.*

Before you read his thoughts on that dedication, discuss with classmates what you would expect survivors of such a deadly battle to feel and how you would expect the survivors to express their patriotism.

ON OKINAWA TODAY, Flag Day will be observed with an extraordinary ceremony: two groups of elderly men, one Japanese, the other American, will gather for a solemn rite. 1

They could scarcely have less in common. Their motives are mirror images; each group honors the memory of men who tried to slay the men honored by those opposite them. But theirs is a common grief. After forty-two years the ache is still there. They are really united by death, the one great victor in modern war. 2

They have come to Okinawa to dedicate a lovely monument in remembrance of the Americans, Japanese and Okinawans killed there in the last and bloodiest battle of the Pacific war. More than 200,000 perished in the 82-day struggle—twice the number of Japanese lost at Hiroshima and more American blood than had been shed at Gettysburg. My own regiment—I was a sergeant in the 29th Marines—lost more than 80 percent of the men who had landed on April 1, 1945. Before the battle was over, both the Japanese and American commanding generals lay in shallow graves. 3

322

Okinawa lies 330 miles southwest of the southernmost Japanese   4
island of Kyushu; before the war, it was Japanese soil. Had there been
no atom bombs—and at that time the most powerful Americans, in
Washington and at the Pentagon, doubted that the device would work—
the invasion of the Nipponese homeland would have been staged from
Okinawa, beginning with a landing on Kyushu to take place November
1. The six Marine divisions, storming ashore abreast, would lead the
way. President Truman asked General Douglas MacArthur, whose estimates of casualties on the eve of battles had proved uncannily accurate,
about Kyushu. The general predicted a million Americans would die in
that first phase.

Given the assumption that nuclear weapons would contribute   5
nothing to victory, the battle of Okinawa had to be fought. No one
doubted the need to bring Japan to its knees. But some Americans came
to hate the things we had to do, even when convinced that doing them
was absolutely necessary; they had never understood the bestial, monstrous and vile means required to reach the objective—an unconditional
Japanese surrender. As for me, I could not reconcile the romanticized
view of war that runs like a red streak through our literature—the glowing aura of selfless patriotism that had led us to put our lives at forfeit—
with the wet, green hell from which I had barely escaped. Today, I
understand. I was there, and twice wounded. This is the story of what
I knew and when I knew it.

To our astonishment, the Marine landing on April 1 was uncon-   6
tested. The enemy had set a trap. Japanese strategy called first for kamikazes to destroy our fleet, cutting us off from supply ships; then
Japanese troops would methodically annihilate the men stranded ashore
using the trench-warfare tactics of World War I—cutting the Americans
down as they charged heavily fortified positions. One hundred and ten
thousand Japanese troops were waiting on the southern tip of the island.
Intricate entrenchments, connected by tunnels, formed the enemy's defense line, which ran across the waist of Okinawa from the Pacific Ocean
to the East China Sea.

By May 8, after more than five weeks of fighting, it became clear   7
that the anchor of this line was a knoll of coral and volcanic ash, which
the Marines christened Sugar Loaf Hill. My role in mastering it—the
crest changed hands more than eleven times—was the central experience
of my youth, and of all the military bric-a-brac that I put away after the
war, I cherish most the Commendation from General Lemuel C. Shepherd, Jr., U.S.M.C., our splendid division commander, citing me for
"gallantry in action and extraordinary achievement," adding, "Your
courage was a constant source of inspiration . . . and your conduct

throughout was in keeping with the highest tradition of the United States Naval Service."

The struggle for Sugar Loaf lasted ten days; we fought under the worst possible conditions—a driving rain that never seemed to slacken, day or night. (I remember wondering, in an idiotic moment—no man in combat is really sane—whether the battle could be called off, or at least postponed, because of bad weather.)   8

Newsweek called Sugar Loaf "the most critical local battle of the war." *Time* described a company of Marines—270 men—assaulting the hill. They failed; fewer than 30 returned. Fletcher Pratt, the military historian, wrote that the battle was unmatched in the Pacific war for "closeness and desperation." Casualties were almost unbelievable. In the 22d and 29th Marine regiments, two out of every three men fell. The struggle for the dominance of Sugar Loaf was probably the costliest engagement in the history of the Marine Corps. But by early evening on May 18, as night thickened over the embattled armies, the 29th Marines had taken Sugar Loaf, this time for keeps.   9

On Okinawa today, the ceremony will be dignified, solemn, seemly. It will also be anachronistic. If the Japanese dead of 1945 were resurrected to witness it, they would be appalled by the acceptance of defeat, the humiliation of their emperor—the very idea of burying Japanese near the barbarians from across the sea and then mourning them together. Americans, meanwhile, risen from their graves, would ponder the evolution of their own society, and might wonder, What ever happened to patriotism?   10

When I was a child, a bracket was screwed to the sill of a front attic window; its sole purpose was to hold the family flag. At first light, on all legal holidays—including Election Day, July 4, Memorial Day and, of course, Flag Day—I would scamper up to show it. The holidays remain, but mostly they mean long weekends.   11

In the late 1920s, during my childhood, the whole town of Attleboro, Massachusetts, would turn out to cheer the procession on Memorial Day. The policemen always came first, wearing their number-one uniforms and keeping perfect step. Behind them was a two-man vanguard—the mayor and, at his side, my father, hero of the 5th Marines and Belleau Wood, wearing his immaculate dress blues and looking like a poster of a Marine, with one magnificent flaw: the right sleeve of his uniform was empty. He had lost the arm in the Argonne. I now think that, as I watched him pass by, my own military future was already determined.   12

The main body of the parade was led by five or six survivors of   13 the Civil War, too old to march but sitting upright in open Pierce-Arrows and Packards, wearing their blue uniforms and broad-brimmed hats. Then, in perfect step, came a contingent of men in their fifties, with their blanket rolls sloping diagonally from shoulder to hip—the Spanish–American War veterans. After these—and anticipated by a great roar from the crowd—came the doughboys of World War I, some still in their late twenties. They were acclaimed in part because theirs had been the most recent conflict, but also because they had fought in the war that—we then thought—had ended all wars.

Americans still march in Memorial Day parades, but attendance is 14 light. One war has led to another and another and yet another, and the cruel fact is that few men, however they die, are remembered beyond the lifetimes of their closest relatives and friends. In the early 1940s, one of the forces that kept us on the line, under heavy enemy fire, was the conviction that this battle was of immense historical import, and that those of us who survived it would be forever cherished in the hearts of Americans. It was rather diminishing to return in 1945 and discover that your own parents couldn't even pronounce the names of the islands you had conquered.

But what of those who *do* remain faithful to patriotic holidays? 15 What are they commemorating? Very rarely are they honoring what actually happened, because only a handful know, and it's not their favorite topic of conversation. In World War II, 16 million Americans entered the armed forces. Of these, fewer than a million saw action. Logistically, it took nineteen men to back up one man in combat. All who wore uniforms were called veterans, but more than 90 percent of them are as uninformed about the killing zones as those on the home front.

If all Americans understood the nature of battle, they might be 16 vulnerable to truth. But the myths of warfare are embedded deep in our ancestral memories. By the time children have reached the age of awareness, they regard uniforms, decorations and Sousa marches as exalted, and those who argue otherwise are regarded as unpatriotic.

General MacArthur, quoting Plato, said: "Only the dead have seen 17 the end of war." One hopes he was wrong, for war, as it had existed for over four thousand years, is now obsolete. As late as the spring of 1945, it was possible for one man, with a rifle, to make a difference, however infinitesimal, in the struggle to defeat an enemy who had attacked us and threatened our West Coast. The bomb dropped on Hiroshima made the man ludicrous, even pitiful. Soldiering has been relegated to Sartre's theater of the absurd. The image of the man as protector and defender of the home has been destroyed (and I suggest that that seed of thought eventually led women to re-examine their own role in society).

Until nuclear weapons arrived, the glorifying of militarism was   18
the nation's hidden asset. Without it, we would almost certainly have been defeated by the Japanese, probably by 1943. In 1941 American youth was isolationist and pacifist. Then war planes from Imperial Japan destroyed our fleet at Pearl Harbor on December 7, and on December 8 recruiting stations were packed. Some of us later found fighting rather different from what had been advertised. Yet in combat these men risked their lives—and often lost them—in hope of winning medals. There is an old soldier's saying: "A man won't sell you his life, but he'll give it to you for a piece of colored ribbon."

Most of the men who hit the beaches came to scorn eloquence.   19
They preferred the 103-year-old "Word of Cambronne." As dusk darkened the Waterloo battlefield, with the French in full retreat, the British sent word to General Pierre Cambronne, commander of the Old Guard. His position, they pointed out, was hopeless, and they suggested he capitulate. Every French textbook reports his reply as "The Old Guard dies but never surrenders." What he actually said was *"Merde."*

If you mention this incident to members of the U.S. 101st Air-   20
borne Division, they will immediately understand. "Nuts" was not Brigadier General Anthony C. McAuliffe's answer to the Nazi demand that he hoist a white flag over Bastogne. Instead, he quoted Cambronne.

The character of combat has always been determined by the weap-   21
ons available to men when their battles were fought. In the beginning they were limited to hand weapons—clubs, rocks, swords, lances. At the Battle of Camlann in 539, England's Arthur—a great warrior, not a king—led a charge that slew 930 Saxons, including their leader.

It is important to grasp the fact that those 930 men were not killed   22
by snipers, grenades or shells. The dead were bludgeoned or stabbed to death, and we have a pretty good idea how this was done. One of the facts withheld from civilians during World War II was that Kabar fighting knives, with seven-inch blades honed to such precision that you could shave with them, were issued to Marines and that we were taught to use them. You never cut downward. You drove the point of your blade into a man's lower belly and ripped upward. In the process, you yourself became soaked in the other man's gore. After that charge at Camlann, Arthur must have been half drowned in blood.

The Battle of Agincourt, fought nearly one thousand years later,   23
represented a slight technical advance: crossbows and long bows had appeared. All the same, Arthur would have recognized the battle. Like

all engagements of the time, this one was short. Killing by hand is hard work, and hot work. It is so exhausting that even men in peak condition collapse once the issue of triumph or defeat is settled. And Henry V's spear carriers and archers were drawn from social classes that had been undernourished for as long as anyone could remember. The duration of medieval battles could have been measured in hours, even minutes.

The Battle of Waterloo, fought exactly four hundred years later, 24 is another matter. By 1815, the Industrial Revolution had begun cranking out appliances of death, primitive by today's standards, but revolutionary for infantrymen of that time. And Napoleon had formed mass armies, pressing every available man into service. It was a long step toward total war, and its impact was immense. Infantrymen on both sides fought with single-missile weapons—muskets or rifles—and were supported by (and were the target of) artillery firing cannonballs.

The fighting at Waterloo continued for three days; for a given 25 regiment, however, it usually lasted one full day, much longer than medieval warfare. A half century later, Gettysburg lasted three days and cost 43,497 men. Then came the marathon slaughters of 1914–1918, lasting as long as ten months (Verdun) and producing hundreds of thousands of corpses lying, as F. Scott Fitzgerald wrote afterward, "like a million bloody rugs." Winston Churchill, who had been a dashing young cavalry officer when Victoria was queen, said of the new combat: "War, which was cruel and magnificent, has become cruel and squalid."

It may be said that the history of war is one of men packed to- 26 gether, getting closer and closer to the ground and then deeper and deeper into it. In the densest combat of World War I, battalion frontage—the length of the line into which the 1,000-odd men were squeezed—had been 800 yards. On Okinawa, on the Japanese fortified line, it was less than 600 yards—about 18 inches per man. We were there and deadlocked for more than a week in the relentless rain. During those weeks we lost nearly 4,000 men.

And now it is time to set down what this modern battlefield was 27 like.

All greenery had vanished; as far as one could see, heavy shellfire 28 had denuded the scene of shrubbery. What was left resembled a cratered moonscape. But the craters were vanishing, because the rain had transformed the earth into a thin porridge—too thin even to dig foxholes. At night you lay on a poncho as a precaution against drowning during the barrages. All night, every night, shells erupted close enough to shake the mud beneath you at the rate of five or six a minute. You could hear the cries of the dying but could do nothing. Japanese infiltration was always imminent, so the order was to stay put. Any man who stood up was cut in half by machine guns manned by fellow Marines.

By day, the mud was hip deep; no vehicles could reach us. As you   29
moved up the slope of the hill, artillery and mortar shells were bursting
all around you, and if you were fortunate enough to reach the top, you
encountered the Japanese defenders, almost face to face, a few feet away.
To me, they looked like badly wrapped brown paper parcels someone
had soaked in a tub. Their eyes seemed glazed. So, I suppose, did ours.

Japanese bayonets were fixed; ours weren't. We used the knives,   30
or, in my case, a .45 revolver and M1 carbine. The mud beneath our
feet was deeply veined with blood. It was slippery. Blood is very slippery. So you skidded around, in deep shock, fighting as best you could
until one side outnumbered the other. The outnumbered side would
withdraw for reinforcements and then counterattack.

During those ten days I ate half a candy bar. I couldn't keep any-   31
thing down. Everyone had dysentery, and this brings up an aspect of
war even Robert Graves, Siegfried Sassoon, Edmund Blunden and Ernest Hemingway avoided. If you put more than a quarter million men
in a line for three weeks, with no facilities for the disposal of human
waste, you are going to confront a disgusting problem. We were fighting and sleeping in one vast cesspool. Mingled with the stench was
another—the corrupt and corrupting odor of rotting human flesh.

My luck ran out on June 5, more than two weeks after we had   32
taken Sugar Loaf Hill and killed the seven thousand Japanese soldiers
defending it. I had suffered a slight gunshot wound above the right knee
on June 2, and had rejoined my regiment to make an amphibious landing
on Oroku Peninsula behind enemy lines. The next morning several of
us were standing in a stone enclosure outside some Okinawan tombs
when a six-inch rocket mortar shell landed among us.

The best man in my section was blown to pieces, and the slime of   33
his viscera enveloped me. His body had cushioned the blow, saving my
life; I still carry a piece of his shinbone in my chest. But I collapsed, and
was left for dead. Hours later corpsmen found me still breathing, though
blind and deaf, with my back and chest a junkyard of iron fragments—
including, besides the piece of shinbone, four pieces of shrapnel too
close to the heart to be removed. (They were not dangerous, a Navy
surgeon assured me, but they still set off the metal detector at the Buffalo airport.)

Between June and November I underwent four major operations   34
and was discharged as 100 percent disabled. But the young have strong
recuperative powers. The blindness was caused by shock, and my vision
returned. I grew new eardrums. In three years I was physically fit. The
invisible wounds remain.

Most of those who were closest to me in the early 1940s had left   35

New England campuses to join the Marines, knowing it was the most dangerous branch of the service. I remember them as bright, physically strong and inspired by an idealism and love of country they would have been too embarrassed to acknowledge. All of us despised the pompousness and pretentiousness of senior officers. It helped that, almost without exception, we admired and respected our commander in chief. But despite our enormous pride in being Marines, we saw through the scam that had lured so many of us to recruiting stations.

Once we polled a rifle company, asking each man why he had 36 joined the Marines. A majority cited *To the Shores of Tripoli*, a marshmallow of a movie starring John Wayne, Randolph Scott and Maureen O'Hara. Throughout the film the uniform of the day was dress blues; requests for liberty were always granted. The implication was that combat would be a lark, and when you returned, spangled with decorations, a Navy nurse like Maureen O'Hara would be waiting in your sack. It was peacetime again when John Wayne appeared on the silver screen as Sergeant Stryker in *Sands of Iwo Jima*, but that film underscores the point; I went to see it with another ex-Marine, and we were asked to leave the theater because we couldn't stop laughing.

After my evacuation from Okinawa, I had the enormous pleasure 37 of seeing Wayne humiliated in person at Aiea Heights Naval Hospital in Hawaii. Only the most gravely wounded, the litter cases, were sent there. The hospital was packed, the halls lined with beds. Between Iwo Jima and Okinawa, the Marine Corps was being bled white.

Each evening, Navy corpsmen would carry litters down to the 38 hospital theater so the men could watch a movie. One night they had a surprise for us. Before the film the curtains parted and out stepped John Wayne, wearing a cowboy outfit—ten-gallon hat, bandanna, checkered shirt, two pistols, chaps, boots and spurs. He grinned his aw-shucks grin, passed a hand over his face and said, "Hi ya, guys!" He was greeted by a stony silence. Then somebody booed. Suddenly everyone was booing.

This man was a symbol of the fake machismo we had come to 39 hate, and we weren't going to listen to him. He tried and tried to make himself heard, but we drowned him out, and eventually he quit and left. If you liked *Sands of Iwo Jima*, I suggest you be careful. Don't tell it to the Marines.

And so we weren't macho. Yet we never doubted the justice of 40 our cause. If we had failed—if we had lost Guadalcanal, and the Navy's pilots had lost the Battle of Midway—the Japanese would have invaded Australia and Hawaii, and California would have been in grave danger. In 1942 the possibility of an Axis victory was very real. It is possible for me to loathe war—and with reason—yet still honor the brave men, many of them boys, really, who fought with me and died beside me. I have been haunted by their loss these forty-two years, and I shall mourn them until my own death releases me. It does not seem too much to ask that they be remembered on one day each year. After all, they sacrificed their futures that you might have yours.

Yet I will not be on Okinawa for the dedication today. I would 41 enjoy being with Marines; the ceremony will be moving, and we would be solemn, remembering our youth and the beloved friends who died there.

Few, if any, of the Japanese survivors agreed to attend the cere- 42 mony. However, Edward L. Fox, chairman of the Okinawa Memorial Shrine Committee, capped almost six years' campaigning for a monument when he heard about a former Japanese naval officer, Yoshio Yazaki—a meteorologist who had belonged to a four-thousand-man force led by Rear Admiral Minoru Ota—and persuaded him to attend.

On March 31, 1945, Yazaki-san had been recalled to Tokyo, and 43 thus missed the battle of Okinawa. Ten weeks later—exactly forty-two years ago today—Admiral Ota and his men committed seppuku, killing themselves rather than face surrender. Ever since then Yazaki has been tormented by the thought that his comrades have joined their ancestors and he is here, not there.

Finding Yazaki was a great stroke of luck for Fox, for whom an 44 Okinawa memorial had become an obsession. His own division commander tried to discourage him. The Japanese could hardly be expected to back a memorial on the site of their last great military defeat. But Yazaki made a solution possible.

If Yazaki can attend, why can't I? I played a role in the early stages 45 of Buzz Fox's campaign and helped write the tribute to the Marines that is engraved on the monument. But when I learned that Japanese were also participating, I quietly withdrew. There are too many graves between us, too much gore, too many memories of too many atrocities.

In 1978, revisiting Guadalcanal, I encountered a Japanese business- 46 man who had volunteered to become a kamikaze pilot in 1945 and was turned down at the last minute. Mutual friends suggested that we meet. I had expected no difficulty; neither, I think did he. But when we confronted each other, we froze.

I trembled, suppressing the sudden, startling surge of primitive 47 rage within. And I could see, from his expression, that this was difficult for him, too. Nations may make peace. It is harder for fighting men. On simultaneous impulse we both turned and walked away.

I set this down in neither pride nor shame. The fact is that some 48 wounds never heal. Yazaki, unlike Fox, is dreading the ceremony. He does not expect to be shriven of his guilt. He knows he must be there but can't say why. Men are irrational, he explains, and adds that he feels very sad.

So do I, Yazaki-san, so do I.   49

Content Considerations

1. How does Manchester characterize patriotism? How does his characterization resemble your own?
2. Manchester claims that the nature of battle "has always been determined by the weapons available to men when their battles were fought" (paragraph 21). In what ways might the peace that follows war be determined by the nature of battle?
3. How do the author's thoughts about and emotions toward Okinawa emerge from his combat experience? What do his thoughts and feelings suggest about the individual soldier's ability to reconcile the self with war? With peace?

Shell Shock

The proper way for a soldier to act during combat is bravely and, when war ends, the soldier is supposed to resume a normal life, working and living as if he had never known horror.

But it doesn't always work that way; it never has.

Armies have always had deserters; deserting has usually been viewed as the conscious action of a coward. Although armies have always had soldiers who suffer mental breakdowns, such breakdowns were seen as weaknesses that could be overcome if the soldier tried hard enough.

But that isn't always true; it never has been.

Roger J. Spiller teaches history at the U.S. Army Command and General Staff College in Fort Leavenworth, Kansas. In the following essay, originally appearing in American Heritage May/June 1990, *Spiller looks at the history of war-related disorders, disorders that have been known as* neurasthenia, shell shock, war neurosis, combat fatigue, *and* post-traumatic stress syndrome. *Before you begin reading Spiller's history, write a page or so about the kinds of events that occur in a war that might have lasting effects on the combatants.*

LET'S CALL HIM FRANK. "He was in the war" is how adults explained Frank's odd behavior a generation ago. As he walked through the small town then, his gait was clumsy, his clothes disheveled, and he seemed to go nowhere in particular. One could drive through any part of town and chance to see Frank on the corner, his face at once drawn and blank, as he was waiting to cross a street where traffic never ceased. Sometimes he carried a paper bag, clutched as though it were filled with precious things. Frank was ghostly, but in an odd way, never threatening. After all, he wasn't quite there. 1

One day, in direct contravention of parental orders, a child approached Frank and asked him questions. Was he really in the war? Frank said yes. What did he do? He *fought*, he said, in the *Pacific*. Already a devotee of war movies, the child knew what that meant: jungle combat against the most fearsome of enemies, the Japanese. The child's eyes widened, and the questions came tumbling out. 2

Frank answered quietly. He described crawling though the jungle, looking for signs of enemy snipers. What signs? asked the child. Rice, 3

Frank said, at the foot of tall jungle trees. Why? Because, Frank replied, rice down below meant a sniper in the tree above.

Then what did you do? asked the child. Then, Frank said almost inaudibly, then I went up and got him. And after that Frank's eyes seem to turn inward. Sensing that he had hurt Frank, the child clumsily did his best to turn the conversation to harmless matters.

I saw Frank's look again on television not so long ago, during one of several specials on those Vietnam veterans who suffer from what is now called PTSD, or posttraumatic stress disorder. I had been thinking a good deal lately about Frank and his kind, and then all of a sudden here was a man, roughly my own age, staring that look at me from the screen. Strangely, I remembered that I had always thought of Frank as being old.

The Veterans' Administration hospital in my hometown had many Franks; they all seemed old, but none could have been more than thirty at the time. The VA hospitals still have their Franks. They are the old ghosts of battle. They have been with us for years, perhaps even for centuries, inextricably linked by their suffering. PTSD's ancestors reach back at least to the American Civil War. Before this century Russian medical scholars were discussing "diseases of the soul" among their soldiery. Their American counterparts wrote at length about "neurasthenia," but not until the First World War did they apply their knowledge to the military world. During and after that war "neurasthenia" was overtaken by "shell shock" and then by the slightly more sophisticated "war neurosis." The "war neurosis" of World War I gave way in World War II to the even more imposing "neuropsychiatric casualty" or the slightly more understanding "combat fatigue." Indeed, the history of soldiering in the last century and a half can be illuminated by these terms and what they represent.

The man I saw on the television screen was telling the interviewer about his unsuccessful life. Not that he was unable to provide for his family; it was only that he often felt estranged, detached from everyone who cared about him. And when the dreams from the old days in Vietnam were so terrible he could not sleep for fear of having them again, he retreated to his own personal redoubt, a small, dimly lit room, filled with relics of his war, that he had cobbled together in his garage. There he spent the night with his demons. Exhausted at dawn, he would climb into his car and commute to work with the rest of us. None of his fellow workers ever knew of his torments. Had he not presented himself to a veterans' counselor, those torments would be private still.

There were other men on the television program, new Franks all. Several of them had withdrawn altogether from society. Unable to adjust to the civil rhythms of life after their wars in Southeast Asia, they had made their homes in the mountains of the Pacific Northwest, sometimes prowling armed and camouflaged through the night forests. Nearly all were combating a past scarred by drug and alcohol abuse and brushes with the law. They commuted nowhere.

Since the end of the war in Vietnam, Americans have been engaged   9
in a subtle and long-standing negotiation with the memory of that divisive conflict. It was perhaps the most ambiguous of our wars, and its aftermath has been no less so. "Back in the world" after their tours in Vietnam, veterans encountered indifference and sometimes outright hostility.

Even during the war, warnings were being sounded that this con-   10
flict, apparently so different in other ways, could also be different in its mental aftereffects. VA psychiatrists began to speak of PVS, a post-Vietnam syndrome, behavioral disorders that were supposed to have been created uniquely by the war. Robert Jay Lifton, a noted psychiatrist and a passionate critic of the war, told Congress in 1970 that the injustice and immorality of Vietnam were sure to stimulate rage, hate, and guilt among those who had been coerced into fighting it. No wonder veterans had difficulty adjusting, given the character of the war; in Lifton's view, these reactions were normal and appropriate. Lifton thought PVS was so elastic and widely abused as to be useless as a diagnosis. Nevertheless, when his own study of Vietnam veterans, *Home from the War,* was published in 1973, he had to admit that the term was "used by almost everyone."

What had happened was that the post–Vietnam syndrome had   11
slipped out of its professional confines and into public usage, a transformation that mirrored American attitudes toward the conduct of the war itself. As the public definition of the syndrome evolved, the post-Vietnam syndrome became another means by which Americans tried to make sense of the war itself.

At first, of course, there was an orgy of forgetfulness. "Putting   12
the war behind us" became a common refrain in the seventies, when the nation was beset with other domestic and international problems. If remembered at all, the conflict was seen as evidence of a kind of pathological international behavior; those who had fought in it were regarded in much the same way.

But intrusions upon our forgetfulness began as early as 1973, when   13
a group of Vietnam veterans at Southern Illinois University conducted a self-study that found an "emotional malaise" common to all veterans of the war. A *New York Times* survey the following year showed higher patterns of drug abuse among veterans than the national average. By 1978 the VA was reporting that about 20 percent of all Vietnam veterans were "having difficulty adjusting" to civilian life. Less than a year later

the U.S. Department of Justice released figures showing that a majority of the fifty-eight thousand men with service records then in prison had been in Vietnam, a statistic that was sure to make headlines but that alone proved little.

The daily news did not improve the Vietnam veteran's image. Across the country dramatic incidents were reported in which veterans of the war killed themselves, loved ones, and others, had shoot-outs with the police, took hostages, and were implicated in other criminal activities. What made these crimes different was the veterans' trial defense: Their wartime experiences absolved them of responsibility for their actions. The courts were often sympathetic. In widely publicized cases vets were acquitted on the ground that they were suffering "combat flashbacks" at the time of their crime, a modern military variant of "not guilty by reason of temporary insanity."

Meanwhile, the post-Vietnam syndrome was losing ground to a more sophisticated understanding of the problem. Increasingly, veterans' readjustment was made the subject of private and government-sponsored research. One of the earlier studies, published in 1979 by the Center for Policy Research, found that 40 percent of all Vietnam vets suffered some sort of emotional distress and that 75 percent struggled with recurrent nightmares and marital and job problems. Other terms—"delayed stress syndrome," "posttraumatic neurosis," and "traumatic war neurosis," to name a few—began to supplant PVS in both professional and public literature. The inevitable disintegration of the fragile public consensus about the war's effects on its soldiers hinted at a new stage in America's negotiations with its memories of the war. When Jan Scruggs launched his campaign for a Vietnam veterans' war memorial in the nation's capital in the spring of 1979, a good deal more was at stake than the eventual building of a monument. After six years of repressing the experiences of the Vietnam War, America began to face the public and private wounds that still cried out for healing.

In professional medical circles an accepted term of psychiatric reference for these postwar behavior disorders was established in 1980 with the publication of the third edition of the American Psychiatric Association's *Diagnostic and Statistical Manual of Mental Disorders,* known as *DSM-III* for short. Having based their work for the past decade upon outmoded diagnostic guidance within a highly charged social atmosphere, analysts, clinicians, and psychological self-help groups could now turn to *DSM-III*'s new definition of posttraumatic stress disorder.

In the hands of *DSM-III*'s authors, the shock of combat was only one of several possible causes of PTSD. Posttraumatic stress disorder was now defined as a behavioral disorder that set in after "a person has experienced an event that is outside the range of usual human experience and that would be markedly distressing to almost anyone." Significantly, the new definition avoided suggesting that PTSD victims had personalities that made them especially susceptible. *DSM-III* merely referred to "several studies" that assigned a more important role to "preexisting psychopathological conditions," but it carefully emphasized that if the stress was sufficiently extreme, anyone could succumb to the disorder. Natural disasters, catastrophic accidents, victimization by criminal or state action, the death of a loved one, and, of course, combat—any of these experiences were regarded as capable of invoking PTSD in even the best-adjusted people.

Three symptomatic complexes composed the disorder: a tendency [18] to relive the traumatic event through recollections, dreams, hallucinations, or symbols; a general feeling of disaffection in which the victim avoided any situation that threatened to recall the original events of the shock; and finally, what was called increased arousal, or a combination of sleep disturbances, irritability or anger, inability to concentrate, hyperalertness, and what laymen would call jumpiness.

Even now the number of war veterans suffering from PTSD is [19] difficult to gauge. Posttraumatic stress disorder or a milder variant less intractable to treatment, posttraumatic stress syndrome, is estimated by veterans' groups to have affected as many as 500,000, perhaps as many as 800,000, ex-combatants. A recent study by the Research Triangle Institute's William Schlenger found that PTSD sufferers now make up about one-third of the 38 percent of Vietnam veterans exposed to combat action. Translated into raw numbers, Schlenger's figures amount to about 470,000 PTSD casualties. And there are suggestions that the numbers are increasing as time goes by.

Moreover, PTSD casualties are in one sense *new* casualties of the [20] war. Certain aspects of the war, such as the episodic tempo of fire base–oriented fighting, the one-year tour of duty, and the soldiers' access to alcohol and drugs—self-medication, in essence—meant that the fighting soldier could tough it out. Of course, a serious wound enabled a soldier to escape the fighting sooner, but physical wounds and stress disorders routinely coexist, and early evacuation clearly does not protect soldiers from the threat of PTSD. Most victims of the disorder fought their war without resorting to medical treatment for any but physical wounds, went home, and were discharged, only to find that while they had left the war, the war had not left them. Official figures show that during the war, "combat stress reactions," the term of choice at the time, amounted to only 1.2 percent of American casualties, far lower than comparable figures for World War II (23 percent) and the Korean War (12 percent). One wartime psychiatrist reported that only 5 percent of psychiatric admissions were legitimate combat fatigue, whereas 40 percent of all recorded cases were simply psychiatric disorders common to civil life. Earlier wars appear to have contained their psychiatric casualties, and anyway, the declaration of peace seemed a proper prescription for any discontent. But the most prominent feature of the Vietnam War's psychological history seems to have been its postponement.

The more common explanations of Vietnam's lingering psychological effect were born in our judgments on the war as it was being fought. Vietnam was conceived as somehow unique, an aberration of America's military experience, somehow un-American. Convenient as such a judgment might be, it cannot withstand scrutiny. Except insofar as any historical event is unique, our military experience in Vietnam was hardly unusual. The same is true of PTSD.   21

For most Americans the standard upon which Vietnam has been judged—and found wanting—has been the Second World War, a conflict that makes a much more compelling claim to uniqueness than Vietnam ever could. We have fought revolutionary wars, guerrilla wars, punitive wars, imperial wars, limited wars for the finer points of policy, wars marked by low and grudging social support, wars that consumed disproportionately younger men, wars whose supposed nobility was spoiled by atrocity, wars in which the rhythms of life at home were hardly interrupted, and wars in which the soldiers had only the most meager idea of why they were fighting. Indeed, the Vietnam War has been described in all these ways. By contrast, World War II's image is so gratifying that few of these descriptions have ever been applied to that conflict. Indeed, World War II's image is so appealing to the national memory that it has overshadowed the intervening war in Korea, a conflict that in some respects was at least as unsatisfying as Vietnam. If we are forced to remember any war fondly, World War II is always the conflict of choice.   22

Yet none of these traditional standards of judgment are at all likely to tell us what we need to know to understand PTSD. PTSD belongs to the soldier's history of war, a history that until recently has been hidden from view, seldom celebrated, poorly documented, hardly remembered, almost never studied. Because the soldier's history of war does not readily submit to the orderly requirements of history, and because, when uncovered, it often challenges the orderly traditions by which military history has shaped our understanding of the warfare, the soldier's war has been the great secret of military history. And within this special, secret history of war, the darkest corner of all has had to do with war's essential, defining feature: combat—what it is like to have lived through it and to have lived with one's own combat history for the rest of one's life.   23

Throughout history the sustaining picture we have been given of   24 the soldier in combat is his anonymity and his changelessness. Only a heroic act may elevate a solider from the ranks; otherwise he never escapes from the great uniformed masses, turned this way and that, charging here, retreating there. Let a writer describe the career of an ordinary solider at war and he will show us a man who, nervous at first, usually rises to the immediate occasion and does his duty. Purified by his baptism of fire, he attains a state of soldierly grace in which each succeeding combat experience hardens him and protects him from misfortune. If he survives his war, he disappears into manly retirement. Along the way some fail the test of combat. And because the way in which a society conducts war follows in some respects its most deeply held values, those who fail are outcasts.

Though in vogue for centuries, this simplistic view of the soldier at war was at last challenged by the Industrial Revolution. Mechanical advancements enabled combatants to fire their weapons faster, more accurately, and at greater ranges than ever before, forcing the once densely packed battle formations to disperse, to seek intermittent cover from enemy fire, and to adjust their methods of command. 25

What was a good deal less obvious, however, was that there had been a corresponding transformation during the nineteenth century in human relationships and sensibilities: a democratic as well as an industrial revolution had occurred. The modern ways of war sprang not only from deadly new machinery but from a new importance and appreciation of the individual man on the battlefield. If military technology now influenced the conduct of war with an unprecedented force, so, too, did the individual soldier's performance in combat. On the eve of his own death in the Franco-Prussian War, the French officer Ardant du Picq had concluded in his classic *Études sur le combat* that the human cost of combat was going up. "Man is capable of but a given quality of fear. Today one must swallow in five minutes the dose that one took in an hour in Turenne's day," he wrote. 26

Du Picq was precocious. At the time only a few observers perceived the higher human burdens of modern battle. Instead, military commanders and soldiers, very like the societies from which they emerged, saw warfare in Homeric terms, as a matter of valor, courage, manliness, sacrifice, and, on occasion, the intervention of the gods. At all events, whatever a soldier did or did not do on the field of battle was believed to be the result of his absolute and conscious control over his own actions. Men chose to be heroes, and they chose to be cowards. 27

The persistence of the romantic view of warfare is remarkable, to say the least, when it is cast against the military history of the last century. Certainly the experience of our own Civil War should have spelled the doom of romance, but as Gerald Linderman's recent study 28

Embattled Courage has shown, the reality of combat was repressed by the war's veterans. Had soldiers of the Civil War suffered mental break-downs because of their combat experiences, either during the war or afterward? If so—and there can be little doubt that they had—the terms upon which society and soldiers alike regarded warfare ensured that their experiences would remain hidden from notice, ignored or confused with other ailments.

Society was protected from these uncomfortable questions not only   29
by its own beliefs but by the state of medical knowledge in the mid-nineteenth century. Psychological treatises of the time belonged more to the realm of philosophy than medicine. Medical practice aimed at the alleviation of obvious physical complaints, and upon the outbreak of the war, military surgeons, overwhelmed by the massive number of soldiers torn apart by shot and shell, would not have been sympathetic toward soldiers who complained of suffering invisible wounds. In any case, neither society nor medicine provided a means by which such soldiers' complaints could be understood.

Only two diagnoses of mental disorder were available to the field   30
surgeon: If a soldier's behavior was sufficiently bizarre and dramatic, he could simply be classified as one of the 2,603 cases of insanity recorded in the Federal army during the war. But if a soldier was chronically morose, lost his appetite and physical stamina, and was unable to func-tion as well as his comrades, he became a candidate for the more opaque diagnosis of "nostalgia." Described by surgeons as a particularly de-bilitating form of homesickness, nostalgia was regarded chiefly as a "camp disease," marked by lassitude of the spirit, complicated by the boredom of long bivouacs and the rigors of marching. But neither nostalgia nor any other mental ailment was ever attributed to the rigors of combat itself. On the contrary, T.J. Calhoun, an assistant surgeon with the Army of the Potomac, advised his colleagues that if the soldier could not be "laughed out of it by his comrades" or by "appeals to his man-hood," then a good dose of battle was the best "curative."

At only one Federal hospital could a soldier suffering from what   31
modern clinicians would diagnose as a stress disorder expect any sort of treatment. At Turner's Lane Hospital in Philadelphia Dr. S. Weir Mitch-ell investigated neurological traumas that were later recorded in his clas-sic *Gunshot Wounds and Other Injuries of Nerves.* Several of Mitchell's case narratives portray wounded soldiers, suffering from a paralysis that Mitchell and his colleagues had difficulty understanding. Although these cases arrived because of their physical wounds—one patient had fallen from a tree, while another had had part of a tree fall on him—their paralysis seems to have had little connection to their wounds. Mitchell would eventually become a novelist as well as a pioneer neurologist; in

his very first attempt at fiction, a short story in the *Atlantic Monthly* based upon his experiences at Turner's Lane, Mitchell wrote of a soldier, unwounded, who had been made "dumb by explosion."

Since neither society nor medicine could quite comprehend that   32 the shock of combat caused mental as well as physical damage, soldiers took other measures to alleviate their complaints. An enormous number of them—about two hundred thousand on each side—simply deserted. During combat soldiers could always join the unofficial army of stragglers that attended active campaigning. In battle, units seemed to melt away, only to reconstitute themselves once the fighting had stopped. Hidden away among these numbers were no doubt men who in later wars would have been discovered, diagnosed, and treated for combat stress of one sort or another.

Yet the traditional conceptions of human behavior in combat were   33 nothing if not persistent. Each war seemed to provide proof anew that how men acted in battle depended on heroic virtue. Very much in the manner that a star shines brightest before its extinction, the traditional conception of human conduct in battle took on an intense glow in the years between the Civil War and the First World War. At the very time when foundations were being laid for new psychological understanding of human behavior, there appeared within the world of military thought a set of beliefs that held that no matter what the weaponry, the spirit of the soldier, properly inspired and managed by his courageous officers, would inevitably triumph in battle.

Ironically, this crusade of self-deception was being mounted in   34 those very nations where the greatest advances in psychology were being made. In Paris, where Jean-Martin Charcot's studies in hysteria at the Salpêtrière attracted the young Sigmund Freud, French military savants would argue before long that *élan vital*—indomitable will—was the key to victory in battle. While in Germany and Britain theoretical debates over psychology routinely appeared in the medical journals, army officers often spoke of the high casualties that would necessarily be purchased by direct assaults on enemy lines and the corresponding need for men of good breeding and character to lead them.

After the Civil War American clinicians found another diagnosis   35 for mental disorders, one that reached a peak of social and medical popularity by the turn of the century. "Neurasthenia"—literally a loss of the finite amount of nervous energy supposed to be inherent in each person—was promoted by Dr. George Beard and found an especially receptive clientele among the upper classes of the industrial Northeast. Neurasthenia was marked by chronic physical weakness, fatigue, stomach disorders, and anxiety. In private practice after the war, Weir Mitchell himself routinely diagnosed neurasthenia in his well-born Philadelphia patients and prescribed a "rest cure" that he had first tried on Civil War soldiers. But the compartmentalization of the medical and military worlds persisted; both Mitchell and Beard had been wartime surgeons, but neither ever seemed to look to combat as a causative factor in his patients' complaints. Nor, for that matter, did anyone else.

Only a few researchers had an inkling that psychology was an 36 important new means of understanding combat. Before the turn of the century, articles in obscure medical journals in St. Petersburg and Moscow discussed what was called hysteria in soldiers on campaign. From the Sino-Japanese Naval War of 1894-95 came medical reports of "traumatic delirium" among Japanese troops who had been "wounded in the neighborhood of the places where enormous shells had exploded." Toward the end of 1900 Morgan Finucane, a British army contract surgeon at Aldershot, treating soldiers evacuated from the Boer War, speculated in a *Lancet* article that artillery fire might be responsible for the mental disorientation he found in some of his patients. And an American army medical officer, Capt. R. L. Richards, observing combat during the Russo-Japanese War, reported hospital wards and evacuation trains from the front filled with troops, physically untouched, who were mentally impaired and no longer any good for soldiering. None of these reports seem to have made the least impression upon either medical or military thought. The notion that normal men could be mentally as well as physically wounded by the stresses of modern combat could not, as yet, challenge society's long and dearly held misconceptions about what it was really like to be trapped inside a battle.

And then came August 1914. Playing the general too much, some 37 writers have characterized the opening stages of the Great War as a period of free maneuver, and indeed, from the strategic to the tactical levels, the combatant armies did contend with one another in ways that corresponded to the fondest imaginings of any staff-college student contemplating paper victories. But this war was not the lark many anticipated. By the time the maneuvering was definitively finished in December 1914, the French Army alone had suffered more than 350,000 casualties, and on other parts of the front the numbers were sufficient to crush even the sturdiest optimism, save, of course, that of the high commands.

Apart from the vast numbers of troops engaged, the most imme- 38 diately noticeable feature of this new war was the antagonists' relentlessly industrial delivery of fire upon their enemies. And as time passed, their skill at deploying stupendous, unprecedented quantities of shell improved by quantum leaps. Less than a year after the war began, more artillery shells were fired at the Battle of Neuve-Chapelle than had been fired in all of the Boer War.

The sheer magnitude of this shellfire early on produced rumors 39 that men died from that effect alone. *The Times History of the War* reports that as early as the Battle of the Marne, "dead men had been found standing in the trenches . . . [and] every, normal attitude of life was imitated by these dead men" who had no signs of physical injury. Observers lucky enough to retain their wits thought it inconceivable that men could live through such experiences unaffected.

Soon enough, all the warring nations began to receive soldiers   40
evacuated from the front who had become mentally disabled. In Germany the psychologist Karl Birnbaum drew a clinical picture from the first six months of the war in which nervous conditions arose from the fatigue and exhaustion of fighting that included "great weariness and profuse weeping, even in otherwise strong men." One of Birnbaum's colleagues reported soldiers who had lost their voices, who were unable to walk steadily, who were easily startled, and who had difficulty controlling their emotions.

An American psychiatrist, Clarence A. Neymann, who served with   41
the German Red Cross in Heidelberg from the earliest days of the war, saw no cases at all until after the Battle of the Marne had halted the initial German Army offensive. Then, Neymann recognized, "Hardly a transport of sick and wounded . . . did not contain its quota of mental cases." At first such cases were regarded as nuisances by hard-pressed surgeons and were sent farther to the rear, where after a period of "stagnation" they were returned to the front lines. One immediately noticeable class of mental case, marked by tremors, difficulty in standing, and chronic indigestion, quickly acquired the informal diagnosis of *Granatfieber,* or grenade fever. To these were added a growing number of casualties who had suffered "especially trying experiences" at the front. Soon, Neymann reported, his wards became so crowded that the overflow of patients had to be shunted to base hospitals for warehousing.

The *British Medical Journal* for December 1914 carried an article by   42
Dr. T.R. Elliott, then a lieutenant serving with the Royal Army Medical Corps, who reported several cases of "transient paraplegia from shell explosions." Elliott's patients had sustained no physical wounds, but their legs were temporarily paralyzed. He did not discount entirely the possibility that shellfire had created a hysterical condition in his patients, but like a good many of his colleagues, he saw in these cases a physical origin, and shellfire provided a fertile ground in which to look. Elliott thought many cases were misdiagnosed as hysterical when, in fact, these soldiers had suffered physical injuries from being concussed, buried, blown up. He also took note of a diagnostic trend that attributed these complaints to the carbon monoxide and nitric oxide released by high explosives, but he could find no evidence for this in conversations with returning soldiers. Only a month before, in the very same journal, an-

other doctor had forecast, "I do not think that the psychologists will get many cases."

On the contrary, in the months and years of war that lay ahead, there was nothing short of what one scholar has called "a mass epidemic of mental disorders" along the fighting lines, disorders that inspired a huge body of literature on the psychology of combat. At the same time Elliott's article appeared, the British army received a report from lines at Boulogne that 7 to 10 percent of all officer patients and 3 to 4 percent of patients from the other ranks were suffering nervous breakdowns. By the end of 1914 more than nineteen hundred such cases had been reported in the British army alone. The next year that number increased tenfold. By the end of the war, the British army had treated more than eighty thousand frontline men for mental disorders, variously classified. 43

The classification, diagnosis, and treatment of the mental wreckage of combat posed unprecedented and, indeed, unanticipated problems for the medical profession in all the countries at war. Early in 1915 C.S. Myers, writing in *The Lancet,* introduced a classification for these disorders that was—as it happened—all too appropriate to the epidemic then overwhelming battalion surgeons: shell shock. Ironically, Myers thought that hysteria, not concussion, was responsible for shell shock. Another British neurologist, Sir Frederick Mott, quickly entered the debate to agree with Elliot. And so began a veritable flood of articles in the professional journals and in popular literature. For better or worse, *shell shock* was enshrined as a term of public usage. 44

Shell shock had a convoluted career both during the war and after. The diagnosis was so obligingly broad that it could be applied to any number of mental ailments, and before long shell shock aroused suspicion in medical as well as—not surprisingly—military circles. By 1916 physicians only reluctantly employed the popular term, preferring to rely instead on more conventional diagnoses such as neurasthenia and war neurosis, and most of the medical elite understood that whatever lay at the bottom of shell shock, the concussions of high explosives and their gases were entirely too simplistic an explanation. 45

While the medical debates progressed, however, a war was on, and commanding officers interpreted shell shock in accordance with their own unambiguous professional values. In the early days of the war soldiers found wandering about behind the combat lines were simply shot for cowardice. Others who funked their duty were court-martialed. One commander flatly "refused to allow" shell-shock cases in his battalion, while in one particular infantry division anyone who evinced symptoms of shell shock was tied to the barbed-wire lines that protected the trenches. 46

This approach might have become more widespread but for the remarkable numbers of "all-round good sporting chaps" among the of- 47 ficer classes who broke down. Faced with mounting shell-shock casualties, not to mention the terrifying realities of the carnage on the Western front, the armies in time conceded that mental stresses, however classified, could easily debilitate their soldiers. One official estimate showed more than two hundred thousand British soldiers discharged during the war because of shell shock.

One of the most public cases of shell shock was that of the poet Siegfried Sassoon. As a young officer in the Royal Welsh Fusiliers from 1915 on, Sassoon was a model soldier, well liked by his men and so avid a trench raider that he was nicknamed Mad Jack. Having already won the Military Cross, Sassoon was convalescing from his latest wound when in the summer of 1917 he wrote "A Soldier's Declaration," which protested the conduct of the war and announced that he would no longer contribute to the massacre. And just to make sure he was heard, he sent copies of the protest to his commanding officer and the House of Commons. "A Soldier's Declaration" was published in the *Times* of London at the end of July, but by then Sassoon had already met an army medical board and been packed off as a shell-shock case to the Craiglockhart War Hospital near Edinburgh. [48]

At Craiglockhart Sassoon was fortunate to be entrusted to Dr. W.H.R. Rivers, a young Freudian whose realistic understanding of shell shock was founded upon an unromantic view of the battlefield rather than on rarefied theories. Rivers soon decided that the young officer only needed rest, but he could have fallen into the clutches of other physicians who advocated a so-called disciplinary treatment for shell shock that included painful electrical shocks, isolation, and unsympathetic handling; all intended to encourage the reappearance of the soldier's "normal" self. [49]

Sassoon was familiar with such rough-and-ready treatment, part of which encouraged shell-shocked soldiers to repress their memories of the trenches, shake themselves out of their depression, and carry on manfully. In "Repression of War Experience," a poem published after his experience at Craiglockhart, Sassoon made savage fun of "disciplinary treatment" and the outmoded social view that inspired it: [50]

> And it's been proved that soldiers don't go mad
> Unless they lose control of ugly thoughts
> That drive them out to jabber among the trees.

Eventually discharged by Rivers, Sassoon returned to the front, his views on the war unchanged. There he fought until July 1918, when he was wounded again and invalided home for good. But to say that Sassoon's war was over would be a mistake. In the form of restlessness, [51] irritability, guilt over surviving, and, above all, battle dreams, Sassoon's war remained alive for years afterward. His memoirs recalled his time at Craiglockhart and his fellow patients there: "Shell shock. How many a brief bombardment had its long-delayed after-effect in the minds of these survivors, many of whom had looked at their companions and laughed while inferno did its best to destroy them. Not then was their evil hour; but now; now, in the sweating suffocation of nightmare, in paralysis of limbs, in the stammering of dislocated speech. . . . "

Sassoon was right. The "long-delayed after-effect" of the war was [52] to be an essential part of European postwar life. The war had blasted a great demographic hole in all the combatant nations. In Germany, where thirty-one per thousand of that nation's population were killed during the war, another 10 percent of the population—disabled veterans, widows, and dependent families—six million in all, were victimized by it. The French lost even more: thirty-four killed for every thousand citizens. Great Britain's war dead was less—sixteen per thousand of population—but that nation confronted the same problems of human reconstruction as the other Europeans. Ten years afterward more than two million British veterans were receiving some sort of government assistance. Sixty-five thousand of these were still in mental hospitals, suffering from what was then classified as "chronic neurasthenia."

The fortunes of shell-shocked veterans depended more upon social [53] views than medical advances. Even though some German psychiatrists advanced highly sophisticated explanations for war-related nervous disorders, German society at large resisted the idea that war alone caused nervous disability. Less than 2 percent of all German casualties treated during the war had been diagnosed as nervous disorders. Either a shell-shocked veteran was insane or his suffering had to do with heredity. That being so, the war bore no responsibility for his mental state. True to this form, six years after the war's end only 5,410 German veterans were drawing pensions on diagnoses of insanity as a result of their service.

While a highly conservative medical opinion held sway in Ger- [54] many, in Britain the whole question of shell shock became a matter for heated public discussion. As early as 1915 members of Parliament, fearful that shell-shock victims returning from the front would be consigned to lunatic asylums, moved to prevent shell-shock cases from being confused with ordinary cases of insanity. Parliament's concerns were real enough: one doctor estimated that more than 20 percent of all the shell-shock victims at one of the army's main hospitals were committed to asylums. Moreover, quite without regard to what the doctors or the army (whose medical service had forbidden use of shell shock as a diagnosis in 1917) thought, the British public readily accepted shell shock as a war-related nervous disorder that could afflict anyone at all. During the ten years immediately following the war, pension authorities examined 114,000 shell-shocked veterans. On the eve of World War II, the British Ministry of Pensions was still paying two million pounds a year to shell-shocked pensioners from the 1914–18 war.

The veterans of the Great War phrased their complaints in much   55
the same way as Vietnam veterans more than half a century later. Front-line troops often resented all but their own kind, and especially their countrymen on the home front. When soldiers returned home to find scant appreciation or understanding of their wartime trials, their resentment could easily deepen into bitterness and outright alienation. A German veteran's lament, written in 1925, could pass for some veteran's complaint today: 'The . . . army returned home . . . after doing its duty and was shamefully received. There were no laurel wreaths; hate-filled words were hurled at the soldiers. Military decorations were torn from the soldiers' . . . uniforms. . . .'' Weimar Germany struck no medals commemorating war service as in times past. Not until six years after the armistice was there an official memorial service for the war dead.

But these were public manifestations of much more private trials.   56
Sassoon's Craiglockhart psychiatrist, Rivers, believed that society did no good at all by asking, "What's it really like?" and then insisting that soldiers "banish all thoughts of war from their minds." Torn between a conflicting desire to retrieve the past and to avoid its pain, the soldiers found their inchoate memories had become an essential part of their identities. Rivers thought that the best course of action lay somewhere between the outright repression of one's war experiences and an unhealthy fixation upon the past.

This was more easily said than done. Veterans who recorded their   57
postwar experiences often mentioned nightmares, vivid battle dreams that persisted for years, sometimes for decades. Certain events unexpectedly called forth memories of the war. Armistice Day celebrations meant reliving a murderous chaos in Delville Wood for one veteran— "hand-to-hand fighting with knives and bayonets, cursing and brutality on both sides, mud and stench, dysentery and unattended wounds. . . .'' Unable to come to terms with a peaceful, indifferent society, another veteran escaped to the country: "I realized that this was what I needed. Silence. Isolation. Now that I could let go, I broke down, avoided strangers, cried easily and had terrible nightmares."

Steering a course between repression and fixation proved difficult   58
for the armies as well, for when the Second World War began, much of what had been discovered in the Great War about the stresses of combat had been repressed all too well. Valuable insights into the management of combat stress, the diagnosis and treatment of soldiers suf-

fering from nervous disorders, and the vast professional organization required to tend such cases, not to mention a substantial body of medical and military knowledge—all were seemingly forgotten by the outbreak of World War II. The United States had suffered only a glancing blow in the Great War when compared with other nations, yet in 1942 some 58 percent of all the patients in VA hospitals were World War I shell-shock cases, now twenty-four years older. Ignoring experience, knowledge, and memory, the U.S. Army followed a now familiar cycle of mystification, suspicion, diagnostic confusion, a competition between military and medical authorities for the power to determine how such cases fitted within the business of war, a grudging reconciliation with the unavoidable facts of combat fatigue, and, by war's end, a pragmatic approach to neuropsychiatric battle casualties.

In the period between the two world wars, medical authorities in the American army, confident that "proper psychiatric screening of the mentally unfit at induction was the basic solution for eliminating the psychiatric disorders of military service," managed to institute psychiatric exams of soldiers when they enlisted. Of 5.2 million American men called to the recruiting stations after Pearl Harbor, 1.6 million were prevented from enlisting because of various "mental deficiencies." But the widespread faith in psychiatric screening that one American army psychiatrist observed could only be "equated with the use of magic" was again tested by combat. In the American army alone the enlistee rejection rate for this war was more than seven and a half times that of World War I, yet before the war was over, the psychiatric discharge rate soared to 250 percent of that earlier conflict. 59

Since U.S. Army medical authorities were slow to recognize the problem that awaited them—the Surgeon General's Office of the U.S. Army did not even appoint a psychiatric consultant until well after the war began—the troops were in effect defenseless against combat stress in the first years of the war. Field commanders once again adopted the rough-and-ready approach so prevalent in the Great War, and which Gen. George Patton's celebrated slapping incident showed was still in vogue in some fighting units. On the besieged island of Malta in 1942, when air attacks were at their most intense, antiaircraft artillery crews were officially advised that "anxiety neurosis was the term employed by the medical profession to commercialize fear, that if a soldier was a man he would not permit his self-respect to admit an anxiety neurosis or to show fear." 60

Knowing very well that most physicians had little training in or understanding of psychiatric disorders in civil life, much less the special permutations that combat stress could produce, psychiatrists were anxious to find their way to the front lines, a journey whose difficulties 61

were compounded by a less than warm reception from military authorities. One board-certified psychiatrist who was to accompany the Americans' Western Task Force as it invaded North Africa in the summer of
1942 was assigned to latrine inspection duties before shipping out. After
he landed in North Africa, he was given guard duty on medical-supply
convoys.

The U.S. Army had its baptism of fire in North Africa at Kasserine   62
and Faïd passes in February 1943. Up to 34 percent of all casualties were
"mental." Worse yet, only 3 percent of these soldiers were ever returned
to frontline duty. Despite the experience of World War I, when it was
discovered that shell shock intensified if the patient was evacuated from
the combat zones, neuropsychiatric casualties were shuffled through an
evaluation system that took them hundreds of miles to the rear. One
American psychiatrist, working in the rear areas, reported that most of
these cases presented a "bizarre clinical picture, which included dramatic
syndromes of terror states with mutism, dissociative behavior, marked
tremulousness and startle reaction, partial or complete amnesia, severe
battle dreams, and even hallucinatory phenomena." Unable to return to
combat or even to noncombat duty, these soliders could only be sent
home. At one point the number of soldiers evacuated from North Africa
as neuropsychiatric casualties equaled the number of replacements arriving in that theater of operations.

The experiences of North Africa were repeated elsewhere, and during   63
the entire war. Fighting in the South Pacific at New Georgia, the American
43d Infantry Division virtually disintegrated under fire. More than 40 percent of the 4,400 battle losses sustained by the soldiers of this division were
diagnosed as psychiatric cases. During one forty-four-day period of fighting along the Gothic Line in Italy, the 1st Armored Division's psychiatric
casualties amounted to a startling 54 percent of all losses. Even toward the
end of the war, the 6th Marine Division on Okinawa suffered 2,662
wounded in a ten-day period—as well as 1,289 psychiatric casualties. Nearly
a half-million American soldiers were battle casualties during the fighting
in Europe; by 1945 another 111,000 neuropsychiatric cases—then usually
called combat fatigue—had been treated. Worse yet, these statistics must
be regarded as the minimum credible figures. Still more cases were no
doubt masked by an imperfect medical accounting system, command resistance, actual wounds, susceptibility to disease, self-inflicted wounds, de-
sertions, and even frostbite cases.

During the course of the war, frontline soldiers and medics alike   64
had come to agree that everyone in combat had his breaking point if he
fought long enough. As early as 1943 consulting psychiatrists in the
Army's II Corps had persuaded their commanding general, Omar Bradley, to order that all breakdowns in combat be initially diagnosed simply

as exhaustion, putting to rest the notion that only the mentally weak were susceptible to the stresses of combat. Eventually a vast network of psychiatric care was constructed in the Army; each fighting division had its own psychiatrist, and some younger practitioners even found their way to the fighting battalions. Whether the enlightened view of combat fatigue and its real causes ever triumphed is a good deal more problematical.

The Second World War produced an unprecedented body of 65 knowledge about human behavior in combat, knowledge that has for the most part been little studied outside professional medical circles. One compendium of medical literature, published in 1954, shows 1,166 articles on the subject of combat fatigue. There was, of course, a great diversity of interpretations regarding the cause, character, and treatment of the disorder, but in one respect all agreed that combat fatigue was "transient." They may well have been wrong.

Wartime psychiatry, no less than wartime medicine in general, had 66 as its official objective the prompt treatment and return to duty of the wounded soldier. Psychiatrists in uniform took pride in turning in the highest "return to duty" rates they could manage, and indeed, wounded soldiers were often anxious to get back to their buddies on the fighting lines. Combat fatigue was meant to be transient; when a soldier's condition intensified, military psychiatry had failed its primary purpose of maintaining the fighting strength of the army in the field. A cure was hardly the point. Perfectly well-adjusted soliders were not required for combat. The adjustments, if they occurred, were postponed until after the victory parades.

The best known of all World War II's heroes and the quintessential 67 infantryman, Audie Murphy, had a celebrated homecoming. But he was also lucky. When Murphy was invited to Hollywood by the actor James Cagney, his fatigued appearance so alarmed Cagney that he gave the young soldier the use of his pool house for a year. Despite his advantages, Murphy never really got over his war. Twenty-two years after his last combat experiences, Murphy slept with the lights on and a loaded .45 by his bed.

As the American memory commemorated the image of the Second 68 World War, other veterans picked up their lives again and took on the comfortable identity that so characterizes them today: children of the Depression generation who went off to wage a victorious defense of freedom and humanity—tough, uncomplaining, irrepressible in their pursuit of the American Dream. If there were those, like my childhood friend Frank, who did not quite fit the image, they never seemed to interrupt the public consciousness. They lived on with their torments or in the clinical quiet of VA hospitals.

In 1951 two psychiatrists working at the Los Angeles VA Hospi-   69
tal's mental-hygiene clinic published a disturbing report in the *American
Journal of Psychiatry*. For the preceding five years Samuel Futterman and
Eugene Pumpian-Mindlin had been treating two hundred veterans who
exhibited persistent symptoms of intense anxiety, battle dreams, tension, depression, guilt, and aggressive reactions and who were easily
startled by minor noises. The psychiatrist's general impression of their
patients was of a "well-adjusted individual who broke down in [the]
face of an overwhelming trauma." More disturbing still, Futterman and
Pumpian-Mindlin wrote, "even at this late date we still encounter fresh
cases that have never sought treatment until the present time." And
although some veterans responded to treatment, they added, for others
"it is as if they live in the ever present repetition of the traumatic experience that so overwhelmed them."

Nearly fifteen years after the Los Angeles psychiatrists' report,   70
another article appeared in the *Archives of General Psychiatry*. Working
in a VA outpatient mental-health clinic near San Francisco, Herbert Archibald and Read Tuddenham had been "struck with the persistence and
severity of the combat syndrome" in their patients. A systematic study
of these cases revealed "a clear-cut picture . . . of the combat veteran's
chronic stress syndrome" consisting of precisely the same complaints as
those identified in 1951. Nor, in the authors' judgment, were these mild
cases; most were "severely disabling . . . chronic, highly persistent over
long intervals and resistant to modification." As in the earlier investigation, some of the men who saw Archibald and Tuddenham had never
before sought treatment. The article concluded on a forbidding note:
"Perhaps the most disturbing in the latest reports is the suggestion that
the incidence of the syndrome is increasing, as aging makes manifest the
symptoms of traumatic stress which have been latent since the war."

Just two months before this report was published, President Lyn-   71
don Johnson ordered the U.S. Marines to South Vietnam. The cycle of
war experience, and the repression of it, was about to begin anew. Maybe
this is what Frank saw, so far away.

Content Considerations

1. In what ways did medical knowledge affect the diagnosis and treatment
   of war-related disorders?
2. What causes the disorders Spiller describes?
3. Respond to this article, focusing on what war-related disorders reveal
   about the nature of war, of society, and of the individual.

Displaced Persons

The peace that comes after a war is, in most instances, an uneasy one. Those who fled invasion or combat often have no homes to which they can return, for their country has been bombed and burned. Sometimes they do not return because of politics—having resisted a certain party or power or having suffered horribly at its hands, they have no trust that the ruling government will allow them to live freely. Such displaced persons often live for years in refugee camps waiting for a government or independent agency to resolve their fates.

In the following essay, Janet Flanner (1892–1978) writes about a refugee camp outside of Aschaffenburg, Bavaria, in 1948, one of about 300 camps operated by the International Refugee Organization after World War II. Flanner, born in Indianapolis, moved to Paris in 1922 and began contributing to the New Yorker *in 1925, the first year of its publication. She is the author of several books.*

Before you read her essay, write several paragraphs recalling what you already know about displaced persons and refugee camps. As you read, notice how the information she provides corroborates or contradicts what you have written.

ASCHAFFENBURG, OCTOBER 20, 1948. After more than three years 1
of peace, three-quarters of a million uprooted European human beings
are still living in the American Zone of Germany, all of them willing to
go anywhere on earth except home. In the course of this suspended
period of time, these people have turned into statistics and initials. Five
hundred and ninety-eight thousand of them have been formally meta-
morphosed into D.P.s, or Displaced Persons, and are living in some
three hundred International Refugee Organization camps. (The remaining hundred and fifty thousand, because of their hazy D.P. status, are
not entitled to full camp care, or, because of their realism or energy,
have merged with the Germans—who guiltily hate them—and are
struggling for jobs in the midst of German unemployment and weath-
ering the dog-eat-dog existence of Germany's present-day economy.)
What the camp D.P.s are really living in is three hundred limbos—
chiefly former Wehrmacht garrisons, now ironically housing what is
left of the expatriate nationals whom the Nazis maneuvered around Europe as doomed inferiors. One of the camps is outside the town of

Aschaffenburg, in Bavaria, in a quadrangle of barracks on a hill. Another camp is in Würzburg, where there are two garrisons, one on each
side of the Main River, near the bombed remains of the famous fif-
teenth-century statue-inhabited bridge. Wherever these camps are, they
tend to be monotonously alike—modern, German, military establishments. Typically, a camp is a quarter-mile square of harsh, four-story
green stucco buildings that show signs of Allied bombings and D.P.
repairs. According to I.R.O. rules, each building must house a minimum of three hundred D.P.s, in rows of communal bedrooms, all furnished out of salvaged materials and all smelling of smeared cleanliness,
hallroom cooking, and cramped decencies. Every D.P. is theoretically
entitled to forty-five square feet of living space. Sometimes a honey-
moon pair is allowed to enjoy it. Otherwise, there may be in one room
a couple, two children, and a mother-in-law, or three unrelated adults,
with maybe a curtain for privacy. The beds are cots, and a packing case
is likely to serve as a table. In such circumstances, the D.P.s dwell, eat,
breed, wait, and ponder their futures, living a simulacrum of life that
has no connection with the world outside except through the world's
callousness and charity.

Like a well-functioning imitation of a town, each camp has its   2
D.P. mayor, police chief, rival political leaders, teachers, and garbage
collectors, and one socially superior barracks, where the bourgeois remnants maintain the familiar notion of a select neighborhood, and where
they cling together among fewer odors and try to keep up their French.
Each camp is a microcosm of capitalistic society outside; D.P. shoe-
makers, tailors, and carpenters ply their trades, participating in financial
transactions for which the medium of exchange is now the Deutsche
Mark but for which American baby foods, cigarettes, and canned goods,
black-marketed by our occupying Army, provided the currency at the
beginning.

Each of the three hundred limbos also enjoys the Old World in-   3
gredient of arrogant nationalisms and religions. At Camp Wildflecken,
a former training school for Hitler's S.S., there are ten thousand Roman
Catholic Poles; at Giebelstadt, a former Luftwaffe airfield, there are seventeen hundred Jews, mainly Polish; at Aschaffenburg, six thousand
Orthodox Catholic Ukrainians; at Würzburg, a colony of Protestant
Estonians; at Schweinfurt, two thousand Catholic Lithuanians. In the
Orthodox Catholic camps, a church is usually set up in a barracks attic,
on the ecclesiastical principle that no human activity in a building may
take place on a higher level than the service to God does. On Sundays,
the Aschaffenburg garret church is currently decked with gaudy dahlias
from the camp gardens, a magnificent choir of twenty-four young males

sings, and the altar, constructed of embroidery-covered American canned-food boxes, is piously served.

To maintain peace and cut down the number of fist fights, the 4 I.R.O. tries to arrange matters so that each camp—or, at a minimum, each barracks—houses only one religion or nationality. There is a ferocious patriotic dreg that still bubbles up in jealousy and pride as to which nationals have suffered most in the war. The numerically dominating Polish D.P.s, some Jewish and some Catholic, point out that they are the only nationals who engaged in forced labor for the Nazis and who resisted Germans and Russians alike. The Balts, who mostly resisted only the Russians, brag least. The bouncy Ukrainians, who are the second-largest national group, claim that serving in Hitler's Army, which they did on a big scale, was merely a smart way of being anti-Russian. The Ukrainians are the most obstreperously nationalistic of the lot. Recently grown contemptuous of the Saturday-night folk dancing with which other groups keep their national memories warm, the Ukrainian D.P. Scientific Society of Aschaffenburg gave six soirée lectures on Tripilla Culture, and its prehistoric fishing habits and pottery. The Society handed out a pamphlet explaining, in English, that "Tripilla is a peculiar rich culture five thousand years before our times in the Don River town of Tripilla by Kiev. Tripilla Culture, we admit, constituted for the coming into existence of Ukrainians." The D.P. Ukrainians snoozed through the lectures, and loved them.

Reality is further drained from D.P. camp life by the fact that 5 many of the dulled, amiable-looking inhabitants have been through hegiras and immeasurable tragedies that in ordinary existence could prove heroism or lift morale but that in D.P. circles have merely levelled everyone to the cruel, flat surface of commonplace destiny. Some of them have smelled their families burning in crematories, have borne children in beet fields, or have been castrated like calves. Some have walked halfway across Europe on feet that became splayed, have suffered tortures like martyrs, have been beaten like slaves, have been tattooed with serial numbers. Almost all of them have not only survived their frightful experience but have physically recovered. Now the one remaining drama is the hope of emigration tomorrow or, as part of yesterday, of finding that some of their family is still alive, in another D.P. camp, and painstakingly getting their relatives, after months of red tape, into their camp, their barracks, the bed beside their own. Among the Slavs, especially, the family is precious flesh, to be reunited even unto the most remote, broken-down cousinship. This spring, a mysterious, fierce, silent little Polish girl, aged about thirteen, was picked up in Berlin by the German police and sent to an I.R.O. children's camp near Heidelberg. She disappeared, to hunt for somebody who turned

out to be a D.P. great-aunt. By last month, the girl had fished out seven
more apparently legitimate remote relatives, from camps all over the
American Zone; she now has them with her at Aschaffenburg. She refuses to tell how she travelled or got her clues. The D.P. grapevine is
the best and most alert underground communication system in Western
Europe today.

Of all those now homeless in this foreign land, the Jews are the   6
cheeriest—a situation without precedent in the Jewish people's sad, roving history. Ninety per cent of the Jewish D.P.s in the American Zone
have signed up to go to Israel. Their leaders squabble, as a matter of
principle, with the I.R.O., because it has a policy of not sending anyone
to a war zone. The Jewish Agency for Palestine is sending the D.P.s
out anyway, and with particular speed if they are healthy and under
forty-five, the military age limit. Many of the Jewish camps are clus-
tered near Bayreuth, with its operatic echoes of Hitler's favorite, Aryan
composer. The swellest Jewish camp is made up of Luftwaffe officers'
homes at the Giebelstadt Airdrome. Like the inmates of several other
Jewish camps, the Giebelstadt D.P.s are being supplied with various
raw materials, for manufacture, by the American Jewish Joint Distribution Committee. In a bombed-out airfield machine shop, they are
turning out jaunty caps and warm overcoats, and what are probably
Europe's finest work shoes, of superb brown leather, with decorative
steel brads and a slice of thin steel in the heels. The workers are careful
to say that they do not know where these goods go, but the coats could
be useful against Jerusalem's winter chill and the sturdy shoes are suited
to Palestine's rocky fields. Some Giebelstadt D.P.s are earning enough
money to pay German villagers to cut their wood and do their chores—
a bitterly pleasant change.

The hardest blows to D.P. morale have been the long delay by   7
the United States in passing a refugee-immigration bill and then the
nature of the act recently passed. The D.P.s know that America has
generously fed their stomachs. They feel that its immigration bill starves
their hopes. The act disfavors the predominating D.P. Polish Catholics
and Jews; favors the minority Protestant Balts, as a weak insult to Russia; demands almost a Thomas Committee screening of D.P. convictions, characters, bodies, and literacies; and requires, for those accepted,
assurance, from sponsors, of jobs, and "safe and sanitary housing without displacing some other person from such housing"—maybe brand-new
mansions in the skies. The I.R.O., which views itself as self-liquidating,
figures that, with today's limited shipping, it can get seventy-five thousand D.P.s to our welcoming shores by midsummer next year. Those
of the two hundred and five thousand allowed under the bill who fail

to enter by July, 1950, can mildew to death in the camps, unless our congressmen think again.

As the London *Times* has noted, there is a whiff of the slave market 8 in the invitations to D.P.s to enter most countries—including England, which cheerfully calls her D.P. immigration scheme Westward Ho! The D.P.s say cynically, "What is wanted is the pounds of flesh—young, strong, male, and single." Few countries want wives, children, or old begetters. In fact, only Belgium has put into practice a humane scheme— she is admitting twenty thousand D.P. miners and, after three months' work, their entire families. Iraq's recent request for ten doctors without wives is merely the smallest and most candid national project. During the I.R.O.'s last fiscal year, which ended in July, it was able to settle all over the world only the equal of what the United States can legally admit in the next two years, idealist America having up to now admitted fewer D.P.s, proportionately, than any other large power. After all the humanitarian talk, the world's offers to save the D.P.s have been mean.

Most of the D.P.s now in camps have, through delay, lost their 9 sense of choice in regard to what remains of life. From U.N.R.R.A., they attained their peak of "relief and rehabilitation" three years ago. Except for the Jews, whose faces are finally turned again toward Israel, the D.P.s are indeed unconnected with reality. Their favorite reading matter is the pictures in the advertisements in old Army copies of the *Saturday Evening Post,* which they naïvely believe are photographs of miracles of human comfort, justice, and liberty, probably obtained by pressing an electric button. They want to go to the America of their dreams; they fear that the Argentine is too far, Morocco too hot, Canada too cold, England too harsh, Australia too full of horned toads—which it is, according to a startled convoy of D.P. Lithuanians who lately arrived there. And Sweden is too close to Moscow. A psychoanalyst's recent report on certain D.P.s in this district should qualify them for immediate American citizenship. What these D.P.s most fear is insecurity and Russia.

Content Considerations

1. In what ways did the societal structure of the camp mirror the larger society? Why?
2. What problems caused by war persisted into the peace? Was peace achieved in the camp of which Flanner writes? How so?
3. Respond to Flanner's comments regarding the physical and spiritual healing of the refugees. How is such healing achieved? What prevents or delays it?

Painful Questions

On Kristallnacht, "the night of broken glass," November 9, 1938, the persecution of Jews in Germany took one of its most openly violent turns. Jews
were driven from their homes, arrested, deported, beaten, murdered. Their
homes and businesses were plundered, burned, destroyed.

That night marked one of the most public of injustices and brutalities
against the Jews. After that night, concentration camps began to fill quickly,
mostly with Jews but also with sympathizers and others whose political or
religious views were not in line with those of the National Socialist (Nazi)
party and those whose ethnic or national background the Nazis thought inferior.

Helmut Kohl, Chancellor of the Federal Republic of German, authored
the following piece for the fiftieth commemoration of Kristallnacht; it was
published in the March/April 1989 issue of Society. If you were he, what
would you say in commemoration of an event such as Kristallnacht?

FIFTY YEARS AGO synagogues throughout Germany were set on
fire: the houses of prayer built in honor of the one Creator who is
worshiped by Jews and Christians alike. The name given to that occasion, "the night of broken glass," is both cynical and trivializing and
conceals what really happened then.

On November 9, 1938, the National Socialist terror against Jewish
citizens acquired a new dimension. Tens of thousands of them were
arrested and deported to concentration camps, thousands were mal-
treated, hundreds murdered or driven to their death. The pogrom of
that night was a foreboding of the deliberate, systematic, and merciless
persecution of the Jews to come. Then at the latest everyone ought to
have realized that anti-Semitism was a central element of National Socialist ideology, that it was not just one of many means of exercising
power and certainly not a merely coincidental phenomenon of the dic-
tatorship. Countless people suffered as a result of the National Socialist
terror. Many of them were persecuted on account of their political or
religious convictions. But the hatred for the Jews—men, women and
children alike—went even further. The mere fact that someone was of
Jewish descent constituted a capital crime.

Yet fifty years ago most people were still not able to imagine that
the National Socialist racial hatred would shortly lead to even greater

atrocities, that it would in its ultimate, most dreadful form amount to the genocide of European Jews. Human imagination will never be sufficient to picture what lies behind the abstract figures and plain statistics. But looking back we can state one thing with certainty: Auschwitz and Treblinka, Maidanek and Bergen-Belsen—these dreadful sites were from the outset inherent in that godless ideology which idolized a single race.

Today we wonder why so few people objected when the emerging despots solicited support for their inhuman program, initially in back rooms and later out in the streets. This is a painful question, but it is even more painful to ask why there was no widespread protest when the Jews in Germany were ridiculed and harassed, isolated and persecuted. For it is incontestable that from the very first day, from January 30, 1933, onward, Jewish citizens were discriminated against: politically, morally and then legally, with growing brutality and before the eyes of the public. This state terror became more and more common, reaching everyone's immediate neighborhood. The legal system served less and less to protect the weak and was increasingly used for oppressing them. Injustice was translated into law; a particularly abhorrent example of this are the racist Nuremberg Laws of 1935.

The November pogroms were by no means a spontaneous outburst of so-called public wrath. Instead they constituted a scheme that was centrally initiated and locally organized. From today's vantage point it is difficult to understand—and this continues to be a cause of deep shame—why the majority of the population remained silent on November 9 and 10, 1938. Various factors played a role: a lack of personal courage or even paralyzing fear on the part of some, apathy on the part of others. Some were stunned, while others eased their consciences with all sorts of arguments, for example, with the widespread preconception that it was necessary to curb and eliminate "Jewish influence." Some felt personally affected by the suffering of their fellow-citizens, whereas others pretended that it did not concern them. Some watched with great schadenfreude, took part or even benefited in business terms. But we must not forget those who voiced their disapproval or even tried to help as far as possible. Today we recall with great respect and gratitude those bold men and women who, fifty years ago and afterward, helped Jewish citizens in various ways, thus risking their own lives and often the safety of their families as well: for example, by assisting them in finding a hiding place or fleeing abroad.

The *Kristallnacht* day of remembrance raises many questions. The younger generation, too, should honestly consider what they would have done or failed to do in such a situation. In stating that they do so "honestly," I mean above all—without self-righteousness. I am firmly convinced that people today are no better or bolder than people were then. The only difference is that today we are not faced with the choice of, on the one hand, becoming guilty by looking away or by taking part or, on the other, endangering ourselves and others by offering resistance.

Under the rule of law we are spared this dreadful test which would probably overtax many of us today, too. This knowledge teaches us to be modest, indeed humble. It teaches us to be grateful for being able to live in a liberal democracy. And it warns us to be vigilant at all times against anything that might pave the way for totalitarian rule. I feel this is what Dr. Galinski meant recently at the joint memorial ceremony of German and French troops at the site of the Dachau concentration camp: "Preventing people from forgetting is also an important means of making them realize how much they should treasure democracy." 6

Although the genocide of European Jews perpetrated by Germans was unique, we must always ensure everywhere that nothing similar recurs. The warning of this day must therefore never go unheeded. It is an appeal to each of us to reconsider his own thoughts time and again. Although legal guarantees are a precondition for ensuring that there is no return to barbarity, our liberal democracy must also be embedded in our hearts, and not only in our minds. We must always remember that wherever the dignity of a fellow-being is violated, our own dignity is also harmed. Only if we preserve this ability to share suffering, to identify with the victims, can we succeed in the long run in shaping a just society in which people of different origin and with different political convictions can live together in peace and freedom. 7

Respect for the inalienable dignity of each fellow-being requires that we, speaking in biblical terms, do not create an image of him, but let him be what he actually is. Max Frisch, who has dealt in a particularly cogent manner with the factors and effects of anti-Semitic prejudice, once said that all of us are "responsible in a secret and inescapable way" for the face that the other shows us. By forcing our ideas on him, we deny him "the entitlement of everything living that remains impalpable." We must therefore unconditionally accept each fellow-being in his uniqueness and his dissimilarity and not confront him with the choice of either conformity or isolation. This is genuine pluralism, as envisioned by the architects of our constitution. 8

The men and women who deliberated on our constitution in the Parliamentary Council forty years ago were able to retrieve the value and dignity of responsibly exercised freedom not least because they mustered the strength to bear the burden of the past. The truth is that Germans became guilty as individuals, but the injustice perpetrated under the National Socialist tyranny is part of our common history. This history has been entrusted to us in its entirety. By freely facing up to it, 9 we can turn the burden into an opportunity—the opportunity of discovering ourselves and opening up avenues toward a better future.

It would be dishonest to pick out only the favorable parts of German history. This history is indivisible—both the good and the bad aspects are ours. I therefore welcome the fact that the GDR government has of late shown a readiness to acknowledge the responsibility resting on us Germans as a whole, even if only by symbolic gestures. This responsibility includes in particular solidarity with Israel's interests regarding its existence, freedom, and security. This solidarity is not jeopardized by differences of opinion in day-to-day political activities. These discussions relate to political details. Our solidarity, however, always concerns fundamental matters. It is not least that solidarity which reflects the change made by the German nation after 1945.   10

Just as it is not possible to evade the burden of the past, we must time and again recall the best, liberal traditions of German history—traditions to which numerous Jews contributed as well. I need only mention Gabriel Riesser, vice president of the National Assembly convened in St. Paul's Church in Frankfurt, and Hugo Preuss, who played a major part in drafting the Weimar Constitution. I would also like to name with particular gratitude those Jewish citizens who after 1945 were ready to look to the future, to help build a free society. I should also like to emphasize that today there are young Jewish men and women who consciously participate in our free polity with a particularly keen sense of civic duty.   11

We—Jews, Christians, and all liberal-minded people in this country—are faced with a great task for the future: at the end of this century with all its atrocities, with untold human suffering, we are building (1) a Europe founded on the values shared by Jews and Christians, (2) a Europe liberating itself from the scourge of nationalism, and (3) a Europe which is intended to bring people and nations from East and West together in common freedom.   12

Let us not forget those people and nations who are still denied the chance to determine their own destiny. There is not only a temptation to cast aside the past; it is equally wrong to close one's eyes to the suffering of one's contemporaries, to the suffering of those people who still are unable to enjoy freedom.   13

The *Kristallnacht* day of commemoration is not least a reminder that Jews and Christians are in agreement on basic moral issues. All too often we hear, even from well-meaning people, the devious theory of an alleged "revengeful attitude stemming from the Old Testament." Unthinkingly we speak of "Christian charity" and forget that the Torah itself states: "Love thy neighbor as thyself."   14

It is necessary to dispel the notion that Jews have stood on the   15 sidelines in Western history. The opposite is true: They have stood in the very center of the great traditions shaping Europe's and America's political cultures. In many countries Jews were at the forefront of the struggle for human dignity and civil rights, for pluralism and the rule of law, for democracy and self-determination. Heinrich Heine rightly spoke of the pride he took in the fact "that his ancestors belonged to the noble house of Israel, that he was a descendant of those martyrs who gave the world one God and one set of morals and who fought and suffered on all battlefields of the intellect."

The National Socialists claimed that they wanted to save our Eu- 16 ropean culture. In reality, their ideology amounted to an attack on the very values that have shaped this culture. These are only a few of the convictions which Jews and Christians share and which have paved the way intellectually for human rights, the rule of law and pluralistic democracy:

- the conviction that man was created in the image of God, is unique, and is endowed with inalienable dignity;
- the belief that Creation is entrusted to us so that we preserve and develop it as God's assistants and companions—to use Martin Buber's words;
- the prohibition of idolatry, which protects us against the temptation of worshiping power or regarding any ideology as being the absolute truth.

Since Judaism is intrinsically antitotalitarian, totalitarianism is, as 17 Manes Sperber once wrote, "anti-Judaistic wherever it occurs." Jews and Christians are, so to speak, natural allies in opposing all ideological or political claims to the absolute truth. Making as many people as possible aware of this recognition is, in my view, one of the decisive tasks of the Christian-Jewish dialogue. I therefore recall with particular gratitude that ten years ago the secretariat of the International Council of Christians and Jews was transferred from London to the Martin Buber House in Heppenheim.

The pogrom of November 9, 1938, remains present in our minds. 18 It is a distressing and shameful part of our present: Many who were persecuted then still live in our midst. They carry with them harrowing memories, and we know that their pain cannot be expressed in words. Those who witnessed the pogrom fifty years ago as children, adolescents, or adults also have oppressive memories—memories that fill us with shame.

This must not mean that when the last witnesses die, remembrance 19 also ceases. Instead it is our duty to hand on to the generation of our children and grandchildren the awareness that being able to live in freedom and dignity cannot be taken for granted. Coming generations do not, fortunately, know from their own experience what nonfreedom and discrimination actually mean. Nor should they ever have to experience this. For this reason it is our duty to remember—not for the sake of the victims alone, but also for the sake of our children and grandchildren.

I finish with a personal remark addressed to the Jewish citizens in the Federal Republic of Germany: The fact that you live here is a sign of trust which deeply touches us, the non-Jewish majority. We certainly did not have any entitlement to such trust, considering everything that happened in Germany before and after November 9, 1938. It is a precious gift—one of the most precious given to us after 1945. It is also a fragile gift. I realize that your trust can easily be shaken—by the baseness of those who are incorrigible and sometimes even by the thoughtlessness of well-meaning people. Fellow-citizens, the free polity that was created on German soil some forty years ago is our common home. Let us jointly protect and develop it further. This requires the dedicated participation of all people of good will. May I ask you, too, to participate.

20

Content Considerations

1. According to Kohl, what questions does the remembrance of Kristallnacht raise for contemporary society? What are your answers to those questions?
2. Of what value is the past to the present and future?
3. Respond to Kohl's insistence on "the inalienable dignity of each fellow-being" (paragraph 8). How is respect for that dignity demonstrated? Using your knowledge of current American society and any other sources that would help you develop support, evaluate how well Americans currently demonstrate respect for the dignity of fellow-beings.

CYNTHIA OZICK

Why I Won't Go to Germany

Personal reconciliations after a war may be hard not only for soldiers and civilians who survive a particular war or battle but also for people linked by blood or heart to those who have suffered. Such is the case for many Jewish Americans: The Holocaust and its implications haunt their lives, they remain forever shadows into which a life or a nation could be pulled. The following letter was adapted by Harper's *(February 1989) from a letter originally published in the May 1988 issue of the* Quarterly.

Its author, Cynthia Ozick, is a Jewish American born in New York in 1928; she has written essays, novels, and several volumes of short stories. In her letter, Ozick refuses an invitation to a conference on German-Jewish relations. Before you read her refusal, try to imagine what she might say. Write a paragraph focusing on whether you would attend a meeting in a country that had singled out and killed more than six million people of your ethnic, racial, or religious group.

DEAR PROFESSOR X:

Thank you for your letter inviting me to Germany to participate   1
in a conference on current "German-Jewish relations" in the aftermath
of the Holocaust, initiated and organized by distinguished Jewish Americans, yourself among them, and joined on your letterhead by other
Americans of distinction and by prominent Germans of goodwill. It is
very kind of you to have had me in mind; I am touched by your generosity and trust. I wish my response could have been simpler than it is
destined to be.

Professor X, I am a Jew who does not, will not, cannot, set foot   2
in Germany. This is a private moral imperative; I don't think of it as a
"rule," and I don't apply it to everyone, particularly not to German-
born Jews, who as refugees or survivors have urgencies and exigencies
different from my own. Not to set foot in Germany is for me, and I
think for many garden–variety Jewish Americans like myself, one of the
few possible memorials; and it seems to me unsurprising that in this
connection a memorial should take the form of a negation, a turning
away.

But there is another point of view as well, one that may be more   3

362

relevant here. Yours is the fourth invitation I have had to go to Germany. Each was issued with the best will in the world: a German hand reaching out in peace from a democratic German polity—a remembering hand, never a forgetful one. The hand of the "new generation." The more that hand reaches out in its remembering remorsefulness, in its hopeful goodwill, the more resistant my heart becomes.

Here is why. I believe that all this—the conscientious memorializing of what happened four and five decades ago to the Jewish citizens of Germany and of Europe—is in the nature of things an insular and parochial German task. It is something for the Germans to do, independently, in the absence of Jews—the absence of Jews in contemporary Germany being precisely the point. The German task is, after all, a kind of "liberation" (of conscience into history), or emancipation, and the only genuine emancipation—as we know from many other national, social, and cultural contexts—is auto-emancipation. So when Germans want to reflect on German-Jewish "reconciliation," or—skirting that loaded word—German-Jewish "relations," it seems to me they are obligated to do it on their own. Does that strike you as impossible, if not absurd? A hand held out in friendship to someone who isn't there? How can "relations" with Jews be achieved in the absence of Jews? Well, that's exactly the difficulty, isn't it? Europe no longer has what it used to call its "Jewish problem," the Germans having solved it with finality. But there remains now a German problem—the ongoing, perhaps infinitely protracted, problem of the German national conscience—and its gravamen is that the Jews aren't there.

It appears that what Germans of goodwill have been doing lately— and more and more they are doing it with the aid and counsel of American Jewish organizations—is evading the tumultuous epicenter of the problem, even as they struggle to offer more and more evidence that they are facing it. There are no native-born Jews over fifty to achieve "relations" with. Germany is a Jewish museum: apartments, furniture, old neighborhoods newly populated, the old headstones that survived vandalism in the museum-cemeteries or were heaped up as rubble barriers against tanks. Not the old synagogues, though; these were mainly burned. If an old volume by a popular author of the twenties turns up, it has the antiquarian interest of a rare book: books by Jewish writers were burned in every public square—who doesn't know this? The notion of a Jew as a kind of surprising vestige or anachronism—as, in fact, an actual museum piece—is apparently pervasive in Germany, and was once brought home to me by a representative of a German publisher who, after a conversation in New York, wrote me a warmly intended letter: *My time with you was different from any other experience; it was like a visit to a museum.*

The German solution to this perplexity—to the absence of native-   6
born Jews of my generation—has been to behave in a manner inspired,
perhaps, by the straightforward realm of international economics, of
demand and scarcity. If you have depleted through your own folly your
native (and plentiful) supply of Jews, and now you feel remorseful, what
do you do? You put an order in to America—which, rather than de-
pleting its supply of Jewish citizens, has nourished and multiplied it—
and you import living foreign Jews to stand in for the native missing
Jews.

I am afraid that all such programs—wherein Jewish Americans   7
offer themselves (always out of the ideals of humaneness, reconciliation,
hope for the future) to stand in for the murdered Jews of Europe—are
mistaken at the core and, in any case, cannot help the Germans. The
Germans must undertake memorial explorations under their given condition of scarcity—the absence of native Jews. Why must an American
writer, a Jewish citizen of the United States, be imported for a conference on "German-Jewish relations"? Only because there is no German-
born Jewish writer of her own age who is alive to speak. So a foreign
surrogate must do.

But it seems to me that this principle of surrogacy is conceived in   8
profound error. Who will dare to suggest that any living Jew can offer
reconciliation—or even simple human presence—on behalf of the
murdered?

Then let Germans of goodwill do it on their own. They, not   9
American Jewish sponsors, should be the organizing spirits behind Holocaust conferences on German soil—conferences by and for Germans.
The Final Solution was applied to Jews—Jews were its victims; but the
barbarities of the Nazi era are by no means a Jewish issue. They are an
issue of German culture and certainly appropriate for examination by
German institutions and conferences, but not, in my view, with the
assistance or participation of foreign Jews. Here is an instance where
"reconciliation" and "relations" may not, cannot, be a collaborative act,
i.e., a project between Germans and Jews, belonging equally (or even
unequally) to both. Because if it appears to be collaborative, the act
becomes a lie. The Germans in truth have no one to "collaborate" with
but phantoms—the missing, the murdered, the Jews *not there*.

Living Jewish Americans can't serve as surrogates. Anne Frank,   10
before the Annex, before the flight to Holland, was a German Jew: had
Germany not given its allegiance to the criminals and programs that
murdered her, who can doubt that she would today have been a lumi-
nary of German letters? Which American writer can stand in for Anne
Frank, gassed in adolescence? Human beings are not bauxite; one bundle
of Jews is not interchangeable with another bundle. The Nazis objecti-

fied Jews and made them interchangeable bundles. Ah, the bitterness of the irony that, in the name of "German-Jewish relations," in the name of goodwill and the hope of present and future humaneness, the interchangeability of one group of Jews with another is still being pursued on German soil!

That, I think, is the German dilemma; and that is what the "concerned Germans and Americans" on your letterhead need to come to grips with. When Jewish Americans go to Germany to "help"—i.e., to supply Jewish representation at a Holocaust conference—they aren't making it easier for the Germans to see into the soul of the dilemma, namely the loss of *German-Jewish* representation; the Americans are confusing the question by abetting the tragic and degrading falsehood of human interchangeability.

I am very sorry to be so astringent. I have thought about these matters for a long time, and with growing distress as the decades pass and more and more American Jewish organizations fly to Germany in search of similar collaborative objectives. Your letter, by the way, arrived on the very day another letter came to me, this one from a German university—a warm and impressive and earnest letter from an extremely able Ph.D. student (I judge this from the intelligent voice of her fine English sentences) who is interested in fiction written by Jewish Americans, and who has settled on my work as the subject of her dissertation. A self-described "special case" because of her preoccupation with American Jewish writing, she sketched her family background: "My father became a soldier when he was seventeen. His father was a theologian of the Protestant Church and had the position of superintendent. Even though my father's father began to mistrust the National Socialists quite early in the thirties, he was a patriot and thus sent four sons into the war. Three of them were killed." Three dead uncles. I grieve at the obtuseness of this. With all the goodwill in the world, my young correspondent (born in 1955) remains incapable of understanding that a German "patriot" would, at least in his heart if not in his (by then, let us try to concede, coerced) actions, acknowledge that to fight for Hitler was not German patriotism but a betrayal of Germany. And this from a "theologian of the Protestant Church" in an atmosphere of rampant official anti-Semitism. To whom, I can't help wondering, did this theologian give his vote? Was his "mistrust" of the Nazis "early in the thirties" a feeling of immediate alarm and peril, or one of ballot-box regret after the damage was done? My correspondent is clearly engaged, from her point of view, in an intellectual project of remorse and restitution; and yet she cannot recognize the most fundamental first necessity—an understanding of what patriotism means: that it is something you do for yourself, by yourself, out of obligation to the moral im-

11

12

provement of your country; that it is above all a dream of self-transfor-
mation. It would be better all around if she would neglect the study of
"American Jewish fiction" and begin a cultural meditation on her grand-
father's mind.

Content Considerations

1. What is Ozick's point about "human interchangeability" (paragraph 10)?
    What does it have to do with her refusal to go to Germany?
2. To what extent do you agree with Ozick that the examination of Ger-
    man-Jewish relations or reconciliation is a "German problem—the on-
    going, perhaps infinitely protracted, problem of the German conscience"
    (paragraph 4)?
3. How is patriotism connected to war for Ozick? How is it connected to
    peace and reconciliation? How are her ideas about these connections
    different from or similar to your own?

Some Lover of Freedom!

The Persian Gulf war was short. After Iraq invaded Kuwait in August 1990, America began to mass her troops. After the U.N. deadline for Iraq's withdrawal passed in mid-January, the United States and its allies began bombing. A cease-fire took effect February 28, 1991.

Before that war began, many people questioned its necessity. Their questions intensified during the war's duration and continued after its conclusion. Others, of course, questioned how the war could be avoided, believing that Iraq must be driven from Kuwait and believing that the United States must help accomplish that goal.

A war's end signifies peace but often signifies civil unrest as well. A defeat weakens a country's government. It often highlights the citizens' dissatisfactions with the powers that led them into war, and that dissatisfaction is strengthened by the poverty, illness, and starvation that often linger to plague the people of a defeated nation. Such has been the case with the Persian Gulf war, where various groups in Iraq have voiced their discontent and tried to remedy its causes.

In the following article, published in the May 7, 1991, issue of the New American, writer John F. McManus looks at the civil unrest that continued to disrupt Iraq long after the Gulf war ended. Before you read, write several paragraphs focused on what responsibility a victorious country bears toward the people of a country it has defeated.

APPROVAL RATINGS for George Bush have taken a nose dive. Much 1 of the cheering was nothing more than a sign of relief as the war ended. Pollsters who sought an opinion of the President were hard-pressed to find anyone turning in his yellow ribbon and seeming to oppose the troops.

Now that normalcy has returned, cooler heads wonder if there 2 was ever any need to wreak such devastation on Iraq. Was there a need to kill so many Iraqi soldiers when many were eagerly surrendering? Why did the President order U.S. field commanders to let two full Iraqi divisions escape—the very troops who have been crushing Iraqi resistance to Hussein? Also, was it worth even one American life to put the dictatorial Emir of Kuwait back on his throne?

BETRAYING THE KURDS

There can be no denying that our nation's President repeatedly [3] urged Iraq's Kurdish people—and others in Iraq—to rise up and topple Saddam Hussein in the wake of his humiliating defeat. Mr. Bush even broadcast a promise to keep Iraqi helicopter gunships grounded, precisely the help the Kurds needed to succeed. But the gunships continued to fly.

Having been lured into open revolt against the "Butcher of Baghdad" by Bush promises, the Kurds—with no defense against air power— [4] have been slaughtered. They believed that an American president who would mount a huge campaign against Saddam's brutality in Kuwait could be trusted to aid their cause against Saddam's cruelty to them.

Once before, in 1975, the Kurds were urged by the U.S. to rebel [5] against the same Saddam Hussein. But we provided no help. Then, only a few years ago, Hussein used poison gas against these independence-minded people. The Reagan Administration reacted by blocking a Senate move to impose sanctions against the Iraqi government. The Kurds should have known that the U.S. couldn't be trusted. But like Americans who believed in and voted for George Bush, they read his lips and failed to recall the past.

UNMISTAKABLE PARALLELS

In August 1944, a Polish underground army in Warsaw received [6] a similar assurance of aid from Soviet forces advancing toward their Nazi-held city. Believing that the Soviets would join them in routing the retreating Germans, General Bor-Komorowski's 40,000-man army surfaced and took on the heavily armed Nazis with little more than small arms.

But the Soviets deliberately sat on their hands 10 miles east of [7] Warsaw. Nazi artillery, tanks, and planes slaughtered the brave Poles, destroyed their city, and left over 250,000 men, women, and children dead. Four months after the uprising began, the Soviets occupied the devastated Polish capital.

Before General Bor's forces were completely annihilated, U.S. and [8] British forces sought landing rights in Soviet-held territory, hoping to ferry supplies to the Poles. The Soviets repeatedly denied their requests. When the Nazis destroyed what would have been organized resistance to communist rule, the Soviets installed their puppet leaders and had a clear field for creating a Soviet-dominated Poland.

In 1961, the Kennedy Administration half-heartedly backed an invasion of Castro's Cuba at the Bay of Pigs. When promised air cover [9] was cancelled, the invasion became a complete failure. Not only were the 1,400 anti-Castro invaders rounded up, the anti-communist Cuban underground that had been lured into the open was also an easy target for Castro's militia.

Who would have predicted that George Bush would do for Saddam Hussein exactly what Stalin and Lolotov did for Polish communists and the Kennedy Administration did for Castro?

SECRET UNDERSTANDINGS?

Columnist William Safire has speculated that the President "was reminded by Moscow or Riyadh of secret prewar understandings not to overturn Hussein." Prewar understandings? Wasn't it Mr. Bush who likened Hussein to Hitler? Didn't he tell us he was sending half a million troops into battle to rid the world of its worst tyrant? Wasn't combatting Saddam important enough to embrace Syria's Assad, make Gorbachev look like Prince Valiant, and add tens of billions to the U.S. deficit? Now we are led to believe there might have been "secret prewar understandings."

Why would George Bush betray the Kurds and help Hussein stay in power? The likely answer begins with the realization that the President's rhetoric about Saddam was no more believable than the pledge he gave to the Kurds or the pledge of "no new taxes!" he gave to Americans.

But there is a single way to explain this strange war and the even stranger post-war policies that are keeping Hussein in power. Mr. Bush frequently uttered it over the past few months. It is his desire to "reinvigorate" the United Nations and bring on his "new world order." The war certainly did boost the UN, and now that it is over and Saddam is still killing fellow humans, the UN is assuming a new "peacekeeping" role. The war in the Middle East and its aftermath could become known as the gateway to world government under the UN.

Has Saddam Hussein been a willing participant in this UN-boosting activity? Who knows for sure? But when world government under the UN is the goal, and there's a need for an archcriminal like Hussein to sacrifice the well-being of his nation to speed its creation, why should anyone put it past the Iraqi leader?

What then might all this say about George Bush? Start seeking an answer to that by asking the Kurds.

Content Considerations

1. What does McManus suggest about the necessity of the Persian Gulf war? Where do his sympathies lie?
2. McManus compares the situation of the Kurds with several others in which the United States was involved. What does McManus accomplish by doing so? How important are the comparisons to his argument?
3. What does this article suggest about what leaders say? About how leaders make decisions? About hidden agendas?

A Perilous New Order

*After war, boundaries are often redrawn. New alliances are formed. New vows
of security are made and improved plans for defense argued as the world rebuilds
its supply of arms in readiness for the next round of hostilities.*

*Although only about 7 percent of the weapons used by the United States
and its allies in the Persian Gulf war were high-tech, that 7 percent received
the world's attention. Since the Gulf war ended, many nations have inventoried
their weapons supply and found it lacking; hence a ready market of nations is
clamoring to buy the weapons that defeated Iraq. Other nations have perfected
or are seeking the technology that will enable them to build their own.*

*One aftermath of war, then, appears to be a gradual building toward the
next war and the determination not to be caught short when it occurs. The
next article, written by columnist and author Tom Wicker and published in
March 1991, looks at re-arming and arms buildup as a consequence of war.
Before you read his comments, write a paragraph about the drawbacks of re-
arming in the period immediately following war.*

NEW YORK—Wouldn't it be ironic if the resounding defeat of   1
Iraq, led by the high-tech forces of the U.S., resulted in a Third World
newly armed to the teeth with smart bombs, ballistic and cruise missiles,
helicopter gunships, Patriot-style interceptors and radar-invisible aircraft?

That would make wars between Third World rivals more likely,   2
if one thought it had gained a qualitative advantage over another. Such
wars would be more lethal and destructive, and might be more likely
to draw in forces from industrialized nations guarding their interests or
promoting their weaponry.

Even without wars, the increased cost of arms buildups and rival-   3
ries would divert resources that could better be spent to encourage economic growth and fight endemic poverty.

Yet, just such a Third World race for the latest and best in lethal   4
devices seems in prospect—encouraged, in all probability, by the Bush
administration's decision to aid U.S. military contractors in promoting
overseas sales of their hardware.

The war itself, of course, has done the most to stir interest in the   5
acquisition of high-tech weapons. Even the most backward national leader
can hardly be unaware that Iraq's vaunted war machine was quickly

blown to pieces by the advanced armaments used by the U.S. and its allies.

Prime Minister Nawaz Sharif of Pakistan drew the obvious lesson. 6 "To undermine the science, technology, research and modern advances in defense is disastrous," he said in a speech in which he emphasized the need to make Pakistan "an impregnable fortress."

The U.S. director of naval intelligence, Adm. T.A. Brooks, has 7 said at least 40 nations are seeking radar-evading "stealth" technologies, and that by the end of the century nine more states will join the six that already deploy reconnaissance satellites. Many countries now have the ability to build cruise missiles and their guidance systems.

Israel is acquiring submarines from Germany. France does an ac- 8 tive arms-export business. China and others have ballistic missile programs, and the Chinese are willing to sell. The Soviets continue to make available advanced jets and other weapons to Third World countries.

But name-calling does little good, for Uncle Sam is one of the 9 world's biggest arms merchants—peddling $10.8 billion in conventional arms in 1989, second only to Moscow's $11.7 billion. These two accounted for $22.5 billion in such sales out of a world total of $31.8 billion.

Now the Bush administration has told Congress it wants to sell 10 high-tech weapons worth $18 billion—including F-16s, Patriots, M-1 tanks and multiple rocket launchers—to five Persian Gulf allies. With such weapons going to Arab nations, Israel's defense worries are bound to increase, and Israel already is one of the largest recipients of the Pentagon's grants and low-interest loans.

The administration also is siding with arms contractors who have 11 been lobbying for restoration of government authority—unavailable since the late 1970s—to underwrite up to $1 billion in arms sales abroad. The proposal, if approved by Congress, would permit the Export-Import Bank to guarantee commercial bank loans made to overseas buyers of U.S.-made arms.

Administration spokesmen insist there's no conflict with its stated 12 aim of limiting arms sales to the Third World. The guarantees, they say, would be available only to the NATO allies, Japan, Israel, and Australia, unless—a very big unless—the president found it in the national interest to include other nations.

Those spokesmen must be kidding. Only a few years ago, Presi- 13 dent Reagan found it in the national interest to sell arms to Iran. U.S. weapons sold to legally authorized countries, moreover, often have been resold to unauthorized third parties.

Any way you look at it, the Bush proposal would encourage the 14 proliferation of weapons—including high-tech weapons, perhaps ultimately to Third World nations.

How can that help Bush build that stable new world order to   15
which he pays such ardent lip service?

Content Considerations

1. What is Wicker's attitude toward arms sales? How is it expressed?
2. What problems do arm sales to Third World countries present?
3. Wicker says that the United States and the Soviet Union are the two "biggest arms merchants." Why are they? Locate other sources to help you determine how a nation benefits by selling weapons.

— *Ideas for Discussion, Writing, and Research* —

1. Using the pieces by Manchester and Spiller, discuss how combat may affect soldiers once war has ceased.

2. What common issues are raised by Flanner, Kohl, and Ozick? What can you conclude about the aftermath of war from these essays?

3. Select any four of the pieces in this chapter to help you explain what a civilian's life might be like following war.

4. Both Ozick and Manchester comment on patriotism. How do their comments differ? How are they similar? Use both in an explanation of your beliefs about patriotism.

5. Although they focus differently, both McManus and Wicker speak of the time after war as a time when nations prepare for a new war. What is your response to their claims?

6. Flanner writes about the displacement of civilians as one of the long-lasting effects of war. Locate more information on that topic, focusing on the displacement of civilians from a particular area as a result of a particular war.

7. Using any three of the essays in this chapter, discuss how politics help determine how people fare after war.

8. What concerns or practices in the modern world might help avert future wars? Information in the pieces by Manchester, McManus, Kohl, and Spiller as well as your own knowledge and beliefs might help as you construct an answer.

9. Both Manchester and Flanner present first-person narratives of war and/or its aftermath, Manchester as a soldier and Flanner as a journalist. How effective are their narratives? How does the first-person view affect their credibility? Investigate other first-hand accounts of war in order to help you determine what would be lost if stories such as these were never told.

10. With classmates, investigate and share information about shell shock, refugee camps, arms sales, or war damage to the environment. Locate people to interview as well as printed sources to consult for your information.

7

The War without End

SGT. BRUCE BIGGS and his four-man fire team of Company C watched as the sampan with two black-clad figures aboard floated down the stream to the coast. They were patrolling for Viet Cong supply boats, which had been bringing in munitions to the area around Tuy Hoa, South Vietnam, on the South China Sea. When the men aboard the sampan ignored shouted commands to direct their boat to shore, Biggs ordered one of his riflemen to fire his grenade launcher. The grenade destroyed the sampan, and Biggs saw the apparently lifeless body of one of the occupants floating in the water.

Biggs, who, contrary to regulations, was a non-swimmer, handed his M-16 rifle to a companion and waded into the water to retrieve the body. It was not the first action he had seen. The 19-year-old from south Missouri had been in-country three months and already had been in numerous firefights from the central highlands to the Cambodian border, operating for weeks at a time in the stifling heat, the razor-sharp elephant grass, the clammy, dense jungles of a world half a globe away from the varsity basketball court he had played on just two years earlier.

The water was deeper than he anticipated: within a few feet he was up to his chest. Face upward, the body drifted toward him, and

Biggs reached out to grab a collar. Suddenly, the man turned in the water and leaped toward Biggs with a knife in his hand. The sergeant, stunned, could only fall backward with the suspected Viet Cong on top of him, holding him under the water. One of the riflemen on the bank, seeing the unexpected attack, fired and killed the man. A shaken Sgt. Biggs, gasping for air, slogged his way back to land.

Twenty-five years later, the incident still disturbs Biggs. He doesn't like to be near water. And other things about his war affect him. His face changes, his voice alters, when asked about his thirteen months as a combat infantryman in South Vietnam. He doesn't carry change in his pockets (rattling coins signaled their positions to enemy troops); he awakens drenched in sweat after dreaming of being overrun by Vietnamese troops; an avid hunter before the war, he generally avoids guns today.

Biggs now has a daughter in college, and when her English teacher assigned her to interview a Vietnam veteran, he talked to her about the war for the first time.

For Bruce Biggs and millions of others, the Vietnam War has never really ended.

The Vietnam War continues to shape our society today. It became a national nightmare, an eight-year quagmire whose effects will be felt for years. Born of Cold War fears and nurtured on national pride mixed with a touch of arrogance, it brought out both the best and the worst in Americans.

The Vietnam War started at least 1,000 years ago. That's how long the Vietnamese battled Chinese warlords attempting to take over their country. The French assumed control of the region in the 1860s, and the Vietnamese battled them. Their climactic battle was at Bien Dien Phu in 1954. When the French collapsed, the United States was slowly drawn into the region, first with military "advisors," then eventually with more than a half-million combat and support troops.

Explaining the Vietnam War is virtually impossible: it was part of the containment policy of every U.S. administration since World War II, a policy founded on the belief that the Communists had to be held at bay before they reached San Francisco. Vietnam became an obsession: we would not lose to a third-rate nation of peasants. And it became a symbol, spawning a generation of bumper stickers: America—Love it or Leave it; Make Love Not War. What emerges from any attempt to study the war is a series of isolated images, like the photos that appeared daily in the 1960s and early 1970s: a Vietnamese general summarily executing a suspected Viet Cong in Saigon; a young girl, naked and badly burned from American napalm, screaming down a road; bandaged buddies helping each other to an evacuation helicopter.

We talk today of the "lessons of Vietnam," but few could articulate what those lessons were. In part, the lessons learned depend on which side one favored in the war. Those who opposed the conflict speak of not becoming involved in civil wars, of not committing U.S. troops to wars a half-world away, of learning more about cultures before sending troops and materiel, of not supporting dictators who abuse their own people, of the might of protesters to end a war. Supporters of the war say the United States should never ask its soldiers to fight anything less than an all-out war, that the country needs to be solidly behind any troop commitment, that protests should not be tolerated when combat begins, that war news should be carefully monitored.

There were other lessons, already touched on in other chapters in this book: the morality and efficacy of an all-volunteer army versus an army of draftees; the blurring of civilians and combatants in a guerrilla war; the need for carefully articulated national goals and national interests; the need for suspicious news media to examine issues in any war, rather than merely report actions; the limitations of and consequences of technology.

But the Vietnam War was a war that in many ways was unlike any other in which the United States has been involved. It was the first televised war, one in which the carnage and daily misery were brought home each evening on the national news. It was the first war in which Americans fought a conventional war against guerrilla troops. It was the first war America lost. Issues arose that had not come up before and that face us still. In the chapter on technology you read about the widespread use of defoliants in Vietnam in an effort to eliminate cover in the tactics of the guerrilla army of Vietnamese. There now is concern that the exposure of troops to the defoliants has adversely affected their health, as reports of high incidence of cancer among Vietnam veterans and civilians surface.

In sharp contrast to the joyous homecoming given Operation Desert Storm veterans, most Vietnam vets came home to a divided country and to widespread criticism of their role in a controversial war. This lack of recognition and respect for what most assumed to be their patriotic duty left many feeling ashamed and bitter, and their inability to articulate their experiences has resulted in Delayed Stress Syndrome, a variation of earlier battle fatigue. Additionally, many studies show the continuing inability of many Vietnam veterans to focus, to give any sort of meaning to their lives, to readjust to a saner world. Some recent studies even suggest that 'Nam vets earn less money than other war veterans and non-veterans, have more marital problems, and cope less well with stress.

What the United States ended up with from the Vietnam War was an enormous wall of black granite, the most personal of all war memorials in our nation's history. The Wall, as it has come to be known, annually draws more visitors than any other monument in the capitol; millions of average Americans stand mute before the 58,000 names inscribed there.

For Sgt. Bruce Biggs, the Wall is someplace he will visit someday: he is not yet ready. There he will seek out the names of those youngsters he served with, including one young soldier in his squad killed the day before his scheduled rotation home. The war affected us all: civilians and soldiers, combatants and war protesters, veterans and survivors, politicians and parents, children and grandparents. The lessons learned from the longest of American wars will change over time, to be sure. The response of those of the Vietnam generation will surely be different from those of the Persian Gulf war generation, but those differences may be understood if we understand the individuals and the issues.

When Biggs's replacement, another 19 year old, showed up at his fire base, Biggs handed him his Kabar knife, wished him good luck, and jumped aboard a Huey bound for Saigon. He thought then his war was over. Now he knows it is the war that won't ever end.

U.S. Misadventure in Vietnam

The United States was involved in the Vietnam War from 1961 until its withdrawal of troops in 1973 after a negotiated cease-fire; it maintained an official presence in Vietnam until 1975. As the years of that war rolled by, American discontent increased: many people could make no sense of the country's involvement. Many opposed it vehemently; many argued with and criticized the U.S. position and the military actions that grew from it. Others, of course, supported American involvement, believed it justified, and urged its continuance. Others supported the troops but not the war. Others reviled the troops, the government, the military. The Vietnam War divided America.

*The nature of that war and criticisms of it are presented in the next essay by Hans J. Morgenthau (1904–1980), a professor and author (*Politics Among Nations*) who came to the United States from Germany in 1937. The essay originally appeared in* Current History *in 1968 and was reprinted in the same journal in January, 1989. Before you read, work with classmates to decide how a military war differs from a political war and what might be the difficulties of fighting each.*

THE POLICIES the United States is pursuing in Vietnam are open to criticism on three grounds: they do not serve the interests of the United States; they run counter to American interests; and the United States objectives are not attainable, if they are attainable at all, without unreasonable moral liabilities and military risks. 1

In order to understand the rationale underlying our involvement in Southeast Asia one must go back to the spring of 1947 when the postwar policies of the United States were formulated and put into practice—the policy of containment, the Truman doctrine and the Marshall Plan. These policies pursued one single aim by different means: the containment of communism. That aim is derived from two assumptions: the unlimited expansionism of the Soviet Union as a revolutionary power, and the monolithic direction and control the Soviet Union exerted over the world Communist movement. 2

It is against this background that one must consider the involvement of the United States in Southeast Asia. For the modes of thought and action growing from the specific European experiences of the postwar period still dominate today the foreign policies of the United States, 3 paradoxically enough not so much in Europe as elsewhere throughout the world. The Administration consistently justifies its Asian policies by analogy with European experiences. The United States thinks of Asia in 1968 as it thought of Europe in 1947, and the successes of its European policies have become the curse of the policies the United States is pursuing in Asia. For the problems Americans are facing in Asia are utterly different from those they dealt with in Europe two decades ago, and the political world in Europe has been radically transformed.

The active involvement of the United States in Southeast Asia is a response to the Korean War. That war was interpreted by the United States government as the opening shot in a military campaign for world conquest under the auspices of the Soviet Union. In view of this interpretation, it was consistent for the United States to defend South Korea against the North Korean Communists, as it would have defended Western Europe against the Red Army had it stepped over the 1945 line of demarcation. Similarly, it was consistent for the United States to support with massive financial and material aid the French military effort to defeat the Vietnamese Communists. When France was threatened with defeat in 1954, it was consistent for Secretary of State John Foster Dulles and Admiral Arthur Radford, then chairing the Joint Chiefs of Staff, to recommend that President Dwight Eisenhower intervene with American airpower on the side of France. Finally, it was a logical application of this policy of containing communism in Asia to establish and support an anti-Communist regime in South Vietnam, after the division of the country in 1954. However, when the disintegration of this regime became acute the United States continued this policy of containment as though the nature of world communism had not changed since 1950 and as though the political disintegration of South Vietnam posed for the United States an issue similar to the North Korean invasion of South Korea. It was at this point that our policy went astray. 4

While it was plausible—even though it has proven to be historically incorrect—to attribute the outbreak of the Korean War to a worldwide Communist conspiracy, there is no historical evidence whatsoever to interpret in that manner what has happened in Vietnam since 1960. The period of history since (Soviet General Secretary) Nikita Khrushchev's denunciation of Josef Stalin in 1956 has been characterized by the disintegration of the Communist bloc into its national components, each pursuing to a greater or lesser degree its own particular national policy within a common framework of Communist ideology and institutions. The influence that the Soviet Union and China are still able to exert over Communist governments and movements is not the automatic result of their common Communist character, but of the convergence of national interests and of particular power relations. 5

This has always been true of the Vietnamese Communists. Many 6
of them were nationalists before they became Communists, and it was
only the indifference or hostility of the West that made them embrace
communism. Even under the most unfavorable conditions of war with
the United States, the government of North Vietnam has been able to
retain a considerable measure of independence vis-à-vis both the Soviet
Union and China by playing one off against the other. The Vietnamese
Communists are not mere agents of either the Soviet Union or China.
The sources of their strength and their arms are indigenous and must
be judged on their merits.

This being the case, the professed United States war aim, "to stop 7
communism" in South Vietnam, reveals itself as an empty slogan. It
must be made concrete by raising the questions: what kind of communism is the United States fighting in South Vietnam? and what is the
relationship of that communism to the United States interest in containing the Soviet Union and China? The answers to those questions reveal
the unsoundness of American policy. The fate of communism in South
Vietnam is irrelevant to the containment of Soviet or Chinese communism since Vietnamese communism is not controlled by either of them.
The United States fight against the South Vietnamese Communists is
relevant only to its relations with South Vietnam, which, even if she
were governed by Communists, could not affect the balance of power
in Asia.

It is to be held as an axiom, derived from the experience of many 8
guerrilla wars, that a guerrilla war supported, or at least not actively
opposed, by the indigenous population cannot be won, short of the
physical destruction of that population. In the nature of things, the guerrilla is indistinguishable from the rest of the population, and in truth the
very distinction is tenuous in a situation where the guerrilla is an organic
element of the social structure.

In Vietnam, what makes "counter-insurgency" so futile an under- 9
taking is the difference between the motivation of the guerrillas and that
of the professional army fighting them. No professional army could
have withstood the punishment Americans have inflicted on the South
Vietnamese guerrillas since the beginning of 1965.

The United States government recognizes implicitly that there are 10
two wars in South Vietnam—a military war and a political war—and
that victory in the latter will be decisive. In order to win that political
war, the United States has embarked on a massive program of political,
social, and economic reconstruction in South Vietnam. It is the purpose
of that program to establish the government of South Vietnam as a new
focus that will attract the loyalties of the large mass of South Vietnamese
who are indifferent to either side, as well as the disenchanted supporters

of the Viet Cong. This program is up against three obstacles which, in the aggregate, appear insurmountable.

First, the government of South Vietnam is a military government 11 and has remained so in spite of the democratic gloss which carefully circumscribed and managed elections have tried to put on it. The foundation of the government's power is the army, both in terms of the administrative structure and of what there is of loyal support. Yet the army is regarded by large masses of the population not as the expression of the popular will but as its enemy. This is so because of the oppressive behavior of the army toward the peasants and more particularly, because there is reportedly no officer in the South Vietnamese army above the rank of lieutenant colonel who did not fight on the side of the French against his own people.

Second, this impression of an army fighting against its own people 12 is reinforced by the massive presence of foreign armed forces without whom neither that army nor the government it supports could survive. Regardless of professed and actual American intention, the United States military presence, with its destructive economic, social, and moral results in South Vietnam, appears to an ever-increasing number of South Vietnamese as an evil to be eliminated at any price.

Finally, the hoped-for radical change in political loyalties requires 13 radical social, economic, and political reforms, especially with regard to the distribution of land. The achievement of such reforms has indeed earned the Viet Cong the allegiance of large masses of peasants. Both in its composition and policies, the government of South Vietnam represents the interests of a small group of absentee land owners and members of the urban upper middle class who would lose their economic, social and political privileges were that government really trying to counter the social revolution of the Viet Cong with radical social reforms of its own.

The universally recognized weaknesses of the government in South 14 Vietnam—corruption, inefficiency, apathy, lack of public spirit, low military performance, a staggering desertion rate—result irremediably from the nature of that government. They are not to be remedied by American appeals to the South Vietnamese government to do more for the country or to let the South Vietnamese army take over a larger share of the fighting and pacification. A government imposed on an unwilling or at best indifferent people by a foreign power to defend the status quo against a national and social revolution is by dint of its very nature precluded from doing what Americans expect it to do. That nature dooms all efforts at politically effective reconstruction.

The third policy the United States is pursuing in Vietnam is the 15 bombing of the North, to win the war in the South by interdicting the influx of men and material from the North, and to force the government of North Vietnam to the conference table by making it too costly for it to continue the war. Both purposes derive from a faulty perception of reality. The United States assumes that what it faces in South Vietnam is the result of foreign aggression and that there would be no unmanageable trouble in the South if only, in Secretary of State Dean Rusk's often repeated phrase, North Vietnam would leave her neighbor alone. It follows logically from this assumption that internal peace could be restored to South Vietnam if one could insulate South Vietnam from the North or compel the North to cease her assistance to the South. However, this assumption does not square with historical reality.

The roots of the trouble are in the South. They were deeply   16
embedded in the nature of the Ngo Dinh Diem regime (1954–1963), which combined a fierce nationalism with a totalitarian defense of the economic and social status quo. Nobody doubts that the government of North Vietnam welcomed and aided and abetted the progressive disintegration of the Diem regime. But it did not cause it, nor was its support responsible for the Viet Cong's success. When, at the beginning of 1965, the government of South Vietnam was close to defeat at the hands of the Viet Cong, according to official estimates 90 percent of the Viet Cong weapons were of American origin and the annual infiltration from the North amounted to no more than a few thousand men, mostly of Southern origin. Only a total of a few hundred were regulars of the North Vietnamese army.

It is precisely because we have been unable to win the war in the   17
South that we continue to assume that the source of the war is in the North and that victory can be won by bombing the North. However, the day is close at hand when everything that appears to be worth bombing will have been bombed and the war in the South will still not be won. The next logical step will be the invasion of North Vietnam; for if North Vietnam is responsible for the war, then the conquest of North Vietnam will end the war. While it will not accomplish that end, it will conjure up the likelihood of a United States military confrontation with the Soviet Union or China or both. The Soviet Union has assured the United States that it will not stand idly by while the government of North Vietnam is destroyed, and China has made it clear that she will intervene, as she did in the Korean War, when a hostile army approaches her frontiers.

However, if the war in the South lasts long enough, the United   18
States has a good chance of winning it. The United States is not likely to win the war in the traditional way by breaking the enemy's will to resist, but rather by killing so many enemies that there is no one left to resist. Killing in war has traditionally been a means to a psychological

end. In this war, killing becomes an end in itself. The physical elimination of the enemy and victory become synonymous. Hence, the "body
count," however fictitious, is the sole measure of our success.

No civilized nation can wage such a war without suffering incal- 19
culable moral damage. This damage is particularly grave since the nation
can realize no plausible military or political benefit which could justify
this killing for killing's sake. And it is particularly painful for a nation
like the United States—founded as a novel experiment in government,
morally superior to those who preceded it—which has throughout history thought of itself as performing a uniquely beneficial mission not
only for itself but for all mankind.

Why, then, is the United States evidently resolved to continue 20
fighting a war which appears politically aimless, militarily unpromising
and morally dubious? The answer is to be found in the concern for
American prestige. If the United States should leave Vietnam without
having won a victory, so it is argued, the credibility of its commitments
throughout the world would suffer, Communist revolutions throughout
the world would be encouraged, and the reputation of American invincibility would be impaired.

Not only does the containment of Vietnamese communism not 21
further the interests of the United States but, paradoxical as it may seem,
it is even detrimental to those interests. The United States has a legitimate interest in the containment of China and its involvement in Vietnam is frequently explained in terms of this interest. But Vietnamese
nationalism has been for a millennium a barrier to the expansion of
Chinese power into Southeast Asia. There is no patriotic Vietnamese,
North or South, Communist or non-Communist, Buddhist or Catholic,
who does not regard China as the hereditary enemy of Vietnam. Yet to
the degree that the United States weakens Vietnam as a national entity
through the destruction of her human and material resources, it creates
a political, military, and social vacuum into which either the United
States must move in virtual permanence or into which the Soviet Union
or China will move.

What about American prestige? Its decline because of the liquida- 22
tion of United States involvement in Vietnam is a matter for speculation:
its drastic decline by virtue of the involvement is a matter of fact. In the
eyes of most of the world, the most powerful nation on earth is trying
to force a nation of primitive peasants into submission by the massive
use of all the modern means of mass destruction (with the exception of
biological and nuclear weapons) and it is unable either to win or to
liquidate that war. The champion of the "free world" is protecting the
people of South Vietnam from communism by destroying them. And

in the process, the world is moved closer and closer to an unwinnable war with China, if not to the cataclysm of nuclear war.

If the United States were to liquidate the war, the damage to its 23 prestige would at least in some measure be repaired. The United States would show that it is wise and strong enough to admit a mistake and correct it. The liquidation of the misadventure need not affect its future policies.

What the argument about prestige really amounts to is a concern 24 for the prestige not of the United States but of those who are responsible for its involvement in Vietnam. But those who are responsible for the straits in which the nation finds itself today should bear the consequences of their ideological blindness and political and military miscalculations. They ought not to ask the nation to suffer for their false pride.

Content Considerations

1. What support does Morgenthau offer for his three criticisms of the Vietnam War? Summarize them and then explain how convincing they are.
2. What is it about the nature of the Vietnam War that Morgenthau says makes it almost impossible to win? What does he say about how it could be won?
3. Respond to the way in which the author structures his argument. How does he do it? How does it build toward the notion of prestige in the last three paragraphs?

Setting the Stage

The following essay is an excerpt from Lyndon Johnson's War *(1989) by Larry Berman, author of* Planning A Tragedy: The Americanization of the War in Vietnam, The New American Presidency, *and* The Office of Management and Budget and the Presidency, 1921–1979. *In this selection, Berman looks at the administrative misgivings, disagreements, and determinations that occurred preceding the huge increase of American troops in Vietnam.*

By February, 1966, 184,000 troops had been deployed; the administration decided to increase that number to 429,000 by the end of that year. It had doubts that its objectives in the war would ever be met. The Pacification and Revolutionary Development Program wasn't working well—the hearts and minds of the Vietnamese were still alienated. Operation Rolling Thunder— the air campaign over North Vietnam—was not producing the desired effect. In short, the war was not going well and no one quite knew how to fix it.

Before you read Berman's account of differing administrative perspectives, write a few paragraphs about how governments make decisions in war. Work with classmates to gather more views and possibilities.

If you're in one, stop digging.

—DENIS HEALEY, *Law of Holes*

IN JULY 1965 Lyndon Johnson chose to Americanize the war in 1 Vietnam. Faced with the prospects of losing South Vietnam to the Communists, the president announced that U.S. combat strength in Vietnam would immediately be increased from 75,000 to 125,000 and that additional U.S. forces would be sent when requested by field commander General William Westmoreland. The level of forces needed would be achieved through substantial increases in monthly draft calls but Reserve units would not be called into service. "Now," Johnson wrote in his memoirs, "we were committed to major combat in Vietnam. We had determined not to let that country fall under Communist rule as long as we could prevent it."[1]

Just seven months following the July 1965 decision, President 2

Johnson traveled to Honolulu in February 1966 for a first-hand assessment on the war's progress from General William Westmoreland and to secure commitments for political reform from South Vietnam's prime minister Nguyen Cao Ky. Johnson was accompanied by Secretary of State Dean Rusk, Secretary of Defense Robert McNamara, Chairman of the Joint Chiefs of Staff General Earle Wheeler, Special Assistant for National Security McGeorge Bundy, Secretary of Health, Education and Welfare John Gardner, and Secretary of Agriculture Orville Freeman. In Honolulu they were met by a 28-member South Vietnamese delegation headed by Ky and Chief of State Nguyen Van Thieu. Also waiting in Honolulu were General Westmoreland and Pacific Commander Admiral Ullysses S. Grant Sharp, Jr.

The visit to Honolulu was Johnson's first trip outside the North American continent since becoming president. The decision was made hastily and for political reasons—Senator J. William Fulbright, Democratic senator from Arkansas and chairman of the Senate Foreign Relations Committee, had scheduled televised committee hearings on the war. Johnson outfoxed his political adversary by putting the principal witnesses on *Air Force I* and flying to Honolulu. The president's trip galvanized public attention and South Vietnam's premier Ky was featured on the cover of *Time* magazine. Fulbright was left to question retired General James Gavin and diplomat George Kennan—critics of the war but neither holding an official position in government. **3**

At Honolulu, Johnson learned from General Westmoreland that the July deployments had staved off defeat in the South, but additional troops would now be needed to take the military initiative. President Johnson reluctantly agreed to a dramatic increase in U.S. troop strength from the 184,000 currently deployed to 429,000 by the end of the year. In exchange for the increase LBJ, utilizing his favorite exhortation, told Westmoreland to "nail the coonskin to the wall" by reaching the crossover point by December 1966. **4**

LBJ also told Ky he expected results, especially a plan for a new constitution and free elections. To underscore these expectations, the president related a story for South Vietnam's premier. "There was once two poker players and the first player asked 'What do you have?' 'Aces,' said the second. 'How many aces?' asked the first. 'One aces,' answered the second." Looking directly at Ky the president said, "I hope we don't find out we only had one aces."[2] **5**

Nailing the coonskin proved to be elusive, however, and doubts within the administration on the feasibility of achieving U.S. objectives in Vietnam had begun to surface as early as November 1965. Among the doubters was Secretary of Defense Robert McNamara—the god- **6** father of the Pentagon's computerized methodology and systems analysis that had originally forecast an end to the war within a reasonable period of time.

It was Robert Strange McNamara's exuberance for statistical analysis as a method for finding the code to break Ho's will that was discredited during the war. McNamara had utilized statistics and management/systems analysis to solve tough problems throughout his distinguished public career. A graduate of Harvard Business School, he was best known for almost single-handedly reviving Ford Motor Company and for his meteoric rise at Ford from manager to vice-president and, in 1960, to president—the first person outside the Ford family to hold that title. At Ford, as he would later do at the Pentagon, McNamara surrounded himself with a remarkably talented group of young, energetic, and similarly committed individuals who at various times were referred to as the "quiz kids," "whiz kids," "computer jockeys," "technipols," or "McNamara's band."

McNamara's entire public career had been a success story. After serving only one month as president of Ford, McNamara had accepted John Kennedy's offer to run the Pentagon. Following Kennedy's assassination, and during the period in which President Johnson became preoccupied with the legitimacy of transition and then the 1964 election, responsibility for running the war (which was still a relatively small commitment) had fallen to the civilian secretary of defense. Vietnam was then referred to in laudatory terms as "McNamara's war." President Johnson trusted McNamara and respected him for his ability to get things done. General Westmoreland later recalled that "Mr. McNamara came from American business and he was very statistically oriented. He was very anxious to fight this war as efficiently as possible. I have heard him say that he wanted to end the war without having great stockpiles of material as we had in World War II."[3]

McNamara became an open target for southern conservatives on the Armed Services Committee and military hawks who blamed the military stalemate on the secretary of defense. In part this reaction reflected the belief that more bombing would accomplish what a great amount of bombing and a great number of troops had failed to do—bring security and stability to South Vietnam and convince Hanoi to seek negotiations. The attacks on McNamara also manifested the desire by his political opponents to take that smart son-of-a-gun down a peg or two.

McNamara's initial doubts had surfaced following the battle at Ia Drang Valley in November 1965. The battle had pitted the Army's First Cavalry Division against regimental-size formations of North Vietnamese. In direct confrontation with the enemy, premium firepower had smashed large enemy formations. The battle had left 1200 Communists killed-in-action compared with approximately 200 for the United States. Westmoreland believed that the size of enemy casualties validated the concept of attrition as a military strategy.[4]

McNamara, however, doubted that the enemy would stand toe-to-toe very frequently, and a war of attriting the enemy's manpower base would take time, possibly too long for the American public. The secretary subsequently pressed his case for what became a 37-day Christmas bombing pause and at one point told Johnson that the United States could not win the war in Vietnam. During a December 18, 1965, White House meeting, President Johnson asked McNamara, "Then, no matter what we do in the military field there is no sure victory?" McNamara responded, "That's right. We have been too optimistic." When the bombing pause failed to produce fruitful negotiations, the bombing program was accelerated.

By 1967–68 the Joint Chiefs were in open revolt against the civilians in the Pentagon, and President Johnson, who had always been suspicious of the military, now lost faith in his dovish defense secretary. Vitriolic perceptions of "McNamara's band" permeated the inner war councils. Admiral Sharp later wrote, "We could have flattened every war-making facility in North Vietnam. But the handwringers had center stage. . . . The most powerful country in the world did not have the willpower needed to meet the situation."[5] General John Paul McConnel charged that "I didn't think Mr. McNamara understood air power nor its application very well. . . . In fact, I don't think there was at that time anybody in the Office of the Secretary of Defense who understood the application of tactical and strategic powers. At least, not the way I understood it."[6] Admiral Thomas Moorer added, "I thought that McNamara didn't know what the hell he was talking about because they were claiming that the bombing wasn't effective, see."[7]

THE PROGNOSIS IS BAD—OCTOBER 1966

By the final quarter of 1966 the crossover point was nowhere in sight. At President Johnson's behest Secretary McNamara visited Vietnam in October 1966. It had been twelve months since McNamara's last visit—a period during which U.S. troop deployments had more than doubled. The secretary spent his first two days in formal briefings with military commanders and then visited military posts in the field.

Signs of an inconclusive military stalemate were already evident. Military defeat had been prevented, but little progress had been made in rooting out Communist forces and destroying their infrastructure in South Vietnam. Moreover, while unremitting but selective application of air and naval power had inflicted serious damage to war-supporting targets in North Vietnam, it had not reduced Hanoi's capacity to support or direct military operations in the South.

On October 14, 1966 Secretary McNamara wrote LBJ that despite   15 significant increases in U.S. troop deployments and in the intensity of the bombing campaign, Hanoi "knows we can't achieve our goals. The prognosis is bad in that the war can be brought to a satisfactory conclusion within the next two years." The U.S. military escalation had blunted Communist military initiatives, but had not diminished the enemy's will to continue. "Any military victory in South Vietnam the Viet Cong may have had in mind 18 months ago has been thwarted by our emergency deployments and actions. And our program of bombing the North has exacted a price. My concern continues, however, in other respects. This is because I see no reasonable way to bring the war to an end soon." McNamara apparently recognized the limits of U.S. military force in a war with political ends. According to McNamara, Hanoi had adopted a strategy of "attriting our national will."

McNamara identified shortcomings in a military strategy that was   16 seemingly detached from its original political goals. "In essence, we find ourselves—from the point of view of the important war (for the complicity of the people)—no better, and if anything worse off. This important war must be fought and won by the Vietnamese themselves. We have known this from the beginning. But the discouraging truth is that, as was the case in 1961 and 1963 and 1965, we have not found the formula, the catalyst, for training and inspiring them into effective action." The Pacification and Revolutionary Development program—aimed at gaining the hearts and minds of the population—was "thoroughly stalled." Pacification had been a central objective of U.S. policy in Vietnam. It had involved the military, political, economic, and social establishment of local government with the participation of the Vietnamese people. For pacification to succeed, it was necessary to achieve sustained periods of territorial security, economic activity, and political control, yet the Viet Cong political infrastructure still thrived in the South's countryside and provided an enormous intelligence advantage for the enemy. In McNamara's words, "full security exists nowhere (not even behind the US Marines' lines and in Saigon); in the countryside, the enemy almost completely controls the night." The people in rural areas believed that the government of South Vietnam "when it comes will not stay but that the VC will." Moreover, people believed that those who cooperated with the Government of Vietnam (GVN) would be punished by the Viet Cong (VC) and that the GVN was indifferent to the people's welfare. The United States could not do the job of pacification and security for the Vietnamese. "All we can do is massage the heart," warned McNamara.

October 1966 was not, however, the time to pull back or even out. Instead, faced with this unpromising state of affairs, McNamara endorsed a policy of redefining U.S. strategy. "We must continue to press the enemy militarily; we must make demonstrable progress in pacification; at the same time, we must add a new ingredient forced on us by the facts. Specifically, we must improve our position by getting ourselves into a military posture that we credibly would maintain indefinitely—a posture that makes trying to 'wait us out' less attractive." In order to achieve the political objectives of changing Hanoi's long-term strategy, McNamara recommended stabilizing U.S. forces at 470,000. "It is my view that this is enough to punish the enemy at the large-unit operations level and to keep the enemy's main forces from interrupting pacification. I believe also that even many more than 470,000 would not kill the enemy off in such numbers as to break their morale so long as they think they can wait us out." A stabilized U.S. force level would put the United States in a position where negotiations would more likely be productive.

Secretary McNamara also recommended in his report that a portion of the 470,000 troops—perhaps 10,000 to 20,000—should be devoted to the construction and maintenance of an infiltration barrier. This interdiction system would cost $1 billion dollars and be constructed with fences, wires, acoustic sensors, and mines. McNamara also recommended that Rolling Thunder★ attack sorties on the North be stabilized. Approximately 12,000 sorties a month were currently directed against the North—double the amount of the previous year—yet, in Secretary McNamara's opinion, the JCS could not show what effect the sorties had had on Viet Cong infiltration into the South. "Furthermore, it is clear that, to bomb the North sufficiently to make a radical impact upon Hanoi's political, economic and social structure, would require an effort which we could make but which would not be stomached either by our own people or by world opinion; and it would involve a serious risk of drawing us into open war with China."[8]

The Joint Chiefs of Staff quickly responded to McNamara's recommendations. Chairman Earle Wheeler, the country's highest ranking uniformed soldier, wrote directly to the secretary that the chiefs agreed with McNamara that "we cannot predict with confidence that the war can be brought to an end in two years." Accordingly, for political, military, and psychological reasons, it would be necessary to prepare openly for a long-term, sustained military effort. Wheeler warned McNamara that the enemy strategy "appears to be to wait it out; in

17

18

19

other words, communist leaders in both North and South Vietnam expect to win this war in Washington, just as they won the war with France in Paris."

But, while the JCS agreed with McNamara's diagnosis, they vehemently rejected the secretary's proposed treatment. A stable and sustainable force level of 470,000 was substantially less than the military envisioned. The JCS were even less enamored with McNamara's plans for an infiltration barrier which was privately derided as an "Alice-in-Wonderland solution to insurgency." Barriers properly installed and defended by ground and air effort could indeed impede infiltration into South Vietnam, but McNamara's air-raid munitions barrier could not accomplish this goal and the diversion of funds would impair ongoing military programs throughout the world.

The very premise for stabilizing Rolling Thunder as a carrot to induce negotiations was rejected by the chiefs. Instead, they claimed that the air campaign needed to be accelerated. "Our experiences with pauses in bombing and resumption have not been happy ones," Wheeler wrote. "Additionally, the Joint Chiefs of Staff believe that the likelihood of the war being settled by negotiation is small; and that, far from inducing negotiations, another bombing pause will be regarded by North Vietnamese leaders, and our Allies, as renewed evidence of lack of US determination to press the war to a successful conclusion. The bombing campaign is one of the two trump cards in the hands of the President (the other being the presence of US troops in SVN). It should not be given up without an end to the NVN aggression in SVN."

General Wheeler concluded with a clear statement that the chiefs believed the war had reached a critical stage in which "decisions taken over the next sixty days can determine the outcome of the war and, consequently, can affect the over-all security interests of the United States for years to come." Wheeler acknowledged the admirable goals of trying to settle the war by peaceful means. "Certainly, no one—American or foreigner—except those who are determined not to be convinced, can doubt the sincerity, the generosity, the altruism of US actions and objectives. In the opinion of the Joint Chiefs of Staff the time has come when further overt actions and offers on our part are not only nonproductive, they are counterproductive. A logical case can be made that the American people, our Allies, and our enemies alike are increasingly uncertain as to our resolution to pursue the war to a successful conclusion."[9]

*Rolling Thunder was the code name for U.S. air operations over North Vietnam. The program was closely monitored from the White House by President Johnson and his civilian advisors. This interdiction program started in March 1965 as an attempt to destroy North Vietnamese transportation routes and thereby slow infiltration of personnel and supplies from North to South Vietnam. Rolling Thunder was expanded in July 1966 to include ammunition dumps and oil storages, and in the spring of 1967 it was further expanded to include power plants, factories, and airfields in the Hanoi-Haiphong area. The Rolling Thunder program was substantially reduced in April 1968 and terminated on November 1, 1968. In the three years of Rolling Thunder, 643,000 tons of bombs were dropped on North Vietnam.

END NOTES

1. Lyndon Baines Johnson, *The Vantage Point: Perspectives on the Presidency, 1963–1969* (New York: Popular Library, 1971), p. 383.
2. See *Time,* February 18, 1966; *Newsweek,* February 18, 1966 and February 11, 1966; Johnson, *The Vantage Point,* p. 244.
3. William Westmoreland, trial testimony and deposition. For insights into McNamara see David Halberstam, *The Best and the Brightest* (New York: Random House, 1969); Henry Trewitt, *McNamara* (New York: Harper and Row, 1971); William Kaufman, *The McNamara Strategy* (New York: Harper and Row, 1964); Douglas Kinnard, *The War Managers* (Hanover, NH: University Press of New England, 1977); Jonathan Rinehart, "The Man Who Wields Power," *USA.1* (May 1967); Stewart Alsop, "McNamara: The Light that Failed," *Saturday Evening Post* (November 18, 1967); Stewart Alsop, "Vietnam: How Wrong Was McNamara?" *Saturday Evening Post* (March 12, 1966); Neil Sheehan, "You Don't Know Where Johnson Ends and McNamara Begins," *New York Times Magazine* (October 22, 1967); Tom Wicker, "The Awesome Twosome," *New York Magazine* (January 30, 1966).
4. See Krepinevich, *The Army and Vietnam,* pp. 168–72.
5. See Sharp, *Strategy for Defeat,* p. 164.
6. General John Paul McConnel, "Oral history transcript" (Johnson Library).
7. Admiral Thomas Moorer, "Oral history transcript" (Johnson Library).
8. McNamara to the president, "Actions recommended for Vietnam," October 14, 1966.
9. Wheeler to McNamara, "Actions recommended for Vietnam," October 14, 1966.

Content Considerations

1. Review and summarize the information the essay presents about McNamara. What purpose is served by focusing so much on him? What seems to be Berman's attitude toward him?
2. What kind of concerns seemed to have interfered with the decision-making of the officials Berman writes about?
3. In what instances did officials ignore advice? Was it wise for them to have done so? Using the information in this essay as well as your own knowledge for support, discuss some of the ways in which government decisions are made and explain a citizen's part in those decisions.

CLARENCE PAGE

Comparing Wars Does Veterans of Both a Disservice

As American forces blazed a path of victory in the Persian Gulf war, comparisons of that war with the Vietnam War appeared with increasing regularity. The Gulf war came to be seen as a sort of exorcism of the nation's Vietnam ghosts: anguish, defeat, disillusion, civil unrest and protest, death and disability. But columnist Clarence Page takes exception to that comparison in the following essay published in March, 1991.

In his essay, Page disputes some of the facts on which such comparisons rest and explains what he sees as their inherent danger. Before you read what he has to say, work with classmates to compile a list of lessons the country may have learned from its experiences in the Vietnam War. Then list what lessons are emerging from the Persian Gulf war.

CHICAGO—I never expected it to happen, but I feel my Vietnam-era chauvinism rising.   1

As our exuberance over Desert Storm pushes aside the bad memories of Vietnam, the defining war of my generation, I can't help but feel the mixed emotions a World War I veteran feels who has lived long enough to see memories of his generation's sacrifices supplanted by more recent conflicts.   2

It appears I am not alone. "I'm happy to see America finally come around to welcoming troops home the way they should be welcomed," says Richard K. Kolb, editor of the Veterans of Foreign Wars magazine in Kansas City. "But there's also no doubt in my mind that, even as they join in the celebrations, Vietnam veterans can't help but feel a little envy."   3

Kolb ought to know. He served with the 4th Infantry and 101st Airborne divisions in Vietnam, only to face shame, derision, embarrassment and indifference back home. By contrast, as one Washington wit observed, the Gulf War may be the first time Americans welcome the troops home and spit on the news reporters.   4

That's fine, but some armchair analysts already are making unkind comparisons between the troops of the two wars, including implications   5 that the allies won in the gulf because America's all-volunteer troops had the right stuff while our largely drafted Vietnam force didn't.

As early as mid-December, an AP report noted the absence from Saudi Arabia of "the 'booze, broads and drugs' synonymous with Vietnam" and said, "The draftees of Vietnam and their hatred of the military establishment are long gone."   6

A Dec. 23 *Washington Post* story observed, "Vietnam also was fought mostly by draftees, amateurs . . . some of them reluctant soldiers disgusted and demoralized by a war without end."   7

U.S. News & World Report correspondent Mike Tharp, a Vietnam veteran, in February recalled the dope smoking and massage parlors of Vietnam and concluded, "The bottom line drawn in the sand is this: American troops are preparing for their first big ground combat in nearly 20 years and they're going into it straight, sober and focused."   8

The armchair analysts are wrong. The Vietnam force was more "volunteer," better educated and more well-adjusted than most people appear to realize. As Kolb reported in a Jan. 25 *Wall Street Journal* op-ed essay, draftees constituted only 25 percent of the 2.6 million Americans who served in Vietnam (and 27 percent of Vietnam's combat deaths), compared to 66 percent in World War II. Some 76 percent came from lower-, middle- or working-class backgrounds, and 79 percent had high school educations or better.   9

As for their behavior, 97 percent of Vietnam-era veterans earned honorable discharges, and only 15 percent have experienced some form of emotional stress, according to a 1988 Centers for Disease Control study, compared to a third of World War II veterans, according to a 1965 study by the National Academy of Sciences.   10

The real bottom line drawn in the sand is this: When we make frivolous comparisons between the two wars, we do the veterans of both a disservice. We also risk overinflating our nation's ability to be the world's police officer in future wars.   11

George Bush was right when he said Desert Storm would not be another Vietnam. Kuwait had no jungle, no village-to-village fighting, no indigenous population that was sympathetic with the enemy and no need to "win the hearts and minds of the people." Nor, as in Korea, did it have a looming superpower like China or the Soviet Union threatening to strike back if we charged too far.   12

Instead, for eight long years Vietnam was a war without clear goals or a conceivable end. Our forces took hills as ordered, at a terrible cost of life, only to give them up inexplicably, to be retaken by the enemy. No wonder our troops were dispirited. Yet they fought well to the bitter end.   13

Desert Storm had a coalition of allies, U.N. support, congressional   14
support and a clear goal: Kick Saddam Hussein out of Kuwait.

The Bush administration wisely defined the end of Desert Storm   15
before it began, even though it meant Saddam would live, perhaps to
fight another day.

"By God," Bush gushed triumphantly to Congress on March 1,   16
"we've kicked the Vietnam syndrome once and for all."

If so, I'll miss it. My Vietnam-era pride is showing. If memories   17
of that ugly war caused our leaders to be extra careful as they laid the
groundwork for Desert Storm, then its hard lessons have served us well.
We must never forget those lessons, or the men who paid their terrible
price.

Content Considerations

1. What is Page's argument against comparing the Vietnam and Gulf wars?
    How persuasive is his argument?
2. Respond to Page's assertion that "frivolous comparisons between the
    two wars" create the possibility that we "risk overinflating our nation's
    ability to be the world's police officer in future wars" (paragraph 11).
    How might the assertion be true? What situations might occur if the
    nation did over-estimate its "ability to be the world's police officer"?
    What does it mean for a nation to become the world's police officer?
3. What are the lessons Page hopes America learned from the Vietnam
    War? How did the Persian Gulf war illustrate how well the country had
    learned them?

A Refugee

In her book Ten Vietnamese *(1967), writer Susan Sheehan presents extended interviews with Vietnamese people, describing their lives, their adjustment to a sequence of regimes and political changes, their perspectives. The
next selection is a chapter from that book. It focuses on a fifty-year-old man
who lives in a refugee camp after fleeing the hamlet in which he had been
born. That refugee, Duong Tam, lived peacefully until 1945 when the Viet
Minh, the main political-military organization that fought the French for independence (1946–1954), began to dominate the area of Tam's hamlet. Then
his life and that of his family became more difficult.*

*Before you read about his life, write several paragraphs about what war—
a series of wars, actually—might mean in the life of a farmer who cannot read
or write and who has little knowledge of the world beyond his own village.*

DUONG TAM IS A REFUGEE. He fled his native hamlet, Gia Hoi,   1
in the spring of 1965, and now lives ninety-four miles from Gia Hoi in
a refugee camp on the outskirts of Qui Nhon, a city on the central coast
of South Viet Nam, two hundred and seventy miles northeast of Saigon.

Tam was born in Gia Hoi, one of the eleven hamlets in Loc Chau,   2
a village in Binh Dinh province, in March, 1917, when it was part of
the French protectorate of Annam. His parents worked in the rice fields
for landlords; they were never able to buy or rent land. They were too
poor to send Tam, his younger brother, or his two younger sisters to
school. Tam is a little sorry now that he cannot read or write, but he
wasn't sorry then; he recalls his childhood as the happiest time of his
life precisely because he didn't have to go to school. He went to work
in the rice fields when he was ten. In his teens he got bored with planting
and plowing and decided to try another trade. He went to live with an
uncle who ran an ox-cart transportation service in Ban Me Thuot, a city
in the central highlands. He earned more money than he had at home
and at first enjoyed his new way of life. Then memories of the rice fields
began to haunt him and he realized he could never voluntarily stay away
from them. After about six years, he returned home.

Tam's family was Catholic. When he was twenty-two, his parents   3
arranged a marriage for him with a sixteen-year-old girl from Gia Hoi;
he stole a few glances at his fiancée after they became engaged, but he

didn't speak to her until after their church wedding. Of the many children Tam and his wife have had over the years, eight have survived, six boys and two girls. The oldest child is a married daughter of twenty-two, the youngest is a one-year-old boy. Tam hopes he will have no more children. "Eight is enough," he says. At forty-nine, Tam is a diminutive man with curly hair, who wears short-length pants and an overblouse of coarse grayish-brown cotton. The sun and hard work have weathered his face and hands and made them wrinkled and dark. His eyes have a pronounced squint, but Tam says he has had the squint since birth and that he sees very well. His vision has never been tested.

Tam and his wife both worked in the rice fields after their marriage. They worked very hard and they prospered. In time, they bought four acres of riceland and built a large brick house. Their life was peaceful until 1945. French troops had occasionally marched past their village before then, but had never harmed it. Tam had seen some Japanese troops in the early forties; he had had no contact with them. The Viet Minh, however, made their presence known and felt. Tam had some bad experiences with the Viet Minh from the day he first became aware of them in 1945. "They were always asking me to do some work for them for three days and they always kept me working a month," he says. "I wouldn't want the French to return to Viet Nam, but life under the French was better than under the Viet Minh. The French let us alone. The Viet Minh interfered too much in our lives, making us destroy bridges and making us listen to propaganda. They never kept their promises. My younger brother swallowed the Viet Minh propaganda and joined them. He was killed in a clash with French troops in the late forties. I succeeded in evading the Viet Minh draft. Things never got bad enough for me to leave my hamlet for very long. I paid taxes to both sides and went on planting rice."

In 1954, most of the Viet Minh in Tam's area went North after the Geneva Agreements and Gia Hoi was tranquil again. Three years later, trouble started between the government and the Viet Cong. In the late fifties and early sixties, a number of Loc Chau villagers fled to the safer towns and cities. Most of the villagers were Buddhists, but the majority of those who fled were Catholics; eventually the priests left and returned only periodically to say mass for the Catholics who remained. Many villagers, including a few of Tam's friends—but none of his relatives—joined the Viet Cong. In the late fifties, Tam joined the government Self-Defense Corps for three years, "for fun and to protect my hamlet." He gave it up because it took too much time from his field work.

Tam thinks that some people joined or cooperated with the Viet Cong because of a particular grievance against the government, but that others simply sided with the predominant force as the security situation fluctuated. They joined the government side when the government troops were in the area and seemed able to protect them, and the VC when the government troops weren't around. More wound up with the VC because the VC were a much more constant presence, especially at night. "I was one of the only people to make a conscious choice," Tam says. "I had many reasons for not joining the Viet Cong. I knew that Catholics and Communists could not live together. I found the Viet Cong arguments unconvincing. The VC claimed that life in North Viet Nam was much better than life in the South, but I didn't believe them. If that was true, why did so many people come south in 1954 and 1955 after only a few years under Communism? No one felt the need to leave the South except the Viet Minh. The VC said that in a Communist state everyone was equal and enjoyed the same rights and the same material benefits as everyone else. Personally, I wouldn't like that sort of set-up. Sameness doesn't appeal to me. If I work hard, I will do well. If I don't work, I won't eat. That's as it should be. I also didn't join the Viet Cong because I could never bring myself to terrorize people—to kill even my own relatives. This war is much worse than the last one. The fighting is far more widespread and it's harder to keep out of it and to stay put. People don't know which side to take to feel safe. There are so many families with relatives on both sides. I've seen government hamlet chiefs murdered by Viet Cong guerrillas led by their own nephews. It breaks your heart to see Vietnamese families killing each other like that."

In 1962, Gia Hoi became a strategic hamlet. The peasants in Gia Hoi had heard that the Americans had supplied money and barbed wire for the project. When they had to contribute money for the barbed wire and to work without pay to build a fence around the hamlet, they assumed that the American aid went into the pockets of corrupt officials. The Viet Cong were quiescent for a while. After President Diem's death, VC attacks on the hamlet started again. Two of Tam's relatives who had been in the Self-Defense Corps were kidnapped and murdered by the Viet Cong as a part of their campaign of terrorism in the village. Five of his nephews who had been in the Self-Defense Corps were captured by the VC and have disappeared. In early 1964, when Viet Cong pressure on the hamlet became very great, Tam sent his two oldest sons, aged fifteen and seventeen, to Qui Nhon, the provincial capital of Binh Dinh, and one of the only secure places in the province. He feared they would be drafted by the Viet Cong if they stayed at home. His oldest daughter and her husband, who was just as afraid of being drafted by the VC, also went to Qui Nhon.

By November, 1964, Tam seriously contemplated fleeing his hamlet. He knew that the Viet Cong had it in for him: he'd been in the Self-Defense Corps, he was a Catholic, he wouldn't join them, and he even resisted paying taxes to them. He hesitated for a few months. He couldn't quite face losing everything he had worked so hard for and also the hamlet chief urged him to stay on. One night in mid-February, 1965, while he was still hesitating, the VC attacked Gia Hoi. They wiped out four platoons of popular forces and two platoons of ARVN troops then stationed in the hamlet; some of the soldiers were captured but most, including six of Tam's closest friends, were killed. The hamlet chief was also murdered. On the night of the attack, the Viet Cong came to Tam's house and took him prisoner. They held him in a mountain hideout about seven and a half miles from his hamlet for two months. Rice was scarce and when the shortage became acute, the VC allowed Tam to return to his hamlet. A day or two after he got back, some government planes dropped leaflets over the village. The leaflets said that government airborne troops were soon coming to the area for an operation, and urged the population to stand by if they wanted to follow the troops out of the area. That night, the VC again came to kidnap Tam just a few hours before the government troops reached the hamlet. His wife and children were also taken prisoner and held at a VC base at the foot of the mountain, but they were released in a day; the Viet Cong had presumably decided they wouldn't leave the hamlet alone. When Tam got to the mountain hideout for his second stay, the VC told him he had been tried and sentenced to death. A few days after Tam had been captured, one of his fellow prisoners became very ill. Tam and three other prisoners asked the Viet Cong to let them carry the man down to the plain, where he could get decent food and medical treatment. The VC allowed them to go. Tam isn't sure why the VC released him when they had a rice shortage the first time, or why the VC let the sick man be taken down the mountain the second time. He guesses they like to kill people at a chosen moment and in their own way, rather than have them die of illness or starvation. Shortly before Tam and the other prisoners reached the VC camp at the foot of the mountain with the sick man, they stopped for a rest. Tam broke away from the others and sped off in the direction of his hamlet. The first five and a half miles of the way were through an area under complete VC control; he walked nonchalantly, pretending to be a casual stroller. The last two miles were through contested ground. It took Tam several hours to cover these last two miles, darting from bush to bush, and praying he wouldn't fall into a VC booby trap or be shot at by government troops. He got to Gia Hoi safely and learned that the government airborne troops were still in the vicinity and that his hamlet was temporarily quite secure. He decided he would flee Gia Hoi and go to Qui Nhon, where many of his friends and relatives were already living in refugee camps, whenever the first opportunity presented itself; he didn't discuss the plan with anyone. One morning about ten days later, he found that the road from Gia Hoi to the district capital, nine miles away, had been cleared by a government convoy. He hired three tandem bicycles and three men to help peddle the bicycles. He then told his immediate family that they were going to leave Gia Hoi that afternoon. The news pleased his wife. Tam informed only three other people of his decision—his mother, his mother-in-law, and his younger sister (his father, his father-in-law, and his other younger sister were no longer alive). His younger sister wanted very much to go to Qui Nhon, but she and her husband couldn't bear abandoning their house and the land they had worked for. Tam's mother and mother-in-law wouldn't accompany him because they didn't want to die outside their native hamlet. Tam didn't dare tell anyone else of his imminent departure, not even the airborne troops in the village who might have helped him leave. He suspected that the Army was infiltrated by the Viet Cong and in any case he'd had some nasty experiences with the soldiers. They had often stolen his chickens and coconuts and had stolen the door to his house within the past week. "They made a table out of it," Tam says. "I didn't mind. I was preparing to leave everything behind anyway."

Tam and his family set off in the afternoon, on schedule. His wife ⁹ and the two youngest children rode on one bicycle, three more children rode on the second bicycle, and Tam rode on the third, carrying a few bundles of clothing. The clothes and seven hundred piasters were all Tam took; he left his rice fields, his house, his furniture, and his cooking utensils. He had no gold and seven hundred piasters was the only money he had. The bicycle caravan met some Viet Cong on the road who asked Tam where he and his family were going. Tam said he had two sons in the government Army in Qui Nhon and that he was traveling there to talk them into deserting and returning home. The Viet Cong, who weren't very strong in the area right after the road-clearing operation, may or may not have believed this lie; at any rate they allowed the family to proceed. Tam and his wife, children, and clothes reached the outskirts of the district capital as night was falling. He paid the bicycle peddlers their fee—one hundred piasters each—and let them go; the family took a Lambretta (thirty piasters, for the seven of them) to the main church of the town. Tam knew a priest there who gave the family dinner. There were already many refugees camping on the church grounds. Tam and his family spent the night on the church floor. They left early the next morning, by bus, for Qui Nhon because Tam felt

that even the district capital wasn't very secure. The bus ride cost three
hundred and fifty piasters. Tam reached Qui Nhon one afternoon in
May, 1965, empty-handed.

    Tam and his family went right to the main church in the city,   10
where they knew a priest who ran several of the many refugee camps
in Qui Nhon. The priest gave him sixty-six pounds of rice for his family
and one loaf of bread for each child. Fortunately, Tam also received two
thousand piasters from the people for whom his two oldest sons had
worked in the year and a half they had been in Qui Nhon. For washing
dishes, carrying water, and doing many other tasks, the boys had been
given room and board, plus wages of fifty piasters a month each, which
had been kept for them. Tam used a little of this money to buy salt,
nuoc mam, and vegetables.

    Tam started working immediately. Some of his friends and rela-   11
tives who had been in Qui Nhon for a while took him out with them
to collect firewood in the nearby mountain woods. He figured he could
average eighty piasters a day at the most, collecting firewood, and that
he and his family couldn't live on that. After ten days of collecting
firewood, he found a job as a laborer, which he still has. Tam works
for a Vietnamese construction firm, carrying bricks and sand and breaking up stones. He works six days a week (Sundays are for church and
for resting) and earns one hundred and fifteen piasters a day. "I would
make much more if I worked for an American construction firm," Tam
says. "The Americans have many soldiers stationed in Qui Nhon and
they are doing a lot of building. Workers for the American firms are
hired by Vietnamese. If you want a job, you have to bribe them at least
three thousand piasters. I can't afford that amount. If I worked for the
Americans, I'd make the same basic pay I do now, but I'd earn several
hundred more piasters a week by selling the beer cans and soda bottles
the Americans leave around. There's one source of money I haven't yet
tapped—I haven't had time to take part in digging up any of the wreck-
ages of the American planes that have crashed in the Qui Nhon area.
When a plane crashes, the Americans take away only its engines. Some
people I know have made two thousand piasters selling pieces of the
wings. My family is living from hand to mouth now. I'm the only rice-
winner in the family. The minimum we need for food, firewood, cooking oil, clothes, and school for three of my children is three thousand
piasters a month—just about what I'm earning. When someone in the
family gets sick, or we have to buy some clothes, we have to cut down
on what we eat. That wouldn't be necessary if rice in Qui Nhon were
sold at the official price. The rice dealers always say there's no rice
available at the official price and I have to buy it on the black market
for three times as much."

Tam and his family spent their first night in Qui Nhon at the 12 homes of relatives. On their second day, they moved into one of the reception rooms the priests maintain for new arrivals. The original large refugee camps around the main church were full, but when Tam was walking to the mountains to look for firewood, his first week in the city, he noticed that there were some smaller, newer refugee camps on the outskirts of Qui Nhon and realized there were still some tiny plots of land available. He secured the priest's permission to build a hut on one of the plots. It took him a month to build his hut; when it was finished, he moved into it. He had to buy all the necessary building materials himself, which took the last of his sons' two thousand piasters. Tam's one-room hut measures ten feet by ten feet. Cooking is done in a small area in front of the hut. Three sides of the hut are woven bamboo. The fourth side, which is attached to the wall of the hut next door, is made of paper cartons. The roof is corrugated steel. The only furniture Tam has room for is a hammock and two beds. He bought the hammock and one bed and borrowed the other bed from a nephew. Tam's wife and their three youngest children sleep on one bed; he sleeps on the second bed with the three other children who still live at home. Tam's married daughter and her husband live in their own hut with their first child; Tam's oldest son has joined the popular forces and lives in a garrison. There are about two hundred families in Tam's refugee camp, which is situated on a stretch of treeless, sandy land. There is only one well in the camp, and not a single latrine.

"My former kitchen in Gia Hoi was better than this whole hut," 13 Tam says. "At home, my large brick house had many rooms, filled with furniture. I worked hard in my rice fields, though not as hard as I work here. My cash income was lower, but I was able to save about two thousand piasters a year. I didn't spend one piaster for going to the theater, or to a movie, or for keeping a concubine, and we had our own rice, fish, and vegetables. Here, we have to buy everything. At home, the soil was rich and the vegetation was green. There was lots of water and it was less hot and dusty than Qui Nhon. The worst thing about this camp is the complete lack of sanitation facilities. But we have no complaints, even though our living conditions aren't very good and I have to work harder than I did before. We can eat and sleep in peace without worrying that the VC will make us go out and dig up roads, or take us prisoner. I was terrified when the Viet Cong told me I'd been sentenced to death. When I left my hamlet, all I wanted to do was get away from the Communists. I was quite prepared to accept any hardships. I just wanted to save my skin. After I made my escape, I thought I'd been born a second time."

Before he left Gia Hoi, Tam was afraid the Viet Cong would win 14 the war. Since he has come to Qui Nhon, he no longer thinks the government side will lose, for the simple reason that it is not on its own. He has seen many American and South Korean troops in Qui Nhon and he is impressed by their planes and equipment. Some GIs occasionally come to the refugee camp to play with the children; Tam can't talk to them because he doesn't speak English. "People have told me that the United States is the richest, the strongest, and the biggest country in the world," he says. "And I've heard that there are many peasants in the United States, but their lot is better than ours because the American peasants have machines to help them with their field work." Tam has never heard of Prime Minister Ky. He has heard of Ho Chi Minh. Tam approves of the bombing of North Viet Nam and of Viet Cong targets in South Viet Nam. "We must bomb North Viet Nam much harder and destroy everything up there, so that we can end this war as quickly as possible," he says. "There must be many more airstrikes in South Viet Nam, too, even if some civilians are killed by the bombs. Let whoever is afraid of getting killed flee to secure areas. We must crush the Communists. I'm sure I'd be killed if the Communists won. I'm in favor of invading North Viet Nam because I think that all the people there who hate Communism would join us if we gave them the opportunity. I want to see the country reunified, but that can't be done until we crush the Communists."

Although he now believes in ultimate victory over the Communists, Tam has a few worries. "I'm afraid that the VC will infiltrate this camp," he says. "I think they're trying to do it. The priest here told me there are a million refugees in South Viet Nam, about a hundred thousand in Binh Dinh province alone, and that some of them were leaving their homes because of the bombing and fighting and not because of the Viet Cong. I'm also afraid that the government will uproot us. This camp was built on government land. It seems that the government wants the land back and the priests have their hands full persuading the government to let us stay here. We heard that the government, with American aid, was supposed to help the refugees. It doesn't look that way. But what I worry about most is whether I'll see my hamlet again. I've never tried to contact my mother or mother-in-law by mail; it would be futile. I've had word that they are still alive and that the VC came to chew them out after I took off, but they didn't beat them. My mother and mother-in-law are both over eighty. They are too old to beat. I imagine my sister and her husband are having to pay heavy taxes to the Viet Cong and to obey them. I'm sure the VC have taken over my land. I don't miss the social life in my hamlet very much because I don't trust anybody there. I only miss my mother and my mother-in-law and my old way of life. I'd rather return to Gia Hoi than go anywhere in the world. I've never been to Saigon. I don't care to go there. I can't go home now, because I have nothing to go home to. When the war is over, perhaps I'll be able to go home again, but perhaps it won't be possible. I don't like to think that I'll have to live in a refugee camp forever."

Content Considerations

1. How do the political changes in Vietnam affect Tam's life? Which sort of regime does he prefer? Why?
2. What kind of adjustments did Tam make in order to survive? What sense does he make of the series of circumstances in which he lives?
3. In what ways do the attitudes and practices of civilians affect how a war is waged? What must a military force consider when it determines civilian policies?

Coming Home

Coming to terms with the Vietnam War was a slow process. Not until the early 1980s did that war and what it meant to its combatants, its civilians, and its sponsoring nations begin to receive the fullest of attention and close examination. Movies about the war proliferated; novels and short stories reconstructed events, emotions, and consequences whose nuances were never quite projected through straight news reports. Autobiographical accounts by those who served in the war, those who covered it, those who traveled to Vietnam to aid its people or the American military showed, through the reflections they contained, just how widely and deeply that war affected Americans. The Wall was built in Washington, its black granite surface etched with the names of the more than 58,000 Americans who were killed and lost in that war—a memorial that made the wages of war personal, individual, chilling.

Twenty-two years after he returned from his year serving as an infantry lieutenant in the Army in Vietnam, H. W. Weldon, Jr., published this account of his homecoming. Before you read it, write a paragraph about what thoughts of home combatants might have in the far removes of a war zone.

To all who see these presents, greeting: The President of the United States of America authorized by Act of Congress July 9, 1918, has awarded The Silver Star to First Lieutenant Hugh W. Weldon, Jr., 05343367, Infantry, United States Army, for Gallantry In Action while engaged in close combat with an armed hostile force in the Republic of Vietnam on 26 March 1969.

THE POWERFUL THRUST of the jet engines drove me deep into my seat as the plane rose into the Georgia night. It was July 15, 1969, and 35 minutes was all that remained of a journey that had begun two days earlier and a world away. First Lt. Hugh Weldon, Infantry, United States Army, was coming home from Vietnam.

The face that stared vacantly at the disappearing Atlanta lights was different from the fun-loving youngster who had reversed this route a year earlier. Tonight—thanks to an unrelenting tropical sun—my skin tone was darker. And I was more subdued—a hair-raising episode or two had a way of impressing on young lieutenants the merits of a low profile. Finally, baby fat had given way to a leaner body—restful nights for junior infantry officers were few, and the food, well, let's just say that nobody goes to war for the cuisine.

My tour had changed me. And although it was unknown to me at that precise moment, the experience wasn't over. The most important lesson was ahead. 4

This trip had been the focus of my life for the past year; the anticipation started from day one. As with every soldier in every war, there was but one overpowering desire: to go home. To those of us in Vietnam, "home" took on an almost magical air. We spoke of it in reverent terms and built it up to mythical proportions. We called it "The World." 5

Although each of us had a personal view of The World, we generally agreed on the following: The World is a special place where people sleep in real beds; take hot showers every day; and do not have to keep their steel helmet, flak vest, and M-16 rifle within lunging distance. The lazy late breakfasts feature hot, fresh-brewed coffee; and the chocolate desserts are so creamy you need a spoon. In The World, buddies have nothing better to do than pack sandwiches and go on daylong hunting trips together. And last, The World is a distant land where pretty girls smell nice and wear dresses. 6

Except for specific military duties, everything centered around going home. For one year we dreamed, discussed, and planned on getting back to The World. If you wanted to start a conversation with anybody, all you had to do was ask, "Hey, what are you gonna do when you get back to The World?" And then get comfortable. 7

If you've never come home from a war, picture it like this: Assume that all your life you've dreamed of being rich. Of course, all along you knew there was not much chance of its actually happening, but it was fun to while away the hours, daydreaming about how you'd spend the money. Then out of nowhere, a huge inheritance. All of a sudden, your dreams come true. But after concentrating on the dream so long, it's tough to separate the dream from the reality. In a word, it's disorienting. That's what coming home from a war is like. 8

There had already been one culture shock. That morning, while I was passing through San Francisco International Airport, it struck me that nobody had a gun. The entire airport was defenseless. It would be a piece of cake for a few Viet Cong to slip up to the airport doors, blow them—scratch that, the blasted things would open automatically—and enter unopposed. 9

I nervously sat there awaiting my flight, eyes glued to the door, and worked out in detail what I'd do if they showed up before I could get out of there. And the odd thing was that I knew I was being silly. But my eyes never left the door. Yeah, you could call me disoriented. Caught between worlds. 10

The twinkling town of Augusta, Georgia, silently passed beneath   11
us as we crossed from Georgia into South Carolina. Then the pilot
reduced power for landing. The trip so far—Bien Hoa to Travis Air
Base near Oakland to Atlanta—had taken 38 hours. It had been an emotional roller coaster. And it wasn't over yet.

It was 10:30 p.m. when the plane's tires squealed touchdown in   12
Columbia. Sometime during the long glide in, I had started crying softly
into my handkerchief. Here was this infantry officer, his chest covered
with combat and service award ribbons, crying. Fortunately, the plane
was almost deserted. Nobody was watching.

Deep breathing helped, and as we pulled to a stop I regained con-   13
trol. After the rolling stairway was in position, the door swung open
and the few passengers quietly filed out. I had not moved. Not a twitch.

Coming home is not something infantry lieutenants take lightly.   14
While outwardly we were all like John Wayne, in quiet moments we
acknowledged the awful truth: infantry lieutenants had the highest mor-
tality rate of any army group. For example, in my first unit there were
three lieutenants. I alone came home. I was an extraordinarily lucky
person.

Out came the handkerchief again. I knew I couldn't stay on this   15
plane forever. Slowly, I made it to the front of the plane—still out of
sight of the terminal—and peered out into the brightly lit runway area.

There appeared to be about a dozen steps to the ground and then   16
50 yards to the terminal. And there, behind the security barricades,
stood a small quiet group of people. They were staring at this airplane.

I had to do something. With a deep breath, I stood straight, tugged   17
at my wrinkled khaki shirt, and stepped out of the plane's darkness onto
the illuminated top step of the stairway. The five people behind the
barricades went nuts.

Momentarily I froze, uncertain about what to do next. Then, de-   19
liberately, I groped my way down the stairs. One hand held the briefcase
containing my army separation papers, and the other—white knuckles
showing—was attached to the railing.

As the distance narrowed, I began to recognize faces. There was   20
Mom, her eyes scanning me as she went through the age old Mother's
Checklist: two eyes, two arms, two legs, no limp, no scars or wounds,
moving under his own power. . . .

Dad stood beside her, his arm around her waist. From experience   21
in World War II, he knew there was often more to wartime homecom-
ings than met the eye. His expression said, "He looks fine, but I wonder
. . . ?" As usual, he was close to the mark.

My two rotten little brothers were the most animated. They knew   22
high drama when they saw it, and they were milking this scene for all

it was worth. But somehow they seemed less rotten and certainly less little.

Next to them was the stuff of every soldier's dreams. She was 23 wearing a red plaid skirt and waving wildly. I was tired, but I wasn't dead—now *that* was something.

Halfway between the plane and the terminal, I slowed to a stop, 24 unable to continue. All this was just too much.

Out of the worst comes the best. Our most cherished values are 25 forged in the fires of troubled times. Like the seriously ill man who comes to appreciate everyday things, the prisoner who comes to prize freedom, and the soldier under fire who comes to know the calming power of prayer, I was about to make a terrible experience worthwhile.

It hit me. We had all been wrong. Every trooper who had viewed 26 The World as some thing or some place was wrong. It never was hot showers, or soft beds. And it had nothing to do with hunting trips or chocolate cakes.

We had missed the point. 27

The World was the people—our loved ones—who wrote us, prayed 28 for us, and waited for us. They were what was good. They were what was important. And my world was standing behind the barricade 25 yards away.

With that understanding came the end to a long year. I was with 29 the people I cared for and, once again, everything was as it should be. I had made it. My war was finally over.

I started forward again, slowly, one foot in front of the other. 30 Then a little faster. And faster. And faster. . . .

Epilogue—July 15, 1990

I'm pleased to tell you that in the years which followed, I found 31 The World to be to my liking and well-worth the price we paid.

To this day I love to sleep in a soft bed, appreciate hot showers, 32 and seldom pass on the desserts. More important, our family is close; I speak to my parents almost daily, and the whole gang gathers on all the traditional days. And after 20 years of marriage, that pretty girl in the red plaid skirt is still the brightest light in every room.

So my luck continues; I remain the most fortunate of men. But I 33 never go hunting anymore.

Content Considerations

1. What did "home" mean to Weldon during his year in Vietnam? What did it come to mean to him?

2. In what ways was Weldon's trip home disorienting? What were his misgivings?

3. How did a year in Vietnam change Weldon? For what reasons might he consider himself "the most fortunate of men"?

— Ideas for Discussion, Writing, and Research —

1. Morgenthau and Berman address the policies of the Vietnam war. How do they focus differently? In what ways do their essays overlap? What idea of war policy can you construct from their comments?
2. What were the components of U.S. military strategy in the war? What do Morgenthau, Berman, and the U.S. Army Center of Military History (pp. 281) say about those components?
3. Using the essays by Berman, Morgenthau, Sheehan, and any other sources you find useful, explore the pacification program and its purposes. Include some comment on the ways culture may affect war.
4. Weldon and Page suggest that the effects of the Vietnam war on Americans have been long lasting. Examine some of those effects.
5. How do Morgenthau's comments concerning the causes and nature of the Vietnam war fit with comments made by Bower (p. 5), Howard (p. 13), Halperin (p. 26), Sidel (p. 163), Snow (p. 212), Sheehan (p. 397), Kovic (p. 244), or Jervis (p. 191)?
6. Use the pieces by Spiller (p. 332) and Kovic (p. 244) as well as the essays by Morgenthau, Page, and Weldon in this chapter to make preliminary comment upon how war affected soldiers once they returned to civilian life. Then gather information from other sources, including interviews and oral histories.
7. Investigate the aftermath of the Vietnam war for the Vietnamese; focus on the role the United States played in forming the current situation.
8. Explain your position on the Vietnam war: Should the United States have fought the war? Should it have waged a different kind of war? Should it have stayed out entirely? Gather the information you need from selections in this book and elsewhere; devote some part of your explanation to how this long-past war may have some effect on your own life.
9. About a decade after the Vietnam war ended, American popular culture was inundated with movies, books, and television shows about the conflict. Why did it take so long for this reaction? What might be the causes of the awakened interest? Select and examine a particular movie or novel about Vietnam to see what it says about the war, then interview a Vietnam combat veteran to gain another perspective on the movie or book.
10. Much has been written and discussed about "the lessons of Vietnam." However, what those lessons were depends on whom you ask. Interview a veteran, a political scientist, a politician, or any others you believe might be helpful and write an essay about what U.S. society learned from the war in Vietnam.

8

Is Peace Possible?

WHAT IF THEY HELD A WAR and nobody came? That was a popular slogan in the 1970s, in the waning days of the Vietnam war. The peace movement was in full flower: massive demonstrations, anti-war parades by former veterans, efforts by Congress to end the carnage. President Richard Nixon had vowed "peace with honor," and promised to bring the last of the troops home by 1973. He did, but since then American soldiers have died in Grenada, Panama, Lebanon, and Kuwait. We are ready to ring the doorbell of the twenty-first century, and in many ways we approach the door of a stranger. Who will be there? Is a century of peace even possible?

The history of humanity has been a history of war. Among early peoples, wars were a common means of expanding territory, eliminating potential enemies, securing markets. In the past, resplendent kings rode into battle with their troops, often at the head of armies of several hundred thousand soldiers. Alexander the Great spent nearly half his short life on campaign; war was his *raison d'être*. As late as the nineteenth century, Napoleon sought glory for France (and himself) by overseeing his soldiers on battlefields across Europe. Today, national leaders may strut and posture, may affect bemedaled uniforms and ensure photo opportunities of themselves with military hardware, but they almost never are found on the front lines, never squeeze the trigger of a rifle or heave a grenade in anger. Has this distance of leaders from harm's way affected the national policy of modern nations? Is war more likely in states whose leaders—whether elected or acclaimed—never see the carnage of battle firsthand?

Is war merely an instrument of national policy, one more trick for achieving goals in the national leaders' bag? Or is there something that individuals can do, something we can do, something you can do? That's not a question one would want to put to Henry David Thoreau or M.K. Gandhi or the Rev. Martin Luther King, Jr. Or how about Seth Laughlin, a Quaker who lived during the American Civil War? Laughlin was drafted, but he was steadfastly opposed to violence and refused either to serve or to pay the government the fee for a deferment, knowing that would mean someone else would have to fight in his place. He was arrested and forced at bayonet point to stand without moving for a day and a night. When that failed to break his resistance, he was hanged by his thumbs, beaten, tortured. Finally, a panel of Union officers ordered him shot. When twelve troops lined up to carry out the sentence, Laughlin prayed aloud—not for himself, but for the firing squad. The troops, aware of his iron stance and resistance to torture, refused to shoot. The officers who had condemned Laughlin relented, ordering him to prison instead. He died there as a result of the beatings inflicted on him.

Laughlin became a martyr for the peace movement, but let's face it, very few of us are willing to accept capital punishment as the consequence of opposing war. Are there other options? Resistance to conscription is possible only during a draft, so how else does someone oppose war and work for peace?

There are many causes of war, of course, and as many ways to work for peace. Thoreau, who was incensed not only by the U.S.-Mexican War but also by the enslavement of blacks, insisted that a single person who publicly opposed either could change the course of history. His views were adopted a century later by Gandhi and still later by King, and the viability of non-violent resistance was proved.

In the war in the Persian Gulf, many of the weapons used by Iraq were manufactured in the United States and other industrialized nations of the West. Most of those companies are funded by capital invested by individuals who seldom see beyond their portfolios. But what if everyone simply agreed not to invest in corporations that manufacture weapons or the other hardware of war? In 1983, thirteen Roman Catholic congregations in the Chicago area withdrew $1.8 million in stocks from companies that had contracts with the Department of Defense or other ties with the nuclear weapons industry. Similar movements, often led by religious groups, have divested millions of dollars of war-industry stocks and bonds and diverted the money to "peace investments." It remains to be seen how a concerted, nation-wide attempt to boycott weapons' businesses might affect the future of peace.

Even more basic to any meaningful attempt to engage in peace is overhauling the language. There is a tendency, at least in the United States, to revert to war metaphors for sports, politics, law enforcement, and even programs designed to promote social justice. For weeks of Sundays each autumn, modern-day gladiators wearing shoulder pads and helmets entertain millions while their athletic skills and achievements are described in the language of war novels: the bomb, blitzing, walking wounded, total war. "It's trench warfare out there today, Dan."

Politicians declare war on each other, on the opposite party, on a variety of issues. We have "wars" against drugs, against crime, against inflation. Perhaps the most poignant is the war on poverty. There is a growing clamor within the peace organizations for new, non-battle-related metaphors.

A loosely structured amalgam of individuals and organizations is calling for an end to national sovereignty—at least that part of sovereignty that enables wars. Wars are armed conflicts between nations; if one cannot eliminate arms, how about nations? Actually, the idea is not as utopian as it sounds. One way to peace may be to surrender the power to wage war to an international peace-keeping organization, whose duty it will be to police the world and, perhaps, to sue for global social justice. Most of these groups do not seek the end of nation-states but the end of the power of nations to declare and wage battle.

Nationalism is a powerful force in history, certainly one of the past reasons for war. At one point it seemed that consolidation was the order of the day; nations were banding together into unions—political or economic—and few new states were being born. Then came the shake-up in the Union of Soviet Socialist Republics, followed quickly by civil war in Yugoslavia and renewed calls for independence by the Kurds and for a national homeland for the Palestinians. That nationalism is alive and well in the United States was evidenced by the bumper crop of bumper stickers during the showdown with Iraq. We were besieged with a flood of red, white, and blue stickers, and opposition was overwhelmed by millions of yellow ribbons. Almost no one asked why we had sold arms to Iraq just six months earlier, or why a blockade was scrapped in favor of battle.

The unraveling of the former Soviet Union was mind-boggling in its swiftness. Those whose entire lives had been spent as citizen-soldiers in the campaigns of the Cold War were both gratified and anxious. The immediate threat of nuclear war seemed at first glance to be considerably lessened; after all, the United States was now left as the only legitimate Super Power, and the fragmented nations of the loosely aligned Commonwealth of Independent States could hardly be construed as a military threat. But what about those 27,000 nuclear warheads still intact across the former Soviet Union? Who is in charge of those missiles now?

But nuclear war was never the danger that smaller, so-called "brushfire wars" presented to the nations of the world. The United States has found itself embroiled in armed conflict in Korea, Vietnam, and a halfdozen other small countries since the end of World War II; the Russians rolled their tanks into Hungary, put down revolts in Czechoslovakia and Romania, became mired in Afghanistan; England and Argentina exchanged blows over a few islands in the South Atlantic; Cuban troops campaigned in African countries; Maoist guerrillas strike throughout Peru; religious factions slug it out in Lebanon; Palestinians and Israelis continue to torment each other. Because of the complexity of the world today, with its global economy and ideological web, conflagrations in any locale are potentially devastating.

The causes of war are many, and the voices for peace are often drowned in the rumble of war drums. It remains to be seen whether the George Franklins, the Joan Sargeants, the Bruce Biggses, the Alyce Lorenzes or the Seth Laughlins of the past and present will be summoned to war again, or whether, instead, we shall have learned from the wars of the past, and shall enter a century of peace in the year 2000. We hope so.

Turning against the Military Life They Once Chose

Among the assumptions one can reasonably make about a volunteer army such as the one instituted by the United States is that only those who want to join will join. Another is that enlistees are fully aware that their enlistments put them in positions of risk, that their lives may be disrupted and endangered if war should break out.

But some volunteers, in both regular and reserve units, took a look at the Persian Gulf war and declined. Some say that they had not realized that their enlistment might actually shove them into combat zones. Some say that they enlisted after recruiting officials misrepresented military service. Some say that they had not thought much about killing other human beings until the war jolted them squarely into reality. A number of these volunteer soldiers simply refused deployment to the war zone; some filed for conscientious objector discharges when hostilities loomed.

The following article appeared in the New York Times *on January 14, 1991, just a couple of days before the ground war began in the Gulf. In it, author Katherine Bishop interviews military personnel who had decided to resist war. Write a paragraph before you begin about the necessity of keeping agreements, of fulfilling obligations such as those of enlistment; then write a paragraph about whether changing conditions or circumstances might alter an obligation to keep such an agreement.*

SAN FRANCISCO, JAN. 13—Growing up in the rural community 1 of Hollister, about 125 miles south of here, Jeffrey A. Paterson decided that joining the Marines after graduation would be a way to "break away from being a high school kid."

Nearly four years later, as his unit was about to board a plane for 2 Saudi Arabia, Corporal Paterson, 22 years old, sat down on the tarmac at Kaneohe Marine Corps Air Station near Honolulu and became the first marine to refuse deployment in the Persian Gulf crisis.

On a runway that had been strafed in the Japanese attack on Pearl 3 Harbor in 1941, his unit marched around him while his sergeant called him a coward and a disgrace to his country.

Mr. Paterson was later discharged, and since his defiance in August 4 he has become one of the most vocal of a new breed of war resisters: Those who say they have become conscientious objectors to the armed forces they voluntarily joined.

WIDELY DIVERSE REACTIONS

To many Americans, the decisions to seek discharges may seem hypocritical at best and craven at worst. But in interviews, it becomes clear that the soldiers' reasons are as diverse as their backgrounds.

The Defense Department says the 202 applications for conscientious objector status through December 1990 were up only slightly over the previous year. But antiwar organizations like the American Friends Service Committee say they are counseling hundreds of war resisters. Most say that until they heard of Mr. Paterson's action they did not know they had a right to file for discharge on the ground that since joining the military they had developed what the Defense Department calls "a sincere objection to all wars."

In interviews, many acknowledged they were naive to think they would not have to face the issue of combat. And all say it was the imminence of war that forced them to act on the intense struggles of conscience that had troubled them for months or years.

'I KNEW KILLING WAS WRONG'

"The shock of being sent to a possible combat zone is often what gets people thinking more about what they are actually doing," James E. Summers, Jr., a 20-year-old Marine reservist from Jacksonville, Fla., who turned himself in after being absent without leave for a month, wrote in his conscientious-objector application. "I didn't start actually sharing my thoughts with people until I was faced with the possibility of killing another human being."

The new war resisters are likely to have a hard time proving such arguments to the military. "It's pretty darn condescending to imply they didn't know what the job was," said Barbara Sorensen, a spokeswoman for the Army Recruiting Command. "One of our recruiters from New York told me: 'Come on, from the second grade on we know about being a soldier. We learned about George Washington's troops wrapping their feet in paper to keep from freezing to death. We knew being a soldier meant sacrifice. To think otherwise is selfish.' "

But many resisters say they are willing to suffer severe consequences for a greater good, preventing war. Capt. David Wiggins, a 28-year-old Army flight surgeon who is a graduate of West Point, has spent the last month on a hunger strike in Saudi Arabia after his conscientious-objector application was denied. While he said he now believed that war was "an unnecessary evil," Captain Wiggins is continuing on duty for now.

LIKE SIGNING A DEATH WARRANT

And Dr. Yolanda Huet-Vaughn, a 39-year-old captain in the Army   11
reserve, said in a telephone interview that her ethical obligation as a doctor and her belief that nuclear weapons would be used in the gulf caused her to go AWOL when her unit was deployed from Fort Riley, Kan. "It is insanity," she said. "It is basically signing the death warrant of the troops, the civilian population and the environment."

Like many other war resisters, Mr. Paterson said he embraced the   12
Marines with enthusiasm at first. But on duty in South Korea and the Philippines, he said, he became disillusioned by the poverty and prostitution he saw and soon became active in political causes while he waited for his tour of duty to be up last December. But in August, shortly after Iraq invaded Kuwait, his unit was deployed.

Mr. Paterson's application for discharge as a conscientious objector   13
was denied, and he appealed the ruling to a Federal District Court. At the same time the Marines began court-martial proceedings against him. But in December, the Marines agreed to discharge him and Mr. Paterson dropped his court appeal. "I figure I made my point," he said.

RELIGIOUS REASONS ARE CITED

Other war resisters base their request for discharge solely on reli-   14
gious grounds. Demetrio R. Perez, Jr., a Marine reservist who is Mr. Summers's college roommate went AWOL with him, and is also confined at Camp Le Jeune, N.C. He told of applying for a job at a car wash in Florida.

Mr. Perez, 21, wrote in his application that the name of the car   15
wash, Agape, the Greek word for spiritual love, stood "for God's utmost love, and this car wash belongs to Him and I am His servant." He began worshiping at a pacifist Mennonite church. "Warfare," Mr. Perez wrote, "is the most grievous sin against God."

Many resisters criticize the military's sophisticated recruitment ef-   16
fort, saying they were "lured" with benefits like college tuition. At a news conference in Oakland, Calif., last month, two Army reservists whose unit has not been activated announced their application for conscientious-objector status. The reservists, Azania Howse, 35, and Farcia De Toles, 21, said their recruiters had promised them they "would never be anywhere near a war zone" because they were women.

Ms. Sorensen, the Army spokeswoman, denied that recruiters 17
misrepresent military service. "Every Army commercial on television
shows soldiers in combat fatigues," she said.

And other resisters blame no one but themselves for grasping the 18
opportunities that the military seemed to offer without thinking through
all the possible consequences.

Earlier this month, Specialist Joel P. Smith, a reporter for the base 19
newspaper at Sixth Army Headquarters at the Presidio in San Francisco,
whose unit has not yet been assigned to the gulf, stood in a small Meth-
odist church here. In a soft voice breaking with emotion he told of his
decision to file for a conscientious-objector discharge.

With his wife, Mary, and small son, Dylan, beside him, the 29- 20
year-old former diesel truck mechanic from Liberty, W. Va., told how
his study of Buddhism and becoming a vegetarian had helped lead him
to the decision that he cannot kill any living thing.

"I have not been treated unfairly by the military in any way," Mr. 21
Smith said. "I couldn't say I was naive. I just intentionally struck myself
blind."

Content Considerations

1. What reasons do soldiers give for becoming conscientious objectors?
   How sound are their arguments?
2. Explore the reasons that a person who has no desire to participate in
   combat might volunteer for military duty.
3. Explain your own position regarding whether volunteer soldiers have
   a right to refuse combat assignments.

Resistance to Civil Government

Best known as the author of Walden, *a panegyric to simple living, Henry David Thoreau (1817–1862) was also a war protester and an opponent of slavery. In this famous essay, Thoreau writes of the power within each individual to effect change through virtue. He advocates peaceful resistance to government policies that one perceives to be immoral or unjust, a position that later found powerful practitioners in M.K. Gandhi and Martin Luther King, Jr. As you read this, consider how Thoreau makes his case for resistance and what factors might prevent such a stance from devolving into anarchy.*

I HEARTILY ACCEPT THE MOTTO,—"That government is best which governs least;" and I should like to see it acted up to more rapidly and systematically. Carried out, it finally amounts to this, which also I believe,—"That government is best which governs not at all;" and when men are prepared for it, that will be the kind of government which they will have. Government is at best but an expedient; but most governments are usually, and all governments are sometimes, inexpedient. The objections which have been brought against a standing army, and they are many and weighty, and deserve to prevail, may also at last be brought against a standing government. The standing army is only an arm of the standing government. The government itself, which is only the mode which the people have chosen to execute their will, is equally liable to be abused and perverted before the people can act through it. Witness the present Mexican war, the work of comparatively a few individuals using the standing government as their tool; for, in the outset, the people would not have consented to this measure.

This American government,—what is it but a tradition, though a recent one, endeavoring to transmit itself unimpaired to posterity, but each instant losing some of its integrity? It has not the vitality and force of a single living man; for a single man can bend it to his will. It is a sort of wooden gun to the people themselves; and, if ever they should use it in earnest as a real one against each other, it will surely split. But it is not the less necessary for this; for the people must have some complicated machinery or other, and hear its din, to satisfy that idea of government which they have. Governments show thus how successfully men can be imposed on, even impose on themselves, for their own advantage. It is excellent, we must all allow; yet this government never of itself furthered any enterprise, but by the alacrity with which it got out of its way. *It* does not keep the country free. *It* does not settle the West. *It* does not educate. The character inherent in the American people has done all that has been accomplished; and it would have done somewhat more, if the government had not sometimes got in its way. For government is an expedient by which men would fain succeed in letting one another alone; and, as has been said, when it is most expedient, the governed are most let alone by it. Trade and commerce, if they were not made of India rubber, would never manage to bounce over the obstacles which legislators are continually putting in their way; and, if one were to judge these men wholly by the effects of their actions, and not partly by their intentions, they would deserve to be classed and punished with those mischievous persons who put obstructions on the railroads.

But, to speak practically and as a citizen, unlike those who call themselves no-government men, I ask for, not at once no government, but *at once* a better government. Let every man make known what kind of government would command his respect, and that will be one step toward obtaining it.

After all, the practical reason why, when the power is once in the hands of the people, a majority are permitted, and for a long period continue, to rule, is not because they are most likely to be in the right, nor because this seems fairest to the minority, but because they are physically the strongest. But a government in which the majority rule in all cases cannot be based on justice, even as far as men understand it. Can there not be a government in which majorities do not virtually decide right and wrong, but conscience?—in which majorities decide only those questions to which the rule of expediency is applicable? Must the citizen ever for a moment, or in the least degree, resign his conscience to the legislator? Why has every man a conscience, then? I think that we should be men first, and subjects afterward. It is not desirable to cultivate a respect for the law, so much as for the right. The only obligation which I have a right to assume, is to do at any time what I think right. It is truly enough said, that a corporation has no conscience; but a corporation of conscientious men is a corporation *with* a conscience. Law never made men a whit more just; and, by means of their respect for it, even the well-disposed are daily made the agents of injustice. A common and natural result of an undue respect for law is, that you may see a file of soldiers, colonel, captain, corporal, privates, powder-monkeys and all, marching in admirable order over hill and dale to the wars, against their wills, aye, against their common sense and consciences, which makes it very steep marching indeed, and produces a palpitation of the heart. They have no doubt that it is a damnable business in which they are concerned; they are all peaceably inclined. Now, what are they? Men at all? or small moveable forts and magazines, at the service of some unscrupulous man in power? Visit the Navy Yard, and behold a marine, such a man as an American government can make, or such as it can make a man with its black arts, a mere shadow and reminiscence of humanity, a man laid out alive and standing, and already, as one may say, buried under arms with funeral accompaniments, though it may be

> "Not a drum was heard, nor a funeral note,
> As his corse to the ramparts we hurried;
> Not a soldier discharged his farewell shot
> O'er the grave where our hero we buried."

The mass of men serve the State thus, not as men mainly, but as   5 machines, with their bodies. They are the standing army, and the militia, jailers, constables, *posse comitatus,* &c. In most cases there is no free exercise whatever of the judgment or of the moral sense; but they put themselves on a level with wood and earth and stones; and wooden men can perhaps be manufactured that will serve the purpose as well. Such command no more respect than men of straw, or a lump of dirt. They have the same sort of worth only as horses and dogs. Yet such as these even are commonly esteemed good citizens. Others, as most legislators, politicians, lawyers, ministers, and office-holders, serve the State chiefly with their heads; and, as they rarely make any moral distinctions, they are as likely to serve the devil, without intending it, as God. A very few, as heroes, patriots, martyrs, reformers in the great sense, and *men,* serve the State with their consciences also, and so necessarily resist it for the most part; and they are commonly treated by it as enemies. A wise man will only be useful as a man, and will not submit to be "clay," and "stop a hole to keep the wind away," but leave that office to his dust at least:—

> "I am too high-born to be propertied,
> To be a secondary at control,
> Or useful serving-man and instrument
> To any sovereign state throughout the world."

He who gives himself entirely to his fellow-men appears to them   6 useless and selfish; but he who gives himself partially to them is pronounced a benefactor and philanthropist.

How does it become a man to behave toward this American government to-day? I answer that he cannot without disgrace be associated with it. I cannot for an instant recognize that political organization as *my* government which is the *slave's* government also.

All men recognize the right of revolution; that is, the right to refuse allegiance to and to resist the government, when its tyranny or its inefficiency are great and unendurable. But almost all say that such is not the case now. But such was the case, they think, in the Revolution of '75. If one were to tell me that this was a bad government because it taxed certain foreign commodities brought to its ports, it is most probable that I should not make an ado about it, for I can do without them: all machines have their friction; and possibly this does enough good to counterbalance the evil. At any rate, it is a great evil to make a stir about it. But when the friction comes to have its machine, and oppression and robbery are organized, I say, let us not have such a machine any longer. In other words, when a sixth of the population of a nation which has undertaken to be the refuge of liberty are slaves, and a whole country is unjustly overrun and conquered by a foreign army, and subjected to military law, I think that it is not too soon for honest men to rebel and revolutionize. What makes this duty the more urgent is the fact, that the country so overrun is not our own, but ours is the invading army.

Paley, a common authority with many on moral questions, in his chapter on the "Duty of Submission to Civil Government," resolves all civil obligation into expediency; and he proceeds to say, "that so long as the interest of the whole society requires it, that is, so long as the established government cannot be resisted or changed without public inconveniency, it is the will of God that the established government be obeyed, and no longer."—"This principle being admitted, the justice of every particular case of resistance is reduced to a computation of the quantity of the danger and grievance on the one side, and of the probability and expense of redressing it on the other." Of this, he says, every man shall judge for himself. But Paley appears never to have contemplated those cases to which the rule of expediency does not apply, in which a people, as well as an individual, must do justice, cost what it may. If I have unjustly wrested a plank from a drowning man, I must restore it to him though I drown myself. This, according to Paley, would be inconvenient. But he that would save his life, in such a case, shall lose it. This people must cease to hold slaves, and to make war on Mexico, though it cost them their existence as a people.

In their practice, nations agree with Paley; but does any one think that Massachusetts does exactly what is right at the present crisis?

"A drab of state, a cloth-o'-silver slut,
To have her train borne up, and her soul trail in the dirt."

Practically speaking, the opponents to a reform in Massachusetts are not a hundred thousand politicians at the South, but a hundred thousand merchants and farmers here, who are more interested in commerce and agriculture than they are in humanity, and are not prepared to do justice to the slave and to Mexico, *cost what it may.* I quarrel not with far-off foes, but with those who, near at home, cooperate with, and do the bidding of those far away, and without whom the latter would be harmless. We are accustomed to say, that the mass of men are unprepared; but improvement is slow, because the few are not materially wiser or better than the many. It is not so important that many should be as good as you, as that there be some absolute goodness somewhere; for that will leaven the whole lump. There are thousands who are *in opinion* opposed to slavery and to the war, who yet in effect do nothing to put an end to them; who, esteeming themselves children of Washington and Franklin, sit down with their hands in their pockets, and say that they know not what to do, and do nothing; who even postpone the question of freedom to the question of free-trade, and quietly read the prices-current along with the latest advices from Mexico, after dinner, and, it may be, fall asleep over them both. What is the price-current of an honest man and patriot to-day? They hesitate, and they regret, and sometimes they petition; but they do nothing in earnest and with effect. They will wait, well disposed, for others to remedy the evil, that they may no longer have it to regret. At most, they give only a cheap vote, and a feeble countenance and God-speed, to the right, as it goes by them. There are nine hundred and ninety-nine patrons of virtue to one virtuous man; but it is easier to deal with the real possessor of a thing than with the temporary guardian of it.

All voting is a sort of gaming, like chequers or backgammon, with   11
a slight moral tinge to it, a playing with right and wrong, with moral questions; and betting naturally accompanies it. The character of the voters is not staked. I cast my vote, perchance, as I think right; but I am not vitally concerned that that right should prevail. I am willing to leave it to the majority. Its obligation, therefore, never exceeds that of expediency. Even voting *for the right* is *doing* nothing for it. It is only expressing to men feebly your desire that it should prevail. A wise man will not leave the right to the mercy of chance, nor wish it to prevail through the power of the majority. There is but little virtue in the action of masses of men. When the majority shall at length vote for the abolition of slavery, it will be because they are indifferent to slavery, or because there is but little slavery left to be abolished by their vote. *They*

will then be the only slaves. Only *his* vote can hasten the abolition of slavery who asserts his own freedom by his vote.

I hear of a convention to be held at Baltimore, or elsewhere, for 12 the selection of a candidate for the Presidency, made up chiefly of editors, and men who are politicians by profession; but I think, what is it to any independent, intelligent, and respectable man what decision they may come to, shall we not have the advantage of his wisdom and honesty, nevertheless? Can we not count upon some independent votes? Are there not many individuals in the country who do not attend conventions? But no: I find that the respectable man, so called, has immediately drifted from his position, and despairs of his country, when his country has more reason to despair of him. He forthwith adopts one of the candidates thus selected as the only *available* one, thus proving that he is himself *available* for any purposes of the demagogue. His vote is of no more worth than that of any unprincipled foreigner or hireling native, who may have been bought. Oh for a man who is a *man*, and, as my neighbor says, has a bone in his back which you cannot pass your hand through! Our statistics are at fault: the population has been returned too large. How many *men* are there to a square thousand miles in this country? Hardly one. Does not America offer any inducement for men to settle here? The American had dwindled into an Odd Fellow,—one who may be known by the development of his organ of gregariousness, and a manifest lack of intellect and cheerful self-reliance; whose first and chief concern, on coming into the world, is to see that the alms-houses are in good repair; and, before yet he has lawfully donned the virile garb, to collect a fund for the support of the widows and orphans that may be; who, in short, ventures to live only by the aid of the mutual insurance company, which has promised to bury him decently.

It is not a man's duty, as a matter of course, to devote himself to 13 the eradication of any, even the most enormous wrong; he may still properly have other concerns to engage him; but it is his duty, at least, to wash his hands of it, and, if he gives it no thought longer, not to give it practically his support. If I devote myself to other pursuits and contemplations, I must first see, at least, that I do not pursue them sitting upon another man's shoulders. I must get off him first, that he may pursue his contemplations too. See what gross inconsistency is tolerated. I have heard some of my townsmen say, "I should like to have them order me out to help put down an insurrection of the slaves, or to march to Mexico,—see if I would go;" and yet these very men have each, directly by their allegiance, and so indirectly, at least, by their money, furnished a substitute. The soldier is applauded who refuses to serve in an unjust war by those who do not refuse to sustain the unjust government which makes the war; is applauded by those whose own act and authority he disregards and sets at nought; as if the State were penitent to that degree that it hired one to scourge it while it sinned, but not to that degree that it left off sinning for a moment. Thus, under the name of order and civil government, we are all made at last to pay homage to and support our own meanness. After the first blush of sin, comes its indifference; and from immoral it becomes, as it were, *un*moral, and not quite unnecessary to that life which we have made.

The broadest and most prevalent error requires the most disinter- 14
ested virtue to sustain it. The slight reproach to which the virtue of patriotism is commonly liable, the noble are most likely to incur. Those who, while they disapprove of the character and measures of a government, yield to it their allegiance and support, are undoubtedly its most conscientious supporters, and so frequently the most serious obstacles to reform. Some are petitioning the State to dissolve the Union, to disregard the requisitions of the President. Why do they not dissolve it themselves,—the union between themselves and the State,—and refuse to pay their quota into its treasury? Do not they stand in the same relation to the State, that the State does to the Union? And have not the same reasons prevented the State from resisting the Union, which have prevented them from resisting the State?

How can a man be satisfied to entertain an opinion merely, and 15
enjoy *it?* Is there any enjoyment in it, if his opinion is that he is aggrieved? If you are cheated out of a single dollar by your neighbor, you do not rest satisfied with knowing that you are cheated, or with saying that you are cheated, or even with petitioning him to pay you your due; but you take effectual steps at once to obtain the full amount, and see that you are never cheated again. Action from principle,—the perception and the performance of right,—changes things and relations; it is essentially revolutionary, and does not consist wholly with any thing which was. It not only divides states and churches, it divides families; aye, it divides the *individual,* separating the diabolical in him from the divine.

Unjust laws exist: shall we be content to obey them, or shall we 16
endeavor to amend them, and obey them until we have succeeded, or shall we transgress them at once? Men generally, under such a government as this, think that they ought to wait until they have persuaded the majority to alter them. They think that, if they should resist, the remedy would be worse than the evil. But it is the fault of the government itself that the remedy *is* worse than the evil. *It* makes it worse. Why is it not more apt to anticipate and provide for reform? Why does it not cherish its wise minority? Why does it cry and resist before it is

hurt? Why does it not encourage its citizens to be on the alert to point out its faults, and *do* better than it would have them? Why does it always crucify Christ, and excommunicate Copernicus and Luther, and pronounce Washington and Franklin rebels?

One would think, that a deliberate and practical denial of its authority was the only offence never contemplated by government; else, why has it not assigned its definite, its suitable and proportionate penalty? If a man who has no property refuses but once to earn nine shillings for the State, he is put in prison for a period unlimited by any law that I know, and determined only by the discretion of those who placed him there; but if he should steal ninety times nine shillings from the State, he is soon permitted to go at large again. 17

If the injustice is part of the necessary friction of the machine of government, let it go, let it go: perchance it will wear smooth,—certainly the machine will wear out. If the injustice has a spring, or a pulley, or a rope, or a crank, exclusively for itself, then perhaps you may consider whether the remedy will not be worse than the evil; but if it is of such a nature that it requires you to be the agent of injustice to another, then, I say, break the law. Let your life be a counter friction to stop the machine. What I have to do is to see, at any rate, that I do not lend myself to the wrong which I condemn. 18

As for adopting the ways which the State has provided for remedying the evil, I know not of such ways. They take too much time, and a man's life will be gone. I have other affairs to attend to. I came into this world, not chiefly to make this a good place to live in, but to live in it, be it good or bad. A man has not every thing to do, but something; and because he cannot do *every thing,* it is not necessary that he should do *something* wrong. It is not my business to be petitioning the governor or the legislature any more than it is theirs to petition me; and, if they should not hear my petition, what should I do then? But in this case the State has provided no way: its very Constitution is the evil. This may seem to be harsh and stubborn and unconciliatory; but it is to treat with the utmost kindness and consideration the only spirit that can appreciate or deserves it. So is all change for the better, like birth and death which convulse the body. 19

I do not hesitate to say, that those who call themselves abolitionists should at once effectually withdraw their support, both in person and property, from the government of Massachusetts, and not wait till they constitute a majority of one, before they suffer the right to prevail through them. I think that it is enough if they have God on their side, without waiting for that other one. Moreover, any man more right than his neighbors, constitutes a majority of one already. 20

I meet this American government, or its representative the State 21 government, directly, and face to face, once a year, no more, in the person of its tax-gatherer; this is the only mode in which a man situated as I am necessarily meets it; and it then says distinctly, Recognize me; and the simplest, the most effectual, and, in the present posture of affairs, the indispensablest mode of treating with it on this head, of expressing your little satisfaction with and love for it, is to deny it then. My civil neighbor, the tax-gatherer, is the very man I have to deal with,—for it is, after all, with men and not with parchment that I quarrel,—and he has voluntarily chosen to be an agent of the government. How shall he ever know well what he is and does as an officer of the government, or as a man, until he is obliged to consider whether he shall treat me, his neighbor, for whom he has respect, as a neighbor and well-disposed man, or as a maniac and disturber of the peace, and see if he can get over this obstruction to his neighborliness without a ruder and more impetuous thought or speech corresponding with his action? I know this well, that if one thousand, if one hundred, if ten men whom I could name,—if ten *honest* men only,—aye, if *one* HONEST man, in this State of Massachusetts, *ceasing to hold slaves,* were actually to withdraw from this copartnership, and be locked up in the county jail therefor, it would be the abolition of slavery in America. For it matters not how small the beginning may seem to be: what is once well done is done for ever. But we love better to talk about it: that we say is our mission. Reform keeps many scores of newspapers in its service, but not one man. If my esteemed neighbor, the State's ambassador, who will devote his days to the settlement of the question of human rights in the Council Chamber, instead of being threatened with the prisons of Carolina, were to sit down the prisoner of Massachusetts, that State which is so anxious to foist the sin of slavery upon her sister,—though at present she can discover only an act of inhospitality to be the ground of a quarrel with her,—the Legislature would not wholly waive the subject the following winter.

Under a government which imprisons any unjustly, the true place   22
for a just man is also a prison. The proper place to-day, the only place which Massachusetts has provided for her freer and less desponding spirits, is in her prisons, to be put out and locked out of the State by her own act, as they have already put themselves out by their principles. It is there that the fugitive slave, and the Mexican prisoner on parole, and the Indian come to plead the wrongs of his race, should find them; on that separate, but more free and honorable ground, where the State places those who are not *with* her but *against* her,—the only house in a slave-state in which a free man can abide with honor. If any think that their influence would be lost there, and their voices no longer afflict the ear of the State, that they would not be as an enemy within its walls,

they do not know by how much truth is stronger than error, nor how much more eloquently and effectively he can combat injustice who has experienced a little in his own person. Cast your whole vote, not a strip of paper merely, but your whole influence. A minority is powerless while it conforms to the majority; it is not even a minority then; but it is irresistible when it clogs by its whole weight. If the alternative is to keep all just men in prison, or give up war and slavery, the State will not hesitate which to choose. If a thousand men were not to pay their tax-bills this year, that would not be a violent and bloody measure, as it would be to pay them, and enable the State to commit violence and shed innocent blood. This is, in fact, the definition of a peaceable revolution, if any such is possible. If the tax-gatherer, or any other public officer, asks me, as one has done, "But what shall I do?" my answer is, "If you really wish to do any thing, resign your office." When the subject has refused allegiance, and the officer has resigned his office, then the revolution is accomplished. But even suppose blood should flow. Is there not a sort of blood shed when the conscience is wounded? Through this wound a man's real manhood and immortality flow out, and he bleeds to an everlasting death. I see this blood flowing now.

I have contemplated the imprisonment of the offender, rather than the seizure of his goods,—though both will serve the same purpose,— because they who assert the purest right, and consequently are most dangerous to a corrupt State, commonly have not spent much time in accumulating property. To such the State renders comparatively small service, and a slight tax is wont to appear exorbitant, particularly if they are obliged to earn it by special labor with their hands. If there were one who lived wholly without the use of money, the State itself would hesitate to demand it of him. But the rich man—not to make any invidious comparison—is always sold to the institution which makes him rich. Absolutely speaking, the more money, the less virtue; for money comes between a man and his objects, and obtains them for him; and it was certainly no great virtue to obtain it. It puts to rest many questions which he would otherwise be taxed to answer; while the only new question which it puts is the hard but superfluous one, how to spend it. Thus his moral ground is taken from under his feet. The opportunities of living are diminished in proportion as what are called the "means" are increased. The best thing a man can do for his culture when he is rich is to endeavour to carry out those schemes which he entertained when he was poor. Christ answered the Herodians according to their condition. "Show me the tribute-money," said he;—and one took a penny out of his pocket;—If you use money which has the image of Caesar on it, and which he has made current and valuable, that is, *if you*

23

are men of the State, and gladly enjoy the advantages of Caesar's government, then pay him back some of his own when he demands it: "Render therefore to Caesar that which is Caesar's, and to God those things which are God's,"—leaving them no wiser than before as to which was which; for they did not wish to know.

When I converse with the freest of my neighbors, I perceive that, whatever they may say about the magnitude and seriousness of the question, and their regard for the public tranquillity, the long and the short of the matter is, that they cannot spare the protection of the existing government, and they dread the consequences of disobedience to it to their property and families. For my own part, I should not like to think that I ever rely on the protection of the State. But, if I deny the authority of the State when it presents its tax-bill, it will soon take and waste all my property, and so harass me and my children without end. This is hard. This makes it impossible for a man to live honestly and at the same time comfortably in outward respects. It will not be worth the while to accumulate property; that would be sure to go again. You must hire or squat somewhere, and raise but a small crop, and eat that soon. You must live within yourself, and depend upon yourself, always tucked up and ready for a start, and not have many affairs. A man may grow rich in Turkey even, if he will be in all respects a good subject of the Turkish government. Confucius said,—"If a State is governed by the principles of reason, poverty and misery are subjects of shame; if a State is not governed by the principles of reason, riches and honors are the subjects of shame." No: until I want the protection of Massachusetts to be extended to me in some distant southern port, where my liberty is endangered, or until I am bent solely on building up an estate at home by peaceful enterprise, I can afford to refuse allegiance to Massachusetts, and her right to my property and life. It costs me less in every sense to incur the penalty of disobedience to the State, than it would to obey. I should feel as if I were worth less in that case.

Some years ago, the State met me in behalf of the church, and commanded me to pay a certain sum toward the support of a clergyman whose preaching my father attended, but never I myself. "Pay it," it said, "or be locked up in the jail." I declined to pay. But, unfortunately, another man saw fit to pay it. I did not see why the schoolmaster should be taxed to support the priest, and not the priest the schoolmaster; for I was not the State's schoolmaster, but I supported myself by voluntary subscription. I did not see why the lyceum should not present its tax-bill, and have the State to back its demand, as well as the church. However, at the request of the selectmen, I condescended to make some such statement as this in writing:—"Know all men by these presents, that I, Henry Thoreau, do not wish to be regarded as a member of any incorporated society which I have not joined." This I gave to the town-clerk;

24

25

and he has it. The State, having thus learned that I did not wish to be regarded as a member of that church, has never made a like demand on me since; though it said that it must adhere to its original presumption that time. If I had known how to name them, I should then have signed off in detail from all the societies which I never signed on to; but I did not know where to find a complete list.

I have paid no poll-tax for six years. I was put into a jail once on this account, for one night; and, as I stood considering the walls of solid stone, two or three feet thick, the door of wood and iron, a foot thick, and the iron grating which strained the light, I could not help being struck with the foolishness of that institution which treated me as if I were mere flesh and blood and bones, to be locked up. I wondered that it should have concluded at length that this was the best use it could put me to, and had never thought to avail itself of my services in some way. I saw that, if there was a wall of stone between me and my townsmen, there was a still more difficult one to climb or break through, before they could get to be as free as I was. I did not for a moment feel confined, and the walls seemed a great waste of stone and mortar. I felt as if I alone of all my townsmen had paid my tax. They plainly did not know how to treat me, but behaved like persons who are underbred. In every threat and in every compliment there was a blunder; for they thought that my chief desire was to stand the other side of that stone wall. I could not but smile to see how industriously they locked the door on my meditations, which followed them out again without let or hindrance, and *they* were really all that was dangerous. As they could not reach me, they had resolved to punish my body; just as boys, if they cannot come at some person against whom they have a spite, will abuse his dog. I saw that the State was half-witted, that it was timid as a lone woman with her silver spoons, and that it did not know its friends from its foes, and I lost all my remaining respect for it, and pitied it.

Thus the State never intentionally confronts a man's sense, intellectual or moral, but only his body, his senses. It is not armed with superior wit or honesty, but with superior physical strength. I was not born to be forced. I will breathe after my own fashion. Let us see who is the strongest. What force has a multitude? They only can force me who obey a higher law than I. They force me to become like themselves. I do not hear of *men* being *forced* to live this way or that by masses of men. What sort of life were that to live? When I meet a government which says to me, "Your money or your life," why should I be in haste to give it my money? It may be in a great strait, and not know what to do: I cannot help that. It must help itself; do as I do. It is not worth the while to snivel about it. I am not responsible for the successful working of the machinery of society. I am not the son of the engineer. I perceive that, when an acorn and a chestnut fall side by side, the one does not remain inert to make way for the other, but both obey their own laws, and spring and grow and flourish as best they can, till one, perchance, overshadows and destroys the other. If a plant cannot live according to its nature, it dies; and so a man.

The night in prison was novel and interesting enough. The prisoners in their shirt-sleeves were enjoying a chat and the evening air in the door-way, when I entered. But the jailer said, "Come, boys, it is time to lock up;" and so they dispersed, and I heard the sound of their steps returning into the hollow apartments. My room-mate was introduced to me by the jailer, as "a first-rate fellow and a clever man." When the door was locked, he showed me where to hang my hat, and how he managed matters there. The rooms were whitewashed once a month; and this one, at least, was the whitest, most simply furnished, and probably the neatest apartment in the town. He naturally wanted to know where I came from, and what brought me there; and, when I had told him, I asked him in my turn how he came there, presuming him to be an honest man, of course; and, as the world goes, I believe he was. "Why," said he, "they accuse me of burning a barn; but I never did it." As near as I could discover, he had probably gone to bed in a barn when drunk, and smoked his pipe there; and so a barn was burnt. He had the reputation of being a clever man, had been there some three months waiting for his trial to come on, and would have to wait as much longer; but he was quite domesticated and contented, since he got his board for nothing, and thought that he was well treated.

He occupied one window, and I the other; and I saw, that, if one stayed there long, his principal business would be to look out the window. I had soon read all the tracts that were left there, and examined where former prisoners had broken out, and where a grate had been sawed off, and heard the history of the various occupants of that room; for I found that even here there was a history and a gossip which never circulated beyond the walls of the jail. Probably this is the only house in the town where verses are composed, which are afterward printed in a circular form, but not published. I was shown quite a long list of verses which were composed by some young men who had been detected in an attempt to escape, who avenged themselves by singing them.

I pumped my fellow-prisoner as dry as I could, for fear I should never see him again; but at length he showed me which was my bed, and left me to blow out the lamp.

It was like traveling into a far country, such as I had never expected to behold, to lie there for one night. It seemed to me that I never had heard the town-clock strike before, nor the evening sounds of the village; for we slept with the windows open, which were inside the grating. It was to see my native village in the light of the middle ages, and our Concord was turned into a Rhine stream, and visions of knights and castles passed before me. They were the voices of old burghers that I heard in the streets. I was an involuntary spectator and auditor of whatever was done and said in the kitchen of the adjacent village-inn,— a wholly new and rare experience to me. It was a closer view of my native town. I was fairly inside of it. I never had seen its institutions before. This is one of its peculiar institutions; for it is a shire town. I began to comprehend what its inhabitants were about.

In the morning, our breakfasts were put through the hole in the door, in small oblong-square tin pans, made to fit, and holding a pint of chocolate, with brown bread, and an iron spoon. When they called for the vessels again, I was green enough to return what bread I had left; but my comrade seized it, and said that I should lay that up for lunch or dinner. Soon after, he was let out to work at haying in a neighboring field, whither he went every day, and would not be back till noon; so he bade me good-day, saying that he doubted if he should see me again.   32

When I came out of prison,—for some one interfered, and paid the tax,—I did not perceive that great changes had taken place on the common, such as he observed who went in a youth, and emerged a tottering and gray-headed man; and yet a change had to my eyes come over the scene,—the town, and State, and country,—greater than any that mere time could effect. I saw yet more distinctly the State in which I lived. I saw to what extent the people among whom I lived could be trusted as good neighbors and friends; that their friendship was for summer weather only; that they did not greatly purpose to do right; that they were a distinct race from me by their prejudices and superstitions, as the Chinamen and Malays are; that, in their sacrifices to humanity, they ran no risks, not even to their property; that, after all, they were not so noble but they treated the thief as he had treated them, and hoped, by a certain outward observance and a few prayers, and by walking in a particular straight though useless path from time to time, to save their souls. This may be to judge my neighbors harshly; for I believe that most of them are not aware that they have such an institution as the jail in their village.   33

It was formerly the custom in our village, when a poor debtor came out of jail, for his acquaintances to salute him, looking through their fingers, which were crossed to represent the grating of a jail window, "How do ye do?" My neighbors did not thus salute me, but first looked at me, and then at one another, as if I had returned from a long journey. I was put into jail as I was going to the shoemaker's to get a shoe which was mended. When I was let out the next morning, I pro-   34 ceeded to finish my errand, and, having put on my mended shoe, joined a huckleberry party, who were impatient to put themselves under my conduct; and in half an hour,—for the horse was soon tackled,—was in the midst of a huckleberry field, on one of our highest hills, two miles off; and then the State was nowhere to be seen.

This is the whole history of "My Prisons."   35

I have never declined paying the highway tax, because I am as   36
desirous of being a good neighbor as I am of being a bad subject; and, as for supporting schools, I am doing my part to educate my fellow-countrymen now. It is for no particular item in the tax-bill that I refuse to pay it. I simply wish to refuse allegiance to the State, to withdraw and stand aloof from it effectually. I do not care to trace the course of my dollar, if I could, till it buys a man, or a musket to shoot one with,— the dollar is innocent,—but I am concerned to trace the effects of my allegiance. In fact, I quietly declare war with the State, after my fashion, though I will still make what use and get what advantage of her I can, as is usual in such cases.

If others pay the tax which is demanded of me, from a sympathy   37
with the State, they do but what they have already done in their own case, or rather they abet injustice to a greater extent than the State re-quires. If they pay the tax from a mistaken interest in the individual taxed, to save his property or prevent his going to jail, it is because they have not considered wisely how far they let their private feelings inter-fere with the public good.

This, then, is my position at present. But one cannot be too much   38
on his guard in such a case, lest his action be biassed by obstinacy, or an undue regard for the opinions of men. Let him see that he does only what belongs to himself and to the hour.

I think sometimes, Why, this people mean well; they are only   39
ignorant; they would do better if they knew how: why give your neigh-bors this pain to treat you as they are not inclined to? But I think, again, this is no reason why I should do as they do, or permit others to suffer much greater pain of a different kind. Again, I sometimes say to myself, When many millions of men, without heat, without ill-will, without personal feeling of any kind, demand of you a few shillings only, with-out the possibility, such is their constitution, of retracting or altering their present demand, and without the possibility, on your side, of ap-peal to any other millions, why expose yourself to this overwhelming brute force? You do not resist cold and hunger, the winds and the waves, thus obstinately; you quietly submit to a thousand similar necessities. You do not put your head into the fire. But just in proportion as I regard this as not wholly a brute force, but partly a human force, and consider that I have relations to those millions as to so many millions

of men, and not of mere brute or inanimate things, I see that appeal is possible, first and instantaneously, from them to the Maker of them, and, secondly, from them to themselves. But, if I put my head deliberately into the fire, there is no appeal to fire or to the Maker of fire, and I have only myself to blame. If I could convince myself that I have any right to be satisfied with men as they are, and to treat them accordingly, and not according, in some respects, to my requisitions and expectations of what they and I ought to be, then, like a good Mussulman and fatalist, I should endeavor to be satisfied with things as they are, and say it is the will of God. And, above all, there is this difference between resisting this and a purely brute or natural force, that I can resist this with some effect; but I cannot expect, like Orpheus, to change the nature of the rocks and trees and beasts.

I do not wish to quarrel with any man or nation. I do not wish to 40
split hairs, to make fine distinctions, or set myself up as better than my neighbors. I seek rather, I may say, even an excuse for conformity to the laws of the land. I am but too ready to conform to them. Indeed I have reason to suspect myself on this head; and each year, as the tax-gatherer comes round, I find myself disposed to review the acts and position of the general and state governments, and the spirit of the people, to discover a pretext for conformity. I believe that the State will soon be able to take all my work of this sort out of my hands, and then I shall be no better a patriot than my fellow countrymen. Seen from a lower point of view, the Constitution, with all its faults, is very good; the law and the courts are very respectable; even this State and this American government are, in many respects, very admirable and rare things, to be thankful for, such as a great many have described them; but seen from a point of view a little higher, they are what I have described them; seen from a higher still, and the highest, who shall say what they are, or that they are worth looking at or thinking of at all?

However, the government does not concern me much, and I shall 41
bestow the fewest possible thoughts on it. It is not many moments that I live under a government, even in this world. If a man is thought-free, fancy-free, imagination-free, that which *is not* never for a long time appearing *to be* to him, unwise rulers or reformers cannot fatally interrupt him.

I know that most men think differently from myself; but those 42
whose lives are by profession devoted to the study of these or kindred subjects, content me as little as any. Statesmen and legislators, standing so completely within the institution, never distinctly and nakedly behold it. They speak of moving society, but have no resting place without it. They may be men of a certain experience and discrimination, and have no doubt invented ingenious and even useful systems, for which we

sincerely thank them; but all their wit and usefulness lie within certain
not very wide limits. They are wont to forget that the world is not
governed by policy and expediency. Webster never goes behind government, and so cannot speak with authority about it. His words are
wisdom to those legislators who contemplate no essential reform in the
existing government; but for thinkers, and those who legislate for all
time, he never once glances at the subject. I know of those whose serene
and wise speculations on this theme would soon reveal the limits of his
mind's range and hospitality. Yet, compared with the cheap professions
of most reformers, and the still cheaper wisdom and eloquence of politicians in general, his are almost the only sensible and valuable words,
and we thank Heaven for him. Comparatively, he is always strong,
original, and, above all, practical. Still his quality is not wisdom, but
prudence. The lawyer's truth is not Truth, but consistency, or a consistent expediency. Truth is always in harmony with herself, and is not
concerned chiefly to reveal the justice that may consist with wrong-
doing. He well deserves to be called, as he has been called, the Defender
of the Constitution. There are really no blows to be given by him but
defensive ones. He is not a leader, but a follower. His leaders are the
men of '87. "I have never made an effort," he says, "and never propose
to make an effort; I have never countenanced an effort, and never mean
to countenance an effort, to disturb the arrangement as originally made,
by which the various States came into the Union." Still thinking of the
sanction which the Constitution gives to slavery, he says, "Because it
was a part of the original compact,—let it stand." Notwithstanding his
special acuteness and ability, he is unable to take a fact out of its merely
political relations, and behold it as it lies absolutely to be disposed of by
the intellect,—what, for instance, it behoves a man to do here in America to-day with regard to slavery, but ventures, or is driven, to make
some such desperate answer as the following, while professing to speak
absolutely, and as a private man,—from which what new and singular
code of social duties might be inferred?—"The manner," says he, "in
which the government of those States where slavery exists are to regulate it, is for their own consideration, under their responsibility to their
constituents, to the general laws of propriety, humanity, and justice,
and to God. Associations formed elsewhere, springing from a feeling of
humanity, or any other cause, have nothing whatever to do with it.
They have never received any encouragement from me, and they never
will."

They who know of no purer sources of truth, who have traced up   43
its stream no higher, stand, and wisely stand, by the Bible and the
Constitution, and drink at it there with reverence and humility; but they
who behold where it comes trickling into this lake or that pool, gird up

their loins once more, and continue their pilgrimage toward its fountain-head.

No man with a genius for legislation has appeared in America. 44
They are rare in the history of the world. There are orators, politicians, and eloquent men, by the thousand; but the speaker has not yet opened his mouth to speak, who is capable of settling the much-vexed questions of the day. We love eloquence for its own sake, and not for any truth which it may utter, or any heroism it may inspire. Our legislators have not yet learned the comparative value of free-trade and of freedom, of union, and of rectitude, to a nation. They have no genius or talent for comparatively humble questions of taxation and finance, commerce and manufactures and agriculture. If we were left solely to the wordy wit of legislators in Congress for our guidance, uncorrected by the season-able experience and the effectual complaints of the people, America would not long retain her rank among the nations. For eighteen hundred years, though perchance I have no right to say it, the New Testament has been written; yet where is the legislator who has wisdom and practical talent enough to avail himself of the light which it sheds on the science of legislation?

The authority of government, even such as I am willing to submit 45
to,—for I will cheerfully obey those who know and can do better than I, and in many things even those who neither know nor can do so well,—is still an impure one: to be strictly just, it must have the sanction and consent of the governed. It can have no pure right over my person and property but what I concede to it. The progress from an absolute to a limited monarchy, from a limited monarchy to a democracy, is a progress toward a true respect for the individual. Is a democracy, such as we know it, the last improvement possible in government? Is it not possible to take a step further towards recognizing and organizing the rights of man? There will never be a really free and enlightened State, until the State comes to recognize the individual as a higher and inde-pendent power, from which all its own power and authority are derived, and treats him accordingly. I please myself with imagining a State at last which can afford to be just to all men, and to treat the individual with respect as a neighbor; which even would not think it inconsistent with its own repose, if a few were to live aloof from it, not meddling with it, nor embraced by it, who fulfilled all the duties of neighbors and fellow-men. A State which bore this kind of fruit, and suffered it to drop off as fast as it ripened, would prepare the way for a still more perfect and glorious State, which also I have imagined, but not yet anywhere seen.

Content Considerations

1. Thoreau writes, "Under a government which imprisons any unjustly, the true place for a just man is also prison (paragraph 22)." Evaluate his argument that sovereignty of the individual is greater than that of the government.
2. What is the tone of this work? Are you attracted to Thoreau's ideas or put off by his tone?
3. In what ways might a government official respond to Thoreau's arguments against governmental authority?

The War Prayer

The most famous American humorist is Samuel Clemens, better known, of course, as Mark Twain, who in Tom Sawyer *and* Huckleberry Finn *wrote with insight, wit, and scalding irony. Later in his career, his white suits, unruly white hair, and prominent mustache became trademarks as he took his humorous sketches on the road.*

A less well-known aspect of Twain's life was his short career as a soldier. During the Civil War, he served for about three months as a lieutenant in a confederate company of Missouri volunteers before deciding that war was too dangerous. He deserted and went west.

Late in his life he became militantly opposed to all war. "The War Prayer" was written during the hoopla that drove the United States to war with Spain in 1898. Before you read it, consider how public opinion is shaped before and during war.

IT WAS A TIME of great and exalting excitement. The country was   1
up in arms, the war was on, in every breast burned the holy fire of
patriotism; the drums were beating, the bands playing, the toy pistols
popping, the bunched firecrackers hissing and spluttering; on every hand
and far down the receding and fading spread of roofs and balconies a
fluttering wilderness of flags flashed in the sun; daily the young volunteers marched down the wide avenue gay and fine in their new uniforms, the proud fathers and mothers and sisters and sweethearts cheering
them with voices choked with happy emotion as they swung by; nightly
the packed mass meetings listened, panting, to patriot oratory which
stirred the deepest deeps of their hearts and which they interrupted at
briefest intervals with cyclones of applause, the tears running down their
cheeks the while; in the churches the pastors preached devotion to flag
and country and invoked the God of Battles, beseeching His aid in our
good cause in outpouring of fervid eloquence which moved every listener. It was indeed a glad and gracious time, and the half-dozen rash
spirits that ventured to disapprove of the war and cast a doubt upon its
righteousness straightway got such a stern and angry warning that for
their personal safety's sake they quickly shrank out of sight and offended
no more in that way.

Sunday morning came—next day the battalions would leave for   2 the front; the church was filled; the volunteers were there, their young faces alight with martial dreams—visions of the stern advance, the gathering momentum, the rushing charge, the flashing sabers, the flight of the foe, the tumult, the enveloping smoke, the fierce pursuit, the surrender!—then home from the war, bronzed heroes, welcomed, adored, submerged in golden seas of glory! With the volunteers sat their dear ones, proud, happy, and envied by the neighbors and friends who had no sons and brothers to send forth to the field of honor, there to win for the flag or, failing, die the noblest of noble deaths. The service proceeded; a war chapter from the Old Testament was read; the first prayer was said; it was followed by an organ burst that shook the building, and with one impulse the house rose, with glowing eyes and beating hearts, and poured out that tremendous invocation—

God the all-terrible! Thou who ordainest,
Thunder thy clarion and lightning thy sword!

Then came the "long" prayer. None could remember the like of it for passionate pleading and moving and beautiful language. The burden of its supplication was that an ever-merciful and benignant Father of us all would watch over our noble young soldiers and aid, comfort, and encourage them in their patriotic work; bless them, shield them in the day of battle and the hour of peril, bear them in His mighty hand, make them strong and confident, invincible in the bloody onset; help them to crush the foe, grant to them and to their flag and country imperishable honor and glory—

An aged stranger entered and moved with slow and noiseless step 3 up the main aisle, his eyes fixed upon the minister, his long body clothed in a robe that reached to his feet, his head bare, his white hair descending in a frothy cataract to his shoulders, his seamy face unnaturally pale, pale even to ghastliness. With all eyes following him and wondering, he made his silent way; without pausing, he ascended to the preacher's side and stood there, waiting. With shut lids the preacher, unconscious of his presence, continued his moving prayer, and at last finished it with the words, uttered in fervent appeal, "Bless our arms, grant us the victory, O Lord our God, Father and Protector of our land and flag!"

The stranger touched his arm, motioned him to step aside—which 4 the startled minister did—and took his place. During some moments he surveyed the spellbound audience with solemn eyes in which burned an uncanny light; then in a deep voice he said:

"I come from the Throne—bearing a message from Almighty 5 God!" The words smote the house with a shock; if the stranger perceived it he gave no attention. "He has heard the prayer of His servant your shepherd and will grant it if such shall be your desire after I, His messenger, shall have explained to you its import—that is to say, its full import. For it is like unto many of the prayers of men, in that it asks for more than he who utters it is aware of—except he pause and think.

"God's servant and yours has prayed his prayer. Has he paused and taken thought? Is it one prayer? No, it is two—one uttered, the other not. Both have reached the ear of Him Who heareth all supplications, the spoken and the unspoken. Ponder this—keep it in mind. If you would beseech a blessing upon yourself, beware! lest without intent you invoke a curse upon a neighbor at the same time. If you pray for the blessing of rain upon your crop which needs it, by that act you are possibly praying for a curse upon some neighbor's crop which may not need rain and can be injured by it. 6

"You have heard your servant's prayer—the uttered part of it. I am commissioned of God to put into words the other part of it—that part which the pastor, and also you in your hearts, fervently prayed silently. And ignorantly and unthinkingly? God grant that it was so! You heard these words: 'Grant us the victory, O Lord our God!' That is sufficient. The *whole* of the uttered prayer is compact into those pregnant words. Elaborations were not necessary. When you have prayed for victory you have prayed for many unmentioned results which follow victory—*must* follow it, cannot help but follow it. Upon the listening spirit of God the Father fell also the unspoken part of the prayer. He commandeth me to put it into words. Listen! 7

"O Lord our Father, our young patriots, idols of our hearts, go forth to battle—be Thou near them! With them, in spirit, we also go forth from the sweet peace of our beloved firesides to smite the foe. O Lord our God, help us to tear their soldiers to bloody shreds with our shells; help us to cover their smiling fields with the pale forms of their patriot dead; help us to drown the thunder of the guns with the shrieks of their wounded, writhing in pain; help us to lay waste their humble homes with a hurricane of fire; help us to wring the hearts of their unoffending widows with unavailing grief; help us to turn them out roofless with their little children to wander unfriended the wastes of their desolated land in rags and hunger and thirst, sports of the sun flames of summer and the icy winds of winter, broken in spirit, worn with travail, imploring Thee for the refuge of the grave and denied it— for our sakes who adore Thee, Lord, blast their hopes, blight their lives, protract their bitter pilgrimage, make heavy their steps, water their way with their tears, stain the white snow with the blood of their wounded 8 feet! We ask it, in the spirit of love, of Him Who is the Source of Love, and Who is the ever-faithful refuge and friend of all that are sore beset and seek His aid with humble and contrite hearts. Amen.

(*After a pause*) "Ye have prayed it; if ye still desire it, speak! The   9
messenger of the Most High waits."

It was believed afterward that the man was a lunatic, because there   10
was no sense in what he said.

Content Considerations

1. Twain's title is a paradox. How would this piece be different if it were called "The Peace Prayer"?
2. What audience is intended for this "prayer"? Describe such an audience and how it might have been motivated to pray for war. What factors influence people to support wars?
3. Why did Twain include the last sentence in this work? Write your own last sentence, replacing Twain's, and explain to classmates why you wrote it.

THOMAS HARDY

The Man He Killed

Wars are conflicts between nations, but the fighting is always done by individuals, people who do not always have a clear idea of why they are fighting nor of whom they are trying to kill. Thomas Hardy (1840–1928) captured the essence of the universal soldier in this poem.

Hardy, who was never a soldier, described himself as a meliorist, one who believes that changes can be made for the better if humans try hard enough.

Before you read this poem, take a minute and describe any enemy soldier in any war against the United States. What was the motivation for his fighting? What were his goals?

HAD HE AND I BUT MET
By some old ancient inn,
We should have sat us down to wet
Right many a nipperkin!

But ranged as infantry,
And staring face to face,
I shot at him as he at me,
And killed him in his place.

I shot him dead because—
Because he was my foe.
Just so: my foe of course he was;

That's clear enough; although
He thought he'd list, perhaps,
Off-hand like—just as I—
Was out of work—had sold his traps—
No other reason why.

Yes; quaint and curious war is!
You shoot a fellow down
You'd treat, if met where any bar is,
Or help to half-a-crown.

Content Considerations

1. Describe the speaker in Hardy's poem. What sort of person is he? Why is he willing to kill his enemy, whom he indicates is probably much like himself?

2. This poem is written in the first person, yet the title uses the third-person pronoun. How does this shift affect the way you make meaning of this poem?

3. What does this poem suggest about the nature of war?

Casualties of War

Publishing in their April, 1991, issue, the editors of Washington Monthly looked back at the Persian Gulf war and their initial opposition to it. Their hindsight confirmed their original response. That confirmation appears next. In it, the editors consider some of the reasons given for the war and explain their abiding belief that those reasons were neither sound nor sufficient cause to wage war.

 Economic sanctions against Iraq had been in effect months before the war began in an effort to persuade Saddam Hussein to withdraw from Kuwait. Yet the beginning of war was prefaced with the idea that the sanctions were having no effect. It was also prefaced with tales of Iraqi cruelty to Kuwaitis and predictions that Hussein might well launch his variety of nuclear, chemical, and biological weapons against various Middle Eastern nations.

 Before you read the editors' argument, write several paragraphs focusing on when military measures should be used to bring about solutions to what the editors call "foreign policy headaches" (paragraph 12).

THINK ABOUT IT: Saddam's threat to the region ended, the price 1
of oil stabilized, Arabs kissing Americans in the streets of Kuwait City. Three hundred twenty-three American troops dead—a tragedy, certainly, but in relative terms a miracle. Do we at the *Monthly* regret counseling patience, diplomacy, and sanctions rather than war in the Persian Gulf?

Don't bet on it. We continue to believe that this war was wrong 2
both in principle and in practice: in principle, because war should be the last and not the first resort; in practice, because when the United States does go to war, all Americans should be in some way involved, but in this conflict most of us had to bear no burden and pay no price.

For anyone who remembers the Chinese invasion of Tibet, the 3
Soviet invasions of Czechoslovakia and Afghanistan, or the Turkish invasion of Cyprus, the notion that the U.S. has some moral obligation to defend by force of arms any "legitimate government" against foreign aggression is too silly to merit consideration. But there are two arguments against our opposition in principle that we find compelling: 1) "While the coalition patiently waited for sanctions to work, wouldn't Iraqi troops have continued to torture Kuwaitis?" 2) "Wasn't war nec-

essary to wipe out Saddam Hussein's chemical, biological, and nuclear threat?"

The litany of horror coming out of Kuwait certainly does make the blood boil. (Tragically, the litany hasn't ended with the Americans' arrival, since the Iraqi crimes have set in motion the familiar cycle of atrocity, with Kuwaitis carrying out reprisals against collaborators—and against agitators for democracy.) But consider the other side of the ledger. Estimates of the number of dead Iraqi soldiers—not counting civilians—range from between 25,000 and 50,000 *(The New York Times)* to 150,000 (NBC, drawing on Pentagon sources); *Time* and *Newsweek* put the number at around 100,000.

Whatever the precise figure, "there were," as General Schwarzkopf put it, "a very, very large number of dead in these units, a very, very large number of dead." Many of these soldiers were draftees, often ignorant and illiterate and—judging from the mass surrenders to any Americans they could find, including journalists—generally unwilling to fight. If, as Bush repeatedly said, "Our quarrel is not with the Iraqi people," we sure had a strange way of showing it. The Kuwaitis were horribly mistreated. But dropping fuel-air explosives and cluster bombs on starving conscripts is a miserable way to alleviate human suffering.

Don't get us wrong. Unlike isolationists of the right and the left who maintain it was wrong for the U.S. to intervene at all in the Middle East, we consider it a wonder and a delight to hear an arch-realpolitician like George Bush forcefully invoke human rights in the conduct of foreign policy. America during the Cold War tended to be less than zealous in its efforts to protect human rights abroad, as our prewar relations with Iraq amply demonstrate. Bush had eight years as vice president, one and a half years as president, and plenty of evidence to deduce that Saddam Hussein was a killer who had to be contained, not coddled. Were his atrocities really less horrifying when he committed them against his "legitimate" subjects?

Still, Saddam looks like a mere neighborhood bully compared to some of the monsters we've left alone. If there was ever a case to be made for a world policeman, the Khmer Rouge made it in Cambodia. Economic sanctions would never have restrained Pol Pot, whose chief goal was to drive his country backward in time to his proclaimed "Year Zero." Along the way, his forces butchered more than a million in a truly Hitlerian bloodbath. But we did nothing. It took the Vietnamese invasion on Christmas Day, 1978, to stop the killing. (Would Bush have done something? We can find some indication in the fact that his administration is now aiding Khmer Rouge rebels, still apparently commanded by Pol Pot; after all, the Vietnamese installed an illegitimate government.)

The past decade is replete with cases in which the U.S. looked the other way. The Ugandan army murdered up to 200,000 civilians in 1984 alone, according to estimates by the State Department; the U.S. grumbled and did nothing. Over the course of the eighties, 400,000 people died in fighting in Mozambique. How many "Save Mozambique" rallies did you attend, or even see on the news? The most notorious incident on Bush's watch was the murder of dissident students by the Chinese government two years ago. But while the U.S. chose to hunt down Manuel Noriega, other, more banal examples of evil went ignored: in El Salvador, Guatemala, South Africa, Liberia, Sri Lanka.

During the Capitol Hill debate on the war, prowar congressmen   9
frequently quoted an Amnesty International Report, also cited by Bush, on atrocities in Kuwait. We hope they will take the same interest in acting upon other reports from Amnesty. They might turn, for example, to the evaluations of some of our allies. In Saudi Arabia, according to Amnesty's 1990 report, "Torture was reportedly common. . . . Sentences of amputation and flogging continued to be imposed and carried out." In Syria, "thousands of political prisoners, including hundreds of prisoners of conscience, continued to be detained under state-of-emergency legislation in force since 1963. . . . Torture of prisoners was said to be widespread and routine. . . ." The methods of torture sound highly Iraqi: In Egypt, the head of psychiatry at Cairo's Palestinian Red Crescent Hospital was subjected to "persistent and savage torture," including "suspension, beating, and electric shocks. He was also threatened that he would be killed if he ever spoke out about his torture."

That others commit atrocities by no means mitigates the Iraqis'   10
crimes. It does, however, add a pragmatic edge to the moral argument against military force as the means for protecting human rights. Securing a new world order will require first and foremost consistency: consistent moral leadership and consistent application of international law. Clearly, every time some tinpot dictator strings up a dissident, we can't send in the Marines. But we also can't look the other way.

The same logic applies to the argument that we had to use force   11
to wipe out Iraq's "weapons of mass destruction." The fact that Saddam never used such weapons during the conflict—despite confident predictions from assorted military analysts that he would—undermines the credibility of the unconventional threat he posed to his neighbors, but, again, let's assume it was for real. Between 16 and 28 nations have chemical weapons; at least 10 developing nations already have or are trying to produce biological ones, and, according to U.S. intelligence estimates, 15 will have ballistic missiles by the year 2000. Should we bomb Pakistan? India? Brazil? Burma? We can't hope to use the Air Force to stop them all. But we also can't look the other way.

The Gulf war model, like the Panama model, is dangerous not   12

only because it played up the efficacy and even glamor of military rem-
edies for foreign policy headaches but because it denigrated the effectiveness of nonviolent means. To control the spread of unconventional
weapons and the behavior of renegade states, we have to come up with
and then stick to reusable international punishments; the U.S. military,
for moral and practical reasons, just isn't right for the job.

Contrary to the Bush administration line, sanctions were working   13
against Iraq, as evidenced by Saddam's urgent demand that they be lifted
as part of Gorbachev's peace package. But economic means are slow
and politically risky. George Bush is a hero for stomping a fourth-rate
power, while Jimmy Carter is still reviled for slapping a grain embargo
on the Soviets after their invasion of Afghanistan. Nevertheless, in the
past, we have seen that economic weapons, example, and diplomacy
can more humanely accomplish our goals, if given the time to work:
They did so in the cases of Nicaragua and Rhodesia—and in the liberation of Eastern Europe. Certainly, there will be countries that pose
such an immediate, lethal threat that prompt military action is the only
means to head it off. But Iraq was not such a country. A peaceful means
for securing the new world order was the first casualty on January 16.

Content Considerations

1. What do the authors of this piece mean when they say that the "war
   was wrong both in principle and in practice"? To what extent do you
   agree with them?
2. Summarize the support the authors give when they say that Iraqi atrocities against Kuwaiti citizens was not a good enough reason for America
   to fight. Then summarize their logic and support for not accepting as
   a reason Saddam Hussein's weaponry and threat to use them. How
   compelling are their arguments?
3. The authors repeatedly claim that they are not urging the United States
   to "look the other way," to ignore problems in and with other countries. What is the effect of that repetition? What courses of action do
   the authors suggest as alternatives to military action?

The War Is Won but Peace Is Not

*Frank A. Rodgers, a lawyer and member of the Canadian Human Rights
Foundation, delivered the following speech in Saint John, New Brunswick,
Canada, on March 10, 1991, to the Veterans Against Nuclear Arms. As you
might suspect from its title and the date on which it was made, the speech
reflects upon the Gulf war and what is signified by its conclusion.*

*Central to Rodgers's speech is the idea of sovereignty, a word that denotes
a supreme power, autonomy, freedom from outside control. Before you read his
comments, write a paragraph identifying who or what is sovereign in the
United States and in several other nations about which you have some knowledge. Then write a paragraph describing some of the effects of the sovereignty
you identified.*

WHEN I WAS invited here to speak, I was asked to say a few words   1
about the World Court and its relationship to world peace. I have deliberately avoided any reference to the Court, because I believe that in
any mature political society, a Court should have legitimate authority
from the people to interpret laws properly enacted.

Therefore, I wish instead to talk about a more fundamental concept   2
of Democracy. Let me assure you that if we can get over the first hurdle
and see a need for a federation of nations, the Court will take its rightful
place.

In 1952, writing in a Japanese magazine Albert Einstein wrote: 3

To my mind, to kill in war is not a whit better than to commit   4
ordinary murder.

He went on to state,   5

As long as nations are not resolved to abolish war through   6
common actions and solve their conflicts and protect their interests
by peaceful decisions on a legal basis they feel compelled to prepare
for war.

I want to talk to you today and have you think about what com-   7

449

mon actions can be taken and the importance of a legal basis for peace. But first we have to overcome the emotional attachment associated with national interests. In short, there has to be a conversion of the human passions and the human intellect.

The title of this speech is "The War is Won but Peace is Not," and the peace is not, because peace can only be achieved by a legal order, by a sovereign source of law, and a democratically controlled government with independent executive, legislative and judiciary bodies. I believe that through law there is a tendency towards peace. It is an unforgivable false conception to believe that force without the pre-existence of law can give us peace. Running through this speech is a term I am asking you to pay particular attention to. It is the term sovereignty.   8

To understand sovereignty in the political sense, we should not ignore completely what poets have said: From Whitman's *By Blue Ontario's Shore:*   9

> I swear nothing is good to me now that ignores individuals,   10
> The American compact is altogether with individuals,
> The only government is that which makes minute of individuals,
> The whole theory of the universe is directed unerringly to one single individual—namely to You. . . .

I believe our very existence depends upon the correct interpretation and application of sovereignty. This is not a theoretical debate but a question more vital than wages, prices, taxes, food, or any other major issue of immediate interest to the common person everywhere. Because in the final analysis, the solution of all the everyday problems of all human beings depends upon the solution of the central problem of war. In other words, we need a new world order, but there cannot be a new world order until we understand sovereignty.   11

The recent war in the Gulf should make most people realize that human beings are exceptionally perverted and ferocious creatures, capable of murdering, torturing, persecuting and exploiting each other more ruthlessly than any other species in this world. While this fact about our barbaric action has been driven home by the extensive news media and television coverage of the war scenes, the insight is not new. More than twenty-five hundred years ago, Aristotle said: 12

> As man is the most noble of animals if he be perfect in virtue,   13
> so he is the lowest of all if he has been severed from law and justice.

On the international scene, the anarchy that exists between na-   14 tions, severs us from law and justice. We are living in a world without public law, and the so-called new world order we hear about, cannot take us one step closer to peace until we come to understand the term sovereignty and then create a new social unit with legitimate power and authority that stands higher and broader than the nation-state.

The seventeenth century English philosopher Thomas Hobbes, pointed out in the 1650's, that sovereign nations are always at war with one another, either waging the cold war of intrigue and diplomacy or the hot war of steel and shell. "War," says Hobbes, "consists not in battle only or in the act of fighting." In other words, it exists wherever men cannot settle their differences without recourse to violence in the last resort. 15

Human nature is such that man does not accept rules unless they are imposed upon him by constituted authority. As human political society developed, the constituted authority of a supernatural God or the absolute Monarch gradually gave way to a revolutionary social idea from the sixteenth and seventeenth centuries—an idea which proclaimed the principle that the sovereign lawgiving authority was the people and that sovereignty resides in the community. 16

According to John Locke and other English as well as French philosophers of the seventeenth and eighteenth century, the democratic conception of sovereignty meant that sovereign rights properly belonged with the people rather than one man, the King. 17

In the democratic sense, sovereignty resides in the community. By community, Locke and others meant the totality of people. Under the conditions of the sixteenth and seventeenth century, the widest horizon of these forebearers of democracy was the nation. When they proclaimed the sovereignty of the nation, they meant the sovereignty of the community, but they also meant sovereignty to have the broadest possible basis. 18

As the world is organized today, sovereignty does not reside in the community, but is exercised in an absolute way by groups of individuals we call nations. This is a total contradiction to the original democratic conception of sovereignty. Today, sovereignty has far too narrow a basis, it no longer has the power it should and is meant to have. We are living in complete anarchy, because in a small world, interrelated in every other respect, there are over one hundred separate sources of law—over one hundred sovereignties. 19

Having come to realize and understand the tremendous benefits mankind has received from the rule of law within nations, the leaders of the democratic countries should be more honest with the people when they talk about the rule of law as a foundation for a new world order. The law that presently exists on the international scene, is at best prim- 20 itive without the legitimate authority and force that comes from sovereignty. We should start understanding and appreciating the fact that the rule of law is the only foundation of a democratic society yet discovered. We should not distort that fact in the interest of parochial national sentiments.

In trying to understand what is needed to push us in the right 21 direction, we should not be afraid of the expression "surrendering sovereignty." The problem is not negative and does not involve giving up something we already have. The problem is positive—creating something we lack, something we have never had, something that we now need. I believe that the creation of institutions with sovereign power beyond national boundaries is merely another phase of the same process in the development of human history, an extension of law and order into another field of human association which up until now has remained unregulated and in anarchy. Man's political nature has expressed itself in a variety of ways in the course of history: the family, tribe or clan, the feudal fief, the religious sect, the city state, the dynasty or empire and the nation state.

Historical circumstances have led people to fulfill their political 22 needs in different ways but the basic needs of security and protection have never changed. Nationalism is only the most recent way in which people have tried to meet them.

Sovereignty is an instrument necessary to create law and order in 23 the relations of people. Sovereignty finds expression in institutions. In the true democratic sense, institutions derive this sovereignty from where sovereignty truly resides, from the people. Those who talk of surrendering the sovereignty of the United States, of Great Britain, of France, of Canada, or any other democratic country, simply do not understand the meaning of sovereignty. The real source of sovereign power cannot be emphasized too strongly and must never be lost sight of, if we are to understand the political problems surrounding national interests.

The nation-states as they were set up in the eighteenth century, 24 and as they are organized in the democracies today, are nothing but instruments of the sovereign people created for a specific purpose of achieving certain objectives—to protect their citizens, to guarantee security to their people, to maintain law and order. Should the people realize and come to the conclusion that in certain fields such as defence, trade, citizenship, and the environment, they will be better protected by delegating and shifting part of their sovereignty from the nations-state to another institution made up of a federation of nations, nothing will be surrendered. Rather, something will be created for the better protection of the lives and liberties of all the people. We should not be afraid to take this step. The residual sovereignty will continue to reside in the people in accordance with the original conception of democracy.

To transfer certain aspects of our sovereign rights from national   25
legislative and judiciary bodies or offices to equally democratically elected
and democratically controlled legislative and judiciary bodies or offices
in order to create, apply and execute the rule of law for the regulation
of human relationships in a field where such a law has never existed, is
not surrender. It is simply the recognition that government is necessary
for peace.

When in the seventeenth and eighteenth century the sovereignty   26
of the community as a supreme source of democratic law became dom-
inante, the world was still very large and still an exclusively agricultural
planet with economic conditions scarcely different from those of antiq-
uity. So a substitute presented itself which permitted the new doctrine
of democratic society to find immediate practical expression. That substitute was the nation-state.

As the twentieth century draws to a close, we are living in an era   27
of absolute political feudalism in which nation states have assumed a
similar role as was assumed by the feudal Barons a thousand years ago.

One meaning of tyranny is to live under a system of law, the   28
creation of which an individual does not participate. In the nation state
system we are unable to participate in the creation of law in any part of
human society beyond our own country. It is therefore a self-delusion
to say that Americans, Englishmen, Frenchmen, and Canadians are free
people. They can be attacked by other nations and forced into war at
any time. What can we do about it?

We have to have the courage to take steps and to show that in   29
some very important respects, the nation-state is obsolete. We have to
destroy the political system of nation feudalism and establish a social
order based on the sovereignty of the community as it was seen by the
forefathers of democracy. In other words, we need a more perfect union.

A few blocks from the White House in Washington, D.C., there   30
exists an organization known as the Association to Unite the Democracies. This organization came into existence nearly fifty years ago through
the writing of Clarence Streit. Mr. Streit approached the problems of
organizing a world government by suggesting we start with a nucleus
made up of ten or fifteen existing democracies based on belief in the
democratic principle that government is made by the people. That association through the writings of Mr. Streit, played a major role in the
formation of NATO, the European Common Market, GATT, the European Parliament and other related institutions. The evolution continues today. But an organization such as the United Nations under its
present setup is only a halfway measure.

We are still waiting for a more perfect union—a more perfect union   31
with institutions containing their sovereignty from the people so that
matters such as defence, citizenship, trade, the value of money, and the

protection of the environment comes under the jurisdiction of a new social unit standing above the individual nation-states. The delegating of sovereignty to better serve the people in those areas of need for which the nation-state is now obsolete, should do nothing detrimental to the cultural pluralism and the diversity of institutions which should be preserved and tolerated within nations right down to the local neighborhood of any city, town or village.

The sovereignty of the people supported by the fundamental political principles of western democracy, transferred to a new institution, would by its very nature, create independent lawmaking, judiciary and executive institutions expressing the sovereignty of the people. Can it be done? There is a ray of hope.   32

The leaders of the democratic countries are talking more frequently about the rule of law and its application to the conduct between nations. Such talk and formal discourse should eventually lead the intellect and minds of these leaders to a truth which they will not be able to ignore. At that point hopefully, reason will rule. Immanuel Kant, the German philosopher of the eighteenth century, writing in his essay on *Perpetual Peace* in 1795 said: 33

> At the tribunal of reason, there is but one way of extricating states from this turbulent situation, in which they are constantly menaced by war, namely, to renounce like individuals, the anarchic liberty of savages, in order to submit themselves to coercive laws, and thus form a society of peoples which would gradually embrace all the peoples of the earth.   34

I hope I have showed that war is not inevitable. If however, it is inevitable, I hope I have showed that it is because of human institutions, not human nature.   35

Content Considerations

1. Upon what institution does peace rest, according to Rodgers? Summarize the argument he makes.
2. Expand upon the role of the individual in Rodgers's plan. How sound is his reasoning?
3. Explain Rodgers's idea for how to attain world peace and then respond to it. Do you agree with it? Would it achieve the goal of peace? Would it produce any bad effects? Is peace desirable? How would his plan affect your life, now and in the future?

Visions of Peace

The possibilities of peace in the twenty-first century depend on individuals who believe in the power of change, and on their commitment to changing the ways in which we resolve conflicts at all levels. The husband-and-wife team of Iliff and Smith present here a vision in which new, creative ways of conflict resolution, beginning in the home, will make wars relics of the human past.

Instead of dichotomies, of "either/or" solutions, alternative positions that need not be cast in stone should be sought. Iliff, a peace studies professor at Park College in Parkville, Missouri, and Smith, a parenting consultant, present a hopeful vision of the future in their assessment of the possibilities for eliminating violence.

Before you read this, consider a confrontational situation in which you have been a participant. How was the conflict resolved?

War begins in the minds of human beings. Since this is so, the
minds of human beings must also be capable of ending war.
—Preamble to the Constitution of UNESCO

What will peace look like in the 21st century?

PEACE IS A TRICKY CONCEPT because for so long we have used it to mean the opposite of war. However peace can no longer be defined simply as the absence of war; its definition must include the presence of social and economic justice. The violent characteristics of repression are the same as warfare, so there is no peace unless repression and oppression are eliminated. For example, the Jim Crow laws of the 1930's and 1940's in the US South decreased violence, but true peace was not achieved because an entire race of people was oppressed. Peace for one side of a conflict is not real peace. The same is true in current-day South Africa. No war has erupted between whites and blacks, but the repression of the blacks under the apartheid system is not peaceful by any means.

Charles Mader, formerly with The Center for the Study of Peace Strategies, provides an updated definition of peace. "Peace is an active and affirmative recognition of the fact that our world is all one system. Peace is health in which each organ receives from and contributes to the larger body of which it is a part." This concept opens up our perspective so that peace now includes harmony in such far-flung areas as business, education, healthcare, the environment, government and international relations.

We are used to seeing peace as a goal—something to be achieved. But we realize now that it is also a way of thinking, a way of seeing the world and ourselves in it. Suddenly it becomes our vision, our goal and our process. Mader's idea is that we see "holism as a fact, and as a strategy." 3

Another problem in looking at peace in the 21st century is that within that very long block of time, peace will look vastly different at any given point. From this writing in 1992, we think of the turn of the century and long for quick and rewarding progress by then. But we must recognize that tendency to think in terms of achievement rather than growth. The change in America's thinking about smoking in public over the last decade serves as a good example. The mark of success was not the tally of non-smoking areas in restaurants and airplanes, but in the changed way of thinking about smoking and the acceptance of it in public. 4

Peacemakers predict that there will be a marked difference in the awareness of how pervasive peace issues are, and that this will pave the way for rapid and steady growth toward peace and justice throughout the century. We seem to be on the threshold of an awakening period comparable to those in medical progress or computer technology in the last half of this century. So just as we are amazed when we detail the medical breakthroughs in any given 10-year period over the last hundred years, we expect to see giant steps in peacemaking in the next hundred. And just as in the medical field, we are constantly aware that it is a process. We will never be through. 5

Hope lies in changing the norm of behavior and thought. We don't expect all violence to end nor do we expect that everyone will adopt this new way of looking at peace. The mark of success is when the *norm* of thinking changes. Scientists call it the theory of critical mass: When a limited number of people learn a new perspective, society as a whole is converted. Ten years ago, the norm in this country was that smokers could smoke almost anywhere at any time. Now that smoking is controlled, smoking is *perceived* as a life-shortening and dirty habit. It's not that everyone changed their minds about smoking, but the norm has changed. In the words of Margaret Mead, "Never doubt that a small group of thoughtful, committed citizens can change the world. Indeed, it's the only thing that ever has." 6

Ken Kesey Jr.'s story, "The 100th Monkey," often told by peace activists, illustrates the same phenomenon. Kesey relates that on an is- 7 land in the Pacific in the 1950's, scientists observed the behavior of monkeys eating sweet potatoes dropped in sand. One young monkey learned to wash off the sand in the ocean, making the potato more enjoyable. She taught her parents and other young monkeys this technique. Gradually, the technique spread throughout the island from young monkey to young monkey. At a certain point, once a sizable minority, say 100, had learned the technique, practically all the monkeys on the island began washing their sweet potatoes. Plus, at the same time, monkeys on other islands acquired the skill. Critical mass was achieved with the hundredth monkey.

We see the 100th Monkey phenomenon in the recent change of attitudes about drunk driving. Fifteen to twenty years ago, no one approved of drunk driving but it was accepted and tolerated. Hair-raising stories about driving while intoxicated were thought of as entertaining. Today, even though drunk driving still occurs in our society, we are now outraged, largely through the efforts of Mothers Against Drunk Driving and Students Against Drunk Driving. Again, as in the monkey culture, we find the youth instrumental in leading the movement. 8

Recognizing that perfection (that is, 100% justice) is not the goal of peacemaking, outrage steps in as a satisfying replacement. When outrage is the reaction to injustice, oppression, and violence on all levels, society will be moving in the right direction. 9

A friend tells how shocked she was to see a Dick Van Dyke Show re-run where Rob and Laura Petrie met their new neighbor. He explained his wife's absence with joke after joke about beating her. Rob and Laura's mildly perplexed—though far from outraged—reactions and that of the laugh-track (as much as the lines themselves), showed the social consciousness of the times. There was simply no awareness of the fact that domestic violence is violence, and no laughing matter. 10

What moves us toward peace?

It's encouraging for those of us hoping to live in the 21st century that so many of the characteristics of future peace will come from trends that are not only visible now but in fact are thriving. 11

Unity Perspective

The first characteristic is a unity perspective. Whether dealing with another person, another nation, or the environment, the idea is to train ourselves to see the similarities between us rather than the differences. In use, this outlook carries enormous power toward finding shared values and common ground, reducing fear, and promoting collaboration. When we see how alike we are, we are less likely to see malicious intent. We are able to imagine shared goals, dreams, insecurities, fears. We 12 become more likely to ask questions for information rather than as a way of vying for position. And finally, this process makes us more likely to see that we are on parallel journeys with that other person, the other nation, and even the environment.

Strides taken in using the unity perspective parallel a long period 13 of improvement in family-building techniques. Let's imagine a "getting along" spectrum to mark the progress over the years.

At one end of the spectrum lies criticizing. A wife tells her hus- 14 band, "You've tracked mud on the carpet. I've just cleaned up in here, and now I have to do this all over. I don't know why you can't wipe your feet before you come in like I do." So, while we have a clear naming of the problem and suggestion of a solution, we also have a dividing line. The wife's words imply that she is good; the husband is bad. The problem is obvious to her; he has to be told. She works toward clean (i.e., good); he messes up. This does not necessarily come from a desire to nag. The genuinely well-intentioned thinking often goes like this: "If I just tell you what you're doing wrong, tell you why it's wrong and point out to you every time you do it, pretty soon you'll quit."

Next on the spectrum is labeling. "You're a mess!" The implied 15 message is that this incident is just like every other one he is involved in. He is incapable of different behavior. This is his only identity: he is a mess, nothing more. Her intentions, while steeped in emotion, probably have to do with naming the problem so that it can change. Her thinking may be, "I'll just identify the problem and you'll be aware of it and will change."

Then we thought we took a huge step when we found praise on 16 the spectrum. "I like the way you wiped your feet before you came in," certainly has a sweeter ring to it than the previous choices, and subsequent interaction is not tainted by such an obvious drawing of battle-lines. But the underlying message comes from the selective choosing of the behaviors to notice and the manipulative nature of commenting on it. A pattern of this kind of manipulative praise often causes a patronizing feeling as well. This poor woman just can't win! Her thoughts might be, "My naming and judging your behavior in a positive way will motivate you to seek out my approval in the future."

With every move toward improvement, we failed to realize that 17 in each of these approaches lies the common thread of outside judgment on someone's behavior. The wife's effort concentrated on having her voice control her husband's actions. Her words got in the way of his taking responsibility for his own actions. Also, because most people say they don't want to sound like a nag or be in charge of somebody else, this woman's words stood in the way of her taking responsibility for her own actions.

Finally we reached the step of encouragement. The key to en- 18 couragement is that it recognizes effort. When she sees her husband wiping his feet, this time the wife says, "It's really muddy out there, isn't it?" Now there are no battlelines drawn and the couple is free to talk about the mud or any other topic from the same vantage point.

This step was made possible only because of many changes in 19 thinking. Jean Illsley Clarke, author and educator, tells us simply that children are not extensions of their parents. Rather, they are whole people, deserving and possessing their own lives, thoughts and feelings. A parent's most important role in a child's life is not as decision-maker or judge, but as ally. Someone to stand by and offer support, encouragement, and resources—wouldn't we all like to have someone like that!

It is as judge that we are most likely to draw dividing lines between 20 ourselves and others. Resisting that temptation enables us to "be on the same team" and to be available to work with others to reach both our own goals and theirs.

The only life we truly have control of is our own. The most pow- 21 erful role we can *justly* have in another's life is that of ally. Through encouragement, we celebrate the process, the hard work, and the problem-solving, while never presuming that we have a right to judge any journey but our own.

Allowing others to lead their own lives does not mean saving them 22 from the consequences of their actions. Our hapless husband may have to clean his tracks off the carpet or he may live with muddy carpet or he may find himself divorced, or countless other possibilities. A child may fall and bleed. A nation may elect a cruel leader. But by dealing with the consequences, each person or group learns more about the choices and the power they do have.

This trend has extensive parallels in both interpersonal communi- 23 cation (spousal relationships, parenting, management in the workplace) and in international relations.

When we see ourselves as separate but similar, we enhance the 24 bonds of community by communicating those ideas, and ideas about future and building and dreams and feelings. Language can be an immensely powerful tool in the building of a unity perspective.

Language

"Our very language includes win-lose, true-false, good-bad dicho- 25 tomies which see the world as a battleground. A new approach. . . . [is needed] to replace our present thought system with one which sees language as an aid to community or wholeness. . . . Present forms of language have developed as a means either of fighting against something or of showing divisions. Our present language forms were not created for the purpose of unifying. A new set of language forms should be constructed and should be taught in a new language arts curriculum which is at least as different from the old as is the new math from the old mathematics." With these words, Charles Mader reminds us that we are parts of a single system.

Noticing similarities and celebrating them will not bring us to a   26
stage where we are all the same. We will always be individuals, whether on a personal or global level. Our cultures, our histories, our goals, our talents will be unique and varied.

Respect of Differences

So what do we do about these differences? We start by acknowl-   27
edging and respecting them. The difference between our left hand and our right hand gives us an ability to hold and manipulate things that would be severely hindered if our hands were the same. So as individuals or as nations we need to place our efforts on understanding how to enhance our coexistence, rather than on trying to all be the same. It is this idea of respect that allows us to let other nations make what seem to us to be monumental mistakes.

Questions abound when we consider this philosophy. What of the   28
extreme cases? Certainly our outrage would lead us to intervene in the case of another nation's torturing of its citizens? What about the treatment of women in the Islamic world? Here we see the issues for peacework. But notice the progress. We are no longer asking if peace is possible. We are not asking under what conditions would we allow torture, nor who does not deserve equality. The work of today and tomorrow will be the natural outgrowth of the steps that have been taken before.

Having taken these steps and finding ourselves a little less prey to   29
the fear of "other," we see a wondrous opportunity to celebrate the richness of the variety we find around us. This idea is what we embrace when we enjoy the environment, meet new friends, learn a new language, play a team sport. Mader's words again guide us. "Our new vision of peace values the diversity of gifts and recognizes that our differences are a great source of benefit . . . [in] their fullest expression."

The expression of these gifts is promising when we think of in-   30
ternational relations in the 21st century and the possibilities of multiculturalism. At the most basic of levels we've already begun to prepare for peace in the next century. Many preschools are designed around a format that includes world festivals, from authentic dress to food and entertainment. Grade school children in many countries learn multiple languages. Worldwide, travellers participate in a new type of diplomacy by visiting people in other countries who have the same careers or hob-

bies. Dianne Smith, Professor of Education at a midwestern university, invites her students to broaden their definition of world-travel. According to her, every time we read a book set in another place or time, talk to someone raised in a different location, or learn anything about another culture, we are world-travelling. The idea that everyone is the same and everyone is different may be quickly reaching critical mass.

A contradictory note finds the melting pot of European cultures, 31 present-day America, engaged in struggles that seem to ignore both the strides we're making on the abovementioned fronts and also the hard-won internal and external battles since its birth. While our dealing with our ever-evolving black/white issues is far from exemplary, a truly baffling case is the complicated situation in Florida and the southwestern states with South and Central American immigrants, both legal and illegal. To a lesser degree, we see similar conditions surrounding immigrants from Southeast Asia and Arab nations. While we can enumerate the many factors that turn this into a sticky matter (beginning with too few jobs, economic strife, overcrowding, disease), this country was settled by emigrants. 19th century racial problems concerned mixing the blood of different European people. There were family feuds and riots protesting the same conditions—too few jobs, disease—all the way down the list. There was prejudice based on looks, color, culture, and language. Now those cultures are so blended in our country that they stand, indistinct, in the effort to bar the mixing of the blood, the language, the cultures of "Americans" and Hispanics, Arabs, and Orientals.

When heartwarming, apple-pie family dinners often include a list- 32 ing of the attributes of the English side of the family and of the Scottish side of the family, and when we remember that, historically, the English and the Scots were once mortal enemies, we have a true appreciation of how different and how alike we are as a people.

Surely it is a sense of isolation in time that makes us forget that 33 we are not the first generation to deal with the "horror" of mixing blood or of "stolen" jobs, and in fact that the struggles began so many generations ago that we can now boast of our noble and multi-cultured ancestors. How ungrateful we must seem to so neglect the legacy of our forefathers and mothers! Could it be that when we are all dead and buried, our descendants will casually climb from branch to branch in their family trees, blending Arab leaves with Oriental and Hispanic and Native American and European and all the other possibilities as they sit over family dinner? Most assuredly they will.

Empowerment

The Big Dent Theory is an illustration that we, the authors, have 34 created to discuss empowerment. When Tom and Carol sleep in their waterbed, Tom makes a bigger dent than Carol. Equidistant from the center line and lying flat on their backs, Carol rolls toward the dent produced by Tom. Having identified these conditions, they began jockeying for comfortable sleeping positions and started their snooze in companionable equal power—each with space and balance. When Carol turns over and shifts her weight, Tom is unaffected, but when Tom shifts his weight at all, he moves the dent (which Carol has accommodated in her initial position), and now she falls either toward the dent or toward the wooden bed frame. Her balance has been affected. Here we see that Tom has more power: he can choose and adopt a variety of comfortable sleeping positions on his own timetable. Carol can do that once but then loses the power as soon as he changes. She has lost control of her comfort and her timetable in a single movement from someone else. Not only can her comfort level be affected by an outside force, but she has no ability to predict it or prepare for it. (In terms of power against each other, he can affect her balance, but she cannot affect his. However, this is not real power because that is not truly what the goal of either person is; both are really seeking comfortable positions.)

In the first few ever-so-polite weeks of married life, Tom and Carol dealt with The Big Dent in different ways, most of them punctuated by sheepish grins and more and more exasperated sighs. A turning point came when Tom said that he was sorry that this happened, but of course there was nothing for him to do: He weighed more; his dent was bigger. Carol had a completely different point of view: He could turn more gently, stabilizing the water as he turned; he could tell her conversationally, if they were still awake, that the dent would be shifting and let her prepare to accommodate. To his credit, Tom did not view these ideas as petty and tried them out. The new system means that each individual has his/her own responsibilities. Because she weighs less, she accommodates the big dent. Because he weighs more, he communicates more and chooses more careful movements. By making these changes, they are both empowered.

An interesting result occurred. They now have equal, but different, power and skills (Tom knows more about how to turn and stabilize the water at the same time, Carol knows more about how to react to a slope.) Their power didn't come from being the same or from having the same rules, but from working together to see that all needs were met.

A point that bears stressing is that when Tom discovered that he and Carol did not have equal power, he did not think he could equalize it. He thought in terms of having to *give* her power, in this case, weight, which he could not do. Only when they worked to discover where else besides weight did power exist (and here they found it in communication and looking for gentler actions), did they find a way to bring power to each of them.

A relatively new frontier of empowerment presents itself with children. Here is a very easy place to start out thinking that the power is unequal and the only cure for that is for the child to grow up. Unfortunately, if we let a child wait that long to be empowered, she risks being calloused from the struggle, and to the issues, and often does not have the skills to cope with adult power until years into adulthood, if ever. 38

Again body language and mechanics can be most useful for our study. The typical picture of parent and child standing together shows adult standing straight with hands down to the side, and child reaching up to hold hands. Gender makes no difference in this traditional starting point: both moms and dads treated their sons and daughters the same way. Our picture makes sense until we realize that while dad might be standing comfortably erect with arms relaxed, little Mary Jane usually has to reach over her head to place her hand in his. With new eyes, we can now see entire generations of children spending hours in a slightly skewed position with the blood draining out of their arms, and parents obviously enjoying the warm feeling of that tiny hand tucked in theirs long after the little fingers have turned icy from lack of circulation! 39

But what can be done? There's no denying that there are situations that require hand-holding. Alerted to the dilemma, creative parents have found solutions. The most widely used is for Mary Jane to wrap her hand around the extended index finger of the father. Not only is this a few inches lower than the previous position, but it lets her have control of the pressure of the grasp. (Note too, that the child determines whether there is a grasp. Now the father's efforts must be directed toward Mary Jane's compliance rather than his own ability to control.) Other parents have a child hold their coat pocket or skirt. Some have an older child hold the side of the stroller of a sibling. The key to finding the solution is to think in terms of what each party wants. The list may include comfort, physical safety, emotional security, freedom, and space. In the old hand-holding picture, we could hold a child's hand with no training of the child, but we increased our own comfort when we taught her not to wiggle, not to hang on our hands, how to pace herself to match our paces, etc. The new ideas require not more training, but different training. 40

Similarly, we may pick a child up when to do so makes our lives easier but takes power from the child. Coaches often wrap their hands around their young soccer players' shoulders at practice to lift them up and turn them around rather than take the time to translate their own thoughts into "child-speak." Nurturing adults may pick up a crying 41 toddler and hold him on their laps, hoping to comfort, when to kneel and hug might afford the same comfort and leave his power intact. One step farther is the case of a child already sitting on the lap of the parent who is then tipped back into the parent's arms. Now we have a child who has no more power to control his own movements than a turtle on its back. That brings us back full circle to another adult issue. For decades in this country, women have protested the "traditional" child-birth position, saying that their lying powerless on their backs serves no purpose except to make the doctor more comfortable, and in fact loses the benefit of gravity. Even casual study shows that what is called the traditional position is not as traditional as a more crouched position which is still used in more "primitive" cultures.

Non-acceptance of violence

Non-acceptance of violence is a crucial part of the move toward peace because it is a way of re-setting the limits. When we find ourselves at an impasse in negotiations with another, the choices are not whether to fight or to give up, but how to struggle together toward resolution. A new perception of the options and the relationships is required.   42

A simplified model of the evolution of body language in the field of mediation gives us an example. Mediators began with the two parties sitting across from one another, eye to eye, with the issues between them. This afforded them both access to the material but was a rather confrontational position which emphasized their initial fears: "We're on opposite sides on this." To improve the dynamics, savvy mediators positioned their clients next to each other with the issues in front of them, presenting the idea that now we're two people together facing a problem before us. But to make direct eye contact while discussing the issues, each party had to make an obvious effort to turn toward the other, and when the angle became uncomfortable or when the need for emotional distance arose, it was just as obvious an effort to turn away and often came across as an afront or as rejection. Finally, mediators placed clients at right angles to each other, bringing the best of all worlds: they still viewed the problem from the same side, but now were af-forded comfortable and subtle choices about eye contact and connecting. Here are people who no longer have to view an issue within limits set by someone else after they cease to serve a useful purpose.   43

Eliminating violence as an option increases our motivation to find alternatives. Often, we fail to see that one of these alternatives is to act in a positive, nonviolent way. Nonviolent action is more than just pas-sively allowing other people (or nations) to have their way in a disa-greement. Nonviolent action, as taught by Martin Luther King, Jr. and Mohandas Gandhi, can be confrontive in demanding justice.   44

Gene Sharp, another activist who speaks of the practical side of 45 nonviolence, tells the story of Norwegian teachers during World War II. The teachers refused to work when, during Nazi occupation, they were ordered to teach fascist philosophy. Nine thousand of 12,000 teachers refused the commands, even though 1,000 of them were sent to concentration camps. They continued to hold classes in private homes when the Nazis closed schools. After eight months of this nonviolent action, the Nazis gave in, rescinded the order to promote fascism, and allowed them back into the schoolrooms. The teachers' action was spontaneous and relatively unorganized. They had no advance knowledge of nonviolent techniques or preparation in how to use them. Yet, along with countless other unheralded incidents throughout history, their struggle for justice through nonviolent means was successful. Nonviolence, claims Sharp, is not only ethical (moral), but more importantly, it is practical. Most of the incidents of successful nonviolent actions were, as in Norway, spur of the moment and unstructured. It is staggering to imagine how effective the struggle for justice could be if we prepared for nonviolent action with the same energy and resources we use for war.

Using nonviolent action in the face of violence is important for 46 another reason. Beyond War, an organization established to change ways of thinking about war, claims that humanity is challenged with the need to bring about a world that settles its conflicts in new ways. With nuclear warfare looming over our heads, we are simply beyond war. We have come too far for it to be an option, and we must go on to find new ways to live together.

In the words of Martin Luther King, Jr., "If we assume that life 47 is worth living and that man has a right to survival, then we must find an alternative to war." Author Herman Wouk continues this thought, "War is an old habit of thought, an old frame of mind, an old political technique, that must now pass as human sacrifice and human slavery have passed."

Conflict Resolution Skills

Another characteristic of peace after the turn of the century is that 48 people will be skilled in conflict resolution. The next generation will have a greater need for conflict resolution skills than any generation before them, and as with so many of the other categories, the study and use of them is already thriving. Skills such as reflective listening, assertion and creative problem solving are being taught at all levels of education now, ranging from curriculum in elementary schools to college-level courses. Businesses bring in conflict resolution consultants to teach these skills to their employees. A group of schools in San Francisco and

Kansas City even pioneer a program of playground mediation in which students are taught a process to mediate their own conflicts.

The characteristics discussed earlier, the unity perspective, respect   49
of differences, empowerment, and alternatives to violence all can be addressed with listening skills. If we take our mediators' clients and place them in their carefully considered places, we can expect them to first use listening skills in their attempt to resolve conflict. Active listening takes the listener out of the passive role and makes him responsible for listening not only for content, but for feelings and underlying issues. When his partner stops talking, he will use paraphrasing (reflecting), and clarifying questions to verify any impressions he has gotten. The goal of active listening is to achieve a complete understanding of the issues involved. The parties alternate roles until they are satisfied that they have been understood.

Finding and looking for more common ground at this point is both   50
the result and the challenge of active listening. Usually the conflicts that bring us to battlefields or mediation tables are based on incompatibility of positions, rather than incompatibility of values. Value is sometimes defined as what we want deep down inside and position is what we think we have to do to get it. If you and I have had a fender bender that was your fault, I may jump out of my car, livid, demanding your insurance card, shouting demands that my car be returned to its original condition. You may refuse to give your card to me, fearing that your insurance premiums will go up and knowing you are barely managing your regular payments. If we think we are talking options at this point, we can only identify two (give me the card or don't give me the card). If we recognize that we are talking position, and start searching for values, we might discover that your value and mine can be perfectly met by a position you suggest that is agreeable to me. You hand me cash to cover the repair and our conflict is resolved.

This story also shows creative problem solving. Seldom does a   51
problem only have two possible solutions. But finding ourselves trapped in the language filled with dichotomies which Mader described, we often face a dilemma and look for an "either/or" answer. Creative problem solving will train us to look for seemingly bizarre alternatives, generate as many as we possibly can—without judging or editing them in this initial step. Creative problem solving gets us in the habit of questioning old limits. Celebrating other cultures or points of view becomes easier when we can temporarily question our own point of view or the context of it.

The next step is to try to find a workable solution. Perfect solu-   52
tions are mythological creatures that spring from dichotomy language. "Good enough" is what we're looking for now. Because we remember

that peace and life and relationships are processes, we know that we make a good enough decision now and are free to make a different good enough decision tomorrow. This revolving-door-access connects us to the reality of such solutions as the Jim Crow laws. Yes, they virtually ended the violence, but the value of peace was not met. Re-negotiating is an important element of conflict resolution and, done with the original conscientious guidelines, serves to empower both parties.

Parenting

The concentrated effort to prepare society's children to live in a world of peace, in fact to settle for nothing less, is a significant characteristic of future peace. As parents dedicated to creating a world that is all one system, we are charged with raising children's expectations to that level. We must give clear messages to the next generation and every one thereafter. They must not see oppression as normal, so it is important that we start by empowering them, showing them both what it feels like to be empowered (they must not allow themselves to be oppressed in the future) and showing them skills for empowering others. Resisting the urge to let might make right becomes a challenge with far-reaching implications. Clearly we are cautioned not to use violence of any kind, but the message just as deeply given is that we have a "because I said so" mentality. Flexible and questioning thinking should be encouraged. (Remember children are on their own journey and parents may not always understand or agree.)   53

Giving children power right from the start is important for many reasons. It is by far the safest alternative; they are sure to acquire more power at some point and they are better off practicing with parents who love them and will protect them (but not save them!) than with strangers.   54

Teaching every new generation of children the concepts above as a normal part of growing up, just as we know we will do with computer skills, becomes vital. They must have these lessons to survive in the world of the future. That's what the world they're facing requires.   55

The astounding thing about what we'll need in the 21st century for peace is that in every case the elements are already flourishing. The fact that they exist at a grassroots level makes it easier to discover that there are hundreds of examples all around us.   56

"No matter how small a thing you do, it is vitally important that you do it."

—MOHANDAS GANDHI

How can you practice peacemaking?

All of us may be practicing peacemaking without realizing it. Surely 57
in the way we interact with others but also in the way we talk and
think, we change the norm of thinking about peace. We know now that
practicing peacemaking is not just preventing war, but it is an even
bigger job. This is a stage of both challenge and comfort. There is great
hope, here on the brink of the 21st century. Hope comes from the
knowledge that peace is happening all around us, from the smallest
personal interaction to international negotiations.

The work of peace is being done now. The peace visionaries listed 58
here are not elite experts, but work to affect the situations around them.
Realize that the movers and shakers in peacework come from the grassroots levels and from all walks of life. They are not government leaders
or corporate executives, but teachers, parents, friends, and co-workers.
Almost any field produces its own peacemakers.

Charles Mader, for example, is the vice president of a Midwest 59
hospital, stressing that healthcare must be seen from a peacemaking perspective. Jean Illsley Clarke trains parents to use a blend of structure and
nurture that unites parent and child for the important job of learning
about life. Dianne Smith teaches educators how to bring multi-cultur-
alism into the classroom and explores with her students the problems
of a dominant culture which does not empower others. Margaret Mead
represents the many people who show us the importance of how we
relate to each other and to time. We cannot plot peace without an appreciation of what came before our efforts.

Finding our own personal paths toward peace today should prove 60
no more difficult than finding our favorite movies at the video store.
The key is to discover our personal passions—toe holds. Trends named
here and trailblazers mentioned, can become mile markers. But be fore-
warned: We must be prepared, for once we begin, once we are aware,
momentum may sweep us up in a whirlwind.

As generations of the future, we acknowledge that we must be 61
flexible, question, use new perceptions, new language, new definitions,
and, however we may add to them, keep our visions of peace.

Content Considerations

1. How do Iliff and Smith approach the issue of peace? What are their
   assumptions about peace and its attainment?
2. The authors present numerous examples throughout their essay to illustrate concepts. Are these examples effective?
3. What audience does this article assume? Does the audience affect the
   tone?

— *Ideas for Discussion, Writing, and Research* —

1. Using the essays by Rodgers and the *Washington Monthly* editors, discuss alternatives to war. With two or three classmates, write a position paper in which you synthesize these alternatives and present your own ideas about how nations can avoid armed conflict.

2. Research individual resistance to war. What is its history? How effective is such resistance?

3. How do Twain and Hardy personalize war? How does Thoreau treat the dehumanization of soldiers? Locate other literature that centers on soldiering; in an essay, present examples of the literature and the conclusions you form from them about societal attitudes toward war.

4. After reading the Bishop essay (p. 412), interview a war resister—someone opposed to all wars or a specific war—and present his or her views to your class. Discuss whether such a viewpoint is antithetical to a democracy, or whether a democracy depends on opposing voices to exist.

5. Use any four pieces in this chapter to help you formulate or support your own position regarding war. Under what circumstances would you support war?

6. Consider the article by Rodgers and those in chapter 1 by Bower and Howard. Research further the question of whether conflict and aggression are innately human.

7. With several classmates, present a program to your class about the effects of war on a country's population. Consider the use of films such as I.F. Stone's "Hearts and Minds."

8. Peace, according to the Iliff and Smith, is not just the absence of war. What, then, is peace? Use interviews and printed material to help you form a definition.

9. Research a particular country such as Vietnam or Iraq or Germany to learn how long it took for peace to be attained after hostilities ceased.

10. What are the possibilities for peace in the future? What obstacles to peace must be overcome? In the next fifty years, what areas of the globe are the most likely locations for armed conflict, and why? What can be done now to avert such conflict?

Credits *(continued from copyright page)*

Page 48. "How Presidents Take Nations into War" Copyright © 1945/87/90★ by the New York Times Company. Reprinted by permission.

Page 52. "Unlocking the Promise of Freedom" *Vital Speeches of the Day* Vol. 57 #15. May 15, 1991.

Page 60. "S. Hussein" *Vital Speeches of the Day* Vol. 57 #11. March 15, 1991.

Chapter 2

Page 73. "Muddling the Issue of Women in War" Copyright © 1991 by Suzanne Fields, distributed by the Los Angeles Times Syndicate.

Page 76. "Soldier Boys, Soldier Girls" Reprinted by permission of *The New Republic*, © 1990, The New Republic, Inc.

Page 79. "Drafting Daughters" © 1980, The Boston Globe Newspaper Company/Washington Post Writers Group. Reprinted with permission.

Page 82. "Racial Inequity in the Military" Nuclear Times, Inc. Spring 1991: 19–20, Sonia Shah, Managing Editor. Nuclear Times magazine quarterly. $15./year. Subscription to: P.O. Box 351, Kenmore Station, Boston, MA 02215.

Page 87. "Black Leaders vs. Desert Storm" Reprinted from *Commentary*, May 1991, by permission; all rights reserved.

Page 102. "The Fairness Doctrine" © 1991 The Economist Newspaper Limited. January 12, 1991: 21–22. Reprinted with permission.

Page 105. "The Rich Don't Serve—So What?" Reprinted with permission from *The Washington Monthly*. Copyright by The Washington Monthly Company, 611 Connecticut Avenue, N.W., Washington, D.C. 20009 (202) 462-0128.

Page 109. "Claim You're Gay, Avoid the Military" Copyright © 1945/87/90★ by the New York Times Company. Reprinted by permission.

Page 112. "War and Conscience" Reprinted by permission of Macmillan Publishing Company from *A Conflict of Loyalties* edited by James Finn. Copyright © 1968 by Macmillan Publishing Company. Originally published by Western Publishing, Inc.

Chapter 3

Page 127. "Atomic Bombing of Nagasaki Told by Flight Member" Copyright © 1945/87/90★ by The New York Times Company. Reprinted by permission.

Page 134. "Thank God for the Atom Bomb" Copyright © 1988 by Paul Fussell. Reprinted by permission of Summit Books, a division of Simon & Schuster.

Page 149. "The U.S. Was Wrong" Copyright © 1945/87/90★ by The New York Times Company. Reprinted by permission.

Page 152. "War's New Science" From *Newsweek*, February 18. © 1991, Newsweek, Inc. All rights reserved. Reprinted by permission.

Page 155. ". . . And the Dirty Little Weapons" From the *Bulletin of the Atomic Scientists*. Copyright © 1991 by the Educational Foundation for Nuclear Science, 6042 South Kimbark, Chicago, IL 60637, USA. A one-year subscription is $30.

Page 163. "Biological Weapons Research and Physicians: Historical and Ethical Analysis" Published in *Physicians for Social Responsibility*, March 1991. Vol 1, issue 1:31–42.

Page 184. "Battlefields of Ashes and Mud" With permission from *Natural History*, November 1990; Copyright © the American Museum of Natural History, 1990.

Page 188. "Environmental Destruction Is an Ancient Tool of War" © The Washington Post.

Page 191. "Arms Control, Stability, and Causes of War" reprinted by permission of *Daedalus*, Journal of the American Academy of Arts and Sciences, from the issue entitled, "Arms Control: Thirty Years On," Winter 1991, Vol. 120/1.

Chapter 4

Page 209. "Killing Civilians" Excerpt from *The Collected Essays, Journalism and Letters of George Orwell*, Volume 3 by Sonia Orwell and Ian Angus, copyright © 1968 by Sonia Brownell Orwell, reprinted by permission of Harcourt Brace Jovanovich, Inc.

Page 212. "Barkinson's Law on Bombing" The Columbia University Forum Anthology. Atheneum, 1968:309–314.

Page 217. "Smart Versus Nuclear Bombs" Air & Space, June/July 1991:4.

Page 220. "War at Nine Years Old" From *The War According to Anna: A Paean to My Mother*. Seven Stones Press, 1986:75–86. Copyright Kamilla C. Chadwick.

Page 231. "Enemy Aliens: Scare on the Coast" Copyright 1942 Time Warner Inc. Reprinted by permission.

Page 234. "Korematsu *v*. United States" © Encyclopaedia Britannica 1969.

Page 244. "On Patrol" From *Born on the Fourth of July* by Ron Kovic. Copyright 1976 by McGraw-Hill Publishing Company. Reproduced with permission.

Chapter 5

Page 255. "The First Casualty" Excerpt "War Is Fun 1954–1975" from *The First Casualty: From Crimea to Vietnam: The War Correspondent as Hero, Propagandist, and Myth Maker*, copyright © 1975 by Phillip Knightley, reprinted by permission of Harcourt Brace Jovanovich, Inc.

Page 281. "The Media in Vietnam" From Government Printing Office Publication number 80001.

Page 286. "Read Some About It" Reprinted by permission of *The New Republic*, © 1991, The New Republic, Inc.

Page 292. "Eyeballing the Nintendo Apocalypse" By Christopher Dickey from *Rolling Stone* 3/7/91 #599. By Straight Arrow Publishers, Inc. © 1991. All Rights Reserved. Reprinted by Permission.

Page 297. "TV's Clean Little War" From the *Bulletin of the Atomic Scientists*. Copyright © 1991 by the Educational Foundation for Nuclear Science, 6042 South Kimbark, Chicago, IL 60637, USA. A one-year subscription is $30.

Page 304. "Another Front" Reprinted from the *Columbia Journalism Review*, May/June, © 1991.

Page 307. "M★U★S★H," by Margaret Spillane from *The Nation*: February 25, 1991:237–239.

Page 314. "New & Improved Postwar Press Guidelines" Reprinted by permission: Tribune Media Services.

Chapter 6

Page 322. "Okinawa: The Bloodiest Battle of All" Reprinted by permission of Don Congdon Associates, Inc. Copyright © 1987 by William Manchester.

Page 332. "Shell Shock" Reprinted with permission from *American Heritage* Volume 41, Number 4. Copyright 1990 by American Heritage, a Division of Forbes, Inc.

Page 351. "Displaced Persons" From *Janet Flanner's World: Uncollected Writings 1932–1975* by Janet Flanner, copyright © 1979 by Natalia Danesi Murray, reprinted by permission of Harcourt Brace Jovanovich, Inc.

Page 356. "Painful Questions" From *Society*, March/April 1989:7–9. Copyright 1989. Item fee code 0147-2011/183.

Page 362. "Why I Won't Go to Germany" Reprinted by permission of Cynthia Ozick and her agents, Raines & Raines, 71 Park Avenue, New York, NY 10016. Copyright © 1988 by Cynthia Ozick.

Page 367. "Some Lover of Freedom" Published with permission of *The New American* magazine. This article appeared in *The New American*, May 7, 1991.

Page 371. "A Perilous New Order" Copyright © 1945/87/90★ by The New York Times Company. Reprinted by permission.

Chapter 7

Page 379. "U.S. Misadventure in Vietnam" Reprinted with permission from *Current History*. © 1968 *Current History, Inc.*

Page 386. "Setting the Stage" Reprinted from *Lyndon Johnson's War, The Road to Stalemate in Vietnam*, by Larry Berman, by permission of W.W. Norton & Company, Inc. Copyright © 1989 by Larry Berman.

Page 394. "Comparing Wars Does Veterans of Both a Disservice" Reprinted by permission: Tribune Media Services.

Page 397. "A Refugee" Excerpted from *Ten Vietnamese* by Susan Sheehan, published by Alfred A. Knopf. Copyright © 1966, 1967, by Susan Sheehan.

Page 406. "Coming Home" Reprinted from *The Saturday Evening Post* © 1991.

Chapter 8

Page 416. "Turning against the Military Life" Copyright © 1945/87/90★ by The New York Times Company. Reprinted by permission.

Page 445. "Casualties of War" Reprinted with permission from *The Washington Monthly*. Copyright by The Washington Monthly Company, 1611 Connecticut Avenue, N.W., Washington, D.C. 20009. (202) 462-0128.

Page 449. "The War Is Won but Peace Is Not" *Vital Speeches of the Day*. Vol. 57 #14, May 1, 1991.

MyAccountingLab

S0-BNX-619

■ Web-based tutorial and assessment software where students have more "I Get It" moments.

■ Flexible for instructors to easily integrate into their course.

For Instructors

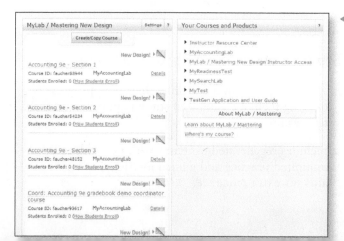

Powerful Homework and Test Manager

■ Homework assignments, quizzes, and tests that directly correlate to the textbook.

■ Homework guided solutions to help students understand concepts.

■ Multiple assignment options including time limits, proctoring, and maximum number of attempts allowed.

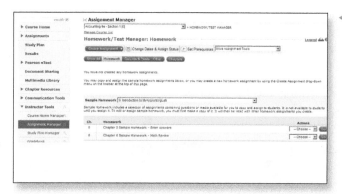

Comprehensive Gradebook Tracking

■ Automatic grading that tracks students' results on tests, homework, and tutorials.

■ Flexible Gradebook with numerous student data views, weighted assignments, choice on which attempts to include when calculating scores, and the ability to omit results of individual assignments.

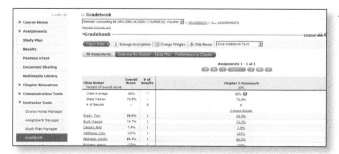

Department-Wide Solutions

■ Simplified for departmental implementation with the use of Coordinator Courses—make changes once and they ripple down to all members.

View a guided tour of MyAccountingLab at
http://www.myaccountinglab.com/support/tours

For Students

Interactive Tutorial Exercises

■ Homework and practice exercises with additional algorithmic–generated problems for more practice.

■ Personalized interactive learning—guided solutions and learning aids for point-of-use help and immediate feedback.

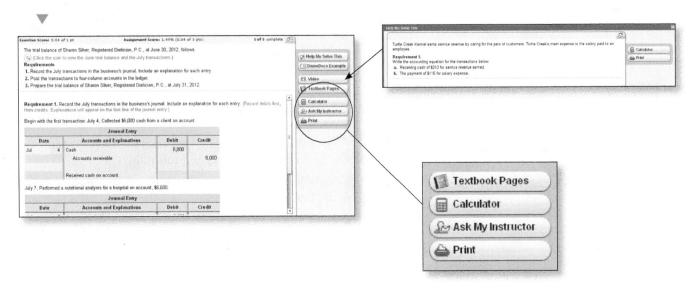

Study Plan for Self-Paced Learning

■ Assists students in monitoring their own progress by offering them a customized study plan based on their test results.

■ Includes regenerated exercises with new values for unlimited practice and guided multimedia learning aids for extra guidance.

PEARSON

ALWAYS LEARNING

Jeffrey Slater

College Accounting
A Practical Approach

Custom Edition for Portland Community College

Taken from:
*College Accounting, Chapters 1-12 with Study Guide
and Working Papers,* Twelfth Edition
by Jeffrey Slater

Cover Art: Courtesy of Glowimages/Getty Images.

Taken from:

College Accounting, Chapters 1-12 with Study Guide and Working Papers, Twelfth Edition
by Jeffrey Slater
Copyright © 2013 by Pearson Education, Inc.
Published by Prentice Hall
Upper Saddle River, New Jersey 07458

All rights reserved. No part of this book may be reproduced, in any form or by any means, without permission in writing from the publisher.

This special edition published in cooperation with Pearson Learning Solutions.

All trademarks, service marks, registered trademarks, and registered service marks are the property of their respective owners and are used herein for identification purposes only.

Pearson Learning Solutions, 501 Boylston Street, Suite 900, Boston, MA 02116
A Pearson Education Company
www.pearsoned.com

Printed in the United States of America

1 2 3 4 5 6 7 8 9 10 V0UD 18 17 16 15 14

000200010271897338

DS

ISBN 10: 1-269-94804-0
ISBN 13: 978-1-269-94804-3

BRIEF CONTENTS

CONTENTS

8   Paying, Recording, and Reporting Payroll and Payroll Taxes: The Conclusion of the Payroll Process 289

9   Sales and Cash Receipts 335

GAME PLAN FOR SUCCESS
FROM ACCOUNTING COACH
JEFF SLATER...

COACHING SUCCESS WITH IN-CHAPTER LEARNING TOOLS

- **Learning Unit Reviews:** Each chapter is organized into small, bite-sized units. Students are introduced to a new concept in the learning unit, and then they can immediately test their understanding in the learning unit review.
- **Instant Replay:** This feature, located in the self-review quiz at the end of each learning unit for the first five chapters, is like a private tutoring session with the author, as he anticipates students' questions and walks them through the provided solution, step by step. These Instant Replay sections are the key to retention.
- **Chapter Opening Game Plan:** Each chapter introduces students to the key concepts that they will learn in the chapter using student-friendly companies and examples.
- **Coaching Tips:** Short, sweet, and to the point. They're not found on every page; instead they are provided only when students may need some coaching.
- **In-Text Practice Set:** The in-text Sullivan Realty Practice Set (Chapter 5) enables students to complete two cycles of transactions (either manually or with Peachtree or Quickbooks).

END-OF-CHAPTER PRACTICE MATERIAL

- **Demonstration Problems:** Demonstration problems walk students through a sample problem as if they were getting one-on-one help from their instructor.
- **Blueprint:** This is a visual summary of the chapter. Students can use it as a roadmap to review what they have learned. It stresses when to perform specific activities.
- **Concept Checks:** Short exercises can be assigned or used in class for difficult topics.
- **Learning Objectives:** A learning objective number and the average time to complete each exercise is now included for all end-of-chapter material.
- **Group A and New Group B Exercises:** Short exercises can be assigned or used in class to focus on building skills. B exercises were added to the text in this edition.
- **Group A and Group B Problems:** All of the problems have been updated for this edition.
- **Financial Report Problem:** Students use the annual financial report of Kellogg Company to apply theory and applications completed in the chapter.
- **Discussion Questions:** These include ethical questions and critical-thinking questions.
- **Computerized Accounting:** Selected end-of-chapter problems can be completed with Peachtree or Quickbooks.

- **Continuing Problem: On The Job: Sanchez Computer Center:** Students follow the activities of a single company and then are asked to apply concepts to solve specific accounting problems for the company. Problems can be found in Chapters 1–12 and can be solved manually or by using Peachtree or Quickbooks.
- **Computer Workshops:** This book contains seven computer workshops (for the most recent versions of Peachtree and QuickBooks) with detailed step-by-step instructions on how to take a manual problem from the end of the chapter and use both types of software.

Students need to do accounting manually before they can use the computer. These workshops allow the student to see how fast accounting procedures can be done on the computer. They will need these computer skills when applying for jobs in the business.

These workshops assume no computer knowledge and facilitate a step-by-step teaching package. Each step provides the student (or instructor) with detailed explanations. Initial instructions appear in the textbook itself, and then students are directed to the computer to do the actual work online.

MyAccountingLab

NEW TO THIS EDITION

MyAccountingLab® is Web-based tutorial and assessment software for accounting that not only gives students more "I Get It" moments, but also gives instructors the flexibility to make technology an integral part of their course.

With MyAccountingLab students will have...

- **Personalized help** when they need it with the interactive "Help Me Solve This" tool that automatically generates algorithmic versions of the problem the student is working on and provides step-by-step assistance until the solution is obtained. The "Help Me Solve This" tool is personal tutorials to help students understand how to work through accounting problems.
- **Dynamic learning resources** that work with students' individual learning styles. *All Learning Aids can be turned off by the instructor.*
- **Interactive Tutorial Exercises**—found in MyAccountingLab's homework and practice questions—that are correlated to students' Pearson textbook.
- **A personalized Study Plan** for self-paced learning that links students directly to interactive tutorial exercises on the topics they have yet to master.
- **An easy-to-navigate system** so the focus is on what matters the most—learning accounting!
- **Chapter resources** that are in one spot for students so they can quickly access all learning tools associated with each chapter of the book they are using. Examples of the chapter resources include audio PowerPoints, videos, MP3 summaries, e-Study guide, Check Figure for Cost Accounting, working papers, etc.

MyAccountingLab is also reshaping accounting courses for instructors by...

- **Providing flexibility** for any course through its robust course management tools and adaptable course materials.
- **Offering several choices** when it comes to scheduling, item analysis, questions and problems, and grading and assessment.
- **Simplifying instructor and student experiences** from set-up and through day-to-day activity with its easy-to-use interface.
- **Motivating students** by providing learning tools that engage, stimulate, and help students connect online and in the classroom.

Chapter Changes

All Chapters:

- New Accounting Coach feature, which assesses students' understanding of key concepts.
- New chapter summaries which summarize key concepts and terms. This feature provides students with an all-in-one review tool for each chapter.
- All problems and exercises are updated. MyAccountingLab contains an exact match of the A and B sets in the text. In addition, MyAccountingLab provides three additional sets of problems and exercises for endless practice and assignment opportunities.
- An additional set of exercises (Set B) has been added to the text.
- Classroom Demonstration Exercises have been renamed "Concept Checks" and are reproduced in MyAccountingLab.
- The "Play by Play: Extra Help" explanation of solutions to Learning Unit quizzes has been retitled "Instant Replay."

Chapter 1 Accounting Concepts and Procedures
- New chapter opener entitled "Game Plan" with new company information on eBay

Chapter 2 Debits and Credits: Analyzing and Recording Business Transactions
- New chapter opener entitled "Game Plan" with new company information on Subway

Chapter 3 Beginning the Accounting Cycle
- New chapter opener entitled "Game Plan" with new company information on American Airlines

Chapter 4 The Accounting Cycle Continued
- New chapter opener entitled "Game Plan" with new company information on General Motors

Chapter 5 The Accounting Cycle Completed
- New chapter opener entitled "Game Plan" with new company information on Disney
- Updated 2010 numbers for the Sullivan Realty Mini-Practice Set

Chapter 6 Banking Procedure and Control of Cash
- New chapter opener entitled "Game Plan" with a banking example about the latest banking procedures
- Updated information on trends in banking and accounting procedures for debit and credit cards

Chapter 7 Calculating Pay and Payroll Taxes: The Beginning of the Payroll Process
- New chapter opener entitled "Game Plan" with new company information on Sears
- Updated figures and tables throughout include 2010 rates
- Footnote on OASDI rate used and explained
- Continued focus on integrating role of employee and employer

Chapter 8 Paying, Recording, and Reporting Payroll and Payroll Taxes: The Conclusion of the Payroll Process
- New chapter opener entitled "Game Plan" with new company information on Google
- Updated figures and tables throughout include 2010 payroll tax rates
- Updated tax forms

Chapter 9 Sales and Cash Receipts
- New chapter opener entitled "Game Plan" with new company information on Home Depot

Chapter 10 Purchases and Cash Payments
- New chapter opener entitled "Game Plan" with new company information on Best Buy
- Special journal appendix problems included in MyAccountingLab

Chapter 11 Preparing a Worksheet for a Merchandise Company
- New chapter opener entitled "Game Plan" with new company information on Apple

Chapter 12 Completion of the Accounting Cycle for a Merchandise Company
- New chapter opener entitled "Game Plan" with new company information on Toys "R" Us
- New Computer Workshop after Chapter 12

FOR INSTRUCTORS

Instructor's Resource Center (IRC): Register. Redeem. Login.

At www.pearsonhighered.com/slater instructors can access a variety of print, media, and presentation resources available with this text in downloadable, digital format. For most texts, resources are also available for course management platforms such as Blackboard, WebCT, and Course Compass.

It gets better. Once you register, you will not have additional forms to fill out or multiple usernames and passwords to remember to access new titles and/or editions. As a registered faculty member, you can log in directly to download resource files and receive immediate access and instructions for installing course management content to your campus server.

Need help? Our dedicated technical support team is ready to assist instructors with questions about the media supplements that accompany this text. Visit http://247pearsoned.custhelp.com for answers to frequently asked questions and toll-free user support phone numbers.

The following supplements are available to adopting instructors. For detailed descriptions, please visit www.pearsonhighered.com/slater.

Instructor's Resource Center (IRC) online: Login at www.pearsonhighered.com/slater.
Chapters 1–12 with Study Guide and Working Papers: 0-13-277217-5
Study Guide and Working Papers (Chapters 1–12): 0-13-277215-9
Study Guide and Working Papers (Chapters 13–25): 0-13-277216-7
Instructor's Solutions Manual: 0-13-277207-8
Instructor's Manual: Visit the IRC for this supplement.
TestGen Test Generating Software: Visit the IRC for this supplement.
Test Item File: Visit the IRC for this supplement.
Working Papers in Excel format: Visit the IRC for this supplement.
PowerPoint Presentation Slides: Visit the IRC for this supplement.

FOR STUDENTS

Textbook Volumes

Textbook Chapters 1–25: ISBN 0-13-277206-X *Includes payroll and additional blank worksheets
Textbook Chapters 1–12: ISBN 0-13-277217-5 *Includes study guide and working papers for Chapters 1–12

Print Study Aids

Study Guide and Working Papers Chapters 1–12: ISBN 0-13-277215-9
Study Guide and Working Papers Chapters 13–25: ISBN 0-13-277216-7
Who Dun It? Practice Set: ISBN 0-13-277253-1

Online Resources

Valuable resources for both students and professors can be found at www.pearsonhighered.com/slater.

REVIEWERS

Terry Aime, *Delgado Community College*
Cornelia Alsheimer, *Santa Barbara City College*
Julia Angel, *North Arkansas College*
Julie Armstrong, *St. Clair County Community College*
Marjorie Ashton, *Truckee Meadows Community College*
John Babich, *Kankakee Community College*
Cecil Battiste, *Valencia Community College*
Donald Benoit, *Mitchell College*
Peggy A. Berrier, *Ivy Technical State College*
Michelle Berube, *Everest University*
Anne Bikofsky, *College of Westchester*
Michael Bitting, *John A. Logan College*
David Bland, *Cape Fear Community College*
Suzanne Bradford, *Angelina College*
Beverly Bugay, *Tyler Junior College*
Gary Bumgarner, *Mountain Empire Community College*
Betsy Crane, *Victoria College*
Noel Craven, *El Camino College*
Don Curfman, *McHenry County College*
John Daugherty, *Pitt Community College*
Susan Davis, *Green River Community College*
Michael Discello, *Pittsburgh Technical Institute*
Sylvia Dorsey, *Florence-Darlington Technical College*
Sid Downey, *Cochise College*
Donna Eakman, *Great Falls College of Technology*
Steven Ernest, *Baton Rouge Community College*
John Evanson, *Williston State College*
Marilyn Ewing, *Seward County Community College*
Nancy Fallon, *Albertus Magnus College*
Nicole Fife, *Bucks County Community College*
Brian Fink, *Danville Area Community College*
Paul Fisher, *Rogue Community College*
Carolyn Fitzmorris, *Hutchinson Community College*
Trish Glennon, *Central Florida Community College*
Nancy Goehring, *Monterey Peninsula College*
Jane Goforth, *North Seattle Community College*
Lori Grady, *Bucks County Community College*
Gretchen Graham, *Community College of Allegheny County*
Marina Grau, *Houston Community College*
Mary Jane Green, *Des Moines Area Community College*
Joyce Griffin, *Kansas City Kansas Community College*
Becky Hancock, *El Paso Community College*
Toni Hartley, *Laurel Business Institute*
Raymond Hartman, *Triton Community College*
Scott Hays, *Central Oregon Community College*

Kathy Hebert, *Louisiana Technical College*
Sueanne Hely, *West Kentucky Community & Technical College*
Maggie Hilgart, *Mid-State Technical College*
Michele Hill, *Schoolcraft College*
Michelle Hoeflich, *Elgin Community College*
Mary Hollars, *Vincennes University*
Donna Jacobs, *University of New Mexico-Gallup*
Judy Jager, *Pikes Peak Community College*
Jane Jones, *Mountain Empire Community College*
Jenny Jones, *Central Kentucky Technical College*
Patrick Jozefowicz, *Southwest Wisconsin Technical College*
Nancy Kelly, *Middlesex Community College*
Karen Kettelson, *Western Wisconsin Technical College*
Elizabeth King, *Sacramento City College*
Ken Koerber, *Bucks County Community College*
David Krug, *Johnson County Community College*
Christy Land, *Catawba Valley Community College*
Ronald Larner, *John Wood Community College*
Lee Leksell, *Lake Superior College*
Lolita Lockett, *Florida Community College at Jacksonville*
Sue Mardock, *Colby Community College*
John Masserwick, *Five Towns College*
Pam Mattson, *Tulsa Community College*
Bonnie Mayer, *Lakeshore Technical College*
Sally McMillin, *Katharine Gibbs School*
John Miller, *Metropolitan Community College*
Susan L. Miller, *Delaware County Community College*
Cora Newcomb, *Technical College of Lowcountry*
Jon Nitschke, *Great Falls Technical College*
Lorinda Oliver, *Vermont Technical College*
Barbara Pauer, *Gateway Technical College*
Nicholas Peppes, *St. Louis Community College*
Richard Pettit, *Mountain View College*
Lisa Phillips, *City College*
Margaret Pollard, *American River College*
Shirley Powell, *Arkansas State University*
Linda Prescott, *Hillsborough Community College*
Claudia Quinn, *San Joaquin Delta College*
Jerry Rhodes, *Daymar College*
Ed Richter, *Southeast Technical Institute*
Alberta Robinson, *Indiana Business College*
Beth Sanders, *Hawaii Community College*
Bob Sanner, *Central Community College*
Debra Schmidt, *Cerritos College*
Karen Scott, *Bates Technical College*

Carolyn Seefer, *Diablo Valley College*

Jeri Spinner, *Idaho State University*

Alice Steljes, *Illinois Valley Community College*

Jack Stone, *Linn-Benton Community College*

Rick Street, *Spokane Community College*

Domenico Tavella, *Pittsburgh Technical Institute*

Bill Taylor, *Cossatot Community College*

Mary J. Tobaben, *Collin County Community College*

Ron J. Trucks, *Jefferson College*

Elaine Tuttle, *Bellevue Community College*

Ski Vanderlaan, *Delta College*

Andy Williams, *Edmonds Community College*

Jack Williams, *Tulsa Community College*

Supplement Authors and Invaluable Assistance

Test Item File: William Jefferson, *Metropolitan Community College;* Brenda Mattison, *TriCounty Technical College*

PowerPoint Presentations: Robin Turner, *Rowan-Cabarrus Community College*

Computerized Workshops: Terri Brunsdon

End-of-chapter Peachtree/QuickBooks problems: Terri Brunsdon

Who Dun It? Practice Set: Toni Hartley, *Laurel Business Institute*

Update of Chapters 7, 8, and Continuing Problem Corner Dress Shop and Who Dun It? Practice Sets: Richard Pettit, *Mountain View College*

Text Accuracy Checkers: Richard Pettit, *Mountain View College;* Cornelia Alsheimer-Barthel, *Santa Barbara City College*

Solutions Manual Update: Judith Zander, *Grossmont Community College*

Supplement Quality Assurance: Richard Pettit, *Mountain View College;* Michele Hill, *Schoolcraft College*

I WANT TO HEAR FROM YOU

How to "get to me": Please e-mail me at jeffslater@aol.com, and I promise to get back to you within 24 hours or less. You are my customer, and I want to provide you with the best service possible.

Accounting Concepts and Procedures

THE GAME PLAN

Did you ever think about how a business with millions of sales each day keeps track of them and why it needs to? When you purchase an item on eBay, accounting surrounds each transaction.

You have a record of your purchase in your PayPal account, and at the same time, eBay tracks the sale in its version of a PayPal account, called the Revenue account. In this chapter, we will see how eBay records all these transactions and how eBay communicates its sales to the business world. If you want to run your own business one day, it is important to understand accounting—"the language of business"—so that you can communicate your performance in the business world like eBay.

LEARNING OBJECTIVES

- **1.** Defining and listing the functions of accounting.
- **2.** Recording transactions in the basic accounting equation.
- **3.** Seeing how revenue, expenses, and withdrawals expand the basic accounting equation.
- **4.** Preparing an income statement, a statement of owner's equity, and a balance sheet.

ACCOUNTING AND BUSINESS

Companies like eBay have to comply with many federal statutes. The Sarbanes-Oxley Act is a federal statute passed to prevent fraud at public companies. This act requires a closer look at the internal controls and the accuracy of the financial results of a company.

> **Accounting** A system that measures the business's activities in financial terms, provides written reports and financial statements about those activities, and communicates these reports to decision makers and others.

Accounting is the language of business; it provides information to managers, owners, investors, government agencies, and others inside and outside the organization. Accounting provides answers and insights to questions like these:

- Should I invest in Google or Apple stock?
- How will increasing fuel costs affect American Airlines?
- Can United Airlines pay its debt obligations?
- What percentage of the Amazon marketing budget is allocated to e-business? How does that percentage compare with the competition? What is the overall financial condition of Amazon?

Smaller businesses also need answers to their financial questions:

- At a local Walgreens, did business increase enough over the last year to warrant hiring a new assistant?
- Should Local Auto Detailing Co. spend more money to design, produce, and send out new brochures in an effort to create more business?
- What role should the Internet play in the future of business spending?

Accounting is as important to individuals as it is to businesses; it answers questions like these:

- Should I take out a loan to buy a new Chevy Volt or wait until I can afford to pay cash for it?
- Would my money work better in a money market or in the stock market?

The accounting process analyzes, records, classifies, summarizes, reports, and interprets financial information for decision makers—whether individuals, small businesses, large corporations, or governmental agencies—in a timely fashion. It is important that students understand the "whys" of this accounting process. Just knowing the mechanics is not enough.

Types of Business Organization

The four main categories of business organization are (1) sole proprietorships, (2) partnerships, (3) corporations, and (4) limited liability corporations. Let's define each of them and look at their advantages and disadvantages. This information also appears in Table 1.1.

> **Sole proprietorship** A type of business organization that has one owner. The owner is personally liable for paying the business's debts.

Sole Proprietorship A sole proprietorship, such as Mona's Nail Care, is a business that has one owner. That person is both the owner and the manager of the business. An advantage of a sole proprietorship is that the owner makes all the decisions for the business. A disadvantage is that if the business cannot pay its obligations, the business owner must pay them, which means that the owner could lose some of his or her personal assets (e.g., house or savings).

Sole proprietorships are easy to form. They end if the business closes or when the owner dies.

> **Partnership** A form of business organization that has at least two owners. The partners usually are personally liable for the partnership's debts.

Partnership A partnership, such as Hope and Sam, is a form of business ownership that has at least two owners (partners). Each partner acts as an owner of the company, which is an advantage because the partners can share the decision making and the risks of the business usually outlined in a partnership agreement. A disadvantage is that, as in a sole proprietorship, the partners' personal assets could be lost if the partnership cannot meet its obligations.

Partnerships are easy to form. They end when a partner dies or leaves the partnership, or when the partners decide to close the business.

TABLE 1.1 Types of Business Organizations

	Sole Proprietorship (Mona's Nail Care)	Partnership (Hope and Sam)	Corporation (eBay)	Limited Liability Corporations (LLC)
Ownership	Business owned by one person.	Business owned by more than one person.	Business owned by stockholders.	Business owned by a limited number of stockholders.
Formation	No formal filing or agreement necesssary to form.	Requires a partnership agreement to define the terms of partnership.	Requires filing with the state to be recognized.	Requires filing with the state a document called articles of incorporation.
Liability	Owner could lose personal assets to meet obligations of business.	Partners could lose personal assets to meet obligations of partnership.	Limited personal risk. Stockholders' loss is limited to their investment in the company.	Limited personal risk. Stockholders' loss is limited to their investment.
Closing	Ends with death of owner or closing of business.	Ends with death of partner or closing of business.	Can continue indefinitely.	May end with death of shareholder.

Corporation A corporation, such as eBay, is a business owned by stockholders. The corporation may have only a few stockholders, or it may have many stockholders. The stockholders are not personally liable for the corporation's debts, and they usually do not have input into the business decisions.

Corporations are more difficult to form than sole proprietorships or partnerships as the corporation must file with the state in order to gain the protections provided by this form of business. Corporations can exist indefinitely.

Liability Corporations (LLC) A limited liability corporation, such as the law firm of Battista, Tucker and Sam, LLC, is a business owned by a few stockholders. The stockholders are liable only to the extent of their investment in the firm and, unlike a corporation, have input in the business decisions. Like corporations, the LLC must file with the state in which it does business in order to gain the liability protection of this form of business.

Classifying Business Organizations

Whether we are looking at a sole proprietorship, a partnership, or a corporation, the business can be classified by what the business does to earn money. Companies are categorized as service, merchandise, or manufacturing businesses.

A limo service is a good example of a service company because it provides a service. The first part of this book focuses on service businesses.

Gap and JCPenney sell products. They are called merchandise companies. Merchandise companies can either make their own products or sell products that are made by another supplier. Companies such as Intel and Ford Motor Company that make their own products are called manufacturers. (See Table 1.2, p. 4.)

Definition of Accounting

Accounting (also called the accounting process) is a system that measures the activities of a business in financial terms. It provides reports and financial statements that show how the various transactions the business undertook (e.g., buying and

Corporation A type of business organization that is owned by stockholders. Stockholders usually are not personally liable for the corporation's debts.

Service company Business that provides a service.

Merchandise company Business that buys a product from a manufacturing company to sell to its customers.

Manufacturer Business that makes a product and sells it to its customers.

L01

TABLE 1.2 Examples of Service, Merchandise, and Manufacturing Businesses

Service Businesses	Merchandise Businesses	Manufacturing Businesses
Mona's Nail Care	Sears	Hershey's
eBay	JCPenney	Ford Motor Company
Dr. Wheeler, M.D.	Amazon.com	Toro
Accountemps	Home Depot	Levi's
Langley Landscaping	Gap	Intel

selling goods) affected the business. This accounting process performs the following functions:

- **Analyzing:** Looking at what happened and how the business was affected.
- **Recording:** Putting the information into the accounting system.
- **Classifying:** Grouping all the same activities (e.g., all purchases) together.
- **Summarizing:** Totaling the results.
- **Reporting:** Issuing the statements that tell the results of the previous functions.
- **Interpreting:** Examining the statements to determine how the various pieces of information they contain relate to each other.
- **Communication:** Providing the reports and financial statements to people who are interested in the information, such as the business's decision makers, investors, creditors, and government agencies (e.g., the Internal Revenue Service).

As you can see, a lot of people use these reports. A set of procedures and guidelines were developed to make sure that everyone prepares and interprets them the same way. These guidelines are known as generally accepted accounting principles (GAAP). International Financial Reporting Standards (IFRS) are a group of guidelines developed by the International Accounting Standards Board. The United States is considering a change from GAAP to IFRS. No final decisions have been made.

Now let's look at the difference between bookkeeping and accounting. Keep in mind that we use the terms *accounting* and the *accounting process* interchangeably.

Difference between Bookkeeping and Accounting

Confusion often arises concerning the difference between bookkeeping and accounting. Bookkeeping is the recording (record keeping) function of the accounting process; a bookkeeper enters accounting information in the company's books. An accountant takes that information and prepares the financial statements that are used to analyze the company's financial position. Accounting involves many complex activities. Often, it includes the preparation of tax and financial reports, budgeting, and analyses of financial information.

Today, computers are used for routine bookkeeping operations that used to take weeks or months to complete. This book explains how the advantages of the computer can be applied to a manual accounting system by using hands-on knowledge of how accounting works. Basic accounting knowledge is needed even though computers can do routine tasks. QuickBooks, Excel, and Peachtree are popular software packages in use today.

LEARNING UNIT 1-1 THE ACCOUNTING EQUATION
Assets, Liabilities, and Equities

Let's begin our study of accounting concepts and procedures by looking at a small business: Mia Wong's law practice. Mia decided to open her practice at the end of August. She consulted her accountant before she made her decision, and he gave her some important information. First, he told her the new business would be considered a separate business entity whose finances had to be kept separate and distinct from

Generally accepted accounting principles (GAAP) The procedures and guidelines that must be followed during the accounting process.

International Financial Reporting Standards (IFRS) A group of accounting standards and procedures that if adopted by the US, could replace GAAP.

Bookkeeping The recording function of the accounting process.

Mia's personal finances. The accountant went on to say that all transactions can be analyzed using the basic accounting equation: Assets = Liabilities + Owner's Equity.

Mia had never heard of the basic accounting equation. She listened carefully as the accountant explained the terms used in the equation and how the equation works.

Assets Cash, land, supplies, office equipment, buildings, and other properties of value *owned* by a firm are called assets.

Equities The rights of financial claim to the assets are called equities. Equities belong to those who supply the assets. If you are the only person to supply assets to the firm, you have the sole rights or financial claims to them. For example, if you supply the law firm with $6,000 in cash and $8,000 in office equipment, your equity in the firm is $14,000.

Relationship between Assets and Equities The relationship between assets and equities is

Assets = Equities
(Total value of items *owned* by business)   (Total claims against the assets)

The total dollar value of the assets of your law firm will be equal to the total dollar value of the financial claims to those assets, that is, equal to the total dollar value of the equities.

The total dollar value is broken down on the left-hand side of the equation to show the specific items of value owned by the business and on the right-hand side to show the types of claims against the assets owned.

Liabilities A firm may have to borrow money to buy more assets; when it does, it *buys assets on account* (buy now, pay later). Suppose the law firm purchases a new computer for $3,000 on account from Dell, and the company is willing to wait 10 days for payment. The law firm has created a liability: an obligation to pay that comes due in the future. Dell is called the creditor. This liability—the amount owed to Dell—gives the store the right, or the financial claim, to $3,000 of the law firm's assets. When Dell is paid, the store's rights to the assets of the law firm will end because the obligation has been paid off.

Basic Accounting Equation To best understand the various claims to a business's assets, accountants divide equities into two parts. The claims of creditors—outside persons or businesses—are labeled *liabilities*. The claim of the business's owner is labeled owner's equity. Let's see how the accounting equation looks now.

Assets =   Equities

1. Liabilities: rights of creditors
2. Owner's equity: rights of owner

Assets = Liabilities + Owner's Equity

The total value of all the assets of a firm equals the combined total value of the financial claims of the creditors (liabilities) and the claims of the owners (owner's equity). This calculation is known as the basic accounting equation. The basic accounting equation provides a basis for understanding the conventional accounting system of a business. The equation records business transactions in a logical and orderly way that shows their impact on the company's assets, liabilities, and owner's equity.

Importance of Creditors Another way of presenting the basic accounting equation is

Assets − Liabilities = Owner's Equity

This form of the equation stresses the importance of creditors. The owner's rights to the business's assets are determined after the rights of the creditors are subtracted. In other words, creditors have first claim to assets. If a firm has no

Assets Properties (resources) of value owned by a business (cash, supplies, equipment, land).

Equities The rights or financial claim of creditors (liabilities) and owners (owner's equity) who supply the assets to a firm.

Liabilities Obligations that come due in the future. Liabilities are the financial rights or claims of creditors to assets.

Creditor Someone who has a claim to assets.

Owner's equity Rights or financial claims to the assets of a business (in the accounting equation, assets minus liabilities).

L02

Basic accounting equation Assets = Liabilities + Owner's Equity.

Capital The owner's investment of equity in the company.

liabilities—therefore no creditors—the owner has the total rights to assets. Another term for the owner's current investment, or equity, in the business's assets is capital.

As Mia Wong's law firm engages in business transactions (paying bills, serving customers, and so on), changes will take place in the assets, liabilities, and owner's equity (capital). Let's analyze some of these transactions.

> ✗ ➔ ○
> **COACHING TIP**

In accounting, capital does not mean cash. Capital is the owner's current investment, or equity, in the assets of the business.

Transaction A Aug. 28: Mia invests $6,000 in cash and $200 of office equipment into the business.

On August 28, Mia withdraws $6,000 from her personal bank account and deposits the money in the law firm's newly opened bank account. She also invests $200 of office equipment in the business. She plans to be open for business on September 1. With the help of her accountant, Mia begins to prepare the accounting records for the business. We put this information into the basic accounting equation as follows:

Assets				= Liabilities + Owner's Equity
Cash	+	Office Equipment	=	Mia Wong, Capital
$6,000	+	$200	=	$6,200
			$6,200 = $6,200	

Note that the total value of the assets, cash, and office equipment—$6,200—is equal to the combined total value of liabilities (none, so far) and owner's equity ($6,200). Remember, Mia has supplied all the cash and office equipment, so she has the sole financial claim to the assets. Note how the heading "Mia Wong, Capital" is written under the owner's equity heading. The $6,200 is Mia's investment, or equity, in the firm's assets.

Transaction B Aug. 29: Law practice buys office equipment for cash, $500.

From the initial investment of $6,000 cash, the law firm buys $500 worth of office equipment (such as a computer desk), which lasts a long time, whereas supplies (such as pens) tend to be used up relatively quickly.

Supplies One type of asset acquired by a firm; it has a much shorter life than equipment.

	Assets				= Liabilities + Owner's Equity
	Cash	+	Office Equipment	=	Mia Wong, Capital
Beginning Balance	$6,000	+	$200	=	$6,200
Transaction	−500		+500		
Ending Balance	$5,500	+	$700	=	$6,200
				$6,200 = $6,200	

Shift in assets A shift that occurs when the composition of the assets has changed but the total of the assets remains the same.

Shift in Assets As a result of the last transaction, the law office has less cash but has increased its amount of office equipment. This shift in assets indicates that the makeup of the assets has changed, but the total of the assets remains the same.

Suppose you go food shopping at Walmart with $100 and spend $60. Now you have two assets, food and money. The composition of your assets has *shifted*—you have more food and less money than you did—but the *total* of the assets has not increased or decreased. The total value of the food, $60, plus the cash, $40, is still $100. When you borrow money from the bank, on the other hand, you increase cash (an asset) and increase liabilities at the same time. This action results in an increase in assets, not just a shift.

An accounting equation can remain in balance even if only one side is updated. The key point to remember is that the left-hand-side total of assets must always equal the right-hand-side total of liabilities and owner's equity.

Transaction C Aug. 30: Buys additional office equipment on account, $300.

The law firm purchases an additional $300 worth of chairs and desks from Wilmington Company. Instead of demanding cash right away, Wilmington agrees to deliver the equipment and to allow up to 60 days for the law practice to pay the invoice (bill).

This liability, or obligation to pay in the future, has some interesting effects on the basic accounting equation. Wilmington Company accepts as payment a partial claim against the assets of the law practice. This claim exists until the law firm pays off the bill. This unwritten promise to pay the creditor is a liability called accounts payable.

Accounts payable Amounts owed to creditors that result from the purchase of goods or services on account—a liability.

Assets			=	Liabilities	+	Owner's Equity	
Cash	+	Office Equipment	=	Accounts Payable	+	Mia Wong, Capital	
$5,500	+	$ 700	=			$6,200	Beginning Balance
		+300		+$300			Transaction
$5,500	+	$1,000	=	$300	+	$6,200	Ending Balance
			$6,500 = $6,500				

When this information is analyzed, we can see that the law practice increased what it owes (accounts payable) as well as what it owns (office equipment) by $300. The law practice gains $300 in an asset but also takes on an obligation to pay Wilmington Company at a future date.

The owner's equity remains unchanged. This transaction results in an increase of total assets from $6,200 to $6,500.

Finally, note that after each transaction the basic accounting equation remains in balance.

LEARNING UNIT 1-1 REVIEW

AT THIS POINT you should be able to do the following:

- Define and explain the purpose of the Sarbanes-Oxley Act.
- Define and explain the differences between sole proprietorships, partnerships, and corporations.
- Explain the difference between GAAP and IFRS.
- List the functions of accounting.
- Compare and contrast bookkeeping and accounting.
- Explain the role of the computer as an accounting tool.
- State the purpose of the accounting equation.
- Explain the difference between liabilities and owner's equity.
- Define capital.
- Explain the difference between a shift in assets and an increase in assets.

To test your understanding of this material, complete Instant Replay: Self-Review Quiz 1-1. The blank forms you need for all Self-Review quizzes and end-of-chapter material throughout the textbook can be found in the *Study Guide and Working Papers*. The solution to the quiz immediately follows here in the text. If you have difficulty doing the problems, review Learning Unit 1-1 and the solution to the quiz along with a detailed explanation called Play by Play: Extra Help on Self-Review Quiz with Jeff Slater, your author. Be sure to check the Slater Web site for student study aids.

Keep in mind that learning accounting is like learning to type: The more you practice, the better you become. You will not be an expert in one day. Be patient. It will all come together.

Instant Replay Self-Review Quiz 1-1

Record the following transactions in the basic accounting equation:

1. Gracie Ryan invests $17,000 cash to begin a real estate company.
2. The real estate company buys $600 of computer equipment from Walmart for cash.
3. The real estate company buys $800 of additional computer equipment on account from Best Buy.

Solution to Instant Replay: Self-Review Quiz 1-1

	Assets			=	Liabilities	+	Owner's Equity
	Cash	+	Computer Equipment	=	Accounts Payable	+	Gracie Ryan, Capital
	+$17,000						+$17,000
1. Balance	17,000			=			17,000
	−600		+$600				
2. Balance	16,400	+	600	=			17,000
			+800		+$800		
3. Ending Balance	$16,400	+	$1,400	=	$800	+	$17,000

$17,800 = $17,800

PLAY BY PLAY: EXTRA HELP ON SELF-REVIEW QUIZ 1-1

Let's review first: The left side of the accounting equation shows what is owned by the business and the right side of the equation shows you who supplied those assets to a business. Now let's look at the transactions in the solution:

Transaction 1: In your head you must say to yourself, "What did the business get and how did it get it?" The business is getting or increasing its cash by $17,000 and that cash is being supplied by Gracie Ryan. Think of Gracie as increasing her rights in the business since she is supplying cash. Keep in mind that capital does not mean cash. Instead it is what the owner supplies to the business. (Gracie may in the future supply other items to the business.)

So the end result is to put $17,000 on the left side of the equation under cash and put $17,000 under Gracie Ryan, Capital on the right side. The sum of the left side must equal the sum on the right side.

Transaction 2: Here we are NOT looking at the personal finances of Gracie. You must focus on the business. What did the business get and who supplied it to the business?

In this transaction the business is getting $600 of computer equipment by using some of its cash. *It is shifting its assets: more equipment for less cash*. Note that capital is not affected since Gracie has not invested anything new into the business.

Note that the right side of the equation is not touched, but the equation still remains in the balance. We are just rearranging the composition of the assets.

Transaction 3: Now the business is getting more equipment but is not paying cash. The equipment is being supplied by a creditor called Accounts Payable. Hopefully in the future the business will be able to pay the creditor back the $800 that it owes. The end result is that the business now has $1,400 in equipment. Note that capital is not affected since no new investments were made by Gracie into the business.

Summary: At the end of these three transactions this company is made up of two assets, Cash $16,400 and Computer Equipment $1,400. The total of the assets was supplied by creditors $800 and the owner Gracie Ryan, Capital $17,000. The sum of the left side ($17,800) must equal the sum of the right side ($17,800).

COACHING TIP

$17,800 $17,800

LEARNING UNIT 1-2 THE BALANCE SHEET

In the first learning unit, the transactions for Mia Wong's law firm were recorded in the accounting equation. The transactions we recorded occurred before the law firm opened for business. A statement called a balance sheet or statement of financial position can show the financial position of a company before it opened. The balance sheet is a formal statement that presents the information from the ending balances of both sides of the accounting equation. Think of the balance sheet as a snapshot of the business's financial position as of a particular date.

Let's look at the balance sheet of Mia Wong's law practice for August 31, 201X, shown in Figure 1.1. The figures in the balance sheet come from the ending balances of the accounting equation for the law practice as shown in Learning Unit 1-1.

Balance sheet A statement, as of a particular date, that shows the amount of assets owned by a business as well as the amount of claims (liabilities and owner's equity) against these assets. Also known as statement of financial position.

COACHING TIP

The balance sheet shows the company's financial position as of a particular date. (In our example, that date is at the end of August.)

FIGURE 1.1
The Balance Sheet

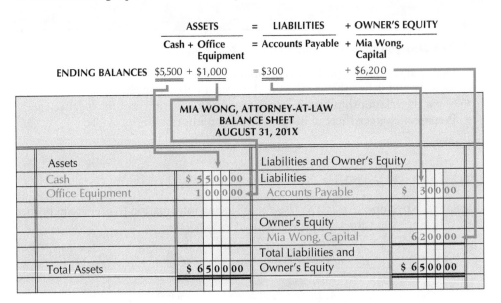

Note in Figure 1.1 that the assets owned by the law practice appear on the left-hand side and that the liabilities and owner's equity appear on the right-hand side. Both sides equal $6,500. This *balance* between left and right gives the balance sheet its name. In later chapters we look at other ways to set up a balance sheet.

Points to Remember in Preparing a Balance Sheet

The Heading The heading of the balance sheet provides the following information:

- The company name: Mia Wong, Attorney-at-Law
- The name of the statement: Balance Sheet
- The date for which the report is prepared: August 31, 201X

Use of the Dollar Sign Note that the dollar sign is not repeated each time a figure appears. As shown in Figure 1.2, the balance sheet for Mia Wong's law practice, it usually is placed to the left of each column's top figure and to the left of the column's total.

Distinguishing the Total When adding numbers down a column, use a single line above the total and a double line beneath it. A single line means that the numbers above it have been added or subtracted. A double line indicates a total. It is important to align the numbers in the column; many errors occur because these figures are not lined up. These rules are the same for all accounting reports.

The balance sheet gives Mia the information she needs to see the law firm's financial position before it opens for business. This information does not tell her, however, whether the firm made a profit.

FIGURE 1.2 Partial Balance Sheet

MIA WONG, ATTORNEY-AT-LAW BALANCE SHEET AUGUST 31, 201X		
Assets		
Cash	$ 5 5 0 0 00	A single line means the numbers above it have been added or subtracted.
Office Equipment	1 0 0 0 00	
Total Assets	$ 6 5 0 0 00	A double line indicates a total.

LEARNING UNIT 1-2 REVIEW

AT THIS POINT you should be able to do the following:

- Define and state the purpose of a balance sheet.
- Identify and define the elements making up a balance sheet.
- Show the relationship between the accounting equation and the balance sheet.
- Prepare a balance sheet in proper form from information provided.

Instant Replay ○ Self-Review Quiz 1-2

The date is November 30, 201X. Use the following information to prepare in proper form a balance sheet for Janning Company:

Accounts Payable	$40,000
Cash	18,000
A. Janning, Capital	9,000
Office Equipment	31,000

Solution to Instant Replay: Self-Review Quiz 1-2

JANNING COMPANY BALANCE SHEET NOVEMBER 30, 201X										
Assets				Liabilities and Owner's Equity						
Cash	$18	0	00	00	Liabilities					
Office Equipment	31	0	00	00	Accounts Payable	$ 40	0	0	00	
					Owner's Equity					
					A. Janning, Capital	9	0	0	00	
					Total Liabilities and					
Total Assets	$ 4 9	0	00	00	Owner's Equity	$ 49	0	0	00	

FIGURE 1.3
Balance Sheet

Capital does not mean cash. The capital amount is the owner's current investment of assets in the business.

PLAY BY PLAY: EXTRA HELP ON SELF-REVIEW QUIZ 1-2

Let's review first: A photo of your family is like a balance sheet: It gives you a history of your family as of a particular date. The balance sheet is a formal report that lists assets, liabilities, and owner's equity for a business as of a particular date.

Before preparing the report, identify whether each item is an asset, liability, or owner's equity. Accounts payable is a liability. Hopefully the business will be able to pay. Cash is an asset, or something of value owned by the business. A. Janning, Capital is owner's equity, representing the value of the assets which the owner is supplying to the business.

The heading of a balance sheet answers three questions:

Who? Janning Company

What report? Balance Sheet

When? November 30, 201X

The left side of the balance sheet lists out the assets: cash, and office equipment.

The right side lists out who supplies the assets to the business: creditors (accounts payable) or the owner, A. Janning, Capital. Use single lines to add and double lines for totals. The sum of the left side must equal the sum of the right side.

LEARNING UNIT 1-3 THE ACCOUNTING EQUATION EXPANDED:
Revenue, Expenses, and Withdrawals

● L03

As soon as Mia Wong's office opened on September 1, she began performing legal services for her clients and earning revenue for the business. At the same time, as a part of doing business, she incurred various expenses such as rent.

When Mia asked her accountant how these transactions fit into the accounting equation, she began by defining some terms.

Revenue

A service company earns revenue when it provides services to its clients. Mia's law firm earned revenue when she provided legal services to her clients for legal fees. When revenue is earned, owner's equity is increased. In effect, revenue is a subdivision of owner's equity.

Revenue An amount earned by performing services for customers or selling goods to customers; it can be in the form of cash or accounts receivable. A subdivision of owner's equity: As revenue increases, owner's equity increases.

Accounts receivable An asset that indicates amounts owed by customers.

Assets are increased. The increase is in the form of cash if the client pays right away. If the client promises to pay in the future, the increase is called accounts receivable. When revenue is earned, the transaction is recorded as an increase in revenue and an increase in assets (either as cash or as accounts receivable, depending on whether it was paid right away or will be paid in the future).

Expenses

Expense A cost incurred in running a business by consuming goods or services in producing revenue. A subdivision of owner's equity.

A business's expenses are the costs the company incurs in carrying on operations in its effort to create revenue. Expenses are also a subdivision of owner's equity; when expenses are incurred, they *decrease* owner's equity. Expenses can be paid for in cash or they can be charged.

Net Income/Net Loss

Net income When revenue totals more than expenses, the result is net income.

When revenue totals more than expenses, net income is the result; when expenses total more than revenue, net loss is the result.

Net loss When expenses total more than revenue, the result is net loss.

Withdrawals

Withdrawals A subdivision of owner's equity that records money or other assets an owner withdraws from a business for personal use.

At some point Mia Wong may need to withdraw cash or other assets from the business to pay living or other personal expenses that do not relate to the business. We will record these transactions in an account called withdrawals. Sometimes this account is called the *owner's drawing account*. Withdrawals is a subdivision of owner's equity that records personal expenses not related to the business. Withdrawals decrease owner's equity (see Figure 1.4 below).

It is important to remember the difference between expenses and withdrawals. Expenses relate to business operations; withdrawals are the result of personal needs outside the normal operations of the business.

Now let's analyze the September transactions for Mia Wong's law firm using an expanded accounting equation that includes withdrawals, revenues, and expenses.

Expanded accounting equation Assets = Liabilities + Capital – Withdrawals + Revenue – Expenses.

Expanded Accounting Equation

Transaction D Sept. 1–30: Provided legal services for cash, $2,000.

Transactions A, B, and C were discussed earlier, when the law office was being formed in August. See Learning Unit 1.1.

FIGURE 1.4
Owner's Equity

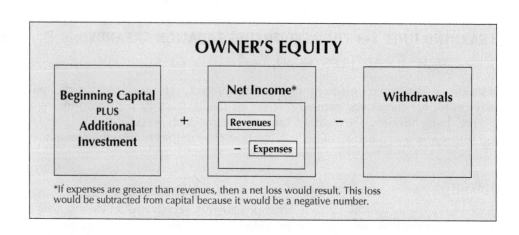

Assets			=	Liabilities	+		Owner's Equity			
Cash	+ Accts. Rec.	+ Office Equip.	= Accts. Pay.	+ M. Wong, Capital	– M. Wong, Withdr.	+ Revenue	– Expenses		
$5,500		+ $1,000	= $300	+ $6,200					Balance Forward
+2,000						+ $2,000			
$7,500		+ $1,000	= $300	+ $6,200		+ $2,000			Ending Balance
		$8,500 = $8,500							

In the law firm's first month of operation, a total of $2,000 in cash was received for legal services performed. In the accounting equation, the asset Cash is increased by $2,000. Revenue is also increased by $2,000, resulting in an increase in total owner's equity.

A revenue column was added to the basic accounting equation. Amounts are recorded in the revenue column when they are earned. They are also recorded in the assets column under Cash and/or Accounts Receivable (see also Transaction E below). Do not think of revenue as an asset. It is part of owner's equity. It is the revenue that creates an inward flow of cash and accounts receivable.

COACHING TIP

Remember: Accounts receivables result from earning revenue even when cash is not yet received.

Record an expense when it is incurred, whether it is paid immediately or is to be paid later.

Transaction E Sept. 1–30: Provided legal services on account, $3,000.

Assets			=	Liabilities	+		Owner's Equity			
Cash	+ Accts. Rec.	+ Office Equip.	= Accts. Pay.	+ M. Wong, Capital	– M. Wong, Withdr.	+ Revenue	– Expenses		
$7,500		+ $ 1,000	= $ 300	+ $6,200		+ $2,000			Bal. for. Trans.
	+$3,000					+ 3,000			
$7,500	+ $3,000	+ $ 1,000	= $ 300	+ $6,200		+ $5,000			End. Bal.
		$11,500	= $11,500						

Mia's law practice performed legal work on account for $3,000. The firm did not receive the cash for these earned legal fees; it accepted an unwritten promise from these clients that payment would be received in the future.

Transaction F Sept. 1–30: Received $900 cash as partial payment from previous services performed on account.

During September some of Mia's clients who had received services and promised to pay in the future decided to reduce what they owed the practice by making payment of $900. This decision is shown as follows on the expanded accounting equation:

Assets			=	Liabilities	+		Owner's Equity			
Cash	+ Accts. Rec.	+ Office Equip.	= Accts. Pay.	+ M. Wong, Capital	– M. Wong, Withdr.	+ Revenue	– Expenses		
$7,500	+ $3,000	+ $ 1,000	= $ 300	+ $6,200		+ $5,000			Bal. for. Trans.
+900	–900								
$8,400	+ $2,100	+ $ 1,000	= $ 300	+ $6,200		+ $5,000			End. Bal.
		$11,500	= $11,500						

The law firm increased the asset Cash by $900 and reduced another asset, Accounts Receivable, by $900. The *total* of assets does not change. The right-hand side of the expanded accounting equation has not been touched because the total on the left-hand side of the equation has not changed. The revenue was recorded when it was earned (see Transaction E), and the *same revenue cannot be recorded twice*. This transaction analyzes the situation *after* the revenue has been previously earned and recorded. Transaction F shows a shift in assets resulting in more cash and less accounts receivable.

Transaction G Sept. 1–30: Paid salaries expense, $700.

	Assets			= Liabilities	+			Owner's Equity		
	Cash	+ Accts. Rec.	+ Office Equip.	= Accts. Pay.	+ M. Wong, Capital	– M. Wong, Withdr.	+ Revenue	– Expenses
Bal. for Trans.	$8,400	+ $2,100	+ $ 1,000	= $ 300	+ $6,200		+ $5,000	
	–700							+ $700
End. Bal.	$7,700	+ $2,100	+ $ 1,000	= $ 300	+ $6,200		+ $5,000	– $700
			$10,800	=	$10,800			

As expenses increase, they decrease owner's equity. This incurred expense of $700 reduces the cash by $700. Although the expense was paid, the total of our expenses to date has *increased* by $700. Keep in mind that owner's equity decreases as expenses increase, so the accounting equation remains in balance, because expenses are deducted from Owner's Equity.

Transaction H Sept. 1–30: Paid rent expense, $400.

	Assets			= Liabilities	+			Owner's Equity		
	Cash	+ Accts. Rec.	+ Office Equip.	= Accts. Pay.	+ M. Wong, Capital	– M. Wong, Withdr.	+ Revenue	– Expenses
Bal. for Trans.	$7,700	+ $2,100	+ $ 1,000	= $ 300	+ $6,200		+ $5,000	– $700
	–400							+400
End. Bal.	$7,300	+ $2,100	+ $ 1,000	= $ 300	+ $6,200		+ $5,000	– $1,100
			$10,400	=	$10,400			

During September the practice incurred rent expenses of $400. This rent was not paid in advance; it was paid when it came due. The payment of rent reduces the asset Cash by $400 as well as increases the expenses of the firm, resulting in a decrease in owner's equity. The firm's expenses are now $1,100.

Transaction I Sept. 1–30: Incurred advertising expenses of $200, to be paid next month.

	Assets			= Liabilities	+			Owner's Equity		
	Cash	+ Accts. Rec.	+ Office Equip.	= Accts. Pay.	+ M. Wong, Capital	– M. Wong, Withdr.	+ Revenue	– Expenses
Bal. for Trans.	$7,300	+ $2,100	+ $ 1,000	= $ 300	+ $6,200		+ $5,000	– $1,100
				+200				+200
End. Bal.	$7,300	+ $2,100	+ $ 1,000	= $ 500	+ $6,200		+ $5,000	– $1,300
			$10,400	=	$10,400			

Mia ran an ad in the local newspaper and incurred an expense of $200. This increase in expenses caused a corresponding decrease in owner's equity. Because Mia has not paid the newspaper for the advertising yet, she owes $200. Thus her liabilities (Accounts Payable) increase by $200. Eventually, when the bill comes in and is paid, both Cash and Accounts Payable will be decreased.

Transaction J Sept. 1–30: Mia withdrew $100 for personal use.

	Assets		= Liabilities	+		Owner's Equity			
Cash	+ Accts. Rec.	+ Office Equip.	= Accts. Pay.	+ M. Wong, Capital	– M. Wong, Withdr.	+ Revenue	– Expenses		
$7,300	+ $2,100	+ $ 1,000	= $ 500	+ $6,200		+ $5,000	– $1,300		Bal. for. Trans.
–100					+$100				
$7,200	+ $2,100	+ $ 1,000	= $ 500	+ $6,200	– $100	+ $5,000	– $1,300		End. Bal.
		$10,300	= $10,300						

By taking $100 for personal use, Mia *increased* her withdrawals from the business by $100 and decreased the asset Cash by $100. Note that as withdrawals increase, the owner's equity *decreases*. Keep in mind that a withdrawal is *not* a business expense. It is a subdivision of owner's equity that records money or other assets an owner withdraws from the business for *personal* use.

Subdivision of Owner's Equity   Take a moment to review the subdivisions of owner's equity:

- As capital increases, owner's equity increases (see transaction A).
- As withdrawals increase, owner's equity decreases (see transaction J).
- As revenue increases, owner's equity increases (see transaction D and E).
- As expenses increase, owner's equity decreases (see transaction G through I).

Mia Wong's Expanded Accounting Equation   The following is a summary of the expanded accounting equation for Mia Wong's law firm.

			Mia Wong Attorney-at-Law Expanded Accounting Equation: A Summary						
Assets			**= Liabilities**	**+**		**Owner's Equity**			
Cash	+ Accts. Rec.	+ Office Equip.	= Accts. Pay.	+ M. Wong, Capital	– M. Wong, Withdr.	+ Revenue	– Expenses		
$6,000		+$200 =		+$6,200					A.
6,000		+ 200 =		6,200					Balance
–500		+500							B.
5,500		+ 700 =		6,200					Balance
		+300	+$300						C.
5,500 +		1,000 =	300 +	6,200					Balance
+2,000						+$2,000			D.
7,500		+ 1,000 =	300 +	6,200		+ 2,000			Balance
	+ $3,000					+3,000			E.
7,500 +	3,000 +	1,000 =	300 +	6,200		+ 5,000			Balance
+900	–900								F.
8,400 +	2,100 +	1,000 =	300 +	6,200		+ 5,000			Balance

(continued on page 16)

	Assets			= Liabilities	+			Owner's Equity		
	Cash +	Accts. Rec.	+ Office Equip.	= Accts. Pay.	+ M. Wong, Capital	− M. Wong, Withdr.	+	Revenue	−	Expenses
G.	−700									+$700
Balance	7,700 +	2,100 +	1,000 =	300 +	6,200		+	5,000	−	700
H.	−400									+400
Balance	7,300 +	2,100 +	1,000 =	300 +	6,200		+	5,000	−	1,100
I.				+200						+200
Balance	7,300 +	2,100 +	1,000 =	500 +	6,200		+	5,000	−	1,300
J.	−100					+$100				
End Balance	$7,200 +	$2,100 +	$1,000 =	$500 +	$6,200 −	$100 +		$5,000	−	$1,300

Mia Wong
Attorney-at-Law
Expanded Accounting Equation: A Summary

$$\$10,300 = \$10,300$$

LEARNING UNIT 1-3 REVIEW

AT THIS POINT you should be able to do the following:

- Define and explain the difference between revenue and expenses.
- Define and explain the difference between net income and net loss.
- Explain the subdivisions of owner's equity.
- Explain the effects of withdrawals, revenue, and expenses on owner's equity.
- Record transactions in an expanded accounting equation and balance the basic accounting equation as a means of checking the accuracy of your calculations.

Instant Replay ◌ Self-Review Quiz 1-3

Record the following transactions into the expanded accounting equation for the Bing Company. Note that all titles have a beginning balance.

1. Received cash revenue, $4,000.
2. Billed customers for services rendered, $6,000.
3. Received a bill for telephone expenses (to be paid next month), $125.
4. Bob Bing withdrew cash for personal use, $500.
5. Received $1,000 from customers in partial payment for services performed in transaction 2.

Solution to Instant Replay Self-Review Quiz 1-3

	Assets			= Liabilities	+			Owner's Equity		
	Cash +	Accts. Rec.	+ Cleaning Equip.	= Accts. Pay.	+ B. Bing, Capital	− B. Bing, Withdr.	+	Revenue	−	Expenses
Beg. Balance	$10,000 +	$2,500 +	$6,500 =	$1,000 +	$11,800 −	$ 800 +		$9,000	−	$2,000
1.	+4,000							+4,000		
Balance	14,000 +	2,500 +	6,500 =	1,000 +	11,800 −	800 +		13,000	−	2,000
2.		+6,000						+6,000		
Balance	14,000 +	8,500 +	6,500 =	1,000 +	11,800 −	800 +		19,000	−	2,000
3.				+125						+125
Balance	14,000 +	8,500 +	6,500 =	1,125 +	11,800 −	800 +		19,000	−	2,125

(continued on page 17)

Assets			= Liabilities		+	Owner's Equity				
Cash	+ Accts. Rec.	+ Cleaning Equip.	= Accts. Pay.	+ B. Bing, Capital	– B. Bing, Withdr.	+ Revenue	– Expenses			
–500					+$500			4.		
13,500	+ 8,500 +	6,500 =	1,125 +	11,800 –	1,300 +	19,000 –	2,125	Balance		
+1,000	–1,000							5.		
$14,500	+ $7,500 +	$6,500 =	$1,125 +	$11,800 –	$1,300 +	$19,000 –	$2,125	End. Balance		
		$28,500 = $28,500								

PLAY BY PLAY: EXTRA HELP ON SELF-REVIEW QUIZ 1-3

Let's review first: You only record revenue when it is earned. What can the business get? Cash and/or promises from customers called Accounts Receivable. Revenue is not an asset but does provide an inward flow of assets into the business. Revenue is part of owner's equity. Think of expenses as always increasing in a business. The end result will be a decrease in owner's equity. Expenses are recorded when they happen and can be paid for by cash or charged as Accounts Payable.

Withdrawals work just like expenses as they also are deducted from Owner's Equity, but they represent personal withdrawals by the owner. Expenses and withdrawals are not recorded together. Each has a separate title.

Transaction 1: The company has done the work. It now records revenue of $4,000 in the revenue column (we only put numbers in this column when we do the work). This time the inward flow of assets from the revenue is all in the form of cash of $4,000.

Transaction 2: This time the company does the work but is not getting the cash. It is receiving promises that it will be paid in the future. You record the $6,000 in the revenue column because you did the work. The inward flow from this revenue is not cash but promises called Accounts Receivable. Thus, the Accounts Receivable column is increased by $6,000.

Transaction 3: An expense has happened and should be recorded whether money is paid or not. The expenses for telephone have INCREASED by $125, resulting in the total expenses rising to $2,125. As expenses in a business rise, the end result is a reduction in owner's equity.

Since the expense was charged, the $125 is recorded under Accounts Payable because hopefully the expense will be paid in the future. At this point this telephone expense has created a liability. Remember that an expense is not a liability.

Transaction 4: This transaction relates to a personal transaction and does not affect any expenses in the business. Bob Bing takes $500 cash from the business. Think of Bob as receiving the $500, but in reality his owner's rights will be reduced. This is shown by a $500 increase under withdrawals, which now results in a total of $1,300 (a reduction to owner's equity) and a decrease to cash. Note that expenses are not affected since this is a personal transaction.

Transaction 5: No new work is done, so we do not earn or record any new revenue. Here customers are paying part of what they owe. The result is that company cash increased by $1,000 and Accounts Receivable is reduced by $1,000. This is a shift in assets: more cash, less accounts receivable.

Summary: Note the four subdivisions of owner's equity: Capital, Withdrawals, Revenues, and Expenses. As capital and revenue increases, owner's equity will increase. As expenses and withdrawals increase, owner's equity will decrease. Revenue is not an asset. Rather, it provides assets in the form of cash and/or accounts receivable. Only record revenue when work is done. Only record expenses when they happen, regardless of whether cash is paid.

COACHING TIP

Revenue is shown when earned, not when cash is received.

◯ LO4   LEARNING UNIT 1-4 PREPARING FINANCIAL STATEMENTS

Mia Wong would like to be able to find out if her firm is making a profit, so she asks her accountant if he can measure the firm's financial performance on a monthly basis. Her accountant replies that a number of financial statements that he can prepare, such as the income statement, will show Mia how well the law firm has performed over a specific period of time. The accountant can use the information in the income statement to prepare other reports.

The Income Statement

Income statement An accounting statement that details the performance of a firm (revenue minus expenses) for a specific period of time.

An income statement is an accounting statement that shows business results in terms of revenue and expenses. If revenues are greater than expenses, the report shows net income. If expenses are greater than revenues, the report shows net loss. An income statement typically covers 1, 3, 6, or 12 months. It cannot cover more than one year. The statement shows the result of all revenues and expenses throughout the entire period and not just as of a specific date. The income statement for Mia Wong's law firm is shown in Figure 1.5.

Points to Remember in Preparing an Income Statement

Heading The heading of an income statement tells the company's name, the name of the statement, and the period of time the statement covers.

COACHING TIP

The income statement is prepared from data found in the revenue and expense columns of the expanded accounting equation. The inside column of numbers ($700, $400, $200) is used to subtotal all expenses ($1,300) before subtracting from revenue.

The Setup As you can see on the income statement, the inside column of numbers ($700, $400, and $200) is used to subtotal all expenses ($1,300) before subtracting them from revenue ($5,000 − $1,300 = $3,700).

FIGURE 1.5
The Income Statement

MIA WONG, ATTORNEY-AT-LAW INCOME STATEMENT FOR MONTH ENDED SEPTEMBER 30, 201X		
Revenue:		
Legal Fees		$ 5 0 0 0 00
Operating Expenses:		
Salaries Expense	$ 7 0 0 00	
Rent Expense	4 0 0 00	
Advertising Expense	2 0 0 00	
Total Operating Expenses		1 3 0 0 00
Net Income		$ 3 7 0 0 00

Operating expenses may be listed in alphabetical order, in order of largest amounts to smallest, or in a set order established by the accountant.

The Statement of Owner's Equity

Statement of owner's equity A financial statement that reveals the change in capital. The ending figure for capital is then placed on the balance sheet.

As we said, the income statement is a business statement that shows business results in terms of revenue and expenses, but how does net income or net loss affect owner's equity? To find out, we have to look at a second type of statement, the statement of owner's equity.

The statement of owner's equity shows for a certain period of time what changes occurred in Mia Wong, Capital. The statement of owner's equity is shown in Figure 1.6.

The capital of Mia Wong can be

Increased by: Owner Investment
Net Income (Revenue – Expenses) and Revenue Greater Than Expenses
Decreased by: Owner Withdrawals
Net Loss (Revenue – Expenses) and Expenses Greater Than Revenue

---

Remember, a withdrawal is *not* a business expense and thus, is not involved in the calculation of net income or net loss on the income statement. It appears on the statement of owner's equity. The statement of owner's equity summarizes the effects of all the subdivisions of owner's equity (revenue, expenses, withdrawals) on beginning capital. The ending capital figure ($9,800) will be the beginning figure in the next statement of owner's equity.

Suppose Mia's law firm had operated at a loss in the month of September. Suppose that instead of net income, a $400 net loss occurred and an additional investment of $700 was made on September 15. Figure 1.7 shows how the statement would look with this net loss and additional investment.

COACHING TIP

If this statement of owner's equity is omitted, the information will be included in the owner's equity section of the balance sheet.

FIGURE 1.6
Statement of Owner's Equity—Net Income

MIA WONG, ATTORNEY-AT-LAW STATEMENT OF OWNER'S EQUITY FOR MONTH ENDED SEPTEMBER 30, 201X		
Mia Wong, Capital, September 1, 201X		$ 6 2 0 0 00
Net Income for September	$ 3 7 0 0 00	
Less Withdrawals for September	1 0 0 00	
Increase in Capital		3 6 0 0 00
Mia Wong, Capital, September 30, 201X		$ 9 8 0 0 00

Comes from Income Statement

FIGURE 1.7
Statement of Owner's Equity—Net Loss

MIA WONG, ATTORNEY-AT-LAW STATEMENT OF OWNER'S EQUITY FOR MONTH ENDED SEPTEMBER 30, 201X		
Mia Wong, Capital, September 1, 201X		$ 6 2 0 0 00
Additional Investment, September 15, 201X		7 0 0 00
Total Investment for September*		$ 6 9 0 0 00
Less: Net Loss for September	$ 4 0 0 00	
Withdrawals for September	1 0 0 00	
Decrease in Capital		5 0 0 00
Mia Wong, Capital, September 30, 201X		$ 6 4 0 0 00

*Beginning capital and additional investments.

The Balance Sheet

Now let's look at how to prepare a balance sheet from the expanded accounting equation (see Figure 1.8, p. 20). As you can see, the asset accounts (cash, accounts receivable, and office equipment) appear on the left side of the balance sheet.

Accounts payable and Mia Wong, Capital appear on the right side. Notice that the $9,800 of capital can be calculated within the accounting equation or can be read from the statement of owner's equity.

FIGURE 1.8
The Accounting Equation and the Balance Sheet

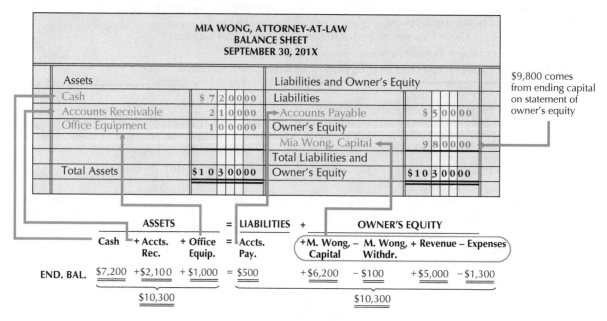

Main Elements of the Income Statement, the Statement of Owner's Equity, and the Balance Sheet

In this chapter we have discussed three financial statements: the income statement, the statement of owner's equity, and the balance sheet. A fourth statement, called the statement of cash flows, will not be covered at this time. Let us review what elements of the expanded accounting equation go into each statement and the usual order in which the statements are prepared. Figure 1.8 presents a diagram of the accounting equation and the balance sheet. Table 1.3 summarizes the following points:

- The income statement is prepared first; it includes revenues and expenses and shows net income or net loss. This net income or net loss is used to update the next statement, the statement of owner's equity.
- The statement of owner's equity is prepared second; it includes beginning capital and any additional investments, the net income or net loss shown on the income statement, withdrawals, and the total, which is the ending capital. The balance in Capital comes from the statement of owner's equity.

Ending capital Beginning Capital + Additional Investments + Net Income Withdrawals = Ending Capital. Or: Beginning Capital + Additional Investments – Net Loss – Withdrawals = Ending Capital.

TABLE 1.3 What Goes on Each Financial Statement

	Income Statement	Statement of Owner's Equity	Balance Sheet
Assets			X
Liabilities			X
Capital* (beg.)		X	
Capital (end)		X	X
Withdrawals		X	
Revenues	X		
Expenses	X		

*Note: Additional Investments go on the statement of owner's equity.

COACHING TIP

Net income is reported separately from capital on the balance sheet in the equity section in both QuickBooks and Peachtree.

- The balance sheet is prepared last; it includes the final balances of each of the elements listed in the accounting equation under Assets and Liabilities. The balance in Capital comes from the statement of owner's equity.

LEARNING UNIT 1-4 REVIEW

AT THIS POINT you should be able to do the following:

- Define and state the purpose of the income statement, the statement of owner's equity, and the balance sheet.
- Discuss why the income statement should be prepared first.
- Show what happens on a statement of owner's equity when a net loss occurs.
- Compare and contrast these three financial statements.
- Calculate a new figure for capital on the statement of owner's equity and the balance sheet.

Instant Replay ⊙ Self-Review Quiz 1-4

From the balances listed next for Rusty Realty prepare the following:

1. Income statement for the month ended November 30, 201X.
2. Statement of owner's equity for the month ended November 30, 201X.
3. Balances as of November 30, 201X.

Cash	$4,000	R. Rusty, Capital	
Accounts Receivable	1,370	November 1, 201X	$5,000
Store Furniture	1,490	R. Rusty, Withdrawals	100
Accounts Payable	900	Commissions Earned	1,500
		Rent Expense	200
		Advertising Expense	150
		Salaries Expense	90

Solution to Instant Replay: Self-Review Quiz 1-4

FIGURE 1.9
Financial Statements

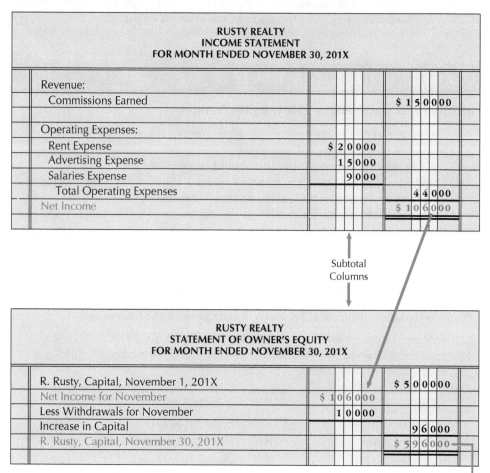

FIGURE 1.9
Financial Statements

RUSTY REALTY
INCOME STATEMENT
FOR MONTH ENDED NOVEMBER 30, 201X

Revenue:		
Commissions Earned		$ 1 5 0 0 00
Operating Expenses:		
Rent Expense	$ 2 0 0 00	
Advertising Expense	1 5 0 00	
Salaries Expense	9 0 00	
Total Operating Expenses		4 4 0 00
Net Income		$ 1 0 6 0 00

Subtotal
Columns

RUSTY REALTY
STATEMENT OF OWNER'S EQUITY
FOR MONTH ENDED NOVEMBER 30, 201X

R. Rusty, Capital, November 1, 201X		$ 5 0 0 0 00
Net Income for November	$ 1 0 6 0 00	
Less Withdrawals for November	1 0 0 00	
Increase in Capital		9 6 0 00
R. Rusty, Capital, November 30, 201X		$ 5 9 6 0 00

RUSTY REALTY
BALANCE SHEET
NOVEMBER 30, 201X

Assets		Liabilities and Owner's Equity	
Cash	$ 4 0 0 0 00	Liabilities	
Accounts Receivable	1 3 7 0 00	Accounts Payable	$ 9 0 0 00
Store Furniture	1 4 9 0 00		
		Owner's Equity	
		R. Rusty, Capital	5 9 6 0 00
		Total Liabilities and	
Total Assets	$ 6 8 6 0 00	Owner's Equity	$ 6 8 6 0 00

PLAY BY PLAY: EXTRA HELP ON SELF-REVIEW QUIZ 1-4

Let's review first: The first formal report is the income statement, which is made up of only revenues and expenses. This report shows how a company is performing for a specific period of time. The second report is the statement of the owner's equity. This report shows how capital has changed from its beginning balance during this period of time. The net income is added to the beginning balance less any personal withdrawals resulting in a new figure for capital, which will also be placed in the balance sheet. This third report, the balance sheet, is made up of assets, liabilities, and the new figure for capital. The balance sheet shows the history of the company as of a particular date.

The Income Statement: Commissions earned is the revenue for Rusty Realty. It is listed to the right since it is the only revenue. The inside column will be used for a subtotal if there is more than one revenue.

Rent, Advertising, and Salaries are expenses that are listed on the income statement. Note that we use the inside column to subtotal them and then list the final figure as total operating expenses of $440 in the right column. The difference between revenue ($1,500) and the total operating expenses ($440) results in a net income of $1,060. Keep in mind that net income is not cash. Remember that some revenue may not have resulted in cash and some of the expenses may not have been paid for in cash.

Statement of Owner's Equity: The beginning balance of Rusty, Capital is $5,000. We place this to the right because it is one number. We then use the inside column to add net income from the income statement ($1,060) and subtract any withdrawals ($100) to get an increase in capital of $960, which is placed in the right column. This figure is then added to beginning capital to arrive at Rusty, Capital (ending) of $5,960.

Balance Sheet: All the assets are listed on the left (cash, accounts receivable, and store furniture), for a total of $6,860. The liability of $900 for accounts payable is listed on the right and will be added to the new figure for Rusty, Capital of $5,960 from the statement of owner's equity.

Summary: The income statement lists out revenue and expenses. No withdrawals are found on this report. The statement of owner's equity will show how capital changes by net income, net loss, and/or withdrawals. The balance shows the new history of the company's assets, liabilities, and a new figure for capital.

x ——→ C
COACHING TIP

The balance sheet shows the latest or ending balance in capital.

DEMONSTRATION PROBLEM

MyAccountingLab

 **LO2,3,4**

Michael Brown opened his law office on June 1, 201X. During the first month of operations, Michael conducted the following transactions:

a. Invested $6,000 in cash into the law practice.
b. Paid $600 for office equipment.
c. Purchased additional office equipment on account, $1,000.
d. Received cash for performing legal services for clients, $2,000.
e. Paid salaries, $800.
f. Performed legal services for clients on account, $1,000.
g. Paid rent, $1,200.
h. Withdrew $500 from his law practice for personal use.
i. Received $500 from customers in partial payment for legal services performed, transaction 6.

(continued on page 24)

Requirements

1. Record these transactions in the expanded accounting equation.
2. Prepare the financial statements at June 30 for Michael Brown, Attorney-at-Law.

Demonstration Problem Solutions

Requirement 1
Record these transactions in the expanded accounting equation.

Part 1	Part 2	Demonstration Problem Complete

	Assets			= Liabilities +			Owner's Equity		
A.	Cash	+ Accts. Rec.	+ Office Equip.	= Accounts Payable	+ M. Brown, Capital	− M. Brown, Withdr.	+ Legal Fees	− Expenses
a.	+$6,000				+$6,000			
BAL.	6,000		=		6,000			
b.	−600		+$600					
BAL.	5,400	+	600 =		6,000			
c.			+1,000	+$1,000				
BAL.	5,400	+	1,600 =	1,000 +	6,000			
d.	+2,000						+$2,000	
BAL.	7,400	+	1,600 =	1,000 +	6,000		+ 2,000	
e.	−800							+$800
BAL.	6,600	+	1,600 =	1,000 +	6,000		+ 2,000	− 800
f.	+$1,000						+1,000	
BAL.	6,600 +	1,000 +	1,600 =	1,000 +	6,000		+ 3,000	− 800
g.	−1,200							+1,200
BAL.	5,400 +	1,000 +	1,600 =	1,000 +	6,000		+ 3,000	− 2,000
h.	−500					+$500		
BAL.	4,900 +	1,000 +	1,600 =	1,000 +	6,000	− 500	+ 3,000	− 2,000
i.	+500	−500						
End. Bal.	$5,400 +	$500 +	$1,600 =	$1,000 +	$6,000	− $500	+ $3,000	− $2,000

$$\$7,500 = \$7,500$$

Solution Tips to Expanded Accounting Equation

- **Transaction a:** The business increased its Cash by $6,000. Owner's Equity (capital) increased when Michael supplied the cash to the business. Note how the equation is now in balance.
- **Transaction b:** A shift in assets occurred when the equipment was purchased. The business lowered its Cash by $600, and a new column—Office Equipment—was increased for the $600 of equipment that was bought. The amount of capital is not touched because the owner did not supply any new funds. You do not have to touch both sides of the equation to make it balance.
- **Transaction c:** When creditors supply $1,000 of additional equipment, the business Accounts Payable shows the debt. The business had increased what it *owes* the creditors. The end result is an increase in an asset and an increase in a liability.
- **Transaction d:** Legal Fees, a subdivision of Owner's Equity, is increased when the law firm provides a service even if no money is received. The service provides an inward flow of $2,000 to Cash, an asset. Remember that Legal Fees is *not* an asset. As Legal Fees revenue increase, Owner's Equity increases. Keep in mind that revenue can provide an inflow of cash and/or accounts receivable. Cash and accounts receivable are assets. The revenue is part of Owner's Equity.

- **Transaction e:** The salary paid by Michael creates an $800 increase in Expenses and a corresponding decrease in Owner's Equity as well as a decrease in Cash. Keep in mind that as the expenses increase they do in fact lower Owner's Equity.
- **Transaction f:** Michael did the work and earned the $1,000. That $1,000 is recorded as revenue. This time the legal fees create an inward flow of assets called Accounts Receivable for $1,000. Remember that Legal Fees is *not* an asset. It is a subdivision of Owner's Equity.
- **Transaction g:** The $1,200 rent expense reduces Owner's Equity as well as Cash. Remember to think of expenses as increasing. This increase in expenses then causes Owner's Equity to decrease.
- **Transaction h:** Withdrawals are for personal use. Here the business decreases Cash by $500 while Michael's withdrawals increase by $500. Withdrawals decrease the Owner's Equity. Remember to think of withdrawals as increasing. This is the amount withdrawn by the owner for personal use, decreasing Owner's Equity.
- **Transaction i:** This transaction does not reflect new revenue in the form of Legal Fees. It is only a shift in assets: more Cash and less Accounts Receivable.

Requirement 2

Prepare the financial statements at June 30 for Michael Brown, Attorney-at-Law.

Part 1	Part 2	Demonstration Problem Complete

Solution Tips to Financial Statements

a. The income statement lists only revenues and expenses for a period of time. The inside column is for subtotaling. Withdrawals are not listed here.

b. The statement of owner's equity takes the net income figure of $1,000 and adds it to beginning capital less any withdrawals. This new capital figure of $6,500 will go on the balance sheet. This statement shows changes in capital for a period of time.

c. The $5,400, $500, $1,600 (Assets) and $1,000 (Liabilities) came from the totals of the expanded accounting equation. The capital figure of $6,500 came from the statement of owner's equity. This balance sheet reports assets, liabilities, and a new figure for capital at a specific date.

A
MICHAEL BROWN, ATTORNEY-AT-LAW
INCOME STATEMENT
FOR MONTH ENDED JUNE 30, 201X

Revenue:		
Legal Fees		$3,000
Operating Expenses:		
Salaries Expense	$ 800	
Rent Expense	1,200	
Total Operating Expenses		2,000
Net Income		$1,000

B
MICHAEL BROWN, ATTORNEY-AT-LAW
STATEMENT OF OWNER'S EQUITY
FOR MONTH ENDED JUNE 30, 201X

Michael Brown, Capital, June 1, 201X		$6,000
Net income for June	$1,000	
Less withdrawls for June	500	
Increase in Capital		500
Michael Brown, Capital, June 30, 201X		$6,500

(continued on page 26)

C

MICHAEL BROWN, ATTORNEY-AT-LAW
BALANCE SHEET
JUNE 30, 201X

Assets		Liabilities and Owner's Equity	
Cash	$5,400	Liabilities	
Accounts Receivable	500	Accounts Payable	$1,000
Office Equipment	1,600	Owner's Equity	
		M. Brown, Capital	$6,500
Total Assets	$7,500	Total Liabilities and Owner's Equity	$7,500

Part 1	Part 2	Demonstration Problem Complete

BLUEPRINT: FINANCIAL STATEMENTS

❶ Income Statement
Measuring performance

Revenue:		XXX	
Operating Expenses	XX		
Other Expenses	XX	XXX	
Net Income		XXX	

❷ Statement of Owner's Equity
Calculating new figure for capital

Beginning Capital		XXX
Additional Investments		XXX
Total Investments		XXX
Net Income (or loss)	XXX	
Less Withdrawals	XXX	
Increase in Capital (or decrease)		XXX
Ending Capital		XXX

❸ Balance Sheet
Where do we now stand

	Assets		Liabilities and Owner's Equity	
		XXX	Liabilities	XXX
		XXX	Owner's Equity	
		XXX	Ending Capital	XXX
	Total Assets	XXX	Total Liab. + OE	XXX

ACCOUNTING COACH

The following Coaching Tips are from Learning Units 1-1 to 1-4. Take the Pre-Game Checkup and use the Check Your Score at the bottom of the page to see how you are doing. The Accounting Coach provides tips before each Checkup to help you avoid common accounting errors.

LU 1-1 The Accounting Equation

Pre-Game Tips: After a transaction is recorded in the accounting equation, the sum of all the assets must equal the total of all the liabilities and owner's equity.

Pre-Game Checkup

Answer true or false to the following statements.

1. Capital is cash.
2. Accounts Payable is a liability.
3. A shift in assets means liabilities will increase.
4. Assets – Liabilities = Owner's Equity.
5. Assets represent what is owned by the business.

LU 1-2 The Balance Sheet

Pre-Game Tips: The Balance Sheet is a formal report listing assets, liabilities, and owner's equity as of a particular date.

Pre-Game Checkup

Answer true or false to the following statements.

1. Cash is a liability.
2. Office Equipment is an asset.
3. Accounts Payable is listed under assets.
4. Capital is listed under liabilities.
5. A heading of a financial report has no particular date.

LU 1-3 The Expanded Accounting Equation

Pre-Game Tips: Revenue is recorded when earned even if cash is not received. Expenses are recorded when they happen (incurred) whether they are paid or to be paid later.

Pre-Game Checkup

Answer true or false to the following statements.

1. Revenue is an asset.
2. Withdrawals increase owner's equity.
3. As expenses go down, owner's equity goes down.
4. An advertising bill incurred but unpaid is recorded as an increase in Advertising Expense and a decrease in liability.
5. Revenue inflows can only be in the form of cash.

LU 1-4 Financial Reports

Pre-Game Tips: Net income from the income statement is used to update the statement of owner's equity. The ending figure for capital on the statement of owner's equity is the one used to update the balance sheet.

Pre-Game Checkup

Answer true or false to the following statements.

1. Net income occurs when expenses are greater than revenue.
2. Withdrawals will reduce owner's capital on the income statement.
3. The balance sheet lists assets, liabilities, and expenses.
4. Withdrawals are listed on the income statement.
5. Assets are listed on the income statement.

CHECK YOUR SCORE: Answers to the Pre-Game Checkup

LU 1-1
1. False—Capital represents the owner's claim to the assets.
2. True.
3. False—A shift in assets means liabilities will stay the same.
4. True.
5. True.

LU 1-2
1. False—Cash is an asset.
2. True.
3. False—Accounts Payable is listed under liabilities.
4. False—Capital is listed under owner's equity.
5. False—A heading of a financial report does have a particular date.

LU 1-3
1. False—Revenue is part of owner's equity.
2. False—Withdrawals decrease owner's equity.
3. False—As expenses go down, owner's equity goes up.
4. False—An advertising bill incurred but unpaid is recorded as an increase in Advertising Expense and an increase in liability.
5. False—Revenue inflows can be in the form of cash and/or accounts receivable.

LU 1-4
1. False—Net income occurs when expenses are less than revenue.
2. False—Withdrawals will reduce owner's capital on the statement of owner's equity.
3. False—Expenses are listed on the income statement.
4. False—Withdrawals are listed on the statement of owner's equity.
5. False—Assets are listed on the balance sheet.

Chapter Summary

MyAccountingLab

Here are all the key concepts and equations to help you understand the concepts of this chapter and prepare you for your exam. After completing this review, go to MyAccountingLab for more practice opportunities.

Concepts You Should Know	Key Terms

LO1 **Defining and listing the functions of accounting.**
 	
1. The functions of accounting involve analyzing, recording, classifying, summarizing, reporting, and interpreting financial information.
 	
2. Forms of business organization:
 	
  a. A sole proprietorship is a business owned by one person.
 	
  b. A partnership is a business owned by two or more persons.
 	
  c. A corporation is a business owned by stockholders.
 	
  d. An LLC is owned by a limited number of stockholders.
 	
3. The Sarbanes-Oxley Act helps prevent fraud at trading companies.
 	
4. GAAP and IFRS are guidelines established by U.S. (GAAP) and international (IFRS) accounting standard boards.
	Accounting (p. 2)
	Assets (p. 5)
	Bookkeeping (p. 4)
	Corporation (p. 3)
	Creditor (p. 5)
	Equities (p. 5)
	Generally accepted accounting principles (GAAP) (p. 4)
	International Financial Reporting Standards (IFRS) (p. 4)
	Liabilities (p. 5)
	Manufacturer (p. 3)
	Merchandise company (p. 3)
	Owner's equity (p. 5)
	Partnership (p. 2)
	Sole proprietorship (p. 2)
	Service company (p. 3)

LO2 **Recording transactions in the basic accounting equation.** 1. Assets = Liabilities + Owner's Equity is the basic accounting equation. 2. Liabilities represent amounts owed to creditors. 3. Capital does not mean cash. 4. In a shift of assets the composition of assets changes but the total of assets does not change.	Accounts payable (p. 7) Balance sheet (p. 9) Basic accounting equation (p. 5) Capital (p. 6) Shift in assets (p. 6) Supplies (p. 6) Statement of financial position (p. 9) Assets = Liabilities + Owner's Equity (p. 5)

Seeing how revenue, expenses, and withdrawals expand the basic accounting equation.

1. Revenue generates an inward flow of assets. Expenses generate an outward flow of assets or a potential outward flow.

2. When revenue totals more than expenses, net income is the result; when expenses total more than revenue, there is a net loss.

3. Owner's equity can be subdivided into four elements: capital, withdrawals, revenue, and expenses.

4. Withdrawals and expenses will decrease owner's equity.

Accounts receivable (p. 12)

Expanded accounting equation (p. 12)

Expense (p. 12)

Net income (p. 12)

Net loss (p. 12)

Revenue (p. 11)

Withdrawals (p. 12)

Assets = Liabilities + Capital − Withdrawals + Revenue − Expenses (p. 12)

○ **L03**

Preparing an income statement, a statement of owner's equity, and a balance sheet.

1. The income statement is a statement written for a specific period of time that lists earned revenue and expenses incurred to produce the earned revenue.

2. The statement of owner's equity is a statement written for a specific period of time that reveals the causes of a change in capital. The ending figure for capital will be used on the balance sheet.

3. The balance sheet is a statement written for a specific point of time that uses the ending balances of assets and liabilities from the accounting equation and the capital from the statement of owner's equity.

4. The income statement should be prepared first because the information on it about net income or net loss is used to prepare the statement of owner's equity, which in turn provides information about capital for the balance sheet.

Ending capital (p. 20)

Income statement (p. 18)

Statement of owner's equity (p. 18)

○ **L04**

Discussion Questions and Critical Thinking/Ethical Case

1. What are the functions of accounting?

2. Define, compare, and contrast sole proprietorships, partnerships, and corporations.

3. How are businesses classified?

4. What is the relationship of bookkeeping to accounting?

5. List the three elements of the basic accounting equation.

6. Define capital.

7. The total of the left-hand side of the accounting equation must equal the total of the right-hand side. True or false? Please explain.

8. A balance sheet tells a company where it is going and how well it performs. True or false? Please explain.

9. Revenue is an asset. True or false? Please explain.

10. Owner's equity is subdivided into what categories?

11. A withdrawal is a business expense. True or false? Please explain.

12. As expenses increase they cause owner's equity to increase. Defend or reject.

13. What does an income statement show?

14. The statement of owner's equity only calculates ending withdrawals. True or false? Please explain.

15. Paul Kloss, accountant for Lowe & Co., traveled to New York on company business. His total expenses came to $350. Paul felt that because the trip extended over the weekend he would "pad" his expense account with an additional $100 of expenses. After all, weekends represent his own time, not the company's. What would you do? Write your specific recommendations to Paul.

MyAccountingLab ## Concept Checks

● L01 *(5 MIN)*   **Classifying Accounts**

1. Classify each of the following items as an Asset (A), Liability (L), or part of Owner's Equity (OE).

   a. Computer Tablet   _____
   b. Accounts Payable   _____
   c. Accounts Receivable   _____
   d. Cash   _____
   e. A. Jones, Capital   _____
   f. Verizon Cell Phone   _____

● L01 *(5 MIN)*   **The Accounting Equation**

2. Complete the following statements.
   a. _____: rights of the creditors
   b. _____ are total value of items owned by a business.
   c. _____ _____ is an unwritten promise to pay the creditor.

Shift versus Increase in Assets

LO1 *(5 MIN)*

3. Identify which transaction results in a shift in assets (S) and which transaction causes an increase in assets (I).
   a. Target bought computer equipment on account.
   b. Macy's bought office equipment for cash.

The Balance Sheet

LO2, 4 *(5 MIN)*

4. From the following, calculate what would be the total of assets on the balance sheet.

B. Fleese, Capital	$12,000
Computer Equipment	21,000
Accounts Payable	8,000
Cash	34,000

The Accounting Equation Expanded

LO3 *(5 MIN)*

5. From the following, which are subdivisions of owner's equity?
   a. Trees _____
   b. J. Penny, Capital _____
   c. Accounts Payable _____
   d. J. Penny, Withdrawals _____
   e. Accounts Receivable _____
   f. Advertising Expense _____
   g. Taxi Fees Earned _____
   h. Computer Equipment _____

Identifying Assets

6. Identify which of the following are *not* assets.
   a. DVD Player _____
   b. Accounts Receivable _____
   c. Accounts Payable _____
   d. Grooming Fees Earned _____

The Accounting Equation Expanded

7. Which of the following statements are false?
   a. _____ Revenue provides only outward flows of cash.
   b. _____ Revenue is a subdivision of Assets.
   c. _____ Revenue provides an inward flow of cash or accounts receivable.
   d. _____ Expenses are part of Total Assets.

Preparing Financial Statements

8. Indicate whether the following items would appear on the income statement (IS), statement of owner's equity (OE), or balance sheet (BS).
   a. _____ Tutoring Fees Earned
   b. _____ Office Equipment
   c. _____ Accounts Receivable
   d. _____ Office Supplies
   e. _____ Legal Fees Earned

(continued on page 32)

f. _____ Advertising Expenses

g. _____ J. Earl, Capital (Beg.)

h. _____ Accounts Payable

Preparing Financial Statements

9. Indicate next to each statement whether it refers to the income statement (IS), statement of owner's equity (OE), or balance sheet (BS).

a. _____ Withdrawals found on it

b. _____ List total of all assets

c. _____ Statement that is prepared last

d. _____ Statement listing net income

MyAccountingLab   Exercises

Set A

● LO2 *(5 MIN)*   **1A-1.** Complete the following table:

	Assets	=	Liabilities	+	Owner's Equity
a.	$27,000	=	?	+	$18,000
b.	?	=	$6,000	+	$69,000
c.	$35,000	=	$10,000	+	?

● LO2 *(5 MIN)*   **1A-2.** Record the following transactions in the basic accounting equation. Treat each one separately.

Assets = Liabilities + Owner's Equity

a. Micheal invests $112,000 in company.

b. Bought equipment for cash, $1500.

c. Bought equipment on account, $750.

●○ LO2, 4 *(10 MIN)*   **1A-3.** From the following, prepare a balance sheet for Rauscher Co. Cleaners at the end of April 201X: Cash, $52,000; Equipment, $28,000; Accounts Payable, $14,000; B. Rauscher, Capital.

● LO3 *(15 MIN)*   **1A-4.** Record the following transactions in the expanded accounting equation. The running balance may be omitted for simplicity.

Assets			=	Liabilities	+			Owner's Equity		
Cash + Accounts	+ Computer		=	Accounts	+ B. Baker,	–	B. Baker,	+ Revenues		
Receivable	Equipment			Payable	Capital		Withdrawals	– Expenses		

a. Baker invested $90,000 in a computer company.

b. Bought computer equipment on account, $10,200.

c. Baker paid personal telephone bill from company checkbook, $50.

d. Received cash for services rendered, $13,700.

e. Billed customers for services rendered for month, $29,000.

f. Paid current rent expense, $4,200.

g. Paid supplies expense, $1,510.

● LO4 *(20 MIN)*   **1A-5.** From the following account balances, prepare in proper form for September (a) an income statement, (b) a statement of owner's equity, and (c) a balance sheet for Frechette Realty.

Cash	$5,700	S. Frechette, Withdrawals	$ 225
Accounts Receivable	990	Professional Fees	3,500
Office Equipment	7,200	Salaries Expense	600
Accounts Payable	10,000	Utilities Expense	150
S. Frechette, Capital, Sep 1, 201X	1,840	Rent Expense	475

Set B

1B-1. Complete the following table:

LO2 *(5 MIN)*

	Assets	=	Liabilities	+	Owner's Equity
a.	$ 30,000	=	?	+	$ 15,000
b.	?	=	$ 10,000	+	$ 55,000
c.	$		15,000 = $3,000	+	?

1B-2. Record the following transactions in the basic accounting equation. Treat each one separately.
  a. Morgan invests $118,000 in company.
  b. Bought equipment for cash, $1,100.
  c. Bought equipment on account, $800.

LO2 *(5 MIN)*

1B-3. From the following, prepare a balance sheet for Rauscher Co. Cleaners at the end of April 201X: Cash, $18,000; Equipment, $40,000; Accounts Payable, $25,000; B. Rauscher, Capital.

LO2, 4 *(10 MIN)*

1B-4. Record the following transactions in the expanded accounting equation. The running balance may be omitted for simplicity.
  a. Baker invested $60,000 in a computer company.
  b. Bought computer equipment on account, $10,000.
  c. Baker paid personal telephone bill from company checkbook, $150.
  d. Received cash for services rendered, $14,000.
  e. Billed customers for services rendered for month, $30,000.
  f. Paid current rent expense, $3,500.
  g. Paid supplies expense, $1,470.

LO3 *(15 MIN)*

1B-5. From the following account balances, prepare in proper form for September (a) an income statement, (b) a statement of owner's equity, and (c) a balance sheet for Frechette Realty.

LO4 *(20 MIN)*

Cash	$ 7,050	S. Frechette, Withdrawals	$ 800
Accounts Receivable	1,060	Professional Fees	4,000
Office Equipment	6,700	Salaries Expense	400
Accounts Payable	2,000	Utilities Expense	360
S. Frechette, Capital, September 1, 201X	10,770	Rent Expense	400

Problems

MyAccountingLab

Set A

1A-1. Mike Ackerman decided to open Mike's Nail Spa. Mike completed the following transactions:
  a. Invested $17,000 cash from his personal bank account into the business.
  b. Bought store equipment for cash, $3,900.
  c. Bought additional store equipment on account, $6,100.
  d. Paid $700 cash to partially reduce what was owed from transaction C.

Based on this information, record these transactions into the basic accounting equation.

LO2 *(15 MIN)*

Check Figure:
Cash $22,400

1A-2. Bob Shire is the accountant for Shire's Internet Service. From the following information, his task is to construct a balance sheet as of September 30, 201X, in proper form. Could you help him?

LO2, 4 *(15 MIN)*

Building	$30,000	Cash	$35,000
Accounts Payable	17,000	Equipment	29,000
Shire, Capital	77,000		

Check Figure:
Total Assets $94,000

LO3 *(20 MIN)*

Check Figure:
Total Assets $24,925

1A-3. At the end of September, Ron Ferlito decided to open his own typing service. Analyze the following transactions he completed by recording their effects in the expanded accounting equation.

a. Invested $15,000 in his typing service.
b. Bought new office equipment on account, $6,500.
c. Received cash for typing services rendered, $900.
d. Performed typing services on account, $3,600.
e. Paid secretary's salary, $325.
f. Paid office supplies expense for the month, $150.
g. Rent expenses for office due but unpaid, $900.
h. Withdrew cash for personal use, $600.

LO4 *(30 MIN)*

Check Figure:
Total Liabilities and
Owner's Equity $3,575

1A-4. Johann Wheldon, owner of Wheldon Stenciling Service, has requested that you prepare from the following balances (a) an income statement for November 201X, (b) a statement of owner's equity for November, and (c) a balance sheet as of November 30, 201X.

Cash	$1,900	Stenciling Fees	$2,600
Accounts Receivable	650	Advertising Expense	110
Equipment	1,025	Repair Expense	20
Accounts Payable	250	Travel Expense	225
J. Wheldon, Capital, Nov. 1, 201X	2,510	Supplies Expense	155
J. Wheldon, Withdrawals	900	Rent Expense	375

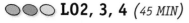

LO2, 3, 4 *(45 MIN)*

PT/QB

1A-5. Jerry Trickett, a retired army officer, opened Trickett's Catering Service. As his accountant, analyze the transactions listed next and present them in proper form.

a. The analysis of the transactions by using the expanded accounting equation.
b. A balance sheet showing the position of the firm before opening for business on March 31, 201X.
c. An income statement for the month of April.
d. A statement of owner's equity for April.
e. A balance sheet as of April 30, 201X.

Check Figure:
Total Assets,
Apr. 30 $51,400

201X

Mar. 25   Jerry Trickett invested $45,000 in the catering business from his personal savings account.

27   Bought equipment for cash from Small Co., $1,600.

28   Bought additional equipment on account from Aiden Co., $2,200.

29   Paid $100 to Aiden Co. as partial payment of the March 28 transaction.

(You should now prepare your balance sheet as of March 31, 201X.)

Apr.   1   Catered a graduation and immediately collected cash, $1,900.

5   Paid salaries of employees, $700.

8   Prepared desserts for customers on account, $150.

10   Received $75 cash as partial payment of April 8 transaction.

15   Paid telephone bill, $120.

17   Paid his home electric bill from the company's checkbook, $80.

20   Catered a wedding and received cash, $2,700.

25   Bought additional equipment on account, $1000.

28   Rent expense due but unpaid, $500.

30   Paid supplies expense, $550.

Set B

MyAccountingLab

1B-1. Mike Ackerman decided to open Mike's Nail Spa. Mike completed the following transactions:

L02 *(15 MIN)*

a. Invested $24,000 cash from his personal bank account into the business.
b. Bought store equipment for cash, $3,700.
c. Bought additional store equipment on account, $6,100.
d. Paid $900 cash to partially reduce what was owed from transaction C.

Check Figure:
Ending Balance Cash $29,200

Record these transactions into the basic accounting equation.

1B-2. Bob Shire is the accountant for Shire's Internet Service. From the following information, his task is to construct a balance sheet as of September 30, 201X, in proper form. Can you help him?

L02, 4 *(15 MIN)*

Building	$ 55,000
Accounts Payable	15,000
Shire, Capital	142,000
Cash	48,000
Equipment	54,000

Check Figure:
Total Assets $157,000

1B-3. At the end of September, Ron Ferlito decided to open his own typing service. Analyze the following transactions he completed by recording their effects into the expanded accounting equation.

L03 *(20 MIN)*

a. Invested $30,000 in his typing business.
b. Bought new office equipment on account, $5,000.
c. Received cash for typing services rendered, $400.
d. Performed typing services on account, $3,100.
e. Paid secretary's salary, $425.
f. Paid office supplies expense for the month, $130.
g. Rent expenses for office due but unpaid, $750.
h. Withdrew cash for personal use, $500.

Check Figure:
Total Assets $37,445

1B-4. Johann Wheldon, owner of Wheldon Stenciling Service, has requested that you prepare from the following balances (a) an income statement for November 201X, (b) a statement of owner's equity for November, and (c) a balance sheet as of November 30, 201X.

L03 *(30 MIN)*

Cash	$2,400	Stenciling Fees	$3000
Accounts Receivable	650	Advertising Expense	110
Equipment	685	Repair Expense	50
Accounts Payable	850	Travel Expense	550
J. Wheldon, Capital, Nov. 1, 201X	1,125	Supplies Expense	55
J. Wheldon, Withdrawals	300	Rent Expense	175

Check Figure:
J. Weldon, Capital, $2,885
Nov. 1, 201X

1B-5. Jerry Trickett, a retired army officer, opened Trickett's Catering Service. As his accountant, analyze the transactions listed and present them in proper form.

a. The analysis of the transactions by using the expanded accounting equation.
b. A balance sheet showing the financial position of the firm before opening on March 31, 201X.
c. An income statement for the month of April.
d. A statement of owner's equity for April.
e. A balance sheet as of April 30, 201X.

(continued on page 36)

201X		
Mar.	25	Jerry Trickett invested $30,000 in the catering business from his personal savings account.
	27	Bought equipment for cash from Lucas Co., $700.
	28	Bought additional equipment on account from Gavin Co., $3,000.
	29	Paid $1,000 to Gavin Co. as partial payment of the March 28 transaction.
Apr.	1	Catered a graduation and collected cash, $2,500.
	5	Paid salaries of employees, $1,500.
	8	Prepared desserts for customers on account, $200.
	10	Received $100 cash as partial payment of September 8 transaction.
	15	Paid telephone bill, $60.
	17	Paid his home electric bill from the company's checkbook, $90.
	20	Catered a wedding and received cash, $1,400.
	25	Bought additional equipment on account, $900.
	28	Rent expense due but unpaid, $900.
	30	Paid supplies expense, $250.

Check Figure:
Total Liabilities and
Owner's Equity
Apr. 30 $35,100

○○**LO2, 4** *(5 MIN)*   **Financial Report Problem**

Reading the Kellogg's Annual Report

Go to http://investor.kelloggs.com/annuals.cfm, to access the Kellogg's 2010 Annual Report. Find the balance sheet and calculate the following: How much did cash increase in 2010 from 2009?

MyAccountingLab   **ON** the Job |||||||||||||||||||||||||||||

○○**LO3, 4** *(45 MIN)*   **SANCHEZ COMPUTER CENTER**

The following problem continues from one chapter to the next, carrying the balances of each month forward. Each chapter focuses on the learning experience of the chapter, adds information as the business grows and shows how critical the knowledge of accounting is to the performance of a business decision-maker.

Assignment

1. Set up an expanded accounting equation spreadsheet using the following accounts:

Assets	Liabilities	Owner's Equity
Cash	Accounts Payable	Freedman, Capital
Supplies		Freedman, Withdrawal
Computer Shop		Service Revenue
Equipment		Expenses (notate type)
Office Equipment		

2. Analyze and record each transaction in the expanded accounting equation.

3. Prepare the financial statements ending July 31 for Sanchez Computer Center.

On July 1, 201X, Tony Freedman decided to begin his own computer service business. He named the business the Sanchez Computer Center. During the first month Tony conducted the following business transactions:

a.   Invested $4,500 of his savings into the business.

b.   Paid $1,200 (check #8095) for the computer from Multi Systems, Inc.

c.   Paid $600 (check #8096) for office equipment from Office Furniture, Inc.

d.   Set up a new account with Office Depot and purchased $250 in office supplies on credit.

e.   Paid July rent, $400 (check #8097).

f.   Repaired a system for a customer and collected $250.

g.   Collected $200 for system upgrade labor charge from a customer.

h.   Electric bill due but unpaid, $85.

i.   Collected $1,200 for services performed on Taylor Golf computers.

j.   Withdrew $100 (check #8098) to take his wife, Carol, out in celebration of opening the new business.

SUBWAY CASE

A Fresh Start

LO4 *(20 MIN)*

"Hey, Stan the man!" a loud voice boomed. "I never thought I'd see you making sandwiches!" Stan Hernandez stopped layering lettuce in a foot-long submarine sandwich and grinned at his old college buddy, Ron.

"Neither did I. But then again," said Stan, "I never thought I'd own a profitable business either."

That night, catching up on their lives over dinner, Stan told Ron how he became the proud owner of a Subway sandwich restaurant.

"After working like crazy at Xellent Media for five years and *finally* making it to marketing manager, then wham . . . I got laid off," said Stan. "That very day I was having my lunch at the local Subway as usual, when. . . ."

"Hmmm, wait a minute! I did notice you've lost quite a bit of weight," Ron interrupted and began to hum the bars of Subway's latest ad featuring Clay Henry, yet another hefty male who lost weight on a diet of Subway sandwiches.

"Right!" Stan quipped, "Not only was I laid off, but I was 'downsizing!' *Anyway,* I was eating a Dijon horseradish melt when I opened up an *Entrepreneur* magazine someone had left on the table—right to the headline 'Subway Named #1 Franchise in All Categories for 11th Time in 15 Years.'"

Well, to make a foot-long submarine sandwich story short, Stan realized his long-time dream of being his own boss by owning a business with a proven product and highly successful business model. When you look at Stan's restaurant, you are really seeing two businesses. Even though Stan is the sole proprietor of his business, he operates under an agreement with Subway of Milford, Connecticut. Subway supplies the business know-how and support (like training at Subway University, national advertising, and gourmet bread recipes). Stan supplies capital (his $12,500 investment) and his food preparation, management, and elbow grease. Subway and Stan operate interdependent businesses, and both rely on accounting information for their success.

Subway, in business since 1965, has grown dramatically over the years and now has more than 18,000 locations in 73 countries. It has even surpassed McDonald's in the number of locations in the United States and Canada. To manage this enormous service business requires careful control of each of its stores. At a Subway regional office, Mariah Washington, a field consultant for Stan's territory, monitors Stan's restaurant closely. In addition to making monthly visits to check whether Stan is complying with Subway's model in everything from décor to uniforms to food quality and safety, she also looks closely at Stan's weekly sales and inventory reports. When Stan's sales go up, Subway's do too, because each Subway franchisee, like Stan, pays Subway, the franchiser, a percentage of sales in the form of royalties.

Why does headquarters require accounting reports? Accounting reports give the information both Stan and the company need to make business decisions in a number of vital areas. For example:

- Before Stan could buy his Subway restaurant, the company needed to know how much cash Stan had and his assets and liabilities (such as credit card debt). Stan prepared a personal balance sheet to give them this information.
- Stan must have the right amount of supplies on hand. If he has too few, he can't make the sandwiches. If he has too many for the amount he expects to sell, items such as sandwich meats and bread dough may spoil. The inventory report tells Mariah what supplies are on hand. In combination with the sales report, it also alerts Mariah to potential red flags: If Stan is reporting that he is using far too much bread dough for the amount of sandwiches he is selling, a problem would be indicated.
- Although Subway does not require its restaurant owners to report operating costs and profit information, Subway gives them the option and most franchisees take it. Information on profitability helps Mariah and Stan make decisions such as whether and when to remodel or buy new equipment.

So that its restaurant owners can make business decisions in a timely manner, Subway requires them to submit the weekly sales and inventory report to headquarters electronically every Thursday by 2:00 P.M. Stan has his latest report in mind as he makes a move to pay the bill for his dinner with Ron. "We had a great week. Let me get this," he says. "Thanks, Stan the Man. I'm going to keep in touch because I may just be ready for a business opportunity of my own!"

Discussion Questions

1. What makes Stan a sole proprietor?
2. Why are Stan and Subway interdependent businesses?
3. Why did Stan have to share his personal balance sheet with Subway? Do you think most interdependent businesses operate this way?
4. What does Subway learn from Stan's weekly sales and inventory reports?

Debits and Credits: Analyzing and Recording Business Transactions

THE GAME PLAN

Do you ever wonder when making a purchase at the mall how a shop will know if the cash taken in at the register will equal the sales at the end of the day? For example, if you go to Subway and purchase a sub, how will Subway know that the money collected for your sale will equal the amount in the register at day's end? In this chapter, we learn how businesses small and large like Subway are required to use the accounting equation to ensure this balance. By following the rules associated with the accounting equation, investors and creditors, when reviewing financial statements, can have confidence that businesses like Subway are accurately reporting their financial activities.

LEARNING OBJECTIVES

- **1.** Setting up and organizing a chart of accounts.
- **2.** Recording transactions in T accounts according to the rules of debit and credit.
- **3.** Preparing a trial balance.
- **4.** Preparing financial statements from a trial balance.

In Chapter 1 we used the expanded accounting equation to document the financial transactions performed by Mia Wong's law firm. Remember how long it was: The cash column had a long list of pluses and minuses, with no quick system of recording and summarizing the increases and decreases of cash or other items. Can you imagine the problem Subway would have if it used the expanded accounting equation to track the thousands of business transactions it makes each day?

LEARNING UNIT 2-1 THE T ACCOUNT

Account An accounting device used in bookkeeping to record increases and decreases of business transactions relating to individual assets, liabilities, capital, withdrawals, revenue, expenses, and so on.

Let's look at the problem a little more closely. Each business transaction is recorded in the accounting equation under a specific account. Different accounts are used for each of the subdivisions of the accounting equation: asset accounts, liabilities accounts, expense accounts, revenue accounts, and so on. What is needed is a way to record the increases and decreases in specific account *categories* and yet keep them together in one place. The answer is the standard account form (see Figure 2.1). A standard account is a formal account that includes columns for date, item, posting reference, debit, and credit. Each account has a separate form, and all transactions affecting that account are recorded on the form. All the business's account forms (which often are referred to as *ledger accounts*) are then placed in a ledger. Each page of the ledger contains one account. The ledger may be in the form of a bound or a loose-leaf book. If computers are used, the ledger may be part of a computer file. For simplicity's sake, we use the T account form. This form got its name because it looks like the letter T. Generally, T accounts are used for demonstration purposes. Each T account contains three basic parts:

Standard account A formal account that includes columns for date, explanation, posting reference, debit, and credit.

Ledger A group of accounts that records data from business transactions.

T account A skeleton version of a standard account, used for demonstration purposes.

$$
\begin{array}{c}
1\\
\text{Title of Account}\\
\hline
2\quad\text{Left side} \quad\bigg|\quad \text{Right side}\quad 3
\end{array}
$$

All T accounts have this structure.

In accounting, the left side of any T account is called the debit side.

$$
\begin{array}{c|c}
\text{Left side} & \\
\text{Dr. (debit)} & \\
\end{array}
$$

Debit The left-hand side of any account. A number entered on the left side of any account is said to be debited to an account.

Just as the word *left* has many meanings, the word *debit* for now in accounting means a position, the left side of an account. Do not think of it as good (+) or bad (−).

Amounts entered on the left side of any account are said to be *debited* to an account. The abbreviation for debit, Dr., is from the Latin *debere*.

The right side of any T account is called the credit side.

$$
\begin{array}{c|c}
 & \text{Right side}\\
 & \text{Cr. (credit)}\\
\end{array}
$$

Credit The right-hand side of any account. A number entered on the right side of any account is said to be credited to an account.

Amounts entered on the right side of an account are said to be *credited* to an account. The abbreviation for credit, Cr., is from the Latin *credere*.

At this point do not associate the definition of debit and credit with the words *increase* or *decrease*. Think of debit or credit as only indicating a *position* (left or right side) of a T account.

Balancing an Account

No matter which individual account is being balanced, the procedure used to balance it is the same.

Account Title							Account No.	
Date	Item	PR	Debit	Date	Item	PR	Credit	

FIGURE 2.1
The Standard Account Form Is the Source of the T Account's Shape

COACHING TIP

If the balance is greater on the credit side, that is the side the ending balance would be on.

	Dr.	Cr.
Entries ⟶	5,000	400
	600	500
Footings ⟶	5,600	900
Balance 4,700		

In the "real" world, the T account would also include the date of the transaction. The date would appear to the left of the entry:

	Dr.		Cr.
4/2	5,000	4/3	400
4/20	600	4/25	500
	5,600		900
Bal 4,700			

Footings The totals of each side of a T account.

Ending balance The difference between footings in a T account.

Note that on the debit (left) side the numbers add up to $5,600. On the credit (right) side the numbers add up to $900. The $5,600 and the $900 written in small type are called footings. Footings help in calculating the new (or ending) balance. The ending balance ($4,700) is placed on the debit or left side, because the balance of the debit side is greater than that of the credit side.

Remember that the ending balance does not tell us anything about increase or decrease. It only tells us that we have an ending balance of $4,700 on the debit side.

LEARNING UNIT 2-1 REVIEW

AT THIS POINT you should be able to do the following:

- Define ledger.
- State the purpose of a T account.
- Identify the three parts of a T account.
- Define debit.
- Define credit.
- Explain footings and calculate the balance of an account.

↙ Instant Replay ◎ Self-Review Quiz 2-1

Respond True or False to the following:

1.

Dr.	Cr.
3,000	200
200	600

The balance of the account is $2,400 Cr.

(continued on page 42)

2. A credit always means increase.
3. A debit is the left side of any account.
4. A ledger can be prepared manually or by computer.
5. Footings replace the need for debits and credits.

Solutions to Instant Replay: Self-Review Quiz 2-1

1. False
2. False
3. True
4. True
5. False

PLAY BY PLAY: EXTRA HELP ON SELF-REVIEW QUIZ 2-1

Let's review first: "Debit" does not mean good or bad. Instead, it represents a position, the left side of any account. "Credit" does not mean good or bad either. It represents a position, the right side of any account.

1. It is false because if you add the two debits of 3,000 and 200 you get 3,200 on the debit, or left side. A dr. + dr. = Debit balance. Now if you add the credit side of 200 and 600 you get a balance of 800 on the credit side. A cr. + cr. = Credit balance. To find the ending balance we take 3,200 less the 800 to arrive at a balance that is still larger on the DEBIT side by 2,400.
2. A credit is a position. It is the right side of any account.
3. Yes, the debit is always the left side of any account. It does not mean good or bad.
4. In the past, the ledger, a group of accounts, was prepared manually; however, today most ledgers are prepared (not only updated) by computer software.
5. Footings are used to add debits and credits to arrive at a new balance. Think of footings as the totals of a column.

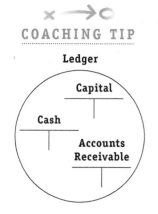

COACHING TIP

LEARNING UNIT 2-2 RECORDING BUSINESS TRANSACTIONS:
Debits and Credits

Can you get a queen in checkers? In a baseball game, does a runner rounding first base skip second base and run over the pitcher's mound to get to third? No; most of us don't do such things because we follow the rules of the game. Usually we learn the rules first and reflect on the reasons for them afterward. The same is true in accounting.

Instead of first trying to understand all the rules of debit and credit and how they were developed in accounting, it is easier to learn the rules by "playing the game."

T Account Entries for Accounting in the Accounting Equation

Have patience. Learning the rules of debit and credit is like learning to play any game: The more you play, the easier it becomes. Table 2.1 shows the rules for the side on which you enter an increase or a decrease for each of the separate accounts in the accounting equation. For example, an increase is entered on the debit side in the asset account but on the credit side for a liability account.

TABLE 2.1 Rules of Debit and Credit

Account Category	Increase (Normal Balance)	Decrease
Assets	Debit	Credit
Liabilities	Credit	Debit
Owner's Equity		
Capital	Credit	Debit
Withdrawals	Debit	Credit
Revenue	Credit	Debit
Expenses	Debit	Credit

It might be easier to visualize these rules of debit and credit if we look at them in the T account form, using + to show increase and – to show decrease.

> **Normal balance of an account**
> The side of an account that increases by the rules of debit and credit.

Assets		=	Liabilities		+	Owner's Equity											
						– Capital –		+ Withdrawals +		Revenue –		Expenses					
Dr.	Cr.		Dr.	Cr.	+	Dr.	Cr.	Dr.	Cr.	Dr.	Cr.	Dr.	Cr.				
+	–		–	+		–	+	+	–	–	+	+	–				

Rules for Assets Work in the Opposite Direction to Those for Liabilities When you look at the equation you can see that the rules for assets work in the opposite direction to those for liabilities. That is, for assets the increases appear on the debit side and the decreases are shown on the credit side; the opposite is true for liabilities. As for the owner's equity, the rules for withdrawals and expenses, which *decrease* owner's equity, work in the opposite direction to the rules for capital and revenue, which *increase* owner's equity.

Assets		+	Withdrawals		+	Expenses		=	Liabilities		+	Capital		+	Revenue	
Dr.	Cr.		Dr.	Cr.		Dr.	Cr.		Dr.	Cr.		Dr.	Cr.		Dr.	Cr.
+	–		+	–		+	–		–	+		–	+		–	+

This setup may help you visualize how the rules for withdrawals and expenses are just the opposite of those for capital and revenue.

A normal balance of an account is the side that increases by the rules of debit and credit. For example, the balance of cash is a debit balance, because an asset is increased by a debit. We discuss normal balances further in Chapter 3.

Balancing the Equation It is important to remember that any amount(s) entered on the debit side of a T account or accounts also must appear on the credit side of another T account or accounts. This approach ensures that the total amount added to the debit side will equal the total amount added to the credit side, thereby keeping the accounting equation in balance.

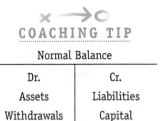

COACHING TIP

Normal Balance	
Dr.	Cr.
Assets	Liabilities
Withdrawals	Capital
Expenses	Revenue

L01

Chart of accounts A numbering system of accounts that lists the account titles and account numbers to be used by a company.

Chart of Accounts Our job is to analyze Mia Wong's business transactions—the transactions we looked at in Chapter 1—using a system of accounts guided by the rules of debit and credit that will summarize increases and decreases of individual accounts in the ledger. The goal is to prepare an income statement, statement of owner's equity, and balance sheet for Mia Wong. Sound familiar? If this system works, the rules of debit and credit and the use of accounts will give us the same answers as in Chapter 1, but with greater ease.

Mia's accountant developed what is called a chart of accounts. The chart of accounts is a numbered list of all of the business's accounts. It allows accounts to be located quickly. In Mia's business, for example, 100s are assets, 200s are liabilities, and so on. As you see in Table 2.2, each separate asset and liability account has its own number. Note that the chart may be expanded as the business grows.

TABLE 2.2 Chart of Accounts for Mia Wong, Attorney-at-Law

Balance Sheet Accounts	
Assets	**Liabilities**
111 Cash	211 Accounts Payable
112 Accounts Receivable	**Owner's Equity**
121 Office Equipment	311 Mia Wong, Capital
	312 Mia Wong, Withdrawals

Income Statement Accounts	
Revenue	**Expenses**
411 Legal Fees	511 Salaries Expense
	512 Rent Expense
	513 Advertising Expense

The Transaction Analysis: Five Steps

We will analyze the transactions in Mia Wong's law firm using a teaching device called a *transaction analysis chart* to record these five steps. (Keep in mind that the transaction analysis chart is not a part of any formal accounting system.) The five steps to analyzing each business transaction include the following:

STEP 1: Determine which accounts are affected. Example: Cash, Accounts Payable, Rent Expense. A transaction always affects at least two accounts.

STEP 2: Determine which categories the accounts belong to: assets, liabilities, capital, withdrawals, revenue, or expenses. Example: Cash is an asset.

STEP 3: Determine whether the accounts increase or decrease. Example: If you receive cash, that account increases.

STEP 4: What do the rules of debit and credit say (Table 2.1)?

STEP 5: What does the T account look like? Place amounts into accounts either on the left or right side depending on the rules in Table 2.1.

The following chart shows the five-step analysis from another perspective.

COACHING TIP

Remember that the rules of debit and credit only tell us on which side to place information. Whether the debit or credit represents increases or decreases depends on the account category: assets, liabilities, capital, and so on. Think of a business transaction as an exchange: You get something and you give or part with something.

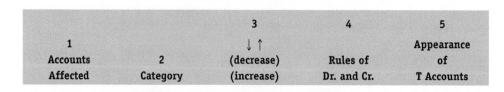

1		3	4	5
		↓ ↑		Appearance
Accounts	2	(decrease)	Rules of	of
Affected	Category	(increase)	Dr. and Cr.	T Accounts

Let us emphasize a major point: *Do not try to debit or credit an account until you go through the first three steps of the transaction analysis.*

Applying the Transaction Analysis to Mia Wong's Law Practice

Transaction A August 28: Mia Wong invests $6,000 cash and $200 of office equipment in the business.

---

1 Accounts Affected	2 Category	3 ↓ ↑	4 Rules of Dr. and Cr.	5 Appearance of T Accounts
Cash	Asset	↑	Dr.	Cash 111
				(A) 6,000 |
Office Equipment	Asset	↑	Dr.	Office Equipment 121
				(A) 200 |
Mia Wong, Capital	Capital	↑	Cr.	Mia Wong, Capital 311
				| 6,200 (A)

COACHING TIP

Note that in column 3 of the chart it doesn't matter if both arrows go up, as long as the sum of the debits equals the sum of the credits in the T accounts in column 5.

Note again that every transaction affects at least two T accounts and that the total amount added to the debit side(s) must equal the total amount added to the credit side(s) of the T accounts of each transaction.

Analysis of Transaction A

STEP 1: Which accounts are affected? The law firm receives its cash and office equipment, so three accounts are involved: Cash, Office Equipment, and Mia Wong, Capital. These account titles come from the chart of accounts.

STEP 2: Which categories do these accounts belong to? Cash and Office Equipment are assets. Mia Wong, Capital is capital.

STEP 3: Are the accounts increasing or decreasing? Cash and Office Equipment, both assets, are increasing in the business. The rights or claims of Mia Wong, Capital are also increasing because she invested money and office equipment in the business.

STEP 4: What do the rules say? According to the rules of debit and credit, an increase in assets (Cash and Office Equipment) is a debit. An increase in Capital is a credit. Note that the total dollar amount of debits will equal the total dollar amount of credits when the T accounts are updated in column 5.

STEP 5: What does the T account look like? The amount for Cash and Office Equipment is entered on the debit side. The amount for Mia Wong, Capital goes on the credit side.

A transaction that involves more than one debit or more than one credit is called a compound entry. This first transaction of Mia Wong's law firm is a compound entry; it involves a debit of $6,000 to Cash and a debit of $200 to Office Equipment (as well as a credit of $6,200 to Mia Wong, Capital).

The name for this double-entry analysis of transactions, where two or more accounts are affected and the total of debits and credits is equal, is double-entry bookkeeping. This double-entry system helps in checking the recording of business transactions.

As we continue, the explanations will be brief, but do not forget to apply the five steps in analyzing and recording each business transaction.

Compound entry A transaction involving more than one debit or credit.

Double-entry bookkeeping An accounting system in which the recording of each transaction affects two or more accounts and the total of the debits is equal to the total of the credits.

Transaction B Aug. 29: Law practice bought office equipment for cash, $500.

---

1 Accounts Affected	2 Category	3 ↓ ↑	4 Rules of Dr. and Cr.	5 T Account Update
Office Equipment	Asset	↑	Dr.	Office Equipment 121
				(A) 200
				(B) 500
Cash	Asset	↓	Cr.	Cash 111
				(A) 6,000 | 500 (B)

Analysis of Transaction B

STEP 1: The law firm paid $500 cash for the office equipment it purchased. The accounts involved in the transaction are Cash and Office Equipment.

STEP 2: The accounts belong to these categories: Office Equipment is an asset; Cash is an asset.

STEP 3: The asset Office Equipment is increasing. The asset Cash is decreasing; it is being reduced to buy the office equipment.

STEP 4: An increase in the asset Office Equipment is a debit; a decrease in the asset Cash is a credit.

STEP 5: When the amounts are placed in the T accounts, the amount for Office Equipment is entered on the debit side and the amount for Cash on the credit side.

Transaction C Aug. 30: Bought more office equipment on account, $300.

---

1 Accounts Affected	2 Category	3 ↓ ↑	4 Rules of Dr. and Cr.	5 T Account Update
Office Equipment	Asset	↑	Dr.	Office Equipment 121
				(A) 200
				(B) 500
				(C) 300
Accounts Payable	Liability	↑	Cr.	Accounts Payable 211
				300 (C)

Analysis of Transaction C

STEP 1: The law firm receives office equipment totaling $300 by promising to pay in the future. An obligation or liability, Accounts Payable, is created. The accounts affected are Office Equipment and Accounts Payable.

STEP 2: Office Equipment is an asset. Accounts Payable is a liability.

STEP 3: The asset Office Equipment is increasing; the liability Accounts Payable is increasing because the law firm is increasing what it owes.

STEP 4: An increase in the asset Office Equipment is a debit. An increase in the liability Accounts Payable is a credit.

STEP 5: Enter the amount for Office Equipment on the debit side of the T account. The amount for the Accounts Payable goes on the credit side.

Transaction D Sept. 1–30: Provided legal services for cash, $2,000.

1 Accounts Affected	2 Category	3 ↓ ↑	4 Rules of Dr. and Cr.	5 T Account Update			
Cash	Asset	↑	Dr.	Cash 111			
				(A)	6,000	500	(B)
				(D)	2,000		
Legal Fees	Revenue	↑	Cr.	Legal Fees 411			
						2,000	(D)

Analysis of Transaction D

STEP 1: The firm earned revenue from legal services and received $2,000 in cash. The accounts affected are Legal Fees and Cash.

STEP 2: Cash is an asset. Legal Fees is revenue.

STEP 3: Cash, an asset, is increasing. Legal Fees, or revenue, is also increasing.

STEP 4: An increase in Cash, an asset, is debited. An increase in Legal Fees, or revenue, is credited.

STEP 5: Enter the amount for Cash on the debit side of the T account. Enter the amount for Legal Fees on the credit side.

Transaction E Sept. 1–30: Provided legal services on account, $3,000.

1 Accounts Affected	2 Category	3 ↓ ↑	4 Rules of Dr. and Cr.	5 T Account Update			
Accounts Receivable	Asset	↑	Dr.	Accounts Receivable 112			
				(E)	3,000		
Legal Fees	Revenue	↑	Cr.	Legal Fees 411			
						2,000	(D)
						3,000	(E)

Analysis of Transaction E

STEP 1: The law practice has earned revenue of $3,000 but has not yet received payment (cash). The amounts owed by these clients are called Accounts Receivable. Revenue is earned at the time the legal services are provided, whether payment is received then or will be received some time in the future. The accounts affected are Accounts Receivable and Legal Fees.

STEP 2: Accounts Receivable is an asset. Legal Fees is revenue.

STEP 3: Accounts Receivable is increasing because the law practice increased the amount owed to it for legal fees earned but not yet paid. Legal Fees, or revenue, is increasing.

STEP 4: An increase in the asset Accounts Receivable is a debit. An increase in Revenue is a credit.

STEP 5: Enter the amount for Accounts Receivable on the debit side of the T account. The amount for Legal Fees goes on the credit side.

Transaction F Sept. 1–30: Received $900 cash from clients for services rendered previously on account.

---

1 Accounts Affected	2 Category	3 ↓ ↑	4 Rules of Dr. and Cr.	5 T Account Update			
Cash	Asset	↑	Dr.	Cash 111			
				(A) 6,000	500	(B)	
				(D) 2,000			
				(F) 900			
Accounts Receivable	Asset	↓	Cr.	Accounts Receivable 112			
				(E) 3,000	900	(F)	

Analysis of Transaction F

STEP 1: The law firm collects $900 in cash from previous revenue earned. Because the revenue is recorded at the time it is earned, and not when the collection is received, in this transaction we are concerned only with the collection, which affects the Cash and Accounts Receivable accounts.

STEP 2: Cash is an asset. Accounts Receivable is an asset.

STEP 3: Because clients are paying what is owed, Cash (asset) is increasing and the amount owed (Accounts Receivable) is decreasing (the total amount owed by clients to Wong is going down). This transaction results in a shift in assets, more Cash for less Accounts Receivable.

STEP 4: An increase in Cash, an asset, is a debit. A decrease in Accounts Receivable, an asset, is a credit.

STEP 5: Enter the amount for Cash on the debit side of the T account. The amount for Accounts Receivable goes on the credit side.

Transaction G Sept. 1–30: Paid salaries expense, $700.

---

1 Accounts Affected	2 Category	3 ↓ ↑	4 Rules of Dr. and Cr.	5 T Account Update			
Salaries Expense	Expense	↑	Dr.	Salaries Expense 511			
				(G) 700			
Cash	Asset	↓	Cr.	Cash 111			
				(A) 6,000	500	(B)	
				(D) 2,000	700	(G)	
				(F) 900			

Analysis of Transaction G

STEP 1: The law firm pays $700 of salaries expense by cash. The accounts affected are Salaries Expense and Cash.

STEP 2: Salaries Expense is an expense. Cash is an asset.

STEP 3: The Salaries Expense of the law firm is increasing, which results in a decrease in Cash.

STEP 4: An increase in Salaries Expense, an expense, is a debit. A decrease in Cash, an asset, is a credit.

STEP 5: Enter the amount for Salaries Expense on the debit side of the T account. The amount for Cash goes on the credit side.

Transaction H Sept. 1–30: Paid rent expense, $400.

1 Accounts Affected	2 Category	3 ↓ ↑	4 Rules of Dr. and Cr.	5 T Account Update			
Rent Expense	Expense	↑	Dr.	Rent Expense 512			
				(H)	400		
Cash	Asset	↓	Cr.	Cash 111			
				(A)	6,000	500	(B)
				(D)	2,000	700	(G)
				(F)	900	400	(H)

Analysis of Transaction H

STEP 1: The law firm's rent expenses of $400 are paid in cash. The accounts affected are Rent Expense and Cash.

STEP 2: Rent is an expense. Cash is an asset.

STEP 3: The Rent Expense increases the expenses, and the payment for the Rent Expense decreases the cash.

STEP 4: An increase in Rent Expense, an expense, is a debit. A decrease in Cash, an asset, is a credit.

STEP 5: Enter the amount for Rent Expense on the debit side of the T account. Place the amount for Cash on the credit side.

Transaction I Sept. 1–30: Received a bill for Advertising Expense (to be paid next month), $200.

1 Accounts Affected	2 Category	3 ↓ ↑	4 Rules of Dr. and Cr.	5 T Account Update			
Advertising Expense	Expense	↑	Dr.	Advertising Expense 513			
				(I)	200		
Accounts Payable	Liability	↑	Cr.	Accounts Payable 211			
						300	(C)
						200	(I)

Analysis of Transaction I

STEP 1: The advertising bill in the amount of $200 has come in and payment is due but has not yet been made. Therefore, the accounts involved here are Advertising Expense and Accounts Payable; the expense has created a liability.

(continued on page 50)

STEP 2: Advertising Expense is an expense. Accounts Payable is a liability.

STEP 3: Both the expense and the liability are increasing.

STEP 4: An increase in an expense is a debit. An increase in a liability is a credit.

STEP 5: Enter the amount for Advertising Expense on the debit side of the T account. Enter the amount for Accounts Payable on the credit side.

Transaction J Sept. 1–30: Wong withdrew cash for personal use, $100.

1 Accounts Affected	2 Category	3 ↓ ↑	4 Rules of Dr. and Cr.	5 T Account Update
Mia Wong, Withdrawals	Withdrawals	↑	Dr.	Mia Wong, Withdrawals 312 (J) 100 |
Cash	Asset	↑	Cr.	Cash 111 (A) 6,000 | 500 (B) (D) 2,000 | 700 (G) (F) 900 | 400 (H) | 100 (J)

Analysis of Transaction J

STEP 1: Mia Wong withdraws $100 cash from business for *personal* use. This withdrawal is not a business expense. The accounts affected are Withdrawals and Cash.

STEP 2: This transaction affects the Withdrawals and Cash accounts.

STEP 3: Mia has increased what she has withdrawn from the business for personal use. The business cash decreased.

STEP 4: An increase in Withdrawals is a debit. A decrease in Cash is a credit. (*Remember:* Withdrawals go on the statement of owner's equity; expenses go on the income statement.)

STEP 5: Enter the amount for Mia Wong, Withdrawals, on the debit side of the T account. The amount for Cash goes on the credit side.

COACHING TIP

Withdrawals are always increased by debits.

Summary of Transactions for Mia Wong										
Assets		=	**Liabilities**	+				**Owner's Equity**		
Cash 111		=	Accounts	+	Capital	−	Withdrawals	+	Revenue	−	Expenses
(A) 6,000	500 (B)		Payable 211		Mia Wong,		Mia Wong,		Legal		Salaries
(D) 2,000	700 (G)	=	300 (C)	+	Capital 311	−	Withdrawals 312	+	Fees 411	−	Expense 511
(F) 900	400 (H)		200 (I)		6,200 (A)		(J) 100 |		2,000 (D) 3,000 (E)		(G) 700 |
	100 (J)										
Accounts Receivable 112											Rent Expense 512
(E) 3,000	900 (F)										(H) 400 |
Office Equipment 121											Advertising Expense 513
(A) 200											(I) 200 |
(B) 500											
(C) 300											

LEARNING UNIT 2-2 REVIEW

AT THIS POINT you should be able to do the following:

- State the rules of debit and credit.
- List the five steps of a transaction analysis.
- Fill out a transaction analysis chart.
- Explain double-entry bookkeeping.

Instant Replay ◎ Self-Review Quiz 2-2

King Company uses the following accounts from its chart of accounts: Cash (111), Accounts Receivable (112), Equipment (121), Accounts Payable (211), Jamie King, Capital (311), Jamie King, Withdrawals (312), Professional Fees (411), Utilities Expense (511), and Salaries Expense (512).

Record the following transactions into transaction analysis charts.

- **a.** Jamie King invested in the business $1,000 cash and equipment worth $700 from his personal assets.
- **b.** Billed clients for services rendered, $12,000.
- **c.** Utilities bill due but unpaid, $150.
- **d.** Withdrew cash for personal use, $120.
- **e.** Paid salaries expense, $250.

Solution to Instant Replay: Self-Review Quiz 2-2

a.

1 Accounts Affected	2 Category	3 ↓ ↑	4 Rules of Dr. and Cr.	5 T Account Update
Cash	Asset	↑	Dr.	Cash 111
				(A) 1,000
Equipment	Asset	↑	Dr.	Equipment 121
				(A) 700
Jamie King, Capital	Capital	↑	Cr.	Jamie King, Capital 311
				1,700 (A)

b.

1 Accounts Affected	2 Category	3 ↓ ↑	4 Rules of Dr. and Cr.	5 T Account Update
Accounts Receivable	Asset	↑	Dr.	Accounts Receivable 112
				(B) 12,000
Professional Fees	Revenue	↑	Cr.	Professional Fees 411
				12,000 (B)

(continued on page 52)

c.

1 Accounts Affected	2 Category	3 ↓ ↑	4 Rules of Dr. and Cr.	5 T Account Update
Utilities Expense	Expense	↑	Dr.	Utilities Expense 511
				(C) 150 |
Accounts Payable	Liability	↑	Cr.	Accounts Payable 211
				| 150 (C)

d.

1 Accounts Affected	2 Category	3 ↓ ↑	4 Rules of Dr. and Cr.	5 T Account Update
Jamie King, Withdrawals	Withdrawals	↑	Dr.	Jamie King, Withdrawals 312
				(D) 120 |
Cash	Asset	↓	Cr.	Cash 111
				(A) 1,000 | 120 (D)

e.

1 Accounts Affected	2 Category	3 ↓ ↑	4 Rules of Dr. and Cr.	5 T Account Update
Salaries Expense	Expense	↑	Dr.	Salaries Expense 512
				(E) 250 |
Cash	Asset	↓	Cr.	Cash 111
				(A) 1,000 | 120 (D)
				| 250 (E)

PLAY BY PLAY: EXTRA HELP ON SELF-REVIEW QUIZ 2-2

Let's review first: Make up a note card of the rules of debit and credit from Table 2.1. You will notice that assets, withdrawals, and expenses increase when you put amounts on the left, or debit, side of these accounts. The accounting system balances because liabilities, capital, and revenue increase when you put amounts on the right, or credit, side of these accounts. The increase side of any account will represent its normal balance. Think of a chart of accounts as a roadmap to all account titles a company will use. *All accounts affected must come from the chart of accounts.*

Transaction A: In column 1 all titles must come from the chart of accounts. The order listed does not matter as long as the sum of the left side equals the sum of the right side. In this transaction we see that accounts affected include Cash, Equipment, and Jamie King, Capital. Cash and Equipment are assets, while Capital is categorized as capital. Remember that the six category choices are as follows:

assets	liabilities
capital	withdrawals
revenue	expenses

The cash and equipment in business are increasing (thus arrows up) and because the owner supplied them Jamie King, Capital rights are increasing. Assets are increased by putting amounts on the debit side and capital is increased by putting amounts on the credit side (See table 2.3).

TABLE 2.3 Rules of Debit and Credit

Account Category	Increase (Normal Balance)	Decrease
Assets	Debit	Credit
Liabilities	Credit	Debit
Owner's Equity		
Capital	Credit	Debit
Withdrawals	Debit	Credit
Revenue	Credit	Debit
Expenses	Debit	Credit

Transaction B: Here we do the work but do not get the money yet. We see from the chart of accounts that revenue is called Professional Fees and customers owing money is called Accounts Receivable. Revenue for King Co. is going up, and customers owe the company more money. Increase in an asset is a debit, and increase in revenue is a credit.

Transaction C: Here we record Utilities Expense before it is paid. The expenses have increased for King Co. and it has increased what it owes the utility company. An increase in an expense is a debit and an increase in a liability is a credit. Here an expense has created a liability.

Transaction D: This is not a business expense since this is a personal withdrawal of cash by the owner. Jamie King, Withdrawals are increasing since King is taking the withdrawal but the business is lowering its cash from the withdrawal. An increase in withdrawal is a debit and a decrease in cash is a credit. Note the "dr" in the middle of "withdrawal." A withdrawal always increases by a debit.

Transaction E: In this transaction the business has another expense increasing and is paying for it in cash. The end result is that expenses increase on the debit side and cash, which is an asset, decreases on the credit side. Remember that we record expenses when they happen whether they are paid or not. Here they were paid. In transaction C they were not paid.

Summary: The transaction analysis charts are a great way to organize your information before deciding on what to debit or credit. Column 1 must come from the chart of accounts. In the category column you have six choices: assets, liabilities, capital, revenue, withdrawals, and expenses. The arrows tell you if the business accounts are increasing or decreasing. Note in column 5 that if an account is repeated a running summary of all transactions is accumulated in the account.

LEARNING UNIT 2-3 THE TRIAL BALANCE AND PREPARATION OF FINANCIAL STATEMENTS

Let us look at all the transactions we have discussed, arranged by T accounts and recorded using the rules of debit and credit. This grouping of accounts is much easier to use than the expanded accounting equation because all the transactions that affect a particular account are in one place.

Summary of Transactions of Mia Wong							
Assets	= Liabilities	+			Owner's Equity		

Cash 111		=	Accounts	+	Capital	− Withdrawals	+ Revenue	− Expenses

Cash 111

(A)	6,000	500 (B)
(D)	2,000	700 (G)
(F)	900	400 (H)
		100 (J)
8,900		1,700
7,200		

→ **Footings**
→ **New Balance**

Accounts Receivable 112

(E)	3,000	900 (F)
2,100		

Office Equipment 121

(A)	200	
(B)	500	
(C)	300	
1,000		

= Accounts Payable 211

	300 (C)
	200 (I)
	500

+ Mia Wong, Capital 311

	6,200 (A)

− Mia Wong, Withdrawals 312

(J) 100	

Legal Fees 411

	2,000 (D)
	3,000 (E)
	5,000

− Salaries Expenses 511

(G) 700	

− Rent Expense 512

(H) 400	

− Advertising Expense 513

(I) 200	

As we saw in Learning Unit 2-2, when all the transactions are recorded in the accounts, the total of all the debits should be equal to the total of all the credits. (If they are not, the accountant must go back and find the error by checking the numbers and adding every column again.)

● L03   ## The Trial Balance

Footings are used to obtain the totals of each side of every T account that has more than one entry. The footings are used to find the ending balance. The ending balances are used to prepare a trial balance. The trial balance is not a financial statement, although it is used to prepare financial statements. The trial balance lists all the accounts with their balances in the same order as they appear in the chart of accounts. It proves the accuracy of the ledger. For example, look at the preceding Cash account. The footing for the debit side is $8,900, and the footing for the credit side is $1,700. Because the debit side is larger, we subtract $1,700 from $8,900 to arrive at an *ending debit balance* of $7,200. Now look at the Rent Expense account. It doesn't need a footing because it has only one entry. The amount itself is the ending balance. When the ending balance has been found for every account, we should be able to show that the total of all debits equals the total of all credits.

Trial balance A list of the ending balances of all the accounts in a ledger. The total of the debits should equal the total of the credits.

In the ideal situation, businesses would take a trial balance every day. The large number of transactions most businesses conduct each day makes this impractical. Instead, trial balances are prepared periodically.

Keep in mind that the figure for Capital might not be the beginning figure if any additional investment has taken place during the period. You can tell by looking at the Capital account in the ledger.

A more detailed discussion of the trial balance is provided in the next chapter. For now, notice the heading, how the accounts are listed, the debits in the left column, the credits in the right, and that the total of debits is equal to the total of credits.

A trial balance of Mia Wong's accounts is shown in Figure 2.2.

FIGURE 2.2
Trial Balance for Mia Wong's
Law Firm

MIA WONG, ATTORNEY-AT-LAW
TRIAL BALANCE
SEPTEMBER 30, 201X

	Dr.	Cr.
Cash	7 2 0 0 00	
Accounts Receivable	2 1 0 0 00	
Office Equipment	1 0 0 0 00	
Accounts Payable		5 0 0 00
Mia Wong, Capital		6 2 0 0 00
Mia Wong, Withdrawals	1 0 0 00	
Legal Fees		5 0 0 0 00
Salaries Expense	7 0 0 00	
Rent Expense	4 0 0 00	
Advertising Expense	2 0 0 00	
Totals	11 7 0 0 00	11 7 0 0 00

COACHING TIP

Because this statement is not a formal one, it doesn't need dollar signs; the single and double lines under subtotals and final totals, however, are still used for clarity.

Preparing Financial Statements

● L04

The trial balance is used to prepare the financial statements. The diagram in Figure 2.3 (p. 56) shows how financial statements can be prepared from a trial balance. Statements do not have debit or credit columns. The left column is used only to subtotal numbers.

LEARNING UNIT 2-3 REVIEW

AT THIS POINT you should be able to do the following:

- Explain the role of footings.
- Prepare a trial balance from a set of accounts.
- Prepare financial statements from a trial balance.

Instant Replay ◎ Self-Review Quiz 2-3

As the bookkeeper of Pam's Hair Salon, you are to prepare from the accounts that follow on June 30, 201X (1) a trial balance as of June 30, (2) an income statement for the month ended June 30, (3) a statement of owner's equity for the month ended June 30, and (4) a balance sheet as of June 30, 201X.

Cash 111	
4,500	300
2,000	100
1,000	1,200
300	1,300
	2,600

Accounts Payable 211	
300	700

Salon Fees 411	
	3,500
	1,000

Accounts Receivable 121	
1,000	300

Pam Jay, Capital 311	
	4,000*

Rent Expense 511	
1,200	

Salon Equipment 131	
700	

Pam Jay, Withdrawals 321	
100	

Salon Supplies Expense 521	
1,300	

Salaries Expense 531	
2,600	

*No additional investments.

(solution page 57)

FIGURE 2.3
Steps in Preparing Financial Statements
from a Trial Balance

MIA WONG, ATTORNEY-AT-LAW
INCOME STATEMENT
FOR MONTH ENDED SEPTEMBER 30, 201X

Revenue:		
Legal Fees		$5 0 0 00
Operating Expenses:		
Salaries Expense	$7 0 0 00	
Rent Expense	4 0 0 00	
Advertising Expense	2 0 0 00	
Total Operating Expenses		1 3 0 0 00
Net Income		$3 7 0 0 00

MIA WONG, ATTORNEY-AT-LAW
TRIAL BALANCE
SEPTEMBER 30, 201X

	Dr.	Cr.
Cash	7 2 0 0 00	
Accounts Receivable	2 1 0 0 00	
Office Equipment	1 0 0 0 00	
Accounts Payable		5 0 0 00
Mia Wong, Capital		6 2 0 0 00
M. Wong, Withdrawals	1 0 0 00	
Legal Fees		5 0 0 0 00
Salaries Expense	7 0 0 00	
Rent Expense	4 0 0 00	
Advertising Expense	2 0 0 00	
Totals	11 7 0 0 00	11 7 0 0 00

MIA WONG, ATTORNEY-AT-LAW
STATEMENT OF OWNER'S EQUITY
FOR MONTH ENDED SEPTEMBER 30, 201X

Mia Wong, Capital		
September 1, 201X		$6 2 0 0 00
Net Income for September	$3 7 0 0 00	
Less Withdrawals		
for September	1 0 0 00	
Increase in Capital		3 6 0 0 00
Mia Wong, Capital		
September 30, 201X		$9 8 0 0 00

MIA WONG, ATTORNEY-AT-LAW
BALANCE SHEET
SEPTEMBER 30, 201X

Assets		Liabilities and Owner's Equity	
Cash	$7 2 0 0 00	Liabilities	
Accts. Receivable	2 1 0 0 00	Accounts Payable	$5 0 0 00
Office Equipm.	1 0 0 0 00	Owner's Equity	
		M. Wong, Capital	9 8 0 0 00
		Total Liab. and	
Total Assets	$10 3 0 0 00	Owner's Eq.	$10 3 0 0 00

Solution to Instant Replay: Self-Review Quiz 2-3

FIGURE 2.4

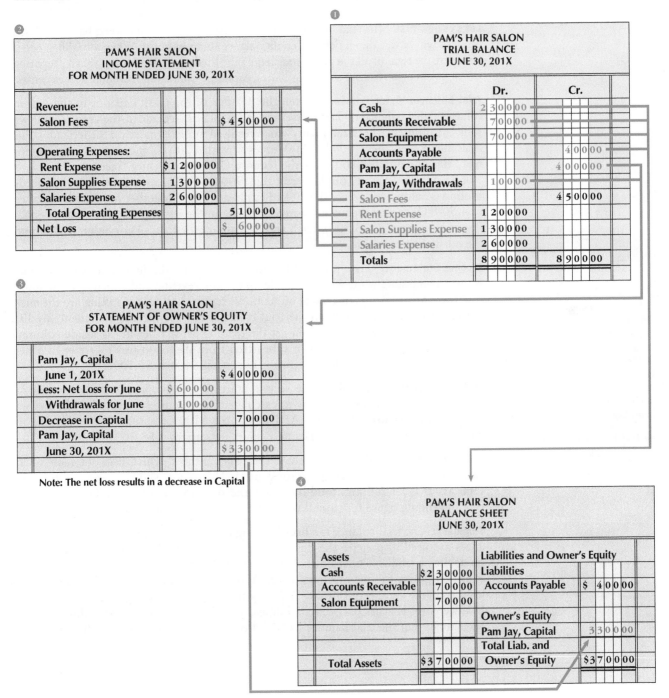

②

PAM'S HAIR SALON
INCOME STATEMENT
FOR MONTH ENDED JUNE 30, 201X

Revenue:			
Salon Fees			$ 4 5 0 0 00
Operating Expenses:			
Rent Expense	$1 2 0 0 00		
Salon Supplies Expense	1 3 0 0 00		
Salaries Expense	2 6 0 0 00		
Total Operating Expenses		5 1 0 0 00	
Net Loss		$ 6 0 0 00	

①

PAM'S HAIR SALON
TRIAL BALANCE
JUNE 30, 201X

	Dr.	Cr.
Cash	2 3 0 0 00	
Accounts Receivable	7 0 0 00	
Salon Equipment	7 0 0 00	
Accounts Payable		4 0 0 00
Pam Jay, Capital		4 0 0 0 00
Pam Jay, Withdrawals	1 0 0 00	
Salon Fees		4 5 0 0 00
Rent Expense	1 2 0 0 00	
Salon Supplies Expense	1 3 0 0 00	
Salaries Expense	2 6 0 0 00	
Totals	8 9 0 0 00	8 9 0 0 00

③

PAM'S HAIR SALON
STATEMENT OF OWNER'S EQUITY
FOR MONTH ENDED JUNE 30, 201X

Pam Jay, Capital			
June 1, 201X		$ 4 0 0 0 00	
Less: Net Loss for June	$ 6 0 0 00		
Withdrawals for June	1 0 0 00		
Decrease in Capital		7 0 0 00	
Pam Jay, Capital			
June 30, 201X		$ 3 3 0 0 00	

Note: The net loss results in a decrease in Capital

④

PAM'S HAIR SALON
BALANCE SHEET
JUNE 30, 201X

Assets		Liabilities and Owner's Equity	
Cash	$2 3 0 0 00	Liabilities	
Accounts Receivable	7 0 0 00	Accounts Payable	$ 4 0 0 00
Salon Equipment	7 0 0 00		
		Owner's Equity	
		Pam Jay, Capital	3 3 0 0 00
		Total Liab. and	
Total Assets	$3 7 0 0 00	Owner's Equity	$3 7 0 0 00

PLAY BY PLAY: EXTRA HELP ON SELF-REVIEW QUIZ 2-3

Let's review first: The trial balance is a list of accounts and their ending balances. Each account will have either a debit or credit balance (but not both). When a trial balance is complete the total of all the debits must equal the total of all the credits. When preparing a trial balance you list out assets, liabilities, capital, withdrawals, revenue, and expenses.

Trial balance: After you have taken the balance of the Cash account in the ledger, it has a debit balance of 2,300 (we added the debits, we added the credits, and we took the difference between them, which resulted in 2,300 more on the left side). For Accounts Receivable 1,000 less 300 leaves us with a 700 debit balance. Salon Equipment has one number, so that is the balance (700 debit). Once Accounts Payable is balanced it is 400 larger on the credit side (700–300). The only other title that needs footing is Salon Fees, so the 3,500 and 1,000 are added together for a credit balance of 4,500. Once each balance is listed the sum on the left (8,900) does indeed equal the sum on the right (8,900). Each ending balance for Pam's Hair Salon ends up on the normal balance side.

Income Statement: Once the trial balance is complete, the first statement to make is the income statement, which is made up of only revenue and expense. Remember that there are no debits or credits on financial reports. All we are taking are the ending balances of each title from the trial balance. For the income statement, we list salon fees as the revenue and then list the three expense titles in the inside column. Total operating expenses are then subtracted from the salon fees to arrive at a net loss. Here revenue is less than operating expenses ($4,500–$5,100).

Statement of Owner's Equity: The second statement to prepare is the statement of owner's equity, which shows how to calculate a new figure for capital. Note that in this case the net loss of $600 is ADDED to the $100 of withdrawals, resulting in a decrease of $700 to capital. The new figure for capital is $3,300 ($4,000–$700).

Balance Sheet: The third statement is the balance sheet, which lists out each asset, each liability, and the new figure for capital. This report shows that as of June 30 total assets is $3,700 and total liabilities and owner's equity is $3,700. Remember that the ending figure for capital comes from the statement of owner's equity.

Summary: The trial balance is a list of ending balances of ledger accounts. These balances are used to prepare the three financial statements. Financial statements have no debits or credits. The inside columns are used to subtotal numbers. Revenue and expenses go on the income statement. Withdrawals and either net income or net loss go on the statement of owner's equity to calculate a new figure for capital. The balance sheet is a list of assets, liabilities, and the new amount for ending capital. Remember that the trial balance has debit or credits, not the financial statements.

COACHING TIP

	Dr.	Cr.
Cash	x	
Acc. Rec.	x	
Salon Equip.	x	
Accounts Pay.		x
Pam Jay, Cap.		x
Pam Jay, Withd.	x	
Salon Fees		x
Rent Expense	x	
Salon Supp. Exp.	x	
Salaries Exp.	x	

Note that titles on the trial balance are not indented.

DEMONSTRATION PROBLEM

MyAccountingLab

Debits and Credits: Analyzing and Recording Business Transactions

◖◖◖◖◯ LO1, 2, 3, 4

The chart of accounts of Mel's Delivery Service includes the following: Cash, 111; Accounts Receivable, 112; Office Equipment, 121; Delivery Trucks, 122; Accounts Payable, 211; Mel Free, Capital, 311; Mel Free, Withdrawals, 312; Delivery Fees Earned, 411; Advertising Expense, 511; Gas Expense, 512; Salaries Expense, 513; and Telephone Expense, 514. The following transactions resulted for Mel's Delivery Service during the month of July:

Transaction A:	Mel invested $10,000 in the business from his personal savings account.
Transaction B:	Bought delivery trucks on account, $17,000.
Transaction C:	Advertising bill received but unpaid, $700.
Transaction D:	Bought office equipment for cash, $1,200.
Transaction E:	Received cash for delivery services rendered, $15,000.
Transaction F:	Paid salaries expense, $3,000.
Transaction G:	Paid gas expense for company trucks, $1,250.
Transaction H:	Billed customers for delivery services rendered, $4,000.
Transaction I:	Paid telephone bill, $300.
Transaction J:	Received $3,000 as partial payment of transaction H.
Transaction K:	Mel paid home telephone bill from company checkbook, $150.

Requirements

As Mel's newly employed accountant, you must do the following:

1. Set up T accounts in a ledger.

2. Record transactions in the T accounts. (Place the letter of the transaction next to the entry.)

3. Foot and take the balance of each account where appropriate.

4. Prepare a trial balance at the end of July.

5. Prepare from the trial balance, in proper form, (a) an income statement for the month of July, (b) a statement of owner's equity, and (c) a balance sheet as of July 31, 201X.

Demonstration Problem Solution

Requirements 1, 2, 3, 4

Set up T accounts, record transactions, foot each account, and prepare a trial balance.

Part 1	Part 2	Demonstration Problem Complete

GENERAL LEDGER

Cash 111				Accts. Payable 211			Advertising Expense 511	
(A)	10,000	1,200	(D)		17,000	(B)	(C)	700
(E)	15,000	3,000	(F)		700	(C)		
(J)	3,000	1,250	(G)		17,700			
		300	(I)					
		150	(K)					
	28,000	5,900						
	22,100							

Accts. Receivable 112				Mel Free, Capital 311			Gas Expense 512	
(H)	4,000	3,000	(J)		10,000	(A)	(G)	1,250
	1,000							

Office Equipment 121		Mel Free, Withdrawals 312		Salaries Expense 513	
(D)	1,200	(K)	150	(F)	3,000

Delivery Trucks 122		Delivery Fees Earned 411			Telephone Expense 514	
(B)	17,000		15,000	(E)	(I)	300
			4,000	(H)		
			19,000			

Solution Tips to Recording Transactions

A. Cash	A	↑	Dr.
Mel Free, Capital	Cap.	↑	Cr.
B. Delivery Trucks	A	↑	Dr.
Accts. Payable	L	↑	Cr.
C. Advertising Expense	Exp.	↑	Dr.
Accts. Payable	L	↑	Cr.
D. Office Equipment	A	↑	Dr.
Cash	A	↓	Cr.
E. Cash	A	↑	Dr.
Del. Fees Earned	Rev.	↑	Cr.
F. Salaries Expense	Exp.	↑	Dr.
Cash	A	↓	Cr.
G. Gas Expense	Exp.	↑	Dr.
Cash	A	↓	Cr.
H. Acc. Receivable	A	↑	Dr.
Del. Fees Earned	Rev.	↑	Cr.
I. Tel. Expense	Exp.	↑	Dr.
Cash	A	↓	Cr.
J. Cash	A	↑	Dr.
Accts. Receivable	A	↓	Cr.
K. Mel Free, Withd.	Withd.	↑	Dr.
Cash	A	↓	Cr.

Mel's Delivery Service
Trial Balance
July 31, 201X

	Dr.	Cr.
Cash	22,100	
Accounts Receivable	1,000	
Office Equipment	1,200	
Delivery Trucks	17,000	
Accounts Payable		17,700
Mel Free, Capital		10,000
Mel Free, Withdrawals	150	
Delivery Fees Earned		19,000
Advertising Expense	700	
Gas Expense	1,250	
Salaries Expense	3,000	
Telephone Expense	300	
TOTALS	46,700	46,700

Solution Tips to Taking the Balance of an Account and Preparation of a Trial Balance

3. Footings: Cash   Add left side, $28,000.

Add right side, $5,900.

Take difference, $22,100, and stay on side that is larger.

Accounts Payable Add $17,000 + $700 and stay on same side.

Total is $17,700.

4. Trial balance is a list of the ledger's ending balances. The list is in the same order as the chart of accounts. Each title has only one number listed either as a debit or credit balance.

Requirement 5

Prepare an Income Statement, Statement of Owner's Equity, and a Balance Sheet from the Trial Balance.

Part 1	Part 2	Demonstration Problem Complete

FIGURE 2.5
Financial Statements

5a.

MEL'S DELIVERY SERVICE INCOME STATEMENT FOR MONTH ENDED JULY 31, 201X								
Revenue:								
Delivery Fees Earned						$19 0 0	0 00
Operating Expenses:								
Advertising Expense	$	7 0 0	00					
Gas Expense	1	2 5 0	00					
Salaries Expense	3	0 0 0	00					
Telephone Expense		3 0 0	00					
Total Operating Expenses					5 2 5	0 00		
Net Income					$13 7 5	0 00		

b.

MEL'S DELIVERY SERVICE STATEMENT OF OWNER'S EQUITY FOR MONTH ENDED JULY 31, 201X						
Mel Free, Capital						
July 1, 201X				$10 0 0	0 00	
Net Income for July	$13 7 5 0	00				
Less Withdrawals for July	1 5 0	00				
Increase in Capital				$13 6 0	0 00	
Mel Free, Capital						
July 31, 201X				$23 6 0	0 00	

c.

MEL'S DELIVERY SERVICE BALANCE SHEET JULY 31, 201X					
Assets			Liabilities and Owner's Equity		
Cash	$22 1 0 0 00		Liabilities		
Accounts Receivable	1 0 0 0 00		Accounts Payable	$17 7 0 0 00	
Office Equipment	1 2 0 0 00				
Delivery Trucks	17 0 0 0 00				
			Owner's Equity		
			Mel Free, Capital	23 6 0 0 00	
			Total Liab. and		
Total Assets	$41 3 0 0 00		Owner's Equity	$41 3 0 0 00	

Solution Tips to Prepare Financial Statements from a Trial Balance

Trial Balance

		Dr.	Cr.
Balance Sheet	Assets	X	
	Liabilities		X
Statement of Equity	Capital		X
	Withdrawals	X	
Income Statement	Revenues		X
	Expenses	X	
		XX	XX

Net income of $13,750 on the income statement goes on the statement of owner's equity.

Ending capital of $23,600 on the statement of owner's equity goes on the balance sheet as the new figure for capital.

Note: Financial statements do not show debits or credits. The inside column is used for subtotaling.

Part 1	Part 2	Demonstration Problem Complete

BLUEPRINT: PREPARING FINANCIAL STATEMENTS FROM A TRIAL BALANCE

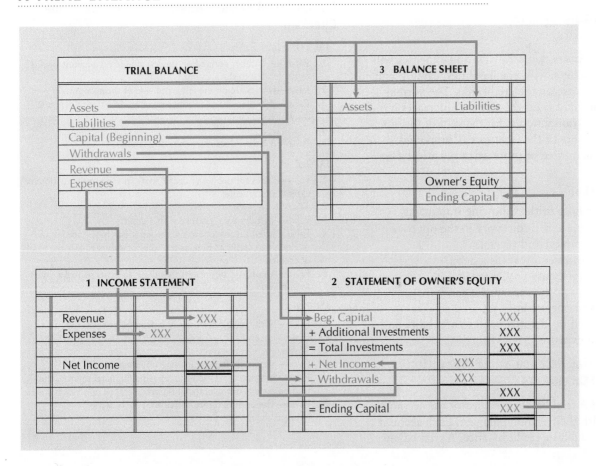

ACCOUNTING COACH

The following Coaching Tips are from Learning Units 2-1 to 2-3. Take the Pre-Game Checkup and use the Check Your Score at the bottom of the page to see how you are doing. The Accounting Coach provides tips before each Checkup to help you avoid common accounting errors.

LU 2-1 The T Account

Pre-Game Tips: Think of "debit" or "credit" as only indicating a position (left or right). To balance an account, total the left (debit) side and the right (credit) side and take the difference between the two totals. This ending balance is placed on the side that is greater. Do not think at this point of "debit" or "credit" as being good or bad. They simply indicate a position, left or right.

Pre-Game Checkup

Answer true or false to the following statements.

1. A number entered on the left side of an account is said to be credited to the account.
2. Debits always are positive.
3. Footings are always a credit balance.
4. "Credit" always means the number should be put on the right side.
5. A ledger does not use debits or credits.

LU 2-2 Recording Business Transactions: Debits and Credits

Pre-Game Tips: Assets, withdrawals, and expenses will increase on the debit side, while liabilities, capital, and revenues will increase on the credit side. The normal balance of an account is on the side that increases it. The goal of each transaction is for the sum of the left side to equal the sum of the right side. Compound entries result when three or more accounts affect a transaction.

Pre-Game Checkup

Answer true or false to the following statements.

1. Rules for debit and credit work in the opposite direction as capital and revenue.
2. Increase in an asset always is a debit.
3. Withdrawals increase with a credit.
4. After a transaction is recorded it can have only one debit and one credit.
5. An unpaid bill results in a debit to a liability and a credit to an expense.

LU 2-3 The Trial Balance and Preparation of Financial Statements

Pre-Game Tips: A trial balance is a list of the accounts in the ledger with their ending balances. Each account can only have a debit or credit balance. A trial balance will list assets, liabilities, capital, withdrawals, revenue, and expenses. When the financial statements are prepared there are no debits or credits on the financial reports. It is the ending balance of each account that is listed. The inside columns of financial reports are used for subtotaling.

Pre-Game Checkup

Answer true or false to the following statements.

1. Withdrawals are usually a credit balance on the trial balance.
2. A balance sheet will list only debit accounts.
3. The balance sheet is always prepared before the income statement.
4. Subtotaling is only used on the trial balance.
5. The beginning balance of capital is shown on the balance sheet.

CHECK YOUR SCORE: Answers to the Pre-Game Checkup

LU 2-1

1. False—A number entered on the left side of an account is said to be debited to the account.
2. False—Debits are on the left-hand side of the account.
3. False—Whether or not footings are a credit balance depends on which side is larger after balancing.
4. True.
5. False—A ledger does use debits and credits.

LU 2-2

1. False—Rules for debit and credit work in the same direction as capital and revenue.
2. True.
3. False—Withdrawals increase with a debit.
4. False—After a transaction is recorded it can have more than one debit or credit as long as the total of debits equals the total of credits.
5. False—An unpaid bill results in a debit to expense and a credit to liability.

LU 2-3

1. False—Withdrawals are usually a debit balance on the trial balance.
2. True.
3. False—prepared after the income statement.
4. False—Subtotaling is used in preparing financial reports; the trial balance is not a financial report.
5. False—The ending figure for capital is shown on the balance sheet.

Chapter Summary

Here are all the key concepts and equations to help you understand the concepts of this chapter and prepare you for your exam. After completing this review, go to MyAccountingLab for more practice opportunities.

MyAccountingLab

Concepts You Should Know	Key Terms	
Setting up and organizing a chart of accounts. 1. A T account is a simplified version of a standard account. 2. A ledger is a group of accounts. 3. A debit is the left-hand position (side) of an account, and a credit is the right-hand position (side). 4. A footing is the total of one side of an account. The ending balance is the difference between the footings.	Chart of accounts (p. 44) Compound entry (p. 45) Double-entry book-keeping (p. 45)	⬤ **L01**
Recording transactions in T accounts according to the rules of debit and credit. 1. A chart of accounts lists the account titles and their numbers for a company. 2. The transaction analysis chart is a teaching device. 3. A compound entry is a transaction involving more than one debit or credit. 4. In double-entry bookkeeping, the recording of each business transaction affects two or more accounts, and the total of debits equals the total of credits. 5. A trial balance is a list of the ending balances of all accounts, listed in the same order as the chart of accounts. 6. Any additional investments during the period result in the Capital balance on the trial balance not being the beginning figure. 7. No debit or credit columns are used in the three financial statements.	Account (p. 40) Credit (p. 40) Debit (p. 40) Ending balance (p. 41) Footings (p. 41) Ledger (p. 40) Normal balance of an account (p. 43) Standard account (p. 40) T account (p. 40)	⬤ **L02**
Preparing a trial balance. 1. A trial balance is a list of the ending balances of all accounts, listed in the same order as chart of accounts. 2. Any additional investments during the period result in the Capital balance on the trial balance not being the beginning figure.	Trial balance (p. 54)	⬤ **L03**
Preparing financial statements from a trial balance. 1. No debit or credit columns are used in the three financial statements. 2. To prepare the financial statements, take the balances of each ledger account to prepare the income statement, statement of owner's equity, and balance sheet.		◯ **L04**

Discussion Questions and Critical Thinking/Ethical Case

1. Define a ledger.

2. Why is the left-hand side of an account called a debit?

3. Footings are used in balancing all accounts. True or false? Please explain.

4. What is the end product of the accounting process?

5. What do we mean when we say that a transaction analysis chart is a teaching device?

6. What are the five steps of the transaction analysis chart?

7. Explain the concept of double-entry bookkeeping.

8. A trial balance is a formal statement. True or false? Please explain.

9. Why are there no debit or credit columns on financial statements?

10. Compare the financial statements prepared from the expanded accounting equation with those prepared from a trial balance.

11. Audrey Flet, the bookkeeper of ALN Co., was scheduled to leave on a three-week vacation at 5:00 on Friday. She couldn't get the company's trial balance to balance. At 4:30, she decided to put in fictitious figures to make it balance. Audrey told herself she would fix it when she got back from her vacation. Was Audrey right or wrong to do this? Why?

MyAccountingLab   ## Concept Checks

○○ **LO1, 2** *(5 MIN)*   **The T Account**

1.   From the following, foot and balance each account.

Cash 110				Ken Dalton, Capital 311	
7/24	3,000	7/25	100	7/3	11,000
7/26	11,000			7/11	6,000
				7/21	7,000

○ **LO2** *(5 MIN)*   **Transaction Analysis**

2.   Complete the following:

Account	Category	↑	↓	Normal Balance
A. Accounts Payable				
B. Taxable Fees Earned				
C. Accounts Receivable				
D. M. Blanc, Capital				
E. M. Blanc, Withdrawals				
F. Prepaid Advertising				
G. Rent Expense				

Transaction Analysis

L02 *(5 MIN)*

3. Record the following transaction in the transaction analysis chart: Provided legal fees for $5,000, receiving $500 cash with the remainder to be paid next month.

Accounts Affected	Category	↓	↑	Rules of Dr. and Cr.	T Accounts

Trial Balance

L04 *(5 MIN)*

4. Rearrange the following titles in the order they would appear on a trial balance:

B. O'Mally, Withdrawals   Hair Salon Fees Earned

Accounts Receivable   Selling Expense

Cash   Salary Expense

B. O'Mally, Capital   Advertising Expense

Office Equipment   Accounts Payable

Trial Balance/Financial Statements

L03 *(10 MIN)*

5. From the following trial balance, identify which statement each title will appear on:

- Income statement (IS)
- Statement of owner's equity (OE)
- Balance sheet (BS)

Bradford Co.
Trial Balance
Nov. 30, 201X

		Dr.	Cr.
A. _____	Cash	600	
B. _____	Computer	100	
C. _____	Computer Equipment	1,000	
D. _____	Accounts Payable		800
E. _____	L. Bradford, Capital		200
F. _____	L. Bradford, Withdrawals	500	
G. _____	Legal Fees Earned		1,500
H. _____	Consulting Fees Earned		300
I. _____	Wage Expense	200	
J. _____	Supplies Expense	250	
K. _____	Internet Advertising Expense	150	
	Totals	2,800	2,800

MyAccountingLab   Exercises

Set A

LO1 *(10 MIN)*   **2A-1.** From the following, prepare a chart of accounts.

Panasonic HD Television	Legal Fees
Salary Expense	L. Janas, Capital
Accounts Payable	Cash
Accounts Receivable	Advertising Expense
Repair Expense	L. Janas, Withdrawals

LO2 *(5 MIN)*   **2A-2.** Record the following transaction in the transaction analysis chart: Shaylin Princeton bought a new piece of computer equipment for $26,000, paying $9,000 down and charging the rest.

LO2 *(5 MIN)*   **2A-3.** Complete the following table. For each account listed on the left, fill in what category it belongs to, whether increases and decreases in the account are marked on the debit or credit sides, and on which financial statement the account appears. A sample is provided.

Accounts Affected	Category	↑	↓	Appears on Which Financial Statements
Computer Supplies	Asset	Dr.	Cr.	Balance Sheet
Legal Fees Earned				
P. Roy, Withdrawals				
Accounts Payable				
Salaries Expense				
Auto				

LO2 *(20 MIN)*   **2A-4.** Given the following accounts, complete the table by inserting appropriate numbers next to the individual transaction to indicate which account is debited and which account is credited.

1. Cash
2. Accounts Receivable
3. Equipment
4. Accounts Payable
5. B. Barker, Capital
6. B. Barker, Withdrawals
7. Plumbing Fees Earned
8. Salaries Expense
9. Advertising Expense
10. Supplies Expenses

			Rules	
	Transaction		Dr.	Cr.
Example: **A.**	Paid salaries expense.		8	1
B.	Bob paid personal utilities bill from the company checkbook.			
C.	Advertising bill received but unpaid.			
D.	Received cash from plumbing fees.			
E.	Paid supplies expense.			
F.	Bob invested in additional equipment for the business.			
G.	Billed customers for plumbing services rendered.			
H.	Received one-half the balance from transaction G.			
I.	Bought equipment on account.			

2A-5. From the following trial balance of Hill's Cleaners (Figure 2.6), prepare the following: ⬤ **L04** *(20 MIN)*

- Income statement
- Statement of owner's equity
- Balance sheet

FIGURE 2.6

HILL'S CLEANERS
TRIAL BALANCE
MAY 31, 201X

	Dr.	Cr.
Cash	8 0 0 00	
Equipment	7 0 0 00	
Accounts Payable		5 0 0 00
J. Hill, Capital		1 0 8 6 00
J. Hill, Withdrawals	2 3 0 00	
Cleaning Fees		4 1 5 00
Salaries Expense	1 0 0 00	
Utilities Expense	1 7 1 00	
Totals	2 0 0 1 00	2 0 0 1 00

Set B

2B-1. From the following, prepare a chart of accounts. ⬤ **L01** *(10 MIN)*

Copy machine	Legal Fees Earned
Salary Expense	L. Jones, Capital
Accounts Payable	Cash
Accounts Receivable	Advertising Expense
Rent Expense	L. Jones, Withdrawals

2B-2. Record the following transaction in the transaction analysis chart: Sally Pallermo bought a new piece of computer equipment for $11,000, paying $10,000 down and charging the rest. ⬤ **L02** *(5 MIN)*

2B-3. Complete the following table. For each account listed on the left, fill in what category it belongs to, whether increases and decreases in the account are marked on the debit or credit sides, and on which financial statement the account appears. A sample is provided. ⬤ **L02** *(5 MIN)*

Accounts Affected	Category	Increases	Decreases	Appears on Which Financial Statement
Office Supplies	Asset	Dr.	Cr.	Balance Sheet
Rental Fees Earned				
A. Troy, Withdrawals				
Accounts Payable				
Wage Expense				
Computer				

2B-4. Given the following accounts, complete the table by inserting appropriate numbers next to the individual transaction to indicate which account is debited and which account is credited. ⬤ **L02** *(20 MIN)*

1. Cash
2. Accounts Receivable
3. Furniture
4. Accounts Payable
5. B. Martin, Capital

6. B. Martin, Withdrawals
7. Photography Fees Earned
8. Salaries Expense
9. Advertising Expense
10. Supplies Expenses

		Transaction	Rules Dr.	Cr.
Example:	A.	Paid salaries expense.	8	1
	B.	Bill paid personal utilities bill from the company checkbook.		
	C.	Advertising bill received but unpaid.		
	D.	Received cash from photography fees.		
	E.	Paid supplies expense.		
	F.	Bill invested in additional furniture for the business.		
	G.	Billed customers for photography services rendered.		
	H.	Received one-half the balance from transaction G.		
	I.	Bought furniture on account.		

LO4 *(20 MIN)*

2B-5. From the following trial balance of Hill's Cleaners (Figure 2.7), prepare the following:

- Income statement
- Statement of owner's equity
- Balance sheet

FIGURE 2.7

HILL'S CLEANERS
TRIAL BALANCE
MAY 31, 201X

	Dr.	Cr.
Cash	8 0 0 00	
Equipment	7 0 0 00	
Accounts Payable		5 0 0 00
J. Hill, Capital		1 0 8 6 00
J. Hill, Withdrawals	2 3 0 00	
Cleaning Fees		4 1 5 00
Salaries Expense	1 0 0 00	
Utilities Expense	1 7 1 00	
Totals	2 0 0 1 00	2 0 0 1 00

MyAccountingLab   ## Problems

Set A

LO2 *(20 MIN)*

2A-1. The following transactions occurred in the opening and operation of Bryce's Delivery Service.

a. Bryce Orwell opened the delivery service by investing $28,000 from his personal savings account.
b. Purchased used delivery trucks on account, $12,000.
c. Rent expense due but unpaid, $1,200.
d. Received cash for delivery, $2,100.
e. Billed a client on account, $300.
f. Bryce withdrew cash for personal use, $800.

Check Figure:
After F:

Cash	
(A) 28,000	800 (F)
(D) 2,100	

Complete a transaction analysis chart for each of the transactions. The chart of accounts includes Cash; Accounts Receivable; Delivery Trucks; Accounts Payable; Bryce Orwell, Capital; Bryce Orwell, Withdrawals; Delivery Fees Earned; and Rent Expense.

2A-2. Brian Pud opened a consulting company, and the following transactions resulted:

● **L02** *(20 MIN)*

a. Brian invested $40,000 in the consulting agency.

b. Bought office equipment on account, $7,000.

c. Agency received cash for consulting work that it completed for a client, $2,000.

d. Brian paid a personal bill from the company checkbook, $150.

e. Paid advertising expense for the month, $300.

f. Rent expense for the month due but unpaid, $1,000.

g. Paid $1,100 as partial payment of what was owed from transaction B.

As Brian's accountant, analyze and record the transactions in T account form. Set up the T accounts and label each entry with the letter of the transaction.

Check Figure:
After G:

Cash

(A)	40,000	150	(D)
(C)	2,000	300	(E)
		1,100	(G)

Chart of Accounts

Assets	**Revenue**
Cash 111	Consulting Fees Earned 411
Office Equipment 121	
Liabilities	**Expenses**
Accounts Payable 211	Advertising Expense 511
	Rent Expense 512
Owner's Equity	
Brian Pud, Capital 311	
Brian Pud, Withdrawals 312	

2A-3. From the following T accounts of Brad's Cleaning Service, (a) record and foot the balances, and (b) prepare a trial balance in proper form for October 31, 201X.

● **L03** *(20 MIN)*

Cash 111			
(A)	10,000	(D)	300
(G)	4,000	(E)	400
		(F)	200
		(H)	300
		(I)	1,000

Accounts Payable 211			
(D)	300	(C)	2,300

Cleaning Fees Earned 411		
	(B)	7,000

Check Figure:
Trial Balance Total $19,000

Accounts Receivable 112			
(B)	7,000	(G)	4,000

Brad Joy, Capital 311		
	(A)	10,000

Rent Expense 511	
(F)	200

Office Equipment 121	
(C)	2,300
(H)	300

Brad Joy, Withdrawals 312	
(I)	1,000

Utilities Expense 512	
(E)	400

2A-4. From the trial balance of Gail Lucas, Attorney-at-Law (Figure 2.8), prepare (a) an income statement for the month of May, (b) a statement of owner's equity for the month ended May 31, and (c) a balance sheet at May 31, 201X.

● **L04** *(40 MIN)*

PT/QB

FIGURE 2.8

Check Figure:
Total Assets $7,350

GAIL LUCAS, ATTORNEY-AT-LAW TRIAL BALANCE MAY 31, 201X		
	Dr.	Cr.
Cash	5 0 0 0 00	
Accounts Receivable	1 1 0 0 00	
Office Equipment	1 2 5 0 00	
Accounts Payable		3 0 0 0 00
Salaries Payable		7 6 0 00
G. Lucas, Capital		3 6 9 0 00
G. Lucas, Withdrawals	6 0 0 00	
Revenue from Legal Fees		1 6 5 0 0 0
Utilities Expense	3 5 0 00	
Rent Expense	6 5 0 00	
Salaries Expense	1 5 0 00	
Totals	9 1 0 0 00	9 1 0 0 00

L02, 3, 4 *(60 MIN)*

Check Figure:
Total Trial Balance $45,200

2A-5. The chart of accounts for Annis's Delivery Service is as follows:

Chart of Accounts

Assets	**Revenue**
Cash 111	Delivery Fees Earned 411
Accounts Receivable 112	**Expenses**
Office Equipment 121	Advertising Expense 511
Delivery Trucks 122	Gas Expense 512
Liabilities	Salaries Expense 513
Accounts Payable 211	Telephone Expense 514
Owner's Equity	
Avery Annis, Capital 311	
Avery Annis, Withdrawals 312	

Annis's Delivery Service completed the following transactions during the month of August:

Transaction A:	Avery Annis invested $29,000 in the delivery service from her personal savings account.
Transaction B:	Bought delivery trucks on account, $12,000.
Transaction C:	Bought office equipment for cash, $600.
Transaction D:	Paid advertising expense, $650.
Transaction E:	Collected cash for delivery services rendered, $2,300.
Transaction F:	Paid drivers' salaries, $600.
Transaction G:	Paid gas expense for trucks, $1,600.
Transaction H:	Performed delivery services for a customer on account, $1,700.
Transaction I:	Telephone expense due but unpaid, $200.
Transaction J:	Received $250 as partial payment of transaction H.
Transaction K:	Avery withdrew cash for personal use, $300.

As Avery's newly hired accountant, you must perform the following:

1. The T accounts in the ledger have been set up for you. Record transactions in the T accounts. (Place the letter of the transaction next to the entry.)
2. Foot the T accounts where appropriate.
3. Prepare a trial balance at the end of August.
4. Prepare from the trial balance, in proper form, (a) an income statement for the month of August, (b) a statement of owner's equity, and (c) a balance sheet as of August 31, 201X.

CHAPTER 2 Debits and Credits: Analyzing and Recording Business Transactions 73

Set B

2B-1. The following transactions occurred in the opening and operation of Bryon's Delivery Service. Complete a transaction analysis chart for each of the transactions.

Transaction A:	Bryon Orn opened the delivery service by investing $50,000 from his personal savings account.
Transaction B:	Purchased used delivery trucks on account, $7,000.
Transaction C:	Rent expense due but unpaid, $1,200.
Transaction D:	Received cash for delivery, $1,700.
Transaction E:	Billed a client on account, $150.
Transaction F:	Bryon withdrew cash for personal use, $100.

The chart of accounts for the shop includes Cash; Accounts Receivable; Delivery Truck; Accounts Payable; Bryon Orn, Capital; Bryon Orn, Withdrawals; Delivery Fees Earned; and Rent Expense.

2B-2. Brian Pud opened a consulting company, and the following transactions resulted. As Brian's accountant, analyze and record the transactions in T account form. Label each entry with the letter of the transaction.

Transaction A:	Brian invested $18,000 in the consulting agency.
Transaction B:	Bought office equipment on account, $4,000.
Transaction C:	Agency received cash for consulting work that it completed for a client, $2,400.
Transaction D:	Brian paid a personal bill from the company checkbook, $50.
Transaction E:	Paid advertising expense for the month, $200.
Transaction F:	Rent expense for the month due but unpaid, $1,200.
Transaction G:	Paid $900 as partial payment of what was owed from transaction B.

The chart of accounts includes Cash, 111; Office Equipment, 121; Accounts Payable, 211; Brian Pud, Capital, 311; Brian Pud, Withdrawals, 312; Consulting Fees Earned, 411; Advertising Expense, 511; and Rent Expense, 512.

2B-3. From the following T accounts of Brad's Cleaning Service, (a) record and foot the balances, and (b) prepare a trial balance in proper form for October 31, 201X.

Cash 111			
(A)	12,000	(D)	1,000
(G)	3,500	(E)	150
		(F)	100
		(H)	250
		(I)	600

Accounts Receivable 112			
(B)	14,000	(G)	3,500

Office Equipment 121		
(C)	1,400	
(H)	250	

Accounts Payable 211			
(D)	1,000	(C)	1,400

Brad Joy, Capital 311		
	(A)	12,000

Brad Joy, Withdrawals 312		
(I)	600	

Cleaning Fees Earned 411		
	(B)	14,000

Rent Expense 511		
(F)	100	

Utilities Expense 512		
(E)	150	

Check Figure:
After F:

Cash

(A) 50,000	100 (F)
(D) 1,700	

Check Figure:
After G:

Cash

(A) 18,000	50 (D)
(C) 2,400	200 (E)
	900 (G)

Check Figure:
Trial Balance Total $26,400

LO2 *(20 MIN)*

LO2 *(20 MIN)*

LO3 *(20 MIN)*

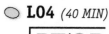

L04 *(40 MIN)*

2B-4. From the trial balance of Gail Lucas, Attorney-at-Law (Figure 2.9), prepare (a) an income statement for the month of May, (b) a statement of owner's equity for the month ended May 31, and (c) a balance sheet at May 31, 201X.

FIGURE 2.9

Check Figure:
Total Assets $8,000

GAIL LUCAS, ATTORNEY-AT-LAW TRIAL BALANCE MAY 31, 201X				
		Debit		Credit
Cash		6 0 0 0 00		
Accounts Receivable		7 5 0 00		
Office Equipment		1 2 5 0 00		
Accounts Payable				6 2 0 0 00
Salaries Payable				7 7 0 00
G. Lucas, Capital				1 1 8 0 00
G. Lucas, Withdrawals		8 0 0 00		
Revenue from Legal Fees				1 8 0 0 00
Utilities Expense		1 5 0 00		
Rent Expense		5 0 0 00		
Salaries Expense		5 0 0 00		
Totals		9 9 5 0 00		9 9 5 0 00

L02, 3, 4 *(60 MIN)*

Check Figure:
Trial Balance Total $33,700

2B-5. The chart of accounts of Annis's Delivery Service is as follows: Cash, 111; Accounts Receivable, 112; Office Equipment, 121; Delivery Trucks, 122; Accounts Payable, 211; Avery Annis, Capital, 311; Avery Annis, Withdrawals, 312; Delivery Fees Earned, 411; Advertising Expense, 511; Gas Expense, 512; Salaries Expense, 513; and Telephone Expense, 514. Annis's Delivery Service completed the following transactions during the month of August:

Transaction A:	Avery invested $17,000 in the delivery service from her personal savings account.
Transaction B:	Bought delivery trucks on account, $11,000.
Transaction C:	Bought office equipment for cash, $600.
Transaction D:	Paid advertising expense, $350.
Transaction E:	Collected cash for delivery services rendered, $3,500.
Transaction F:	Paid drivers' salaries, $900.
Transaction G:	Paid gas expense for trucks, $1,700.
Transaction H:	Performed delivery services for a customer on account, $1,600.
Transaction I:	Telephone expense due but unpaid, $600.
Transaction J:	Received $400 as partial payment of transaction H.
Transaction K:	Avery withdrew cash for personal use, $250.

As Avery's newly hired accountant, you must perform the following:

1. The T accounts in the ledger have been set up for you. Record transactions in the T accounts. (Place the letter of the transaction next to the entry.)
2. Foot the T accounts where appropriate.
3. Prepare a trial balance at the end of August.
4. Prepare from the trial balance, in proper form, (a) an income statement for the month of August, (b) a statement of owner's equity, and (c) a balance sheet as of August 31, 201X.

Financial Report Problem

Reading the Kellogg's Annual Report

○ **LO4** (5 min)

Go to http://investor.kelloggs.com/annuals.cfm, to access the Kellogg's 2010 Annual Report and find the balance sheet of Kellogg's. Did Kellogg's Accounts Payable go up or down from 2009 to 2010? What does this change mean? Into what category does Accounts Payable fall by rules of debit and credit? Which side of the T account would make Accounts Payable increase?

ON the JOB ||||||||||||||||||||||||||||

MyAccountingLab

SANCHEZ COMPUTER CENTER

●●○ **LO2, 3, 4** (60 MIN)

The Sanchez Computer Center created its chart of accounts as follows:

Chart of Accounts as of July 1, 201X

Assets		Revenue	
1000	Cash	4000	Service Revenue
1020	Accounts Receivable	**Expenses**	
1030	Supplies	5010	Advertising Expense
1080	Computer Shop Equipment	5020	Rent Expense
1090	Office Equipment	5030	Utilities Expense
Liabilities		5040	Phone Expense
2000	Accounts Payable	5050	Supplies Expense
Owner's Equity		5060	Insurance Expense
3000	Freedman, Capital	5070	Postage Expense
3010	Freedman, Withdrawals		

You will use this chart of accounts to complete the Continuing Problem.

The following problem continues from Chapter 1. The balances as of July 31 have been brought forward in the working papers that accompany this text.

Assignment

1. Set up T accounts in a ledger.

2. Record transactions k through s in the appropriate T accounts.

3. Foot and take the balances of the T accounts where appropriate.

4. Prepare a trial balance at the end of August.

5. Prepare from the trial balance an income statement, statement of owner's equity, and a balance sheet for the two months ending with August 31, 201X.

    k. Received the phone bill for the month of July, $155.

    l. Paid $150 (check #8099) for insurance for the month.

    m. Paid $200 (check #8100) of the amount due from transaction d in Chapter 1.

    n. Paid advertising expense for the month, $1,400 (check #8101).

    o. Billed a client (Jeannine Sparks) for services rendered, $850.

    p. Collected $900 for services rendered.

    q. Paid the electric bill in full for the month of July (check #8102, transaction h, Chapter 1).

    r. Paid cash (check #8103) for $50 in stamps.

    s. Purchased $200 worth of supplies from Computer Connection on credit.

SUBWAY CASE

Debits on the Left . . .

When Stan took the big leap from being an employee to a Subway owner, the thing that terrified him most was *not* the part about managing people—that was one of his strengths as a marketing manager. Why, at Xellent Media, 40 sales reps reported to him! No, Stan was terrified of having to manage the accounts. Subway restaurant owners have so many accounts to deal with: food costs, payroll, rent, utilities, supplies, advertising, promotion, and, biggest of all, cash. It's critical for them to keep debits and credits straight. If not, both they and Subway could lose a lot of money, quickly.

● **LO2** *(20 MIN)*

Even though Stan got some intense training in accounting and bookkeeping at Subway University, he still felt shaky about doing his own books. When he confided his fears to Mariah Washington, his field consultant, she suggested he hire an accountant. "You need to play to your strengths," said Mariah, and she told Stan, "More and more owners are using accountants, and almost all owners of multiple franchises do. In fact, some accountants actually specialize in handling Subway accounts for these multirestaurant owners."

Even though Stan decided to hire his cousin, Lila, to do his accounting, he still needs to feed her the right data so she can calculate his T accounts. Like many small business owners, Stan enters data into an accounting software program such as QuickBooks or Peachtree, which he then uploads to his accountant, who edits it and reviews it for accuracy. Several times in the beginning Stan mistakenly debited both cash and supplies when he paid for orders of paper cups, bread dough, and other supplies.

Lila urged Stan to review the rules for recording debits and credits. She even told him to practice for a while using a paper ledger. "On the computer debits and credits are not as visible as they are with your paper system. Since you only enter the payables, the computer does the other side of the balance sheet. So you have to bone up on debits and credits to ensure that your Peachtree data are correct."

Discussion Questions

1. Why is the cash account so important in Stan's business?
2. Why do you think that most owners of the larger shops use accountants to do their books instead of doing the accounting themselves?
3. Is the difference between debits and credits important to Subway restaurant owners who don't do their own books?

Beginning the Accounting Cycle 3

THE GAME PLAN

Did you ever go to the airport late at night and wonder how an airline gets all its planes ready and safe for the next day's flights? American Airlines completes a checklist for its airplanes' maintenance and cleaning. Day in and day out, these checklists must be followed. Just like the American Airlines maintenance and cleaning procedures, specific steps must be completed in accounting for American Airlines to properly maintain its accounting records over a period of time. These procedures or steps are referred to as the **accounting cycle**. Once one cycle is completed (usually called a fiscal year), another cycle is begun. Learning the accounting procedures necessary during an accounting cycle will help you understand how businesses like American Airlines maintain consistent accounting records.

LEARNING OBJECTIVES

◎ **1.** Journalizing: analyzing and recording business transactions into a journal.

◎ **2.** Posting: transferring information from a journal to a ledger.

◎ **3.** Preparing a trial balance.

Accounting cycle For each accounting period, the process that begins with the recording of business transactions or procedures into a journal and ends with the completion of a post-closing trial balance.

Accounting period The period of time for which an income statement is prepared.

Calendar year The 12-month period a business chooses for its accounting year. Alternatively known as fiscal year and natural business year.

Interim reports Financial statements that are prepared for a month, quarter, or some other portion of the fiscal year.

Companies like American Airlines have to perform certain accounting procedures. The normal accounting procedures that are performed over a period of time are called the accounting cycle. The accounting cycle takes place in a period of time called an accounting period. An accounting period is the period of time covered by the income statement. Although it can be any time period up to one year (e.g., one month or three months), most businesses use a one-year accounting period. The year can be either a calendar year (January 1 through December 31) or a fiscal year.

A fiscal year is an accounting period that runs for any 12 consecutive months, so it can be the same as a calendar year. Big Dollar and Aeropostale, Inc., end their accounting periods on January 31. A business can choose any fiscal year that is convenient. For example, some retailers may decide to end their fiscal year when inventories and business activity are at a low point, such as after the Christmas season. This period is called a natural business year. Using a natural business year allows the business to count its year-end inventory when it is easiest to do so.

Businesses would not be able to operate successfully if they only prepared financial reports at the end of their calendar or fiscal year. For more timely information, most businesses prepare interim reports on a monthly, quarterly, or semiannual basis.

In this chapter, as well as in Chapters 4 and 5, we follow Brenda Clark's new business, Clark's Word Processing Services. We follow the normal accounting procedures that the business performs over a period of time. Clark has chosen to use a fiscal period of January 1 to December 31, which also is the calendar year.

● LO1   LEARNING UNIT 3-1 ANALYZING AND RECORDING BUSINESS TRANSACTIONS INTO A JOURNAL: Steps 1 and 2 of the Accounting Cycle

The General Journal

Chapter 2 taught us how to analyze and record business transactions into T accounts, or ledger accounts. Recording a debit in an account on one page of the ledger and recording the corresponding credit on a different page of the ledger, however, can make it difficult to find errors. It would be much easier if all the business's transactions were located in the same place. That is the function of the journal or general journal. Transactions are entered in the journal in chronological order (January 1, 8, 15, etc.), and then this recorded information is used to update the ledger accounts. In computerized accounting, a journal may be stored on disk.

We will use a general journal, the simplest form of a journal, to record the transactions of Clark's Word Processing Services. A transaction [debit(s) + credit(s)] that has been analyzed and recorded in a journal is called a journal entry. The process of recording the journal entry into the journal is called journalizing.

Journal A listing of business transactions in chronological order. The journal links on one page the debit and credit parts of transactions. Alternatively known as general journal.

Journal entry The transaction (debits and credits) that is recorded into a journal once it is analyzed.

Journalizing The process of recording a transaction entry into the journal.

Book of original entry Book that records the first formal information about business transactions. Example: a journal.

Book of final entry Book that receives information about business transactions from a book of original entry (a journal). Example: a ledger.

The journal is called the book of original entry because it contains the first formal information about the business transactions. The ledger is known as the book of final entry because the information the journal contains will be transferred to the ledger. Like the ledger, the journal may be a bound or loose-leaf book. Each of the journal pages looks like or similar to the one in Figure 3.1. The pages of the journal are numbered consecutively from page 1. Keep in mind that the journal and the ledger are separate books.

Relationship between the Journal and the Chart of Accounts The accountant must refer to the business's chart of accounts for the account name that is to be used in the journal. Every company has its own "unique" chart of accounts.

The following chart of accounts for Clark's Word Processing Services lists the accounts used in the business. By the end of Chapter 5, we will have discussed each of these accounts.

CLARK'S WORD PROCESSING SERVICES GENERAL JOURNAL				
				Page 1
Date	Account Titles and Description	PR	Dr.	Cr.

FIGURE 3.1
The General Journal

Note that we will continue to use transaction analysis charts as a teaching aid in the journalizing process.

Clark's Word Processing Services
Chart of Accounts

Assets (100–199)

111 Cash
112 Accounts Receivable
114 Office Supplies
115 Prepaid Rent
121 Word Processing Equipment
122 Accumulated Depreciation,
     Word Processing Equipment

Liabilities (200–299)

211 Accounts Payable
212 Salaries Payable

Owner's Equity (300–399)

311 Brenda Clark, Capital
312 Brenda Clark, Withdrawals
313 Income Summary

Revenue (400–499)

411 Word Processing Fees

Expenses (500–599)

511 Office Salaries Expense
512 Advertising Expense
513 Telephone Expense
514 Office Supplies Expense
515 Rent Expense
516 Depreciation Expense,
     Word Processing Equipment

Journalizing the Transactions of Clark's Word Processing Services Certain formalities must be followed in making journal entries:

- The debit portion of the transaction always is recorded first.
- The credit portion of a transaction is indented a ½ inch and placed below the debit portion.
- The explanation of the journal entry follows immediately after the credit and is indented 1 inch from the date column.
- A one-line space follows each transaction and explanation. This makes the journal easier to read, and there is less chance of mixing transactions.
- Each transaction must affect at least two different accounts.
- Finally, as always, the total amount of debits must equal the total amount of credits. The same format is used for each of the entries in the journal.

MAY 1, 201X: BRENDA CLARK BEGAN THE BUSINESS BY INVESTING $10,000 IN CASH			
1	2	3	4
Accounts Affected	Category	↓↑	Rules of Dr. and Cr.
Cash	Asset	↑	Dr.
Brenda Clark, Capital	Capital	↑	Cr.

FIGURE 3.2
Owner Investment

✗ ──→◦
COACHING TIP

For now the PR (posting reference) column is blank; we discuss it later.

CLARK'S WORD PROCESSING SERVICES
GENERAL JOURNAL

Page 1

Date		Account Titles and Description	PR	Dr.	Cr.
201X May	1	Cash		10 0 0 0 00	
		Brenda Clark, Capital			10 0 0 0 00
		Initial investment of cash by owner			

Let's now look at the structure of this journal entry (Figure 3.2). The entry contains the following information:

1. Year of the journal entry   201X
2. Month of the journal entry   May
3. Day of the journal entry   1
4. Name(s) of accounts debited   Cash
5. Name(s) of accounts credited   Brenda Clark, Capital
6. Explanation of transaction   Investment of cash
7. Amount of debit(s) $10,000
8. Amount of credit(s) $10,000

MAY 1: PURCHASED WORD PROCESSING EQUIPMENT FROM BEN CO. FOR $6,000, PAYING $1,000 AND PROMISING TO PAY THE BALANCE WITHIN 30 DAYS

1	2	3	4
Accounts Affected	Category	↓↑	Rules of Dr. and Cr.
Word Processing Equipment	Asset	↑	Dr.
Cash	Asset	↓	Cr.
Accounts Payable	Liability	↑	Cr.

This transaction affects three accounts. When a journal entry has more than two accounts, it is called a compound journal entry.

In this entry (Figure 3.3), only the day is entered in the date column because the year and month were entered at the top of the page from the first transaction. This information doesn't need to be repeated until a new page is needed or a change of months occurs.

Compound journal entry A journal entry that affects more than two accounts.

FIGURE 3.3
Purchase of Equipment

	1	Word Processing Equipment		6 0 0 0 00	
		Cash			1 0 0 0 00
		Accounts Payable			5 0 0 0 00
		Purchase of equipment from Ben Co.			

MAY 1: RENTED OFFICE SPACE, PAYING $1,200 IN ADVANCE FOR THE FIRST THREE MONTHS

1	2	3	4
Accounts Affected	Category	↓↑	Rules of Dr. and Cr.
Prepaid Rent	Asset	↑	Dr.
Cash	Asset	↓	Cr.

✗ ──→◦
COACHING TIP

Rent paid in advance is an asset.

In this transaction (Figure 3.4) Clark gains an asset called prepaid rent and gives up an asset, cash. The prepaid rent does not become an expense until it expires.

		1	Prepaid Rent		1 2 0 0 00		
			Cash			1 2 0 0 00	
			Rent paid in advance—(3 months)				

FIGURE 3.4
Paid Rent in Advance

MAY 3: PURCHASED OFFICE SUPPLIES FROM NORRIS CO. ON ACCOUNT, $600

1	2	3	4
Accounts Affected	**Category**	**↓↑**	**Rules of Dr. and Cr.**
Office Supplies	Asset	↑	Dr.
Accounts Payable	Liability	↑	Cr.

COACHING TIP

Supplies become an expense when used up.

Remember, supplies are an asset when they are purchased. Once they are used up or consumed in the operation of business, they become an expense (Figure 3.5).

FIGURE 3.5
Purchased Supplies on Account

		3	Office Supplies		6 0 0 00		
			Accounts Payable			6 0 0 00	
			Purchase of supplies on account				
			from Norris				

MAY 7: COMPLETED SALES PROMOTION PIECES FOR A CLIENT AND IMMEDIATELY COLLECTED $3,000

1	2	3	4
Accounts Affected	**Category**	**↓↑**	**Rules of Dr. and Cr.**
Cash	Asset	↑	Dr.
Word Processing Fees	Revenue	↑	Cr.

		7	Cash		3 0 0 0 00		
			Word Processing Fees			3 0 0 0 00	
			Cash received for services rendered				

FIGURE 3.6
Services Rendered

MAY 13: PAID OFFICE SALARIES, $650

1	2	3	4
Accounts Affected	**Category**	**↓↑**	**Rules of Dr. and Cr.**
Office Salaries Expense	Expense	↑	Dr.
Cash	Asset	↓	Cr.

		13	Office Salaries Expense		6 5 0 00		
			Cash			6 5 0 00	
			Payment of office salaries				

FIGURE 3.7
Paid Salaries

MAY 18: ADVERTISING BILL FROM AL'S NEWS CO. COMES IN BUT IS NOT PAID, $250

1	2	3	4
Accounts Affected	**Category**	**↓↑**	**Rules of Dr. and Cr.**
Advertising Expense	Expense	↑	Dr.
Accounts Payable	Liability	↑	Cr.

COACHING TIP

Remember, expenses are recorded when they are incurred, no matter when they are paid.

FIGURE 3.8
Received Advertising Bill

	18	Advertising Expense		2 5 0 00	
		Accounts Payable			2 5 0 00
		Bill in but not paid from Al's News			

COACHING TIP

Keep in mind that as withdrawals increase, owner's equity decreases.

MAY 20: BRENDA CLARK WROTE A CHECK ON THE BANK ACCOUNT OF THE BUSINESS TO PAY HER HOME MORTGAGE PAYMENT OF $625

1	2	3	4
Accounts Affected	**Category**	↓↑	**Rules of Dr. and Cr.**
Brenda Clark, Withdrawals	Withdrawals	↑	Dr.
Cash	Asset	↓	Cr.

FIGURE 3.9
Personal Withdrawal

	20	Brenda Clark, Withdrawals		6 2 5 00	
		Cash			6 2 5 00
		Personal withdrawal of cash			

COACHING TIP

Reminder: Revenue is recorded when it is earned, no matter when the cash is actually received.

MAY 22: BILLED MORRIS COMPANY FOR A SOPHISTICATED WORD PROCESSING JOB, $5,000

1	2	3	4
Accounts Affected	**Category**	↓↑	**Rules of Dr. and Cr.**
Accounts Receivable	Asset	↑	Dr.
Word Processing Fees	Revenue	↑	Cr.

FIGURE 3.10
Fees Earned

	22	Accounts Receivable		5 0 0 0 00	
		Word Processing Fees			5 0 0 0 00
		Billed Morris Co. for fees earned			

MAY 27: PAID OFFICE SALARIES, $650

1	2	3	4
Accounts Affected	**Category**	↓↑	**Rules of Dr. and Cr.**
Office Salaries Expense	Expense	↑	Dr.
Cash	Asset	↓	Cr.

FIGURE 3.11
Paid Salaries

			CLARK'S WORD PROCESSING SERVICES **GENERAL JOURNAL**				
							Page 2
	Date		Account Titles and Description	PR	Dr.		Cr.
	201X May	27*	Office Salaries Expense		6 5 0 00		
			Cash				6 5 0 00
			Payment of office salaries				

*Note that this is a new page, so the year and month are repeated.

MAY 28: PAID HALF THE AMOUNT OWED FOR WORD PROCESSING EQUIPMENT PURCHASED MAY 1 FROM BEN CO., $2,500

1	2	3	4
Accounts Affected	**Category**	**↓↑**	**Rules of Dr. and Cr.**
Accounts Payable	Liability	↓	Dr.
Cash	Asset	↓	Cr.

28	Accounts Payable		2 5 0 0 00		
	Cash			2 5 0 0 00	
	Paid half the amount owed Ben Co.				

FIGURE 3.12
Partial Payment

MAY 29: RECEIVED AND PAID TELEPHONE BILL, $220

1	2	3	4
Accounts Affected	**Category**	**↓↑**	**Rules of Dr. and Cr.**
Telephone Expense	Expense	↑	Dr.
Cash	Asset	↓	Cr.

29	Telephone Expense		2 2 0 00		
	Cash			2 2 0 00	
	Paid telephone bill				

FIGURE 3.13
Paid Telephone Bill

This concludes the journal transactions of Clark's Word Processing Services for the month of May.

LEARNING UNIT 3-1 REVIEW

AT THIS POINT you should be able to do the following:

- Define an accounting cycle.
- Define and explain the relationship of the accounting period to the income statement.
- Compare and contrast a calendar year to a fiscal year.
- Explain the term *natural business year.*
- Explain the function of interim reports.
- Define and state the purpose of a journal.
- Compare and contrast a book of original entry to a book of final entry.
- Differentiate between a chart of accounts and a journal.
- Journalize a business transaction.
- Explain a compound entry.

↙ Instant Replay ◎ Self-Review Quiz 3-1

The following are the transactions of Lowe's Repair Service for the month of June 201X. Journalize the transactions in proper form. The chart of accounts includes Cash; Accounts Receivable; Prepaid Rent; Repair Supplies; Repair Equipment; Accounts Payable; A. Lowe, Capital; A. Lowe, Withdrawals; Repair Fees Earned; Salaries Expense; Advertising Expense; and Supplies Expense.

201X

June 1   A. Lowe invested $7,000 cash and $5,000 of repair equipment in the business.

1   Paid two months' rent in advance, $1,200.

4   Bought repair supplies from Melvin Co. on account, $600. (These supplies have not yet been consumed or used up.)

15   Performed repair work, received $600 in cash, and had to bill Doe Co. for remaining balance of $300.

18   A. Lowe paid his home telephone bill, $50, with a check from the company.

20   Advertising bill for $400 from Jones Co. received but payment not due yet. (Advertising has already appeared in the newspaper.)

24   Paid salaries, $1,400.

Solution to Instant Replay: Self-Review Quiz 3-1

FIGURE 3.14
Transactions Journalized

LOWE'S REPAIR SERVICE
GENERAL JOURNAL

Page 1

Date			Account Titles and Description	PR	Dr.	Cr.
201X June	1		Cash		7 0 0 0 00	
			Repair Equipment		5 0 0 0 00	
			A. Lowe, Capital			12 0 0 0 00
			Owner investment			
	1		Prepaid Rent		1 2 0 0 00	
			Cash			1 2 0 0 00
			Rent paid in advance—2 mos.			
	4		Repair Supplies		6 0 0 00	
			Accounts Payable			6 0 0 00
			Purchase on account from Melvin Co.			
	15		Cash		6 0 0 00	
			Accounts Receivable		3 0 0 00	
			Repair Fees Earned			9 0 0 00
			Performed repairs for Doe Co.			
	18		A. Lowe, Withdrawals		5 0 00	
			Cash			5 0 00
			Personal withdrawal			
	20		Advertising Expense		4 0 0 00	
			Accounts Payable			4 0 0 00
			Advertising bill from Jones Co.			
	24		Salaries Expense		1 4 0 0 00	
			Cash			1 4 0 0 00
			Paid salaries			

PLAY BY PLAY: EXTRA HELP ON SELF-REVIEW QUIZ 3-1

Let's review first: When recording transactions into a general journal, the accounts debited will be aligned to the date column and the credit(s) will be indented. These titles will come from the chart of accounts. The explanation line will then be indented below the last credit entry. The sum of the left side (Dr.) must equal the sum of the right side (Cr.) for each transaction.

Here are the transaction analysis charts for each transaction. Be sure to remember that the accounts affected come from the chart of accounts. You have six categories: assets, liabilities, capital, withdrawals, revenues, and expenses. You must ask yourself what the company is getting and how it is getting it. Remember to think of expenses and withdrawals as increasing, resulting in a decrease to owner's equity.

June 1	Cash	Asset	↑	Dr.
	Repair Equip.	Asset	↑	Dr.
	A. Lowe, Cap.	Capital	↑	Cr.

Debits are listed first against the date column and credits are indented. This is an investment by the owner. The month is written because the month starts a new page.

| 1 | Prepaid Rent | Asset | ↑ | Dr. |
| | Cash | Asset | ↓ | Cr. |

This is a shift in assets, more rent paid in advance by cash. Note that the month is not repeated.

| 4 | Repair Supplies | Asset | ↑ | Dr. |
| | Accounts Payable | Liability | ↑ | Cr. |

This is an example of buy now and pay later. Supplies will not be an expense until they are used up.

15	Cash	Asset	↑	Dr.
	Acc. Receiv.	Asset	↑	Dr.
	Rep. Fees Earn.	Revenue	↑	Cr.

Here we did the work and got some money as well as some promises that the customer will pay later. Note how the two debits are against the date column and the credit is indented.

| 18 | A. Lowe, Withd. | Withdr. | ↑ | Dr. |
| | Cash | Asset | ↓ | Cr. |

The owner increases her withdrawals for personal use, and the end result is that the business has less cash.

| 20 | Advertising Exp. | Expense | ↑ | Dr. |
| | Accounts Pay. | Liability | ↑ | Cr. |

An expense has been incurred but is not paid for. This expense has created a liability. Think of expenses as always increasing.

| 24 | Salaries Exp. | Expense | ↑ | Dr. |
| | Cash | Asset | ↓ | Cr. |

Here the expense is increasing and it is being paid for in cash.

COACHING TIP

The journal (green) is the book of original entry and the ledger (blue) is the book of final entry.

● **LO2**   **LEARNING UNIT 3-2 POSTING TO THE LEDGER:**
Step 3 of the Accounting Cycle

The general journal serves a particular purpose: It puts every transaction the business does in one place. It cannot do certain things, though. For example, if you were asked to find the balance of the cash account from the general journal, you would have to go through the entire journal and look for only the cash entries. Then you would have to add up the debits and credits for the Cash account and determine the difference between the two.

Posting The transferring, copying, or recording of information from a journal to a ledger.

What we really need to do to find balances of accounts is to transfer the information from the journal to the ledger. This process is called posting. In the ledger we accumulate an ending balance for each account so that we can prepare financial statements.

FIGURE 3.15
Four-Column Account

Accounts Payable							Account No. 211	
						Balance		
Date	Explanation	Post. Ref.	Debit		Credit	Debit	Credit	
201X May 1		GJ1			5 0 0 0 00		5 0 0 0 00	
3		GJ1			6 0 0 00		5 6 0 0 00	
18		GJ1			2 5 0 00		5 8 5 0 00	
28		GJ2	2 5 0 0 00				3 3 5 0 00	

COACHING TIP

$5,000 Cr. + $600 Cr. = $5,600 Cr.

In Chapter 2 we used the T account form to make our ledger entries. T accounts are simple, but they are not used in the real business world; they are only used for demonstration purposes. In practice, accountants often use a four-column account form that includes a column for the business's running balance. Figure 3.15 shows a standard four-column account. We use this format in the text from now on.

Four-column account A running balance account that records debits and credits and has a column for an ending balance (debit or credit). It replaces the standard two-column account we used earlier.

Posting

Now let's look at how to post the transactions of Clark's Word Processing Services from its journal. The diagram in Figure 3.16 shows how to post the cash line from the journal to the ledger. The steps in the posting process are numbered and illustrated in the figure.

STEP 1: In the Cash account in the ledger, record the date (May 1, 201X) and the amount of the entry ($10,000).

STEP 2: Record the page number of the journal "GJ1" in the posting reference (PR) column of the Cash account.

STEP 3: Calculate the new balance of the account. To keep a running balance in each account, as you would in your personal checkbook, take the present balance in the account on the previous line and add or subtract the transaction as necessary to arrive at your new balance.

STEP 4: Record the account number of Cash (111) in the posting reference (PR) column of the journal. This listing is known as cross-referencing.

Cross-referencing Adding to the PR column of the journal the account number of the ledger account that was updated from the journal.

The same sequence of steps occurs for each line in the journal. In a manual system like Clark's, the debits and credits in the journal may be posted in the order they were recorded, or all the debits may be posted first and then all the credits. If Clark's used a computer with an accounting software the program menu would post at the press of a button.

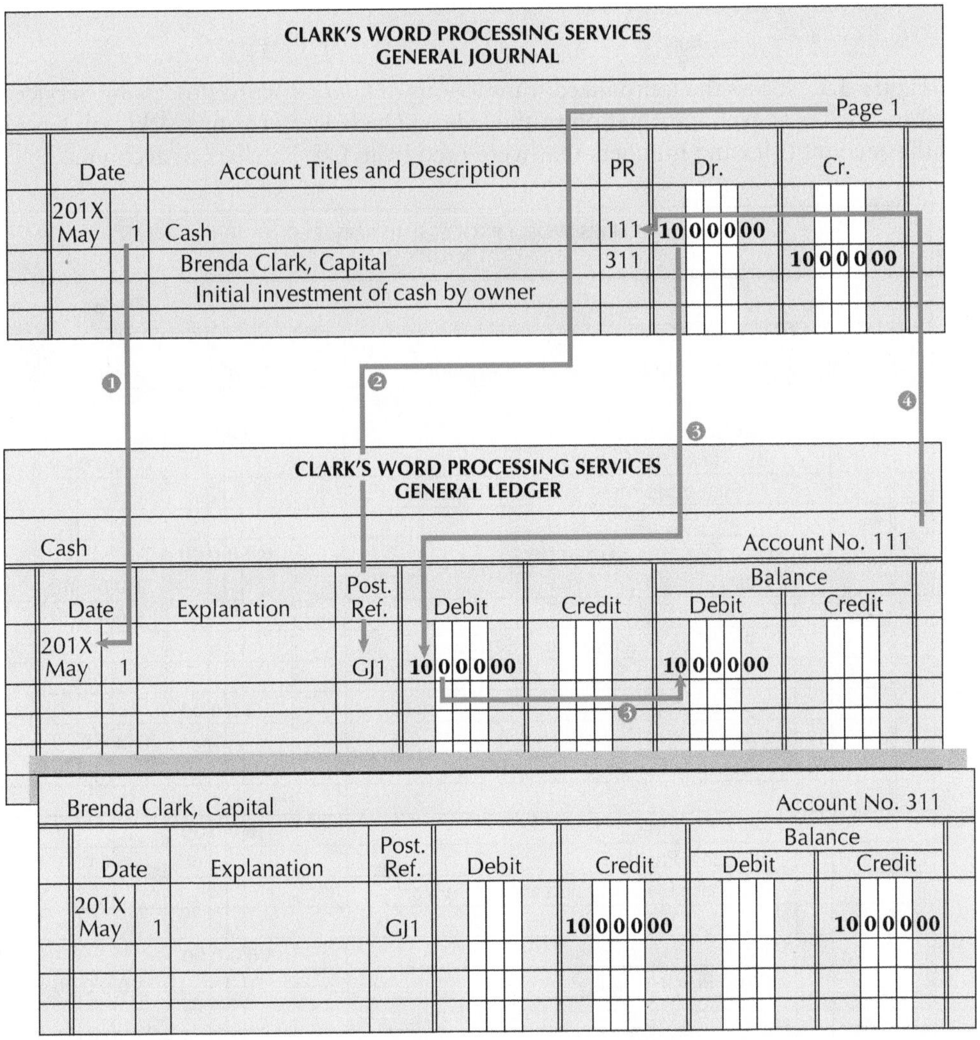

FIGURE 3.16
How to Post from Journal to Ledger

Using Posting References The posting references are helpful. In the journal, the PR column tells us which transactions have or have not been posted and also to which accounts they were posted. In the ledger, the posting reference leads us back to the original transaction in its entirety, so we can see why the debit or credit was recorded and what other accounts were affected. (It leads us back to the original transaction by identifying the journal and the page in the journal from which the information came.)

LEARNING UNIT 3-2 REVIEW

AT THIS POINT you should be able to do the following:

- State the purpose of posting.
- Discuss the advantages of the four-column account.
- Identify the elements to be posted.
- From journalized transactions, post to the general ledger.

Instant Replay ◌ Self-Review Quiz 3-2

Figure 3.17 shows the journalized transactions of Clark's Word Processing Services. Your task is to post information to the ledger. The ledger in your workbook has all the account titles and numbers that were used from Clark's chart of accounts.

FIGURE 3.17
Journalized Entries

		CLARK'S WORD PROCESSING SERVICES GENERAL JOURNAL				
						Page 1
Date		Account Titles and Description	PR	Dr.	Cr.	
201X May	1	Cash		10000 00		
		Brenda Clark, Capital			10000 00	
		Initial investment of cash by owner				
	1	Word Processing Equipment		6000 00		
		Cash			1000 00	
		Accounts Payable			5000 00	
		Purchase of equip. from Ben Co.				
	1	Prepaid Rent		1200 00		
		Cash			1200 00	
		Rent paid in advance (3 months)				
	3	Office Supplies		600 00		
		Accounts Payable			600 00	
		Purchase of supplies on acct. from Norris				
	7	Cash		3000 00		
		Word Processing Fees			3000 00	
		Cash received for services rendered				
	13	Office Salaries Expense		650 00		
		Cash			650 00	
		Payment of office salaries				
	18	Advertising Expense		250 00		
		Accounts Payable			250 00	
		Bill received but not paid from Al's News				
	20	Brenda Clark, Withdrawals		625 00		
		Cash			625 00	
		Personal withdrawal of cash				
	22	Accounts Receivable		5000 00		
		Word Processing Fees			5000 00	
		Billed Morris Co. for fees earned				

FIGURE 3.17 (continued)

CLARK'S WORD PROCESSING SERVICES
GENERAL JOURNAL

Page 2

Date		Account Titles and Description	PR	Dr.	Cr.
201X May	27	Office Salaries Expense		65000	
		Cash			65000
		Payment of office salaries			
	28	Accounts Payable		250000	
		Cash			250000
		Paid half the amount owed Ben Co.			
	29	Telephone Expense		22000	
		Cash			22000
		Paid telephone bill			

Solution to Instant Replay: Self-Review Quiz 3-2

FIGURE 3.18
Posting from Journal to the Ledger
Using PR Columns

CLARK'S WORD PROCESSING SERVICES
GENERAL JOURNAL

Page 1

Date		Account Titles and Description	PR	Dr.	Cr.
201X May	1	Cash	111	1000000	
		Brenda Clark, Capital	311		1000000
		Initial investment of cash by owner			
	1	Word Processing Equipment	121	600000	
		Cash	111		100000
		Accounts Payable	211		500000
		Purchase of equip. from Ben Co.			
	1	Prepaid Rent	115	120000	
		Cash	111		120000
		Rent paid in advance (3 months)			
	3	Office Supplies	114	60000	
		Accounts Payable	211		60000
		Purchase of supplies on acct. from Norris			
	7	Cash	111	300000	
		Word Processing Fees	411		300000
		Cash received from services rendered			
	13	Office Salaries Expense	511	65000	
		Cash	111		65000
		Payment of office salaries			
	18	Advertising Expense	512	25000	
		Accounts Payable	211		25000
		Bill received but not paid from Al's News			

FIGURE 3.18 (continued)

CLARK'S WORD PROCESSING SERVICES
GENERAL JOURNAL

Page 1

Date		Account Titles and Description	PR	Dr.	Cr.
	20	Brenda Clark, Withdrawals	312	625 00	
		Cash	111		625 00
		Personal withdrawal of cash			
	22	Accounts Receivable	112	5000 00	
		Word Processing Fees	411		5000 00
		Billed Morris Co. for fees earned			

CLARK'S WORD PROCESSING SERVICES
GENERAL JOURNAL

Page 2

Date		Account Titles and Description	PR	Dr.	Cr.
201X May	27	Office Salaries Expense	511	650 00	
		Cash	111		650 00
		Payment of office salaries			
	28	Accounts Payable	211	2500 00	
		Cash	111		2500 00
		Paid half the amount owed Ben Co.			
	29	Telephone Expense	513	220 00	
		Cash	111		220 00
		Paid telephone bill			

FIGURE 3.18 (continued)

CLARK'S WORD PROCESSING SERVICES
PARTIAL GENERAL LEDGER

Cash   Account No. 111

Date		Explanation	Post. Ref.	Debit	Credit	Balance Debit	Balance Credit
201X May	1		GJ1	10000 00		10000 00	
	1		GJ1		1000 00	9000 00	
	1		GJ1		1200 00	7800 00	
	7		GJ1	3000 00		10800 00	
	13		GJ1		650 00	10150 00	
	20		GJ1		625 00	9525 00	
	27		GJ2		650 00	8875 00	
	28		GJ2		2500 00	6375 00	
	29		GJ2		220 00	6155 00	

Accounts Receivable   Account No. 112

Date		Explanation	Post. Ref.	Debit	Credit	Balance Debit	Balance Credit
201X May	22		GJ1	5000 00		5000 00	

FIGURE 3.18 *(continued)*

Office Supplies — Account No. 114

Date	Explanation	Post. Ref.	Debit	Credit	Balance Debit	Balance Credit
201X May 3		GJ1	600 00		600 00	

Prepaid Rent — Account No. 115

Date	Explanation	Post. Ref.	Debit	Credit	Balance Debit	Balance Credit
201X May 1		GJ1	1 200 00		1 200 00	

Word Processing Equipment — Account No. 121

Date	Explanation	Post. Ref.	Debit	Credit	Balance Debit	Balance Credit
201X May 1		GJ1	6 000 00		6 000 00	

Accounts Payable — Account No. 211

Date	Explanation	Post. Ref.	Debit	Credit	Balance Debit	Balance Credit
201X May 1		GJ1		5 000 00		5 000 00
3		GJ1		600 00		5 600 00
18		GJ1		250 00		5 850 00
28		GJ2	2 500 00			3 350 00

Brenda Clark, Capital — Account No. 311

Date	Explanation	Post. Ref.	Debit	Credit	Balance Debit	Balance Credit
201X May 1		GJ1		10 000 00		10 000 00

Brenda Clark, Withdrawals — Account No. 312

Date	Explanation	Post. Ref.	Debit	Credit	Balance Debit	Balance Credit
201X May 20		GJ1	625 00		625 00	

Word Processing Fees — Account No. 411

Date	Explanation	Post. Ref.	Debit	Credit	Balance Debit	Balance Credit
201X May 7		GJ1		3 000 00		3 000 00
22		GJ1		5 000 00		8 000 00

FIGURE 3.18 *(continued)*

Office Salaries Expense — Account No. 511

Date		Explanation	Post. Ref.	Debit	Credit	Balance Debit	Balance Credit
201X May	13		GJ1	650 00		650 00	
	27		GJ2	650 00		1300 00	

Advertising Expense — Account No. 512

Date		Explanation	Post. Ref.	Debit	Credit	Balance Debit	Balance Credit
201X May	18		GJ1	250 00		250 00	

Telephone Expense — Account No. 513

Date		Explanation	Post. Ref.	Debit	Credit	Balance Debit	Balance Credit
201X May	29		GJ2	220 00		220 00	

PLAY BY PLAY: EXTRA HELP ON SELF-REVIEW QUIZ 3-2

Let's review first: The PR column of the journal will show to which account information has been posting. The PR column in the ledger accounts show from which page of the journal the information came. When updating ledger accounts, two debits added equals a debit balance. Two credits added would be a credit balance. If you have a debit and a credit, take the difference between them; whichever side is larger is the balance (be it a debit or credit).

Partial General Ledger:

Cash: There are nine postings from the journal to the cash account. GJ1 means that posting came from the general journal, page 1. In the second line the credit of 1,000 is subtracted from the debit balance in line 1 (10,000) to show a new balance of 9,000 in line 2. In line 3 the 1,200 credit is then subtracted from the 9,000 debit for a current balance of 7,800. Normally the balance is on the side that causes it to increase. Thus cash is normally a debit balance.

Accounts Payable: In this account the first three postings were credits from the general journal. Note that the month is written only once. Since all three are credits we add each together, arriving at a credit balance of 5,850. On May 28 a debit of 2,500 is posted and we take the difference between a 5,850 credit balance and a 2,500 debit balance to arrive at a 3,350 ending credit balance.

Office Salaries Expense: Note that here we have two debit postings, so they are added together to arrive at a 1,300 debit balance.

Summary: Posting is copying from the journal to the ledger. The ledger will accumulate information in the form of debits and credits. The last line in the balance column will show whether it is a debit or credit balance. The general journal does not show a running balance like the ledger accounts do.

COACHING TIP

Posting is done from journal (green) to ledger (blue).

LEARNING UNIT 3-3 PREPARING THE TRIAL BALANCE:
Step 4 of the Accounting Cycle

● **LO3**

Did you note in Quiz 3-2 how each account had a running balance figure? Did you know the normal balance of each account in Clark's ledger? As we discussed in Chapter 2, the list of the individual accounts with their balances taken from the ledger is called a trial balance.

Trial balance An informal listing of the ledger accounts and their balances in the ledger to aid in proving the equality of debits and credits.

The trial balance shown in Figure 3.19 was developed from the ledger accounts of Clark's Word Processing Services that were posted and balanced in Quiz 3-2. If the information is journalized or posted incorrectly, the trial balance will not be correct.

TRIAL BALANCE

Debits	Credits
Assets	Liabilities
Expenses	Revenue
Withdrawals	Capital

The trial balance will not show everything:

- The capital figure on the trial balance may not be the beginning capital figure. For instance, if Brenda Clark had made additional investments during the period, the additional investment would have been journalized and posted to the Capital account. The only way to tell if the capital balance on the trial balance is the original balance is to check the ledger Capital account to see whether any additional investments were made. This confirmation of beginning capital will be important when we make financial reports.

FIGURE 3.19
Trial Balance

CLARK'S WORD PROCESSING SERVICE TRIAL BALANCE MAY 31, 201X	Debit	Credit
Cash	6 1 5 5 00	
Accounts Receivable	5 0 0 0 00	
Office Supplies	6 0 0 00	
Prepaid Rent	1 2 0 0 00	
Word Processing Equipment	6 0 0 0 00	
Accounts Payable		3 3 5 0 00
Brenda Clark, Capital		10 0 0 0 00
Brenda Clark, Withdrawals	6 2 5 00	
Word Processing Fees		8 0 0 0 00
Office Salaries Expense	1 3 0 0 00	
Advertising Expense	2 5 0 00	
Telephone Expense	2 2 0 00	
Totals	21 3 5 0 00	21 3 5 0 00

The trial balance lists the accounts in the same order as in the ledger. The $6,155 figure of cash came from the ledger.

- Even careful cross-referencing does not guarantee that transactions have been properly recorded. For example, the following errors would remain undetected: (1) a transaction that may have been omitted in the journalizing process, (2) a transaction incorrectly analyzed and recorded in the journal, and (3) a journal entry journalized or posted twice.

x ⟶ ○
COACHING TIP

The totals of a trial balance can balance and yet be incorrect.

What to Do If a Trial Balance Doesn't Balance

The trial balance of Clark's Word Processing Services shows that the total of debits is equal to the total of credits. What happens, however, if the trial balance is in balance but the correct amount is not recorded in each ledger account? Accuracy in the journalizing and posting process will help ensure that no errors are made.

Even if you find an error, the first rule is "don't panic." Everyone makes mistakes, and accepted ways of correcting them are available. Once an entry has been made in ink, correcting an error in it must always show that the entry has been changed and who changed it. Sometimes the change has to be explained.

Some Common Mistakes

If the trial balance does not balance, the cause could be something relatively simple. Here are some common errors and how they can be fixed:

- If the difference (the amount you are off) is 10, 100, 1,000, and so forth, it is probably a mathematical error in addition.
- If the difference is equal to an individual account balance in the ledger, the amount could have been omitted. It is also possible the figure was not posted from the general journal.
- Divide the difference by two, then check to see whether a debit should have been a credit, or vice versa, in the ledger or trial balance. Example: $150 difference ÷ 2 = $75 means you may have placed $75 as a debit to an account instead of a credit, or vice versa.
- If the difference is evenly divisible by nine, a slide or transposition may have occurred. A slide is an error resulting from adding or deleting zeros in writing numbers. For example, $4,175.00 may have been copied as $41.75. A transposition is the accidental rearrangement of digits of a number. For example, $4,175 might have been accidentally written as $4,157.
- Compare the balances in the trial balance with the ledger accounts to check for copying errors.
- Recompute balances in each ledger account.
- Trace all postings from journal to ledger.

If you cannot find the error after taking all these steps, take a coffee break. Then start all over again.

Making a Correction Before Posting

Before posting, error correction is straightforward. Simply draw a line through the incorrect entry, write the correct information above the line, and write your initials near the change. Keep in mind that accounting software may provide their own methods for making corrections.

Correcting an Error in an Account Title Figure 3.20 shows an error and its correction in an account title:

Slide The error that results in adding or deleting zeros in the writing of a number. Example: 79,200 → 7,920.

Transposition The accidental rearrangement of digits of a number. Example: 152 → 125.

FIGURE 3.20
Account Error

		1	Word Processing Equipment		6 0 0 0 00					
			Cash ~~Accounts Payable~~ *amp*					1 0 0 0 00		
			~~Accounts Receivable~~					5 0 0 0 00		
			Purchase of equipment from Ben Co.							

Correcting a Numerical Error Numbers are handled the same way as account titles, as the next change from 520 to 250 in Figure 3.21 shows:

18	Advertising Expense		2 5 0 00		
	Accounts Payable			*amp* ~~5 2 0~~ 2 5 0 00	
	Bill from Al's News				

FIGURE 3.21
Number Error

Correcting an Entry Error If a number has been entered in the wrong column, a straight line is drawn through it. The number is then written in the correct column, as shown in Figure 3.22:

1	Word Processing Equipment		6 0 0 0 00	
	Cash			1 0 0 0 00
	Accounts Payable	*amp* **5 0 0 0 00**	5 0 0 0 00	
	Purchase of equip. from Ben Co.			

FIGURE 3.22
Correcting Entry

Making a Correction After Posting

It is also possible to correct an amount that is correctly entered in the journal but posted incorrectly to the ledger of the proper account. The first step is to draw a line through the error and write the correct figure above it. The next step is changing the running balance to reflect the corrected posting. Here, too, a line is drawn through the balance and the corrected balance is written above it. Both changes must be initialed, as shown in Figure 3.23.

FIGURE 3.23
Correction After Posting

						Balance	
			Word Processing Fees			Account No. 411	
Date	Explanation	Post. Ref.	Debit	Credit	Debit	Credit	
201X May 7		GJ1		2 5 0 0 00		2 5 0 0 00	
22		GJ1		~~4 1 0 0 00~~ ~~1 0 0 00~~ *amp*		~~6 6 0 0 00~~ ~~2 6 0 0 00~~ *amp*	

Correcting an Entry Posted to the Wrong Account

Drawing a line through an error and writing the correction above it is possible when a mistake has occurred within the proper account, but when an error involves a posting to the wrong account, the journal must include a correction accompanied by an explanation. In addition, the correct information must be posted to the appropriate ledgers.

Suppose, for example, that as a result of tracing postings from journal entries to ledgers you find that a $180 telephone bill was incorrectly debited as an advertising expense. The following illustration shows how this correction is done.

STEP 1: The journal entry is corrected and the correction is explained (Figure 3.24):

FIGURE 3.24
Corrected Entry for Telephone

	Date		Account Titles and Description	PR	Dr.	Cr.
	201X May	29	Telephone Expense	513	1 8 0 0 0	
			Advertising Expense	512		1 8 0 0 0
			To correct error in which			
			Advertising Exp. was debited			
			for charges to Telephone Exp.			

GENERAL JOURNAL — Page 3

STEP 2: The Advertising Expense ledger account is corrected (Figure 3.25):

FIGURE 3.25
Ledger Update for Advertising

Advertising Expense — Account No. 512

	Date		Explanation	Post. Ref.	Debit	Credit	Balance Debit	Balance Credit
	201X May	18		GJ1	1 7 5 00		1 7 5 00	
		23		GJ1	1 8 0 00		3 5 5 00	
		29	Correcting entry	GJ3		1 8 0 00	1 7 5 00	

STEP 3: The Telephone Expense ledger is corrected (Figure 3.26):

FIGURE 3.26
Ledger Update for Telephone

Telephone Expense — Account No. 513

	Date		Explanation	Post. Ref.	Debit	Credit	Balance Debit	Balance Credit
	201X May	29		GJ3	1 8 0 00		1 8 0 00	

LEARNING UNIT 3-3 REVIEW

AT THIS POINT you should be able to do the following:

- Prepare a trial balance with a ledger, using four-column accounts.
- Analyze and correct a trial balance that doesn't balance.
- Correct journalizing and posting errors.

Instant Replay ○ Self-Review Quiz 3-3

1.
MEMO

TO: Al Vincent
FROM: Professor Jones
RE: Trial Balance
You have submitted to me an incorrect trial balance (Figure 3.28). Could you please rework and turn in to me before next Friday?
Note: Individual amounts look OK.

A. RICE TRIAL BALANCE OCTOBER 31, 201X	Dr.	Cr.
Cash		8 0 6 0 00
Operating Expenses		1 7 0 0 00
A. Rice, Withdrawals		4 0 0 00
Service Revenue		5 4 0 0 00
Equipment	5 0 0 0 00	
Accounts Receivable	3 5 4 0 00	
Accounts Payable	2 0 0 0 00	
Supplies	3 0 0 00	
A. Rice, Capital		11 6 0 0 00

FIGURE 3.27
Incorrect Trial Balance

2. An $8,000 debit to Office Equipment was mistakenly journalized and posted on June 9, 201X, to Office Supplies. Prepare the appropriate journal entry to correct this error.

Solution to Instant Replay: Self-Review Quiz 3-3

1.

A. RICE TRIAL BALANCE OCTOBER 31, 201X	Dr.	Cr.
Cash	8 0 6 0 00	
Accounts Receivable	3 5 4 0 00	
Supplies	3 0 0 00	
Equipment	5 0 0 0 00	
Accounts Payable		2 0 0 0 00
A. Rice, Capital		11 6 0 0 00
A. Rice, Withdrawals	4 0 0 00	
Service Revenue		5 4 0 0 00
Operating Expenses	1 7 0 0 00	
Totals	19 0 0 0 00	19 0 0 0 00

FIGURE 3.28
Correct Trial Balance

2.

	Date		Account Titles and Description	PR	Dr.	Cr.
	201X June	9	Office Equipment		8 0 0 0 0 0	
			Office Supplies			8 0 0 0 0 0
			To correct error in which office supplies			
			had been debited for purchase of			
			office equipment			

GENERAL JOURNAL — Page 4

FIGURE 3.29
Correcting Entry

PLAY BY PLAY: EXTRA HELP ON SELF-REVIEW QUIZ 3-3

Let's review first: Items in a trial balance are listed in the same order as in the ledger or chart of accounts. Expect each account to have its normal balance (either a debit or credit). No title in the trial list balance can have both a debit and credit balance.

List the ending balance of each ledger account (last number listed in the balance columns) and list them in the order of the ledger. They should follow this pattern:

Assets	Dr.
Liabilities	Cr.
Capital	Cr.
Withdrawals	Dr.
Revenues	Cr.
Expenses	Dr.

When complete, the total of all debits will equal the total of the credits. In this case the total is 19,000.

Summary: The trial balance lists the accounts in the same order as the ledger. Be sure to refer to the learning unit for what to do if the trial balance does not balance. It could be a posting mistake or just a math error.

DEMONSTRATION PROBLEM

LO1,2,3

Journalizing Transaction, Posting, and Preparing a Trial Balance

In March, Abby's Employment Agency had the following transactions:

201X

Mar.	1	Abby Todd invested $5,000 cash in the new employment agency.
	4	Bought equipment for cash, $200.
	5	Earned employment fee commission, $200, but payment from Blue Co. will not be received until June.
	6	Paid wages expense, $300.
	7	Abby paid her home utility bill from the company checkbook, $75.
	9	Placed Rick Wool at VCR Corporation, receiving $1,200 cash.
	15	Paid cash for supplies, $200.
	28	Telephone bill received but not paid, $180.
	29	Advertising bill received but not paid, $400.

The chart of accounts includes Cash, 111; Accounts Receivable, 112; Supplies, 131; Equipment, 141; Accounts Payable, 211; A. Todd, Capital, 311; A. Todd, Withdrawals, 321; Employment Fees Earned, 411; Wage Expense, 511; Telephone Expense, 521; and Advertising Expense, 531.

Requirements

Your tasks are to do the following:

1. Journalize business transactions in General Journal (all page 1).

2. Set up a ledger based on the chart of accounts.

3. Journalize (all page 1) and post transactions.

4. Prepare a trial balance for March 31.

Demonstration Problem Solution

Requirements 1 and 2

Set up ledger based on chart of accounts. Journalize (all page 1) and post transactions.

Part 1	Part 2	Demonstration Problem Complete

a.

FIGURE 3.30
General Ledger

Cash   111

Date		PR	Dr.	Cr.	Balance Dr.	Balance Cr.
201X Mar.	1	GJ1	5,000		5,000	
	4	GJ1		200	4,800	
	6	GJ1		300	4,500	
	7	GJ1		75	4,425	
	9	GJ1	1,200		5,625	
	15	GJ1		200	5,425	

Accounts Receivable   112

Date		PR	Dr.	Cr.	Balance Dr.	Balance Cr.
201X Mar.	5	GJ1	200		200	

Supplies   131

Date		PR	Dr.	Cr.	Balance Dr.	Balance Cr.
201X Mar.	15	GJ1	200		200	

Equipment   141

Date		PR	Dr.	Cr.	Balance Dr.	Balance Cr.
201X Mar.	4	GJ1	200		200	

Accounts Payable   211

Date		PR	Dr.	Cr.	Balance Dr.	Balance Cr.
201X Mar.	28	GJ1		180		180
	29	GJ1		400		580

A. Todd, Capital   311

Date		PR	Dr.	Cr.	Balance Dr.	Balance Cr.
201X Mar.	1	GJ1		5,000		5,000

A. Todd, Withdrawals   321

Date		PR	Dr.	Cr.	Balance Dr.	Balance Cr.
201X Mar.	7	GJ1	75		75	

Employment Fees Earned   411

Date		PR	Dr.	Cr.	Balance Dr.	Balance Cr.
201X Mar.	5	GJ1		200		200
	9	GJ1		1,200		1,400

Wage Expense   511

Date		PR	Dr.	Cr.	Balance Dr.	Balance Cr.
201X Mar.	6	GJ1	300		300	

Telephone Expense   521

Date		PR	Dr.	Cr.	Balance Dr.	Balance Cr.
201X Mar.	28	GJ1	180		180	

Advertising Expense   531

Date		PR	Dr.	Cr.	Balance Dr.	Balance Cr.
201X Mar.	29	GJ1	400		400	

b.

FIGURE 3.31
Journal Entries and Post References

	Date		Account Titles and Description	PR	Dr.	Cr.
	201X Mar.	1	Cash	111	5 0 0 0 00	
			A. Todd, Capital	311		5 0 0 0 00
			Owner investment			
		4	Equipment	141	2 0 0 00	
			Cash	111		2 0 0 00
			Bought equipment for cash			
		5	Accounts Receivable	112	2 0 0 00	
			Employment Fees Earned	411		2 0 0 00
			Fees on account from Blue Co.			
		6	Wage Expense	511	3 0 0 00	
			Cash	111		3 0 0 00
			Paid wages			
		7	A. Todd, Withdrawals	321	7 5 00	
			Cash	111		7 5 00
			Personal withdrawals			
		9	Cash	111	1 2 0 0 00	
			Employment Fees Earned	411		1 2 0 0 00
			Cash fees			
		15	Supplies	131	2 0 0 00	
			Cash	111		2 0 0 00
			Bought supplies for cash			
		28	Telephone Expense	521	1 8 0 00	
			Accounts Payable	211		1 8 0 00
			Telephone bill owed			
		29	Advertising Expense	531	4 0 0 00	
			Accounts Payable	211		4 0 0 00
			Advertising bill received			

ABBY'S EMPLOYMENT AGENCY — Page 1

Solution Tips to Journalizing

1. When journalizing, the PR column is not filled in.
2. Write the name of the debit against the date column. Indent credits and list them below debits. Be sure total debits for each transaction equal total credits.
3. Skip a line between each transaction.

The Analysis of the Journal Entries

Mar.	1	Cash	A	↑	Dr.	$5,000	
		A. Todd, Capital	Capital	↑	Cr.	$5,000	
	4	Equipment	A	↑	Dr.	$ 200	
		Cash	A	↓	Cr.	$ 200	
	5	Accts. Receivable	A	↑	Dr.	$ 200	
		Empl. Fees Earned	Rev.	↑	Cr.	$ 200	
	6	Wage Expense	Exp.	↑	Dr.	$ 300	
		Cash	A	↓	Cr.	$ 300	
	7	A. Todd, Withdrawals	Withd.	↑	Dr.	$ 75	
		Cash	A	↓	Cr.	$ 75	
	9	Cash	A	↑	Dr.	$1,200	
		Empl. Fees Earned	Rev.	↑	Cr.	$1,200	
	15	Supplies	A	↑	Dr.	$ 200	
		Cash	A	↓	Cr.	$ 200	
	28	Telephone Expense	Exp.	↑	Dr.	$ 180	
		Accounts Payable	L	↑	Cr.	$ 180	
	28	Advertising Expense	Exp.	↑	Dr.	$ 400	
		Accounts Payable	L	↑	Cr.	$ 400	

COACHING TIP

This analysis is what should be going through your head before determining debit or credit.

Solution Tips to Posting

The PR column in the ledger cash account tells you from which page journal information came. After the ledger cash account is posted, account number 111 is put in the PR column of the journal for cross-referencing.

Note how we keep a running balance in the cash account. A $5,000 debit balance and a $200 credit entry result in a new debit balance of $4,800.

Requirement 3

Preparing a Trial Balance from the Ledger

Part 1	Part 2	Demonstration Problem Complete

FIGURE 3.32

ABBY'S EMPLOYMENT AGENCY
TRIAL BALANCE
MARCH 31, 201X

	Dr.	Cr.
Cash	5 4 2 5 00	
Accounts Receivable	2 0 0 00	
Supplies	2 0 0 00	
Equipment	2 0 0 00	
Accounts Payable		5 8 0 00
A. Todd, Capital		5 0 0 0 00
A. Todd, Withdrawals	7 5 00	
Employment Fees Earned		1 4 0 0 00
Wage Expense	3 0 0 00	
Telephone Expense	1 8 0 00	
Advertising Expense	4 0 0 00	
Totals	6 9 8 0 00	6 9 8 0 00

Solution Tip to Trial Balance

The trial balance lists the ending balances of the titles in the order in which they appear in the ledger. The total of 6,980 on the left equals 6,980 on the right in Figure 3.33.

Part 1	Part 2	**Demonstration Problem Complete**

BLUEPRINT OF FIRST FOUR STEPS OF ACCOUNTING CYCLE

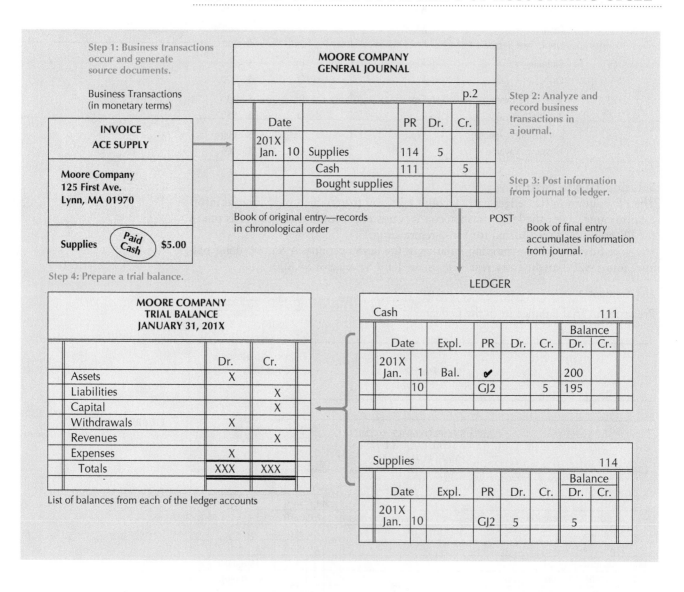

ACCOUNTING COACH

The following Coaching Tips are from Learning Units 3-1 to 3-3. Take the Pre-Game Checkup and use the Check Your Score at the bottom of the page to see how you are doing. The Accounting Coach provides tips before each Checkup to help you avoid common accounting errors.

LU 3-1 Analyzing and Recording Business Transactions into a Journal: Steps 1 and 2 of the Accounting Cycle

Pre-Game Tips: When journalizing transactions be sure to use the Chart of Accounts. It provides the specific titles you will use for either debit(s) or credit(s). You will not use the Chart of Accounts for the explanations in the journal. In the journal, the debit portion of the transaction is listed first, followed by the credit portion. Remember that these titles come from the Chart of Accounts. The total of all debits must equal the total of all credits for each individual transaction.

Pre-Game Checkup
1. The ledger is the book of original entry.
2. Compound journal entries must have no more than three credits.
3. Billing a company for services on account would result in a debit to cash.
4. When you journalize, the PR column must be completed.
5. Rent paid in advance is an expense.

LU 3-2 Posting to the Ledger: Step 3 of the Accounting Cycle

Pre-Game Tips: Posting is transferring information from the journal to the ledger. The ledger accounts keep a running balance of each title, while the journal does not. Cross-referencing helps to fill in the PR column of the journal to show the account number that was posted from that line. With computer software, today's posting could be just a click away.

Pre-Game Checkup
1. Posting can only be done manually.
2. Posting means transferring information from the ledger to the journal.
3. Cross-referencing means the PR column in the ledger is up to date.
4. Posting can only be done once a month.
5. Posting results in information being accumulated in the journal.

LU 3-3 Preparing the Trial Balance: Step 4 of the Accounting Cycle

Pre-Game Tips: The trial balance is listed in the same order as the general ledger. Only one balance is shown for each account in the trial balance. Keep in mind that the trial balance could be in balance and still be incorrect due to posting twice, missing transactions, or analyzing them incorrectly.

Pre-Game Checkup
1. The trial balance is in the same order as the journal.
2. A trial balance can have two balances for some accounts.
3. Slides and transpositions can help locate errors in the trial balance.
4. If a journal entry is posted, no corrections can be made.
5. Account titles that have credit balances are indented.

CHECK YOUR SCORE: Answers to the Pre-Game Checkup

LU 3-1
1. False—The ledger is the book of final entry.
2. False—Compound journal entries must have more than two accounts.
3. False—Billing a company for services on account would result in a debit to accounts receivable.
4. False—When you post, the PR column is completed.
5. False—Rent paid in advance is an asset.

LU 3-2
1. False—Posting can be done by computer.
2. False—Posting means transferring information from the journal to the ledger.

3. False—Cross-referencing means the PR column is updated in the journal.
4. False—Posting can be done at various times.
5. False—Posting results in information being accumulated in the ledger.

LU 3-3
1. False—The trial balance is in the same order as the ledger.
2. False—A trial balance can have only one balance per title.
3. True.
4. False—If a journal entry is posted, corrections can still be made.
5. False—All account titles are listed with no indentations.

Chapter Summary

MyAccountingLab

Here are all the key concepts and equations to help you understand the concepts of this chapter and prepare you for your exam. After completing this review, go to MyAccountingLab for more practice opportunities.

Concepts You Should Know	Key Terms
L01 Journalizing: analyzing and recording business transactions into a journal.	Accounting cycle (p. 78)

L01

Journalizing: analyzing and recording business transactions into a journal.

1. The accounting cycle is a sequence of accounting procedures that are usually performed during an accounting period.

2. An accounting period is the time period (up to one year) for which the income statement is prepared.

3. A calendar year is from January 1 to December 31. The fiscal year is any 12-month period.

4. Interim statements are statements that are usually prepared for a portion of the business's calendar or fiscal year.

5. A general journal is a book that records transactions in chronological order. It is the book of original entry.

6. The ledger is a collection of accounts in which information is accumulated from the postings of the journal. The ledger is the book of final entry.

7. Journalizing is the process of recording journal entries.

8. The chart of accounts provides the specific titles of accounts to be entered in the journal.

9. When journalizing, the post reference (PR) column is left blank.

10. A compound journal entry occurs when more than two accounts are affected in the journalizing process of a business transaction.

Key Terms

Accounting cycle (p. 78)

Accounting period (p. 78)

Book of final entry (p. 78)

Book of original entry (p. 78)

Calendar year (p. 78)

Compound journal entry (p. 80)

Fiscal year (p. 78)

General journal (p. 78)

Interim reports (p. 78)

Journal (p. 78)

Journal entry (p. 78)

Journalizing (p. 78)

Natural business year (p. 78)

Posting: transferring information from a journal to a ledger.

1. Posting is the process of transferring information from the journal to the ledger.

2. The journal and ledger contain the same information but in a different form.

3. The four-column account aids in keeping a running balance of an account.

4. The normal balance of an account will be located on the side that increases it according to the rules of debit and credit.

5. The mechanical process of posting requires care in transferring to the appropriate account the dates, post references, and amounts.

Cross-referencing (p. 86)

Four-column account (p. 86)

Posting (p. 86)

● **L02**

Preparing a trial balance

1. A trial balance can balance but be incorrect.

2. If a trial balance doesn't balance, check for errors in addition, omission of postings, slides, transpositions, copying errors, and so on.

Slide (p. 94)

Trial balance (p. 93)

Transposition (p. 94)

● **L03**

Discussion Questions and Critical Thinking/Ethical Case

1. Explain the concept of the accounting cycle.

2. An accounting period is based on the balance sheet. Agree or disagree?

3. Compare and contrast a calendar year versus a fiscal year.

4. What are interim statements?

5. Why is the ledger called the book of final entry?

6. How do transactions get "linked" in a general journal?

7. What is the relationship of the chart of accounts to the general journal?

8. What is a compound journal entry?

9. Posting means updating the journal. Agree or disagree? Please comment.

10. The side that decreases an account is the normal balance. True or false?

11. The PR column of a general journal is the last item to be filled in during the posting process. Agree or disagree?

12. Discuss the concept of cross-referencing.

13. What is the difference between a transposition and a slide?

14. Jay Simons, the accountant of See Co., would like to buy a new software package for his general ledger. He couldn't do it because all funds were frozen for the rest of the fiscal period. Jay called his friend at Joor Industries and asked whether he could copy its software. Comment on why it is or is not okay for Jay to make such a request.

MyAccountingLab

Concept Checks

L01 (5 MIN)   General Journal

1. Complete the following from the general journal of Mueller Co.:
    a. Year of journal entry   _____
    b. Month of journal entry   _____
    c. Day of journal entry   _____
    d. Name(s) of accounts debited _____
    e. Name(s) of accounts credited _____
    f. Explanation of transaction   _____
    g. Amount of debit(s)   _____
    h. Amount of credit(s)   _____
    i. Page of journal   _____

FIGURE 3.33
General Journal

		MUELLER COMPANY GENERAL JOURNAL				Page 1
Date		Account Titles and Descriptions	PR	Dr.	Cr.	
201X Oct.	3	Cash		9 0 0 0 00		
		Equipment		37 0 0 0 00		
		B. Mueller, Capital			46 0 0 0 00	
		Initial Investment by Owner				

General Journal

◯ **LO2** *(5 MIN)*

2. Provide the explanation for each of the general journal entries in Figure 3.34.

FIGURE 3.34
Journal Entries

	Date		Account Titles and Descriptions	PR	Debit	Credit
	201X Jan.	10	Cash		7000000	
			Computer Equipment		1000000	
			B. Babson, Capital			1700000
			(A)			
		11	Cash		4000	
			Accounts Receivable		6000	
			Consulting Fees Earned			10000
			(B)			
		14	Advertising Expense		17000	
			Accounts Payable			17000
			(C)			

GENERAL JOURNAL — Page 4

Posting and Balancing

◯ **LO2** *(5 MIN)*

3. Balance this four-column account. What function does the PR column serve? When will Account 111 be used in the journalizing and posting process?

		Cash			Acct. 111 Balance	
Date	Explanation	PR	Dr.	Cr.	Dr.	Cr.
201X						
Nov.	7	GJ 1	70			
	10	GJ 1	12			
	18	GJ 2		3		
	22	GJ 3	20			

The Trial Balance

◯ **LO4** *(15 MIN)*

4. The following trial balance (Figure 3.35) was prepared *incorrectly*.

   a. Rearrange the accounts in proper order.

FIGURE 3.35

TIMMONY CO.
TRIAL BALANCE
DECEMBER 31, 201X

	Dr.	Cr.
D. Timmony, Capital	4800	
Equipment	1600	
Rent Expense		2500
Advertising Expense		500
Accounts Payable		800
Taxi Fees	1600	
Cash	1500	
D. Timmony, Withdrawals	—	1100
Totals	9500	4900

b. Calculate the total of the trial balance. (Small numbers are used intentionally so that you can do the calculations in your head.) Assume each account has a normal balance.

● LO3 *(5 MIN)*   **Correcting Entry**

5. On June 1, 2010, a telephone expense for $250 was debited to Repair Expense. On June 10, 2010, this error was found. Prepare the corrected journal entry. When would a correcting entry *not* be needed?

MyAccountingLab   **Exercises**

Set A

● LO1 *(10 MIN)*   **3A-1.** Prepare journal entries for the following transactions that occurred during July:

201X		
July 1	Jodi Wills invested $90,000 cash and $11,000 of equipment into her new business.	
3	Purchased building for $120,000 on account.	
12	Purchased a truck from Liberty Co. for $9,000 cash.	
18	Bought supplies from McVey Co. on account, $800.	

● LO1 *(10 MIN)*   **3A-2.** Record the following into the general journal of Raymond's Auto Shop.

201X		
Jan. 1	Raymond Tucci invested $100,000 cash in the auto shop.	
5	Paid $12,000 for auto equipment.	
8	Bought from Leominster Co. auto equipment for 1,000 on account.	
14	Received $1,500 for repair fees earned.	
18	Billed Thompson Co. $900 for services rendered.	
20	Raymond withdrew $150 for personal use.	

● LO2 *(10 MIN)*   **3A-3.** Post the transactions in Figure 3.36 to the ledger of Koskorous Company. The partial ledger of Koskorous Company is Cash, 111; Equipment, 121; Accounts Payable, 211; and A. Koskorous, Capital, 311. Please use four-column accounts in the posting process.

FIGURE 3.36
Journal Entries

Date 201X			PR	Dr.	Cr.
					Page 4
Jan.	6	Cash		9 0 0 0 00	
		A. Koskorous, Capital			9 0 0 0 00
		Cash investment			
	14	Equipment		3 7 0 0 00	
		Cash			3 0 0 0 00
		Accounts Payable			7 0 0 00
		Purchase of equipment			

3A-4. From the following transactions for Long Company for the month of January, (a) prepare journal entries (assume that it is page 1 of the journal), (b) post to the ledger (use a four-column account), and (c) prepare a trial balance.

●●● **L01, 2, 3** (20 MIN)

201X		
Jan. 1	Jan Long invested $12,000 in the business.	
4	Bought from Mesa Co. equipment on account, $2,300.	
15	Billed Buddy Co. for services rendered, $1,000.	
18	Received $2,000 cash for services rendered.	
24	Paid salaries expense, $1,400.	
28	Jan withdrew $500 for personal use.	

A partial chart of accounts includes Cash, 111; Accounts Receivable, 112; Equipment, 121; Accounts Payable, 211; J. Long, Capital, 311; J. Long, Withdrawals, 312; Fees Earned, 411; and Salaries Expense, 511.

3A-5. You have been hired to correct the trial balance in Figure 3.37 that has been recorded improperly from the ledger to the trial balance.

● **L03** (15 MIN)

FIGURE 3.37
Incorrect Trial Balance

SANDY CO. TRIAL BALANCE JANUARY 31, 201X	Dr.	Cr.
Accounts Payable	9 0 0 00	
A. Sandy, Capital		9 2 5 0 00
A. Sandy, Withdrawals		2 5 0 00
Services Earned		5 1 0 0 00
Concessions Earned	1 4 0 0 00	
Rent Expense	7 0 0 00	
Salaries Expense	2 1 0 0 00	
Miscellaneous Expense		1 2 0 0 00
Cash	10 0 0 0 00	
Accounts Receivable		2 4 0 0 00
Totals	15 1 0 0 00	18 2 0 0 00

3A-6. On February 6, 201X, Mark Sullivan made the journal entry in Figure 3.38 to record the purchase on account of office equipment priced at $1,200. This transaction had not yet been posted when the error was discovered. Make the appropriate correction.

● **L03** (10 MIN)

FIGURE 3.38
Recording Error

	GENERAL JOURNAL			
Date	Account Titles and Description	PR	Dr.	Cr.
201X Feb. 6	Office Equipment		8 0 0 00	
	Accounts Payable			8 0 0 00
	Purchase of office equip. on account			

Set B

LO1 (10 MIN)

3B-1. Prepare journal entries for the following transactions that occurred during March:

201X		
Mar. 1	Jordan Doxbury invested $50,000 cash and $5,000 of equipment into her new business.	
3	Purchased building for $20,000 on account.	
12	Purchased a truck from Lancaster Co. for $15,000 cash.	
18	Bought supplies from Roger Co. on account, $1,000.	

LO1 (10 MIN)

3B-2. Record the following into the general journal of Rick's Auto Shop.

201X	
Sep. 1	Rick Stone invested $110,000 cash in the auto shop.
5	Paid $9,000 for auto equipment.
8	Bought from Lexington Co. auto equipment for $8,000 on account.
14	Received $1,600 for repair fees earned.
18	Billed Franklin Co. $675 for services rendered.
20	Rick withdrew $200 for personal use.

LO2 (10 MIN)

3B-3. Post the transactions to the ledger of Koskorous Company. The partial ledger of Koskorous Company is Cash, 111; Equipment, 121; Accounts Payable, 211; and A. Koskorous, Capital, 311. Please use four-column accounts in the posting process.

	Date			PR	Dr.	Cr.		Page 4
	201X Feb.	6	Cash		3000 00			
			A. Koskorous, Capital			3000 00		
			Cash investment					
		14	Equipment		600 00			
			Cash			300 00		
			Accounts Payable			300 00		
			Purchase of equipment					

LO1, 2, 3 (20 MIN)

3B-4. From the following transactions for Long Company for the month of January,
  a. prepare journal entries (assume that it is page 1 of the journal),
  b. post to the ledger (use a four-column account), and
  c. prepare a trial balance.

A partial chart of accounts includes

Cash, 111
Accounts Receivable, 112
Equipment, 121
Accounts Payable, 211

J. Long, Capital, 311
J. Long, Withdrawals, 312
Fees Earned, 411
Salaries Expense, 511

201X

Jan.	1	Jan Long invested $25,000 in the business.
	4	Bought from Lind Co. equipment on account, $800.
	15	Billed Parent Co. for services rendered, $5,000.
	18	Received $8,000 cash for services rendered.
	24	Paid salary expense, $1,200.
	28	Jan withdrew $800 for personal use.

3B-5. You have been hired to correct the trial balance below that has been recorded improperly from the ledger to the trial balance.

● **LO3** *(15 MIN)*

SANDY CO.
TRIAL BALANCE
JANUARY 31, 201X

	Dr.	Cr.
Accounts Payable	1 7 00	
A. Sandy, Capital		5 7 5 0
A. Sandy, Withdrawals		9 5 0
Services Earned		8 0 0 0
Concessions Earned	1 8 00	
Rent Expense	6 00	
Salaries Expense	2 4 00	
Miscellaneous Expense		8 00
Cash	1 1 0 00	
Accounts Receivable		1 5 00
Totals	1 7 5 00	1 7 0 00

3B-6. On February 6, 201X, Morris Sanford made the journal entry below to record the purchase on account of office equipment priced at $1,000.

● **LO3** *(10 MIN)*

GENERAL JOURNAL

Date	Account Titles and Description	PR	Dr.	Cr.
201X Feb. 6	Office Equipment		9 00	
	Accounts Payable			9 00
	Purchase of office equipment on account			

MyAccountingLab

Problems

Set A

LO1 *(30 MIN)*

3A-1. Jarome Tacks operates Jarome's Cleaning Service. As the bookkeeper, you have been requested to journalize the following transactions:

201X	
Aug. 1	Paid rent for two months in advance, $10,000.
6	Purchased cleaning equipment on account from Aiden's Supply House, $5,000.
12	Purchased cleaning supplies from Lowell's Wholesale for $200 cash.
14	Received $1,400 cash from cleaning fees earned.
20	Jarome withdrew $900 for his personal use.
21	Advertising bill received from *Sary News* but unpaid, $500.
25	Paid electrical expense, $50.
28	Paid salaries expense, $1,100.
29	Performed cleaning work for $2,500, but payment will not be received until April.
30	Paid Aiden's Supply House half the amount owed from Aug. 6 transaction.

Check Figure:
Aug. 21
Dr. Advertising expense $500
Cr. Accounts Payable $500

Your task is to journalize the preceding transactions. The chart of accounts for Jarome's Cleaning Service is as follows:

Chart of Accounts

Assets		Owner's Equity	
111	Cash	311	Jarome Tacks, Capital
112	Accounts Receivable	312	Jarome Tacks, Withdrawals
114	Prepaid Rent	**Revenue**	
116	Cleaning Supplies	411	Cleaning Fees Earned
120	Cleaning Equipment	**Expenses**	
121	Office Equipment	511	Advertising Expense
Liabilities		512	Electrical Expense
211	Accounts Payable	514	Salaries Expense

LO1, 2, 3 *(45 MIN)*

3A-2. On November 1, 201X, Barbie Riley opened Barbie's Art Studio. The following transactions occurred in November:

201X	
Nov. 1	Barbie Riley invested $6,000 in the art studio.
1	Paid three months' rent in advance, $3,600.
3	Purchased $1,800 of equipment from Brasa Co. on account.
5	Received $8,000 cash for art-training workshop for teachers.
8	Purchased $350 of art supplies for cash.
9	Billed Walter Co. $4,000 for group art lesson for its employees.
10	Paid salaries of assistants, $500.
15	Barbie withdrew $300 from the business for her personal use.
28	Paid electrical bill, $130.
29	Paid telephone bill for November, $210.

Your tasks are to do the following:

   a. Set up the ledger based on the following chart of accounts.

   b. Journalize (journal is page 1) and post the November transactions.

   c. Prepare a trial balance as of November 30, 201X.

Check Figure:
Trial Balance
Total $19,800

The chart of accounts for Barbie's Art Studio is as follows:

Chart of Accounts

Assets		Owner's Equity	
111	Cash	311	Barbie Riley, Capital
112	Accounts Receivable	312	Barbie Riley, Withdrawals
114	Prepaid Rent	**Revenue**	
121	Art Supplies	411	Art Fees Earned
131	Equipment	**Expenses**	
Liabilities		511	Electrical Expense
211	Accounts Payable	521	Salaries Expense
		531	Telephone Expense

3A-3. The following transactions occurred in November 201X for A. Glover's Placement Agency:

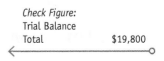 **L01, 2, 3** *(45 MIN)*

201X		
Nov. 1	A. Glover invested $6,000 cash in the placement agency.	
1	Bought equipment on account from Cinder Co., $2,100.	
3	Earned placement fees of $2,000, but payment will not be received until December.	
5	A. Glover withdrew $400 for his personal use.	
7	Paid wages expense, $1,400.	
9	Placed a client on a local TV show, receiving $5,000 cash.	
15	Bought supplies on account from Holly Co., $400.	
28	Paid telephone bill for November, $110.	
29	Advertising bill from Shimmer Co. received but not paid, $800.	

Check Figure:
Tiral Balance
Total $16,300

The chart of accounts for A. Glover Placement Agency is as follows:

Chart of Accounts

Assets		Owner's Equity	
111	Cash	311	A. Glover, Capital
112	Accounts Receivable	312	A. Glover, Withdrawals
131	Supplies	**Revenue**	
141	Equipment	411	Placement Fees Earned
Liabilities		**Expenses**	
211	Accounts Payable	511	Wage Expense
		521	Telephone Expense
		531	Advertising Expense

Your tasks are to do the following:

   a. Set up the ledger based on the chart of accounts.

   b. Journalize (page 1) and post the November transactions.

   c. Prepare a trial balance as of November 30, 201X.

Set B

L01 *(30 MIN)*

3B-1. Jarome Tacks operates Jarome's Cleaning Service. As the bookkeeper, you have been requested to journalize the following transactions:

201X		
Aug.	1	Paid rent for two months in advance, $3,000.
	6	Purchased cleaning equipment on account from Brian's Supply House, $15,000.
	12	Purchased cleaning supplies from Liberty's Wholesale for $700 cash.
	14	Received $1,800 cash from cleaning fees earned.
	20	Jason withdrew $150 for his personal use.
	21	Advertising bill received from *Morning News* but unpaid, $500.
	25	Paid electrical expense, $60.
	28	Paid salaries expense, $500.
	29	Performed cleaning work for $1,900, but payment will not be received until April.
	30	Paid Brian's Supply House half the amount owed from the Aug. 6 transaction.

Check Figure:
Aug. 21
Dr. Advertising expense $500
Cr. Accounts payable $500

The chart of accounts for Jarome's Cleaning Service includes Cash, 111; Accounts Receivable, 112; Prepaid Rent, 114; Cleaning Supplies, 116; Cleaning Equipment, 120; Office Equipment, 121; Accounts Payable, 211; Jarome Tacks, Capital, 311; Jarome Tacks, Withdrawals, 312; Cleaning Fees Earned, 411; Advertising Expense, 511; Electrical Expense, 512; and Salaries Expense, 514.

3B-2. On November 1, 201X, Barbie Riley opened Barbie's Art Studio. The following transactions occurred in November.

L01, 2, 3 *(45 MIN)*

201X		
Nov.	1	Barbie Riley invested $8,000 in the art studio.
	1	Paid ten months' rent in advance, $2,800.
	3	Purchased $1,200 of equipment from Omni Co. on account.
	5	Purchased $900 cash for art-training workshop for teachers.
	8	Purchased $450 of art supplies for cash.
	9	Billed Howie Co. $2,500 for group art lessons for its employees.
	10	Paid salaries of assistants, $1,300.
	15	Barbie withdrew $100 from the business for personal use.
	28	Paid electrical bill, $110.
	29	Paid telephone bill for November, $140.

Check Figure:
Total Trial Balance $12,600

Your tasks are to do the following:

a. Set up a ledger.

b. Journalize (all page 1) and post the November transactions.

c. Prepare a trial balance as of November 30, 201X.

The chart of accounts includes Cash, 111; Accounts Receivable, 112; Prepaid Rent, 114; Art Supplies, 121; Equipment, 131; Accounts Payable, 211; Barbie Riley, Capital, 311; Barbie Riley, Withdrawals, 312; Art Fees Earned, 411; Electrical Expense, 511; Salaries Expense, 521; and Telephone Expense, 531.

3B-3. The following transactions occurred in November 201X for A. Glover's
Placement Agency:

○○○ **L01, 2, 3** *(45 MIN)*

201X		
Nov.	1	A. Glover invested $5,000 cash in the placement agency.
	1	Bought equipment on account from Tinker Co., $1,200.
	3	Earned placement fees of $2,500, but payment from Avon Co. will not be received until July.
	5	A. Glover withdrew $1,000 for his personal use.
	7	Paid wages expense, $1,300.
	9	Placed a client on a local TV show, receiving $900 cash.
	15	Bought supplies on account from Reindeer Co., $300.
	28	Paid telephone bill for November, $190.
	29	Advertising bill from Shimmer Co. received but not paid, $400.

Check Figure:
Total Trial Balance $10,300

The chart of accounts includes Cash, 111; Accounts Receivable, 112;
Supplies, 131; Equipment, 141; Accounts Payable, 211; A. Glover, Capital,
311; A. Glover, Withdrawals, 312; Placement Fees Earned, 411; Wage
Expense, 511; Telephone Expense, 521; and Advertising Expense, 531.

Your task is to do the following:

a. Set up a ledger based on the chart of accounts.

b. Journalize (all page 1) and post the November transactions.

c. Prepare a trial balance at November 30, 201X.

Financial Report Problem

Reading the Kellogg's Annual Report

Go to http://investor.kelloggs.com/annuals.cfm, to access the Kellogg's 2010 Annual
Report, and find the statement of earnings. Sales are the revenue for a merchandise
company. How much did Kellogg's sales increase or decrease from 2009 to 2010?
What inward flows could result from these net sales?

● **L03** *(5 MIN)*

 **ON the JOB**

MyAccountingLab

SANCHEZ COMPUTER CENTER

○○○ **L01, 2, 3** *(45 MIN)*

Tony's computer center is picking up in business, so he has decided to expand his
bookkeeping system to a general journal/ledger system. The balances from August
have been forwarded to the ledger accounts.

Assignment

1. Use the chart of accounts in Chapter 2 to record the following transactions in Figures 3.39 through 3.49.

FIGURE 3.39
Prepaid Rent

Sanchez Computer Center   8104
385 N. Escondido Blvd.
Escondido CA 92025   *September 1, --201X-----*

Pay
To the
Order of— *Capital Management* --- $ *1200.00* -------
          One thousand two hundred and 001100

First Union Bank
322 Glen Ave.
Escondido, CA 92025
memo *Prepaid Rent—Aug. Sept. Oct.** ---------*Tony Freedman* --------
0611 062 78 72

*One check is written for 3 months' rent on September 1. That included August rent. For this problem, consider it all prepaid.

FIGURE 3.40
Service Revenue

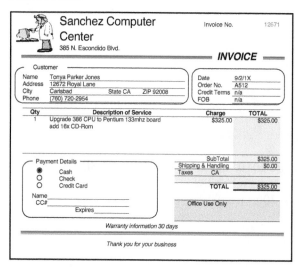

FIGURE 3.41
Service Revenue

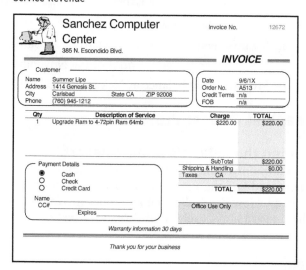

FIGURE 3.42
Phone Bill

Sanchez Computer Center   8105
385 N. Escondido Blvd.
Escondido CA 92025   *September 8, --201X-----*

Pay
To the
Order of— *Pacific Bell* ------------------------------------ $ *155.00* -----
          One hundred fifty five and 001100

First Union Bank
322 Glen Ave.
Escondido, CA 92025
memo *August phone bill transaction (k) Chpt. 2* -------*Tony Freedman* -------
0611 062 78 72

Refer back to Chapter 2, transaction k.

FIGURE 3.43
Sparks Collection

Jeannine Sparks   251
1919 Sierra St.
Escondido CA 92025   *September 12, --201X-----*

Pay
To the
Order of— *Sanchez Computer Center* ------------------------------ $ *850.00* -----
          Eight hundred fifty dollars and 001100

Bank First
322 Cardiff Ave.
Escondido, CA 92025
memo *Computer Fixed, Transaction (o) Chpt. 2* ------*Jeannine Sparks* ------
0611 062 78 72

Refer back to Chapter 2, transaction o.

FIGURE 3.44
Paid Computer Connection

FIGURE 3.45
Purchased Computer Equipment

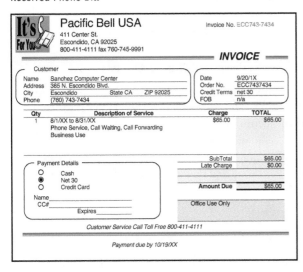

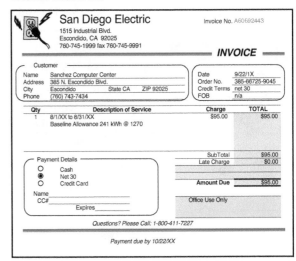

Refer back to Chapter 2, transaction s.

FIGURE 3.46
Received Phone Bill

FIGURE 3.47
Received Electric Bill

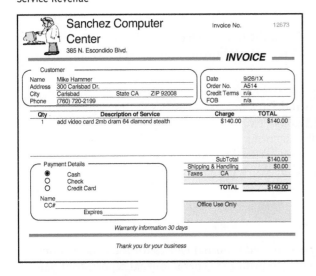

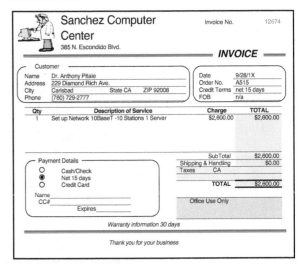

FIGURE 3.48
Service Revenue

FIGURE 3.49
Service Revenue

2. Post all transactions to the general ledger accounts (the Prepaid Rent Account #1025 has been added to the chart of accounts).

3. Prepare a trial balance for September 30, 201X.

4. Prepare the financial statements for the three months ended September 30, 201X.

PEACHTREE COMPUTER WORKSHOP

COMPUTERIZED ACCOUNTING APPLICATION FOR CHAPTER 3

Preparing to use Peachtree Complete Accounting

Before starting this assignment, visit the multimedia library of the MyAccountingLab Web site and read the following PDF documents for your version of Peachtree.

1. An Introduction to Computerized Accounting
2. Installing Peachtree Complete Accounting and Student Data Files
3. An Introduction to Peachtree Complete Accounting
4. Correcting Peachtree Transactions
5. How to Repeat or Restart a Peachtree Assignment
6. Backing Up and Restoring Your Work in Peachtree

Workshop 1:

Journalizing, Posting, General Ledger, Trial Balance, and Chart of Accounts

In this workshop you enter, post, and edit journal entries for the Atlas Company using Peachtree Complete Accounting. You will also print the general journal report, trial balance, and chart of accounts.

Instructions and data files for completing this assignment are in the multimedia library of the MyAccountingLab Web site. Open the *Workshop 1 Atlas Company* PDF document for your version of Peachtree and download the *Atlas Company* data file for your version of Peachtree.

QUICKBOOKS COMPUTER WORKSHOP

COMPUTERIZED ACCOUNTING APPLICATION FOR CHAPTER 3

Preparing to use QuickBooks Pro

Before starting this assignment, visit the multimedia library of the MyAccountingLab Web site and read the following PDF documents for your version of QuickBooks.

1. An Introduction to Computerized Accounting
2. Installing QuickBooks Pro and Student Data Files
3. An Introduction to QuickBooks Pro
4. Correcting QuickBooks Transactions
5. How to Repeat or Restart a QuickBooks Assignment
6. Backing Up and Restoring Your Work in QuickBooks

Workshop 1:

Journalizing, Posting, General Ledger, Trial Balance, and Chart of Accounts

In this workshop, you enter, post, and edit journal entries for the Atlas Company using QuickBooks Pro. You will also print the general journal report, trial balance, and chart of accounts.

Instructions and data files for completing this assignment are in the multimedia library of the MyAccountingLab Web site. Open the *Workshop 1 Atlas Company* PDF document for your version of QuickBooks and download the *Atlas Company* data file for your version of QuickBooks.

The Accounting Cycle Continued

THE GAME PLAN: THE ACCOUNTING CYCLE CONTINUED

When driving a new car like the Chevrolet Volt, do you ever wonder how many steps it takes to design a car from the idea to the finished product? Designers at General Motors first sketched the concept of the Volt using design software and then considered how this new electrical car could be manufactured. While accountants do not design cars, they do use a sketch pad called a worksheet to make changes and adjustments to the trial balance and financial statements. Today, whether in the accounting department at General Motors or a small business, these "design sheets" or worksheets are "sketched" by accounting software. Laying out a worksheet will provide you with a tool to aid you in understanding the "design"—the financial statements generated by your computerized accounting software. Using these worksheets, you will learn how to complete the accounting cycle.

LEARNING OBJECTIVES

1. Adjustments: prepaid rent, office supplies, depreciation on equipment, and accrued salaries.

2. Preparing the adjusted trial balance on the worksheet.

3. Preparing the income statement and balance sheet sections of the worksheet.

4. Preparing financial statements from the worksheet.

Each year General Motors completes an accounting cycle. In Figure 4.1, steps 1–4 show the parts of the manual accounting cycle that were completed for Clark's Word Processing Services in the previous chapter. This chapter continues the cycle with steps 5–6: the preparation of a worksheet and the three financial statements.

LEARNING UNIT 4-1 STEP 5 OF THE ACCOUNTING CYCLE:
Preparing a Worksheet

Worksheet A columnar device used by accountants to aid them in completing the accounting cycle—often just referred to as "spreadsheet." It is not a formal report.

An accountant uses a worksheet to organize and check data before preparing financial statements necessary to complete the accounting cycle. When an accounting software package is used, a worksheet is not needed. The most important function of the worksheet is to allow the accountant to find and correct errors before financial statements are prepared. In a way, a financial statement acts as the accountant's scratch pad. No one sees the worksheet once the financial statements are prepared. A sample worksheet is shown in Figure 4.2.

The accounts listed on the far left of the worksheet are taken from the ledger. The rest of the worksheet has five sections: the trial balance, adjustments, adjusted trial balance, income statement, and balance sheet. Each of these sections is divided into debit and credit columns.

The Trial Balance Section

We discussed how to prepare a trial balance in Chapter 2. Some companies prepare a separate trial balance; others, such as Clark's Word Processing Services, prepare the trial balance directly on the worksheet. A trial balance is taken on every account listed in the ledger that has a balance. Additional titles from the ledger are added as they are needed. (We will show how to add account titles later.)

● L01   The Adjustments Section

Chapters 1–3 discussed transactions that occurred with outside suppliers and companies. In a business, also inside transactions occur during the accounting cycle.

FIGURE 4.1

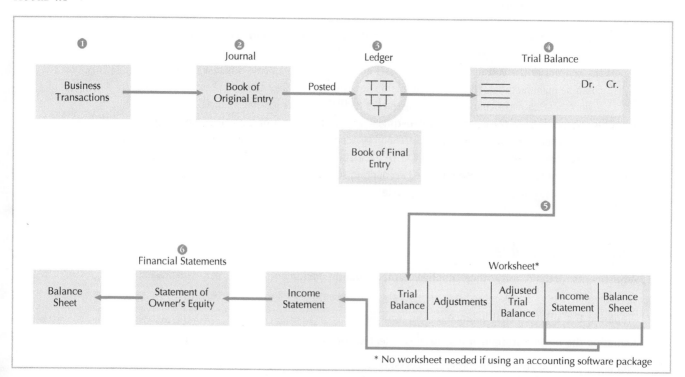

* No worksheet needed if using an accounting software package

FIGURE 4.2
Sample Worksheet

CLARK'S WORD PROCESSING SERVICES **WORKSHEET** **FOR MONTH ENDING MAY 31, 201X**									
Account Titles	Trial Balance		Adjustments		Adjusted Trial Balance		Income Statement	
	Dr.	Cr.	Dr.	Cr.	Dr.	Cr.	Dr.	Cr.
Cash	6 1 5 5 00							
Accounts Receivable	5 0 0 0 00							
Office Supplies	6 0 0 00							
Prepaid Rent	1 2 0 0 00							
Word Processing Equipment	6 0 0 0 00							
Accounts Payable		3 3 5 0 00						
Brenda Clark, Capital		10 0 0 0 00						
Brenda Clark, Withdrawals	6 2 5 00							
Word Processing Fees		8 0 0 0 00						
Office Salaries Expense	1 3 0 0 00							
Advertising Expense	2 5 0 00							
Telephone Expense	2 2 0 00							
	21 3 5 0 00	21 3 5 0 00						

These transactions must be recorded, too. At the end of the worksheet process, the accountant will have all of the business's accounts up-to-date and ready to be used to prepare the formal financial reports. The Sarbanes-Oxley Act specifically states the need to have accurate financial statements. By analyzing each of Clark's accounts on the worksheet, the accountant will be able to identify specific accounts that must be adjusted to bring them up-to-date. The accountant for Clark's Word Processing Services needs to adjust the following accounts:

a. Office Supplies
b. Prepaid Rent
c. Word Processing Equipment
d. Office Salaries Expense

Let's look at how to analyze and adjust each of these accounts.

A. Adjusting the Office Supplies Account

On May 31, the accountant found out that the company had only $100 worth of office supplies on hand. When the company had originally purchased the $600 of office supplies, they were considered an asset. As the supplies were used up, they became an expense.

- Office supplies available: $600 on trial balance.
- Office supplies left or on hand as of May 31: $100 will end up on adjusted trial balance.
- Office supplies used up in the operation of the business for the month of May: $500 is shown in the adjustments column.

As a result, the asset Office Supplies is too high on the trial balance (it should be $100, not $600). At the same time, if we don't show the additional expense of supplies used, the company's *net income* will be too high.

If Clark's accountant does not adjust the trial balance to reflect the change, the company's net income will be too high on the income statement and both sides (Assets and Owner's Equity) of the balance sheet will be too high.

COACHING TIP

Worksheets can be completed on Excel spreadsheets.

Adjusting The process of calculating the latest up-to-date balance of each account at the end of an accounting period.

Now let's look at the adjustment for office supplies in terms of the transaction analysis chart.

Will go on income statement

Accounts Affected	Category	↓↑	Rules
Office Supplies Expense	Expense	↑	Dr.
Office Supplies	Asset	↑	Cr.

Will go on balance sheet

Office Supplies Exp. 514
500

This amount is supplies used up.

Office Supplies 114	
600	500
100	

↑
This amount is supplies on hand.

The Office Supplies Expense account comes from the chart of accounts in Chapter 3. Because it is not listed in the account titles, it must be listed below the trial balance. Let's see how we enter this adjustment in the worksheet in Figure 4.3.

Place $500 in the debit column of the adjustments section on the same line as Office Supplies Expense. Place $500 in the credit column of the adjustments section on the same line as Office Supplies. The numbers in the adjustment column show what is used, *not* what is on hand.

COACHING TIP

The adjustment for supplies deals with the amount of supplies *used up*.

FIGURE 4.3

Note: Amount "used up" for supplies, $500, goes in adjustments section.

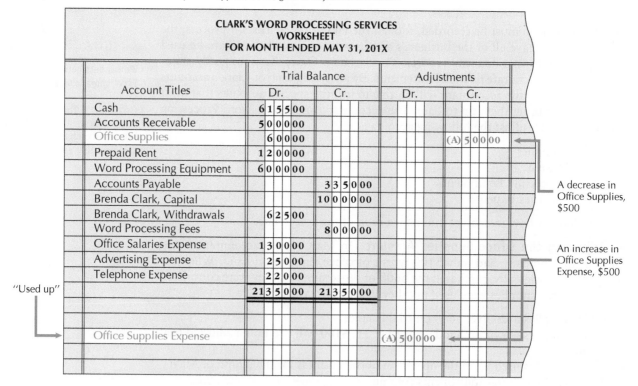

"Used up"

A decrease in Office Supplies, $500

An increase in Office Supplies Expense, $500

B. Adjusting the Prepaid Rent Account Back on May 1, Clark's Word Processing Services paid three months' rent in advance. The accountant realized that the rent expense would be $400 per month ($1,200 ÷ 3 months = $400).

Remember, when rent is paid in advance, it is considered an asset called *prepaid rent*. When the asset, prepaid rent, begins to expire or be used up, it becomes an expense. Now it is May 31, and one month's prepaid rent has become an expense.

How is this type of rent handled? Should the account be $1,200, or is only $800 of prepaid rent left as of May 31? What do we need to do to bring Prepaid Rent to the "true" balance? The answer is that we must increase Rent Expense by $400 and decrease Prepaid Rent by $400 (so that there is only $800 left (see Figure 4.4)).

Without this adjustment, the expenses for Clark's Word Processing Services for May will be too low, and the asset prepaid rent will be too high. If unadjusted amounts were used in the formal reports, the net income shown on the income statement would be too high, and both sides (Assets and Owner's Equity) would be too high on the balance sheet. In terms of our transaction analysis chart, the adjustment would look like this:

Will go on income statement

Accounts Affected	Category	↓↑	Rules
Rent Expense	Expense	↑	Dr.
Prepaid Rent	Asset	↓	Cr.

Will go on balance sheet

```
        Rent Expense 515              Prepaid Rent 115
            400 |                    1200  |  400
                                      800  |
```

Like the Office Supplies Expense account, the Rent Expense account comes from the chart of accounts in Chapter 3.

Figure 4.4 shows how to enter an adjustment to Prepaid Rent.

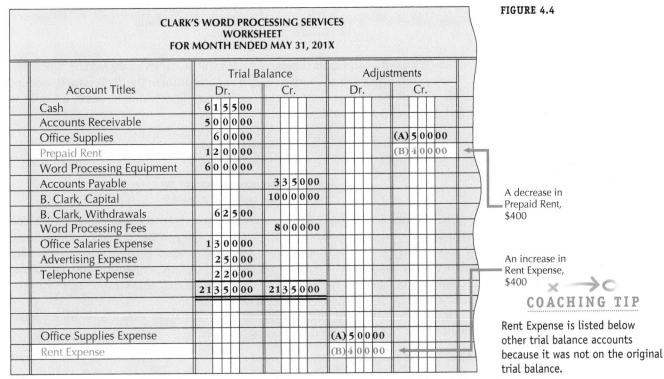

FIGURE 4.4

CLARK'S WORD PROCESSING SERVICES
WORKSHEET
FOR MONTH ENDED MAY 31, 201X

Account Titles	Trial Balance Dr.	Trial Balance Cr.	Adjustments Dr.	Adjustments Cr.
Cash	6 1 5 5 00			
Accounts Receivable	5 0 0 0 00			
Office Supplies	6 0 0 00			(A) 5 0 0 00
Prepaid Rent	1 2 0 0 00			(B) 4 0 0 00
Word Processing Equipment	6 0 0 0 00			
Accounts Payable		3 3 5 0 00		
B. Clark, Capital		10 0 0 0 00		
B. Clark, Withdrawals	6 2 5 00			
Word Processing Fees		8 0 0 0 00		
Office Salaries Expense	1 3 0 0 00			
Advertising Expense	2 5 0 00			
Telephone Expense	2 2 0 00			
	21 3 5 0 00	21 3 5 0 00		
Office Supplies Expense			(A) 5 0 0 00	
Rent Expense			(B) 4 0 0 00	

A decrease in Prepaid Rent, $400

An increase in Rent Expense, $400

COACHING TIP

Rent Expense is listed below other trial balance accounts because it was not on the original trial balance.

C. Adjusting the Word Processing Equipment Account for Depreciation The life of the asset affects how it is adjusted. The two accounts we just discussed, Office Supplies and Prepaid Rent, involve things that are used up relatively quickly. Equipment—like word processing equipment—is expected to last much longer. Equipment is expected to help produce revenue over a longer period. For that reason accountants treat it differently. The balance sheet reports the historical cost, or original cost, of the equipment. The original cost also is reflected in the ledger. The adjustment shows how the cost of the equipment is allocated (spread) over its expected useful life. This spreading is called depreciation.

LO2

Historical cost The actual cost of an asset at time of purchase.

Depreciation The allocation (spreading) of the cost of an asset (such as an auto or equipment) over its expected useful life.

x ——→○
COACHING TIP

Original cost of $6,000 for word processing equipment remains *unchanged* after adjustments.

To depreciate the equipment, we have to figure out how much its cost goes down each month. Then we have to keep a running total of how that depreciation mounts up over time. The Internal Revenue Service (IRS) issues guidelines, tables, and formulas that must be used to estimate the amount of depreciation. Different methods can be used to calculate depreciation. We will use the simplest method—straight-line depreciation—to calculate the depreciation of Clark's Word Processing Services' equipment. Under the straight-line method, equal amounts are taken over successive periods of time. Table 4-1 shows how some companies estimate life of equipment using the straight-line method.

The calculation of depreciation for the year for Clark's Word Processing Services is as follows:

$$\frac{\text{Cost of Equipment} - \text{Residual Value}}{\text{Estimated Years of Usefulness}} = (\text{Trade-In or Salvage Value})$$

According to the IRS, word processing equipment has an expected life of five years. At the end of that time, the property's value is called its "residual value." Think of residual value as the estimated value of the equipment at the end of the fifth year. For Clark, the equipment has an estimated residual value of $1,200.

$$\frac{\$6,000 - \$1,200}{5 \text{ Years}} = \frac{\$4,800}{5} = \$960 \text{ Depreciation per Year}$$

Residual value Estimated value of an asset after all the allowable depreciation has been taken.

Our trial balance is for one month, so we must determine the adjustment for that month:

$$\frac{\$960}{12 \text{ Months}} = \$80 \text{ Depreciation per Month}$$

This $80 is known as depreciation expense, which will be shown on the income statement.

Next, we create a new account to keep a running total of the depreciation amount separate from the original cost of the equipment. The "running total" account is called Accumulated Depreciation.

Accumulated Depreciation A contra-asset account that summarizes or accumulates the amount of depreciation that has been taken on an asset.

Accumulated Depreciation	
Dr.	Cr.

is a contra-asset account found on the balance sheet. A credit will increase it.

The Accumulated Depreciation account shows the relationship between the original cost of the equipment and the amount of depreciation that has been taken or accumulated over a period of time. This *contra-asset* account has the opposite balance of an asset such as equipment. Accumulated Depreciation will summarize, accumulate, or build up the amount of depreciation that is taken on the word processing equipment over its estimated useful life.

Figure 4.5 shows how this calculation of depreciation would look on a partial balance sheet of Clark's Word Processing Services.

TABLE 4.1 How Companies Estimate Useful Life

Company	Method of Depreciation	Estimated Life of Equipment
Claire's Stores	Straight-Line	Furniture: 3–25 years
Merck	Straight-Line	Building: 10–50 years
		Office Equip.: 3–15 years
Big Lots	Straight-Line	Building: 40 years
		Equipment: 3–15 years
Dollar General	Straight-Line	Building: 39–40 years
		Furniture: 3–10 years

FIGURE 4.5

① Historical cost of $6,000 of equipment is not changed.

② Amount of accumulated depreciation is $80 after one month.

③ This figure shows the unused amount of the equipment that may be depreciated in future periods of time. This figure, the cost of the asset less its accumulated depreciation, is often termed *book value* or *carrying value*.

CLARK'S WORD PROCESSING SERVICES
BALANCE SHEET
MAY 31, 201X

Assets		
- - - - - - -		XXXX
Word Processing Equip.	$6,000	
Less Accumulated Depreciation	80	5,920

Let's summarize the key points before going on to mark the adjustment on the worksheet:

1. Depreciation Expense goes on the income statement, which results in

   - an increase in total expenses,
   - a decrease in net income, and, therefore,
   - less to be paid in taxes.

2. Accumulated Depreciation is a contra-asset account found on the balance sheet next to its related equipment account. Accumulated depreciation increases with a credit.

3. The original cost of equipment is not reduced; it stays the same until the equipment is sold or removed.

4. Each month the amount in the Accumulated Depreciation account grows larger while the cost of the equipment remains the same.

Now, let's analyze the adjustment on the transaction analysis chart:

Will go on income statement

Accounts Affected	Category	↓↑	Rules
Depreciation Expense, Word Processing Equipment	Expense	↑	Dr.
Accumulated Depreciation, Word Processing Equipment	Contra-Asset	↑	Cr.

Will go on balance sheet

Dep. Expense, W. P. 516	Accum. Dep., W. P. 122
80			80

Remember, the original cost of the equipment never changes: (1) The Equipment account is not included among the affected accounts because the original cost of equipment remains the same, and (2) the original cost does not change. As the accumulated depreciation increases (as a credit), the equipment's book value decreases.

Figure 4.6 (p. 126) shows how we enter the adjustment for depreciation of word processing equipment.

Because it is a new business, neither account had a previous balance. Therefore, neither is listed in the account titles of the trial balance. We need to list both accounts below Rent Expense in the account titles section. On the worksheet, put $80 in the debit column of the adjustments section on the same line as Depreciation Expense, W. P. Equipment, and put $80 in the credit column of the adjustments section on the same line as Accumulated Depreciation, W. P. Equipment.

Next month, on June 30, $80 would be entered under Depreciation Expense and Accumulated Depreciation would show a balance of $160. Remember, in May, Clark's was a new company so no previous depreciation had been taken.

Now let's look at the last adjustment for Clark's Word Processing Services.

COACHING TIP

Note that the original cost of the equipment on the worksheet has *not* been changed ($6,000).

Book value Cost of equipment less accumulated depreciation.

FIGURE 4.6

CLARK'S WORD PROCESSING SERVICES **WORKSHEET** **FOR MONTH ENDED MAY 31, 201X**							
Account Titles	Trial Balance		Adjustments				
	Dr.	Cr.	Dr.	Cr.			
Cash	6 1 5 5 00						
Accounts Receivable	5 0 0 0 00						
Office Supplies	6 0 0 00			(A) 5 0 0 00			
Prepaid Rent	1 2 0 0 00			(B) 4 0 0 00			
Word Processing Equipment	6 0 0 0 00						
Accounts Payable		3 3 5 0 00					
B. Clark, Capital		10 0 0 0 00					
B. Clark, Withdrawals	6 2 5 00						
Word Processing Fees		8 0 0 0 00					
Office Salaries Expense	1 3 0 0 00						
Advertising Expense	2 5 0 00						
Telephone Expense	2 2 0 00						
	21 3 5 0 00	21 3 5 0 00					
Office Supplies Expense			(A) 5 0 0 00				
Rent Expense			(B) 4 0 0 00				
Depreciation Exp., W. P. Equip.			(C) 8 0 00				
Accum. Deprec., W. P. Equip.				(C) 8 0 00			

An increase in Depreciation Expense, W. P. Equipment

An increase in Accumulated Depreciation, W. P. Equipment

×　━━▶○
COACHING TIP

Note that accounts listed below the trial balance are always *increasing*.

×　━━▶○
COACHING TIP

An expense can be incurred without being paid as long as it helped create earned revenue for a period of time.

Accrued salaries payable
Salaries that are earned by employees but unpaid and unrecorded during the period (and thus need to be recorded by an adjustment) and will not come due for payment until the next accounting period.

D. Adjusting the Salaries Accrued Account Clark's Word Processing Services paid $1,300 in office salaries expense (see the trial balance of any previous worksheet in this chapter). The last salary checks for the month were paid on May 27. How can we update this account to show the salary expense as of May 31?

John Murray worked for Clark on May 28, 29, 30, and 31 (see Figure 4.7). His next paycheck is not due until June 3. John earned $350 for these four days. Is the $350 an expense to Clark in May when it was earned, or in June when it is due and is paid?

Think back to Chapter 1, in which we first discussed revenue and expenses. We noted then that revenue is recorded when it is earned and expenses are recorded when they are incurred, not when they are actually paid. This principle will be discussed further in a later chapter. For now, it is enough to remember that we record revenue and expenses when they occur because we want to match earned revenue with the expenses that resulted in earning those revenues. In this case, by working those four days, John Murray created some revenue for Clark in May. Therefore, the office salaries expense must be shown in May—the month the revenue was earned.

The results are as follows:

- Office Salaries Expense is increased by $350. This unpaid and unrecorded expense for salaries for which payment is not yet due is called accrued salaries payable. In effect, we now show the true expense for salaries ($1,650 instead of $1,300):

Office Salaries Expense	
1,300	
350	

- Salaries Payable is also increased by $350. Clark's created a liability called salaries payable, which means that the firm owes money for salaries. When the firm pays John Murray, it will reduce its liability salaries payable as well as decrease its cash.

FIGURE 4.7

May						
Sunday	Monday	Tuesday	Wednesday	Thursday	Friday	Saturday
						1
2	3	4	5	6	7	8
9	10	11	12	13	14	15
16	17	18	19	20	21	22
23	24	25	26	27	28	29
30	31					

In terms of the transaction analysis chart, the following would be done:

Will go on income statement

Accounts Affected	Category	↓↑	Rules	
Office Salaries Expense	Expense	↑	Dr.	
Salaries Payable	Liability	↑	Cr.	

Will go on balance sheet

Office Salaries Exp. 511	Salaries Payable 212
1,300	350
350	

How the adjustment for accrued salaries is entered in the worksheet is shown in Figure 4.8.

FIGURE 4.8

CLARK'S WORD PROCESSING SERVICES
WORKSHEET
FOR MONTH ENDED MAY 31, 201X

Account Titles	Trial Balance Dr.	Trial Balance Cr.	Adjustments Dr.	Adjustments Cr.
Cash	6 1 5 5 00			
Accounts Receivable	5 0 0 0 00			
Office Supplies	6 0 0 00			(A) 5 0 0 00
Prepaid Rent	1 2 0 0 00			(B) 4 0 0 00
Word Processing Equipment	6 0 0 0 00			
Accounts Payable		3 3 5 0 00		
B. Clark, Capital		10 0 0 0 00		
B. Clark, Withdrawals	6 2 5 00			
Word Processing Fees		8 0 0 0 00		
Office Salaries Expense	1 3 0 0 00		(D) 3 5 0 00	
Advertising Expense	2 5 0 00			
Telephone Expense	2 2 0 00			
	21 3 5 0 00	21 3 5 0 00		
Office Supplies Expense			(A) 5 0 0 00	
Rent Expense			(B) 4 0 0 00	
Depreciation Exp., W. P. Equip.			(C) 8 0 00	
Accum. Deprec., W. P. Equip.				(C) 8 0 00
Salaries Payable				(D) 3 5 0 00

An increase in Office Salaries Expense, $350

An increase in Salaries Payable, $350

The account Office Salaries Expense is already listed in the account titles, so $350 is placed in the debit column of the adjustments section on the same line as Office Salaries Expense. However, because Salaries Payable is not listed in the account titles, it is added below the trial balance after Accumulated Depreciation, W. P. Equipment. The amount $350 is also placed in the credit column of the adjustments section on the same line as Salaries Payable.

Now that we have finished all the adjustments that we intended to make, we total the adjustments section, as shown in Figure 4.9.

FIGURE 4.9
The Adjustments Section
of the Worksheet

CLARK'S WORD PROCESSING SERVICES
WORKSHEET
FOR MONTH ENDED MAY 31, 201X

Account Titles	Trial Balance Dr.	Trial Balance Cr.	Adjustments Dr.	Adjustments Cr.
Cash	6 1 5 5 00			
Accounts Receivable	5 0 0 0 00			
Office Supplies	6 0 0 00			(A) 5 0 0 00
Prepaid Rent	1 2 0 0 00			(B) 4 0 0 00
Word Processing Equipment	6 0 0 0 00			
Accounts Payable		3 3 5 0 00		
B. Clark, Capital		10 0 0 0 00		
B. Clark, Withdrawals	6 2 5 00			
Word Processing Fees		8 0 0 0 00		
Office Salaries Expense	1 3 0 0 00		(D) 3 5 0 00	
Advertising Expense	2 5 0 00			
Telephone Expense	2 2 0 00			
	21 3 5 0 00	21 3 5 0 00		
Office Supplies Expense			(A) 5 0 0 00	
Rent Expense			(B) 4 0 0 00	
Depreciation Exp., W. P. Equip.			(C) 8 0 00	
Accum. Deprec., W. P. Equip.				(C) 8 0 00
Salaries Payable				(D) 3 5 0 00
			1 3 3 0 00	1 3 3 0 00

The Adjusted Trial Balance Section

The adjusted trial balance is the next section on the worksheet. To fill it out we must summarize the information in the trial balance and adjustments sections, as shown in Figure 4.10 (p. 129).

Note that when the numbers are brought across from the trial balance to the adjusted trial balance, two debits will be added together and two credits will be added together. If the numbers include a debit and a credit, take the difference between the two and place it on the side that is larger.

Now that we have completed the adjustments and adjusted trial balance sections of the worksheet, it is time to move on to the income statement and the balance sheet sections. Before we tackle the statements, look at the chart shown in Table 4.2. This table should be used as a reference to help you in filling out the next two sections of the worksheet.

Keep in mind that the numbers from the adjusted trial balance are carried over to one of the last four columns of the worksheet before the bottom section is completed.

L03   The Income Statement Section

As shown in Figure 4.11 (p. 130), the income statement section lists only revenue and expenses from the adjusted trial balance. Note that Accumulated Depreciation and Salaries Payable do not go on the income statement. Accumulated Depreciation is a contra-asset found on the balance sheet. Salaries Payable is a liability found on the balance sheet.

The revenue ($8,000) and all the individual expenses are listed in the income statement section. The revenue is placed in the credit column of the income statement section because it has a credit balance. The expenses have debit balances so

FIGURE 4.10
The Adjusted Trial Balance Section of the Worksheet

CLARK'S WORD PROCESSING SERVICES
WORKSHEET
FOR MONTH ENDED MAY 31, 201X

Account Titles	Trial Balance Dr.	Trial Balance Cr.	Adjustments Dr.	Adjustments Cr.	Adjusted Trial Balance Dr.	Adjusted Trial Balance Cr.
Cash	6155 00				6155 00	
Accounts Receivable	5000 00				5000 00	
Office Supplies	600 00			(A) 500 00	100 00	
Prepaid Rent	1200 00			(B) 400 00	800 00	
Word Processing Equipment	6000 00				6000 00	
Accounts Payable		3350 00				3350 00
Brenda Clark, Capital		10000 00				10000 00
Brenda Clark, Withdrawals	625 00				625 00	
Word Processing Fees		8000 00				8000 00
Office Salaries Expense	1300 00		(D) 350 00		1650 00	
Advertising Expense	250 00				250 00	
Telephone Expense	220 00				220 00	
	21350 00	21350 00				
Office Supplies Expense			(A) 500 00		500 00	
Rent Expense			(B) 400 00		400 00	
Depreciation Exp., W. P. Equip.			(C) 80 00		80 00	
Accum. Deprec., W. P. Equip.				(C) 80 00		80 00
Salaries Payable				(D) 350 00		350 00
			1330 00	1330 00	21780 00	21780 00

Annotations:

If no adjustment is made, just carry over amount from trial balance on same side.

Supplies were $600, but we used up $500, leaving us with a $100 balance (on hand) in Supplies. *Note:* If the account lists both a debit and a credit, take the *difference* between the two and place it on the side that is larger.

Note: Equipment is *not* adjusted here.

Two debits are added together. If there were two credits, they also would be added together.

Carry these amounts over to adjusted trial balance in the same positions.

Note: The total of the left (debit) must equal the total of the right (credit) ($21,780).

TABLE 4.2 Normal Balances and Account Categories

Account Titles	Category	Normal Balance on Adjusted Trial Balance	Income Statement		Balance Sheet	
			Dr.	Cr.	Dr.	Cr.
Cash	Asset	Dr.			X	
Accounts Receivable	Asset	Dr.			X	
Office Supplies	Asset	Dr.			X	
Prepaid Rent	Asset	Dr.			X	
Word Proc. Equip.	Asset	Dr.			X	
Accounts Payable	Liability	Cr.				X
Brenda Clark, Capital	Capital	Cr.				X
Brenda Clark, Withdrawals	Withdrawal	Dr.			X	
Word Proc. Fees	Revenue	Cr.		X		
Office Salaries Exp.	Expense	Dr.	X			
Advertising Expense	Expense	Dr.	X			
Telephone Expense	Expense	Dr.	X			
Office Supplies Exp.	Expense	Dr.	X			
Rent Expense	Expense	Dr.	X			
Dep. Exp., W. P. Equip.	Expense	Dr.	X			
Acc. Dep., W. P. Equip.	Contra-Asset	Cr.				X
Salaries Payable	Liability	Cr.				X

FIGURE 4.11
The Income Statement Section of the Worksheet

	Adjusted Trial Balance		Income Statement	
Account Titles	Dr.	Cr.	Dr.	Cr.
Cash	6 1 5 5 00			
Accounts Receivable	5 0 0 0 00			
Office Supplies	1 0 0 00			
Prepaid Rent	8 0 0 00			
Word Processing Equipment	6 0 0 0 00			
Accounts Payable		3 3 5 0 00		
B. Clark, Capital		10 0 0 0 00		
B. Clark, Withdrawals	6 2 5 00			
Word Processing Fees		8 0 0 0 00		8 0 0 0 00
Office Salaries Expense	1 6 5 0 00		1 6 5 0 00	
Advertising Expense	2 5 0 00		2 5 0 00	
Telephone Expense	2 2 0 00		2 2 0 00	
Office Supplies Expense	5 0 0 00		5 0 0 00	
Rent Expense	4 0 0 00		4 0 0 00	
Depreciation Exp., W. P. Equip.	8 0 00		8 0 00	
Accum. Deprec., W. P. Equip.		8 0 00		
Salaries Payable		3 5 0 00		
	21 7 8 0 00	21 7 8 0 00	3 1 0 0 00	8 0 0 0 00
Net Income			4 9 0 0 00	
			8 0 0 0 00	8 0 0 0 00

CLARK'S WORD PROCESSING SERVICES
WORKSHEET
FOR MONTH ENDED MAY 31, 201X

$8,000
−3,100
$4,900

they are placed in the debit column of the income statement section. The following steps must be taken after the debits and credits are placed in the correct columns:

STEP 1: Total the debits and credits.

STEP 2: Calculate the balance between the debit and credit columns and place the difference on the smaller side.

STEP 3: Total the columns.

The worksheet in Figure 4.11 shows that the label Net Income is added in the account title column on the same line as $4,900. When the figures result in a net income, it will be placed in the debit column of the income statement section of the worksheet. A net loss is placed in the credit column. The $8,000 total indicates that the two columns are in balance.

The Balance Sheet Section

To fill out the balance sheet section of the worksheet, the following are carried over from the adjusted trial balance section: assets, contra-assets, liabilities, capital, and withdrawals. Because the beginning figure for Capital* is used on the worksheet, Net Income is brought over to the credit column of the balance sheet so both columns balance.

Let's now look at the completed worksheet in Figure 4.12 (p. 132) to see how the balance sheet section is completed. Note how the Net Income of $4,900 is brought over to the credit column of the balance sheet section. The figure for Capital is also in the credit column while the figure for Withdrawals is in the debit column. By placing Net Income in the credit column, both sides total $18,680. If a net loss were to occur it would be placed in the debit column of the balance sheet section.

Now that we have completed the worksheet, we can go on to the three financial statements. But first let's summarize our progress.

COACHING TIP

The difference between $3,100 Dr. and $8,000 Cr. indicates Net Income of $4,900. The $4,900 is placed in the debit column to balance both columns to $8,000. Actually, the credit side is larger by $4,900.

COACHING TIP

Remember: The ending figure for Capital is not on the worksheet.

LEARNING UNIT 4-1 REVIEW

AT THIS POINT you should be able to do the following:

- Define and explain the purpose of a worksheet.
- Explain the need as well as the process for adjustments.
- Explain the concept of depreciation.
- Explain the difference between depreciation expense and accumulated depreciation.
- Prepare a worksheet from a trial balance and adjustment data.

*We assume no additional investments during the period.

CLARK'S WORD PROCESSING SERVICES
WORKSHEET
FOR MONTH ENDED MAY 31, 201X

Account Titles	Trial Balance Dr.	Trial Balance Cr.	Adjustments Dr.	Adjustments Cr.	Adjusted Trial Balance Dr.	Adjusted Trial Balance Cr.	Income Statement Dr.	Income Statement Cr.	Balance Sheet Dr.	Balance Sheet Cr.
Cash	6155 00				6155 00				6155 00	
Accounts Receivable	5000 00				5000 00				5000 00	
Office Supplies	600 00			(A) 500 00	100 00				100 00	
Prepaid Rent	1200 00			(B) 400 00	800 00				800 00	
Word Processing Equipment	6000 00				6000 00				6000 00	
Accounts Payable		3350 00				3350 00				3350 00
B. Clark, Capital		10000 00				10000 00				10000 00
B. Clark, Withdrawals	625 00				625 00				625 00	
Word Processing Fees		8000 00				8000 00		8000 00		
Office Salaries Expense	1300 00		(D) 350 00		1650 00		1650 00			
Advertising Expense	250 00				250 00		250 00			
Telephone Expense	220 00				220 00		220 00			
	21350 00	21350 00								
Office Supplies Expense			(A) 500 00		500 00		500 00			
Rent Expense			(B) 400 00		400 00		400 00			
Depreciation Exp., W. P. Equip.			(C) 80 00		80 00		80 00			
Accum. Deprec., W. P. Equip.				(C) 80 00		80 00				80 00
Salaries Payable				(D) 350 00		350 00				35 00
			1330 00	1330 00	21780 00	21780 00	3100 00	8000 00	18680 00	13780 00
Net Income							4900 00			4900 00
							8000 00	8000 00	18680 00	18680 00

"Original cost of $6,000 is not adjusted"

"Used up"

"On hand"

contra-asset

FIGURE 4.12

Instant Replay ⊙ Self-Review Quiz 4-1

From the accompanying trial balance and adjustment data in Figure 4.13 and the adjustment data below, complete a worksheet for P. Logan Co. for the month ended Dec. 31, 201X. (You can use the blank fold-out worksheet located at the end of the textbook.)

Note: The numbers used on this quiz may seem impossibly small, but we have done that on purpose, so that at this point you don't have to worry about arithmetic, just about preparing the worksheet correctly.

Adjustment Data

a. Depreciation Expense, Store Equipment, $1.
b. Insurance Expired, $2.
c. Supplies on hand, $1.
d. Salaries owed but not paid to employees, $3.

FIGURE 4.13

P. LOGAN COMPANY TRIAL BALANCE DECEMBER 31, 201X	Dr.	Cr.
Cash	15 00	
Accounts Receivable	3 00	
Prepaid Insurance	3 00	
Store Supplies	5 00	
Store Equipment	6 00	
Accumulated Depreciation, Store Equipment		4 00
Accounts Payable		2 00
P. Logan, Capital		14 00
P. Logan, Withdrawals	3 00	
Revenue from Clients		25 00
Rent Expense	2 00	
Salaries Expense	8 00	
	45 00	45 00

Solution to Instant Replay: Self-Review Quiz 4-1

Don't adjust this line! Store Equipment always contains the historical cost.

Amount used up

Note that supplies on hand end up on the adjusted trial balance.

P. LOGAN COMPANY
WORKSHEET
FOR MONTH ENDED DECEMBER 31, 201X

Account Titles	Trial Balance Dr.	Trial Balance Cr.	Adjustments Dr.	Adjustments Cr.	Adjusted Trial Balance Dr.	Adjusted Trial Balance Cr.	Income Statement Dr.	Income Statement Cr.	Balance Sheet Dr.	Balance Sheet Cr.
Cash	1500				1500				1500	
Accounts Receivable	300				300				300	
Prepaid Insurance	300			(B) 200	100				100	
Store Supplies	500			(C) 400	100				100	
Store Equipment	600				600				600	
Accum. Depr., Store Equipment		400		(A) 100		500				500
Accounts Payable		200				200				200
P. Logan, Capital		1400				1400				1400
P. Logan, Withdrawals	300				300				300	
Revenue from Clients		2500				2500		2500		
Rent Expense	200				200		200			
Salaries Expense	800		(D) 300		1100		1100			
	4500	4500								
Depr. Exp., Store Equipment			(A) 100		100		100			
Insurance Expense			(B) 200		200		200			
Supplies Expense			(C) 400		400		400			
Salaries Payable				(D) 300		300				300
			1000	1000	4900	4900	2000	2500	2900	2400
Net Income							500			500
							2500	2500	2900	2900

Note that Accumulated Depreciation is listed in the trial balance because the company is not new. Store Equipment has already been depreciated $4.00 from earlier periods.

FIGURE 4.14

PLAY BY PLAY: EXTRA HELP ON SELF-REVIEW QUIZ 4-1

Let's review first: When completing a worksheet, we list the original trial balance, add adjustments, complete an adjusted trial balance, and then decide which titles go on the income statement and balance sheet. Since we do not have columns for statement of owner's equity, withdrawals and net income will be placed on the balance sheet columns. Remember, it is the old figure for Capital that is placed on the worksheet.

Account title column: Any item not listed on the original trial balance will be listed below the trial balance. This will happen when we make adjustments. Note that when we list each title below the trial balance it will be increasing in value.

Adjustment column:

A. Depreciation:

In this adjustment Accumulated Depreciation is already listed on the trial balance so we only have to add Depreciation Expense below the trial balance. Here is the transaction analysis chart for this adjustment:

Depr. Exp. Store Equipm.	Expense	↑	Dr. $1
Acc. Deprec. Store Equip.	Contra-asset	↑	Cr. $1

Note that the original cost of Store Equipment of $6 is not touched.

B. Insurance Expired:

In this adjustment Prepaid Insurance is already listed on the trial balance so we only have to add Insurance Expense below the trial balance. Here is the transaction analysis chart for this adjustment:

Insurance Expense	Expense	↑	Dr. $2
Prepaid Insurance	Asset	↓	Cr. $2

Expired means used up and thus we use the amount of $2.

C. Supplies On Hand:

In this adjustment we have to calculate the amount of supplies used up. We take the beginning amount of supplies of $5 less the amount on hand of $1 to find the amount used up of $4. This is the amount of the adjustment. Since we have Office Supplies listed on the trial balance we only have to add Supplies Expense below the trial balance. Here is the transaction analysis chart for this adjustment:

Supplies Expense	Expense	↑	Dr. $4
Office Supplies	Asset	↓	Cr. $4

D. Salaries Owed:

In this adjustment we have Salaries Expense already listed on the trial balance. Here we have to add Salaries Payable below the trial balance. The following transaction analysis chart shows the new expense that has been incurred but has not been paid:

Salaries Expense	Expense	↑	Dr. $3
Salaries Payable	Liability	↑	Cr. $3

The sum of all the debits on the adjustments equals the sum of the credits.

COACHING TIP

Think of the person as an asset and the dog as a contra-asset. They both stick together (like an asset and a contra-asset on the balance sheet) but have opposite personalities. The dog's name is AC—always a credit.

Adjusted Trial Balance Columns: Accounts that were not adjusted or added below the trial balance have their balances carried over to the adjusted trial balance. Accounts that were adjusted will have their combined balances carried over to the adjusted trial balance.

For example, Salaries Expense is adjusted by adding the debit balance of $8 and the adjustment of $3 to equal an $11 debit balance on the adjusted trial balance. Every account in the adjusted trial balance will end up either on the Income Statement or Balance Sheet columns of the worksheet.

Income Statement Columns: From the adjusted trial balance, all revenue and expense accounts are listed. Note that when we total the debit and credit columns they do not equal each other until we calculate the difference between revenues and expenses. In this case, the ($5) difference will be added to the debit column of the income statement section so both columns will total $25.

Balance Sheet Columns: From the adjusted trial balance, assets and withdrawals will end up in the debit column. The old figures for Capital, liabilities, and contra-assets are in the credit column. Note that the totals of the columns will not balance until a net income of $5 is placed under the $24. This is done because we use the old figure for Capital on the worksheet and there is no column on the worksheet for the statement of owner's equity.

Summary: On the worksheet, items in accounts listed below the trial balance are increasing. Adjustments for supplies must be used up. The original cost of equipment is never touched in the adjustment process. Capital is the old balance on the worksheet. Net income is the difference between revenue and expenses and is carried over to the credit column of the balance sheet. Net losses will be in opposite columns. Income Statement columns and Balance Sheet columns will be out of balance by the amount of Net Income.

LO4   LEARNING UNIT 4-2 STEP 6 OF THE ACCOUNTING CYCLE:
Preparing the Financial Statements from the Worksheet

The formal financial statements can be prepared from the worksheet completed in Learning Unit 4-1. Before beginning, we must check that the entries on the worksheet are correct and in balance. To ensure the accuracy of the figures, we double-check that (1) all entries are recorded in the appropriate column, (2) the correct amounts are entered in the proper places, (3) the addition is correct across the columns (i.e., from the trial balance to the adjusted trial balance to the financial statements), and (4) the columns are added correctly.

Preparing the Income Statement

The first statement to be prepared for Clark's Word Processing Services is the income statement. When preparing the income statement it is important to remember the following:

1. Every figure on the formal statement is on the worksheet. Figure 4.15 (p. 137) shows where each of these figures goes on the income statement.
2. No debit or credit columns appear on the formal statement.
3. The inside column on financial statements is used for subtotaling.
4. Withdrawals do not go on the income statement; they go on the statement of owner's equity.

FIGURE 4.15 From Worksheet to Income Statement

CLARK'S WORD PROCESSING SERVICES INCOME STATEMENT FOR MONTH ENDED MAY 31, 201X		
Revenue:		
Word Processing Fees		$8 0 0 0 00
Operating Expenses:		
Office Salaries Expense	$1 6 5 0 00	
Advertising Expense	2 5 0 00	
Telephone Expense	2 2 0 00	
Office Supplies Expense	5 0 0 00	
Rent Expense	4 0 0 00	
Depreciation Expense, W. P. Equipment	8 0 00	
Total Operating Expenses		3 1 0 0 00
Net Income		$4 9 0 0 00

Account Titles	Income Statement	
	Dr.	Cr.
Cash		
Accounts Receivable		
Office Supplies		
Prepaid Rent		
Word Processing Equipment		
Accounts Payable		
Brenda Clark, Capital		
Brenda Clark, Withdrawals		
Word Processing Fees		8 0 0 0 00
Office Salaries Expense	1 6 5 0 00	
Advertising Expense	2 5 0 00	
Telephone Expense	2 2 0 00	
Office Supplies Expense	5 0 0 00	
Rent Expense	4 0 0 00	
Depreciation Expense, W. P. Equip.	8 0 00	
Accum. Deprec., W. P. Equip.		
Salaries Payable		
	3 1 0 0 00	8 0 0 0 00
Net Income	4 9 0 0 00	
	8 0 0 0 00	8 0 0 0 00

FIGURE 4.16 Completing a Statement of Owner's Equity

CLARK'S WORD PROCESSING SERVICES STATEMENT OF OWNER'S EQUITY FOR MONTH ENDED MAY 31, 201X		
Brenda Clark, Capital, May 1, 201X		$1 0 0 0 0 00
Net Income for May	$4 9 0 0 00	
Less Withdrawals for May	6 2 5 00	
Increase in Capital		4 2 7 5 00
Brenda Clark, Capital, May 31, 201X		$1 4 2 7 5 00

→ Balance Sheet Cr. column on worksheet

→ From income statement, Net Income on worksheet (or from formal report just prepared)

→ Balance Sheet Dr. column on worksheet

→ This figure is not on the worksheet. It is calculated here and used to prepare the balance sheet. Note that no additional investments were made during May.

Take a moment to look at the income statement in Figure 4.15. Note where items go from the income statement section of the worksheet onto the formal statement.

Preparing the Statement of Owner's Equity

Figure 4.16 (p. 137) is the statement of owner's equity for Clark's. The figure shows where the information comes from on the worksheet. It is important to remember that if additional investments were made, the figure on the worksheet for Capital would not be the beginning figure for Capital in the Statement of Owner's Equity. Checking the ledger account for Capital will tell you whether the amount is correct. Note how Net Income and Withdrawals aid in calculating the new figure for Capital.

Preparing the Balance Sheet

In preparing the balance sheet (Figure 4.17, p. 139), remember that the balance sheet section totals on the worksheet ($18,680) do *not* match the totals on the formal balance sheet ($17,975). This information is grouped differently on the formal statement. First, in the formal report Accumulated Depreciation ($80) is subtracted from Word Processing Equipment, reducing the balance. Second, Withdrawals ($625) are subtracted from Owner's Equity, reducing the balance further. These two reductions (−$80 − $625 = −$705) represent the difference between the worksheet total and the total on the formal of the balance sheet ($17,975 − $18,680 = −$705). Figure 4.17 shows how to prepare the balance sheet from the worksheet.

LEARNING UNIT 4-2 REVIEW

AT THIS POINT you should be able to do the following:

- Prepare the three financial statements from a worksheet.
- Explain why totals of the formal balance sheet don't match totals of balance sheet columns on the worksheet.

Instant Replay ⊙ Self-Review Quiz 4-2

From the worksheet for P. Logan (p. 134), please prepare (1) an income statement for December, (2) a statement of owner's equity, and (3) a balance sheet for December 31, 201X. No additional investments took place during the period. Solution is on page 140.

FIGURE 4.17
From Worksheet to Balance Sheet

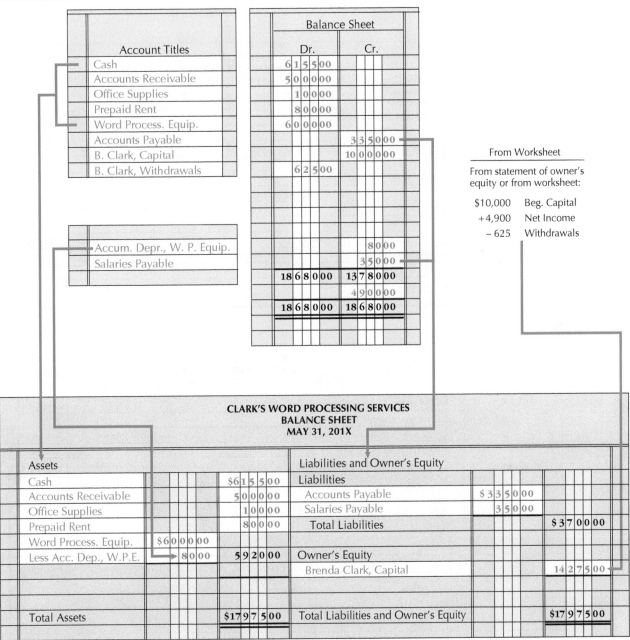

Account Titles	Balance Sheet Dr.	Balance Sheet Cr.
Cash	6 1 5 5 00	
Accounts Receivable	5 0 0 0 00	
Office Supplies	1 0 0 00	
Prepaid Rent	8 0 0 00	
Word Process. Equip.	6 0 0 0 00	
Accounts Payable		3 3 5 0 00
B. Clark, Capital		10 0 0 0 00
B. Clark, Withdrawals	6 2 5 00	
Accum. Depr., W. P. Equip.		8 0 00
Salaries Payable		3 5 0 00
	18 6 8 0 00	13 7 8 0 00
		4 9 0 0 00
	18 6 8 0 00	18 6 8 0 00

From Worksheet

From statement of owner's equity or from worksheet:

$10,000	Beg. Capital
+4,900	Net Income
− 625	Withdrawals

CLARK'S WORD PROCESSING SERVICES
BALANCE SHEET
MAY 31, 201X

Assets			Liabilities and Owner's Equity		
Cash		$6 1 5 5 00	Liabilities		
Accounts Receivable		5 0 0 0 00	Accounts Payable	$ 3 3 5 0 00	
Office Supplies		1 0 0 00	Salaries Payable	3 5 0 00	
Prepaid Rent		8 0 0 00	Total Liabilities		$ 3 7 0 0 00
Word Process. Equip.	$6 0 0 0 00				
Less Acc. Dep., W.P.E.	8 0 00	5 9 2 0 00	Owner's Equity		
			Brenda Clark, Capital		14 2 7 5 00
Total Assets		$17 9 7 5 00	Total Liabilities and Owner's Equity		$17 9 7 5 00

Solution to Instant Replay: Self-Review Quiz 4-2

FIGURE 4.18

P. LOGAN COMPANY
INCOME STATEMENT
FOR THE MONTH ENDED DECEMBER 31, 201X

Revenue:			
Revenue from clients			$ 25 00
Operating Expenses:			
Rent Expense	$ 2 00		
Salaries Expense	11 00		
Depreciation Expense, Store Equipment	1 00		
Insurance Expense	2 00		
Supplies Expense	4 00		
Total Operating Expenses		20 00	
Net Income		$ 5 00	

P. LOGAN COMPANY
STATEMENT OF OWNER'S EQUITY
FOR THE MONTH ENDED DECEMBER 31, 201X

P. Logan, Capital, December 1, 201X			$ 14 00
Net Income for December	$ 5 00		
Less Withdrawals for December	3 00		
Increase in Capital		2 00	
P. Logan, Capital, December 31, 201X		$ 16 00	

P. LOGAN COMPANY
BALANCE SHEET
DECEMBER 31, 201X

Assets				Liabilities and Owner's Equity			
Cash		$ 15 00		Liabilities			
Accounts Receivable		3 00		Accounts Payable	$ 2 00		
Prepaid Insurance		1 00		Salaries Payable	3 00		
Store Supplies		1 00		Total Liabilities		$ 5 00	
Store Equipment	$ 6 00			Owner's Equity			
Less Acc. Dep., St. Eq.	5 00	1 00		P. Logan, Capital		16 00	
				Total Liabilities and			
Total Assets		$ 21 00		Owner's Equity		$ 21 00	

PLAY BY PLAY: EXTRA HELP ON SELF-REVIEW QUIZ LU4-2

Let's review first: There are no debits or credits on the formal financial statements. The three financial statements are made from the last four columns of the worksheet.

Income Statement: The income statement is made up of revenues and expenses. Use the inside column for subtotaling. All numbers found on the income statement are also found on the worksheet.

Statement of Owner's Equity: The net income of $5 is used from the income statement to update the statement of owner's equity. Note that the $14 is the old figure from the worksheet. The increase in capital of $2 is not found on the worksheet. Logan's ending figure of $16 is not found on the worksheet.

Balance Sheet: Logan's ending figure of $16 from the statement of owner's equity is used as the Capital figure on the balance sheet. Note under Assets how the inside column is used to calculate store equipment less accumulated depreciation. Note that the totals of $21 from the balance sheet are not found on the worksheet. When the financial statement is prepared there are no debits or credits.

Summary: The worksheet was prepared in terms of debits and credits, not the formal financial statements. The inside column of the financial statements is for subtotaling. The worksheet used the old figure for Capital while the balance sheet uses the figure from the statement of owner's equity for the new figure of Capital. Many of the numbers on the statement of owner's equity and balance sheet will not be found on the worksheet since there are no debits or credits on formal financial statements.

DEMONSTRATION PROBLEM

Preparing a Worksheet and Financial Statements

From the following trial balance and adjustment data complete (1) a worksheet and (2) the three financial statements (numbers are intentionally small so you may concentrate on the theory).

 **L01, 2, 3, 4**

FROST COMPANY
TRIAL BALANCE
DECEMBER 31, 201X

	Dr.	Cr.
Cash	14	
Accounts Receivable	4	
Prepaid Insurance	5	
Plumbing Supplies	3	
Plumbing Equipment	7	
Accumulated Depreciation, Plumbing Equipment		5
Accounts Payable		1
J. Frost, Capital		12
J. Frost, Withdrawals	3	
Plumbing Fees		27
Rent Expense	4	
Salaries Expense	5	
Totals	45	45

Adjustment Data

a. Insurance Expired, $3.
b. Plumbing Supplies on hand, $1.
c. Depreciation Expense, Plumbing Equipment, $1.
d. Salaries owed but not paid to employees, $2.

Requirements:

1. Prepare a worksheet
2. Prepare financial statments

Demonstration Problem Solutions

Requirement 1

Preparing a worksheet

Part 1	Part 2	Demonstration Problem Complete

Adjustments

a.

Insurance Expense	Expense	↑	Dr.	$3
Prepaid Insurance	Asset	↓	Cr.	$3

Expired means used up.

b.

Plumbing Supplies Expense	Expense	↑	Dr.	$2
Plumbing Supplies	Asset	↓	Cr.	$2

$3 − 1 = $2 *used up*

c.

Depreciation Expense, Plumbing Equipment	Expense	↑	Dr.	$1
Contra-Asset Accumulated Depreciation, Plumbing Equipment	Contra-Asset	↑	Cr.	$1

The original cost of equipment of $7 is not "touched."

d.

Salaries Expense	Expense	↑	Dr.	$2
Salaries Payable	Liability	↑	Cr.	$2

FIGURE 4.19
Solution to Worksheet

FROST COMPANY
WORKSHEET
FOR MONTH ENDED DECEMBER 31, 201X

Account Titles	Trial Balance Dr.	Trial Balance Cr.	Adjustments Dr.	Adjustments Cr.	Adjusted Trial Balance Dr.	Adjusted Trial Balance Cr.	Income Statement Dr.	Income Statement Cr.	Balance Sheet Dr.	Balance Sheet Cr.
Cash	1400				1400				1400	
Accounts Receivable	400				400				400	
Prepaid Insurance	500			(A) 300	200				200	
Plumbing Supplies	300			(B) 200	100				100	
Plumbing Equipment	700				700				700	
Accum. Depr., Plumb. Equip.		500		(C) 100		600				600
Accounts Payable		100				100				100
J. Frost, Capital		1200				1200				1200
J. Frost, Withdrawals	300				300				300	
Plumbing Fees		2700				2700		2700		
Rent Expense	400				400		400			
Salaries Expense	500		(D) 200		700		700			
	4500	4500								
Insurance Expense			(A) 300		300		300			
Plumbing Supplies Expense			(B) 200		200		200			
Depr. Exp. Plumb. Equip.			(C) 100		100		100			
Salaries Payable				(D) 200		200				200
			800	800	4800	4800	1700	2700	3100	2100
Net Income							1000			1000
							2700	2700	3100	3100

Original cost not adjusted

"Used up"   "On hand"

The last four columns of the worksheet (Figure 4.19) are prepared from Adjusted Trial Balance.

Capital of $12 is the old figure. Net income of $10 (revenue – expenses) is brought over to same side as Capital on the balance sheet Cr. column to balance columns. This is done because the worksheet contains the old figure for Capital.

Requirement 2

Preparing financial statements

Part 1	**Part 2**	Demonstration Problem Complete

FROST COMPANY
INCOME STATEMENT
FOR MONTH ENDED DECEMBER 31, 201X

Revenue:		
Plumbing Fees		$27
Operating Expenses:		
Rent Expense	$4	
Salaries Expense	7	
Insurance Expense	3	
Plumbing Supplies Expense	2	
Depreciation Expense, Plumbing Equipment	1	
Total Operating Expenses		17
Net Income		$10

FROST COMPANY
STATEMENT OF OWNER'S EQUITY
FOR MONTH ENDED DECEMBER 31, 201X

J. Frost, Capital, Dec. 1, 201X		$12
Net Income for December	$10	
Less Withdrawals for December	3	
Increase in Capital		7
J. Frost, Capital, Dec. 31, 201X		$19

FROST COMPANY
BALANCE SHEET
DECEMBER 31, 201X

Assets			Liabilities and Owner's Equity		
Cash		$14	Liabilities		
Accounts Receivable		4	Accounts Payable	$1	
Prepaid Insurance		2	Salaries Payable	2	
Plumbing Supplies		1	Total Liabilities		$3
Plumbing Equipment	$7				
Less Accumulated Dep.	6	1	Owner's Equity		
			J. Frost, Capital		19
			Total Liabilities and		
Total Assets		$22	Owner's Equity		$22

Solution Tips for Preparing Financial Statements from a Worksheet

The inside columns of the three financial statements are used for subtotaling. No debits or credits appear on the formal statements.

	Statements
Income Statement	From Income Statement columns of worksheet for revenue and expenses.
Statement of Owner's Equity	Beginning figure for Capital from Balance Sheet worksheet Cr. column. Net Income from income statement. Withdrawal figure from Balance Sheet worksheet Dr. column.
Balance Sheet	Assets from Balance Sheet worksheet Dr. column. Liabilities and Accumulated Depreciation from Balance Sheet worksheet Cr. Column. New figure for Capital from statement of owner's equity.

Note how Plumbing Equipment $7 and Accumulated Depreciation $6 are rearranged on the formal balance sheet. The Total Assets of $22 is not on the worksheet. Remember, no debits or credits appear on formal statements.

Part 1	Part 2	**Demonstration Problem Complete**

Blueprint of Steps 5 and 6 of the Accounting Cycle

Prepare Worksheet

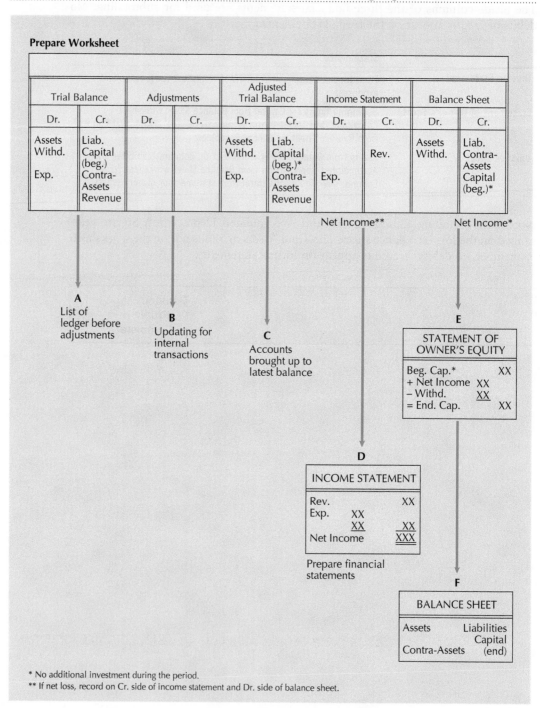

Trial Balance		Adjustments		Adjusted Trial Balance		Income Statement		Balance Sheet	
Dr.	Cr.	Dr.	Cr.	Dr.	Cr.	Dr.	Cr.	Dr.	Cr.
Assets Withd. Exp.	Liab. Capital (beg.) Contra-Assets Revenue			Assets Withd. Exp.	Liab. Capital (beg.)* Contra-Assets Revenue	Exp.	Rev.	Assets Withd.	Liab. Contra-Assets Capital (beg.)*

Net Income**   Net Income*

A
List of ledger before adjustments

B
Updating for internal transactions

C
Accounts brought up to latest balance

E
STATEMENT OF OWNER'S EQUITY

Beg. Cap.*   XX
+ Net Income XX
– Withd.   XX
= End. Cap.   XX

D
INCOME STATEMENT

Rev.   XX
Exp.   XX
          XX   XX
Net Income   XXX

Prepare financial statements

F
BALANCE SHEET

Assets   Liabilities
                Capital
Contra-Assets   (end)

* No additional investment during the period.
** If net loss, record on Cr. side of income statement and Dr. side of balance sheet.

ACCOUNTING COACH

The following Coaching Tips are from Learning Units 4-1 and 4-2. Take the Pre-Game Checkup and use the Check Your Score at the bottom of the page to see how you are doing. The Accounting Coach provides tips before each Checkup to help you avoid common accounting errors.

LU 4-1 Step 5 of the Accounting Cycle: Preparing a Worksheet

Pre-Game Tips: When preparing adjustments on a worksheet, the accounts listed below the trial balance will always be increasing. In the adjustment for supplies, the adjustment is the amount of supplies used—not what is on hand. Keep in mind that for the adjustment for depreciation the original cost of the asset is not touched. The adjustment is an increase in Depreciation Expense and an increase in Accumulated Depreciation. Depreciation Expense goes on the income statement as an expense, and accumulated depreciation goes on the balance sheet as a contra-asset account. Keep in mind that the original costs of the asset and accumulated depreciation are both listed on the balance sheet.

Pre-Game Checkup
Answer true or false to the following statements.

1. A worksheet is a formal report.
2. Accumulated Depreciation is a contra-liability.
3. The adjustment for supplies is the amount of supplies on hand.
4. The normal balance of Accumulated Depreciation is a debit.
5. The old figure for Capital is on the worksheet, so Net Income must be brought over at the bottom to the balance sheet credit column so totals will balance.

LU 4-2 Step 6 of the Accounting Cycle: Preparing the Financial Statements from the Worksheet

Pre-Game Tips: The worksheet uses debits and credits; however, when the three formal financial statements are prepared they do not use debits and credits. The worksheet uses the beginning figure for Capital (no additional investment during the month), but when the financial statements are complete the formal balance sheet will list the figure for ending Capital from the statement of owner's equity.

Pre-Game Checkup
Answer true or false to the following statements.

1. Subtotaling is not used in preparing the formal financial statements from a worksheet.
2. Withdrawals are listed on the income statement.
3. Accumulated Depreciation is added to the cost of the asset on the balance sheet.
4. Debits are the inside column on the formal reports.
5. Totals on the formal balance sheet will match totals on the worksheet.

CHECK YOUR SCORE: ANSWERS TO THE PRE-GAME CHECKUP

LU 4-1
1. False—A worksheet is an informal report.
2. False—Accumulated Depreciation is a contra-asset.
3. False—The adjustment for Supplies is the amount of supplies used up.
4. False—The normal balance of Accumulated Depreciation is a credit.
5. True.

LU 4-2
1. False—Subtotaling *is* used in preparing the formal financial statements from a worksheet.
2. False—Withdrawals are listed on the statement of owner's equity.
3. False—Accumulated depreciation is subtracted from the cost of the asset on the balance sheet.
4. False—There are no debits or credits on financial statements.
5. False—Totals on formal reports do not match totals on the worksheet since there are no debits and credits on financial reports and subtotaling is used.

Chapter Summary

MyAccountingLab

Here are all the key concepts and equations to help you understand the concepts of this chapter and prepare you for your exam. After completing this review, go to MyAccountingLab for more practice opportunities.

Concepts You Should Know	Key Terms
L01 **Preparing Adjustments: prepaid rent, office supplies, depreciation on equipment, and accrued salaries.** 1. The worksheet is not a formal statement. 2. Adjustments update certain accounts so that they will reflect their latest balance before financial statements are prepared. 3. Adjustments will affect both the income statement and the balance sheet. 4. The original cost of a piece of equipment is not adjusted; historical cost is not lost. 5. Depreciation is the process of spreading the original cost of the asset over its expected useful life. 6. Accumulated depreciation is a contra-asset on the balance sheet.	**Adjusting** (p. 121) **Worksheet** (p. 120)
L02 **Preparing the adjusted trial balance on the worksheet.** 1. Accounts listed below the account titles on the trial balance of the worksheet are increasing. Supplies adjustment is amount used up. Rent adjustment is amount expired. Original cost of equipment is not adjusted.	**Accrued salaries payable** (p. 126) **Accumulated Depreciation** (p. 124) **Book value** (p. 125) **Depreciation** (p. 123) **Historical cost** (p. 123) **Residual value** (p. 124)
L03 **Preparing the income statement and balance sheet sections of the worksheet.** 1. Revenue and expenses go on income statement sections of the worksheet. 2. Assets, contra-assets, liabilities, capital, and withdrawals go on balance sheet sections of the worksheet.	
L04 **Preparing financial statements from the worksheet.** 1. The formal statements prepared from a worksheet do not have debit or credit columns. 2. Revenue and expenses go on the income statement. 3. Beginning capital plus net income less withdrawals (or, beginning capital minus net loss less withdrawals) go on the statement of owner's equity. 4. Assets, contra-assets, liabilities, and the new figure for capital go on the balance sheet.	

Discussion Questions and Critical Thinking/Ethical Case

1. Worksheets are required in every company's accounting cycle. Please agree or disagree and explain why.

2. What is the purpose of adjusting accounts?

3. What is the relationship of internal transactions to the adjusting process?

4. Explain how an adjustment can affect both the income statement and balance sheet. Please give an example.

5. Why do we need the Accumulated Depreciation account?

6. Depreciation expense goes on the balance sheet. True or false. Why?

7. Each month Accumulated Depreciation grows while Equipment goes up. Agree or disagree? Defend your position.

8. Define the term *accrued salaries*.

9. Why don't the formal financial statements contain debit or credit columns?

10. Explain how the financial statements are prepared from the worksheet.

11. Janet Fox, president of Angel Co., went to a tax seminar. One of the speakers at the seminar advised the audience to put off showing expenses until next year because doing so would allow them to take advantage of a new tax law. When Janet returned to the office, she called in her accountant, Frieda O'Riley. She told Frieda to forget about making any adjustments for salaries in the old year so more expenses could be shown in the new year. Frieda told her that putting off these expenses would not follow generally accepted accounting procedures. Janet said she should do it anyway. You make the call. Write your specific recommendations to Frieda.

Concept Check

MyAccountingLab

Adjustment for Supplies

● **L01** *(5 MIN)*

1. *Before Adjustment*

Computer Supplies	Computer Supplies Expense
750	

Given: At year end, an inventory of Computer Supplies showed $200.
a. How much is the adjustment for Computer Supplies?
b. Complete a transaction analysis box for this adjustment.
c. What will the balance of Computer Supplies be on the adjusted trial balance?

Adjustment for Prepaid Rent

● **L01** *(10 MIN)*

2. *Before Adjustment*

Prepaid Rent	Rent Expense
500	

Given: At year end, rent expired is $50.
a. How much is the adjustment for Prepaid Rent?
b. Complete a transaction analysis box for this adjustment.
c. What will be the balance of Prepaid Rent on the adjusted trial balance?

LO1 *(10 MIN)*   **Adjustment for Depreciation**

3.   *Before Adjustment*

Equip.	Acc. Dep., Equip.	Dep. Exp., Equip.
10,200	1,000	

Given: At year end, depreciation on Equipment is $700.

a. Which of these three T accounts is not affected?
b. Which account is a contra-asset?
c. Draw a transaction analysis box for this adjustment.
d. What will be the balance of these three accounts on the adjusted trial balance?

LO1 *(10 MIN)*   **Adjustment for Accrued Salaries**

4.   *Before Adjustment*

Salaries Expense	Salaries Payable
1,800	

Given: Accrued Salaries, $50.

a. Complete a transaction analysis box for this adjustment.
b. What will be the balance of these two accounts on the adjusted trial balance?

LO2, 3 *(15 MIN)*   **Worksheet**

5.   From the following adjusted trial balance titles of a worksheet, identify in which column each account will be listed on the last four columns of the worksheet:

(ID) Income Statement Dr. Column
(IC) Income Statement Cr. Column
(BD) Balance Sheet Dr. Column
(BC) Balance Sheet Cr. Column

	ATB		IS	BS
A. Ex: Legal Fees	~	~	IC	
B. Accts. Payable	~	~		
C. Cash	~	~		
D. Prepaid Advertising	~	~		
E. Salaries Payable	~	~		
F. Dep. Expense	~	~		
G. V., Capital	~	~		
H. V., Withdrawals	~	~		
I. Computer Supplies	~	~		
J. Rent Expense	~	~		
K. Supplies Payable	~	~		
L. Advertising Expense	~	~		
M. Accum. Depreciation	~	~		
N. Wages Payable	~	~		

6. From the following balance sheet (which was made from the worksheet and other financial statements), explain why the lettered numbers were not found on the worksheet. *Hint:* No debits or credits appear on the formal financial statements.

◯ **L04** *(15 MIN)*

		LAZE CO. BALANCE SHEET DECEMBER 31, 201X		
Assets		**Liabilities and Owner's Equity**		
Cash	$6	Liabilities		
Acc. Receivable	2	Accounts Payable	$2	
Supplies	2	Salaries Payable	1	
Equipment	$10	Total Liabilities		$3 (B)
Less Acc. Dep.	4 6 (A)	Owner's Equity		
		J. Laze, Capital		13
		Total Liabilities and		
Total Assets	$16	**Owner's Equity**		$16

◑◐ **L02, 3** *(15 MIN)*

		H. WELLS BALANCE SHEET DECEMBER 31, 201X		
Assets		**Liabilities and Owner's Equity**		
Cash	$6	Liabilities		
Acc. Receivable	2	Accounts Payable	$2	
Supplies	2	Salaries Payable	1	
Equipment	$10	Total Liabilities		$3
Less Acc. Dep.	4 6	Owner's Equity		
		H. Wells, Capital		13 (B)
		Total Liabilities and		
Total Assets	$16 (A)	**Owner's Equity**		$16

Exercises

MyAccountingLab

Set A

4A-1. Complete the following table.

◯ **L04** *(5 MIN)*

Account	Category	Normal Balance	Which Financial Statement(s) Found
Accounts Payable			
Prepaid Rent			
Office Equipment			
Depreciation Expense			
B. Reel, Capital			
B. Reel, Withdrawals			
Wages Payable			
Accumulated Depreciation			

LO1 *(10 MIN)* **4A-2.** Use transaction analysis charts to analyze the following adjustments:

    a. Depreciation on equipment, $500.

    b. Rent expired, $200.

LO1 *(10 MIN)* **4A-3.** From the following adjustment data, calculate the adjustment amount and record appropriate debits or credits:

    a. Supplies purchased, $1,300.
       Supplies on hand, $100.

    b. Office equipment, $10,500.
       Accumulated depreciation before adjustment, $1,200.
       Depreciation expense, $800.

LO3 *(20 MIN)* **4A-4.** From the following trial balance (Figure 4.20) and adjustment data, complete a worksheet for J. Tripp as of October 31, 201X:

    a. Depreciation expense, equipment, $1.

    b. Insurance expired, $5.

    c. Store supplies on hand, $7.

    d. Wages owed, but not paid for (they are an expense in the old year), $6.

FIGURE 4.20

J. TRIPP
TRIAL BALANCE
OCTOBER 31, 201X

	Dr.	Cr.
Cash	3200	
Accounts Receivable	200	
Prepaid Insurance	900	
Store Supplies	800	
Store Equipment	1000	
Accumulated Depreciation, Equipment		500
Accounts Payable		1000
J. Tripp, Capital		4100
J. Tripp, Withdrawals	1000	
Revenue from Clients		2700
Rent Expense	1000	
Wage Expense	200	
	8300	8300

LO4 *(20 MIN)* **4A-5.** From the completed worksheet in Exercise 4A-4, prepare

    a. an income statement for October.

    b. a statement of owner's equity for October.

    c. a balance sheet as of October 31, 201X.

Set B

LO4 *(5 MIN)* **4B-1.** Complete the following table.

Account	Category	Normal Balance	Which Financial Statement(s) Found
Accounts Payable			
Prepaid Insurance			
Computer Equipment			
Depreciation Expense			
B. Free, Capital			
B. Free, Withdrawals			
Salaries Payable			
Accumulated Depreciation			

4B-2. Use transaction analysis charts to analyze the following adjustments: ● **L01** *(5 MIN)*
   a. Depreciation on equipment, $700.
   b. Rent expired, $300.

4B-3. From the following adjustment data, calculate the adjustment amount and   ● **L01** *(10 MIN)*
   record appropriate debits or credits:

   Data Table

   a. Supplies purchased, $900.
      Supplies on hand, $150.
   b. Office equipment, $14,500.
      Accumulated depreciation before adjustment, $600.
      Depreciation expense, $1,100.

4B-4. From the following trial balance (Figure 4.21) and adjustment data, complete   ● **L03** *(20 MIN)*
   a worksheet for J. Tripp as of October 31, 201X:

   More Info

   a. Depreciation expense, equipment, $3.
   b. Insurance expired, $3.
   c. Store supplies on hand, $4.
   d. Wages owed but not paid for (they are an expense in the old year), $10.

   Data Table

J. TRIPP TRIAL BALANCE OCTOBER 31, 201X	Dr.	Cr.
Cash	6 00	
Accounts Receivable	2 00	
Prepaid Insurance	4 00	
Store Supplies	7 00	
Store Equipment	9 00	
Accumulated Depreciation, Equipment		3 00
Accounts Payable		4 00
J. Tripp, Capital		1 0 00
J. Tripp, Withdrawals	9 00	
Revenue from Clients		2 5 00
Rent Expense	3 00	
Wage Expense	2 00	
	4 2 00	4 2 00

4B-5. From the completed worksheet in Exercise 4B-4, prepare   ○ **L04** *(20 MIN)*
   a. an income statement for October.
   b. a statement of owner's equity for October.
   c. a balance sheet as of October 31, 201X.

Problems

MyAccountingLab

Set A

●● **L01, 2** *(15 MIN)*

4A-1. Use the following adjustment data on December 31 to complete a partial
   worksheet (Figure 4.22, p. 154) up to the adjusted trial balance.
   a. Fitness supplies on hand, $2,700.
   b. Depreciation taken on fitness equipment, $500.

FIGURE 4.22

JEANETTE'S FITNESS CENTER TRIAL BALANCE MARCH 31, 201X		
	Debit	Credit
Cash in Bank	10 5 00 00	
Accounts Receivable	5 8 00 00	
Fitness Supplies	5 7 00 00	
Fitness Equipment	11 2 0 00	
Accumulated Depreciation, Fitness Equipment		5 5 00 00
J. Woodrich, Capital		14 5 7 5 00
J. Woodrich, Withdrawals	1 5 00 00	
Fitness Fees		15 3 0 0 00
Rent Expense	4 5 0 00	
Advertising Expense	2 2 5 00	
	35 3 7 5 00	35 3 7 5 00

Check Figure:
Total of adjusted
trial balance $35,875

L02, 3 *(30 MIN)*

4A-2. Update the trial balance for Lancing Landscaping Service (Figure 4.23) for March 31, 201X.

Adjustment Data to Update the Trial Balance

   a. Rent expired, $350.
   b. Landscaping supplies on hand (remaining), $150.
   c. Depreciation expense, Landscaping equipment, $400.
   d. Wages earned by workers but not paid or due until April, $600.

FIGURE 4.23

LANCING'S LANDSCAPING SERVICE TRIAL BALANCE MARCH 31, 201X		
	Dr.	Cr.
Cash in Bank	6 7 0 0 00	
Accounts Receivable	4 0 0 00	
Prepaid Rent	1 6 0 0 00	
Landscaping Supplies	1 1 2 2 00	
Landscaping Equipment	1 6 0 0 00	
Accumulated Depreciation, Landscaping Equipment		1 0 2 0 00
Accounts Payable		1 0 3 2 00
A. Lancing, Capital		2 4 0 5 00
Landscaping Revenue		8 7 0 0 00
Heat Expense	2 7 5 00	
Advertising Expense	1 0 0 00	
Wage Expense	1 3 6 0 00	
	13 1 5 7 00	13 1 5 7 00

Check Figure:
Adjusted Trial Balance total $14,157

Your task is to prepare a worksheet for Lancing's Landscaping Service for the month of March.

L01 *(60 MIN)*

4A-3. Update the trial balance for Kyler's Moving Co. (Figure 4.24, p. 155) for January 31, 201X.

Adjustment Data to Update Trial Balance

   a. Insurance expired, $550.
   b. Moving supplies on hand, $700.

c. Depreciation on moving truck, $400.

d. Wages earned but unpaid, $200.

Your task is to

1. complete a worksheet for Kyler's Moving Co. for the month of January.

2. prepare an income statement for January, a statement of owner's equity for January, and a balance sheet as of January 31, 201X.

FIGURE 4.24

KYLER'S MOVING CO. TRIAL BALANCE JANUARY 31, 201X		
	Dr.	Cr.
Cash	2 0 0 0 00	
Prepaid Insurance	2 0 0 0 00	
Moving Supplies	1 7 0 0 00	
Moving Truck	11 0 0 0 00	
Accumulated Depreciation, Moving Truck		6 0 0 00
Accounts Payable		2 2 0 9 00
K. Hilton, Capital		8 6 0 0 00
K. Hilton, Withdrawals	1 9 0 0 00	
Revenue from Moving		8 6 0 0 00
Wage Expense	3 1 5 0 00	
Rent Expense	5 5 0 00	
Advertising Expense	7 0 3 00	
	23 0 0 3 00	23 0 0 3 00

Check Figure:
Net Income $2,047

4A-4. The trial balance for Daniel's Repair Service appears in Figure 4.25.

Adjustment Data to Update Trial Balance

a. Insurance expired, $450.

b. Repair supplies on hand, $2,300.

c. Depreciation on repair equipment, $200.

d. Wages earned but unpaid, $400.

Your task is to

1. complete a worksheet for Daniel's Repair Service for the month of April.

2. prepare an income statement for April, a statement of owner's equity for April, and a balance sheet as of April 30, 201X.

●●○ **LO2, 3, 4**
(60 MIN)

PT/QB

FIGURE 4.25

DANIEL'S REPAIR SERVICE TRIAL BALANCE APRIL 30, 201X		
	Dr.	Cr.
Cash	2 4 0 0 00	
Prepaid Insurance	3 5 0 0 00	
Repair Supplies	5 0 0 0 00	
Repair Equipment	7 0 0 0 00	
Accumulated Depreciation, Repair Equipment		1 1 0 0 00
Accounts Payable		5 5 7 0 00
D. Heines, Capital		5 5 2 0 00
Revenue from Repairs		8 4 0 0 00
Wages Expense	1 9 0 0 00	
Rent Expense	7 2 0 00	
Advertising Expense	7 0 00	
	20 5 9 0 00	20 5 9 0 00

Check Figure:
Net Income $1,960

MyAccountingLab

Set B

⬤◯ **L01, 2** *(15 MIN)*

4B-1. Please complete a partial worksheet (Figure 4.26) up to the adjusted trial balance for Jeremy's Fitness Center using the following adjustment data:

   a. Fitness supplies on hand, $2,900.
   b. Depreciation taken on fitness equipment, $1,000.

FIGURE 4.26

Check Figure:
Total of Adjusted
Trial Balance $32,725

JEREMY'S FITNESS CENTER TRIAL BALANCE OCTOBER 31, 201X	Dr.	Cr.
Cash	9 5 0 0 00	
Accounts Receivable	6 1 0 0 00	
Fitness Supplies	5 8 0 0 00	
Fitness Equipment	7 2 0 0 00	
Accumulated Depreciation, Fitness Equipment		4 5 0 0 00
J. Wickers, Capital		13 9 2 5 00
J. Wickers, Withdrawals	2 2 5 0 00	
Fitness Fees		13 3 0 0 00
Rent Expense	7 5 0 00	
Advertising Expense	1 2 5 00	
	31 7 2 5 00	31 7 2 5 00

⬤⬤ **L02, 3** *(30 MIN)*

4B-2. Given the trial balance in Figure 4.27 and adjustment data of Lan's Landscaping Service, your task is to prepare a worksheet for the month of October.

Adjustment Data to Update the Trial Balance

   a. Rent expired, $650.
   b. Landscaping supplies on hand (remaining), $300.
   c. Depreciation expense, landscaping equipment, $150.
   d. Wages earned by workers but not paid or due until November, $550.

FIGURE 4.27

Check Figure:
Adjusted Trial Balance total $13,620

LAN'S LANDSCAPING SERVICE TRIAL BALANCE OCTOBER 31, 201X	Dr.	Cr.
Cash in Bank	4 6 0 0 00	
Accounts Receivable	1 0 0 0 00	
Prepaid Rent	1 0 0 0 00	
Landscaping Supplies	1 1 9 5 00	
Landscaping Equipment	3 2 0 0 00	
Accumulated Depreciation, Landscaping Equipment		7 8 0 00
Accounts Payable		1 0 7 5 00
A. Lan, Capital		3 3 6 5 00
Landscaping Revenue		7 7 0 0 00
Heat Expense	3 2 5 00	
Advertising Expense	1 6 0 00	
Wage Expense	1 4 4 0 00	
	12 9 2 0 00	12 9 2 0 00

4B-3. Using the trial balance in Figure 4.28, and adjustment data of Kyler's Moving Co., prepare

L01 *(60 MIN)*

1. a worksheet for the month of January.
2. an income statement for January, a statement of owner's equity for January, and a balance sheet as of January 31, 201X.

Adjustment Data to Update Trial Balance

  a. Insurance expired, $450.
  b. Moving supplies on hand, $400.
  c. Depreciation on moving truck, $350.
  d. Wages earned but unpaid, $180.

FIGURE 4.28

KYLER'S MOVING CO. TRIAL BALANCE JANUARY 31, 201X	Dr.	Cr.
Cash	11 000 00	
Prepaid Insurance	1 800 00	
Moving Supplies	1 000 00	
Moving Truck	16 000 00	
Accumulated Depreciation, Moving Truck		5 500 00
Accounts Payable		2 700 00
K. Hilton, Capital		19 228 00
K. Hilton, Withdrawals	1 300 00	
Revenue from Moving		8 300 00
Wages Expense	3 150 00	
Rent Expense	775 00	
Advertising Expense	703 00	
	35 728 00	35 728 00

Check Figure:
Net Income $2,092

4B-4. As the bookkeeper of Daniel's Repair Service, use the information in Figure 4.29 (p. 158), to prepare

L02, 3, 4
(60 MIN)

1. a worksheet for the month of April.
2. an income statement for April, a statement of owner's equity for April, and a balance sheet as of April 30, 201X.

Adjustment Data to Update Trial Balance

  a. Insurance expired, $200.
  b. Repair supplies on hand, $2,600.
  c. Depreciation on repair equipment, $500.
  d. Wages earned but unpaid, $180.

FIGURE 4.29

DANIEL'S REPAIR SERVICE TRIAL BALANCE APRIL 30, 201X		
	Dr.	Cr.
Cash	3 4 0 0 00	
Prepaid Insurance	5 0 0 0 00	
Repair Supplies	4 9 0 0 00	
Repair Equipment	3 5 0 0 00	
Accumulated Depreciation, Repair Equipment		9 0 0 00
Accounts Payable		5 0 4 0 00
D. Heins, Capital		5 7 4 0 00
Revenue from Repairs		7 6 0 0 00
Wages Expense	1 5 0 0 00	
Rent Expense	7 5 0 00	
Advertising Expense	2 3 0 00	
	19 2 8 0 00	19 2 8 0 00

Check Figure:
Net Income $1,940

Financial Report Problem

LO1 *(20 MIN)*

Reading the Kellogg's Annual Report

Go to http://investor.kelloggs.com/annuals.cfm, to access the Kellogg's 2010 Annual Report, and look at Note 1 under Property. Find out how Kellogg's depreciates its equipment. How is the equipment recorded?

MyAccountingLab

ON the JOB

LO2, 3, 4
(45 MIN)

SANCHEZ COMPUTER CENTER

At the end of September, Tony took a complete inventory of his supplies and found the following:

 5 dozen ¼" screws at a cost of $8.00 a dozen

 2 dozen ½" screws at a cost of $5.00 a dozen

 2 cartons of computer inventory paper at a cost of $14 a carton

 3 feet of coaxial cable at a cost of $4.00 per foot

After speaking to his accountant, he found that a reasonable depreciation amount for each of his long-term assets is as follows:

Computer purchased July 5, 201X	Depreciation $33 a month
Office equipment purchased July 17, 201X	Depreciation $10 a month
Computer workstations purchased Sept. 17, 201X	Depreciation $20 a month

Tony uses the straight-line method of depreciation and declares no salvage value for any of the assets. If any long-term asset is purchased in the first 15 days of the month, he will charge depreciation for the full month. If an asset is purchased on the 16th of the month, or later, he will not charge depreciation in the month it was purchased.

August and September's rent has now expired.

ASSIGNMENT

Use your trial balance from the completed problem in Chapter 3 and the adjusting information given here to complete the worksheet for the three months ended September 30, 201X. From the worksheets, prepare the financial statements.

SUBWAY CASE

Where the Dough Goes . . .

○○○ **L01, 2, 3** *(20 MIN)*

No matter how harried Stan Hernandez feels as the owner of his own Subway restaurant, the aroma of his fresh-baked gourmet breads *always* perks him up. However, the sales generated by Subway's line of gourmet seasoned breads perks Stan up even more. Subway restaurants introduced freshly baked bread in 1983, a practice that made it stand out from other fast-food chains and helped build its reputation for made-to-order freshness. Since then Subway franchisees have introduced many types of gourmet seasoned breads—such as Hearty Italian or Monterey Cheddar—according to a schedule determined by headquarters.

Stan was one month into the "limited-time promotion" for the chain's new Roasted Garlic seasoned bread when his bake oven started faltering. "The temperature controls just don't seem quite right," said his employee and "sandwich artist," Rashid. "It's taking incrementally longer to bake the bread."

"This couldn't happen at a worse time," moaned Stan. "We're baking enough Roasted Garlic bread to keep a whole town of vampires away, but if we don't get it out of the oven fast enough, we'll keep our customers away!"

That very day Stan called his field consultant, Mariah, to discuss what to do about his bake oven. Mariah reminded Stan that his oven trouble illustrated the flip side of buying an existing store from a retired franchisee—having to repair or replace worn or old equipment. After receiving a rather expensive repair estimate and considering the age of the oven, Stan ultimately decided it would make sense for him to purchase a new one. Mariah concurred, "At the rate your sales are going, Stan, you're going to need that roomier new model."

"Wow, do you realize how much this new bake oven is going to cost me?—$3,000!" Stan exclaimed while meeting with his cousin-turned-Subway-accountant, Lila Hernandez. "Yes, it's a lot to lay out, Stan," said Lila, "but you'll be depreciating the cost over a period of 10 years, which will help you at tax time. Let's do the adjustment on your worksheet, so you can see it."

The two of them were sitting in Stan's small office behind the Subway kitchen, and they pulled up this month's worksheet on Stan's Peachtree program. Lila laughed, "I'm sure glad you started entering your worksheets on Peachtree again! The figures on those old ones were so doodled over and crossed out that I could barely decipher them! We may need your worksheets at tax time."

"Anything for you, *mi prima*," Stan said. "I may depreciate my bake oven, but my gratitude for your accounting skills only appreciates with time!"

Discussion Questions

1. If you are using a straight-line method of depreciation and Stan's bake oven has a residual value of $1,000, how much depreciation will he account for each year and what would the adjustment be for each month?
2. Where does Lila get the information on the useful life of Stan's bake oven and the estimate for its residual value? Why do you think she gets her information from this particular source?
3. Why is a clear worksheet helpful even after that month's statements have been prepared?

PEACHTREE COMPUTER WORKSHOP

COMPUTERIZED ACCOUNTING APPLICATION FOR CHAPTER 4

Refresher on using Peachtree Complete Accounting

Before starting this assignment, you may want to refresh your memory by reading the following PDF documents found in the multimedia library on the MyAccountingLab Web site. Remember to choose the PDF document for your version of Peachtree.

1. An Introduction to Peachtree Complete Accounting
2. Correcting Peachtree Transactions
3. How to Repeat or Restart a Peachtree Assignment
4. Backing Up and Restoring Your Work in Peachtree

You also should have completed Workshop 1 for the Atlas Company in Chapter 3.

Workshop 2:

Compound Journal Entries, Adjusting Entries, and Financial Reports

In this workshop you will post compound journal entries and adjusting journal entries for Zell Company using Peachtree. You will also print the general journal report, trial balance, income statement, and balance sheet.

Instructions and the data file for completing this assignment are in the multimedia library of the MyAccountingLab Web site. Open the *Workshop 2 Zell Company* PDF document for your version of Peachtree and download the *Zell Company* data file for your version of Peachtree.

QUICKBOOKS COMPUTER WORKSHOP

COMPUTERIZED ACCOUNTING APPLICATION FOR CHAPTER 4

Refresher on using QuickBooks Pro

Before starting this assignment, you may want to refresh your memory by reading the following PDF documents found in the multimedia library on the MyAccountingLab Web site. Remember to choose the PDF document for your version of QuickBooks.

1. An Introduction to Computerized Accounting
2. Installing QuickBooks Pro and Student Data Files
3. An Introduction to QuickBooks Pro
4. Correcting QuickBooks Transactions
5. How to Repeat or Restart a QuickBooks Assignment
6. Backing Up and Restoring Your Work in QuickBooks. You also should have completed Workshop 1 for the Atlas Company in Chapter 3.

Workshop 2:

Compound Journal Entries, Adjusting Entries, and Financial Reports

In this workshop you will post compound journal entries and adjusting journal entries for Zell Company using Quickbooks. You will also print the general journal report, trial balance, income statement, and balance sheet.

Instructions and the data file for completing this assignment are in the multimedia library of the MyAccountingLab Web site. Open the *Workshop 2 Zell Company* PDF document for your version of Quickbooks and download the *Zell Company* data file for your version of Quickbooks.

The Accounting Cycle Completed

THE GAME PLAN

By April 15 of every year, you send in your Federal Income Tax form to the IRS. What a relief! But the truth is that you have to go through this process year after year. Each year you gather your financial information and provide a report of your earnings and expenses to the government. The same concept holds true in accounting for companies as well. For example, Disney must report to investors and government regulators how operations performed during its accounting cycle. When one accounting cycle is closed the next one begins. This period of time is called the fiscal year. Many companies end their fiscal years in March, July, or October. Other companies, like retailers, end on December 31 so holiday sales can be included in the final results. No matter when companies end their fiscal years, the accounting cycle must be completed and financial reports prepared so that companies can report to the appropriate governmental authorities, like the SEC and IRS, investors, and creditors.

LEARNING OBJECTIVES

- 1. Journalizing and posting adjusting entries.
- 2. Journalizing and posting closing entries.
- 3. Preparing a post-closing trial balance.

Each accounting cycle completed by Disney will end with the preparation of a post-closing trial balance. In Chapters 3 and 4 we completed these steps of the manual accounting cycle for Clark's Word Processing Services:

STEP 1: Business transactions occurred and generated source documents.

STEP 2: Business transactions were analyzed and recorded in a journal.

STEP 3: Information was posted or transferred from journal to ledger.

STEP 4: A trial balance was prepared.

STEP 5: A worksheet was completed.

STEP 6: Financial statements were prepared.

This chapter covers the following steps to complete Clark's accounting cycle for the month of May:

STEP 7: Journalizing and posting adjusting entries.

STEP 8: Journalizing and posting closing entries.

STEP 9: Preparing a post-closing trial balance.

LO1   LEARNING UNIT 5-1 JOURNALIZING AND POSTING ADJUSTING ENTRIES:
Step 7 of the Accounting Cycle

Recording Journal Entries from the Worksheet

The information in the worksheet is up-to-date. The financial reports prepared from that information can give the business's management and other interested parties a good idea of where the business stands as of a particular date. However, the worksheet is only an informal report. The information concerning the adjustments has not been placed into the journal or posted to the ledger accounts yet, which means that the books are not up-to-date and ready for the next accounting cycle to begin. For example, the ledger shows $1,200 of Prepaid Rent, but the balance sheet we prepared in Chapter 4 shows an $800 balance. Essentially, the worksheet is a tool for preparing financial statements. Now we must use the adjustment columns of the worksheet as a basis for bringing the ledger up-to-date. To update the ledger, we use adjusting journal entries (see Figures 5.1 and 5.2). Again, the updating must be done before the next accounting period starts. For Clark's Word Processing Services, the next period begins on June 1.

Adjusting journal entries
Journal entries that are needed in order to update specific ledger accounts to reflect correct balances at the end of an accounting period.

Figure 5.2 shows the adjusting journal entries for Clark's taken from the adjustments section of the worksheet. Once the adjusting journal entries are posted to the ledger, the accounts making up the financial statements that were prepared from the worksheet will equal the updated ledger. (Keep in mind that we are using the same journal and ledger as in the previous chapters.) Let's look at some simplified T accounts to show how Clark's ledger looked before and after the adjustments (A–D) were posted.

Adjustment (A)

	Before Posting:	Office Supplies 114	Office Supplies Expense 514
		600	
	After Posting:	Office Supplies 114	Office Supplies Expense 514
		600 | 500	500

Account Titles	Trial Balance		Adjustments	
	Dr.	Cr.	Dr.	Cr.
Cash	6 1 5 5 00			
Accounts Receivable	5 0 0 0 00			
Office Supplies	6 0 0 00			(A) 5 0 0 00
Prepaid Rent	1 2 0 0 00			(B) 4 0 0 00
Word Processing Equipment	6 0 0 0 00			
Accounts Payable		3 3 5 0 00		
Brenda Clark, Capital		1 0 0 0 0 00		
Brenda Clark, Withdrawals	6 2 5 00			
Word Processing Fees		8 0 0 0 00		
Office Salaries Expense	1 3 0 0 00		(D) 3 5 0 00	
Advertising Expense	2 5 0 00			
Telephone Expense	2 2 0 00			
	2 1 3 5 0 00	2 1 3 5 0 00		
Office Supplies Expense			(A) 5 0 0 00	
Rent Expense			(B) 4 0 0 00	
Depreciation Exp., W. P. Equip.			(C) 8 0 00	
Accum. Deprec., W. P. Equip.				(C) 8 0 00
Salaries Payable				(D) 3 5 0 00
			1 3 3 0 00	1 3 3 0 00

FIGURE 5.1
Adjustments A–D in the Adjustments Section of the Worksheet Must Be Recorded in the Journal and Posted to the Ledger.

CLARK'S WORD PROCESSING SERVICES
GENERAL JOURNAL

Page 2

Date		Account Titles and Description	PR	Dr.	Cr.
		Adjusting Entries			
May	31	Office Supplies Expense	514	5 0 0 00	
		Office Supplies	114		5 0 0 00
	31	Rent Expense	515	4 0 0 00	
		Prepaid Rent	115		4 0 0 00
	31	Depreciation Expense, W. P. Equip.	516	8 0 00	
		Accumulated Depreciation, W. P. Equip.	122		8 0 00
	31	Office Salaries Expense	511	3 5 0 00	
		Salaries Payable	212		3 5 0 00

FIGURE 5.2
Journalizing and Posting Adjustments from the Adjustment Section of the Worksheet

COACHING TIP

Each adjustment affects both the income statement and balance sheet.

Adjustment (B)

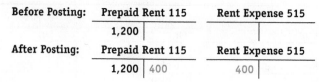

Adjustment (C)

Before Posting:

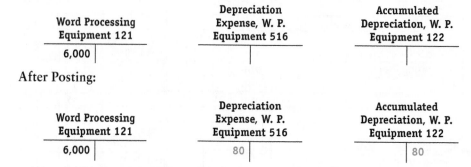

After Posting:

Word Processing Equipment 121	Depreciation Expense, W. P. Equipment 516	Accumulated Depreciation, W. P. Equipment 122
6,000	80	80

   The first adjustment in (C) shows the same balances for Depreciation Expense and Accumulated Depreciation. However, in subsequent adjustments the Accumulated Depreciation balance will keep getting larger, but the debit to Depreciation Expense and the credit to Accumulated Depreciation will stay the same. We will see why in a moment.

Adjustment (D)

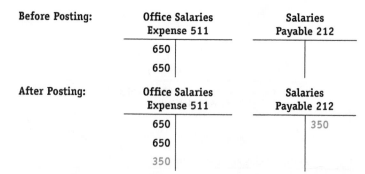

LEARNING UNIT 5-1 REVIEW

AT THIS POINT you should be able to do the following:

- Define and state the purpose of adjusting entries.
- Journalize adjusting entries from the worksheet.
- Post journalized adjusting entries to the ledger.
- Compare specific ledger accounts before and after posting of the journalized adjusting entries.

Instant Replay ⊙ Self-Review Quiz 5-1

Turn to the worksheet for P. Logan Company (Figure 4.14, p. 134 in Chapter 4) and (1) journalize and post the adjusting entries and (2) compare the adjusted ledger accounts before and after the adjustments are posted. T accounts are provided in your study guide with beginning balances.

Solution to Instant Replay: Self-Review Quiz 5-1

Date		Account Titles and Description	PR	Dr.	Cr.
		Adjusting Entries			
Dec.	31	Depreciation Expense, Store Equip.	511	1 00	
		Accumulated Depreciation, Store Equip.	122		1 00
	31	Insurance Expense	516	2 00	
		Prepaid Insurance	116		2 00
	31	Supplies Expense	514	4 00	
		Store Supplies	114		4 00
	31	Salaries Expense	512	3 00	
		Salaries Payable	212		3 00

Page 2

FIGURE 5.3
Journalized Adjusting Entries

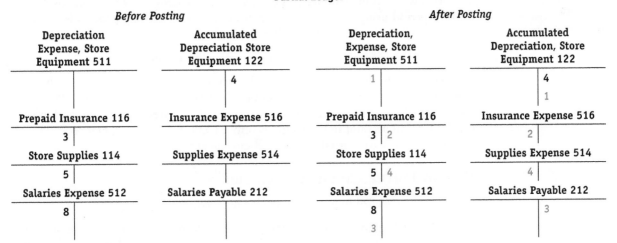

Partial Ledger

PLAY BY PLAY: **EXTRA HELP ON SELF-REVIEW QUIZ 5-1**

Let's review first: Once the financial statements are prepared from the worksheet our ledger is still not up-to-date. Information about the adjustments on the worksheet have not been journalized or posted to the ledger.

How to update the ledger with adjustments on the worksheet: Using the worksheet of Logan Company, go to the adjustments section and journalize the four adjusting entries. Once the adjustments are journalized they must be posted to the ledger. When the postings are complete, the titles for depreciation expense, accumulated depreciation, insurance expense, prepaid insurance, supplies expense, store supplies, salaries expense, and salaries payable will have the latest, up-to-date balances.

Summary: The ending balances in the ledger after posting adjustments will be the same amounts that were found on the adjusted trial balance.

⬤ LO2   **LEARNING UNIT 5-2 JOURNALIZING AND POSTING CLOSING ENTRIES:**
Step 8 of the Accounting Cycle

To make recording of the next period's transactions easier, a mechanical step, called *closing*, is taken by Clark's accountant. Closing is intended to end—or close off—the revenue, expense, and withdrawal accounts at the end of the accounting period. The information needed to complete closing entries will be found in the income statement and balance sheet sections of the worksheet.

To make it easier to understand this process, we will first look at the difference between temporary (nominal) accounts and permanent (real) accounts.

Here is the expanded accounting equation we used in an earlier chapter:

$$\text{Assets} = \text{Liabilities} + \text{Capital} - \text{Withdrawals} + \text{Revenues} - \text{Expenses}$$

Three of the items in that equation—Assets, Liabilities, and Capital—are known as real or permanent accounts because their balances are carried over from one accounting period to another. The other three items—Withdrawals, Revenues, Expenses, and Income Summary—are called nominal or temporary accounts because their balances are not carried over from one accounting period to another. Instead, their "balances" are reset at zero at the beginning of each accounting period by closing their balances at the end of the prior period. This process allows us to accumulate new data about revenue, expenses, and withdrawals in the new accounting period. The process of closing summarizes the effects of the temporary accounts on Capital for that period using closing journal entries. When the closing process is complete, the accounting equation will be reduced to

$$\text{Assets} = \text{Liabilities} + \text{Ending Capital}$$

If you look back to Figure 4.16 in Chapter 4, you will see that we already calculated the new capital on the balance sheet to be $14,275 for Clark's Word Processing Services. Before the mechanical closing procedures are journalized and posted, Clark's Capital account in the ledger is only $10,000 (Chapter 3, Figure 3.19). Let's look now at how to journalize and post closing entries.

How to Journalize Closing Entries

Four steps are needed in journalizing closing entries:

> **STEP 1:** Clear to zero the revenue balance and transfer it to Income Summary. Income Summary is a temporary account in the ledger needed for closing. At the end of the closing process, Income Summary will no longer hold a balance.

$$\text{Revenue} \rightarrow \text{Income Summary}$$

> **STEP 2:** Clear to zero the individual expense balances and transfer them to Income Summary.

$$\text{Expenses} \rightarrow \text{Income Summary}$$

> **STEP 3:** Clear to zero the balance in Income Summary and transfer it to Capital.

$$\text{Income Summary} \rightarrow \text{Capital}$$

> **STEP 4:** Clear to zero the balance in Withdrawals and transfer it to Capital.

$$\text{Withdrawals} \rightarrow \text{Capital}$$

Permanent (real) accounts
Accounts whose balances are carried over to the next accounting period. Examples: Assets, Liabilities, Capital.

Temporary (nominal) accounts Accounts whose balances at the end of an accounting period are not carried over to the next accounting period.

Closing journal entries
Journal entries that are prepared to (a) reset all temporary accounts to a zero balance and (b) update Capital to a new balance.

Income Summary A temporary account in the ledger that summarizes revenue and expenses and transfers the balance (net income or net loss) to Capital. This account does not have a normal balance, i.e. it could have a debit or a credit balance.

COACHING TIP

After all closing entries are journalized and posted to the ledger, all temporary accounts have a zero balance in the ledger. Closing is a step-by-step process.

Figure 5.4 is a visual representation of these four steps. Keep in mind that this information must first be journalized and then posted to the appropriate ledger accounts. The worksheet presented in Figure 5.5 contains all the figures we will need for the closing process.

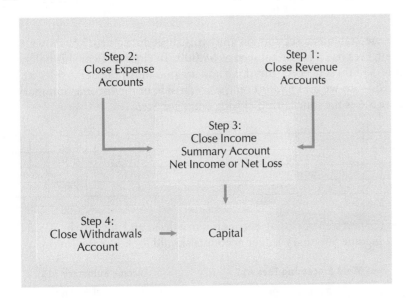

FIGURE 5.4
Four Steps in Journalizing Closing Entries (All numbers can be found on the worksheet in Figure 5.5.)

COACHING TIP

Don't forget two goals of closing:

1. Clear all temporary accounts in ledger.

2. Update Capital to a new balance that reflects a summary of all the temporary accounts.

FIGURE 5.5
Closing Figures on the Worksheet

Account Titles	Income Statement		Balance Sheet	
	Dr.	Cr.	Dr.	Cr.
Cash			6 1 5 5 00	
Accounts Receivable			5 0 0 0 00	
Office Supplies			1 0 0 00	
Prepaid Rent			8 0 0 00	
Word Processing Equipment			6 0 0 0 00	
Accounts Payable				3 3 5 0 00
B. Clark, Capital		For Step 1		10 0 0 0 00
B. Clark, Withdrawals	For Step 2		6 2 5 00	
Word Processing Fees		8 0 0 0 00		
Office Salaries Expense	1 6 5 0 00		For Step 4	
Advertising Expense	2 5 0 00			
Telephone Expense	2 2 0 00			
Office Supplies Expense	5 0 0 00			
Rent Expense	4 0 0 00			
Depreciation Exp., W. P. Equip.	8 0 00			
Acc. Depreciation, W. P. Equip.		For Step 3		8 0 00
Salaries Payable				3 5 0 00
	3 1 0 0 00	8 0 0 0 00	18 6 8 0 00	13 7 8 0 00
Net Income	4 9 0 0 00			4 9 0 0 00
	8 0 0 0 00	8 0 0 0 00	18 6 8 0 00	18 6 8 0 00

COACHING TIP

All numbers used in the closing process can be found on the worksheet.

Step 1: Clear Revenue Balance and Transfer to Income Summary Here is what is in the ledger before closing entries are journalized and posted:

Word Processing Fees 411	Income Summary 313
8,000	

The income statement section on the worksheet in Figure 5.5 shows that Word Processing Fees has a credit balance of $8,000. To close or clear this balance to zero, a debit of $8,000 is needed. But if we add an amount to the debit side, we must also add a credit—so we add $8,000 on the credit side of the Income Summary.

Figure 5.6 is the journalized closing entry for Step 1:

FIGURE 5.6
Closing Revenue to Income Summary

	May	31	Word Processing Fees	411	8 0 0 0 00	
			Income Summary	313		8 0 0 0 00

After the first step of closing entries is journalized and posted, the Word Processing Fees and Income Summary ledger accounts should look like the following:

Word Processing Fees 411		Income Summary 313
8,000	8,000	8,000
Closing	Revenue	Revenue

Note that the revenue balance is cleared to zero and transferred to Income Summary, a temporary account also located in the ledger.

Step 2: Clear Individual Expense Balances and Transfer the Total to Income Summary The ledger for each expense account is shown here before closing entries are journalized and posted. Each expense is listed on the worksheet in the debit column of the income statement section in Figure 5.5.

Office Salaries Expense 511	Advertising Expense 512
650	250
650	
350	

Telephone Expense 513	Office Supplies Expense 514
220	500

Rent Expense 515	Depreciation Expense, W. P. Equipment 516
400	80

The income statement section of the worksheet lists all the expenses as debits. If we want to reduce each expense to zero, each one must be credited.

Figure 5.7 is the journalized closing entry for Step 2:

FIGURE 5.7
Closing Each Expense Account Balance to Income Summary

		31	Income Summary	313	3 1 0 0 00	
			Office Salaries Expense	511		1 6 5 0 00
			Advertising Expense	512		2 5 0 00
			Telephone Expense	513		2 2 0 00
			Office Supplies Expense	514		5 0 0 00
			Rent Expense	515		4 0 0 00
			Depreciation Expense, W. P. Equip.	516		8 0 00

COACHING TIP

Remember, the worksheet is a tool. The accountant realizes that the information about the total of the expenses will be transferred to the Income Summary account.

COACHING TIP

The $3,100 is the total of all expense account balances.

Individual expenses and Income Summary accounts should look like the following after closing entries are journalized and posted:

Office Salaries Expense 511		
650	Closing	1,650
650		
350		

Advertising Expense 512		
250	Closing	250

Telephone Expense 513		
220	Closing	220

Office Supplies Expense 514		
500	Closing	500

Rent Expense 515		
400	Closing	400

Depreciation Expense, W. P. Equipment 516		
80	Closing	80

Income Summary 313	
Expenses	Revenue
Step 2 3,100	8,000 Step 1

Step 3: Clear Balance in Income Summary (Net Income) and Transfer It to Capital

The Income Summary and B. Clark, Capital accounts look this way before Step 3:

Income Summary 313		B. Clark, Capital 311	
3,100	8,000		10,000
	4,900		

Note that the balance of Income Summary (Revenues minus Expenses, or $8,000 Cr − $3,100 Dr = $4,900 Cr. We must clear that amount from the Income Summary account and transfer to the B. Clark, Capital account.

In order to transfer the Credit Balance of $4,900 from Income Summary to Capital, it will be necessary to debit Income Summary for $4,900 and credit or increase Capital of B. Clark for $4,900.

Figure 5.8 is the journalized closing entry for Step 3:

	31	Income Summary	313	4 9 0 0 00	
		B. Clark, Capital	311		4 9 0 0 00

FIGURE 5.8
Closing Net Income to B. Clark, Capital

The Income Summary and B. Clark, Capital accounts will look like the following in the ledger after the closing entries of Step 3 are journalized and posted:

	Income Summary 313		B. Clark, Capital 311	
Total of Expenses →	3,100	8,000 ← Revenue	10,000	
Debit to close account →	4,900	4,900 ← Net Income		4,900 ← Net Income

COACHING TIP

At the end of these three steps, the Income Summary has a zero balance. If we had a net loss, the end result would be to decrease Capital. The entry would be debit Capital and credit Income Summary for the loss.

Step 4: Clear the Withdrawals Balance and Transfer It to Capital

Next, we must close the Withdrawals account. The B. Clark, Withdrawals and B. Clark, Capital accounts currently look like this:

B. Clark, Withdrawals 312		B. Clark, Capital 311	
625			10,000
			4,900

To bring the Withdrawals account to a zero balance and summarize its effect on Capital, we must credit Withdrawals and debit Capital.

Remember, withdrawals are a nonbusiness expense and thus are not transferred to Income Summary. The closing entry is journalized as shown in Figure 5.9.

FIGURE 5.9
Closing Withdrawal to
B. Clark, Capital

	31	B. Clark, Capital	311	6 2 5 00		
		B. Clark, Withdrawals	312			6 2 5 00

At this point the B. Clark, Withdrawals and B. Clark, Capital accounts would look this way in the ledger.

COACHING TIP

Note that the $10,000 is a beginning balance because no additional investments were made during the period.

B. Clark, Withdrawals 312

625	Closing 625

B. Clark, Capital 311

→ 625	10,000 ↖
Withdrawals	Beg. Balance
	4,900 ↖
	Net Income

Now let's look at a summary of the closing entries in Figure 5.10.

FIGURE 5.10
Four Closing Entries

		SUMMARY OF CLOSING ENTRIES				
Date		Account Titles and Description	PR	Dr.	Cr.	
		Closing Entries				
201X						
May	31	Word Processing Fees	411	8 0 0 0 00		
		Income Summary	313		8 0 0 0 00	← Step 1
	31	Income Summary	313	3 1 0 0 00		
		Office Salaries Expense	511		1 6 5 0 00	
		Advertising Expense	512		2 5 0 00	
		Telephone Expense	513		2 2 0 00	← Step 2
		Office Supplies Expense	514		5 0 0 00	
		Rent Expense	515		4 0 0 00	
		Depreciation Expense, W. P. Equip.	516		8 0 00	
	31	Income Summary	313	4 9 0 0 00		
		B. Clark, Capital	311		4 9 0 0 00	← Step 3
	31	B. Clark, Capital	311	6 2 5 00		
		B. Clark, Withdrawals	312		6 2 5 00	← Step 4

The following figure shows the complete ledger for Clark's Word Processing Services (see Figure 5.11). Note how "adjusting" or "closing" is written in the explanation column of individual ledgers, as, for example, in the one for Office Supplies. If the goals of closing have been achieved, only permanent accounts will have balances carried to the next accounting period. All temporary accounts should have zero balances.

FIGURE 5.11
Complete Ledger

CLARK'S WORD PROCESSING SERVICES
GENERAL LEDGER

Cash   Account No. 111

Date		Explanation	Post. Ref.	Debit	Credit	Balance Debit	Balance Credit
201X May	1		GJ1	10 00 0 00		10 00 0 00	
	1		GJ1		1 00 0 00	9 00 0 00	
	1		GJ1		1 20 0 00	7 80 0 00	
	7		GJ1	3 00 0 00		10 80 0 00	
	15		GJ1		65 0 00	10 15 0 00	
	20		GJ1		62 5 00	9 52 5 00	
	27		GJ2		65 0 00	8 87 5 00	
	28		GJ2		2 50 0 00	6 37 5 00	
	29		GJ2		2 20 0 00	6 15 5 00	

Accounts Receivable   Account No. 112

Date		Explanation	Post. Ref.	Debit	Credit	Balance Debit	Balance Credit
201X May	22		GJ1	5 00 0 00		5 00 0 00	

Office Supplies   Account No. 114

Date		Explanation	Post. Ref.	Debit	Credit	Balance Debit	Balance Credit
201X May	3		GJ1	60 0 00		60 0 00	
	31	Adjusting	GJ2		50 0 00	10 0 00	

(Continued on next page)

Figure 5.11 (continued)

Prepaid Rent — Account No. 115

Date		Explanation	Post. Ref.	Debit	Credit	Balance Debit	Balance Credit
201X May	1		GJ1	1 20 0 00		1 20 0 00	
	31	Adjusting	GJ2		40 0 00	80 0 00	

Word Processing Equipment — Account No. 121

Date		Explanation	Post. Ref.	Debit	Credit	Balance Debit	Balance Credit
201X May	1		GJ1	6 00 0 00		6 00 0 00	

Accumulated Depreciation, Word Processing Equipment — Account No. 122

Date		Explanation	Post. Ref.	Debit	Credit	Balance Debit	Balance Credit
201X May	31	Adjusting	GJ2		80 00		80 00

Accounts Payable — Account No. 211

Date		Explanation	Post. Ref.	Debit	Credit	Balance Debit	Balance Credit
201X May	1		GJ1		5 00 0 00		5 00 0 00
	3		GJ1		60 0 00		5 60 0 00
	18		GJ1		25 0 00		5 85 0 00
	28		GJ2	2 50 0 00			3 35 0 00

Salaries Payable — Account No. 212

Date		Explanation	Post. Ref.	Debit	Credit	Balance Debit	Balance Credit
201X May	31	Adjusting	GJ2		35 0 00		35 0 00

Note how this amount is same ending balance as Figure 4.16 (p. 137).

Brenda Clark, Capital — Account No. 311

Date		Explanation	Post. Ref.	Debit	Credit	Balance Debit	Balance Credit
201X May	1		GJ1		10 00 0 00		10 00 0 00
	31	Closing (Net Income)	GJ2		4 90 0 00		14 90 0 00
	31	Closing (Withdrawals)	GJ2	6 25 00			14 27 5 00

Figure 5.11 *(continued)*

Brenda Clark, Withdrawals Account No. 312

Date		Explanation	Post. Ref.	Debit	Credit	Balance Debit	Balance Credit
201X May	20		GJ1	6 2 5 00		6 2 5 00	
	31	Closing	GJ2		6 2 5 00	—	—

Income Summary Account No. 313

Date		Explanation	Post. Ref.	Debit	Credit	Balance Debit	Balance Credit
201X May	31	Closing (Revenue)	GJ2		8 0 0 0 00		8 0 0 0 00
	31	Closing (Expenses)	GJ2	3 1 0 0 00			4 9 0 0 00
	31	Closing (Net Income)	GJ2	4 9 0 0 00		—	—

Word Processing Fees Account No. 411

Date		Explanation	Post. Ref.	Debit	Credit	Balance Debit	Balance Credit
201X May	7		GJ1		3 0 0 0 00		3 0 0 0 00
	22		GJ1		5 0 0 0 00		8 0 0 0 00
	31	Closing	GJ2	8 0 0 0 00		—	—

Office Salaries Expense Account No. 511

Date		Explanation	Post. Ref.	Debit	Credit	Balance Debit	Balance Credit
201X May	13		GJ1	6 5 0 00		6 5 0 00	
	27		GJ2	6 5 0 00		1 3 0 0 00	
	31	Adjusting	GJ2	3 5 0 00		1 6 5 0 00	
	31	Closing	GJ2		1 6 5 0 00	—	—

Advertising Expense Account No. 512

Date		Explanation	Post. Ref.	Debit	Credit	Balance Debit	Balance Credit
201X May	18		GJ1	2 5 0 00		2 5 0 00	
	31	Closing	GJ2		2 5 0 00	—	—

Figure 5.11 *(continued)*

Telephone Expense							Account No. 513	
		Post.				Balance		
Date	Explanation	Ref.	Debit	Credit	Debit		Credit	
201X May 29		GJ2	2 2 0 00		2 2 0 00			
31	Closing	GJ2		2 2 0 00	—		—	

Office Supplies Expense							Account No. 514	
		Post.				Balance		
Date	Explanation	Ref.	Debit	Credit	Debit		Credit	
201X May 31	Adjusting	GJ2	5 0 0 00		5 0 0 00			
31	Closing	GJ2		5 0 0 00	—		—	

Note: Accounts 312 to 516 are temporary and are closed to zero.

Rent Expense							Account No. 515	
		Post.				Balance		
Date	Explanation	Ref.	Debit	Credit	Debit		Credit	
201X May 31	Adjusting	GJ2	4 0 0 00		4 0 0 00			
31	Closing	GJ2		4 0 0 00	—		—	

Depreciation Expense, Word Processing Equipment							Account No. 516	
		Post.				Balance		
Date	Explanation	Ref.	Debit	Credit	Debit		Credit	
201X May 31	Adjusting	GJ2	8 0 00		8 0 00			
31	Closing	GJ2		8 0 00	—		—	

LEARNING UNIT 5-2 REVIEW

AT THIS POINT you should be able to do the following:

- Define the goals of the closing process.
- Differentiate between temporary (nominal) and permanent (real) accounts.
- List the four mechanical steps of closing.
- Explain the role of the Income Summary account.
- Explain the role of the worksheet in the closing process.

Instant Replay ⟳ Self-Review Quiz 5-2

Go to the worksheet for P. Logan in Figure 4.14 (p. 134 in Chapter 4). Then (1) journalize and post the closing entries and (2) calculate the new balance for P. Logan, Capital.

Solution to Instant Replay: Self-Review Quiz 5-2

		Closing Entries					
Dec.	31	Revenue from Clients	410	25 00			
		Income Summary	312			25 00	
	31	Income Summary	312	20 00			
		Rent Expense	518			2 00	
		Salaries Expense	512			11 00	
		Depreciation Expense, Store Equip.	510			1 00	
		Insurance Expense	516			2 00	
		Supplies Expense	514			4 00	
	31	Income Summary	312	5 00			
		P. Logan, Capital	310			5 00	
	31	P. Logan, Capital	310	3 00			
		P. Logan, Withdrawals	311			3 00	

FIGURE 5.12
Closing Entries for Logan

Partial Ledger

P. Logan, Capital 310
3 | 14
| 5
| 16

Revenue from Clients 410
25 | 25

Supplies Expense 514
4 | 4

P. Logan, Withdrawals 311
3 | 3

Dep. Exp., Store Equip. 510
1 | 1

Insurance Expense 516
2 | 2

Income Summary 312
20 | 25
5 | 5

Salaries Expense 512
11 | 11

Rent Expense 518
2 | 2

P. Logan, (Beginning) Capital		$14
Net Income	$5	
Less Withdrawals	3	
Increase in Capital		2
P. Logan, Capital (ending)		$16

PLAY BY PLAY: EXTRA HELP ON SELF-REVIEW QUIZ 5-2

Let's review first: Why are closing entries necessary? In the ledger we need to get the new balance in the Capital account. When financial statements were prepared, the ledger for Capital had only the old balance. Also, to get ready for the next accounting period we must close all temporary accounts to zero so they will be ready to collect new data regarding revenues, expenses, and withdrawals. Without the closing process each year, financial statements would run into the next period and financial analysis would be difficult. Keep in mind that the Income Summary account that will be used in the closing process is a temporary account (like a storage area for revenues and expenses).

Why use four steps to closing?

Because you need to do the following:

1. Clear all temporary accounts to zero.
2. Update the Capital account in the ledger to its new balance.

Steps to closing:

1. Close revenue account(s) to Income Summary.
2. Close each INDIVIDUAL expense to Income Summary.
3. Remove the balance in Income Summary (net income or net loss) and transfer it to the Capital account.
4. Close any withdrawals directly to Capital.

All the closing entries can be journalized directly from the last four columns of the worksheet. Each individual expense along with the total of expenses is found on the worksheet. Once these four closing entries are journalized and posted, all temporary accounts have a zero balance and P. Logan, Capital now has an ending balance of $16. This is same amount of ending capital that was used to make the formal balance sheet.

Summary: If you look at the T account in the solution you will see four numbers in Income Summary. Can you explain them?

20...this represents the total of all the expenses.

25...this represents the total revenue of all the revenues.

5 on the credit side...this is net income (25–20).

5 on the debit side...this comes from the third closing entry, which transfers the balance in Income Summary to Capital.

COACHING TIP

Sweep or clear all revenue and expenses into a dustpan (Income Summary) and then place the balance into a barrel (like Capital).

● L03   LEARNING UNIT 5-3 THE POST-CLOSING TRIAL BALANCE: Step 9 of the Accounting Cycle and the Cycle Reviewed

Preparing a Post-Closing Trial Balance

Post-closing trial balance The final step in the accounting cycle that lists only permanent accounts in the ledger and their balances after adjusting and closing entries have been posted.

The last step in the accounting cycle is the preparation of a post-closing trial balance, which lists only permanent accounts in the ledger and their balances after adjusting and closing entries have been posted. This post-closing trial balance aids in checking whether the ledger is in balance. This checking is important because so many new postings go to the ledger from the adjusting and closing process.

The procedure for taking a post-closing trial balance is the same as for a trial balance, except that, because closing entries have closed all temporary accounts, the post-closing trial balances will contain only permanent accounts (balance sheet). We will walk through this procedure in the Learning Unit 5-3 quiz coming up after we review the accounting cycle.

The Accounting Cycle Reviewed

Table 5.1 lists the steps we completed in the manual accounting cycle for Clark's Word Processing Services for the month of May.

TABLE 5.1 Steps of the Manual Accounting Cycle

Steps	Explanation
1. Collect source documents from business transactions as they occur.	Cash register tape, sales tickets, bills, checks, payroll cards
2. Analyze and record business transactions in a journal.	Called journalizing
3. Post or transfer information from journal to ledger.	Copying the debits and credits of the journal entries into the ledger accounts
4. Prepare a trial balance.	Summarizing each individual ledger account and listing those accounts to test for mathematical accuracy in recording transactions
5. Prepare a worksheet.	A multicolumn form that summarizes accounting information to complete the accounting cycle
6. Prepare financial statements.	Income statement, statement of owner's equity, and balance sheet
7. Journalize and post adjusting entries.	Using figures in the adjustment columns of worksheet
8. Journalize and post closing entries.	Using figures in the income statement and balance sheet sections of worksheet
9. Prepare a post-closing trial balance.	Proving the mathematical accuracy of the adjusting and closing process of the accounting cycle

COACHING TIP

Remember: No worksheet is needed when using accounting software.

Insight Most companies journalize and post adjusting and closing entries only at the end of their fiscal year. A company that prepares interim statements may complete only the first six steps of the cycle. Worksheets allow the preparation of interim reports without the formal adjusting and closing of the books. In this case, footnotes on the interim report will indicate the extent to which adjusting and closing were completed.

LEARNING UNIT 5-3 REVIEW

AT THIS POINT you should be able to do the following:

- Prepare a post-closing trial balance.
- Explain the relationship of interim statements to the accounting cycle.

Instant Replay Self-Review Quiz 5-3

From the ledger in Figure 5.11 (p. 171), prepare a post-closing trial balance.

Solution to Instant Replay: Self-Review Quiz 5-3

FIGURE 5.13
Post-Closing Trial Balance for Clark's
Word Processing Services

	Dr.	Cr.
CLARK'S WORD PROCESSING SERVICES **POST-CLOSING TRIAL BALANCE** **MAY 31, 201X**		
Cash	6 1 5 5 00	
Accounts Receivable	5 0 0 0 00	
Office Supplies	1 0 0 00	
Prepaid Rent	8 0 0 00	
Word Processing Equipment	6 0 0 0 00	
Accumulated Depreciation, Word Processing Equip.		8 0 00
Accounts Payable		3 3 5 0 00
Salaries Payable		3 5 0 00
Brenda Clark, Capital		14 2 7 5 00
Totals	18 0 5 5 00	18 0 5 5 00

COACHING TIP

Each day when the park closes,
the employees clean and restock
it to get ready for the next "cycle"
of customers.

PLAY BY PLAY: EXTRA HELP ON SELF-REVIEW QUIZ 5-3

Let's review first: The post-closing trial balance contains only permanent accounts because all temporary accounts have been closed. All temporary accounts are summarized in the Capital account. Remember that Income Summary is a temporary account.

Post-Closing Trial Balance: Once all the closing entries have been journalized and posted we can then prepare a post-closing trial balance. Since only permanent accounts are left after closing, the structure of the post-closing trial balance should look as follows:

Assets .... Dr.

Contra-Assets .... Cr.

Liabilities .... Cr.

Ending Capital .... Cr.

Summary: To begin the next accounting cycle, only permanent accounts with balances are brought forward. In the new cycle transactions will be journalized and posted. Adjustments will be made and new financial statements will be prepared. By the end of the cycle all temporary accounts will be closed to get a new ending figure for capital in the ledger. The end result will be to prepare a new post-closing trial balance.

DEMONSTRATION PROBLEM

MyAccountingLab

◯◯◯ L01, 2, 3

Requirements:

1. Journalize transactions and post to ledger.
2. Prepare a worksheet.
3. Prepare financial statements.
4. Journalize adjusting and closing entries and prepare a post-closing trial balance.

Assets	**Owner's Equity**
111 Cash	311 Rolo Kern, Capital
112 Accounts Receivable	312 Rolo Kern, Withdrawals
114 Prepaid Rent	313 Income Summary
115 Office Supplies	**Revenue**
121 Office Equipment	411 Fees Earned
122 Accumulated Depreciation, Office Equipment	**Expenses**
Liabilities	511 Salaries Expense
211 Accounts Payable	512 Advertising Expense
212 Salaries Payable	513 Rent Expense
	514 Office Supplies Expense
	515 Depreciation Expense, Office Equipment

COACHING TIP

Note: Accounts 312 to 515 are temporary accounts.

We will use unusually small numbers to simplify calculation and emphasize the theory.

201X

Jan.	1	Rolo Kern invested $1,200 cash and $100 of office equipment to open Rolo Co.
	1	Paid rent for three months in advance, $300.
	4	Purchased office equipment on account, $50.
	6	Bought office supplies for cash, $40.
	8	Collected $400 for services rendered.
	12	Rolo paid his home electric bill from the company checkbook, $20.
	14	Provided $100 worth of services to clients who will not pay until next month.
	16	Paid salaries, $60.
	18	Advertising bill received for $70 but will not be paid until next month.

Adjustment Data on January 31

a. Supplies on hand, $6.
b. Rent expired, $100.
c. Depreciation, Office Equipment, $20.
d. Salaries accrued, $50.

Demonstration Problem Solutions

Requirement 1
Journalize transactions and post to ledger

Part 1	Part 2	Part 3	Part 4	Demonstration Problem Complete

FIGURE 5.14
Journal Entries for Rolo Company

General Journal					Page 1
Date	Account Titles and Description	PR	Dr.	Cr.	
201X Jan 1	Cash	111	1 2 0 0 00		
	Office Equipment	121	1 0 0 00		
	R. Kern, Capital	311		1 3 0 0 00	
	Initial Investment				
1	Prepaid Rent	114	3 0 0 00		
	Cash	111		3 0 0 00	
	Rent Paid in Advance—3 months				
4	Office Equipment	121	5 0 00		
	Accounts Payable	211		5 0 00	
	Purchased Equipment on Account				
6	Office Supplies	115	4 0 00		
	Cash	111		4 0 00	
	Supplies purchased for cash				
8	Cash	111	4 0 0 00		
	Fees Earned	411		4 0 0 00	
	Services rendered				
12	R. Kern, Withdrawals	312	2 0 00		
	Cash	111		2 0 00	
	Personal payment of a bill				
14	Accounts Receivable	112	1 0 0 00		
	Fees Earned	411		1 0 0 00	
	Services rendered on account				
16	Salaries Expense	511	6 0 00		
	Cash	111		6 0 00	
	Paid salaries				
18	Advertising Expense	512	7 0 00		
	Accounts Payable	211		7 0 00	
	Advertising bill, but not paid				

Solution Tips to Journalizing and Posting Transactions

Jan 1	Cash	Asset	↑	Dr.	$1,200
	Office Equipment	Asset	↑	Dr.	$ 100
	R. Kern, Capital	Capital	↑	Cr.	$1,300

1	Prepaid Rent	Asset	↑	Dr.	$300	
	Cash	Asset	↓	Cr.	$300	
4	Office Equipment	Asset	↑	Dr.	$ 50	
	Accounts Payable	Liability	↑	Cr.	$ 50	
6	Office Supplies	Asset	↑	Dr.	$ 40	
	Cash	Asset	↓	Cr.	$ 40	
8	Cash	Asset	↑	Dr.	$400	
	Fees Earned	Revenue	↑	Cr.	$400	
12	R. Kern, Withdrawals	Withdrawals	↑	Dr.	$ 20	
	Cash	Asset	↓	Cr.	$ 20	
14	Accounts Receivable	Asset	↑	Dr.	$100	
	Fees Earned	Revenue	↑	Cr.	$100	
16	Salaries Expense	Expense	↑	Dr.	$ 60	
	Cash	Asset	↓	Cr.	$ 60	
18	Advertising Expense	Expense	↑	Dr.	$ 70	
	Accounts Payable	Liability	↑	Cr.	$ 70	

Note: All account titles come from the chart of accounts. When journalizing, the PR column of the general journal is blank. It is in the posting process that we update the ledger. The PR column in the ledger accounts tells us from what journal page the information came. After the title in the ledger is posted to, we fill in the PR column of the journal, telling us to what account number the information was transferred.

Requirement 2
Preparing a worksheet (Figure 5.15, p. 183)

Part 1	**Part 2**	Part 3	Part 4	Demonstration Problem Complete

Solution Tips to the Trial Balance and Completion of the Worksheet
After the posting process is complete from the journal to the ledger, we take the ending balance in each account and prepare a trial balance on the worksheet (see Figure 5.15). If a title has no balance, it is not listed on the trial balance. New titles on the worksheet will be added as needed.

Adjustments

Office Supplies Expense	Expense	↑	Dr.	$ 34	($40 – $6)
Office Supplies	Asset	↓	Cr.	$ 34	
Rent Expense	Expense	↑	Dr.	$100	
Prepaid Rent	Asset	↓	Cr.	$100	

COACHING TIP

Supplies on hand of $6 is not the adjustment. You need to calculate amount used up.

Do not touch original cost of equipment.	Depr. Exp., Office Equip.	Expense	↑	Dr.	$ 20
	Accum. Dep., Office Equip.	Contra-Asset	↑	Cr.	$ 20
	Salaries Expense	Expense	↑	Dr.	$ 50
	Salaries Payable	Liability	↑	Cr.	$ 50

Note: This information on the worksheet has *not* been updated in the ledger. (Updating happens when we journalize and post adjustments at the end of the cycle.)

Note that the last four columns of the worksheet come from numbers on the adjusted trial balance.

On the worksheet we copy the Net Income of $166 to the Balance Sheet credit column in order to make it balance, because the Capital figure there is the old one, hence the net income has not yet been included.

FIGURE 5.15
Completed Worksheet for Rolo Company

ROLO CO.
WORKSHEET
FOR MONTH ENDED JANUARY 31, 201X

Account Titles	Trial Balance Dr.	Trial Balance Cr.	Adjustments Dr.	Adjustments Cr.	Adjusted Trial Balance Dr.	Adjusted Trial Balance Cr.	Income Statement Dr.	Income Statement Cr.	Balance Sheet Dr.	Balance Sheet Cr.
Cash	118000				118000				118000	
Accounts Receivable	10000				10000				10000	
Prepaid Rent	30000			(B) 10000	20000				20000	
Office Supplies	4000			(A) 3400	600				600	
Office Equipment	15000				15000				15000	
Accounts Payable		12000				12000				12000
R. Kern, Capital		130000				130000				130000
R. Kern, Withdrawals	2000				2000				2000	
Fees Earned		50000				50000		50000		
Salaries Expense	6000		(D) 5000		11000		11000			
Advertising Expense	7000				7000		7000			
	192000	192000								
Office Supplies Expense			(A) 3400		3400		3400			
Rent Expense			(B) 10000		10000		10000			
Depr. Exp., Office Equip.			(C) 2000		2000		2000			
Acc. Dep., Office Equip.				(C) 2000		2000				2000
Salaries Payable				(D) 5000		5000				5000
			20400	20400	199000	199000	33400	50000	165600	149000
Net Income							16600			16600
							50000	50000	165600	165600

Supplies used up
Supplies on hand

Requirement 3
Preparing the financial statements

Part 1	Part 2	**Part 3**	Part 4	Demonstration Problem Complete

FIGURE 5.16
Income Statement for Rolo Company

ROLO CO.
INCOME STATEMENT
FOR MONTH ENDED JANUARY 31, 201X

Revenue:			
Fees Earned			$5 0 0 00
Operating Expenses			
Salaries Expense	$1 1 0 00		
Advertising Expense	7 0 00		
Office Supplies Expense	3 4 00		
Rent Expense	1 0 0 00		
Depreciation Expense, Office Equipment	2 0 00		
Total Operating Expenses		3 3 4 00	
Net Income		$1 6 6 00	

FIGURE 5.17
Statement of Owner's Equity for Rolo Company

ROLO CO.
STATEMENT OF OWNER'S EQUITY
FOR MONTH ENDED JANUARY 31, 201X

R. Kern, Capital, January 1, 201X		$1 3 0 0 00
Net Income for January	$1 6 6 00	
Less Withdrawals for January	2 0 00	
Increase in Capital		1 4 6 00
R. Kern, Capital, January 31, 201X		$1 4 4 6 00

FIGURE 5.18
Balance Sheet for Rolo Company

ROLO CO.
BALANCE SHEET
JANUARY 31, 201X

Assets			Liabilities & Owner's Equity		
Cash		$1 1 8 0 00	Liabilities		
Accounts Receivable		1 0 0 00	Accounts Payable	$1 2 0 00	
Prepaid Rent		2 0 0 00	Salaries Payable	5 0 00	
Office Supplies		6 00	Total Liabilities		$ 1 7 0 00
Office Equipment	$1 5 0 00		Owner's Equity		
Less Accum. Depr.	2 0 00	1 3 0 00	R. Kern, Capital		1 4 4 6 00
			Total Liabilities &		
Total Assets		$1 6 1 6 00	Owner's Equity		$1 6 1 6 00

Solution Tips to Preparing the Financial Statements

The statements are prepared from the worksheet. (Many of the ledger accounts are not up-to-date.) The income statement (Figure 5.16) lists revenue and expenses. The Net Income figure of $166 is used to update the statement of owner's equity. The statement of owner's equity (Figure 5.17) calculates a new figure for Capital, $1,446 (Beginning Capital + Net Income − Withdrawals). This new figure is then listed on the balance sheet (Figure 5.18) (Assets, Liabilities, and a new figure for Capital).

Requirement 4

Journalize and post adjusting and closing entries and prepare a post-closing trial balance (Figure 5.19).

Part 1	Part 2	Part 3	**Part 4**	Demonstration Problem Complete

FIGURE 5.19
Adjusting and Closing Entries Journalized and Posted

General Journal					Page 2
Date		Account Titles and Description	PR	Dr.	Cr.
		ADJUSTING ENTRIES			
Jan.	31	Office Supplies Expense	514	3 4 00	
		Office Supplies	115		3 4 00
	31	Rent Expense	513	1 0 0 00	
		Prepaid Rent	114		1 0 0 00
	31	Depr. Expense, Office Equipment	515	2 0 00	
		Accum. Depr., Office Equip.	122		2 0 00
	31	Salaries Expense	511	5 0 00	
		Salaries Payable	212		5 0 00
		CLOSING ENTRIES			
	31	Fees Earned	411	5 0 0 00	
		Income Summary	313		5 0 0 00
	31	Income Summary	313	3 3 4 00	
		Salaries Expense	511		1 1 0 00
		Advertising Expense	512		7 0 00
		Office Supplies Expense	514		3 4 00
		Rent Expense	513		1 0 0 00
		Depr. Expense, Office Equip.	515		2 0 00
	31	Income Summary	313	1 6 6 00	
		R. Kern, Capital	311		1 6 6 00
	31	R. Kern, Capital	311	2 0 00	
		R. Kern, Withdrawals	312		2 0 00

Step 1 → (Fees Earned / Income Summary)
Step 2 → (Income Summary / expenses)
Step 3 → (Income Summary / R. Kern, Capital)
Step 4 → (R. Kern, Capital / R. Kern, Withdrawals)
Closing

Solution Tips to Journalizing and Posting Adjusting and Closing Entries

Adjustments

The adjustments from the worksheet are journalized (same journal as transactions) and posted to the ledger. Now ledger accounts will be brought up-to-date. Remember, we have already prepared the financial statements from the worksheet. Our goal now is to get the ledger up-to-date.

Closing

Note that Income Summary is a temporary account located in the ledger.

Goals

1. Wipe out all temporary accounts in the ledger to zero balances.
2. Get a new figure for Capital in the ledger.

Steps in the Closing Process

STEP 1: Close revenue accounts to Income Summary.

STEP 2: Close expense accounts to Income Summary.

STEP 3: Close balance of Income Summary to Capital. (This amount really is the Net Income and equal to the figure on the worksheet.)

STEP 4: Close balance of Withdrawals to Capital.

All the journal closing entries are posted. (No new calculations are needed because all figures are on the worksheet.) The result in the ledger is that all temporary accounts have a zero balance (Figure 5.20).

FIGURE 5.20
General Ledger for Rolo Company

GENERAL LEDGER

Cash					111
				Balance	
Date	PR	Dr.	Cr.	Dr.	Cr.
1/1	GJ1	1,200		1,200	
1/1	GJ1		300	900	
1/6	GJ1		40	860	
1/8	GJ1	400		1,260	
1/12	GJ1		20	1,240	
1/16	GJ1		60	1,180	

Accounts Receivable					112
				Balance	
Date	PR	Dr.	Cr.	Dr.	Cr.
1/14	GJ1	100		100	

Accumulated Depreciation, Equipment					122
				Balance	
Date	PR	Dr.	Cr.	Dr.	Cr.
1/31 Adj.	GJ2		20		20

Accounts Payable					211
				Balance	
Date	PR	Dr.	Cr.	Dr.	Cr.
1/4	GJ1		50		50
1/18	GJ1		70		120

Salaries Payable					212
				Balance	
Date	PR	Dr.	Cr.	Dr.	Cr.
1/31 Adj.	GJ2		50		50

FIGURE 5.20 *(Continued)*

Prepaid Rent					114
Date	PR	Dr.	Cr.	Balance Dr.	Balance Cr.
1/1	GJ1	300		300	
1/31 Adj.	GJ2		100	200	

Rolo Kern, Capital					311
Date	PR	Dr.	Cr.	Balance Dr.	Balance Cr.
1/1	GJ1		1,300		1,300
1/31 Clos.	GJ2		166		1,466
1/31 Clos.	GJ2	20			1,446

Office Supplies					115
Date	PR	Dr.	Cr.	Balance Dr.	Balance Cr.
1/6	GJ1	40		40	
1/31 Adj	GJ2		34	6	

Rolo Kern, Withdrawals					312
Date	PR	Dr.	Cr.	Balance Dr.	Balance Cr.
1/12	GJ1	20		20	
1/31 Clos.	GJ2		20	—	

Office Equipment					121
Date	PR	Dr.	Cr.	Balance Dr.	Balance Cr.
1/1	GJ1	100		100	
1/4	GJ1	50		150	

Income Summary					313
Date	PR	Dr.	Cr.	Balance Dr.	Balance Cr.
1/31 Clos.	GJ2		500		500
1/31 Clos.	GJ2	334			166
1/31 Clos.	GJ2	166		—	

Fees Earned					411
Date	PR	Dr.	Cr.	Balance Dr.	Balance Cr.
1/8	GJ1		400		400
1/14	GJ1		100		500
1/31 Clos.	GJ2	500			—

Rent Expense					513
Date	PR	Dr.	Cr.	Balance Dr.	Balance Cr.
1/31 Adj.	GJ2	100		100	
1/31 Clos.	GJ2		100	—	

Salaries Expense					511
Date	PR	Dr.	Cr.	Balance Dr.	Balance Cr.
1/16	GJ1	60		60	
1/31 Adj.	GJ2	50		110	
1/31 Clos.	GJ2		110	—	

Office Supplies Expense					514
Date	PR	Dr.	Cr.	Balance Dr.	Balance Cr.
1/31 Adj.	GJ2	34		34	
1/31 Clos.	GJ2		34	—	

Advertising Expense					512
Date	PR	Dr.	Cr.	Balance Dr.	Balance Cr.
1/18	GJ1	70		70	
1/31 Clos.	GJ2		70	—	

Depreciation Expenses Office Equipment					515
Date	PR	Dr.	Cr.	Balance Dr.	Balance Cr.
1/31 Adj.	GJ2	20		20	
1/31 Clos.	GJ2		20	—	

Solution Tips for the Post-Closing Trial Balance

The post-closing trial balance is a list of the ledger *after* adjusting and closing entries have been completed. Note that the figure for Capital, $1,446, is the new figure (see Figure 5.21).

FIGURE 5.21
Post-Closing Trial Balance for Rolo Company

COACHING TIP

The post-closing trial balance contains all permanent accounts.

ROLO CO. POST-CLOSING TRIAL BALANCE JANUARY 31, 201X		
	Dr.	Cr.
Cash	1 1 8 0 00	
Accounts Receivable	1 0 0 00	
Prepaid Rent	2 0 0 00	
Office Supplies	6 00	
Office Equipment	1 5 0 00	
Accum. Dep., Office Equipment		2 0 00
Accounts Payable		1 2 0 00
Salaries Payable		5 0 00
R. Kern, Capital		1 4 4 6 00
TOTAL	1 6 3 6 00	1 6 3 6 00

Beginning Capital	$1,300
+ Net Income	166
– Withdrawals	20
= Ending Capital	$1,446

The post-closing trial balance is made up of permanent accounts only. Next accounting period we will enter new amounts in the Revenues, Expenses, and Withdrawal accounts.

Part 1	Part 2	Part 3	Part 4	**Demonstration Problem Complete**

BLUEPRINT OF CLOSING PROCESS FROM THE WORKSHEET

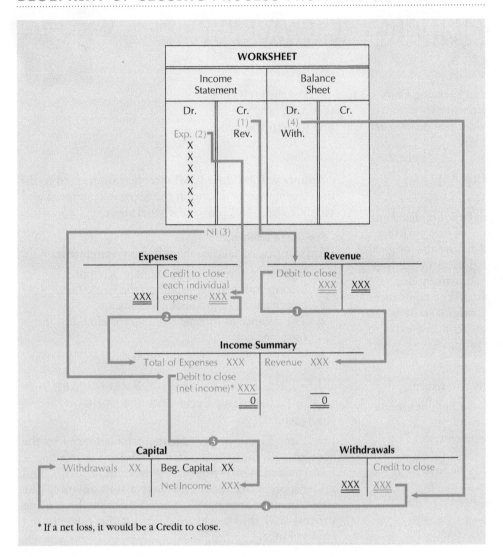

* If a net loss, it would be a Credit to close.

The Closing Steps

1. Close revenue ($) balance to Income Summary.
2. Close each *individual* expense and transfer *total* of all expenses to Income Summary.
3. Transfer balance in Income Summary (net income or net loss) to Capital.
4. Close Withdrawals to Capital.

ACCOUNTING COACH

The following Coaching Tips are from Learning Units 5-1 to 5-3. Take the Pre-Game Checkup and use the Check Your Score at the bottom of the page to see how you are doing. The Accounting Coach provides tips before each Checkup to help you avoid common accounting errors.

LU 5-1 Journalizing and Posting Adjusting Entries: Step 7 of the Accounting Cycle

Pre-Game Tips: All adjustments can be journalized and posted from the adjustments section of the worksheet. Remember that all accounts listed below the original trial balance are increasing. The adjustment for supplies is the amount used up. The adjustment for rent is the amount of rent that has expired. The adjustment for depreciation does not affect the original cost of the asset. The adjustment for salaries shows a new expense creating a liability because it is not yet paid.

Pre-Game Checkup
Answer true or false to the following statements.

1. After the adjustment is posted, the Supplies ledger account shows the amount on hand.
2. After posting, Accumulated Depreciation has a debit balance.
3. Adjustments on a worksheet do not have to be journalized and posted.
4. After the adjustment is posted, Prepaid Rent shows the amount expired.
5. Depreciation Expense is a contra-asset.

LU 5-2 Journalizing and Posting Closing Entries: Step 8 of the Accounting Cycle

Pre-Game Tips: The goal of closing is to update the ledger for the next accounting cycle. All temporary accounts need to be cleared, and a new figure for capital results. In the process, Income Summary is a temporary account that helps closing revenues and expenses to Capital. Withdrawals will be closed directly to Capital since it is not a business expense. When the closing process is complete, all temporary accounts will be closed. All information needed to do the closing can be found in the income statement and balance sheet sections of the worksheet.

Pre-Game Checkup
Answer true or false to the following statements.

1. Income Summary is a permanent account.
2. Income Summary is found on the worksheet.
3. Expenses are permanent accounts.
4. The balance in Income Summary is closed to the Cash account.
5. Income Summary has a normal debit balance.

LU 5-3 The Post-Closing Trial Balance: Step 9 of the Accounting Cycle and the Cycle Reviewed

Pre-Game Tips: The post-closing trial balance lists the accounts of the ledger after all closing entries have been posted. Only permanent accounts remain, and all temporary accounts now have a zero balance. The title "Income Summary" is used only in the closing process and thus never ends up on the post-closing trial balance.

Pre-Game Checkup
Answer true or false to the following statements.

1. Income Summary is listed on the post-closing trial balance.
2. Interim reports are always prepared each month.
3. Capital on the post-closing trial balance is the beginning balance for the next accounting cycle.
4. Accumulated Depreciation is a temporary account.
5. Supplies on the post-closing trial balance represent the amount of supplies used up.

CHECK YOUR SCORE: Answers to the Pre-Game Checkup

LU 5-1
1. True.
2. False—After posting, Accumulated Depreciation has a credit balance.
3. False—Adjustments on a worksheet have to be journalized and posted.
4. False—After the adjustment is posted, Prepaid Rent shows the amount that has not expired yet.
5. False—Depreciation Expense is an expense.

LU 5-2

1. False—Income Summary is a temporary account.
2. False—Income Summary is not found on the worksheet.
3. False—Expenses are temporary accounts.
4. False—The balance in Income Summary is closed to Capital.
5. False—Income Summary has no normal balance.

LU 5-3

1. False—Income Summary is a temporary account and thus not listed on the post-closing trial balance since it is closed.
2. False—Interim reports are only optional and there is no set requirement for when or how often they are prepared.
3. True.
4. False—Accumulated Depreciation is a permanent account.
5. False—Supplies on the post-closing trial balance represents the amount of supplies on hand.

Chapter Summary

Here are all the key concepts and equations to help you understand the concepts of this chapter and prepare you for your exam. After completing this review, go to MyAccountingLab for more practice opportunities.

MyAccountingLab

Concepts You Should Know	Key Terms	
Journalizing and posting adjusting entries. 1. After formal financial statements have been prepared, the ledger has still not been brought up-to-date. 2. Information for journalizing adjusting entries comes from the adjustments section of the worksheet.	Adjusting journal entries (p. 162)	● **L01**
Journalizing and posting closing entries. 1. Closing is a mechanical process that aids the accountant in recording transactions for the next period. 2. Assets, Liabilities, and Capital are permanent (real) accounts; their balances are carried over from one accounting period to another. Withdrawals, Revenue, and Expenses are temporary (nominal) accounts; their balances are not carried over from one accounting period to another. 3. Income Summary is a temporary account in the general ledger and does not have a normal balance. It will summarize revenue and expenses and transfer the balance to Capital. Withdrawals do not go into Income Summary. 4. All information for closing can be obtained from the worksheet or ledger. 5. When closing is complete, all temporary accounts in the ledger will have a zero balance, and all this information will be updated in the Capital account.	Closing journal entries (p. 166) Income Summary (p. 166) Permanent (real) accounts (p. 166) Temporary (nominal) accounts (p. 166)	● **L02**
Preparing a post-closing trial balance. 1. Closing entries are usually done only at year-end. Interim reports can be prepared from worksheets that are prepared monthly, quarterly, or at some other regular interval. 2. The post-closing trial balance is prepared from the ledger accounts after the adjusting and closing entries have been posted. 3. The accounts on the post-closing trial balance are all permanent titles.	Post-closing trial balance (p. 176)	● **L03**

Discussion and Critical Thinking Questions/Ethical Case

1. When a worksheet is completed, what balances are found in the general ledger?

2. Why must adjusting entries be journalized even though the formal statements have already been prepared?

3. "Closing slows down the recording of next year's transactions." Defend or reject this statement with supporting evidence.

4. What is the difference between temporary and permanent accounts?

5. What are the two major goals of the closing process?

6. List the four steps of closing.

7. What is the purpose of Income Summary and where is it located?

8. How can a worksheet aid the closing process?

9. What accounts are usually listed on a post-closing trial balance?

10. Closing entries are always prepared once a month. Agree or disagree? Why?

11. Todd Silver is the purchasing agent for Moore Co. One of his suppliers, Gem Co., offers Todd a free vacation to France if he buys at least 75% of Moore's supplies from Gem Co. Todd, who is angry because Moore Co. has not given him a raise in over a year, is considering the offer. Write your recommendation to Todd.

Concept Checks

MyAccountingLab

● **L01** *(5 MIN)*

Journalizing and Posting Adjusting Entries

1. Post the following adjusting entries that came from the adjustments section of the worksheet to the T accounts and be sure to cross-reference back to the journal. (Use Figure 5.22.)

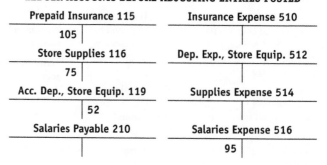

LEDGER ACCOUNTS BEFORE ADJUSTING ENTRIES POSTED

Prepaid Insurance 115	Insurance Expense 510
105	
Store Supplies 116	**Dep. Exp., Store Equip. 512**
75	
Acc. Dep., Store Equip. 119	**Supplies Expense 514**
52	
Salaries Payable 210	**Salaries Expense 516**
	95

FIGURE 5.22
Journalized Adjusting Entries

Date		Account Titles and Description	PR	Dr.	Cr.
Aug.	31	Insurance Expense		8 00	
		Prepaid Insurance			8 00
	31	Supplies Expense		2 5 00	
		Store Supplies			2 5 00
	31	Depr. Exp., Store Equipment		1 5 00	
		Accum. Depr., Store Equipment			1 5 00
	31	Salaries Expense		8 2 00	
		Salaries Payable			8 2 00

General Journal — Page 3

Steps of Closing and Journalizing Closing Entries

LO2 *(10 MIN)*

2. Explain the four steps of the closing process given the following:

Aug. 31 ending balance, before closing	
Fees Earned	$1,000
Rent Expense	150
Advertising Expense	110
J. Roulette, Capital	5,000
J. Roulette, Withdrawals	50

Journalizing Closing Entries

LO2 *(15 MIN)*

3. From the following accounts, journalize the closing entries (assume January 31).

Max Benson, Capital 310	Gas Expense 510
250	5

Max Benson, Withdr. 312	Advertising Exp. 512
105	101

Income Summary 314	Dep. Exp., Taxi 516
	6

Taxi Fees 410
115

Posting to Income Summary

LO2 *(10 MIN)*

4. Draw a T account of Income Summary and post to it all entries from Question 3 that affect it. Is Income Summary a temporary or permanent account?

Posting to Capital

LO2 *(10 MIN)*

5. Draw a T account for Max Benson, Capital, and post to it all entries from Question 3 that affect it. What is the final balance of the Capital account?

MyAccountingLab   Exercises

● **L01** (15 MIN)   **Set A**

5A-1. From the adjustments section of a worksheet presented in Figure 5.23, prepare adjusting journal entries for the end of July.

FIGURE 5.23
Adjustments on Worksheet

	Adjustments	
	Dr.	Cr.
Prepaid Rent		(A) 1 2 0 0 00
Office Supplies		(B) 3 5 0 00
Accumulated Depreciation, Equipment		(C) 2 2 5 00
Salaries Payable		(D) 4 0 0 00
Rent Expense	(A) 1 2 0 0 00	
Office Supplies Expense	(B) 3 5 0 00	
Depreciation Expense, Equipment	(C) 2 2 5 00	
Salaries Expense	(D) 4 0 0 00	
	2 1 7 5 00	2 1 7 5 00

●● **L01, 2** (10 MIN)   **5A-2.** Complete the following table by placing an X in the correct column.

	Temporary	Permanent	Will Be Closed
Ex. Accounts Receivable		X	
1. Income Summary			
2. Jen Rich, Capital			
3. Salary Expense			
4. Jen Rich, Withdrawals			
5. Fees Earned			
6. Accounts Payable			
7. Cash			

● **L02** (15 MIN)   **5A-3.** From the following T accounts, journalize the four closing entries on December 31, 201X.

J. Konnor, Capital		Rent Expense	
	18,800	7,000	

J. Konnor, Withdrawals		Wage Expense	
2,500		8,200	

Income Summary		Insurance Expense	
		2,800	

Fees Earned		Dep. Expense, Office Equipment	
	40,000	2,800	

5A-4. From the following posted T accounts, reconstruct the closing journal entries for July 31, 201X.

L02 *(20 MIN)*

M. Fitzgerald, Capital	
Withdrawals 1,700	5,000 (July 1)
	1,000 Net Income

Insurance Expense	
250	Closing 250

M. Fitzgerald, Withdrawals	
1,700	Closing 1,700

Wage Expense	
900	Closing 900

Income Summary	
Expenses 2,800	Revenue 3,800
Closing 1,000	

Rent Expense	
1,400	Closing 1,400

Salon Fees	
Closing 3,800	3,800

Depreciation Expense, Equipment	
250	Closing 250

5A-5. From the following accounts (not in order), prepare a post-closing trial balance for Winter Co. on October 31, 201X. *Note:* These balances are *before* closing.

L03 *(20 MIN)*

Accounts Receivable	$19,950	P. Winter, Capital	$45,300
Legal Supplies	9,700	P. Winter, Withdrawals	3,000
Office Equipment	54,400	Legal Fees Earned	28,000
Repair Expense	2,700	Accounts Payable	48,000
Salaries Expense	1,550	Cash	30,000

Set B

5B-1. From the adjustments section of a worksheet presented in Figure 5.24, prepare adjusting journal entries for the end of January.

L01 *(15 MIN)*

FIGURE 5.24
Adjustments Section of Worksheet

	Adjustments	Dr.	Cr.
	Prepaid Rent		(A) 1 7 00
	Office Supplies		(B) 5 00
	Accumulated Depreciation, Equipment		(C) 4 2 5
	Salaries Payable		(D) 1 0 00
	Rent Expense	(A) 1 7 00	
	Office Supplies Expense	(B) 5 00	
	Depreciation Expense, Equipment	(C) 4 2 5	
	Salaries Expense	(D) 1 0 00	
		3 6 2 5	3 6 2 5

LO1, 2 *(10 MIN)*   **5B-2.** Complete the following table by placing an X in the correct column.

		Temporary	Permanent	Will Be Closed
Ex.	Accounts Receivable		X	
1.	Income Summary			
2.	Jan Ralls, Capital			
3.	Rent Expense			
4.	Jan Ralls, Withdrawals			
5.	Fees Earned			
6.	Accounts Payable			
7.	Cash			

LO2 *(15 MIN)*   **5B-3.** From the following T accounts, journalize the four closing entries on January 31, 201X.

J. Kris, Capital		Rent Expense	
	37,000	10,000	

J. Kris, Withdrawals		Wage Expense	
5,000		8,300	

Income Summary		Insurance Expense	
		1,300	

Fees Earned		Depr. Expense, Office Equipment	
	42,000	2,500	

LO2 *(20 MIN)*   **5B-4.** From the following posted T accounts, reconstruct the closing journal entries for December 31, 201X.

M. Ferron, Capital		Insurance Expense	
Withdrawals 700	4,000 (Dec. 1)	275	Closing 275
	2,425 Net Income		

M. Ferron, Withdrawals		Wage Expense	
	700 Closing 700	200	Closing 200

Income Summary		Rent Expense	
Expenses 2,375	Revenue 4,800	1,400	Closing 1,400
Closing 2,425			

Salon Fees		Depreciation Expense, Equipment	
Closing 4,800	4,800	500	Closing 500

5B-5. From the following accounts (not in order), prepare a post-closing trial balance for Winter Co. on October 31, 201X. *Note:* These balances are *before* closing.

● **L03** *(20 MIN)*

Accounts Receivable	$ 28,500	P. Winter, Capital	$ 47,790
Legal Supplies	5,300	P. Winter, Withdrawals	6,000
Office Equipment	28,500	Legal Fees Earned	8,000
Repair Expense	1,740	Accounts Payable	47,000
Salaries Expense	1,750	Cash	31,000

Problems

MyAccountingLab

Set A

5A-1. Consider the data in Figure 5.25 for Daisy's Dance Studio:

●●**L01, 2** *(40 MIN)*

FIGURE 5.25
Trial Balance for Daisy's Dance Studio

DAISY'S DANCE STUDIO TRIAL BALANCE SEPTEMBER 30, 201X	Dr.	Cr.
Cash	60 0 0 00	
Accounts Receivable	11 0 0 0 00	
Prepaid Insurance	8 0 0 00	
Dance Supplies	1 4 0 0 00	
Dance Equipment	19 0 0 0 00	
Accumulated Depreciation, Dance Equipment		10 2 0 0 00
Accounts Payable		18 0 0 0 00
D. Dalia, Capital		45 5 0 0 00
D. Dalia, Withdrawals	4 0 0 00	
Dance Fees Earned		21 8 0 0 00
Salaries Expense	1 7 0 0 00	
Telephone Expense	7 0 0 00	
Advertising Expense	5 0 0 00	
	95 5 0 0 00	95 5 0 0 00

Check Figure:
Net Income $15,500

Adjustment Data

    a. Insurance expired, $100.
    b. Dance supplies on hand, $1,100.
    c. Depreciation on dance equipment, $2,000.
    d. Salaries earned by employees but not to be paid until October, $1,000.

Your task is to do the following:

1. Prepare a worksheet.
2. Journalize adjusting and closing entries.

(35 MIN)

Check Figure:
Post-closing
trial balance $4,094

5A-2. Enter the beginning balance in each account in your working papers from the Trial Balance columns of the worksheet (Figure 5.26, p. 199). From that worksheet, (1) journalize and post adjusting and closing entries and (2) prepare from the ledger a post-closing trial balance for the month of January.

5A-3. As the bookkeeper of Parker's Plowing, you have been asked to complete the entire accounting cycle for Parker from the following information.

(150 MIN)

201X

Jan.	1	Parker invested $14,000 cash and $9,000 worth of snow equipment into the plowing company.
	1	Paid rent for five months in advance for garage space, $3,500.
	4	Purchased office equipment on account from Liliis Corp., $12,600.
	6	Purchased snow supplies for $500 cash.
	8	Collected $15,000 from plowing local shopping centers.
	12	Parker Muroney withdrew $5,000 from the business for his own personal use.
	20	Plowed Holiday Co. parking lots, payment not to be received until March, $7,000.
	26	Paid salaries to employees, $1,400.
	28	Paid Liliis Corp. one-half amount owed for office equipment.
	29	Advertising bill received from Carter Co. but will not be paid until March, $600.
	30	Paid telephone bill, $200.

Use the following chart of accounts.

Chart of Accounts

Assets	Owner's Equity
111 Cash	311 Parker Muroney, Capital
112 Accounts Receivable	312 Parker Muroney, Withdrawals
114 Prepaid Rent	313 Income Summary
115 Snow Supplies	**Revenue**
121 Office Equipment	411 Plowing Fees
122 Accumulated Depreciation, Office Equipment	**Expenses**
123 Snow Equipment	511 Salaries Expense
124 Accumulated Depreciation Snow Equipment	512 Advertising Expense
Liabilities	513 Telephone Expense
211 Accounts Payable	514 Rent Expense
212 Salaries Payable	515 Snow Supplies Expense
	516 Depreciation Expense, Office Equipment
	517 Depreciation Expense, Snow Equipment

Problem 5A-3 continued on p. 200.

FIGURE 5.26
Worksheet for Palmer Cleaning Service

PALMER CLEANING SERVICE
WORKSHEET
FOR MONTH ENDED JANUARY 31, 201X

Account Titles	Trial Balance Dr.	Trial Balance Cr.	Adjustments Dr.	Adjustments Cr.	Adjusted Trial Balance Dr.	Adjusted Trial Balance Cr.	Income Statement Dr.	Income Statement Cr.	Balance Sheet Dr.	Balance Sheet Cr.
Cash	50000				50000				50000	
Prepaid Insurance	52000			(A) 26000	26000				26000	
Cleaning Supplies	29000			(B) 24600	4400				4400	
Auto	329000				329000				329000	
Accum. Depr., Auto		46000		(C) 75000		121000				121000
Accounts Payable		38400				38400				38400
B. Palmer, Capital		441000				441000				441000
B. Palmer, Withdrawals	101000				101000				101000	
Cleaning Fees		586000				586000		586000		
Salaries Expense	99000		(D) 16000		115000		115000			
Telephone Expense	11000				11000		11000			
Advertising Expense	22500				22500		22500			
Gas Expense	21000				21000		21000			
	714500	714500								
Insurance Expense			(A) 26000		26000		26000			
Cleaning Supplies Expense			(B) 24600		24600		24600			
Depr. Expense, Auto			(C) 75000		75000		75000			
Salaries Payable				(D) 16000		16000				16000
			141600	141600	805500	805500	295100	586000	510400	219500
Net Income							290900			290900
							586000	586000	510400	510400

Adjustment Data

a. Snow supplies on hand, $400.
b. Rent expired, $700.
c. Depreciation on office equipment, $210: ($12,600/5 yr. = $2,520/12 mo. = $210).
d. Depreciation on snow equipment, $150: ($9,000/5 yr. = $1,800/12 mo. = $150).
e. Accrued salaries, $380.

Check Figure:
Net Income $18,260

MyAccountingLab

L01, 2 *(40 MIN)*

Set B

5B-1.

MEMO

TO:	*Matt Kaminsky*
FROM:	*Abby Ellen*
RE:	*Accounting Needs*

Please prepare ASAP from the following information (Figure 5.27 on the following page) (1) a worksheet along with (2) journalized adjusting and closing entries.

Check Figure:
Net Income $18,500

Adjustment Data

a. Insurance expired, $700.

b. Dance supplies on hand, $300.

c. Depreciation on dance equipment, $400.

d. Salaries earned by employees but not due to be paid until October, $1,000.

FIGURE 5.27
Trial Balance for Daisy's
Dance Studio

DAISY'S DANCE STUDIO TRIAL BALANCE SEPTEMBER 30, 201X	Dr.	Cr.
Cash	30 0 0 0 00	
Accounts Receivable	8 0 0 0 00	
Prepaid Insurance	8 0 0 00	
Dance Supplies	1 0 0 0 00	
Dance Equipment	21 0 0 0 00	
Accumulated Depreciation, Dance Equipment		8 9 0 0 00
Accounts Payable		27 0 0 0 00
D. Dalia, Capital		4 5 0 0 00
D. Dalia, Withdrawals	9 0 0 00	
Dance Fees Earned		23 8 0 0 00
Salaries Expense	1 1 0 0 00	
Telephone Expense	5 0 0 00	
Advertising Expense	9 0 0 00	
	64 2 0 0 00	64 2 0 0 00

L01, 2 *(35 MIN)*

Check Figure:
Post-closing
Trial Balance $4,674

5B-2. Enter the beginning balance in each account in your working papers from the Trial Balance columns of the worksheet (Figure 5.28, p. 201). From the worksheet, (1) journalize and post adjusting and closing entries and (2) prepare from the ledger a post-closing trial balance at the end of September.

FIGURE 5.28
Worksheet for Palmer Cleaning Service

PALMER CLEANING SERVICE
WORKSHEET
FOR MONTH ENDED JANUARY 31, 201X

Account Titles	Trial Balance Dr.	Cr.	Adjustments Dr.	Cr.	Adjusted Trial Balance Dr.	Cr.	Income Statement Dr.	Cr.	Balance Sheet Dr.	Cr.
Cash	50000				50000				50000	
Prepaid Insurance	74000			(A) 31000	43000				43000	
Cleaning Supplies	32600			(B) 15200	17400				17400	
Auto	357000				357000				357000	
Accumulated Depreciation, Auto		44000		(C) 85000		129000				129000
Accounts Payable		61000				61000				61000
B. Palmer, Capital		193600				193600				193600
B. Palmer, Withdrawals	71000				71000				71000	
Cleaning Fees		468000				468000		468000		
Salaries Expense	105000		(D) 21000		126000		126000			
Telephone Expense	17000				17000		17000			
Advertising Expense	31000				31000		31000			
Gas Expense	29000				29000		29000			
	766600	766600								
Insurance Expense			(A) 31000		31000		31000			
Cleaning Supplies Expense			(B) 15200		15200		15200			
Depreciation Expense, Auto			(C) 85000		85000		85000			
Salaries Payable				(D) 21000		21000				21000
			152200	152200	872600	872600	334200	468000	538400	404600
Net Loss							133800			133800
							468000	468000	538400	538400

LO1, 2, 3
(150 MIN)

PT/QB

Check Figure:
Net Income $10,880

5B-3. From the following transactions as well as additional data, please complete the entire accounting cycle for Parker's Plowing (use the chart of accounts for 5A-3).

201X

Jan. 1   Parker invested $10,000 cash and $12,000 worth of snow equipment into the plowing company.

1   Paid rent for six months in advance for garage space, $6,000.

4   Purchased office equipment on account from Lumen Corp., $12,600.

6   Purchased snow supplies for $800 cash.

8   Collected $14,000 from plowing local shopping centers.

12   Parker Muroney withdrew $4,000 from the business for his own personal use.

20   Plowed Alton Co. parking lots, payment not to be received until May, $1,500.

26   Paid salaries to employees, $1,900.

28   Paid Lumen Corp. one-half amount owed for office equipment.

29   Advertising bill received from Washington Co. but will not be paid until May, $700.

30   Paid telephone bill, $130.

Adjustment Data

a. Snow supplies on hand, $700.

b. Rent expired, $1,000.

c. Depreciation on office equipment, $210: ($12,600/5 yr = $2,520/12 mo. = $210).

d. Depreciation on snow equipment, $200: ($12,000/5 yr = $2,400/12 mo. = $200).

e. Accrued salaries, $380.

Financial Report Problem

LO3 *(15 MIN)*

Reading the Kellogg's Annual Report

Go to http://investor.kelloggs.com/annuals.cfm, to access the Kellogg's 2010 Annual Report and find Note 1 in Basis of Presentation. What is the fiscal year for Kellogg's Company?

MyAccountingLab

LO1, 2, 3
(60 MIN)

ON the JOB ||||||||||||||||||||||||

SANCHEZ COMPUTER CENTER

Tony decided to end the Sanchez Computer Center's first year as of September 30, 201X. Following is an updated chart of accounts.

Assets	Revenue
1000 Cash	4000 Service Revenue
1020 Accounts Receivable	**Expenses**
1025 Prepaid Rent	5010 Advertising Expense
1030 Supplies	5020 Rent Expense
1080 Computer Shop Equip.	5030 Utilities Expense
1081 Accum. Depr., C.S. Equip.	5040 Phone Expense
1090 Office Equipment	5050 Supplies Expense
1091 Accum. Depr., Office Equip.	5060 Insurance Expense
Liabilities	5070 Postage Expense
2000 Accounts Payable	5080 Depr. Exp., C.S. Equip.

Assets	Revenue
Owner's Equity	5090 Depr. Exp., Office Equip.
3000 T. Freedman, Capital	
3010 T. Freedman, Withdrawals	
3020 Income Summary	

Assignment

1. Journalize the adjusting entries from Chapter 4.
2. Post the adjusting entries to the ledger.
3. Journalize the closing entries.
4. Post the closing entries to the ledger.
5. Prepare a post-closing trial balance.

SUBWAY CASE

Closing Time

○○ LO2, 3 *(20 MIN)*

"You wait and see," Stan told his new sandwich artist Wanda Kurtz. "Everything will fall into place soon." Wanda had a tough time serving customers quickly enough, and Stan was in the middle of giving her a pep talk when the phone rang.

"I'll let the machine pick up," Stan reassured Wanda, as he proceeded to train her in some crucial POS touch-screen maneuvers.

"Stan!" an urgent voice came over the message machine. "I think you've forgotten something!" Stan picked up the phone and said, "Lila, can I get back to you tomorrow? I'm in the middle of an important talk with Wanda." One of Stan's strong points as an employer was his ability to focus 100 percent on his employees' concerns. Yet, Lila simply would not wait.

"Stan," Lila said impatiently, "you absolutely must get me your worksheet by noon tomorrow so I can close your books. Tomorrow's the 31st of March and we close on the last day of the month!"

"*Ay caramba!*" Stan sighed. "Looks like I'm going to be up till the wee hours," he confided to Wanda when he put down the phone.

Although Subway company policy doesn't require a closing every month, closing the books is a key part of their accounting training for all new franchisees. By closing their books, business owners can clearly measure their net profit and loss for each period separate from all other periods. This practice makes activities such as budgeting and comparing performance with similar businesses (or performance over time) possible.

At 9:00 A.M. the next morning, an exhausted Stan opened up the restaurant and e-mailed his worksheet to Lila. He was feeling quite pleased with himself—that is, until he heard Lila's urgent-sounding voice coming over the message machine 10 minutes later.

"I've been over and over this," said Lila after Stan picked up, "and I can't get it to balance. I know it's hard for you to do this during working hours, but I need you to go back over the figures."

Stan opened up Peachtree and pored over his worksheets. Errors are hard to find when closing the books and, unfortunately, the process doesn't offer a set way to detect errors or any set place to start. Stan chose payroll because it is one of the largest expenses and because of the new hire.

At 11:45 he called Lila, who sounded both exasperated and relieved to hear from him. "I think I've got it! It looks like I messed up on adjusting the Salaries Expense account. I looked at the payroll register and compared the total to the Salaries Payable account. It didn't match! When I hired Wanda Kurtz on the 26th, I should have increased both the Salaries Expense and the Salaries Payable lines because she has accrued wages."

"Yes," said Lila, "Salaries Expense is a debit and Salaries Payable is a credit, and you skipped the payable. Great! With this adjusting entry in the general journal, the worksheet will balance."

Stan's sigh of relief turned into a big yawn, and they both laughed. "I guess I just find it easier to hire people and train them than to account for them," said Stan.

Discussion Questions

1. How would the adjustment be made if Wanda Kurtz received $7.00 per hour and worked 25 additional hours? Where do you place her accrued wages?
2. Stan bought three new Subway aprons and hats for Wanda Smith for $20 each but forgot to post it to the Uniforms account. How much will the closing balance be off? In what way will it be off?
3. Put yourself in Stan's shoes: What is the value of doing a monthly closing, no matter how much—or little—business you do?

Mini Practice Set

Sullivan Realty

Est Time 5 hours

Reviewing the Accounting Cycle Twice

This comprehensive review problem requires you to complete the accounting cycle for Sullivan Realty twice. This practice set allows you to review Chapters 1–5 while reinforcing the relationships between all parts of the accounting cycle. By completing two cycles, you will see how the ending June balances in the ledger are used to accumulate data in July.

First, look at the chart of accounts for Sullivan Realty.

Sullivan Realty
Chart of Accounts

Assets	Revenue
111 Cash	411 Commissions Earned
112 Accounts Receivable	**Expenses**
114 Prepaid Rent	511 Rent Expense
115 Office Supplies	512 Salaries Expense
121 Office Equipment	513 Gas Expense
122 Accumulated Depreciation, Office Equipment	514 Repairs Expense
123 Automobile	515 Telephone Expense
124 Accumulated Depreciation, Automobile	516 Advertising Expense
Liabilities	517 Office Supplies Expense
211 Accounts Payable	518 Depreciation Expense, Office Equipment
212 Salaries Payable	519 Depreciation Expense, Automobile
Owner's Equity	524 Miscellaneous Expense
311 John Sullivan, Capital	
312 John Sullivan, Withdrawals	
313 Income Summary	

On June 1, 201X, John Sullivan opened a real estate office called Sullivan Realty. The following transactions were completed for the month of June:

201X

June 1   John Sullivan invested $9,000 cash in the real estate agency along with $4,000 of office equipment.

———| **DEPOSIT TICKET** |———

SULLIVAN REALTY (213)478-3584
8200 SUNSET BOULEVARD
Los Angeles, CA 90028

DATE _____ *June 1* _____ *201X* _____

SIGN HERE IN PRESENCE OF TELLER FOR CASH RET'D FROM DEP.

BAY BANK
Box 1739 Terminal Annex
Los Angeles, CA 90052

⑊⅃2200066⅃⅃⅃⅃4OO⋯O3857⋯O⅃362⑊

CASH	CURRENCY	9,000	00
	COIN		
LIST CHECKS SINGLY			
TOTAL FROM OTHER SIDE			
TOTAL		9,000	00
LESS CASH RECEIVED			
NET DEPOSIT		9,000	00

16-66/1220

A hold for uncollected funds may be placed on funds deposited by check or similar instruments. This could delay your ability to withdraw such funds. The delay if any would not exceed the period of time permitted by law.

June 1   Rented and paid three months rent in advance to Miller Property Management, $3,000.

SULLIVAN REALTY (213) 478-3584   0001

8200 SUNSET BOULEVARD
LOS ANGELES, CA 90028   *June 1*   *201X*

PAY TO THE
ORDER OF *Miller Property Mgmt Co.* $ | 3,000 $\frac{XX}{100}$ |

~~~ *Three Thousand and* $\frac{XX}{100}$ ~~~~~ DOLLARS

BAY BANK
Box 1739 Terminal Annex
Los Angeles, CA 90052

MEMO *Rent June–Aug. 201X*   *John Sullivan*

June   1   Bought an automobile on account from Volvo West, $14,000.

	Volvo West	1 Salem St. Los Angeles, CA 90052 (213) 639-1917		**INVOICE**

INVOICE NO. 1113

DATE: June 1/1X

TERMS: Net 90

To: SULLIVAN REALTY
8200 Sunset Blvd.
Los Angeles, CA 90028

QUANTITY	DESCRIPTION		UNIT PRICE	AMOUNT
1	ONLY	1999 Z75 4-Door Automatic	$12,000.00	$14,000.00

Make all checks payable to Volvo West	SUBTOTAL	14,000.00
	FREIGHT	
	TAX	
	TOTAL DUE	$14,000.00

THANK YOU FOR YOUR BUSINESS!

June   4   Purchased office supplies from Office Supply Direct for cash, $300.

Office Supply Direct   **INVOICE**

1 Ferncroft Rd.   **DATE:**   June 4/1X
Los Angeles, CA 90052   **NUMBER:**   D198795
Phone (213) 631-0288   **TERMS:**   Cash

SOLD TO:	SHIPPED TO:
Sullivan Realty 8200 Sunset Blvd. Los Angeles, CA 90028	Sullivan Realty 8200 Sunset Blvd. Los Angeles, CA 90028

DATE	DESCRIPTION	UNIT PRICE	AMOUNT
Jun 4/1X	Office supplies PAYMENT RECEIVED - - CHK #0002 - THANK YOU		$300.00
		Subtotal	300.00
		Total	$300.00

Business Number: 115555559

THANK YOU FOR YOUR BUSINESS

PLEASE PAY THE ABOVE

SULLIVAN REALTY (213) 478-3584   0002

8200 SUNSET BOULEVARD   *June 4*   *201X*
LOS ANGELES, CA 90028

PAY TO THE
ORDER OF   *Office Supply Direct* $ *300 $\frac{XX}{100}$*

Three Hundred and $\frac{XX}{100}$ DOLLARS

BAY BANK
Box 1739 Terminal Annex
Los Angeles, CA 90052

MEMO   *Office supplies*   *John Sullivan*

June 5 Purchased additional office supplies from Office Supply Direct on account, $150.

Office Supply Direct INVOICE

1 Ferncroft Rd.
Los Angeles, CA 90052
Phone (213) 631-0288

DATE: June 5/1X
NUMBER: D198825
TERMS: net 60

SOLD TO:

Sullivan Realty
8200 Sunset Blvd.
Los Angeles, CA 90028

SHIPPED TO:

Sullivan Realty
8200 Sunset Blvd.
Los Angeles, CA 90028

DATE	DESCRIPTION	UNIT PRICE	AMOUNT
Jun 5/1X	Office supplies		$150.00
		Subtotal	150.00
		Total	$150.00

Business Number: 115555559

THANK YOU FOR YOUR BUSINESS

PLEASE PAY
THE ABOVE

June 6 Sold a house to Bill Barnes and collected a $6,000 commission.

⊢ DEPOSIT TICKET ⊣

SULLIVAN REALTY (213)478-3584
8200 SUNSET BOULEVARD
Los Angeles, CA 90028

DATE _____ June 6 _____ 201X _____

SIGN HERE IN PRESENCE OF TELLER FOR CASH RET'D FROM DEP.

BAY BANK
Box 1739 Terminal Annex
Los Angeles, CA 90052

⑈12200066⑈1⑈1400⑈03857⑈0136 2⑈

CASH	CURRENCY		
	COIN		
LIST CHECKS SINGLY 250-99		6,000	00
TOTAL FROM OTHER SIDE			
TOTAL			
LESS CASH RECEIVED			
NET DEPOSIT		6,000	00

16-66/1220

A hold for uncollected funds may be placed on funds deposited by check or similar instruments. This could delay your ability to withdraw such funds. The delay if any would not exceed the period of time permitted by law.

SULLIVAN REALTY COMMISSION REPORT				*Date:* June 6, 201X
Name: Bill Barnes				
Date:	*Sales Description*	*Sales No.*	*Commission Amount*	
Jun 6/1X	Home at 66 Sullivan St.	A1001	$6,000.00	Paid in full.
C001		*Remarks:*		

June   8   Paid gas bill to Petro Petroleum, $22.

SULLIVAN REALTY (213) 478-3584	0003
8200 SUNSET BOULEVARD LOS ANGELES, CA 90028	*June 8* *201X*
PAY TO THE ORDER OF *Petro Petroleum*	$ *22 XX/100*
Twenty-two and XX/100 ——————————— DOLLARS	
BAY BANK Box 1739 Terminal Annex Los Angeles, CA 90052	
MEMO *Gas Bill – June 6*	*John Sullivan*

June   15   Paid Betty Long, office secretary, $350.

SULLIVAN REALTY (213) 478-3584	0004
8200 SUNSET BOULEVARD LOS ANGELES, CA 90028	*June 15* *201X*
PAY TO THE ORDER OF *Betty Long*	$ *350 XX/100*
Three Hundred fifty and XX/100 ——————————— DOLLARS	
BAY BANK Box 1739 Terminal Annex Los Angeles, CA 90052	
MEMO *Salary – June 1–15*	*John Sullivan*

June   17   Sold a building lot to West Land Developers and earned a commission, $6,500; payment to be received on July 8.

SULLIVAN REALTY COMMISSION REPORT				**Date:** June 17, 201X
Name: West Land Developers				
Date:	**Sales Description**	**Sales No.**	**Commission Amount**	
Jun 17/1X	Lot at 8 Ridge Rd.	A1002	$6,500.00	
C002		**Remarks:** Payment due July 8, 201X		

June   20   John Sullivan withdrew $1,000 from the business to pay personal expenses.

SULLIVAN REALTY (213) 478-3584	0005

8200 SUNSET BOULEVARD
LOS ANGELES, CA 90028

June 20   201X

PAY TO THE
ORDER OF   John Sullivan $ 1,000 XX/100

One Thousand and XX/100 ———————————— DOLLARS

BAY BANK
Box 1739 Terminal Annex
Los Angeles, CA 90052

MEMO   Withdrawal   John Sullivan

June   21   Sold a house to Laura Harrison and collected a $3,500 commission.

— DEPOSIT TICKET —

SULLIVAN REALTY (213)478-3584
8200 SUNSET BOULEVARD
Los Angeles, CA 90028

DATE   June 21   201X

SIGN HERE IN PRESENCE OF TELLER FOR CASH RET'D FROM DEP. →

BAY BANK
Box 1739 Terminal Annex
Los Angeles, CA 90052

⑆122000661⑆1400⑈03857⑈01362⑈

CASH	CURRENCY		
	COIN		
LIST CHECKS SINGLY 270-88		3,500	00
TOTAL FROM OTHER SIDE			
TOTAL			
LESS CASH RECEIVED			
NET DEPOSIT		3,500	00

16-66/1220

A hold for uncollected funds may be placed on funds deposited by check or similar instruments. This could delay your ability to withdraw such funds. The delay if any would not exceed the period of time permitted by law.

SULLIVAN REALTY
COMMISSION REPORT   **Date:**   June 21, 201X

Name: Ms. Laura Harrison

Date:	Sales Description	Sales No.	Commission Amount	
Jun 21/1X	Home at 666 Jersey St.	A1003	$3,500.00	Paid in full.
C003		**Remarks:**		

June   22   Paid gas bill, $25, to Petro Petroleum.

SULLIVAN REALTY (213) 478-3584   0006

8200 SUNSET BOULEVARD
LOS ANGELES, CA 90028   *June 22   201X*

PAY TO THE
ORDER OF *Petro Petroleum* $ *25 XX/100*

Twenty-five and XX/100 ———————————— DOLLARS

BAY BANK
Box 1739 Terminal Annex
Los Angeles, CA 90052

MEMO *Gas Bill–June 22*   *John Sullivan*

June   24   Paid Volvo West $600 to repair automobile.

Volvo West   1 Salem St.
Los Angeles, CA 90052
(213) 639-1917

INVOICE

INVOICE NO. 1184
DATE: June 24/1X
TERMS: Cash

To: SULLIVAN REALTY   Ship To:
8200 Sunset Blvd.
Los Angeles, CA 90028   Pickup

QUANTITY	DESCRIPTION	UNIT PRICE	AMOUNT
1	ONLY Z75 Air conditioning repair		$ 600.00

Make all checks payable to Volvo West | | SUBTOTAL | 600.00 |
| | | FREIGHT | |
PAYMENT RECEIVED - Check #0007 | | TAX | |
| | | TOTAL DUE | $ 600.00 |

THANK YOU FOR YOUR BUSINESS!

SULLIVAN REALTY (213) 478-3584   0007

8200 SUNSET BOULEVARD
LOS ANGELES, CA 90028   *June 24   201X*

PAY TO THE
ORDER OF *Volvo West* $ *600 XX/100*

Six Hundred and XX/100 ———————————— DOLLARS

BAY BANK
Box 1739 Terminal Annex
Los Angeles, CA 90052

MEMO *Auto Repairs – Inv. 1184*   *John Sullivan*

June 30   Paid Betty Long, office secretary, $350.

SULLIVAN REALTY (213) 478-3584   0008

8200 SUNSET BOULEVARD
LOS ANGELES, CA 90028   _June 30_   _201X_

PAY TO THE
ORDER OF _Betty Long_ $ | 350 XX/100

Three Hundred fifty and XX/100 ———————— DOLLARS

BAY BANK
Box 1739 Terminal Annex
Los Angeles, CA 90052

MEMO _Salary – June 16–30_   _John Sullivan_

June 30   Paid CellService Inc. June telephone bill, $510.

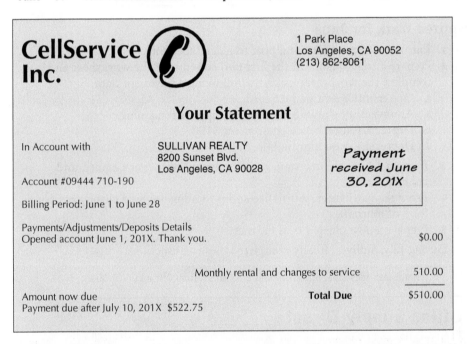

CellService Inc.

1 Park Place
Los Angeles, CA 90052
(213) 862-8061

Your Statement

In Account with   SULLIVAN REALTY
8200 Sunset Blvd.
Los Angeles, CA 90028

Account #09444 710-190

Billing Period: June 1 to June 28

Payment received June 30, 201X

Payments/Adjustments/Deposits Details
Opened account June 1, 201X. Thank you. $0.00

Monthly rental and changes to service   510.00

Amount now due   **Total Due** $510.00
Payment due after July 10, 201X $522.75

SULLIVAN REALTY (213) 478-3584   0009

8200 SUNSET BOULEVARD
LOS ANGELES, CA 90028   _June 30_   _201X_

PAY TO THE
ORDER OF _CellService Inc._ $ | 510 XX/100

Five Hundred Ten and XX/100 ———————— DOLLARS

BAY BANK
Box 1739 Terminal Annex
Los Angeles, CA 90052

MEMO _June Phone Bill_   _John Sullivan_

June   30   Received advertising bill for June, $1,200, from Salem News. The bill is to be paid on July 2.

Salem News
1 Main St., Los Angeles, CA 90052
(213) 744-1000
I N V O I C E

SOLD TO:	Sullivan Realty 8200 Sunset Blvd. Los Angeles, CA 90028	Invoice No.: Date: Due Date:	4879 June 30, 201X July 2, 201X

DATE	DESCRIPTION		AMOUNT
June 26/1X	Advertising in Salem News during June 201X		$1,200.00
		SUBTOTAL	1,200.00
Business Number 944122338		TOTAL	$1,200.00

MAKE ALL CHECKS PAYABLE TO SALEM NEWS

Required Work for June

1. Journalize transactions and post to ledger accounts.
2. Prepare a trial balance in the first two columns of the worksheet and complete the worksheet using the following adjustment data:
   a. One month's rent had expired.
   b. An inventory shows $50 of office supplies remaining.
   c. Depreciation on office equipment, $100.
   d. Depreciation on automobile, $200.
3. Prepare a June income statement, statement of owner's equity, and balance sheet.
4. From the worksheet, journalize and post adjusting and closing entries (p. 3 of journal).
5. Prepare a post-closing trial balance.

Check Figure:
June post closing
trial balance $38,893

During July, Sullivan Realty completed these transactions:

July   1   Purchased additional office supplies on account from Office Supply Direct, $700.

Office Supply Direct   INVOICE

1 Ferncroft Rd.
Los Angeles, CA 90052
Phone (213) 631-0288

DATE: Jul 1/1X
NUMBER: D1996035
TERMS: Net 60

SOLD TO:	SHIPPED TO:
Sullivan Realty 8200 Sunset Blvd. Los Angeles, CA 90028	Sullivan Realty 8200 Sunset Blvd. Los Angeles, CA 90028

DATE	DESCRIPTION	UNIT PRICE	AMOUNT
Jul 2/1X	Office supplies		$700.00
		Subtotal	700.00
		Total	$700.00

Business Number: 115555559

THANK YOU FOR YOUR BUSINESS

PLEASE PAY
THE ABOVE

July   2   Paid Salem News advertising bill for June.

SULLIVAN REALTY (213) 478-3584	0010
8200 SUNSET BOULEVARD LOS ANGELES, CA 90028	_July 2_ _201X_

PAY TO THE ORDER OF _Salem News_ $ | _1,200 $\frac{XX}{100}$_

One Thousand Two Hundred and $\frac{XX}{100}$ ———————— DOLLARS

BAY BANK
Box 1739 Terminal Annex
Los Angeles, CA 90052

MEMO _Invoice # 4879_   _John Sullivan_

⑈12200066⑈⑆1400⑈03857⑈01362⑈0010

July   3   Sold a house to Melissa King and collected a commission of $6,600.

SULLIVAN REALTY COMMISSION REPORT				**Date:** July 3, 201X
Name:	Melissa King			
Date:	**Sales Description**	**Sales No.**	**Commission Amount**	
July 3/1X	Home at 800 Rose Ave.	A1004	$6,600.00	Paid in full.
C004		**Remarks:**		

⊢ **DEPOSIT TICKET** ⊢			

SULLIVAN REALTY (213) 478-3584
8200 SUNSET BOULEVARD
Los Angeles, CA 90028

	CURRENCY		
CASH			
	COIN		
LIST CHECKS SINGLY 278-92		6,600	00
TOTAL FROM OTHER SIDE			
TOTAL			
LESS CASH RECEIVED			
NET DEPOSIT		6,600	00

16-66/1220

A hold for uncollected funds may be placed on funds deposited by check or similar instruments. This could delay your ability to withdraw such funds. The delay if any would not exceed the period of time permitted by law.

DATE _July 3_   _201X_

SIGN HERE IN PRESENCE OF TELLER FOR CASH RET'D FROM DEP.

BAY BANK
Box 1739 Terminal Annex
Los Angeles, CA 90052

⑈12200066⑈⑆1400⑈03857⑈01362⑈

July   6   Paid gas bill to Petro Petroleum, $29.

SULLIVAN REALTY (213) 478-3584	0011
8200 SUNSET BOULEVARD LOS ANGELES, CA 90028	July 6 201X

PAY TO THE ORDER OF _Petro Petroleum_ $ | 29 XX/100 |

Twenty-nine and XX/100 ——————————————— DOLLARS

BAY BANK
Box 1739 Terminal Annex
Los Angeles, CA 90052

MEMO _Gas Bill – July 6_   _John Sullivan_

July   8   Collected commission from West Land Developers for sale of building lot on June 17.

—| DEPOSIT TICKET |—

SULLIVAN REALTY (213)478-3584
8200 SUNSET BOULEVARD
Los Angeles, CA 90028

DATE   _July 8   201X_

SIGN HERE IN PRESENCE OF TELLER FOR CASH RET'D FROM DEP.

BAY BANK
Box 1739 Terminal Annex
Los Angeles, CA 90052

⑆ 1 2 2 0 0 0 6 6 ⑈ ⑆ 1 4 0 0 ⑉ 0 3 8 5 7 ⑉ 0 1 3 6 2 ⑈

	CURRENCY		
CASH	COIN		
LIST CHECKS SINGLY 228-114		6,500	00
TOTAL FROM OTHER SIDE			
TOTAL			
LESS CASH RECEIVED			
NET DEPOSIT		6,500	00

16-66/1220

A hold for uncollected funds may be placed on funds deposited by check or similar instruments. This could delay your ability to withdraw such funds. The delay if any would not exceed the period of time permitted by law.

July   12   Paid $300 to Regan Realtors Assoc. to send employees to realtors' workshop.

SULLIVAN REALTY (213) 478-3584	0012
8200 SUNSET BOULEVARD LOS ANGELES, CA 90028	July 12 201X

PAY TO THE ORDER OF _Regan Realtors Assoc._ $ | 300 XX/100 |

Three Hundred and XX/100 ——————————————— DOLLARS

BAY BANK
Box 1739 Terminal Annex
Los Angeles, CA 90052

MEMO _Workshop Registration_   _John Sullivan_

July 15 Paid Betty Long, office secretary, $350.

SULLIVAN REALTY (213) 478-3584	0013
8200 SUNSET BOULEVARD LOS ANGELES, CA 90028	July 15 201X

PAY TO THE ORDER OF Betty Long $ 350 XX/100

Three Hundred fifty and XX/100 ——————————— DOLLARS

BAY BANK
Box 1739 Terminal Annex
Los Angeles, CA 90052

MEMO Salary July 1–15   John Sullivan

July 17 Sold a house to Matt Karminsky and earned a commission of $2,400. Commission to be received on August 10.

SULLIVAN REALTY COMMISSION REPORT				Date:	July 17, 201X
Name:	Matt Karminsky				
Date:	**Sales Description**	**Sales No.**	**Commission Amount**		
July 17/1X	Home at RR2, Site 3	A1010	$2,400.00		
C005		**Remarks:** Payment due August 10, 201X			

July 18 Sold a building lot to DiBiasi Builders and collected a commission of $7,000.

——| DEPOSIT TICKET |——	
SULLIVAN REALTY (213)478-3584 8200 SUNSET BOULEVARD Los Angeles, CA 90028	

CASH	CURRENCY		
	COIN		
LIST CHECKS SINGLY 269-10		7,000	00
TOTAL FROM OTHER SIDE			
TOTAL			
LESS CASH RECEIVED			
NET DEPOSIT		7,000	00

DATE July 18 201X

SIGN HERE IN PRESENCE OF TELLER FOR CASH RET'D FROM DEP.

16-66/1220

A hold for uncollected funds may be placed on funds deposited by check or similar instruments. This could delay your ability to withdraw such funds. The delay if any would not exceed the period of time permitted by law.

BAY BANK
Box 1739 Terminal Annex
Los Angeles, CA 90052

⑆122000661⑆1400⑈03857⑈013 62⑆

SULLIVAN REALTY					
COMMISSION REPORT				**Date:**	July 18, 201X
Name:	DiBiasi Builders				
Date:	**Sales Description**	**Sales No.**	**Commission Amount**		
July 18/1X	Building lot at 5004 King St. E	A1005	$7,000.00	Paid in full.	
C006			**Remarks:**		

July   22   Sent a check to Catholic Charities for $40 to help sponsor a local road race to aid the poor. (This amount is not to be considered an advertising expense; it is a business expense and is posted to Miscellaneous Expense.)

SULLIVAN REALTY (213) 478-3584	0014
8200 SUNSET BOULEVARD	
LOS ANGELES, CA 90028	*July 22 201X*
PAY TO THE ORDER OF *Catholic Charities*	$ *40 XX/100*
Forty and XX/100 ————————————	DOLLARS
BAY BANK	
Box 1739 Terminal Annex	
Los Angeles, CA 90052	
MEMO *Aid to Poor*	*John Sullivan*

⑆122000661⑆1400⑈03857⑉0136 2⑆0014

July   24   Paid Volvo West $590 for repairs to automobile due to accident.

Volvo West	1 Salem St. Los Angeles, CA 90052 (213) 639-1917	**INVOICE**
		INVOICE NO. 2119
		DATE: July 24/1X
		TERMS: Cash
To:	SULLIVAN REALTY 8200 Sunset Blvd. Los Angeles, CA 90028	

QUANTITY	DESCRIPTION	UNIT PRICE	AMOUNT
	Accident Repairs		$ 590.00
Make all checks payable to Volvo West		SUBTOTAL	590.00
		FREIGHT	
PAYMENT RECEIVED - Check #0015		TAX	
		TOTAL DUE	$ 590.00

SULLIVAN REALTY (213) 478-3584   0015

8200 SUNSET BOULEVARD   July 24   201X
LOS ANGELES, CA 90028

PAY TO THE   *Volvo West* $ 590 XX/100
ORDER OF

Five Hundred Ninety and XX/100 ———————————— DOLLARS

BAY BANK
Box 1739 Terminal Annex
Los Angeles, CA 90052

MEMO *Auto Repairs – Inv. 2119*   *John Sullivan*

July   28   John Sullivan withdrew $1,800 from the business to pay personal expenses.

SULLIVAN REALTY (213) 478-3584   0016

8200 SUNSET BOULEVARD   July 28   201X
LOS ANGELES, CA 90028

PAY TO THE   *John Sullivan* $ 1,800 XX/100
ORDER OF

One Thousand Eight hundred and XX/100 ——————— DOLLARS

BAY BANK
Box 1739 Terminal Annex
Los Angeles, CA 90052

MEMO *Withdrawal*   *John Sullivan*

July   30   Paid Betty Long, office secretary, $350.

SULLIVAN REALTY (213) 478-3584   0017

8200 SUNSET BOULEVARD   July 30   201X
LOS ANGELES, CA 90028

PAY TO THE   *Betty Long* $ 350 XX/100
ORDER OF

Three Hundred fifty and XX/100 ——————————— DOLLARS

BAY BANK
Box 1739 Terminal Annex
Los Angeles, CA 90052

MEMO *Salary – July 16–31*   *John Sullivan*

July 30 Paid CellService Inc. telephone bill, $590.

CellService Inc.

1 Park Place
Los Angeles, CA 90052
(213) 862-8061

Your Statement

In Account with

SULLIVAN REALTY
8200 Sunset Blvd.
Los Angeles, CA 90028

Payment received July 30, 201X

Account #09444 710-190

Billing Period: July 1 to July 28

Payments/Adjustments/Deposits Details	$590.00
Payment Received July 2. Thank you.	−590.00
Monthly rental and changes to service	590.00
Amount now due	**Total Due** $590.00
Payment due after August 10, 201X $610.75	

SULLIVAN REALTY (213) 478-3584   0018

8200 SUNSET BOULEVARD
LOS ANGELES, CA 90028   *July 30   201X*

PAY TO THE
ORDER OF   *CellService Inc.* $ 590 XX/100

Five Hundred Ninety and XX/100 ——————————— DOLLARS

BAY BANK
Box 1739 Terminal Annex
Los Angeles, CA 90052

MEMO *July Phone Bill*   *John Sullivan*

July 30 Advertising bill from *Salem News* for July, $1,400. The bill is to be paid on August 2.

Salem News
1 Main St., Los Angeles, CA 90052
(213) 744-1000

I N V O I C E

SOLD TO: Sullivan Realty
8200 Sunset Blvd.
Los Angeles, CA 90028

Invoice No.: 5400
Date: July 30, 201X
Due Date: August 2, 201X

DATE	DESCRIPTION	AMOUNT
July 30/1X	Advertising in Salem News during July 201X	$1,400.00
	SUBTOTAL	1,400.00
Business Number 944122338	TOTAL	$1,400.00

MAKE ALL CHECKS PAYABLE TO SALEM NEWS

Required Work for July

1. Journalize transactions in a general journal (p. 4) and post to ledger accounts.
2. Prepare a trial balance in the first two columns of a blank, fold-out worksheet located at the end of your textbook and complete the worksheet using the following adjustment data:
   a. One month's rent had expired.
   b. An inventory shows $90 of office supplies remaining.
   c. Depreciation on office equipment, $100.
   d. Depreciation on automobile, $200.
3. Prepare a July income statement, statement of owner's equity, and balance sheet.
4. From the worksheet, journalize and post adjusting and closing entries (p. 6 of journal).
5. Prepare a post-closing trial balance.

PEACHTREE COMPUTER WORKSHOP

COMPUTERIZED ACCOUNTING APPLICATION FOR CHAPTER 5

Refresher on using Peachtree Complete Accounting

Before starting this assignment, you may want to refresh your memory by reading the following PDF documents in the multimedia library of the MyAccountingLab Web site. Remember to choose the PDF document for your version of Peachtree.

1. An Introduction to Peachtree Complete Accounting
2. Correcting Peachtree Transactions
3. How to Repeat or Restart a Peachtree Assignment
4. Backing Up and Restoring Your Work in Peachtree

You also should have completed the following workshops:

1. Workshop 1 Atlas Company from Chapter 3
2. Workshop 2 Zell Company from Chapter 4

Workshop 3:

Accounting Cycle Mini Practice Set

In this workshop you will complete the June and July accounting cycles for Sullivan Realty using Peachtree. Tasks include posting journal entries and adjusting journal entries, printing reports and financial statements, and closing the accounting period.

Instructions and the data file for completing this assignment are in the multimedia library of the MyAccountingLab Web site. Open the *Workshop 3 Sullivan Realty* PDF document for your version of Peachtree and download the *Sullivan Realty* data file for your version of Peachtree.

QUICKBOOKS COMPUTER WORKSHOP

COMPUTERIZED ACCOUNTING APPLICATION FOR CHAPTER 5

Refresher on using QuickBooks Pro

Before starting this assignment, you may want to refresh your memory by reading the following PDF documents in the multimedia library of the MyAccountingLab Web site. Remember to choose the PDF document for your version of QuickBooks.

1. An Introduction to QuickBooks Pro
2. Correcting QuickBooks Transactions
3. How to Repeat or Restart a QuickBooks Assignment
4. Backing Up and Restoring Your Work in QuickBooks

You also should have completed the following workshops:

1. Workshop 1 Atlas Company from Chapter 3
2. Workshop 2 Zell Company from Chapter 4

Workshop 3:

Accounting Cycle Mini Practice Set

In this workshop you will complete the June and July accounting cycles for Sullivan Realty using QuickBooks. Tasks include posting journal entries and adjusting journal entries, printing reports and financial statements, and closing the accounting period.

Instructions and the data file for completing this assignment are in the multimedia library of the MyAccountingLab Web site. Open the *Workshop 3 Sullivan Realty* PDF document for your version of QuickBooks and download the *Sullivan Realty* data file for your version of QuickBooks.

Banking Procedure and Control of Cash

THE GAME PLAN

Denied. Have you ever been shopping and given the clerk your credit or debit card, only to be told that the transaction has been denied for lack of funds? You cannot understand it since you just sent a check to the credit card company yesterday! You know you have a zero dollar balance on your card but the credit card company shows a negative balance. How could this happen? In this chapter, we will look at banking procedures, the reconciliation of bank statements with company accounting records, and the control of cash. Maintaining accurate records of transactions, rather than just relying on bank-prepared statements, is important to the control of cash and shows the importance of accounting in business.

LEARNING OBJECTIVES

● **1.** Depositing, writing, and endorsing checks for a checking account.

● **2.** Reconciling a bank statement.

● **3.** Establishing and replenishing a petty cash fund; setting up an auxiliary petty cash record.

○ **4.** Establishing and replenishing a change fund.

● **5.** Handling transactions involving cash short and over.

Bank Rate, Inc., helps you monitor how interest rates change. Be it in business or your personal life, you need to make wise financial decisions. In the first five chapters of this book, we analyzed the accounting cycle for businesses that perform personal services (e.g., word processing or legal services). In this chapter we turn our attention to Becca's Jewelry Store, a merchandising company that earns revenue by selling goods (or merchandise) to customers. When Becca's business began to increase, she became concerned that she was not monitoring the business's cash closely. She understood that a business with good internal control systems safeguards cash. Cash is the asset that is most easily stolen, lost, or mishandled. Therefore, it is important to protect all cash receipts and to control cash payments so that payments are made only for authorized business purposes.

After studying the situation carefully, Becca began a series of procedures that were to be followed by all company employees. The new company policies that Becca's Jewelry Store put into place are as follows:

Internal control system
Procedures and methods to control a firm's assets as well as monitor its operations.

1. Responsibilities and duties of employees will be divided. For example, the person receiving the cash, whether at the register or by opening the mail, will not record this information into the accounting records. The accountant will not be handling the cash receipts.
2. All cash receipts of Becca's Jewelry Store will be deposited into the bank the same day they arrive.
3. All cash payments will be made by check (except petty cash, which is discussed later in this chapter).
4. Employees will be rotated. This change allows workers to become acquainted with the work of others as well as to prepare for a possible changeover of jobs.
5. Becca Baker will sign all checks after receiving authorization to pay from the departments concerned.
6. At time of payment, all supporting invoices or documents will be stamped "paid." The stamp will show when the invoice or document is paid as well as the number of the check used.
7. All checks will be prenumbered. Periodically, the number of the checks that were issued and the numbers of the blank check forms remaining will be verified to make sure that all check numbers are accounted for. This change will control the use of checks and make it difficult to use a check fraudulently without its being revealed at some point.
8. Monthly bank statements will be sent to and reconciled by someone other than the employees who handle, record, or deposit the cash.

● LO1   LEARNING UNIT 6-1 BANK PROCEDURES, CHECKING ACCOUNTS, AND BANK RECONCILIATION

Becca knew that a checking account is one of the most useful and common banking services available, but she had many questions and decisions to make. She wanted to know about account options, monthly service charges, check-printing charges, minimum balance requirements, interest paid on the account, availability of automatic teller machines (ATMs), line of credit, and debit cards. Before Becca's Jewelry opened on April 1, 201X, she met with the manager of Sunshine Bank to discuss opening and using a checking account for the company.

Opening a Checking Account

Signature card A form signed by a bank customer that the bank uses to verify signature authenticity on all checks.

COACHING TIP

A signature card is another safeguard.

The bank manager gave Becca a signature card to fill out. The bank uses the signature card to verify the authenticity of the signature on company checks. Because Becca would be signing all the checks for her company, she was the only person who needed to sign the card.

The bank account enabled Becca to implement two of the basic internal control procedures. First, all revenue sources (cash and checks from cash sales and accounts receivable collections as well as credit card and debit card proceeds) were deposited in the bank account. Second, all withdrawals were to be made by check.

After Becca completed the initial paperwork, she received deposit slips and a set of checks. A deposit slip is a form that is used when making deposits of currency, coins, or checks in a bank or other financial institution. When filling out a deposit slip, you list the total amount of currency, coins, and checks that you are depositing (see Figure 6.1, p. 224).

You list each check that you are depositing individually. Also, alongside each check you list its American Bankers Association (ABA) code. The ABA code is found in the upper-right corner of each check, below the check number. In Figure 6.1, the *16* identifies the large city or state the bank is located in, and the *21* identifies the bank. The *112* is split into two parts: *1* represents the First Federal Reserve District, and *12* is a routing number used by the Federal Reserve Bank. When completing a deposit slip, only the first two numbers are required.

When a deposit is completed, the depositor receives a copy of the deposit slip as a receipt or proof of the transaction. The deposit should also be recorded on the current check stub. The bank manager told Becca that she could give the deposits to a bank teller or she could use an ATM. Often, Becca makes her deposits after business hours when the bank is closed. At those times, she puts the deposit into a locked bag (provided by the bank) and places the bag in the night depository. The bank will credit Becca's account when the deposit is processed. Becca plans to make all business payments by written check (except petty cash) and deposit all money received (cash and checks) in the bank account.

Check Endorsement

Checks have to be *endorsed* (signed) by the person to whom the check is made out before they can be deposited or cashed. Endorsement is the signing or stamping of one's name on the back left-hand side of the check. This signature means that the payee has transferred the right to deposit or cash the check to someone else (the bank). The bank can then collect the money from the person or company that issued the check.

Three different types of endorsement can be used (see Figure 6.2, p. 225). The first is a *blank endorsement*. A blank endorsement does not specify that a particular person or firm must endorse it. It can be further endorsed by someone else. The bank will pay the last person who signs the check. This type of endorsement is not very safe. If the check is lost, the person who finds it can sign it and get the money.

The second type of endorsement is a *full endorsement*. The person or company signing (or stamping) the back of the check indicates the name of the company or the person to whom the check is to be paid. Only the person or company named in the endorsement can transfer the check to someone else.

Restrictive endorsements, the third type of endorsement, are the safest for businesses. Becca's Jewelry Store stamps the back of the check so that it must be deposited in the firm's account. This stamp limits any further use of the check.

Deposit slip A form provided by a bank for use in depositing money or checks into a checking account.

COACHING TIP

When a bank credits your account, it is increasing the balance.

Endorsement *Blank:* Could be further endorsed. *Full:* Restricts further endorsement to only the person or company named. *Restrictive:* Restricts any further endorsement.

COACHING TIP

Endorsements can be made by using a rubber stamp instead of a handwritten signature.

COACHING TIP

The regulations require the endorsement to be within the top 1½ inches to speed up the check-clearing process.

FIGURE 6.1
Deposit Slip

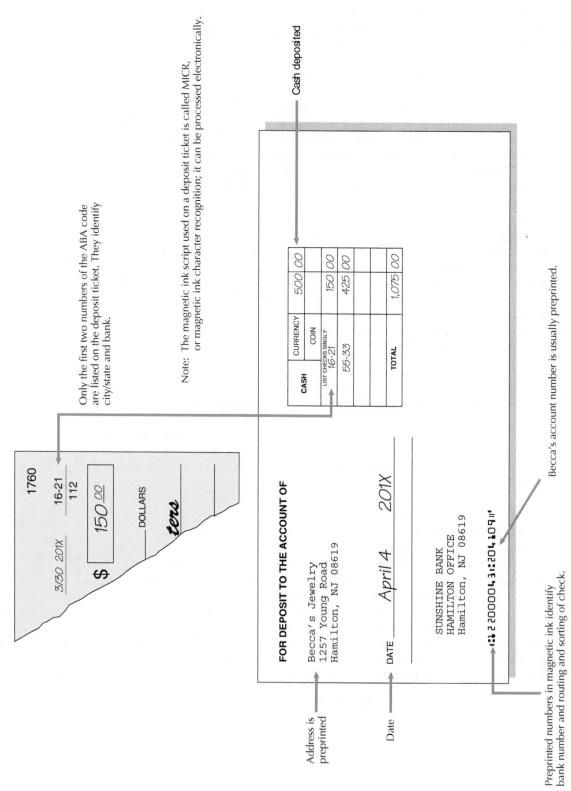

Cash deposited

Only the first two numbers of the ABA code are listed on the deposit ticket. They identify city/state and bank.

Note: The magnetic ink script used on a deposit ticket is called MICR, or magnetic ink character recognition; it can be processed electronically.

CASH	CURRENCY	500	00
	COIN		
LIST CHECKS SINGLY	16-21	150	00
	55-33	425	00
TOTAL		1,075	00

1760

$\dfrac{16\text{-}21}{112}$

3/30 201X

$ 150 $\frac{00}{}$

_____ DOLLARS

_____ *tens*

FOR DEPOSIT TO THE ACCOUNT OF

Becca's Jewelry
1257 Young Road
Hamilton, NJ 08619

DATE _____ *April 4   201X*

SUNSHINE BANK
HAMILTON OFFICE
Hamilton, NJ 08619

⑆ ⑈ 200004 ⑆ ⑇ 204 ⑈ 09 ⑈

Becca's account number is usually preprinted.

Preprinted numbers in magnetic ink identify bank number and routing and sorting of check.

Address is preprinted

Date

Types of Check Endorsement

FIGURE 6.2
Types of Check Endorsement

Blank Endorsement

Becca Baker

204109

A signature on the back left side of a check of the person or firm the check is payable to. This check can be *further* endorsed by someone else; the bank will give the money to the last person who signs the check. This type of endorsement is not very safe. If the check is lost, anyone who picks it up can sign it and get the money.

Full Endorsement

Pay to the order of
Sunshine Bank

Becca's Jewelry Store
204109

This type of endorsement is safer than a simple signature, because the person or company signing (or stamping) the back of the check indicates the name of the company or person to whom the check is to be paid. Only the person or company named in the endorsement can transfer the check to someone else.

Restrictive Endorsement

Payable to the order of
Sunshine Bank
for deposit only.

Becca's Jewelry Store
204109

This endorsement is the safest for businesses. Becca's Jewelry Store stamps the back of the check so that it must be deposited in the firm's account. This endorsement limits any further use of the check (it can only be deposited in the specified account).

In the past and to a lesser extent in the present the primary sources of cash were cash sales and the collection of company accounts receivable. The journal entries to record the collection and deposit of cash in a bank vary only by the source. If the deposit is composed of the proceeds of cash sales, the journal entry is as follows (see Figure 6.3).

Date	Accounts	PR	Dr.	Cr.
	Cash		500 00	
	Sales			500 00

If the deposit is composed of collections of company accounts receivable, the journal entry would be as follows:

Date	Accounts	PR	Dr.	Cr.
	Cash		750 00	
	Accounts Receivable			750 00

There are two other sources of revenue that have taken on greater importance to businessmen and businesswomen: the credit card and the debit card. There are two categories of credit cards: those issued by financial institutions and those issued by credit card companies. Many of those issued by financial institutions, such as MasterCard, VISA, and Discover, are co-branded by other institutions such as airlines, NFL teams, and colleges and universities. These credit cards offer revolving credit facilities. Other credit cards such as American Express are issued by credit card companies. These companies generally extend credit for 30 days at a time. There are several good reasons for a merchant to accept credit cards in payment for its goods or services. The seller does not have to make a decision as to whether it should grant credit or the amount of the credit to be granted. The seller also avoids the risk that the purchaser cannot or will not pay. Additionally, the seller does not have to maintain an accounts receivable system. Credit cards offer a greater number of repayment plans than do merchants, and this may actually increase sales. A credit card may facilitate purchases over the phone or Internet as cash does not need to change hands at the time of sale, and the seller usually receives payment to the company's bank account within 24 hours from VISA, MasterCard, or Discover. American Express typically takes longer than one day to credit the merchant's bank account. A drawback is that merchants typically must pay a service fee associated with the cost of processing the credit card transaction. The following example reflects a 1.5% service charge (Figure 6.4).

FIGURE 6.4
Journal Entry to Record the Deposit of the Proceeds of Credit Card Sales

Date	Account	PR	Dr.	Cr.
	Cash		985 00	
	Service Charge Expense		15 00	
	Sales			1000 00

A debit card is an instrument very similar to the credit card that is used by the buyer to purchase goods and services. Debit cards are issued by banks, savings and loan institutions, and credit unions on behalf of depositors having an account with the institution. In addition, a debit card is not an extension of credit, as the debit card holder cannot spend more than the balance currently in his or her institutional account. As far as the merchant accepting the card is concerned, a debit card, with minor exceptions, is the same as a credit card. Both eliminate the need for the buyer to carry cash or checks to complete a purchase. Within 24 hours the merchant usually receives payment that is reduced by the amount of the service charge fee associated with the debit card transaction. The journal entry to record a debit card transaction is the same as the one shown in Figure 6.4.

The Checkbook

Check A form used to indicate a specific amount of money that is to be paid by the bank to a named person or company.

Drawer Person who writes a check.

Drawee Bank that drawer has an account with.

Payee The person or company to whom the check is payable.

When Becca opened her business's checking account, she received checks. These checks can be used to buy items for the business or to pay bills or salaries.

A check is a written order signed by a drawer (the person who writes the check) instructing a drawee (the person who pays the check) to pay a specific sum of money to the payee (the person to whom the check is payable). Figure 6.5 shows a check issued by Becca's Jewelry Store. Becca Baker is the drawer, Sunshine Bank is the drawee, and Ziegler Wholesalers is the payee.

Look at the check in Figure 6.5. Notice that certain features, such as the company's name and address and the check number, are preprinted. Also notice (1) the line drawn after xx/100, which is to fill up the empty space and ensure that the amount cannot be changed, and (2) the word *and*, which should be used only to differentiate between dollars and cents.

Figure 6.5 includes a check stub. The check stub is used to record transactions, and it is kept for future reference. The information found on the stub includes the beginning balance ($3,441), the amount of any deposits ($0), the total amount in the account ($3,441), the amount of the check being written ($580), and the ending balance ($2,861). The check stub should be filled out before the check is written.

FIGURE 6.5
A Company Check

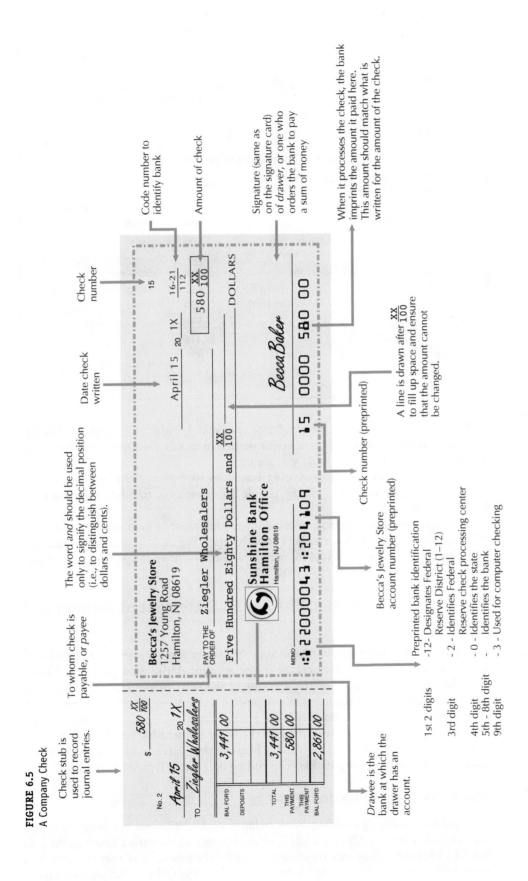

Check stub is used to record journal entries.

To whom check is payable, or payee

The word *and* should be used only to signify the decimal position (i.e., to distinguish between dollars and cents).

Code number to identify bank

Amount of check

Check number

Date check written

Signature (same as on the signature card) of *drawer*, or one who orders the bank to pay a sum of money

When it processes the check, the bank imprints the amount it paid here. This amount should match what is written for the amount of the check.

A line is drawn after $\frac{XX}{100}$ to fill up space and ensure that the amount cannot be changed.

Check number (preprinted)

Check number (preprinted)

Becca's Jewelry Store account number (preprinted)

Preprinted bank identification
-12- Designates Federal Reserve District (1–12)
- 2 - Identifies Federal Reserve check processing center
- 0 - Identifies the state
- Identifies the bank
- 3 - Used for computer checking

1st 2 digits
3rd digit
4th digit
5th - 8th digit
9th digit

Drawee is the bank at which the drawer has an account.

FIGURE 6.6
Transaction (In-Company Records)
Affecting Checkbook Balance

Bank Deposits Made for April		
Date of Deposit	**Amount**	**Received From**
Apr. 1	$5,000	Becca Baker, Capital
4	340	Jennifer Leung
16	89	Mary Figueroa
27	117	Carl Jones
28	900	Cash Sales
Total deposits for month:	$6,446	

Checks Written for the Month of April					
Date	**Check No.**	**Payment To**	**Amount**	**Description**	
Apr. 2	10	Quality Insurance	$ 500	Insurance paid in advance	
7	11	ABC Wholesalers	400	Merchandise	
9	12	Payroll	800	Salaries	
10	13	Times Newspaper	100	Advertising	
12	14	Verizon	99	Telephone	
15	15	Ziegler Wholesalers	580	Merchandise	
15		ATM Withdrawal	50	Postage	
Total Amount of Checks Written:			$2,529		
Deposits and Credits			$6,446		
Withdrawals and Fees			−2,529		
Balance in Account			$3,917		

COACHING TIP

Figure 6.7 shows one format for
a bank statement. Different banks
use different formats.

If the written amount on the check does not match the amount expressed in figures, Sunshine Bank may pay the amount written in words, return the check unpaid, or contact the drawer to see what was meant.

Many companies use check-writing machines to type out the information on the check. These machines prevent people from making fraudulent changes on handwritten checks.

During the same time period, in-company records must be kept for all transactions affecting Becca's Jewelry Store's checkbook balance. Figure 6.6 shows these records. Note that the bank deposits ($6,446) minus the checks written ($2,529) give an ending checkbook balance of $3,917.

Monthly Recordkeeping: The Bank's Statement of Account and In-Company Records

Each month, Sunshine Bank will send Becca's Jewelry Store a statement of account. This statement reflects all the activity in the account during that period. It begins with the beginning balance of the account at the start of the month, along with the checks the bank has paid and any deposits received (see Figure 6.7). Any other charges or additions to the bank balance are indicated by codes found on the statement. All checks that have been paid by the bank are sent back to Becca's Jewelry Store. They are called cancelled checks because they have been processed by the bank and are no longer negotiable. The ending balance in Figure 6.7 is $3,592.

Cancelled check A check that
has been processed by a bank and is
no longer negotiable.

● **LO2**

The Bank Reconciliation Process

COACHING TIP

Online banking and computer
software has made the reconciliation process even easier.

The problem is that the ending bank balance of $3,592 does not agree with the amount in Becca's checkbook, $3,917, or the balance in the cash amount in the ledger, $3,917. Such differences are caused partly by the time a bank takes to process a company's transactions. A company records a transaction when it occurs, but a bank

FIGURE 6.7
A Bank Statement

Sunshine Bank

Becca's Jewelry Store
1257 Young Road
Hamilton, NJ 08619

ACCOUNT
NUMBER 20 410 9

CLOSING
PERIOD 4/30/1X

AMOUNT
ENCLOSED $_____

RETURN THIS PORTION WITH YOUR PAYMENT IF YOU ARE NOT USING OUR AUTOMATIC PAYMENT PLAN   Address Correction on Reverse Side ☐

CHECKING ACCOUNT

ON	YOUR BALANCE WAS	NO.	WE SUBTRACTED CHECKS TOTALING	LESS SERVICE CHARGE	NO.	WE ADDED DEPOSITS OF	MAKING YOUR PRESENT BALANCE
	0	5	1,949.00	5.00	4	5,546.00	3,592.00

DATE	CHECKS • WITHDRAWALS • PAYMENTS			DEPOSITS • INTEREST • ADVANCES	BALANCE
4/1				5,000.00	5,000.00
4/2	500.00				4,500.00
4/4				340.00	4,840.00
4/7	400.00				4,440.00
4/9	800.00				3,640.00
4/10	100.00				3,540.00
4/12	99.00				3,441.00
4/15				89.00	3,530.00
4/15	50.00 ATM				3,480.00
4/27				117.00	3,597.00
4/30	5.00 SC				3,592.00

FIGURE 6.8
Bank Reconciliation Using Back of the Bank Statement

CHECKS OUTSTANDING	
NUMBER	AMOUNT
15	580	00
TOTAL OF CHECKS OUTSTANDING	580	00

1. Enter balance shown on this statement — 3,592 | 00

2. If you have made deposits since the date of this statement add them to the above balance. — 900 | 00

3. SUBTOTAL — 4,492 | 00

4. Deduct total of checks outstanding — 580 | 00

5. ADJUSTED BALANCE This should agree with your checkbook. — 3,912 | 00*

COACHING TIP

Keep in mind that both the bank and the depositor can make mistakes that will not be discovered until the reconciliation process.

TO VERIFY YOUR CHECKING BALANCE
1. Sort checks by number or by date issued and compare with your check stubs and prior outstanding list. Make certain all checks paid have been recorded in your checkbook. If any of your checks were not included with this statement, list the numbers and amounts under "CHECKS OUTSTANDING."
2. Deduct the Service Charge as shown on the statement from your checkbook balance.
3. Review copies of charge advices included with this statement and check for proper entry in your checkbook.

IF THE ADJUSTED BALANCE DOES NOT AGREE WITH YOUR CHECKBOOK BALANCE, THE FOLLOWING SUGGESTIONS ARE OFFERED FOR YOUR ASSISTANCE.

- Recheck additions and subtractions in your checkbook and figures to the left.
- Make certain checkbook balances have been carried forward properly.
- Verify deposits recorded on statement against deposits entered in checkbook.
- Compare amount on each checkbook stub.

*Note that the $5 service charge is included

cannot record a deposit until it receives that deposit, and it cannot pay a check until the check is presented by the payee. In addition, the bank statement will report fees and transactions that the company did not know about.

Becca's accountant has to find out why there is a $325 difference between the balances and how the records can be brought into balance. The process of reconciling the bank balance on the bank statement versus the company's checkbook balance is called a bank reconciliation. Bank reconciliations involve several steps, including calculating the deposits in transit and the outstanding checks. The bank reconciliation usually is done on the back of the bank statement (see Figure 6.8). However, it can also be done by computer software.

Bank reconciliation The process of reconciling the checkbook balance with the bank balance given on the bank statement.

Bank statement A report sent by a bank to a customer indicating the previous balance, atm transactions, nonsufficient funds, individual checks processed, individual deposits received, service charges, and ending bank balance.

Deposits in Transit In comparing the list of deposits received by the bank with the checkbook, the accountant notices that a deposit made on April 28 for $900 was not on the bank's statement. The accountant realizes that to prepare this statement, the bank only included information about Becca's Jewelry Store up to April 27. This deposit made by Becca was not shown on the monthly bank statement because it arrived at the bank after the statement was printed after April 30. Thus, timing becomes a consideration in the reconciliation process. Deposits not yet added to the bank balance are called deposits in transit. This deposit needs to be added to the bank balance shown on the bank statement. Becca's check-book is not affected, because the deposit has already been added to its balance. The bank has no way of knowing that the deposit is coming until it receives it.

Deposits in transit Deposits that were made by customers of a bank but did not reach, or were not processed by, the bank before the preparation of the bank statement.

COACHING TIP

Check no. 15 is outstanding in Figure 6.8.

Outstanding checks Checks written by a company or person that were not received or not processed by the bank before the preparation of the bank statement.

Outstanding Checks The first thing the accountant does when the bank statement is received is put the checks in numerical order (1, 2, 3, etc.). In doing so, the accountant notices that one payment was not made by the bank and check no. 15 was not returned by the bank.

Becca's books showed that this check had been deducted from the checkbook balance. The outstanding check, however, had not yet been presented to the bank for payment or deducted from the bank balance. When this check does reach the bank, the bank will reduce the amount of the balance.

Service Charges Becca's accountant also notices a bank service charge of $5. Becca's book balance will be lowered by $5.

Nonsufficient Funds While Becca's Jewelry Store did not experience either of the following two transactions, both may occur in the normal course of business. An NSF (nonsufficient funds) check is a check that has been returned because the drawer did not have enough money in its account to pay the check. Accountants are continually on the lookout for NSF checks. An NSF check means less money in the checking account than was thought. Becca will have to (1) lower the checkbook balance and (2) try to collect the amount from the customer. The bank will notify Becca's Jewelry of an NSF check (or other deductions) by a debit memorandum. Think of a <u>de</u>bit memorandum as a <u>de</u>duction from the account holder's balance.

NSF (nonsufficient funds) Notation indicating that a check has been written on an account that lacks sufficient funds to back it up.

Debit memorandum Decrease in depositor's balance.

Credit memorandum Increase in depositor's balance.

If the bank acts as a collecting agent for Becca's Jewelry, say in collecting notes, it will charge Becca a small fee and the net amount collected will be added to Becca's bank balance. The bank will send to Becca a credit memorandum verifying the increase in the depositor's balance.

A journal entry is also needed to bring the ledger accounts of Cash and Service Charge expense up-to-date. Any adjustment to the checkbook balance results in a journal entry. The entry in Figure 6.9 was made to accomplish this step.

FIGURE 6.9
Service Charge Journalized

Apr.	30	Service Charge Expense				5	00					
		Cash								5	00	
		Bank service charge for April										

It is important for Becca to prepare a bank reconciliation when she receives her bank statement every month as part of the cash control procedure. It verifies the amount of cash in her checking account. Another important reason to do a bank reconciliation is that it may uncover irregularities such as employee theft of funds.

Here are step-by-step instructions for preparing a bank reconciliation:

1. **Prepare a list of deposits in transit.** Compare the deposits listed on your bank statement with the bank deposits shown in your checkbook. On your bank reconciliation, list any deposits that have not yet cleared the bank statement. Also, take a look at the bank reconciliation you prepared last month. Did all of last month's deposits in transit clear on this month's bank statement? If not, you should find out what happened.

2. **Prepare a list of outstanding checks.** In your checkbook, mark each check that cleared the bank statement this month. On your bank reconciliation, list all the checks in your checkbook that did not clear. Also, take a look at the bank reconciliation you prepared last month. Did any checks outstanding from last month still not clear the bank? If so, be sure they are on your list of outstanding checks this month. If a check is several months old and still has not cleared the bank, you may want to investigate further.

3. **Record any bank charges or credits.** Take a close look at your bank statement. Are all special charges made by the bank recorded in your books? If not, journalize them now as if you had just written a check for that amount. By the same token, any credits made to your account by the bank should be journalized as well. Post the entries to your general ledger.

4. **Compute the cash balance per your books.**

5. **Enter bank balance on the reconciliation.** At the top of the bank reconciliation statement, enter the ending balance from the bank statement.

6. **Total the deposits in transit.** Add up the deposits in transit and enter the total on the reconciliation. Add the total deposits in transit to the bank balance to arrive at a subtotal.

7. **Total the outstanding checks.** Add up the outstanding checks, and enter the total on the reconciliation.

8. **Compute the balance per the reconciliation.** Subtract the total outstanding checks (see step 7) from the subtotal in step 6. The result should equal the balance shown in your general ledger.

Before we look at a more comprehensive bank statement, let's look at trends in banking.

Trends in Banking

The Internet is changing how people bank. In the past, banking took place on the main street of your town. The branches were open from 9 A.M. to 3 P.M. Monday through Thursday. They were probably open from 9 A.M. to 6 P.M. on Friday and possibly from 9 A.M. to noon on Saturday. These times were not always convenient for people who worked full time.

Many financial institutions have developed ways to transfer funds electronically, without the use of paper checks. Such systems are called electronic funds transfers (EFTs). Most EFTs are established to save money and avoid theft.

Financial institutions use powerful computer networks to automate millions of daily transactions. Today, banks are able to use computer technology to give you the option of bypassing the time-consuming, paper-based aspects of traditional banking so that you can manage your finances more quickly and efficiently.

The first step toward online banking, automatic teller machines (ATMs), were first installed in banks about 40 years ago. For the first time, customers could make deposits, withdraw money, and obtain account balances without having to stand in line during the times that the bank was open. Today, customers are able to use an ATM in banks, supermarkets, malls, and possibly even at a college student center.

×——→◯
COACHING TIP

Adjustments to the checkbook balance must be journalized and posted. These steps keep the depositor's ledger accounts (especially Cash) up-to-date. This charge could be recorded as a miscellaneous expense.

Electronic funds transfer (EFT) An electronic system that transfers funds without the use of paper checks.

ATM Automatic teller machine that allows for depositing, withdrawal, and advanced banking transactions.

x ──→ ○
COACHING TIP

Internet Banking is expanding rapidly.

Call centers were the next major step forward for banks. Customers could now telephone the center using either a toll-free number or local number and find out information about their accounts without leaving their home.

The latest development in banking is internet or online banking. Most of the large banks offer fully secure, fully functional online banking for free or for a small fee. Some smaller banks offer limited access; for instance, you may be able to view your account balance and history but may not be able to initiate transactions online. As more banks succeed online and more customers use their sites, fully functional online banking is becoming as common as ATMs.

With a debit card and personal identification number (PIN), you can use an ATM to withdraw cash, make deposits, or transfer funds between accounts. Some ATMs charge a fee if you are not a member of their ATM network or are making a transaction at a remote location.

Retail purchases can also be made with a debit card. You enter your PIN or sign for the purchase. Some banks that issue debit cards are charging customers a fee for a debit card purchase made with a PIN. Although a debit card looks like a credit card, the money for the purchase is transferred from your bank account to the store's account at the time of the purchase. The purchase will be shown on your bank account statement.

Immediately call the card issuer when you suspect a debit card may be lost or stolen. Most companies have toll-free numbers and a 24-hour service to deal with such emergencies. Although federal law limits your liability for a stolen credit card to $50, your liability for unauthorized use of your ATM or debit card can be much greater—depending on how quickly you report the loss. Also, it is important to remember that when you use a debit card, federal law does not give you the right to stop payment. You must resolve the problem with the seller.

If you don't mind foregoing the teller window and the lobby cookie, a virtual bank or e-bank, such as Virtual Bank or Giant Bank, may save you real money. Virtual banks are banks without bricks. They exist entirely online and offer much of the same range of services and adhere to the same regulations as your corner bank. Virtual banks pass the money that they save on overhead, such as buildings and tellers, along to you in the form of higher yields and lower fees. Banking is available everywhere, all the time. Your finances are at your fingertips. With the advent of "smart phones" such as the iPhone, Droid, Nexus, and Palm Pre, internet banking is available regardless of location. Almost every major and many minor bank has developed "banking apps," which are provided to enable customers to access their accounts from almost any location.

Advantages of Online Banking Customers who use online banking services enjoy many advantages. They can do almost everything from the comfort of their own homes at convenient times and without standing in long lines.

- *Convenience:* Unlike your corner site, online banks never close. They are available 24 hours a day, seven days a week.
- *Availability:* If you are out of state or even out of the country when a money problem arises, you can log on instantly to your online bank and take care of business, 24/7.
- *Transaction speed:* Online bank sites generally execute and confirm transactions as quickly or even faster than ATM processing speeds.
- *Efficiency:* You can access and manage all of your bank accounts, including IRAs and CDs, from one secure site.
- *Effectiveness:* Many online banking sites now offer sophisticated tools to help you manage all of your assets more effectively. Most of these tools are compatible with money managing programs such as Quicken and Microsoft Money.

Disadvantages of Online Banking Although online banking has many advantages, it also has some disadvantages.

- *Start-up may take time:* In order to register for your bank's online program, you will probably have to provide some personal identification and sign a form at a branch bank.
- *Learning curve:* Banking sites can be difficult to navigate at first. Plan to invest time to read the tutorials in order to become comfortable in your virtual lobby.
- *Bank site changes:* Even the largest banks periodically upgrade their online programs, adding new features in unfamiliar places. In some cases, you may need to reenter account information.
- *Trust:* For many people, the biggest hurdle to online banking is learning to trust it. Did my transaction go through? Did I push the transfer button once or twice? Best bet: Always print the transaction receipt and keep it with your bank records until it shows up on your personal site or your bank statement.

When problems arise, it is usually much easier to sort them out face to face rather than to use e-mail or the telephone. Perhaps the biggest problem with online banking is security. It is important to keep passwords safe and to be aware of fake e-mails arriving in your inbox. These e-mails pretend to be from your bank and attempt to obtain log in information from you. This kind of fraud is called phishing.

Phishing Fake e-mails that attempt to obtain information about online banking customers.

Fraudulent practices can happen at cash registers when you make a purchase or at restaurants when you pay with a credit card and the waiter is out of your sight. Skimming is the theft of credit card information used in an otherwise legitimate debit card or credit card transaction. Skimming at ATMs can be much more damaging because of the number of accounts and the amount of money that can be quickly accessed. Card-based purchases—online, debit, and credit—are convenient for consumers. For example, tens of thousands of ATMs are swipe-based. The large number of ATMs contributes to the skimming problem. In a way, we've become victims of the convenience we demand.

Here are some tips to help you avoid becoming a skimming victim.

- Keep your PIN safe. Don't give it to anyone.
- Watch out for people who try to "help" you at an ATM.
- Look at the ATM before using it. If it doesn't look right, don't use it.
- If an ATM has any unusual signage, don't use it. No bank would hang a sign that says, "Swipe your ATM here before inserting it in the card reader" or something to that effect.
- If your card is not returned after the transaction or after pressing cancel, immediately contact the institution that issued the card.
- Check your statement to be sure that no unusual withdrawals appear on it.

Check Truncation (Safekeeping) Some banks do not return cancelled checks to the depositor but instead use a procedure called check truncation or safekeeping. This practice is increasing rapidly. The bank holds a cancelled check for a specific period of time (usually 90 days) and then keeps a microfilm copy handy and destroys the original check. In Texas, for example, some credit unions and savings and loan institutions do not send back checks. Instead, the check date, number, and amount are listed on the bank statement. If the customer needs a copy of a check, the bank will provide the check or a photocopy for a small fee. (Photocopies are accepted as evidence in Internal Revenue Service tax returns and audits.)

Check truncation (safekeeping) Procedure whereby checks are not returned to the drawer with the bank statement but are instead kept at the bank for a certain amount of time before being first transferred to microfilm and then destroyed.

Truncation cuts down on the amount of "paper" that is returned to customers and thus provides substantial cost savings. It is estimated that more than 80 million checks are written each day in the United States.

Example of a More Comprehensive Bank Statement The bank reconciliation of Becca's Jewelry was not as complicated as it is for many companies, even using today's computer technology. Let's look at a reconciliation for Matty's Supermarket (Figures 6.10 and 6.11), which is based on the following business transactions:

Matty's checkbook balance	$13,176.84
Bank balance	23,726.04
Leased space to Subway	8,456.00
Leased space to Dunkin' Donuts	3,616.12
Both lease payments are deposited by electronic transfer.	
Matty pays a health insurance payment each month by electronic transfer	1,444.00
Deposits in transit 5/30	6,766.52

Checks outstanding

Ck # 738	$1,144.00
739	1,277.88
740	332.00
741	812.56
742	1,834.12
	1,440.00

Check # 734 was overstated in company's books

FIGURE 6.10
Bank Statement for Matty's Supermarket

Ranger Bank
1 Left St.
Marblehead, MA 01945

ACCOUNT STATEMENT

Matty's Supermarket
20 Sullivan St.
Lynn, MA 01917

Checking Account: 775800061

Checking Account Summary as of 6/30/1X

Beginning Balance	Total Deposits	Total Withdrawals	Service Charge	Ending Balance
$26,224.48	$17,410.56	$19,852.00	$57.00	$23,726.04

Checking Accounts Transactions

Deposits	Date	Amount
Deposit	6/05	4,000.00
Deposit	6/05	448.00
Deposit	6/09	778.40
EFT leasing: Dunkin' Donuts	6/18	3,616.12
EFT leasing: Subway	6/27	8,456.00
Interest	6/30	112.04

Charges	Date	Amount
Service charge: Check printing	6/30	57.00
EFT: Blue Cross/Blue Shield	6/21	1,444.00
NSF	6/21	208.00

Checks				Daily Balance			
Number	Date	Amount		Date	Balance	Date	Balance
401	6/07	400.00		5/28	26,224.48	6/18	21,059.00
733	6/13	12,000.00		6/05	30,464.48	6/21	19,615.00
734	6/13	600.00		6/07	29,664.48	6/28	28,071.00
735	6/11	400.00		6/09	30,442.88	6/30	23,726.04
736	6/18	400.00		6/11	30,042.88		
737	6/30	4,400.00		6/13	17,442.88		

Note that in Figure 6.11 each adjustment to Matty's checkbook is the reconciliation process that would result in general journal entries in the company's accounting records.

FIGURE 6.11
Bank Reconciliation for Matty's Supermarket

MATTY'S SUPERMARKET
Bank Reconciliation as of June 30, 201X

Checkbook balance			Bank balance		
Matty's checkbook balance		$13,176.84	Bank balance		$23,726.04
Add:			Add:		
EFT leasing: Dunkin' Donuts	$ 3,616.12		Deposits in transit, 5/30		6,766.52
					$30,492.56
EFT leasing: Subway	8,456.00				
Interest	112.04				
Error: Overstated check no. 734	1,440.00	13,624.16			
		$26,801.00			
Deduct:			Deduct:		
Service charge	$ 57.00		Outstanding checks:		
NSF check	208.00		No. 738	$1,144.00	
EFT health insurance payment	1,444.00	1,709.00	No. 739	1,277.88	
			No. 740	332.00	
			No. 741	812.56	
			No. 742	1,834.12	5,400.56
Reconciled balance		$25,092.00	Reconciled balance		$25,092.00

LEARNING UNIT 6-1 REVIEW

AT THIS POINT you should be able to do the following:

- Define and explain the need for deposit slips.
- Explain where the American Bankers Association transit number is located on the check and what its purpose is.
- List as well as compare and contrast the three common types of check endorsements.
- Explain the structure of a check.
- Define and state the purpose of a bank statement.
- Explain deposits in transit, checks outstanding, service charge, and NSF checks.
- Explain the difference between a debit memorandum and a credit memorandum.
- Prepare a bank reconciliation.
- Explain electronic funds transfer and check truncation.
- Explain the advantages and disadvantages of online banking.

Instant Replay ◉ Self-Review Quiz 6-1

Indicate, by placing an X under it, the heading that describes the appropriate action in a bank reconciliation for each of the following situations:

Situation	Add to Bank Balance	Deduct from Bank Balance	Add to Checkbook Balance	Deduct from Checkbook Balance
1. Check printing charge				
2. Deposits in transit				

(continued on page 236)

Situation	Add to Bank Balance	Deduct from Bank Balance	Add to Checkbook Balance	Deduct from Checkbook Balance
3. NSF check				
4. A $75 check was written and recorded by the company as $85				
5. Proceeds of a note collected by the bank				
6. Check outstanding				
7. Forgot to record ATM withdrawal				
8. Forgot to record direct deposit				

Solution to Instant Replay: Self-Review Quiz 6-1

Situation	Add to Bank Balance	Deduct from Bank Balance	Add to Checkbook Balance	Deduct from Checkbook Balance
1				X
2	X			
3				X
4			X	
5			X	
6		X		
7				X
8			X	

Deposits in transit are added to the bank balance, whereas checks outstanding are subtracted from the bank balance.

 **L03**

LEARNING UNIT 6-2 THE ESTABLISHMENT OF PETTY CASH AND CHANGE FUNDS

Becca realized how time-consuming and expensive it would be to write checks for small amounts to pay for postage, small supplies, and so forth, so she set up a petty cash fund. Similarly, she established a *change fund* to make cash transactions more convenient. This unit explains how to manage petty cash and change funds.

Setting Up the Petty Cash Fund

The petty cash fund is an account dedicated to paying small day-to-day expenses. These petty cash expenses are recorded in an auxiliary record and later summarized, journalized, and posted. Becca estimated that the company would need a fund of $60 to cover small expenditures during the month of May. This petty cash was not expected to last longer than one month. She gave one of her employees responsibility for overseeing the fund. This person is called the *custodian*.

Petty cash fund Fund (source) that allows payment of small amounts without the writing of checks.

COACHING TIP

Petty Cash is an asset on the balance sheet that is established by writing a new check. The Petty Cash account is debited only once unless a greater or lesser amount of petty cash is needed on a regular basis.

CHAPTER 6 Banking Procedure and Control of Cash **237**

Becca named her office manager, John Sullivan, as custodian. In other companies, the cashier or secretary may be in charge of petty cash. Check no. 6 was drawn to the order of the custodian and cashed to establish the fund. John keeps the petty cash fund in a small tin box in the office safe.

Shown here is the transaction analysis chart for the establishment of a $60 petty cash fund, which would be journalized on May 1, 201X, as shown in Figure 6.12.

Accounts Affected	Category	↓ ↑	Rules
Petty Cash	Asset	↑	Dr.
Cash (checks)	Asset	↓	Cr.

Note that the new asset called Petty Cash, which was created by writing check no. 6, reduced the asset Cash. In reality, the total assets stay the same; what has occurred is a shift from the asset Cash (check no. 6) to a new asset account called Petty Cash.

The Petty Cash account is not debited or credited again if the size of the fund is not changed. If the $60 fund is used up quickly, the fund should be increased. If the fund is too large, the Petty Cash account should be reduced. We take a closer look at this issue when we discuss replenishment of petty cash.

	GENERAL JOURNAL			Page 1	
Date	Account Title and Description	PR	Dr.	Cr.	
201X May 1	Petty Cash		60 00		
	Cash			60 00	
	Establishment of petty cash and change fund.				

FIGURE 6.12
Establishing Petty Cash

Making Payments from the Petty Cash Fund

John Sullivan has the responsibility for filling out a petty cash voucher for each cash payment made from the petty cash fund. The petty cash vouchers are numbered in sequence.

Note that when the voucher (shown in Figure 6.13, p. 238) is completed, it will include

- the voucher number (which will be in sequence),
- the date,
- the person or organization to whom the payment was made,
- the amount of payment,
- the reason for payment (in this case, cleaning),
- the signature of the person who approved the payment,
- the signature of the person who received the payment from petty cash, and
- the account to which the expense will be charged.

The completed vouchers are placed in the petty cash box. No matter how many vouchers John Sullivan fills out, the total of the vouchers in the box and the cash on hand should equal the original amount of petty cash with which the fund was established ($60).

Petty cash voucher A petty cash form to be completed when money is taken out of petty cash.

COACHING TIP

The check for $60 is usually drawn to the order of the custodian and is cashed, and the proceeds are turned over to John Sullivan, the custodian.

FIGURE 6.13
Petty Cash Voucher

Petty Cash Voucher No. 1

Date:　May 2, 201X　　　　　　　　　　　Amount: $3.00
Paid To:　Al's Cleaning
For:　　Cleaning Package

Approved By:　*John Sullivan*

Payment Received By:　*Al Smith*

Debit Account No.:　619

Assume that at the end of May the following items are documented by petty cash vouchers in the petty cash box as having been paid by John Sullivan:

201X
May
2　Cleaning package, $3.00

5　Postage stamps, $9.00

8　First-aid supplies, $15.00

9　Delivery expense, $6.00

14　Delivery expense, $15.00

27　Postage stamps, $6.00

Auxiliary petty cash record
A supplementary record for summarizing petty cash information.

John records this information in the auxiliary petty cash record shown in Figure 6.14. It is not a required record but is an aid to John. In other words, it is an auxiliary record that is not essential but that is quite helpful as part of the petty cash system. You may want to think of the auxiliary petty cash record as an optional worksheet. Let's look at how to replenish the petty cash fund.

FIGURE 6.14
Auxiliary Petty Cash Record

Date		Voucher No.	Description	Receipts	Payments	Postage Expense	Delivery Expense	Sundry Account	Sundry Amount
							Category of Payments		
201X May	1		Establishment	60 00					
	2	1	Cleaning		3 00			Cleaning	3 00
	5	2	Postage		9 00	9 00			
	8	3	First Aid		15 00			Misc.	15 00
	9	4	Delivery		6 00		6 00		
	14	5	Delivery		15 00		15 00		
	27	6	Postage		6 00	6 00			
			Total	60 00	54 00	15 00	21 00		18 00

How to Replenish the Petty Cash Fund

No postings are done from the auxiliary record because it is not a journal. At some point the summarized information found in the auxiliary petty cash record is used as a basis for a journal entry in the general journal and eventually posted to appropriate ledger accounts to reflect up-to-date balances.

The $54 of expenses (see Figure 6.14) is recorded in the general journal (Figure 6.15) and a new check, no. 17, for $54 is cashed and returned to John Sullivan. In replenishment, old expenses are updated in the journal and ledger to show where money has gone. The petty cash box now once again reflects $60 cash. The old vouchers that were used are stamped to indicate that they have been processed and the fund replenished.

Note that in the replenishment process the debits are a summary of the totals (except sundry, because individual items are different) of expenses or other items from the auxiliary petty cash record. Posting these specific expenses will ensure that the expenses will not be understated on the income statement. The credit to Cash allows us to draw a check for $54 to put money back in the petty cash box. The $60 in the box now agrees with the Petty Cash account balance. The end result is that our petty cash box is filled, and we have justified for which accounts the petty cash money was spent. Think of replenishment as a single, summarizing entry.

COACHING TIP

A new check, which is payable to the custodian and is cashed by John, is written in the replenishment process, and the cash is placed in the petty cash box.

FIGURE 6.15
Establishment and Replenishment of Petty Cash Fund

			GENERAL JOURNAL			Page 1	
	Date		Account Title and Description	PR	Dr.	Cr.	
Petty cash is an asset. →	201X May	1	Petty Cash		60 00		
			Cash			60 00	
			Establishment				
Note that the Petty Cash account is not listed in replenishment unless we raise or lower the basic amount. To raise it we would debit it; to lower it we would credit it. →		31	Postage Expense		15 00		
			Delivery Expense		21 00		
			Cleaning Expense		3 00		
			Miscellaneous Expense		15 00		
			Cash			54 00	
			Replenishment				

Remember that if at some point the petty cash fund is to be greater than $60, a check can be written that will increase Petty Cash and decrease Cash. If the Petty Cash account balance is to be reduced, we can credit or reduce Petty Cash. For our present purpose, however, Petty Cash will remain at $60.

The auxiliary petty cash record after replenishment would look as shown in Figure 6.16, p. 240 (keep in mind that no postings are made from the auxiliary).

FIGURE 6.16
Auxiliary Petty Cash Record with Replenishment

									Category of Payments				
											Sundry		
Date	Voucher No.	Description	Receipts		Payments		Postage Expense		Delivery Expense		Account	Amount	
201X May 1		Establishment	60 00										
2	1	Cleaning			3 00						Cleaning	3 00	
5	2	Postage			9 00		9 00						
8	3	First Aid			15 00						Misc.	15 00	
9	4	Delivery			6 00				6 00				
14	5	Delivery			15 00				15 00				
27	6	Postage			6 00		6 00						
		Total	60 00		54 00		15 00		21 00			18 00	
		Ending Balance			6 00								
			60 00		60 00								
		Ending Balance	6 00										
31		Replenishment	54 00										
31		Balance (New)	60 00										

Figure 6.17 may help you put the sequence together.

FIGURE 6.17
Which Transactions Involve Petty Cash and How to Record Them

Date	Description	New Check Written	Petty Cash Voucher Prepared	Recorded in Auxiliary Petty Cash Record	
201X May 1	Establishment of petty cash for $60	X		X	} Dr. Petty Cash Cr. Cash
2	Paid salaries, $2,000	X			
10	Paid $10 from petty cash for Band-Aids		X	X	} No journal entries
19	Paid $8 from petty cash for postage		X	X	
24	Paid light bill, $200	X			
29	Replenishment of petty cash to $60	X		X	} Dr. individual expenses Cr. Cash

Has nothing to do with petty cash (amounts too great)

In this step the old expenses are listed in the general journal and a new check is written to replenish. All old vouchers are removed from the petty cash box.

Before concluding this unit, let's look at how Becca will handle setting up a change fund and problems with cash shortages and overages.

Setting Up a Change Fund and Insight into Cash Short and Over

 **LO4**

If a company such as Becca's Jewelry expects to have many cash transactions occurring, it may be a good idea to establish a change fund. This fund is placed in the cash register drawer and used to make change for customers who pay cash. Becca decides to put $120 in the change fund, made up of various denominations of bills and coins. Let's look at a transaction analysis chart and the journal entry (Figure 6.18) for this sort of transaction.

Change fund Fund made up of various denominations that are used to make change for customers.

COACHING TIP

Accounts Affected	Category	↓ ↑	Rules
Change Fund	Asset	↑	Dr.
Cash	Asset	↓	Cr.

Beg. change fund
+ Cash register total
= Cash should have on hand
− Counted cash
= Shortage or overage of cash

Apr.	1	Change Fund		1 2 0 00	
		Cash			1 2 0 00
		Establish change fund			

FIGURE 6.18
Change Fund Established

At the close of the business day, Becca will place the amount of the change fund back in the safe in the office. She will prepare the change fund (the same $120) in the appropriate denominations for the next business day. She will deposit in the bank the *remainder* of the cash taken in for the day.

In the next section, we look at how to record errors that are made in making change, called cash short and over.

Cash Short and Over In a local pizza shop the total sales for the day did not match the amount of cash on hand. Errors often happen in making change. To record and summarize the differences in cash, an account called *Cash Short and Over* is used. This account records both overages (too much money) and shortages (not enough money). Let's first look at the account (in T account form).

 **LO5**

Cash Short and Over The account that records cash shortages and overages. If the ending balance is a debit, it is recorded on the income statement as a miscellaneous expense; if it is a credit, it is recorded as miscellaneous income.

Cash Short and Over

Dr.	Cr.
shortage	overage

All shortages will be recorded as debits and all overages will be recorded as credits. This account is temporary. If the ending balance of the account is a debit (a shortage), it is considered a miscellaneous expense that would be reported on the income statement. If the balance of the account is a credit (an overage), it is considered as other-income reported on the income statement. Let's look at how the Cash Short and Over account could be used to record shortages or overages in sales as well as in the petty cash process.

Example 1: Shortages and Overages in Sales On December 5 a pizza shop rang up sales of $560 for the day but only had $530 in cash.

Accounts Affected	Category	↓ ↑	Rules
Cash	Asset	↑	Debit $530
Cash Short and Over	Misc. Exp.	↑	Debit $30
Sales	Revenue	↑	Credit $560

The journal entry would be as shown in Figure 6.19

FIGURE 6.19
Cash Shortage

Dec.	5	Cash	5 3 0 00			
		Cash Short and Over	3 0 00			
		Sales			5 6 0 00	
		Cash shortage				

Note that the shortage of $30 is a debit and would be recorded on the income statement as a miscellaneous expense.

What would the entry look like if the pizza shop showed a $50 overage, i.e. if the cash at the end of the day was $610?

Accounts Affected	Category	↓ ↑	Rules
Cash	Asset	↑	Debit $610
Cash Short and Over	Other Income	↑	Credit $50
Sales	Revenue	↑	Credit $560

The journal entry would be as shown in Figure 6.20.

FIGURE 6.20
Cash Overage

Dec.	5	Cash	6 1 0 00			
		Cash Short and Over			5 0 00	
		Sales			5 6 0 00	
		Cash overage				

Note that the Cash Short and Over account would be reported as other income on the income statement. Now let's look at how to use this Cash Short and Over account to record petty cash transactions.

Example 2: Cash Short and Over in Petty Cash A local computer company established petty cash for $200. On November 30, the petty cash box had $160 in vouchers as well as $32 in coin and currency. What would be the journal entry to replenish petty cash? Assume the vouchers were made up of $90 for postage and $70 for supplies expense.

If you add up the vouchers and cash in the box, cash is short by $8.

COACHING TIP

NOTE: The account Petty Cash is not used since the level in petty cash is not raised or lowered.

Accounts Affected	Category	↓ ↑	Rules
Postage Expense	Expense	↑	Debit $90
Supplies Expense	Expense	↑	Debit $70
Cash Short and Over	Misc. Expense	↑	Debit $8
Cash	Asset	↓	Credit $168

The journal entry is shown in Figure 6.21

FIGURE 6.21
Petty Cash Replenished with
Shortage

Nov.	30	Postage Expense	9 0 00			
		Supplies Expense	7 0 00			
		Cash Short and Over	8 00			
		Cash			1 6 8 00	

In the case of an overage, the Cash Short and Over would be a credit as other income. The solution to Instant Replay: Self Review Quiz 6-2 shows how a fund shortage would be recorded in the auxiliary record.

LEARNING UNIT 6-2 REVIEW

AT THIS POINT you should be able to do the following:

- State the purpose of a petty cash fund.
- Prepare a journal entry to establish a petty cash fund.
- Prepare a petty cash voucher.
- Explain the relationship of the auxiliary petty cash record to the petty cash process.
- Prepare a journal entry to replenish Petty Cash to its original amount.
- Explain why individual expenses are debited in the replenishment process.
- Explain how a change fund is established.
- Explain how Cash Short and Over could be a miscellaneous expense.

Instant Replay ◦ Self-Review Quiz 6-2

As the custodian of the petty cash fund, it is your task to prepare journal entries to establish the fund on October 1 as well as to replenish the fund on October 31. Please keep an auxiliary petty cash record.

201X			
Oct.	1	Establish petty cash fund for $90, check no. 8.
	5	Voucher 11, delivery expense, $21.
	9	Voucher 12, delivery expense, $15.
	10	Voucher 13, office repair expense, $24.
	17	Voucher 14, general expense, $12.
	30	Replenishment of petty cash fund, $78, check no. 108. (Check would be payable to the custodian.)

COACHING TIP

How to calculate shortage: $21 + $15 + $24 + $12 = $72 of vouchers. Replenished with $78 check. Thus there was a $6 shortage. Note how cash short and over was entered in the auxiliary petty cash record.

Solution to Instant Replay: Self-Review Quiz 6-2

FIGURE 6.22
Establishment and Replenishment of Petty Cash

	GENERAL JOURNAL		Page 6	
Date	Account Title and Description	PR	Dr.	Cr.
201X Oct. 1	Petty Cash		90 00	
	Cash			90 00
	Establishment, Check 8			

31	Delivery Expense		36 00	
	General Expense		12 00	
	Office Repair Expense		24 00	
	Cash Short and Over		6 00	
	Cash			78 00
	Replenishment, Check 108			

FIGURE 6.23
Auxiliary Petty Cash Received

								Category of Payments			
										Sundry	
Date	Voucher No.	Description	Receipts		Payments		Delivery Expense	General Expense		Account	Amount
201X Oct. 1		Establishment	90 00								
5	11	Delivery			21 00		21 00				
9	12	Delivery			15 00		15 00				
10	13	Repairs			24 00					Office Repair	24 00
17	14	General			12 00				12 00		
25		Fund Shortage			6 00					Cash Short and Over	6 00
		Totals	90 00		78 00		36 00		12 00		30 00
		Ending Balance			12 00						
					90 00						
30		Ending Balance	12 00								
31		Replenishment	78 00								
Nov. 1		New Balance	90 00								

BLUEPRINT: A BANK RECONCILIATION

Checkbook Balance	**Bank Balance**
+ EFT (electronic funds transfer)	+ Deposits in transit
+ Interest earned	− Outstanding checks
+ Notes collected	± Bank errors
+ Direct deposits	
− ATM withdrawals	
− Check redeposits	
− NSF check	
− Online fees	
− Automatic withdrawals	
− Overdrafts	
− Service charges	
− Stop payments	
± Book errors*	
+ Credit Memo—adds to balance	
− Debit Memo—deducts from balance	

*If a $60 check is recorded as $50, we must decrease the checkbook balance by $10.

ACCOUNTING COACH

The following Coaching Tips are from Learning Units 6-1 and 6-2. Take the Pre-Game Checkup and use the Check Your Score at the bottom of the page to see how you are doing. The Accounting Coach provides tips before each Checkup to help you avoid common accounting errors.

LU 6-1 Bank Procedures, Checking Accounts, and Bank Reconciliation

Pre-Game Tips: When reconciling a bank statement, timing is a key consideration. Deposits in transit would be added to the bank balance while checks outstanding would be subtracted. Sometimes on the bank statement, interest is shown and must be updated on the checkbook side. If you forget to record a withdrawal from an ATM, you must update your book balance. Keep in mind that any adjustments to the checkbook will require journal entries so the cash ledger account will be correct. Today, online banking is taking over many of the manual tasks, but the accounting theory remains the same.

Pre-Game Checkup
Answer true or false to the following statements.

1. A credit memo from the bank means that it is decreasing your balance.
2. NSF results in an increase to your checkbook balance.
3. Blank endorsements are the safest type of endorsement.
4. The drawer is the one receiving a check.
5. A service charge must be adjusted on the bank balance.

LU 6-2 The Establishment of Petty Cash and Change Funds

Pre-Game Tips: Petty cash is an asset. When petty cash is replenished to the same level, all of the old expenses are shown and a new check is written. The account Petty Cash is not touched. When a new level of petty cash is desired, the account Petty Cash will be debited to increase it or credited to decrease it. Keep in mind that the account Cash Short and Over is a miscellaneous account found on the income statement. A debit balance on Cash Short and Over means that you have a shortage, and a credit balance means you have an overage.

Pre-Game Checkup

Answer true or false to the following statements.

1. Petty cash is an expense.
2. Increasing the Petty Cash account means that you have to credit it.
3. In the replenishment process, cash is not involved.
4. When petty cash is established, the Petty Cash account is debited.
5. A shortage in the Cash Short and Over account results in a credit balance.

CHECK YOUR SCORE: Answers to the Pre-Game Checkup

LU 6-1
1. False—A credit memo from the bank means that it is increasing your balance.
2. False—NSF results in a decrease to your checkbook balance.
3. False—Restrictive endorsements are the safest type of endorsement.
4. False—The payee is to whom a check is payable.
5. False—A service charge must be adjusted on the checkbook balance.

LU 6-2
1. False—Petty cash is an asset.
2. False—Increasing the Petty Cash account means that you have to debit it.
3. False—In the replenishment process, a new check (cash) needs to be written.
4. True.
5. False—A shortage in the Cash Short and Over account results in a debit balance.

Chapter Summary

MyAccountingLab

Here are all the key concepts and equations to help you understand the concepts of this chapter and prepare you for your exam. After completing this review, go to MyAccountingLab for more practice opportunities.

Concepts You Should Know	Key Terms
L01 Depositing, writing, and endorsing checks for a checking account.	Check (p. 226)
	Cancelled check (p. 228)
1. Restrictive endorsement limits any further negotiation of a check.	Deposit slip (p. 223)
2. The payee is the person to whom the check is payable. The drawer is the one who orders the bank to pay a sum of money. The drawee is the bank with which the drawer has an account.	Drawee (p. 226)
	Drawer (p. 226)
	Endorsement (p. 223)
	Internal control system (p. 222)
	Payee (p. 226)
	Signature card (p. 222)
L02 Reconciling a bank statement.	ATM (p. 231)
1. The process of reconciling the bank balance with the company's cash balance is called the bank reconciliation.	Bank reconciliation (p. 230)
2. Deposits in transit are added to the bank balance.	Bank statement (p. 230)
3. Checks outstanding are subtracted from the bank balance.	Credit memorandum (p. 230)
4. NSF means that a check previously deposited has non-sufficient funds to be credited (deposited) to a checking account; therefore, the amount is not included in the bank balance and thus the checking account balance is lowered.	Check truncation (safekeeping) (p. 233)
	Debit memorandum (p. 230)
5. When a bank debits your account, it is deducting an amount from your balance. A credit to the account is an increase to your balance.	Deposits in transit (p. 230)
6. All adjustments to the checkbook balance require journal entries.	Electronic funds transfer (EFT) (p. 231)
7. The Internet has created online banking options.	NSF (nonsufficient funds) (p. 230)
	Outstanding checks (p. 230)
	Phishing (p. 233)

Establishing and replenishing a petty cash fund; setting up an auxiliary petty cash record.

1. Petty Cash is an asset found on the balance sheet.

2. The auxiliary petty cash record is an auxiliary book; therefore, no postings are done from this record.

3. When a petty cash fund is established, the amount is entered as a debit to Petty Cash and a credit to Cash.

4. At the time of replenishment of the petty cash fund, all expenses are debited (by category) and a credit to Cash (a new check) results. This replenishment, when journalized and posted, updates the ledger from the journal.

5. The only time the Petty Cash account is used is to establish the fund initially or to bring the fund to a higher or lower level.

Auxiliary petty cash record (p. 238)

Petty cash fund (p. 236)

Petty cash voucher (p. 237)

● **L03**

Establishing and replenishing a change fund.

1. A change fund is an asset that is used to give change to cash customers.

Change fund (p. 241)

○ **L04**

Handling transactions involving cash short and over.

1. Cash Short and Over is an account that is either a miscellaneous expense or miscellaneous income, depending on whether the ending balance is a shortage or overage.

Cash Short and Over (p. 241)

● **L05**

Discussion Questions and Critical Thinking/Ethical Case

1. What is the purpose of internal control?

2. What is the advantage of having preprinted deposit slips?

3. Explain the difference between a blank endorsement and a restrictive endorsement.

4. Explain the difference between payee, drawer, and drawee.

5. Why should check stubs be filled out first, before the check itself is written?

6. A bank statement is sent twice a month. True or false? Please explain.

7. Explain the end product of a bank reconciliation.

8. Why are outstanding checks subtracted from the bank balance?

9. An NSF check results in a bank issuing the depositor a credit memorandum. Agree or disagree? Please explain your response.

10. Why do adjustments to the checkbook balance in the reconciliation process need to be journalized?

11. What is EFT?

12. What are the major advantages and disadvantages of online banking?

13. What is meant by check truncation or safekeeping?

14. Petty cash is a liability. Agree or disagree? Explain.

15. Explain the relationship of the auxiliary petty cash record to the recording of the cash payment.

16. At the time of replenishment, why are the totals of individual expenses debited?

17. Explain the purpose of a change fund.

18. Explain how Cash Short and Over can be a miscellaneous expense.

19. Sean Nah, the bookkeeper of Revell Co., received a bank statement from Lone Bank. Sean noticed a $250 mistake made by the bank in the company's favor. Sean called his supervisor, who said that as long as it benefits the company, he should not tell the bank about the error. You make the call. Write your specific recommendations to Sean.

Concept Checks

🔘 **L02** *(10 MIN)*   **Bank Reconciliation**

1. Indicate what effect (#1 – 4) each situation (#a – f) will have on the bank reconciliation process.
   1. Add to bank balance.
   2. Deduct from bank balance.
   3. Add to checkbook balance.
   4. Deduct from checkbook balance.
      _____ **a.** Check no. 150 was outstanding for $120.
      _____ **b.** $200 deposit in transit.
      _____ **c.** $155 NSF check.
      _____ **d.** A check written for $15 was recorded in the company's books as $25.
      _____ **e.** Bank collected a $1,000 note less a $50 collection fee.
      _____ **f.** $12 bank service charge.

Journal Entries in Reconciliation Process

⬤ **LO2** *(5 MIN)*

2.   Which of the transactions in Exercise 1 would require a journal entry?

Bank Reconciliation

⬤ **LO2** *(10 MIN)*

3.   From the following, construct a bank reconciliation for King Co. as of November 30, 201X.

Checkbook balance	$1,907.10
Bank statement balance	1,938.20
Deposits in transit	283.70
Outstanding checks	389.50
Bank service charge	15.80
NSF check	58.90

Petty Cash

⬤ **LO3** *(10 MIN)*

4.   Indicate what effects (#1 – 4) each situation (#a – f) will have. (Note: There might be more than one effect applicable for a situation.)

1. New check written.
2. Recorded in general journal.
3. Petty cash voucher prepared.
4. Recorded in auxiliary petty cash record.
   _____ a. Established petty cash.
   _____ b. Paid $1,200 bill.
   _____ c. Paid $3 for Band-Aids from petty cash.
   _____ d. Paid $4 for stamps from petty cash.
   _____ e. Paid electric bill, $270.
   _____ f. Replenished petty cash.

Replenishment of Petty Cash

⬤ **LO3** *(15 MIN)*

5.   Petty cash was originally established for $25. During the month, $4 was paid out for stamps and $5 for floor wax. During replenishment, the custodian discovered that the balance in petty cash was $8. Record, using a general journal entry, the replenishment of petty cash back to $25.

Increasing Petty Cash

⬤ **LO3** *(10 MIN)*

6.   In Exercise 5, if the custodian decided to raise the level of petty cash to $35, what would be the journal entry to replenish? (Use a general journal entry.)

Exercises

Set A

6A-1. From the following information, construct a bank reconciliation for Zing Co. as of March 31, 201X. Then prepare journal entries if needed.

⬤ **LO2** *(15 MIN)*

Checkbook balance	$1,851	Outstanding checks	$642
Bank statement balance	1,400	Bank service charge	55
Deposits (in transit)	1,000	NSF: Mia Kaminsky's check in payment of account was returned for insufficient funds.	38

LO3 *(15 MIN)*   **6A-2.** In general journal form, prepare journal entries to establish a petty cash fund on October 1 and replenish it on October 31.

201X		
Oct.	1	A $109 petty cash fund is established.
	31	At the end of the month, $23 cash plus the following paid vouchers exist: donations expense, $23; postage expense, $19; office supplies expense, $27; miscellaneous expense, $17.

LO3 *(15 MIN)*   **6A-3.** If in Exercise 6A-2 cash on hand is $17, prepare the entry to replenish the petty cash on October 31.

LO3 *(15 MIN)*   **6A-4.** If in Exercise 6A-2 cash on hand is $29, prepare the entry to replenish the petty cash on October 31.

LO5 *(15 MIN)*   **6A-5.** At the end of the day the clerk for Bill's Variety Shop noticed an error in the amount of cash he should have. Total cash sales from the sales tape were $1,190, whereas the total cash in the register was $1,149. Bill keeps a $21 change fund in his shop. Prepare an appropriate general journal entry to record the cash sale as well as reveal the cash shortage.

Set B

LO2 *(15 MIN)*   **6B-1.** From the following information, construct a bank reconciliation for Zing Co. as of March 31, 201X. Then prepare journal entries if needed.

Checkbook balance	$1,563	Outstanding checks	$654
Bank statement balance	1,200	Bank service charge	45
Deposits (in transit)	900	NSF: Mia Kaminsky's check in payment of account was returned for insufficient funds.	72

LO3 *(15 MIN)*   **6B-2.** In general journal form, prepare journal entries to establish a petty cash fund on January 1 and replenish it on January 31.

201X		
Jan.	1	A $107 petty cash fund is established.
	31	At the end of the month, $32 cash plus the following paid vouchers exist: donations expense, $22; postage expense, $13; office supplies expense, $22; miscellaneous expense, $18.

LO3 *(15 MIN)*   **6B-3.** If in Exercise 6B-2 cash on hand is $29, prepare the entry to replenish the petty cash on January 31.

LO3 *(15 MIN)*   **6B-4.** If in Exercise 6B-2 cash on hand is $35, prepare the entry to replenish the petty cash on January 31.

LO5 *(15 MIN)*   **6B-5.** At the end of the day the clerk for Jack's Variety Shop noticed an error in the amount of cash he should have. Total cash sales from the sales tape were $1,208, whereas the total cash in the register was $1,156. Jack keeps a $28 change fund in his shop. Prepare an appropriate general journal entry to record the cash sale as well as reveal the cash shortage.

Problems

Set A

6A-1. Slacks.com received a bank statement from Italian Bank indicating a bank balance of $7,600. Based on Slacks.com's check stubs, the ending checkbook balance was $8,767. Your task is to prepare a bank reconciliation for Slacks.com as of July 31, 201X, from the following information (journalize entries as needed):

LO2 *(20 MIN)*

Check Figure:
Reconciled Balance $8,500

   a. Checks outstanding: no. 122, $810; no. 130, $690.
   b. Deposits in transit, $2,400.
   c. Slacks.com forgot to record a $1,260 equipment purchase made with a debit card.
   d. Bank service charges, $40.
   e. Italian Bank collected a note for Slacks.com, $1,040, less a $7 collection fee.

6A-2. From the following bank statement, please (1) complete the bank reconciliation for Jimmy's Deli found on the reverse of the following bank statement and (2) journalize the appropriate entries as needed.

LO2 *(20 MIN)*

Check Figure:
Reconciled Balance $4,720

   a. A deposit of $1,600 is in transit.
   b. Jimmy's Deli has an ending checkbook balance of $5,730.
   c. Checks outstanding: no. 111, $450; no. 119, $1,400; no. 121, $390.
   d. Jim Rice's check for $1,000 bounced due to lack of sufficient funds.
   e. Bank Service Charge $10.

Bourne National Bank
Rio Mean Branch
Bugna, Texas
Jimmy's Deli
8811 2nd St.
Bugna, Texas

Old Balance	Checks and Other Withdrawals in Order of Payment		Deposits	Date	New Balance
6,700				2/2	6,700
	60.00	200.00		2/3	6,440
	90.00		320.00	2/10	6,670
	630.00		620.00	2/15	6,660
	1,000.00	NSF	240.00	2/20	5,900
	1,250.00		1,180.00	2/24	5,830
	680.00	10.00 SC	220.00	2/28	5,360

6A-3. The following transactions occurred in April for Joyous Co.:

LO3 *(30 MIN)*

Check Figure:
Cash Replenishment $69

201X
Apr.

  1 Issued check no. 14 for $125 to establish a petty cash fund.

  5 Paid $13 from petty cash for postage, voucher no. 1.

  8 Paid $16 from petty cash for office supplies, voucher no. 2.

  15 Issued check no. 15 to Real Bell Corp. for $240 from past purchases on account.

  17 Paid $16 from petty cash for office supplies, voucher no. 3.

  20 Issued check no. 16 to Angell Corp., $625 for past purchases on account.

  24 Paid $13 from petty cash for postage, voucher no. 4.

  26 Paid $11 from petty cash for local church donation, voucher no. 5 (a miscellaneous payment).

  28 Issued check no. 17 to Jay Moon to pay for office equipment, $725.

  30 Replenished petty cash, check no. 18.

Your tasks are to do the following:

1. Record the appropriate entries in the general journal as well as the auxiliary petty cash record as needed.
2. Replenish the petty cash fund on April 30 (check no. 18).

L03, 4, 5 *(40 MIN)*

6A-4. From the following, record the transactions in Burbanks's auxiliary petty cash record and general journal as needed:

Check Figure:
Cash Replenishment $137

201X		
Oct.	1	A check was drawn (no. 444) payable to Jane Janiak, petty cashier, to establish a $180 petty cash fund.
	5	Paid $26 for postage stamps, voucher no. 1.
	9	Paid $10 for delivery charges on goods for resale, voucher no. 2.
	12	Paid $18 for donation to a church (miscellaneous expense), voucher no. 3.
	14	Paid $12 for postage stamps, voucher no. 4.
	17	Paid $21 for delivery charges on goods for resale, voucher no. 5.
	27	Purchased computer supplies from petty cash for $18; voucher no. 6.
	28	Paid $20 for postage, voucher no. 7.
	29	Drew check no. 592 to replenish petty cash and a $12 shortage.

Set B

L02 *(20 MIN)*

6B-1. Slacks.com received a bank statement from French Bank indicating a balance of $8,200. Based on Slacks.com's check stubs, the ending checkbook balance was $9,000. Your task is to prepare a bank reconciliation for Slacks.com as of July 31, 201X, from the following information (journalize as needed):

Check Figure:
Reconciled Balance $8,730

a. Checks outstanding: no. 122, $850; no. 130, $720.
b. Deposits in transit, $2,100.
c. Slacks.com forgot to record a $1,300 equipment purchase made with a debit card.
d. Bank service charges, $55.
e. French bank collected a note for Slacks.com, $1,090, less a $5 collection fee.

L02 *(20 MIN)*

6B-2. From the following statement, please (1) complete the bank reconciliation for Jimmy's Deli found on the reverse of the bank statement and (2) journalize the appropriate entries as needed.

a. A deposit of $2,300 is in transit.
b. Jimmy's Deli has an ending checkbook balance of $4,470.
c. Checks outstanding: no. 111, $950; no. 119, $1,600; no. 121, $280.
d. Stanley Pennant's check for $1,500 bounced due to lack of sufficient funds.

Check Figure:
Reconciled Balance $2,910

Bourne National Bank
Rio Mean Branch
Bugna, Texas
Jimmy's Deli
8811 2nd St.
Bugna, Texas

Old Balance	Checks and Other Withdrawals in Order of Payment		Deposits	Date	New Balance
5,300				2/2	5,300
	70.00	230.00		2/3	5,000
	110.00		360.00	2/10	5,250
	540.00		530.00	2/15	5,240
	1,500.00	NSF	270.00	2/20	4,010
	1,350.00		1,250.00	2/24	3,910
	570.00	60.00 SC	160.00	2/28	3,440

6B-3. The following transactions occurred in April for Joyous Co.:

● **LO3** (*30 MIN*)

201X		
Apr.	1	Issued check no. 14 for $120 to establish a petty cash fund.
	5	Paid $10 from petty cash for postage, voucher no. 1.
	8	Paid $16 from petty cash for office supplies, voucher no. 2.
	15	Issued check no. 15 to Upright Corp. for $240 for past purchases on account.
	17	Paid $17 from petty cash for office supplies, voucher no. 3.
	20	Issued check no. 16 to Federer Corp. $500 for past purchases on account.
	24	Paid $15 from petty cash for postage, voucher no. 4.
	26	Paid $12 from petty cash for local church donation, voucher no. 5 (a miscellaneous payment).
	28	Issued check no. 17 to Josh Loon to pay for office equipment, $600.
	30	Replenished petty cash, check no. 18.

Check Figure:
Cash Replenishment $70

Your tasks are to do the following:

a. Record the appropriate entries in the general journal as well as the auxiliary petty cash record as needed

b. Be sure to replenish the petty cash fund on April 30 (check no. 18).

6B-4. From the following, record the transactions in Burbank's auxiliary petty cash record and general journal as needed:

●○○● **LO3, 4, 5** (*40 MIN*)

201X		
Oct.	1	A check was drawn (no. 444) payable to Eileen Cooper, petty cashier, to establish a $200 petty cash fund.
	5	Paid $20 for postage stamps, voucher no. 1.
	9	Paid $11 for delivery charges on goods for resale, voucher no. 2.
	12	Paid $16 for donation to a church (miscellaneous expense), voucher no. 3.
	14	Paid $10 for postage stamps, voucher no. 4.
	17	Paid $20 for delivery charges on goods for resale, voucher no. 5.
	27	Purchased computer supplies from petty cash for $25, voucher no. 6.
	28	Paid $13 for postage, voucher no. 7.
	29	Drew check no. 715 to replenish petty cash and a $5 shortage.

Check Figure:
Cash Replenishment $120

Financial Report Problem

● **LO2** (*15 MIN*)

Reading the Kellogg's Annual Report

Go to http://investor.kelloggs.com/annuals.cfm, to access the Kellogg's 2010 Annual Report. How often do you think Kellogg's reconciles its bank statement? What type of security control may be in place? Support your position.

ON the JOB |||||||||||||||||||||||||

MyAccountingLab

SANCHEZ COMPUTER CENTER

○○○ **LO2, 3, 4** (*60 MIN*)

The books have been closed for the first year of business for Sanchez Computer Center. The company ended up with a marginal profit for the first three months in operation. Tony expects faster growth as he enters a busy season.

Following is a list of transactions for the month of October. Petty Cash account #1010 and Miscellaneous Expense account #5100 have been added to the chart of accounts.

Oct.	1	Paid rent for November, December, and January, $1,200 (check no. 8108).
	2	Established a petty cash fund for $100.
	4	Collected $3,600 from a cash customer for building five systems.
	5	Collected $2,600, the amount due from A. Pitale's invoice no. 12674, customer on account.
	6	Purchased $25 worth of stamps using petty cash voucher no. 101.
	7	Withdrew $2,000 (check no. 8109) for personal use.
	8	Purchased $22 worth of supplies using petty cash voucher no. 102.
	12	Paid the newspaper carrier $10 using petty cash voucher no. 103.
	16	Paid the amount due on the September phone bill, $65 (check no. 8110).
	17	Paid the amount due on the September electric bill, $95 (check no. 8111).
	22	Performed computer services for Taylor Golf; billed the client $4,200 (invoice no. 12675).
	23	Paid $20 for computer paper using petty cash voucher no. 104.
	30	Took $15 out of petty cash for lunch, voucher no. 105.
	31	Replenished the petty cash. Coin and currency in drawer total $8.

Because Tony was so busy trying to close his books, he forgot to reconcile his last three months of bank statements. A list of all deposits and checks written for the past three months (each entry is identified by chapter, transaction date, or transaction letter) and the bank statements for July through September are provided. The statement for October won't arrive until the first week of November.

Assignment

1. Record the transactions in general journal or petty cash format.

2. Post the transactions to the general ledger accounts.

3. Prepare a trial balance.

4. Compare the Computer Center's deposits and checks with the bank statements and complete a bank reconciliation as of September 30, 201X.

Sanchez Computer Center Summary of Deposits and Checks

Chapter	Transaction	Payor/Payee	Amount
		Deposits	
1	a	Tony Freedman	$4,500
1	f	Cash customer	250
1	i	Taylor Golf	1,200
1	g	Cash customer	200
2	p	Cash customer	900
3	Sept. 2	Tonya Parker Jones	325
3	Sept. 6	Summer Lipe	220
3	Sept. 12	Jeannine Sparks	850
3	Sept. 26	Mike Hammer	140

Chapter	Transaction	Check #	Payor/Payee	Amount
			Checks	
1	b	8095	Multi Systems, Inc.	$1,200
1	c	8096	Office Furniture, Inc.	600
1	e	8097	Capital Management	400
1	j	8098	Tony Freedman	100
2	l	8099	Insurance Protection, Inc.	150
2	m	8100	Office Depot	200
2	n	8101	Computer Edge Magazine	1,400
2	q	8102	San Diego Electric	85
2	r	8103	U.S. Postmaster	50
3	Sept. 1	8104	Capital Management	1,200
3	Sept. 8	8105	Pacific Bell USA	155
3	Sept. 15	8106	Computer Connection	200
3	Sept. 16	8107	Multi Systems, Inc.	1,200

Bank Statement

First Union Bank 322 Glen Ave. Escondido, CA 92025

Sanchez Computer Center			Statement Date: July 22, 201X	
Checks Paid:			Deposits and Credits:	
Date paid	Number	Amount	Date received	Amount
7-4	8095	1,200.00	7-1	4,500.00
7-7	8096	600.00	7-10	250.00
7-15	8097	400.00	7-20	1,200.00
			7-21	200.00
Total 3 checks paid for $2,200.00			Total Deposits	$6,150.00
Ending balance on July 22—$3,950.00				

Received statement July 29, 201X.

Bank Statement

First Union Bank 322 Glen Ave. Escondido, CA 92025

Sanchez Computer Center			Statement Date: August 21, 201X	
Checks Paid:			Deposits and Credits:	
Date paid	Number	Amount	Date received	Amount
8-2	8098	100.00	8-12	900.00
8-3	8099	150.00		
8-10	8100	200.00		
8-15	8101	1,400.00		
8-20	8102	85.00		
Total 5 checks paid for $1,935.00			Total Deposits	$900.00
Beginning balance on July 22—$3,950.00			Ending balance on August 21—$2,915.00	

Received statement August 27, 201X.

Bank Statement

First Union Bank 322 Glen Ave. Escondido, CA 92025				
Sanchez Computer Center			**Statement Date: September 20, 201X**	
Checks Paid:			Deposits and Credits:	
Date paid	Number	Amount	Date received	Amount
9-2	8103	50.00	9-4	325.00
9-6	8104	1,200.00	9-7	220.00
9-12	8105	155.00	9-14	850.00
Total 3 checks paid for $1,405.00			Total Deposits	$1,395.00
Beginning balance on August 21			Ending balance on September 20	
$2,915.00			$2,905.00	

Received statement September 29, 201X.

SUBWAY CASE

Counting Down the Cash

Subway now requires all of its franchisees to submit their weekly sales and inventory reports electronically using new point-of-sale (POS) touch-screen cash registers. With the new POS registers, clerks use a touch screen to punch in the number and type of items bought. Franchisees can quickly reconfigure prices and products to match new promotions. Not only is this POS method faster than using the old cash registers, but it also allows franchisees to view every transaction as it occurs—from their own back office computers or even from home. Also, individual POS terminals within the restaurant are linked, so franchisees are able to see consolidated data quickly.

L01,2,3,4
(20 MIN)

The transition to electronic reporting and networked POS terminals, however, has not been without bumps, as Stan can testify. About six months before the deadline for all Subway franchisees to "go electronic," Stan attended a heated meeting on the topic at his local chapter of the North American Association of Subway Franchisees (NAASF). The NAASF is an independent organization of franchisees that serves as an advisory council on Subway policies and issues of common concern. Everyone seemed to be talking at once.

"I just don't trust these machines. What am I supposed to do when the system crashes?" complained one man.

"Yeah, and I don't like the idea of a bunch of kids knowing more about how to run the software than I do," said one older franchisee.

"Don't be so quick to assume that our sandwich artists will love POS," said one woman. "I overheard one of my employees say to another, 'POS means Peeking Over Shoulders.' These young kids we hire have more reason to be resistant than we do!"

"I'll say they do!" rejoined Jay Harden, the president of Stan's local NAASF. "Employee theft is one of the largest problems we face as franchisees. I, for one, really welcome the cash control we get with POS."

Stan had to agree with Jay. Training staff to record every sale and record it correctly is a critical component of a cash business such as Subway. In Stan's view, the POS machines would only make that training easier. Cash control is built into the new system, which also provides the owners with information that will help them spot problems—such as employee theft—and track trends. Of course, thought Stan, the chore of counting down the cash at the end of a shift remained. No matter what type of computer program you install, cash still must be counted down and rectified with the register tape at the end of each shift.

As the voices rang louder around him, Stan thought about what had happened that day when Ellen closed out her cash register drawer. He had spent hours figuring out a discrepancy between the cash in the drawer and the register tape. Ellen had forgotten to void a mistaken entry for $99.99. Stan had first suspected that she had made a huge error in counting change.

Thinking of errors in counting brought him back to the topic of the meeting. Stan raised his hand to speak.

"One thing that concerns me is the potential for accounting errors. I still have to key in data from the POS terminals into my Peachtree accounting software. Every time I have to reenter data, the potential for error multiplies."

"That shows good foresight, Stan," said Jay Harden. "We're actually exploring computer programs that will feed the data directly from the POS terminals into our accounting programs." Even some of the technophobes and POS skeptics in the group had to agree that it would be a great idea.

Discussion Questions

1. What is an advisory council? Why do you think franchisees need one?
2. Why do you think some small business owners fear computerization?
3. How would Stan catch a discrepancy in the Cash account? How would he record a loss?
4. Why does Subway invest time, money, and effort in investigating new cash handling systems such as its new POS terminals?

The internal control policies of a company will depend on things such as number of employees, company size, sources of cash, and usage of the Internet.

Calculating Pay and Payroll Taxes: The Beginning of the Payroll Process

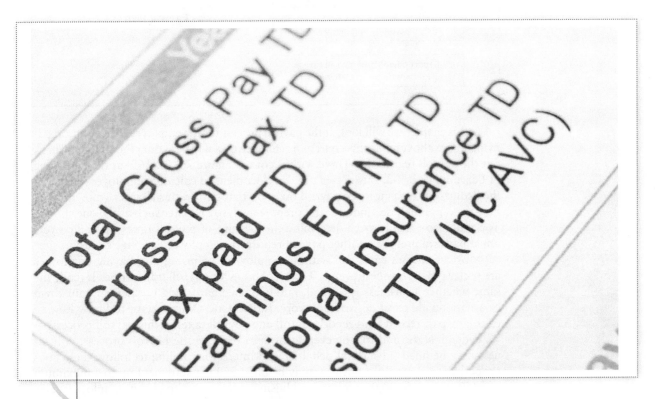

THE GAME PLAN

Wow! You just got your first paycheck from your new job at Sears. You had expected a check for $500 but were disappointed when you saw the check was for much less. You had forgotten about all the taxes withheld from your paycheck. Sears, like many other companies, has payroll departments that prepare its payrolls, which calculate employee earnings and proper amounts to be withheld for Social Security and Medicare, as well as state and federal income tax. Through the understanding of the payroll process in this chapter, you will learn the difference between gross pay and net pay. Generally speaking, gross pay is what you wish you had and net pay is what you actually get!

LEARNING OBJECTIVES

○ 1. Calculating gross pay, employee payroll tax deductions for federal income tax withholding, state income tax withholding, FICA (OASDI, Medicare), and net pay.

○ 2. Preparing a payroll register.

○ 3. Maintaining an employee earnings record.

○ 4. Calculating employer taxes for FICA (OASDI, Medicare), FUTA, SUTA, and workers' compensation insurance.

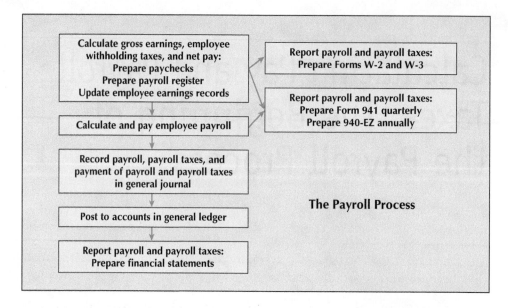

In this chapter we will look at the payroll process for the employer (see the accompanying figure above). Use this chart as a reference tool when reading the chapter. Check out the payroll register for Travelwithus.com in Figure 7.3 (p. 269) at the beginning of Learning Unit 7-2. Businesses use this document to calculate employees' pay and the deductions for employee payroll taxes on that pay. In this chapter you will learn how to compute these amounts and prepare a payroll register such as the one shown. You will also learn how to determine the amount of payroll taxes that employers must pay and prepare another payroll report, the employee earnings record.

Most businesses can't run without employees, so hiring and paying employees are pretty typical business events. The accounting for payroll transactions is really the same whether a business is a small, family-owned gardening business in your town or a nationwide retail department store. Either way, it's important to know how to calculate, pay, record, and report payroll and payroll taxes in this payroll process.

Federal, state, and maybe even local laws regulate the payroll process. A business may be fined substantial penalties and interest for failing to follow these laws properly. For example, a business may be fined $50 per statement up to a maximum of $250,000, or $100,000 for a small business, for failing to give its employees their W-2 forms, Wage and Tax Statements after August 31 of the calendar year following the tax year. Because of this, there are many companies, such as ADP, Paychex, and Ceridian, that will handle payroll for a fee. However, it is often less costly for the business to do these tasks itself.

In this chapter we take a close look at the employees of Travelwithus.com, a new Internet-based company that makes travel arrangements for its customers, to see how a payroll is figured and recorded. Travelwithus.com specializes in two types of travel, cruises and business travel. We look at how its payroll is affected by federal, state, and local taxes and how the accountant at Travelwithus.com handles payroll transactions for the company.

LO1   LEARNING UNIT 7-1 CALCULATION OF GROSS EARNINGS, EMPLOYEE WITHHOLDING TAXES, AND NET PAY

Katherine Kurtz is the accountant for Travelwithus.com who calculates and records each payroll for the company. Several parts of Katherine's job are especially important. First, Katherine must be accurate in everything she does, because any mistake she makes in working with the payroll may affect both the employee and the company. Second, Katherine needs to be on time when working on the company's payroll so that employees get their paychecks as expected and governments receive payroll taxes when due. Third, Katherine must at all times obey the appropriate federal, state, and local laws governing payroll matters. Fourth, because processing payroll involves personal employee information such as pay rates and marital status, Katherine always needs to keep payroll data confidential.

Gross Earnings

To begin the payroll process, Katherine must first calculate the earnings for Travelwithus.com's employees. To make the correct calculations, Katherine must know how each employee has been classified for payroll purposes. As a rule, a company will classify every employee either as "hourly" or "salaried." If an employee is an hourly employee, that employee only will be paid for the hours he or she worked. Employees classified as salaried employees receive a fixed dollar amount for the time period worked.

Travelwithus.com classified three of its six employees as hourly. For these three employees, Katherine must compute the hours they worked during a specific time period known as a pay period; the number of hours determines how much each has earned. For payroll purposes, pay periods are defined as daily, weekly, biweekly (every two weeks), semimonthly (twice each month), monthly, quarterly, or annually. A pay period can start on any day of the week and must end after the specified period of time has passed. Most companies use weekly, biweekly, semimonthly, or monthly pay periods when calculating their payrolls.

Companies can use different pay periods for different groups of employees. Travelwithus.com chose a biweekly pay period for its hourly employees and a monthly pay period for its salaried employees. The biweekly pay period starts on Monday and ends two weeks later on a Sunday. Hourly employees actually receive their paychecks on the following Friday because it takes Katherine a few days to calculate all of the amounts involved in paying an hourly payroll. The monthly pay period starts on the first day of the calendar month and ends on the last day of that month. Salaried employees will be paid on the last day of the month. Because they receive a fixed amount of pay, Katherine is able to calculate these payroll amounts much faster than the hourly ones and can even start these calculations before the month ends.

Now that Katherine knows the pay period for Travelwithus.com's hourly employees, she calculates their total or gross earnings. Gross earnings are calculated by adding the regular earnings for an employee for the period to any overtime earnings the employee has earned for that period.

Overtime earnings must be computed according to federal law. The federal law that governs overtime earnings is called the Fair Labor Standards Act and is sometimes referred to as the **Federal Wage and Hour Law.** An employer must follow the Fair Labor Standards Act if it is involved in interstate commerce, in other words, if it is doing business in more than one state. For most employers, this law says that an hourly employee must be paid at least one and a half times his or her regular pay rate for any hours he or she works over 40 in one workweek. A workweek, according to the law, is a seven-day (or 168-hour) period that can start at any time, but once the starting time for the week is determined, it must stay the same for each week.

It is important to know that some states also have payroll laws that need to be followed in determining pay. For example, California requires employers to pay overtime pay to hourly employees who have worked more than 8 hours in any day, even if they work less than 40 hours total for that week. Employers must follow both sets of laws, and in this case, Travelwithus.com would pay overtime if an employee works more than 8 hours in one day and if an employee works more than 40 hours in one week.

Hourly employees of Travelwithus.com have two workweeks in each biweekly pay period. Travelwithus.com's hourly workweek starts on Monday morning at 12:01 A.M. each week and ends seven days later on Sunday evening at 12:00 midnight. Thus, Katherine must calculate overtime pay for any employee who worked more than 40 hours in each week of this two-week period.

Stephanie Higuera is one of the three hourly employees working for Travelwithus. com. Travelwithus.com's most recent biweekly pay period began on Monday, October 16, at 12:01 A.M. and ended on Sunday, October 29 at 12:00 midnight. The first week of this period ended on Sunday, October 22, and during this week Stephanie worked 44 hours. During the second week that ended on October 29, Stephanie worked 38 hours.

Pay or payroll period A length of time used by an employer to calculate the amount of an employee's earnings. Pay periods can be daily, weekly, biweekly (once every two weeks), semimonthly (twice each month), monthly, quarterly, or annual.

Gross earnings (gross pay) Amount of pay received before any deductions.

Fair Labor Standards Act (Federal Wage and Hour Law) A law the majority of employers must follow that contains rules stating the minimum hourly rate of pay and the maximum number of hours a worker will work before being paid time and a half for overtime hours worked. This law also has other rules and regulations that employers must follow for payroll purposes.

Interstate commerce A test that is applied to determine whether an employer must follow the rules of the Fair Labor Standards Act. If an employer communicates or does business with another business in some other state, it is usually considered to be involved in interstate commerce.

Workweek A seven-day (168-hour) period used to determine overtime hours for employees. A workweek can begin on any given day, but must end seven days later.

How much should she be paid? Katherine will answer this question by first calculating both Stephanie's regular hours and her overtime hours. According to the federal law, Katherine must look at each week separately. Stephanie worked 44 hours during the first week, which means that she worked 40 regular hours and 4 overtime hours. Because she worked fewer than 40 hours in the second week, all of these hours are regular hours.

Week No.	Week Ending	Regular Hours	Overtime Hours	Total Hours
1	October 22	40	4	44
2	October 29	38	0	38
Total		78	4	82

Stephanie earns $11.40 for each hour she works, so Katherine computes Stephanie's pay as follows:

$11.40 regular rate × 1.5 = $17.10 overtime rate
78 regular hours × $11.40 regular rate = $889.20 regular earnings
4 overtime hours × $17.10 overtime rate =   68.40 overtime earnings
$889.20 regular earnings + $68.40 overtime earnings = $957.60 gross earnings

Or, Katherine could figure Stephanie's pay this way: [SAME]

$11.40 regular rate × 0.5 = $5.70 extra pay for
    each overtime hour
82 total hours × $11.40 regular rate = $934.80 earnings at the regular rate
4 overtime hours × $5.70 extra pay for each
    overtime hour =   22.80 extra earnings
$934.80 earnings at the regular rate + $22.80
    extra earnings = $957.60 gross earnings

Notice that either way, Katherine computed exactly the same amount of gross earnings. The advantage of using the first method is that it clearly shows the amount of extra money that Stephanie earned from working those additional overtime hours. The advantage of the second is that it shows the effect of being paid at a higher, overtime rate for those extra hours worked.

Julia Regan also works for Travelwithus.com. She, however, is a salaried employee, and earns $4,875 per month. As a salaried (one example of an exempt) employee, she is not eligible for overtime pay, and Katherine will list her total earnings for the month of October as $4,875. To be considered a salaried employee, Julia must qualify as a salaried employee according to the specifics of the Fair Labor Standards Act. Thus, Travelwithus.com can't decide to classify employees as salaried just to avoid paying the overtime pay; these employees must be salaried persons according to this law.

Federal Income Tax Withholding

After Katherine determines Stephanie's and Julia's gross earnings, she figures out how much each of them will actually receive in their paychecks after several different taxes have been withheld. These taxes are called payroll taxes and must be paid by the employees. Employees pay these amounts by having them taken out, or withheld, from their paychecks. Their employer then sends them to the Internal Revenue Service (IRS), state governments, and maybe even local governments so they count against the amount of federal, state, and possible local income taxes that the employees will owe for the year.

In this way, Stephanie and Julia pay their taxes on a "pay as you go basis." In other words, when Stephanie and Julia complete their federal income tax returns at the end of the year, they will deduct the amount of income tax withheld during the year from the total amount owed for the year. How and when Travelwithus.com turns these amounts over to the federal, state, and local governments will be discussed in Chapter 8. Katherine computes the amount of taxes to be withheld based on each employee's gross earnings for the pay period.

Katherine starts figuring out how much to withhold from each employee's pay by looking at the W-4 that he or she completed. The IRS Form W-4, Employee's Withholding Allowance Certificate, is completed by every employee and provides information that will be used to determine the amount of federal income tax (FIT) withholdings. Figure 7.1 (p. 264) is Stephanie's W-4 form. Notice that it shows Stephanie's marital status and total number of allowances she claims for federal income tax purposes. Usually, an employee may claim one allowance for himself or herself, one for his or her spouse, and one for each of his or her dependents, such as a child. Employees who want more withheld from their paychecks can claim fewer allowances than they really have. However, they are not allowed to claim more allowances than they really have to avoid underpaying taxes owed, which may also result in them owing the government amounts for penalties and interest.

To look up the amount of federal income tax that needs to be withheld from Stephanie's paycheck, Katherine uses Stephanie's marital status and the number of claimed allowances listed on her Form W-4. She also uses Stephanie's gross earnings for the pay period and the length of the pay period. The amount of federal income tax that needs to be withheld is listed in a wage bracket table that can be found in the IRS publication called Circular E, *Employer's Tax Guide*, also known as Publication 15. Check out one of the tables from the Circular that's shown in Figure 7.2. Notice from the heading "SINGLE Persons—BIWEEKLY Payroll Period" that this table applies to single persons who are paid biweekly. Wage bracket tables are prepared according to marital status and pay period; Circular E has a similar table for married persons who are paid biweekly, as well as tables for single and married persons who are paid daily, weekly, monthly, semimonthly, monthly, quarterly, and annually. Also notice that the table has rows for different ranges of gross pay, starting from lower amounts of pay in the top rows of the table to higher amounts in the bottom rows.

Katherine determines the amount of federal income tax that needs to be withheld from Stephanie's paycheck by first locating the correct table in Circular E. She finds the table for single persons who are paid biweekly. Then, she locates the row that says "At least $940 but less than $960." Stephanie's gross pay for this pay period is $957.60, so this row applies to her. Katherine traces this row to the column for one withholding allowance, and finds that the amount of withholding tax is $93. Based on Stephanie's gross earnings of $957.60 and her one claimed allowance, Katherine will withhold $93 in federal income taxes from Stephanie's pay.

What if Stephanie had earned $960 instead of 957.60? Would the amount of federal income tax withheld be the same? No, Katherine would have withheld $96. To see this, check out the heading for the columns showing the wages. Notice that it says, "If the wages are—." Katherine will look at the rows of wage ranges, stopping when she sees the line that says, "At least $940 but less than $960." If Stephanie's gross wages are exactly $960—not less than $960—Katherine must go to the next line, which says, "At least $960 but less than $980" and withhold the amount in the column for one withholding allowance, which is $96.

State Income Tax Withholding

Most states also charge their residents an income tax based on the amount of money they earn from their employers. In 2011, only Alaska, Florida, Nevada, South Dakota, Texas, Washington, and Wyoming do not. (Technically, New Hampshire and Tennessee also do not have a state income tax; it is only imposed on interest and dividends.) So, in addition to withholding federal income taxes, Katherine may also have to determine amounts for state income tax (SIT) withholding. Fortunately for Katherine, the process for withholding state income tax is much the same as it is for withholding federal income tax. In many states, withholding amounts are based on the same information that is listed in the employee's W-4, although some states do have their own versions of this form that are used instead. Employers use state publications similar to the federal Publication 15 to figure the amount to be withheld

Form W-4 (Employee's Withholding Allowance Certificate) A form filled out by employees and used by employers to supply needed information about the number of allowances claimed, marital status, and so forth. The form is used for payroll purposes to determine federal income tax withholding from an employee's paycheck.

Federal income tax (FIT) withholding Amount of federal income tax withheld by the employer from the employee's gross pay; the amount withheld is determined by the employee's gross pay, the pay period, the number of allowances claimed by the employee on the W-4 form, and the marital status indicated on the W-4 form.

Allowances (also called exemptions) Certain dollar amounts of a person's income tax that will be considered nontaxable for income tax withholding purposes.

Circular E An IRS tax publication of tax tables.

Wage bracket table One of various charts in IRS Circular E that provide information about deductions for federal income tax based on earnings and data supplied on the W-4 form.

State income tax (SIT) withholding Amount of state income tax withheld by the employer from the employee's gross pay.

FIGURE 7.1
Completed Form W-4

Form **W-4**	*Cut here and give Form W-4 to your employer. Keep the top part for your records.*	
Department of the Treasury Internal Revenue Service	**Employee's Withholding Allowance Certificate** ▲ **Whether you are entitled to claim a certain number of allowances or exemption from withholding is subject to review by the IRS.** Your employer may be required to send a copy of this form to the IRS.	OMB No. 1545-0074 **201X**

1 Type or print your first name and middle initial.	Last name	2 Your social security number
Stephanie A.	*Higuera*	123 : 45 : 6789

Home address (number and street or rural route)	3 ☒ Single ☐ Married ☐ Married, but withhold at higher Single rate.
104 Inverness Way	Note. If married, but legally separated, or spouse is a nonresident alien, check the "Single" box.
City or town, state, and ZIP code	4 If your last name differs from that shown on your social security card, check here. You must call 1-800-772-1213 for a new card. ▲ ☐
Southside, MA 01945	

5	Total number of allowances you are claiming (from line **H** above **or** from the applicable worksheet on page 2)	5	*1*
6	Additional amount, if any, you want withheld from each paycheck	6	$
7	I claim exemption from withholding for 2006, and I certify that I meet **both** of the following conditions for exemption.		
	• Last year I had a right to a refund of **all** federal income tax withheld because I had **no** tax liability **and**		
	• This year I expect a refund of **all** federal income tax withheld because I expect to have **no** tax liability.		
	If you meet both conditions, write "Exempt" here ▲	7	

Under penalties of perjury, I declare that I have examined this certificate and to the best of my knowledge and belief, it is true, correct, and complete.
Employee's signature
(Form is not valid unless you sign it.) ▲ *Stephanie A. Higuera*   Date ▲ *January 3, 201X*

8	Employer's name and address (Employer: Complete lines 8 and 10 only if sending to the IRS.)	9 Office code (optional)	10 Employer identification number (EIN)

For Privacy Act and Paperwork Reduction Act Notice, see page 2.   Cat. No. 10220Q   Form **W-4** (201X)

for state income taxes. However, because the 43 states can differ significantly in the way they calculate income tax, we will keep our discussion simple by assuming that state income tax is a fixed percentage of employee earnings. For our example we use an 8% tax rate. So Katherine calculates Stephanie's SIT withholding at $76.61.

Other Income Tax Withholding

We pointed out previously that employees would have state income taxes withheld from their paychecks if they live in one of the 43 states that charges such a tax. In addition, many cities and counties tax employee earnings. Sometimes the tax will be a percentage of gross earnings much like federal income tax, or it may be a fixed dollar amount that the employer will withhold from every pay period. These cities and counties have their own rules regarding payroll tax deposits and tax reports for this type of withholding tax. A state tax rate of 8% will be used in the example in this chapter.

FIGURE 7.2

Wage Bracket Tables: Single Persons—Biweekly Payroll Period

(For Wages Paid through December 2011)

And the wages are –		And the number of withholding allowances claimed is —										
At least	But less than	0	1	2	3	4	5	6	7	8	9	10
		The amount of income tax to be withheld is —										
$800	$820	$93	$72	$50	$30	$16	$2	$0	$0	$0	$0	$0
820	840	96	75	53	32	18	4	0	0	0	0	0
840	860	99	78	56	35	20	6	0	0	0	0	0
860	880	102	81	59	38	22	8	0	0	0	0	0
880	900	105	84	62	41	24	10	0	0	0	0	0
900	920	108	87	65	44	26	12	0	0	0	0	0
920	940	111	90	68	47	28	14	0	0	0	0	0
940	960	114	93	71	50	30	16	2	0	0	0	0
960	980	117	96	74	53	32	18	4	0	0	0	0
980	1,000	120	99	77	56	35	20	6	0	0	0	0
1,000	1,020	123	102	80	59	38	22	8	0	0	0	0
1,020	1,040	126	105	83	62	41	24	10	0	0	0	0
1,040	1,060	129	108	86	65	44	26	12	0	0	0	0
1,060	1,080	132	111	89	68	47	28	14	0	0	0	0
1,080	1,100	135	114	92	71	50	30	16	1	0	0	0
1,100	1,120	138	117	95	74	53	32	18	3	0	0	0
1,120	1,140	141	120	98	77	56	34	20	5	0	0	0
1,140	1,160	144	123	101	80	59	37	22	7	0	0	0
1,160	1,180	147	126	104	83	62	40	24	9	0	0	0
1,180	1,200	150	129	107	86	65	43	26	11	0	0	0
1,200	1,220	153	132	110	89	68	46	28	13	0	0	0
1,220	1,240	156	135	113	92	71	49	30	15	1	0	0
1,240	1,260	159	138	116	95	74	52	32	17	3	0	0
1,260	1,280	162	141	119	98	77	55	34	19	5	0	0
1,280	1,300	165	144	122	101	80	58	37	21	7	0	0
1,300	1,320	168	147	125	104	83	61	40	23	9	0	0
1,320	1,340	171	150	128	107	86	64	43	25	11	0	0
1,340	1,360	174	153	131	110	89	67	46	27	13	0	0
1,360	1,380	177	156	134	113	92	70	49	29	15	1	0
1,380	1,400	180	159	137	116	95	73	52	31	17	3	0
1,400	1,420	183	162	140	119	98	76	55	34	19	5	0
1,420	1,440	188	165	143	122	101	79	58	37	21	7	0
1,440	1,460	193	168	146	125	104	82	61	40	23	9	0
1,460	1,480	198	171	149	128	107	85	64	43	25	11	0
1,480	1,500	203	174	152	131	110	88	67	46	27	13	0
1,500	1,520	208	177	155	134	113	91	70	49	29	15	1
1,520	1,540	213	180	158	137	116	94	73	52	31	17	3
1,540	1,560	218	183	161	140	119	97	76	55	33	19	5
1,560	1,580	223	188	164	143	122	100	79	58	36	21	7
1,580	1,600	228	193	167	146	125	103	82	61	39	23	9
1,600	1,620	233	198	170	149	128	106	85	64	42	25	11
1,620	1,640	238	203	173	152	131	109	88	67	45	27	13
1,640	1,660	243	208	176	155	134	112	91	70	48	29	15
1,660	1,680	248	213	179	158	137	115	94	73	51	31	17
1,680	1,700	253	218	182	161	140	118	97	76	54	33	19
1,700	1,720	258	223	187	164	143	121	100	79	57	36	21
1,720	1,740	263	228	192	167	146	124	103	82	60	39	23
1,740	1,760	268	233	197	170	149	127	106	85	63	42	25
1,760	1,780	273	238	202	173	152	130	109	88	66	45	27
1,780	1,800	278	243	207	176	155	133	112	91	69	48	29
1,800	1,820	283	248	212	179	158	136	115	94	72	51	31
1,820	1,840	288	253	217	182	161	139	118	97	75	54	33
1,840	1,860	293	258	222	187	164	142	121	100	78	57	36
1,860	1,880	298	263	227	192	167	145	124	103	81	60	39
1,880	1,900	303	268	232	197	170	148	127	106	84	63	42
1,900	1,920	308	273	237	202	173	151	130	109	87	66	45
1,920	1,940	313	278	242	207	176	154	133	112	90	69	48
1,940	1,960	318	283	247	212	179	157	136	115	93	72	51
1,960	1,980	323	288	252	217	182	160	139	118	96	75	54
1,980	2,000	328	293	257	222	186	163	142	121	99	78	57
2,000	2,020	333	298	262	227	191	166	145	124	102	81	60
2,020	2,040	338	303	267	232	196	169	148	127	105	84	63
2,040	2,060	343	308	272	237	201	172	151	130	108	87	66
2,060	2,080	348	313	277	242	206	175	154	133	111	90	69
2,080	2,100	353	318	282	247	211	178	157	136	114	93	72

$2,100 and over   Use Table 2(a) for a **SINGLE** person on page 36. Also see the instructions on page 35.

Employee Withholding for Social Security Taxes

In addition to withholding federal and, probably, state income tax, Katherine must also compute and withhold Social Security tax from Travelwithus.com employees. Social Security tax is also known as FICA because it was created by a 1935 federal law called the Federal Insurance Contribution Act. The law became effective in 1937. Ever since then, employers have been required to withhold amounts from employees' pay and turn them over to the federal government. The government then uses these amounts to make the following payments:

- Monthly retirement benefits for persons over 62 years old
- Medical benefits for persons over 65 years old
- Benefits for persons who have become disabled
- Benefits for families of deceased workers who were covered by this law

Before the amount of taxes withheld from employees' pay can be calculated, we need to know a few things about the Social Security (or FICA) tax. First, the tax is really two taxes. One tax is called the old-age, survivor's, and disability insurance (OASDI) tax and the other is known as Medicare. Sometimes people talk about the two taxes as though they were one, but it is key to know that they are actually separate, because each tax is calculated differently. Also know that OASDI puts a limit on the amount of tax that an employee must pay by setting a maximum dollar amount of earnings that can be taxed, and this amount is called the wage base. The same is not true of Medicare; all wages earned are subject to the Medicare tax. The OASDI and Medicare tax rates and the OASDI wage base amount are all set by the federal government; the OASDI wage base increases as the federal government calculated cost-of-living increases in each calendar year. The amounts for 2011 are as follows:

Tax	2011 Tax Rate	2011 Wage Base**
OASDI	6.2%*	$106,800
Medicare	1.45%	None

Katherine begins to calculate the amount of Social Security tax that needs to be withheld from Stephanie's pay by looking at Stephanie's current and year-to-date (YTD) gross earnings. She needs to know the amount of earnings from the current pay period so that she can calculate the current amount of taxes. However, she also needs to know the YTD earnings so that she can see whether Stephanie has reached the maximum amount of OASDI tax yet or if Stephanie will reach it in this pay period. So far in this calendar year, Stephanie has earned a total of $19,471.20. This amount includes the $957.60 that she has earned for the most recent biweekly pay period.

Katherine calculates Stephanie's OASDI and Medicare taxes as follows:

$957.60 gross earnings × 6.2% OASDI tax rate = $59.37 OASDI tax

$957.60 gross earnings × 1.45% Medicare tax rate = $13.89 Medicare tax

Because Stephanie has earned less than the wage base limit of $106,800, all of her earnings for the current pay period are taxable. But what if Stephanie had earned more this year so far? Suppose she had earned $106,140 before this pay period. With her current earnings of $957.60, she would have earned a total of $107,097.60 for the year thus far, which is more than the wage base limit of $106,800. In that case, Katherine would have calculated the amount of OASDI tax to be withheld from Stephanie's pay by first calculating the amount of taxable earnings for the current period:

Stephanie's YTD earnings before this pay period	$106,140.00
Plus: Stephanie's current earnings	957.60
Stephanie's YTD earnings after this pay period	$107,097.60

FICA (Federal Insurance Contributions Act) Part of the Social Security Act of 1935, this law taxes both the employer and employee up to a certain maximum rate and wage base for OASDI tax purposes. It also taxes both the employer and employee for Medicare purposes, but this tax has no wage base maximum.

Calendar year A one-year period beginning on January 1 and ending on December 31. Employers must use a calendar year for payroll purposes, even if the employer uses a fiscal year for financial statements and for any other reason.

COACHING TIP

Medicare unlike OASDI does not have a wage base, all gross earnings are subject to taxation.

---

*The OASDI employee tax rate has been reduced to 4.2% for calendar year 2011 as a part of an economic stimulus plan. All calculations in this textbook will be based on the tax rate of 6.2%.

**The OASDI wage base in 2011 is $106,800 and is scheduled to increase to $110,100 on January 1, 2012.

Less: 2011 OASDI tax wage base limit	106,800.00
Stephanie's earnings above the limit, and thus, not taxable	$297.60 ◄
Stephanie's current earnings	$957.60
Less: Stephanie's earnings above the limit, and thus, not OASDI taxable	297.60 ◄
Stephanie's current OASDI taxable earnings	$660.00

Now Katherine would calculate the amount of OASDI tax as follows:

$660.00 current taxable earnings × 6.2% OASDI tax rate = $40.92 OASDI tax

Stephanie has now reached the maximum amount of taxable wages (taxable earnings), which means she is done paying OASDI tax for the calendar year. What if Stephanie had already earned $106,800 or more before the current pay period? In that case, none of Stephanie's current gross earnings would be subject to OASDI tax. In other words, Stephanie would already have paid her maximum OASDI tax for the year by paying tax on the money she made up to this $106,800 wage base limit. What about next year? Both Social Security taxes are calculated on a calendar year basis, and Stephanie would have to start paying the OASDI tax again until she reached the maximum for that year.

What about the Medicare tax? Would the current amount tax that Stephanie needs to pay for this tax change too? No. Because the Medicare tax does not limit the amount of earnings that can be taxed, all of Stephanie's earnings will be taxable. In other words, even if Stephanie had already earned $106,800 this year, all of her current earnings of $957.60 would be taxable and she would still have $13.89 withheld from her current paycheck for the Medicare tax.

Taxable earnings Shows amount of earnings subject to a tax. The tax itself is not shown.

Other Withholdings

Sometimes employees have additional amounts withheld from their paychecks for various reasons. For example, they may choose to buy medical insurance for themselves and maybe even their spouse and dependents through an insurance plan offered by their employer. Sometimes the employer pays the premium for this insurance coverage, or at least pays for the part of the premium that covers the employee. Even if the employer pays some of the premium, however, it is common for the employee to pay the rest. The employee pays this premium by having it withheld from his or her pay, just as the employee pays income and Social Security taxes by having these amounts withheld by the employer. Travelwithus.com currently offers this opportunity to its employees, and the cost to the hourly employee is $33 for each pay period. Other companies may allow their employees to have funds withheld from their paychecks for union dues, retirement plan contributions, or lfe insurance premiums.

Medical insurance Health care insurance for which premiums may be paid through a deduction from an employee's paycheck.

Net Pay

Katherine's next step in the payroll accounting process is to calculate the amount of pay that Stephanie will actually receive as her paycheck; this amount is called net pay. At this point, Katherine has computed all of the amounts necessary to determine Stephanie's net pay. Now she simply needs to combine them as follows:

Net pay Gross earnings, less deductions. Net pay, or take-home pay, is what the worker actually takes home.

Gross earnings for the current biweekly pay period:		$957.60
Deductions for employee withholding taxes:		
Federal income tax	$93.00	
State income tax	76.61	
OASDI tax	59.37	
Medicare tax	13.89	
Medical insurance	33.00	
Total deductions		275.87
Net pay		$681.73

LEARNING UNIT 7-1 REVIEW

AT THIS POINT you should be able to do the following:

- Explain the purpose of the Fair Labor Standards Act (i.e., the Federal Wage and Hour Law).
- Calculate regular, overtime, and total gross pay.
- Complete a W-4 form.
- Discuss the term *claiming an allowance*.
- Use a wage-bracket tax table to determine the amount of federal income tax withholding.
- Define the purpose of the Social Security (FICA) taxes, OASDI, and Medicare.
- Calculate withholdings for OASDI and Medicare taxes.
- Calculate net pay.

Instant Replay · Self-Review Quiz 7-1

Tony Kagaragis is an hourly software engineer who is paid biweekly. He earns $23.00 per hour. In the first week of the most recent pay period, he worked 39 hours, and during the second week of the period he worked 46 hours. Please calculate his regular, overtime, and gross earnings.

Solutions to Instant Replay: Self-Review Quiz 7-1

1. $23.00 regular rate × 79 regular hours = $1,817.00 regular earnings
2. $23.00 regular rate × 1½ = $34.50 overtime rate. $34.50 overtime rate × 6 overtime hours = $207.00 overtime earnings
3. $1,817.00 + $207.00 = $2,024.00 gross earnings

LEARNING UNIT 7-2 PREPARING A PAYROLL REGISTER AND EMPLOYEE EARNING RECORDLO3. $34.50 overtime rate

At this point, Katherine Kurtz, the accountant for Travelwithus.com, knows how much each of the three hourly employees earned for the most recent biweekly pay period and how many dollars of taxes need to be withheld from their paychecks. She now needs to enter this information into the accounting records for the company. Two primary records are used in accounting systems to keep track of payroll information for a company. The first of these records is a worksheet, known as a payroll register, which shows all information related to an entire pay period. The second record is called the employee earnings record and is used to keep track of an individual employee's payroll history for an entire calendar year.

⬤ LO2   The Payroll Register

Payroll register A multicolumn form that is used to record payroll data.

Katherine enters information about the current payroll period for hourly employees in a payroll register. The register includes each employee's gross earnings, employee withholding taxes, net pay, taxable earnings, cumulative earnings, and the accounts to be charged (Business Scheduling or Cruise Scheduling) for the salary and wage expense for that pay period. Travelwithus.com will actually have two registers, a biweekly one for its hourly employees and a monthly one for its salaried personnel. Figure 7.3 shows the completed payroll register for the hourly payroll covering the biweekly pay period from October 16 through October 29.

FIGURE 7.3
Payroll Register

TRAVELWITHUS.COM INC.
HOURLY EMPLOYEE PAYROLL REGISTER
OCTOBER 16 – 29

Employee / Social Security No.	Allowances and Marital Status	Previous Earnings (YTD)	Current Earnings — Regular			Current Earnings — Overtime			Gross	Current Earnings (YTD)
			Hours	Rate	Amount	Hours	Rate	Amount		
Higuera, Stephanie 123-45-6789	S-1	1851360	78	1140	88920	4	1710	6840	95760	1947120
Sui, Annie 123-45-6788	S-0	2112100	80	1515	121200	4	2273	9090	130290	342390
Taylor, Harold 123-45-6787	S-2	1904370	78	1210	94380	4	1815	7260	101640	2006010
TOTALS					304500			23190	327690	4295520

Marital Status and No. of allowances are from Employee's W-4.
Previous YTD earnings = the employee's total earnings for the year before this pay period.
Regular Hours x Regular Rate = Regular Amount.
Overtime Hours x Overtime Rate = Overtime Amount.
Regular Amount + Overtime Amount = Gross Current Earnings.
Previous YTD Earnings + Gross Current Earnings = Current YTD Earnings.

Taxable Earnings, FUTA/SUTA = Gross Current Earnings < FUTA/SUTA limit of $7,000.
Taxable Earnings, OASDI = GrossCurrent Earnings < OASDI Limit of $$106,800.
FIT = FIT from wage Bracket Table in Circular E.
SIT = Gross Current Earnings x 8%.
FICA, OASDI = Taxable Earnings, OASDI x 6.2%.
FICA, Medicare =Gross Current Earnings x 1.45%.
Medical Insurance = $33 per employee.
Net Pay = Gross Current Earnings – FIT – SIT – OASDI – Medicare – Medical Insurance.

TRAVELWITHUS.COM INC.
HOURLY EMPLOYEE PAYROLL REGISTER
OCTOBER 16 – 29

Employee / Social Security No.	Taxable Earnings — FUTA/SUTA	Taxable Earnings — OASDI	Deductions — FIT	Deductions — SIT	Deductions — FICA OASDI	Deductions — FICA Medicare	Deductions — Medical Insurance	Net Pay	Check No.	Account Charged — Business Scheduling Expense	Account Charged — Cruise Scheduling Expense
Higuera, Stephanie 123-45-6789	—	95760	9300	7661	5937	1389	3300	68173	820	95760	
Sui, Annie 123-45-6788	130290	130290	16800	10423	8078	1889	3300	89800	821		130290
Taylor, Harold 123-45-6787	—	101640	8000	8131	6302	1474	3300	74433	822		101640
TOTALS	130290	327690	34100	26215	20317	4752	9900	232406		95760	231930

⬤ LO3   The Employee Earnings Record

After Katherine prepares the payroll register for the period, and in order to comply with all applicable employment laws and regulations, she also completes a payroll record known as the individual employee earnings record. This record provides a summary of each employee's earnings, withholding taxes, net pay, and cumulative earnings during each calendar year, as shown in Figure 7.4 on page 271. Katherine uses the information summarized in this record to prepare quarterly and annual payroll tax reports. Thus, the employee earnings record is split into calendar quarters, with each quarter being 13 weeks long.

Individual employee earnings record An accounting document that summarizes the total amount of wages paid and the deductions for the calendar year. It aids in preparing governmental reports. A new record is prepared for each employee each year.

COACHING TIP

The Payroll Register is prepared first and provides data for the preparation of the Employee Earnings Record.

LEARNING UNIT 7-2 REVIEW

AT THIS POINT you should be able to do the following:

- Explain and prepare a payroll register.
- Explain the purpose of the taxable earnings columns of the register and explain how they relate to the cumulative earnings column.
- Update an individual employee earnings record.

↙ Instant Replay ◔ Self-Review Quiz 7-2

Mike Chen is an hourly employee who is paid biweekly. He is paid overtime at a rate of 1½ times his hourly rate for any hours he works over 40 in a workweek. Mike worked many overtime hours this year to develop a Web site for his employer, and as of December 10 his cumulative earnings total $105,578.06. For the pay period ending on December 24, Mike's gross earnings are $1,940.85. Calculate Mike's net pay based on the following facts:

- Mike is single and claims three withholding allowances per his Form W-4. Use the tax table in Figure 7.2 on page 265. to find Mike's federal income tax withholding amount.
- The state income tax rate is 8% with no wage base limit.
- The OASDI tax rate is 6.2% with a wage base limit of $106,800 for the year; the Medicare rate is 1.45% with no wage base limit.
- Mike pays $44.00 for medical insurance for the pay period.

Solutions to Instant Replay: Self-Review Quiz 7-2

1. Federal income tax = $212.00 (Look at the "At least $1,940" line and trace it into the "3" withholding allowance column.)
2. State income tax is $155.27 ($1,940.85 × .08)
3. FICA OASDI tax is $75.76 ($106,800 − $105,578.06 = $1,221.94 taxable; $1,221.94 × .062)
4. FICA Medicare tax is $28.14 ($1,940.85 × .0145)
5. Mike Chen's net pay is $1,425.68 ($1,940.85 − $212.00 − $155.27 − $75.76 − $28.14 − $44.00)

⬤ LO4   LEARNING UNIT 7-3 EMPLOYER PAYROLL TAX EXPENSE

Employer Payment for Social Security Taxes

As we discussed, employees pay payroll taxes including federal income tax, Social Security taxes, probably state income tax, and maybe even a city or county income tax. It surprises some employees to find that their employers pay payroll taxes, too. As a matter of fact, employers pay exactly the same amount of Social Security

FIGURE 7.4
Employee Earnings Record

TRAVELWITHUS.COM INC.
EMPLOYEE EARNINGS RECORD
Stephanie Higuera   Social Security No. 123-45-6789

Pay Period	Hours Regular	Hours Overtime	Earnings Regular	Earnings Overtime	Gross	FIT	SIT	FICA OASDI	FICA Medicare	Medical Insurance	Net Pay	Check No.	YTD Earnings
10/2–10/15	80	0	912 00	0 00	912 00	87 00	72 96	56 54	13 22	33 00	649 27	806	18513 60
10/16–10/29	78	4	889 20	68 40	957 60	93 00	76 61	59 37	13 89	33 00	681 73	820	19471 20
10/30–11/12	76	0	866 40	0 00	866 40	81 00	69 31	53 72	12 56	33 00	616 81	825	20337 60
11/13–11/26	80	2	912 00	34 20	946 20	93 00	75 70	58 66	13 72	33 00	672 12	839	21283 80
11/27–12/10	80	4	912 00	68 40	980 40	99 00	78 43	60 78	14 22	33 00	694 57	844	22264 20
12/11–12/24	80	0	912 00	0 00	912 00	87 00	72 96	56 54	13 22	33 00	647 28	858	23176 20
12/25–12/31	48	0	547 20	0 00	547 20	33 00	43 78	33 93	7 93	33 00	395 56	863	23723 40
4th Quarter Totals			5950 80	171 00	6121 80	573 00	489 75	379 54	88 76	231 00	4357 34		
YTD Totals			23142 00	581 40	23723 40	2248 86	1897 87	1470 85	343 99	858 00	16903 83		

taxes (OASDI and Medicare) for each employee as the employee pays. In 2011 the employee's OASDI rate was decreased from 6.2% to 4.2% as part of an economic stimulus plan. The employer's rate remained at 6.2%. The reduced employee rate is not used in any calculations in this text. In addition to paying OASDI and Medicare taxes for each employee, employers also pay unemployment taxes that are used to provide unemployed workers with benefits while they are looking for work.

As Travelwithus.com's accountant, Katherine calculates the amount of Social Security taxes that the company must pay as an employer much the same way that she calculated them for each employee. She first determines the amount of current gross earnings for all employees that fall below the wage base limit of $106,800. She looks at the OASDI Taxable Earnings total in the payroll register for the current period. She then multiplies this total by the OASDI tax rate of 6.2% to determine the OASDI tax that Travelwithus.com must pay:

$3,276.90 gross earnings × 6.2% OASDI tax rate = $203.17 OASDI tax

Katherine then calculates Travelwithus.com's Medicare tax by taking the current gross earnings for all employees and multiplying this total by the Medicare tax rate of 1.45%. Remember that the amount of Medicare tax for each employee is not subject to any limit; every dollar that an employee earns is taxed at the Medicare tax rate of 1.45%.

$3,276.90 gross earnings × 1.45% Medicare tax rate = $47.52 Medicare tax

The way Katherine computes these taxes differs in only one way compared to how she computed them for each employee. Because Katherine is now calculating Travelwithus.com's share of these taxes, Katherine uses current gross earnings for the company in total instead of using each employee's current gross earnings as she did when she was determining the amount to withhold from each employee's paycheck.

FUTA and SUTA

In addition to paying its employer share of FICA taxes, Travelwithus.com must also pay unemployment taxes. Unemployment tax, or unemployment insurance as it is sometimes called, was created by the same 1935 law that created Social Security. This federal law requires all 50 states, the District of Columbia, and U.S. territories to run unemployment compensation programs that are approved and monitored by the federal government. Unemployment taxes are paid by employers based on wages paid to employees. Federal Unemployment Tax Act (FUTA) taxes pay the costs of administering the federal and state programs but do not pay benefits to employees. State Unemployment Tax Act (SUTA) taxes pay the benefits to unemployed persons.

Currently, employers pay FUTA tax at a rate of 6.2%* on wages earned by each employee up to a wage base limit of $7,000. However, the federal government allows employers to take a tax credit for SUTA tax against this tax, up to a maximum credit of 5.4%.

COACHING TIP

Only employers, not employees, must calculate and pay both FUTA and SUTA taxes.

FUTA tax rate	6.2%
Less: Normal FUTA tax credit	5.4%
Net FUTA tax rate	0.8%

---

*Effective July 1, 2011, the federal unemployment tax rate decreased from 6.2% to 6.0% and the FUTA portion rate decreased from 0.8% to 0.6%. The expiring levy of 0.2% was established as a surcharge in 1977 and has been extended several times since that date. At present it is not known if the surcharge will be extended. The IRS is in the process of revising the Form 940 (Employer's Annual Federal Unemployment [FUTA] tax return to accommodate the two different FUTA tax rates for 2011. However, it is possible that the surcharge will be extended at a later date in 2011, retroactive to July 1, 2011.

Because of the uncertainty associated with the extension of the surcharge and the complexity that may be added to the Form 940, the author has decided to treat FUTA in the text and the associated problems as though the surcharge has not expired. The federal unemployment tax rate will remain at 6.2% and the FUTA portion will remain at 0.8%.

Employers are allowed to take this credit as long as they have paid all amounts that they owe for SUTA taxes and have paid them on time. In other words, the federal law essentially says to employers, "Comply with your state's unemployment tax laws and your total tax will not exceed a maximum of 6.2%: 0.8% to the federal government and a state rate that will vary up to maximum of 5.4%." Remember that employers alone are responsible for paying FUTA tax; it is never withheld from the earnings of employees.

Katherine calculates FUTA tax by referring to the FUTA Taxable Earnings total in the current payroll register. This column tells her how much, in total, Travelwithus.com's employees have earned this period that falls below the FUTA wage base limit of $7,000. She uses this amount to calculate the FUTA tax by multiplying it by the net FUTA tax rate as follows:

$1,302.90 FUTA taxable earnings × 0.8% FUTA tax rate = $10.42 FUTA tax

Because states run their own unemployment programs, each state may use a different SUTA wage base limit. These amounts are based on the needs of the unemployment funds in each state. In 2011 the wage base limits for states ranged from $7,000 to $37,300. Different states have different SUTA tax rates for the same reason that the wage base limits vary; they are based on the needs of the unemployment funds in each state.

Additionally, the SUTA tax rate can vary from employer to employer within a state. In any state, an employer's SUTA tax rate will be based on how many dollars it contributes to the state unemployment fund and the dollar amount of claims that its employees make against that fund. In other words, the rate is tied to the employer's employment history. The more frequently an employer lays off its employees, the more unemployment benefits the state will have to pay and the higher the tax rate for that employer. In other words, employers who rarely lay off their workers will be charged a lower SUTA rate than employers who lay off workers often. In this way, the SUTA tax rate motivates employers to stabilize their workforce.

Travelwithus.com's current SUTA rate is 5.4% and the wage base limit for the state in which it is located is $7,000. Katherine calculates Travelwithus.com's SUTA tax similar to the way she calculated its FUTA tax. She first looks at the SUTA Taxable Earnings total in the current payroll register to see how much, in total, Travelwithus.com's employees earned this period below the SUTA wage base limit of $7,000. She then calculates the SUTA tax by multiplying this amount by the SUTA tax rate as follows:

$1,302.90 SUTA taxable earnings × 5.4% SUTA tax rate = $70.36

Workers' Compensation Insurance

Workers' compensation insurance insures employees against losses they may incur due to work caused injury or death while on the job. Each employer must purchase this insurance either through an insurance broker or state agency. In most states, this tax is paid completely by the employer, not the employee.

Travelwithus.com's premium for this insurance is based on its total estimated gross payroll, and the rate is calculated for each $100 of weekly payroll. By estimating payroll before the beginning of the year, the insurance company can determine the amount of the premium to charge Travelwithus.com. If actual payroll for the year turns out to differ from estimated payroll, then the insurance company will either credit Travelwithus.com for any overpayment or bill it for any underpayment. The rate for Travelwithus.com is based on the type of work that its employees perform as well as the amount and extent of any on-the-job injuries that its employees experience.

Travelwithus.com has two groups of employees: travel schedulers and managers. It estimated that it would have $50,000 of gross payroll for its schedulers in the next year, and its rate is $1.80 for every $100 of this payroll. The company also estimated

Workers' compensation insurance A benefit plan required by federal regulations in which employers must purchase insurance to protect their employees against losses due to injury or death incurred while on the job.

COACHING TIP

Workers' Compensation Insurance is based on the type of work each employee performs (more hazardous jobs have higher rates) and the extent of any previous on-the-job injuries.

that it will incur $190,000 of payroll for managers, and its rate for this group is $.22 for every $100 of payroll. Travelwithus.com then calculated its premium as follows:

Workers' compensation premium for schedulers:	*$50,000/$100 = 500*	*500 × $1.80 =*	*$ 900.00*
Workers' compensation premium for managers:	*$190,000/$100 = 1,900*	*1,900 × $.22 =*	*418.00*
Total workers' compensation premium =			*$1,318.00*

Suppose, however, that at the end of the year, Travelwithus.com's scheduler payroll totaled $57,977.14 and its manager payroll totaled $220,648.16. The actual premiums for the year would be calculated in the following manner:

Workers' compensation premium for schedulers:	*$57,977.14/$100 = 580*	*580 × $1.80 =*	*$1,044.00*
Workers' compensation premium for managers:	*$220,648.16/$100 = 2,206*	*2,206 × $.22 =*	*485.32*
Total workers' compensation premium =			*$1,529.32*

Travelwithus.com would then owe an additional amount of premium:

Workers' compensation premium based on actual gross payroll	*$1,529.32*
Workers' compensation premium based on estimated gross payroll	*1,318.00*
Additional workers' compensation premium owed =	*$ 211.32*

LEARNING UNIT 7-3 REVIEW

AT THIS POINT you should be able to do the following:

- Explain the use of the taxable earnings column of the payroll register in calculating the employer's payroll tax expense.
- Calculate the employer's payroll taxes of OASDI, Medicare, FUTA, and SUTA.
- Explain the difference between FUTA and SUTA taxes.
- Understand the purpose of workers' compensation insurance.
- Calculate the estimated premium for workers' compensation insurance.

Instant Replay Self-Review Quiz 7-3

Given the following, calculate the employer FICA OASDI, FICA Medicare, FUTA, and SUTA for Farmington Co. for the weekly payroll of July 8. Assume the following:

- FUTA tax is paid at the net rate of 0.8% on the first $7,000 of earnings.
- SUTA tax is paid at a rate of 5.6% on the first $7,000 of earnings.
- FICA tax rate for Social Security is 6.2% on $106,800, and Medicare is 1.45% on all earnings.

Employee	Cumulative Pay Before This Week's Payroll	Gross Pay for Week
Bill Jones	$6,000	$800
Julie Warner	$6,600	$400
Al Brooks	$7,900	$700

Solutions to Instant Replay: Self-Review Quiz 7-3

1. FICA OASDI   = $1,900 × .062 = $117.80
2. FICA Medicare = $1,900 × .0145 = $27.55
3. FUTA   = $1,200 × .008 = $9.60
4. SUTA   = $1,200 × .056 = $67.20

Blueprint for Recording Transactions in a Payroll Register

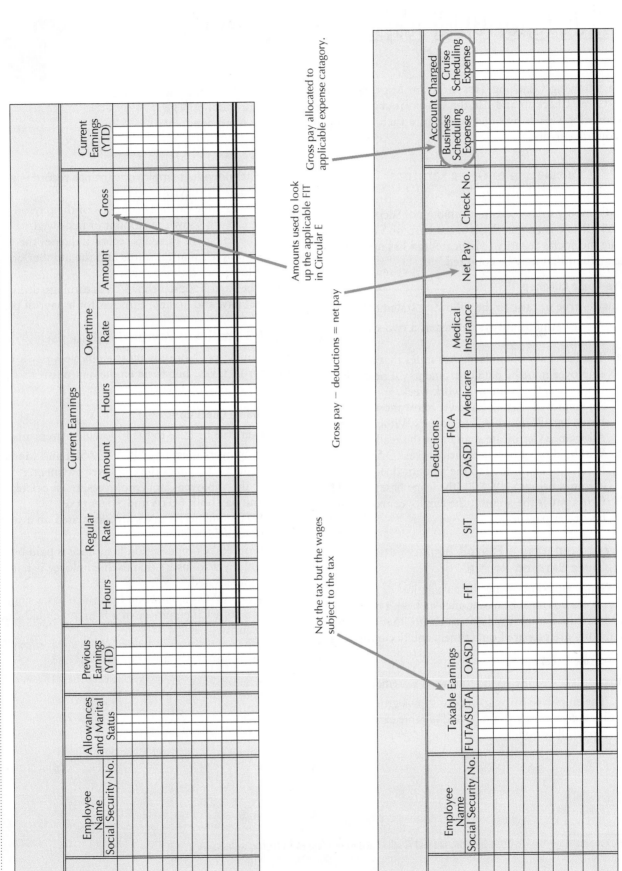

Amounts used to look up the applicable FIT in Circular E

Gross pay – deductions = net pay

Gross pay allocated to applicable expense category.

Not the tax but the wages subject to the tax

ACCOUNTING COACH

The following Coaching Tips are from Learning Units 7-1 through 7-3. Take the Pre-Game Checkup and use the Check Your Score to see how you are doing. The Accounting Coach provides tips before each Checkup to help you avoid common accounting errors.

LU 7-1 Calculation of Gross Earnings, Employee Withholding, Taxes, and Net Pay

Pre-Game Tips: The maximum amount of Social Security (OASDI) tax is capped by a wage base of $106,800*, while the Social Security (Medicare) tax has no limit on the amount that may be collected.

Pre-Game Checkup

Answer true or false to the following statements.

1. A pay period is always defined as a two-week period.
2. The Fair Labor Standards Act states that an employee must be paid overtime pay if he or she works over 40 hours in a work week.
3. An employee may claim fewer allowances on his or her IRS Form-4, Employee's Withholding Allowance Certificate than he or she really has.
4. Withholding of Social Security taxes (OASDI and Medicare) are limited to the amount due on all earnings below $106,800 (the wage base) in 2011.
5. Gross pay is the amount the employee receives in his or her paycheck.

LU 7-2 Preparing a Payroll Register and Employee Earning Record

Pre-Game Tips: Following the calculation of gross and net pay, records must be maintained on both a pay period and individual employee basis to ensure that appropriate reports are prepared on a timely and accurate basis.

Pre-Game Checkup

Answer true or false to the following statements.

1. The employee earnings record shows gross earnings, deductions, net pay, and taxable earnings for a payroll period.
2. The individual employee earnings record is used to update the payroll register.
3. The taxable earnings columns of the payroll register do not show the amount of tax owed.
4. The employee earnings record indicates the employee's marital status and the number of allowances claimed.
5. The payroll register shows gross earnings, deductions, net pay, and taxable earnings for a payroll period.

LU 7-3 Employer Payroll Tax Expense

Pre-Game Tips: Not only must employees pay a variety of payroll taxes, but their employers must also pay a number of payroll taxes.

Pre-Game Checkup

Answer true or false to the following statements.

1. Employers must pay FICA (OASDI and Medicare) equal to 1½ times the employee payment.
2. Only employers, not employees, must calculate and pay both FUTA and SUTA taxes.
3. FUTA and SUTA taxes are calculated on a wage base of $106,800.
4. Workers' Compensation Insurance is paid by the employer to insure that each employee is fairly compensated.
5. Workers' Compensation Insurance has a single rate for each employee of a firm, much like Social Security.

---

*The OASDI Wage base in 2011 is $106,800 and is scheduled to increase to $110,100 on January 1, 2012.

CHECK YOUR SCORE: Answers to the Pre-Game Checkup

LU 7-1

1. False—Pay periods are defined as daily, weekly, biweekly, semi-monthly, monthly, quarterly, or annually.
2. True.
3. True.
4. False—(OASDI) tax is limited by a wage base of $106,800. (Medicare) tax does not have a wage base limit therefore all wages earned are subject to the Medicare tax.
5. False—Gross pay is the amount calculated as earned by the employee before employee withholdings such as FIT, SIT and FICA (OASDI and Medicare). After these deductions from gross pay, the employee receives his or her net pay.

LU 7-2

1. False—The employee earnings record shows gross earnings, deductions, and net pay for the employee for each calendar quarter and the entire calendar year.
2. False—The payroll register is used to update the employee earnings record.
3. True. They show the amount of earnings to be taxed for unemployment taxes and Social Security (OASDI).
4. False—The employee's marital status and the number of allowances are found on the payroll register.
5. True.

LU 7-3

1. False—The employer pays exactly the same amount of Social Security taxes (OASDI and Medicare) as do its employees.
2. True.
3. False—Both FUTA and SUTA are calculated on a wage base of $7,000 for each employee.
4. False—Workers' Compensation Insurance is paid by the employer to insure employees against work related death or injury.
5. False—The rate paid by the employer is based on the type of work each employee performs (more hazardous jobs have higher rates) and the extent of any previous on-the-job injuries or deaths.

Chapter Summary

MyAccountingLab Here are all the key concepts and equations to help you understand the concepts of this chapter and prepare you for your exam. After completing this review, go to MyAccountingLab for more practice opportunities.

Concepts You Should Know	Key Terms
L01 Calculating gross pay, employee payroll tax deductions for federal income tax withholding, state income tax withholding, FICA (OASDI, Medicare), and net pay. 1. The Fair Labor Standards Act states that hourly workers will receive a minimum of one and a half times their regular hourly rate of pay for all hours they work over 40 hours during a workweek. 2. Salaried employees are employees who are classified as salaried according to the provisions of the Fair Labor Standards Act. 3. For the rules of the Fair Labor Standards Act to apply to an employer, the employer must be involved in interstate commerce. 4. Employees and employers pay equal amounts of Social Security tax. Note that Social Security, or FICA tax, is made up of two taxes: OASDI and Medicare. The OASDI tax is based on a tax rate and wage base amount that is set for each calendar year. 5. Gross earnings minus deductions equals net pay. 6. Federal income tax withholding amounts are listed in tax tables found in IRS Circular E, Employer's Tax Guide, also known as Publication 15.	Allowances (also called exemptions) (p. 263) Calendar year (p. 266) Circular E (p. 263) Fair Labor Standards Act (Federal Wage and Hour Law) (p. 261) Federal income tax (FIT) withholding (p. 263) FICA (Federal Insurance Contributions Act) (p. 266) Form W-4 (Employee's Withholding Allowance Certificate) (p. 263) Gross earnings (gross pay) (p. 261) Interstate commerce (p. 261) Medical insurance (p. 267) Net pay (p. 267) Pay or payroll period (p. 261) State income tax (SIT) withholding (p. 263) Taxable earnings (p. 267) Wage bracket table (p. 263) Workweek (p. 261)
L02 Preparing a payroll register. 1. The two primary accounting records used to keep track of payroll amounts are the payroll register and employee earnings record. The payroll register shows gross earnings, deductions, net pay, and taxable earnings for a payroll period. 2. The taxable earnings columns of the payroll register do not show the tax. They show the amount of earnings to be taxed for unemployment taxes, OASDI, and Medicare.	Payroll register (p. 268)

● **L03**

Maintaining an employee earnings record.

1. The employee earnings record shows the gross earnings, deductions, and net pay for an employee for an entire calendar year.

2. The individual employee earnings records are updated soon after the payroll register is prepared.

Individual employee earnings record (p. 270)

● **L04**

Calculating employer taxes for FICA (OASDI, Medicare), FUTA, SUTA, and workers' compensation insurance.

1. The payroll tax expense for an employer is made up of FICA OASDI, FICA Medicare, FUTA, and SUTA.

2. The OASDI tax rate for 2011 is 6.2%, and the wage base limit for this year is $106,800.

3. Medicare has no wage base limit, so an employee and employer will pay this tax on all of an employee's earnings during the calendar year, at a rate of 1.45% for 2011.

4. The maximum amount of credit given for state unemployment taxes paid against the FUTA tax is 5.4%. This figure is known as the normal FUTA tax credit. The normal FUTA tax credit typically results in employers paying 0.8% for FUTA tax.

5. Employers pay workers' compensation insurance premiums based on estimated payroll. At the end of the year, estimated payroll is compared to actual payroll, and the employer either pays any additional premium or receives a credit for any overpayment of premium.

Workers' compensation insurance (p. 273)

Discussion and Critical Thinking Questions/Ethical Case

1. What is the purpose of the Fair Labor Standards Act (also called the Federal Wage and Hour Law)?

2. Explain how to calculate overtime pay.

3. Explain how a W-4 form, called the Employee's Withholding Allowance Certificate, is used to determine Federal Income Tax (FIT) withheld.

4. The more allowances an employee claims on a W-4 form, the more take-home pay the employee gets with each paycheck. Agree or disagree?

5. Explain how federal and state income tax withholdings are determined.

6. Explain why a business should prepare a payroll register before employees are paid.

7. The taxable earnings column of a payroll register records the amount of tax due. Agree or disagree?

8. Define and state the purpose of FICA taxes.

9. Explain how to calculate OASDI and Medicare taxes.

10. The employer doesn't have to contribute to Social Security. Agree or disagree? Please explain.

11. What purpose does the individual employee earnings record serve?

12. Please draw a diagram showing how the following items relate to each other: (a) weekly payroll, (b) payroll register, (c) individual employee earnings record, and (d) general journal entries for payroll.

13. If you earned $130,000 this year, you would pay more OASDI and Medicare than your partner who earned $75,000. Do you agree or disagree? Please provide calculations to support your answer.

14. Explain how an employer can receive a credit against the FUTA tax due.

15. Explain what an experience or merit rating is and how it affects the amount paid by an employer for state unemployment insurance.

16. Who pays workers' compensation insurance, the employee or the employer? What types of benefits does this insurance provide? How are premiums calculated?

17. An employee for Repairs to Go, Inc., works different numbers of hours each week depending on the needs of the business. To simplify the accounting, the bookkeeper for Repairs to Go classifies this employee as a salaried person. Is this practice appropriate? Please explain.

Concept Check

Calculating Gross Earnings

⬤ **L01** *(10 MIN)*

1. Calculate the total wages earned (assume an overtime rate of time and a half over 40 hours).

Employee	Hourly Rate	No. of Hours Worked
Karen Black	$14	30
Peter Rogers	$12	50

FIT and FICA

⬤ **L01** *(15 MIN)*

2. Devon Mark, single, claiming one exemption, has cumulative earnings before this biweekly pay period of $105,800. If he is paid $1,940 this period, what will his deductions be for FIT and FICA (OASDI and Medicare)? The FICA tax rate for Social Security is 6.2% on $106,800 and Medicare is 1.45% on all earnings.

Net Pay

⬤ **L01** *(15 MIN)*

3. From Exercise 2, calculate Devon's net pay. The state income tax rate is 5% and health insurance is $35.

Payroll Register

⬤ **L02** *(10 MIN)*

4. Match the following:
   1. Total gross pay
   2. A deduction
   3. Net pay
      a. _____ Office Salary
      b. _____ FICA OASDI Payable
      c. _____ FICA Medicare
      d. _____ Federal Income Tax
      e. _____ Medical Insurance
      f. _____ Wages and Salaries

Employer and Employee Taxes

⬤ **L02** *(10 MIN)*

5. Identify which of the following taxes are paid by the employee (EE) and which are paid by the employer (ER):
   a. _____ FICA Medicare
   b. _____ FIT
   c. _____ FUTA
   d. _____ SUTA

Exercises

Set A

7A-1. Calculate the total wages earned for each hourly employee assuming an overtime rate of time and a half over 40 hours.

⬤ **L01** *(15 MIN)*

Employee	Hourly Rate	No. of Hours Worked
Lucky Mars	$13	32
Pam Valley	$14	44
Louis Jones	$15	44

L01 *(20 MIN)*   **7A-2.** Compute the net pay for each employee using the federal income tax withholding table in Figure 7.2. Assume that FICA OASDI tax is 6.2% on a wage base limit of $106,800, Medicare is 1.45% on all earnings, the payroll is paid biweekly, and no state income tax applies.

Employee	Status	Allowances	Cumulative Pay	Biweekly Pay
Zhu Rui	Single	2	$61,000	$1,670
Tilla Palmer	Single	1	$58,500	$1,620

L04 *(20 MIN)*   **7A-3.** From the following information, calculate the payroll tax expense for Gray Company for the payroll of August 9:

Employee	Cumulative Earnings before Weekly Payroll	Gross Pay for the Week
U. Acorn	$3,900	$875
F. Jackson	6,100	825
R. Robins	7,100	300

The FICA tax rate for OASDI is 6.2% on the first $106,800 earned, and Medicare is 1.45% on all earnings. Federal unemployment tax is 0.8% on the first $7,000 earned by each employee. The SUTA tax rate for Gray is 5.2% on the first $7,000 of employee earnings for state unemployment purposes.

L04 *(15 MIN)*   **7A-4.** Refer to Exercise 7A-3 and assume that the state changed Gray's SUTA tax rate to 4.0%. What effect would this change have on the total payroll tax expense?

L04 *(15 MIN)*   **7A-5.** Refer to Exercise 7A-3. If R. Robins earned $2,500 for the week instead of $300, what effect would this change have on the total payroll tax expense?

L02 *(20 MIN)*   **7A-6.** The total wage expense for Carol Co. was $156,000. Of this total, $28,000 was above the OASDI wage base limit and not subject to this tax. All earnings are subject to Medicare tax, and $59,000 was above the federal and state unemployment wage base limits and not subject to unemployment taxes. Please calculate the total payroll tax expense for Carol Co. given the following rates and wage base limits:

a. FICA tax rate: OASDI, 6.2% with a wage base limit of $106,800; Medicare, 1.45% with no wage base limit

b. State unemployment tax rate: 5.5% with a wage base limit of $7,000

c. Federal unemployment tax rate (after credit): 0.8% with a wage base limit of $7,000

L04 *(20 MIN)*   **7A-7.** At the end of the first quarter of 201X, you are asked to determine the FUTA tax liability for Carter Company. The FUTA tax rate is 0.8% on the first $7,000 each employee earns during the year (assuming 13 weeks for the first quarter) and each employee earned the same gross weekly pay for all 13 weeks).

Employee	Gross Pay Per Week
R. Frank	$680
G. Jill	810
L. Peter	600
Y. Ralph	410

7A-8. From the following data, estimate the annual premium for workers' compensation insurance:

L04 *(10 MIN)*

Type of Work	Estimated Payroll	Rate per $100
Office	$20,000	$0.17
Repairs	80,000	1.82

Set B

7B-1. Calculate the total wages earned for each employee assuming an overtime rate of time and a half over 40 hours.

L01 *(15 MIN)*

Employee	Hourly Rate	No. of Hours Worked
Lucky Mars	$17	39
Pam Valley	$16	42
Louis Jones	$20	45

7B-2. Compute the net pay for each employee using the federal income tax withholding table included. Assume that FICA OASDI tax is 6.2% on a wage base limit of $106,800; Medicare is 1.45% on all earnings, the payroll is paid biweekly, and no state income tax applies.

L01 *(20 MIN)*

Employee	Status	Allowances	Cumulative Pay	Biweekly Pay
Chen Rong	Single	1	$63,300	$1,710
Mary Pinney	Single	0	$63,700	$1,630

7B-3. From the following information, calculate the payroll tax expense for Aim Company for the payroll of June 9:

L04 *(20 MIN)*

Employee	Cumulative Earnings Before Weekly Payroll	Gross Pay for the Week
O. Barns	$3,300	$800
O. Hienze	6,200	650
D. Toll	7,800	320

The FICA tax rate for OASDI is 6.2% on the first $106,800 earned, and Medicare is 1.45% on all earnings. Federal unemployment tax is 0.8% on the first $7,000 earned by each employee. The SUTA tax rate for Aim is 5.1% on the first $7,000 of earnings for state unemployment purposes.

7B-4. Refer to Exercise 7B-3 and assume that the state changed Aim's SUTA tax rate to 3.5%. What effect would this change have on the total payroll tax expense?

L04 *(15 MIN)*

7B-5. Refer to Exercise 7B-3. If D. Toll earned $3,000 for the week instead of $320, what effect would this change have on the total payroll tax expense?

L04 *(15 MIN)*

7B-6. The total wage expense for Orange Co. was $150,000. Of this total, $26,000 was above the OASDI wage base limit and not subject to this tax. All earnings are subject to Medicare tax, and $62,000 was above the federal and state unemployment wage base limits and not subject to unemployment

L02 *(20 MIN)*

taxes. Please calculate the total payroll tax expense for Orange Co. given the following rates and wage base limits:

a. FICA tax rate: OASDI, 6.2% with a wage base limit of $106,800; Medicare, 1.45% with no wage base limit.

b. State unemployment tax rate 5.6% with a wage base limit of $7,000.

c. Federal unemployment tax rate (after credit): 0.8% with a wage base limit of $7,000.

LO4 *(20 MIN)*   **7B-7.** At the end of the first quarter of 201X, you are asked to determine the FUTA tax liability for Ali Company. The FUTA tax rate is 0.8% on the first $7,000 each employee earns during the year (assuming 13 weeks for the first quarter and each employee earned the same gross weekly pay for all 13 weeks).

Employee	Gross Pay Per Week
T. Bork	$650
G. Jill	770
L. Steven	590
Q. Watson	420

LO4 *(10 MIN)*   **7B-8.** From the following data, estimate the annual premium for worker's compensation insurance:

Type of Work	Estimated Payroll	Rate per $100
Office	$28,000	$0.15
Repairs	85,000	1.86

MyAccountingLab   ## Problems

Set A

LO1 *(20 MIN)*   **7A-1.** From the following information, please complete the chart for gross earnings for the week. (Assume an overtime rate of time and a half over 40 hours.)

Check Figure:
Dave Johnson: $1,016.50 Gross Earnings

Employee	Hourly Rate	No. of Hours Worked	Gross Earnings
Jaden Vasquez	$10	48	
Lucy Ferris	$14	37	
Nicolette Patt	$13	39	
Dave Johnson	$19	49	

LO1 *(30 MIN)*   **7A-2.** May Company has five salaried employees. Your task is to use the following information to calculate net pay for each employee:

Employee	Allowance and Marital Status	Cumulative Earnings before This Payroll	Biweekly Salary	Department
Dixie, Dylan	S-1	$46,000	$1,100	Customer Service
Fry, Marc	S-1	28,000	1,250	Office
Ricard, Alison	S-2	59,200	1,300	Office
Hammel, Audrey	S-3	105,880	1,690	Customer Service
Clinton, Lionel	S-3	26,000	1,110	Customer Service

Assume the following:

1. FICA OASDI is 6.2% on $106,800; FICA Medicare is 1.45% on all earnings.
2. Each employee contributes $45 biweekly for medical insurance.
3. State income tax is 4% of gross pay.
4. FIT is calculated from Figure 7.2.

Check Figure:
Total Net Pay $4,905.30

7A-3. The bookkeeper of Samba Co. gathered the following data from individual employee earnings records and daily time cards. Your task is to complete a payroll register on March 17.

⬤⬤ **LO1, 2** *(40 MIN)*

Employee	Allowance and Marital Status	Cumulative Earnings before This Payroll	Daily Time M	T	W	T	F	Hourly Rate of Pay	FIT
Keys, Pam	M-1	$64,100	6	6	13	6	10	$11	$27
Hale, Don	S-0	14,000	8	12	7	12	7	16	113
Dean, Ria	M-3	70,000	7	8	13	6	13	25	118
Vent, Jane	S-1	22,500	10	5	9	11	5	19	91

Assume the following:

1. FICA OASDI is 6.2% on $106,800; FICA Medicare is 1.45% on all earnings.
2. Federal income tax has been calculated from a weekly table for you.
3. Each employee contributes $26 weekly for health insurance.
4. Overtime is paid at a rate of time and a half over 40 hours.
5. Keys and Dean work in the office; the other employees work in sales.

Check Figure:
Total Net Pay $2,560.37

7A-4. You gathered the following data from time cards and individual employee earnings records. Your tasks are as follows:

1. On December 5, 201X, prepare a payroll register for this biweekly payroll.
2. Calculate the employer taxes of FICA OASDI, FICA Medicare, FUTA, and SUTA.

⬤⬤⬤◯ **LO1, 2, 3, 4** *(40 MIN)*

Employee	Allowance and Marital Status	Cumulative Earnings before This Payroll	Biweekly Salary	Check No.	Department
Abood, John	S-3	$36,900	$1,580	30	Production
Gallant, Nicki	S-1	47,600	2,010	31	Office
Malone, Jeff	S-2	64,800	2,090	32	Production
Scott, Paul	S-1	4,800	900	33	Office

Assume the following:

1. FICA OASDI is 6.2% on $106,800; FICA Medicare is 1.45% on all earnings.
2. Federal income tax is calculated from Figure 7.2.
3. State income tax is 8% of gross pay.
4. Union dues are $13 biweekly.
5. The SUTA rate is 5.4% and the FUTA rate is 0.8% on earnings up to $7,000.

Check Figure:
Total Net Pay $4,685.22

Set B

7B-1. From the following information, please complete the chart for gross earnings for the week. (Assume an overtime rate of time and a half over 40 hours.)

⬤ **LO1** *(20 MIN)*

Employee	Hourly Rate	No. of Hours Worked	Gross Earnings
Jacoby Vasquez	$15	47	
Leena Ferris	$13	45	
Nicolette Patt	$17	42	
Danyl Johnson	$18	50	

Check Figure:
Danyl Johnson Gross Pay $990

LO1 *(30 MIN)*

7B-2. October Company employs five salaried employees. Your task is to use the following information to calculate net pay for each employee:

Employee	Allowance and Marital Status	Cumulative Earnings before This Payroll	Biweekly Salary	Department
Bristow, Dylan	S-0	$45,000	$1,500	Customer Service
Herman, Marc	S-0	30,000	1,350	Office
Sears, Alison	S-1	54,700	1,050	Office
Flaherty, Audrey	S-3	105,800	1,790	Customer Service
Ackerman, Lionel	S-3	34,000	860	Customer Service

Check Figure:
Total Net Pay $4,966.39

Assume the following:

1. FICA OASDI is 6.2% on $106,800; FICA Medicare is 1.45% on all earnings.
2. Each employee contributes $20 biweekly for medical insurance.
3. State income tax is 5% of gross pay.
4. FIT is calculated from Figure 7.2.

LO1, 2 *(40 MIN)*

7B-3. The bookkeeper of Coast Co. gathered the following data from individual employee earnings records and daily time cards. Your task is to complete a payroll register on November 17.

Employee	Allowance and Marital Status	Cumulative Earnings before This Payroll	M	T	W	T	F	Hourly Rate of Pay	FIT
Ryan, Pam	M-1	$65,400	9	10	6	5	5	$17	$40
Badu, Don	S-0	17,500	8	7	12	11	3	13	65
Dean, Ria	M-3	107,150	9	8	11	6	9	16	37
Gray, Jane	S-1	21,000	8	10	6	9	7	20	104

Check Figure:
Total Net Pay $2,130.19

Assume the following:

1. FICA OASDI is 6.2% on $106,800; FICA Medicare is 1.45% on all earnings.
2. Federal income tax has been calculated from a weekly table for you.
3. Each employee contributes $28 weekly for health insurance.
4. Overtime is paid at a rate of time and a half over 40 hours.
5. Ryan and Dean work in the office; the other employees work in sales.

LO1, 2, 3, 4
(40 MIN)

PT/QB

7B-4. You gathered the following data from time cards and individual employee earnings records. Your tasks are as follows:

1. On December 5, 201X, prepare a payroll register for this biweekly payroll.
2. Calculate the employer taxes of FICA OASDI, FICA Medicare, FUTA, and SUTA.

Employee	Allowance and Marital Status	Cumulative Earnings before This Payroll	Biweekly Salary	Check No.	Department
Alvin, John	S-3	$37,400	$1,510	30	Production
Gale, Nicki	S-1	47,500	2,040	31	Office
Malone, Jeff	S-2	64,800	2,080	32	Production
Seaver, Paul	S-1	4,600	810	33	Office

Check Figure:
Total Net Pay $4,886.13

Assume the following:

1. FICA OASDI is 6.2% on $106,800; FICA Medicare is 1.45% on all earnings.
2. Federal income tax is calculated from Figure 7.2.
3. State income tax is 3% of gross pay.
4. Union dues are $18 biweekly.
5. The SUTA rate is 5.4%, and the FUTA rate is 0.8% on earnings below $7,000.

Financial Report Problem

◐◐ **LO1, 2** *(10 MIN)*

Reading the Kellogg's Annual Report

Go to http://investor.kelloggs.com/annuals.cfm, to access the Kellogg's 2010 Annual Report. Go to Notes to Consolidated Financial Statements and calculate from Note 16 how much Advertising Expense has increased from 2009 to 2010.

ON the JOB ||||||||||||||||||||||||||

SANCHEZ COMPUTER CENTER

◐ **LO1** *(60 MIN)*

During the month of November the following transactions occurred.

Assignment

1. Record the following transactions in the general journal and post them to the general ledger.

2. Prepare a trial balance as of November 30, 201X.

Assume the following transactions:

Nov.	1	Billed Vita Needle Company $6,800, invoice no. 12675, for services rendered.
	3	Billed Accu Pac, Inc., $3,900, invoice no. 12676, for services rendered.
	5	Purchased new shop benches for $1,400 on account from System Design Furniture.
	9	Received the phone bill, $150.
	12	Collected $500 of the amount due from Taylor Golf.
	18	Collected $800 of the amount due from Taylor Golf.
	20	Purchased a fax machine for the office from Multi Systems, Inc., on credit, $450.00.

SUBWAY CASE

Payroll Records: A Full-Time Job?

◐◐◐◐ **LO1, 2, 3, 4**
(30 MIN)

Like every Subway restaurant owner, Stan needs to keep a master file of important employee information. This file contains every employee's name, address, phone number, Social Security number, rate of pay, hours worked per week, and W-4 form.

Stan employs two part-time "sandwich artists" and no full-time managers—yet. If his sales continue to be high, he'll need to hire someone to manage operations so that he can spend more time analyzing the financials—with Lila's help—and growing his business. Most restaurants hire primarily part-timers with a core of full-time employees, but the numbers vary from restaurant to restaurant. Benefits vary too. Stan, for instance, plans to offer health and dental benefits when he hires a manager. He knows what a great incentive these benefits are, with health costs so high. He pays his sandwich artists, Rashid and Ellen, the minimum wage because they both have less than a year's experience. However, he's talking to Mariah Washington about creating some incentives to keep them motivated. If Rashid and Ellen are with him for a full year, they'll see a nice raise in their biweekly paychecks. Both the frequency of pay and the tax rates vary by state and sometimes by city or county.

Stan must record all this vital information and report it to the various state, local, and federal authorities. In addition, Stan includes total payroll expenses on the weekly sales and inventory report, which he submits electronically to headquarters from his point-of-sale (POS) screen.

Scheduling workers and keeping payroll records are the bane of Stan's existence. These tasks are so incredibly time consuming. He was pleased to hear, then, at the last meeting of his local North American Association of Subway Franchisees (NAASF) that the new POS terminals will soon offer an electronic scheduling package.

"Wow! That will really help," said Stan cheerfully to another franchisee. "No more different colors of ink just to keep track of who will work when! Now I can plan around Rashid and Ellen's exam schedules without a hassle. Scheduling might just become my favorite module in the new system."

"Sure," said Javier Gonzalez, another owner. "Now you can concentrate on payroll records. What fun!"

"Ay. Que lata," Stan groaned. What a drag!

Discussion Questions

1. What payroll records does Stan need to keep for his Subway restaurant?
2. What other information might Stan want in order to schedule working hours for each employee?
3. How does the payroll register help Stan prepare the payroll? (Consult the process outlined at the beginning of the chapter.)

Paying, Recording, and Reporting Payroll and Payroll Taxes: The Conclusion of the Payroll Process

THE GAME PLAN

Every month or every two weeks you might receive a paycheck. When reviewing all the deductions, did you ever wonder what they were for? Your company must report these deductions in order to meet its state and federal reporting requirements. For example, Google must take taxes out of its employees' paychecks and report the amounts to the federal and state authorities. By law, Google will have to make periodic payroll deposits of these taxes along with some matching requirements like Social Security. Google and other companies also are required by law to contribute to unemployment programs. This chapter will focus on the payroll reporting responsibilities of the employer. For both small and large businesses the payroll process is an inseparable part of the accounting process.

LEARNING OBJECTIVES

- **1.** Recording payroll and payroll taxes.
- **2.** Recording the payroll and the paying of the payroll taxes.
- **3.** Recording employer taxes for FICA OASDI, FICA Medicare, FUTA, SUTA, and workers' compensation insurance.
- **4.** Preparing Forms W-2, W-3, 941, and 940.
- **5.** Paying FUTA, SUTA, and workers' compensation insurance.

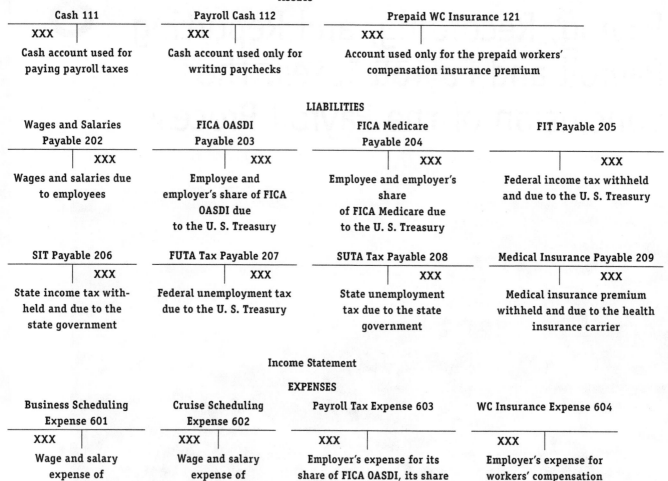

Balance Sheet

ASSETS

Cash 111	Payroll Cash 112	Prepaid WC Insurance 121
XXX	XXX	XXX
Cash account used for paying payroll taxes	Cash account used only for writing paychecks	Account used only for the prepaid workers' compensation insurance premium

LIABILITIES

Wages and Salaries Payable 202	FICA OASDI Payable 203	FICA Medicare Payable 204	FIT Payable 205
XXX	XXX	XXX	XXX
Wages and salaries due to employees	Employee and employer's share of FICA OASDI due to the U. S. Treasury	Employee and employer's share of FICA Medicare due to the U. S. Treasury	Federal income tax withheld and due to the U. S. Treasury

SIT Payable 206	FUTA Tax Payable 207	SUTA Tax Payable 208	Medical Insurance Payable 209
XXX	XXX	XXX	XXX
State income tax withheld and due to the state government	Federal unemployment tax due to the U. S. Treasury	State unemployment tax due to the state government	Medical insurance premium withheld and due to the health insurance carrier

Income Statement

EXPENSES

Business Scheduling Expense 601	Cruise Scheduling Expense 602	Payroll Tax Expense 603	WC Insurance Expense 604
XXX	XXX	XXX	XXX
Wage and salary expense of employees scheduling business travel	Wage and salary expense of employees scheduling cruises	Employer's expense for its share of FICA OASDI, its share of FICA Medicare, FUTA, and SUTA	Employer's expense for workers' compensation insurance

Google has many thousands of employees. With the aid of computers, the accounting department of Google must monitor as well as complete in a timely manner its employer tax responsibilities. In Chapter 7 we learned how to calculate gross earnings, employee withholding taxes, net pay, and employer payroll taxes. We now look at how businesses pay, record, and report these amounts. The journal entries necessary to record all of the payroll transactions for Travelwithus.com appear in the next section. Use the preceding T accounts as a reference guide. They will be covered as part of our discussion on completing the payroll process.

L01   LEARNING UNIT 8-1 RECORDING PAYROLL AND PAYROLL TAX EXPENSE AND PAYING THE PAYROLL

At this point in the payroll process, Katherine Kurtz, the accountant for Travelwithus.com, has calculated gross earnings, deductions for employee withholding taxes, and net pay for each of Travelwithus.com's employees. She entered these amounts into two accounting records for Travelwithus.com called the payroll register and the employee earnings record. She also computed the amount of payroll taxes that Travelwithus.com must pay as an employer. At this point, Katherine must record these payroll amounts in the accounts of Travelwithus.com by making journal entries in the general journal and posting these entries to accounts in the general ledger. By entering these amounts into Travelwithus.com's accounting system, Travelwithus. com's financial statements will include these payroll transactions.

Recording Payroll

Before we discuss how payroll transactions are recorded, let's first review the accounts that we will be using and the rules for increasing and decreasing these accounts:

Accounts Affected	Category	↑↓	Rules	Financial Statement
Business Scheduling Expense	Expense	↑	Dr.	Income Statement
Cruise Scheduling Expense	Expense	↑	Dr.	Income Statement
Payroll Tax Expense	Expense	↑	Dr.	Income Statement
Workers' Compensation	Expense	↑	Dr.	Income Statement
Insurance Expense	Expense	↑	Dr.	Income Statement
Payroll Cash	Asset	↑	Dr.	Balance Sheet
Prepaid Workers' Compensation Insurance	Asset	↑	Dr.	Balance Sheet
FICA OASDI Payable	Liability	↑	Cr.	Balance Sheet
FICA Medicare Payable	Liability	↑	Cr.	Balance Sheet
FIT Payable	Liability	↑	Cr.	Balance Sheet
SIT Payable	Liability	↑	Cr.	Balance Sheet
FUTA Payable	Liability	↑	Cr.	Balance Sheet
SUTA Payable	Liability	↑	Cr.	Balance Sheet
Medical Insurance Payable	Liability	↑	Cr.	Balance Sheet
Wages and Salaries Payable	Liability	↑	Cr.	Balance Sheet

Katherine needs to record the expense of wages and salaries. The information needed to make these journal entries comes from the hourly and salaried payroll registers. Figure 8.1 shows the hourly payroll register for the current payroll period. Katherine locates this register and uses totals from it to make the following journal entry:

		GENERAL JOURNAL			
Date			PR	Dr.	Cr.
201X					
Oct.	29	Business Scheduling Expense		9 5 7 60	
		Cruise Scheduling Expense		2 3 1 9 30	
		FIT Payable			3 4 1 00
		SIT Payable			2 6 2 15
		FICA OASDI Payable			2 0 3 17
		FICA Medicare Payable			4 7 52
		Medical Insurance Payable			9 9 00
		Wages and Salaries Payable			2 3 2 4 06
		To record payroll for the pay period			
		ending October 29, 201X			

FIGURE 8.1 Payroll Register

TRAVELWITHUS.COM INC.
HOURLY EMPLOYEE PAYROLL REGISTER
OCTOBER 16–29

Employee / Social Security No.	Allowances and Marital Status	Previous Earnings (YTD)	Regular Hours	Regular Rate	Regular Amount	Overtime Hours	Overtime Rate	Overtime Amount	Gross	Current Earnings (YTD)
Higuera, Stephanie 123-45-6789	S-1	1851360	78	1140	88920	4	1710	6840	95760	1947120
Sui, Annie 123-45-6788	S-0	212100	80	1515	121200	4	22725	9090	130290	342390
Taylor, Harold 123-45-6787	S-2	1904370	78	1210	94380	4	1815	7260	101640	2006010
TOTALS					304500			23190	327690	4295520

TRAVELWITHUS.COM INC.
HOURLY EMPLOYEE PAYROLL REGISTER
OCTOBER 16–29

Employee / Social Security No.	Taxable Earnings FUTA/SUTA	Taxable Earnings OASDI	FIT	SIT	FICA OASDI	FICA Medicare	Medical Insurance	Net Pay	Check No.	Account Charged Business Scheduling Expense	Account Charged Cruise Scheduling Expense
Higuera, Stephanie 123-45-6789	—	95760	9300	7661	5937	1389	3300	68173	820	95760	
Sui, Annie 123-45-6788	130290	130290	16800	10423	8078	1889	3300	89800	821		130290
Taylor, Harold 123-45-6787	—	101640	8000	8131	6302	1474	3300	74433	822		101640
TOTALS	130290	327690	34100	26215	20317	4752	9900	232406		95760	231930

A couple things may be surprising about the journal entry. First, notice that the gross earnings, not the net pay, are recorded as expenses for the two different departments that the employees worked in. This total amount of earnings is the real expense to Travelwithus.com. Employees will actually only receive the lower, net pay; the difference relates to deductions that are made for OASDI, HI, FIT, state and local income taxes, and other deductions authorized by the employee.

Also notice that the amounts of taxes withheld are recorded in "Payable" accounts, which means that they are liabilities of Travelwithus.com. How can Travelwithus.com be liable for these taxes if the taxes are paid by employees? The answer is that Travelwithus.com collects these amounts by withholding them from the paychecks of its employees and then turns them over to the federal and, in this case, state governments. In other words, Travelwithus.com is the intermediary in this process. Until it does pay these amounts to the governments, Travelwithus.com owes these taxes to the governments. The same is true of the medical insurance premiums that the employees pay; the company collects them and then pays them to the insurance company.

Recording Payroll Tax Expense

Katherine's next task is to record the employer payroll taxes for Travelwithus.com. The entry to record the taxes for the current hourly payroll follows:

GENERAL JOURNAL					
Date			PR	Dr.	Cr.
201X					
Oct.	29	Payroll Tax Expense		3 3 1 47	
		FICA OASDI Payable			2 0 3 17
		FICA Medicare Payable			4 7 52
		FUTA Payable			1 0 42
		SUTA Payable			7 0 36
		To record payroll tax expense for the			
		pay period ending October 29, 201X			

Notice that FICA OASDI, FICA Medicare, FUTA, and SUTA were recorded in separate liability accounts because they are different taxes and, except for the FICA taxes, are paid to different government agencies. Also note that the amount of all of these taxes are added together and recorded as one amount for Travelwithus.com's payroll tax expense. These amounts are an expense to Travelwithus.com because they represent the cost of the payroll taxes that it must pay as an employer.

Payroll tax expense The cost to employers that includes the total of the employer's FICA OASDI, FICA Medicare, FUTA, and SUTA taxes.

Paying the Payroll and Recording the Payment

● **L02**

Katherine next must record the payment of payroll to Travelwithus.com's employees:

GENERAL JOURNAL					
Date			PR	Dr.	Cr.
201X					
Nov.	3	Wages and Salaries Payable		2 3 2 4 06	
		Payroll Cash			2 3 2 4 06
		To record the payment of hourly payroll			
		for the pay period ending October 29,			
		201X			

Travelwithus.com, like most companies, uses a special checking account for paying its payroll. This account is called Payroll Cash and only paychecks are written from this account. A company with a substantial number of employees might want to use an extra account just for payroll for a number of reasons. First, having a separate account just for paychecks provides much better internal control over the funds deposited to pay employees. Also, because only payroll checks are written from this account, it is easier to reconcile it to the bank statement each month and determine whether someone has not cashed his or her paycheck for some reason. Finally, the business can still manage its cash effectively even with this extra bank account; the business simply deposits the total net pay amount in this account and thus has enough money to pay every paycheck without leaving extra in the account that could be used for other purposes.

The paychecks that Travelwithus.com gives to its employees are, like the paychecks of most companies, attached to pay stubs that show the employee's gross earnings, deductions for employee withholding taxes, and net pay. Stephanie Higuera's current paycheck and stub look like this:

Travelwithus.com Inc.

Employee	Social Security	Check	Net Pay	Pay Date	Marital Status	Allowances
Stephanie Higuera	123-45-6789	820	$681.73	11/03/201X	S	1

Earnings	Current			Deductions		
	Pay Rate	Hours	Earnings	Item	Current	YTD
Regular Earnings	11.40	78	889.20	FIT	93.00	2,067.00
Overtime Earnings	17.10	4	68.40	SIT	76.61	1,557.70
Current Gross Earnings			957.60	OASDI	59.37	1,207.21
				Medicare	13.89	282.33
				Medical insurance	33.00	693.00
				Total	275.87	6,807.24

Travelwithus.com Inc.   No. 820
504 Washington Blvd.   11-325/1210
Salem, MA 01970   November 3,   201X

PAY TO THE
ORDER OF   Stephanie Higuera $681.73

Six hundred eighty one and 73/100 _____ DOLLARS

    BC   Bank of Commerce

MEMO October 16–29 payroll   *Julia Regan*

LEARNING UNIT 8-1 REVIEW

AT THIS POINT you should be able to do the following:

- Explain how to use the payroll register to record the payroll.
- Journalize the payroll.
- Journalize the employer's payroll tax expense.
- Journalize the payment of a payroll.

Instant Replay ⊙ Self-Review Quiz 8-1

Given the following information, prepare the general journal entry to record the payroll tax expense for Bill Co. for the weekly payroll of Oct 29. Assume the following:

- SUTA tax is paid at a rate of 5.6% on the first $7,000 of earnings.
- FUTA tax is paid at the net rate of 0.8% on the first $7,000 of earnings.
- FICA tax rate for OASDI is 6.2% on $106,800, and Medicare is 1.45% on all earnings.

Employee	Cumulative Pay Before This Week's Payroll	Gross Pay for the Week
Bill Jones	$6,000	$800
Julie Warner	$6,600	$400
Al Brooks	$7,900	$700

Solution to Instant Replay: Self-Review Quiz 8-1

		GENERAL JOURNAL							
Date		Account	PR	Dr.			Cr.		
201X									
Oct. 29		Payroll Tax Expense		2 2 2 15					
		FICA OASDI Payable					1 1 7 80		
		FICA Medicare Payable					2 7 55		
		FUTA Payable					9 60		
		SUTA Payable					6 7 20		
		To record payroll tax expense for the							
		pay period ending October 29, 201X							

FICA OASDI	= $1,900 × 0.062	= $117.80
FICA Medicare	= $1,900 × 0.0145	= $ 27.55
FUTA	= $1,200 × 0.008	= $ 9.60
SUTA	= $1,200 × 0.056	= $ 67.20

COACHING TIP

Remember that OASDI and Medicare are employer payroll taxes even though employees pay these taxes, too.

LEARNING UNIT 8-2 PAYING FIT AND FICA TAXES AND COMPLETING THE EMPLOYER'S QUARTERLY FEDERAL TAX RETURN, FORM 941

As we discussed in Chapter 7, both employers and employees pay payroll taxes. Employees pay these amounts not by writing checks to the different levels of government, but by having the amounts of these taxes taken out, or withheld, from

Employer identification number (EIN) A number assigned by the IRS that is used by an employer when recording and paying payroll and income taxes.

Form SS-4 The form filled out by an employer to get an EIN. The form is sent to the IRS, which assigns the number to the business.

Federal Insurance Contribution Act (FICA) Part of the Social Security law that requires employees and employers to pay OASDI taxes and Medicare taxes.

● **L03**

Federal Unemployment Tax Act (FUTA) A tax paid by employers to the federal government. The current rate is 0.8% on the first $7,000 of earnings of each employee after the normal SUTA tax credit is applied.

Calendar quarter A three-month, 13-week time period. Four calendar quarters occur during a calendar year that runs from January 1 through December 31. The first quarter is January through March, the second is April through June, the third is July through September, and the fourth is October through December.

the amount of pay that they actually receive. Employers withhold these amounts, report them and the related earnings to federal, state, and sometimes local governments, and then turn them over to those levels of government. Let's now discuss how Travelwithus.com carries out these responsibilities.

For Travelwithus.com, the process began when the business opened. When opening a business, every employer must get a federal identification number. This number is also called an employer identification number (EIN) and is like a Social Security number for businesses in the sense that it identifies businesses to the government. To get an EIN, an employer fills out Form SS-4, much like individuals fill out Form SS-5 to get a Social Security number. Travelwithus.com will use its EIN, 58-1213479, to report employee earnings and payroll taxes.

Travelwithus.com must next determine when its payroll taxes are due to the government. Due dates vary according to the type of tax being paid.

Paying FIT and FICA Taxes

As required by law, Travelwithus.com withholds federal income tax from employees' paychecks, along with Social Security (OASDI) and Medicare taxes as established by the Federal Insurance Contributions Act or FICA. As the employer, Travelwithus.com reports and pays these taxes to the federal government. The Federal Unemployment Tax Act (FUTA) tax is the unemployment tax paid and reported separately that employers pay to the federal government. To see how Travelwithus.com reports the FIT and FICA taxes to the federal government, let's look at its payroll information for the last calendar quarter of the year, which covers October, November, and December.

To comply with federal law, Travelwithus.com must do two things: First, it must determine when FIT and FICA taxes need to be paid to the federal government and make this payment on time. Second, it must report these taxes on Form 941, the Employer's Quarterly Federal Tax Return. Figure 8.2 contains a worksheet that Katherine prepared from payroll registers to make sure that these two tasks happen the way they should.

FIGURE 8.2 Form 941 Worksheet

TRAVELWITHUS.COM INC.
Form 941 Taxes
4th Quarter

| Payroll Period | | Pay Check Date | Earnings | FIT | Taxable FICA Wages for | | FICA | | Total Tax | Cumulative Tax |
					OASDI	Medicare	OASDI EE + ER*	Medicare EE + ER		
October	2–15	Oct. 20	3680 75	393 84	3680 75	3680 75	456 41	106 74	956 99	956 99
October	16–29	Nov. 3	3276 90	341 00	3276 90	3276 90	406 34	95 04	842 38	1799 37
October	31	Oct. 31	18387 33	3493 59	18387 33	18387 33	2280 03	533 23	6306 85	8106 22
Oct./Nov.	30–12	Nov. 17	3276 90	352 00	3276 90	3276 90	406 34	95 03	853 37	8959 59
November	13–26	Dec. 1	3870 02	414 09	3870 02	3870 02	479 88	112 23	1006 20	9965 79
November	30	Nov. 30	18387 33	3493 59	18387 33	18387 33	2280 03	533 23	6306 85	16272 64
Nov./Dec.	27–10	Dec. 15	3340 60	357 44	3340 60	3340 60	414 23	96 88	868 55	17141 19
December	11–24	Dec. 29	3214 50	343 95	3214 50	3214 50	398 60	93 22	835 77	17976 96
December	25–31	Dec. 29	1578 90	168 94	1578 90	1578 90	195 78	45 79	410 51	18387 47
December	31	Dec. 29	18387 33	3493 59	16887 33	18387 33	2094 03	533 23	6120 85	24508 32
4th Quarter Totals			77400 56	12852 03	75900 56	77400 56	9411 67	2244 62	24508 32	24508 32
			(a)	(b)	(c)	(d)	(e)	(f)	(g)	(h)

*EE stands for employee; ER stands for employer

Notice a few things about this worksheet. First, look at the payroll period dates and see that some cover two-week periods and others show the last day of the month. Remember that the two types of dates relate to the two types of payroll that Travelwithus.com has, hourly and salaried. Next, observe that the quarter is 13 weeks long. By putting 13 weeks into each quarter, companies report all 52 weeks of a calendar year. Also, FIT and FICA are shown in separate columns because the IRS wants those amounts reported separately. Finally, notice that for the December 31 monthly payroll not all of the wages earned are taxable for OASDI, because an employee has reached the $106,800 wage base limit by this point in the year.

The total amount of taxes due must be transmitted to the Treasury Department using the Electronic Federal Tax Payment System (EFTPS) unless the quarterly deposit is less than $2,500. If the quarterly payment is less than $2,500 the deposit may be paid by check submitted with the quarterly Form 941.

Types of Payroll Tax Depositors To determine when payroll taxes are due, for payroll tax deposit purposes, employers are usually classified as either monthly or semiweekly depositors. Rarely a company will owe less than $2,500 in total taxes for the quarter, but in this case the taxes may be deposited quarterly. A monthly depositor is an employer who has to deposit Form 941 taxes (federal income tax withholdings, OASDI, and Medicare) on the 15th day of the month following the payday(s). Semiweekly depositors must deposit their Form 941 taxes once or twice each week, depending on when payroll is paid. These classifications last for an entire calendar year, and employers are reevaluated every year.

Employers are classified according to the dollar amount of the Form 941 taxes that they have paid in the past. The IRS developed a rule known as the look-back period rule to determine how to classify an employer for payroll tax deposits. Under this rule, the IRS looks back to a one-year time period that begins on July 1 and ends the following June 30 of the previous year. If during this look-back period an employer paid less than $50,000 of Form 941 taxes, then it is classified as a monthly depositor. Alternately, if the employer paid $50,000 or more during this period, then it is considered a semiweekly depositor. New companies are automatically classified as monthly depositors until they have been in business long enough to have a look-back period that can be used to classify them. Figure 8.3 shows how the look-back period works.

Travelwithus.com is a semiweekly depositor because it made more than $50,000 of FIT and FICA deposits during the most recent look-back period.

Rules for Monthly Depositors If an employer is classified as a monthly depositor, the FIT and both the employee and employer OASDI and Medicare taxes accumulated during any month must be deposited by the 15th day of the next month. If the 15th is a Saturday, Sunday, or bank holiday, then the deposit must be made on the next banking day.

Form 941, Employer's Quarterly Federal Tax Return A tax report that a business will complete after the end of each calendar quarter indicating the total FICA (OASDI and Medicare) taxes owed plus the amount of FIT withheld from employees' pay for the quarter. If federal tax deposits have been made correctly and on time, the total amount deposited should equal the amount due on Form 941. Any difference results in a payment due or a refund.

Form 941 taxes Another term used to describe FIT, OASDI, and Medicare. This name comes from the form used to report these taxes.

Monthly depositor A business classified as a monthly depositor will make its payroll tax deposits only once each month for the amount of Form 941 taxes due from the prior month.

Semiweekly depositor A business classified as a semiweekly depositor may have to make its payroll tax deposits up to twice in one week, depending on when payroll is paid.

Look-back period A period of time used to determine whether a business should make its Form 941 tax deposits on a monthly or semiweekly basis. The IRS defines this period as July 1 through June 30 of the year prior to the year in which Form 941 tax deposits will be made.

Banking day A banking day is any day that a bank is open to the public for business. Generally, a banking day will end at 2:00 or 3:00 P.M. local time. Banking business transacted after this time is usually considered to be the next day's business. Saturdays, Sundays, and federal holidays are usually not considered banking days.

FIGURE 8.3
Look-Back Illustration

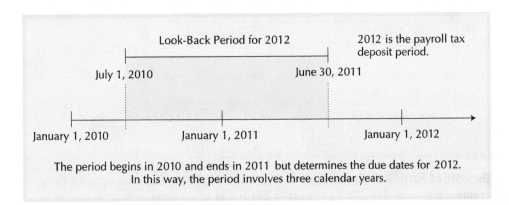

Look-Back Period for 2012

2012 is the payroll tax deposit period.

July 1, 2010   June 30, 2011

January 1, 2010   January 1, 2011   January 1, 2012

The period begins in 2010 and ends in 2011 but determines the due dates for 2012. In this way, the period involves three calendar years.

Rules for Semiweekly Depositors If an employer is classified as a semiweekly depositor, as a general rule it always has three banking days to make its payroll tax deposit. However, semiweekly depositors like Travelwithus.com may have to make up to two payroll tax deposits every week, depending on when they pay their employees. According to the IRS, for this purpose, each week begins on Wednesday and ends on the following Tuesday. This week is broken into two parts, Wednesday through Friday, and Saturday through Tuesday. If the company's payday is a Wednesday, Thursday, or Friday, the payroll tax deposit is due on the following Wednesday. If the company's payday is a Saturday, Sunday, Monday, or Tuesday, the payroll tax deposit is due on the following Friday.

Thus, if an employer pays its employees on a Thursday and a Monday, it must make two payroll tax deposits, one on Wednesday for the Thursday payday, and one on Friday for the Monday payday. If a bank holiday occurs between a payday and the day when the payroll tax deposit is due, the employer gets an extra day to make the deposit. So, a deposit due on a Wednesday will be due on Thursday, or a Friday deposit will be due on the following Monday.

The diagram in Figure 8.4 shows how these rules work:

FIGURE 8.4
Semiweekly Deposit Rules
Illustration

	Sat	Sun	Mon	Tues	Wed	Thurs	Fri	Sat	Sun	Mon	Tues	Wed
If payday is												
Then deposit is due												

See Figure 8.5 to see how the rules apply to Travelwithus.com. Remember that Travelwithus.com's hourly payroll is always paid on a Friday. Because Travelwithus.com is a semiweekly payroll tax depositor, its FIT, OASDI and Medicare tax deposits for its hourly payroll are due on the following Wednesday. Because its hourly payroll is paid on a biweekly, or every other week, basis, Travelwithus.com will need to make a deposit every other Wednesday. However, if we look at week 52, the payday for this week is Friday, December 29, which is two days before New Year's Day. Under the law, January 1 is a federal holiday, so Katherine must apply the rule regarding a holiday that falls between a payday and a tax deposit day and will make the Form 941 tax deposit not on Wednesday but on Thursday, January 4, of the next year.

Travelwithus.com also has a salaried payroll, and this payroll is paid on the last day of the month. In October, the last day of the month is a Tuesday, so Travelwithus.com will make its Form 941 tax deposit for this payroll on the following Friday.

FIGURE 8.5
Third Quarter Payroll Calendar
for Travelwithus.com

October						
Sun	Mon	Tues	Wed	Thu	Fri	Sat
1	2	3	4	5	6	7
8	9	10	11	12	13	14
15	16	17	18	19	20	21
22	23	24	25	26	27	28
29	30	31				

November						
Sun	Mon	Tues	Wed	Thu	Fri	Sat
			1	2	3	4
5	6	7	8	9	10	11
12	13	14	15	16	17	18
19	20	21	22	23	24	25
26	27	28	29	30		

December						
Sun	Mon	Tues	Wed	Thu	Fri	Sat
					1	2
3	4	5	6	7	8	9
10	11	12	13	14	15	16
17	18	19	20	21	22	23
24	25	26	27	28	29	30
31						

= Hourly payroll paydays

= Salaried payroll paydays

☐ = Payroll tax deposit due dates

Deposit of Form 941 Taxes Prior to December 31, 2010, employers paying the government less than $200,000 per year in Form 941 taxes were permitted to pay these taxes (FICA and FIT) by check. The IRS required the employer to use Form 8901,

Federal Tax Deposit Coupon to make these deposits. The Form 8901 is very similar to a deposit slip used to make a deposit in a bank account. Employers owing more than $200,000 of deposits of Form 941 taxes in a year were required to pay these taxes using the Electronic Federal Tax Payment System (EFTPS).

Effective January 1, 2011, all employers paying Form 941 taxes must use the Electronic Federal Tax Payment System (EFTPS) except for those that owe less than $2,500 per quarter. Failure to use the EFTPS could result in a 10% failure-to-deposit penalty. Those employers owing less than $2,500 per quarter will be permitted to remit Form 941 taxes with their quarterly or annual Form 941 submission.

The EFTPS is a communications network that facilitates the direct transfer of funds from the employer's bank to the Treasury Department. These transfers may be transacted by touchtone phone, by personal computer, or online. The EFTPS requirement does not change existing rules for determining a depositor's status as either a monthly or semiweekly depositor for employment taxes.

Enrollment in the EFTPS program is accomplished online at http://www.eftps.gov. It takes several days to obtain the necessary documentation in the mail. Once enrolled in the program the employer can use either of the following two methods to make the required deposit. The employer may instruct the Treasury Financial Agent for that area to withdraw funds from the employer's bank account and route them to the Treasury's account at the Federal Reserve Bank. The employer may also instruct his or her bank to send each payment directly to the Treasury's account at the Federal Reserve Bank.

Once Travelwithus.com has enrolled in EFTPS, all Katherine needs to do is contact the IRS via either the Internet or phone. Katherine must notify the IRS before 8:00 p.m., at least one day in advance of the payment due date, of the amount to be transferred. The EFTPS will provide Travelwithus.com with a confirmation number called an "EFT Number," which guarantees the depositor that the tax deposit has been scheduled and allows the transaction to be traced if necessary.

The last task that Katherine must perform is to record the payment of the FIT and FICA taxes. The journal entry that she makes looks like this:

	GENERAL JOURNAL				
Date		PR	Dr.	Cr.	
201X					
Nov. 8	FICA OASDI Payable		406 34		
	FICA Medicare Payable		95 04		
	FIT Payable		341 00		
	Cash			842 38	
	To record payment of FIT and FICA				
	taxes for pay period ending				
	October 29, 201X				

To get a better idea of how payroll tax amounts appear in the accounting system of Travelwithus.com, let's check out its general ledger for the FICA OASDI Payable and FICA Medicare Payable accounts:

FICA OASDI Payable						Account No. 203
Date		PR	Dr.	Cr.	Cr. Bal.	
201X						
Oct.	15	GJ28		456 41	456 41	
	25	GJ28	456 41		0	
	29	GJ29		406 34	406 34	
	31	GJ29		2280 03	2686 37	
Nov.	3	GJ29	2280 03		406 34	
	8	GJ30	406 34		0	

FICA Medicare Payable						Account No. 204
Date		PR	Dr.	Cr.	Cr. Bal.	
201X						
Oct.	15	GJ28		106 74	106 74	
	25	GJ28	106 74		0	
	29*	GJ29		95 04	95 04	
	31	GJ29		533 23	628 27	
Nov.	3	GJ29	533 23		95 04	
	8	GJ30	95 04		0	

*This represents both the employee and employer deductions.

Notice several things about the ledger accounts. First, the entries on October 29 crediting the FICA OASDI Payable and FICA Medicare Payable accounts came from the general journal entries on this date because the payroll and payroll taxes were recorded on this date. These amounts represent both the employee and employer's shares of OASDI and Medicare. Also notice that the entries on November 8 debiting FICA OASDI Payable for $406.34 and FICA Medicare Payable for $95.04 came from the general journal. They are part of the payment that Travelwithus.com deposited with the Form 941 taxes. To summarize, journal entries crediting these accounts record tax liabilities, and journal entries debiting these accounts record payments of these taxes.

Completing the Employer's Quarterly Federal Tax Return, Form 941

Form 944, Employer's Annual Federal Tax Return The form used by employers to report FICA (OASDI and Medicare) taxes and FIT. This version will be filed by January 31 following the end of the year and can be used by employers who owe $1,000 or less for theses taxes and who have been told by the IRS that they must file this form.

The IRS requires all employers to complete tax returns reporting FICA OASDI, FICA Medicare, and FIT taxes. If these taxes total less than $1,000 for a calendar year, then employers will prepare Form 944, Employer's Annual Federal Tax Return. This form is due from employers by January 31 of the following year. Employers will complete this return only if the IRS notifies them that it is the form that they must use. If, however, taxes total more than $1,000 for a calendar year, then employers must instead complete Form 941, Employer's Quarterly Federal Tax Return, and submit it to the IRS for every quarter in a calendar year. Katherine Kurtz, the accountant for Travelwithus.com, used the worksheet in Figure 8.2 to prepare Form 941 for the last quarter of the year because Travelwithus.com's taxes exceeded $1,000.

The top section of Travelwithus.com's fourth quarter Form 941 in Figure 8.6 identifies the taxpayer, Travelwithus.com, and lists its address, the date that the quarter ended, and its EIN. Refer back to the worksheet in Figure 8.2 and use the letters below the column totals to follow amounts from this worksheet to the Form 941. Line-by-line instructions for completing the Form 941 are as follows:

Part 1:   *Answering questions that relate to the current quarter.*

Line 1:   This line is used to show how many employees were paid during the quarter.

2: This line is used to report total gross earnings for the quarter, which is $77,400.56 per column (a) of the worksheet in Figure 8.2.

3: Total income tax withheld is $12,852.03, which comes from column (b).

4: No entry is needed here; this line is only used for special situations.

5a, Column 1: The wages subject to FICA OASDI tax are the total taxable earnings of $75,900.56, which match column (c). The amount on this line is different from the line 2 amount because one employee reached the OASDI wage base limit of $106,800.

5a, Column 2: Katherine multiplies the amount on line 5a, Column 1, by 12.4%, which is the 6.2% rate for employees and the 6.2% rate for employers, to get the tax of $9,411.67 entered here. Notice that this amount matches column (e) of the worksheet.

5b: This line is used to report taxable tips that employees might have received. Travelwithus.com employees did not receive any tips, so this line is left blank.

5c, Column 1: The wages subject to Medicare tax are the total taxable earnings of $77,400.56, which match column (d). The amount on this line is the same as the line 2 amount because the Medicare tax has no wage base limit.

5c, Column 2: Katherine multiplies the amount on line 5c, Column 1, by 2.9%, which is the 1.45% rate for employees and the 1.45% rate for employers, to get the tax of $2,244.62 entered here. Notice that this amount matches column (f) of the worksheet.

FIGURE 8.6 Completed Form 941

Form **941 for 201X:** Employer's **QUARTERLY** Federal Tax Return
(Rev. January 2010)   Department of the Treasury — Internal Revenue Service

950110

OMB No. 1545-0029

(EIN)
Employer identification number   5 8 – 1 2 1 3 4 7 9

Name (not your trade name)   Travelwithus.com

Trade name (if any)

Address   10 Lovett Road
Number   Street   Suite or room number

Salem   MA   01970
City   State   ZIP code

Report for this Quarter of 2009
(Check one.)

☐ **1:** January, February, March

☐ **2:** April, May, June

☐ **3:** July, August, September

✓ **4:** October, November, December

Read the separate instructions before you complete Form 941. Type or print within the boxes.

Part 1: Answer these questions for this quarter.

1	Number of employees who received wages, tips, or other compensation for the pay period including: *Mar. 12* (Quarter 1), *June 12* (Quarter 2), *Sept. 12* (Quarter 3), *Dec. 12* (Quarter 4)	1	6
2	Wages, tips, and other compensation	2	77,400.56
3	Income tax withheld from wages, tips, and other compensation	3	12,852.03
4	If no wages, tips, and other compensation are subject to social security or Medicare tax	☐ Check and go to line 6.	
5	Taxable social security and Medicare wages and tips:		

		Column 1		Column 2
5a	Taxable social security wages	75,900.56	× .124 =	9,411.67
5b	Taxable social security tips	.	× .124 =	.
5c	Taxable Medicare wages & tips	77,400.56	× .029 =	2,244.62

5d	Total social security and Medicare taxes (*Column 2,* lines 5a + 5b + 5c = line 5d) .	5d	11,656.29
6	Total taxes before adjustments (lines 3 + 5d = line 6)	6	24,508.32
7	**CURRENT QUARTER'S ADJUSTMENTS,** for example, a fractions of cents adjustment. See the instructions.		
7a	Current quarter's fractions of cents		.
7b	Current quarter's sick pay		.
7c	Current quarter's adjustments for tips and group-term life insurance		.
7d	**TOTAL ADJUSTMENTS.** Combine all amounts on lines 7a through 7c	7d	.
8	Total taxes after adjustments. Combine lines 6 and 7d	8	24,508.32
9	Advance earned income credit (EIC) payments made to employees	9	.
10	Total taxes after adjustment for advance EIC (line 8 – line 9 = line 10)	10	24,508.32
11	Total deposits for this quarter, including overpayment applied from a prior quarter and overpayment applied from Form 941-X or Form 944-X		24,508.32
12a	COBRA premium assistance payments (see instructions)		.
12b	Number of individuals provided COBRA premium assistance reported on line 12a		
13	Add lines 11 and 12a	13	24,508.32
14	**Balance due.** If line 10 is more than line 13, write the difference here For information on how to pay, see the instructions.	14	.
15	**Overpayment.** If line 13 is more than line 10, write the difference here		.

☐ Apply to next return.
Check one ☐ Send a refund.

▶ You **MUST** complete both pages of Form 941 and **SIGN** it.

Next ➡

For Privacy Act and Paperwork Reduction Act Notice, see the back of the Payment Voucher.   Cat. No. 17001Z   Form **941** (Rev. 1-2010)

FIGURE 8.6 *(Continued)*

950210

Name *(not your trade name)*	Employer identification number (EIN)
Travelwithus.com	58-1213479

Part 2: Tell us about your deposit schedule and tax liability for this quarter.

If you are unsure about whether you are a monthly schedule depositor or a semiweekly schedule depositor, see *Pub. 15 (Circular E)*, section 11.

16 [M] [A]   Write the state abbreviation for the state where you made your deposits OR write "MU" if you made your deposits in *multiple* states.

17 Check one: ☐ Line 10 is less than $2,500. Go to Part 3.

☐ You were a monthly schedule depositor for the entire quarter. Enter your tax liability for each month. Then go to Part 3.

Tax liability: Month 1 ☐ .

Month 2 ☐ .

Month 3 ☐ .

Total liability for quarter ☐ .   Total must equal line 10.

☑ You were a semiweekly schedule depositor for any part of this quarter. Complete *Schedule B (Form 941): Report of Tax Liability for Semiweekly Schedule Depositors,* and attach it to Form 941.

Part 3: Tell us about your business. If a question does NOT apply to your business, leave it blank.

18 If your business has closed or you stopped paying wages . . . . ☐ Check here, and

enter the final date you paid wages [/   /   ] .

19 If you are a seasonal employer and you do not have to file a return for every quarter of the year . ☐ Check here.

Part 4: May we speak with your third-party designee?

Do you want to allow an employee, a paid tax preparer, or another person to discuss this return with the IRS? See the instructions for details.

☐ Yes. Designee's name and phone number [   ]   ([   ]) – [   ]

Select a 5-digit Personal Identification Number (PIN) to use when talking to the IRS. ☐ ☐ ☐ ☐ ☐

☑ No.

Part 5: Sign here. You MUST complete both pages of Form 941 and SIGN it.

Under penalties of perjury, I declare that I have examined this return, including accompanying schedules and statements, and to the best of my knowledge and belief, it is true, correct, and complete. Declaration of preparer (other than taxpayer) is based on all information of which preparer has any knowledge.

X **Sign your name here** *Katherine C. Kurtz* | Print your name here | Katherine C. Kurtz |
| Print your title here | Controller |

Date [1 / 31 / 201X+1]   Best daytime phone (978) 555 – 4040

Paid preparer's use only

Check if you are self-employed . . . . ☐

Preparer's name		Preparer's SSN/PTIN	
Preparer's signature		Date	/ /
Firm's name (or yours if self-employed)		EIN	
Address		Phone	( ) –
City		State		ZIP code	

5d: The total of OASDI tax of $9,411.67 and Medicare tax of $2,244.62 is $11,656.29.

6: This line is used to report the total income tax, OASDI tax, and Medicare tax withheld of $24,507.32. It is the sum of lines 3 and 5d. Notice that it matches column (g).

7a–h: These lines are used to report special tax adjustments. None apply to Travelwithus.com, so these lines are left blank.

8: This line reports total tax after adjustments, so it is the same as line 6.

9: If Travelwithus.com advanced any earned income credit to its employees, it would deduct these amounts on this line.

10: This line is the difference between lines 8 and 9.

11: This line shows the total of the Form 941 deposits that Travelwithus.com made for the last quarter, $24,508.32. This amount includes the last deposit that Travelwithus.com made for the quarter on Thursday, January 4, because it applies to the December 31 biweekly and monthly payrolls.

12 and 13: Travelwithus.com's deposits exactly total the Form 941 taxes for the quarter, which means it does not have any balance due, nor has it overpaid its taxes.

Part 2: *Providing information about the deposit schedule.*

Line 14: Katherine indicates the abbreviation of the state in which Travelwithus.com has made its deposits.

Line 15: As a semiweekly depositor, Travelwithus.com checks this box and completes and attaches Schedule B: Report of Tax Liability for Semiweekly Schedule Depositors. By showing each day of the quarter, this schedule requires employers to present tax liability amounts on a day-by-day basis. The IRS requires employers to complete this schedule because, by comparing the dates of the tax liabilities to the dates that the deposits were made, it easily allows them to determine whether deposits were made on time. (Schedule B is not shown here.) The amounts for each day are added together to show the total for each month, and these monthly totals together should equal the total liability on line 10.

Part 3: *Indicating specific situations that relate to the business.*

Lines 16 and 17: If a business has not closed and is not a seasonal employer, these lines do not apply. Katherine leaves them blank.

Part 4: *Indicating whether the business would allow an employee, paid tax preparer, or another person to discuss the return with the IRS..* Katherine checks "No."

Part 5: *Signing the return.* Katherine signs the return on behalf of Travelwithus.com.

LEARNING UNIT 8-2 REVIEW

AT THIS POINT you should be able to do the following:

- Explain the purpose of Form SS-4.
- Explain which taxes are reported on Form 941.
- Understand how employers are classified as payroll tax depositors.
- Summarize Form 941 payroll tax deposit rules for monthly depositors.
- Summarize Form 941 payroll tax deposit rules for semiweekly depositors.
- Record the general journal entry to pay FIT, FICA OASDI, and FICA Medicare when a payroll tax deposit is made.
- Understand how the general journal entries recording FICA OASDI and FICA Medicare and the payment of these taxes are posted into the general ledger.
- Complete a Form 941, Employer's Quarterly Federal Tax Return, from a worksheet.

Instant Replay ◎ Self-Review Quiz 8-2

Carol Ann's Import Chalet is a business that employs five full-time employees and four part-time employees. The accountant for Carol Ann's determined that the business is a monthly depositor. The accountant prepared a worksheet showing the following payroll tax liabilities for the month of October:

Payday	OASDI EE + ER	Medicare EE + ER	FIT
10/7	$486.56	$169.05	$829.00
10/14	$632.15	$165.01	$901.00
10/21	$579.43	$131.05	$734.00
10/28	$389.99	$142.24	$765.00
Totals	$2,088.13	$607.35	$3,229.00

1. What is the dollar amount of the Form 941 tax deposit that must be made, and when must it be made according to the monthly deposit rule? Use Figure 8.5 for the date.
2. Now assume that Carol Ann is classified as a semiweekly depositor. Please calculate the amount of each Form 941 tax deposit and its due date by completing the following table (use Figure 8.5 for the dates):

Payday	Date of Deposit	Amount of Deposit
10/7	?	?
10/14	?	?
10/21	?	?
10/28	?	?

COACHING TIP

The tax for Form 941 is
FICA OASDI: employee and employer
FICA Medicare: employee and employer
FIT: employee only

Solutions to Instant Replay: Self-Review Quiz 8-2

1. As a monthly depositor, Carol Ann's deposit date is Wednesday, November 15. The total amount of the deposit is $5,924.48 ($2,088.13 + $607.35 + $3,229.00).
2. As a semiweekly depositor, Carol Ann's deposit schedule is completed as follows:

Payday	Date of Deposit	Amount of Deposit	
10/7	10/13	$1,484.61	($486.56 + $169.05 + $829.00)
10/14	10/20	$1,698.16	
10/21	10/27	$1,444.48	
10/28	11/3	$1,297.23	

LEARNING UNIT 8-3 PREPARING FORMS W-2 AND W-3, PAYING FUTA TAX AND COMPLETING THE EMPLOYER'S ANNUAL UNEMPLOYMENT TAX RETURN, FORM 940, AND PAYING SUTA TAX AND WORKERS' COMPENSATION INSURANCE

Preparing Form W-2: Wage and Tax Statement

◯ **LO4**

The Internal Revenue Service requires that each calendar year employers complete a Form W-2, Wage and Tax Statement, a multipart form. The IRS requires Travelwithus. com to give or mail copies of Form W-2 to each person who worked for the company in the past year. These forms must be distributed by January 31 of the following year.

Employees use the amount on this form to prepare their income tax returns and calculate the amounts of income tax they owe. They must attach one copy of the form to their federal income tax return, and other copies are attached to any state or local income tax returns that they may be required to file. Taxpayers who file electronically do not attach a copy of their W-2 but must furnish a copy if requested by the IRS.

Figure 8.7 shows the W-2 that Stephanie Higuera received from Travelwithus. com. Travelwithus.com prepares the W-2s by using information from Stephanie's employee earnings record. Note that OASDI wages and taxes are shown separately from the amounts reported for Medicare wages and taxes because of the wage base limit for the OASDI tax that does not apply to the Medicare tax.

If an employee stops working for Travelwithus.com during the year, he or she may ask for a W-2 before the year ends. Travelwithus.com must provide the W-2 within 30 days of the last paycheck or the date of the request, whichever is later. Travelwithus.com must also give copies of the W-2s for all employees to the Social Security Administration and state and local governments. It will also keep a copy for its own records.

Form W-2, Wage and Tax Statement A form completed by the employer at the end of the calendar year to provide a summary of gross earnings and deductions to each employee. At least three copies go to the employee, one copy to the IRS, one copy to any state where employee income taxes have been withheld, one copy to the Social Security Administration, and one copy into the records of the business.

FIGURE 8.7 Completed Form W-2

a Control number 22222 Void ☐	For Official Use Only ▶ OMB No. 1545-0008	
b Employer identification number (EIN) 58-1213479	1 Wages, tips, other compensation 23 723.40	2 Federal income tax withheld 2 241.86
c Employer's name, address, and ZIP code TRAVELWITHUS.COM 10 LOVETT ROAD SALEM, MA 01970	3 Social security wages 23 723.40	4 Social security tax withheld 1 470.85
	5 Medicare wages and tips 23 723.40	6 Medicare tax withheld 343.99
	7 Social security tips	8 Allocated tips
d Employee's social security number 123-45-6789	9 Advance EIC payment	10 Dependent care benefits
e Employee's first name and initial STEPHANIE A. Last name HIGUERA Suff.	11 Nonqualified plans	12a See instructions for box 12
1014 INVERNESS WAY SOUTHSIDE, MA 01945	13 Statutory employee ☐ Retirement plan ☐ Third-party sick pay ☐	12b
	14 Other	12c
		12d
f Employee's address and ZIP code		

15 State Employer's state ID number MA 621-8966-4	16 State wages, tips, etc. 23 723.40	17 State income tax 1 897.87	18 Local wages, tips, etc.	19 Local income tax	20 Locality name

Form **W-2** Wage and Tax Statement   **201X**

Copy A For Social Security Administration — Send this entire page with Form W-3 to the Social Security Administration; photocopies are **not** acceptable.

Department of the Treasury—Internal Revenue Service
For Privacy Act and Paperwork Reduction Act Notice, see back of Copy D.

Cat. No. 10134D

Do Not Cut, Fold, or Staple Forms on This Page — Do Not Cut, Fold, or Staple Forms on This Page

Preparing Form W-3: Transmittal of Income and Tax Statements

The IRS also requires Travelwithus.com to prepare its Form W-3, Transmittal of Wage and Tax Statements. Employers such as Travelwithus.com send this form to the Social Security Administration along with copies of the W-2s for all employees (see Figure 8.8). Form W-3 reports the total amounts of wages, tips, and compensation paid to employees, the total OASDI and Medicare taxes withheld, and some other information. The information used to complete Form W-3 came from a summary of the individual employee earnings records that Katherine prepared soon after the year ended. (See Figure 8.9).

Form W-3, Transmittal of Income and Tax Statement A form completed by the employer to verify the number of W-2s and amounts withheld as shown on them. This form is sent to the Social Security Administration data processing center along with copies of each employee's W-2 forms.

FIGURE 8.8 Completed Form W-3

DO NOT STAPLE

a Control number		33333	For Official Use Only ▶ OMB No. 1545-0008		

b	941 [X]	Military [ ] 943 [ ]	944 [ ]	1 Wages, tips, other compensation 286 425.30	2 Federal income tax withheld 48 063.67
Kind of Payer ▶	CT-1 [ ]	Hshld. emp. [ ] Medicare govt. emp. [ ]	Third-party sick pay [ ]	3 Social security wages 284 925.30	4 Social security tax withheld 17655.37

c Total number of Forms W-2 6	d Establishment number	5 Medicare wages and tips 286 425.30	6 Medicare tax withheld 4153.17

e Employer identification number (EIN) 58-1213479	7 Social security tips	8 Allocated tips

f Employer's name TRAVELWITHUS.COM	9 Advance EIC payments	10 Dependent care benefits
	11 Nonqualified plans	12 Deferred compensation
10 LOVETT ROAD SALEM, MA 01970	13 For third-party sick pay use only	
	14 Income tax withheld by payer of third-party sick pay	

g Employer's address and ZIP code

h Other EIN used this year

15 State MA	Employer's state ID number 621-8966-4	16 State wages, tips, etc. 286 425.30	17 State income tax 22 914.02
		18 Local wages, tips, etc.	19 Local income tax

Contact person KATHERINE C. KURTZ	Telephone number (978)555 4040	For Official Use Only
Email address KKURTZ@TRAVELWITH.US	Fax number (978)555 4040	

Under penalties of perjury, I declare that I have examined this return and accompanying documents, and, to the best of my knowledge and belief, they are true, correct, and complete.

Signature ▶ *Katherine C. Kurtz*   Title ▶ CONTROLLER   Date ▶ 2/28/201X

Form W-3 Transmittal of Wage and Tax Statements   201X   Department of the Treasury Internal Revenue Service

Send this entire page with the entire Copy A page of Form(s) W-2 to the Social Security Administration. Photocopies are not acceptable.

Do not send any payment (cash, checks, money orders, etc.) with Forms W-2 and W-3.

Employers send Form W-2 and Form W-3 to the Social Security Administration for FICA tax purposes. The Social Security Administration, under a special agreement with the IRS, makes all information found on individual W-2 forms electronically available to the IRS so that it can check the accuracy of the employer's 941 forms and individual employees' federal income tax returns.

L05   Paying FUTA Tax

If the total FUTA tax owed for the calendar year is less than $500, an employer must pay the tax to the IRS by the end of January of the next year. If the total amount owed is more than $500, then it is due by the end of the month following the end of the calendar quarter. If the employer is required to make Form 941 tax payments by EFTPS, then it must also deposit FUTA tax by this method.

By the end of the year, all of Travelwithus.com's employees earned more than the $7,000 wage base limit, so its total FUTA tax will be calculated as follows:

6 employees × $7,000 FUTA taxable earnings × 0.08%* FUTA tax rate = $336 FUTA tax

---

*Normal FUTA Tax credit 6.2%–5.4%.

FIGURE 8.9 W-3 Worksheet

Employee	Total Earnings	FICA Taxable Earnings		FICA Tax		FIT
		OASDI	Medicare	OASDI	Medicare	
Goldman, Ernie	103 500 00	102 000 00	103 500 00	6 324 00	1 500 75	20 097 00
Higuera, Stephanie	23 723 40	23 723 40	23 723 40	1 470 85	343 99	2 241 86
Kurtz, Katherine	66 448 16	66 448 16	66 448 16	4 119 79	963 50	12 625 15
Regan, Julia	58 500 00	58 500 00	58 500 00	3 627 00	848 25	9 945 00
Sui, Annie	8 287 14	8 287 14	8 287 14	513 80	120 16	1 077 33
Taylor, Harold	25 966 60	25 966 60	25 966 60	1 609 93	376 52	2 077 33
Total	286 425 30	284 925 30	286 425 30	17 665 37	4 153 17	48 063 67

Because this amount is less than $500, Katherine does not need to make a deposit during the year and will deposit the taxes by the end of January of the following year. She then makes the following journal entry to record the payment of FUTA tax.

GENERAL JOURNAL					
Date			PR	Dr.	Cr.
201X+1					
Jan.	31	FUTA Payable		3 36 00	
		Cash			3 36 00
		To record payment of the 201X FUTA			
		tax			

Completing the Employer's Annual Federal Unemployment (FUTA) Tax Return, Form 940

Businesses must complete Form 940, Employer's Annual Federal Unemployment (FUTA) Tax Return. Employers must file Form 940 by January 31 of the following year; however, if all taxes owed for the year were deposited by January 31, then the business has until February 10 to file its return.

To make sure that Travelwithus.com makes its FUTA deposits on time, Katherine keeps track of the amount of FUTA tax owed. Katherine prepared the worksheet in Figure 8.10 to determine the amount of FUTA taxes that Travelwithus.com owes for the first quarter of the year. Notice that she calculates the FUTA tax on the total wages because reporting the FUTA tax for each individual employee is not required. Also notice that Annie Sui has no earnings for the first quarter and therefore no earnings that are taxable for FUTA purposes because she was hired after the quarter began. Finally, notice that Ernie Goldman, Katherine Kurtz, and Julia Regan's first quarter earnings are greater than their FUTA taxable earnings because they earned more than $7,000 during the first quarter, and only the first $7,000 of earnings is taxable.

Although Travelwithus.com's other payroll amounts have been shown for the last quarter of the year, showing FUTA tax calculations for this quarter would not be very helpful. Almost all employees will have made more than the $7,000 FUTA limit by the start of the fourth quarter, and Travelwithus.com would only owe FUTA taxes for one employee, Annie Sui, who was hired just before the fourth quarter began.

Form 940, Employer's Annual Federal Unemployment Tax Return This form is used by employers at the end of the calendar year to report the amount of unemployment tax due for the year. If more than $500 is cumulatively owed at the end of a quarter, it should be paid one month after the end of that quarter. Normally, the report is due January 31 after the calendar year, or February 10 if an employer has already made all deposits.

At the end of the calendar year, Katherine prepares the Form 940 in Figure 8.11. Line-by-line instructions follow:

Part 1:

Line 1a: This line is used to show the state in which payments are made if only one state is involved.

1b is used by employers who pay state unemployment in more than one state.

Part 2:   *Reporting taxable wages and FUTA tax.*

Line 3:   Katherine shows the total wages and salaries paid during the year, $286,425.30, as shown on the W-3 worksheet.

4: This line is used to show any payments that are exempt from FUTA taxes, and does not apply to Travelwithus.com.

5: This line shows the amount of wages and salaries above the $7,000 limit, which is $244,425.30. Because the six employees all reached the $7,000 limit, the total limit is $42,000. Total wages and salaries of $286,425.30 minus taxable wages and salaries of $42,000 equals $244,425.30.

6: Katherine adds the total of lines 4 and 5 and gets $244,425.30.

7: Katherine subtracts line 6 from line 3 to determine the taxable amount of wages and salaries, $42,000.

8: Katherine multiplies line 7, $42,000, by the FUTA tax rate of .008 to get the total FUTA tax of $336.00 for the year.

Part 3 is used to determine adjustments to the FUTA tax calculated in line 8, if any.

Part 4 is used to calculate your FUTA tax.

12: This is the amount of FUTA tax less any adjustments made in Part 3. Travelwithus.com did not have any adjustments.

13: This line shows the amount of FUTA tax that Travelwithus.com paid for the year.

14 and 15: Travelwithus.com paid exactly the right amount of FUTA tax for the year; therefore, no balance is due and no overpayment was made.

Part 5:   *Showing the tax liability by quarter.*

Katherine does not have to complete this section because Travelwithus.com's FUTA tax liability for the year was less than $500.

FIGURE 8.10
FUTA Worksheet

TRAVELWITHUS.COM INC. FUTA Taxes 1st Quarter				
Employee	1st Quarter Earnings	FUTA Taxable Earnings	FUTA Tax Rate	FUTA Tax
Goldman, Ernie	23 9 25 00	7 0 00 00		
Higuera, Stephanie	5 9 28 00	5 9 28 00		
Kurtz, Katherine	16 6 12 04	7 0 00 00		
Regan, Julia	14 6 25 00	7 0 00 00		
Sui, Annie				
Taylor, Harold	5 3 25 59	5 3 25 59		
Total	66 4 15 63	32 2 53 59	0 008	2 5 8 03

FIGURE 8.11 Completed Form 940

Form **940 for 201X:** **Employer's Annual Federal Unemployment (FUTA) Tax Return**   850110

Department of the Treasury — Internal Revenue Service   OMB No. 1545-0028

(EIN)
Employer identification number   5 5 – 1 2 1 3 4 7 9

Name *(not your trade name)*   Travelwithus.com

Trade name *(if any)*

Address   10 Lovett Road
Number   Street   Suite or room number

Salem   MA   01970
City   State   ZIP code

Type of Return
(Check all that apply.)

☐ **a.** Amended
☐ **b.** Successor employer
☐ **c.** No payments to employees in 2010
☐ **d.** Final: Business closed or stopped paying wages

Read the separate instructions before you fill out this form. Please type or print within the boxes.

Part 1: Tell us about your return. If any line does NOT apply, leave it blank.

1 If you were required to pay your state unemployment tax in ...

    1a One state only, write the state abbreviation . . . . **1a** | M | A |

    - OR -

    1b More than one state (You are a multi-state employer) . . . . **1b** ☐ Check here. Fill out Schedule A.

2 If you paid wages in a state that is subject to **CREDIT REDUCTION** . . . . **2** ☐ Check here. Fill out Schedule A (Form 940), Part 2.

Part 2: Determine your FUTA tax before adjustments for 2010. If any line does NOT apply, leave it blank.

3 Total payments to all employees . . . . **3** | 286425.30 |

4 Payments exempt from FUTA tax . . . . **4** | 0. |

    Check all that apply: **4a** ☐ Fringe benefits   **4c** ☐ Retirement/Pension   **4e** ☐ Other
    4b ☐ Group-term life insurance   **4d** ☐ Dependent care

5 Total of payments made to each employee in excess of $7,000 . . . . **5** | 244,425.30 |

6 Subtotal (line 4 + line 5 = line 6) . . . . **6** | 244,425.00 |

7 Total taxable FUTA wages (line 3 – line 6 = line 7) . . . . **7** | 42,000.00 |

8 FUTA tax before adjustments (line 7 × .008 = line 8) . . . . **8** | 336.00 |

Part 3: Determine your adjustments. If any line does NOT apply, leave it blank.

9 If ALL of the taxable FUTA wages you paid were excluded from state unemployment tax, multiply line 7 by .054 (line 7 × .054 = line 9). Then go to line 12 . . . . **9** | 0. |

10 If SOME of the taxable FUTA wages you paid were excluded from state unemployment tax, OR you paid ANY state unemployment tax late (after the due date for filing Form 940), fill out the worksheet in the instructions. Enter the amount from line 7 of the worksheet . . . . . **10** | 0. |

11 If credit reduction applies, enter the amount from line 3 of Schedule A (Form 940) . . . . **11** | . |

Part 4: Determine your FUTA tax and balance due or overpayment for 2010. If any line does NOT apply, leave it blank.

12 Total FUTA tax after adjustments (lines 8 + 9 + 10 + 11 = line 12) . . . . **12** | 336.00 |

13 FUTA tax deposited for the year, including any overpayment applied from a prior year . **13** | 336.00 |

14 Balance due (If line 12 is more than line 13, enter the difference on line 14.)
    • If line 14 is more than $500, you must deposit your tax.
    • If line 14 is $500 or less, you may pay with this return. For more information on how to pay, see the separate instructions . . . . **14** | . |

15 Overpayment (If line 13 is more than line 12, enter the difference on line 15 and check a box below.) . . . . **15** | . |

Check one: ☐ Apply to next return.
                 ☐ Send a refund.

▶ You **MUST** fill out both pages of this form and **SIGN** it.

Next ▶

For Privacy Act and Paperwork Reduction Act Notice, see the back of Form 940-V, Payment Voucher.   Cat. No. 11234O   Form **940** (2010)

FIGURE 8.11 (*Continued*)

850210

Name (not your trade name)	Employer identification number (EIN)
Travelwithus.com	58-1213479

Part 5: Report your FUTA tax liability by quarter only if line 12 is more than $500. If not, go to Part 6.

16   Report the amount of your FUTA tax liability for each quarter; do **NOT** enter the amount you deposited. If you had no liability for a quarter, leave the line blank.

     16a   **1st quarter** (January 1 – March 31) . . . . **16a**   [.   ]

     16b   **2nd quarter** (April 1 – June 30) . . . . **16b**   [.   ]

     16c   **3rd quarter** (July 1 – September 30) . . . . **16c**   [.   ]

     16d   **4th quarter** (October 1 – December 31) . . . . **16d**   [.   ]

17   **Total tax liability for the year** (lines 16a + 16b + 16c + 16d = line 17) **17**   [.   ]   **Total must equal line 12.**

Part 6: May we speak with your third-party designee?

Do you want to allow an employee, a paid tax preparer, or another person to discuss this return with the IRS? See the instructions for details.

☐ **Yes.**   Designee's name and phone number   [   ]   [   ]

       Select a 5-digit Personal Identification Number (PIN) to use when talking to IRS   [ ] [ ] [ ] [ ] [ ]

☑ **No.**

Part 7: Sign here. You MUST fill out both pages of this form and SIGN it.

Under penalties of perjury, I declare that I have examined this return, including accompanying schedules and statements, and to the best of my knowledge and belief, it is true, correct, and complete, and that no part of any payment made to a state unemployment fund claimed as a credit was, or is to be, deducted from the payments made to employees. Declaration of preparer (other than taxpayer) is based on all information of which preparer has any knowledge.

X **Sign your name here**   *Katherine C. Kurtz*

Print your name here   **Katherine C. Kurtz**

Print your title here   **Controller**

Date   2/10/201X+1

Best daytime phone   **(978) 555-4040**

Paid preparer use only   Check if you are self-employed . . . . ☐

Preparer's name		PTIN	
Preparer's signature		Date	/ /
Firm's name (or yours if self-employed)		EIN	
Address		Phone	
City	State	ZIP code	

Paying SUTA Tax

State Unemployment Tax Act (SUTA) taxes are paid to the government of the state in which a business is located and are typically due by the end of the month following each calendar quarter. Employers also usually are required to complete a state unemployment tax report, much like they complete Form 940. Using the first quarter earnings (see Figure 8.10), Katherine calculates the SUTA tax due for the first quarter as follows:

$32,253.59 SUTA taxable earnings × 5.4% SUTA tax rate = $1,741.69

The journal entry to record the payment of SUTA follows:

GENERAL JOURNAL				
Date		PR	Dr.	Cr.
201X				
Apr. 30	SUTA Payable		1 7 4 1 69	
	Cash			1 7 4 1 69
	To record payment of the SUTA			
	tax for the quarter ending March 31,			
	201X			

Paying Workers' Compensation Insurance

Remember from Chapter 7 that the premium for workers' compensation insurance is paid at the beginning of the year based on estimated gross payroll for the year, and the journal entry to record this payment is as follows:

GENERAL JOURNAL				
Date		PR	Dr.	Cr.
201X				
Jan. 5	Prepaid Workers' Compensation Insurance		1 3 1 8 00	
	Cash			1 3 1 8 00
	To record payment of the workers'			
	compensation insurance premium			
	for 201X			

Like any prepaid amount, this amount will gradually be transferred from the Prepaid Workers' Compensation Insurance account, an asset, to the Workers' Compensation Insurance Expense account in the month-end adjusting entries for 201X.

At the end of the year, if Travelwithus.com owes an additional premium because actual gross payroll was higher than estimated gross payroll, the payment of the additional premium would be recorded as follows:

GENERAL JOURNAL				
Date		PR	Dr.	Cr.
201X				
Dec. 31	Workers' Compensation Insurance Expense		2 2 8 48	
	Cash			2 2 8 48
	To record payment of the additional			
	workers' compensation insurance			
	premium for 201X			

State Unemployment Tax Act (SUTA) A tax usually paid only by employers to the state for employee unemployment insurance.

Workers' compensation insurance Insurance paid, in advance by an employer to protect its employees against loss due to accidental death or injury incurred during employment.

LEARNING UNIT 8-3 REVIEW

AT THIS POINT you should be able to do the following:

- Prepare a Form W-2 and a Form W-3.
- Explain the difference between a Form W-2 and a Form W-3.
- Prepare Form 940.
- Explain when FUTA and SUTA taxes are paid.
- Explain when workers' compensation insurance premiums are paid.
- Record the payment of FUTA, SUTA, and workers' compensation insurance amounts.

Instant Replay Self-Review Quiz 8-3

Are the following statements true or false?

1. Employees must receive W-4s by January 31 of the following year.
2. Form W-3 is sent to the Social Security Administration yearly.
3. A Form 940 can only be prepared by a business that employs workers in only one state.
4. The Employer's Annual Federal Unemployment Tax Return reports the employer's FICA and FIT tax liabilities.
5. A FUTA tax liability of $500 or more must be paid 10 days after the quarter ends.
6. Premiums for workers' compensation insurance may be adjusted based on actual payroll figures.

Solutions to Instant Replay: Self-Review Quiz 8-3

COACHING TIP

Remember that the employee completes a W-4 when hired. The employer completes a W-2 for the employee at the end of the year.

1. False. W-2 forms must be sent to each employee by January 31 of the following year. The W-4 form is filled out by a new employee and is used for calculating federal and state income taxes.
2. True.
3. False. Form 940 can be prepared by a business that employs workers in one or more states.
4. False. The Employee's Annual Federal Unemployment Tax Return, Form 940, reports the FUTA tax liability. Form 941 reports the FICA and FIT tax liabilities.
5. False. A FUTA tax liability of $500 or more must be paid one month after the quarter ends.
6. True.

BLUEPRINT: FORM 941 TAX DEPOSIT RULES

Ten Frequently Asked Questions and Answers About Depositing OASDI, Medicare, and FIT to the Government

Here is a summary of questions and answers to help you understand the payroll tax deposit rules for Form 941 taxes:

1. **What are Form 941 taxes?** The term *Form 941 taxes* is used to describe the amount of FIT, OASDI, and Medicare paid by employees and the amount of OASDI and Medicare taxes that are matched and paid by an employer. The total of these taxes is known as Form 941 taxes because it is reported on Form 941 each quarter.

2. **When does an employer deposit Form 941 taxes?** How often an employer deposits Form 941 taxes depends on how the employer is classified for this purpose. The IRS usually classifies an employer as either a monthly or semiweekly depositor based on the amount of Form 941 taxes paid during a time period known as a look-back period.

3. **When is a look-back period?** A look-back period is a fiscal year that begins on July 1 and ends on June 30 of the year before the calendar year when the deposits will be made. For example, for the 2012 calendar year, an employer's look-back period will begin on July 1, 2010, and end on June 30, 2011.

4. **What is the dollar amount used to classify an employer for Form 941 tax deposits?** The key dollar amount used to determine whether an employer is a monthly or semiweekly depositor is $50,000 in Form 941 taxes. Two rules apply here:
    a. If the total amount deposited in Form 941 taxes is less than $50,000 during the look-back period, the employer is considered a monthly tax depositor.
    b. If the total amount deposited in Form 941 taxes is $50,000 or more during the look-back period, the employer is considered a semiweekly tax depositor.

5. **How do employers deposit Form 941 taxes?** Unless an employer pays Form 941 taxes of less than $2,500 per quarter the employer must utilize the Electronic Federal Tax Payment System (EFTPS) to deposit the Form 941 taxes. If the amount of Form 941 taxes owed is less than $2,500 per quarter, payment may be made by check at the time of the submission of the Form 941.

6. **When do monthly depositors make their deposits?** A monthly depositor will figure the total amount of Form 941 taxes owed in a calendar month and then pay this amount by the 15th of the next month. If an employer owes $3,125 in Form 941 taxes for the month of June, it will deposit this same amount no later than July 15 of the same year.

7. **When do semiweekly depositors make their deposits?** The rules for making deposits are a little more complicated for a semiweekly depositor. The depositor may have to make up to two Form 941 deposits each week. When a tax deposit is due depends on when the employees are paid. To keep the rules consistent, the IRS has taken a calendar week and divided it into two payday time periods. It is easiest to think of a two-week period of time when discussing these periods: Wednesday through Friday of week 1, and Saturday of week 1 through Tuesday of week 2.

    Two deposit rules apply to these two time periods. We can call these rules the Wednesday and Friday rules.
    a. Wednesday rule: If employees are paid during the Wednesday through Friday of week 1 period, the tax deposit will be due on Wednesday of week 2.
    b. Friday rule: If employees are paid anytime from Saturday of week 1 through Tuesday of week 2, the tax deposit will be due on Friday of week 2.

These rules mean that the payroll tax deposit will be due three banking days after the payday time period ends. For the Wednesday rule, the deposit is due three banking days after Friday of week 1, on the following Wednesday in week 2. For the Friday rule, the deposit is due three banking days after Tuesday of week 2, on Friday of week 2. The following illustration shows how this timing works.

	Week 1							Week 2						
	Sun	Mon	Tues	Wed	Thur	Fri	Sat	Sun	Mon	Tues	Wed	Thur	Fri	Sat
If payday is														
Then deposit is due														

8. **What is a banking day?** The term *banking day* refers to any day that banks are open to the public for business. Saturdays, Sundays, and legal holidays are not banking days.

9. **How do legal holidays affect payroll tax deposits?** If a legal holiday occurs after the last day of a payday time period, the employer will get one extra day to make its Form 941 tax deposit as follows:

    a. For monthly depositors: If the 15th of the month is a Saturday, Sunday, or legal holiday, the deposit will be due and payable on the next banking day.

    b. For semiweekly depositors: A deposit due on Wednesday will be due on Thursday of the same week, and a Friday deposit will be due on Monday of the following week. Remember that the employer will always have three banking days after the last day of either payday time period to make its payroll tax deposit.

10. **What happens if an employer is late with its Form 941 tax deposit?** If a Form 941 tax deposit is not made the day it should be deposited, the employer may be assessed a fine for lateness and may even be charged interest, depending on how late the deposit is.

ACCOUNTING COACH

The following Coaching Tips are from Learning Units 8-1 through 8-3. Take the Pre-Game Checkup and use the Check Your Score at the bottom of the page to see how you are doing. The Accounting Coach provides tips before each Checkup to help you avoid common accounting errors.

LU 8-1 Recording Payroll and Payroll Tax Expense and Paying the Payroll

Pre-Game Tips: The FICA (OASDI and Medicare) payable accounts contain both employee deductions and the employer's OASDI and Medicare payments.

Pre-Game Checkup

Answer true or false to the following statements.

1. The payroll register is the source of the data used to journalize the payroll in the general journal.
2. The FICA (OASDI and Medicare) payable accounts reflect the tax liability of only the employer.
3. Deductions for payroll withholding taxes represent a liability of the employees until the taxes are paid by the employer.
4. Workers' compensation insurance is paid by the employer to ensure that employees are compensated if they lose their job.
5. Very few companies use a special checking account for paying their payroll.

LU 8-2 Paying FIT and FICA Taxes and Completing the Employer's Quarterly Federal Tax Return, Form 941

Pre-Game Tips: Federal Form 941 reports the FIT, OASDI, and Medicare taxes withheld from employees, as well as reports the OASDI and Medicare taxes due from the employer.

Pre-Game Checkup

Answer true or false to the following statements.

1. If an employer owed less than $50,000 in total taxes during the look-back period it would be classified as a quarterly depositor.
2. The majority of businesses normally make their payroll tax deposits to pay their Form 941 taxes either monthly or semiweekly.

3. FIT, OASDI, Medicare, and FUTA taxes are known as Form 941 taxes.
4. Regardless of the amount of taxes owed, an employer must pay its Form 941 taxes using Electronic Federal Payment (EFTPS).
5. Journal entries crediting accounts OASDI Payable and FIT Payable record the payment of these taxes.

LU 8-3 Preparing Forms W-2 and W-3, Paying FUTA Tax and Completing the Employer's Annual Unemployment Tax Return, Form 940, and Paying SUTA Tax and Workers' Compensation Insurance

Pre-Game Tips: Employers send Form W-2 and Form W-3 to the Social Security Administration, which shares this information with the Internal Revenue Service (IRS).

Pre-Game Checkup

Answer true or false to the following statements.

1. If the amount of FUTA tax is less that $500 during a given quarter, no deposit is required until the FUTA tax liability reaches $500 or until the year ends.
2. The Employer's Annual Federal Unemployment (FUTA) Tax Return, Form 1040 is not due until January 31. However, the due date is extended to February 10 if all taxes owed were paid by January 31.
3. Form W-2s must be distributed to employees no later than February 10.
4. The cost of workers' compensation insurance is charged as an expense when it is paid at the beginning of the calendar year.
5. Employers send Form W-2s and Form W-3s to the Social Security Administration so employees' individual federal income tax returns may be checked.

CHECK YOUR SCORE: Answers to the Pre-Game Checkup

LU 8-1

1. True.
2. False—The FICA (OASDI and Medicare) payable accounts accumulate FICA taxes from both the employees and the employer.
3. False—The employee's liability for FICA (OASDI and Medicare) cease the moment the employer deducts the taxes from the employee's gross pay. Those taxes then become the responsibility of the employer.
4. False—Workers' compensation insurance premiums are paid by the employer to insure the employee against work-related injury or death.
5. False—Almost all large companies establish a special account for paying their payroll. It strengthens cash control, simplifies check reconciliation, and reduces the likelihood of an overdraft.

LU 8-2

1. False—If an employer owed less than $50,000 in total taxes during the look-back period it would be classified as a monthly depositor.
2. True.
3. False—FIT, OASDI, and Medicare taxes are known as Form 941 taxes. FUTA is not a Form 941 tax; it is paid using a Form 940, Employer's Annual Federal Unemployment (FUTA) Tax Return.
4. False—An employer is required to use EFTPS only if the employer owes more than $2,500 in a quarter.
5. False—Debits to the accounts OASDI Payable and FIT Payable record the payments of these taxes. Credits to these accounts record tax liabilities.

LU 8-3

1. True.
2. True.
3. False—Form W-2s must be distributed to employees by January 31.
4. False—When workers' compensation insurance premiums are paid at the beginning of the calendar year it is recorded as Prepaid Workers' Compensation Insurance, an asset. Like any prepaid account, Prepaid Workers' Compensation Insurance will be gradually adjusted over the course of the year to Workers' Compensation Insurance Expense.
5. True.

Chapter Summary

Here are all the key concepts and equations to help you understand the concepts of this chapter and prepare you for your exam. After completing this review, go to MyAccountingLab for more practice opportunities.

MyAccountingLab

Concepts You Should Know	Key Terms	
Recording payroll and payroll taxes. 1. The payroll register provides the data for journalizing the payroll in the general journal. 2. Deductions for payroll withholding taxes represent liabilities of the employer until paid. 3. The Accounts Charged columns in the payroll register indicate which accounts will be debited to record the total wages and salaries expense when a journal entry is prepared.	Payroll tax expense (p. 293)	● **L01**
Recording the payroll and the paying of the payroll. 1. Paying a payroll results in debiting Wages and Salaries Payable and crediting Cash or Payroll Cash.	Employer identification number (EIN) (p. 296) Form SS-4 (p. 296)	● **L02**
Recording employer taxes for FICA OASDI, FICA Medicare, FUTA, SUTA, and workers' compensation insurance. 1. The accounts FICA OASDI Payable and FICA Medicare Payable accumulate the tax liabilities of both the employer and the employee for OASDI and Medicare taxes.	Banking day (p. 297) Calendar quarter (p. 296) Federal Insurance Contributions Act (FICA) (p. 296) Federal Unemployment Tax Act (FUTA) (p. 296) Form 944, Employer's Annual Federal Tax Return (p. 300) Form 941, Employer's Quarterly Federal Tax Return (p. 297) Form 941 taxes (p. 297) Look-back period (p. 297) Monthly depositor (p. 297) Semiweekly depositor (p. 297)	● **L03**

L04   Preparing Forms W-2, W-3, 941, and 940.

1.   Federal Form 941 is prepared and filed no later than one month after the calendar quarter ends. It reports the amount of FIT, OASDI, and Medicare tax withheld from employees and the OASDI and Medicare taxes due from the employer for the calendar quarter.

2.   FIT, OASDI, and Medicare taxes are known as Form 941 taxes.

3.   The total amount of Form 941 taxes paid by a business during a specific period of time determines how often the business will have to make its payroll tax deposits. This time period is called a look-back period.

4.   Businesses will normally make their payroll tax deposits to pay their Form 941 taxes either monthly or semiweekly.

5.   Different deposit rules apply to monthly and semiweekly depositors and these rules determine when deposits are due.

6.   Form 941 payroll tax deposits must be made by EFTPS unless the total tax liability for the quarter is <$2,500, in which case the employer can submit the payment together with Form 944.

7.   Information to prepare W-2 forms can be obtained from the individual employee earnings records.

8.   Form W-3 is used by the Social Security Administration in verifying that taxes have been withheld as reported on individual employee W-2 forms.

9.   Form 940 is prepared by January 31, after the end of the previous calendar year. This form can be filed by February 10 if all required deposits have been made by January 31.

10. If the amount of FUTA taxes is equal to or more than $500 during any calendar quarter, the deposit must be made no later than one month after the quarter ends. If the amount is less than $500, no deposit is required until the liability reaches the $500 point or until the year ends, when any tax due must be paid by January 31 of the following year.

11. The premium for workers' compensation insurance based on estimated payroll for the year is paid at the beginning of the year by the employer to protect against potential losses to its employees due to accidental death or injury incurred while on the job. However, after the year is over and the exact amount of the payroll is known, the insurance premium is recalculated and there may be an adjustment in the year's insurance premium.

Form W-2, Wage and Tax Statement (p. 305)

Form W-3, Transmittal of Income and Tax Statements (p. 305)

L05   Paying FUTA, SUTA, and workers' compensation insurance.

1.   FUTA is for federal unemployment and SUTA is for state unemployment. States will have different rates depending on their unemployment history.

Form 940, Employer's Annual Federal Unemployment Tax Return (p. 307)

State Unemployment Tax Act (SUTA) (p. 311)

Workers' compensation insurance (p. 311)

Discussion and Critical Thinking Questions/Ethical Case

1. What taxes are recorded when recording Payroll Tax Expense?

2. What is a calendar year?

3. An employer must always use a calendar year for payroll purposes. Agree or disagree?

4. Why does payroll information center on 13-week quarters?

5. How is an employer classified as a monthly or semiweekly depositor for Form 941 tax purposes?

6. How are Form 941 taxes paid to the Treasury Department?

7. How often is Form 941 completed?

8. Under what circumstance(s) does the amount on line 15 of Form 941 match the amount found on line 10?

9. Bill Smith leaves his job on July 9. He requests a copy of his W-2 form when he leaves. His boss tells him to wait until January of next year. Please discuss whether Bill's boss is correct in making this statement.

10. Why would one employer prepare a Form 940 completing Part 1, line 1a, but another would prepare a Form 940 Part 1, line 1b?

11. Employer A has a FUTA tax liability of $67.49 on March 31 of the current year. When does the employer have to make the deposit for this liability?

12. Employer B has a FUTA tax liability of $553.24 on January 31 of the current year. When does the employer have to make the deposit for this liability?

13. Who completes Form W-4? Form W-2? Form W-3? When is each form completed?

14. Why is the year-end adjusting entry needed for workers' compensation insurance?

15. Happy Carpet Cleaning, Inc., collects FIT, OASDI, and Medicare from its employees by withholding these taxes from its employees' pay. However, Happy does not pay these amounts to the federal government until the end of the calendar year so that it can maximize its cash during the year. Because it will be paying these amounts to the government, it believes that this practice does not affect its employees. Please comment on this practice.

Concept Check

MyAccountingLab

Account Classifications

1. Complete the following table. Indicate whether a debit or credit results in an increase to the account balance

⬤ **L01** *(10 MIN)*

Accounts Affected	Category	↑↓	Rules
a. Payroll Tax Expense			
b. FICA OASDI Payable			
c. SIT Payable			
d. SUTA Payable			
e. Prepaid Workers' Compensation Insurance			

LO1, 2, 3 *(10 MIN)*   **Look-Back Periods**

2.   Label the following look-back periods for 200C by months.

A	B	C	D
200A		200B	

LO1, 2, 3 *(15 MIN)*   **Monthly versus Semiweekly Depositor**

3.   In December 200B, Mary is trying to find out whether she is a monthly or semiweekly depositor for FICA (OASDI and Medicare) and federal income tax for 200C. Please advise based on the following taxes owed:

200A	Quarter 3	$29,000
	Quarter 4	16,000
200B	Quarter 1	3,500
	Quarter 2	10,700

LO1, 2, 3 *(15 MIN)*   **Paying the Tax**

4.   Complete the following table:

Depositor	4-Quarter Look-Back Period Tax Liability	Payroll Paid	Tax Paid by
Monthly	$28,000	November	a.
Semiweekly	$66,000	On Wednesday	b.
		On Thursday	c.
		On Friday	d.
		On Saturday	e.
		On Sunday	f.
		On Monday	g.

LO1, 2, 3 *(15 MIN)*   **Payroll Account**

5.   Indicate which of the following items apply to the following account titles.
    1. An asset
    2. A liability
    3. An expense
    4. Appears on the income statement
    5. Appears on the balance sheet

        _____ a. FICA OASDI Payable

        _____ b. Office Salaries Expense

        _____ c. Federal Income Tax Payable

        _____ d. FICA Medicare Payable

        _____ e. Wages and Salaries Payable

Exercises

Set A

8A-1.   Complete the table.

LO1, 2 *(10 MIN)*

Item	Account Category	Normal Balance	Account Appears on Which Financial Statements?
Medical Insurance Payable			
Wages and Salaries Payable			
Office Salaries Expense			
Market Wages Expense			
FICA OASDI Payable			
Federal Income Tax Payable			
State Income Tax Payable			

8A-2.   The following amounts were taken from the weekly payroll register for the Wu Lake Company on September 9, 201X. Using the same account title headings used in this chapter, please prepare the general journal entry to record the payroll for the Wu Lake Company for September 9.

LO1, 2 *(20 MIN)*

Plant Wages Expense	$7,148.00
Office Salaries Expense	3,194.00
Deduction for FICA OASDI	538.24
Deduction for FICA Medicare	124.22
Deduction for federal income tax	2,168.55
Deduction for state income tax	502.64
Deduction for union dues	890.00

8A-3.   Use the information from Exercise 8A-2 and the following information to prepare the general journal entry to record the payroll tax expense for the weekly payroll of September 9, 201X:

LO1, 2, 3 *(20 MIN)*

Wages below the FUTA tax wage base limit	$900.00
FUTA tax rate	0.8%
Wages below the SUTA tax wage base limit	$900.00
SUTA tax rate	5.4%

8A-4.   At the end of December 201X, the total amount of OASDI, $540, and Medicare, $180, was withheld as tax deductions from the employees of Falls, Inc. Federal income tax of $2,920 was also deducted from their paychecks. Falls is classified as a monthly depositor of Form 941 taxes. Indicate when this payroll tax deposit is due and provide a general journal entry to record the payment.

LO1, 2, 3 *(20 MIN)*

LO1, 2 *(15 MIN)*   **8A-5.** The following payroll journal entry was prepared by Palmdale Company from its payroll register. Which columns of the payroll register have the data come from? How do the taxable earnings columns of the payroll register relate to this entry?

			GENERAL JOURNAL			
	Date			PR	Dr.	Cr.
	201X					
	Oct.	15	Customer Service Expense		1 2 0 0 00	
			FIT Payable			1 3 2 00
			SIT Payable			7 2 00
			FICA OASDI Payable			7 4 40
			FICA Medicare Payable			1 7 40
			Payroll Cash			9 0 4 20
			To record payroll			

LO1, 2, 3 *(20 MIN)*   **8A-6.** Meghan's Grocery Store made the following Form 941 payroll tax deposits during the look-back period of July 1, 201A, through June 30, 201B:

Quarter Ended	Amount Paid in 941 Taxes
September 30, 201A	$15,780.31
December 31, 201A	13,892.45
March 31, 201B	13,600.12
June 30, 201B	14,020.42

Should Meghan's Grocery Store make Form 941 tax deposits monthly or semiweekly for 201C?

LO1, 2, 3 *(15 MIN)*   **8A-7.** If Meghan's Grocery Store downsized its operation during the second quarter of 201B and, as a result, paid only $6,119.83 in Form 941 taxes for the quarter that ended on June 30, 201B, should Meghan's Grocery make its Form 941 payroll tax deposits monthly or semiweekly for 201C?

LO1, 2, 3 *(15 MIN)*   **8A-8.** From the following T accounts, record the following: (a) the July 3 payment for FICA (OASDI and Medicare) and federal income taxes, (b) the July 30 payment of SUTA tax, and (c) the July 30 deposit of any FUTA tax that may be required.

FICA OASDI Payable 203			FICA Medicare Payable 204	
	June 30 380 (EE)			June 30 190 (EE)
	380 (ER)			190 (ER)

FIT Payable 205			FUTA Tax Payable 206	
	June 30 3,001			June 30 143

SUTA Tax Payable 207	
	June 30 610

Set B

8B-1. Complete the table.

Item	Account Category	Normal Balance	Account Appears on Which Financial Statements?
Health Insurance Payable			
Wages and Salaries Payable			
Office Salaries Expense			
Sales Salaries Expense			
FICA OASDI Payable			
Federal Income Tax Payable			
State Income Tax Payable			

8B-2. The following amounts were taken from the weekly payroll register for the Wu Vale Company on August 9, 201X. Please prepare the general journal entry to record the payroll for the Wu Vale Company for August 9.

Plant Wages Expense	$7,128.00
Office Salaries Expense	3,114.00
Deduction for FICA OASDI	546.00
Deduction for FICA Medicare	100.30
Deduction for federal income tax	2,362.31
Deduction for state income tax	494.36
Deduction for union dues	920.00

8B-3. Use the information from Exercise 8B-2 and the following information to prepare the general journal entry to record the payroll tax expense for the weekly payroll of August 9, 201X.

Wages below the FUTA tax wage base limit	$900.00	Wages below the SUTA tax wage base limit	$900.00
FUTA tax rate	0.8%	SUTA tax rate	5.4%

8B-4. At the end of March 201X, the total amount of OASDI, $500, and Medicare, $220, was withheld as tax deductions from the employees of River, Inc. Federal income tax of $2,940 was also deducted from their paychecks. River is classified as a monthly depositor of Form 941 taxes. Indicate when this payroll tax deposit is due and provide a general journal entry to record the payment.

8B-5. The following payroll journal entry was prepared by Palmdale Company from its payroll register. Which columns of the payroll register have the data come from? How do the taxable earnings columns of the payroll register relate to this entry?

General Journal				
Date	Accounts	PR	Debit	Credit
201X				
Oct. 15	Customer Service Expense		2,000.00	
	FIT Payable			220.00
	SIT Payable			120.00
	FICA OASDI Payable			124.00
	FICA Medicare Payable			29.00
	Payroll Cash			1,507.00
	To record payroll			

○○○ **LO1, 2, 3** *(20 MIN)*   **8B-6.** Louise's Grocery Store made the following Form 941 payroll tax deposits during the look-back period of July 1, 201A, through June 30, 201B:

Quarter Ended	Amount Paid in 941 Taxes
September 30, 201A	$15,781.31
December 31, 201A	13,892.04
March 31, 201B	13,601.26
June 30, 201B	14,021.08

Should Louise's Grocery Store make Form 941 tax deposits monthly or semi-weekly for 201C?

○○○ **LO1, 2, 3** *(15 MIN)*   **8B-7.** If Louise's Grocery Store downsized its operation during the second quarter of 201B and, as a result paid only $6,120.07 in Form 941 taxes for the quarter that ended on June 30, 201B, should Louise's Grocery Store make Form 941 tax deposits monthly or semi-weekly for 201C?

○○○ **LO1, 2, 3** *(15 MIN)*   **8B-8.** From the following T-accounts, record the following: (a) the July 3 payment for FICA (OASDI and Medicare) and federal income taxes, (b) the July 30 payment of SUTA tax, and (c) the July 30 deposit of any FUTA tax that may be required.

FICA OASDI Payable 203

	June 30 450 (EE)
	450 (ER)

FICA Medicare Payable 204

	June 30 180 (EE)
	180 (ER)

FIT Payable 205

	June 30 3,007

FUTA Tax Payable 206

	June 30 142

SUTA Tax Payable 207

	June 30 606

MyAccountingLab   ## Problems

○○○ **LO1, 2, 3** *(30 MIN)*   ### Set A

8A-1. For the biweekly pay period ending on April 10 at Eva's Pet Store, the following partial payroll summary was taken from the individual employee earnings records. Use it to do the following:

1. Complete the table. Use the federal income tax withholding table in Figure 7.2 to figure the amount of income tax withheld.
2. Prepare a journal entry to record the payroll tax expense for Eva's. Please show the calculations for FICA taxes.

| Employee | Allowance and Marital Status | Gross | FICA | | Federal Income Tax |
			OASDI	Medicare	
Apple Edge	S-1	$1,058			
Mike Johnson	S-0	912			
Nat Lane	S-2	1,000			
Derek Poole	S-0	1,266			
Dan Tarantino	S-2	1,580			

Check Figure:
Payroll Tax Expense
$694.85

Assume that the FICA tax rate for OASDI is 6.2% up to $106,800 in earnings (no one earned this much as of April 10), and Medicare is 1.45% on all earnings. The state unemployment tax rate is 5.1% on the first $7,000 of earnings, and the federal unemployment tax rate is 0.8% of the first $7,000 of earnings. (Only Dan Tarantino earned more than $7,000 as of April 10.) In cases where the amount of FICA tax calculates to one-half cent, round up to the next cent.

8A-2. The following is the monthly payroll of Johnson Company, owned by Dan Johnson. Employees are paid on the last day of each month.

L01, 2, 3 *(50 MIN)*

JANUARY

| Employee | Monthly Earnings | YTD Earnings | FICA | | Federal Income Tax |
			OASDI	Medicare	
Saul Fish	$1,940	$1,940	$120.28	$ 28.13	$ 258.00
Jade Bryant	3,250	3,250	201.50	47.13	363.00
Amy Hess	3,760	3,760	233.12	54.52	496.00
	$8,950	$8,950	$554.90	$129.78	$1,117.00

FEBRUARY

| Employee | Monthly Earnings | YTD Earnings | FICA | | Federal Income Tax |
			OASDI	Medicare	
Saul Fish	$2,110	$ 4,050	$130.82	$ 30.60	$ 302.00
Jade Bryant	3,370	6,620	208.94	48.87	319.00
Amy Hess	3,800	7,560	235.60	55.10	426.00
	$9,280	$18,230	$575.36	$134.57	$1,047.00

MARCH

| Employee | Monthly Earnings | YTD Earnings | FICA | | Federal Income Tax |
			OASDI	Medicare	
Saul Fish	$2,050	$ 6,100	$127.10	$ 29.73	$ 590.00
Jade Bryant	2,475	9,095	153.45	35.89	560.00
Amy Hess	4,150	11,710	257.30	60.18	543.00
	$8,675	$26,905	$537.85	$125.80	$1,693.00

Check Figure:
Deposit of SUTA Tax
$1,145.70

Johnson Company is located at 2 Square Street, Marblehead, Massachusetts 01945. Its employer identification number is 29-3458822. The FICA tax rate for Social Security is 6.2% up to $106,800 in earnings during the year, and Medicare is 1.45% on all earnings. The SUTA tax rate is 5.7% on the first $7,000. The FUTA tax rate is 0.8% on the first $7,000 of earnings. Johnson Company is classified as a monthly depositor for Form 941 taxes.

Your tasks are to do the following:

1. Journalize the entries to record the employer's payroll tax expense for each pay period in the general journal.

2. Journalize entries for the payment of each tax liability in the general journal.

LO1, 2, 3 *(50 MIN)*

Check Figure:
Total Liability for
Quarter $7,973.52
∘――――――――――→

8A-3. John Andrews, the accountant for Johnson Company, must complete Form 941 for the first quarter of the current year. John gathered the needed data as presented in Problem 8A-2. Suddenly called away to an urgent budget meeting, John requested that you assist him by preparing the Form 941 for the first quarter. Please note that the difference in the tax liability, a few cents, should be adjusted on line 7a; this difference is due to the rounding of FICA tax amounts.

LO1, 2, 3 *(60 MIN)*

Check Figure:
Dec. 31 Payroll Tax
Expense $880.07
∘――――――――――→

8A-4. The following is the monthly payroll for the last three months of the year for Smith's Sporting Goods Shop, 2 Boat Road, Lynn, Massachusetts 01945. The shop is a sole proprietorship owned and operated by Bill Smith. The employer ID number for Smith's Sporting Goods is 28-9311893.

The employees at Smith's are paid once each month on the last day of the month. Paula Bush is the only employee who has contributed the maximum into Social Security. None of the other employees will reach the social security wage-base limit by the end of the year. Assume the rate for social security to be 6.2% with a wage-base maximum of $106,800, and the rate for Medicare to be 1.45% on all earnings. Smith's is classified as a monthly depositor for Form 941 payroll tax deposit purposes.

Your tasks are to do the following:

1. Journalize the entries to record the employer's payroll tax expense for each period in the general journal.

2. Journalize the payment of each tax liability in the general journal.

3. Complete Form 941 for the fourth quarter of the current year.

OCTOBER

| Employee | Monthly Earnings | YTD Earnings | FICA | | Federal Income Tax |
			OASDI	Medicare	
Paula Bush	$ 2,820	$100,650	$174.84	$ 40.89	$ 530.00
Joe Lapine	3,540	39,700	219.48	51.33	422.00
Gina Vale	3,780	44,200	234.36	54.81	537.00
	$10,140	$184,550	$628.68	$147.03	$1,489.00

NOVEMBER

| Employee | Monthly Earnings | YTD Earnings | FICA | | Federal Income Tax |
			OASDI	Medicare	
Paula Bush	$ 3,040	$103,690	$188.48	$ 44.08	$ 595.00
Joe Lapine	3,860	43,560	239.32	55.97	464.00
Gina Vale	3,660	47,860	226.92	53.07	556.00
	$10,560	$195,110	$654.72	$153.12	$1,615.00

DECEMBER

Employee	Monthly Earnings	YTD Earnings	FICA OASDI	FICA Medicare	Federal Income Tax
Paula Bush	$ 4,240	$107,930	$192.82	$ 61.48	$ 871.00
Joe Lapine	3,860	47,420	239.32	55.97	476.00
Gina Vale	4,320	52,180	267.84	62.64	708.00
	$12,420	$207,530	$699.98	$180.09	$2,055.00

8A-5. Using the information from Problem 8A-4, please complete a Form 940 for Smith's Sporting Goods for the current year. Additional information needed to complete the form is as follows:

   a. SUTA rate: 5.7%

   b. State reporting number: 025-319-2

   c. No FUTA tax deposits were made for this year.

   d. Smith's three employees for the year all earned over $7,000.

LO4, 5 *(20 MIN)*

Check Figure:
Total Exempt Payments
$186,530

Set B

8B-1. For the biweekly pay period ending on April 10 at Clark's Pet Store, the following partial payroll summary is taken from the individual employee earnings records. Use it to do the following:

   1. Complete the table. Use the federal income tax withholding table in Figure 7.2 to figure the amount of income tax withheld.

   2. Prepare a journal entry to record the payroll tax expense for Clark's. Please show the calculations for FICA taxes.

LO1, 2, 3 *(30 MIN)*

Check Figure:
Payroll Tax Expense
$694.57

Employee	Allowance and Marital Status	Gross	FICA OASDI	FICA Medicare	Federal Income Tax
Bill Apple	S-1	$ 1,042			
Homer Gomez	S-0	902			
William New	S-2	1,012			
John Taft	S-0	1,278			
Dan Tarantino	S-2	1,580			

Assume that the FICA tax rate for OASDI is 6.2% up to $106,800 in earnings (no one has earned this much as of April 10), and Medicare is 1.45% on all earnings. The state unemployment tax rate is 5.1% on the first $7,000 of earnings, and the federal unemployment tax rate is 0.8% of the first $7,000 of earnings. (Only Dan Tarantino earned more than $7,000 as of April 10.) In cases where the amount of FICA tax calculates to one-half cent, round up to the next cent.

8B-2. The following is the monthly payroll of Black Company, owned by Devin Black. Employees are paid on the last day of each month.

LO1, 2, 3 *(50 MIN)*

Check Figure:
Deposit of SUTA tax
$1,154.54

JANUARY

| Employee | Monthly Earnings | YTD Earnings | FICA | | Federal Income Tax |
			OASDI	Medicare	
Sam Fish	$1,970	$1,970	$122.14	$ 28.57	$ 264.00
Justine Bryant	3,210	3,210	199.02	46.55	357.00
Alison Pickens	3,800	3,800	235.60	55.10	506.00
	$8,980	$8,980	$556.76	$130.22	$1,127.00

FEBRUARY

| Employee | Monthly Earnings | YTD Earnings | FICA | | Federal Income Tax |
			OASDI	Medicare	
Sam Fish	$2,110	$ 4,080	$130.82	$ 30.60	$ 296.00
Justine Bryant	3,360	6,570	208.32	48.72	327.00
Alison Pickens	3,850	7,650	238.70	55.83	418.00
	$9,320	$18,300	$577.84	$135.15	$1,041.00

MARCH

| Employee | Monthly Earnings | YTD Earnings | FICA | | Federal Income Tax |
			OASDI	Medicare	
Sam Fish	$ 2,175	$ 6,255	$134.85	$ 31.54	$ 592.00
Justine Bryant	2,525	9,095	156.55	36.61	558.00
Alison Pickens	4,050	11,700	251.10	58.73	543.00
	$ 8,750	$27,050	$542.50	$126.88	$1,693.00

Black Company is located at 2 Square Street, Marblehead, Massachusetts 01945. Its employer identification number is 29-3458822. The FICA tax rate for Social Security is 6.2% up to $106,800 in earnings during the year, and Medicare is 1.45% on all earnings. The SUTA tax rate is 5.7% on the first $7,000 of earnings. The FUTA tax rate is 0.8% on the first $7,000 of earnings. Black Company is classified as a monthly depositor for Form 941 taxes.

Your tasks are to do the following:

1. Journalize the entries to record the employer's payroll tax expense for each pay period in the general journal.

2. Journalize entries for the payment of each tax liability in the general journal.

L01, 2, 3 *(50 MIN)*

Check Figure:
Liability for Quarter
$7,999.68

8B-3. Ted Chase, the accountant for Black Company, must complete Form 941 for the first quarter of the current year. Ted gathered the needed data as presented in Problem 8B-2. Suddenly called away to an urgent budget meeting, Ed requested that you assist him by preparing the Form 941 for the first quarter. Please note that the difference in the tax liability, a few cents, should be adjusted on line 7a; this difference is due to the rounding of FICA tax amounts.

L01, 2, 3 *(60 MIN)*

8B-4. The following is the monthly payroll for the last three months of the year for Brown's Sporting Goods Shop, 2 Boat Road, Lynn, Massachusetts 01945. The shop is a sole proprietorship owned and operated by Bill Brown. The employer ID number for Brown's Sporting Goods is 28-9311893.

The employees at Brown's are paid once each month on the last day of the month. David Clark is the only employee who has contributed the maximum into Social Security. None of the other employees will reach the Social Security wage-base limit by the end of the year. Assume the rate for Social Security to be 6.2% with a wage-base maximum of $106,800, and the rate for Medicare to be 1.45% on all earnings. Brown's is classified as a monthly depositor for Form 941 payroll tax deposit purposes.

Your tasks are to do the following:

1. Journalize the entries to record the employer's payroll tax expense for each period in the general journal.

2. Journalize the payment of each tax liability in the general journal.

3. Complete Form 941 for the fourth quarter of the current year.

OCTOBER

Employee	Monthly Earnings	YTD Earnings	FICA OASDI	Medicare	Federal Income Tax
David Clark	$ 3,020	$101,800	$187.24	$ 43.79	$ 532.00
Jack Johnson	3,560	39,400	220.72	51.62	431.00
Hector Walker	3,800	43,900	235.60	55.10	531.00
	$10,380	$185,100	$643.56	$150.51	$1,494.00

NOVEMBER

Employee	Monthly Earnings	YTD Earnings	FICA OASDI	Medicare	Federal Income Tax
David Clark	$ 2,950	$104,750	$182.90	$ 42.78	$ 596.00
Jack Johnson	3,780	43,180	234.36	54.81	470.00
Hector Walker	3,880	47,780	240.56	56.26	556.00
	$10,610	$195,710	$657.82	$153.85	$1,622.00

DECEMBER

Employee	Monthly Earnings	YTD Earnings	FICA OASDI	Medicare	Federal Income Tax
David Clark	$ 4,160	$108,910	$127.10	$ 60.32	$ 870.00
Jack Johnson	3,740	46,920	231.88	54.23	843.00
Hector Walker	4,460	52,240	276.52	64.67	702.00
	$12,360	$208,070	$635.50	$179.22	$2,055.00

Check Figure:
Dec. 31 Payroll Tax Expense $814.72

8B-5. Using the information from Problem 8B-4, please complete a Form 940 for Brown's Sporting Goods for the current year. Additional information needed to complete the form is as follows:

⬭⬤ **L04, 5** *(20 MIN)*

a. SUTA rate: 5.7%

b. State reporting number: 025-319-2

c. No FUTA tax deposits were made for this year.

d. Brown's three employees for the year all earned over $7,000.

Check Figure:
Line 4 Total Exempt Payments $182,000

Financial Report Problem

LO4 *(20 MIN)*

Reading the Kellogg's Annual Report

Go to http://investor.kelloggs.com/annuals.cfm, to access the Kellogg's 2010 Annual Report. Go to Notes to Consolidated Financial Statements and find Note 8: Pension Benefits. How much did Kellogg's spend to fund the 401(k) plans and similar saving plans?

MyAccountingLab **ON the JOB** |||||||||||||||||||||||||

SANCHEZ COMPUTER CENTER

In preparing for next year, on December 1 Tony Freedman hired two hourly employees to assist with some troubleshooting and repair work.

1. Prepare a payroll register for the three pay periods.

2. Record the following transactions in the general journal and post them to the general ledger.

Assume the following transactions:

Dec. 7 Paid employee wages: Lance Kumm, 38 hours, and Anthony Hall, 42 hours.

Dec. 14 Paid employee wages: Lance Kumm, 25 hours, and Anthony Hall, 36 hours.

Dec. 21 Paid employee wages: Lance Kumm, 26 hours, and Anthony Hall, 35 hours.

a. The following accounts have been added to the chart of accounts: Wages Payable #2010, FICA OASDI Payable #2020, FICA Medicare Payable #2030, FIT Payable #2040, State Income Tax Payable #2050, FUTA Tax Payable 2060, SUTA Tax Payable #2070, 2010 Wages Expense #5110, and Payroll Tax Expense #5120.

b. Assume FICA OASDI is taxed at 6.2% up to $106,800 in earnings and Medicare is taxed at at 1.45% on all earnings.

c. State income tax is 2% of gross pay.

d. None of the employees has federal income tax taken out of his or her pay.

e. Each employee earns $10 an hour and is paid 1½ times salary for hours worked in excess of 40 weekly.

As December comes to an end, Tony Freedman wants to take care of his payroll obligations. He will complete Form 941 for the fourth quarter of the current year and Form 940 for federal unemployment taxes. Tony will make the necessary deposits and payments associated with his payroll.

Assignment

1. Using the information in the Chapter 7 problem, record the December payrolls and the payment of the payrolls in the general journal and post them to the general ledger.

2. Using the information in this chapter, record the payroll tax expense for the fourth quarter in the general journal. Use December 31 as the date of the journal entry to record the payroll tax expense for the entire quarter. Post the entry to the general journal.

3. Record the payment of each tax liability in the general journal and post each entry to the general ledger. Sanchez Computer Center is classified as a quarterly depositor. The company wishes to pay all payroll taxes on December 31 even if no deposits are required.

4. Prepare Form 941 for the fourth quarter. Sanchez Computer Center's employer identification number is 35-4132588.

5. Complete Form 940 for Sanchez Computer Center. The FUTA tax ceiling is $7,000, and the SUTA tax ceiling is $7,000 in cumulative wages for each employee. The Sanchez Computer Center's FUTA rate is 0.8% and the SUTA rate is 2.7%. The state reporting number is 025-025-2.

Hint: Sometimes the amount of Social Security taxes paid by the employee for the quarter will not equal the employee's tax liability because of rounding. Any overage or difference should be reported on line 7a of Form 941.

SUBWAY CASE

Hold the Lettuce, Withhold the Taxes

○○○○○ **L01, 2, 3, 4**
(30 MIN)

"As an employer, Stan, what are your tax responsibilities?" asked Angel Tavarez, president of the Los Palmos Kiwanis club. They were at one of the luncheons sponsored by the club every month, and Stan had been asked to join a discussion on the role of small business in the local economy. Fortunately, Angel had told the panelists the questions in advance, so Stan had his answers ready.

"Well, of course, I pay city, state, and U.S. government taxes myself. I also have to file city, state, and federal withholding taxes for each of my two employees. I have to withhold state unemployment taxes, as well as FICA, which is another name for OASDI and Medicare taxes, for each of them. I pay workers' compensation, too," said Stan.

"That's strange," said a voice from the audience. "My brother-in-law has a Subway restaurant in the southern part of the state, and he doesn't pay any city taxes. What's going on here?"

"Naturally, the situation is slightly different for Subway owners in different cities in our state—and across the country," said Stan confidently. "Not all cities have city income taxes. Different states have different regulations about workers' comp as well."

"Oh, right," said the voice, sounding embarrassed.

"So, Stan, how often do you have to pay taxes?" asked Angel Tavarez, shifting the topic diplomatically.

Stan picked up a piece of chalk and drew four large circles on the blackboard. Then he wrote the word "ASPIRIN" in each of the circles. A murmur of "Huh" and "What" went around the room.

"The average employee working for a company pays taxes once a year on April 15 and has one big tax headache. As an employer," Stan said, "I file tax returns on a quarterly basis, so I have four big tax headaches a year! Rather than filling out the 1040-EZ, I complete the Form 941, the Employer's Quarterly Federal Return, to report and pay payroll taxes to the IRS. Yet, while the form is due quarterly, I actually need to deposit the tax money into a Federal Reserve Bank once a month. In addition, I have to file the 940 at the end of each year to pay my federal and state unemployment taxes. Then, for each employee...."

"Stan," Angel interrupted, "I'm afraid time is running out for your segment of the panel discussion. We'll move on to Pamela Pudelle, who is going to tell us about advertising her new pet-grooming parlor."

Later, during the reception, Stan tapped Angel on the shoulder, "Sorry I went over my time limit," he said. "You didn't really go over," said Angel, "but you were getting a little too technical for the audience." While Stan was sorry to have let the discussion veer off course, he felt a little burst of pride: Who would have thought a year ago that he would be willing—and able—to expound about the tax burden of a small business owner!

Discussion Questions

1. What are the taxes called "Form 941 taxes"?
2. Why is Stan classified as a monthly depositor of Form 941 taxes?
3. Assume Stan owed $2,069.90 in Form 941 taxes for March. When would it be due? What would happen if that day were a Sunday?

PEACHTREE COMPUTER WORKSHOP

COMPUTERIZED ACCOUNTING APPLICATION FOR CHAPTER 8

Refresher on using Peachtree Complete Accounting

Before starting this assignment, you may want to refresh your memory by reading the following PDF documents in the multimedia library of the MyAccountingLab Web site. Remember to choose the PDF document for your version of Peachtree.

1. An Introduction to Peachtree Complete Accounting
2. Correcting Peachtree Transactions
3. How to Repeat or Restart a Peachtree Assignment
4. Backing Up and Restoring Your Work in Peachtree

You also should have completed the following workshops:

1. Workshop 1 Atlas Company from Chapter 3
2. Workshop 2 Zell Company from Chapter 4
3. Workshop 3 Sullivan Realty from Chapter 5

Workshop 4:

Payroll Mini Practice Set

In this workshop you will prepare January, February, and March payroll for Pete's Market using Peachtree. Tasks include entering payroll data, producing paychecks, and remitting payroll taxes. You will also print payroll reports.

Instructions and the data file for completing this assignment are in the multimedia library of the MyAccountingLab Web site. Open the *Workshop 4 Pete's Market* PDF document for your version of Peachtree and download the *Pete's Market* data file for your version of Peachtree.

QUICKBOOKS COMPUTER WORKSHOP

COMPUTERIZED ACCOUNTING APPLICATION FOR CHAPTER 8

Refresher on using QuickBooks Pro

Before starting this assignment, you may want to refresh your memory by reading the following PDF documents in the multimedia library of the MyAccountingLab Web site. Remember to choose the PDF document for your version of QuickBooks.

1. An Introduction to QuickBooks Pro
2. Correcting QuickBooks Transactions
3. How to Repeat or Restart a QuickBooks Assignment
4. Backing Up and Restoring Your Work in QuickBooks

You also should have completed the following workshops:

1. Workshop 1 Atlas Company from Chapter 3
2. Workshop 2 Zell Company from Chapter 4
3. Workshop 3 Sullivan Realty from Chapter 5

Workshop 4:

Payroll Mini Practice Set

In this workshop you will prepare January, February, and March payroll for Pete's Market using QuickBooks. Tasks include entering payroll data, producing paychecks, and remitting payroll taxes. You will also print payroll reports.

Instructions and the data file for completing this assignment are in the multimedia library of the MyAccountingLab Web site. Open the *Workshop 4 Pete's Market* PDF document for your version of QuickBooks and download the *Pete's Market* data file for your version of QuickBooks.

Sales and Cash Receipts

THE GAME PLAN

It's after the holidays. The lines to return or exchange gifts in stores are very long. Did you ever stop to think about how stores keep track of all the returns? How do they know what merchandise was discounted or not? Home Depot, like other companies, uses the accounting process to gather information about all sales made, whether cash or credit. Individual customer accounts are updated continually. Home Depot must monitor its inventory in order to ensure enough stock so that it does not run out of an item and miss the sales opportunity. In this chapter, in addition to accounting for returns, we will focus on how credit terms and sales tax may affect how we record the return.

LEARNING OBJECTIVES

1. Recording and posting sales transactions to the general and accounts receivable subsidiary ledger.

2. Preparing, journalizing, and posting a credit memorandum.

3. Recording and posting cash receipts transactions.

4. Recording to the accounts receivable subsidiary ledger.

5. Preparing a schedule of accounts receivable.

When you shop in Home Depot, a merchandise company, you will see a wide variety of products in the store. Let's first look at Chou's Toy Shop to get an overview of merchandise terms and journal entries.

LEARNING UNIT 9-1 CHOU'S TOY SHOP:
Seller's View of a Merchandise Company

Retailers Merchants who buy goods from wholesalers for resale to customers.

Merchandise Goods brought into a store for resale to customers.

Chou's Toy Shop, owned by Chou Li, is a retailer. It buys toys, games, bikes, and similar items from manufacturers and wholesalers and resells these goods (or merchandise) to its customers. The shelving, display cases, and so forth are called "fixtures" or "equipment." These items are not for resale.

Gross Sales

Each cash or charge sale made at Chou's Toy Shop is rung up at the register. Suppose the shop had $3,000 in sales on July 18. Of that amount, $1,800 was cash sales and $1,200 was charges. The account that recorded those sales would be

● **LO1**

Sales	
Dr.	Cr.
	3,000 ◄────── Revenue account with a credit balance

This account is a revenue account with a credit balance and will be found on the income statement. Figure 9.1 shows the journal entry for the day. *Note:* We talk about sales tax later. Lets look at a transaction analysis chart of this transaction before we journalize.

Accounts Affected	Category	↑↓	Rules	T Account Update
Cash	Asset	↑	Dr.	**Cash**
				1,800 |
Accounts Receivable	Asset	↑	Dr.	**Accounts Receivable**
				1,200 |
Sales	Revenue	↑	Cr.	**Sales**
				| 3,000

FIGURE 9.1
Recording Cash and Charge Sales for the Day

July	18	Cash		1 8 0 0 00		
		Accounts Receivable		1 2 0 0 00		
		Sales				3 0 0 0 00
		Sales for July 18				

Sales Returns and Allowances

Sales Returns and Allowances (SRA) account A contra-revenue account that records price adjustments and allowances granted on merchandise that is defective and has been returned.

It would be great for Chou if all the customers were completely satisfied, but that rarely is the case. On July 19, Michelle Reese brought back a doll she bought on account for $50. She told Chou that the doll was defective and that she wanted either a price reduction or a new doll. They agreed on a $10 price reduction. Michelle now owes Chou $40. The account called Sales Returns and Allowances (SRA) would record this information.

Sales Returns and Allowances

Contra-revenue ———————▶ Dr. | Cr.
account with   10 |
a debit balance

This account is a contra-revenue account with a debit balance. It will be recorded on the income statement. Figure 9.2 shows how the journal entry would look. Let's first look at a transaction analysis chart of this transaction before we journalize.

Accounts Affected	Category	↑↓	Rules	T Account Update
Sales Returns and Allowances	Contra-revenue	↑	Dr.	**Sales Ret. & Allow.**
				Dr. | Cr.
				10 |
Accounts Receivable, Michelle Reese	Asset	↓	Cr.	**Accounts Receivable**
				Dr. | Cr.
				1,200 | 10

Look at how the sales returns and allowances increase.

	July	19	Sales Returns and Allowances			1 0 00			
			Accounts Receivable, Michelle Reese					1 0 00	
			Issued credit memorandum						

FIGURE 9.2
Issuing a Credit Memorandum in the General Journal

Sales Discount

Chou gives a 2% sales discount to credit customers who pay their invoice early. He wants his customers to know about this policy, so he posted the following sign at the cash register:

Sales discount Amount a customer is allowed to deduct from the bill total for paying a bill during the discount period.

Sales Discount Policy

2/10, n/30	*2% discount is allowed off price of bill if paid within the first 10 days or full amount is due within 30 days.*
n/10, EOM	*No discount. Full amount of bill is due within 10 days after the end of the month.*

Note that the discount period is the time when a discount is granted. The discount period is less time than the credit period, which is the length of time allowed to pay the amount owed on the invoice.

If Michelle pays her $40 bill early, she will get an $0.80 discount. This information is recorded in the Sales Discount account as follows:

Discount period A period shorter than the credit period when a discount is available to encourage early payment of bills.

Credit period Length of time allowed for payment of goods sold on account.

Sales Discount account A contra-revenue account that records cash discounts granted to customers for payments made within a specific period of time.

Sales Discount

Contra-revenue ———————▶ Dr. | Cr.
account with a   0.80 |
debit balance

Michelle's discount is calculated as follows:

$$2\% \times \$40 = \$0.80$$

Michelle pays her bill on July 24. She is entitled to the discount because she paid her bill within 10 days. Figure 9.3 shows how Chou would record this payment on his books. Let's first look at a transaction analysis chart before we journalize.

x ——→ o
COACHING TIP

Gross Sales
– Sales discount
– SRA
= Net sales

Accounts Affected	Category	↑↓	Rules	T Account Update
Cash	Asset	↑	Dr.	**Cash**
				Dr. 39.20 | Cr.
Sales Discount	Contra-revenue	↑	Dr.	**Sales Discount**
				Dr. 0.80 | Cr.
Accounts Receivable	Asset	↓	Cr.	**Accounts Receivable**
				Dr. 1,200 | Cr. 40

FIGURE 9.3
Recording Sales Discount

	July	24	Cash			3 9 20				
			Sales Discount			80				
			Accounts Receivable, Michelle Reese					4 0 00		
			Payment from Sale on Account							

Net sales Gross sales less sales returns and allowances less sales discounts.

Gross sales The revenue earned from sale of merchandise to customers.

Although Michelle pays $39.20, her Accounts Receivable is credited for the full amount, $40.

In the examples so far we have not shown any transactions with sales tax. Note that the actual or net sales for Chou would be gross sales less sales returns and allowances less any sales discounts. Let's look at how Chou would record his monthly sales if the sales tax were charged.

Sales Tax Payable

Sales Tax Payable account An account in the general ledger that accumulates the amount of sales tax owed. It has a credit balance.

None of the preceding examples shows state sales tax. Still, like it or not, Chou must collect that tax from his customers and send it to the state. Sales tax represents a liability to Chou. The amount Chou must pay to the state is recorded in the Sales Tax Payable account.

Assume the state Chou's is located in charges a 5% sales tax. Remember that Chou's sales on July 18 were $3,000. Chou must figure out the sales tax on the purchases. For this purpose, let's assume only two sales were made on that date: the cash sale ($1,800) and the charge sale ($1,200).

The sales tax on the cash purchase is calculated as follows:

$$\$1,800 \times 0.05 = \$90 \text{ Tax}$$
$$\$1,800 + \$90 \text{ tax} = \$1,890 \text{ Cash}$$

Here is how the sales tax on the charge sale is computed:

$$\$1,200 \times 0.05 = \$60 \text{ Tax} + \$1,200 \text{ Charge} = \$1,260 \text{ Accounts Receivable}$$

It would be recorded as shown in Figure 9.4. Let's first look at a transaction analysis chart of this transaction before we journalize.

Accounts Affected	Category	↑↓	Rules	T Account Update
Cash	Asset	↑	Dr.	**Cash**
Accounts Receivable	Asset	↑	Dr.	**Accounts Receivable**
Sales Tax Payable	Liability	↑	Cr.	**Sales Tax Payable**
Sales	Revenue	↑	Cr.	**Sales**

Cash

Dr.	Cr.
1,890	

Accounts Receivable

Dr.	Cr.
1,260	

Sales Tax Payable

Dr.	Cr.
	90
	60

Sales

Dr.	Cr.
	3,000

July	18	Cash	1 8 9 0 00		
		Accounts Receivable	1 2 6 0 00		
		Sales Tax Payable			1 5 0 00
		Sales			3 0 0 0 00
		July 18 Sales			

FIGURE 9.4
Sales with Sales Tax

In Learning Unit 9-2, we will look in detail at Art's Wholesale Company.

LEARNING UNIT 9-1 REVIEW

AT THIS POINT you should be able to do the following:

- Explain the purpose of a contra-revenue account.
- Explain how to calculate net sales.
- Define, journalize, and explain gross sales, sales returns and allowances, and sales discounts.
- Journalize an entry for a sale including sales tax payable.

Instant Replay ☼ Self-Review Quiz 9-1

Respond true or false to the following:

1. Sales Returns and Allowances is a contra-asset account.
2. Sales Discount has a normal balance of a debit.
3. Sales Tax Payable is a liability.
4. Sales Discount is a contra-asset.
5. Accounts Receivable is a revenue.

Solutions to Instant Replay: Self-Review Quiz 9-1

1. False—it is a contra-revenue account.
2. True
3. True
4. False—it is a contra-revenue account.
5. False—it is an asset.

COACHING TIP

Sales: Revenue	↑	Cr.
SRA: Contra-revenue	↑	Dr.
SD: Contra-revenue	↑	Dr.

LEARNING UNIT 9-2 RECORDING AND POSTING SALES TRANSACTIONS ON ACCOUNT* FOR ART'S WHOLESALE CLOTHING COMPANY: Introduction to Subsidiary Ledgers and Credit Memorandum

Wholesalers Merchants who buy goods from suppliers and manufacturers for sale to retailers.

Art's Wholesale Clothing Company, as a wholesaler, buys merchandise from suppliers and sells the items to retailers, who in turn sell it to individual consumers.

The following transactions occurred in April for Art's Wholesale Clothing Company:

201X

Apr.	3	Sold on account merchandise to Hal's Clothing, $800; terms 2/10, n/30.
	6	Sold on account merchandise to Bevan's Company, $1,600; terms 2/10, n/30.
	12	Credit memo #1 to Bevan's Company for returned merchandise, $600.
	18	Sold on account merchandise to Roe Company, $2,000; terms 2/10, n/30.
	24	Sold on account merchandise to Roe Company, $500; terms 2/10, n/30.
	28	Sold on account merchandise to Mel's Department Store, $900; terms 2/10, n/30.
	29	Sold on account merchandise to Mel's Department Store, $700; terms 2/10, n/30.

Sales invoice A bill sent to customer(s) reflecting a credit sale.

Let's look closer at the April 3 transaction of Art selling to Hal's Clothing. Figure 9.5 shows the actual bill on the sales invoice for this sale:

April 3   Sold on account merchandise to Hal's Clothing, $800. Terms 2/10, n/30.

Here is an analyis of the transaction by the transaction analysis chart.

Accounts Affected	Category	↑↓	Rules	Amount
Accounts Receivable, Hal's Clothing	Asset	↑	Dr.	$800
Sales	Revenue	↑	Cr.	$800

FIGURE 9.5
Sales Invoice

*At the end of Chapter 10, Appendix A shows an alternative method that uses a special journal to record transactions. Your instructor will let you know if this will be covered in your course.

The general journal is shown in Figure 9.6.

	Date		Account Titles and Description	PR	Dr.	Cr.
	201X					
	Apr.	3	Accounts Receivable, Hal's Clothing		80 00	
			Sales			80 00
			Sale on account to Hal's			

ART'S WHOLESALE CLOTHING COMPANY
GENERAL JOURNAL   Page 2

FIGURE 9.6
Merchandise Sold and Accounts Receivable

Accounts Receivable Subsidiary Ledgers

So far in this text, the only title we have used for recording amounts owed to the seller has been Accounts Receivable. Art could have replaced the Accounts Receivable title in the general ledger with the following list of customers who owe him money:

- Accounts Receivable, Bevans Company
- Accounts Receivable, Hal's Clothing
- Accounts Receivable, Mel's Department Store
- Accounts Receivable, Roe Company

As you can see, this system would not be manageable if Art had 1,000 credit customers. To solve this problem, Art sets up a separate accounts receivable subsidiary ledger. Such a special ledger, often simply called a subsidiary ledger, contains a single type of account, such as credit customers. An account is opened for each customer, and the accounts are arranged alphabetically.

The diagram in Figure 9.7 shows how the accounts receivable subsidiary ledger fits in with the general ledger. To clarify the difference in updating the general ledger versus the subsidiary ledger, we will *post* to the general ledger and *record* to the subsidiary ledger. The word *post* refers to information that is moved from the journal to the general ledger; the word *record* refers to information that is transferred from the journal into the individual customer's account in the subsidiary ledger.

Accounts receivable subsidiary ledger A book or file that contains the individual records, in alphabetical order, of amounts owed by various credit customers.

Subsidiary ledger A ledger that contains accounts of a single type. Example: The accounts receivable subsidiary ledger records all credit customers.

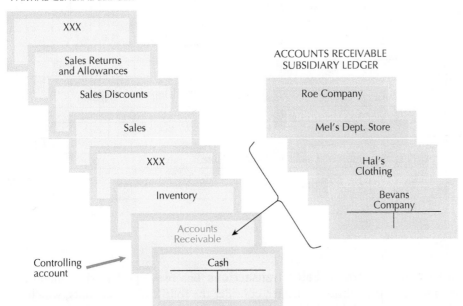

PARTIAL GENERAL LEDGER

XXX

Sales Returns and Allowances

Sales Discounts

Sales

XXX

Inventory

Accounts Receivable

Controlling account → Cash

ACCOUNTS RECEIVABLE SUBSIDIARY LEDGER

Roe Company

Mel's Dept. Store

Hal's Clothing

Bevans Company

FIGURE 9.7
Partial General Ledger of Art's Wholesale Clothing Company and Accounts Receivable Subsidiary Ledger

COACHING TIP

Proving: At the end of the month, the sum of the accounts receivable subsidiary ledger will equal the ending balance in Accounts Receivable, the controlling account in the general ledger.

COACHING TIP

The general ledger is not in the same book as the accounts receivable subsidiary ledger.

Controlling account—Accounts Receivable The Accounts Receivable account in the general ledger, after postings are complete, shows a firm the total amount of money owed to it. This figure is broken down in the accounts receivable subsidiary ledger, where it indicates specifically who owes the money.

The accounts receivable subsidiary ledger, or any other subsidiary ledger, can be in the form of a card file, a binder notebook, or computer tapes or disks. It will not have page numbers. The accounts receivable subsidiary ledger is organized alphabetically based on customers' names and addresses; new customers can be added and inactive customers deleted.

When using an accounts receivable subsidiary ledger, the account title Accounts Receivable in the general ledger is called the controlling account—Accounts Receivable because it summarizes or controls the accounts receivable subsidiary ledger. At the end of the month the total of the individual accounts in the accounts receivable ledger will equal the ending balance in Accounts Receivable in the general ledger.

Figure 9.8 shows how the general journal looks for Art before posting and recording this month's sales transactions on account.

FIGURE 9.8

Before Posting and Recording Sales Transactions

		ART'S WHOLESALE CLOTHING COMPANY GENERAL JOURNAL			Page 2		
Date		Account Titles and Description	PR	Dr.		Cr.	
201X							
Apr.	3	Accounts Receivable, Hal's Clothing		8 0 0 00			
		Sales				8 0 0 00	
		Sale on account to Hal's					
	6	Accounts Receivable, Bevan's Company		1 6 0 0 00			
		Sales				1 6 0 0 00	
		Sale on account to Bevan's					
	12	Sales Returns and Allowances		6 0 0 00			
		Accounts Receivable, Bevan's Company				6 0 0 00	
		Issued credit memo no. 1					
	18	Accounts Receivable, Roe Company		2 0 0 0 00			
		Sales				2 0 0 0 00	
		Sale on account to Roe					
	24	Accounts Receivable, Roe Company		5 0 0 00			
		Sales				5 0 0 00	
		Sale on account to Roe					
	28	Accounts Receivable, Mel's Dept. Store		9 0 0 00			
		Sales				9 0 0 00	
		Sale on account to Mel's					
	29	Accounts Receivable, Mel's Dept. Store		7 0 0 00			
		Sales				7 0 0 00	
		Sale on account to Mel's					

Posting and Recording Sales Transactions Before we post to the general ledger and record to the subsidiary ledger, consider the following T accounts, which show what each title would look like.

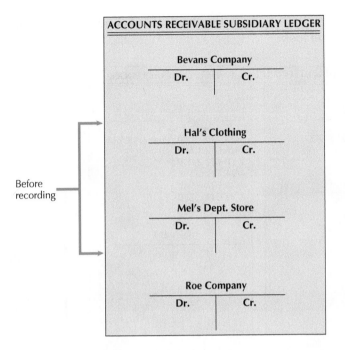

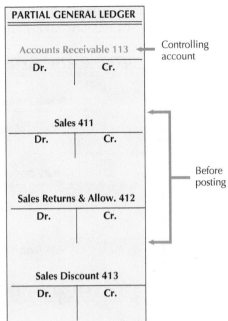

Figure 9.9 shows how the April 3 transaction is posted and recorded.

For this transaction we *post* to the general ledger Accounts Receivable and Sales accounts. Note how the account numbers of 113 and 411 are entered into the PR column of the general journal. We must also *record* to Hal's Clothing in the accounts receivable subsidiary ledger. The amount is placed on the debit side because Hal owed Art the money. When the subsidiary ledger is updated, a (✔) is placed in the PR column of the general journal. The following is how the accounts receivable subsidiary ledger and partial general ledger would look after postings.

		GENERAL JOURNAL			Page 2	
Date		Account Titles and Description	PR	Dr.	Cr.	
201X						
Apr.	3	Accounts Receivable, Hal's Clothing	113 ✔	8 0 0 00		
		Sales	411		8 0 0 00	
		Sale on account to Hal's				

FIGURE 9.9
Transaction for April 3 Posted and Recorded

PARTIAL ACCOUNTS RECEIVABLE SUBSIDIARY LEDGER

Hal's Clothing

Dr.	Cr.
4/3 GJ2 800	

PARTIAL GENERAL LEDGER

Accounts Receivable 113

Dr.	Cr.
4/3 GJ2 800	

Sales 411

Dr.	Cr.
	800 4/3 GJ2

Now lets look at how the complete Accounts Receivable Subsidary Ledger and Partial General Ledger would look.

FIGURE 9.9 (continued)

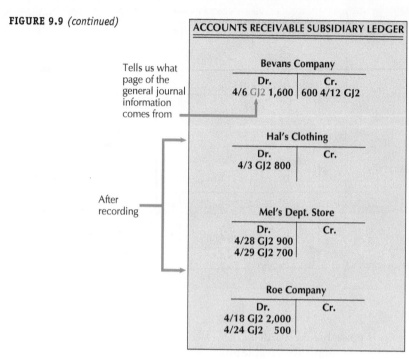

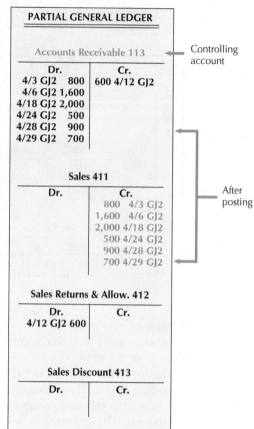

● **LO2**   The Credit Memorandum

Credit memorandum A piece of paper sent by the seller to a customer who has returned merchandise previously purchased on credit. The credit memorandum indicates to the customer that the seller is reducing the amount owed by the customer.

Companies usually handle sales returns and allowances by means of a credit memorandum. Credit memoranda inform customers that the amount of the goods returned or the amount allowed for damaged goods has been subtracted (credited) from the customer's ongoing account with the company.

A sample credit memorandum from Art's Wholesale Clothing Company appears in Figure 9.10. It shows that on April 12, Credit Memorandum No. 1 was issued to Bevans Company for defective merchandise that had been returned.

FIGURE 9.10

Art's Wholesale
Clothing Co.
1528 Belle Ave.
New York, NY 10022

Credit
Memorandum No. _1_
Date: April 12, 201X
Credit to Bevans Company
           110 Aster Rd.
           Cincinnati, Ohio 45227
We credit your account as follows:
Merchandise returned 60 model 8 B men's dress gloves—$600

Let's look at a transaction analysis chart before we journalize, record, and post this transaction.

Accounts Affected	Category	↑↓	Rules
Sales Returns and Allowances	Contra-revenue account	↑	Dr.
Accounts Receivable, Bevans Co.	Asset	↓	Cr.

Journalizing, Recording, and Posting the Credit Memorandum

The credit memorandum results in two postings to the general ledger and one recording to the accounts receivable subsidiary ledger (see Figure 9.11).

×———○
COACHING TIP

Remember: Sales discounts are not taken on returns.

FIGURE 9.11
Postings and Recordings for the Credit Memorandum into the Subsidiary and General Ledgers

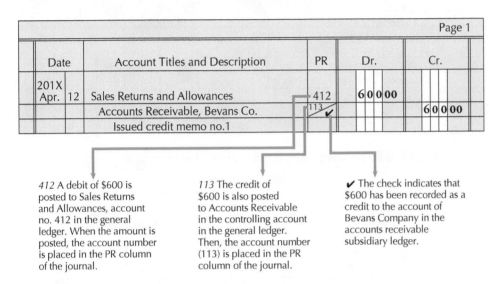

Note that in the PR column next to Accounts Receivable, Bevans Co., a diagonal line separates the account number 113 above and a ✔ below. This notation shows that the amount of $600 has been credited to Accounts Receivable in the controlling account in the general ledger *and* credited to the account of Bevans Company in the accounts receivable subsidiary ledger.

LEARNING UNIT 9-2 REVIEW

AT THIS POINT you should be able to do the following:

- Define and state the purposes of the accounts receivable subsidiary ledger.
- Define and state the purpose of the controlling account, Accounts Receivable.
- Journalize, record, or post sales on account to a general journal and its related accounts receivable and general ledgers.
- Explain, journalize, post, and record a credit memorandum.

Instant Replay ○ Self-Review Quiz 9-2

Journalize, post to the general ledger, and record to accounts receivable subsidiary ledger the following transactions of Bernie Company.

201X		
May	10	Sold merchandise on account to Ring Company, $600; terms 2/10, n/30.
	18	Sold merchandise on account to Lee Corp., $900; terms 2/10, n/30.
	25	Issued credit memo #1 to Ring Company for returned merchandise, $200.

Solution to Instant Replay: Self-Review Quiz 9-2

<table>
<tr><td colspan="6" align="center">BERNIE COMPANY
GENERAL JOURNAL</td><td align="right">Page 4</td></tr>
<tr><td colspan="2">Date</td><td>Account Titles and Description</td><td>PR</td><td>Dr.</td><td>Cr.</td></tr>
<tr><td>201X</td><td></td><td></td><td></td><td></td><td></td></tr>
<tr><td>May</td><td>10</td><td>Accounts Receivable, Ring Clothing</td><td>141 ✓</td><td>600 00</td><td></td></tr>
<tr><td></td><td></td><td>Sales</td><td>310</td><td></td><td>600 00</td></tr>
<tr><td></td><td></td><td>Sale on account to Ring Co.</td><td></td><td></td><td></td></tr>
<tr><td></td><td></td><td></td><td></td><td></td><td></td></tr>
<tr><td></td><td>18</td><td>Accounts Receivable, Lee Corp.</td><td>141 ✓</td><td>900 00</td><td></td></tr>
<tr><td></td><td></td><td>Sales</td><td>310</td><td></td><td>900 00</td></tr>
<tr><td></td><td></td><td>Sale on account to Lee Corp.</td><td></td><td></td><td></td></tr>
<tr><td></td><td></td><td></td><td></td><td></td><td></td></tr>
<tr><td></td><td>25</td><td>Sales Returns and Allowances</td><td>312</td><td>200 00</td><td></td></tr>
<tr><td></td><td></td><td>Accounts Receivable, Ring Co.</td><td>141 ✓</td><td></td><td>200 00</td></tr>
<tr><td></td><td></td><td>Issued credit memo no. 1</td><td></td><td></td><td></td></tr>
</table>

ACCOUNTS RECEIVABLE SUBSIDIARY LEDGER

Lee Corp.

Dr.	Cr.
5/18 GJ4 900	

Ring Co.

Dr.	Cr.
5/10 GJ4 600	200 5/25 GJ4

PARTIAL GENERAL LEDGER

Accounts Receivable 141

Dr.	Cr.
5/10 GJ4 600	200 5/25 GJ4
5/18 GJ4 900	

Sales 310

Dr.	Cr.
	600 5/10 GJ4
	900 5/18 GJ4

Sales Returns & Allow. 312

Dr.	Cr.
5/25 GJ4 200	

● L03   LEARNING UNIT 9-3 RECORDING AND POSTING CASH RECEIPT TRANSACTIONS FOR ART'S WHOLESALE:

Schedule of Accounts Receivable

The following cash receipts transactions occurred for Art's Wholesale Clothing in April:

201X		
Apr.	1	Art Newner invested $8,000 in the business.
	4	Received check from Hal's Clothing for payment of invoice no. 1, less 2% discount.
	15	Cash sales for first half of April, $900.
	16	Received check from Bevans Company in settlement of invoice no. 2, less returns and 2% discount.
	22	Received check from Roe Company for payment of invoice no. 3, less 2% discount.
	27	Sold store equipment, $500.
	30	Cash sales for second half of April, $1,200.

Figure 9.12 provides a closer look at how the April 4 transaction would be journalized. Let's first look at the transaction analysis chart before showing the journalized transaction.

Accounts Affected	Category	↑↓	Rules	T Account Update
Cash	Asset	↑	Dr.	Cash
Sales Discount	Contra-revenue	↑	Dr.	Sales Discount
Accounts Receivable, Hal's Clothing	Asset	↓	Cr.	Acc. Rec. Hal's Clothing

Cash

Dr.	Cr.
784	

Sales Discount

Dr.	Cr.
16	

Acc. Rec.

Dr.	Cr.
800	800

Hal's Clothing

Dr.	Cr.
800	800

COACHING TIP

Hal's Clothing is located in the accounts receivable subsidiary ledger.

Apr.	4	Cash		784 00		
		Sales Discount		16 00		
		Accounts Receivable, Hal's Clothing			800 00	

FIGURE 9.12
Recording Sales Discount in General Journal

Figure 9.13 shows the complete set of April cash receipts transactions for Art's Wholesale journalized for the month, followed by a complete posting to the general ledger and recordings to the accounts receivable subsidiary ledger. (Remember from the past unit that we posted all the sales on account information.)

FIGURE 9.13
Journalized Cash Receipts Transactions

		GENERAL JOURNAL			Page 2
Date		Account Titles and Description	PR	Dr.	Cr.
201X					
Apr.	1	Cash	111	8000 00	
		Art Newner, Capital	311		8000 00
		Owner Investment			
	4	Cash	111	784 00	
		Sales Discount	413	16 00	
		Accounts Receivable, Hal's Clothing	113 ✓		800 00
		Hal's paid invoice no. 1			
	15	Cash	111	900 00	
		Sales	411		900 00
		Cash sales for first half of April			
	16	Cash	111	980 00	
		Sales Discount	413	20 00	
		Accounts Receivable, Bevan's Company	113 ✓		1000 00
		Bevan paid invoice no. 2			
	22	Cash	111	1960 00	
		Sales Discount	413	40 00	
		Accounts Receivable, Roe Co.	113 ✓		2000 00
		Roe paid invoice no. 3			

(continued)

FIGURE 9.13
(continued)

	27	Cash	111	5 0 0 0 0		
		Store Equipment	121		5 0 0 0 0	
		Sold store equipment				
	30	Cash	111	1 2 0 0 0 0		
		Sales	411		1 2 0 0 0 0	
		Cash sales for second half of April				

L04

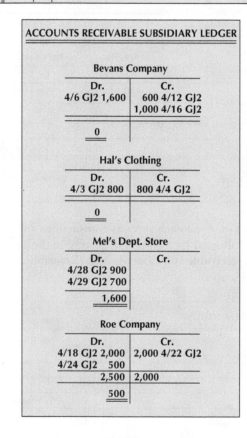

ACCOUNTS RECEIVABLE SUBSIDIARY LEDGER

Bevans Company

Dr.	Cr.
4/6 GJ2 1,600	600 4/12 GJ2
	1,000 4/16 GJ2
0	

Hal's Clothing

Dr.	Cr.
4/3 GJ2 800	800 4/4 GJ2
0	

Mel's Dept. Store

Dr.	Cr.
4/28 GJ2 900	
4/29 GJ2 700	
1,600	

Roe Company

Dr.	Cr.
4/18 GJ2 2,000	2,000 4/22 GJ2
4/24 GJ2 500	
2,500	2,000
500	

PARTIAL GENERAL LEDGER

Cash 111

Dr.	Cr.
4/1 GJ2 8,000	
4/4 GJ2 784	
4/15 GJ2 900	
4/16 GJ2 980	
4/22 GJ2 1,960	
4/27 GJ2 500	
4/30 GJ2 1,200	
14,324	

Accounts Receivable 113 ← Controlling account

Dr.	Cr.
4/3 GJ2 800	800 4/4 GJ2
4/16 GJ2 1,600	600 4/12 GJ2
4/18 GJ2 2,000	1,000 4/16 GJ2
4/24 GJ2 500	2,000 4/22 GJ2
4/28 GJ2 900	4,400
4/29 GJ2 700	
6,500	
Bal. 2,100	

Store Equipment 121

Dr.	Cr.
4/1 Bal. 24,000	500 4/27 GJ2
23,500	

Art Newner, Capital 311

Dr.	Cr.
	8,000 4/1 GJ2
	8,000

Sales 411

Dr.	Cr.
	800 4/3 GJ2
	1,600 4/6 GJ2
	900 4/15 GJ2
	2,000 4/18 GJ2
	500 4/24 GJ2
	900 4/28 GJ2
	700 4/29 GJ2
	1,200 4/30 GJ2
	8,600

Sales Discount 413

Dr.	Cr.
4/4 GJ2 16	
4/16 GJ2 20	
4/22 GJ2 40	
76	

Schedule of Accounts Receivable

The schedule of accounts receivable is an alphabetical list of the companies that have an outstanding balance in the accounts receivable subsidiary ledger. This total should be equal to the balance of the Accounts Receivable controlling account in the general ledger at the end of the month.

Let's examine the schedule of accounts receivable for Art's Wholesale Clothing Company in Figure 9.14.

ART'S WHOLESALE CLOTHING COMPANY SCHEDULE OF ACCOUNTS RECEIVABLE APRIL 30, 201X	
Mel's Dept. Store	$1 6 0 0 00
Roe Company	5 0 0 00
Total Accounts Receivable	$2 1 0 0 00

The balance of the controlling account, Accounts Receivable ($2,100), in the general ledger does indeed equal the sum of the individual customer balances in the accounts receivable ledger ($2,100) as shown in the schedule of accounts receivable. The schedule of accounts receivable can help forecast potential cash inflows as well as possible credit and collection decisions.

LO5

COACHING TIP

Schedule of Accounts Receivable is listed in alphabetical order.

FIGURE 9.14
Schedule of Accounts Receivable

Schedule of accounts receivable A list of the customers, in alphabetical order, that have an outstanding balance in the accounts receivable subsidiary ledger. This total should be equal to the balance of the Accounts Receivable controlling account in the general ledger at the end of the month.

LEARNING UNIT 9-3 REVIEW

AT THIS POINT you should be able to do the following:

- Journalize cash receipts transactions.
- Record and post cash receipts transactions to the accounts receivable subsidiary ledger and general ledger.
- Prepare a schedule of accounts receivable.

Instant Replay ⊙ Self-Review Quiz 9-3

Journalize, post to the general ledger, and record to the accounts receivable subsidiary ledger the following transactions of Mabel Corporation, given the following balances.

Accounts Receivable Subsidiary Ledger

Name	Balance	Invoice No.
Irene Welch	$500	1
Janis Fross	200	2

Partial General Ledger

	Acct. No.	Balance
Cash	110	$600
Accounts Receivable	120	700
Store Equipment	130	600
Sales	410	700
Sales Discount	420	

201X

May	1	Received check from Irene Welch for invoice no. 1, less 2% discount.
	8	Cash sales collected, $200.
	15	Received check from Janis Fross for invoice no. 2, less 2% discount.
	19	Sold store equipment at cost, $300.

Solution to Instant Replay: Self-Review Quiz 9-3

	Date			PR	Dr.	Cr.
			MABEL CORPORATION **GENERAL JOURNAL**			Page 3
	201X					
	May	1	Cash	110	4 9 0 00	
			Sales Discount	420	1 0 00	
			Accounts Receivable, Irene Welch	120 ✔		5 0 0 00
			Received payment from Irene Welch			
		8	Cash	110	2 0 0 00	
			Sales	410		2 0 0 00
			Cash sale			
		15	Cash	110	1 9 6 00	
			Sales Discount	420	4 00	
			Accounts Receivable, Janis Fross	120 ✔		2 0 0 00
			Received payment from Janis Fross			
		19	Cash	110	3 0 0 00	
			Store Equipment	130		3 0 0 00
			Sold store equipment			

ACCOUNTS RECEIVABLE SUBSIDIARY LEDGER

Janis Fross

Dr.	Cr.
Bal. 200	200 5/15 GJ3

Irene Welch

Dr.	Cr.
Bal. 500	500 5/1 GJ3

PARTIAL GENERAL LEDGER

Cash 110

Dr.	Cr.
Bal. 600	
5/1 GJ3 490	
5/8 GJ3 200	
5/15 GJ3 196	
5/19 GJ3 300	

Accounts Receivable 120

Dr.	Cr.
Bal. 700	500 5/1 GJ3
	200 5/15 GJ3

Store Equipment 130

Dr.	Cr.
Bal. 600	300 5/19 GJ3

Sales 410

Dr.	Cr.
	700 Bal.
	200 5/8 GJ3

Sales Discount 420

Dr.	Cr.
5/1 GJ3 10	
5/15 GJ3 4	

BLUEPRINT: TRANSFERRING INFORMATION FROM THE GENERAL JOURNAL

Post → General Ledger (account #)
Record → Subsidiary Ledger (✓)

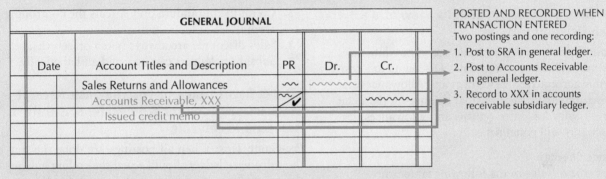

Issuing a Credit Memo without Sales Tax Recorded in a General Journal

POSTED AND RECORDED WHEN TRANSACTION ENTERED
Two postings and one recording:

1. Post to SRA in general ledger.

2. Post to Accounts Receivable in general ledger.

3. Record to XXX in accounts receivable subsidiary ledger.

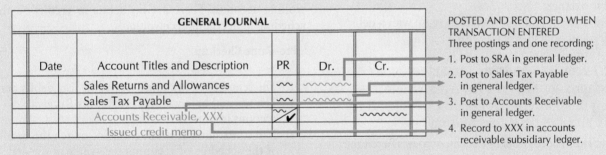

Issuing a Credit Memo with Sales Tax Recorded in a General Journal

POSTED AND RECORDED WHEN TRANSACTION ENTERED
Three postings and one recording:

1. Post to SRA in general ledger.

2. Post to Sales Tax Payable in general ledger.

3. Post to Accounts Receivable in general ledger.

4. Record to XXX in accounts receivable subsidiary ledger.

The following Coaching Tips are from Learning Units 9-1 to 9-3. Take the Pre-Game Checkup and use the Check Your Score to see how you are doing. The Accounting Coach provides tips before each Checkup to help you avoid common accounting errors.

LU 9-1 Chou's Toy Shop: Seller's View of a Merchandise Company

Pre-Game Tips: Sales is a revenue account, while Sales Returns and Allowances and Sales Discounts are contra-revenue accounts. Sales Returns and Allowances and Sales Discounts have their normal balance on the debit side. Gross sales less sales returns and allowances, less sales discounts will equal net sales.

Pre-Game Checkup
Answer true or false to the following statements.

1. Net sales and gross sales are the same.
2. Sales Tax Payable is an asset.
3. Sales Discounts is a revenue account with a debit balance.
4. Sales Returns and Allowances increase with a debit.
5. Sales Discounts increase with a credit.

LU 9-2 Recording and Posting Sales Transactions on Account for Art's Wholesale Clothing Company: Introduction to Subsidiary Ledgers and Credit Memorandum

Pre-Game Tips: The controlling account, Accounts Receivable, in the general ledger will equal the sum of Accounts Receivable in the subsidiary ledger at the end of the month. If a credit memorandum is issued, Sales Returns and Allowances will increase with a debit, and an Accounts Receivable controlling account, as well as the specific subsidiary ledger, will be reduced. The normal balance of each account in the subsidiary ledger is a debit balance.

Pre-Game Checkup
Answer true or false to the following statements.

1. The controlling account is located in the subsidiary ledger.
2. A checkmark in the posting reference column means the controlling account has been updated.
3. Credit memorandum only affects the controlling account.
4. Sales discounts are always taken on returns.
5. Subsidiary ledgers can be listed alphabetically.

LU 9-3 Recording and Posting Cash Receipt Transactions for Arts Wholesale: Schedule of Accounts Receivable

Pre-Game Tips: When all postings are done the sum of the subsidiary ledger should equal the ending balance in the controlling account. It is the schedule of accounts receivable that lists each customer with its ending balance. This total in the schedule of accounts receivable is the one that matches the ending balance in the controlling account. There are no debits or credits on the schedule of accounts receivable.

Pre-Game Checkup
Answer true or false to the following statements.

1. The schedule of accounts receivable lists debits first.
2. The normal balance of an Accounts Receivable account is a credit.
3. The controlling account does not match the total of the schedule of accounts receivable at the end of the month.
4. Sales Discounts is a contra-asset.
5. The schedule of accounts receivable shows what we owe vendors.

CHECK YOUR SCORE: Answers to the Pre-Game Checkup

LU 9-1

1. False—Net sales is gross sales less allowances and any discounts.
2. False—Sales Tax Payable is a liability.
3. False—Sales Discounts is a contra-revenue account with a debit balance.
4. True.
5. False—Sales Discounts increase with a debit.

LU 9-2

1. False—The controlling account is located in the general ledger.
2. False—A checkmark in the posting reference column means the subsidiary ledger has been updated.
3. False—Credit memorandum affects both the controlling account and the subsidiary ledger.
4. False—Sales discounts are never taken on returns.
5. True.

LU 9-3

1. False—There are no debits on the schedule of accounts receivable.
2. False—The normal balance of an Accounts Receivable account is a debit.
3. False—The controlling account does match the total of the schedule of accounts receivable at the end of the month.
4. False—Sales Discounts is a contra-revenue account.
5. False—The schedule of accounts receivable shows the amount vendors owe the seller.

Chapter Summary

MyAccountingLab

Here are all the key concepts and equations to help you understand the concepts of this chapter and prepare you for your exam. After completing this review, go to MyAccountingLab for more practice opportunities.

Concepts You Should Know	Key Terms
L01 Recording and posting sales transactions. 1. Sales Returns and Allowances and Sales Discount are contra-revenue accounts. 2. Net Sales = Gross Sales – Sales Returns and Allowances – Sales Discounts. 3. Sales Tax Payable is a liability account.	Accounts receivable subsidiary ledger (p. 341) Controlling account—Accounts Receivable (p. 342) Credit period (p. 337) Discount period (p. 337) Gross sales (p. 338) Merchandise (p. 336) Net sales (p. 338) Retailers (p. 336) Sales discount (p. 337) Sales Discount account (p. 337) Sales invoice (p. 340) Sales Returns and Allowances (SRA) account (p. 336) Sales Tax Payable account (p. 338) Subsidiary ledger (p. 341) Wholesalers (p. 340)
L02 Preparing, journalizing, and posting a credit memorandum. 1. When a credit memorandum is issued, the result is that Sales Returns and Allowances increases and Accounts Receivable decreases. 2. When we record this entry into the general journal, all parts of the transaction will be posted to the general ledger and recorded in the subsidiary ledger.	Credit memorandum (p. 344)
L03 Recording and posting cash receipts transactions. 1. Sales result in an inflow of cash and/or accounts receivable. All cash receipts transactions result in an inward flow of cash.	

Recording to the accounts receivable subsidiary ledger.

L04

1. The normal balance of the accounts receivable subsidiary ledger is a debit.

2. A ✓ in the PR of the general journal means that the subsidiary ledger has been updated.

3. The accounts receivable subsidiary ledger is not in the same book as Accounts Receivable, the controlling account in the general ledger.

Preparing a schedule of accounts receivable.

Schedule of accounts receivable (p. 349)

L05

1. The schedule of accounts receivable is an alphabetical list of companies with an outstanding balance.

2. At the end of the month, the total of all customers' ending balances in the accounts receivable subsidiary ledger should be equal to the ending balance in Accounts Receivable, the controlling account in the general ledger.

Discussion Questions and Critical Thinking Questions/ Ethical Case

1. Explain the purpose of a contra-revenue account.

2. What is the normal balance of Sales Discount?

3. Give two examples of contra-revenue accounts.

4. What is the difference between a discount period and a credit period?

5. Explain the terms:

   a. 2/10, n/30

   b. n/10, EOM

6. What category is Sales Discount in?

7. Compare and contrast the Controlling Account—Accounts Receivable to the accounts receivable subsidiary ledger.

8. Why is the accounts receivable subsidiary ledger organized in alphabetical order?

9. When is a (✓) used?

10. What is an invoice? What purpose does it serve?

11. Why is sales tax a liability to the business?

12. Sales discounts are taken on sales tax. Agree or disagree? Explain why.

13. When a seller issues a credit memorandum (assume no sales tax), what accounts will be affected?

14. Amy Jak is the National Sales Manager of Land.com. To get sales up to the projection for the old year, Amy asked the accountant to put the first two weeks' sales in January back into December. Amy told the accountant that this secret would only be between them. Should Amy move the new sales into the old sales year? You make the call. Write down your specific recommendations to Amy.

MyAccountingLab

Concept Checks

LO1 *(5 MIN)*   **Overview**

1. Complete the following table for Sales, Sales Returns and Allowances, and Sales Discounts.

Accounts Affected	Category	Rules to Increase Account	Temporary or Permanent

LO1 *(5 MIN)*   **Calculating Net Sales**

2. Given the following, calculate net sales:

Gross Sales	$38
Sales Returns and Allowances	12
Sales Discounts	3

General Journal

●●○ **LO1, 3, 4** *(10 MIN)*

3. Match the following activities to the three business transactions (more than one number can be used).
   1. Record to the accounts receivable subsidiary ledger.
   2. Journalize the transaction.
   3. Post to the general ledger.
   a. _____ Sold merchandise on account to Lee Co., invoice no. 1, $60.
   b. _____ Sold merchandise on account to Flynn Co., invoice no. 2, $1,500.
   c. _____ Issued credit memorandum no. 1 to Flynn Co. for defective merchandise, $50.

Credit Memorandum

● **LO2** *(10 MIN)*

4. Complete the transactional analysis box for the following transaction: Issued credit memorandum to Fox.com for defective merchandise, $206.

Journalize Transactions

●●● **LO1, 2, 3** *(15 MIN)*

5. Journalize the following transactions:
   a. Sold merchandise on account to Weis Co., invoice no. 10, $32.
   b. Received check from Phair Co., $1000, less 2% discount.
   c. Cash Sales, $99.
   d. Issued credit memorandum no. 2 to Weis Co. for defective merchandise, $19.

6. From the following, prepare a schedule of accounts receivable for Pine Co. for May 31, 201X.

● **LO5** *(15 MIN)*

Accounts Receivable Subsidiary Ledger

James Co.

	Dr.	Cr.
5/6 GJ1	99	

Noel Co.

	Dr.	Cr.	
5/20 GJ1	28	13	5/27 GJ1

Rose Co.

	Dr.	Cr.
5/9 GJ1	11	

General Ledger

Accounts Receivable

	Dr.	Cr.	
5/31 GJ1	138	13	5/31 GJ1

MyAccountingLab   Exercises

Set A

LO1, 4 *(10 MIN)*   **9A-1.** From the general journal in Figure 9.15, record to the accounts receivable subsidiary ledger and post to the general ledger accounts as appropriate.

FIGURE 9.15
General Journal, Subsidiary Ledger, and Partial General Ledger

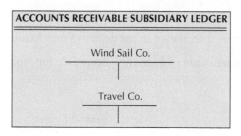

General Journal					
Date			PR	Dr.	Cr.
201X					
Nov.	18	Accounts Receivable, Wind Sail Co.		6 2 0 00	
		Sales			6 2 0 00
		Sold merchandise to Wind Sail Co.			
	19	Accounts Receivable, Travel Co.		9 3 0 00	
		Sales			9 3 0 00
		Sold merchandise to Travel Co.			

ACCOUNTS RECEIVABLE SUBSIDIARY LEDGER
Wind Sail Co.
Travel Co.

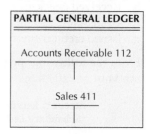

PARTIAL GENERAL LEDGER
Accounts Receivable 112
Sales 411

LO1, 2, 4 *(10 MIN)*   **9A-2.** Journalize, record, and post when appropriate the following transactions in the general journal (all sales carry terms of 1/10, n/30):

201X		
May	16	Sold merchandise on account to Pearl Co., invoice no. 1, $900.
	18	Sold merchandise on account to Glenda Co., invoice no. 2, $1,900.
	20	Issued credit memorandum no. 1 to Glenda Co. for defective merchandise, $710.

Use the following account numbers: Accounts Receivable, 112; Sales, 411; Sales Returns and Allowances, 412.

LO3, 4 *(10 MIN)*   **9A-3.** From Exercise 9-2, journalize the receipt of a check from Pearl Co. for payment of invoice no. 1 on May 24.

LO4, 5 *(20 MIN)*   **9A-4.** From the following transactions for Andrew Co., journalize, record, post, and prepare a schedule of accounts receivable when appropriate. You will have to set up your own accounts receivable subsidiary ledger and partial general ledger as needed. All sales terms are 4/10, n/30.

201X		
Oct.	1	Andrew Albright invested $2,600 in the business.
	1	Sold merchandise on account to Greenfield Co., invoice no. 1, $750.
	2	Sold merchandise on account to Robert Co., invoice no. 2, $900.
	3	Cash sale, $215.
	8	Issued credit memorandum no. 1 to Greenfield Co. for defective merchandise, $150.
	10	Received check from Greenfield Co. for invoice no. 1, less returns and discount.
	15	Cash sale, $430.
	18	Sold merchandise on account to Greenfield Co., invoice no. 3, $650.

9A-5. From the following facts calculate what Cara Dock paid Hollow Co. for the purchase of a dining room set. Sale terms are 2/10, n/30.
    a. Sales ticket price before tax, $10,000, dated April 5.
    b. Sales tax, 8%.
    c. Returned one defective chair for credit of $800 on April 8.
    d. Paid bill on April 13.

◯ **LO2** *(10 MIN)*

Set B

9B-1. From the general journal in Figure 9.16, record to the accounts receivable subsidiary ledger and post to the general ledger accounts as appropriate.

◗◯ **LO1, 4** *(10 MIN)*

FIGURE 9.16
The General Journal, Subsidiary Ledger, and Partial General Ledger

	General Journal				
Date	Account Titles and Explanations	PR	Dr.	Cr.	
201X					
Aug. 18	Accounts Receivable, Wind Sail Co.		560 00		
	Sales				
	Sold merchandise to Wind Sail Co.			560 00	
19	Accounts Receivable, Travel Co.		860 00		
	Sales				
	Sold merchandise to Travel Co.			860 00	

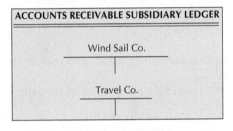

ACCOUNTS RECEIVABLE SUBSIDIARY LEDGER

Wind Sail Co.

Travel Co.

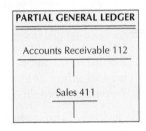

PARTIAL GENERAL LEDGER

Accounts Receivable 112

Sales 411

9B-2. Journalize, record, and post when appropriate the following transactions in the general journal (all sales carry terms of 5/10, n/30):

◗◗◯ **LO1, 2, 4** *(10 MIN)*

201X

Nov. 16 Sold merchandise on account to Pearl Co., invoice no. 1, $920.
    18 Sold merchandise on account to Glenda Co., invoice no. 2, $1,600.
    20 Issued credit memorandum no. 1 to Glenda Co. for defective merchandise, $690. Use the following account numbers: Accounts Receivable, 112; Sales, 411; Sales Returns and Allowances, 412.

9B-3. From Exercise 9B-2, journalize the receipt of a check from Pearl Co. for payment of invoice no.1 on November 24.

◗◯ **LO3, 4** *(10 MIN)*

9B-4. From the following transactions for Andrew Co., journalize, record, post, and prepare a schedule of accounts receivable when appropriate. The accounts receivable subsidiary ledger and partial general ledger have been set up for you. All sales terms are 4/10, n/30.

◗● **LO4, 5** *(20 MIN)*

201X

Oct. 1 Andrew Albright invested $3,200 in the business.
    1 Sold merchandise on account to Greenfield Co., invoice no. 1, $800.
    2 Sold merchandise on account to Robert Co., invoice no. 2, $920.
    3 Cash sale, $210.
    8 Issued credit memorandum no. 1 to Greenfield Co. for defective merchandise, $200.
    10 Received check from Greenfield Co. for invoice no. 1, less returns and discount.
    15 Cash sale, $420.
    18 Sold merchandise on account to Greenfield Co., invoice no. 3, $700.

LO2 *(10 MIN)*

9B-5. From the following facts calculate what Uriah Jones paid Jade Co. for the purchase of a dining room set. Sale terms are 1/10, n/30.
  a. Sales ticket price before tax, $12,000, date April 5.
  b. Sales tax 2%.
  c. Returned one defective chair for credit of $500 on April 8.
  d. Paid bill on April 13.

MyAccountingLab

Problems

Group A

LO1, 2, 4, 5
(40 MIN)

9A-1. Bill Hass has opened Ciabatta and Whatnot, a wholesale grocery and bread company. The following transactions occurred in January:

201X		
Jan.	1	Sold grocery merchandise to Cindi Co. on account, $500, invoice no. 1.
	4	Sold bread merchandise to Common Law Co. on account, $850, invoice no. 2.
	8	Sold grocery merchandise to Canadian Co. on account, $750, invoice no. 3.
	10	Issued credit memorandum no. 1 to Cindi Co. for $210 of grocery merchandise returned due to spoilage.
	15	Sold bread merchandise to Common Law Co. on account, $300, invoice no. 4.
	19	Sold grocery merchandise to Canadian Co. on account, $800, invoice no. 5.
	25	Sold bread merchandise to Cindi Co. on account, $150, invoice no. 6.

Check Figure:
Schedule of accounts
receivable $3,140

Required
  1. Journalize the transactions.
  2. Record to the accounts receivable subsidiary ledger and post to the general ledger as appropriate.
  3. Prepare a schedule of accounts receivable for the end of January.

LO1, 2, 4, 5
(50 MIN)

9A-2. The following transactions of Jack's Auto Supply occurred in November (Balances as of November 1 are given for general ledger and accounts receivable ledger accounts: Danielson $400 Dr.; Wallace $550 Dr.; Whitnall $400; Accounts Receivable $1,350 Dr.; Sales Tax Payable $1,900 Cr. Be sure to enter these balances in your working papers before beginning.):

201X		
Nov.	1	Sold auto parts merchandise to R. Danielson on account, $1,600, invoice no. 50, plus 6% sales tax.
	5	Sold auto parts merchandise to J. Wallace on account, $850, invoice no. 51, plus 6% sales tax.
	8	Sold auto parts merchandise to Lance Whitnall on account, $9,000, invoice no. 52, plus 6% sales tax.
	10	Issued credit memorandum no. 12 to R. Danielson for $850 for defective auto parts merchandise returned from Nov. 1 transaction. (Be careful to record the reduction in Sales Tax Payable as well.)
	12	Sold auto parts merchandise to J. Wallace on account, $750, invoice no. 53, plus 6% sales tax.

Check Figure:
Schedule of accounts
receivable $13,381

Required

1. Journalize the transactions.
2. Record to the accounts receivable subsidiary ledger and post to the general ledger as appropriate.
3. Prepare a schedule of accounts receivable for the end of November.

9A-3. Mike Patten owns Patten's Sneaker Shop. (Balances as of May 1 are provided for the accounts receivable and general ledger accounts as follows: Donati $375 Dr.; Lindall $850 Dr.; Pilar $550 Dr.; Zamora $650 Dr.; Cash $15,000 Dr.; Accounts Receivable $2,425 Dr.; sneaker rack equipment $850 Dr.; Mike Patten, Capital $39,000 Cr.; Sales $2,200 Cr. Be sure to put beginning balances in your working papers.) The following transactions occurred in May:

○○○○●L01, 2, 3, 4, 5 *(70 MIN)*

201X

May	1	Mike Patten invested an additional $14,500 in the sneaker store.
	3	Sold $900 of merchandise on account to B. Donati, sales ticket no. 60; terms 2/10, n/30.
	4	Sold $700 of merchandise on account to Ron Lindall, sales ticket no. 61; terms 2/10, n/30.
	9	Sold $400 of merchandise on account to Jim Zamora, sales ticket no. 62; terms 2/10, n/30.
	10	Received cash from B. Donati in payment of May 3 transaction, sales ticket no. 60, less discount.
	20	Sold $3,000 of merchandise on account to Pilar Pry, sales ticket no. 63; terms 2/10, n/30.
	22	Received cash payment from Ron Lindall in payment of May 4 transaction, sales ticket no. 61.
	23	Collected cash sales, $2,400.
	24	Issued credit memorandum no. 1 to Pilar Pry for $2,200 of merchandise returned from May 20 sales on account.
	26	Received cash from Pilar Pry in payment of May 20, sales ticket no. 63. (Don't forget about the credit memo and discount.)
	28	Collected cash sales, $6,800.
	30	Sold sneaker rack equipment for $350 cash. (Beware.)
	30	Sold merchandise priced at $4,000, on account to Ron Lindall, sales ticket no. 64; terms 2/10, n/30.
	31	Issued credit memorandum no. 2 to Ron Lindall for $700 of merchandise returned from May 30 transaction, sales ticket no. 64.

Check Figure:
Schedule of accounts
receivable $6,125

Required

1. Journalize the transactions.
2. Record to the accounts receivable subsidiary ledger and post to the general ledger as needed.
3. Prepare a schedule of accounts receivable for the end of May.

L01, 2, 3, 4, 5 *(75 MIN)*

9A-4. Gary Wilcox opened Gary's Cosmetic Market on October 1. A 6% sales tax is calculated and added to all cosmetic sales. Gary offers no sales discounts. The following transactions occurred in October:

201X		
Oct.	1	Gary Wilcox invested $8,500 in the Cosmetic Market from his personal savings account.
	5	From the cash register tapes, lipstick cash sales were $4,800, plus sales tax.
	5	From the cash register tapes, eye shadow cash sales were $2,500, plus sales tax.
	8	Sold lipstick on account to Fione Tay Co., $500, sales ticket no. 1, plus sales tax.
	9	Sold eye shadow on account to Marika Sanford Co., $1,500, sales ticket no. 2, plus sales tax.
	15	Issued credit memorandum no. 1 to Fione Tay Co. for $300 for lipstick returned. (Be sure to reduce Sales Tax Payable for Gary's.)
	19	Marika Sanford Co. paid half the amount owed from sales ticket no. 2, dated October 9.
	21	Sold lipstick on account to Mary Ruvolo Co., $550, sales ticket no. 3, plus sales tax.
	24	Sold eye shadow on account to Peter Melnyk Co., $700, sales ticket no. 4, plus sales tax.
	25	Issued credit memorandum no. 2 to Mary Ruvolo Co. for $150 for lipstick returned from sales ticket no. 3, dated October 21.
	29	Cash sales taken from the cash register tape showed the following: 1. Lipstick: $1,300 + $78 sales tax collected. 2. Eye shadow: $2,600 + $156 sales tax collected.
	29	Sold lipstick on account to Marika Sanford Co., $500, sales ticket no. 5, plus sales tax.
	30	Received payment from Marika Sanford Co. of sales ticket no. 5, dated October 29.

Check Figure:
Schedule of accounts
receivable $2,173

Required
1. Journalize the transactions.
2. Record to the accounts receivable subsidiary ledger and post to the general ledger when appropriate.
3. Prepare a schedule of accounts receivable for the end of October.

MyAccountingLab

L01, 2, 4, 5 *(40 MIN)*

Group B

9B-1. Bill Haas has opened Ciabatta and Whatnot, a wholesale grocery and bread company. The following transactions occurred in January:

201X		
Jan.	1	Sold grocery merchandise to Cindi Co. on account, $900, invoice no. 1.
	4	Sold bread merchandise to Common Law Co. on account, $550, invoice no. 2.
	8	Sold grocery merchandise to Canadian Co. on account, $1,000, invoice no. 3.
	10	Issued credit memorandum no. 1 to Cindi Co. for $160 of grocery merchandise returned due to spoilage.
	15	Sold bread merchandise to Common Law Co. on account, $300, invoice no. 4.
	19	Sold grocery merchandise to Canadian Co. on account, $400, invoice no. 5.
	25	Sold bread merchandise to Cindi Co. on account, $500, invoice no. 6.

Check Figure:
Schedule of accounts
receivable $3,490

Required
1. Journalize the transactions.
2. Record to the accounts receivable subsidiary ledger and post to the general ledger as appropriate.
3. Prepare a schedule of accounts receivable for the end of January.

9B-2. The following transactions of Jack's Auto Supply occurred in November (Balances as of November 1 are given for general ledger and accounts receivable ledger accounts: Danielson $1,100 Dr.; Wallace $250 Dr.; Whitnall $500; Accounts Receivable $1,850 Dr.; Sales Tax Payable $2,000 Cr. Be sure to enter these balances in your working papers before beginning.):

 **L01, 2, 4, 5**
(50 MIN)

201X

Nov. 1   Sold auto parts merchandise to R. Danielson on account, $600, invoice no. 30, plus 8% sales tax.

5   Sold auto parts merchandise to J. Wallace on account, $900, invoice no. 31, plus 8% sales tax.

8   Sold auto parts merchandise to Lance Whitnall on account, $9,000, invoice no. 32, plus 8% sales tax.

10   Issued credit memorandum no. 12 to R. Danielson for $450 for defective auto parts merchandise returned from January 1 transaction. (Be careful to record the reduction in Sales Tax Payable as well.)

12   Sold auto parts merchandise to J. Wallace on account, $450, invoice no. 33, plus 8% sales tax.

Required

1. Journalize the transactions.
2. Record to the accounts receivable subsidiary ledger and post to the general ledger as appropriate.
3. Prepare a schedule of accounts receivable for the end of November.

Check Figure:
Schedule of accounts
receivable $13,190

9B-3. Mike Pattern owns Pattern's Sneaker Shop. (Balances as of May 1 are provided for the accounts receivable and general ledger accounts as follows: Donati $325 Dr.; Lindall $800 Dr.; Pry $500 Dr.; Zamora $700 Dr.; Cash $14,000 Dr.; Accounts Receivable $2,325 Dr.; sneaker rack equipment $1,300 Dr.; Mike Pattern, Capital $39,000 Cr.; Sales $2,500 Cr. Be sure to put them in your working papers.) The following transactions occurred in May:

L01, 2, 3, 4, 5 *(70 MIN)*

201X

May   1   Mike Pattern invested an additional $11,000 in the sneaker store.

3   Sold $800 of merchandise on account to B. Donati, sales ticket no. 70; terms 1/10, n/30.

4   Sold $600 of merchandise on account to Ron Lindall, sales ticket no. 71; terms 1/10, n/30.

9   Sold $300 of merchandise on account to Jim Zamora, sales ticket no. 72; terms 1/10, n/30.

10   Received cash from B. Donati in payment of May 3 transaction, sales ticket no. 70, less discount.

20   Sold $2,000 of merchandise on account to Pilar Pry, sales ticket no. 73; terms 1/10, n/30.

22   Received cash payment from Ron Lindall in payment of May 4 transaction, sales ticket no. 71.

23   Collected cash sales, $2,000.

24   Issued credit memorandum no. 1 to Pilar Pry for $1,800 of merchandise returned from May 20 sales on account.

26   Received cash from Pilar Pry in payment of May 20 sales ticket no. 73. (Don't forget about the credit memo and discount.)

28   Collected cash sales, $7,000.

30   Sold sneaker rack equipment for $150 cash. (Beware.)

30   Sold merchandise priced at $5,000 on account to Ron Lindall, sales ticket no. 74, terms 1/10, n/30.

31   Issued credit memorandum no. 2 to Ron Lindall for $875 of merchandise returned from May 30 transaction, sales ticket no. 74.

Check Figure:
Schedule of accounts
receivable $6,750

Required

1. Journalize the transactions.
2. Record to the accounts receivable subsidiary ledger and post to the general ledger as needed.
3. Prepare a schedule of accounts receivable for the end of May.

 LO1, 2, 3, 4, 5 *(75 MIN)*

9B-4. Gary Wilcox opened Gary's Cosmetic Market on October 1. A 4% sales tax is calculated and added to all cosmetic sales. Gary offers no sales discounts. The following transactions occurred in April:

201X		
Oct.	1	Gary Wilcox invested $9,500 in the Cosmetic Market from his personal savings account.
	5	From the cash register tapes, lipstick cash sales were $4,900, plus sales tax.
	5	From the cash register tapes, eye shadow cash sales were $2,500, plus sales tax.
	8	Sold lipstick on account to Fione Tay Co., $500, sales ticket no. 1, plus sales tax.
	9	Sold eye shadow on account to Marika Sanford Co., $600, sales ticket no. 2, plus sales tax.
	15	Issued credit memorandum no. 1 to Marika Sanford Co. for $50 for lipstick returned. (Be sure to reduce Sales Tax Payable for Gary's.)
	19	Marika Sanford Co. paid half the amount owed from sales ticket no. 2, dated October 9.
	21	Sold lipstick on account to Mary Ruvolo Co., $500, sales ticket no. 3, plus sales tax.
	24	Sold eye shadow on account to Peter Melnyk Co., $800, sales ticket no. 4, plus sales tax.
	25	Issued credit memorandum no. 2 to Mary Ruvolo Co. for $300 for lipstick returned from sales ticket no. 3, dated October 21.
	29	Cash sales taken from the cash register tape showed the following: 1. Lipstick: $700 + $28 sales tax collected. 2. Eye shadow: $3,500 + $140 sales tax collected.
	29	Sold lipstick on account to Marika Sanford Co., $500, sales ticket no. 5, plus sales tax.
	30	Received payment from Marika Sanford Co. of sales ticket no. 5, dated October 29.

Check Figure:
Schedule of accounts
receivable $1,820

Required

1. Journalize, record, and post as appropriate.
2. Prepare a schedule of accounts receivable for the end of October.

⬤ **LO1** *(15 MIN)*

Reading the Kellogg's Annual Report

Go to http://investor.kelloggs.com/annuals.cfm, to access the Kellogg's 2010 Annual Report, Note 1, Revenue Recognition, and find out what account records the promotional package inserts.

MyAccountingLab

⬤ON the JOB ||||||||||||||||||||||||||||||

SANCHEZ COMPUTER CENTER

To assist you in recording these transactions for the month of January, at the end of this problem is the schedule of accounts receivable as of December 31 and an updated chart of accounts with the current balance listed for each account.

Assignment

1. Journalize the transactions.
2. Record in the accounts receivable subsidiary ledger and post to the general ledger as appropriate. A partial subsidiary ledger is included in the working papers that accompany this text.

3. The following accounts have been added to the chart of accounts: Sales #4010, Sales Returns and Allowances #4020, and Sales Discounts #4030.
4. Prepare a schedule of accounts receivable as of January 31, 201X.

The January transactions are as follows:

Jan.	1	Sold $700 worth of merchandise to Taylor Golf on credit, sales invoice no. 5000; terms 2/10, n/30.
	10	Sold $3,000 worth of merchandise on account to Anthony Pitale, sales invoice no. 5001; terms 2/10, n/30.
	11	Received $3,000 from Accu Pac, Inc., toward payment of its balance; no discount allowed.
	12	Collected $2,000 cash sales.
	19	Sold $4,000 worth of merchandise on account to Vita Needle, sales invoice no. 5002; terms 4/10, n/30.
	20	Collected balance in full from invoice no. 5001, Anthony Pitale.
	29	Issued credit memorandum to Taylor Golf for $400 worth of merchandise returned, invoice no. 5000.
	29	Collected full payment from Vita Needle, invoice no. 5002.

Schedule of Accounts Receivable
Sanchez Computer Center
December 31, 201X

Taylor Golf	$ 2,900.00
Vita Needle	6,800.00
Accu Pac	3,900.00
Total Amount Due	$13,600.00

Chart of Accounts and Current Balances as of 12/31/1X

Account #	Account Name	Debit Balance	Credit Balance
1000	Cash	$ 3,336.64	
1010	Petty Cash	100	
1020	Accounts Receivable	13,600	
1025	Prepaid Rent	1,600	
1030	Supplies	90	
1040	Merchandise Inventory	0	
1080	Computer Shop Equipment	3,800	
1081	Accumulated Dep., C.S. Equip.		$ 99
1090	Office Equipment	1,050	
1091	Accumulated Dep., Office Equip.		20
2000	Accounts Payable		2,050
2010	Wages Payable		0
2020	FICA—Social Security Payable		0
2030	FICA—Medicare Payable		0
2040	FIT Payable		0
2050	SIT Payable		0
2060	FUTA Payable		0
2070	SUTA Payable		0
3000	Freedman, Capital		7,406
3010	Freedman, Withdrawals	2,015	

(continued)

Chart of Accounts and Current Balances as of 12/31/1X

Account #	Account Name	Debit Balance	Credit Balance
3020	Income Summary		0
4000	Service Revenue		18,500
4010	Sales		0
4020	Sales Returns and Allowances	0	
4030	Sales Discounts	0	
5010	Advertising Expense	0	
5020	Rent Expense	0	
5030	Utilities Expense	0	
5040	Phone Expense	150	
5050	Supplies Expense	42	
5060	Insurance Expense	0	
5070	Postage Expense	25	
5080	Dep. Exp., C.S. Equipment	0	
5090	Dep. Exp., Office Equipment	0	
5100	Miscellaneous Expense	10	
5110	Wage Expense	2,030	
5120	Payroll Tax Expense	226.36	
5130	Interest Expense	0	
5140	Bad Debt Expense	0	
6000	Purchases	0	
6010	Purchases Returns and Allowances		0
6020	Purchases Discounts		0
6030	Freight In	0	

Purchases and Cash Payments

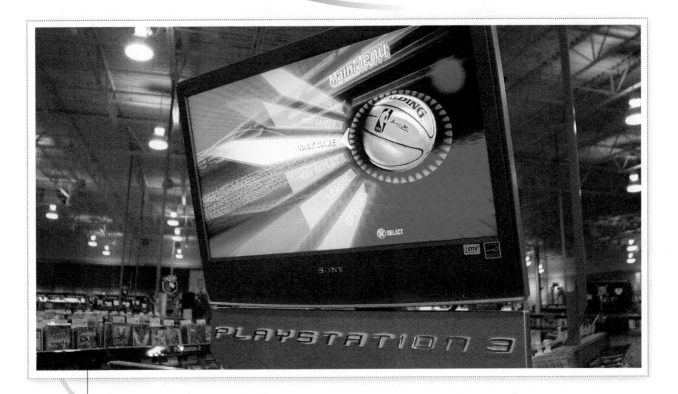

THE GAME PLAN

So you have decided to buy a Sony high-definition, 3D television. You know the exact model you want; however, there is only a limited supply available. You visit Best Buy and ask the salesperson if this model is in stock. The salesperson goes to the computer and searches the inventory. Yes, there is one left in stock. You buy it and now that item is reported temporarily out of stock. In this chapter you will learn how inventory is accounted for when purchased by the company and sold to a buyer.

LEARNING OBJECTIVES

- **1.** Recording and posting purchase transactions.
- **2.** Recording to accounts payable subsidiary ledger.
- **3.** Preparing, journalizing, and posting a debit memorandum.
- **4.** Recording and posting cash payment transactions.
- **5.** Preparing a schedule of accounts payable.
- **6.** Journalizing transactions for a perpetual accounting system.

⬤ **L01**   **LEARNING UNIT 10-1 CHOU'S TOY SHOP:**
Buyer's View of a Merchandise Company

Purchases

Purchases Merchandise for resale. It is a cost.

When you go into your local Target do you ever wonder how a store records all of the merchandise it purchases from a company like Sony? First, let us look at Chou's Toy Shop. Chou brings merchandise into his toy store for resale to customers. The account that records the cost of this merchandise is called Purchases. Suppose Chou buys $4,000 worth of Barbie dolls on account from Mattel Manufacturing on July 6. The Purchases account records all merchandise bought for resale.

	Purchases	
Purchases is a cost.	Dr.	Cr.
The rules work the same as an expense.	4,000	

This account has a debit balance and is classified as a cost. Purchases represent costs that are directly related to bringing merchandise into the store for resale to customers. The July 6 entry would be analyzed and journalized as in Figure 10.1.

COACHING TIP

If Chou's purchased a new display case for the store, it would not show up in the Purchases account. The case is considered equipment that is not for resale to customers.

Accounts Affected	Category	↑↓	Rules	T Account Update			
Purchases	Cost	↑	Dr.	**Purchases**			
				Dr.	Cr.		
				4,000			
Accounts Payable, Mattel	Liability	↑	Cr.	**Acc. Payable**		**Mattel**	
				Dr.	Cr.	Dr.	Cr.
					4,000		4,000

Keep in mind that we would have to record to Mattel in the accounts payable subsidiary ledger. We talk about the subsidiary ledger in Learning Unit 10-2.

FIGURE 10.1
Purchased Merchandise on Account

Jul.	6	Purchases			4 0 0 0 00		
		Accounts Payable, Mattel				4 0 0 0 00
		Purchases on account				

Purchases Returns and Allowances

Purchases Returns and Allowances A contra-cost account in the ledger that records the amount of defective or unacceptable merchandise returned to suppliers and/or price reductions given for defective items.

Chou noticed that some of the dolls he received were defective, and he notified the manufacturer of the defects. On July 9, Mattel issued a credit memorandum indicating that Chou would get a $500 reduction from the original selling price. Chou then agreed to keep the dolls. The account that records a decrease to a buyer's cost is a contra-cost account called Purchases Returns and Allowances. The account lowers the cost of purchases.

Purchases Returns and Allowances	
Dr.	Cr.
	500 ◄——— **Normal balance is a credit.**

Let's analyze this reduction to cost and prepare a general journal entry (Figure 10.2).

Accounts Affected	Category	↑↓	Rules	T Account Update			
Accounts Payable, Mattel	Liability	↓	Dr.	**Acc. Payable**		**Mattel**	
				Dr.	Cr.	Dr.	Cr.
				500	4,000	500	4,000
Purchases Returns and Allowances	Contra-cost	↑	Cr.	**Purchases Ret. & Allow.**			
				Dr.	Cr.		
					500		

When posted to general ledger accounts as well as recorded to Mattel in the accounts payable subsidiary ledger, Chou owes $500 less.

Jul.	9	Accounts Payable, Mattel			5 0 0 00				
		Purchases Returns and Allowances					5 0 0 00		
		Received credit memorandum							

FIGURE 10.2
Credit Memorandum Received

Purchases Discount Now let's look at the analysis and journal entry when Chou pays Mattel. Mattel offers a 2% cash discount if the invoice is paid within 10 days. To take advantage of this cash discount, Chou sent a check to Mattel on July 15. The discount is taken after the allowance.

$$\$4,000$$
$$\underline{- 500 \text{ allowance}}$$
$$\$3,500 \times 0.02 = \$70 \text{ purchases discount}$$

The account that records this discount is called Purchases Discount. It, too, is a contra-cost account because it lowers the cost of purchases.

Purchases Discount	
Dr.	Cr.
	70 ◄——— **Normal balance is a credit.**

Let's analyze and prepare a general journal entry (Figure 10.3).

Jul.	15	Accounts Payable, Mattel			3 5 0 0 00				
		Purchases Discount					7 0 00		
		Cash					3 4 3 0 00		
		Paid Mattel balance owed							

COACHING TIP

Remember: For Chou it is a purchases discount, whereas for Mattel it is a sales discount.

Purchases Discount A contra-cost account in the general ledger that records discounts offered by vendors of merchandise for prompt payment of purchases by buyers.

COACHING TIP

Remember: Purchases are debits; purchases discounts are credits.

FIGURE 10.3
Purchase Discount Journalized

Accounts Affected	Category	↑↓	Rules	T Account Update			
Accounts Payable, Mattel	Liability	↓	Dr.	**Acc. Payable**		**Mattel**	
				Dr.	Cr.	Dr.	Cr.
				500	4,000	500	4,000
				3,500		3,500	
Purchases Discount	Contra-cost	↑	Cr.	**Purchases Discount**			
				Dr.	Cr.		
					70		
Cash	Asset	↓	Cr.	**Cash**			
				Dr.	Cr.		
					3,430		

After the journal entry is posted and recorded to Mattel, the result will show that Chou saved $70 and totally reduced what he owed to Mattel. The actual—or net—cost of his purchase is $3,430, calculated as follows:

Purchases	$4,000
− Purchases Returns and Allowances	500
− Purchases Discounts	70
= Net Purchases	$3,430

F.O.B. destination *Seller* pays or is responsible for the cost of freight to purchaser's location or destination.

Freight charges are not taken into consideration in calculating net purchases. Still, they are important. If the seller is responsible for paying the shipping cost until the goods reach their destination, the freight charges are F.O.B. destination. (F.O.B. stands for "free on board" the carrier.) For example, if a seller located in Boston sold goods F.O.B. destination to a buyer in New York, the seller would have to pay the cost of shipping the goods to the buyer.

F.O.B. shipping point *Purchaser* pays or is responsible for the shipping costs from seller's shipping point to purchaser's location.

If the buyer is responsible for paying the shipping costs, the freight charges are F.O.B. shipping point. In this situation, the seller will sometimes prepay the freight charges as a matter of convenience and will add it to the invoice of the purchaser, as in the following example:

Bill amount ($800 + $80 prepaid freight)	$880
Less 5% cash discount (0.05 × $800)	40
Amount to be paid by buyer	$840

Purchases discounts are not taken on freight. The discount is based on the purchase price.

If the seller ships goods F.O.B. shipping point, legal ownership (title) passes to the buyer *when the goods are shipped*. If goods are shipped by the seller F.O.B. destination, title will change *when goods have reached their destination*. (See Exhibit 10.1.)

EXHIBIT 10.1

FOB shipping point   **FOB destination**

FOB shipping point: Title changes hands at the shipping point, and buyer owns the goods while they are in transit. So, the buyer pays the shipping costs.

FOB destination: Title changes hands at the destination point, and seller owns the goods while they are in transit. So, the seller, not the buyer, pays the shipping costs.

LEARNING UNIT 10-1 REVIEW

AT THIS POINT you should be able to do the following:

- Explain and calculate purchases, purchases returns and allowances, and purchases discounts.
- Calculate net purchases.
- Explain why purchases discounts are not taken on freight.
- Compare and contrast F.O.B. destination with F.O.B. shipping point.

Instant Replay ⊙ Self-Review Quiz 10-1

Respond true or false to the following:

1. Net purchases = Purchases − Purchases Returns and Allowances − Purchases Discount.
2. Purchases is a contra-cost.
3. F.O.B. destination means the seller covers shipping cost and retains title until goods reach their destination.
4. Purchases discounts are not taken on freight.
5. Purchases Discount is a contra-cost account.

Solutions to Instant Replay: Self-Review Quiz 10-1

1. True   2. False   3. True   4. True   5. True

LEARNING UNIT 10-2 RECORDING AND POSTING PURCHASES TRANSACTIONS ON ACCOUNT FOR ART'S WHOLESALE CLOTHING COMPANY:
Introduction to Subsidiary Ledgers and Debit Memorandum

201X		
Apr.	3	Purchased merchandise on account, $5,000, and freight, $50, from Abby Blake Co.; terms 2/10, n/60.
	4	Purchased equipment on account, $4,000, from Joe Francis Co.
	6	Purchased merchandise on account, $800, from Thorpe Co.; terms 1/10, n/30.
	7	Purchased merchandise on account, $980, from John Sullivan Co.; terms n/10, EOM.
	9	Art's issued debit memo #1, $200, to Thorpe for defective merchandise.
	12	Purchased merchandise on account, $600, from Abby Blake Co.; terms 1/10, n/30.
	25	Purchased $500 of supplies on account from John Sullivan Co.

Let's look at the steps Art's Wholesale Clothing Company took when it ordered goods from Abby Blake Company on April 3.

Purchase requisition A
form used within a business by
the requesting department asking
the purchasing department of the
business to buy specific goods.

Step 1: Prepare a Purchase Requisition at Art's Wholesale Clothing Company The inventory clerk notes a low inventory level of ladies' jackets for resale, so the clerk sends a purchase requisition to the purchasing department. A duplicate copy is sent to the accounting department. A third copy remains with the department that initiated the request to be used as a check on the purchasing department.

Step 2: Purchasing Department of Art's Wholesale Clothing Company Prepares a Purchase Order After checking various price lists and suppliers' catalogs, the purchasing department fills out a form called a purchase order. This form gives Abby Blake Company the authority to ship the ladies' jackets ordered by Art's Wholesale Clothing Company (see Figure 10.4).

Purchase order A form used in
business to place an order for the
buying of goods from a seller.

FIGURE 10.4
Purchase Order

PURCHASE ORDER NO. 1
ART'S WHOLESALE CLOTHING COMPANY
1528 BELLE AVE.
NEW YORK, NY 10022

Purchased From:	Abby Blake Company 12 Foster Road Englewood Cliffs, NJ 07632		Date: April 1, 201X Shipped VIA: Freight Truck Terms: 2/10, n/60 FOB: Englewood Cliffs
Quantity	Description	Unit Price	Total
100	Ladies' Jackets Code 14-0	$50	$5,000
			Art's Wholesale By: Bill Joy

Purchase order number must appear on all invoices.

Step 3: Sales Invoice Prepared by Abby Blake Company Abby Blake Company receives the purchase order and prepares a sales invoice. The sales invoice for the seller is the purchase invoice for the buyer. A sales invoice is shown in Figure 10.5.

The invoice shows that the goods will be shipped F.O.B. Englewood Cliffs. Thus, Art's Wholesale Clothing Company is responsible for paying the shipping costs.

The sales invoice also shows a freight charge. Thus, Abby Blake prepaid the shipping costs as a matter of convenience. Art's will repay the freight charges when it pays the invoice.

Purchase invoice The seller's
sales invoice, which is sent to the
purchaser.

Receiving report A business
form used to notify the appropriate
people of the ordered goods received
along with the quantities and specific
condition of the goods.

Step 4: Receiving the Goods When goods are received, Art's Wholesale inspects the shipment and completes a receiving report. The receiving report verifies that the exact merchandise that was ordered was received in good condition.

FIGURE 10.5
Sales Invoice

SALES INVOICE NO. 228
ABBY BLAKE COMPANY
12 FOSTER ROAD
ENGLEWOOD, CLIFFS, NJ 07632

Sold To:	Art's Wholesale Clothing Co. 1528 Belle Ave. New York, NY 10022		Date: April 3, 201X Shipped VIA: Freight Truck Terms: 2/10, n/60 Your Order No: 1 FOB: Englewood Cliffs
Quantity	Description	Unit Price	Total
100	Ladies' Jackets Code 14-0 Freight	$50	$5,000 50 $5,050

Step 5: Verifying the Numbers Before the invoice is approved for recording and payment, the accounting department must check the purchase order, invoice, and receiving report to make sure that all are in agreement and that no steps have been omitted. The form used for checking and approval is an invoice approval form (see Figure 10.6).

Invoice approval form Used by the accounting department in checking the invoice and finally approving it for recording and payment.

FIGURE 10.6
Invoice Approval Form

```
┌─────────────────────────────────────────────────────┐
│              INVOICE APPROVAL FORM                    │
│              Art's Wholesale Clothing Co.             │
├────────────────────────────────┬────────────────────┤
│ Purchase Order #               │  _____    │
│ Requisition check              │  _____    │
│ Purchase Order check           │  _____    │
│ Receiving Report check         │  _____    │
│ Invoice check                  │  _____    │
│ Approved for Payment           │  _____    │
└────────────────────────────────┴────────────────────┘
```

Keep in mind that Art's Wholesale Clothing Company does not record this purchase until the *invoice is approved for recording and payment.* Abby Blake Company records this transaction in its records when the sales invoice is prepared, however.

Let's look closer at the April 3 transaction.

201X

Apr. 3 Purchased merchandise on account, $5,000, plus freight, $50, from Abby Blake Co.

THE ANALYSIS			
Accounts Affected	**Category**	**↑↓**	**Rules of Dr. and Cr.**
Purchases	Cost	↑	Dr. $5,000
Freight-In	Cost	↑	Dr. $50
Accounts Payable, Abby Blake Co.	Liability	↑	Cr. $5,050

Figure 10.7 shows how the general journal would look.

COACHING TIP

	Buyer		Seller	
Purchase	Dr. Cost		Sale Cr.	Revenue
PRA	Cr.	Contra-cost	SRA Dr.	Contra-revenue
PD	Cr.	Contra-cost	SD Dr.	Contra-revenue

						Page 2	
	Apr.	3	Purchases		5 0 0 0 00		
			Freight-In		5 0 00		
			Accounts Payable, Abby Blake Co.			5 0 5 0 00	
			Purchased merchandise on account				
			from Abby Blake				

FIGURE 10.7
Merchandise Purchase, Plus Freight Cost

Accounts Payable Subsidiary Ledger

LO2

In the last chapter we saw the accounts receivable subsidiary ledger. It listed customers owing Art's money from sales on account. Now we look at Art's, the buyer, and an accounts payable subsidiary ledger. See Figure 10.8.

Note that the normal balance is a credit for Accounts Payable and its subsidiary ledger, whereas in the last chapter Accounts Receivable had a debit normal balance.

Accounts Payable is the controlling account in the ledger and at the end of the month the sum of the individual amount owed to the creditors should equal the balance in Accounts Payable at the end of the month.

Accounts payable subsidiary ledger A book or file that contains, in alphabetical order, the name of the creditor and amount owed from purchases on account.

Figure 10.9 shows how the general journal looks for Art's before posting and recording this month's purchases on account.

FIGURE 10.8
Partial General Ledger of Art's Wholesale Clothing Company and Accounts Payable Subsidiary Ledger

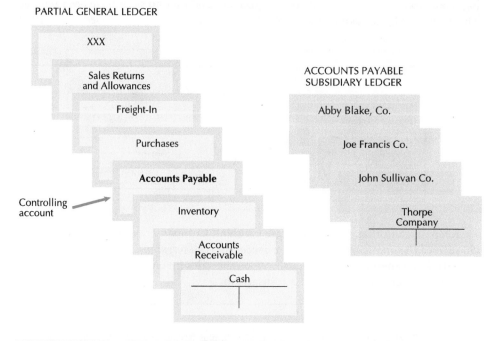

FIGURE 10.9

			GENERAL JOURNAL					
							Page 2	
	Date		Account Titles and Description	PR	Dr.		Cr.	
201X								
Apr.	3		Purchases		5 0 0 00			
			Freight-In		5 0 00			
			Accounts Payable, Abby Blake Co.				5 0 5 0 00	
			Purchased merchandise on account, Blake					
	4		Equipment		4 0 0 0 00			
			Accounts Payable, Joe Francis				4 0 0 0 00	
			Purchased equipment on account, Francis					
	6		Purchases		8 0 0 00			
			Accounts Payable, Thorpe Company				8 0 0 00	
			Purchased merchandise on account, Thorpe					
	7		Purchases		9 8 0 00			
			Accounts Payable, John Sullivan Co.				9 8 0 00	
			Purchased merchandise on account, Sullivan					
	9		Accounts Payable, Thorpe Company		2 0 0 00			
			Purchases Returns and Allowances				2 0 0 00	
			Debit memo no. 1					
	12		Purchases		6 0 0 00			
			Accounts Payable, Abby Blake Co.				6 0 0 00	
			Purchased merchandise on account, Blake					
	25		Supplies		5 0 0 00			
			Accounts Payable, John Sullivan Co.				5 0 0 00	
			Purchased supplies on account, Sullivan					

Posting and Recording Purchases Transactions Before we post to the general ledger and record to the subsidiary ledger, let's first examine the T accounts and what each one would look like.

(Before Recordings)

(Before Postings)

Now let's look at how to post and record the April 3 transaction.

FIGURE 10.10

	Date		Account Titles and Description	PR	Dr.	Cr.
	201X					
	Apr.	3	Purchases	511	5 0 0 0 00	
			Freight-In	514	5 0 00	
			Accounts Payable, Abby Blake Co.	211 ✔		5 0 5 0 00
			Purchased merchandise on account, Blake			

GENERAL JOURNAL   Page 2

PARTIAL ACCOUNTS PAYABLE SUBSIDIARY LEDGER

Abby Blake Co.

Dr.	Cr.
	5,050 GJ2 4/3

PARTIAL GENERAL LEDGER

Accounts Payable 211

Dr.	Cr.
	5,050 GJ2 4/3

Purchases 511

Dr.	Cr.
4/3 GJ2 5,000	

Freight-In 514

Dr.	Cr.
4/3 GJ2 50	

For this transaction we post to the general ledger accounts Purchases, Freight-In, and Accounts Payable. Note how the account numbers 511, 514, and 211 are entered into the PR column of the general journal. We must also *record* to Abby Blake Co. in the accounts payable subsidiary ledger. Note that it is placed on the credit side because we owe Abby the money. When the subsidiary ledger is updated, a (✓) is placed in the PR column of the general journal. Figure 10.10 shows how the accounts payable subsidiary ledger and the partial general ledger would look after posting and recording.

Before concluding this unit, let's take a closer look at the April 9 transaction when Art's issues a debit memorandum to Thorpe Company. We analyze the transaction and show how to post and record it.

● L03   Debit Memorandum

Debit memorandum A memo issued by a purchaser to a seller, indicating that some Purchases Returns and Allowances have occurred and therefore the purchaser now owes less money on account.

In Chapter 9, Art's Wholesale Clothing Company had to handle returned goods as a seller. It did so by issuing credit memoranda to customers who returned or received an allowance on the price. In this chapter, Art's must handle returns as a buyer. It does so by using debit memoranda. A debit memorandum is a piece of paper issued by a customer to a seller. It indicates that a return or allowance has occurred.

On April 6, Art's Wholesale had purchased men's hats for $800 from Thorpe Company. On April 9, 20 hats valued at $200 were found to have defective brims. Art's issued a debit memorandum to Thorpe Company, as shown in Figure 10.11. At some point in the future, Thorpe will issue Art's a credit memorandum. Let's look at how Art's Wholesale Clothing Company handles such a transaction in its accounting records.

FIGURE 10.11
Debit Memorandum

DEBIT MEMORANDUM		No. 1
Art's Wholesale Clothing Company 1528 Belle Ave. New York, NY 10022		
TO: Thorpe Company 3 Access Road Beverly, MA 01915		April 9, 201X
WE DEBIT your account as follows:		
Quantity	Unit Cost	Total
20 Men's Hats Code 827 – defective brims	$10	$200

Journalizing and Posting the Debit Memo First, let's look at a transactional analysis chart.

COACHING TIP

Result of debit memo: debits or reduces Accounts Payable. On seller's books, accounts affected would include Sales Returns and Allowances and Accounts Receivable.

Accounts Affected	Category	↑↓	Rules
Accounts Payable	Liability	↓	Dr.
Purchases Returns and Allowances	Contra-cost	↑	Cr.

Next, let's examine the journal entry for the debit memorandum (Figure 10.12).

FIGURE 10.12
Debit Memorandum Journalized and Posted

			GENERAL JOURNAL			
						Page 2
	Date		Account Titles and Description	PR	Dr.	Cr.
	Apr.	9	Accounts Payable, Thorpe Company	211 ✓	2 0 0 00	
			Purchases Returns and Allowances	513		2 0 0 00
			Debit memo no.1			

The two postings and one recording are the following:

1. 211: Post to Accounts Payable as a debit in the general ledger (account no. 211). When done, place in the PR column the account number, 211, above the diagonal on the same line as Accounts Payable in the journal.
2. ✓: Record to Thorpe Co. in the accounts payable subsidiary ledger to show that Art's doesn't owe Thorpe as much money. When done, place a ✓ in the journal in the PR column below the diagonal line on the same line as Accounts Payable in the journal.
3. 513: Post to Purchases Returns and Allowances as a credit in the general ledger (account no. 513). When done, place the account number, 513, in the PR column of the journal on the same line as Purchases Returns and Allowances. (If equipment was returned that was not merchandise for resale, we would credit Equipment and not Purchases Returns and Allowances.)

The following are the completed accounts payable subsidiary ledger and general ledger for Art's.

COACHING TIP

PURCHASES RETURNS AND ALLOWANCES

Dr.   Cr.

—   +

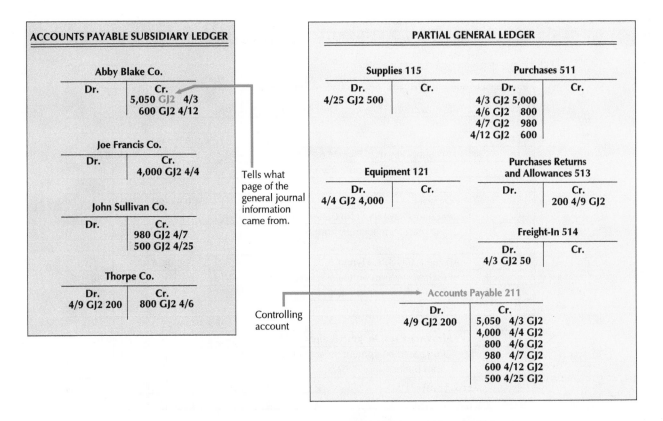

LEARNING UNIT 10-2 REVIEW

AT THIS POINT you should be able to do the following:

- Explain the relationship between a purchase requisition, a purchase order, and a purchase invoice.
- Explain for what purpose a typical invoice approval form may be used.
- Journalize transactions for purchase and cash payments.
- Explain how to record to the accounts payable subsidiary ledger and post to the general ledger from a general journal.
- Explain a debit memorandum and be able to journalize an entry resulting from its issuance.

Instant Replay ⊙ Self-Review Quiz 10-2

Journalize and post the following transactions:

201X		
May	5	Bought merchandise on account from Flynn Co., invoice no. 512, dated May 6, $900; terms 1/10, n/30.
	7	Bought merchandise from John Butler Company, invoice no. 403, dated May 7, $1,000; terms n/10 EOM.
	13	Issued debit memo no. 1 to Flynn Co. for merchandise returned, $300, from invoice no. 512.
	17	Purchased $400 of equipment on account from John Butler Company, invoice no. 413, dated May 18.

Solution to Instant Replay: Self-Review Quiz 10-2

	GENERAL JOURNAL			Page 1
Date	**Account Titles and Description**	**PR**	**Dr.**	**Cr.**
201X				
May 5	Purchases	512	900 00	
	Accounts Payable, Flynn Co.	212 ✓		900 00
	Purchased on account from Flynn			
7	Purchases	512	1000 00	
	Accounts Payable, John Butler Co.	212 ✓		1000 00
	Purchased on account from Butler			
13	Accounts Payable, Flynn Co.	212 ✓	300 00	
	Purchases returns and allowances	513		300 00
	Issued debit memo no. 1			
17	Equipment	121	400 00	
	Accounts Payable, John Butler Co.	212 ✓		400 00
	Purchased equipment on account			
	from Butler			

ACCOUNTS PAYABLE SUBSIDIARY LEDGER

John Butler Co.

Dr.	Cr.
	1,000 5/7 GJ1
	400 5/17 GJ1

Flynn Co.

Dr.	Cr.
5/13 GJ1 300	900 5/5 GJ1

PARTIAL GENERAL LEDGER

Equipment 121

Dr.	Cr.
5/17 GJ1 400	

Purchases 512

Dr.	Cr.
5/5 GJ1 900	
5/7 GJ1 1,000	

Accounts Payable 212

Dr.	Cr.
5/13 GJ1 300	900 5/5 GJ1
	1,000 5/7 GJ1
	400 5/17 GJ1

Purchases Returns and Allowances 513

Dr.	Cr.
	300 5/13 GJ1

LEARNING UNIT 10-3 RECORDING AND POSTING CASH PAYMENTS TRANSACTIONS FOR ART'S WHOLESALE:
Schedule of Accounts Payable

○ **L04**

The following cash payment transactions occurred for Art's Wholesale Clothing Company in April.

201X		
Apr.	2	Issued check no. 1 to Pete Blum for insurance paid in advance, $900.
	7	Issued check no. 2 to Joe Francis Company in payment of its April 4 invoice no. 388.
	9	Issued check no. 3 to Rick Flo Co. for merchandise purchased for cash, $800.
	12	Issued check no. 4 to Thorpe Company in payment of its April 6 invoice no. 414, less the return and 1% discount.
	28	Issued check no. 5, $700, for salaries paid.

Figure 10.13 provides a closer look at how the April 12 transaction would be journalized.

Accounts Affected	Category	↑↓	Rules	T Account Update
Cash	Asset	↓	Cr.	**Cash** Dr. | Cr. | 594
Purchases Discount	Contra-cost	↑	Cr.	**Purchases Discount** Dr. | Cr. | 6
Account Payable, Thorpe Co.	Liability	↓	Dr.	**Accounts Payable** Dr. | Cr. 600 | 600 **Thorpe Co.** Dr. | Cr. 600 | 600

FIGURE 10.13

	Apr.	12	Accounts Payable, Thorpe Co.		6 0 0 00			
			Purchases Discount				6 00	
			Cash				5 9 4 00	
			Paid invoice no. 414					

Figure 10.14 (p. 380) shows the complete set of cash payments transactions journalized for the month, followed by a complete posting to the general ledger and recordings to the accounts payable subsidiary ledger (remember from the past unit that we posted all the purchases on account).

FIGURE 10.14

			GENERAL JOURNAL				Page 2	
	Date		Account Titles and Description	PR	Dr.		Cr.	
201X								
Apr.	2		Prepaid Insurance	116	9 0 0 00			
			Cash	111			9 0 0 00	
			Paid for insurance in advance					
	7		Accounts Payable, Joe Francis Co.	211 ✔	4 0 0 00			
			Cash	111			4 0 0 00	
			Paid invoice no. 388					
	9		Purchases	511	8 0 0 00			
			Cash	111			8 0 0 00	
			Cash purchases					
	12		Accounts Payable, Thorpe Co.	211 ✔	6 0 0 00			
			Purchases Discount	512			6 00	
			Cash	111			5 9 4 00	
			Paid invoice no. 414					
	28		Salaries Expense	611	7 0 0 00			
			Cash	111			7 0 0 00	
			Paid salaries					

(continued on next page)

● L05

Controlling account The account in the general ledger that summarizes or controls a subsidiary ledger. Example: The Accounts Payable account in the general ledger is the controlling account for the accounts payable subsidiary ledger. After postings are complete, it shows the total amount owed from purchases made on account.

Now let's prove that the sum of the accounts payable subsidiary ledger at the end of the month is equal to the controlling account, Accounts Payable, at the end of April for Art's Wholesale Clothing Company. To do so, creditors with an ending balance in Art's accounts payable subsidiary ledger must be listed in the schedule of accounts payable (see Figure 10.15). At the end of the month, the total owed ($7,130) in Accounts Payable, the controlling account in the general ledger, should equal the sum owed the individual creditors that are listed on the schedule of accounts payable. If it doesn't, the journalizing, posting, and recording must be checked to ensure that they are complete. Also, the balances of each title should be checked.

LEARNING UNIT 10-3 REVIEW

AT THIS POINT you should be able to do the following:

- Journalize, post, and record cash payments transactions.
- Prepare a schedule of accounts payable.

Instant Replay ◉ Self-Review Quiz 10-3

For the following transactions, journalize, post to the general ledger, and record to the accounts payable subsidiary ledger.

Accounts Payable Subsidiary Ledger

Name	Balance	Invoice No.
Bob Finkelstein	$300	488
Al Jeep	200	410

(Continued on following page spread on p. 382)

FIGURE 10.14 (*Continued*)

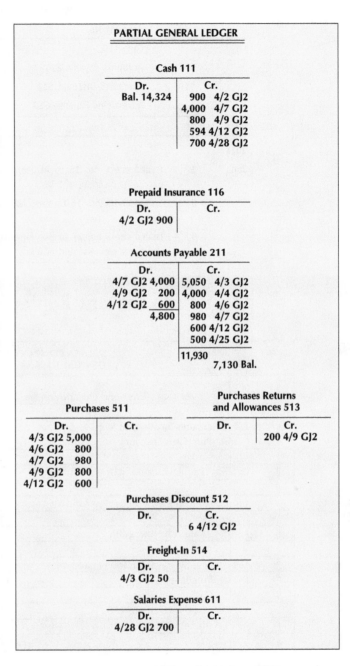

ACCOUNTS PAYABLE SUBSIDIARY LEDGER

Abby Blake Co.

Dr.	Cr.
	5,050 4/3 GJ2
	600 4/12 GJ2

Joe Francis Co.

Dr.	Cr.
4/7 GJ2 4,000	4,000 4/4 GJ1

John Sullivan Co.

Dr.	Cr.
	980 4/7 GJ2
	500 4/25 GJ2

Thorpe Co.

Dr.	Cr.
4/9 GJ1 200	800 4/6 GJ2
4/12 GJ1 600	

PARTIAL GENERAL LEDGER

Cash 111

Dr.	Cr.
Bal. 14,324	900 4/2 GJ2
	4,000 4/7 GJ2
	800 4/9 GJ2
	594 4/12 GJ2
	700 4/28 GJ2

Prepaid Insurance 116

Dr.	Cr.
4/2 GJ2 900	

Accounts Payable 211

Dr.	Cr.
4/7 GJ2 4,000	5,050 4/3 GJ2
4/9 GJ2 200	4,000 4/4 GJ2
4/12 GJ2 600	800 4/6 GJ2
4,800	980 4/7 GJ2
	600 4/12 GJ2
	500 4/25 GJ2
11,930	
	7,130 Bal.

Purchases 511

Dr.	Cr.
4/3 GJ2 5,000	
4/6 GJ2 800	
4/7 GJ2 980	
4/9 GJ2 800	
4/12 GJ2 600	

Purchases Returns and Allowances 513

Dr.	Cr.
	200 4/9 GJ2

Purchases Discount 512

Dr.	Cr.
	6 4/12 GJ2

Freight-In 514

Dr.	Cr.
4/3 GJ2 50	

Salaries Expense 611

Dr.	Cr.
4/28 GJ2 700	

FIGURE 10.15
Schedule of Accounts Payable

ART'S WHOLESALE CLOTHING COMPANY SCHEDULE OF ACCOUNTS PAYABLE APRIL 30, 201X		
Abby Blake Co.	$5 6 5 0 00	
John Sullivan Co.	1 4 8 0 00	
Total Accounts Payable	$7 1 3 0 00	

Partial General Ledger

Account No.	Balance
Cash 110	$700
Accounts Payable 210	500
Purchases Discount 511	—
Advertising Expense 610	—

201X

Jun. 1 Issued check no. 15 to Al Jeep in payment of its May 25 invoice no. 410, less purchases discount of 2%.

8 Issued check no. 16 to Moss Advertising Co. to pay advertising bill due, $75, no discount.

9 Issued check no. 17 to Bob Finkelstein in payment of its May 28 invoice no. 488, less purchases discount of 2%.

Solution to Instant Replay: Self-Review Quiz 10-3

MELISSA COMPANY
GENERAL JOURNAL Page 2

Date		Account Titles and Description	PR	Dr.	Cr.
201X					
Jun.	1	Accounts Payable, Al Jeep	210 ✔	2 0 0 00	
		Purchases Discount	110		4 00
		Cash			1 9 6 00
		Paid invoice no. 410			
	8	Advertising Expense	610	7 5 00	
		Cash	110		7 5 00
		Paid Advertising Bill			
	9	Accounts Payable, Bob Finkelstein	210 ✔	3 0 0 00	
		Purchases Discount	110		6 00
		Cash			2 9 4 00
		Paid invoice no. 488			

ACCOUNTS PAYABLE SUBSIDIARY LEDGER

Bob Finkelstein

Dr.	Cr.
6/1 GJ2 300	300 Bal.

Al Jeep

Dr.	Cr.
6/9 GJ2 200	200 Bal.

PARTIAL GENERAL LEDGER

Cash 110

Dr.	Cr.
Bal. 700	196 6/1 GJ2
	75 6/8 GJ2
	294 6/9 GJ2

Accounts Payable 210

Dr.	Cr.
6/1 GJ2 200	500 Bal.
6/9 GJ2 300	

Purchases Discount 511

Dr.	Cr.
	4 6/1 GJ2
	6 6/9 GJ2

Advertising Expense 610

Dr.	Cr.
6/8 GJ2 75	

LEARNING UNIT 10-4 INTRODUCTION TO A MERCHANDISE COMPANY USING A PERPETUAL INVENTORY SYSTEM

● **L06**

Introduction to the Merchandise Cycle

In this learning unit we will focus on recording transactions using a perpetual inventory system. This is an inventory system that continually monitors its levels of inventory. The previous units were based on a periodic inventory system. This means that at the end of each accounting period the cost of unsold goods is calculated. There is no continual tracking of inventory.

Let's use Walmart as an example as both the buyer and seller. We know that Walmart must buy inventory from suppliers to sell to you, the customer. This inventory is called merchandise inventory. It is an asset sold to you for cash or accounts receivable and represents *sales revenue* or sales for Walmart.

What did it cost Walmart to bring the inventory into the store? The cost of goods sold is the total cost of merchandise inventory brought into the store and sold. These costs do not include any operating expenses such as heat, advertising, and salaries. To find Walmart's profit before operating expenses, we take the sales revenue less cost of goods sold. Figure 10.16 is called *gross profit on sales*.

For example, if Walmart sells a TV for $500 that cost $300 to bring into the store, its gross profit is $200. To find its net income or net loss, Walmart would subtract its operating expenses. Figure 10.17 shows how a merchandiser calculates its net income or net loss.

Note: In step 1 the sales provide an inflow of cash or accounts receivable. Step 2 shows that when the inventory is sold, it is recognized as a cost (cost of goods sold). By subtracting sales less cost of goods sold, we arrive at the gross profit in step 3. Step 4 shows that operating expenses subtracted from gross profit result in a net income or net loss in step 5.

Perpetual inventory system An inventory system that keeps *continual track* of each type of inventory by recording units on hand at beginning, units sold, and the current balance after each sale or purchase.

Periodic inventory system An inventory system that, at the *end* of each accounting period, calculates the cost of the unsold goods on hand by taking the cost of each unit times the number of units of each product on hand.

Merchandise Inventory An asset and perpetual inventory system account that records purchases of merchandise. Discounts and returns are recorded in this account for the buyer.

FIGURE 10.16
Calculating Gross Profit on Sales

Cost of goods sold In a perpetual inventory system, an account that records the cost of merchandise inventory used to make the sale.

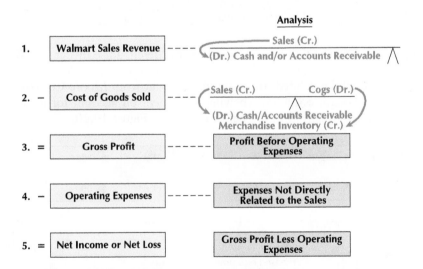

FIGURE 10.17
Introduction to Perpetual Inventory for a Merchandise Company

What Inventory System Walmart Uses

When you pay at Walmart you see the use of bar codes and optical scanners. Walmart keeps detailed records of the inventory it brings into the store and what inventory is sold. With this method, Walmart keeps track of what it costs to make the sale (cost of goods sold) by matching revenues and costs (see Figure 10.18).

FIGURE 10.18
Matching Revenues and Costs

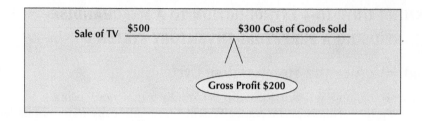

More and more companies, large or small, are using the perpetual inventory system due to increasing computerization. Walmart knows that using the perpetual inventory system will help control stocks of inventory as well as lost or stolen goods.

Recording Merchandise Transactions

Now let's look at Walmart as both a buyer and seller. Let's first focus on Walmart the buyer.

Walmart: The Buyer When Walmart brings merchandise inventory into the stores from suppliers it is recorded in the *Merchandise Inventory account*. Think of this account as purchases of merchandise—for cash or on account—that is for resale to customers. Each order is documented by an invoice for Walmart. Keep in mind that Merchandise Inventory is the cost of bringing the merchandise into the store, not the price at which the merchandise will be sold to customers. Let's assume that on July 9 Walmart bought flat-screen TVs from Sony Corp. for $7,000 with terms 2/10, n/30. Walmart would record the purchase as shown in Figure 10.19.

FIGURE 10.19
Purchase Inventory on Account

Analysis:					
Merchandise Inventory	A	↑	Dr.	$7,000
Accounts Payable	L	↑	Cr.	$7,000

Journal Entry:	Jul.	9	Merchandise Inventory	7 0 0 0 00	
			Accounts Payable/Sony		7 0 0 0 00
			Purchased inventory on account		
			from Sony 2/10, n/30		

Keep in mind that not all purchases will go to Merchandise Inventory. Walmart will buy supplies, equipment, and so forth that are not for resale to customers. These amounts will be debited to the specific account from Moore Co. For example, if Walmart bought $5,000 of shelving equipment on account for its store on November 9, the transaction would be recorded as in Figure 10.20.

FIGURE 10.20
Purchasing of Equipment on Account

Analysis:					
Shelving Equipment	A	↑	Dr.	$5,000
Accounts Payable	L	↑	Cr.	$5,000

Journal Entry:	Nov.	9	Shelving Equipment	5 0 0 0 00	
			Accounts Payable/Moore Co.		5 0 0 0 00
			Purchased equipment on account		

What happens if Walmart finds a defective TV among its purchase from Sony?

Recording Purchases Returns and Allowances Because on July 14 Walmart noticed a damaged TV in the shipment, it issues a debit memorandum. This document notifies Sony, the supplier, that Walmart is reducing what is owed Sony by $600, the cost of the TV (to bring it into the store) and that the TV is being returned. On Walmart's books the analysis and journal entry in Figure 10.21 results.

Analysis:	Accounts Payable	L	↓	Dr.	$600
	Merchandise Inventory	A	↓	Cr.	$600

Journal Entry:		Jul.	14	Accounts Payable/Sony	6 0 0 00	
				Merchandise Inventory		6 0 0 00
				To record debit memo no. 10		

FIGURE 10.21
Recording a Debit Memorandum

Note that the cost of merchandise inventory has been reduced by $600 due to the return. In the perpetual inventory system there is no purchases, returns, and allowances title. The reduction in cost from the return is recorded *directly* into the Merchandise Inventory account. Let's now look at how Walmart would record any cash discounts it receives due to payment of the Sony bill within the discount period.

Recording Purchase Discounts Let's assume that Walmart pays Sony within the first 10 days. Keep in mind that we take no discounts on returned goods (the $600 return). The amount of purchase discount will be recorded as a reduction to the cost of merchandise inventory. Figure 10.22 shows the analysis and journal entry on July 16. A discount lowers the cost of inventory.

Analysis:	Accounts Payable	L	↓	Dr.	$6,400
	Cash	A	↓	Cr.	$6,272
	Merchandise Inventory	A	↓	Cr.	$ 128

FIGURE 10.22
Recording a Purchase Discount

($7,000 – $600 Return)

Journal Entry:		Jul.	16	Accounts Payable/Sony	6 4 0 0 00	
				Cash		6 2 7 2 00
				Merchandise Inventory		1 2 8 00

2% × $6,400

Keep in mind that had Walmart missed the discount period, it would have debited $6,400 to Accounts Payable and credited Cash for $6,400. Merchandise Inventory would not be reduced.

Recording Cost of Freight The cost of freight ($300) is to be paid by Walmart. When the purchaser is responsible for cost of freight, it is added to the cost of merchandise inventory. If the cost of freight is paid by the seller, it could be recorded in an operating expense account called Freight-Out. Figure 10.23 is the analysis and journal entry for freight on July 10.

Analysis:	Merchandise Inventory	A	↑	Dr.	$300
	Cash	A	↓	Cr.	$300

FIGURE 10.23
Recording Cost of Freight

Freight Cost added to Merchandise Inventory

Journal Entry:		Jul.	10	Merchandise Inventory	3 0 0 00	
				Cash		3 0 0 00
				Payment of freight		

Walmart: The Seller Now let's look at Walmart as the *seller* of merchandise.

Recording Sales at Walmart Sales revenues are earned at Walmart when the goods are transferred to the buyer. The earned revenue can be for cash and/or credit. Let's look at the following example of the sale of a TV at Walmart for $950 on credit to customer Jones on August 10, which cost Walmart $600. Keep in mind when using the perpetual inventory system that at the time of the earned sale Walmart will do the following:

At selling price ⟶ 1. *Record the sales (cash and/or credit).*
At cost ⟶   2. *Record the cost of the inventory sold and the*
                     reduction in inventory.

First, let's analyze the transaction in Figure 10.24. Note that we will have two entries, one to record the sale and one to show a new cost and less inventory on hand.

FIGURE 10.24
Recording Sales and Cost of Goods Sold

Selling Price <	**Accounts Receivable**	**Asset**	↑	Dr.	$950
	Sales	**Revenue**	↑	Cr.	$950
Cost to < Make sale	**Cost of Goods Sold**	**Cost**	↑	Dr.	$600
	Merchandise Inventory	**Asset**	↓	Cr.	$600

Journal Entries:

Aug.	10	Accounts Receivable/Jones	9 5 0 00		
		Sales		9 5 0 00
		Charge sales		
	10	Cost of Goods Sold	6 0 0 00	
		Merchandise Inventory		6 0 0 00
		To record cost of		
		merchandise sold on account		

Be sure to go back to steps 1 and 2 of Figure 10.17. These two steps reinforce the preceding journal entries. Remember that if the sale were a cash sale, we would have debited Cash instead of Accounts Receivable. Note also that the Sales account only records sales of goods held for resale.

How Walmart Records Sales Returns Allowances and Sales Discounts Keep in mind that we are now looking at how the *seller* of merchandise records a transaction giving the customer a credit due to an allowance or a return of goods from a previous sale. Usually, the seller will issue a *credit memorandum*, a document informing the customer of the adjustment due to the return or allowance. For example, let's look at a customer, Smith Co., who returned a $950 TV on August 15 that had been purchased at Walmart. On Walmart's books, the analysis and journal entry in Figure 10.25 resulted.

The first entry records the return at the original selling price using the contra-revenue account Sales Returns and Allowances. The second entry records putting the inventory back in Walmart's books at cost and reducing its Cost of Goods Sold because the inventory was not sold. Remember that we only record the Cost of Goods Sold when the sale has been earned. Keep in mind that if the customer kept the TV but at a reduced price, no entry affecting Merchandise Inventory and Cost of Goods Sold would be needed.

FIGURE 10.25
Return of Goods

The Analysis: at Selling Price	Sales Returns and Allowances	Contra-Revenue	↑	Dr.	$950
	Accounts Receivable	Asset	↓	Cr.	$950
At Cost	Merchandise Inventory	Asset	↑	Dr.	$600
	Costs of Goods Sold	Cost	↓	Cr.	$600

Journal Entries:

Aug.	15	Sales Returns and Allowances	9 5 0 00		
		Accounts Receivable*/Smith Co.		9 5 0 00	
		Returned goods			
	15	Merchandise Inventory	6 0 0 00		
		Cost of Goods Sold		6 0 0 00	

*If it were a *cash* customer. cash would be credited.

Let's assume a customer, Smith Co., on August 25 gets a 2% discount for paying for a $950 TV early. The analysis and entry in Figure 10.26 would result on the seller's book:

FIGURE 10.26
Recording Sales Discount

The Analysis:	Cash	Asset	↑	Dr.	$931
	Sales Discount	Contra-Revenue	↑	Dr.	$ 19
	Accounts Receivable	Asset	↓	Cr.	$950

Journal Entry:

Aug.	25	Cash	9 3 1 00		
		Sales Discount	1 9 00		
		Accounts Receivable/Smith Co.		9 5 0 00	

Now let's summarize (Figure 10.27) all the entries for both the buyer and the seller (in this case, Walmart).

FIGURE 10.27

	Walmart the Buyer			Walmart the Seller	
Bought Inventory for Resale on Account	Merchandise Inventory → Accounts Payable	At Cost	Sold Inventory on Account	Accounts Receivable → Sales Cost of Goods Sold → Merchandise Inventory	At Selling Price At Cost
Issued a Debit Memo for Merchandise Returned	Accounts Payable → Merchandise Inventory	At Cost	Issued a Credit Memo for Returned Merchandise	Sales Returns and Allowances → Accounts Receivable Merchandise Inventory → Cost of Goods Sold	At Selling Price At Cost
Recorded a Purchase Discount	Accounts Payable Cash Merchandise Inventory		Recorded a Sales Discount	Cash Sales Discount Accounts Receivable	

Amount of discount ——

Figure 10.28 shows a comparison of Perpetual and Periodic Systems.

FIGURE 10.28 Comparison of Perpetual and Periodic Systems

Transaction	Perpetual System				Periodic System			
(A) Sold merchandise that cost $8,000 on account for $20,000.	Accts. Receivable	20000 00			Accts. Receivable	20000 00		
	Sales		20000 00		Sales		20000 00	
	Cost of Goods Sold	8000 00						
	Merch. Inventory		8000 00					
(B) Purchased $900 of merchandise on account.	Merch. Inventory	900 00			Purchases	900 00		
	Accts. Payable		900 00		Accts. Payable		900 00	
(C) Paid $50 freight charges.	Merch. Inventory	50 00			Freight-In	50 00		
	Cash		50 00		Cash		50 00	
(D) Cash customer returned $200 of merchandise. Cost of merchandise was $100.	Sales Ret. & Allow.	200 00			Sales Ret. & Allow.	200 00		
	Cash*		200 00		Cash*		200 00	
	Merch. Inventory	100 00						
	Cost of Goods Sold		100 00					
(E) Returned $400 of merchandise previously bought on account because of defects.	Accts. Payable	400 00			Accts. Payable	400 00		
	Merch. Inventory		400 00		Pur. Ret. & Allow.		400 00	

* or Accounts Receivable if made to charge customers

LEARNING UNIT 10-4 REVIEW

AT THIS POINT you should be able to do the following:

- Define the terms *merchandise inventory*, *sales*, and *cost of goods sold*.
- Explain how discounts are recorded in a perpetual inventory system.
- Journalize transactions for a merchandise company using a perpetual system.

Instant Replay ◎ Self-Review Quiz 10-4

Pete's Clock Shops completed the following merchandise transactions in the month of June:

201X		
Jun.	1	Purchased merchandise on account from Clock Suppliers, $4,000; terms 2/10, n/30.
	3	Sold merchandise on account, $2,000; terms 2/10, n/30. The cost of the merchandise sold was $1,200.
	4	Received credit from Clock Suppliers for merchandise returned, $400.
	10	Received collections in full, less discounts, from June 3 sales.
	11	Paid Clock Suppliers in full, less discount.
	14	Purchased office equipment for cash, $500.
	15	Purchased $2,800 of merchandise from Abe's Distribution for cash.
	16	Received a refund because of defective merchandise from supplier on cash purchase of $400.
	17	Purchased merchandise from Rose Corp., $6,000, free on board shipping point (buyer pays freight); terms 2/10, n/30. Freight to be paid on June 20.
	18	Sold merchandise for $3,000 cash; the cost of the merchandise sold was $1,600.
	20	Paid freight on June 17 purchase, $180.
	25	Purchased merchandise from Lee Co., $1,400, free on board destination (seller pays freight); terms 2/10, n/30.
	26	Paid Rose Corp. in full, less discount.
	27	Made refunds to cash customers for returned clocks, $300. The cost of the defective clocks was $120.

Pete's Clock Shop accounts included the following:

Cash, 101; Accounts Receivable, 112; Merchandise Inventory, 120; Office Equipment, 124; Accounts Payable, 201; P. Rings, Capital, 301; Sales, 401; Sales Returns and Allowances, 411; Sales Discount, 412; Cost of Goods Sold, 501.

Journalize the transactions using a perpetual inventory system.

Solution to Instant Replay: Self-Review Quiz 10-4

	Date		Account Titles and Description	PR	Dr.	Cr.
	201X		**GENERAL JOURNAL**			Page 2
	Jun.	1	Merchandise Inventory		4 0 0 0 00	
			Accounts Payable			4 0 0 0 00
		3	Accounts Receivable		2 0 0 0 00	
			Sales			2 0 0 0 00
			Cost of Goods Sold		1 2 0 0 00	
			Merchandise Inventory			1 2 0 0 00
		4	Accounts Payable		4 0 0 00	
			Merchandise Inventory			4 0 0 00
		10	Cash		1 9 6 0 00	
			Sales Discount		4 0 00	
			Accounts Receivable			2 0 0 0 00
		11	Accounts Payable		3 6 0 0 00	
			Cash			3 5 2 8 00
			Merchandise Inventory			7 2 00
		14	Office Equipment		5 0 0 00	
			Cash			5 0 0 00
		15	Merchandise Inventory		2 8 0 0 00	
			Cash			2 8 0 0 00
		16	Cash		4 0 0 00	
			Merchandise Inventory			4 0 0 00
		17	Merchandise Inventory		6 0 0 0 00	
			Accounts Payable			6 0 0 0 00
		18	Cash		3 0 0 0 00	
			Sales			3 0 0 0 00
			Cost of Goods Sold		1 6 0 0 00	
			Merchandise Inventory			1 6 0 0 00
		20	Merchandise Inventory		1 8 0 00	
			Cash			1 8 0 00
		25	Merchandise Inventory		1 4 0 0 00	
			Accounts Payable			1 4 0 0 00
		26	Accounts Payable		6 0 0 0 00	
			Cash			5 8 8 0 00
			Merchandise Inventory			1 2 0 00
		27	Sales Returns and Allowances		3 0 0 00	
			Cash*			3 0 0 00
			Merchandise Inventory		1 2 0 00	
			Cost of Goods Sold			1 2 0 00

* If this were a charge customer it would have been Accounts Receivable.

BLUEPRINT: PERIODIC VERSUS PERPETUAL

Periodic		Perpetual
Purchases	⟶	Merchandise Inventory
Purchase Discounts	⟶	Merchandise Inventory
Sales/Accounts Receivable	⟶	Sales/Accounts Receivable Cost of Goods Sold/Merchandise Inventory
Freight-In	⟶	Merchandise Inventory
Sales Discounts	⟶	Sales Discounts
Sales Returns and Allowances	⟶	Sales Returns and Allowances

ACCOUNTING COACH

The following Coaching Tips are from Learning Units 10-1 to 10-4. Take the Pre-Game Checkup and use the Check Your Score at the bottom of the page to see how you are doing. The Accounting Coach provides tips before each Checkup to help you avoid common accounting errors.

LU 10-1 Chou's Toy Shop: Buyers View of a Merchandise Company

Pre-Game Tips: Merchandise for resale to customers is called a purchase. The Purchases account is a cost that will be shown on the income statement. This cost works just like expenses but is directly related to bringing the goods for resale into the store. Purchases Returns and Allowances and Purchases Discounts are contra-cost accounts that will be recorded on the income statement. If shipping terms are FOB destination the seller will pay the cost of freight.

Pre-Game Checkup

Answer true or false to the following statements.

1. The normal balance of Purchases is a debit.
2. Purchases Discounts is a cost.
3. F.O.B. shipping point means that the seller of the goods is responsible for covering the shipping costs.
4. An increase in Purchases Returns and Allowances is a credit.
5. A credit memorandum received will result in an increase in Accounts Payable.

LU 10-2 Recording and Posting Purchases Transactions on Account for Art's Wholesale Clothing Company; Introduction to Subsidiary Ledgers and Debit Memorandum

Pre-Game Tips: The accounts payable subsidiary ledger lists the amounts owed to each customer. It is just the opposite of the accounts receivable subsidiary ledger. The normal balance of the accounts payable subsidiary ledger is a credit. The controlling account, Accounts Payable, is located in the general ledger. The cost of freight is recorded in the Freight-In account, which represents a cost of freight. It has a debit balance. A debit memorandum means the buyer does not owe as much and thus Accounts Payable is reduced and a purchases returns and allowances results. The debit memorandum also reduces what is owed to the customer in the subsidiary ledger.

Pre-Game Checkup

Answer true or false to the following statements.

1. Purchases Returns and Allowances is increased by a debit.
2. Freight-In is a cost that will be shown on the income statement.
3. The controlling account, Accounts Payable, is located in the subsidiary ledger.
4. The normal balance of each customer in the accounts payable subsidiary ledger is a credit.
5. Debit memorandums are issued by the seller.

LU 10-3 Recording and Posting Cash Payments Transactions for Art's Wholesale: Schedule of Accounts Payable

Pre-Game Tips: When a cash payment is made within the discount period from a charge purchase the result is a debit to Accounts Payable and the Subsidiary account and a credit to Purchases Discounts and Cash. Remember that Purchases Discounts is a contra-cost account with a normal credit balance. At the end of the month the total from the schedule of accounts payable should equal the ending balance in Accounts Payable, the controlling account.

Pre-Game Checkup

Answer true or false to the following statements.

1. Purchases Discounts is a contra-revenue account.
2. The schedule of accounts payable is listed by debits and credits.
3. An increase in Purchases Discounts is made by debiting the account.
4. Purchases Discounts are shown on the balance sheet.
5. The normal balance of each customer in the accounts payable subsidiary ledger is a debit.

LU 10-4 Introduction to a Merchandise Company Using a Perpetual Inventory System

Pre-Game Tips: In a perpetual inventory system, all purchases of inventory are recorded in an asset account called Merchandise Inventory. The cost of selling inventory is recorded in the Cost of Goods Sold account. When a sale is made, the company gets cash and/or accounts receivable and a sale is shown. At the same time, the company records the cost of goods to Inventory Sold along with a reduction in Merchandise Inventory since it is sold. Returns to the seller will increase the Merchandise Inventory account. If a seller pays for the cost of freight, it is added to the cost of merchandise inventory.

Pre-Game Checkup

Answer true or false to the following statements.

1. In the perpetual system there are no Purchases, Purchases Discounts, or Purchases Returns and Allowances accounts.

2. The Sales Discount account is not used in a perpetual accounting system.
3. Cost of freight results in a decrease to Merchandise Inventory.
4. Sales plus cost of goods sold equals gross profit.
5. Perpetual systems do not record cash sales.

CHECK YOUR SCORE: Answers to the Pre-Game Checkup

LU 10-1
1. True.
2. False—Purchases Discounts is a contra-cost.
3. False—F.O.B. shipping point means that the buyer of the goods is responsible for covering the shipping costs.
4. True.
5. False—A credit memorandum received by the purchaser will result in a decrease in Accounts Payable.

LU 10-2
1. False—Purchases Returns and Allowances is increased by a credit.
2. True.
3. False—The controlling account, Accounts Payable, is located in the general ledger.
4. True.
5. False—Debit memorandums are issued by the buyer.

LU 10-3
1. False—Purchases Discounts is a contra-cost account.
2. False—The schedule of accounts payable contains no debits or credits.
3. False—An increase in Purchases Discounts is made by crediting the account.
4. False—Purchases Discounts are shown on the income statement.
5. False—The normal balance of each customer in the accounts payable subsidiary ledger is a credit.

LU 10-4
1. True.
2. False—The Sales Discount account is used in a perpetual accounting system.
3. False—Cost of freight results in an increase to Merchandise Inventory because it increases the cost of the inventory.
4. False—Sales minus cost of goods sold equals gross profit.
5. False—Perpetual systems record both cash and charge sales.

Chapter Summary

MyAccountingLab

Here are all the key concepts and equations to help you understand the concepts of this chapter and prepare you for your exam. After completing this review, go to MyAccountingLab for more practice opportunities.

Concepts You Should Know	Key Terms
L01 Recording and posting purchase transactions. 1. Purchases are merchandise for resale. The Purchases account is a cost. 2. Purchases Returns and Allowances and Purchases Discounts are contra-costs. 3. F.O.B. shipping point means that the purchaser of the goods is responsible for covering the shipping costs. 4. Purchases discounts are not taken on freight.	F.O.B. destination (p. 370) F.O.B. shipping point (p. 370) Invoice approval form (p. 373) Purchases (p. 368) Purchases Discount (p. 369) Purchase order (p. 372) Purchase invoice (p. 372) Purchases Returns and Allowances (p. 368) Purchase requisition (p. 372) Receiving report (p. 372)

L02 Recording to accounts payable subsidiary ledger.
 	
1. The steps for buying merchandise from a company may include the following:
 	
  a. The requesting department prepares a purchase requisition.
 	
  b. The purchasing department prepares a purchase order.
 	
  c. The seller receives the order and prepares a sales invoice (a purchase invoice from the buyer).
 	
  d. The buyer receives the goods and prepares a receiving report.
 	
  e. The accounting department verifies and approves the invoice for payment.
 	
2. The accounts payable subsidiary ledger, organized in alphabetical order, is not in the same book as Accounts Payable, the controlling account in the general ledger.
	Accounts payable subsidiary ledger (p. 373)

L03 Preparing, journalizing, and posting a debit memorandum. 1. A debit memorandum (issued by the buyer) indicates that the amount owed from a previous purchase is being reduced because some goods were defective or not up to a specific standard and thus were returned or an allowance requested.	Debit memorandum (p. 376)

Recording and posting cash payment transactions. ◯ **L04**

1. All payments of cash (check) are recorded in the general journal.

2. At the end of the month, the schedule of accounts payable, a list of ending amounts owed individual creditors, should equal the ending balance in Accounts Payable, the controlling account in the general ledger.

Preparing a schedule of accounts payable. ● **L05**

Controlling account (p. 380)

1. The schedule of accounts payable is a list of ending amounts owed individual creditors.

2. At the end of the month, the total amount on the schedule should equal the ending balance in Accounts Payable, the controlling account in the general ledger.

Journalizing transactions for a perpetual accounting system. ◯ **L06**

Cost of goods sold (p. 383)

1. In a perpetual inventory system, whenever a sale is recognized, the cost of goods sold and merchandise inventory must be updated.

Merchandise Inventory (p. 383)

Periodic inventory system (p. 383)

2. Purchases discounts or returns are reflected directly in the Merchandise Inventory account (a debit) for a perpetual inventory system.

Perpetual inventory system (p. 383)

Discussion Questions and Critical Thinking/Ethical Case

1. Explain how net purchases is calculated.

2. What is the normal balance of Purchases Discount?

3. What is a contra-cost?

4. Explain the difference between F.O.B. shipping point and F.O.B. destination.

5. F.O.B. destination means that title to the goods will switch to the buyer when goods are shipped. Do you agree or disagree? Why?

6. What is the normal balance of each creditor in the accounts payable subsidiary ledger?

7. Why could the balance of the controlling account, Accounts Payable, equal the sum of the accounts payable subsidiary ledger during the month?

8. What is the relationship between a purchase requisition and a purchase order?

9. What purpose could a typical invoice approval form serve?

10. Explain the difference between merchandise and equipment.

11. Why would the purchaser issue a debit memorandum?

12. Explain why a trade discount is not a cash discount.

13. What new account is used in a perpetual system compared to the periodic system?

14. What is the normal balance of cost of goods sold?

15. How are discounts recorded in a perpetual system?

16. Spring Co. bought merchandise from All Co. with terms 2/10, n/30. Joanne Ring, the bookkeeper, forgot to pay the bill within the first 10 days. She went to Mel Ryan, the head accountant, who told her to backdate the check so that it looked like the bill was paid within the discount period. Joanne told Mel that she thought they could get away with it. Should Joanne and Mel backdate the check to take advantage of the discount? You make the call. Write down your specific recommendations to Joanne.

MyAccountingLab   Concept Checks

Questions 1–6 are based on a periodic inventory system.

Questions 7–10 are based on a perpetual inventory system.

◍◍◍◍ L01, 2, 3 *(10 MIN)*   **Accounts for Purchase Activities**

1.   Complete the following table:

To the Seller		To the Buyer
Sales	↔	a. _____
Sales returns and allowances	↔	b. _____
Sales discount	↔	c. _____
Credit memorandum	↔	d. _____
Schedule of accounts receivable	↔	e. _____
Accounts receivable subsidiary ledger	↔	f. _____

Accounts

◑ **L01** (*5 MIN*)

2. Complete the following table:

Account	Category	↑↓	Temporary or Permanent
Purchases			
Purchases Returns and Allowances			
Purchases Discount			

Calculating Net Purchases

◑ **L01** (*5 MIN*)

3. Calculate Net Purchases from the following: Purchases, $30; Purchases Returns and Allowances, $4; Purchases Discounts, $1.

General Journal, Recording, and Posting

◔◔◔ **L01, 2, 3** (*10 MIN*)

4. Match the following to the three business transactions (more than one number can be used).

   1. Recorded to the accounts payable subsidiary ledger.

   2. Recorded to the general journal.

   3. Posted to the general ledger.

   ____ a. Bought merchandise on account from Strong.com, invoice no. 12, $160.

   ____ b. Bought equipment on account from Lee Co., invoice no. 13, $150.

   ____ c. Issued debit memo no. 1 to Strong.com for merchandise returned, $60, from invoice no. 12.

Journalizing Transactions

◔◔ **L01, 5** (*15 MIN*)

5. Journalize the following transactions:
   a. Issued credit memo no. 2, $44, to Pam Co.
   b. Cash sales, $184.
   c. Received check from Mark Co., $50, less 1% discount.
   d. Bought merchandise on account from Mellow Co., $36, invoice no. 20; terms 1/10, n/30.
   e. Cash purchase of merchandise, $230.
   f. Issued debit memo to Mellow Co., $12, for merchandise returned from invoice no. 20.

6. From the following prepare a schedule of Accounts Payable for Matthews.com for May 31, 201X:

◑ **L05** (*10 MIN*)

Accounts Payable Subsidiary Ledger

Robertson Co.

Dr.	Cr.	
	55	5/7 GJ1

Brian Co.

	Dr.	Cr.	
5/25 GJ1	8	47	5/20 GJ1

General Ledger

Accounts Payable

	Dr.	Cr.	
5/31 GJ1	8	102	5/31 GJ1

7. Draw a seesaw similar to the one shown in Figure 10.18 and show a sale of $1,000 that cost the store $450. Be sure to label all the accounts.

◑ **L06** (*15 MIN*)

LO6 *(10 MIN)*

8. Bailey C. paid $190 to Porter Co. and received a $25 purchases discount. Journalize the entry.

LO6 *(10 MIN)*

9. Pavel Morse returned $310 of merchandise to Lazlo Co. What would be the journal entry on the books of both the buyer and seller?

LO6 *(10 MIN)*

10. Vintage Co. paid the cost of freight, $90. Journalize the transaction. Assume that Vintage Co. is the buyer.

MyAccountingLab

EXERCISES

Set A

Exercises 10A-1–10A-6 are based on a periodic inventory system.
Exercises 10A-7–10A-10 are based on a perpetual inventory system.

LO1 *(15 MIN)*

10A-1. From the general journal in Figure 10.29, record to the accounts payable subsidiary ledger and post to general ledger accounts as appropriate.

FIGURE 10.29

GENERAL JOURNAL					Page 2
Date		PR	Dr.	Cr.	
201X					
Jun. 3	Purchases		8 5 0 00		
	Accounts Payable, Avril.com			8 5 0 00	
	Purchased merchandise on account				
4	Purchases		6 0 0 00		
	Accounts Payable, Jill.com			6 0 0 00	
	Purchased merchandise on account				
8	Equipment		1 7 0 00		
	Accounts Payable, Pearl.com			1 7 0 00	
	Bought equipment on account				

Partial Accounts Payable Subsidiary Ledger

Avril.com

Dr.	Cr.

Jill.com

Dr.	Cr.

Pearl.com

Dr.	Cr.

Partial General Ledger

Equipment 120

Dr.	Cr.

Accounts Payable 210

Dr.	Cr.

Purchases 510

Dr.	Cr.

LO3 *(15 MIN)*

10A-2. On June 10, 201X, Even Co. issued debit memorandum no. 1 for $360 to Mango Co. for merchandise returned from invoice no. 312. Your task is to journalize, record, and post this transaction as appropriate.

LO4, 5 *(20 MIN)*

10A-3. Journalize, record, and post when appropriate the following transactions into the general journal (p. 2) for Kaden's Clothing. All purchases discounts are 4/10, n/30. If using working papers, be sure to put in beginning balances.

Accounts Payable Subsidiary Ledger

Name	Balance	Invoice No.
A. Jenkins	$1,400	522
B. Foss	700	488
J. Lee	800	562
B. Rodgers	450	821

Partial General Ledger

Account	Balance
Cash 110	$3,500
Accounts Payable 210	3,350
Purchases Discount 511	
Advertising Expense 610	

201X

Apr. 1 Issued check no. 20 to A. Jenkins Company in payment of its March 28 invoice no. 522.

8 Issued check no. 21 to Fios Advertising in payment of its advertising bill, $98, no discount.

15 Issued check no. 22 to B. Foss in payment of his March 25 invoice no. 488.

10A-4. From Exercise 10A-3, prepare a schedule of accounts payable and verify that the total of the schedule equals the amount in the controlling account.

● **L05** *(10 MIN)*

10A-5. Record the following transaction in a transaction analysis chart for the buyer: Bought merchandise for $8,600 on account. Shipping terms were F.O.B. destination. The cost of shipping was $490.

● **L01** *(10 MIN)*

10A-6. Lucy Adams bought merchandise with a list price of $3,600. Lucy was entitled to a 25% trade discount as well as a 3% cash discount. What was Lucy's actual cost of buying this merchandise after the cash discount?

● **L01** *(10 MIN)*

10A-7. Journalize the following transactions:

○ **L06** *(15 MIN)*

201X

Apr. 8 Purchased merchandise on account from Collins Supplies, $10,000; terms 2/10, n/30.

15 Sold merchandise on account, $6,500; terms 2/10, n/30. The cost of merchandise was $5,000.

20 Received credit from Collins Suppliers for merchandise returned, $110.

10A-8. Journalize the following transactions:

○ **L06** *(15 MIN)*

201X

Jan. 4 Sold merchandise for $300 cash. The cost of merchandise was $250.

9 Purchased merchandise from Red Co., $3,500, free on board shipping (buyer pays freight); terms 3/10, n/30. Freight to be paid on January 20.

20 Paid freight on January 9 purchase, $70.

L06 *(15 MIN)*

10A-9. Journalize the following transactions:

201X		
Apr.	5	Sold merchandise for $1,050 cash. The cost of the merchandise was $600.
	16	Made refunds to cash customers for defective merchandise, $90. The cost of defective merchandise was $30.

L06 *(15 MIN)*

10A-10. Journalize the following transactions:

201X		
Jul.	8	Sold merchandise on account, $580, Ring; terms 4/10, n/30. Cost of merchandise was $310.
	12	Purchased office equipment on account from NHB Co., $1,900.
	13	Made refunds to cash customers, $240, for defective merchandise. The cost of defective merchandise was $40.

Set B

L01 *(15 MIN)*

10B-1. From the general journal in Figure 10.30, record to the accounts payable subsidiary ledger and post to the general ledger accounts as appropriate.

FIGURE 10.30

	Journal Entry			
Date	**Accounts**	**PR**	**Debit**	**Credit**
201X				
Jun. 3	Purchases		910	
	Accounts Payable, Avril.com			910
	Purchased merchandise on account			
4	Purchases		590	
	Accounts Payable, Jill.com			590
	Purchased merchandise on account			
8	Equipment		150	
	Accounts Payable, Pearl.com			150
	Bought equipment on account			

Partial Accounts Payable Subsidiary Ledger

Avril.com

Dr.	Cr.

Jill.com

Dr.	Cr.

Pearl.com

Dr.	Cr.

Partial General Ledger

Equipment 120

Dr.	Cr.

Accounts Payable 210

Dr.	Cr.

Purchases 510

Dr.	Cr.

10B-2. On October 10, 201X, Barney Co. issued debit memorandum no. 1 for $420 to Mango Co. for merchandise returned from invoice no. 312. Your task is to journalize, record, and post this transaction as appropriate. Use the periodic inventory system.

⬤ **L03** *(15 MIN)*

10B-3. Journalize, record, and post when appropriate the following transactions into the general journal for Kaden's Clothing. All purchases discounts are 3/10, n/30. Assume the periodic inventory system. If using working papers, be sure to put in beginning balances.

◯⬤ **L04, 5** *(20 MIN)*

201X		
Apr.	1	Issued check no. 20 to A. Jenkins Company in payment of its March 28 invoice no. 522.
	8	Issued check no. 21 to Fios Advertising in payment of its advertising bill, $97, no discount.
	15	Issued check no. 22 to B. Foss in payment of its March 25 invoice no. 488.

Accounts Payable Subsidiary Ledger

Name	Balance	Invoice No.
A. Jenkins	$500	522
B. Foss	100	488
J. Lee	400	562
B. Rodgers	50	821

Partial General Ledger

Account	Balance
Cash 110	$2,800
Accounts Payable 210	1,050
Purchases Discount 511	
Advertising Expense 610	

10B-4. From Exercise 10B-3, prepare a schedule of accounts payable and verify that the total of the schedule equals the amount in the controlling account.

⬤ **L05** *(10 MIN)*

10B-5. Record the following transaction in a transaction analysis chart for the buyer: Bought merchandise for $9,100 on account. Shipping terms were F.O.B. destination. The cost of shipping was $460. Assume the periodic inventory system.

⬤ **L01** *(10 MIN)*

10B-6. Mike Dolan bought merchandise with a list price of $3,000. Angie was entitled to a 30% trade discount as well as a 4% cash discount. What was Mike's actual cost of buying this merchandise after the cash discount?

⬤ **L01** *(10 MIN)*

10B-7. Journalize the following transactions. Assume a perpetual inventory system.

⬤ **L06** *(15 MIN)*

201X		
Apr.	8	Purchased merchandise on account from Young Supplies, $20,000; terms 4/10, n/30.
	15	Sold merchandise on account, $4,000; terms 4/10, n/30. The cost of merchandise was $2,500.
	20	Received credit from Young Supplies for merchandise returned, $200.

L06 *(15 MIN)*

10B-8. Journalize the following transactions. Assume the perpetual inventory system.

201X		
Jan.	4	Sold merchandise for $750 cash. The cost of merchandise was $200.
	9	Purchased merchandise from Rare Co., $2,700, free on board shipping (buyer pays freight); terms 1/10, n/30. Freight to be paid on January 20.
	20	Paid freight on January 9 purchase, $70.

L06 *(15 MIN)*

10B-9. Journalize the following transactions. Assume the perpetual inventory system.

201X		
Apr.	5	Sold merchandise for $1,450 cash. The cost of the merchandise was $725.
	16	Made refunds to cash customers for defective merchandise, $65. The cost of defective merchandise was $30.

L06 *(15 MIN)*

10B-10. Journalize the following transactions. Assume a perpetual inventory system.

201X		
Jul.	8	Sold merchandise on account, $640, Ring; terms 2/10, n/30. Cost of merchandise was $380.
	12	Purchased office equipment on account from TRE Co., $1,300.
	13	Made refunds to cash customers, $150, for defective merchandise. The cost of defective merchandise was $35.

MyAccountingLab

Problems

Set A

L01, 2 *(30 MIN)*

10A-1. Rodney Fey recently opened Rodney's Skate Shop. As the bookkeeper of the company, please journalize, record, and post when appropriate the following transactions (account numbers are Store Supplies, 115; Store Equipment, 121; Accounts Payable, 210; Purchases, 510):

Check Figure:
Accounts payable ending Bal. $8,200

201X		
Jun.	4	Bought $800 of merchandise on account from Adams Co., invoice no. 442, dated June 5; terms 7/10, n/30.
	5	Bought $4,800 of store equipment from Norton Co., invoice no. 502, dated June 6.
	8	Bought $1,200 of merchandise on account from Rolo Co., invoice no. 401, dated June 9; terms 7/10, n/30.
	14	Bought $1,400 of store supplies on account from Adams Co., invoice no. 419, dated June 14.

L01, 2, 5
(45 MIN)

10A-2. The following transactions occurred for Rachel's Natural Food. If using working papers, be sure to put in beginning balances.

201X		
Aug.	8	Purchased $800 of merchandise on account from Airon Co., invoice no. 400, dated August 9; terms 6/10, n/60.
	10	Purchased $1,100 of merchandise on account from Bixby Co., invoice no. 420, dated August 11; terms 6/10, n/60.

12 Purchased $500 of store supplies on account from Mixon Co., invoice no. 510, dated August 13.

14 Issued debit memo no. 8 to Airon Co. for merchandise returned, $400, from invoice no. 400.

17 Purchased $620 of office equipment on account from Ryan Co., invoice no. 810, dated August 18.

Check Figure:
Total schedule of accounts payable $5,470

24 Purchased $500 of additional store supplies on account from Mixon Co., invoice no. 516, dated August 25; terms 6/10, n/30.

Your tasks are to do the following:

1. Journalize the transactions.
2. Post and record as appropriate.
3. Prepare a schedule of accounts payable.

Accounts Payable Subsidiary Ledger

Name	Balance
Airon Co.	$ 450
Bixby Co.	400
Mixon Co.	1,250
Ryan Co.	250

Partial General Ledger

Account	Number	Balance
Store Supplies	110	$ —
Office Equipment	120	—
Accounts Payable	210	2,350
Purchases	510	$16,000
Purchases Returns and Allowances	512	—

Check Figure:
Total of schedule of accounts payable $2,175

10A-3. Wendy Ellis operates a wholesale computer center. The account balances as of October 1, 201X, are as follows. If using working papers, be sure to put in beginning balances.

 **L01, 2, 3, 4, 5**

(45 MIN)

Accounts Payable Subsidiary Ledger

Name	Balance
Andrews Co.	$1,050
Hitch Co.	1,600
Seakale Co.	650
Zeke Co.	1,000

Check Figure:
Total of schedule of accounts payable $2,175

Partial General Ledger

Account	Number	Balance
Cash	110	$18,000
Delivery Truck	150	—
Accounts Payable	210	4,300
Computer Purchases	510	—
Computer Purchases Discount	511	—
Rent Expense	610	—
Utilities Expense	620	—

Your tasks are to do the following:

1. Journalize the following transactions.
2. Record to the accounts payable subsidiary ledger and post to the general ledger as appropriate.
3. Prepare a schedule of accounts payable.

201X

Oct.	1	Paid half the amount owed Hitch Co. from previous purchases of appliances on account, less a 5% purchases discount, check no. 21.
	3	Bought a delivery truck for $9,500 cash, check no. 22, payable to Bill Brown Co.
	6	Bought computer merchandise from Lectro Co., check no. 23, $2,600.
	18	Bought additional computer merchandise from Proton Co., check no. 24, $900.
	24	Paid Zeke Co. the amount owed, less a 5% purchases discount, check no. 25.
	28	Paid rent expense to Prince's Realty Trust, check no. 26, $1,700.
	29	Paid utilities expense to Pumice Utility Co., check no. 27, $290.
	30	Paid half the amount owed Seakale Co., no discount, check no. 28.

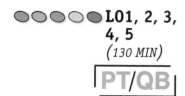

LO1, 2, 3, 4, 5

(130 MIN)

PT/QB

Check Figures:
Total of accounts receivable account. $6,900
    Total of accounts payable account. $9,200

10A-4. Allison Cooper opened Allison's Toy House. As her newly hired accountant, your tasks are to do the following:

1. Journalize the transactions for the month of October.
2. Record to subsidiary ledgers and post to the general ledger as appropriate.
3. Prepare a schedule of accounts receivable and a schedule of accounts payable.

The following is the partial chart of accounts for Allison's Toy House:

Allison's Toy House Chart of Accounts

Assets			Revenue		
110	Cash		410	Toy Sales	
112	Accounts Receivable		412	Sales Returns and Allowances	
114	Prepaid Rent		414	Sales Discounts	
121	Delivery Truck		**Cost of Goods**		
Liabilities			510	Toy Purchases	
210	Accounts Payable		512	Purchases Returns and Allowances	
Owner's Equity			514	Purchases Discount	
310	A. Cooper, Capital		**Expenses**		
			610	Salaries Expense	
			612	Cleaning Expense	

201X

Oct.	1	Allison Cooper invested $8,200 in the toy store.
	1	Paid three months' rent in advance, check no. 1, $3,000.
	1	Purchased merchandise from Sarah Harmitz Company on account, $3,800, invoice no. 410, dated October 2; terms 7/10, n/30.
	3	Sold merchandise to Robert Gibbs on account, $1,100, invoice no. 1; terms 7/10, n/30.
	6	Sold merchandise to Inez Tenenbaum on account, $700, invoice no. 2; terms 7/10, n/30.

8   Purchased merchandise from Sarah Harmitz Co. on account, $1,500, invoice no. 415, dated October 9; terms 7/10, n/30.

9   Sold merchandise to Robert Gibbs on account, $600, invoice no. 3; terms 7/10, n/30.

9   Paid cleaning service, check no. 2, $200.

10   Inez Tenenbaum returned merchandise that cost $300 to Allison's Toy House. Allison issued credit memorandum no. 1 to Inez Tenenbaum for $300.

10   Purchased merchandise from Lane Chipkin on account, $4,000, invoice no. 311, dated October 11; terms 6/15, n/60.

12   Paid Sarah Harmitz Co. invoice no. 410, dated October 2, check no. 3.

13   Sold $1,600 of toy merchandise for cash.

13   Paid salaries, $900, check no. 4.

14   Returned merchandise to Lane Chipkin in the amount of $1,500. Allison's Toy House issued debit memorandum no. 1 to Lane Chipkin.

15   Sold merchandise for $3,800 cash.

16   Received payment from Inez Tenenbaum, invoice no. 2 (less returned merchandise) less discount.

16   Robert Gibbs paid invoice no. 1.

16   Sold toy merchandise to Amanda Reader on account, $3,900, invoice no. 4; terms 7/10, n/30.

20   Purchased delivery truck on account from Sam Katz Garage, $3,100, invoice no. 111, dated October 21 (no discount).

22   Sold to Robert Gibbs merchandise on account, $1,000, invoice no. 5; terms 7/10, n/30.

23   Paid Lane Chipkin balance owed, check no. 5.

24   Sold toy merchandise on account to Amanda Reader, $1,700, invoice no. 6; terms 7/10, n/30.

25   Purchased toy merchandise, $500, check no. 6.

26   Purchased toy merchandise from William Smith on account, $4,600, invoice no. 211, dated October 27; terms 7/10, n/30.

28   Robert Gibbs paid invoice no. 5, dated October 22.

28   Amanda Reader paid invoice no. 6, dated October 24.

28   Allison invested an additional $5,500 in the business.

28   Purchased merchandise from Sarah Harmitz Co., $1,600, invoice no. 436, dated October 29; terms 7/10, n/30.

30   Paid Sarah Harmitz Co. invoice no. 436, check no. 7.

30   Sold merchandise to Bonnie Flow Company on account, $2,400, invoice no. 7; terms 7/10, n/30.

10A-5.   Jasmine's Toy Shop completed the following merchandise transactions in the month of April:

⬤ **L06** (*40 MIN*)

201X

Apr.   2   Purchased merchandise on account from Westland Suppliers, $1,000; terms 1/10, n/30.

4   Sold merchandise on account, $600; terms 1/10, n/30. The cost of the merchandise sold was $300.

4   Received credit from Westland Suppliers for merchandise returned, $100.

10   Received collections in full, less discounts, from April 4 sales.

11   Paid Westland Suppliers in full, less discount.

(continued on next page)

Check Figure:
Journal entry for Apr. 21 transaction.

Dr. Merchandise inventory $90

Cr. Cash $90

14	Purchased store equipment for cash, $270.
15	Purchased $1,500 of merchandise from Collins Distribution for cash.
16	Received a refund due to defective merchandise from supplier on cash purchase of $100.
17	Purchased merchandise from Brown Corp., $5,000, free on board shipping point (buyer pays freight); terms 1/10, n/30. Freight to be paid on April 21.
18	Sold merchandise for $2,500 cash; the cost of merchandise sold was $1,500.
21	Paid freight on April 17 purchase, $90.
25	Purchased merchandise from Aster Co., $1,120, free on board destination (seller pays freight); terms 1/10, n/30.
26	Paid Brown Corp. in full, less discount.
27	Made refunds to cash customers for defective toys, $160. The cost of the defective toys was $90.

Jasmine's Toy Shop accounts included the following: Cash, 101; Accounts Receivable, 112; Merchandise Inventory, 120; Store Equipment; 124; Accounts Payable, 201; J. Jasmine, Capital, 301; Sales, 401; Sales Discounts, 412; Sales Returns and Allowances, 414; Cost of Goods Sold, 501.

Assignment
Journalize the transactions using a perpetual inventory system.

Set B

LO1, 2 *(30 MIN)*

10B-1. Rodney Fey recently opened Rodney's Skate Shop. As the bookkeeper of the company, please journalize, record, and post when appropriate the following transactions:

Check Figure:
Accounts payable ending balance $8,900

201X		
Jun.	4	Bought $700 of merchandise on account from Adams.com, invoice no. 442, dated June 5; terms 5/10, n/30.
	5	Bought $4,600 of store equipment from Norton Co., invoice no. 502, dated June 6.
	8	Bought $2,000 of merchandise on account from Rolo Co., invoice no. 401, dated June 9 terms 5/10, n/30.
	14	Bought $1,600 of store supplies on account from Adam.Com, invoice no. 419, dated June 14.

LO1, 2, 5
(45 MIN)

10B-2. As the accountant of Rachel's Natural Food Store (1) journalize the following transactions into the general journal (p. 2), (2) record and post as appropriate, and (3) prepare a schedule of accounts payable. If using working papers, be sure to put in the following balances: Airon Co. $250; Bixby Co. $750; Mixon Co. $1,200; Ryan Co. $400; Accounts Payable $2,600; Purchases $1,900.

Check Figure:
Total of schedule of accounts payable $6,160

201X		
Aug.	8	Purchased $700 of merchandise on account from Airon Co., invoice no. 400, dated August 9; terms 6/10, n/60.
	10	Purchased $1,350 of merchandise on account from Bixby Co., invoice no. 420, dated August 11; terms 6/10, n/60.
	12	Purchased $550 of store supplies on account from Mixon Co., invoice no. 510, dated August 13.
	14	Issued debit memo no. 8 to Airon Co. for merchandise returned, $450, from invoice no. 400.

17	Purchased $560 of office equipment on account from Ryan Co., invoice no. 810, dated August 18.
24	Purchased $850 of additional store supplies on account from Mixon Co., invoice no. 516, dated August 25; terms 6/10, n/30.

10B-3. Wendy Ellis operates a wholesale computer center and has hired you as her bookkeeper to record the following transactions. She would like you to (1) journalize the following transactions, (2) record to the accounts payable subsidiary ledger and post to the general ledger as appropriate, and (3) prepare a schedule of accounts payable. If using working papers, be sure to put in the following beginning balances: Andrews Co. $1,350; Hitch Co. $1,200; Seakate Co. $700; Cash $17,000; Accounts Receivable $4,650.

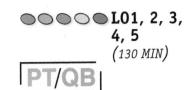

L01, 2, 3, 4, 5
(45 MIN)

201X

Oct.	1	Paid half the amount owed Hitch Co. from previous purchases of appliances on account, less a 5% purchases discount, check no. 21.
	3	Bought a delivery truck for $6,500 cash, check no. 22, payable to Bob Singer Co.
	6	Bought computer merchandise from Lossy Co., check no. 23, $3,100.
	18	Bought additional computer merchandise from Proton Co., check no. 24, $650.
	24	Paid Zeke Co. the amount owed, less a 5% purchases discount, check no. 25.
	28	Paid rent expense to King's Realty Trust, check no. 26, $2,400.
	29	Paid utilities expense to Gravel Utility Co., check no. 27, $280.
	30	Paid half the amount owed Seakate Co., no discount, check no. 28.

Check Figure:
Total of schedule of accounts payable $2,300

10B-4. Allison Cooper opened Allison's Toy House. As her newly hired accountant, your tasks are to do the following:

1. Journalize the transactions for the month of October.
2. Record to subsidiary ledgers and post to the general ledger as appropriate.
3. Prepare a schedule of accounts receivable and a schedule of accounts payable.

(Use the same chart of accounts as in Problem 10A-4. The working papers that accompany this text have all the forms you need to complete this problem.)

L01, 2, 3, 4, 5
(130 MIN)

PT/QB

201X

Oct.	1	Allison Cooper invested $7,400 in the toy store.
	1	Paid three months' rent in advance, check no. 1, $2,900.
	1	Purchased merchandise from Sarah Harmitz Company on account, $3,700, invoice no. 410, dated October 2; terms 7/10, n/30.
	3	Sold merchandise to Robert Gibbs on account, $120, invoice no. 1; terms 7/10, n/30.
	6	Sold merchandise to Inez Tenenbaum on account, $800, invoice no. 2; terms 2/10, n/30.
	8	Purchased merchandise from Sarah Harmitz Co., $900, invoice no. 415, dated October 9; terms 7/10, n/30.
	9	Sold merchandise to Robert Gibbs on account, $100, invoice no. 3; terms 7/10, n/30.
	9	Paid cleaning service, check no. 2, $225.
	10	Inez Tenenbaum returned merchandise that cost $200 to Allison's Toy House. Allison issued credit memorandum no. 1 to Inez Tenenbaum for $200.

Check Figure:
Total of schedule of accounts receivable $7,600; of accounts payable $9,400

(continued on next page)

	10	Purchased merchandise from Lane Chipkin on account, $3,700, invoice no. 311, dated October 11; terms 5/15, n/60.
	12	Paid Lane Chipkin Co. invoice no. 410, dated October 2, check no. 3.
	13	Sold $1,000 of toy merchandise for cash.
	13	Paid salaries, $800, check no. 4.
	14	Returned merchandise to Lane Chipkin in the amount of $1,400. Allison's Toy House issued debit memorandum no. 1 to Lane Chipkin.
	15	Sold merchandise for $3,700 cash.
	16	Received payment from Inez Tenenbaum, invoice no. 2 (less returned merchandise), less discount.
	16	Robert Gibbs paid invoice no. 1.
	16	Sold toy merchandise to Amanda Reader on account, $4,500, invoice no. 4; terms 7/10, n/30.
	20	Purchased delivery truck on account from Sam Katz Garage, $3,100, invoice no. 111, dated October 21 (no discount).
	22	Sold to Robert Gibbs merchandise on account, $500, invoice no. 5; terms 7/10, n/30.
	23	Paid Lane Chipkin balance owed, check no. 5.
	24	Sold toy merchandise on account to Amanda Reader, $1,600, invoice no. 6; terms 7/10, n/30.
	25	Purchased toy merchandise, $1,200, check no. 6.
	26	Purchased toy merchandise from Sanya Burger on account, $5,400, invoice no. 211, dated October 27; terms 7/10, n/30.
	28	Robert Gibbs paid invoice no. 5, dated October 22.
	28	Amanda Reader paid invoice no. 6, dated October 24.
	28	Allison invested an additional $7,500 in the business.
	28	Purchased merchandise from Sarah Harmitz Co., $1,500, invoice no. 436, dated October 29; terms 7/10, n/30.
	30	Paid Sarah Harmitz Co. invoice no. 436, check no. 7.
	30	Sold merchandise to Bonnie Flow Company on account, $3,000, invoice no. 7; terms 7/10, n/30.

⬤⬤⬤⬤◗ **LO1, 2, 3, 4, 5**
(40 MIN)

10B-5.   Julie's Toy Shop completed the following merchandise transactions in the month of April:

201X

Apr.	2	Purchased merchandise on account from Beech Suppliers, $4,000; terms 1/10, n/30.
	4	Sold merchandise on account $500; terms 1/10, n/30. The cost of the merchandise sold was $200.
	4	Received credit from Beech Suppliers for merchandise returned, $500.
	10	Received collections in full, less discounts, from April 4 sales.
	11	Paid Beech Suppliers in full, less discount.
	14	Purchased office equipment for cash, $350.
	15	Purchased $1,600 of merchandise from Kelly Distribution for cash.
	16	Received a refund due for defective merchandise from supplier on cash purchase of $115.
	17	Purchased merchandise from Roy Corp., $3,000, free on board shipping point (buyer pays freight); terms 1/10, n/30. Freight to be paid on April 21.
	18	Sold merchandise for $2,800 cash; the cost of the merchandise sold was $1,700.

Check Figure:
Journal entry for Apr. 21 transaction.

Dr. Merchandise inventory $125
Cr. Cash $125

21	Paid freight on April 17 purchase, $125.
25	Purchased merchandise from Roland Co., $1,150, free on board destination (seller pays freight); terms 1/10, n/30.
26	Paid Roy Corp., in full, less discount.
27	Made refunds to cash customers for defective toys, $210. The cost of the defective toys was $110.

Julie's Toy Shop accounts included the following: Cash, 101; Accounts Receivable, 112; Merchandise Inventory, 120; Office Equipment, 124; Accounts Payable, 201; B. Julie, Capital, 301; Sales, 401; Sales Discounts, 412; Sales Returns and Allowances, 414; Cost of Goods Sold, 501.

Assignment
Journalize the transactions using the perpetual inventory system.

Financial Report Problem

Reading the Kellogg's Annual Report
Go to http://investor.kelloggs.com/annuals.cfm, to access the Kellogg's 2010 Annual Report, and locate the balance sheet. How much has merchandise inventory increased from 2009 to 2010?

 **LO1** *(15 MIN)*

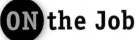the Job ||||||||||||||||||||||||||

MyAccountingLab

SANCHEZ COMPUTER CENTER

◗◗◗○◗ **LO1, 2, 3, 4, 5**
(60 MIN)

The following is an updated schedule of accounts payable as of January 31, 201X.

Schedule of Accounts Payable	
Office Depot	$ 50
System Design Furniture	1,400
Pac Bell	150
Multi Systems, Inc.	450
Total Accounts Payable	$ 2,050

Assignment

1. Journalize the transactions.

2. Record in the accounts payable subsidiary ledger and post to the general ledger as appropriate. A partial general ledger is included in the working papers that accompany this text.

3. The following accounts have been added to the chart of accounts: Purchases #6000, Purchase Returns and Allowances #6010, and Purchase Discounts #6020.

4. Prepare a schedule of accounts payable as of February 28, 201X.

The transactions for the month of February are as follows:

201X		
Feb.	1	Prepaid the rent for the months of February, March, and April, $1,200, check #2585.
	4	Bought merchandise on account from Multi Systems, Inc., purchase order no. 4010, $450; terms 3/10, n/30.
	8	Bought office supplies on account from Office Depot, purchase order no. 4011, $250; terms n/30.
	9	Purchased merchandise on account from Computer Connection, purchase order no. 4012, $500; terms 1/30, n/60.
	15	Paid purchase order no. 4010 in full to Multi Systems, Inc., check #2586.
	21	Issued debit memorandum no. 10 to Computer Connection for merchandise returned from purchase order no. 4012, $100.
	27	Paid for office supplies, $50, check #2587.

PEACHTREE COMPUTER WORKSHOP

COMPUTERIZED ACCOUNTING APPLICATION FOR CHAPTER 10

Refresher on using Peachtree Complete Accounting

Before starting this assignment, you may want to refresh your memory by reading the following PDF documents in the multimedia library of the MyAccountingLab Web site. Remember to choose the PDF document for your version of Peachtree.

1. An Introduction to Peachtree Complete Accounting
2. Correcting Peachtree Transactions
3. How to Repeat or Restart a Peachtree Assignment
4. Backing Up and Restoring Your Work in Peachtree

You also should have completed the following workshops:

1. Workshop 1 Atlas Company from Chapter 3
2. Workshop 2 Zell Company from Chapter 4
3. Workshop 3 Sullivan Realty from Chapter 5
4. Workshop 4 Pete's Market from Chapter 8

Workshop 5:

PART A: Recording Transactions in the Sales, Receipts, Purchases, and Payments Journals

PART B: Accounting Cycle Mini Practice Set with Sales and Purchasing

PART A: In this part of the workshop, you will learn to record customer sales on account, customer credit memos, customer cash receipts, purchases from vendors on account, and payments to vendors for Mars Company using Peachtree. You will also print the aged receivables and aged payables reports and the sales journal, cash receipts journal, purchasing journal, and cash disbursement journals.

Instructions and the data file for completing Part A of the assignment are in the multimedia library of the MyAccountingLab Web site. Open the *Workshop 5 Part A Mars Company* PDF document for your version of Peachtree and download the *Mars Company* data file for your version of Peachtree.

PART B: In this part of the workshop you will complete a mini practice set of March accounting transactions for Abby's Toy House using Peachtree. Transactions include customer sales on account, customer credit memos, customer cash receipts, purchases from vendors on account, payments to vendors, and general journal entries in Peachtree. You will also print the aged receivables and aged payables reports and the general journal and general ledger reports.

Instructions and the data file for completing Part B of the assignment are in the multimedia library of the MyAccountingLab Web site. Open the *Workshop 5 Part B Abby's Toy House* PDF document for your version of Peachtree and download the *Abby's Toy House* data file for your version of Peachtree.

QUICKBOOKS COMPUTER WORKSHOP

COMPUTERIZED ACCOUNTING APPLICATION FOR CHAPTER 10

Refresher on Using QuickBooks Pro

Before starting this assignment, you may want to refresh your memory by reading the following PDF documents in the multimedia library of the MyAccountingLab Web site. Remember to choose the PDF document for your version of QuickBooks.

1. An Introduction to QuickBooks Pro
2. Correcting QuickBooks Transactions
3. How to Repeat or Restart a QuickBooks Assignment
4. Backing Up and Restoring Your Work in QuickBooks

You also should have completed the following workshops:

1. Workshop 1 Atlas Company from Chapter 3
2. Workshop 2 Zell Company from Chapter 4
3. Workshop 3 Sullivan Realty from Chapter 5
4. Workshop 4 Pete's Market from Chapter 8

Workshop 5:

PART A: Recording Transactions in the Sales, Receipts, Purchases, and Payments Journals

PART B: Accounting Cycle Mini Practice Set with Sales and Purchasing

PART A: In this part of the workshop, you will learn to record customer sales on account, customer credit memos, customer cash receipts, purchases from vendors on account, and payments to vendors for Mars Company using QuickBooks. You will also print the aged receivables and aged payables reports and the sales journal, cash receipts journal, purchasing journal, and cash disbursement journals.

Instructions and the data file for completing Part A of the assignment are in the multimedia library of the MyAccountingLab Web site. Open the *Workshop 5 Part A Mars Company* PDF document for your version of QuickBooks and download the *Mars Company* data file for your version of QuickBooks.

PART B: In this part of the workshop, you will complete a mini practice set of March accounting transactions for Abby's Toy House using QuickBooks. Transactions include customer sales on account, customer credit memos, customer cash receipts, purchases from vendors on account, payments to vendors, and general journal entries in Peachtree. You will also print the aged receivables and aged payables reports and the general journal and general ledger reports.

Instructions and the data file for completing Part B of the assignment are in the multimedia library of the MyAccountingLab Web site. ***Open the Workshop 5 Part B Abby's Toy House*** PDF document for your version of QuickBooks and download the *Abby's Toy House* data file for your version of QuickBooks.

Appendix A

SPECIAL JOURNALS WITH PROBLEM MATERIAL

LEARNING OBJECTIVES

● **1.** Identify which special journal or general journal will record a transaction.

● **2.** Record transactions in special journals or a general journal and post to subsidiary and general ledger accounts.

CLASSROOM DEMONSTRATION PROBLEM:
Periodic Method

●● **LO1, 2**

DEMONSTRATION PROBLEM

Journalizing Transactions to Special Journals*; Posting to Subsidiary and General Ledger Accounts from Special Journals

All credit sales are 2/10, n/30. All merchandise purchased on account has 3/10, n/30 credit terms. Assume Periodic Inventory System. Ignore Sales Tax. The company uses Sales Journal, Purchases Journal, Cash Receipt and Cash Payment Journals as well as a General Journal.

Requirements:

1. Identify which special journal or if the general journal will be used to record a transaction.
2. Journalize transactions and post to subsidiary ledgers and general ledgers as appropriate.

201X

Mar.	1	J. Ling invested $2,000 into the business.
	1	Sold merchandise on account to Balder Co., $500, invoice no. 1.
	2	Purchased merchandise on account from Case Co., $500.
	4	Sold $2,000 of merchandise for cash.
	6	Paid Case Co. from previous purchases on account, check no. 1.
	8	Sold merchandise on account to Lewis Co., $1,000, invoice no. 2.
	10	Received payment from Balder for invoice no. 1.
	12	Issued a credit memorandum to Lewis Co. for $200 for faulty merchandise.
	14	Received payment from Lewis Co.
	16	Purchased merchandise on account from Noone Co., $1,000.
	17	Purchased equipment on account from Case Co., $300.
	18	Issued a debit memorandum to Noone Co. for $500 for defective merchandise.
	20	Paid salaries, $300, check no. 2.
	24	Paid Noone balance owed, check no. 3.

---

*All sales on account will go in a Sales Journal. Purchases on account will go in a Purchases Journal. Cash received will go in the Cash Receipts Journal and money paid out will go in the Cash Payments Journal. Transactions that do not fit into these special journals will go into the General Journal.

Demonstration Problem Solution

Part 1	Part 2	Demonstration Problem Complete

Identify which special journal or general journal will record a transaction.

Transaction	What to Do Step-by-Step

201X

Mar.   1   *Money Received:* Record in cash receipts journal. Post immediately to J. Ling, Capital, because it is in sundry.

      1   *Sale on Account:* Record in sales journal. Record immediately to Balder Co. in accounts receivable subsidiary ledger. Place a ✓ in Post. Ref. column of sales journal when subsidiary is updated.

      2   *Buy Merchandise on Account:* Record in purchases journal. Record to Case Co. immediately in the accounts payable subsidiary ledger.

      4   *Money In:* Record in cash receipts journal. No posting needed (put an × in Post. Ref. column).

      6   *Money Out:* Record in cash payments journal. Save $15, which is a Purchases Discount. Record immediately to Case Co. in accounts payable subsidiary ledger (the full amount of $500).

      8   *Sales on Account:* Record in sales journal. Update immediately to Lewis in accounts receivable subsidiary ledger.

    10   *Money In:* Record in cash receipts journal. Because Balder pays within 10 days, it gets a $10 discount. Record the full amount immediately to Balder in the accounts receivable subsidiary ledger.

    12   *Returns:* Record in general journal. Seller issues credit memo resulting in higher sales returns and customers owing less. All postings and recordings are done immediately.

    14   *Money In:* Record in cash receipts journal:

$$\$1,000 - \$200 \text{ returns} = \$800$$
$$\underline{\times\ 0.02}$$
$$\$\ 16 \text{ discount}$$

           Record immediately the $800 to Lewis in the accounts receivable subsidiary ledger.

    16   *Buy Now, Pay Later:* Record in purchases journal. Record immediately to Noone Co. in the accounts payable subsidiary ledger.

    17   *Buy Now, Pay Later:* Record in purchases journal in Sundry. This item is not merchandise for resale. Record and post immediately.

    18   *Returns:* Record in general ledger. Buyer issues a debit memo reducing the Accounts Payable due to purchases return and allowances. Post and record immediately.

    20   *Salaries:* Record in cash payments journal, sundry column. Post immediately to Salaries Expense.

    24   *Money Out:* Record in cash payments journal. Save 3% ($15), a purchases discount. Record immediately to accounts payable subsidiary ledger that you reduce Noone by $500.

Requirement 2

Record transactions in special journals or general journal and post to subsidiary and general ledger accounts.

Part 1	**Part 2**	Demonstration Problem Complete

Record accounts receivable subsidiary ledger immediately.

FIGURE A.1
Sales Journal

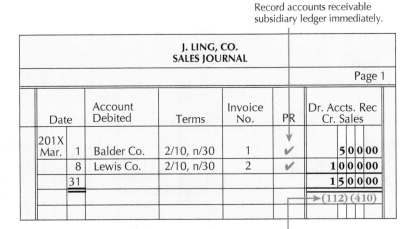

	Date	Account Debited	Terms	Invoice No.	PR	Dr. Accts. Rec Cr. Sales
201X Mar.	1	Balder Co.	2/10, n/30	1	✔	5 0 0 00
	8	Lewis Co.	2/10, n/30	2	✔	1 0 0 0 00
	31					1 5 0 0 00
						(112) (410)

J. LING, CO. SALES JOURNAL — Page 1

COACHING TIP

Remember, the sales journal only records sales on account.

Total posted at end of month to these accounts.

FIGURE A.2
Purchases Journal

J. LING, CO. PURCHASES JOURNAL — Page 1

	Date	Account Credited	Terms	PR	Accounts Payable Cr.	Purchases Dr.	Sundry–Dr. Acct.	PR	Amount
201X Mar.	2	Case Co.	3/10, n/30	✔	5 0 0 00	5 0 0 00			
	16	Noone Co.	3/10, n/30	✔	1 0 0 0 00	1 0 0 0 00			
	17	Case Co.	3/10, n/30	✔	3 0 0 00		Equip.	116	3 0 0 00
	31				1 8 0 0 00	1 5 0 0 00			3 0 0 00
					(210)	(510)			(X)

Record to accounts payable subsidiary ledger immediately.

Post totals at end of month to general ledger.

Post immediately to Equipment in general ledger.

Do not post total.

COACHING TIP

Remember, the purchases journal records buy now, pay later transactions. Purchases are merchandise for resale, while equipment is not for resale.

Post to capital immediately.

FIGURE A.3
Cash Receipts Journal

J. LING, CO. CASH RECEIPTS JOURNAL — Page 1

	Date	Cash Dr.	Sales Discount Dr.	Accts. Receivable Cr.	Sales Cr.	Sundry Account Names	PR	Amount Cr.
201X Mar.	1	2 0 0 0 00				J. Ling, Cap.	310	2 0 0 0 00
	4	2 0 0 00			2 0 0 00	Cash sale	✗	
	10	4 9 0 00	1 0 00	5 0 0 00		Balder Co.	✔	
	14	7 8 4 00	1 6 00	8 0 0 00		Lewis Co.	✔	
	31	5 2 7 4 00	2 6 00	1 3 0 0 00	2 0 0 00			2 0 0 0 00
		(111)	(430)	(112)	(410)			(X)

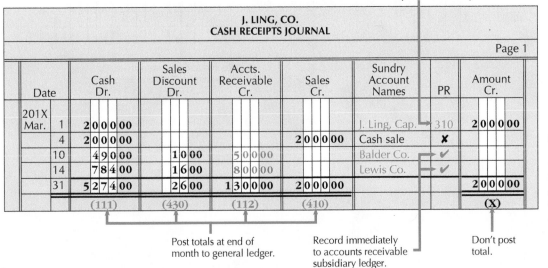

Post totals at end of month to general ledger.

Record immediately to accounts receivable subsidiary ledger.

Don't post total.

COACHING TIP

Remember, the cash receipts journal records any transaction that involves the receipt of cash.

FIGURE A.4
Cash Payments Journal

COACHING TIP

Remember, the cash payment records only transactions that result in the payment of cash.

Record immediately to accounts payable subsidiary ledger.

J. LING, CO.
CASH PAYMENTS JOURNAL

Page 1

Date	Ck. No.	Account Debited	PR.	Sundry Dr.	Accounts Payable Dr.	Purchases Discount Cr.	Cash Cr.
201X Mar. 6	1	Case Co	✔		500 00	15 00	485 00
20	2	Salaries Expense	610	300 00			300 00
24	3	Noone Co.	✔		500 00	15 00	485 00
31				300 00	1000 00	30 00	1270 00
				(X)	(210)	(530)	(111)

Post immediately to Salaries Expense.

Do not post total.

Post totals at end of month to the general ledger.

FIGURE A.5
General Journal

COACHING TIP

Remember, transactions not fitting into the four special journals are recorded in the general journal.

J. LING, CO. GENERAL JOURNAL

Page 1

Date	Account Titles and Description	PR	Dr.	Cr.
201X Mar. 12	Sales Returns and Allowances	420	200 00	
	Accounts Receivable, Lewis Co.	112 ✔		200 00
	Issued credit memo			
18	Accounts Payable, Noone Co.	210 ✔	500 00	
	Purchases Returns and Allowances	520		500 00
	Issued debit memo			

Record and post immediately to subsidiary and general ledgers.

ACCOUNTS RECEIVABLE SUBSIDIARY LEDGER

Balder Company

Date	PR	Dr.	Cr.	Dr. Bal.
201X 3/1	SJ1	500		500
3/10	CRJ1		500	——

Lewis Company

Date	PR	Dr.	Cr.	Dr. Bal.
201X 3/8	SJ1	1,000		1,000
3/12	GJ1		200	800
3/14	CPJ1		800	——

ACCOUNTS PAYABLE SUBSIDIARY LEDGER

Case Company

Date	PR	Dr.	Cr.	Cr. Bal.
201X 3/2	PJ1		500	500
3/6	CPJ1	500		——
3/17	PJ1		300	300

Noone Company

Date	PR	Dr.	Cr.	Cr. Bal.
201X 3/16	PJ1		1,000	1,000
3/18	GJ1	500		500
3/24	CPJ1	500		——

FIGURE A.6
Subsidiary and General Ledgers

COACHING TIP

Note that in the accounts receivable subsidiary ledger (Dr. balance) customers owe the seller, while in the accounts payable subsidiary ledger (Cr. balance) the seller owes the vendors it purchased items from.

GENERAL LEDGER

Cash 111

3/31 CRJ1 5,274	1,270 3/31 CPJ1
Bal. 4,004	

Accounts Receivable 112

3/31 SJ1 1,500	200 3/12 GJ1
Bal. 0	1,300 3/31 CRJ1

Equipment 116

3/17 PJ1 300	

Accounts Payable 210

3/18 GJ1 500	1,800 3/31 PJ1
3/31 CPJ1 1,000	300 Bal.

J. Ling, Capital 310

	2,000 3/1 CRJ1

Sales 410

	1,500 3/31 SJ1
	2,000 3/31 CRJ1
	3,500 Bal.

Sales Returns and Allowances 420

3/12 GJ1 200	

Sales Discount 430

3/31 CRJ1 26	

Purchases 510

3/31 PJ1 1,500	

Purchase Returns and Allowances 520

	500 3/18 GJ1

Purchase Discount 530

	30 3/31 CPJ1

Salaries Expense 610

3/20 CPJ1 300	

COACHING TIP

Remember, in the General Ledger Accounts Receivable and Accounts Payable are the controlling accounts.

SUMMARY OF SOLUTION TIPS

Seller	Buyer
Sales journal	Purchases journal
Cash receipts journal	Cash payments journal
Sales (Cr.)	Purchases (Dr.)
Sales Returns and Allowances (Dr.)	Purchase Returns and Allowances (Cr.)
Sales Discounts (Dr.)	Purchase Discounts (Cr.)
Accounts Receivable (Dr.)	Accounts Payable (Cr.)
Accounts receivable subsidiary ledger	Accounts payable subsidiary ledger
Schedule of accounts receivable	Schedule of accounts payable
Issue a credit memo or receive a debit memo	Receive a credit memo or issue a debit memo

End of Month Post totals (except sundry) of special journal to the general ledger.

Note: In this problem at the end of the month, (1) Accounts Receivable in the general ledger, the controlling account, has a zero balance, as does each title in the accounts receivable subsidiary ledger, and (2) the balance in Accounts Payable (the controlling account) is $300. In the accounts payable subsidiary ledger, J. Ling owes Case $300. The sum of the accounts payable subsidiary ledger does equal the balance in the controlling account at the end of the month.

Part 1	Part 2	**Demonstration Problem Complete**

Appendix A Problems

A-1. Jill Blue opened Food.com, a wholesale grocery and pizza company. Since Jill Blue only sells to retailers, she does not have to charge sales tax to her customers. Jill Blue uses a sales journal for sales on account. The following transactions occurred in June:

201X

June		
	1	Sold grocery merchandise to Duncan Co. on account, $500, invoice no. 1.
	4	Sold pizza merchandise to Sue Moore Co. on account, $600, invoice no. 2.
	8	Sold grocery merchandise to Long Co. on account, $700, invoice no. 3.
	10	Issued credit memorandum no. 1 to Duncan Co. for $150 of grocery merchandise returned due to spoilage.
	15	Sold pizza merchandise to Sue Moore Co. on account, $160, invoice no. 4.
	19	Sold grocery merchandise to Long Co. on account, $300, invoice no. 5.
	25	Sold pizza merchandise to Duncan Co. on account, $1,200, invoice no. 6.

Check Figure:
Schedule of accounts
receivable $3,310

Required

1. Journalize the transactions in the appropriate journals.
2. Record to the accounts receivable subsidiary ledger and post to the general ledger as appropriate.
3. Prepare a schedule of accounts receivable.

A-2. The following transactions of Ted's Auto Supply occurred in November. Ted uses a sales journal to record sales on account (your working papers have balances as of November 1 for certain general ledger and accounts receivable ledger accounts):

201X

Nov.	1	Sold auto parts merchandise to R. Volan on account, $1,000, invoice no. 60, plus 5% sales tax.
	5	Sold auto parts merchandise to J. Seth on account, $800, invoice no. 61, plus 5% sales tax.
	8	Sold auto parts merchandise to Lance Corner on account, $9,000, invoice no. 62, plus 5% sales tax.
	10	Issued credit memorandum no. 12 to R. Volan for $500 for defective auto parts merchandise returned from Nov. 1 transaction. (Be careful to record the reduction in Sales Tax Payable as well.)
	12	Sold auto parts merchandise to J. Seth on account, $600, invoice no. 63, plus 5% sales tax.

Required

1. Journalize the transactions in the appropriate journals.
2. Record to the accounts receivable subsidiary ledger and post to the general ledger as appropriate.
3. Prepare a schedule of accounts receivable.

Check Figure:
Schedule of accounts receivable $13,045

A-3. Abby Kim recently opened Skates.com. Abby uses a purchases journal to record purchases on account. As the bookkeeper of her company, please journalize, record, and post when appropriate the following transactions (account numbers are Store Supplies, 115; Store Equipment, 121; Accounts Payable, 210; Purchases, 510):

201X

June	4	Bought $700 of merchandise on account from Mail.com, invoice no. 442, dated June 5; terms 2/10, n/30.
	5	Bought $4,000 of store equipment from Norton Co., invoice no. 502, dated June 6.
	8	Bought $1,400 of merchandise on account from Rolo Co., invoice no. 401, dated June 9; terms 2/10, n/30.
	14	Bought $900 of store supplies on account from Mail.com, invoice no. 419, dated June 14.

Check Figure:
Total of purchases column in purchases journal: $2,100

A-4. Mabel's Natural Food Store uses a purchases journal and a general journal to record the following transactions (continued from April):

201X

May	8	Purchased $600 of merchandise on account from Aton Co., invoice no. 400, dated May 9; terms 2/10, n/60.
	10	Purchased $1,200 of merchandise on account from Broward Co., invoice no. 420, dated May 11; terms 2/10, n/60.
	12	Purchased $500 of store supplies on account from Midden Co., invoice no. 510, dated May 13.
	14	Issued debit memo no. 8 to Aton Co., for merchandise returned, $400, from invoice no. 400.
	17	Purchased $560 of office equipment on account from Relar Co., invoice no. 810, dated May 18.
	24	Purchased $650 of additional store supplies on account from Midden Co., invoice no. 516, dated May 25; terms 2/10, n/30.

Check Figure:
Total schedule of accounts payable $5,810

The food store decided to keep a separate column for the purchases of supplies in the purchases journal. Your tasks are to do the following:

1. Journalize the transactions.
2. Post and record as appropriate.
3. Prepare a schedule of accounts payable.

A-5. Abby Ellen opened Abby's Toy House. As her newly hired accountant, your tasks are to do the following:

1. Journalize the transactions for the month of March. Abby uses special journals for sales on account, purchases on account, cash receipts and cash payments, as well as a general journal.
2. Record to subsidiary ledgers and post to the general ledger as appropriate.
3. Total and rule the journals.
4. Prepare a schedule of accounts receivable and a schedule of accounts payable.
5. Ignore Sales Tax.

The following is the partial chart of accounts for Abby's Toy House:

<table>
<tr><td colspan="4" align="center">Abby's Toy House Chart of Accounts</td></tr>
<tr><td colspan="2">Assets</td><td colspan="2">Revenue</td></tr>
<tr><td>110</td><td>Cash</td><td>410</td><td>Toy Sales</td></tr>
<tr><td>112</td><td>Accounts Receivable</td><td>412</td><td>Sales Returns and Allowances</td></tr>
<tr><td>114</td><td>Prepaid Rent</td><td>414</td><td>Sales Discounts</td></tr>
<tr><td>121</td><td>Delivery Truck</td><td colspan="2">Cost of Goods</td></tr>
<tr><td colspan="2">Liabilities</td><td>510</td><td>Toy Purchases</td></tr>
<tr><td>210</td><td>Accounts Payable</td><td>512</td><td>Purchases Returns and Allowances</td></tr>
<tr><td colspan="2">Owner's Equity</td><td>514</td><td>Purchases Discount</td></tr>
<tr><td>310</td><td>A. Ellen, Capital</td><td colspan="2">Expenses</td></tr>
<tr><td></td><td></td><td>610</td><td>Salaries Expense</td></tr>
<tr><td></td><td></td><td>612</td><td>Cleaning Expense</td></tr>
</table>

Check Figures:
Total of schedule of accounts receivable $7,600
Total of schedule of accounts payable $9,000

201X

Mar.

1   Abby Ellen invested $8,000 in the toy store.

1   Paid three months' rent in advance, check no. 1, $3,000.

1   Purchased merchandise from Earl Miller Company on account, $4,000, invoice no. 410, dated March 2; terms 2/10, n/30.

3   Sold merchandise to Bill Burton on account, $1,000, invoice no. 1; terms 2/10, n/30.

6   Sold merchandise to Jim Rex on account, $700, invoice no. 2; terms 2/10, n/30.

8   Purchased merchandise from Earl Miller Co. on account, $1,200, invoice no. 415, dated March 9; terms 2/10, n/30.

9   Sold merchandise to Bill Burton on account, $600, invoice no. 3; terms 2/10, n/30.

9   Paid cleaning service, check no. 2, $300.

10 Jim Rex returned merchandise that cost $300 to Abby's Toy House. Abby issued credit memorandum no. 1 to Jim Rex for $300.

10 Purchased merchandise from Minnie Katz on account, $4,000, invoice no. 311, dated March 11; terms 1/15, n/60.

12 Paid Earl Miller Co. invoice no. 410, dated March 2, check no. 3.

13 Sold $1,300 of toy merchandise for cash.

13 Paid salaries, $600, check no. 4.

14 Returned merchandise to Minnie Katz in the amount of $1,000. Abby's Toy House issued debit memorandum no. 1 to Minnie Katz.

15	Sold merchandise for $4,000 cash.
16	Received payment from Jim Rex, invoice no. 2 (less returned merchandise) less discount.
16	Bill Burton paid invoice no. 1.
16	Sold toy merchandise to Amy Rose on account, $4,000, invoice no. 4; terms 2/10, n/30.
20	Purchased delivery truck on account from Sam Katz Garage, $3,000, invoice no. 111, dated March 21 (no discount).
22	Sold to Bill Burton merchandise on account, $900, invoice no. 5; terms 2/10, n/30.
23	Paid Minnie Katz balance owed, check no. 5.
24	Sold toy merchandise on account to Amy Rose, $1,100, invoice no. 6; terms 2/10, n/30.
25	Purchased toy merchandise, $600, check no. 6.
26	Purchased toy merchandise from Woody Smith on account, $4,800, invoice no. 211, dated March 27; terms 2/10, n/30.
28	Bill Burton paid invoice no. 5, dated March 22.
28	Amy Rose paid invoice no. 6, dated March 24.
28	Abby invested an additional $5,000 in the business.
28	Purchased merchandise from Earl Miller Co., $1,400, invoice no. 436, dated March 29; terms 2/10, n/30.
30	Paid Earl Miller Co. invoice no. 436, check no. 7.
30	Sold merchandise to Bonnie Flow Company on account, $3,000, invoice no. 7; terms 2/10, n/30.

SALES AND CASH RECEIPTS JOURNAL USING A PERPETUAL INVENTORY SYSTEM FOR ART'S WHOLESALE CLOTHING

ART'S WHOLESALE CLOTHING COMPANY
SALES JOURNAL

Page 1

Date	Account Debited	Terms	Invoice No.	Post. Ref.	Dr. Acc. Rec Cr. Sales	Cost of Goods Sold Dr. Merchandise Inventory Cr.
201X Apr. 3	Hal's Clothing	2/10, n/30	1	✔	800 00	560 00
6	Bevans Company	2/10, n/30	2	✔	1600 00	1120 00
18	Roe Company	2/10, n/30	3	✔	2000 00	1400 00
24	Roe Company	2/10, n/30	4	✔	500 00	350 00
28	Mel's Dept. Store	2/10, n/30	5	✔	900 00	630 00
29	Mel's Dept. Store	2/10, n/30	6	✔	700 00	490 00
30						
					6500 00	4550 00
					(113) (411)	(510) (114)

FIGURE A.7
A Sales Journal under a Perpetual System

What's new:

In the sales journal: New columns for Cost of Goods Sold (Dr.) and Inventory (Cr.). Each time a charge sale is earned, the Cost of Goods Sold increases and the amount of Inventory at cost is reduced.

In the general ledger: New ledger accounts for Inventory and Cost of Goods Sold.

Example: On April 3, Art's Wholesale sold Hal's Clothing $800 of merchandise on account. This sale cost Art's $560 to bring this merchandise into the store.

FIGURE A.8
A Cash Receipts Journal under a
Perpetual System

Date	Cash Dr.	Sales Discount Dr.	Accounts Receivable Cr.	Sales Cr.	Sundry Account Name	Post. Ref.	Amount Cr.	Costs of Goods Sold Dr. Merchandise Inventory Cr.
201X Apr. 1	8 0 0 0 00				Art Newner, Capital	311	8 0 0 0 00	
4	7 8 4 00	1 6 00	8 0 0 00		Hal's Clothing	✔		
15	9 0 0 00			9 0 0 00	Cash Sales	x		6 3 0 00
16	9 8 0 00	2 0 00	1 0 0 0 00		Bevans Company	✔		
22	1 9 6 0 00	4 0 00	2 0 0 0 00		Roe Company	✔		
27	5 0 0 00				Store Equipment	121	5 0 0 00	
30	1 2 0 0 00			1 2 0 0 00	Cash Sales	x		8 4 0 00
	1 4 3 2 4 00	7 6 00	3 8 0 0 00	2 1 0 0 00			8 5 0 0 00	1 4 7 0 00
	(111)	(413)	(113)	(411)			(X)	(510) (114)

Title row of table:

ART'S WHOLESALE CLOTHING COMPANY
CASH RECEIPTS JOURNAL   Page 1

What's new:
> *In the cash receipts journal:* New columns for Cost of Goods Sold (Dr.) and Inventory (Cr.). Each time a cash sale is earned, the Cost of Goods Sold increases and the amount of Inventory at cost is reduced.

11

Preparing a Worksheet for a Merchandise Company

THE GAME PLAN

Do you ever need to adjust your work schedule so you can do better in class? Companies often have to make adjustments to better serve their customers. For example, when you visit an Apple store, Apple makes adjustments to the inventory so customer demand can be met. In addition, Apple makes other adjustments that customers may not be aware of. These adjustments include supplies, rent, the number of employees, and depreciation. Like the preparation of worksheets of non-merchandising companies that you learned in Chapter 4, to make these adjustments, many merchandise companies will also use a worksheet with some differences. In this chapter you will learn how a merchandising company prepares a worksheet and how it flows to the financial statements.

LEARNING OBJECTIVES

1. Figuring adjustments for merchandise inventory, unearned rent, supplies used, insurance expired, depreciation expense, and salaries accrued.

2. Preparing a worksheet for a merchandise company.

When you shop at the Apple Store, do you ever wonder how Apple controls its inventory? In Chapters 9 and 10 we discussed the subsidiary ledgers as well as entries for a merchandise company. Additional material provided an introduction to perpetual inventory. Now we shift our attention to recording adjustments and completing a worksheet for a merchandise company. Note that the appendix at the end of the chapter shows worksheets for a perpetual system.

● **LO1**

LEARNING UNIT 11-1 ADJUSTMENTS FOR MERCHANDISE INVENTORY AND UNEARNED RENT

The Merchandise Inventory account shows the goods that a merchandise company has available to sell to customers. Companies have several ways to keep track of the cost of goods sold (the total cost of the goods sold to customers) and the quantity of inventory on hand. In this chapter we discuss the periodic inventory system, in which the balance in inventory is updated only at the end of the accounting period.*
This system is used by companies, such as Art's Wholesale Clothing Company, that sell a variety of merchandise with low unit prices.

Assume that Art's Wholesale Clothing Company started the year with $19,000 worth of merchandise. This merchandise is called beginning merchandise inventory or simply beginning inventory. The balance of beginning inventory in the merchandise inventory account never changes during the accounting period. Any purchases of merchandise are recorded in a separate account, the Purchases account. During the accounting period $52,000 worth of such purchases were made and recorded in the Purchases accounts by Art's Wholesale.

At the end of the period, the company takes a physical count of the merchandise in stock; this amount is called ending merchandise inventory or simply ending inventory. It is calculated on an inventory sheet as shown in Figure 11.1. This $4,000 is the ending inventory for this period and will become the beginning inventory for the next period.

When the income statement is prepared, the cost of goods sold section requires two distinct numbers for inventory. The beginning inventory adds to the cost of goods sold, and the ending inventory is subtracted from the cost of goods sold. Remember that the two figures for beginning and ending inventory were calculated months apart. Thus, combining these amounts to come up with one inventory figure would not be accurate.

Note that in the calculation (in the margin) of cost of goods sold a title called Freight-In is shown.

Cost of goods sold Total cost of the goods which were sold to customers.

Periodic inventory system An inventory system that, at the *end of* each accounting period, calculates the cost of the unsold goods on hand by taking the cost of each unit times the number of units on hand of each product.

Beginning merchandise inventory (beginning inventory) The cost of goods on hand in a company to *begin* an accounting period.

Ending merchandise inventory (ending inventory) The cost of goods that remain unsold at the *end* of the accounting period. It is an asset on the new balance sheet.

Freight-In A cost of goods sold account that records the shipping cost to the buyer.

Cost of goods sold

    Beginning inventory

\+   Net purchases

\+   Freight-in

\−   Ending inventory

\=   Cost of goods sold

FIGURE 11.1
Ending Inventory Sheet

ART'S WHOLESALE CLOTHING COMPANY **ENDING INVENTORY SHEET** **AS OF DECEMBER 31, 201X**			
Amount	Explanation	Unit Cost	Total
20	Ladies' Jackets code 14-0	$50	$1,000
10	Men's Hats code 327	10	100
90	Men's Shirts code 423	10	900
100	Ladies' Blouses code 481	20	2,000
			$4,000
Counted by _____	Checked and priced by_____		

Perpetual inventory system An inventory system that keeps *continual track* of each type of inventory by recording units on hand at the beginning, units sold, and the current balance after each sale or purchase.

*For a discussion of the perpetual inventory system, see Chapter 10, Learning Unit 10-4.

Freight-In is a cost of goods sold account that records the shipping cost to the buyer. Note that net sales (gross sales less sales returns and allowances and sales discounts) less cost of goods sold equals gross profit. Subtracting operating expenses from gross profits equals net income.

Gross profit Net sales less cost of goods sold.

Adjustments A and B: Merchandise Inventory, $19,000 Adjusting the Merchandise Inventory account is a two-step process because we must record the beginning inventory and ending inventory amounts separately. The first step deals with beginning merchandise inventory.

Given: Beginning Inventory, $19,000 Our first adjustment removes the old outdated beginning inventory from the asset account (Merchandise Inventory) and transfers it to Income Summary. We do so by crediting Merchandise Inventory for $19,000 and debiting Income Summary for the same amount. This adjustment (A) is shown in the following T account form and on a transaction analysis chart.

COACHING TIP

Note that Income Summary has no normal balance of debit or credit.

Merchandise Inventory 114		Income Summary 313

Bal.	19,000	Adj.	19,000	Adj.	19,000

Adjustment (A)

Accounts Affected	Category	↑↓	Rules
Income Summary	—	—	Dr.
Merchandise Inventory	Asset	↓	Cr.

(This, as well as the following adjusting entries would be recorded first on the worksheet and then in the general journal.)

The second step is entering the amount of ending inventory ($4,000) in the Merchandise Inventory account. This step is done to record the up-to-date amount of goods on hand at the end of the period as an asset and to subtract this amount from the cost of goods sold (because we have not sold this inventory yet). To do so, we debit Merchandise Inventory for $4,000 and credit Income Summary for the same amount. This adjustment (B) is shown in the following T account form.

COACHING TIP

Second adjustment updates Inventory account with a new figure for ending inventory.

Merchandise Inventory 114			Income Summary 313		
Bal.	19,000	Adj.	19,000		
Adj.	4,000		Adj.	19,000	Adj. 4,000

Adjustment (B)

Let's look at how this process or method of recording merchandise inventory is reflected in the balance sheet and income statement (see Figure 11.2). Note that the $19,000 of beginning inventory is assumed sold and is shown on the income statement as part of the cost of goods sold. The ending inventory of $4,000 is assumed not to be sold and is subtracted from the cost of goods sold on the income statement. The ending inventory becomes next month's beginning inventory on the balance sheet. When the income statement is prepared, we will need a figure for beginning inventory as well as a figure for ending inventory. The goal of this adjustment is to wipe out the old inventory (a cost) and show the new inventory (not yet a cost).

COACHING TIP

Beginning inventory	$19,000
+ Net cost of purchases*	50,910
= Cost of goods available for sale	$69,910
− Ending inventory	4,000
= Cost of goods sold	$65,910

*$52,000 Purchases − $860 PD − $680 PRA + $450 Freight-In

Adjustment C: Unearned Rent Another new account we have not seen before is a liability called Unearned Rent or Rent Received in Advance. This account records the amount collected for rent before the service (renting the space) has been provided.

FIGURE 11.2
Recording Inventory on a
Partial Balance Sheet and
Income Statement

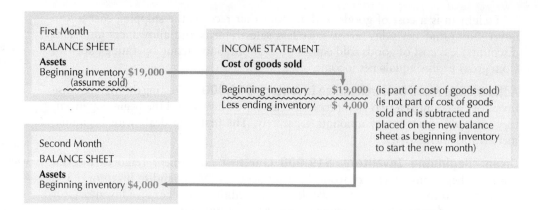

COACHING TIP

Received cash for renting space
in future:

| Cash | Asset | ↑ | Dr. |
| Unearned Rent | Liab. | ↑ | Cr. |

COACHING TIP

The adjustment when rental
income is earned:

| Unearned Rent | Liab. | ↓ | Dr. |
| Rental Income | Rev. | ↑ | Cr. |

Suppose Art's Wholesale Clothing Company is subletting a portion of its space to Jesse Company for $200 per month. Jesse Company sends Art's cash for $600 for three months' rent paid in advance. This unearned rent ($600) is a liability on the balance sheet because Art's Wholesale owes Jesse Company three months' worth of occupancy.

When Art's Wholesale fulfills a portion of the rental agreement—when Jesse Company has been in the space for a period of time—this liability account will be reduced and the Rental Income account will be increased. Rental income is another type of revenue for Art's Wholesale.

Remember that under accrual accounting, revenue is recognized when it is earned, whether payment is received then or not. Here, Art's Wholesale collected cash in advance for a service that it has not yet performed. A liability called Unearned Rent is the result. Art's Wholesale may have the cash, but the rental income is not recorded until it is earned. Examples of other types of unearned revenue besides unearned rent include prepaid subscriptions for magazines, legal fees collected before the work is performed, and prepaid insurance.

LEARNING UNIT 11-1 REVIEW

AT THIS POINT you should be able to do the following:

- Define the periodic system of inventory accounting.
- Explain why beginning and ending inventory are two separate figures in the cost of goods sold section on the income statement.
- Calculate net sales, cost of goods sold, gross profit, and net income.
- Show how to calculate a figure for ending merchandise inventory.
- Explain why Unearned Rent is a *liability* account.

Instant Replay ⚙ Self-Review Quiz 11-1

Given the following, prepare the two *adjusting* entries for Merchandise Inventory on 12/31/1X.

Merchandise Inventory, 1/1/1X	$ 8,000
Purchases	9,000
Purchases Returns and Allowances	3,000
Merchandise Inventory, 12/31/1X	4,000
Cost of Goods Sold	10,000
Unearned Magazine Subscriptions	8,000

Solution to Instant Replay: Self-Review Quiz 11-1

Dec.	31	Income Summary	8 0 0 0 00	
		Merchandise Inventory		8 0 0 0 00
	31	Merchandise Inventory	4 0 0 0 00	
		Income Summary		4 0 0 0 00

FIGURE 11.3
Merchandise Inventory Adjustments

COACHING TIP

Note that Unearned Magazine Subscriptions is a liability and is not involved in the adjustment for Merchandise Inventory.

LEARNING UNIT 11-2 COMPLETING THE WORKSHEET

● LO2

In this unit we prepare a worksheet for Art's Wholesale Clothing Company. For convenience, we reproduce the company's chart of accounts in Figure 11.4.

Figure 11.5 (p. 428) shows the trial balance that was prepared on December 31, 201X, from Art's Wholesale ledger. (Note that it is placed directly in the first two columns of the worksheet.)

In looking at the trial balance, we see many new titles that did not appear in the trial balance which we completed for a service company in Chapter 5. Let's look specifically at these new titles shown in Table 11.1.

Note the following:

- Mortgage Payable is a liability account that records the increases and decreases in the amount of debt owed on a mortgage. We discuss this account more in the next chapter, when financial reports are prepared.

Mortgage Payable A liability account showing amount owed on a mortgage.

FIGURE 11.4
Art's Wholesale Clothing Company Chart of Accounts

CHART OF ACCOUNTS

Assets 100–199
111 Cash
112 Petty Cash
113 Accounts Receivable
114 Merchandise Inventory
115 Supplies
116 Prepaid Insurance
121 Store Equipment
122 Accum. Depreciation, Store Equipment

Liabilities 200–299
211 Accounts Payable
212 Salaries Payable
213 Federal Income Tax Payable
214 FICA—Social Security Payable
215 FICA—Medicare Payable
216 State Income Tax Payable
217 SUTA Tax Payable
218 FUTA Tax Payable
219 Unearned Rent*
220 Mortgage Payable

Owner's Equity 300–399
311 Art Newner, Capital
312 Art Newner, Withdrawals
313 Income Summary

Revenue 400–499
411 Sales
412 Sales Returns and Allowances
413 Sales Discount
414 Rental Income

Cost of Goods Sold 500–599
511 Purchases
512 Purchases Discount
513 Purchases Returns and Allowances
514 Freight-In

Expenses 600–699
611 Salaries Expense
612 Payroll Tax Expense
613 Depreciation Expense, Store Equipment
614 Supplies Expense
615 Insurance Expense
616 Postage Expense
617 Miscellaneous Expense
618 Interest Expense
619 Cleaning Expense
620 Delivery Expense

*Although Unearned Rent is the only term under Liabilities not using payable, it is a liability.

FIGURE 11.5
Trial Balance Section of the
Worksheet

		Trial Balance	
		Dr.	Cr.
Cash		1 2 9 2 0 00	
Petty Cash		1 0 0 00	
Accounts Receivable		1 4 5 0 0 00	
Merchandise Inventory		1 9 0 0 0 00	
Supplies		8 0 0 00	
Prepaid Insurance		9 0 0 00	
Store Equipment		4 0 0 0 00	
Acc. Dep., Store Equipment			4 0 0 00
Accounts Payable			1 7 9 0 0 00
Federal Income Tax Payable			8 0 0 00
FICA—Soc. Sec. Payable			4 5 4 00
FICA—Medicare Payable			1 0 6 00
State Income Tax Payable			2 0 0 00
SUTA Tax Payable			1 0 8 00
FUTA Tax Payable			3 2 00
Unearned Rent			6 0 0 00
Mortgage Payable			2 3 2 0 00
Art Newner, Capital			7 9 0 5 00
Art Newner, Withdrawals		8 6 0 0 00	
Income Summary			
Sales			9 5 0 0 0 00
Sales Returns and Allowances		9 5 0 00	
Sales Discount		6 7 0 00	
Purchases		5 2 0 0 0 00	
Purchases Discount			8 6 0 00
Purchases Returns and Allowances			6 8 0 00
Freight-In		4 5 0 00	
Salaries Expense		1 1 7 0 0 00	
Payroll Tax Expense		4 2 0 00	
Postage Expense		2 5 00	
Miscellaneous Expense		3 0 00	
Interest Expense		3 0 0 00	
		1 2 7 3 6 5 00	1 2 7 3 6 5 00

Interest Expense The cost of borrowing money.

Unearned Revenue A liability account that records amount owed for goods or services in advance of delivery. The Cash account would record the receipt of cash.

- Interest Expense represents a nonoperating expense for Art's Wholesale and thus is categorized as Other Expense. We look at this expense in the next chapter.
- Unearned Revenue is a liability account that records receipt of payment for goods and services in advance of delivery. Unearned Rent is a particular example of this general type of account.

We already discussed the adjustments that make up the two-step process involved in adjusting Merchandise Inventory at the end of the accounting period. Now we show T accounts and transaction analysis charts for other adjustments that need to be made at this point for a merchandise firm, just as they must be made for a service company.

Adjustment C: Rental Income Earned by Art's Wholesale, $200 A month ago, Cash was increased by $600, as was a liability, Unearned Rent. Art's Wholesale received payment in advance but had not earned the rental income.

TABLE 11.1 Summary of New Account Titles

Title	Category	Account Reported on	Normal Balance	Temporary or Permanent
Petty Cash	Asset	Balance Sheet	Dr.	Permanent
Merchandise Inventory* (When sold)	Asset / Cost of Goods Sold	Balance Sheet from prior period / Income Statement of current period	Dr.	Permanent
Federal Income Tax Payable	Liability	Balance Sheet	Cr.	Permanent
FICA—Social Security Payable	Liability	Balance Sheet	Cr.	Permanent
FICA—Medicare Payable	Liability	Balance Sheet	Cr.	Permanent
State Income Tax Payable	Liability	Balance Sheet	Cr.	Permanent
SUTA Tax Payable	Liability	Balance Sheet	Cr.	Permanent
FUTA Tax Payable	Liability	Balance Sheet	Cr.	Permanent
Unearned Rent†	Liability	Balance Sheet	Cr.	Permanent
Mortgage Payable	Liability	Balance Sheet	Cr.	Permanent
Sales	Revenue	Income Statement	Cr.	Temporary
Sales Returns and Allowances	Contra-Revenue	Income Statement	Dr.	Temporary
Sales Discount	Contra-Revenue	Income Statement	Dr.	Temporary
Purchases§	Cost of Goods Sold	Income Statement	Dr.	Temporary
Purchases Discount	Contra-Cost of Goods Sold	Income Statement	Cr.	Temporary
Purchases Returns and Allowances	Contra-Cost of Goods Sold	Income Statement	Cr.	Temporary
Freight-In	Cost of Goods Sold	Income Statement	Dr.	Temporary
Payroll Tax Expense	Expense	Income Statement	Dr.	Temporary
Postage Expense	Expense	Income Statement	Dr.	Temporary
Interest Expense	Other Expense	Income Statement	Dr.	Temporary

*The ending inventory of current period is a contra-cost of goods sold on the income statement and will be an asset on the balance sheet for the next period.

†Referred to as Unearned Revenue.

§Note that the categories for Purchases and Freight-In are Cost of Goods Sold, whereas Purchases Discounts and Purchases Returns and Allowances are Contra-Cost of Goods Sold.

Now, because $200 has been earned, the liability is reduced and Rental Income can be recorded for the $200. This step is shown as follows:

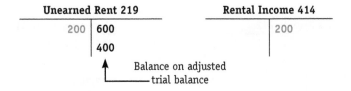

Unearned Rent	Liability	↓	Dr.	$200
Rental Income	Revenue	↑	Cr.	$200

Adjustment D: Supplies on Hand, $300 Because $500 worth of supplies were used up, Supplies Expense is increased, and the asset Supplies is decreased.

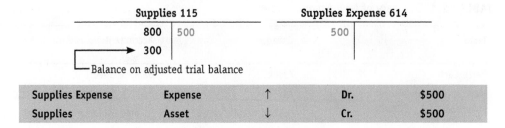

| Supplies Expense | Expense | ↑ | Dr. | $500 |
| Supplies | Asset | ↓ | Cr. | $500 |

Adjustment E: Insurance Expired, $300 Because insurance has expired by $300, Insurance Expense is increased by $300 and the asset Prepaid Insurance is decreased by $300.

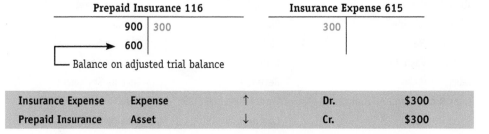

| Insurance Expense | Expense | ↑ | Dr. | $300 |
| Prepaid Insurance | Asset | ↓ | Cr. | $300 |

Adjustment F: Depreciation Expense, $50 When depreciation is taken, Depreciation Expense and Accumulated Depreciation are both increased by $50. Note that the cost of the store equipment remains the same.

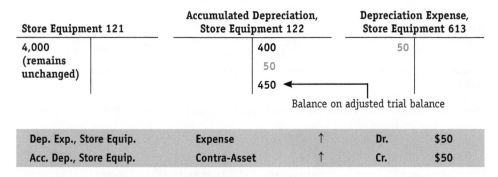

| Dep. Exp., Store Equip. | Expense | ↑ | Dr. | $50 |
| Acc. Dep., Store Equip. | Contra-Asset | ↑ | Cr. | $50 |

Adjustment G: Salaries Accrued, $600 The $600 in accrued salaries causes an increase in Salaries Expense and Salaries Payable.

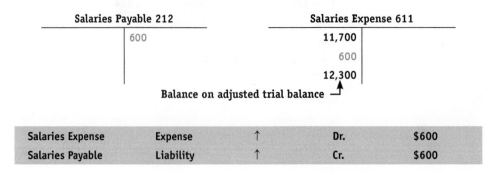

| Salaries Expense | Expense | ↑ | Dr. | $600 |
| Salaries Payable | Liability | ↑ | Cr. | $600 |

Figure 11.6 shows the worksheet with the adjustments and adjusted trial balance columns filled out. Note that the adjustment numbers in the Income Summary from beginning and ending inventory are also carried over to the adjusted trial balance and are not combined.

FIGURE 11.6
Worksheet with Three Columns Filled Out

	Trial Balance		Adjustments		Adjusted Trial Balance	
	Dr.	Cr.	Dr.	Cr.	Dr.	Cr.
Cash	12 92 00 0				12 92 00 0	
Petty Cash	1 00 00				1 00 00	
Accounts Receivable	14 50 00 0		(B)	(A)	14 50 00 0	
Merchandise Inventory	19 00 00 0		4 00 00 0	19 00 00 0	4 00 00 0	
Supplies	8 00 00			(D) 5 00 00	3 00 00	
Prepaid Insurance	9 00 00			(E) 3 00 00	6 00 00	
Store Equipment	4 00 00 0				4 00 00 0	
Acc. Dep., Store Equipment		4 00 00		(F) 5 00 0		4 50 00
Accounts Payable		17 90 00 0				17 90 00 0
Federal Income Tax Payable		8 00 00				8 00 00
FICA—Soc. Sec. Payable		4 54 00				4 54 00
FICA—Medicare Payable		1 06 00				1 06 00
State Income Tax Payable		2 00 00				2 00 00
SUTA Tax Payable		1 08 00				1 08 00
FUTA Tax Payable		3 20 0				3 20 0
Unearned Rent		6 00 00	(C) 2 00 00			4 00 00
Mortgage Payable		2 32 00 0				2 32 00 0
Art Newner, Capital		79 05 00				79 05 00
Art Newner, Withdrawals	8 60 00 0		(A)	(B)	8 60 00 0	
Income Summary			19 00 00 0	4 00 00 0	19 00 00 0	4 00 00 0
Sales		95 00 00 0				95 00 00 0
Sales Returns and Allowances	9 50 00				9 50 00	
Sales Discount	6 70 00				6 70 00	
Purchases	52 00 00 0				52 00 00 0	
Purchases Discount		8 60 00				8 60 00
Purchases Returns and Allowances		6 80 00				6 80 00
Freight-In	4 50 00				4 50 00	
Salaries Expense	11 70 00 0		(G) 6 00 00		12 30 00 0	
Payroll Tax Expense	4 20 00				4 20 00	
Postage Expense	2 50 0				2 50 0	
Miscellaneous Expense	3 00 0				3 00 0	
Interest Expense	3 00 00				3 00 00	
	127 36 5 00	127 36 5 00				
Rental Income				(C) 2 00 00		2 00 00
Supplies Expense			(D) 5 00 00		5 00 00	
Insurance Expense			(E) 3 00 00		3 00 00	
Depreciation Expense, Store Equip.			(F) 5 00 0		5 00 0	
Salaries Payable				(G) 6 00 00		6 00 00
			24 65 0 00	24 65 0 00	132 01 5 00	132 01 5 00

The next step in completing the worksheet is to fill out the income statement columns from the adjusted trial balance, as shown in Figure 11.7.

COACHING TIP

Remember: We do not combine the $19,000 and $4,000 in Income Summary. When we prepare the cost of goods sold section for the formal income statement, we will need both a beginning and an ending figure for inventory.

FIGURE 11.7
Income Statement Section of the Worksheet

$19,000 of beginning inventory is assumed sold during the period and thus is part of the cost of goods sold. By placing it in the debit column of Income Summary we increase the cost of goods sold.

$4,000 is the cost of ending inventory at the end of the period. It is assumed to be unsold and therefore is not part of the cost of goods sold. By placing it in the credit column of Income Summary, we reduce the cost of goods sold.

$95,000 is the credit balance of Sales. The Sales Returns and Allowances, $950, and Sales Discount, $670, are placed on the debit side, which represents a reduction to total sales:
(Cr.) Sales
(Dr.) Less: Sales Returns and Allowances
(Dr.) Less: Sales Discount

The Purchases account, $52,000, is on the debit side, reflecting an increase in costs due to purchasing additional merchandise. The Purchases Discount, $860, and Purchases Returns and Allowances, $680, are on the credit side, which reduces cost of purchases:
(Dr.) Purchases
(Cr.) Less: Purchases Returns and Allowances
(Cr.) Less: Purchases Discount

Freight-In adds to the cost of goods sold.

Rental Income, which falls under the category "other income" for Art's Wholesale, is increased by $200, because the first month's rental agreement has been fulfilled.

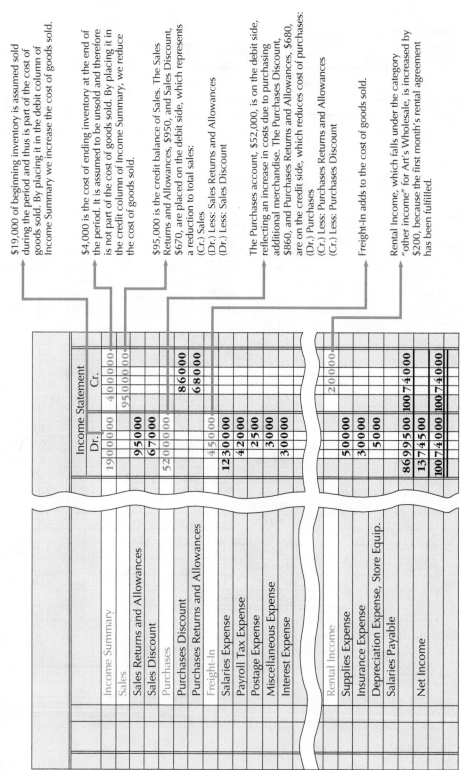

	Income Statement	
	Dr.	Cr.
Income Summary	19 000 00	4 000 00
Sales		95 000 00
Sales Returns and Allowances	9 50 00	
Sales Discount	6 70 00	
Purchases	52 000 00	
Purchases Discount		8 60 00
Purchases Returns and Allowances		6 80 00
Freight-In	4 50 00	
Salaries Expense	12 3 00 00	
Payroll Tax Expense	4 20 00	
Postage Expense	25 00	
Miscellaneous Expense	30 00	
Interest Expense	30 00	
Rental Income		2 00 00
Supplies Expense	5 00 00	
Insurance Expense	3 00 00	
Depreciation Expense, Store Equip.	5 00 00	
Salaries Payable		
	86 9 95 00	100 7 40 00
Net Income	13 7 45 00	
	100 7 40 00	100 7 40 00

The next step in completing the worksheet is to fill out the balance sheet columns (Figure 11.8). Note how ending inventory is carried over to the balance sheet from the adjusted trial balance column. Take time also to look at the placement of the payroll tax liabilities as well as Unearned Rent on the worksheet.

Figure 11.9 (p. 434) is the completed worksheet.

FIGURE 11.8
Balance Sheet Section of the Worksheet

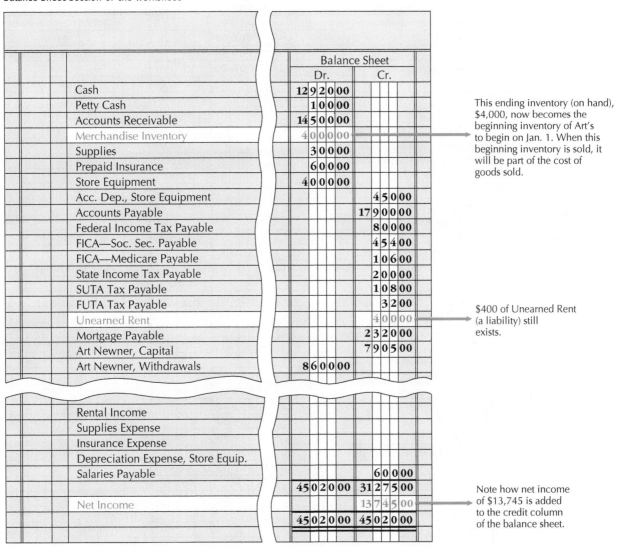

	Balance Sheet	
	Dr.	Cr.
Cash	12 9 2 0 00	
Petty Cash	1 0 0 00	
Accounts Receivable	14 5 0 0 00	
Merchandise Inventory	4 0 0 0 00	
Supplies	3 0 0 00	
Prepaid Insurance	6 0 0 00	
Store Equipment	4 0 0 0 00	
Acc. Dep., Store Equipment		4 5 0 00
Accounts Payable		17 9 0 0 00
Federal Income Tax Payable		8 0 0 00
FICA—Soc. Sec. Payable		4 5 4 00
FICA—Medicare Payable		1 0 6 00
State Income Tax Payable		2 0 0 00
SUTA Tax Payable		1 0 8 00
FUTA Tax Payable		3 2 00
Unearned Rent		4 0 0 00
Mortgage Payable		2 3 2 0 00
Art Newner, Capital		7 9 0 5 00
Art Newner, Withdrawals	8 6 0 0 00	

This ending inventory (on hand), $4,000, now becomes the beginning inventory of Art's to begin on Jan. 1. When this beginning inventory is sold, it will be part of the cost of goods sold.

$400 of Unearned Rent (a liability) still exists.

Rental Income		
Supplies Expense		
Insurance Expense		
Depreciation Expense, Store Equip.		
Salaries Payable		6 0 0 00
	45 0 2 0 00	31 2 7 5 00
Net Income		13 7 4 5 00
	45 0 2 0 00	45 0 2 0 00

Note how net income of $13,745 is added to the credit column of the balance sheet.

FIGURE 11.9
Completed Worksheet

	Trial Balance		Adjustments	
	Dr.	Cr.	Dr.	Cr.
Cash	1292000			
Petty Cash	10000			
Accounts Receivable	1450000			
Merchandise Inventory	1900000		(B)400000	(A)1900000
Supplies	80000			(D)50000
Prepaid Insurance	90000			(E)30000
Store Equipment	400000			
Acc. Dep., Store Equipment		40000		(F)5000
Accounts Payable		1790000		
Federal Income Tax Payable		80000		
FICA—Social Security Payable		45400		
FICA—Medicare Payable		10600		
State Income Tax Payable		20000		
SUTA Tax Payable		10800		
FUTA Tax Payable		3200		
Unearned Rent		60000	(C)20000	
Mortgage Payable		232000		
Art Newner, Capital		790500		
Art Newner, Withdrawals	860000			
Income Summary			(A)1900000	(B)400000
Sales		950000		
Sales Returns and Allowances	95000			
Sales Discount	67000			
Purchases	5200000			
Purchases Discount		86000		
Purchases Returns and Allowances		68000		
Freight-In	45000			
Salaries Expense	1170000		(G)60000	
Payroll Tax Expense	42000			
Postage Expense	2500			
Miscellaneous Expense	3000			
Interest Expense	3000			
	12736500	12736500		
Rental Income				(C)20000
Supplies Expense			(D)50000	
Insurance Expense			(E)30000	
Depreciation Expense, Store Equip.			(F)5000	
Salaries Payable				(G)60000
			2465000	2465000
Net Income				

WORKSHEET
FOR YEAR ENDED DECEMBER 31, 201X

FIGURE 11.9
(continued)

Adjusted Trial Bal. Dr.	Adjusted Trial Bal. Cr.	Income Statement Dr.	Income Statement Cr.	Balance Sheet Dr.	Balance Sheet Cr.
1292000				1292000	
10000				10000	
1450000				1450000	
400000				400000	
30000				30000	
60000				60000	
400000				400000	
	45000				45000
	1790000				1790000
	80000				80000
	45400				45400
	10600				10600
	20000				20000
	10800				10800
	3200				3200
	40000				40000
	232000				232000
	790500				790500
860000				860000	
1900000	400000	1900000	400000		
	9500000		9500000		
95000		95000			
67000		67000			
5200000		5200000			
	86000		86000		
	68000		68000		
45000		45000			
1230000		1230000			
42000		42000			
2500		2500			
3000		3000			
30000		30000			
	20000		20000		
50000		50000			
30000		30000			
5000		5000			
	60000				60000
13201500	13201500	8699500	10074000	4502000	3127500
		1374500			1374500
		10074000	10074000	4502000	4502000

LEARNING UNIT 11-2 REVIEW

AT THIS POINT you should be able to do the following:

- Complete adjustments for a merchandise company.
- Complete a worksheet.

Instant Replay ○ Self-Review Quiz 11-2

From the trial balance shown in Figure 11.10, complete a worksheet for Ray Company. Additional data include the following: (A and B) On December 31, 201X, ending inventory was calculated at $200; (C) Storage Fees Now Earned, $516; (D) Prepaid Rent Expired, $100; (E) Depreciation Expense, Office Equipment, $60; (F) Salaries Accrued, $200.

FIGURE 11.10
Trial Balance of Ray Company

Account Title	Trial Balance Dr.	Trial Balance Cr.
Cash	2 4 8 6 00	
Merchandise Inventory	8 2 4 00	
Prepaid Rent	1 1 5 2 00	
Prepaid Insurance	6 0 00	
Office Equipment	2 1 6 0 00	
Accumulated Depreciation, Office Equipment		5 6 0 00
Unearned Storage Fees		2 5 1 6 00
Accounts Payable		1 0 0 00
B. Ray, Capital		1 9 3 2 00
Income Summary	—	—
Sales		11 0 4 0 00
Sales Returns and Allowances	5 4 6 00	
Sales Discount	2 1 6 00	
Purchases	5 2 5 6 00	
Purchases Returns and Allowances		1 6 8 00
Purchases Discount		1 0 2 00
Salaries Expense	2 0 1 6 00	
Insurance Expense	1 3 9 2 00	
Utilities Expense	9 6 00	
Plumbing Expense	2 1 4 00	
	16 4 1 8 00	16 4 1 8 00

Solution to Instant Replay: Self-Review Quiz 11-2

The solution is shown in Figure 11.11.

COACHING TIP

The ending inventory of $200 becomes next month's beginning inventory.

FIGURE 11.11
Worksheet for Ray Company

RAY COMPANY
WORKSHEET
FOR YEAR ENDED DECEMBER 31, 201X

	Trial Balance Dr.	Trial Balance Cr.	Adjustments Dr.	Adjustments Cr.	Adjusted Trial Balance Dr.	Adjusted Trial Balance Cr.	Income Statement Dr.	Income Statement Cr.	Balance Sheet Dr.	Balance Sheet Cr.
Cash	248600				248600				248600	
Merchandise Inventory	82400		(B) 20000	(A) 82400	20000				20000	
Prepaid Rent	115200			(D) 10000	105200				105200	
Prepaid Insurance	6000				6000				6000	
Office Equipment	216000				216000				216000	
Acc. Dep., Office Equipment		56000		(E) 6000		62000				62000
Unearned Storage Fees		251600	(C) 51600			200000				200000
Accounts Payable		10000				10000				10000
B. Ray, Capital		193200				193200				193200
Income Summary			(A) 82400	(B) 20000	82400	20000	82400	20000		
Sales		1104000				1104000		1104000		
Sales Returns and Allowances	54600				54600		54600			
Sales Discount	21600				21600		21600			
Purchases	525600				525600		525600			
Purchases Returns and Allowances		16800				16800		16800		
Purchases Discount		10200				10200		10200		
Salaries Expense	201600		(F) 20000		221600		221600			
Insurance Expense	139200				139200		139200			
Utilities Expense	9600				9600		9600			
Plumbing Expense	21400				21400		21400			
	1641800	1641800								
Storage Fees Earned				(C) 51600		51600		51600		
Rent Expense			(D) 10000		10000		10000			
Depreciation Expense, Equipment			(E) 6000		6000		6000			
Salaries Payable				(F) 20000		20000				20000
			190000	190000	1687800	1687800	1092000	1202600	595800	485200
Net Income							110600			110600
							1202600	1202600	595800	595800

BLUEPRINT: A WORKSHEET FOR A MERCHANDISE COMPANY

Account Titles	Adjustments Dr.	Adjustments Cr.	Adjusted Trial Balance Dr.	Adjusted Trial Balance Cr.	Income Statement Dr.	Income Statement Cr.	Balance Sheet Dr.	Balance Sheet Cr.
Cash			X				X	
Petty Cash			X				X	
Accounts Receivable			X				X	
Merchandise Inventory	X-E	X-B	X-E				X-E	
Supplies			X				X	
Equipment			X				X	
Acc. Dep., Store Equipment				X				X
Accounts Payable				X				X
Federal Income Tax Payable				X				X
FICA—Social Security Payable				X				X
FICA—Medicare Payable				X				X
State Income Tax Payable				X				X
SUTA Tax Payable				X				X
FUTA Tax Payable				X				X
Unearned Sales				X				X
Mortgage Payable				X				X
A. Flynn, Capital				X				X
A. Flynn, Withdrawals			X				X	
Income Summary*	X-B	X-E	X-B	X-E	X-B	X-E		
Sales				X		X		
Sales Returns and Allow.			X		X			
Sales Discount			X		X			
Purchases			X		X			
Purchases Ret. and Allow.				X		X		
Purchases Discount				X		X		
Freight-In			X		X			
Salaries Expense			X		X			
Payroll Tax Expense			X		X			
Insurance Expense			X		X			
Depreciation Expense			X		X			
Salaries Payable				X				X
Rental Income				X		X		

* Note that the figures for beginning (X-B) and ending inventory (X-E) are never combined on the Income Summary line of the worksheet. When the formal income statement is prepared, two distinct figures for inventory will be used to explain and calculate cost of goods sold. Beginning inventory adds to cost of goods sold; ending inventory reduces cost of goods sold.

ACCOUNTING COACH

The following Coaching Tips are from Learning Units 11-1 and 11-2. Take the Pre-Game Checkup and use the Check Your Score at the bottom of the page to see how you are doing. The Accounting Coach provides tips before each Checkup to help you avoid common accounting errors.

LU 11-1 Adjustments for Merchandise Inventory and Unearned Rent

Pre-Game Tips: The purpose of the adjustment for Merchandise Inventory is to wipe out the beginning inventory and bring on the ending inventory. We assume that the beginning inventory is sold and is part of the cost of goods sold. The ending inventory is not sold and is not part of the cost of goods sold. The ending inventory becomes the new figure for beginning inventory. Unearned Rent is not a revenue account. It is a liability. Revenue will only be recognized when it is earned.

Pre-Game Checkup
Answer true or false to the following statements.

1. Freight-In is a cost of goods sold account.
2. Beginning inventory is subtracted from cost of goods sold.
3. Income Summary is not used to adjust Merchandise Inventory.
4. When unearned rent is earned the liability will go up.
5. The ending inventory of one period can never be the new inventory of the next period.

LU 11-2 Completing the Worksheet

Pre-Game Tips: Before you complete the worksheet, make sure you review this table:

Sales	Revenue	Credit Balance	Income Statement
SRA	Contra Revenue	Debit Balance	Income Statement
Unearned	Liability	Credit Balance	Balance Sheet
Purchases	Cost	Debit Balance	Income Statement
PRA	Contra Cost	Credit Balance	Income Statement

Pre-Game Checkup
Answer true or false to the following statements.

1. Ending inventory goes in the credit column of the balance sheet section of the worksheet.
2. Freight-In goes in the debit column of the balance sheet section of the worksheet.
3. Unearned Rent goes in the debit column of the balance sheet section of the worksheet.
4. Accumulated Depreciation goes in the credit column of the balance sheet section of the worksheet.
5. Income Summary for the beginning inventory goes in the credit column of the income statement.

CHECK YOUR SCORE: Answers to the Pre-Game Checkup

LU 11-1
1. True.
2. False—Beginning inventory is added to cost of goods sold.
3. False—Income Summary is used to adjust Merchandise Inventory.
4. False—When unearned rent is earned the liability will go down.
5. False—The ending inventory of one period always becomes new inventory of the next period.

LU 11-2
1. False—Ending inventory goes in the debit column of the balance sheet section of the worksheet.
2. True—Freight-In goes in the debit column of the income statement.
3. False—Unearned Rent goes in the credit column of the balance sheet section of the worksheet.
4. True.
5. True.

Chapter Summary

MyAccountingLab

Here are all the key concepts and equations to help you understand the concepts of this chapter and prepare you for your exam. After completing this review, go to MyAccountingLab for more practice opportunities.

Concepts You Should Know	Key Terms
L01 Figuring adjustments for merchandise inventory, unearned rent, supplies used, insurance expired, depreciation expense, and salaries accrued. 1. The periodic inventory system updates the record of goods on hand only at the end of the accounting period. 2. In the periodic inventory system, additional purchases of merchandise during the accounting period will be recorded in the Purchases account. The amount in beginning inventory will remain unchanged during the accounting period. At the end of the period, a new figure for ending inventory will be calculated. 3. Beginning inventory from the start of the accounting period becomes part of the cost of goods sold, whereas ending inventory is a reduction to cost of goods sold. 4. The perpetual inventory system keeps a continuous record of inventory. 5. Net sales less cost of goods sold equals gross profit. Gross profit less operating expenses equals net income. 6. Unearned Revenue is a liability account that accumulates revenue that has not been earned yet, although the cash has been received. It represents a liability to the seller until the service or product is performed or delivered.	Beginning merchandise inventory (beginning inventory) (p. 424) Cost of goods sold (p. 424) Ending merchandise inventory (ending inventory) (p. 424) Freight-In (p. 424) Gross profit (p. 425) Periodic inventory system (p. 424) Perpetual inventory system (p. 424)
L02 Preparing a worksheet for a merchandise company. 1. Both the beginning and ending figures for merchandise inventory are shown in the Merchandise Inventory account and Income Summary. The balance sheet debit column shows the ending figure for inventory. 2. Unearned Revenue is a liability on the balance sheet credit column.	Interest Expense (p. 428) Mortgage Payable (p. 427) Unearned Revenue (p. 428)

Discussion Questions and Critical Thinking/Ethical Case

1. What is the function of the Purchases account?

2. Explain why Unearned Revenue is a liability account.

3. In a periodic system of inventory, the balance of beginning inventory will remain unchanged during the period. True or false?

4. What is the purpose of an inventory sheet?

5. Why do many Unearned Revenue accounts have to be adjusted?

6. Explain why figures for beginning and ending inventory are not combined on the Income Summary line of the worksheet.

7. Jim Heary is the custodian of petty cash. Jim, who is short of personal cash, decided to pay his home electrical and phone bills from petty cash. He plans to pay it back next month. Do you feel Jim should do so? You make the call. Write down your specific recommendations to Jim.

Concept Checks

Adjustment for Merchandise Inventory

1. Given the following, journalize the adjusting entries for Merchandise Inventory. Note that ending inventory has a balance of $21,000.

Merchandise Inventory 114		Income Summary 313	
54,000			

Adjustment for Unearned Fees

2. **a.** Given the following, journalize the adjusting entry. By December 31, $230 of the unearned dog walking fees were earned.

Unearned Dog Walking Fees 225		Earned Dog Walking Fees 441	
	890 12/1/1X		5,100 12/1/1X

   b. What is the category of unearned dog walking fees?

Worksheet

3. Match the following:
   1. Located on the Income Statement debit column of the worksheet.
   2. Located on the Income Statement credit column of the worksheet.
   3. Located on the Balance Sheet debit column of the worksheet.
   4. Located on the Balance Sheet credit column of the worksheet.

   _____ **a.** Beginning Merchandise Inventory (amount)
   _____ **b.** Sales Returns and Allowance
   _____ **c.** Salaries Payable
   _____ **d.** Sales
   _____ **e.** Accounts Receivable

MyAccountingLab

● **LO1** *(10 MIN)*

● **LO1** *(15 MIN)*

● **LO2** *(10 MIN)*

● L01 *(10 MIN)*   **Merchandise Inventory Adjustment**

4.   Given beginning merchandise inventory of $1,500 and ending merchandise inventory of $45, what would be the adjusting entries?

● L02 *(10 MIN)*   **Income Summary on the Worksheet**

5.   Given a figure of beginning inventory of $440 and a $920 figure for ending inventory, place these numbers on the Income Summary line of this partial worksheet.

	Adj.		ATB		Income Statement	
	Dr.	Cr.	Dr.	Cr.	Dr.	Cr.
Income Summary	A	B	C	D	E	F

Exercises

Set A

● L01 *(10 MIN)*   **11A-1.** Indicate the normal balance and category of each of the following accounts:

a. Unearned Revenue
b. Merchandise Inventory (beginning of period)
c. Freight-In
d. Payroll Tax Expense
e. Purchases Discount
f. Sales Discount
g. FICA—Social Security Payable
h. Purchases Returns and Allowances

● L01 *(15 MIN)*   **11A-2.** From the following, calculate (a) net sales, (b) cost of goods sold, (c) gross profit, and (d) net income: Sales, $21,800; Sales Discount, $500; Sales Returns and Allowances, $270; Beginning Inventory, $660; Net Purchases, $13,100; Ending Inventory, $560; Operating Expenses, $3,700.

● L01 *(10 MIN)*   **11A-3.** Autumn Co. had the following balances on December 31, 201X:

Cash		Unearned Janitorial Service
2,600		590

Janitorial Service
7,700

The accountant for Autumn has asked you to make an adjustment because $390 of janitorial services has just been performed for customers who had paid for two months. Construct a transaction analysis chart.

●● L01, 2 *(15 MIN)*   **11A-4.** Dixon Co. purchased merchandise costing $430,000. Calculate the cost of goods sold under the following situations:

a. Beginning inventory $37,000 and no ending inventory
b. Beginning inventory $46,000 and a $62,000 ending inventory
c. No beginning inventory and a $31,000 ending inventory

● L02 *(20 MIN)*   **11A-5.** Prepare a worksheet for Morin Co. from the following information using Figure 11.12:

a/b.	Merchandise Inventory, ending	9
c.	Store Supplies on hand	2
d.	Depreciation on Store Equipment	3
e.	Accrued Salaries	2

FIGURE 11.12
Trial Balance for Morin Co.

MORIN CO. TRIAL BALANCE DECEMBER 31, 201X	Dr.	Cr.
Cash	7 00	
Accounts Receivable	2 00	
Merchandise Inventory	1 3 00	
Store Supplies	8 00	
Store Equipment	2 0 00	
Accumulated Depreciation, Store Equipment		8 00
Accounts Payable		7 00
J. Morin, Capital		3 8 00
Income Summary	—	—
Sales		4 4 00
Sales Returns and Allowances	6 00	
Purchases	1 9 00	
Purchases Discount		5 00
Freight-In	2 00	
Salaries Expense	1 3 00	
Advertising Expense	1 2 00	
Totals	1 0 2 00	1 0 2 00

Set B

11B-1. Indicate the normal balance and category of each of the following accounts: **L01** *(10 MIN)*

  a. Salaries Payable
  b. Merchandise Inventory (beginning of period)
  c. Freight-In
  d. Payroll Tax Expense
  e. Purchases Returns and Allowances
  f. Sales Returns and Allowance
  g. FICA—Social Security Payable
  h. Purchases Discounts

11B-2. From the following, calculate (a) net sales, (b) cost of goods sold, (c) gross   **L01** *(15 MIN)*
profit, and (d) net income: Sales, $22,700; Sales Discount, $400; Sales
Returns and Allowances, $370; Beginning Inventory, $760; Net Purchases,
$12,100; Ending Inventory, $460; Operating Expenses, $2,700.

11B-3. Bates Co. had the following balances on December 31, 201X: **L01** *(10 MIN)*

The accountant for Bates has asked you to make an adjustment because
$430 of janitorial services has just been performed for customers who had
paid for two months. Construct a transaction analysis chart.

Cash		Unearned Janitorial Service	
1,800			620
Janitorial Service			
	7,500		

11B-4. Edmond Co. purchased merchandise costing $350,000. Calculate the cost of   **L01, 2** *(15 MIN)*
goods sold under the following situations:
  a. Beginning inventory $37,000 and no ending inventory
  b. Beginning inventory $49,000 and a $64,000 ending inventory
  c. No beginning inventory and a $25,000 ending inventory

● **LO2** *(20 MIN)*

11B-5. Prepare a worksheet for Mitchell Co. from the following information using Figure 11.13.

FIGURE 11.13
Trial Balance for Mitchell Co.

MITCHELL CO. TRIAL BALANCE DECEMBER 31, 201X	Dr.	Cr.
Cash	6 00	
Accounts Receivable	4 00	
Merchandise Inventory	1 1 00	
Store Supplies	9 00	
Store Equipment	1 8 00	
Accumulated Depreciation, Store Equipment		6 00
Accounts Payable		5 00
J. Mitchell, Capital		3 2 00
Income Summary	—	—
Sales		6 6 00
Sales Returns and Allowances	1 2 00	
Purchases	2 1 00	
Purchases Discount		2 00
Freight-In	4 00	
Salaries Expense	1 1 00	
Advertising Expense	1 5 00	
Totals	1 1 1 00	1 1 1 00

a/b. Merchandise Inventory, ending   12
 c. Store Supplies on hand   2
 d. Depreciation on Store Equipment   6
 e. Accrued Salaries   1

MyAccountingLab   ## Problems

Set A

You can also use the foldout worksheets at the end of the working papers that accompany this text.

● **LO1** *(30 MIN)*

Check Figure:
Net income $2,103

11A-1. Based on the following accounts, calculate the following:

a. Net sales
b. Cost of goods sold
c. Gross profit
d. Net income

Accounts Payable	$ 5,900
Operating Expenses	2,100
Kiln Co., Capital	19,800
Purchases	1,700
Freight-In	91
Ending Merchandise Inventory, Dec. 31, 201X	61
Sales	6,300
Accounts Receivable	540
Cash	790
Purchases Discount	54
Sales Returns and Allowances	320
Beg. Merchandise Inventory, Jan. 1, 201X	82
Purchases Returns and Allowances	74
Sales Discount	93

11A-2 From the trial balance in Figure 11.14, complete a worksheet for Jack's Hardware. Assume the following:

a/b. Ending inventory on December 31 is calculated at $320.
  c. Insurance expired, $150.
  d. Depreciation on store equipment, $50.
  e. Accrued wages, $110.

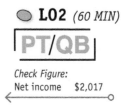

L02 *(60 MIN)*

PT/QB

Check Figure:
Net income $2,017

FIGURE 11.14
Trial Balance for Jack's Hardware

JACK'S HARDWARE TRIAL BALANCE DECEMBER 31, 201X		
	Dr.	Cr.
Cash	7 8 6 00	
Accounts Receivable	1 1 5 2 00	
Merchandise Inventory	6 5 0 00	
Prepaid Insurance	7 2 0 00	
Store Equipment	2 1 7 0 00	
Accumulated Depreciation, Store Equipment		6 4 0 00
Accounts Payable		5 2 5 00
Jack Spool, Capital		1 6 5 6 00
Income Summary	—	—
Hardware Sales		11 1 3 4 00
Hardware Sales Returns and Allowances	5 2 4 00	
Hardware Sales Discount	2 4 0 00	
Purchases	5 2 4 4 00	
Purchases Discount		1 6 0 00
Purchases Returns and Allowances		1 2 6 00
Wages Expense	1 7 5 6 00	
Rent Expense	7 8 4 00	
Telephone Expense	1 0 7 00	
Miscellaneous Expense	1 0 8 00	
Total	14 2 4 1 00	14 2 4 1 00

LO2 *(60 MIN)*

Check Figure:
Net income $5,175

11A-3. The owner of Sonata Company asked you to prepare a worksheet from the trial balance in Figure 11.15.

Additional Data

a/b. Ending merchandise inventory on December 31, $1,845.

c. Office supplies used up, $240.

d. Rent expired, $235.

e. Depreciation expense on office equipment, $575.

f. Office salaries earned but not paid, $320.

FIGURE 11.15
Trial Balance for Sonata Company

SONATA COMPANY TRIAL BALANCE DECEMBER 31, 201X	Dr.	Cr.
Cash	5 2 5 4 00	
Petty Cash	2 0 0 00	
Accounts Receivable	2 4 0 9 00	
Beginning Merchandise Inventory, Jan. 1	4 9 7 2 00	
Prepaid Rent	6 4 9 00	
Office Supplies	9 6 6 00	
Office Equipment	9 1 8 0 00	
Accumulated Depreciation, Office Equipment		7 6 0 0 00
Accounts Payable		5 9 8 2 00
K. Sonata, Capital		5 4 7 6 00
K. Sonata, Withdrawals	5 1 0 0 00	
Income Summary	—	—
Sales		5 2 2 1 8 00
Sales Returns and Allowances	1 0 5 00	
Sales Discount	2 2 0 0 00	
Purchases	2 9 4 2 8 00	
Purchases Discount		1 4 00
Purchases Returns and Allowances		3 4 8 00
Office Salaries Expense	7 3 0 4 00	
Insurance Expense	2 4 7 5 00	
Advertising Expense	8 0 0 00	
Utilities Expense	5 9 6 00	
Total	7 1 6 3 8 00	7 1 6 3 8 00

LO1, 2 *(60 MIN)*

Check Figure:
Net loss $3,574

11A-4. From the trial balance in Figure 11.16 (p. 447) and additional data, complete the worksheet for John's Wholesale Clothing Company.

Additional Data

a/b. Ending merchandise inventory on December 31, $5,500.

c. Supplies on hand, $450.

d. Insurance expired, $450.

e. Depreciation on store equipment, $450.

f. Storage fees earned, $156.

JOHN'S WHOLESALE CLOTHING COMPANY TRIAL BALANCE DECEMBER 31, 201X	Dr.	Cr.
Cash	4 3 5 0 00	
Petty Cash	3 0 0 00	
Accounts Receivable	7 1 0 0 00	
Merchandise Inventory	9 1 0 0 00	
Supplies	9 0 0 00	
Prepaid Insurance	8 9 0 00	
Store Equipment	2 8 0 0 00	
Acc. Dep., Store Equipment		1 2 0 0 00
Accounts Payable		11 0 1 5 00
Federal Income Tax Payable		1 1 0 0 00
FICA—Social Security Payable		4 6 2 00
FICA—Medicare Payable		1 3 0 00
State Income Tax Payable		1 5 0 00
SUTA Tax Payable		1 0 0 00
FUTA Tax Payable		3 6 00
Unearned Storage Fees		2 7 5 00
John Win, Capital		14 0 0 0 00
John Win, Withdrawals	4 2 0 0 00	
Income Summary	—	—
Sales		45 9 0 0 00
Sales Returns and Allowances	1 5 0 0 00	
Sales Discount	1 4 0 5 00	
Purchases	27 0 0 0 00	
Purchases Discount		3 5 0 00
Purchases Returns and Allowances		3 0 0 00
Freight-In	1 5 0 00	
Salaries Expense	14 0 0 0 00	
Payroll Tax Expense	4 1 0 00	
Interest Expense	8 6 5 00	
Total	74 9 7 0 00	74 9 7 0 00

FIGURE 11.16
Trial Balance for John's Wholesale Clothing Company

Set B

11B-1. Based on the following accounts, calculate (a) net sales, (b) cost of goods sold, (c) gross profit, and (d) net income.

MyAccountingLab

● **L01** *(30 MIN)*

Accounts Payable	$ 6,400
Operating Expenses	1,500
Market Co., Capital	19,200
Purchases	1,300
Freight-In	89
Ending Merchandise Inventory, Dec. 31, 201X	65
Sales	5,500
Accounts Receivable	540
Cash	770
Purchases Discounts	50
Sales Returns and Allowances	290
Beginning Merchandise Inventory, Jan 1, 201X	82
Purchases Returns and Allowances	69
Sales Discount	85

Check Figure:
Net income $2,338

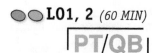

LO1, 2 *(60 MIN)*

Check Figure:
Net income $2,052

FIGURE 11.17
Trial Balance for Jabar's Hardware

11B-2. From the trial balance in Figure 11.17 as well as additional data, complete a worksheet for Jabar's Hardware.

Additional Data

a/b. Ending inventory on December 31 is calculated at $300.
  c. Insurance expired, $170.
  d. Depreciation on store equipment, $70.
  e. Accrued wages, $80.

JABAR'S HARDWARE TRIAL BALANCE DECEMBER 31, 201X	Dr.	Cr.
Cash	791 00	
Accounts Receivable	1177 00	
Merchandise Inventory	575 00	
Prepaid Insurance	675 00	
Store Equipment	2190 00	
Accumulated Depreciation, Store Equipment		660 00
Accounts Payable		493 00
Jabar Spool, Capital		1608 00
Income Summary	—	—
Hardware Sales		11052 00
Hardware Sales Returns and Allowances	568 00	
Hardware Sales Discount	216 00	
Purchases	5232 00	
Purchases Discounts		200 00
Purchases Returns and Allowances		96 00
Wages Expense	1708 00	
Rent Expense	776 00	
Telephone Expense	93 00	
Miscellaneous Expense	108 00	
Total	14109 00	14109 00

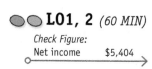

LO1, 2 *(60 MIN)*

Check Figure:
Net income $5,404

11B-3. The owner of Ballad Company asked you to prepare a worksheet from the trial balance shown in Figure 11.18 (p. 449) and additional data.

Additional Data

a/b. Ending merchandise inventory on December 31, $1,785.
  c. Office supplies used up, $200.
  d. Rent expired, $185.
  e. Depreciation expense on office equipment, $450.
  f. Office salaries earned but not paid, $280.

FIGURE 11.18
Trial Balance for Ballad Company

BALLAD COMPANY TRIAL BALANCE DECEMBER 31, 201X	Dr.	Cr.
Cash	5 3 2 1 00	
Petty Cash	2 2 0 00	
Accounts Receivable	2 6 0 8 00	
Beginning Merchandise Inventory, Jan. 1	4 9 5 1 00	
Prepaid Rent	6 4 9 00	
Office Supplies	9 0 0 00	
Office Equipment	9 2 5 0 00	
Accumulated Depreciation, Office Equipment		7 9 0 0 00
Accounts Payable		5 9 1 2 00
K. Ballad, Capital		5 5 0 2 00
K. Ballad, Withdrawals	5 1 0 0 00	
Income Summary	—	—
Sales		5 2 7 3 3 00
Sales Returns and Allowances	9 4 00	
Sales Discount	2 3 0 0 00	
Purchases	2 9 3 1 6 00	
Purchases Discounts		2 4 00
Purchases Returns and Allowances		3 0 0 00
Office Salaries Expense	7 8 2 4 00	
Insurance Expense	2 4 5 0 00	
Advertising Expense	8 0 0 00	
Utilities Expense	5 8 8 00	
Total	7 2 3 7 1 00	7 2 3 7 1 00

11B-4. From the trial balance in Figure 11.19 and additional data, complete the worksheet for Sean's Wholesale Clothing Company.

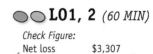

L01, 2 *(60 MIN)*

Check Figure:
Net loss $3,307

Additional Data

a/b. Ending merchandise inventory on December 31, $5,900.
  c. Supplies on hand, $250.
  d. Insurance expired, $600.
  e. Depreciation on store equipment, $500.
  f. Storage fees earned, $216.

FIGURE 11.19
Trial Balance for Sean's Wholesale
Clothing Company

	Dr.	Cr.
SEAN'S WHOLESALE CLOTHING COMPANY **TRIAL BALANCE** **DECEMBER 31, 201X**		
Cash	4 8 9 0 00	
Petty Cash	1 0 0 00	
Accounts Receivable	7 5 0 0 00	
Merchandise Inventory	9 1 0 0 00	
Supplies	7 0 0 00	
Prepaid Insurance	8 3 0 00	
Store Equipment	2 8 0 0 00	
Accumulated Depreciation, Store Equipment		1 3 0 0 00
Accounts Payable		10 9 6 5 00
FIT Payable		1 0 0 0 00
FICA—Social Security Payable		4 5 2 00
FICA—Medicare Payable		1 1 4 00
SIT Payable		1 1 0 00
SUTA Tax Payable		1 1 8 00
FUTA Tax Payable		3 4 00
Unearned Storage Fees		4 0 0 00
Sean Win, Capital		14 0 0 0 00
Sean Win, Withdrawals	3 8 0 0 00	
Income Summary		
Sales		43 3 2 2 00
Sales Returns and Allowances	1 5 2 5 00	
Sales Discount	1 4 0 5 00	
Purchases	25 5 0 0 00	
Purchases Discount		5 0 0 00
Purchases Returns and Allowances		3 5 0 00
Freight-In	2 0 0 00	
Salaries Expense	13 0 0 0 00	
Payroll Tax Expense	4 0 0 00	
Interest Expense	9 1 5 00	
	72 6 6 5 00	72 6 6 5 00

⬤ **LO1** *(10 MIN)*   **Financial Report Problem**

Reading the Kellogg's Annual Report

Go to http://investor.kelloggs.com/annuals.cfm, to access the Kellogg's 2010 Annual Report and find the Consolidated Statement of Earnings. What is the cost of goods sold in 2010?

MyAccountingLab

◑◑ **LO1, 2** *(60 MIN)*   **SANCHEZ COMPUTER CENTER**

The first six months of the year have concluded for Sanchez Computer Center, and Tony wants to make the necessary adjustments to his accounts to prepare accurate financial statements.

Assignment

To prepare these adjustments, use the trial balance in Figure 11.20 and the following inventory that Tony took at the end of March:

Supplies

10 dozen 1/4" screws at a cost of $10 a dozen
5 dozen 1/2" screws at a cost of $7 a dozen
2 feet of coaxial cable at a cost of $5 per foot

Merchandise Inventory

A physical inventory taken on March 31 indicated that merchandise inventory was valued at $300.

Depreciation of Computer Equipment

Computer depreciates at $33 a month; purchased July 5.
Computer workstations depreciate at $20 per month; purchased September 17.
Shop benches depreciate at $25 per month; purchased November 5.

Depreciation of Office Equipment

Office equipment depreciates at $10 per month; purchased July 17.
Fax machine depreciates at $10 per month; purchased November 20.

Expiration of Prepaid Rent

Six months' worth of rent at a rental rate of $400 per month has expired. The following accounts have been added to the chart of accounts: Merchandise Inventory #1050, and Income Summary #3020.

Remember: If any long-term asset is purchased in the first 15 days of the month, Tony will charge depreciation for the full month. If an asset is purchased later than the 15th, he will not charge depreciation in the month it was purchased.

Complete the 10-column worksheet for the six months ended March 31, 201X.

Sanchez Computer
Trial Balance
March 31, 201X

Account Titles	Trial Balance	
	Dr.	Cr.
Cash	13,416.64	
Petty Cash	100.00	
Accounts Receivable	10,900.00	
Prepaid Rent	2,800.00	
Supplies	390.00	
Computer Shop Equipment	3,800.00	
Accum. Dep., C.S. Equip.		99.00
Office Equipment	1,050.00	
Accum. Dep., Office Equip.		20.00
Accounts Payable		2,700.00
T. Freedman, Capital		7,406.00
T. Freedman, Withdrawals	2,015.00	

(continued)

FIGURE 11.20
Trial Balance for Sanchez Computer
March 31, 201X

Sanchez Computer
Trial Balance
March 31, 201X

Income Summary		
Service Revenue		18,500.00
Sales		9,700.00
Sales Returns and Allowances	400.00	
Sales Discounts	220.00	
Advertising Expense		
Rent Expense		
Utilities Expense		
Phone Expense	150.00	
Supplies Expense	42.00	
Insurance Expense		
Postage Expense	25.00	
Miscellaneous Expense	10.00	
Wages Expense	2,030.00	
Payroll Tax Expense	226.36	
Purchases	950.00	
Purchase Returns		100.00
Total	38,525.00	38,525.00

Appendix

A Worksheet for Art's Wholesale Clothing Co. Using a Perpetual Inventory System

What's New: The Merchandise Inventory account (in Figure A.1) does not need to be adjusted. The $4,000 figure for merchandise is the up-to-date balance in the account. The difference between beginning inventory and ending inventory will be part of a new account called *Cost of Goods Sold* on the worksheet.

How the $65,910 of Cost of Goods Sold was calculated from a periodic setup:

	Purchases	$52,000	←	**Assumed sold; part of cost**
+	Merchandise Inventory	$15,000	←	**Beg. Inv. – Ending Inv.** **$19,000 – $4,000**
–	Purchases Discount	860	→	**Reduces costs**
–	Purchases Returns and Allowances	680	↗	
+	Freight-In	450	→	**Adds to cost**
		$65,910		**Cost of Goods Sold**

What's Deleted from the Periodic Worksheet: Account titles for Purchases, Purchases Discounts, Purchases Returns and Allowances, and Freight-In.

Note: Net income is the same on the periodic and the perpetual worksheets.

Problem for Appendix

Using the solution to Instant Replay Self-Review Quiz 11-2 (p. 436) about Ray Company, convert this worksheet to a perpetual inventory system worksheet.

FIGURE A.1
Worksheet for Art's Wholesale Clothing Co. Using a Perpetual Inventory System

ART'S WHOLESALE CLOTHING CO.
WORKSHEET
FOR YEAR ENDED DECEMBER 31, 201X

Account Titles	Trial Balance Dr.	Trial Balance Cr.	Adjustments Dr.	Adjustments Cr.	Adjusted Trial Balance Dr.	Adjusted Trial Balance Cr.	Income Statement Dr.	Income Statement Cr.	Balance Sheet Dr.	Balance Sheet Cr.
Cash	1292000				1292000				1292000	
Petty Cash	10000				10000				10000	
Accounts Receivable	1450000				1450000				1450000	
Merchandise Inventory	400000				400000				400000	
Supplies	80000			(B) 50000	30000				30000	
Prepaid Insurance	90000			(C) 30000	60000				60000	
Store Equipment	400000				400000				400000	
Acc. Dep., Store Equip.		40000		(D) 5000		45000				45000
Accounts Payable		1790000				1790000				1790000
Federal Income Tax		80000				80000				80000
FICA—Social Security		45400				45400				45400
FICA—Medicare		10600				10600				10600
State Income Tax		20000				20000				20000
SUTA Tax		10800				10800				10800
FUTA Tax Payable		3200				3200				3200
Unearned Rent		60000	(A) 20000			40000				40000
Mortgage Payable		232000				232000				232000
Art Newner, Capital		790500				790500				790500
Art Newner, Withdrawal	860000				860000				860000	
Sales		9500000				9500000		9500000		
Sales Returns and Allow.	95000				95000		95000			
Sales Discount	67000				67000		67000			
Cost of Goods Sold	6591000				6591000		6591000			
Salaries Expense	1170000		(E) 60000		1230000		1230000			
Payroll Tax Expense	42000				42000		42000			
Postage Expense	2500				2500		2500			
Miscellaneous Expense	3000				3000		3000			
Interest Expense	30000				30000		30000			
	12582500	12582500								
Rental Income				(A) 20000		20000		20000		
Supplies Expense			(B) 50000		50000		50000			
Insurance Expense			(C) 30000		30000		30000			
Dep. Exp., Store Equip.			(D) 5000		5000		5000			
Salaries Payable				(E) 60000		60000				60000
			165000	165000	12647500	12647500	8145500	9520000	4502000	3127500
Net Income							1374500			1374500
							9520000	9520000	4502000	4502000

FIGURE A.2
Worksheet for Ray Company Using a Perpetual Inventory System

RAY COMPANY
WORKSHEET
FOR YEAR ENDED DECEMBER 31, 201X

Account Titles	Trial Balance Dr.	Trial Balance Cr.	Adjustments Dr.	Adjustments Cr.	Adjusted Trial Balance Dr.	Adjusted Trial Balance Cr.	Income Statement Dr.	Income Statement Cr.	Balance Sheet Dr.	Balance Sheet Cr.
Cash	2 48 6 00				2 48 6 00				2 48 6 00	
Merchandise Inventory	2 0 0 00				2 0 0 00				2 0 0 00	
Prepaid Rent	1 1 5 2 00			(B) 1 0 0 00	1 0 5 2 00				1 0 5 2 00	
Prepaid Insurance	6 0 00			(C) 6 0 00	6 0 00				6 0 00	
Office Equipment	2 1 6 0 00				2 1 6 0 00				2 1 6 0 00	
Accumulated Dep., Off. Equip.		5 6 0 00				6 2 0 00				6 2 0 00
Unearned Storage Fees		2 5 1 6 00	(A) 5 1 6 00			2 0 0 0 00				2 0 0 0 00
Accounts Payable		1 0 0 00				1 0 0 00				1 0 0 00
B. Ray, Capital		1 9 3 2 00				1 9 3 2 00				1 9 3 2 00
Sales		1 1 0 4 0 00				1 1 0 4 0 00		1 1 0 4 0 00		
Sales Returns and Allowances	5 4 6 00				5 4 6 00		5 4 6 00			
Sales Discounts	2 1 6 00				2 1 6 00		2 1 6 00			
COGS*	5 6 1 0 00				5 6 1 0 00		5 6 1 0 00			
Salaries Expense	2 0 1 6 00		(D) 2 0 0 00		2 2 1 6 00		2 2 1 6 00			
Insurance Expense	1 3 9 2 00				1 3 9 2 00		1 3 9 2 00			
Utilities Expense	9 6 00				9 6 00		9 6 00			
Plumbing Expense	2 1 4 00				2 1 4 00		2 1 4 00			
	16 1 4 8 00	16 1 4 8 00								
Storage Fees Earned				(A) 5 1 6 00		5 1 6 00		5 1 6 00		
Rent Expense			(B) 1 0 0 00		1 0 0 00		1 0 0 00			
Dep. Expense, Equip.			(C) 6 0 00		6 0 00		6 0 00			
Salaries Payable				(D) 2 0 0 00		2 0 0 00				2 0 0 00
			8 7 6 00	8 7 6 00	16 4 0 8 00	16 4 0 8 00	10 4 5 0 00	11 5 5 6 00	5 9 5 8 00	4 8 5 2 00
Net Income							1 1 0 6 00			1 1 0 6 00
							11 5 5 6 00	11 5 5 6 00	5 9 5 8 00	5 9 5 8 00

*$624 ($824 − $200) + $5,256 − $168 − $102.

Completion of the Accounting Cycle for a Merchandise Company

THE GAME PLAN

Have you noticed the high price of electronic games for children? Prices seem to be increasing month by month. Stores like Toys"R"Us try to be competitive but they have to make sure that they make a profit as well. Each year, companies prepare financial statements to see how their profit-making operations are performing. Two of the financial statements that they prepare are called the income statement and the balance sheet. In this chapter, you will learn to prepare these two financial statements. The income statement will look at the company's revenues, amount of returns, cost of goods sold, and operating expenses. The balance sheet will provide a look at the company's assets, liabilities, and stockholders' equity on a certain date. The preparation of these financial statements allows stakeholders, such as creditors and investors, to evaluate whether or not they want to do business with a company, whether lending it money or investing in the company stock. Financial statements are an important barometer of a company's success.

LEARNING OBJECTIVES

- 1. Preparing financial statements for a merchandise company.
- 2. Recording adjusting and closing entries for a merchandise company.
- 3. Preparing a post-closing trial balance for a merchandise company.
- 4. Completing reversing entries.

When you buy a toy at Toys"R"Us just keep in mind all the steps Toys"R"Us must take to complete its accounting cycle. In this chapter we discuss the steps involved in completing the accounting cycle for a merchandise company. These steps include preparing financial reports, journalizing and posting adjusting and closing entries, preparing a post-closing trial balance, and reversing entries.

LEARNING UNIT 12-1 PREPARING FINANCIAL STATEMENTS

As we discussed in Chapter 5, when we were dealing with a service company rather than a merchandise company, the three financial statements can be prepared from the worksheet. Let's begin by looking at how Art's Wholesale Clothing Company prepares the income statement.

● L01   The Income Statement

Art is interested in knowing how well his shop performed for the year ended December 31, 201X. What were its net sales? What was the level of returns of goods from dissatisfied customers? What was the cost of the goods brought into the store versus the selling price received? How many goods were returned to suppliers? What is the cost of the goods that have not been sold? What was the cost of the Freight-In? The income statement in Figure 12.1 is prepared from the income statement columns of the worksheet. Note that no debit or credit columns appear on the formal income statement; the inside columns in financial reports are used for subtotaling, not for debit and credit.

The income statement is broken down into several sections. Remembering the sections can help you set it up correctly on your own. The income statement shows the following:

	Net Sales
−	Cost of Goods Sold
=	Gross Profit
−	Operating Expenses
=	Net Income from Operations
+	Other Income
−	Other Expenses
=	Net Income

Let's take these sections one at a time and see where the figures come from on the worksheet.

Revenue Section

Net Sales The first major category of the income statement shows net sales. The figure here—$93,380—is not on the worksheet. Instead, the accountant must combine the amounts for gross sales, sales returns and allowances, and sales discount found on the worksheet to arrive at a figure for net sales. Thus these individual amounts are not summarized in a single figure for net sales until the formal income statement is prepared.

Cost of Goods Sold Section The figures for Merchandise Inventory are shown separately on the worksheet. The $19,000 represents the beginning inventory of the period, and the $4,000, calculated from an inventory sheet, is the ending inventory. Note that on the financial report the cost of goods sold section uses two separate figures for inventory.

Note that the following numbers are not found on the worksheet but are shown on the formal income statement (they are combined by the accountant in preparing the income statement):

- Net Purchases: $50,460 (Purchases – Purchases Discount – Purchases Returns and Allowances)
- Net Cost of Purchases: $50,910 (Net Purchases + Freight-In)
- Cost of Goods Available for Sale: $69,910 (Beginning Inventory + Net Cost of Purchases)
- Cost of Goods Sold: $65,910 (Cost of Goods Available for Sale – Ending Inventory)

COACHING TIP

	Sales
−	Sales Ret. & Allow.
−	Sales Discount
=	Net Sales

COACHING TIP

	Beg. Inventory
+	Net Cost of Purchases
−	Ending Inventory
=	Cost of Goods Sold

FIGURE 12.1
Partial Worksheet and Income Statement

ART'S WHOLESALE CLOTHING COMPANY
INCOME STATEMENT
FOR YEAR ENDED DECEMBER 31, 201X

Revenue:			
Gross Sales			$95,000 00
Less: Sales Ret. and Allow.		$ 950 00	
Sales Discount		670 00	1,620 00
Net Sales			$93,380 00
Cost of Goods Sold:			
Merchandise Inventory, 1/1/1X		$19,000 00	
Purchases	$52,000 00		
Less: Purch. Discount	$ 860 00		
Purch. Ret. and Allow.	680 00	1,540 00	
Net Purchases		$50,460 00	
Add: Freight-In		450 00	
Net Cost of Purchases		50,910 00	
Cost of Goods Available for Sale		$69,910 00	
Less: Merch. Inv., 12/31/1X		4,000 00	
Cost of Goods Sold			65,910 00
Gross Profit			$27,470 00
Operating Expenses:			
Salaries Expense		$12,300 00	
Payroll Tax Expense		420 00	
Dep. Exp., Store Equip.		50 00	
Supplies Expense		500 00	
Insurance Expense		300 00	
Postage Expense		25 00	
Miscellaneous Expense		30 00	
Total Operating Expenses			13,625 00
Net Income from Operations			$13,845 00
Other Income:			
Rental Income		$ 200 00	
Other Expenses:			
Interest Expense		300 00	100 00
Net Income			$13,745 00

ART'S WHOLESALE CLOTHING COMPANY
PARTIAL WORKSHEET
FOR YEAR ENDED DECEMBER 31, 201X

	Income Statement	
	Dr.	Cr.
Income Summary	19,000 00	4,000 00
Sales		95,000 00
Sales Returns and Allowances	950 00	
Sales Discount	670 00	
Purchases	52,000 00	
Purchases Discount		860 00
Purchases Returns and Allowances		680 00
Freight-In	450 00	
Salaries Expense	12,300 00	
Payroll Tax Expense	420 00	
Postage Expense	25 00	
Miscellaneous Expense	30 00	
Interest Expense	300 00	
Rental Income		200 00
Supplies Expense	500 00	
Insurance Expense	300 00	
Depreciation Expense, Store Equip.	50 00	
Salaries Payable		
	86,995 00	100,740 00
Net Income	13,745 00	
	100,740 00	100,740 00

Gross Profit Gross profit ($27,470) is calculated by subtracting the cost of goods sold from net sales ($93,380 – $65,910). This amount is not found on the worksheet.

Operating Expenses Section Like the other figures we have discussed, the business's operating expenses do not appear on the worksheet. To get this figure ($13,625), the accountant adds up all the expenses from the worksheet.

Many operating companies break expenses down into those directly related to the selling activity of the company (selling expenses) and those related to administrative or office activity (administrative expenses or general expenses). Here's a sample list (not connected to example for Art's Wholesale) broken down into these two categories:

Operating Expenses

- Selling Expenses:

  Sales Salaries Expense

  Delivery Expense

  Advertising Expense

  Depreciation Expense, Store Equipment

  Insurance Expense

     Total Selling Expenses

- Administrative Expenses:

  Rent Expense

  Office Salaries Expense

  Utilities Expense

  Office Supplies Expense

  Depreciation Expense, Office Equipment

     Total Administrative Expenses

        Total Operating Expenses

Selling expenses Operating expenses directly related to the sale of goods excluding Cost of Goods Sold.

Administrative expenses (general expenses) Operating expenses such as general office expenses that are incurred indirectly in the selling of goods.

Other income Any revenue other than revenue from sales. It appears in a separate section on the income statement. Examples: Rental Income and Storage Fees.

Other Income (or Other Revenue) Section The other income, or other revenue, section is used to record any revenue other than revenue from sales. For example, Art's Wholesale makes a profit from subletting a portion of a building. The $200 of rental income the company earns from this is recorded in the other income section.

Other expenses Non-operating expenses that do not relate to the main operating activities of the business; they appear in a separate section on the income statement. One example given in the text is Interest Expense, interest owed on money borrowed by the company.

Other Expenses Section The other expenses section is used to record nonoperating expenses, that is, expenses that are not related to the main operating activities of the business. For example, Art's Wholesale owes $300 interest on money it has borrowed. That expense is shown in the other expenses section.

Statement of Owner's Equity

The information used to prepare the statement of owner's equity comes from the balance sheet columns of the worksheet. Keep in mind that the capital account in the ledger should be checked to see whether any additional investments occurred during the period. Figure 12.2 shows how the worksheet aids in this step. The ending figure of $13,050 for Art Newner, Capital is carried over to the balance sheet, which is the final report we look at in this chapter.

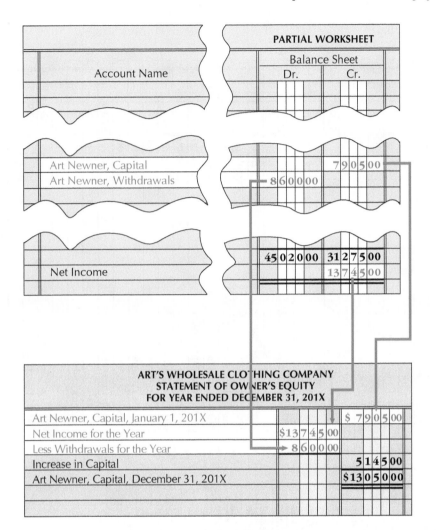

FIGURE 12.2
Preparing Statement of Owner's Equity from the Worksheet

COACHING TIP

Any additional investment by the owner would be added to his or her beginning capital amount.

The Balance Sheet

Figure 12.3 shows how a worksheet is used to aid in the preparation of a classified balance sheet. A classified balance sheet breaks down the assets and liabilities into more detail. Classified balance sheets provide management, owners, creditors, and suppliers with more information about the company's ability to pay current and long-term debts. They also provide a more complete financial picture of the firm.

The categories on the classified balance sheet are as follows:

- Current assets are defined as cash and assets that will be converted into cash or used up during the normal operating cycle of the company or one year, whichever is longer. (Think of the operating cycle as the time period it takes a company to buy and sell merchandise and then collect accounts receivable.)

  Accountants list current assets in order of how easily they can be converted into cash (called *liquidity*). In most cases, Accounts Receivable can be turned into cash more quickly than Merchandise Inventory. For example, it can be quite difficult to sell an outdated computer in a computer store or to sell last year's model car this year.

- Plant and equipment are long-lived assets that are used in the production or sale of goods or services. Art's Wholesale has only one plant asset, store equipment; other plant assets could include buildings and land. The assets are usually listed in order according to how long they will last; the shortest-lived assets are listed first. Land is always the last asset listed (and—keep in mind—land is never depreciated). Note that we still show the cost of the asset less its accumulated depreciation.

Classified balance sheet A balance sheet that categorizes assets as current assets or plant and equipment and groups liabilities as current or long-term liabilities.

Current assets Assets that can be converted into cash or used within one year or the normal operating cycle of the business, whichever is longer.

Operating cycle Average time it takes to buy and sell merchandise and then collect accounts receivable.

Plant and equipment Long-lived assets such as equipment, buildings or land that are used in the production or sale of goods or services.

FIGURE 12.3
Partial Worksheet and Classified Balance Sheet

ART'S WHOLESALE CLOTHING COMPANY
WORKSHEET
FOR YEAR ENDED DECEMBER 31, 201X

	Balance Sheet	
	Dr.	Cr.
Cash	12920 00	
Petty Cash	100 00	
Accounts Receivable	14500 00	
Merchandise Inventory	4000 00	
Supplies	300 00	
Prepaid Insurance	600 00	
Store Equipment	4000 00	
Acc. Dep., Store Equipment		450 00
Accounts Payable		17900 00
Federal Income Tax Payable		800 00
FICA—Social Security Payable		454 00
FICA—Medicare Payable		106 00
State Income Tax Payable		200 00
SUTA Tax Payable		108 00
FUTA Tax Payable		32 00
Unearned Rent		400 00
Mortgage Payable		2320 00
Art Newner, Capital		7905 00
	45020 00	31275 00
Salaries Payable		600 00
Net Income		13745 00
	45020 00	45020 00

ART'S WHOLESALE CLOTHING COMPANY
CLASSIFIED BALANCE SHEET
FOR YEAR ENDED DECEMBER 31, 201X

Assets

Current Assets:			
Cash		$12920 00	
Petty Cash		100 00	
Accounts Receivable		14500 00	
Merchandise Inventory		4000 00	
Supplies		300 00	
Prepaid Insurance		600 00	
Total Current Assets			$32420 00
Plant and Equipment:			
Store Equipment		$4000 00	
Less: Accum. Depreciation		450 00	3550 00
Total Assets			$35970 00

Liabilities

Current Liabilities:			
Mortgage Payable (current portion)		$ 320 00	
Accounts Payable		17900 00	
Federal Income Tax Payable		800 00	
FICA—Social Security Payable		454 00	
FICA—Medicare Payable		106 00	
State Income Tax Payable		200 00	
SUTA Tax Payable		108 00	
FUTA Tax Payable		32 00	
Salaries Payable		600 00	
Unearned Rent		400 00	
Total Current Liabilities			$20920 00
Long-Term Liabilities:			
Mortgage Payable		2000 00	
Total Liabilities			$22920 00

Owner's Equity

Art Newner, Capital, December 31, 201X			13050 00
Total Liabilities and Owner's Equity			$35970 00

- **Current liabilities** are the debts or obligations of Art's Wholesale that must be paid within one year or one operating cycle. The order of listing accounts in this section is not always the same; many times companies will list their liabilities in the order they expect to pay them off. Note that the current portion of the mortgage, $320 (that portion due within one year), is listed before Accounts Payable.
- **Long-term liabilities** are debts or obligations that are not due and payable for a comparatively long period, usually for more than one year. For Art's Wholesale the only long-term liability is Mortgage Payable. The long-term portion of the mortgage is listed here; the current portion, due within one year, is listed under current liabilities.

Current liabilities Obligations that will come due within one year or within the operating cycle, whichever is longer.

COACHING TIP

Mortgage Payable:

$2,320

– 320 current portion

$2,000 long-term liability

Long-term liabilities Obligations that are not due or payable for a long time, usually for more than a year.

LEARNING UNIT 12-1 REVIEW

AT THIS POINT you should be able to do the following:

- Prepare a detailed income statement from the worksheet.
- Explain the difference between selling and administrative expenses.
- Prepare a statement of owner's equity from the worksheet.
- Explain as well as compare current assets with plant and equipment.
- Explain the difference between current and long-term liabilities.
- Prepare a classified balance sheet from a worksheet.

Instant Replay ◦ Self-Review Quiz 12-1

Using the worksheet from Self-Review Quiz 11-2 in Chapter 11 (p. 436), prepare in proper form (1) an income statement, (2) a statement of owner's equity, and (3) a classified balance sheet for Ray Company.

Solutions to Instant Replay: Self-Review Quiz 12-1

1

FIGURE 12.4
Income Statement for Ray Company

RAY COMPANY INCOME STATEMENT FOR YEAR ENDED DECEMBER 31, 201X				
Revenue:				
Sales				$11 04 0 00
Less: Sales Ret. and Allow.			$ 5 4 6 00	
Sales Discount			2 1 6 00	7 6 2 00
Net Sales				$10 27 8 00
Cost of Goods Sold:				
Merchandise Inventory, 1/1/1X			$ 8 2 4 00	
Purchases		$5 2 5 6 00		
Less: Pur. Ret. and Allow.	$ 1 6 8 00			
Purchases Discount	1 0 2 00	2 7 0 00		
Net Purchases			4 9 8 6 00	
Cost of Goods Available for Sale			$ 5 8 1 0 00	
Less: Merchandise Inv., 12/31/1X			2 0 0 00	
Cost of Goods Sold				5 6 1 0 00
Gross Profit				$ 4 6 6 8 00
Operating Expenses:				
Salaries Expense		$ 2 2 1 6 00		
Insurance Expense		1 3 9 2 00		
Utilities Expense		9 6 00		
Plumbing Expense		2 1 4 00		
Rent Expense		1 0 0 00		
Depreciation Exp., Equip.		6 0 00		
Total Operating Expenses				4 0 7 8 00
Net Income from Operations				$ 5 9 0 00
Other Income:				
Storage Fees Earned				5 1 6 00
Net Income				$ 1 1 0 6 00

2

FIGURE 12.5
Statement of Owner's Equity for Ray Company

RAY COMPANY STATEMENT OF OWNER'S EQUITY FOR YEAR ENDED DECEMBER 31, 201X	
B. Ray, Capital, 1/1/1X	$ 1 9 3 2 00
Net Income for the Year	1 1 0 6 00
B. Ray, Capital, 12/31/1X	$ 3 0 3 8 00

3

RAY COMPANY BALANCE SHEET DECEMBER 31, 201X		
Assets		
Current Assets:		
Cash	$2 4 8 6 00	
Merchandise Inventory	2 0 0 00	
Prepaid Rent	1 0 5 2 00	
Prepaid Insurance	6 0 00	
Total Current Assets		$3 7 9 8 00
Plant and Equipment:		
Office Equipment	$2 1 6 0 00	
Less: Accumulated Depreciation	6 2 0 00	1 5 4 0 00
Total Assets		$5 3 3 8 00
Liabilities		
Current Liabilities		
Accounts Payable	$ 1 0 0 00	
Salaries Payable	2 0 0 00	
Unearned Storage Fees	2 0 0 0 00	
Total Liabilities		$2 3 0 0 00
Owner's Equity		
B. Ray, Capital, December 31, 201X		3 0 3 8 00
Total Liabilities and Owner's Equity		$5 3 3 8 00

FIGURE 12.6
Balance Sheet for Ray Company

LEARNING UNIT 12-2 JOURNALIZING AND POSTING ADJUSTING AND CLOSING ENTRIES; PREPARING THE POST-CLOSING TRIAL BALANCE

LO2

Journalizing and Posting Adjusting Entries

From the worksheet of Art's Wholesale (repeated in Figure 12.7 for your convenience), the adjusting entries can be journalized from the adjustments column and posted to the ledger. Keep in mind that the adjustments have been placed only on the worksheet, not in the journal or in the ledger. At this point, the journal does not reflect adjustments and the ledger still contains only unadjusted amounts.

Partial Ledger

Merchandise Inventory 114		Income Summary 313	
Dr.	**Cr.**	**Dr.**	**Cr.**
19,000	19,000 (A)	(A) 19,000	4,000 (B)
(B) 4,000			

FIGURE 12.7
Completed Worksheet

ART'S WHOLESALE CLOTHING CO.
WORKSHEET
FOR YEAR ENDED DECEMBER 31, 201X

	Trial Balance Dr.	Trial Balance Cr.	Adjustments Dr.	Adjustments Cr.
Cash	12 9 2 0 00			
Petty Cash	1 0 0 00			
Accounts Receivable	14 5 0 0 00			
Merchandise Inventory	19 0 0 0 00		(B) 4 0 0 0 00	(A) 19 0 0 0 00
Supplies	8 0 0 00			(D) 5 0 0 00
Prepaid Insurance	9 0 0 00			(E) 3 0 0 00
Store Equipment	4 0 0 0 00			
Acc. Dep., Store Equipment		4 0 0 00		(F) 5 0 00
Accounts Payable		17 9 0 0 00		
Federal Income Tax Payable		8 0 0 00		
FICA—Social Security Payable		4 5 4 00		
FICA—Medicare Payable		1 0 6 00		
State Income Tax Payable		2 0 0 00		
SUTA Tax Payable		1 0 8 00		
FUTA Tax Payable		3 2 00		
Unearned Rent		6 0 0 00	(C) 2 0 0 00	
Mortgage Payable		2 3 2 0 00		
Art Newner, Capital		7 9 0 5 00		
Art Newner, Withdrawals	8 6 0 0 00			
Income Summary			(A) 19 0 0 0 00	(B) 4 0 0 0 00
Sales		95 0 0 0 00		
Sales Returns and Allowances	9 5 0 00			
Sales Discount	6 7 0 00			
Purchases	52 0 0 0 00			
Purchases Discount		8 6 0 00		
Purchases Returns and Allowances		6 8 0 00		
Freight-In	4 5 0 00			
Salaries Expense	11 7 0 0 00		(G) 6 0 0 00	
Payroll Tax Expense	4 2 0 00			
Postage Expense	2 5 00			
Miscellaneous Expense	3 0 00			
Interest Expense	3 0 0 00			
	127 3 6 5 00	127 3 6 5 00		
Rental Income				(C) 2 0 0 00
Supplies Expense			(D) 5 0 0 00	
Insurance Expense			(E) 3 0 0 00	
Depreciation Expense; Store Equip.			(F) 5 0 00	
Salaries Payable				(G) 6 0 0 00
			24 6 5 0 00	24 6 5 0 00
Net Income				

FIGURE 12.7
(continued)

	Adjusted Trial Bal. Dr.	Adjusted Trial Bal. Cr.	Income Statement Dr.	Income Statement Cr.	Balance Sheet Dr.	Balance Sheet Cr.
Cash	12 9 2 0 00				12 9 2 0 00	
Petty Cash	1 0 0 00				1 0 0 00	
Accounts Receivable	14 5 0 0 00				14 5 0 0 00	
Merchandise Inventory	4 0 0 0 00				4 0 0 0 00	
Supplies	3 0 0 00				3 0 0 00	
Prepaid Insurance	6 0 0 00				6 0 0 00	
Store Equipment	4 0 0 0 00				4 0 0 0 00	
Acc. Dep., Store Equipment		4 5 0 00				4 5 0 00
Accounts Payable		17 9 0 0 00				17 9 0 0 00
Federal Income Tax Payable		8 0 0 00				8 0 0 00
FICA—Social Security Payable		4 5 4 00				4 5 4 00
FICA—Medicare Payable		1 0 6 00				1 0 6 00
State Income Tax Payable		2 0 0 00				2 0 0 00
SUTA Tax Payable		1 0 8 00				1 0 8 00
FUTA Tax Payable		3 2 00				3 2 00
Unearned Rent		4 0 0 00				4 0 0 00
Mortgage Payable		2 3 2 0 00				2 3 2 0 00
Art Newner, Capital		7 9 0 5 00				7 9 0 5 00
Art Newner, Withdrawals	8 6 0 0 00				8 6 0 0 00	
Income Summary	19 0 0 00	4 0 0 00	19 0 0 00	4 0 0 00		
Sales		95 0 0 0 00		95 0 0 0 00		
Sales Returns and Allowances	9 5 0 00		9 5 0 00			
Sales Discount	6 7 0 00		6 7 0 00			
Purchases	52 0 0 0 00		52 0 0 0 00			
Purchases Discount		8 6 0 00		8 6 0 00		
Purchases Returns and Allowances		6 8 0 00		6 8 0 00		
Freight-In	4 5 0 00		4 5 0 00			
Salaries Expense	12 3 0 0 00		12 3 0 0 00			
Payroll Tax Expense	4 2 0 00		4 2 0 00			
Postage Expense	2 5 00		2 5 00			
Miscellaneous Expense	3 0 00		3 0 00			
Interest Expense	3 0 0 00		3 0 0 00			
Rental Income		2 0 0 00		2 0 0 00		
Supplies Expense	5 0 0 00		5 0 0 00			
Insurance Expense	3 0 0 00		3 0 0 00			
Depreciation Expense, Store Equip.	5 0 00		5 0 00			
Salaries Payable		6 0 0 00				6 0 0 00
	132 0 1 5 00	132 0 1 5 00	86 9 9 5 00	100 7 4 0 00	45 0 2 0 00	31 2 7 5 00
Net Income			13 7 4 5 00			13 7 4 5 00
			100 7 4 0 00	100 7 4 0 00	45 0 2 0 00	45 0 2 0 00

Supplies 115	
Dr.	Cr.
800	500 (D)

Supplies Expense 614	
Dr.	Cr.
(D) 500	

Prepaid Insurance 116	
Dr.	Cr.
900	300 (E)

Insurance Expense 615	
Dr.	Cr.
(E) 300	

Accum. Dep., Store Equipment 122	
Dr.	Cr.
	400
	50 (F)

Dep. Expense, Store Equip. 613	
Dr.	Cr.
(F) 50	

Salaries Payable 212	
Dr.	Cr.
	600 (G)

Salaries Exp. 611	
Dr.	Cr.
11,700	
(G) 600	

Unearned Rent 219	
Dr.	Cr.
(C) 200	600

Rental Income 414	
Dr.	Cr.
	200 (C)

The journalized and posted adjusting entries are shown in Figure 12.8. Note that the liability Unearned Rent is reduced by $200 and Rental Income has increased by $200.

FIGURE 12.8
Journalized and Posted
Adjusting Entries

ART'S WHOLESALE CLOTHING CO.
GENERAL JOURNAL

Page 2

Date		Account Titles and Description	PR	Dr.	Cr.
		Adjusting Entries			
	31	Income Summary	313	19 0 0 00	
		Merchandise Inventory	114		19 0 0 00
		Transferred beginning inventory			
		to Income Summary			
	31	Merchandise Inventory	114	4 0 0 00	
		Income Summary	313		4 0 0 00
		Records cost of ending inventory			
	31	Unearned Rent	219	2 0 0 00	
		Rental Income	414		2 0 0 00
		Rental income earned			
	31	Supplies Expense	614	5 0 0 00	
		Supplies	115		5 0 0 00
		Supplies consumed			
	31	Insurance Expense	615	3 0 0 00	
		Prepaid Insurance	116		3 0 0 00
		Insurance expired			
	31	Dep. Exp., Store Equipment	613	5 0 00	
		Acc. Dep., Store Equipment	122		5 0 00
		Depreciation on equipment			
	31	Salaries Expense	611	6 0 0 00	
		Salaries Payable	212		6 0 0 00
		Accrued salaries			

Income Summary 313

	Dr.	Cr.	
Adj.	19,000	4,000	Adj.
Clos.	67,995	96,740	Clos.
	86,995	100,740	
Net Income → Clos.	13,745		

COACHING TIP

Note that Income Summary before the closing process contains the adjustments for Merchandise Inventory. The end result is that the net income of $13,745 is closed to the Capital account.

Journalizing and Posting Closing Entries

In Chapter 5, we discussed the closing process for a service company. The goals of closing are the same for a merchandise company. These goals are (1) to clear all temporary accounts in the ledger to zero and (2) to update capital in the ledger to its latest balance. The company must use the worksheet and the steps listed here to complete the closing process.

STEP 1   Close all balances on the income statement credit column of the worksheet, except Income Summary, by debits.
Then credit the total to the Income Summary account.

STEP 2   Close all balances on the income statement debit column of the worksheet, except Income Summary, by credits.
Then debit the total to the Income Summary account.

STEP 3   Transfer the balance of the Income Summary account to the Capital account.

STEP 4   Transfer the balance of the owner's Withdrawals account to the Capital account.

Let's look now at the journalized closing entries in Figure 12.9. When these entries are posted, all the temporary accounts will have zero balances in the ledger, and the Capital account will be updated with a new balance.

Let's take a moment to look at the Income Summary account in T account form:

The Post-Closing Trial Balance

● **L03**

The post-closing trial balance shown in Figure 12.10 (on the following page spread to the right) is prepared from the general ledger. Note first that all temporary accounts have been closed and thus are not shown on this post-closing trial balance. Note also that the ending inventory figure of the last accounting period, $4,000, becomes the beginning inventory figure on January 1, 201X.

FIGURE 12.9
General Journal Closing Entries

	Date	Account Titles and Description	PR	Dr.	Cr.
		ART'S WHOLESALE CLOTHING CO. **GENERAL JOURNAL**			Page 2
		Closing Entries			
	31	Sales	411	95 0 0 00	
		Rental Income	414	2 0 00	
		Purchases Discount	512	8 6 00	
		Purchases Ret. and Allow.	513	6 8 00	
		Income Summary	313		96 7 4 0 00
		Transfers credit account balances			
		on income statement column of			
		worksheet to Income Summary			
	31	Income Summary	313	67 9 9 5 00	
		Sales Returns and Allowances	412		9 5 0 00
		Sales Discount	413		6 7 0 00
		Purchases	511		52 0 0 0 00
		Freight-In	514		4 5 0 00
		Salaries Expense	611		12 3 0 0 00
		Payroll Tax Expense	612		4 2 0 00
		Postage Expense	616		2 5 00
		Miscellaneous Expense	617		3 0 00
		Interest Expense	618		3 0 0 00
		Supplies Expense	614		5 0 0 00
		Insurance Expense	615		3 0 0 00
		Depreciation Expense, Store Equip.	613		5 0 00
		Transfers all expenses, and			
		deductions to Sales are			
		closed to Income Summary			
	31	Income Summary	313	13 7 4 5 00	
		A. Newner, Capital	311		13 7 4 5 00
		Transfer of net income to			
		Capital from Income Summary			
	31	A. Newner, Capital	311	8 6 0 0 00	
		A. Newner, Withdrawals	312		8 6 0 0 00
		Closes withdrawals to			
		Capital Account			

LEARNING UNIT 12-2 REVIEW

AT THIS POINT you should be able to do the following:

- Journalize and post adjusting entries for a merchandise company.
- Explain the relationship of the worksheet to the adjusting and closing process.
- Complete the closing process for a merchandise company.
- Prepare a post-closing trial balance and explain why ending Merchandise Inventory is not a temporary account.

Instant Replay ⊙ Self-Review Quiz 12-2

Using the worksheet from Self-Review Quiz 11-2 in Chapter 11 (p. 436), journalize the closing entries.

FIGURE 12.10
Post-Closing Trial Balance for Art's Wholesale Clothing Company

ART'S WHOLESALE CLOTHING COMPANY POSTCLOSING TRIAL BALANCE DECEMBER 31, 201X	Dr.	Cr.
Cash	12 9 2 0 00	
Petty Cash	1 0 0 00	
Accounts Receivable	14 5 0 0 00	
Merchandise Inventory	4 0 0 0 00	
Supplies	3 0 0 00	
Prepaid Insurance	6 0 0 00	
Store Equipment	4 0 0 0 00	
Accum. Depreciation, Store Equipment		4 5 0 00
Accounts Payable		17 9 0 0 00
Federal Income Tax Payable		8 0 0 00
FICA—Social Security Payable		4 5 4 00
FICA—Medicare Payable		1 0 6 00
State Income Tax Payable		2 0 0 00
SUTA Tax Payable		1 0 8 00
FUTA Tax Payable		3 2 00
Salary Payable		6 0 0 00
Unearned Rent		4 0 0 00
Mortgage Payable		2 3 2 0 00
Art Newner, Capital		13 0 5 0 00
	36 4 2 0 00	36 4 2 0 00

Solution to Instant Replay Self-Review Quiz 12-2

FIGURE 12.11
Closing Entries Journalized

					Page 2	
Date	Account Titles and Description	PR	Dr.	Cr.		
	Closing Entries					
Dec. 31	Sales		11 0 4 0 00			
	Storage Fees Earned		5 1 6 00			
	Purchases Returns and Allowances		1 6 8 00			
	Purchases Discount		1 0 2 00			
	Income Summary			11 8 2 6 00		
31	Income Summary		10 0 9 6 00			
	Sales Returns and Allowances			5 4 6 00		
	Sales Discount			2 1 6 00		
	Purchases			5 2 5 6 00		
	Salaries Expense			2 2 1 6 00		
	Insurance Expense			1 3 9 2 00		
	Utilities Expense			9 6 00		
	Plumbing Expense			2 1 4 00		
	Rent Expense			1 0 0 00		
	Depreciation Exp., Equipment			6 0 00		
31	Income Summary		1 1 0 6 00			
	B. Ray, Capital			1 1 0 6 00		

LO4   LEARNING UNIT 12-3 REVERSING ENTRIES (OPTIONAL SECTION)

Reversing entries Optional bookkeeping technique in which certain adjusting entries are reversed or switched on the first day of the new accounting period so that transactions in the new period can be recorded without referring back to prior adjusting entries.

The accounting cycle for Art's Wholesale Clothing Company is completed. Now let's look at reversing entries, an optional way of handling some adjusting entries. Reversing entries are general journal entries that are the opposite of adjusting entries. Reversing entries help reduce potential errors and simplify the recordkeeping process. If Art's accountant makes reversing entries, routine transactions can be made in the usual steps.

To help explain the concept of reversing entries, let's look at these two adjustments that could be reversed:

1. When an increase occurs in an asset account (no previous balance).

   Example: Interest Receivable

                Interest Income

   (Interest earned but not collected is covered in later chapters.)

2. When an increase occurs in a liability account (no previous balance).

   Example: Salaries Expense

                Salaries Payable

With the exception of businesses in their first year of operation, accounts such as Accumulated Depreciation or Inventory cannot be reduced because they have previous balances.

Art's bookkeeper handles an entry without reversing for salaries at the end of the year (see Figure 12.12). Note that the permanent account, Salaries Payable, carries over to the new accounting period a $600 balance. Remember that the $600 was an expense of the prior year.

FIGURE 12.12
Reversing Entries Not Used

❶ On December 31, an adjusting entry was journalized and posted for $600 of salaries incurred but not paid.

ADJUSTING JOURNAL ENTRY

| | Salaries Expense | 6 0 0 00 | |
| | Salaries Payable | | 6 0 0 00 |

T ACCOUNT UPDATE

Salaries Exp.	Salaries Pay.
11,700	600
600	

❷ On January 8 after closing entries have been journalized and posted, Salaries Expense has a zero balance.

CLOSING JOURNAL ENTRY

| | Income Summary | X X X | |
| | Salaries Expense | | 12 3 0 0 00 |

Salaries Exp.		Salaries Pay.
11,700	12,300	600
600		

On January 8 of the new year, the payroll to be paid is $2,000. If the optional reversing entry is *not* used, the bookkeeper must make the following compound journal entry as shown in Figure 12.13.

FIGURE 12.13
Entry When Optional Reversing Entry Is Not Used

	Salaries Payable	6 0 0 00	
	Salaries Expense	1 4 0 0 00	
	Cash		2 0 0 0 00

| Salaries Exp. | Salaries Pay. | Cash |
| 1,400 | 600 | 600 | | 2,000 |

To do so, the bookkeeper has to refer back to the adjustment on December 31 to determine how much of the salary of $2,000 is indeed a new salary expense and what portion was shown in the old year although not paid. It is easy to see how potential errors can result if the bookkeeper pays the payroll but forgets about the adjustment in the previous year. In this way, reversing entries can help avoid potential errors.

Figure 12.14 shows the four steps the bookkeeper would take if reversing entries were used. Note that steps 1 and 2 are the same whether the accountant uses reversing entries or not.

FIGURE 12.14
Reversing Entries Used

① On December 31, an adjustment for salary was recorded.

② Closing entry on December 31.

③ On January 1 (first day of the following fiscal period), a reverse adjusting entry was made for salary on December 31 (by "flipping" the previous adjustment).

This way, the liability is reduced to 0. We know it will be paid in this new period, but the Salaries Expense has a credit balance of $600 until the payroll is paid. When the payroll of $2,000 is paid, the following results:

④ Paid Payroll $2,000.

Note that the balance of Salaries Expense is indeed only $1,400, the *true* expense in the new year. Reversing results in switching the adjustment the first day of the new period. Also note that each of the accounts ends up with the same balance no matter which method is chosen. Using a reversing entry for salaries, however, allows the accountant to make the normal entry when it is time to pay salaries.

LEARNING UNIT 12-3 REVIEW

AT THIS POINT you should be able to do the following:

- Explain the purpose of reversing entries.
- Complete a reversing entry.
- Explain when reversing entries can be used.

⬐ Instant Replay ◗ Self-Review Quiz 12-3

Explain which of the following situations could be reversed:

1

Supplies Exp.		Supplies	
	200	800	200

2

Wages Exp.		Wages Payable	
3,200			200
200			

3

Sales		Unearned Sales	
	4,000	50	200
	50		

Solutions to Instant Replay: Self-Review Quiz 12-3

1. Not reversed: Asset Supplies is decreasing, not increasing.
2. Reversed: Liability is increasing and no previous balance exists.
3. Not reversed: Liability is decreasing and a previous balance exists.

Blueprint: Financial Statements

(1) INCOME STATEMENT				
Revenue:				
Sales				$ XXX
Less: Sales Ret. and Allow.			$ XXX	
Sales Discount			XXX	XXX
Net Sales				$ XXXX
Cost of Goods Sold:				
Merchandise Inventory, 1/1/1X			$ XXX	
Purchases		$XXX		
Less: Purchases Discount	$XXX			
Purch. Ret. and Allow.	XXX	XXX		
Net Purchases		XXX		
Add: Freight-In		XXX		
Net Cost of Purchases			XXX	
Cost of Goods Avail. for Sale			$XXXX	
Less: Merch. Inv., 12/31/1X			XXX	
Cost of Goods Sold				XXXX
Gross Profit				$XXXX
Operating Expenses:				
~~			$XXX	
~~			XXX	
~~			XXX	
Total Operating Expenses				XXX
Net Income from Operations				$ XXX
Other Income:				
Rental Income			$ XXX	
Storage Fees Income			XXX	
Total Other Income			$ XXX	
Other Expenses:				
Interest Expenses			XXX	XXX
Net Income:				$ XXX

(2) STATEMENT OF OWNER'S EQUITY			
Beginning Capital			$XXX
Additional Investments			XXX
Total Investment			$XXX
Net Income		$XXX	
Less: Withdrawals		XXX	
Increase in Capital			XXX
Ending Capital			$XXX

(3) BALANCE SHEET				
Assets				
Current Assets:				
Cash		$ XXXX		
Acccounts Receivable		XXXX		
Merchandise Inventory		XXXX		
Prepaid Insurance		XXX		
Total Current Assets			$ XXXX	
Plant and Equipment:				
Store Equipment	$XXXX			
Less Accumulated Depreciation	XXXX	$XXXX		
Office Equipment	$XXXX			
Less Accumulated Depreciation	XXX	XXX		
Total Plant and Equipment			XXXX	
Total Assets			$XXXX	
Liabilities				
Current Liabilities:				
Unearned Revenue		$XXX		
Mortgage Payable (current portion)		XXX		
Accounts Payable		XXX		
Salaries Payable		XX		
FICA—Social Security Payable		XX		
FICA—Medicare Payable		XX		
Income Taxes Payable		XX		
Total Current Liabilities			$XXX	
Long-Term Liabilities				
Mortgage Payable			$XXX	
Total Liabilities			$XXXX	
Owner's Equity				
Capital*			XXXX	
Total Liabilities and Owner's Equity			$XXXX	

* From statement of owner's equity

ACCOUNTING COACH 12

The following Coaching Tips are from Learning Units 12-1 to 12-3. Take the Pre-Game Checkup and use the Check Your Score at the bottom of the page to see how you are doing. The Accounting Coach provides tips before each Checkup to help you avoid common accounting errors.

LU 12-1 Preparing Financial Statements

Pre-Game Tips: The financial statements do not have debits and credits. The inside columns are for subtotaling. The totals on the financial statements will not always equal the same total amounts on the worksheet. Net Income will always be the same on the worksheet and income statement.

Purchases along with Merchandise Inventory will be added to Cost of Goods Sold, while Ending Inventory will be subtracted. Revenue less Cost of Goods Sold equals Gross Profit. To get Net Income from Operations, we subtract Gross Profit from Operating Expenses.

Pre-Game Checkup

Answer true or false to the following statements.

1. Freight-In is subtracted from Net Purchases.
2. Sales on the formal income statement has a credit balance.
3. Rental Income is shown on the balance sheet.
4. Accumulated Depreciation is a contra-asset on the balance sheet.
5. Unearned Rent is a revenue on the income statement.

LU 12-2 Journalizing and Posting Adjusting and Closing Entries; Preparing the Post-Closing Trial Balance

Pre-Game Tips: All adjustments can be taken from the adjustments column on the worksheet. Keep in mind that we adjust Inventory through Income Summary. We assume that old inventory is sold and is a cost and that the ending inventory is not a cost until it is sold. Income Summary is a temporary account and will not appear on the post-closing trial balance. The closing process transfers all temporary accounts through Income Summary except Withdrawals, which is closed directly to Capital.

Pre-Game Checkup

Answer true or false to the following statements.

1. Some temporary accounts will go on the post-closing trial balance.
2. Merchandise Inventory (ending) is listed as a debit on the post-closing trial balance.
3. Unearned Rent is a permanent account.
4. The Capital amount on the post-closing trial balance is listed before the closing process.
5. Purchases is listed on the post-closing trial balance.

LU 12-3 Reversing Entries (Optional Section)

Pre-Game Tips: Reversing entries is a way of handling some adjusting entries. By making a reversing entry, the accountant does not have to worry about the past adjustment and will make the normal entry when a transaction occurs. Reversing entries can be done when an increase occurs in an asset (no previous balance) or when an increase occurs in a liability account (no previous balance).

Pre-Game Checkup

Answer true or false to the following statements.

1. Reversing entries are required.
2. Interest Income and Interest Receivables may sometimes use a reversing entry.
3. Reversing entries are made in the old year, not the new.
4. Reversing entries for Salary will show true salary expense in the new year.
5. Regardless of whether reversing entries are used, the same balances will end up in each account.

CHECK YOUR SCORE: Answers to the Pre-Game Checkup

LU 12-1
1. False—Freight-In is added to Net Purchases.
2. False—Sales on the formal income statement has no debits or credits.
3. False—Rental Income is shown on the income statement.
4. True.
5. False—Unearned Rent is a liability on the balance sheet.

LU 12-2
1. False—No temporary accounts will go on the post-closing trial balance.
2. True.
3. True.
4. False—The Capital account on the post-closing trial balance is listed after the closing process.
5. False—Purchases is a temporary account and will not appear on the post-closing trial balance.

LU 12-3
1. False—Reversing entries are optional.
2. True.
3. False—Reversing entries are made in the new year.
4. True.
5. True.

Chapter Summary

MyAccountingLab

Here are all the key concepts and equations to help you understand the concepts of this chapter and prepare you for your exam. After completing this review, go to MyAccountingLab for more practice opportunities.

Concepts You Should Know	Key Equations and Terms
L01 Preparing financial statements for a merchandise company. 1. The formal income statement can be prepared from the income statement columns of the worksheet. 2. No debit or credit columns are used on the formal income statement. 3. The cost of goods sold section has a figure for beginning inventory and a separate figure for ending inventory. 4. Operating expenses could be broken down into selling and administrative expenses of owner's equity. 5. A classified balance sheet breaks assets into current assets and plant and equipment. Liabilities are broken down into current and long term liabilities.	Administrative expenses (general expenses) (p. 458) Classified balance sheet (p. 459) Current assets (p. 459) Current liabilities (p. 461) Long-term liabilities (p. 461) Operating cycle (p. 459) Other expenses (p. 458) Other income (p. 458) Plant and equipment (p. 459) Selling expenses (p. 458)
L02 Recording adjusting and closing entries. 1. The information for journalizing, adjusting, and closing entries can be obtained from the worksheet. 2. In the closing process, the balance of all temporary accounts will be zero and the Capital account is brought up to its new balance. 3. Inventory is not a temporary account. The ending inventory, along with other permanent accounts, will be listed in the post-closing trial balance.	
L03 Preparing a post-closing trial balance. 1. Merchandise Inventory is a permanent account. 2. The ending inventory, along with other permanent accounts, will be listed in the post-closing trial balance.	
L04 Completing reversing entries. 1. Reversing entries are optional. They can aid in reducing potential errors and simplify the recordkeeping process. 2. The reversing entry "flips" the previous adjustment on the first day of a new fiscal period. 3. Reversing entries are only used if (a) assets are increasing and have no previous balance or (b) liabilities are increasing and have no previous balance.	Reversing entries (p. 470)

Discussion Questions and Critical Thinking/Ethical Case

1. Which columns of the worksheet aid in the preparation of the income statement?

2. Explain the components of cost of goods sold.

3. Explain how operating expenses can be broken down into different categories.

4. What is the difference between current assets and plant and equipment?

5. What is an operating cycle?

6. Why journalize adjusting entries *after* the formal reports in a manual system have been prepared?

7. Explain the steps of closing for a merchandise company.

8. Temporary accounts could appear on a post-closing trial balance. Agree or disagree?

9. What is the purpose of using reversing entries? Are they mandatory? When should they be used?

10. Janet Flynn, owner of Reel Company, plans to apply for a bank loan at Petro National Bank. Because the company has a lot of debt on its balance sheet, Janet does not plan to show the loan officer the balance sheet. She plans only to bring the income statement. Do you feel that this move is a sound financial move by Janet? You make the call. Write down your specific recommendations to Janet.

Concept Checks

MyAccountingLab

Calculate Net Sales

● **LO1** *(5 MIN)*

1. From the following, calculate net sales:

Purchases	$101	Sales Discount	$21
Gross Sales	176	Operating Expenses	48
Sales Returns and Allowances	18		

Calculate Cost of Goods Sold

● **LO1** *(5 MIN)*

2. Calculate Cost of Goods Sold:

Freight-In	$ 8	Ending Inventory	$ 7
Beginning Inventory	16	Net Purchases	67

Calculate Gross Profit and Net Income

● **LO1** *(10 MIN)*

3. Using Exercises 1 and 2, calculate the following:
   a. Gross profit
   b. Net income or net loss

L01, 2 *(15 MIN)*   **Classification of Accounts**

4.   Match the following categories to each account listed.

1. Current Asset
2. Plant and Equipment
3. Current Liabilities
4. Long-Term Liabilities

_____ **a.** Petty Cash   _____ **f.** Mortgage Payable (Current)
_____ **b.** Accounts Receivable   _____ **g.** SUTA Payable
_____ **c.** Prepaid Rent   _____ **h.** Accumulated Depreciation
_____ **d.** FICA Payable   _____ **i.** Computer Equipment
_____ **e.** Store Supplies   _____ **j.** Unearned Rent

L04 *(10 MIN)*   **Reversing Entries**

5.   **a.** On January 1, prepare a reversing entry. On January 8, journalize the entry to record the paying of salary expense, $820.
b. What will be the balance in Salaries Expense on January 8 (after posting)?

December 31:

Salaries Expense			Salaries Payable	
Dr.	**Cr.**		**Dr.**	**Cr.**
820	1,170 closing			350 Adj.
Adj. 350				

MyAccountingLab   **Exercises**

Set A

L01 *(15 MIN)*   **12A-1.** From the following accounts, prepare a cost of goods sold section in proper form: Merchandise Inventory, 12/31/1X, $9,040; Purchases Discount, $860; Merchandise Inventory, 12/01/1X, $4,400; Purchases, $60,000; Purchases Returns and Allowances, $1,040; Freight-In, $330.

L01 *(10 MIN)*   **12A-2.** Give the category, the classification, and the report(s) on which each of the following appears (for example: Cash—asset, current asset, balance sheet):

a. Salaries Payable
b. Accounts Payable
c. Mortgage Payable
d. Unearned Legal Fees
e. SIT Payable
f. Office Equipment
g. Land

L02 *(10 MIN)*   **12A-3.** From the partial worksheet in Figure 12.15, journalize the closing entries for December 31 for G. Jackson Co.

L01 *(15 MIN)*   **12A-4.** From the worksheet in Exercise 12A-3, prepare the assets section of a classified balance sheet.

L02, 4 *(30 MIN)*   **12A-5.** On December 31, 2012, $290 of salaries has been accrued. (Salaries before the accrued amount totaled $28,000.) The next payroll to be paid will be on February 3, 2013, for $5,700. Please do the following:

a. Journalize and post the adjusting entry (use T accounts).
b. Journalize and post the reversing entry on January 1.
c. Journalize and post the payment of the payroll. Cash has a balance of $17,000 before the payment of payroll on February 3.

FIGURE 12.15
Worksheet for G. Jackson Co.

	G. JACKSON CO. WORKSHEET FOR YEAR ENDED DECEMBER 31, 201X			
	Income Statement		Balance Sheet	
Account Titles	Dr.	Cr.	Dr.	Cr.
Cash			188 00	
Merchandise Inventory			452 00	
Prepaid Advertising			564 00	
Prepaid Insurance			31 00	
Office Equipment			1062 00	
Accum. Dep., Office Equip.				212 00
Accounts Payable				251 00
G. Jackson, Capital				962 00
Income Summary	358 00	452 00		
Sales		5496 00		
Sales Returns and Allowances	226 00			
Sales Discount	107 00			
Purchases	2628 00			
Purchases Returns and Allow.		38 00		
Purchases Discount		53 00		
Salaries Expense	1086 00			
Insurance Expense	694 00			
Utilities Expense	47 00			
Plumbing Expense	55 00			
Advertising Expense	10 00			
Dep. Expenses, Office Equip.	28 00			
Salaries Payable				72 00
	5239 00	6039 00	2297 00	1497 00
Net Income	800 00			800 00
	6039 00	6039 00	2297 00	2297 00

Set B

12B-1. From the following accounts, prepare a cost of goods sold section in proper form: Merchandise Inventory, 12/31/1X, $8,990; Purchases Discount, $850; Merchandise Inventory, 12/01/1X, $4,200; Purchases, $64,000; Purchases Returns and Allowances, $960; Freight-In $280.

● **L01** *(15 MIN)*

12B-2. Give the category, the classification, and the report(s) on which each of the following appears (for example: Cash—asset, current asset, balance sheet):

● **L01** *(10 MIN)*

a. Wages Payable
b. Accounts Payable
c. Notes Payable
d. Unearned Revenue
e. FIT Payable
f. Office Furniture
g. Land

LO2 *(10 MIN)*   **12B-3.** From the partial worksheet in Figure 12.16, journalize the closing entries for December 31 for G. Jackson Co.

FIGURE 12.16
Worksheet for G. Jackson Co.

	G. JACKSON CO. WORKSHEET FOR YEAR ENDED DECEMBER 31, 201X				
	Income Statement		Balance Sheet		
Account	Debit	Credit	Debit	Credit	
Cash			192 00		
Merchandise Inventory			448 00		
Prepaid Advertising			555 00		
Prepaid Insurance			28 00		
Office Equipment			1083 00		
Accum. Dep., Office Equipment				207 00	
Accounts Payable				252 00	
G. Jackson, Capital				986 00	
Income Summary	362 00	448 00			
Sales		5518 00			
Sales Returns and Allowances	223 00				
Sales Discounts	109 00				
Purchases	2621 00				
Purchases Returns and Allowances		32 00			
Purchases Discount		47 00			
Salaries Expense	1086 00				
Insurance Expense	696 00				
Utilities Expense	43 00				
Plumbing Expenses	54 00				
Advertising Expense	14 00				
Dep. Expenses, Office Equip.	30 00				
Salaries Payable				72 00	
	5238 00	6045 00	2306 00	1499 00	
Net Income	807 00			807 00	
	6045 00	6045 00	2306 00	2306 00	

LO1 *(15 MIN)*   **12B-4.** From the worksheet in Exercise 12B-3, prepare the assets section of a classified balance sheet.

LO2, 4 *(30 MIN)*   **12B-5.** On December 31, 2012, $330 of salaries has been accrued. (Salaries before the accrued amount totaled $28,500.) The next payroll to be paid will be on February 3, 2013, for $6,400. Please do the following:

a. Journalize and post the adjusting entry (use T accounts).
b. Journalize and post the reversing entry on January 1.
c. Journalize and post the payment of the payroll. Cash has a balance of $14,500 before the payment of payroll on February 3.

MyAccountingLab   **Problems**

Set A

LO1 *(30 MIN)*   **12A-1.** Prepare a formal income statement from the partial worksheet for Rose Co. in Figure 12.17.

Check Figure:
Net Income from
operations $659

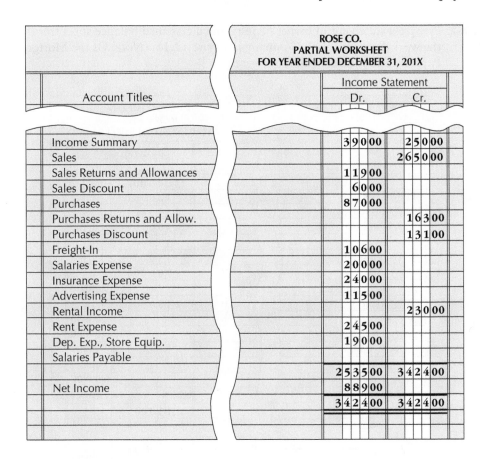

FIGURE 12.17
Partial Worksheet for Rose Co.

ROSE CO.
PARTIAL WORKSHEET
FOR YEAR ENDED DECEMBER 31, 201X

Account Titles	Income Statement Dr.	Income Statement Cr.
Income Summary	3 9 0 00	2 5 0 00
Sales		2 6 5 0 00
Sales Returns and Allowances	1 1 9 00	
Sales Discount	6 0 00	
Purchases	8 7 0 00	
Purchases Returns and Allow.		1 6 3 00
Purchases Discount		1 3 1 00
Freight-In	1 0 6 00	
Salaries Expense	2 0 0 00	
Insurance Expense	2 4 0 00	
Advertising Expense	1 1 5 00	
Rental Income		2 3 0 00
Rent Expense	2 4 5 00	
Dep. Exp., Store Equip.	1 9 0 00	
Salaries Payable		
	2 5 3 5 00	3 4 2 4 00
Net Income	8 8 9 00	
	3 4 2 4 00	3 4 2 4 00

LO1 *(40 MIN)*

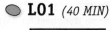

FIGURE 12.18
Partial Worksheet for John's Company

Check Figure:
Total Assets $32,195

12A-2. Prepare a statement of owner's equity and a classified balance sheet from the worksheet for John's Company in Figure 12.18. (*Note:* Of the Mortgage Payable, $220 is due within one year.)

JOHN'S COMPANY
WORKSHEET
FOR YEAR ENDED DECEMBER 31, 201X

| | Balance Sheet | |
Account Titles	Dr.	Cr.
Cash	23 0 0 0 00	
Petty Cash	1 2 0 00	
Accounts Receivable	1 3 5 0 00	
Merchandise Inv.	3 9 0 0 00	
Supplies	3 7 5 00	
Prepaid Insurance	4 5 0 00	
Store Equipment	2 7 0 0 00	
Acc. Dep., Store Eq.		9 0 0 00
Automobile	1 5 0 0 00	
Acc. Dep., Auto.		3 0 0 00
Accounts Payable		2 6 0 0 00
Taxes Payable		2 3 5 0 00
Unearned Rent		19 5 0 0 00
Mortgage Payable		6 0 0 00
H. Johns, Capital		12 0 0 0 00
H. Johns, With.	1 5 0 00	
Salaries Payable		6 0 0 00
	33 5 4 5 00	38 8 5 0 00
Net Loss	5 3 0 5 00	
	38 8 5 0 00	38 8 5 0 00

LO1, 2 *(90 MIN)*

Check Figure:
Net Income $4,570

12A-3. a Complete the worksheet for Joe's Supplies in Figure 12.19 (p. 483).

b. Prepare an income statement, a statement of owner's equity, and a classified balance sheet. (*Note:* The amount of the mortgage due the first year is $820.)

c. Journalize the adjusting and closing entries.

FIGURE 12.19
Worksheet for Joe's Supplies

JOE'S SUPPLIES
WORKSHEET
FOR YEAR ENDED DECEMBER 31, 201X

Account Titles	Trial Balance Dr.	Trial Balance Cr.	Adjustments Dr.	Adjustments Cr.
Cash	1800 00			
Accounts Receivable	3300 00			
Merch. Inventory, 1/1/1X	11300 00	(B)	10100 00	11300 00 (A)
Prepaid Insurance	1900 00			490 00 (E)
Equipment	3700 00			
Accum. Dep., Equipment		1010 00		360 00 (D)
Accounts Payable		5100 00		
Unearned Training Fees		2090 00	(C) 270 00	
Mortgage Payable		1180 00		
P. Joe, Capital		10560 00		
P. Joe, Withdrawals	4290 00			
Income Summary		(A)	11300 00	10100 00 (B)
Sales		95500 00		
Sales Returns and Allowances	3200 00			
Sales Discount	2630 00			
Purchases	63100 00			
Purchases Returns and Allow.		1390 00		
Purchases Discount		3220 00		
Freight-In	2640 00			
Advertising Expense	11400 00			
Rent Expense	9600 00			
Salaries Expense	13700 00			
	132560 00	132560 00		
Training Fees Earned				270 00 (C)
Dep. Exp., Equipment			(D) 360 00	
Insurance Expense			(E) 490 00	
			22520 00	22520 00

12A-4. Using the ledger balances and additional data given, do the following for Cross Lumber for the year ended December 31, 201X:

1. Prepare the worksheet.
2. Prepare the income statement, statement of owner's equity, and balance sheet.

LO1, 2, 3, 4
(150 MIN)

Check Figure:
Net Income $4,466

(continued on page 484)

3. Journalize and post adjusting and closing entries. (Be sure to put beginning balances in the ledger first.)
4. Prepare a post-closing trial balance.
5. Journalize the reversing entry for wages accrued.

Account Balances for Cross Lumber

Acct. No.		
110	Cash	$ 1,390
111	Accounts Receivable	1,380
112	Merchandise Inventory	4,500
113	Lumber Supplies	279
114	Prepaid Insurance	223
121	Lumber Equipment	3,000
122	Accum. Dep., Lumber Equipment	500
220	Accounts Payable	1,190
221	Wages Payable	—
330	J. Cross, Capital	7,097
331	J. Cross, Withdrawals	2,700
332	Income Summary	—
440	Sales	23,000
441	Sales Returns and Allowances	250
550	Purchases	15,100
551	Purchases Discount	305
552	Purchases Returns and Allowances	320
660	Wages Expense	2,300
661	Advertising Expense	430
662	Rent Expense	860
663	Dep. Expense, Lumber Equipment	—
664	Lumber Supplies Expense	—
665	Insurance Expense	—

Additional Data

a./b.	Merchandise inventory, December 31	$5,000
c.	Lumber supplies on hand, December 31	90
d.	Insurance expired	160
e.	Depreciation for the year	270
f.	Accrued wages on December 31	100

Set B

12B-1. From the partial worksheet for Rose Co. shown in Figure 12.20, prepare a formal income statement.

MyAccountingLab

● **L01** (70 MIN)

PT/QB

FIGURE 12.20
Partial Worksheet of Rose Co.

Check Figure:
Net income from
operations $975

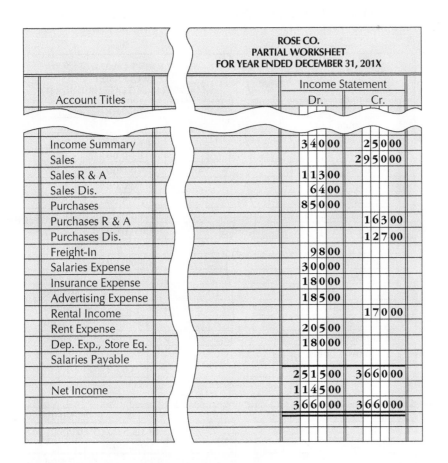

ROSE CO.
PARTIAL WORKSHEET
FOR YEAR ENDED DECEMBER 31, 201X

Account Titles	Income Statement Dr.	Income Statement Cr.
Income Summary	3 4 0 00	2 5 0 00
Sales		2 9 5 0 00
Sales R & A	1 1 3 00	
Sales Dis.	6 4 00	
Purchases	8 5 0 00	
Purchases R & A		1 6 3 00
Purchases Dis.		1 2 7 00
Freight-In	9 8 00	
Salaries Expense	3 0 0 00	
Insurance Expense	1 8 0 00	
Advertising Expense	1 8 5 00	
Rental Income		1 7 0 00
Rent Expense	2 0 5 00	
Dep. Exp., Store Eq.	1 8 0 00	
Salaries Payable		
	2 5 1 5 00	3 6 6 0 00
Net Income	1 1 4 5 00	
	3 6 6 0 00	3 6 6 0 00

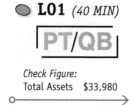

L01 *(40 MIN)*

Check Figure:
Total Assets $33,980

12B-2. From the worksheet shown for John's Company in Figure 12.21, complete the following:

a. Statement of owner's equity

b. Classified balance sheet

(*Note:* Of the Mortgage Payable, $190 is due within one year.)

FIGURE 12.21
Worksheet for John's Company

JOHN'S COMPANY
WORKSHEET
FOR YEAR ENDED DECEMBER 31, 201X

Account Titles	Balance Sheet Dr.	Balance Sheet Cr.
Cash	2 4 0 0 00	
Petty Cash	1 3 0 00	
Accts. Receivable	1 5 0 0 00	
Merch. Inventory	3 7 0 0 00	
Supplies	2 7 5 00	
Prepaid Ins.	5 0 0 00	
Store Equip.	3 0 0 0 00	
Acc. Dep., Store Eq.		9 0 0 00
Automobile	2 0 0 0 00	
Acc. Dep., Auto.		2 2 5 00
Accts. Payable		2 9 0 0 00
Taxes Payable		2 4 5 0 00
Unearned Rent		19 0 0 0 00
Mortgage Payable		6 5 0 00
H. Johns, Capital		12 2 0 0 00
H. Johns, Withd.	5 0 00	
Salaries Payable		7 5 0 00
	35 1 5 5 00	39 0 7 5 00
Net Loss	3 9 2 0 00	
	39 0 7 5 00	39 0 7 5 00

12B-3. From the partial worksheet for Joe's Supplies in Figure 12.22, do the following:

⬤◯ **L01, 2** *(90 MIN)*

1. Complete the worksheet.
2. Prepare the income statement, statement of owner's equity, and classified balance sheet. (*Note:* The amount of the mortgage due the first year is $890.)
3. Journalize the adjusting and closing entries.

Check Figure:
Net Income $4,700
←————————○

FIGURE 12.22
Worksheet for Joe's Supplies

JOE'S SUPPLIES
WORKSHEET
FOR YEAR ENDED DECEMBER 31, 201X

Account Titles	Trial Balance Dr.	Trial Balance Cr.	Adjustments Dr.	Adjustments Cr.
Cash	2 5 0 0 00			
Accounts Receivable	3 1 0 0 00			
Merch. Inventory, 1/1/1X	11 0 0 0 00		(B)10 6 0 0 00	11 0 0 0 00 (A)
Prepaid Insurance	1 9 2 0 00			5 5 0 00 (E)
Equipment	3 1 0 0 00			
Accum. Dep., Equipment		1 0 1 0 00		4 4 0 00 (D)
Accounts Payable		5 0 7 0 00		
Unearned Training Fees		2 1 7 00	(C) 3 0 0 00	
Mortgage Payable		1 3 3 0 00		
P. Joe, Capital		10 5 0 0 00		
P. Joe, Withdrawals	4 2 5 0 00			
Income Summary			(A)11 0 0 0 00	10 6 0 0 00 (B)
Sales		95 6 8 0 00		
Sales Returns and Allowances	3 1 7 0 00			
Sales Discount	2 6 0 0 00			
Purchases	64 1 0 0 00			
Purchases Returns and Allow.		1 3 3 0 00		
Purchases Discounts		3 2 4 0 00		
Freight-In	2 6 6 0 00			
Advertising Expense	1 1 3 0 00			
Rent Expense	9 5 0 0 00			
Salaries Expense	13 1 0 0 00			
	132 3 0 0 00	132 3 0 0 00		
Training Fees Earned				3 0 0 00 (C)
Dep. Exp., Equipment			(D) 4 4 0 00	
Insurance Expense			(E) 5 5 0 00	
			22 8 9 0 00	22 8 9 0 00

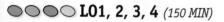 **LO1, 2, 3, 4** *(150 MIN)*

Check Figure:
Net Income $5,608

12B-4. From the ledger balances and additional data given, do the following for Cross Lumber for the year ended December 31, 201X.

1. Prepare the worksheet.
2. Prepare the income statement, statement of owner's equity, and balance sheet.
3. Journalize and post adjusting and closing entries. (Be sure to put beginning balances in the ledger first.)
4. Prepare a post-closing trial balance.
5. Journalize the reversing entry for wages accrued.

Account Balances of Cross Lumber		
Acct. No.		
110	Cash	$ 1,300
111	Accounts Receivable	1,280
112	Merchandise Inventory	4,300
113	Lumber Supplies	267
114	Prepaid Insurance	209
121	Lumber Equipment	3,300
122	Acc. Dep., Lumber Equipment	530
220	Accounts Payable	1,200
221	Wages Payable	—
330	J. Cross, Capital	5,761
331	J. Cross, Withdrawals	2,700
332	Income Summary	—
440	Sales	23,200
441	Sales Returns and Allowances	230
550	Purchases	14,500
551	Purchases Discount	325
552	Purchases Returns and Allowances	340
660	Wages Expense	2,120
661	Advertising Expense	370
662	Rent Expense	780
663	Dep. Exp., Lumber Equipment	—
664	Lumber Supplies Expense	—
665	Insurance Expense	—

Additional Data

a./b.	Merchandise inventory, December 31	$4,700
c.	Lumber supplies on hand, December 31	75
d.	Insurance expired	120
e.	Depreciation for the year	210
f.	Accrued wages on December 31	135

Financial Report Problem

LO2, 3 *(5 MIN)*

Reading the Kellogg's Annual Report

Go to http://investor.kelloggs.com/annuals.cfm, to access the Kellogg's 2010 Annual Report and locate the consolidated statement of earnings. How much has Selling and General Administrative Expense increased from 2009 to 2010?

ON the JOB ||||||||||||||||||||||||||||

MyAccountingLab

SANCHEZ COMPUTER CENTER

●●LO1, 2 *(60 MIN)*

Using the worksheet in Chapter 11 for Sanchez Computer Center, journalize and post the adjusting entries and prepare the financial statements.

Mini Practice Set

The Corner Dress Shop

Reviewing the Accounting Cycle for a Merchandise Company
This practice set will help you review all the key concepts of a merchandise company, along with the integration of payroll, including the preparation of Form 941.

Because you are the bookkeeper of the Corner Dress Shop, we have gathered the following information for you. It will be your task to complete the accounting cycle for March.

THE CORNER DRESS SHOP POST-CLOSING TRIAL BALANCE FEBRUARY 28, 201X	1	2
Cash	2 1 9 3 90	
Accounts Receivable	2 2 0 0 00	
Petty Cash	3 5 00	
Merchandise Inventory	5 6 0 0 00	
Prepaid Rent	1 8 0 0 00	
Delivery Truck	6 0 0 0 00	
Accumulated Depreciation, Truck		1 5 0 0 00
Accounts Payable		1 9 0 0 00
FIT Payable		9 7 5 00
FICA—OASDI Payable		1 3 3 9 20
FICA—Medicare Payable		3 1 3 20
SIT Payable		7 5 6 00
SUTA Payable		9 7 9 20
FUTA Payable		1 6 3 20
Unearned Rent		8 0 0 00
B. Loeb, Capital		9 1 0 3 10
Total	17 8 2 8 90	17 8 2 8 90

Balances in subsidiary ledgers as of March 1 are as follows:

Accounts Receivable		Accounts Payable	
Bing Co.	$2,200	Blew Co.	$1,900
Blew Co.	—	Jones Co.	—
Ronald Co.	—	Moe's Garage	—
		Morris Co.	—

Payroll is paid monthly:

FICA rate	OASDI 6.2% on $106,800
	Medicare 1.45% on all earnings
SUTA rate	4.8% on $7,000
FUTA rate	.8% on $7,000
SIT rate	7%
FIT	Use the table provided at the end of this practice set.

The payroll register for January and February is provided. In March, salaries are as follows:

Mel Case	$3,325
Jane Holl	4,120
Jackie Moore	4,760

Your tasks are to do the following:

1. Set up a general ledger, accounts receivable subsidiary ledger and accounts payable subsidiary ledger, auxiliary petty cash record, and payroll register. (Be sure to update ledger accounts based on information given in the post-closing trial balance for February 28 before beginning.)
2. Journalize the transactions, and prepare the payroll register.
3. Update the accounts payable and accounts receivable subsidiary ledgers.
4. Post to the general ledger.
5. Prepare a trial balance on a worksheet and complete the worksheet.
6. Prepare an income statement, statement of owner's equity, and classified balance sheet.
7. Journalize the adjusting and closing entries.
8. Post the adjusting and closing entries to the ledger.
9. Prepare a post-closing trial balance.
10. Complete Form 941 and sign it as of the last day in April.

Chart of Accounts for the Corner Dress Shop

Assets
110 Cash
111 Accounts Receivable
112 Petty Cash
114 Merchandise Inventory
116 Prepaid Rent
120 Delivery Truck
121 Accumulated Depreciation, Truck

Liabilities
210 Accounts Payable
212 Salaries Payable
214 Federal Income Tax Payable
216 FICA—OASDI Payable
218 FICA—Medicare Payable
220 State Income Tax Payable
222 SUTA Tax Payable
224 FUTA Tax Payable
226 Unearned Rent

Owner's Equity
310 B. Loeb, Capital
320 B. Loeb, Withdrawals
330 Income Summary

Revenue
410 Sales
412 Sales Returns and Allowances
414 Sales Discount
416 Rental Income

Cost of Goods Sold
510 Purchases
512 Purchases Returns and Allowances
514 Purchases Discount

Expenses
610 Sales Salaries Expense
611 Office Salaries Expense
612 Payroll Tax Expense
614 Cleaning Expense
616 Depreciation Expense, Truck
618 Rent Expense
620 Postage Expense
622 Delivery Expense
624 Miscellaneous Expense

THE CORNER DRESS SHOP
PAYROLL REGISTER
JANUARY AND FEBRUARY 201X

Employees	Allow. and Marital Status	Cum. Earnings	Salary	Earnings			Cum. Earnings
				Reg.	O/T	Gross	
Mel Case	M – 2	—	3300 00	3300 00		3300 00	3300 00
Jane Holl	M – 1	—	3400 00	3400 00		3400 00	3400 00
Jackie Moore	M – 0	—	4100 00	4100 00		4100 00	4100 00
Totals for Jan.			10800 00	10800 00		10800 00	10800 00
Mel Case	M – 2	3300 00	3300 00	3300 00		3300 00	6600 00
Jane Holl	M – 1	3400 00	3400 00	3400 00		3400 00	6800 00
Jackie Moore	M – 0	4100 00	4100 00	4100 00		4100 00	8200 00
Totals for Feb.		10800 00	10800 00	10800 00		10800 00	21600 00

PAYROLL REGISTER

Taxable Earnings			Deductions					Ck. No.	Distribution	
	FICA		FICA						Office Salary Expense	Sales Salary Expense
Unemp.	Soc. Sec.	Medicare	OASDI	Medicare	FIT	SIT	Net Pay			
3300 00	3300 00	3300 00	204 60	47 85	233 00	231 00	2583 55		3300 00	
3400 00	3400 00	3400 00	210 80	49 30	297 00	238 00	2604 90			3400 00
4100 00	4100 00	4100 00	254 20	59 45	445 00	287 00	3054 90			4100 00
10800 00	10800 00	10800 00	669 60	156 60	975 00	756 00	8242 80		3300 00	7500 00
3300 00	3300 00	3300 00	204 60	47 85	233 00	231 00	2583 55		3300 00	
3400 00	3400 00	3400 00	210 80	49 30	297 00	238 00	2604 90			3400 00
2900 00	4100 00	4100 00	254 20	59 45	445 00	287 00	3054 90			4100 00
9600 00	10800 00	10800 00	669 60	156 60	975 00	756 00	8242 80		3300 00	7500 00

201X

Mar. 1 Bing paid balance owed, no discount.

2 Purchased merchandise from Morris Company on account, $10,000; terms 2/10, n/30.

2 Paid $6 from the petty cash fund for cleaning package, voucher no. 18 (consider it a cleaning expense).

3 Sold merchandise to Ronald Company on account, $7,000, invoice no. 51; terms 2/10, n/30.

5 Paid $3 from the petty cash fund for postage, voucher no. 19.

6 Sold merchandise to Ronald Company on account, $5,000, invoice no. 52; terms 2/10, n/30.

8 Paid $10 from the petty cash fund for first aid emergency, voucher no. 20.

9 Purchased merchandise from Morris Company on account, $5,000; terms 2/10, n/30.

9 Paid $5 for delivery expense from petty cash fund, voucher no. 21.

9 Sold more merchandise to Ronald Company on account, $3,000, invoice no. 53; terms 2/10, n/30.

9 Paid cleaning service, $300, check no. 110.

(Continued)

(Continued)

10   Ronald Company returned merchandise costing $1,000 from invoice no. 52; the Corner Dress shop issued credit memo no. 10 to Ronald Company for $1,000.

11   Purchased merchandise from Jones Company on account, $10,000; terms 1/15, n/60.

12   Paid Morris Company invoice dated March 2, check no. 111.

13   Sold $7,000 of merchandise for cash.

14   Returned merchandise to Jones Company in amount of $2,000; the Corner Dress Shop issued debit memo no. 4 to Jones Company.

14   Paid $5 from the petty cash fund for delivery expense, voucher no. 22.

15   Paid taxes due for FICA (OASDI and Medicare) and FIT for February payroll, check no. 112.

15   Sold Merchandise for $29,000 cash.

15   Betty withdrew $100 for her own personal expenses, check no. 113.

15   Paid state income tax for February payroll, check no. 114.

16   Received payment from Ronald Company for invoice no. 52, less discount.

16   Ronald Company paid invoice no. 51, $7,000.

16   Sold merchandise to Bing Company on account, $3,200, invoice no. 54; terms 2/10, n/30.

21   Purchased delivery truck on account from Moe's Garage, $17,200.

22   Sold merchandise to Ronald Company on account, $4,000, invoice no. 55; terms 2/10, n/30.

23   Paid Jones Company the balance owed, check no. 115.

24   Sold merchandise to Bing Company on account, $2,000, invoice no. 56; terms 2/10, n/30.

25   Purchased merchandise for $1,000 check no. 116.

27   Purchased merchandise from Blew Company on account, $6,000; terms 2/10, n/30.

27   Paid $2 postage from the petty cash fund, voucher no. 23.

28   Ronald Company paid invoice no. 55 dated March 22, less discount.

28   Bing Company paid invoice no. 54 dated March 16.

29   Purchased merchandise from Morris Company on account, $9,000; terms 2/10, n/30.

30   Sold merchandise to Blew Company on account, $10,000, invoice no. 57; terms 2/10, n/30.

30   Issued check no. 117 to replenish to the same level the petty cash fund.

30   Recorded payroll in payroll register.

30   Journalized payroll entry (to be paid on 31st).

30   Journalized employer's payroll tax expense.

31   Paid payroll checks no. 118, no. 119, and no. 120.

Additional Data

a./b. Ending merchandise inventory, $13,515.

c. During March, rent expired, $600.

d. Truck depreciated, $150.

e. Rental income earned, $200 (one month's rent from subletting).

f. Betty Loeb's dress shop is located at 1 Milgate Rd., Marblehead, MA 01945. Its identification number is 33-4158215.

MARRIED Persons—MONTHLY Payroll Period

(For Wages Paid through December 201X)

And the wages are—		And the number of withholding allowances claimed is—										
At least	But less than	0	1	2	3	4	5	6	7	8	9	10
		The amount of income tax to be withheld is—										
$ 0	$680	$0	$0	$0	$0	$0	$0	$0	$0	$0	$0	$0
680	720	4	0	0	0	0	0	0	0	0	0	0
720	760	8	0	0	0	0	0	0	0	0	0	0
760	800	12	0	0	0	0	0	0	0	0	0	0
2,600	2,640	223	177	135	104	73	42	11	0	0	0	0
2,640	2,680	229	183	139	108	77	46	15	0	0	0	0
2,680	2,720	235	189	143	112	81	50	19	0	0	0	0
2,720	2,760	241	195	149	116	85	54	23	0	0	0	0
2,760	2,800	247	201	155	120	89	58	27	0	0	0	0
2,800	2,840	253	207	161	124	93	62	31	0	0	0	0
2,840	2,880	259	213	167	128	97	66	35	4	0	0	0
2,880	2,920	265	219	173	132	101	70	39	8	0	0	0
2,920	2,960	271	225	179	136	105	74	43	12	0	0	0
2,960	3,000	277	231	185	140	109	78	47	16	0	0	0
3,000	3,040	283	237	191	145	113	82	51	20	0	0	0
3,040	3,080	289	243	197	151	117	86	55	24	0	0	0
3,080	3,120	295	249	203	157	121	90	59	28	0	0	0
3,120	3,160	301	255	209	163	125	94	63	32	2	0	0
3,160	3,200	307	261	215	169	129	98	67	36	6	0	0
3,200	3,240	313	267	221	175	133	102	71	40	10	0	0
3,240	3,280	319	273	227	181	137	106	75	44	14	0	0
3,280	3,320	325	279	233	187	141	110	79	48	18	0	0
3,320	3,360	331	285	239	193	146	114	83	52	22	0	0
3,360	3,400	337	291	245	199	152	118	87	56	26	0	0
$3,400	$3,440	$343	$297	$251	$205	$158	$122	$91	$60	$30	$0	$0
3,440	3,480	349	303	257	211	164	126	95	64	34	3	0
3,480	3,520	355	309	263	217	170	130	99	68	38	7	0
3,520	3,560	361	315	269	223	176	134	103	72	42	11	0
3,560	3,600	367	321	275	229	182	138	107	76	46	15	0
3,600	3,640	373	327	281	235	188	142	111	80	50	19	0
3,640	3,680	379	333	287	241	194	148	115	84	54	23	0
3,680	3,720	385	339	293	247	200	154	119	88	58	27	0
3,720	3,760	391	345	299	253	206	160	123	92	62	31	0
3,760	3,800	397	351	305	259	212	166	127	96	66	35	4
3,800	3,840	403	357	311	265	218	172	131	100	70	39	8
3,840	3,880	409	363	317	271	224	178	135	104	74	43	12
3,880	3,920	415	369	323	277	230	184	139	108	78	47	16
3,920	3,960	421	375	329	283	236	190	144	112	82	51	20
3,960	4,000	427	381	335	289	242	196	150	116	86	55	24
4,000	4,040	433	387	341	295	248	202	156	120	90	59	28
4,040	4,080	439	393	347	301	254	208	162	124	94	63	32
4,080	4,120	445	399	353	307	260	214	168	128	98	67	36
4,120	4,160	451	405	359	313	266	220	174	132	102	71	40
4,160	4,200	457	411	365	319	272	226	180	136	106	75	44
4,200	4,240	463	417	371	325	278	232	186	140	110	79	48
4,240	4,280	469	423	377	331	284	238	192	146	114	83	52
4,280	4,320	475	429	383	337	290	244	198	152	118	87	56
4,320	4,360	481	435	389	343	296	250	204	158	122	91	60
4,360	4,400	487	441	395	349	302	256	210	164	126	95	64
4,400	4,440	493	447	401	355	308	262	216	170	130	99	68
4,440	4,480	499	453	407	361	314	268	222	176	134	103	72
4,480	4,520	505	459	413	367	320	274	228	182	138	107	76
4,520	4,560	511	465	419	373	326	280	234	188	142	111	80
4,560	4,600	517	471	425	379	332	286	240	194	147	115	84
4,600	4,640	523	477	431	385	338	292	246	200	153	119	88
4,640	4,680	529	483	437	391	344	298	252	206	159	123	92
4,680	4,720	535	489	443	397	350	304	258	212	165	127	96
4,720	4,760	541	495	449	403	356	310	264	218	171	131	100
4,760	4,800	547	501	455	409	362	316	270	224	177	135	104
4,800	4,840	553	507	461	415	368	322	276	230	183	139	108
4,840	4,880	559	513	467	421	374	328	282	236	189	143	112
4,880	4,920	565	519	473	427	380	334	288	242	195	149	116
4,920	4,960	571	525	479	433	386	340	294	248	201	155	120
4,960	5,000	577	531	485	439	392	346	300	254	207	161	124
5,000	5,040	583	537	491	445	398	352	306	260	213	167	128
5,040	5,080	589	543	497	451	404	358	312	266	219	173	132
5,080	5,120	595	549	503	457	410	364	318	272	225	179	136
5,120	5,160	601	555	509	463	416	370	324	278	231	185	140
5,160	5,200	607	561	515	469	422	376	330	284	237	191	145

PEACHTREE COMPUTER WORKSHOP

COMPUTERIZED ACCOUNTING APPLICATION FOR CHAPTER 12

Refresher on using Peachtree Complete Accounting

Before starting this assignment, you may want to refresh your memory by reading the following PDF documents in the multimedia library of the MyAccountingLab Web site. Remember to choose the PDF document for your version of Peachtree.

1. An Introduction to Peachtree Complete Accounting
2. Correcting Peachtree Transactions
3. How to Repeat or Restart a Peachtree Assignment
4. Backing Up and Restoring Your Work in Peachtree

You also should have completed the following workshops:

1. Workshop 1 Atlas Company from Chapter 3
2. Workshop 2 Zell Company from Chapter 4
3. Workshop 3 Sullivan Realty from Chapter 5
4. Workshop 4 Pete's Market from Chapter 8
5. Workshop 5 Part A Mars Company from Chapter 10
6. Workshop 5 Part B Abby's Toy House from Chapter 10

Workshop 6:

Accounting Cycle for a Merchandising Company

In this workshop you complete an accounting cycle for a merchandising business owned by the Corner Dress Shop using Peachtree. Tasks include maintaining inventory, recording sales on account, merchandise returns, merchandise purchases, vendor payments, and payroll. You will also prepare inventory reports, aged receivables and aged payable reports, general journal and general ledger reports, a trial balance, and financial statements. Finally, you will close the accounting period.

Instructions and the data file for completing this assignment are in the multimedia library of the MyAccountingLab Web site. Open the *Workshop 6 The Corner Dress Shop* PDF document for your version of Peachtree and download *The Corner Dress Shop* data file for your version of Peachtree.

QUICKBOOKS COMPUTER WORKSHOP

COMPUTERIZED ACCOUNTING APPLICATION FOR CHAPTER 12

Refresher on using QuickBooks Pro

Before starting this assignment, you may want to refresh your memory by reading the following PDF documents in the multimedia library of the MyAccountingLab Web site. Remember to choose the PDF document for your version of QuickBooks.

1. An Introduction to QuickBooks Pro
2. Correcting QuickBooks Transactions
3. How to Repeat or Restart a QuickBooks Assignment
4. Backing Up and Restoring Your Work in QuickBooks

You also should have completed the following workshops:

1. Workshop 1 Atlas Company from Chapter 3
2. Workshop 2 Zell Company from Chapter 4
3. Workshop 3 Sullivan Realty from Chapter 5.
4. Workshop 4 Pete's Market from Chapter 8
5. Workshop 5 Part A Mars Company from Chapter 10
6. Workshop 5 Part B Abby's Toy House from Chapter 10

Workshop 6:

Accounting Cycle for a Merchandising Company

In this workshop you complete an accounting cycle for a merchandising business owned by the Corner Dress Shop using QuickBooks. Tasks include maintaining inventory, recording sales on account, merchandise returns, merchandise purchases, vendor payments, and payroll. You will also prepare inventory reports, aged receivables and aged payable reports, general journal and general ledger reports, a trial balance, and financial statements. Finally, you will close the accounting period.

Instructions and the data file for completing this assignment are in the multimedia library of the MyAccountingLab Web site. Open the *Workshop 6 The Corner Dress Shop* PDF document for your version of Quickbooks and download the *The Corner Dress Shop* data file for your version of Quickbooks.

GLINDEX

A Combined Glossary and Subject Index

time. Banking business transacted after this time is usually considered to be the next day's business. Saturdays, Sundays, and federal holidays are usually not considered banking days, 297, 314

Basic accounting equation. Assets = Liabilities + Owner's Equity, 5

Beginning merchandise inventory (beginning inventory). The cost of goods on hand in a company to begin an accounting period, 424, 440

Blank endorsement, 223

Book of final entry. Book that receives information about business transactions from a book of original entry (a journal). Example: a ledger, 78

Book of original entry. Book that records the first formal information about business transactions. Example: a journal, 78, 103

Book value. Cost of asset (for example, equipment) less accumulated depreciation, 125

Bookkeeping. The recording function of the accounting process, 4. *See also* Double–entry bookkeeping

compared to accounting, 4

Business organizations, 2–3

C

Calendar quarter. A three-month, 13-week time period. Four calendar quarters occur during a calendar year that runs from January 1 through December 31. The first quarter is January through March, the second is April through June, the third is July through September, and the fourth is October through December, 296

Calendar year. (1) A one-year period beginning on January 1 and ending on December 31. Employers must use a calendar year for payroll purposes, even if the employer uses a fiscal year for financial statements and for any other reason. (2) The 12-month period a business chooses for its accounting year. Alternatively known as *fiscal year* and *natural business year*, 78, 266

Call centers (banking), 232

Cancelled check. A check that has been processed by a bank and is no longer negotiable, 228

Capital. The owner's investment of equity in the company, 6, 8. *See also* Ending capital

Capital Account, 93, 169–170

Cash. *See also* Cash receipts; Change fund; Petty cash
monitoring, 222

Cash Account, 92

Cash payment transactions, 379–380, 392, 395
recording, 416

Cash receipts, 354
journal for, 421–422

Cash Short and Over. The account that records cash shortages and overages. If the ending balance is a debit, it is recorded on the income statement as a miscellaneous expense; if it is a credit, it is recorded as miscellaneous income, 241–243, 247

Change fund. Fund made up of various denominations that are used to make change for customers, 236, 241, 245, 247

Chart of accounts. A numbering system of accounts that lists the account titles and account numbers to be used by a company, 44, 65
relationship with journal, 78–79
use for journalizing, 103

Check. A form used to indicate a specific amount of money that is to be paid by the bank to a named person or company, 226. *See also* Cancelled check; NSF (Nonsufficient funds); Outstanding checks
endorsement of, 223
payroll, 294

Check truncation (safekeeping). Procedure whereby checks are not returned to the drawer with the bank statement but are instead kept at the bank for a certain amount of time before being first transferred to microfilm and then destroyed, 233

Checkbooks, 226–228

Checking accounts, 222–223, 245–246
deposits to, 223

Classified balance sheet. A balance sheet that categorizes assets as current assets or plant and equipment and groups liabilities as current or long-term liabilities, 459

Closing journal entries. Journal entries that are prepared to (a) reset all temporary accounts to a zero balance and (b) update Capital to a new balance, 166, 175–176
journalizing and posting, 467

Dollar sign, use of, 10, 55

Double-entry bookkeeping. An accounting system in which the recording of each transaction affects two or more accounts and the total of the debits is equal to the total of the credits, 45, 65

Drawee. Bank that drawer has an account with, 226, 246

Drawer. A person who writes a check, 226, 246

E

e-Banks, 232

Electronic Federal Tax Payment System (EFTPS), 299

Electronic funds transfer (EFT). An electronic system that transfers funds without the use of paper checks, 231

EFT number, 299

Employee earnings record. *See* Individual employee earnings record

Employer identification number (EIN). A number assigned by the IRS that is used by an employer when recording and paying payroll and income taxes, 296

Employer payroll tax expense, 270, 272–273, 276, 304, 317

Employer's Annual Federal Unemployment Tax Return. *See* Form 940, Employer's Annual Federal Unemployment Tax Return

Employer's Quarterly Federal Tax Return. *See* Form 944, Employer's Annual Federal Tax Return

Ending balance. The difference between footings in a T account, 41

Ending capital. Beginning Capital + Additional Investments + Net Income Withdrawals = Ending Capital. Or: Beginning Capital + Additional Investments – Net Loss – Withdrawals = Ending Capital, 20

Ending merchandise inventory (ending inventory). The cost of goods that remain unsold at the end of the accounting period. It is an asset on the new balance sheet, 424

Endorsement. *Blank:* Could be further endorsed. *Full:* Restricts further endorsement to only the person or company named. *Restrictive:* Restricts any further endorsement, 223, 246

Equities. The rights or financial claim of creditors (liabilities) and owners (owner's equity) who supply the assets to a firm, 5

Errors

correcting, 94–96

in trial balance, 93–95

Ethical cases

backdating checks, 396

borrowing from petty cash, 441

bribes from suppliers, 192

concealing debt, 477

copying software, 106

employee classification, 280

following GAAP, 149

moving new sales into old sales year, 356

padding expense account, 30

paying employee withholding tax to government, 319

reporting bank errors, 248

using fictional figures, 66

Expanded accounting equation. Assets = Liabilities + Capital – Withdrawals + Revenue – Expenses, 12

Expense. A cost incurred in running a business by consuming goods or services in producing revenue. A subdivision of owner's equity, 12–13, 17

dating of, 81

F

F.O.B. destination. *Seller* pays or is responsible for the cost of freight to purchaser's location or destination, 370

F.O.B. shipping point. *Purchaser* pays or is responsible for the shipping costs from seller's shipping point to purchaser's location, 370, 394

Fair Labor Standards Act (Federal Wage and Hour Law). A law the majority of employers must follow that contains rules stating the minimum hourly rate of pay and the maximum number of hours a worker will work before being paid time and a half for overtime hours worked. This law also has other rules and regulations that employers must follow for payroll purposes, 261

State Income Tax (SIT) withholding. Amount of state income tax withheld by the employer from the employee's gross pay, 263

State Unemployment Tax Act (SUTA). A tax usually paid only by employers to the state for employee unemployment insurance, 272–273, 311, 315, 317

Statement of account, from bank, 228

Statement of cash flows. A financial report that provides a detailed breakdown of the specific increases and decreases in cash during an accounting period. It helps readers of the statement evaluate past performance as well as predict future cash flows of the business, 20

Statement of financial position, 9. *See also* Balance sheet

Statement of owner's equity. A financial statement that reveals the change in capital. The ending figure for capital is then placed on the balance sheet, 18, 23, 141

for a merchandising company, 458

preparing from worksheet, 138

Subsidiary ledger. A ledger that contains accounts of a single type. Example: The accounts receivable subsidiary ledger records all credit customers, 341, 352, 392

posting to from special journals, 413–418

Supplies. One type of asset acquired by a firm; it has a much shorter life than equipment, 6

as expense, 81

Supplies on Hand, 135, 429, 440

SUTA. *See* State Unemployment Tax Act

T

T account. A skeleton version of a standard account, used for demonstration purposes, 40, 64–65

T account entries, 42–44

Taxable earnings. Shows amount of earnings subject to a tax. The tax itself is not shown, 267

Taxes. *See also* Federal Income Tax (FIT) withholding, paying; Form 941 taxes; IRS Circular E; IRS Forms; Payroll taxes; State Income Tax (SIT) withholding; State Unemployment Tax Act (SUTA); Tax Act of 1989

employee, 304, 313, 315, 317

employer taxes, 313, 315, 317

income tax, 262–264

Medicare tax, 267, 272, 276, 295–296, 304

OASDI taxes, 266–267, 272, 276, 295–296, 304

Temporary (nominal) accounts. Accounts whose balances at the end of an accounting period are not carried over to the next accounting period, 166

Total, distinguishing, 10

Transactions

analysis of, 44–50, 52–53, 65

journalizing, 79–83, 96

merchandise transactions, 384–388

recording, 64

sales transactions on account, 340

Transit number, ABA, 223, 235

Transmittal of Income and Tax Statement. *See* Form W-3, Transmittal of Income and Tax Statement

Transposition. The accidental rearrangement of digits of a number. Example: $152 \rightarrow 125$, 94

Trial balance. (1)A list of the ending balances of all the accounts in a ledger. (2)An informal listing of the ledger accounts and their balances in the ledger to aid in proving the equality of debits and credits, The total of the debits should equal the total of the credits. 53–54, 64–65, 93

indentation of titles on, 58

post-closing, 176

preparation of, 93–96, 103

Truncation. *See* Check truncation

U

Unearned Rent Account, 425–426

adjustments to, 439–440

Unearned Revenue. A liability account that records amount owed for goods or services in advance of delivery. The Cash account would record the receipt of cash, 428, 440

Unemployment taxes, 272–273

CREDITS

Chapter 1, page 1, © Iain Masterton / Alamy

Chapter 2, page 39, © dbimages / Alamy; page 76, Courtesy Subway Restaurants

Chapter 3, page 77, © PSL Images / Alamy

Chapter 4, page 119, © izmostock / Alamy; page 135, © sonya etchison/Shutterstock.com; page 159, Courtesy Subway Restaurants

Chapter 5, page 161, ZUMA Press/Newscom; page 176, © iStockphoto.com/Katja Bone; page 178, © Racheal Grazias/Shutterstock.com; page 203, Courtesy Subway Restaurants

Chapter 6, page 221, © Jeff Greenberg / Alamy; page 256, Courtesy Subway Restaurants

Chapter 7, page 259, © Daisy-Daisy / Alamy; page 287, Courtesy Subway Restaurants

Chapter 8, page 289, © VIEW Pictures Ltd / Alamy; page 331, Courtesy Subway Restaurants

Chapter 9, page 335, St Petersburg Times/ZumaPress/Newscom

Chapter 10, page 367, James Berglie/ZUMA Press/Newscom

Chapter 11, page 423, © Cindy Hopkins / Alamy

Chapter 12, page 455, Andreas Gebert/dpa/picture-alliance/Newscom